CASES AND MATERIALS

# LABOR LAW

THIRTEENTH EDITION

*by*

ARCHIBALD COX
Carl M. Loeb University Professor Emeritus
Harvard Law School

DEREK CURTIS BOK
The 300th Anniversary University Professor and President Emeritus
Harvard University

ROBERT A. GORMAN
Kenneth W. Gemmill Professor of Law Emeritus
University of Pennsylvania

MATTHEW W. FINKIN
Albert J. Harno Professor of Law
University of Illinois

NEW YORK, NEW YORK
**FOUNDATION PRESS**

2001

COPYRIGHT © 1948, 1951, 1954, 1958, 1962, 1965, 1969, 1977, 1981, 1986, 1991, 1996 FOUNDATION PRESS
COPYRIGHT © 2001 By FOUNDATION PRESS

        395 Hudson Street
        New York, NY 10014
        Phone Toll Free 1–877–888–1330
        Fax (212) 367–6799
        fdpress.com

**ISBN** 1–58778–060–7

 *TEXT IS PRINTED ON 10% POST CONSUMER RECYCLED PAPER*

# DEDICATION

To Archibald Cox and Derek Curtis Bok—
who, as influential scholars and public commentators, have
constructively shaped the course of Labor Law and public policy

Robert A. Gorman
Matthew W. Finkin

\*

# PREFACE

Since the Twelfth Edition appeared in 1996, the question of the role of collective representation, in the labor market has pressed to the fore. Studies of union success, *e.g.* TOM JURAVICH & KATE BRONFENBRENNER, RAVENSWOOD: THE STEELWORKERS' VICTORY AND THE REVIVAL OF AMERICAN LABOR (1999) — and failure, *e.g.* JULIUS GETMAN, THE BETRAYAL OF LOCAL 114: PAPERWORKERS, POLITICS & PERMANENT REPLACEMENTS (1998) — have appeared. An extended and analytically powerful survey of managerial and employee desires and opinions has been produced, RICHARD FREEMAN & JOEL ROGERS, WHAT WORKERS WANT (1999). Legal symposia on the labor law of the future have been held, notably at the Indiana University, Columbia University and the University of Pennsylvania law schools, whose proceedings have now been published. Social scientists have attempted to gauge the nature and pace of change in the world of work. And prescriptions for a better social ordering have been written. *See, e.g.*, STEPHEN HERZENBERG, JOHN ALIC & HOWARD WIAL, NEW RULES FOR A NEW ECONOMY: EMPLOYMENT AND OPPORTUNITY IN POSTINDUSTRIAL AMERICA (1998) and PAUL OSTERMAN, SECURING PROSPERITY (1999). The scholarly ferment reflects the economic and social background against which it resonates: of a greater shift toward market mediated systems to deal with issues that used more broadly to be treated by collective representation in the workplace and the impact of rapidly developing information technology, to name but two.

This Thirteenth Edition updates the law of collective representation generated by the National Labor Relations Board, the courts of appeals and the U.S. Supreme Court. It has deleted obsolescent problems for discussion and included problems (and cases) that are at the forefront of change, especially those dealing with e-mail and the internet. It also builds on the prior edition's expansion of materials in labor history and industrial relations; and, it has refined the discussion concerning the contemporary significance of the Labor Act, drawing upon economics, industrial relations and comparative labor law to pose alternatives to the way the United States will deal with the employment relation in the next decade.

In sum, we believe this edition continues to be both attuned to the "march of events" and "teachable." Putting it together would not have been possible without the cheerful, energetic and painstaking secretarial contribution of Linda Payne of the staff of the University of Illinois College of Law to whom a special debt of gratitude is owed.

MATTHEW W. FINKIN
ROBERT A. GORMAN

June, 2001

\*

# BIBLIOGRAPHY

Although the cases, text and problems in this book, coupled with classroom discussion, ought to be sufficient for study of the course, it is important for a law student to become familiar with the books and other publications in the field of labor law. They may be useful in filling up omissions, clarifying problems, and pursuing matters of special interest. Moreover, knowledge of the leading labor law publications and an ability to use them will be valuable in practicing law. One who has taken a course in Labor Law ought at the least to be familiar not only with the publications of the National Labor Relations Board (in particular its annual reports) but also with at least one of the principal labor law research services: these services are important complements to computer-based research.

## A. General Labor Law Texts

J. Getman, B. Pogrebin, & D. Gregory, Labor Management Relations and the Law (2d ed.1999).

R. Gorman, Basic Text on Labor Law: Unionization and Collective Bargaining (1976).

P. Hardin, ed., The Developing Labor Law (3d ed. 1992), with annual supplements.

M. Malin, Individual Rights Within the Union (1988).

D. Ray, C. Sharpe & R. Strassfeld, Understanding Labor Law (1999).

## B. History of Labor Law

I. Bernstein, The New Deal Collective Bargaining Policy (1950).

M. Derber & E. Young (ed.), Labor and the New Deal (1957).

M. Dubofsky, The State and Labor in Modern America (1994).

F. Frankfurter & N. Greene, The Labor Injunction (1930).

J. Gross, The Making of the National Labor Relations Board: A Study in Economics, Politics, and the Law 1933–1937 (1974); The Reshaping of the National Labor Relations Board: National Labor Policy in Transition 1937–1947 (1981); Broken Promise: The Subversion of U.S. Labor Relations Policy 1947–1994 (1995).

## C. Critical Appraisals of American Labor Law

J. Atleson, Values and Assumptions in American Labor Law (1983).

C. Craver, Can Unions Survive? The Rejuvenation of the American Labor Union (1993).

W. Gould, Agenda for Reform: The Future of Employment Relationships and the Law (1993).

C. Tomlins, The State and the Unions: Labor Relations, Law, and the Organized Labor Movement in America, 1880–1960 (1985).

P. Weiler, Governing the Workplace: The Future of Labor and Employment Law (1990).

## D. Labor Arbitration

F. Elkouri & E. Elkouri, How Arbitration Works (5th ed. 1997).

National Academy of Arbitrators, Proceedings of the Annual Meeting (annual series).

T. St. Antoine (ed.), The Common Law of the Workplace (1998).

## E. Articles

The best writing in the field of labor law is found in articles published in various law reviews. The articles which seem most helpful are cited at pertinent points throughout this volume.

## F. Website

The NLRB's website is: www.nlrb.gov. It makes accessible weekly summaries, press releases, opinions of the General Counsel, and other such material in addition to all Board decisions.

## G. Labor Research Services

Computerized research has come to play a significant, perhaps dominant, role in labor law research. It is, however, still useful to be familiar with the comprehensive and frequently published hardcopy research materials. The two principal labor law services are published by Bureau of National Affairs and Commerce Clearing House. Both services, published weekly, provide current decisions of the courts and of the NLRB, generally prior to their publication in official form or in the reporter system. (Court decisions are in full text; NLRB decisions are generally abstracted, with full text provided for the more important cases.) These decisions, supplied initially in looseleaf form for insertion in binders, are periodically bound up into permanent volumes. Each of the services has a looseleaf volume containing case tables, as well as a detailed subject matter index which leads the user into synopses of cases organized by subject matter. The services also publish (and ultimately bind) current decisions in areas closely allied to federal and state labor relations law, such as arbitration decisions and cases dealing with employment discrimination on the basis of race, religion, sex, national origin, disability and age. In addition, the Bureau of National Affairs (BNA) publishes a looseleaf binder of contract clauses, Collective Bargaining Negotiations and Contracts (2 volumes).

## H. General Books

The average law student would be well advised to do supplementary reading in books which increase one's knowledge of the labor movement and one's understanding of labor economics and industrial relations. There are many books which fill this need, ranging from college textbooks through the good biographies of labor leaders to discussions of public labor policy. The volumes listed below are a few among many of equal merit.

1. *Industrial Relations.*

   C. Kerr, J. Dunlop, Harbison & Myers, Industrialism and Industrial Man (1964); Industrialism and Industrial Man Reconsidered (1975).

   T. Kochan (ed.), Challenges and Choices Facing American Labor (1985).

   T. Kochan, Collective Bargaining and Industrial Relations (2d ed. 1988).

   T. Kochan, H. Katz & R. McKersie, The Transformation of American Industrial Relations (Cornell ILR ed. 1994).

   Various proceedings of the Industrial Relations Research Association

2. *Labor Economics.*

   R. Ehrenberg & R. Smith, Modern Labor Economics (6th ed. 1997).

   D. Hamermesh & A. Rees, The Economics of Work and Pay (5th ed. 1992).

   C. Kerr & P. Staudohar, Labor Economics and Industrial Relations (1994).

   A. Rees, The Economics of Trade Unions (3d ed. 1989).

3. *Labor History.*

   I. Bernstein, A History of the American Worker—The Lean Years: 1920–1933 (1960); Turbulent Years: 1933–1941 (1969); A Caring Society: The New Deal, the Workers, and the Great Depression (1985).

   D. Brody, Workers in Industrial America (1980).

   F. Dulles, Labor in America: A History (4th ed. 1984).

   D. Montgomery, The Fall of the House of Labor (1987); Citizen Worker (1993).

4. *Labor Negotiations.*

   C. Stevens, Strategy and Collective Bargaining Negotiations (1978).

R. Walton & R. McKersie, A Behavioral Theory of Labor Negotiations: An Analysis of a Social Interaction System (1965).

5. *Labor Unions.*

D. Bok & J. Dunlop, Labor and the American Community (1970).

R. Freeman & J. Medoff, What Do Unions Do? (1984).

M. Goldfield, The Decline of Organized Labor in the United States (1987).

B. Hirsch & T. Addison, The Economic Analysis of Unions: New Approaches and Evidence (1986).

L. Mishel & P. Voos (eds.), Unions and Economic Competitiveness (1992).

6. *Comparative Labor Law.*

The *Comparative Labor Law and Policy Journal* (the leading periodical).

R. Blanpain (ed.), The International Encyclopedia for Labour Law and Industrial Relations (multi-volume loose-leaf of national and international entries of various dates).

O. Kahn-Freund, Labor and the Law (Davies & Freedland ed. 1983).

W. Keller (ed.), International Labor and Employment Laws (1997) (with supplementary volumes).

R. Locke, T. Kochan & M. Piore (eds.), Employment Relations in a Changing World Economy (1995).

7. *Sociology of Work.*

Economic Policy Institute's annual, The State of Working America (L. Mishel, J. Bornstein and J. Schmitt, eds.).

National Research Council, The Changing Nature of Work (1999).

# SUMMARY OF CONTENTS

# TABLE OF CONTENTS

# TABLE OF CASES

Principal cases are in bold type. Non-principal cases are in roman type. References are to Pages.

# LABOR LAW

*

# INTRODUCTION

## SCOPE OF THE COURSE

Among the more intricate and vital relationships in our society—along with the relationship of individual to family and of citizen to state—is that of a worker to his or her job. Employment is more than a source of income. One's sense of worth and of accomplishment is shaped largely by one's workplace responsibilities, performance and rewards. It is therefore natural for workers to wish to participate in the shaping of the rules that govern the workplace, or at least to be treated "fairly" under those rules. Historically, many workers seeking to achieve these objectives have turned to unionization and collective bargaining, and as an incident on occasion to work stoppages, picketing and boycotts. It is the reaction of lawmaking institutions to these activities that is the basic stuff of the traditional Labor Law course.

One ought not get the impression that the rules that govern the workplace are set exclusively through "private" dealings between labor and management. Indeed, modern labor laws regulate a host of substantive aspects of the work relationship, quite literally from the cradle (medical leaves and insurance coverage for working mothers, and child labor laws) to the grave (retirement and pension plans, and disability and life insurance). State and federal laws regulate minimum wages, working hours, health and safety, pension funding and benefits, discrimination on the basis of race, sex and age, treatment of the disabled and those injured in industrial accidents, benefits for the unemployed and disabled, employment rights of returning members of the armed forces. The United States Department of Labor, alone, is charged with administering some 180 federal statutes governing the employment relationship. State labor laws are also of great importance; among the most striking common law developments in any field of human activity in recent years in the United States has been the emergence of a right to be protected against "unjust dismissal" in an increasing number of circumstances in many jurisdictions.

This network of comprehensive and interlacing federal and state laws regulating the workplace makes very pointed the question, why is the conventional law school course in Labor Law confined to questions centering about union organization and collective bargaining. Perhaps the answer lies principally in history and in habit. But there are sound reasons which justify focusing our attention upon this subject matter even as an original question.

In the first place, collective bargaining has great significance in the governance of workers in American industry—and that is true even though the proportion of workers who are union members or who work for unionized enterprises has been dwindling in the past three decades. Despite all of the detailed regulations mentioned above, the rules which most vitally affect workers in their daily lives are made in each industrial establishment either by the employer unilaterally or by the negotiation and administration of collective agreements. Although legislation may place "floors" under wages and "ceilings" over hours, and otherwise establish minimum guarantees regarding such matters as workplace discrimination or safety, all of the rules that would give employees benefits and rights beyond those statutory minima are determined by private adjustment. That adjustment has historically been effected through collective bargaining in the most significant components of American industry, and that remains true in large degree today. Collective bargaining agreements also routinely afford workers protections that are altogether outside the range of those provided by legislation. The use of seniority as a principal criterion for promotions and for layoffs and recalls, the grant of holiday and vacation pay and other forms of paid leaves of absence, and the provision for bilateral grievance procedures commonly culminating in impartial arbitration, are all examples. Even in the non-union sector of our economy, it is undeniable that wage rates and other workplace benefits and practices have been patterned after those that have been developed in the unionized sector. In short, collective bargaining is an important element—historically and currently—in achieving improved working conditions and worker participation, superimposed though it is upon a framework of significant substantive legal protections.

A second reason for concentrating on issues relating to unionization and collective bargaining is that those issues raise fundamental questions regarding the proper role of government in regulating economic conflict and private economic power. In regulating the relationship between workers and their employers, what aspects should be determined by governmental pronouncement and what should be left to private adjustment? On those matters left to private adjustment, to what extent should government regulate the kinds of peaceful economic pressures that either party may bring to bear upon the other? On those matters meant for governmental regulation, how much should be addressed by detailed legislation—and how much should be left to the administrative agency acting through elucidating regulations and decisions? What role should the courts play? What is the proper sphere of operation of state law in this field, in which there is comprehensive federal legislation and administration?

A third and related reason for the traditional contours of the Labor Law course is that the course, somewhat distinctively, focuses on the rights of groups rather than of individuals. That is obviously so when attention is given to such group devices as strikes, picketing and boycotts in aid of organizing or bargaining. In collective bargaining too, there is the important question of the extent to which the union as the collective representative is properly empowered to exclude access to the employer by individual workers, and is properly empowered to trade off individual benefits for the good of the group. In most associational settings—the church, a political party, a professional organization or social club—the individual can withdraw from the group if he or she would wish to chart a separate, self-interested course. To what extent is that true in the context of bargaining and the related resort to work stoppages and the like, when there is a union which acts as collective representative?

Fourth, the study of unionization and collective bargaining provides an opportunity to consider the procedures, and the strengths and weaknesses, of different kinds of dispute-resolution mechanisms. The normal law school course focuses upon the public judicial system as the preeminent mechanism for resolving conflicts between private parties. Against that context, it may be somewhat strange to deal with a body of law which had its source in a distrust of the judiciary, judges being perceived as both biased against the working class and institutionally incapable of managing disputes between labor and management. In the Labor Law course, one can study the National Labor Relations Board, can compare the Board's functions with those of a judge and jury, and can assess the two different modes of operation which can be utilized by an administrative agency—adjudication and rulemaking. One can also study the contractual grievance procedure—culminating in grievance arbitration—as an alternative, privately created mechanism for resolving labor-management disputes; and one can then appraise the relationship between the arbitration process and the judicial process, and between the arbitrator and the NLRB.

Fifth, although it may be that the traditional Labor Law course cannot lay exclusive claim to this virtue, it does provide a most fertile opportunity to examine issues relating to the responsible practice of the law. It provides any number of opportunities to consider matters of drafting (of statutes and of contracts) and to explore strategic issues surrounding the bargaining process. It also, in a field that is often emotionally charged, invites the consideration of the attorney's ethical responsibilities to the client and to the public interest.

Needless to say, it is difficult to keep these larger themes of Labor Law constantly before the class; the specific substantive problems are much too fascinating. But the possibility is always present, and the thoughtful teacher and student will surely be moved to explore these themes as the course progresses.

# PART ONE

# THE EVOLUTION OF LABOR RELATIONS LAWS

## I. "THE LABOR PROBLEM" AND THE LAW

In the late 1700s, the American Company, an iron "manufactory" in Pennsylvania, imported a group of German iron workers. Peter Hasenclever, the resident manager, explained one of his ensuing difficulties:

> [T]hey pretended to have their wages raised, which I refused. They made bad work; I complained, and reprimanded them; they told me they could not make better work at such low wages; and, if they did not please me, I might dismiss them. I was, therefore, obliged to submit, for it had cost me a prodigious expense to transport them from Germany; and, had I dismissed them, I must have lost these disbursements, and could get no good workmen in their stead.

*Quoted in* P. Paskoff, Industrial Evolution: Organization, Structure, and Growth of the Pennsylvania Iron Industry, 1750–1860, 15 (1983).

Until roughly a century before this episode, the organization of work was not primarily based upon freely-bargained employment relationships: it was, rather, often predicated upon legal systems in which one owned the labor of another, and upon an economic system under which individual artisans were largely sellers not of services but of goods. The employment relationship was perceived in English law as an aspect of domestic relations—of "master and servant"—growing out of the servant's membership in the master's household, in which many of the respective obligations of the parties were not the product of a bargained-for exchange in a labor market, but were fixed by law. In sum, the idea that goods and services would be produced predominantly by persons working under a regime of individual contracts of employment—of "free" or "wage labor" as it was called in the mid-nineteenth century—was an historically novel development. See generally E. Phelps Brown, The Economics of Labor 10 (1962).

4

Hasenclever's confrontation illuminates one aspect of the situation of those engaged for wages upon another's work; that is, the inevitable conflicts that emerge, for example, over what a fair wage or a fair day's work is. To the proponents of the "Scientific Management" movement at the dawn of the twentieth century, such conflict could be obviated by discovery of the "one right way" to perform a task, and of exactly the right amount of work that would maximize both the employer's profits and the employee's income without undue fatigue, in which "scientific" determination the employees in the workplace would have nothing whatsoever to say. But as the economist Phelps Brown has pointed out, disputes over wages and work pace are often manifestations of a deeper underlying conflict, to which, it might be added, the apostles of Scientific Management were indifferent, if not hostile:

> There are work places where the prescription of tasks is undertaken and accepted not as the assertion of authority over subordinates but as part of the organization of a team with whose purposes the individual worker identifies himself. There are temperaments to which directions, rules, and discipline are not irksome: rather they meet a need and provide reassurance. But the record of unrest, protest, and proposed reforms leaves no doubt that many men have felt and still do feel it irksome to be compelled, if they are to get a living, to put themselves under the orders of an employer. His authority appears arbitrary, and a way of exploiting the power that is his by reason of his relative wealth and his control of the access to livelihood. The parties once accepted in English terminology as master and servant have been renamed, in merely functional terms that imply no subordination, employer and employed; but the employed in practice may still speak of the employer as the boss. The issue is one not of amenity, or pay, but of power.

E. Phelps Brown, The Economics of Labor 35–36 (1962).

Hasenclever's confrontation illustrates as well one of several means of resolving such conflict, that is, collective employee action vis-a-vis the employer. (In ancient Egypt, according to Reinhardt Bendix, there is documentary evidence that the slaves building the pyramids protested even under the whip by murmuring in unison.) This is not, however, the sole means by which employees could deal with such potential conflict; nor was the process—one of employer judgment based upon market constraints, unmediated by resort to law—foreordained. Arguably, as Phelps Brown points out, employees could be persuaded simply to accept the relationship as just and the terms and conditions established unilaterally by the employer as fair; or, they could express individual dissent simply by quitting—assuming that the law or their individual undertakings permitted that prerogative. Alternatively, the law—in lieu of allowing the unregulated play of organized collective protest and market forces—could itself establish the terms and conditions of employment (indeed, in a Colonial America plagued by chronic shortages of skilled labor, municipalities often legislated maximum wage rates); or, the law could develop regimes either to prohibit or to protect the kind of collective protest that Hasenclever's crew had made. All of these at one time or another have been reflected in the American experience.

————

In the Federal period, the labor market was a mixture of free and unfree labor, that is, in the latter instance, slaves, apprentices, and a residuum of indentured servants. Manufacture, with the prominent exception of early textile manufacture, was predominantly artisanal: shoes, hats, barrels, and furniture tended to be produced in relatively small workshops by a few apprentices and a journeyman or two working under the supervision of a master craftsman who purchased the raw materials and sold the finished product. To the journeymen of the time, the period of service was expected to be a relatively brief interlude until they would establish themselves in turn as masters; and in the early Federal period such upward mobility was often experienced.

Despite its personal intimacy, the work setting of the time was not without conflict. Dissatisfied apprentices frequently ran away. Journeymen, imbued with pride in and the independence of their craft, demanded—and secured—the right largely to set their own work schedules, often to come and go as they pleased, to control the pace of production, even to drink on the job. "Thurlow Weed, recalling his years as a journeyman printer in New York, remembered that at eleven every morning in the print shop the journeymen would unvariably pause to 'jeff' for beer, often mortgaging 'a large share of their weekly earnings to the local grocery.'" H. Rock, Artisans of the New Republic 296 (1984). In 1817, a group of shipyard workers quit when the owner refused to continue their "grog privileges." Id.

The claim of artisanal independence, enforced by quitting, individually or in groups, rested partly on the ideal of "manhood" prevalent at the time—of the moral sanctity of defending one's rights—and partly on the republican values that had fueled the Revolution. Consequently, the rise of the factory system was thought by many to challenge those values:

> From the beginning, democratic opinion was suspicious of the concentrations of wealth and power private industry required and created. Men and women who had recently fought for liberty from the king could look at the new industrial capitalist and find a "purse proud aristocrat," a "Tory in Disguise." Americans were wedded to the self-sustaining family farm as the norm of social and economic organization and the locus of public virtue. Such a people had an understandably difficult time accommodating the system of production, labor, and rewards that came with the factory. Industrial production radically altered the accustomed link between work and value—between the quantity of work invested and the economic value realized and between the quality of work done and the value of self-esteem. In this new "factory system," initiative,

autonomy, and skill began to be replaced by passive attention, external discipline, and a predetermined, uniform product.

The Philosophy of Manufacturers: Early Debates Over Industrialization in the United States xxii–xxiii (M. Folsom & S. Lubar eds.)(1982)(reference omitted). In early textile manufacture—the proto-typical factory—spontaneous strikes, or "turnouts," were not uncommon, most often in response to a wage reduction or in protest of working conditions. Joseph Ripka, testifying before the Pennsylvania Senate's investigation of working conditions and a strike that had occurred in his mill in 1836, was fast to impute the labor strife as the work of alien ideology and outside agitation—recurrent managerial themes in American labor history:

> If any evil exists in the factory system, it is the principles of the Trades' Union, which has been introduced amongst the laboring classes in general; it has been imparted to this country by English and Irish men within a few years, and has the tendency to destroy the good feeling which has, heretofore, existed between the employer and the workman in this country, and the leaders are men, either of low character or designing politicians. To show that the principle is a bad one, the leaders are always trying to keep the working people in an excitement, to have them always ready for a turn-out, they lay contribution on the working classes, and expend the money amongst themselves, by going about from place to place to make speeches, and encourage them to turn out. When labor is plenty, the workingmen will get good wages and find plenty employment without the aid of the Trades' Union, and in hard times, the Trades' Union cannot keep up wages or find employment for the working classes.

*Quoted in* A. Wallace, Rockdale: The Growth of an American Village in the Early Industrial Revolution 358–359 (1972).

One of the sources of conflict in artisanal manufacture concerned the supply of labor, especially the number of apprentices a master could take on. To masters, apprentices could be a cheap source of labor, especially on "slop work" (production for wholesale rather than made-to-order or "bespoke work") that did not require a high degree of craftsmanship. (And in some trades, masters shirked their responsibilities to teach apprentices the "mysteries" of the craft, so to convert what was supposed to be a period of training into a form of straightforward child labor, as it was in textile manufacture.) To journeymen, the consequence was the prospect of future competition with an increasing supply of labor. Another conflict was over the price the journeymen were to be paid for finished goods, essentially a piece-rate wage.

In a number of cities in the early Federal period the journeymen formed local "trade unions" to attempt to limit the number of apprentices and to regulate the piece price. The manner in which that control was to be achieved was an outgrowth of the traditional claim the skilled craftsmen had asserted: an insistence that the trade union, not the employer, had the prerogative to make the rules, and that the employer's obligation was to hire only union members who were accordingly bound by those rules. In 1836, the bookbinders of Philadelphia returned a price list (piece rates) submitted to the union by the masters with the blanket assertion of their " 'inalienable rights: to affix a price on the only property we have to dispose of: our labor.' " B. Lurie, Artisans Into Workers: Labor in Nineteenth Century America 64 (1989).

The sporadic legal response to such union efforts was to apply the law of criminal conspiracy, borrowed from England, making it an offense to combine to effect an unlawful end or to effect a lawful end by unlawful means. Thus, New York's journeymen shoemakers were convicted in 1810 of forming an association that bound its members by its rules, forbade them to work with non-members, bound them to work only for union-adopted scale, and forbade masters to have more than two apprentices, and for effecting the scheme "by means of what they called a *strike against the shop* ... the offending member ... then termed a *scab*, and wherever he was employed no others of the society were allowed to work." People v. Melvin, 2 Wheeler Crim.Cas. 262, 268 (1810)(italics in original). It was held no defense that the journeymen's efforts were in response to an agreement by the masters to lower the wage, or that the masters were financing the prosecution. (The masters had instigated the action, in part, because although there were as many non-union journeymen as union members, the latter were "all the best workmen" in the city.) So, too, did the court deny the admission of evidence offered by the journeymen that the wages they contended for were reasonable or the profits of the masters excessive. The workers, the court opined, could combine to raise their own wages and refuse to work until their demands were met, but "the means they used [that is, to strike the shop to prevent the hiring of non-union men who would work below union scale] were of a nature too arbitrary or coercive, and which went to deprive their fellow citizens of rights as precious as any they contended for." Id. at 282.

Criminal prosecution fell into disuse by mid-century, partly due to the contrary holding in Commonwealth v. Hunt, 45 Mass. (4 Metc.) 111 (1842), and partly because of public opinion. It is difficult in any event to assess the impact the application of criminal conspiracy law had upon the early trade unions. After the Union Society of Journeymen Cordwainers was successfully prosecuted in Baltimore in August of 1810, resulting in its dissolution, the journeymen printers commenced a strike the very next month; and, in November of that same year, the newly created Union Philanthropic Society of Journeymen Cordwainers was formed and demanded a price increase. C. Steffen, The Mechanics of Baltimore 223–225 (1984).

But other events were unfolding to undermine the independence of the skilled crafts. First, the process of division of labor, abetted by the substitution of power-driven machinery for hand labor, eroded the need for craft skills.

As late as the 1840s the typical New England shoe shop was a 10′ x 10′ cottage housing a handful of skilled workers who made shoes by time-honored hand methods according to their personal, often eccentric, notions of size and fit.... By the 1870s, the shoemaking cottages were empty, and the men who had once been shoemakers now found themselves factory machine operators: beaters, binders, bottomers, buffers, burnishers, channellers, crimpers, cutters, dressers, edge setters, and so on through some thirty or forty subdivided occupations.

D. Rogers, The Work Ethic In Industrial America 1850–1920, 23 (1978). One consequence was a dramatic increase in productivity. For example, factory workers at the end of the century produced nine times as many pairs of shoes per hour as hand craftsmen. But, "it was the machine that stitched; the worker had become a condition of the machine's activity." R. Thomson, The Path to Mechanized Shoe Production in the United States 226 (1989).

The transition to a system of factory production by semi-skilled machine operators varied widely from product to product, and some trades proved resistant to the transition. Paper making, for example, became mechanized, but remained highly skilled, as did the work of machinists in factories under the "American" or "Armory" system of production. While the pace varied, however, the trend was inexorable.

A second consequence of the development of the factory system was the growth in the scale of manufacturing enterprises:

In 1880 there were approximately 2,700,000 wage earners in manufacturing; by 1900 there were 4,500,000; and by 1920, 8,400,-000. Some of these people worked in small establishments and "sweatshops," but the majority found employment in factories and to a growing degree, in factories with more than 500 employees. During the last third of the nineteenth century the "average" plant in 11 of 16 major industries more than doubled in size. In 1870 there were only a handful of large factories, concentrated in textiles. The McCormick plant in Chicago, supposedly one of the nation's largest, had 400–500 names on its payroll. By 1900, however, there were 1,063 factories with 500–1,000 workers and 443 with more than 1,000 wage earners.

D. Nelson, Managers and Workers: Origins of the Factory System in the United States 1880–1920, 4 (1975).

Gone was the relative intimacy of the antebellum shop. The workforce no longer dealt on a personal basis—of "manliness" and rough equality—with an owner-craftsman, but reported to a foreman (or, in some instances, an internal contractor) who could and did hire and fire at will, who could set each worker's piecework rate on an estimate of what he had to pay to get maximum production, and who got that production by threats, intimidation, and summary discharge. " 'Bill,' " said an assistant superintendent to a foreman after the turn of the century, " 'has anyone been fired from this shop today?' 'No,' the foreman meekly replied. 'Well, then, fire a couple of 'em!' barked the assistant superintendent, in a voice that carried. 'It'll put the fear of God in their hearts.' " *Quoted in* S. Jacoby, Employing Bureaucracy: Managers, Unions, and the Transformation of Work in American Industry, 1900–1945, 21 (1985).

A third development was a change in the composition of the working force. Managerial, supervisory, and highly skilled craft work tended to remain native-born, male, and Protestant. But employers encouraged and capitalized upon massive immigration. The performance of unskilled and semi-skilled work, the work of laborers and machine operators trained to a single part of the production process, was very largely immigrant, highly sex-segregated, and in the more menial jobs, black. In 1880, when 13% of the population as a whole was classified as foreign-born, 42% of those engaged in manufacturing and extractive work were first or second generation immigrants. In addition, over a million employees in the workforce of 1880 were domestic servants—overwhelmingly female and either immigrant or black.

Finally, the organization of work under the factory system was accompanied by the employer's plenary exercise of its prerogative unilaterally to make and enforce rules—rules governing tardiness (or absence), production, deportment, and discipline. Fines were imposed for substandard or defective work. Wages were forfeited by failure to give timely notice of quitting. Workers were regulated in when they could take work breaks; in whether they could get a drink of water; they might be forbidden even to talk to one another on the job. See generally D. Montgomery, The Fall of the House of Labor (1987).

The legal prerogative of employers to demand such obedience drew upon two very different sources. First was the claim of contract: that by accepting employment with notice of the rules the employee had given assent and so was bound. The second rested upon the antecedent law of master and servant, which viewed the servant as a dependent, akin to a child, who owed the master a duty of obedience and of respectful subservience. When, for example, a railroad superintendent forbade employees to shop at a particular store, on pain of discharge, the Supreme Court of Tennessee upheld the employer's prerogative, reasoning in part:

> May I not refuse to trade with any one? May I not forbid my family to trade with any one? May I not dismiss my domestic servant for dealing, or even visiting, where I forbid? And if my domestic, why not my farm-hand, or my mechanic, or teamster? And, if one of them, then why not all four? And, if all four, why not a hundred or a thousand of them? The principle is not changed or affected by the number.

Payne v. Western & Atl. Rr. Co., 81 Tenn. 507, 518 (1884). This drew a sharp dissent by two members of the Court:

> It is argued that a man ought to have the right to say where his employees shall trade. I do not recognize any such right. A

father may well control his family in this, but an employer ought to have no such right conceded to him....

\* \* \*

>    In view of the immense development and large aggregations of capital in this favored country—a capital to be developed and aggregated within the life of the present generation more than a hundred fold—giving the command of immense numbers of employees, by such means as we have before us in this case, it is the demand of a sound public policy, for the future more especially, as well as now, that the use of this power should be restrained within legitimate boundaries.

Id. at 542–43. The dissenters saw in the majority's view a threat to "sound public policy", harkening back to the debate over the introduction of "manufactories" a half century earlier and anticipating elements in the debate over labor legislation a half century later:

>    The principle of the majority opinion will justify employers, at any rate allow them to require employees to trade where they may demand, to vote as they may require, or do anything not strictly criminal that [the] employer may dictate, or feel the wrath of [the] employer by dismissal from service. Employment is the means of sustaining life to himself and family to the employee, and so he is morally though not legally compelled to submit. Capital may thus not only find its own legitimate employment, but may control the employment of others to an extent that in time may sap the foundations of our free institutions.

Id. at 543–44. Eventually the employer's ability to set terms and conditions of employment, to hire and fire "at-will" free of legal interference even from the reach of labor protective legislation, was elevated to a constitutional right of "freedom of contract." See *e.g.,* Lochner v. New York, 198 U.S. 45, 25 S.Ct. 539, 49 L.Ed. 937 (1905)(striking down a maximum work hour law for bakers), Adair v. United States, 208 U.S. 161, 28 S.Ct. 277, 52 L.Ed. 436 (1908)(striking down federal law prohibiting the "yellow-dog" contract), Coppage v. Kansas, 236 U.S. 1, 35 S.Ct. 240, 59 L.Ed. 441 (1915)(striking down a similar state law).

---

## II.  THE RISE OF THE LABOR MOVEMENT[a]

The history of the work relationship is paralleled by the history of the organized labor movement. In the 1830s city central "trades unions,"

---

**a.** Convenient histories of the labor movement are found in Perlman, History of Trade Unionism in the United States (1922); Perlman and Taft, History of Labor in the United States, 1896–1932 (1935); Millis and Montgomery, Organized Labor ch. I–V, XI– XII (1945); F.R. Dulles and M. Dubofsky, Labor in America: a History (4th ed. 1984); A. Blum, A History of the American Labor Movement (1972); G. Hildebrand, American Unionism: An Historical and Analytical Survey (1979); D. Montgomery, The Fall of the

federations of local journeymen's unions, began to be formed in a number of cities. The first federation of city centrals, the National Trades Union, was founded in 1834, the main objective of which was the achievement of the ten-hour day. It did not survive the depression (or "panic") of 1837.

The first national craft unions were founded in the 1850s—printers, machinists, molders, and locomotive engineers. Many of these were ushered into being in response to the exponential growth in rail transportation, making the product of one city competitive with the product of another and—to the extent wages comprised a significant part of product cost—making wage competition an element of price competition on a regional or even national basis. At the end of the 1860s more than thirty such national craft unions were in existence with a total membership of perhaps 300,000. The National Labor Union, a loose federation of national unions, city centrals, and local unions, was formed in 1866 to fight for the eight hour day; it lasted about six years. Around 1869, the Knights of Labor was founded:

> The quintessential expression of the labor movement in the Gilded Age was the Noble and Holy Order of the Knights of Labor, the first mass organization of the American working class. Launched as one of several secret societies among Philadelphia artisans in the late 1860s, the Knights grew in spurts by the accretion of miners (1874–79) and skilled urban tradesmen (1879–85). While the movement formally concentrated on moral and political education, cooperative enterprise, and land settlement, members found it a convenient vehicle for trade union action, particularly in the auspicious economic climate following the depression of the 1870s. Beginning in 1883, local skirmishes escalated into highly publicized confrontations with railroad financier Jay Gould, a national symbol of new corporate power. Strikes by Knights of Labor telegraphers and railroad shopmen touched off an unprecedented wave of strikes and boycotts that carried on into the renewed depression in 1884–85 and spread to thousands of previously unorganized semiskilled and unskilled laborers, both urban and rural. The Southwest Strike on Gould's Missouri and Texas–Pacific railroad lines together with massive urban eight-hour campaigns in 1886 swelled a tide of unrest that has become known as the "Great Upheaval." The turbulence aided the efforts of organized labor, and the Knights exploded in size, reaching more than three-quarters of a million members.

L. Fink, Workingmen's Democracy: The Knights of Labor and American Politics xii–xiii (1983).

By the end of the decade, however, the Knights were in steep decline, due in part to a "titanic" lack of leadership (in Professor Fink's phrase),

House of Labor: the Workplace, the State,    (1987).
and American Labor Activism, 1865–1925

internal divisions (perhaps inevitable in an organization committed to racial, sexual, and ethnic equality), high membership turnover, stiffened employer resistance, and disastrous union losses. In its stead rose the American Federation of Labor, founded in 1886 and presided over (save for one year) until his death in 1924 by Samuel Gompers.

The dominant characteristics of the new American Federation of Labor were the reverse of the Knights'. Where the Knights was a humanitarian, reformist movement, the AFL developed what Selig Perlman termed "a philosophy of pure wage consciousness" in order to signify "a labor movement reduced to an opportunistic basis, accepting the existence of capitalism and having for its object the enlarging of the bargaining power of the wage earner in the sale of his labor."

Where the Knights had looked ultimately to political action, the AFL unions relied on economic power. This is not to imply that the AFL did not support social and labor legislation; it did so repeatedly, but it concentrated on short-run objectives, steered clear of political entanglements and refused to allow its energies to be diverted from the task of improving the immediate economic position of its members.

This effort to improve the position of the wage earner "here and now", within the existing economic system, led the AFL unions under Gompers' leadership to put chief reliance on collective bargaining. They realized that the individual employee was usually helpless in dealing with his employer and they sought to increase the workers' bargaining power by substituting collective strength for individual weakness.

After union recognition, the typical AFL collective agreement treated wages, hours and job security as most important. The prevailing conception seems to have been one of a bargain and sale of labor, and it was not until the 1930's when union organization spread into the mass production industries that a philosophy of collective bargaining developed which speaks of "industrial democracy" and sees in the collective agreement and grievance procedures the substantive and procedural rules for the government of industrial workers.

In 1886 the principle of craft organization fitted comfortably into the new philosophy of business unionism. If the bargaining power of the workers was to be increased by substituting collective strength for individual weakness, it was imperative to organize into one group all the workers in the same occupation; they were the ones, and the only ones, who would destroy labor standards by underbidding each other. In addition, by establishing "job ownership" or "job control", the organized workers could achieve a fair degree of security, which must have appealed to many of them not only as a form of insurance against unemployment during hard times but also as a defense against the threatening competition of unskilled labor.

In the AFL philosophy craft autonomy was closely allied to the principle of craft organization. In 1886 and for years thereafter the chief problem of American unionism seemed to be to stay organized. Trade union leaders concluded that the internal solidarity of the craft group should not be risked by the loss of its identity in larger units—the industry, the AFL, the world labor movement—where solidarity would grow less as the size of the unit increased. Nor was a close knit organization required. A national organization of the whole trade union movement was useful chiefly to formulate broad policies, to unite the crafts in spreading organization into new fields, and to act as spokesman, especially on political issues affecting labor. In securing immediate economic objectives experience seemed to show that reliance should be placed on the independent action of the craft unions which had their own solidarity and knew their own needs.

The problem of staying organized also gave rise to the ruthless opposition to dual unionism which has played so important a role in American trade union history. The concurrent existence of the Knights and the trade unions, both in the same field, had resulted in dual authority and divided loyalty, which sapped the trade unions' strength. Thus the AFL became devoted to the principle that in each recognized field of activity there should be but one union, chartered by the AFL, which would have exclusive jurisdiction.

The organizational structure of the American Federation of Labor paralleled its philosophy. As the name implied, it was a federation of trade unions. The dominant units were autonomous International Unions which were "affiliated" with the American Federation of Labor. Under each International were the local unions it had chartered. It was in the locals that individual workers held their membership.

With this philosophy and internal structure, the trade union movement experienced a period of solid, and sometimes spectacular, growth. For ten years after it was founded in 1886, the AFL's membership remained virtually constant. This was a truly remarkable success, for a depression occurred in 1893, and in every previous depression, as Gompers noted in 1899, the trade unions had been "literally mowed down and swept out of existence. Here for the first time the unions manifested their stability and permanence." (American Federation of Labor, Convention Proceedings, 1899, quoted in Perlman, History of Trade Unionism in the United States (1922), 135–136.) In 1897 AFL entered a period of rapid growth. Between 1897 and 1900 membership rose from something less than 275,000 to 548,000. By 1903 the number of members was 1,465,000, five and one half times the membership only a decade before. AFL membership then remained fairly constant until 1910 when it again began to rise. By 1914 there were more than 2,000,000 AFL members.

The increase in membership was concentrated in the skilled trades and a few industries. More than half was attributable to the phenomenal growth of unions among coal miners, railroad workers and building trades employees. The great mass of semi-skilled and unskilled workers remained unorganized. Yet despite this limitation, union membership in 1914 was perhaps nine times greater than in 1869. The post-Civil War era was marked—in Charles A. Beard's phrase—by the "Triumph of Business

Enterprise." But the years are no less significant for the rise of a permanent labor movement.

The AFL was not the only significant labor union during the first two decades of the twentieth century. The Industrial Workers of the World (IWW), popularly known as the Wobblies, presented a major alternative for American workers. See D. Montgomery, Workers' Control in America (1980) (ch. 4); P. Foner, The Industrial Workers of the World, 1905–1917 (Vol. 4 of his History of the Labor Movement in the United States)(1965); P. Brissenden, the IWW: A Study of American Syndicalism (1919). Founded in 1905, the IWW rejected the business unionism and craft organization of the AFL. It refused to limit union goals to improving the condition of workers within a capitalist economy. Drawing upon the European syndicalist tradition, the IWW advocated the abolition of capitalism and the modern political state through the direct action of workers, who would ultimately govern society. Scorning the AFL's reliance on collective negotiations, written agreements, and trade autonomy, the IWW believed in organization from the bottom up. Beginning with unskilled workers, the IWW eventually hoped to create "one big union" of labor solidarity. Its tactics of direct action were dramatic and intensive. The IWW typically responded to labor disputes by organizing highly visible strikes, accompanied by massive picketing and parades. Given their ideological and tactical differences, it is not surprising that the IWW and the AFL were bitter rivals.

The IWW was not a large formal organization. Its membership probably never exceeded more than 25,000. Yet its influence extended far beyond its members. A congressional Commission on Industrial Relations concluded that the "spirit and vocabulary" of the IWW "permeates to a large extent enormous masses of workers," particularly the unskilled. The IWW was most successful among the timber and migratory agricultural workers of the West and the mill workers of the East, groups the AFL did not even attempt to organize.

Despite its influence and visibility in the years preceding World War One, the IWW essentially collapsed during and after the War. The IWW opposed American intervention in World War One, claiming that the war was essentially a product of the capitalist militarism that exploited workers in all countries. These views unleashed vigorous suppression of the IWW by the government. Yet most historians of the IWW believe that it would not have survived anyway. They cite the preference of its leaders for direct action over the more routine work of organization and collective bargaining, its related financial weaknesses, severe internecine feuds, and its hostility toward skilled workers.

The rise of the Knights of Labor, and later of the American Federation of Labor, accompanied by strikes and, in many cases, considerable violence—sometimes triggered and often exacerbated by the use of paramilitary and military force at the behest of employers—brought to the fore widespread debate about "the Labor Question." The idea of wage labor as a brief interlude on the way to economic independence as an autonomous artisan-entrepreneur had been forcefully rebutted by the rise of the factory and of a permanent working class. To some, the very existence of such a class, largely immigrant and thought especially prone to violence and revolutionary tendencies, was a potential threat to the Republic. (Note the construction and architecture of the many Armories of the period that dot American cities.)

Some employers instituted "welfare" plans—health care, recreational facilities, even bonuses or profit sharing—to Americanize and "uplift" their working forces, to reduce labor turnover, to tie the workforce more closely to the firm (psychologically as well as economically), and to keep unions out. *See generally* S. Brandes, American Welfare Capitalism, 1880–1940 (1976); *see, e.g.*, G. Zahavi, Workers, Managers , and Welfare Capitalism (1988). Others experimented with company-sponsored systems of employee representation and works councils. Other curatives were debated from workers' cooperatives to Socialist programs of worker ownership of the means of production. The need for any such reform, however, was strongly resisted by employers who insisted upon "open"—that is, nonunion—shops and the prerogatives of employers. As the industrialist Henry Sage wrote in 1886:

> The remedy for present evils is not in combinations to force from capital already earned, and possessed by somebody, an unjust demand for more wages—that is the freebooter's method; not by cooperative partnerships, not by schemes of social reformers, who assume that they can manage the affairs of all mankind with more wisdom than they have yet acquired, each acting for himself under the pressure of his own interests. The world is not ready yet to accept or even to try the methods of these self-appointed reformers. The remedy is in the moral elevation of men to the point where they are willing to do justly, to perform their contracts, to be true to all their obligations; to be industrious, prudent, saving; to practice self-denial when need be while laying foundations for future wealth and comfort; and to be contented and manly in the sphere wherein God has placed them. These qualities in the laborer, and on the part of the employer such breadth of justice, wisdom, and kindness as we may reasonably expect, will best serve to build up the great industrial interests of this country, and will always insure the rights of both by wise and peaceable methods. Until this moral condition is reached, there is but one other remedy by which turbulence and anarchy, such as now exist in portions of our country, can be suppressed. That is in these three words—*"Enforce the laws!"*

*Quoted in* M. Derber, The American Idea of Industrial Democracy 1865–1965, n. 1 at 60 (1970)(italics in original). Sage's declaration places in issue what the law ought to be.

# III. JUDICIAL INTERVENTION[a]

## A. THE LABOR INJUNCTION IN PRIVATE DISPUTES

Scholars have traced the roots of the basic common law of strikes and picketing far back into the 18th century. The earliest reported American labor case was tried in 1806 when the Philadelphia cordewainers (shoemakers) were indicted for striking for higher wages. Recorder Levy charged the jury that "a combination of workmen to raise their wages may be considered from a two-fold point of view; one is to benefit themselves, the other to injure those who do not join their society. The rule of law condemns both." The Philadelphia Cordwainers' Case, 3 Commons & Gilmore, Doc. Hist.Am.Soc. 59–248. Later, criminal prosecutions fell into disuse partly as the result of the adverse decision in *Commonwealth v. Hunt,* 45 Mass. (4 Metc.) 111 (1842), and partly because of public opinion. On the civil side, however, the volume of labor litigation sharply increased, and although it is impossible to reconstruct the legal atmosphere of the post Civil War period, it seems fair to say that when the labor disputes engendered by the conflict over union organization were taken to the courts, the judges were substantially free, despite the scattered precedents, to create new law appropriate to the new occasion, guided only by the vague "principles" which emerged from rulings upon more familiar situations.

## Vegelahn v. Guntner

167 Mass. 92, 44 N.E. 1077 (1896).

[After a preliminary hearing upon the bill of complaint an injunction issued *pendente lite* restraining the respondents "from interfering with the plaintiff's business by patrolling the sidewalk or street in front or in the vicinity of the premises occupied by him, for the purpose of preventing any person or persons who now are or may hereafter be in his employment, or desirous of entering the same, from entering it, or continuing in it; or by obstructing or interfering with such persons, or any others, in entering or

**a.** See e.g., Sayre, Criminal Conspiracy, 35 Harv.L.Rev. 393 (1922); Landis, Cases on Labor Law (1st ed.), 1–37. Examples of more recent historical scholarship are Holt, Labour Conspiracy Cases in the United States, 1805–1842: Bias and Legitimation in Common Law Adjudication, 22 Osgoode Hall L.J. 591 (1984); Note, Tortious Interference with Contractual Relations in the Nineteenth Century: The Transformation of Property, Contract and Tort, 93 Harv.L.Rev. 1510 (1980); C. Tomlins, Law, Labor, and Ideology in the Early American Republic Pt. 2 (1993). The common law of strikes and picketing was summarized in 4 Restatement, Torts, ch. 38. The summary is far more favorable to the cause of organized labor than the bulk of court decisions.

leaving the plaintiff's said premises; or by intimidating, by threats or otherwise, any person or persons who now are or may hereafter be in the employment of the plaintiff, or desirous of entering the same, from entering it, or continuing in it; or by any scheme or conspiracy among themselves or with others, organized for the purpose of annoying, hindering, interfering with, or preventing any person or persons who now are or may hereafter be in the employment of the plaintiff, or desirous of entering it, or from continuing therein.''']

■ The hearing on the merits was before HOLMES, J., who reported the case for the consideration of the full court, as follows:

"The facts admitted or proved are that, following upon a strike of the plaintiff's workmen, the defendants have conspired to prevent the plaintiff from getting workmen, and thereby to prevent him from carrying on his business unless and until he will adopt a schedule of prices which has been exhibited to him, and for the purpose of compelling him to accede to that schedule, but for no other purpose. If he adopts that schedule he will not be interfered with further. The means adopted for preventing the plaintiff from getting workmen are, (1) in the first place, persuasion and social pressure. And these means are sufficient to affect the plaintiff disadvantageously, although it does not appear, if that be material, that they are sufficient to crush him. I ruled that the employment of these means for the said purpose was lawful, and for that reason refused an injunction against the employment of them. If the ruling was wrong, I find that an injunction ought to be granted.

"(2) I find also, that, as a further means for accomplishing the desired end, threats of personal injury or unlawful harm were conveyed to persons seeking employment or employed, although no actual violence was used beyond a technical battery, and although the threats were a good deal disguised, and express words were avoided. It appeared to me that there was danger of similar acts in the future. I ruled that conduct of this kind should be enjoined.

"The defendants established a patrol of two men in front of the plaintiff's factory, as one of the instrumentalities of their plan. The patrol was changed every hour, and continued from half-past six in the morning until half-past five in the afternoon, on one of the busy streets of Boston. The number of men was greater at times, and at times showed some little inclination to stop the plaintiff's door, which was not serious, but seemed to me proper to be enjoined. The patrol proper at times went further than simple advice, not obtruded beyond the point where the other person was willing to listen, and conduct of that sort is covered by (2) above, but its main purpose was in aid of the plan held lawful in (1) above. I was satisfied that there was probability of the patrol being continued if not enjoined. I ruled that the patrol, so far as it confined itself to persuasion and giving notice of the strike, was not unlawful, and limited the injunction accordingly.

"There was some evidence of persuasion to break existing contracts. I ruled that this was unlawful, and should be enjoined. * * * "

[The final decree was as follows: " * * * that the defendants, and each and every [sic] of them, their agents and servants, be restrained and enjoined from interfering with the plaintiff's business by obstructing or physically interfering with any persons in entering or leaving the plaintiff's premises * * * or by intimidating, by threats, express or implied, of violence or physical harm to body or property, any person or persons who now are or hereafter may be in the employment of the plaintiff, or desirous of entering the same, from entering or continuing in it, or by in any way hindering, interfering with, or preventing any person or persons who now are in the employment of the plaintiff from continuing therein, so long as they may be bound so to do by lawful contract."]

■ Allen, J. * * * The patrol was maintained as one of the means of carrying out the defendants' plan, and it was used in combination with social pressure, threats of personal injury or unlawful harm and persuasion to break existing contracts. It was thus one means of intimidation, indirectly to the plaintiff, and directly to persons actually employed, or seeking to be employed, by the plaintiff, and of rendering such employment unpleasant or intolerable to such persons. Such an act is an unlawful interference with the rights both of employer and of employed. An employer has a right to engage all persons who are willing to work for him, at such prices as may be mutually agreed upon, and persons employed or seeking employment have a corresponding right to enter into or remain in the employment of any person or corporation willing to employ them. These rights are secured by the constitution itself. [Citations omitted.] No one can lawfully interfere by force or intimidation to prevent employers or persons employed or wishing to be employed from the exercise of these rights. It is in Massachusetts, as in some other states, even made a criminal offense for one, by intimidation or force, to prevent, or seek to prevent, a person from entering into or continuing in the employment of a person or corporation. Pub.St. c. 74, § 2. Intimidation is not limited to threats of violence or of physical injury to person or property. It has a broader signification, and there also may be a moral intimidation which is illegal. * * * The patrol was unlawful interference both with the plaintiff and with the workmen, within the principle of many cases; and, when instituted for the purpose of interfering with his business, it became a private nuisance. [Citations omitted.]

The defendants contend that these acts were justifiable, because they were only seeking to secure better wages for themselves, by compelling the plaintiff to accept their schedule of wages. This motive or purpose does not justify maintaining a patrol in front of the plaintiff's premises, as a means of carrying out their conspiracy. A combination among persons merely to regulate their own conduct is within allowable competition, and is lawful, although others may be indirectly affected thereby. But a combination to do injurious acts expressly directed to another, by way of intimidation or constraint, either of himself or of persons employed or seeking to be employed by him, is outside of allowable competition, and is unlawful. * * *

A question is also presented whether the court should enjoin such interference with persons in the employment of the plaintiff who are not bound by contract to remain with him, or with persons who are not under any existing contract, but who are seeking or intending to enter into his employment. A conspiracy to interfere with the plaintiff's business by means of threats and intimidation, and by maintaining a patrol in front of his premises, in order to prevent persons from entering his employment, or in order to prevent persons who are in his employment from continuing therein, is unlawful, even though such persons are not bound by contract to enter into or to continue in his employment; and the injunction should not be so limited as to relate only to persons who are bound by existing contracts. * * * We therefore think that the injunction should be in the form as originally issued. So ordered.

■ FIELD, C.J. (dissenting). * * *

■ HOLMES, J. (dissenting). * * * The important difference between the preliminary and the final injunction is that the former goes further, and forbids the defendants to interfere with the plaintiff's business "by any scheme * * * organized for the purpose of * * * preventing any person or persons who now are or may hereafter be * * * desirous of entering the [plaintiff's employment] from entering it." I quote only a part, and the part which seems to me most objectionable. This includes refusal of social intercourse, and even organized persuasion or argument, although free from any threat of violence, either express or implied. And this is with reference to persons who have a legal right to contract or not to contract with the plaintiff, as they may see fit. Interference with existing contracts is forbidden by the final decree. I wish to insist a little that the only point of difference which involves a difference of principle between the final decree and the preliminary injunction, which it is proposed to restore, is what I have mentioned, in order that it may be seen exactly what we are to discuss. It appears to me that the opinion of the majority turns in part on the assumption that the patrol necessarily carries with it a threat of bodily harm. That assumption I think unwarranted, for the reasons which I have given. Furthermore, it cannot be said, I think, that two men, walking together up and down a sidewalk, and speaking to those who enter a certain shop, do necessarily and always thereby convey a threat of force. I do not think it possible to discriminate, and to say that two workmen, or even two representatives of an organization of workmen, do; especially when they are, and are known to be, under the injunction of this court not to do so. See Stimson, Labor Law, § 60, especially pages 290, 298–300; Reg. v. Shepherd, 11 Cox.Cr.Cas. 325. I may add that I think the more intelligent workingmen believe as fully as I do that they no more can be permitted to usurp the state's prerogative of force than can their opponents in their controversies. But, if I am wrong, then the decree as it stands reaches the patrol, since it applies to all threats of force. With this I pass to the real difference between the interlocutory and the final decree.

I agree, whatever may be the law in the case of a single defendant (Rice v. Albee, 164 Mass. 88, 41 N.E. 122), that when a plaintiff proves that several persons have combined and conspired to injure his business, and have done acts producing that effect, he shows temporal damage and a cause of action, unless the facts disclose or the defendants prove some ground of excuse or justification; and I take it to be settled, and rightly settled, that doing that damage by combined persuasion is actionable, as well as doing it by falsehood or by force. [Citations omitted.]

Nevertheless, in numberless instances the law warrants the intentional infliction of temporal damage, because it regards it as justified. It is on the question of what shall amount to a justification, and more especially on the nature of the considerations which really determine or ought to determine the answer to that question, that judicial reasoning seems to me often to be inadequate. The true grounds of decision are considerations of policy and of social advantage, and it is vain to suppose that solutions can be attained merely by logic and general propositions of law which nobody disputes. Propositions as to public policy rarely are unanimously accepted, and still more rarely, if ever, are capable of unanswerable proof. They require a special training to enable any one even to form an intelligent opinion about them.

In the early stages of law, at least, they generally are acted on rather as inarticulate instincts than as definite ideas, for which a rational defense is ready.

To illustrate what I have said in the last paragraph: It has been the law for centuries that a man may set up a business in a small country town, too small to support more than one, although thereby he expects and intends to ruin some one already there, and succeeds in his intent. In such a case he is not held to act "unlawfully and without justifiable cause," as was alleged in Walker v. Cronin and Rice v. Albee. The reason, of course, is that the doctrine generally has been accepted that free competition is worth more to society than it costs, and that on this ground the infliction of the damage is privileged. Com. v. Hunt, 4 Metc. (Mass.) 111, 134. Yet even this proposition nowadays is disputed by a considerable body of persons, including many whose intelligence is not to be denied, little as we may agree with them.

I have chosen this illustration partly with reference to what I have to say next. It shows without the need of further authority that the policy of allowing free competition justifies the intentional inflicting of temporal damage, including the damage of interference with a man's business by some means, when the damage is done, not for its own sake, but as an instrumentality in reaching the end of victory in the battle of trade. In such a case it cannot matter whether the plaintiff is the only rival of the defendant, and so is aimed at specially, or is one of a class all of whom are hit. The only debatable ground is the nature of the means by which such damage may be inflicted. We all agree that it cannot be done by force or threats of force. We all agree, I presume, that it may be done by persuasion to leave a rival's shop, and come to the defendant's. It may be done by the refusal or withdrawal of various pecuniary advantages, which, apart from this consequence, are within the defendant's lawful control. It may be done by the withdrawal of, or threat to withdraw, such advantages from third persons who have a right to deal or not to deal with the plaintiff, as a means of inducing them not to deal with him either as customers or servants. Com. v. Hunt, 4 Metc. (Mass.) 111, 112, 133; Bowen v. Matheson, 14 Allen, 499; Heywood v. Tillson, 75 Me. 225; Steamship Co. v. McGregor [1892] App.Cas. 25. I have seen the suggestion made that the conflict between employers and employed was not competition, but I venture to assume that none of my brethren would rely on that suggestion. If the policy on which our law is founded is too narrowly expressed in the term "free competition," we may substitute "free struggle for life." Certainly, the policy is not limited to struggles between persons of the same class, competing for the same end. It applies to all conflicts of temporal interests.

I pause here to remark that the word "threats" often is used as if, when it appeared that threats had been made, it appeared that unlawful conduct had begun. But it depends on what you threaten. As a general rule, even if subject to some exceptions, what you may do in a certain event you may threaten to do—that is, give warning of your intention to do—in that event, and thus allow the other person the chance of avoiding the consequence. So, as to "compulsion," it depends on how you "compel." Com. v. Hunt, 4 Metc. (Mass.) 111, 133. So as to "annoyance" or "intimidation." Connor v. Kent, Curran v. Treleaven, 17 Cox, Cr.Cas. 354, 367, 368, 370. In Sherry v. Perkins, 147 Mass. 212, 17 N.E. 307, it was found as a fact that the display of banners which was enjoined was part of a scheme to prevent workmen from entering or remaining in the plaintiff's employment, "by threats and intimidation." The context showed that the words as there used meant threats of personal violence and intimidation by causing fear of it.

So far, I suppose, we are agreed. But there is a notion, which latterly has been insisted on a good deal, that a combination of persons to do what any one of them lawfully might do by himself will make the otherwise lawful conduct unlawful. It would be rash to say that some as yet unformulated truth may not be hidden under this proposition. But, in the general form in which it has been presented and accepted by many courts, I think it plainly untrue, both on authority and principle. Com. v. Hunt, 4 Metc. (Mass.) 111; Randall v. Hazelton, 12 Allen, 412, 414. There was combination of the most flagrant and dominant kind in Bowen v. Matheson, and in the Steamship Co. Case, and combination was essential to the success achieved. [These cases are summarized, pp. 29–30, infra.] But it is not necessary to cite cases. It is plain from the slightest consideration of practical affairs, or the most superficial reading of industrial history, that free competition means combination, and that the organization of the world, now going on so fast, means an ever-increasing might and scope of combination. It seems to me futile to set our faces against this tendency. Whether beneficial on the whole, as I think it, or detrimental, it is inevitable, unless the fundamental axioms of society, and even the fundamental conditions of life, are to be changed.

One of the eternal conflicts out of which life is made up is that between the effort of every man to get the most he can for his services, and that of society, disguised under the name of capital, to get his services for the least possible return. Combination on the one side is patent and powerful. Combination on the other is the necessary and desirable counterpart, if the battle is to be carried on in a fair and equal way. * * *

If it be true that workingmen may combine with a view, among other things, to getting as much as they can for their labor, just as capital may combine with a view to getting the greatest possible return, it must be true that, when combined, they have the same liberty that combined capital has, to support their interests by argument, persuasion, and the bestowal or refusal of those advantages which they otherwise lawfully control. I can remember when many people thought that, apart from violence or breach of contract, strikes were wicked, as organized refusals to work. I suppose that intelligent economists and legislators have given up that notion today. I feel pretty confident that they equally will abandon the idea that an organized refusal by workmen of social intercourse with a man who shall enter their antagonist's employ is unlawful, if it is dissociated from any threat of violence, and is made for the sole object of prevailing, if possible, in a contest with their employer about the rate of wages. The fact that the immediate object of the act by which the benefit to themselves is to be gained is to injure their antagonist does not necessarily make it unlawful, any more than when a great house lowers the price of goods for the purpose and with the effect of driving a smaller antagonist from the business. * * *

---

## PROBLEMS FOR DISCUSSION

**1.** In *Vegelahn v. Guntner,* how would you characterize: (a) the interest of the plaintiff with which the defendants were interfering? (b) the objective of the defendants? (c) the method or conduct utilized by the defendants? Which of these was at the core of the court's finding that a tort had been committed?

**2.** What was the essential point of difference between Mr. Justice Holmes and the court majority? Was the difference one of fact, or of law, or of social policy? What criteria can judges (particularly appellate judges) use to determine how to choose between the Holmes formulation and that of the court?

**3.** Why did the employer in *Vegelahn* seek relief through an injunctive action? What other forms of relief were available? Regarding each possible form of relief, consider whether there are significant differences in: (a) the substantive rules of law applied; (b) the method of proof; (c) the procedural safeguards for the defendants; (d) the mode of enforcement of the remedy. As counsel for the plaintiff, which would you seek? Could you successfully seek more than one?

---

## Plant v. Woods

176 Mass. 492, 57 N.E. 1011 (1900).

Bill in equity, filed in the Superior Court, * * * to restrain the defendants from any acts or the use of any methods tending to prevent the members of the plaintiff association from securing employment or continuing in their employment. * * *

■ HAMMOND, J. This case arises out of a contest for supremacy between two labor unions of the same craft, having substantially the same constitution and by-laws. The chief difference between them is that the plaintiff union is affiliated with a national organization having its headquarters in Lafayette, in the state of Indiana, while the defendant union is affiliated with a similar organization having its headquarters in Baltimore, in the state of Maryland. The plaintiff union was composed of workmen who, in 1897, withdrew from the defendant union. * * *

The contest became active early in the fall of 1898. In September of that year the members of the defendant union declared "all painters not affiliated with the Baltimore headquarters to be nonunion men," and voted "to notify bosses" of that declaration. * * *

A duly authorized agent of the defendants would visit a shop where one or more of the plaintiffs were at work, and inform the employer of the action of the defendant union with reference to the plaintiffs, and ask him to induce such of the plaintiffs as were in his employ to sign applications for reinstatement in the defendant union. As to the general nature of these interviews the master finds that the defendants have been courteous in manner, have made no threats of personal violence, have referred to the plaintiffs as nonunion men, but have not otherwise represented them as men lacking good standing in their craft; that they have not asked that the Lafayette men be discharged, and in some cases have expressly stated that they did not wish to have them discharged, but only that they sign the blanks for reinstatement in the defendant union. The master, however, further finds, from all the circumstances under which those requests were made, that the defendants intended that employers of Lafayette men should fear trouble in their business if they continued to employ such men, * * * and as a means to this end they caused strikes to be instituted in the shops where strikes would seriously interfere with the business of the shops, and in all other shops they made such representations as would lead the proprietors thereof to expect trouble in their business. * * * It is well to see what is the meaning of this threat to strike, when taken in connection with the intimation that the employer may "expect trouble in his business." It means more than that the strikers will cease to work. That is only the preliminary skirmish. It means that those who have ceased to work will by strong, persistent, and organized persuasion and social pressure of every description do all they can to prevent the employer from procuring workmen to take their places. It means much more. It means that, if these peaceful measures fail, the employer may reasonably expect that unlawful physical injury may be done to his property; that attempts in all the ways practiced by organized labor will be made to injure him in his business, even to his ruin, if possible; and that by the use of vile and opprobrious epithets and other annoying conduct, and actual and threatened personal violence, attempts will be made to intimidate those who enter or desire to enter his employ; and that whether or not all this be done by the strikers or only by their sympathizers, or with the open sanction and approval of the former, he will have no help from them in his efforts to protect himself. * * * Such is the nature of the threat, and such the degree of coercion and intimidation involved in it. If the defendants can lawfully perform the acts complained of in the city of Springfield, they can pursue the plaintiffs all over the state in the same manner, and compel them to abandon their trade, or bow to the behests of their pursuers. It is to be observed that this is not a case between the employer and employed, or, to use a hackneyed expression, between capital and labor, but between laborers all of the same craft, and each having the same right as any one of the others to pursue his calling. In this as in every other case of equal rights the right of each individual is to be exercised with due regard to the similar right of all others, and the right of one be said to end where that of another begins. The right involved is the right to dispose of one's labor with full freedom. This is a legal right, and it is entitled to legal protection. * * * The same rule is stated with care and discrimination by Wells, J., in Walker v. Cronin, 107 Mass. 555: "Every one has a right to enjoy the fruits and advantages of his own enterprise, industry, skill and credit. He has no right to be protected against competition, but he has a right to be free from malicious and wanton interference, disturbance, or annoyance. If disturbance or loss come as the result of competition, or the exercise of like rights by others, it is damnum absque injuria, unless some superior right by contract, or otherwise, is interfered with. But if it come from the merely wanton or malicious acts of others, without the justification of competition, or the service of any interest or lawful purpose, it then stands upon a different footing." In this case the acts complained of were calculated to cause damage to the plaintiffs, and did actually cause such damage; and they were intentionally done for that purpose. Unless, therefore, there was justifiable cause, the acts were malicious and unlawful. Walker v. Cronin, ubi supra; Carew v. Rutherford, 106 Mass. 1, and cases cited therein.

* * * In cases somewhat akin to the one at bar this court has had occasion to consider the question how far acts manifestly coercive and intimidating in their nature, which cause damage and injury to the business or property of another, and are done with intent to cause such injury, and partly in reliance upon such coercion, are justifiable. [The court then discussed *Bowen v. Matheson*, 14 Allen 499 (Mass.1867), which is abstracted p. 24, infra.] On the other hand, it was held in Carew v. Rutherford, 106 Mass. 1, that a conspiracy against a mechanic—who is under the necessity of employing workmen in order to carry on his business—to obtain a sum of money from him, which he is under no legal obligation to pay, by inducing his workmen to leave him, or by deterring others from entering into his employ, or by threatening to do this, so that he is induced to pay the money demanded under a reasonable apprehension that he cannot carry on his business without yielding to the demands, is illegal, if not criminal, conspiracy; that the acts done under it are illegal, and that the money thus obtained may be recovered back. Chapman, C.J., speaking for the court, says that "there is no doubt that, if the parties under such circumstances succeed in injuring the business of the mechanic, they are

liable to pay all the damages done to him.'' That case bears a close analogy to the one at bar. The acts there threatened were like those in this case, and the purpose was, in substance, to force the plaintiff to give his work to the defendants, and to extort from him a fine because he had given some of his work to other persons. Without now indicating to what extent workmen may combine, and in pursuance of an agreement may act by means of strikes and boycotts to get the hours of labor reduced, or their wages increased, or to procure from their employers any other concession directly and immediately affecting their own interests, or to help themselves in competition with their fellow workmen, we think this case must be governed by the principles laid down in Carew v. Rutherford, ubi supra. The purpose of these defendants was to force the plaintiffs to join the defendant association, and to that end they injured the plaintiffs in their business, and molested and disturbed them in their efforts to work at their trade. It is true they committed no acts of personal violence, or of physical injury to property, although they threatened to do something which might reasonably be expected to lead to such results. In their threat, however, there was plainly that which was coercive in its effect upon the will. It is not necessary that the liberty of the body should be restrained. Restraint of the mind, provided it would be such as would be likely to force a man against his will to grant the thing demanded, and actually has that effect, is sufficient in cases like this. * * * The necessity that the plaintiffs should join this association is not so great, nor is its relation to the rights of the defendants, as compared with the right of the plaintiffs to be free from molestation, such as to bring the acts of the defendant under the shelter of the principles of trade competition. Such acts are without justification, and therefore are malicious and unlawful, and the conspiracy thus to force the plaintiffs was unlawful. Such conduct is intolerable, and inconsistent with the spirit of our laws. * * *

■ HOLMES, C.J. (dissenting). * * * If the decision in the present case simply had relied upon Vegelahn v. Guntner, I should have hesitated to say anything, although I might have stated that my personal opinion had not been weakened by the substantial agreement with my views to be found in the judgments of the majority of the house of lords in Allen v. Flood. But, much to my satisfaction, if I may say so, the court has seen fit to adopt the mode of approaching the question which I believe to be the correct one, and to open an issue which otherwise I might have thought closed. The difference between my Brethren and me now seems to be a difference of degree, and the line of reasoning followed makes it proper for me to explain where the difference lies.

I agree that the conduct of the defendants is actionable unless justified. May v. Wood, 172 Mass. 11, 14, 51 N.E. 191, and cases cited. I agree that the presence or absence of justification may depend upon the object of their conduct; that is, upon the motive with which they acted. Vegelahn v. Guntner, 167 Mass. 92, 105, 106, 44 N.E. 1077, 35 L.R.A. 722. I agree, for instance, that, if a boycott or a strike is intended to override the jurisdiction of the courts by the action of a private association, it may be illegal. Weston v. Barnicoat, 175 Mass. 454, 56 N.E. 619, 49 L.R.A. 612. On the other hand, I infer that a majority of my Brethren would admit that a boycott or strike intended to raise wages directly might be lawful, if it did not embrace in its scheme or intent violence, breach of contract, or other conduct unlawful on grounds independent of the mere fact that the action of the defendants was combined. A sensible workingman would not contend that the courts should sanction a combination for the purpose of inflicting or threatening violence, or the infraction of admitted rights. To come directly to the point, the issue is narrowed to the question whether, assuming that some purposes would be a justification, the purpose in this case of the threatened boycotts and strikes was such as to justify the threats. That purpose was not directly concerned with wages. It was one degree more remote. The immediate object and motive was to strengthen the defendants' society as a preliminary and means to enable it to make a better fight on questions of wages or other matters of clashing interests.

I differ from my Brethren in thinking that the threats were as lawful for this preliminary purpose as for the final one to which strengthening the union was a means. I think that unity of organization is necessary to make the contest of labor effectual, and that societies of laborers lawfully may employ in their preparation the means which they might use in the final contest.

Although this is not the place for extended economic discussion, and although the law may not always reach ultimate economic conceptions, I think it well to add that I cherish no illusions as to the meaning and effect of strikes. While I think the strike a lawful instrument in the universal struggle of life, I think it pure phantasy to suppose that there is a body of capital of which labor, as a whole, secures a larger share by that means.

The annual product, subject to an infinitesimal deduction for the luxuries of the few, is directed to consumption by the multitude, and is consumed by the multitude always. Organization and strikes may get a larger share for the members of an organization, but, if they do, they get it at the expense of the less organized and less powerful portion of the laboring mass. They do not create something out of nothing.

* * * [S]ubject to the qualifications which I have expressed, I think it lawful for a body of workmen to try by combination to get more than they now are getting, although they do it at the expense of their fellows, and to that end to strengthen their union by the boycott and the strike.

––––––

BOWEN v. MATHESON, 96 Mass. 499 (14 Allen 503) (1867). Plaintiff and defendants were competitors engaged in the business of furnishing seamen to vessels sailing from the Port of Boston. The defendants entered into a combination for the purpose of controlling the entire business and destroying competitors who did not comply with their terms (among which was a prohibition upon furnishing seamen for wages below a stipulated amount); they agreed, among other things, not to furnish seamen to any vessel which shipped men furnished by the plaintiff. On demurrer to these allegations *held,* for defendants. "If the effect is to destroy the business of shipping masters who are not members of the association, it is such a result as in the competition of business often follows from a course of proceeding that the law permits. New inventions and new methods of transacting business often destroy the business of those who adhere to old methods. Sometimes associations break down the business of individuals * * *. As the declaration sets forth no illegal acts on the part of defendants, the demurrer must be sustained."

MOGUL STEAMSHIP COMPANY v. McGREGOR, GOW & CO., 23 Q.B.Div. 598 (1889). Defendants, a number of shipowners, formed themselves into a combination for the purpose of driving the plaintiffs and other competitors from the field and thereby securing control of the carriage of tea from certain Chinese ports. In order to accomplish this object defendants during the tea harvest of 1885 combined to offer very low freight rates with a view to "smashing" the rates and thereby rendering it unprofitable for the plaintiffs to send their ships to those ports. Defendants offered a five per cent rebate to all shippers and agents who would deal exclusively with defendants' vessels, and any agent who broke the condition forfeited his entire rebate on all shipments made on behalf of all his principals during the whole year. Plaintiffs brought this action for damages and an injunction against the continuance of the conspiracy. *Held*, for defendants. Acts which intentionally damage another's trade are actionable if done without just cause or excuse. Here, just cause or excuse is to be found in the defendants' right "to carry on their own trade freely in the mode and manner that best suits them, and which they think best calculated to secure their advantage. * * * It is urged, however, on the part of plaintiffs, that even if the acts complained of would not be wrongful had they been committed by a single individual, they became actionable when they are the result of concerted action among several. * * * [It is impossible] to acquiesce in the view that the English law places any such restriction on the combination of capital as would be involved in the recognition of such a distinction. * * * The truth is, that the combination of capital for purposes of trade and competition is a very different thing from such a combination of several persons against one, with a view to harm him, as falls under the head of an indictable conspiracy. There is no just cause or excuse in the latter class of cases. There is just cause or excuse in the former. There are cases in which the very fact of a combination is evidence of a design to do that which is hurtful without just cause—is evidence—to use a technical expression—of malice. But it is perfectly legitimate, as it seems to me, to combine capital for all the mere purposes of trade for which capital may, apart from combination, be legitimately used in trade. To limit combinations of capital, when used for purposes of competition, in the manner proposed by the argument of the plaintiffs, would in the present day, be impossible—would be only another method of attempting to set boundaries to the tides."

# PROBLEMS FOR DISCUSSION

**1.** In *Plant v. Woods*, how would you characterize: (a) the interest of the plaintiffs with which the defendants were interfering? (b) the objective of the defendants? (c) the method or conduct utilized by the defendants? Which of these was at the core of the court's finding that a tort had been committed?

**2.** What was the essential point of difference between Mr. Justice Holmes and the court majority? Was the difference one of fact, or of law, or of social policy? Is there a narrowing of differences in the four-year period between the *Vegelahn* and *Plant* decisions?

**3.** Does the court in *Plant* help the reader understand why picketing or striking with an object of forcing the plaintiffs to change their union affiliation is tortious and enjoinable? Does Mr. Justice Holmes help the reader to understand why such activity is legal? Does he see certain affirmative values to be served by these forms of pressure? Does he not also concede that there are certain limits to their use? How does he formulate those limits? Can judges formulate those limits?

**4.** Assume that in 1904 a case reaches the Supreme Judicial Court of Massachusetts in which the Stone Masons Union seeks to enjoin the Bricklayers Union from combining and conspiring to interfere with the employment of stone masons in the work of cleaning and pointing brick walls by threatening building contractors with strikes by the bricklayers unless the bricklayers are given not only the work of laying brick but also the cleaning and pointing of brick walls. Assuming *Plant v. Woods* to be binding precedent, what judgment should the court render? (Are the respective interests of the employer, the plaintiff employees, the defendant employees, the public any different? Does that matter in deciding the case?)

**5.** Dainty Garment Company was a manufacturer of women's clothing in New York City. By 1908 its employees and the employees of other New York shops had been organized by the International Ladies Garment Workers. Wage rates were standardized. Average hourly earnings were 50 cents. In 1909 Dainty Garment shut down. Three weeks later a new shop was opened 40 miles up the Hudson in Beacon, New York, by a concern known as Super–Dainty Garments, Inc. All but the qualifying shares of its stock are owned by the brother-in-law of Dainty's owner. Dainty's owner is general manager of the new shop. Super–Dainty is paying 20 cents an hour to inexperienced help and 30 cents is the average hourly earnings of an experienced operator. Labor costs are more than 50 per cent of the total cost of manufacturing.

ILG sent organizers to Beacon. A number of employees became members. Super–Dainty countered by discharging the employees who joined the union and threatening to leave town if the shop was unionized. ILG picketed the shop. There were five instances of name calling and violence during the past week, but the picketing was otherwise peaceful. Nevertheless, the picketing is discouraging many employees from working and interferes with the pick-up and delivery of goods because unionized teamsters refuse to cross the picket lines.

(a) Assume that careful legal research produces neither an applicable statute nor a judicial precedent in a labor controversy. As lawyer for Super–Dainty, would you think that you had a reasonable chance of securing any form of legal relief? What remedies would you seek? What arguments would you present in support of them?

(b) What would be your answering arguments as attorney for ILG?

(c) As judge, how would you go about reaching a decision? What considerations would you deem relevant? What would be your decision?

————

*Development of the "objectives" test.*—As the division of opinion in *Plant v. Woods* suggests, wide divergences can be found in judicial rulings upon the lawfulness of various labor objectives. Although the cases noted immediately below could probably be opposed by contrary rulings from other jurisdictions, they do illustrate the dominant trend in judicial opinions at the time and also the present state of the common law in many jurisdictions (except as modified by constitutional and statutory developments to be discussed later).

In UNITED SHOE MACHINERY CORP. V. FITZGERALD, 237 Mass. 537, 130 N.E. 86 (1921), the plaintiff employer, which had individual contracts with its machinists binding them to work for a year at specified rates, was struck and picketed in support of union demands for collective bargaining. The court held this to be an unlawful objective, and issued an injunction. In HOPKINS V. OXLEY STAVE CO., 83 Fed. 912 (C.C.A.8 1897), the plaintiff installed certain machines for hooping barrels, previously done by hand (more expensively and utilizing more workers). When the company resisted union demands to discontinue the use of these machines, the union notified the plaintiff's customers (suppliers of meat, flour and other commodities) that they must cease purchasing machine-hooped barrels in which to pack their wares, and induced the Trades Assembly of Kansas City to declare a boycott of all products packed in machine-hooped barrels. The district court enjoined any hindering or interfering with the plaintiff's business and customers. The two objects of the defendants—to deprive the plaintiff and its customers of their right freely to conduct their business, and "to deprive the public at large of the advantages to be derived from the use of an invention which was not only designed to diminish the cost of making certain necessary articles, but to lessen the labor of human hands"—were held unlawful. In CENTRAL METAL PRODUCTS CORP. V. O'BRIEN, 278 Fed. 827 (N.D.Ohio 1922), the plaintiff company hired members of the Carpenters Union to install on a construction site the metal doors, frames, transoms and sash that it manufactured, but the Amalgamated Sheet Metal Workers called a strike of its members employed by other contractors at the site when the plaintiff refused to assign the installation work to sheet metal workers instead of to carpenters. The court enjoined the strike and threats to strike.

————

## B.   The Antitrust Laws

### 1.   THE SHERMAN ACT

In 1890, Congress in the Sherman Act declared unlawful "every contract, combination in the form of trust or otherwise, or conspiracy, in restraint of trade or commerce among the several States, or with foreign nations * * *." Violations were made punishable as federal crimes, the Attorney General of the United States was authorized to institute injunction proceedings in federal courts, and persons injured in their business as a result of such unlawful conduct were given the right to sue civilly for treble damages. Although the obvious objective of the legislation was the elimination of agreements between manufacturers or suppliers to fix the price or regulate the supply of goods, or allocate customers or exclude competitors, the Sherman Act was soon applied more often to labor unions than to business corporations. *See* Hovencamp, Labor Conspiracies in American Law, 1880–1930, 66 Texas L.Rev. 919 (1988)(for a fuller explanation of why that was so).

When in 1894 the American Railway Union, organized by Eugene V. Debs, instituted a strike against the Pullman Company to protest a wage cut—a strike which spread over a wide area and generated robbery, violence and property damage—the United States Circuit Court issued an injunction at the request of the Attorney General, invoking the Sherman Antitrust Act. United States v. Debs, 64 Fed. 724 (C.C.Ill.1894). The Supreme Court affirmed, but did not rely on the specific congressional authorization to enjoin given by the Sherman Act. In re Debs, 158 U.S. 564, 15 S.Ct. 900, 39 L.Ed. 1092 (1895). It was not until Loewe v. Lawlor, popularly known as the *Danbury Hatters* case, that the Court squarely considered whether the Sherman Act applied to combinations of workers.

It should be noted that the situation of the hat makers at the turn of the century illustrates some of the developments canvassed earlier. See generally D. Bensman, The Practice of Solidarity: American Hat Finishers in the Nineteenth Century (1985). The hydraulic hat presser, first utilized in 1891, became widespread, resulting in the partial displacement of skilled hat finishers by semi-skilled labor; the steam-powered lathe reduced the labor needed to pounce a hat by twenty-five percent. The Depression of 1893 stimulated employer efforts to take control of the workplace from its organized skilled craftsmen—to hire "helpers" in lieu of skilled journeymen and to pay by the day rather than by the piece. One response of the craft unions of makers and finishers respectively was to merge into a single union in 1896, the United Hatters of North America.

In 1885, the hat finishers had affiliated with the Knights of Labor, but by 1896, the Knights were moribund and the American Federation of Labor, founded in 1886, represented the largest labor federation in America. Moreover, the A.F. of L. was active in promoting a boycott of "unfair" firms, which coincided with the Hatters' plan of boycotting hats that lacked the union label. The United Hatters joined the A.F. of L. and secured its support.

The precipitating event was the union's effort in 1899 to reduce unemployment among its members by enforcing a fifty-five hour work week. The initial target was F. Berg and Company, which agreed the following year to hire only union members (who, by union rules, could not work more than fifty-five hours). That victory convinced other manufacturers of the utility of having the union label (and avoiding the A.F. of L.'s "We Don't Patronize" list); by 1902, only 12 of the Nation's 120 hat manufacturers remained non-union.

According to one historian, the situation of hat making was fairly typical of a number of industries characterized by numerous small competitors and cut-throat competition. To these industries, unions offered the prospect of stabilization: of wringing out those competitors unable to meet union wage and work standards leaving the remaining competitors with higher profit margins and better paid workers. It was a case, as he put it, of "workers organizing capitalists" who, because of competitive conditions, were unable to organize themselves. Colin Gordon, New Deals: Business, Labor and Politics in America, 1920–1935 (1994).

One of those hat manufacturers who refused to be organized was Dietrich E. Loewe, who owned a hat factory in Danbury, Connecticut. Loewe's own workers were apparently content; but the logic of eliminating competition on the basis of wages and working conditions required that he meet union standards—which he could not do and remain in business. Loewe refused to recognize the union and in a walk in the woods with his fellow manufacturer, Charles Hart Merritt, he came up with the idea of an employers' organization—the American Anti–Boycott Association—to combat the boycott in the courts. *See generally* Daniel Ernst, Lawyers Against Labor (1995).

The union set out systematically to persuade retailers and wholesalers not to carry Loewe's hats; local trade union councils were asked to put retailers who carried the product on their local "unfair" lists. Loewe struck back. He turned to the legal counsel to the Anti–Boycott Association, David Davenport, who compiled a list of over 2000 union members and, comparing the real estate and bank records in Danbury, Bethel, and Norwalk, identified over 240 hatters who owned homes or had bank accounts. On September 13, 1903, he had the Sheriff of Fairfield County attach their property, and filed suit against them for treble damages under the Sherman Act—over $240,000. The same day, anticipating public sympathy for the unionists, Loewe published a statement in the *Danbury News*:

> This is a country of liberty, some are Protestants, some Catholics, some believe in unionism, and some do not, but whatever their creed or belief all must be treated with fairness and permitted to earn a livelihood. We are unwilling to blacklist the citizens and youth who do not belong or cannot obtain entrance into the unions. We believe with our honored President, Theodore Roosevelt, that the principle of the open shop is the only true and correct basis for individual liberty.

Before reading the following case, read carefully the text of Sections 1 and 2 of the Sherman Act in the Statutory Supplement. Consider whether that language could reasonably be construed to prohibit: (a) the forming and joining of labor unions; (b) collective bargaining between a union and an employer; (c) peaceful strikes, picketing and boycotts in aid of employee demands. What standards could a court use to determine the proper reach of the statutory ban, a most important question in view of the powerful remedies afforded under the Act?

———

## Loewe v. Lawlor

208 U.S. 274, 28 S.Ct. 301, 52 L.Ed. 488 (1908).

■ Mr. Chief Justice Fuller delivered the opinion of the court:

This was an action brought in the circuit court for the district of Connecticut under § 7 of the antitrust act of July 2, 1890 [26 Stat. at L. 210, chap. 647, U.S.Comp.Stat.1901, p. 3202], claiming three-fold damages for injuries inflicted on plaintiffs by combination or conspiracy declared to be unlawful by the act.

[The complaint alleged that the plaintiffs were hat manufacturers located in Danbury, Connecticut, the bulk of whose business was through wholesalers and retailers in other states. The defendants were members of the United Hatters of North America, which was alleged to have 9000 members in a large number of locals and to be combined with 1,400,000 others in the American Federation of Labor. The objective of the defendants was to unionize the workers employed by all American hat manufacturers and to achieve this by "restraining and destroying" their interstate trade, by "intimidation and threats" made to these manufacturers and their customers, and by boycotting them and their customers by appeals to union members throughout the United States. It was further alleged that of the eighty-two hat manufacturers in the nation, seventy had already been organized, and that a boycott was instituted against the plaintiffs when they refused to recognize the union. The defendants were said to have conspired intentionally and maliciously to interfere with the plaintiffs' production of hats and their distribution in interstate commerce, by inducing a strike at their factories and a boycott of the hats when sold elsewhere, as well as a boycott of the wholesalers selling them and of those who purchased (even hats made by others than the plaintiffs) from those wholesalers. The boycott of the wholesalers and dealers was effected by direct pressure and by distributing circulars, as well as by publicizing the boycott in local newspapers and union publications. The plaintiffs alleged actual damage to their business and property in the amount of $80,000.

[The defendants' demurrer was sustained, and the complaint dismissed, on the ground that the combination stated was not within the Sherman Act. When the case reached the circuit court of appeals, that court certified this question to the Supreme Court: "Upon this state of facts can plaintiffs maintain an action against defendants under § 7 of the anti-trust act of July 2, 1890?"]

In our opinion, the combination described in the declaration is a combination "in restraint of trade or commerce among the several states," in the sense in which those words are used in the act, and the action can be maintained accordingly.

And that conclusion rests on many judgments of this court, to the effect that the act prohibits any combination whatever to secure action which essentially obstructs the free flow of commerce between the states, or restricts, in that regard, the liberty of a trader to engage in business.

The combination charged falls within the class of restraints of trade aimed at compelling third parties and strangers involuntarily not to engage in the course of trade except on conditions that the combination imposes; and there is no doubt that (to quote from the well-known work of Chief Justice Erle on Trade Unions) "at common law every person has individually, and the public also has collectively, a right to require that the course of trade should be kept free from unreasonable obstruction." But the objection here is to the jurisdiction, because, even conceding that the declaration states a case good at common law, it is contended that it does not state one within the statute. Thus, it is said that the restraint alleged would operate to entirely destroy plaintiffs' business and thereby include intrastate trade as well; that physical obstruction is not alleged as contemplated; and that defendants are not themselves engaged in interstate trade.

We think none of these objections are tenable, and that they are disposed of by previous decisions of this court. * * *

In W.W. Montague & Co. v. Lowry, 193 U.S. 38, 48 L.Ed. 608, 24 Sup.Ct.Rep. 307, which was an action brought by a private citizen under § 7 against a combination engaged in the manufacture of tiles, defendants were wholesale dealers in tiles in California, and combined with manufacturers in other states to restrain the interstate traffic in tiles by refusing to sell any tiles to any wholesale dealer in California who was not a member of the association, except at a prohibitive rate. The case was a commercial boycott against such dealers in California as would not or could not obtain membership in the association. The restraint did not consist in a physical obstruction of interstate commerce, but in the fact that the plaintiff and other independent dealers could not purchase their tiles from manufacturers in other states because such manufacturers had combined to boycott them. This court held that this obstruction to the purchase of tiles, a fact antecedent to physical transportation, was within the prohibition of the act. Mr. Justice Peckham, speaking for the court, said, concerning the agreement, that it "restrained trade, for it narrowed the market for the sale of tiles in California from the manufacturers and dealers therein in other states, so that they could only be sold to the members of the association, and it enhanced prices to the nonmember."

The averments here are that there was an existing interstate traffic between plaintiffs and citizens of other states, and that, for the direct purpose of destroying such interstate traffic, defendants combined not merely to prevent plaintiffs from manufacturing articles then and there intended for transportation beyond the state, but also to prevent the vendees from reselling the hats which they had imported from Connecticut, or from further negotiating with plaintiffs for the purchase and intertransportation of such hats from Connecticut to the various places of destination. So that, although some of the means whereby the interstate traffic was to be destroyed were acts within a state, and some of them were, in themselves, as a part of their obvious purpose and effect, beyond the scope of Federal authority, still, as we have seen, the acts must be considered as a whole, and the plan is open to condemnation, notwithstanding a negligible amount of intrastate business might be affected in carrying it out. If the purposes of the combination were, as alleged, to prevent any interstate transportation at all, the fact that the means operated at one end before physical transportation commenced, and, at the other end, after the physical transportation ended, was immaterial.

Nor can the act in question be held inapplicable because defendants were not themselves engaged in interstate commerce. The act made no distinction between classes. It provided that "every" contract, combination, or conspiracy in restraint of trade was illegal. The records of Congress show that several efforts were made to exempt, by legislation, organizations of farmers and laborers from the operation of the act, and that all these efforts failed, so that the act remained as we have it before us.

In an early case (United States v. Workingmen's Amalgamated Council, 26 L.R.A. 158, 4 Inters.Com.Rep. 831, 54 Fed. 994) the United States filed a bill under the Sherman act in the circuit court for the eastern district of Louisiana, averring the existence of "a gigantic and widespread combination of the members of a multitude of separate organizations for the purpose of restraining the commerce among the several states and with foreign countries," and it was contended that the statute did not refer to combinations of laborers. But the court, granting the injunction, said:

> "I think the congressional debates show that the statute had its origin in the evils of massed capital; but, when the Congress came to formulating the prohibition, which is the yardstick for measuring the complainant's right to the injunction, it expressed it in these words: 'Every contract or combination in the form of trust, or otherwise in restraint of trade or commerce among the several states or with foreign nations, is hereby declared to be illegal.' The subject had so broadened in the minds of the legislators that the source of the evil was not regarded as material, and the evil in its entirety is dealt with. They made the interdiction include combinations of labor as well as of capital; in fact, all combinations in restraint of commerce, without reference to the character of the persons who entered into them. It is true this statute has not been much expounded by judges, but, as it seems to me, its meaning, as far as relates to the sort of combinations to which it is to apply, is manifest, and that it includes combinations

which are composed of laborers acting in the interest of laborers. * * *"

We think a case within the statute was set up and that the demurrer should have been overruled.

Judgment reversed and cause remanded with a direction to proceed accordingly.

[The American Federation of Labor called upon the workers of the United States to donate one hour's pay on January 27, 1916, lest the individual defendant hatters lose their homes and bank accounts. The money donated—along with that contributed by the United Hatters—paid the damages. In total, the case had cost the labor movement over $400,000.]

————

## PROBLEMS FOR DISCUSSION

**1.** If the strike at the hat factories in Danbury had been successful in shutting them down, so that no boycott of wholesalers and their customers had been necessary, would the strikers have violated the Sherman Act?

**2.** Is there a material difference between the boycott effected by the manufacturers and wholesalers of tile described in the *Montague* case (discussed in the principal case) and the boycott effected by the laborers in *Loewe v. Lawlor,* such that antitrust liability in the former case would not be controlling in the latter?

**3.** Assume that Super–Dainty Garment Co. (p. 29, supra) was a Philadelphia firm selling in the New York and Chicago markets in competition with New York City manufacturers. If the Pennsylvania courts were unwilling to issue injunctions in labor disputes, would there be any basis for suit in a federal court? (Consider this question again after reading the following Note.)

————

CORONADO COAL CO. v. UNITED MINE WORKERS, 268 U.S. 295, 45 S.Ct. 551, 69 L.Ed. 963 (1925). The plaintiffs were a number of coal companies, interrelated in organization and physical location, controlled by the Bache–Denman Coal Company. They brought an action under the Sherman Act for treble damages against the International of the Mine Workers, its District No. 21 and other locals, for damage to business and property stemming from a violent strike at the plaintiffs' Sebastian County mines in Arkansas. Bache, the manager of the mines—which had been unionized by District 21, a regional mineworkers organization—announced his intention to close them down and then reopen them on a nonunion basis. When the mines were reopened, union members attacked guards there and committed serious injury to persons and property. In a later episode, union sympathizers armed with guns attacked workers, equipment and other property; two persons were killed, and dynamite was used to destroy the mine premises. After a trial resulted in a verdict of $200,000 which was then trebled, the case was remanded by the Supreme Court, since the evidence failed to support a claim under the Sherman Act; the Court found only a "local motive" for the defendants' actions, a protest against the use of nonunion workers at the mines and against the mineowners' breach of contract with the union. In the Court's words, "it was in fact a local strike, local in its origin and motive, local in its waging, and local in its felonious and murderous ending," and although reprehensible such a strike would fall outside the ban of the Sherman Act.

On remand, new evidence was introduced, which demonstrated to the Court that the objective of District 21 was not simply "local" but was directed at so crippling the plaintiffs' nonunion mines as to prevent their competition with unionized mines in adjacent states. Pertinent passages of the Court's opinion follow.

Part of the new evidence was an extract from the convention proceedings of District No. 21 at Ft. Smith, Ark., in February, 1914, in which the delegates discussed the difficulties presented in their maintenance of the union scale in Arkansas, Oklahoma, and Texas because of the keen competition from the nonunion fields of Southern Colorado and the nonunion fields of the South in Alabama and Tennessee. Stewart, the president, called attention to a new field in Oklahoma which he said would be a great competitor of union coal fields, and that District No. 21 would be forced to call a strike to bring in to line certain operators in that section, and in the event that they did so the District would fight such a conflict to the bitter end regardless of cost. * * *

A new witness was one Hanraty, who was for seven years president of District No. 21 * * * He said that he made speeches all through District No. 21 and did not remember a speech in which he did not mention the danger from nonunion coal in taking the markets of union coal and forcing a nonunion scale, and that it was a constant subject of discussion among the officers and members.

* * * The mere reduction in the supply of an article to be shipped in interstate commerce by the illegal or tortious prevention of its manufacture or production is ordinarily an indirect and remote obstruction to that commerce. But when the intent of those unlawfully preventing the manufacture or production is shown to be to restrain or control the supply entering and moving in interstate commerce, or the price of it in interstate markets, their action is a direct violation of the Anti-Trust Act. * * * We think there was substantial evidence at the second trial in this case tending to show that the purpose of the destruction of the mines was to stop the production of nonunion coal and prevent its shipment to markets of other states than Arkansas, where it would by competition tend to reduce the price of the commodity and affect injuriously the maintenance of wages for union labor in competing mines, and that the direction by the District Judge to return a verdict for the defendants other than the International Union was erroneous.

## 2.  THE CLAYTON ACT AND THE DEVELOPMENT OF THE UNIONS, 1890–1930

Throughout the years 1886–1914 there gradually developed, despite the hostile attitude of the courts and the organized opposition of employers, a strong body of opinion which held that workers should be granted the right to organize unions without employer interference, and that employers should be required to recognize and deal with their employees' unions. As early as 1894, the United States Strike Commission, which had been investigating the causes of the Pullman strike, criticized the attitude of some of the courts and urged employers to recognize and bargain with labor organizations. In 1902 a report made by the Industrial Commission to Congress ridiculed the suggestion that individual freedom was lost under a system of collective agreements and stressed their effectiveness in promoting industrial peace. It declared—

"The chief advantage which comes from the practice of periodically determining the conditions of labor by collective bargaining directly between employers and employees is, that thereby each side obtains a better understanding of the actual state of the industry, of the conditions which confront the other side, and of the motives which influence it. Most strikes and lockouts would not occur if each party understood exactly the position of the other. Where representatives of employers and employees can meet personally together and discuss all the considerations on which the wage scale and the conditions of labor would be based, a satisfactory agreement can, in the great majority of instances, be reached. * * *

"It is not to be supposed that the introduction of joint conferences and arbitration committees in a trade will render strikes and lockouts thereafter impossible. * * * Nevertheless experience both in England and in our own country shows that where these practices have once become fairly well established they greatly reduce the number of strikes and lockouts, and in many trades do away with them altogether for long periods of time. Even when a cessation of employment does intervene, the experience of the beneficial effects of peaceful methods usually leads to their reestablishment." (H.R.Doc. No. 380, 57th Cong., 1st Sess. 844–45.)

When Woodrow Wilson was elected in 1912, urging that there be a "New Freedom," the tariff was reduced, the banking and currency system was reformed, and the anti-trust laws were strengthened by the enactment of the Federal Trade Commission and Clayton Antitrust Acts. The Clayton Act also contained two sections inserted at the request of organized labor, which Samuel Gompers hailed as "labor's charter of freedom". Many supposed that they swept out of the federal courts the precedents at common law and under the Sherman Act which had proved so detrimental to the labor movement. It was not until some years later that the hope proved false.

The gains of organized labor under the new spirit of the Wilson Administration were soon strengthened by the emotional fervor of a war to make the world safe for democracy. Widened profit margins and the wartime scarcity of labor also made employers less reluctant to grant wage increases, and the AFL affiliates enhanced their prestige and secured new members by successful strikes. Both employers and the government made important concessions to the labor unions in order to secure their cooperation in increasing industrial output. Possibly the most important factor, however, was the encouragement given to unionization by the federal government's wartime labor policies.

In the autumn of 1917 it became apparent that governmental intervention would be necessary to prevent labor disputes from impeding the production of war materials, and in 1918, President Wilson set up a National War Labor Board which adopted the following principle as one of the policies which would guide its action:

"The right of workers to organize in trade unions and to bargain collectively, through chosen representatives, is recognized and affirmed. This right shall not be denied, abridged, or interfered with by the employers in any manner whatsoever."

This policy was vigorously enforced by the Board and was followed by other government agencies. In several cases the government seized and operated the plants of companies which persisted in anti-union tactics in defiance of the Board's orders.

Thus the ideas expressed in the official reports quoted above became the foundation of the national labor policy. For the first time the right to organize and bargain collectively received effective government protection.

As a result of the favorable economic conditions and government policies which prevailed during the six year period 1914–1920, trade union memberships nearly doubled, to total more than 5 million. The AFL experienced its proportionate share of the growth for its membership increased from 2,000,000 to 4,000,000. Despite the large total increase, however, the increase was concentrated in a few trades. In 1920 two-thirds of all union members were to be found in four groups: 17.6% in building construction; 17% in metals, machinery and shipbuilding; 7.4% in clothing; and 24.9% in transportation and commerce. The trade union movement had not reached the unskilled workers in mass production industry. In 1918 and 1919, the AFL made its greatest attempt to enter this untouched field, through a major drive to organize the basic steel industry, dominated by the giant United States Steel Corporation. Corporate resistance, characterized by mass discharges and violence, precipitated a strike, also characterized by violence, by 343,000 steel workers in the fall of 1919. But the strike failed and union organization in the industry was utterly obliterated.

Organized labor encountered other problems after the end of World War I. President Wilson's efforts to put on a more permanent footing the union-supportive policies of wartime failed, due to employer resistance, and open-shop campaigns gathered popular support. Throughout the 1920's economic conditions were also unfavorable to a labor movement. Trade unions had usually grown strong during a rise in the business cycle when prices were outrunning wages; real wages rose considerably during the

1920's. Large mass production establishments became increasingly dominant especially in such growing industries as iron and steel, automobile, rubber and petroleum. In this adjustment many jobs became routine and employment in the established trades declined. The new unskilled laborers lacked any union tradition. Many of them were immigrants inclined to follow the employers' wishes and when strikes occurred, replacements were easy to find. Some industries, notably cotton textiles, moved south to find cheaper labor which had not been influenced by unionism.

The large corporations were strongholds of anti-unionism, both through traditional weapons and newly developing benevolent personnel practices. "Welfare capitalism" brought profit-sharing plans (usually short-lived), bonus systems, more rational systems of hiring and discipline through more scientific personnel management, and employee welfare plans that attempted to substitute "company consciousness" for loyalty to craft. A most significant feature of this trend was the development of the "company union," or the employee representation plan or works council, typically instigated, financed and controlled by the employer. Already popular during World War I, company unions increased their membership from 403,000 to 1,500,000 between 1919 and 1928, a period in which the American Federation of Labor lost some 400,000 members. Lacking financial strength (apart from employer support) and dependent on employer approval for taking any significant actions, company unions nonetheless built up a company *esprit de corps* and often furnished a bulwark against penetration by an "outside union."

Judicial decisions during the early 1920's were also extremely unfavorable to labor unions. In all but a few liberal courts, notably the New York Court of Appeals, continued reliance was placed on the restrictive tests of "unlawful objectives" and "unlawful means." The Clayton Act, which Samuel Gompers had hailed as labor's "charter of freedom," was rendered impotent by a series of Supreme Court decisions of which *Duplex Printing Press Co. v. Deering* is the leading illustration.

---

## Duplex Printing Press Co. v. Deering

254 U.S. 443, 41 S.Ct. 172, 65 L.Ed. 349 (1921).

■ Mr. Justice Pitney delivered the opinion of the Court.

This was a suit in equity brought by appellant in the District Court for the Southern District of New York for an injunction to restrain a course of conduct carried on by defendants in that district and vicinity in maintaining a boycott against the products of complainant's factory, in furtherance of a conspiracy to injure and destroy its good will, trade, and business— especially to obstruct and destroy its interstate trade. * * * Complainant is a Michigan corporation, and manufactures printing presses at a factory in Battle Creek, in that state, employing about 200 machinists in the factory, in addition to 50 office employees, traveling salesmen, and expert machinists or road men, who supervise the erection of the presses for complainant's customers at their various places of business. * * * [It] conducts its business on the "open shop" policy, without discrimination against either union or non-union men. The individual defendants and the local organizations of which they are the representatives are affiliated with the International Association of Machinists, an unincorporated association having a membership of more than 60,000, and are united in a combination, to which the International Association also is a party, having the object of compelling complainant to unionize its factory and enforce the "closed shop," the eight-hour day, and the union scale of wages, by means of interfering with and restraining its interstate trade in the products of the factory. Complainant's principal manufacture is newspaper presses of large size and complicated mechanism, varying in weight from 10,000 to 100,000 pounds, and requiring a considerable force of labor and a considerable expenditure of time—a week or more—to handle, haul, and erect them at the point of delivery. These presses are sold throughout the United States and in foreign countries; and, as they are especially designed for the production of daily papers, there is a large market for them in and about the city of New York. They are delivered there in the ordinary course of interstate commerce; the handling, hauling, and installation work at destination being done by employees of the purchaser under the supervision of a specially skilled machinist supplied by complainant. The acts complained of and sought to be restrained have nothing to do with the conduct or management of the factory in Michigan, but solely with the installation and operation of the presses by complainant's customers. None of the defendants is or ever was an employee of complainant, and complainant at no time has had relations with either of the organizations that they represent. In August, 1913 (eight months before the filing of the bill), the International Association called a strike at complainant's factory in Battle Creek, as a result of which union machinists to the number of about 11 in the factory and 3 who supervised the erection of presses in the field left complainant's employ. But the defection of so small a number did not materially interfere with the operation of the factory, and sales and shipments in interstate commerce continued.

The acts complained of made up the details of an elaborate programme adopted and carried out by defendants and their organizations in and about the city of New York as part of a country-wide programme adopted by the International Association, for the purpose of enforcing a boycott of complainant's product. The acts embraced the following, with others: Warning customers that it would be better for them not to purchase, or having purchased, not to install, presses made by complainant, and threatening them with loss should they do so; threatening customers with sympathetic strikes in other trades; notifying a trucking company, usually employed by customers to haul the presses, not to do so, and threatening it with trouble if it should; inciting employees of the trucking company, and other men employed by customers of complainant, to strike against their respective employers in order to interfere with the hauling and installation of presses, and thus bring pressure to bear upon the customers; notifying repair shops not to do repair work on Duplex presses; coercing union men, by threatening them with loss of union cards and with being blacklisted as "scabs" if they assisted in installing the presses; threatening an exposition company with a strike if it permitted complainant's presses to be exhibited; and resorting to a variety of other modes of preventing the sale of presses of complainant's manufacture in or about New York City, and delivery of them in interstate commerce, such as injuring and threatening to injure complainant's customers and prospective customers, and persons concerned in hauling, handling, or installing the presses. In some cases the threats were undisguised; in other cases polite in form, but none the less sinister in purpose and effect. * * *

All the judges of the Circuit Court of Appeals concurred in the view that defendants' conduct consisted essentially of efforts to render it impossible for complainant to carry on any commerce in printing presses between Michigan and New York and that defendants had agreed to do and were endeavoring to accomplish the very thing pronounced unlawful by this court in Loewe v. Lawlor, * * * [and] that the interference with interstate commerce was such as ought to be enjoined, unless the Clayton Act of October 15, 1914, forbade such injunction.

* * * [The Court held that the Clayton Act applied to injunction actions that were pending at the time of the Act's passage.]

Looking first to the [Sherman Act] the thing declared illegal by its first section (26 Stat. 209 [Comp.St. § 8820] )is:

"Every contract, combination in the form of trust or otherwise, or conspiracy, in restraint of trade or commerce among the several states, or with foreign nations." * * *

In Loewe v. Lawlor, 208 U.S. 274, 28 Sup.Ct. 301, 52 L.Ed. 488, 13 Ann.Cas. 815, where there was an effort to compel plaintiffs to unionize their factory by preventing them from manufacturing articles intended for transportation beyond the state, and also by preventing vendees from reselling articles purchased from plaintiffs and negotiating with plaintiffs for further purchases, by means of a boycott of plaintiffs' products and of dealers who handled them, this court held that there was a conspiracy in restraint of trade actionable under section 7 of the Sherman Act (section 8829), * * *. And when the case came before the court a second time, 235 U.S. 522, 534, 35 Sup.Ct. 170, 59 L.Ed. 341, it was held that the use of the primary and secondary boycott and the circulation of a list of "unfair dealers," intended to influence customers of plaintiffs and thus subdue the latter to the demands of the defendants, and having the effect of interfering with plaintiffs' interstate trade, was actionable. * * *

Upon the question whether the provisions of the Clayton Act forbade the grant of an injunction under the circumstances of the present case, the Circuit Court of Appeals was divided; the majority holding that under section 20, "perhaps in conjunction with section 6," there could be no injunction. * * *

As to section 6, it seems to us its principal importance in this discussion is for what it does not authorize, and for the limit it sets to the immunity conferred. The section assumes the normal objects of a labor organization to be legitimate, and declares that nothing in the anti-trust laws shall be construed to forbid the existence and operation of such organizations or to forbid their members from *lawfully* carrying out their *legitimate* objects; and that such an organization shall not be held in itself—merely because of its existence and operation—to be an illegal combination or conspiracy in restraint of trade. But there is nothing in the section to exempt such an organization or its members from accountability where it or they depart from its normal and legitimate objects and engage in an actual combination or conspiracy in restraint of trade. And by no fair or permissible construction can it be taken as authorizing any activity otherwise unlawful, or enabling a normally lawful organization to become a cloak for an illegal combination or conspiracy in restraint of trade as defined by the anti-trust laws.

The principal reliance is upon section 20. * * * The first paragraph merely puts into statutory form familiar restrictions upon the granting of injunctions already established and of general application in the equity practice of the courts of the United States. It is but declaratory of the law as it stood before. The second paragraph declares that "no such restraining order or injunction" shall prohibit certain conduct specified—manifestly still referring to a "case between an employer and employees, * * * involving, or growing out of, a dispute concerning terms or conditions of employment," as designated in the first paragraph. It is very clear that the restriction upon the use of the injunction is in favor only of those concerned as parties to such a dispute as is described. * * * If the qualifying words are to have any effect, they must operate to confine the restriction upon the granting of injunctions, and also the relaxation of the provisions of the anti-trust and other laws of the United States, to parties standing in proximate relation to a controversy such as is particularly described.

The majority of the Circuit Court of Appeals appears to have entertained the view that the words "employers and employees," as used in section 20, should be treated as referring to "the business class or clan to which the parties litigant respectively belong," and that, as there had been a dispute at complainant's factory in Michigan concerning the conditions of employment there—a dispute created, it is said, if it did not exist before, by the act of the Machinists' Union in calling a strike at the factory—section 20 operated to permit members of the Machinists' Union elsewhere, some 60,000 in number, although standing in no relation of employment under complainant, past, present, or prospective, to make that dispute their own and proceed to instigate sympathetic strikes, picketing, and boycotting against employers wholly unconnected with complainant's factory and having relations with complainant only in the way of purchasing its product in the ordinary course of interstate commerce, and this where there was no dispute between such employers and their employees respecting terms or conditions of employment.

We deem this construction altogether inadmissible. Section 20 must be given full effect according to its terms as an expression of the purpose of Congress; but it must be borne in mind that the section imposes an exceptional and extraordinary restriction upon the equity powers of the courts of the United States and upon the general operation of the anti-trust laws, a restriction in the nature of a special privilege or immunity to a particular class, with corresponding detriment to the general public; and it would violate rules of statutory construction having general application and far-reaching importance to enlarge that special privilege by resorting to a loose construction of the section, not to speak of ignoring or slighting the qualifying words that are found in it. Full and fair effect will be given to every word if the exceptional privilege be confined—as the natural meaning of the words confines it—to those who are proximately and substantially concerned as parties to an actual dispute respecting the terms or conditions of their own employment, past, present, or prospective. * * *

The qualifying effect of the words descriptive of the nature of the dispute and the parties concerned is further borne out by the phrases defining the conduct that is not to be subjected to injunction or treated as a violation of the laws of the United States, that is to say:

(a) "Terminating any relation of employment, * * * or persuading others by peaceful means so to do;" (b) "attending at any place where any such person or persons may lawfully be, for the purpose of peacefully obtaining or communicating information, or from peacefully persuading any person to work or to abstain from working;" (c) "ceasing to patronize or to employ any party to such dispute, or * * * recommending, advising, or persuading others by peaceful and lawful means so to do;" (d) "paying or giving to, or withholding from, any person engaged in such dispute, any strike benefits; * * * " (e) "doing any act or thing which might lawfully be done in the absence of such dispute by any party thereto."

The emphasis placed on the words "lawful" and "lawfully," "peaceful" and "peacefully," and the references to the dispute and the parties to it, strongly rebut a legislative intent to confer a general immunity for conduct violative of the anti-trust laws, or otherwise unlawful. The subject of the boycott is dealt with specifically in the "ceasing to patronize" provision, and by the clear force of the language employed the exemption is limited to pressure exerted upon a "party to such dispute" by means of "peaceful and *lawful*" influence upon neutrals. There is nothing here to justify defendants or the organizations they represent in using either threats or persuasion to bring about strikes or a cessation of work on the part of employees of complainant's customers or prospective customers, or of the trucking company employed by the customers, with the object of compelling such customers to withdraw or refrain from commercial relations with complainant, and of thereby constraining complainant to yield the matter in dispute. To instigate a sympathetic strike in aid of a secondary boycott cannot be deemed "peaceful and lawful" persuasion. In essence it is a threat to inflict damage upon the immediate employer, between whom and his employees no dispute exists, in order to bring him against his will into a concerted plan to inflict damage upon another employer who is in dispute with his employees.

\* \* \*

The extreme and harmful consequences of the construction adopted in the court below are not to be ignored. The present case furnishes an apt and convincing example. An ordinary controversy in a manufacturing establishment, said to concern the terms or conditions of employment there, has been held a sufficient occasion for imposing a general embargo upon the products of the establishment and a nationwide blockade of the channels of interstate commerce against them, carried out by inciting sympathetic strikes and a secondary boycott against complainant's customers, to the great and incalculable damage of many innocent people far remote from any connection with or control over the original and actual dispute—people constituting, indeed, the general public upon whom the cost must ultimately fall, and whose vital interest in unobstructed commerce constituted the prime and paramount concern of Congress in enacting the anti-trust laws, of which the section under consideration forms after all a part.

Reaching the conclusion, as we do, that complainant has a clear right to an injunction under the Sherman Act as amended by the Clayton Act, it becomes unnecessary to consider whether a like result would follow under the common law or local statutes; there being no suggestion that relief thereunder could be broader than that to which complainant is entitled under the acts of Congress. \* \* \*

■ Mr. Justice Brandeis, dissenting, with whom Mr. Justice Holmes and Mr. Justice Clarke, concur.

The Duplex Company, a manufacturer of newspaper printing presses, seeks to enjoin officials of the machinists' and affiliated unions from interfering with its business by inducing their members not to work for plaintiff or its customers in connection with the setting up of presses made by it. Unlike Hitchman Coal & Coke Co. v. Mitchell, 245 U.S. 229, 38 Sup.Ct. 65, 62 L.Ed. 260, L.R.A.1918C, 497, Ann.Cas.1918B, 461, there is here no charge that defendants are inducing employees to break their contracts. Nor is it now urged that defendants threaten acts of violence. But plaintiff insists that the acts complained of violate both the common law of New York and the Sherman Act, and that, accordingly, it is entitled to relief by injunction under the state law and under section sixteen of the Clayton Act, October 15, 1914, c. 323, 38 Stat. 730, 737.

The defendants admit interference with plaintiff's business but justify on the following ground: There are in the United States only four manufacturers of such presses; and they are in active competition. Between 1909 and 1913 the machinists' union induced three of them to recognize and deal with the union, to grant the eight-hour day, to establish a minimum wage scale, and to comply with other union requirements. The fourth, the Duplex Company, refused to recognize the union; insisted upon conducting its factory on the open shop principle; refused to introduce the eight-hour day and operated, for the most part, ten hours a day; refused to establish a minimum wage scale; and disregarded other union standards. Thereupon two of the three manufacturers, who had assented to union conditions, notified the union that they should be obliged to terminate their agreements with it unless their competitor, the Duplex Company, also entered into the agreement with the union, which, in giving more favorable terms to labor, imposed correspondingly greater burdens upon the employer. Because the Duplex Company refused to enter into such an agreement, and in order to induce it to do so, the machinists' union declared a strike at its factory, and in aid of that strike instructed its members and the members of affiliated unions not to work on the installation of presses which plaintiff had delivered in New York. Defendants insisted that by the common law of New York, where the acts complained of were done, and where this suit was brought, and also by section 20 of the Clayton Act, 38 Stat. 730, 738, the facts constitute a justification for this interference with plaintiff's business.

First. As to the rights at common law: Defendants' justification is that of self-interest. They have supported the strike at the employer's factory by a strike elsewhere against its product. They have injured the plaintiff, not maliciously, but in self-defense. They contend that the Duplex Company's refusal to deal with the machinists' union and to observe its standards threatened the interest, not only of such union members as were its factory employees, but even more of all members of the several affiliated unions employed by plaintiff's competitors and by others whose more advanced standards the plaintiff was, in reality, attacking; and that none of the defendants and no person whom they are endeavoring to induce to refrain from working in connection with the setting up of presses made by the plaintiff is an outsider, an interloper. In other words, that the contest between the company and the machinists' union involves vitally the interest of every person whose co-operation is sought. May not all with a common interest join in refusing to expend their labor upon articles whose very production constitutes an attack upon their standard of living and the institution which they are convinced supports it? Applying common law principles the answer should, in my opinion, be: Yes, if as a matter of fact those who so co-operate have a common interest.

The change in the law by which strikes once illegal and even criminal are now recognized as lawful was effected in America largely without the intervention of legislation. This reversal of a common-law rule was not due to the rejection by the courts of one principle and the adoption in its stead of another, but to a better realization of the facts of industrial life. It is conceded that, although the strike of the workmen in plaintiff's factory injured its business, the strike was not an actionable wrong; because the obvious self-interest of the strikers constituted a justification. See Pickett v. Walsh, 192 Mass. 572, 78 N.E. 753, 6 L.R.A.(N.S) 1067, 116 Am.St.Rep. 272, 7 Ann.Cas. 638. Formerly courts held that self-interests could not be so served. Commons, History of Labor in the United States, vol. 2, c. 5. But even after strikes to raise wages or reduce hours were held to be legal because of the self-interest, some courts held that there was not sufficient causal relationship between a strike to unionize a shop and the self-interest of the strikers to justify injuries inflicted. Plant v. Woods, 176 Mass. 492, 57 N.E. 1011 * * *. But other courts, repeating the same legal formula, found that there was justification, because they viewed the facts differently. National Protective Ass'n v. Cumming, 170 N.Y. 315, 63 N.E. 369 * * *.

When centralization in the control of business brought its corresponding centralization in the organization of workingmen, new facts had to be appraised. A single employer might, as in this case, threaten the standing of the whole organization and the standards of all its members; and when he did so the union, in order to protect itself, would naturally refuse to work on his materials wherever found. When such a situation was first presented to the courts, judges concluded that the intervention of the purchaser of the materials established an insulation through which the direct relationship of the employer and the workingmen did not penetrate; and the strike against the material was considered a strike against the purchaser by unaffected third parties. Burnham v. Dowd, 217 Mass. 351, 104 N.E. 841 * * *. But other courts, with better appreciation of the facts of industry, recognized the unity of interest throughout the union, and that, in refusing to work on materials which threatened it, the union was only refusing to aid in destroying itself. Bossert v. Dhuy, 221 N.Y. 342, 117 N.E. 582 * * *.

So, in the case at bar, deciding a question of fact upon the evidence introduced and matters of common knowledge, I should say, as the two lower courts apparently have said, that the defendants and those from whom they sought cooperation have a common interest which the plaintiff threatened. This view is in harmony with the views of the Court of Appeals of New York. For in New York, although boycotts like that in Loewe v. Lawlor, 208 U.S. 274, 28 Sup.Ct. 301, 52 L.Ed. 488, 13 Ann.Cas. 815, are illegal because they are conducted not against a product but against those who deal in it and are carried out by a combination of persons not united by common interest but only by sympathy, * * * it is lawful for all members of a union by whomever employed to refuse to handle materials whose production weakens the union. * * * "The voluntary adoption of a rule not to work on non-union made material and its enforcement * * * differs entirely from a general boycott of a particular dealer or manufacturer with a malicious intent and purpose to destroy the good will or business of such dealer or manufacturer." Bossert v. Dhuy * * *. In my opinion, therefore, plaintiff had no cause of action by the common law of New York.

Second. As to the anti-trust laws of the United States: [The Clayton Act] was the fruit of unceasing agitation, which extended over more than 20 years and was designed to equalize before the law the position of workingmen and employer as industrial combatants. Aside from the use of the injunction, the chief source of dissatisfaction with the existing law lay in the doctrine of malicious combination, and, in many parts of the country, in the judicial declarations of the illegality at common law of picketing and persuading others to leave work. The grounds for objection to the latter are obvious. The objection to the doctrine of malicious combinations requires some explanation. By virtue of that doctrine, damage resulting from conduct such as striking or withholding patronage or persuading others to do either, which without more might be damnum absque injuria because the result of trade competition, became actionable when done for a purpose which a judge considered socially or economically harmful and therefore branded as malicious and unlawful. It was objected that, due largely to environment, the social and economic ideas of judges, which thus became translated into law, were prejudicial to a position of equality, between workingman and employer; that due to this dependence upon the individual opinion of judges great confusion existed as to what purposes were lawful and what unlawful; and that in any event Congress, not the judges, was the body which should declare what public policy in regard to the industrial struggle demands.

By 1914, the ideas of the advocates of legislation had fairly crystalized upon the manner in which the inequality and uncertainty of the law should be removed. It was to be done by expressly legalizing certain acts regardless of the effects produced by them upon other persons. As to them Congress was to extract the element of injuria from the damages thereby inflicted, instead of leaving judges to determine according to their own economic and social views whether the damage inflicted on an employer in an industrial struggle was damnum absque injuria, because an incident of trade competition, or a legal injury, because in their opinion, economically and socially objectionable. This idea was presented to the committees which reported the Clayton Act. The resulting law set out certain acts which had previously been held unlawful, whenever courts had disapproved of the ends for which they were performed; it then declared that, when these acts were committed in the course of an industrial dispute, they should not be held to violate any law of the United States. In other words the Clayton Act substituted the opinion of Congress as to the propriety of the purpose for that of differing judges; and thereby it declared that the relations between employers of labor and workingmen were competitive relations, that organized competition was not harmful and that it justified injuries necessarily inflicted in its course. Both the majority and the minority report of the House committee indicate that such was its purpose. If, therefore, the act applies to the case at bar, the acts here complained of cannot "be considered or held to be violations of any law of the United States," and hence do not violate the Sherman Act.

The Duplex Company contends that section 20 of the Clayton Act does not apply to the case at bar, because it is restricted to cases "between an employer and employees, or between employers and employees, or between employees, or between persons employed and persons seeking employment, involving, or growing out of, a dispute concerning terms or conditions of employment"; whereas the case at bar arises between an employer in Michigan and workingmen in New York not in its employ, and does not involve their conditions of employment. But Congress did not restrict the provision to employers and workingmen in their employ. By including "employers and employees" and "persons employed and persons seeking employment" it showed that it was not aiming merely at a legal relationship between a specific employer and his employees. * * *

Because I have come to the conclusion that both the common law of a state and a statute of the United States declare the right of industrial combatants to push their struggle to the limits of the justification of self-interest, I do not wish to be understood as attaching any constitutional or moral sanction to that right. All rights are derived from the purposes of the society in which they exist; above all rights rises duty to the community. The conditions developed in industry may be such that those engaged in it cannot continue their struggle without danger to the community. But it is not for judges to determine whether such conditions exist, nor is it their function to set the limits of permissible contest and to declare the duties which the new situation demands. This is the function of the legislature which, while limiting individual and group rights of aggression and defense, may substitute processes of justice for the more primitive method of trial by combat.

---

## PROBLEMS FOR DISCUSSION

**1.** Was the strike at the Duplex plant in Michigan a violation of the Sherman Act? What exactly was done by the defendant Machinists employed by the New York newspapers? Is there any difference in the treatment of this factual issue by Mr. Justice Pitney and Mr. Justice Brandeis?

**2.** What were the critical phrases on the interpretation of which the *Duplex* case turned? As a matter of textual reading which party had the stronger case? What light, if any, did other parts of Section 20 throw upon the issue? See generally Ernst, The Labor Exemption, 1908–14, 74 Iowa L.Rev. 1151 (1989).

**3.** Would Mr. Justice Brandeis have joined in the endorsement of an injunction had the New York machinists gone beyond refusing to work on the "hot" printing presses and had instead refused altogether to work for their newspaper employers? Or had they gone yet further and sought to pressure teamsters to refuse to truck the hot presses or to refuse to work altogether for *their* trucker employers?

---

## IV. LEGISLATIVE AND CONSTITUTIONAL PROTECTIONS

---

### A. THE ENACTMENT OF THE NORRIS–LAGUARDIA ACT

The narrow interpretation put upon Section 20 of the Clayton Act in the *Duplex* case marked, at least for the time being, the failure of the first legislative attempt to curtail the use of the injunction in labor disputes. Throughout the 1920's injunctions were quickly sought and readily obtained under the "means" and "objectives" tests. Nevertheless there were constant additions to the body of opinion which opposed the intervention of the courts into labor disputes and regarded judicial interpretations of the Clayton Act as a frustration of sound legislative policy. In 1932 this policy was adopted by Congress in the Norris–LaGuardia Act, which also served as a model for a number of state anti-injunction statutes.

The classic exposition of what were believed to be the evils of the labor injunction is Frankfurter and Greene, The Labor Injunction (1930). A shorter discussion may be found in Gregory & Katz, Labor and the Law chap. IV (3d ed. 1979). We summarize here the main points made by critics of the labor injunction in advocating legislative curtailment of the power of the courts.

*Substantive considerations.* Many of the criticisms of judicial intervention into labor disputes stemmed from the premise that the courts could neither adjudicate the underlying labor controversy nor adopt measures to remedy the causes of strikes and industrial unrest. Regardless of whether the employees were provoked to strike by the action of their employer, the "means test" applied, and if violence broke out on the picket line, the picketing might be enjoined and the leaders cited for contempt without any inquiry into the occasion which gave rise to their conduct. Much the same was true of the "objectives test." Although in some cases objectives which were held unlawful were objectives which an inquiry into the merits might condemn, there are others in which the courts applied abstract concepts without real consideration of the underlying economic and human problems. In enjoining strikes for the closed shop, the courts did not inquire into the employees' need or lack of need for strengthening their organization; into the union's need or lack of need for security against employer attacks; or into the use to which the union might be expected to put the power which the closed shop gave. In *Duplex Printing Press Co. v. Deering* (p. 37 supra) the courts found no occasion to inquire either into the wages or working conditions prevailing at the Duplex plant or into their effect upon the standards which the defendants were seeking to establish in the plants of the three competitors.

It is not intended to suggest by these illustrations that critics of the labor injunction believed the courts should make such inquiries. Probably the courts were quite unsuited to adjudicating disputes "on their merits"—no one suggested that they should. The point is simply that the grant or denial of an injunction bore no relation to the merits of the underlying social and economic dispute, and that the courts could do nothing about the basic industrial problems stemming from the workers' difficulties in finding a place in the new industrial world.

The solution proposed was union organization and collective bargaining. But the pressure often needed on employees to join unions and on employers to recognize those unions (or simply not to destroy them through coercion and discrimination) took the form of strikes, picketing and boycotts. Judicial intervention which curtailed concerted activities on the part of organized employees tended to thwart the spread of collective bargaining. Organized labor and its supporters also singled out certain specific legal doctrines as especially objectionable.

One such doctrine centered upon what was known to labor and its supporters as the "yellow-dog contract." This was a provision of the employment contract in which the employee promised not to join a union during the period of his or her employment. In HITCHMAN COAL & COKE CO. v. MITCHELL, 245 U.S. 229, 38 S.Ct. 65, 62 L.Ed. 260 (1917), the Supreme Court upheld the issuance of an injunction against union organizers seeking to persuade such employees to become union members. Such otherwise lawful persuasion was, through the yellow-dog contract, converted into an interference with and "an effort to subvert" existing contractual relations. Prior to *Hitchman Coal,* the yellow-dog contract had been chiefly a psychological weapon; but that decision put into the hands of employers a new and powerful instrument which—although it could not be used under the government's wartime labor policies—became after the war a method of virtually fastening a closed, non-union shop on workers by judicial decree. Such restraints upon the solicitation of potential union members were enforced throughout the 1920s. E.g., International Organization, United Mine Workers of America v. Red Jacket Consol. Coal & Coke Co., 18 F.2d 839 (4th Cir.1927).

As a result of such decisions yellow-dog contracts enjoyed wide popularity. But in the end the decisions enforcing such contracts proved self-defeating. They became the focus for aroused opposition to judicial intervention in labor disputes. The reaction reached a peak in 1930, when the Senate voted to reject the nomination of Circuit Judge Parker (the author of the *Red Jacket* decision) to a vacancy on the United States Supreme Court. The same sentiment was largely responsible for the enactment of the Norris–LaGuardia Act by a coalition of Democrats and insurgent Republicans in 1932. The tone of the criticism is perhaps encapsulated in the remarks of Rep. Oliver (75 Cong.Rec. 5481 (1932)):

> It is strange during a period when the loudest outcry from great industrial concerns has been that government has invaded the domain of private business with meddlesome laws, that they themselves have invaded the government in a scandalous way with successful demands for injunctions that strip from labor every natural and constitutional right. It is strange, in the field of American freedom where laws do not govern but men alone reign, that the most powerful impulse of these free rules is toward tyranny.

> This bill says that a Federal court shall not arbitrarily enter the field of the government of men, where the purest liberty ought to prevail, and by the power of the government bring down into slavery those who are attempting to negotiate for what they believe to be the necessities of their lives and the happiness of their children. We are restoring the courts to a government of laws.

\* \* \*

A court issued an injunction against striking miners so that they had to leave their homes, although the State law gave them the right to stay there and contest their rights. The court issued an injunction to the effect that the union could not expend its money to feed them while they were on strike; that it could not help to clothe them and they were evicted from their homes under a Federal injunction, when the dispute was about wages.... [A] court issued an injunction to the effect that no striker might talk to another striker about the strike; that a striker could not publish in the newspapers that there was a strike; that he could not telegraph, telephone or write to anyone in America that there was a strike; that a striker might not ever say there was a "yellow-dog" contract, signed with his name, but coerced from him by his bosses.

The second point on which criticism of the labor injunction tended to focus was the so-called "objectives test," under which the courts decided according to their views of social and economic policy the question whether the employees' demands justified their combining to inflict injury on an employer. The application of this doctrine under decisions like *Plant v. Woods* (p. 23, supra); and *Duplex Printing Press Co. v. Deering* (p. 40, supra) was so severely narrow as to handicap many organizational activities; but perhaps the sharpest accusation was that the courts were applying a "double standard": one law of combination and competition for corporate enterprises, another for labor unions. Some insight into the justice of this accusation may be gained by comparing the decision in *Plant v. Woods* and the abstracts on page 30, supra, with the abstracts of *Bowen v. Matheson* and *Mogul S. S. Co. v. McGregor, Gow & Co.* (pp. 27–28, supra).

An unfortunate characteristic of many American strikes has been the accompanying violence. Labor unions complained that the courts sought to deal with such violence by injunctions and citations for contempt instead of leaving the protection of persons and property to the normal processes of the criminal law. They also complained of the doctrines under which the misconduct of a few individuals was attributed to the labor organization which sponsored a strike or picket line. Under the law of conspiracy as developed in labor cases, unions "were held responsible not for acts of agents who had authority to act, but for every act committed by any member of a union merely because he was a member, or because he had some relation to the union although not authorized by virtue of his position to act for the union in what he did." (Mr. Justice Frankfurter dissenting in United Brotherhood of Carpenters and Joiners v. United States, 330 U.S. 395, 67 S.Ct. 775, 91 L.Ed. 973 (1947).) Under the rule enunciated in the *Debs* case, see United States v. Debs, 64 Fed. 724, 764 (C.C.Ill.1894), aff'd on other grounds, 158 U.S. 564, 15 S.Ct. 900, 39 L.Ed. 1092 (1895), a union which called a strike might be held responsible for violations of the criminal law even though the violations were not shown to have been permitted by union members and the union did everything possible to prevent them. Under either line of reasoning an injunction might be issued and union leaders cited for contempt in such a way as to break a strike merely because of unlawful acts which the union had not authorized and for which it would not be responsible under the normal rules of agency.

*Procedural Objections.* In equity, proceedings for an injunction are usually commenced by presenting to the chancellor a sworn bill of complaint, accompanied by affidavits, on the basis of which the complainant asks for an *ex parte* restraining order binding until both sides can be heard upon the complainant's request for an injunction *pendente lite* (more often known as a preliminary injunction). In the case of a labor dispute a restraining order would be requested to forbid the picketing and other concerted activities which accompany a strike. Since the chancellor made his decision *ex parte,* he heard only the employer's side of the case. And in the highly emotional atmosphere of a labor dispute it was all too easy for the complainant to make allegations which would justify the issuance of a restraining order and to support them with affidavits of misconduct on the part of the defendant union officers and employees.

The *ex parte* restraining order was often the decisive step in the labor dispute, for the strike was likely to be the climax of an organizing drive, and once the strike was halted, the drive could not be revived. The effect of *ex parte* restraining orders was frequently enhanced by protracted delays before the hearing on the merits. A thirty-day delay was not uncommon before the application for a temporary injunction came on to be heard. Even this application might be determined on the papers alone without an opportunity to cross-examine witnesses. The trial came still later—unless the case had been rendered moot by the collapse of the strike and the defeat of the union. The appellate process was even slower.

Severe criticism was also levelled at the obscurity of injunctions written by lawyers but addressed to workingmen. In *Great Northern R. Co. v. Brosseau,* 286 Fed. 414 (D.N.D.1923), Judge Amidon commented—

"During the 30 years that courts have been dealing with strikes by means of injunctions, these orders have steadily grown in length, complexity, and the vehemence of their rhetoric. They are full of the rich vocabulary of synonyms which is a part of our English language. They are also replete with superlative words and the superlative phrases of which the legal mind is fond. The result has been that such writs have steadily become more and more complex and prolix."

The enforcement of labor injunctions also raised cries of abuse. Large corporations imported strike breakers into the community and surrounded them with armed guards furnished by private detective agencies. It was often their affidavits that furnished the basis for injunctive relief. When the decree issued, the guards were sworn in as deputy sheriffs or deputy marshals. The class of plug-uglies from whom the "private detectives" on the rolls of strike-breaking agencies were recruited was not adept at preserving order; perhaps it was only natural that they should be more concerned with breaking the strike.

Under these conditions it seems unlikely that the labor injunction was as useful in maintaining order and protecting property as the ordinary police. But what seemed particularly unfair to the workers was the practice of citing those engaged in violence for contempt of court instead of prosecuting them for breaches of peace or other violations of the criminal law. The respondent was tried by the same judge who issued the injunction and was not entitled to the benefit of a jury of his peers. Consequently, not only did one person seem to be acting as prosecutor and judge, but the strikers lost the protection of a trial before a body which might have been more sympathetic towards their cause and more understanding of the emotional tensions of a labor dispute.

*Considerations of Judicial Administration.* In the eyes of many students of the labor injunction the merits of the contending arguments of management and labor were far less important than its effect on the prestige of the courts. It was plain to anyone that labor cases turned on questions of social and economic policy more suitable for legislative than judicial determination. Since judicial doctrines favored employers and were regarded as highly unfair by union supporters, workers acquired a distrust of the courts which shook their confidence in law and which even today must be taken into account in shaping labor policies.

"The history of the labor injunction in action puts some matters beyond question. In large part, dissatisfaction and resentment are caused, first, by the refusal of courts to recognize that breaches of the peace may be redressed through criminal prosecution and civil action for damages, and, second, by the expansion of a simple, judicial device to an enveloping code of prohibited conduct, absorbing, *en masse,* executive and police functions and affecting the livelihood, and even lives, of multitudes. Especially those zealous for the unimpaired prestige of our courts have observed how the administration of law by decrees which through vast and vague phrases surmount law, undermines the esteem of courts upon which our reign of law depends. Not government, but 'government by injunction', characterized by the consequences of a criminal prosecution without its safeguards, has been challenged." (Frankfurter & Greene, The Labor Injunction 200 (1930).)

*Interpretation of the Act.* It is useful to examine the provisions of the Norris–LaGuardia Act in some detail. (Consult the full text of the statute in the Statutory Supplement.) Consider Section 2 of the Act, and its broad declaration of the need to protect workers in joining unions, pursuing collective bargaining, and resorting to concerted activities. Is Congress suggesting that these are substantive rights to be protected against employer interference—or is the statute simply one that purports to regulate the equity jurisdiction of the federal courts? Consider, in each section, whether Congress was promoting national policy through "procedural" or through "substantive" regulation. What particular abuses in the prior law was each of the sections designed to correct? In what respects do the provisions of the Norris–LaGuardia Act differ from those of Section 20 of the Clayton Act? Consider the substantive labor activity itemized in both statutes and the procedural or remedial provisions as well.

## B. The Sherman Act Reexamined

It will be recalled that in Loewe v. Lawlor, supra p. 33, the Supreme Court held that the Sherman Act applied to combinations of workers. That case was an action for damages, but with the introduction in the Clayton Act of 1914 of the private injunctive action, the federal courts became available to private parties for equity relief against antitrust violations. The Supreme Court affirmed the grant of such relief, at least against the secondary boycott—in the face of the other more labor-protective provisions of the Clayton Act—in the *Duplex* case, at p. 40, supra.

In the course of time, however, the usefulness of the Sherman Act as a strike-breaking weapon was curtailed by decisions holding that certain strikes at manufacturing establishments did not have the necessary relationship to interstate commerce to come under federal authority. Apparently coverage depended upon the strikers' purpose. If a union made up of employees at a manufacturing establishment called a strike for the purpose of raising their wages or improving their working conditions, the combination did not violate the Sherman Act even though shipments in interstate commerce were halted or reduced. *E.g.,* United Leather Workers' v. Herkert & Meisel Trunk Co., 265 U.S. 457, 44 S.Ct. 623, 68 L.Ed. 1104 (1924). However, if a union which had organized some establishments in an industry were to call an organizational strike or institute a boycott in order to organize non-union factories and protect its members against the competition of cheap, non-union goods, then the strike would be unlawful. Coronado Coal Co. v. United Mine Workers, 268 U.S. 295, 45 S.Ct. 551, 69 L.Ed. 963 (1925); Alco–Zander Co. v. Amalgamated Clothing Workers, 35 F.2d 203 (D.C.Pa.1929). Whether this distinction would have survived the expanded concept of interstate commerce which developed after 1937 is uncertain.

By 1940, reexamination of the reach and purposes of the Sherman Act was also appropriate in light of Congress's more hospitable attitude toward unions and toward the stabilization of economic conditions in the labor market. Congressional support for unionization and collective bargaining was declared most conspicuously in the Railway Labor Act of 1926 (amended in 1934) and the National Labor Relations Act of 1935, as well as in the Norris–LaGuardia Act of 1932. A number of New Deal statutes manifested an understanding that wages, hours and other labor conditions are not altogether appropriately determined by competition in the labor market. The Fair Labor Standards Act of 1938 standardized employer practices regarding minimum wages, maximum hours and overtime pay. The Social Security Act of 1935 served as the foundation for a federal program of retirement and disability benefits, survivors' insurance benefits and unemployment compensation. The Davis–Bacon Act of 1931 set minimum wage standards on public projects, and the Walsh–Healey Act of 1936 required contractors with the federal government to meet specified wage and hour standards.

This congressional recognition that standardization of working conditions was sound economic policy—either through unionization or through substantive legislative mandate—was bound to create tensions with the competitive premises underlying the Sherman Act. It is perhaps this realization that accounted for a major reinterpretation of the antitrust laws in the following case.

---

## Apex Hosiery Co. v. Leader

310 U.S. 469, 60 S.Ct. 982, 84 L.Ed. 1311 (1940).

■ MR. JUSTICE STONE delivered the opinion of the Court.

Petitioner, a Pennsylvania corporation, is engaged in the manufacture, at its factory in Philadelphia, of hosiery, a substantial part of which is shipped in interstate commerce. It brought the present suit in the federal district court for Eastern Pennsylvania against respondent Federation, a labor organization, and its officers, to recover treble the amount of damage inflicted on it by respondents in conducting a strike at petitioner's factory alleged to be a conspiracy in violation of the Sherman Anti–Trust Act, 26 Stat. 209, 15 U.S.C. sec. 1, 15 U.S.C.A. sec. 1. * * *

[The Federation, with only eight members among the Apex Company's 2500 workers, instigated a violent strike (aided by employees from other Philadelphia companies) in support of its demands for a closed shop. The plant was forcibly seized and occupied for some seven weeks, during which time the strikers wrecked machinery and did other substantial damage to company property and equipment. For nearly three months, none of Apex's hosiery could be shipped in interstate commerce; the strike prevented the shipment of some $800,000 worth of finished hosiery, 80 percent of which was to be shipped outside the state. A jury trial resulted in a verdict of $237,310, which the district court trebled in entering judgment for the petitioner in excess of $711,000. The court of appeals reversed, concluding that the effect of the strike upon interstate commerce (less than three percent of the total output of the American hosiery industry) was insubstantial and also that the evidence failed to show an intent on the part of the respondents to restrain interstate commerce.]

A point strongly urged in behalf of respondents in brief and argument before us is that Congress intended to exclude labor organizations and their activities wholly from the operation of the Sherman Act. To this the short answer must be made that for the thirty-two years which have elapsed since the decision of Loewe v. Lawlor, 208 U.S. 274, 28 S.Ct. 301, 52 L.Ed. 488, 13 Ann.Cas. 815, this Court, in its efforts to determine the true meaning and application of the Sherman Act has repeatedly held that the words of the act, "Every contract, combination * * * or conspiracy, in restraint of trade or commerce" do embrace to some extent and in some circumstances labor unions and their activities; and that during that period Congress, although often asked to do so, has passed no act purporting to exclude labor unions wholly from the operation of the Act. On the contrary Congress has repeatedly enacted laws restricting or purporting to curtail the application of the Act to labor organizations and their activities, thus recognizing that to some extent not defined they remain subject to it. * * *

While we must regard the question whether labor unions are to some extent and in some circumstances subject to the Act as settled in the affirmative, it is equally plain that this Court has never thought the Act to apply to all labor union activities affecting interstate commerce. The prohibitions of the Sherman Act were not stated in terms of precision or of crystal clarity and the Act itself did not define them. In consequence of the vagueness of its language, perhaps not uncalculated, the courts have been left to give content to the statute, and in the performance of that function it is appropriate that courts should interpret its words in the light of its legislative history and of the particular evils at which the legislation was aimed. * * *

The critical words which circumscribe the judicial performance of this function so far as the present case is concerned are "Every * * * combination * * * or conspiracy, in restraint of trade or commerce." Since in the present case, as we have seen, the natural and predictable consequence of the strike was the restraint of interstate transportation the precise question which we are called upon to decide is whether that restraint resulting from the strike maintained to enforce union demands by compelling a shutdown of petitioner's factory is the kind of "restraint of trade or commerce" which the Act condemns.

In considering whether union activities like the present may fairly be deemed to be embraced within this phrase, three circumstances relating to the history and application of the Act which are of striking significance must first be taken into account. The legislative history of the Sherman Act as well as the decisions of this Court interpreting it, show that it was not aimed at policing interstate transportation or movement of goods and property. * * * It was another and quite a different evil at which the Sherman Act was aimed. It was enacted in the era of "trusts" and of "combinations" of businesses and of capital organized and directed to control of the market by suppression of competition in the marketing of goods and services, the monopolistic tendency of which had become a matter of public concern. The end sought was the prevention of restraints to free competition in business and commercial transactions which tended to restrict production, raise prices or otherwise control the market to the detriment of purchasers or consumers of goods and services, all of which had come to be regarded as a special form of public injury. * * *

A second significant circumstance is that this Court has never applied the Sherman Act in any case, whether or not involving labor organizations or activities unless the Court was of opinion that there was some form of restraint upon commercial competition in the marketing of goods or services and finally this Court has refused to apply the Sherman Act in cases like the present in which local strikes conducted by illegal means in a production industry prevented interstate shipment of substantial amounts of the product but in which it was not shown that the restrictions on shipments had operated to restrain commercial competition in some substantial way. * * *

The common law doctrines relating to contracts and combinations in restraint of trade were well understood long before the enactment of the Sherman law. They were contracts for the restriction or suppression of competition in the market, agreements to fix prices, divide marketing territories, apportion customers, restrict production and the like practices, which tend to raise prices or otherwise take from buyers or consumers the advantages which accrue to them from free competition in the market. Such contracts were deemed illegal and were unenforcible at common law. * * * In enacting the Sherman law [Congress] took over that concept by condemning such restraints wherever they occur in or affect commerce between the states. They extended the condemnation of the statute to restraints effected by any combination in the form of trust or otherwise, or conspiracy, as well as by contract or agreement, having those effects on the competitive system and on purchasers and consumers of goods or services which were characteristic of restraints deemed illegal at common law, and they gave both private and public remedies for the injuries flowing from such restraints. * * *

The question remains whether the effect of the combination or conspiracy among respondents was a restraint of trade within the meaning of the Sherman Act. This is not a case of a labor organization being used by combinations of those engaged in an industry as the means or instrument for suppressing competition or fixing prices. See United States v. Brims, 272 U.S. 549, 47 S.Ct. 169, 71 L.Ed. 403; Local 167 v. United States, 291 U.S. 293, 54 S.Ct. 396, 78 L.Ed. 804. Here it is plain that the combination or conspiracy did not have as its purpose restraint upon competition in the market for petitioner's product. Its object was to compel petitioner to accede to the union demands and an effect of it, in consequence of the strikers' tortious acts, was the prevention of the removal of petitioner's product for interstate shipment. So far as appears the delay of these shipments was not intended to have and had no effect on prices of hosiery in the market * * *

A combination of employees necessarily restrains competition among themselves in the sale of their services to the employer; yet such a combination was not considered an illegal restraint of trade at common law when the Sherman Act was adopted, either because it was not thought to be unreasonable or because it was not deemed a "restraint of trade." Since the enactment of the declaration in § 6 of the Clayton Act that "the labor of a human being is not a commodity or article of commerce * * * nor shall such [labor] organizations or the members thereof, be held or construed to be illegal combinations or conspiracies in restraint of trade, under the antitrust laws", it would seem plain that restraints on the sale of the employee's services to the employer, however much they curtail the competition among employees, are not in themselves combinations or conspiracies in restraint of trade or commerce under the Sherman Act.

* * * Furthermore, successful union activity, as for example consummation of a wage agreement with employers, may have some influence on price competition by eliminating that part of such competition which is based on differences in labor standards. Since, in order to render a labor combination effective it must eliminate the competition from non-union made goods, see American Steel Foundries v. Tri–City Central Trades Council, 257 U.S. 184, 209, 42 S.Ct. 72, 78, 66 L.Ed. 189, 27 A.L.R. 360, an elimination of price competition based on differences in labor standards is the objective of any national labor organization. But this effect on competition has not been considered to be the kind of curtailment of price competition prohibited by the Sherman Act. * * *

[The Court then traced its decisions holding secondary boycotts unlawful under the Sherman Act, including Duplex Printing Press Co. v. Deering, 254 U.S. 443, 41 S.Ct. 172 (1921), page 40, supra, and Bedford Cut Stone Co. v. Journeyman Stone Cutters' Ass'n, 274 U.S. 37, 47 S.Ct. 522 (1927). The Court noted that in Loewe v. Lawlor, page 33, supra, the Court drew an analogy to an unlawful conspiracy to circulate a "blacklist" designed to induce retailers not to deal with specified wholesalers. It then observed that in all such cases of secondary boycotts, "the effort of the union was to compel unionization of an employer's factory, not by a strike in his factory but by restraining by the boycott or refusal to work on the manufactured product purchases of his product in interstate commerce in competition with the like product of union shops."]

It will be observed that in each of these cases where the Act was held applicable to labor unions, the activities affecting interstate commerce were directed at control of the market and were so widespread as substantially to affect it. There was thus a suppression of competition in the market by methods which were deemed analogous to those found to be violations in the non-labor cases. * * * That the objective of the restraint in the boycott cases was the strengthening of the bargaining position of the union and not the elimination of business competition—which was the end in the nonlabor cases—was thought to be immaterial because the Court viewed the restraint itself, in contrast to the interference with shipments caused by a local factory strike, to be of a kind regarded as offensive at common law because of its effect in curtailing a free market and it was held to offend against the Sherman Act because it effected and was aimed at suppression of competition with union made goods in the interstate market.

Both the Duplex Printing Co. and Bedford Stone cases followed the enactment of the Clayton Act and the recognition of the "rule of reason" in the Standard Oil case, supra. The applicability of that rule to restraints upon commerce effected by a labor union in order to promote and consolidate the interests of its union was not considered.[25] But an important point

25. Whether the interest of the labor unions in these cases in maintaining and extending their respective organizations, rendered the restraint reasonable as a means of attaining that end within the common law rule, or brought the restraints within the rule of reason developed and announced in the Standard Oil case, was not discussed and we need not consider it here. * * *

considered and decided by the Court in both cases was that nothing in the Clayton Act precluded the relief granted. We are not now concerned with the merits of either point. The only significance of the two cases for present purposes is that in each the Court considered it necessary, in order to support its decision, to find that the restraint operated to suppress competition in the market.

If, without such effects on the market, we were to hold that a local factory strike, stopping production and shipment of its product interstate, violates the Sherman law, practically every strike in modern industry would be brought within the jurisdiction of the federal courts, under the Sherman Act, to remedy local law violations. The Act was plainly not intended to reach such a result, its language does not require it, and the course of our decisions precludes it. The maintenance in our federal system of a proper distribution between state and national governments of police authority and of remedies private and public for public wrongs is of far-reaching importance. An intention to disturb the balance is not lightly to be imputed to Congress. The Sherman Act is concerned with the character of the prohibited restraints and with their effect on interstate commerce. It draws no distinction between the restraints effected by violence and those achieved by peaceful but oftentimes quite as effective means. Restraints not within the Act, when achieved by peaceful means, are not brought within its sweep merely because, without other differences, they are attended by violence.

[The dissenting opinion is omitted.]

---

## PROBLEMS FOR DISCUSSION

**1.** After *Apex Hosiery,* is it safe to say that all concerted activities by nonemployees with an objective of organizing or securing recognition from a company will be immune from antitrust liability? Is *Coronado Coal* thus overruled?

**2.** After *Apex Hosiery,* is it safe to say that all secondary-boycott activity will be immune from antitrust liability? Is *Loewe v. Lawlor* thus overruled? (Reconsider this question after reading the *Hutcheson* case immediately below.)

**3.** Would the strike and picketing in the Dainty Garment problem (p. 29, supra) violate the Sherman Act as construed by the Supreme Court in *Apex?*

**4.** Does this decision effectively render Sections 6 and 20 of the Clayton Act, and the Norris–LaGuardia Act, unnecessary as protections for peaceful (and indeed even violent) self-interested labor activity?

---

## C.  THE APPLICATION OF THE NORRIS–LAGUARDIA ACT

The ink on the *Apex Hosiery* decision was hardly dry when the Supreme Court—somewhat more controversially—placed drastic restrictions upon the application of the Sherman Act not through a narrowing construction of that Act but rather through an expansive interpretation of the Norris–LaGuardia Act. The *Hutcheson* case, a criminal prosecution, grew out of a program developed in the late 1930s by Assistant Attorney General Thurman Arnold to utilize criminal sanctions under the Sherman Act to combat certain labor union abuses. He assured that there was no intention to prosecute unions for using strikes, picketing, boycotts and other coercion having a reasonable connection to wages, hours, health or safety, or the establishment and maintenance of collective bargaining. The primary targets, rather, were these: (a) union attempts to prevent the use of cheaper material, improved equipment or more efficient methods; (b) union attempts to compel the hiring of useless and unnecessary labor (as distinguished from "reasonable requirements that a minimum amount of labor be hired in the interests of safety and health or of avoidance of undue speeding of the work"); (c) union extortion of businesses; (d) union cooperation with businesses in enforcing price-fixing schemes; and (e) union attempts to wrest work from other unions already in established collective bargaining relationships (jurisdictional disputes). Is all (or any) of this union conduct a proper target for antitrust prosecutions, when tested against the original purposes of the Sherman Act?

---

## United States v. Hutcheson

312 U.S. 219, 61 S.Ct. 463, 85 L.Ed. 788 (1941).

■ MR. JUSTICE FRANKFURTER delivered the opinion of the Court.

\* \* \* Anheuser–Busch, Inc., operating a large plant in St. Louis, contracted with Borsari Tank Corporation for the erection of an additional facility. The Gaylord Container Corporation, a lessee of adjacent property from Anheuser–Busch, made a similar contract for a new building with the Stocker Company. Anheuser–Busch obtained the materials for its brewing and other operations and sold its finished products largely through interstate shipments. The Gaylord Corporation was equally dependent on interstate commerce for marketing its goods, as were the construction companies for their building materials. Among the employees of Anheuser–Busch were members of the United Brotherhood of Carpenters and Joiners of America and of the International Association of Machinists. The conflicting claims of these two organizations, affiliated with the American Federation of Labor, in regard to the erection and dismantling of machinery had long been a source of controversy between them. Anheuser–Busch had had agreements with both organizations whereby the Machinists were given the disputed jobs and the Carpenters agreed to submit all disputes to arbitration. But in 1939 the president of the Carpenters, their general representative, and two officials of the Carpenters' local organization, the four men under indictment, stood on the claims of the Carpenters for the jobs. Rejection by the employer of the Carpenters' demand and the refusal of the latter to submit to arbitration were followed by a strike of the Carpenters, called by the defendants against Anheuser–Busch and the construction companies, a picketing of Anheuser–Busch and its tenant, and a request through circular letters and the official publication of the Carpenters that union members and their friends refrain from buying Anheuser–Busch beer.

These activities on behalf of the Carpenters formed the charge of the indictment as a criminal combination and conspiracy in violation of the Sherman Law. Demurrers denying that what was charged constituted a violation of the laws of the United States were sustained (D.C., 32 F.Supp. 600) and the case came here under the Criminal Appeals Act.

Section 1 of the Sherman Law on which the indictment rested is as follows: "Every contract, combination in the form of trust or otherwise, or conspiracy, in restraint of trade or commerce among the several States, or with foreign nations, is hereby declared to be illegal." The controversies engendered by its application to trade union activities and the efforts to secure legislative relief from its consequences are familiar history. The Clayton Act of 1914 was the result. Act of October 15, 1914, 38 Stat. 730. "This statute was the fruit of unceasing agitation, which extended over more than 20 years and was designed to equalize before the law the position of workingmen and employer as industrial combatants." Duplex Printing Press Co. v. Deering, 254 U.S. 443, 484, 41 S.Ct. 172, 182, 65 L.Ed. 349, 16 A.L.R. 196. Section 20 of that Act * * * withdrew from the general interdict of the Sherman Law specifically enumerated practices of labor unions by prohibiting injunctions against them—since the use of the injunction had been the major source of dissatisfaction—and also relieved such practices of all illegal taint by the catch-all provision, "nor shall any of the acts specified in this paragraph be considered or held to be violations of any law of the United States". The Clayton Act gave rise to new litigation and to renewed controversy in and out of Congress regarding the status of trade unions. By the generality of its terms the Sherman Law had necessarily compelled the courts to work out its meaning from case to case. It was widely believed that into the Clayton Act courts read the very beliefs which that Act was designed to remove. Specifically the courts restricted the scope of § 20 to trade union activities directed against an employer by his own employees. Duplex Printing Press Co. v. Deering, supra. Such a view it was urged, both by powerful judicial dissents and informed lay opinion, misconceived the area of economic conflict that had best be left to economic forces and the pressure of public opinion and not subjected to the judgment of courts. Id., 254 U.S. at pages 485, 486, 41 S.Ct. at page 183, 65 L.Ed. 349, 16 A.L.R. 196. Agitation again led to legislation and in 1932 Congress wrote the Norris–LaGuardia Act. Act of March 23, 1932, 47 Stat. 70, 29 U.S.C. §§ 101–115, 29 U.S.C.A. §§ 101–115.

The Norris–LaGuardia Act removed the fetters upon trade union activities, which according to judicial construction § 20 of the Clayton Act had left untouched, by still further narrowing the circumstances under which the federal courts could grant injunctions in labor disputes. More especially, the Act explicitly formulated the "public policy of the United States" in regard to the industrial conflict and by its light established that the allowable area of union activity was not to be restricted, as it had been in the Duplex case, to an immediate employer-employee relation. Therefore, whether trade union conduct constitutes a violation of the Sherman Law is to be determined only by reading the Sherman Law and § 20 of the Clayton Act and the Norris–LaGuardia Act as a harmonizing text of outlawry of labor conduct.

Were then the acts charged against the defendants prohibited or permitted by these three interlacing statutes? If the facts laid in the indictment come within the conduct enumerated in § 20 of the Clayton Act they do not constitute a crime within the general terms of the Sherman Law because of the explicit command of that section that such conduct shall not be "considered or held to be violations of any law of the United States". So long as a union acts in its self-interest and does not combine with non-labor groups, the licit and the illicit under § 20 are not to be distinguished by any judgment regarding the wisdom or unwisdom, the rightness or wrongness, the selfishness or unselfishness of the end of which the particular union activities are the means. There is nothing remotely within the terms of § 20 that differentiates between trade union conduct directed against an employer because of a controversy arising in the relation between employer and employee, as such, and conduct similarly directed but ultimately due to an internecine struggle between two unions seeking the favor of the same employer. Such strike between competing unions has been an obdurate conflict in the evolution of so-called craft unionism and has undoubtedly been one of the potent forces in the modern development of industrial unions. These conflicts have intensified industrial tension but there is not the slightest warrant for saying that Congress has made § 20 inapplicable to trade union conduct resulting from them.

In so far as the Clayton Act is concerned, we must therefore dispose of this case as though we had before us precisely the same conduct on the part of the defendants in pressing claims against Anheuser–Busch for increased wages, or shorter hours, or other elements of what are called working conditions. The fact that what was done was done in a competition for jobs against the Machinists rather than against, let us say, a company union is a differentiation which Congress has not put into the federal legislation and which therefore we cannot write into it.

It is at once apparent that the acts with which the defendants are charged are the kind of acts protected by § 20 of the Clayton Act. The refusal of the Carpenters to work for Anheuser–Busch or on construction work being done for it and its adjoining tenant, and the peaceful attempt to get members of other unions similarly to refuse to work, are plainly within the free scope accorded to workers by § 20 for "terminating any relation of employment", or "ceasing to perform any work or labor", or "recommending, advising or persuading others by peaceful means so to do". The picketing of Anheuser–Busch premises with signs to indicate that Anheuser–Busch was unfair to organized labor, a familiar practice in these situations, comes within the language "attending at any place where any such person or persons may lawfully be, for the purpose of peacefully obtaining or communicating information, or from peacefully persuading any person to work or to abstain from working". Finally, the recommendation to union members and their friends not to buy or use the product of Anheuser–Busch is explicitly covered by "ceasing to patronize * * * any party to such dispute, or from recommending, advising, or persuading others by peaceful and lawful means so to do."

Clearly, then, the facts here charged constitute lawful conduct under the Clayton Act unless the defendants cannot invoke that Act because outsiders to the immediate dispute also shared in the conduct. But we need not determine whether the conduct is legal within the restrictions which Duplex Printing Press Co. v. Deering gave to the immunities of § 20 of the Clayton Act. Congress in the Norris–LaGuardia Act has expressed the public policy of the United States and defined its conception of a "labor dispute" in terms that no longer leave room for doubt. * * * Such a dispute, § 13(c), 29 U.S.C.A. § 113(c), provides, "includes any controversy concerning terms or conditions of employment, or concerning the association or representation of persons in negotiating, fixing, maintaining, changing, or seeking to arrange terms or conditions of employment, regardless of whether or not the disputants stand in the proximate relation of employer and employee". And under § 13(b) a person is "participating or interested in a labor dispute" if he "is engaged in the same industry, trade, craft, or occupation in which such dispute occurs, or has a direct or indirect interest therein, or is a member, officer, or agent of any association composed in whole or in part of employers or employees engaged in such industry, trade, craft, or occupation".

To be sure, Congress expressed this national policy and determined the bounds of a labor dispute in an act explicitly dealing with the further withdrawal of injunctions in labor controversies. But to argue, as it was urged before us, that the Duplex case still governs for purposes of a criminal prosecution is to say that that which on the equity side of the court is allowable conduct may in a criminal proceeding become the road to prison. It would be strange indeed that although neither the Government nor Anheuser–Busch could have sought an injunction against the acts here challenged, the elaborate efforts to permit such conduct failed to prevent criminal liability punishable with imprisonment and heavy fines. That is not the way to read the will of Congress, particularly when expressed by a statute which, as we have already indicated, is practically and historically one of a series of enactments touching one of the most sensitive national problems. Such legislation must not be read in a spirit of mutilating narrowness. * * * The appropriate way to read legislation in a situation like the one before us, was indicated by Mr. Justice Holmes on circuit: "A statute may indicate or require as its justification a change in the policy of the law, although it expresses that change only in the specific cases most likely to occur in the mind. The Legislature has the power to decide what the policy of the law shall be, and if it has intimated its will, however indirectly, that will should be recognized and obeyed. The major premise of the conclusion expressed in a statute, the change of policy that induces the enactment, may not be set out in terms, but it is not an adequate discharge of duty for the courts to say: We see what you are driving at, but you have not said it, and therefore we shall go on as before." Johnson v. United States, 163 Fed. 30, 32.

The relation of the Norris–LaGuardia Act to the Clayton Act is not that of a tightly drawn amendment to a technically phrased tax provision. The underlying aim of the Norris–LaGuardia Act was to restore the broad purpose which Congress thought it had formulated in the Clayton Act but which was frustrated, so Congress believed, by unduly restrictive judicial construction. This was authoritatively stated by the House Committee on the Judiciary. "The purpose of the bill is to protect the rights of labor in the same manner the Congress intended when it enacted the Clayton Act, October 15, 1914, 38 Stat.L. 738, which act, by reason of its construction and application by the Federal courts, is ineffectual to accomplish the congressional intent." H.Rep. No. 669, 72d Congress, 1st Session, p. 3. The Norris–LaGuardia Act was a disapproval of Duplex Printing Press Co. v. Deering, supra, and Bedford Cut Stone Co. v. Journeyman Stone Cutters' Association, 274 U.S. 37, 47 S.Ct. 522, 71 L.Ed. 916, 54 A.L.R. 791, as the authoritative interpretation of § 20 of the Clayton Act, for Congress now placed its own meaning upon that section. The Norris–LaGuardia Act reasserted the original purpose of the Clayton Act by infusing into it the immunized trade union activities as redefined by the later Act. In this light § 20 removes all such allowable conduct from the taint of being "violations of any law of the United States", including the Sherman Law. * * *

Mr. Justice Murphy took no part in the disposition of this case.

■ Mr. Justice Stone (concurring).

As I think it clear that the indictment fails to charge an offense under the Sherman Act, as it has been interpreted and applied by this Court, I find no occasion to consider the impact of the Norris–LaGuardia Act on the definition of participants in a labor dispute in the Clayton Act, as construed by this Court in Duplex Printing Press Co. v. Deering, 254 U.S. 443, 41 S.Ct. 172, 65 L.Ed. 349, 16 A.L.R. 196—an application of the Norris–LaGuardia Act which is not free from doubt and which some of my brethren sharply challenge. * * *

■ Mr. Justice Roberts. I am of opinion that the judgment should be reversed. [Justice Roberts concluded that there was an illegal secondary boycott which interfered with the interstate shipment of materials to Anheuser–Busch, Borsari and Stocker.] * * *

By a process of construction never, as I think, heretofore indulged by this court, it is now found that, because Congress forbade the issuing of injunctions to restrain certain conduct, it intended to repeal the provisions of the Sherman Act authorizing actions at law and criminal prosecutions for the commission of torts and crimes defined by the anti-trust laws. * * * [T]o attribute to Congress an intent to repeal legislation which has had a definite and well understood scope and effect for decades past, by resurrecting a rejected construction of the Clayton Act and extending a policy strictly limited by the Congress itself in the Norris–LaGuardia Act, seems to me a usurpation by the courts of the function of the Congress not only novel but fraught, as well, with the most serious dangers to our constitutional system of division of powers.

THE CHIEF JUSTICE joins in this opinion.

———

## PROBLEMS FOR DISCUSSION

**1.** What result would the Court have reached had it applied the Sherman Act as construed in *Apex Hosiery?* Given the fact that the Clayton Act had been largely discredited as a protective shield for labor activities, why did Justice Frankfurter invoke it at all? Are you convinced by his correlated interpretation of the Clayton and Norris–LaGuardia Acts?

**2.** In considering the foregoing questions, it is interesting to note that what became the Norris–LaGuardia Act was largely the product of a drafting committee of academics who were invited by a subcommittee of the Senate Judiciary Committee to draft a bill in 1928. A principal draftsman was Professor Frankfurter of the Harvard Law School. After a division emerged within the drafting committee as to whether to accord direct substantive rights to workers or rather to make procedural reforms, Professor Frankfurter wrote as follows to one of his committee colleagues:

> I think one bill should concentrate on the procedural abuses of the injunction to the exclusion of modifications of the substantive law, either civil or criminal. Personally, * * * I should confine this bill to the procedural features governing injunctions. Let's see how far we can get with comprehensive, adequate corrections of the procedural evils. Substantive law can be dealt with separately, so far as necessary. I think there is better chance of passage of a procedural measure and better likelihood of securing its fair interpretation and observation by the courts, if we do not over-load it either with doubtful substantive provisions or, at all events, provisions which run counter to the deeper hostilities of the judges.

See Gorman & Finkin, "The Individual and the Requirement of 'Concert' Under the National Labor Relations Act," 130 U.Pa.L.Rev. 286, 334 (1981). See also Frankfurter & Greene, The Labor Injunction 215–16 (1930)("It is not immunity from legal as distinguished from equitable remedies,—hitherto unlawful conduct remains unlawful."); Frankfurter & Greene, "Congressional Power Over the Labor Injunction," 31 Colum.L.Rev. 385, 408 (1931)("[T]he bill only withdraws the remedy of injunction. Civil action for damages and criminal prosecution remain available instruments. Illegal strikes are not made legal.") Whose approach to the statute is more convincing: the 1930 Professor Frankfurter, or the 1940 Justice Frankfurter?

**3.** Reexamine the list of union activities that the Attorney General's office had targeted for elimination through use of the Sherman Act. Was that program of prosecution tenable any longer after the Supreme Court decision in *Apex Hosiery?* Was it not expressly repudiated by Justice Frankfurter in the *Hutcheson* decision?

**4.** In light of your answer to the question immediately above, might it fairly be said that the Supreme Court went too far in removing legal restraints upon union pressures that would generally be regarded as improper and objectionable? (Through what institutional procedures should "objectionable" be defined?)

---------

## Burlington Northern R.R. Co. v. Brotherhood of Maintenance of Way Employes

481 U.S. 429, 107 S.Ct. 1841, 95 L.Ed.2d 381 (1987).

■ JUSTICE BRENNAN delivered the opinion of the Court.

What began as a dispute over renewal of a collective-bargaining agreement between a small railroad in Maine and some of its employees expanded to picketing and threats of strike activity at railroad facilities around the country. A Federal District Court then enjoined the picketing of any railroads other than those involved in the primary dispute. The question we must decide is whether a federal court has jurisdiction to issue such an injunction.

[Respondent Union, which represents railroad employees nationwide, had a dispute over renewal of a collective-bargaining agreement with a small railroad that is a subsidiary of Guilford Transportation Industries, Inc. (Guilford), which also owns other railroads. After exhausting the settlement procedures mandated by the Railway Labor Act (RLA), the Union instituted a lawful strike against the Guilford railroads. The Union later extended its picketing to other railroads (including petitioners) with which Guilford interchanged traffic. In petitioners' consolidated actions, the Federal District Court entered a preliminary injunction against the Union's picketing of any railroads other than those involved in the primary dispute. The court held that the "substantial alignment" test governs interpretation of the Norris–LaGuardia Act, §§ 1 and 4 of which bar federal courts from issuing injunctions against activities "growing out of" a "labor dispute." Under the test, the scope of lawful strike activity is confined to activities that further the union's economic interests in a labor dispute, and that are directed at the primary employer and other substantially aligned employers—those having an ownership interest in, or providing essential services or facilities to, the primary employer. The court concluded that none of the petitioners was "substantially aligned" with Guilford, and that thus the Union's secondary activity did not grow out of a labor dispute under the Norris–LaGuardia Act and could be enjoined. The Court of Appeals reversed, concluding that the District Court had no jurisdiction to enter an injunction.]

We granted certiorari to resolve the Circuit conflict over the propriety of using the substantial-alignment test to narrow the definition of labor disputes under the Norris–LaGuardia Act, and to address, if necessary, the applicability of the RLA and §§ 1 and 4 of the Norris–LaGuardia Act to secondary picketing.

## II

"The Norris–LaGuardia Act ... expresses a basic policy against the injunction of activities of labor unions." Machinists v. Street, 367 U.S. 740, 772, 81 S.Ct. 1784, 1802, 6 L.Ed.2d 1141 (1961)....

The congressional debates over the Norris–LaGuardia Act disclose that the Act's sponsors were convinced that the extraordinary step of divesting federal courts of equitable jurisdiction was necessary to remedy an extraordinary problem. According to the sponsors, federal courts had refused to abide by the clear command of § 20 of the Clayton Act, which stated in part:

> "[N]o ... restraining order or injunction shall prohibit any person or persons, whether singly or in concert, ... from ceasing to perform any work or labor, or from recommending, advising, or persuading others by peaceful means so to do; or from attending at any place where any such person or persons may lawfully be, for the purpose of [so recommending and persuading]; ... or from peaceably assembling in a lawful manner, and for lawful purposes...." 29 U.S.C. § 52.

The language of the Clayton Act was broad enough to encompass all peaceful strike activity, whether directed at the primary employer or at neutral "secondary" employers. Nevertheless, in Duplex Printing Press Co. v. Deering, 254 U.S. 443, 41 S.Ct. 172, 65 L.Ed. 349 (1921), the Court held that § 20 did not prevent courts from enjoining secondary activity. In *Duplex,* the employees' primary dispute was with a manufacturer of printing presses in Battle Creek, Michigan. Because a strike by only the employees of the manufacturer was unlikely to succeed, the international union representing the employees expanded the strike to those employers who transported, installed, and serviced the presses. The Court held that Congress did not intend § 20 to protect such an expansion. In reaching this conclusion, the Court appeared to rely not only on certain remarks made during the legislative debates, see id., at 475–477, n. 1, 41 S.Ct., at 179–180, n. 1, but also on its more general intuition about the political and economic significance of secondary picketing. Federal courts could enjoin secondary picketing, the Court stated, because "Congress had in mind [the protection of] particular industrial controversies, not a general class war." Id., at 472, 41 S.Ct., at 178. See also Bedford Co. v. Stone Cutters Assn., 274 U.S. 37, 60, 47 S.Ct. 522, 529, 71 L.Ed. 916 (1927)(Brandeis, J., dissenting).

The Norris–LaGuardia Act responded directly to the construction of the Clayton Act in *Duplex,* and to the pattern of injunctions entered by federal judges. "The underlying aim of the Norris–LaGuardia Act was to restore the broad purpose which Congress thought it had formulated in the Clayton Act but which was frustrated, so Congress believed, by unduly restrictive judicial construction." United States v. Hutcheson, 312 U.S. 219, 235–236, 61 S.Ct. 463, 468, 85 L.Ed. 788 (1941). Representative LaGuardia's description of the need for the Act is typical of those offered in the House debate:

"Gentlemen, there is one reason why this legislation is before Congress, and that one reason is disobedience of the law on the part of whom? On the part of organized labor? No. Disobedience of the law on the part of a few Federal judges. If the courts had been satisfied to construe the law as enacted by Congress, there would not be any need of legislation of this kind. If the courts had administered even justice to both employers and employees, there would be no need of considering a bill of this kind now. If the courts had not emasculated and purposely misconstrued the Clayton Act, we would not today be discussing an anti-injunction bill."
75 Cong.Rec. 5478 (Mar. 8, 1932).

The Act thus reflects Congress' decision to "abolis[h], for purposes of labor immunity, the distinction between primary activity between the 'immediate disputants' and secondary activity in which the employer and the members of the union do not stand 'in the proximate relation of employer and employee.' " Woodwork Manufacturers v. NLRB, 386 U.S. 612, 623, 87 S.Ct. 1250, 1257, 18 L.Ed.2d 357 (1967)(quoting H.R.Rep. No. 669, 72d Cong., 1st Sess., 8 (1932)). Moreover, the legislative history leaves no doubt that Congress intended the Norris–LaGuardia Act to cover the railroads. After lengthy debate, punctuated with numerous references to the notorious Pullman Strike of 1894, the House refused an amendment proposed by Representative Beck that would have exempted railroads from the coverage of the Act. See 75 Cong.Rec. 5471–5480, 5501–5512 (1932). The historical background of the Norris–LaGuardia Act thus reveals that Congress intended to preclude courts from enjoining secondary as well as primary activity, and that the railroads were to be treated no differently from other industries in this regard.[7]

### III

We first consider petitioners' argument that § 4's ban on injunctions is inapplicable to this case because the controversy is not one "involving or growing out of" a "labor dispute" under § 4 of the Norris–LaGuardia Act.

Section 13(c) of the Norris–LaGuardia Act states that "[t]he term 'labor dispute' includes any controversy concerning terms or conditions of employment ... regardless of whether or not the disputants stand in the proximate relation of employer and employee." 29 U.S.C. § 113(c). Section 13(a) provides in pertinent part that: "[a] case shall be held to involve or to grow out of a labor dispute when the case involves persons who are engaged in the same industry...." § 113(a). If this statutory language is accorded its plain meaning, BMWE's dispute with Maine Central over the

---

**7.** The Norris–LaGuardia Act was not Congress' last word on secondary picketing. The 1947 Taft–Hartley and 1959 Landrum–Griffin amendments to the National Labor Relations Act provided the National Labor Relations Board with exclusive authority to seek injunctions in federal court against some forms of secondary activity. 29 U.S.C. §§ 158(b)(4), 160. But as we explain, infra, 1852, Congress exempted railroad employers and employees from these amendments, § 152, and so the Norris–LaGuardia Act's prohibition on injunctions applies to railway disputes today, as it did in 1932.

terms and conditions of employment is unquestionably a labor dispute, and the secondary activity against petitioners grows out of that dispute.

Petitioners argue, however, that this Court should adopt a test of "substantial alignment" to narrow the scope of labor disputes under § 13(c). Petitioners rely on several lower court decisions in which the term "labor dispute" has been applied only to disputes where the picketed employer is "substantially aligned" with the primary employer. See Ashley, Drew & N.R. Co. v. United Transportation Union, 625 F.2d, at 1363–1364 (citing cases). * * *

We reject these narrow constructions of § 13(c) for several reasons. First, we have long recognized that "Congress made the definition [of 'labor dispute'] broad because it wanted it to be broad.... Congress attempted to write its bill in unmistakable language because it believed previous measures looking toward the same policy against nonjudicial intervention in labor disputes had been given unduly limited constructions by the Courts." Telegraphers v. Chicago & N.W.R. Co., 362 U.S. 330, 335–336, 80 S.Ct. 761, 764, 4 L.Ed.2d 774 (1960); see also Marine Cooks & Stewards v. Panama S.S. Co., 362 U.S. 365, 369, 80 S.Ct. 779, 783, 4 L.Ed.2d 797 (1960)("The [Act's] language is broad because Congress was intent upon taking the federal courts out of the labor injunction business except in the very limited circumstances left open for federal jurisdiction under the Norris–LaGuardia Act").

Accordingly, we have consistently declined to construe § 13(c) narrowly. For example, we have interpreted § 13(c) to embrace disputes "having their genesis in political protests" as opposed to economic self-interest. Jacksonville Bulk Terminals, Inc. v. Longshoremen, 457 U.S. 702, 711, 102 S.Ct. 2672, 2679, 73 L.Ed.2d 327 (1982).[8] It would be particularly anomalous to adopt a narrowing construction of the phrase "growing out of a labor dispute" in the context of secondary picketing, because Congress' primary motivation in passing the Norris–LaGuardia Act was to immunize such picketing from federal court injunctions. Were we to limit the scope of § 13(c) as petitioners suggest, we would again commit precisely the error that prompted Congress to pass the Act.

Adoption of some variant of the substantial-alignment test would be contrary to the Act in yet another way. The focus of the substantial-alignment test—whether labor activity will "furthe[r] the union's economic interest in a labor dispute," Ashley, Drew, supra, at 1363—requires courts to second-guess which activities are truly in the union's interest. As the Court of Appeals explained:

"No union engages in secondary conduct without expecting to advance its economic interests.... Unions do not lightly call in

---

**8.** See also Marine Cooks & Stewards v. Panama S.S. Co., 362 U.S. 365, 80 S.Ct. 779, 4 L.Ed.2d 797 (1960)(picketing by American seamen of foreign ship with foreign crew to protest loss of American jobs to foreign competition held to grow out of a labor dispute); New Negro Alliance v. Sanitary Grocery Co., 303 U.S. 552, 58 S.Ct. 703, 82 L.Ed. 1012 (1938) (picketing by civic group to induce store to hire Negro employees held to grow out of a labor dispute).

their chips and impose burdens on other workers who find their own pay and working conditions satisfactory.... Under the 'substantial alignment' test of *Ashley, Drew* the court must ... weig[h] the economic gains to the union's members from secondary pressure against the losses the secondary conduct imposes on others in society. It is only a small exaggeration to say that this is exactly what courts were doing before 1932, exactly why Congress passed the Norris–LaGuardia Act." 793 F.2d, at 806.

Finally, nothing in the Norris–LaGuardia Act or the RLA distinguishes permissible from impermissible secondary activity. As we observed in Trainmen v. Jacksonville Terminal Co., 394 U.S. 369, 386–387, 89 S.Ct. 1109, 1120, 22 L.Ed.2d 344 (1969):

> "No cosmic principles announce the existence of secondary conduct, condemn it as an evil, or delimit its boundaries. These tasks were first undertaken by judges, intermixing metaphysics with their notions of social and economic policy. And the common law of labor relations ... has drawn no lines more arbitrary, tenuous, and shifting than those separating 'primary' from 'secondary' activities."

For the railway industry, unlike other industries covered by the NLRA, Congress has provided "neither usable standards nor access to administrative expertise" to facilitate the difficult task of distinguishing primary and secondary activity. Id., at 392, 89 S.Ct., at 1123. Given the inherent indeterminacy of these concepts and the lack of congressional guidance, it is obvious that any judicial attempt to limit the language of § 13 would make "the lawfulness of a strike ... depend upon judicial views of social and economic policy." Jacksonville Bulk Terminals, Inc., supra, 457 U.S., at 715, 102 S.Ct., at 2681. Even if we were confident that our mixture of metaphysics and social policy, unlike that of our predecessors earlier in this century, would produce a construction of § 13(c) that would substantially align with Congress' contemporary views, the fact remains that Congress passed the Norris–LaGuardia Act to forestall judicial attempts to narrow labor's statutory protection. Accordingly, we refuse to narrow the definition of labor dispute under § 13(c) to exclude those battles involving secondary activity.

[In part IV of its opinion, the court considered and rejected a number of arguments by the petitioners in support of their claims that the Railway Labor Act should be read to bar the secondary boycott and that earlier Court decisions should therefore be read to allow an injunction against such a violation of the Act.]

## V

"Th[e] judge-made law of the late 19th and early 20th centuries was based on self-mesmerized views of economic and social theory ... and on statutory misconstruction." Trainmen v. Jacksonville Terminal Co., 394 U.S. 369, 382, 89 S.Ct. 1109, 1117, 22 L.Ed.2d 344 (1969). It may be that the evolution of judicial attitudes toward labor in "the decades since the

Norris–LaGuardia Act was passed has dissipated any legitimate concern about the impartiality of federal judges in disputes between labor and management." Buffalo Forge Co. v. Steelworkers, 428 U.S. 397, 432, 96 S.Ct. 3141, 3159, 49 L.Ed.2d 1022 (1976)(Stevens, J., dissenting). But our decision in this case ultimately turns not on concerns of partiality, but on questions of power. In the Norris–LaGuardia Act, Congress divested federal courts of the power to enjoin secondary picketing in railway labor disputes. Congress has not seen fit to restore that power. Accordingly, we affirm the decision of the Court of Appeals.

————

## PROBLEMS FOR DISCUSSION

**1.**   In January 1980, in response to the Soviet Union's invasion of Afghanistan, the International Longshoremen's Association announced that its members would not handle any cargo bound to, or coming from, the Soviet Union or carried on Russian ships. The President of the ILA stated that the union's members were thereby denouncing the behavior of the Soviet Union: "People are upset and they refuse to continue the business as usual policy as long as the Russians insist on being international bully boys." Members of the ILA refused to load certain chemicals onto ships that were docked at the Jacksonville Terminals in Florida and that were headed for the Soviet Union. The Terminal Company had a collective bargaining agreement with the ILA, which provided that there would be no work stoppage during the contract term. The Company brought an action for breach of contract in the federal court and sought an injunction. The parties agreed that the central question was whether this was a "case involving or growing out of any labor dispute" within the meaning of section 4 of the Norris–LaGuardia Act. How should the court have ruled on that question? See Jacksonville Bulk Terminals, Inc. v. International Longshoremen's Ass'n, 457 U.S. 702, 102 S.Ct. 2672, 73 L.Ed.2d 327 (1982).

**2.**   The Volunteer Trial Lawyers Association is a group of attorneys who, in addition to their usual duties for private law firms, are regularly assigned by the courts of the District of Columbia to serve as counsel to defendants in criminal cases. (The local Defenders Association is inadequately staffed to handle all of the cases.) The attorneys are paid by the District at the hourly rate of $30. After unsuccessfully requesting the District to increase the hourly rate to $40, the VTLA and its members have recently authorized a refusal to take court assignments unless the hourly fee is increased. The District has brought an action for an injunction against the work stoppage. Have the defendants violated the federal antitrust laws? Does a federal court have the power to issue an injunction? See Federal Trade Com'n v. Superior Court Trial Lawyers Ass'n, 493 U.S. 411, 110 S.Ct. 768, 107 L.Ed.2d 851 (1990).

**3.**   The Lyric Theater has a multi-year contract with Declasse Catering to provide food and beverage service during intermissions. The Food Service Workers Union has been attempting to organize the waitstaff at Declasse. It has asked the Lyric to ask Declasse to agree to a "card check," *i.e.* to recognize the union voluntarily as its employees bargaining representative after a neutral agency has counted and verified the signatures on the cards designating the union as the employees' representative. The Lyric has stated that it would have no involvement in a dispute between Declasse and the Union. The Union has now begun to distribute handbills to patrons entering the Lyric. The handbills state *inter alia*: "Lyric out of tune with food service workers' rights! We are the only Lyric workers without a union," and "Ask the people serving you what they think about how the Lyric treats them." It has also written to companies whose key executives serve on the Lyric's governing board to have them remove their executives from the board. The Lyric has moved in federal court to enjoin the Union from "threatening or harassing the Lyric's donors, officers and patrons" and from "engaging in fraudulent or defamatory representations concerning the Lyric." May the injunction issue? *Compare* San Antonio Community Hosp. v. Southern California Dist. Council of Carpenters, 125 F.3d 1230 (9th Cir.1997), *with* Metropolitan Opera Ass'n, Inc. v. Local 100, Hotel Employees and Restaurant Employees Int'l Union, 239 F.3d 172 (2d Cir.2001).

---

## D. LABOR ACTIVITY AND THE CONSTITUTION

At precisely the same time that the Supreme Court in the *Apex Hosiery* and *Hutcheson* cases sounded a dramatic retreat in the application of the antitrust laws to union activity, it went even further by declaring that labor picketing was properly (at least in some cases) to be assimilated to speech that was protected against governmental restrictions by virtue of the First and Fourteenth Amendments to the Federal Constitution. The high water mark in this development was the famous decision that follows.

---

## Thornhill v. Alabama[a]

310 U.S. 88, 60 S.Ct. 736, 84 L.Ed. 1093 (1940).

■ MR. JUSTICE MURPHY delivered the opinion of the Court.

Petitioner, Byron Thornhill, was convicted in the Circuit Court of Tuscaloosa County, Alabama, of the violation of Section 3448 of the State Code of 1923. The Code Section reads as follows: "§ 3448. Loitering or picketing forbidden.—Any person or persons, who, without a just cause or legal excuse therefor, go near to or loiter about the premises or place of business of any other person, firm, corporation, or association of people, engaged in a lawful business, for the purpose or with intent of influencing, or inducing other persons not to trade with, buy from, sell to, have business dealings with, or be employed by such persons, firm, corporation, or association, or who picket the works or place of business of such other

---

**a.** See Cox, Strikes, Picketing and the Constitution, 4 Vand.L.Rev. 574 (1951); Gregory, Constitutional Limitations on the Regulation of Union and Employer Conduct, 49 Mich.L.Rev. 191 (1950); Farmer & Williamson, Picketing and the Injunctive Power of State Courts—From *Thornhill* to *Vogt,* 35 U.Det.L.J. 431 (1958); Cox, The Influence of Mr. Justice Murphy on Labor Law, 48 Mich. L.Rev. 767 (1950); Getman, Labor Law and Free Speech: The Curious Policy of Limited Expression, 43 Md.L.Rev. 4 (1984); Jones, Free Speech: Pickets on the Grass, Alas! Amidst Confusion, a Consistent Principle, 29 S.Cal.L.Rev. 137 (1956); Samoff, Picketing and the First Amendment: "Full Circle" and "Formal Surrender," 9 Lab.L.J. 889 (1958); St. Antoine, Free Speech or Economic Weapon? The Persisting Problem of Picketing, 16 Suffolk U.L.Rev. 883 (1982).

persons, firms, corporations, or associations of persons, for the purpose of hindering, delaying, or interfering with or injuring any lawful business or enterprise of another, shall be guilty of a misdemeanor; but nothing herein shall prevent any person from soliciting trade or business for a competitive business." * * *

The proofs consist of the testimony of two witnesses for the prosecution. It appears that petitioner on the morning of his arrest was seen "in company with six or eight other men" "on the picket line" at the plant of the Brown Wood Preserving Company. Some weeks previously a strike order had been issued by a Union, apparently affiliated with The American Federation of Labor, which had as members all but four of the approximately one hundred employees of the plant. Since that time a picket line with two picket posts of six to eight men each had been maintained around the plant twenty-four hours a day. * * * There is no testimony indicating the nature of the dispute between the Union and the Preserving Company, or the course of events which led to the issuance of the strike order, or the nature of the effort for conciliation.

The Company scheduled a day for the plant to resume operations. One of the witnesses, Clarence Simpson, who was not a member of the Union, on reporting to the plant on the day indicated, was approached by petitioner who told him that "they were on strike and did not want anybody to go up there to work." None of the other employees said anything to Simpson, who testified: "Neither Mr. Thornhill nor any other employee threatened me on the occasion testified to. Mr. Thornhill approached me in a peaceful manner, and did not put me in fear; he did not appear to be mad." "I then turned and went back to the house, and did not go to work." The other witness, J.M. Walden, testified: "At the time Mr. Thornhill and Clarence Simpson were talking to each other, there was no one else present, and I heard no harsh words and saw nothing threatening in the manner of either man." For engaging in some or all of these activities, petitioner was arrested, charged, and convicted as described. [By appropriate motions he raised and the courts below ruled on the constitutional questions considered herein.]

First. The freedom of speech and of the press, which are secured by the First Amendment against abridgment by the United States, are among the fundamental personal rights and liberties which are secured to all persons by the Fourteenth Amendment against abridgment by a state.

The safeguarding of these rights to the ends that men may speak as they think on matters vital to them and that falsehoods may be exposed through the processes of education and discussion is essential to free government. Those who won our independence had confidence in the power of free and fearless reasoning and communication of ideas to discover and spread political and economic truth. Noxious doctrines in those fields may be refuted and their evil averted by the courageous exercise of the right of free discussion. Abridgment of freedom of speech and of the press, however, impairs those opportunities for public education that are essential to effective exercise of the power of correcting error through the processes of popular government. Compare United States v. Carolene Products, 304 U.S. 144, 152, 153n * * *. It is imperative that, when the effective exercise of these rights is claimed to be abridged, the courts should "weigh the circumstances" and "appraise the substantiality of the reasons advanced" in support of the challenged regulations. Schneider v. State, 308 U.S. 147, 161, 162, 60 S.Ct. 146, 150, 151, 84 L.Ed. 155.

Second. The section in question must be judged upon its face. * * *

Third. Section 3448 has been applied by the State courts so as to prohibit a single individual from walking slowly and peacefully back and forth on the public sidewalk in front of the premises of an employer, without speaking to anyone, carrying a sign or placard on a staff above his head stating only that the employer did not employ union men affiliated with the American Federation of Labor; the purpose of the described activity was concededly to advise customers and prospective customers of the relationship existing between the employer and its employees and thereby to induce such customers not to patronize the employer. O'Rourke v. City of Birmingham, 27 Ala.App. 133, 168 So. 206, certiorari denied 232 Ala. 355, 168 So. 209. The statute as thus authoritatively construed and applied leaves room for no exceptions based upon either the number of persons engaged in the proscribed activity, the peaceful character of their demeanor, the nature of their dispute with an employer, or the restrained character and the accurateness of the terminology used in notifying the public of the facts of the dispute.

* * * It is apparent that one or the other of the offenses [defined in Section 3448] comprehends every practicable method whereby the facts of a labor dispute may be publicized in the vicinity of the place of business of an employer. The phrase "without a just cause or legal excuse" does not in any effective manner restrict the breadth of the regulation; the words themselves have no ascertainable meaning either inherent or historical. * * * The vague contours of the term "picket" are nowhere delineated.[18]

---

18. See Hellerstein, Picketing Legislation and the Courts (1931), 10 No.Car.L.Rev. 158, 186n:

"A picketer may: (1) Merely observe workers or customers. (2) Communicate information, e.g., that a strike is in progress, making either true, untrue or libelous statements. (3) Persuade employees or customers not to engage in relations with the employer: (a) through the use of banners, without speaking, carrying true, untrue or libelous legends; (b) by speaking, (i) in a calm, dispassionate manner, (ii) in a heated, hostile manner, (iii) using abusing epithets and profanity, (iv) yelling loudly, (v) by persisting in making arguments when employees or customers refuse to listen; (c) by offering money or similar inducements to strike breakers. (4) Threaten employees or customers: (a) by the mere presence of the picketer; the presence may be a threat of, (i) physical violence, (ii) social ostracism, being branded in the community as a 'scab', (iii) a trade or employees' boycott, i.e., preventing workers from securing employment and refusing to trade with customers, (iv) threatening injury to property; (b) by verbal threats. (5) Assaults and use of violence. (6) Destruction of property. (7) Blocking of entrances and interference with traffic. The picketer may engage in a combination of any of the types of conduct enumerated above. The picketing may be carried on singly or in groups; it may be directed to employees alone or to customers alone or to both. It may involve persons who have contracts with the employer or those who have not or both."

* * * In sum, whatever the means used to publicize the facts of a labor dispute, whether by printed sign, by pamphlet, by word of mouth or otherwise, all such activity without exception is within the inclusive prohibition of the statute so long as it occurs in the vicinity of the scene of the dispute.

Fourth. We think that Section 3448 is invalid on its face.

* * * Freedom of discussion, if it would fulfill its historic function in this nation, must embrace all issues about which information is needed or appropriate to enable the members of society to cope with the exigencies of their period.

In the circumstances of our times the dissemination of information concerning the facts of a labor dispute must be regarded as within that area of free discussion that is guaranteed by the Constitution. Hague v. C.I.O., 307 U.S. 496, 59 S.Ct. 954, 83 L.Ed. 1423; Schneider v. State, 308 U.S. 147, 155, 162, 163, 60 S.Ct. 146, 151, 84 L.Ed. 155. See Senn v. Tile Layers Union, 301 U.S. 468, 478, 57 S.Ct. 857, 862, 81 L.Ed. 1229. It is recognized now that satisfactory hours and wages and working conditions in industry and a bargaining position which makes these possible have an importance which is not less than the interests of those in the business or industry directly concerned. The health of the present generation and of those as yet unborn may depend on these matters, and the practices in a single factory may have economic repercussions upon a whole region and affect widespread systems of marketing. The merest glance at State and Federal legislation on the subject demonstrates the force of the argument that labor relations are not matters of mere local or private concern. Free discussion concerning the conditions in industry and the causes of labor disputes appears to us indispensable to the effective and intelligent use of the processes of popular government to shape the destiny of modern industrial society. The issues raised by regulations, such as are challenged here, infringing upon the right of employees effectively to inform the public of the facts of a labor dispute are part of this larger problem.

* * * It may be that effective exercise of the means of advancing public knowledge may persuade some of those reached to refrain from entering into advantageous relations with the business establishment which is the scene of the dispute. Every expression of opinion on matters that are important has the potentiality of inducing action in the interests of one rather than another group in society. But the group in power at any moment may not impose penal sanctions on peaceful and truthful discussion of matters of public interest merely on a showing that others may thereby be persuaded to take action inconsistent with its interests. Abridgment of the liberty of such discussion can be justified only where the clear danger of substantive evils arises under circumstances affording no opportunity to test the merits of ideas by competition for acceptance in the market of public opinion. We hold that the danger of injury to an industrial

concern is neither so serious nor so imminent as to justify the sweeping proscription of freedom of discussion embodied in Section 3448.

The State urges that the purpose of the challenged statute is the protection of the community from the violence and breaches of the peace, which, it asserts, are the concomitants of picketing. The power and the duty of the State to take adequate steps to preserve the peace and to protect the privacy, the lives, and the property of its residents cannot be doubted. But no clear and present danger of destruction of life or property, or invasion of the right of privacy, or breach of the peace can be thought to be inherent in the activities of every person who approaches the premises of an employer and publicizes the facts of a labor dispute involving the latter. We are not now concerned with picketing en masse or otherwise conducted which might occasion such imminent and aggravated danger to these interests as to justify a statute narrowly drawn to cover the precise situation giving rise to the danger. Compare American Steel Foundries v. Tri–City Council, 257 U.S. 184, 205, 42 S.Ct. 72, 77, 66 L.Ed. 189, 27 A.L.R. 360. Section 3448 in question here does not aim specifically at serious encroachments on these interests and does not evidence any such care in balancing these interests against the interest of the community and that of the individual in freedom of discussion on matters of public concern. * * * The danger of breach of the peace or serious invasion of rights of property or privacy at the scene of a labor dispute is not sufficiently imminent in all cases to warrant the legislature in determining that such place is not appropriate for the range of activities outlawed by Section 3448.

Reversed.

■ MR. JUSTICE MCREYNOLDS is of opinion that the judgment below should be affirmed.

———

## PROBLEMS FOR DISCUSSION

**1.** Is it sound to treat labor picketing as essentially congruent with political speech for purposes of protection against government regulation under the First and Fourteenth Amendments? What arguments can be made by employers to the contrary? Did the Court, by equating picketing with speech, err as much as did the *Vegelahn* court, p. 17 supra, when it equated picketing with violence? (For the application of modern constitutional analysis to invalidate a state mass-picketing statute, see Nash v. Texas, 632 F.Supp. 951 (E.D.Tex.1986).)

**2.** Does *Thornhill* compel the conclusion that effecting a secondary boycott by peaceful picketing is constitutionally protected against federal or state regulation? Similarly, for picketing by a minority union to force the employer into a closed-shop agreement? Similarly, for picketing to force the employer to reassign work from members of one union to members of another? Similarly, for picketing to shut down an employer until it forgoes the use of labor-saving machinery?

Assuming that *Thornhill* were to receive such an expansive interpretation, would that be defensible social policy?

# V.  The Wagner Act[a]

---

## A.  Origins and Constitutionality

---

### Railway Labor Act

The passage of the National Labor Relations Act was the culmination of a long period of development, in which one of the more significant events was the enactment in 1926 of the Railway Labor Act. The provisions of that Act were agreed upon in advance through private negotiations between the railroads and the interested unions, and little change was made by the Congress. In general, the emphasis of the Act was on the peaceful settlement of labor disputes, thus reflecting the strategic importance of the transportation industry in the national economy. Adjustment boards were to be established by agreement of the carriers and the workers to settle differences over the interpretation of contracts and to decide minor disputes over working conditions. More elaborate provisions were included to assist in resolving disputes over the negotiation of wages and working conditions. Section 2 of the Act imposed a duty on both sides to make "every reasonable effort to make and maintain agreements concerning rates of pay, rules, and working conditions * * *." In addition, a mediation board was established consisting of five members appointed by the President. The board was empowered to use mediation in order to assist the unions and the carriers in the event of a breakdown in their negotiations. The mediation board was not to impose a settlement, but could encourage the parties to submit their differences to final and binding arbitration. If these techniques did not result in a settlement, the mediation board was empowered to notify the President if the dispute threatened severely to disrupt interstate commerce, and the President could then appoint a board to investigate and report on the dispute within thirty days; neither party

---

**a.** See the studies of the history of the National Labor Relations Act noted in the bibliography set out on page vii, supra. Some recent appraisals from an historical or economic perspective respectively include Barenberg, The Political Economy of the Wagner Act: Power, Symbol, and Workplace Cooperation, 106 Harv.L.Rev. 1379 (1993), and Dau–Schmidt, A Bargaining Analysis of American Labor Law and the Search for Bargaining Equality and Industrial Peace, 91 Mich. L.Rev. 419 (1992). Some provocative and sometimes controversial historical contribu-

tions should be noted, see e.g., Karren Orren, Belated Feudalism: Labor, the Law, and Liberal Development in the United States (1991); Colin Gordon, New Deals: Business, Labor, and Politics in America, 1920–1935 (1994); Stanley Vitoz, New Deal Labor Policy and the American Industrial Economy (1987). There has also been an extensive debate in the legal periodical literature on the Labor Act from the point of view of advocates of "critical legal studies," feminism, and "law and economics" as well as from critics of these perspectives.

was allowed to change the conditions out of which the dispute arose for an additional thirty days following the making of the report. Thereafter, the parties were free to resort to economic warfare to settle their differences.

The provisions requiring that the status quo be maintained for as much as sixty days represented a substantial concession on the part of the unions. In return, labor obtained a guarantee against interference by the railroads in the process of union organization. Hence, the Act declared that the representatives or parties to railway disputes should be designated "by the respective parties in such manner as may be provided in their corporate organization or unincorporated association, or by other means of collective action, without interference, influence or coercion exercised by either party over the self-organization or designation of representatives by the other." After the enactment of this statute the Texas & N.O.R. Co. resorted to inducement and coercion, including discriminatory discharges, to set up on its lines a company union in lieu of the Brotherhood of Railway and Steamship Clerks. The resulting litigation ended in a landmark decision of the United States Supreme Court. Texas & N.O.R. Co. v. Brotherhood of Railway & S.S. Clerks, 281 U.S. 548, 50 S.Ct. 427, 74 L.Ed. 1034 (1930). The Court, in the following passage, upheld the power of Congress to prohibit interference with self-organization, or with the selection of representatives, for the amicable adjustment of disputes.

We entertain no doubt of the constitutional authority of Congress to enact the prohibition. The power to regulate commerce is the power to enact "all appropriate legislation" for its "protection or advancement". * * * Exercising this authority, Congress may facilitate the amicable settlement of disputes which threaten the service of the necessary agencies of interstate transportation. * * * It has long been recognized that employees are entitled to organize for the purpose of securing the redress of grievances and to promote agreements with employers relating to rates of pay and conditions of work. American Steel Foundries v. Tri–City Central Trade Council, 257 U.S. 184, 209, 42 S.Ct. 72, 66 L.Ed. 189, 27 A.L.R. 360. Congress was not required to ignore this right of the employees but could safeguard it and seek to make their appropriate collective action an instrument of peace rather than of strife. Such collective action would be a mockery if representation were made futile by interferences with freedom of choice. Thus the prohibition by Congress of interference with the selection of representatives for the purpose of negotiation and conference between employers and employees, instead of being an invasion of the constitutional right of either, was based on the recognition of the rights of both. * * * The Railway Labor Act of 1926 does not interfere with the normal exercise of the right of the carrier to select its employees or to discharge them. The statute is not aimed at this right of the employers but at the interference with the right of employees to have representatives of their own choosing. As the carriers subject to the act have no constitutional right to interfere with the freedom of the employees in making their selections, they cannot complain of the statute on constitutional grounds. * * *

As time went on, certain defects in the Railway Labor Act became increasingly apparent to labor. In 1934, therefore, substantial amendments were enacted to meet these objections. First, in an effort to eliminate the device of the "company union" controlled by the employer, the 1934 amendments declared it unlawful (and subject to criminal penalties) for carriers to use their funds to assist company unions or to induce their employees to join such unions. Second, in order to resolve employer challenges to the capacity of union representatives seeking to negotiate, the National Mediation Board was given the added task of conducting elections or using other appropriate methods to determine which union was desired by the employees. Third, in order to eliminate the disparities that developed among different grievance-adjustment boards across the nation, Congress in 1934 created the National Railroad Adjustment Board. The purpose of the Board was (and is) to resolve grievances over the meaning of collective bargaining agreements. It was to be composed of eighteen representatives selected by the carriers and an equal number chosen by the employees, and it was to be divided into four separate divisions, each having jurisdiction over different occupations. Decisions of the Board were made enforceable by the winning party in the federal district courts. With the passage of these amendments—and the extension in 1936 of the Act's coverage to air carriers as well as railroads—the Railway Labor Act assumed the form which has endured, with only minor modifications, until the present day.

--------

## THE WAGNER ACT

In every respect American trade union history after 1933 stood in contrast with the twenties. A few facts epitomize what occurred. In 1933 less than 3,000,000 workers were members of trade unions. Early in the 1940's 12,000,000 workers were organized. Between 1937 and 1940 the great industrial giants of the steel, automobile, rubber and electrical manufacturing industries were forced to begin adapting themselves to the ways of collective bargaining.

These events were part of the New Deal revolution. Their explanation lies in the conditions which gave it birth. The stock market panic of 1929 and the deep depression of the early and middle thirties stirred intellectual, social and economic ferment. During the first third of the century the mass of the American people were not ready to listen to those who criticized existing institutions. The collapse of the economic system after 1929 dispelled the worker's faith in welfare capitalism and made the middle classes more sympathetic towards the objectives of organized labor. Perhaps the two most significant factors in the growth of the union movement beginning in the mid–1930s were: (1) the federal government's policy of giving active encouragement to unionization and collective bargaining and (2) the formation of the Congress of Industrial Organizations.

The impetus for general legislation aiding unionization came from the search for measures to halt the deepening depression. Keynesian economics pointed toward increasing mass purchasing power as a way of speeding up economic activity. One method Congress could have used was to fix minimum wages and maximum hours (to spread employment), and another was to encourage unionization. Measures of the second type offered several advantages: unions might raise wages above the minimum, they could police their contracts without direct governmental regulation of terms of employment, and there was reason to hope that such legislation would not be as vulnerable to constitutional attack as wage and hour laws.

In the National Industrial Recovery Act of 1934, Congress adopted both approaches. Fair labor standards were to be established by raising wages, shortening hours and eliminating industrial homework, child labor and other sweatshop practices. Section 7 of the NIRA declared that "employees shall have the right to organize and bargain collectively through representatives of their own choosing," and shall be free from "interference, restraint, or coercion" by employers in unionizing "or in other mutual aid or protection," and also that no employee or person seeking employment could be required to join a company union or to refrain from joining a union of his own choosing. The NIRA also attempted to organize industry through trade associations and codes of fair competition that would eliminate cut-throat competition and so stabilize prices.

In 1935, the National Industrial Recovery Act collapsed partly as a result of its own weight although the immediate occasion was a Supreme Court decision holding the basic statute unconstitutional. The administration's policy toward business turned away from the philosophy of cartelization to the older tradition of enforced competition, but it scarcely slackened its interest in building up the bargaining power of employees. The Wagner Act of 1935[b] established on a permanent foundation the legally protected right of employees to organize and bargain collectively through representatives of their own choosing. The basic idea reaches back before 1900 but much of its elaboration was the work of the NIRA period.

The heart of the Wagner Act was Section 7, which originally provided—

> "Employees shall have the right to self-organization, to form, join or assist labor organizations, to bargain collectively through representatives of their own choosing, and to engage in concerted

**b.** The official title of the act was the National Labor Relations Act. The colloquial name is used here to distinguish the act in its original form from the present National Labor Relations Act which contains provisions derived from the original act and others added by the Taft–Hartley Act in 1947 and the Landrum–Griffin Act in 1959.

The text of the National Labor Relations Act is printed in the statutory supplement. Students should follow the statutory text in studying these pages.

activities for the purpose of collective bargaining or other mutual aid or protection.''

These three rights—to organize, to bargain collectively and to engage in peaceful strikes and picketing—were to be implemented and enforced through the other provisions of the Act. Section 8(1) of the Wagner Act (now Section 8(a)(1)), outlawing employer coercion of employees in the exercise of their Section 7 rights, covers such antiunion tactics as beating up labor organizers, locking out employees to destroy incipient unions, industrial espionage, threats of economic reprisal and the more subtle techniques of promising or granting economic benefits in order to show that the union has little to offer the employees. Section 8(2) was designed to outlaw company-formed "representation plans" or "work councils" which were carefully controlled so as to give employees the forms of organization without the substance and which were known as "company unions." Section 8(3) forbade discrimination in hiring or firing, and Section 8(4) outlawed such discrimination in the specific case of an employee asserting rights before the NLRB.

While those four subsections have their most common application at the stage when the employees are taking steps to form a union (or when an outside union is seeking to persuade them to organize), Section 8(5) relates primarily to the period after the employees have organized and are seeking to engage in collective bargaining. It imposes upon the employer an affirmative duty to bargain with the union which (under Section 9(a)) has been selected "by the majority of the employees in a unit appropriate for such purposes"; moreover, this union is to be the "exclusive" representative, and the employer may deal with no other employee representative. To determine which group of employees should have a say in the selection of a bargaining representative, and to determine formally whether a labor organization (and which) has majority support, the National Labor Relations Board is given authority by Section 9 of the Act to conduct representation proceedings, culminating in a secret-ballot election and a certification of the results (and of any union receiving a majority of the valid votes cast).

To administer both the unfair labor practice and representation provisions of the Act, Congress established the kind of administrative agency which was becoming an increasingly common method of implementing New Deal legislation. The NLRB was created under Sections 3 and 4, and under Section 10 (which regulates NLRB procedure in unfair labor practice cases) the Board assumed the functions of both prosecutor and judge by issuing complaints of violation, having its staff prosecute the complaints and then passing upon the merits of the case. Judicial enforcement and review were authorized under Section 10(e) and (f) upon petition to an appropriate federal court of appeals. While the courts were authorized to review most questions of law, their power with respect to findings of fact was restricted to determining whether the findings were "supported by evidence." These provisions gave rise to bitter controversy and the Taft–Hartley amendments later made significant changes in both NLRB organization and the scope of judicial review.

Although the Wagner Act was partly an economic measure designed to enable industrial workers to raise their wages and improve their standard of living, it also embodied a conscious, carefully articulated program for minimizing labor disputes. Its sponsors urged that enforcement of the guarantees of the rights to organize and bargain collectively would be the best method of achieving industrial peace without undue sacrifice of personal and economic freedom.

The Act has indeed reduced strikes and other forms of industrial unrest for a number of reasons. Most obviously, the prohibition of employer unfair labor practices and the legal compulsion to recognize and bargain with the union designated by a majority of employees in an appropriate unit will tend to eliminate strikes for those purposes. Moreover, collective bargaining itself tends to reduce the number of strikes and lockouts. Four points may be made in support of this proposition. (1) Collective bargaining enables employers and employees to dig behind their prejudices and exchange their views to such an extent that on many points they reach agreement while on others they discover that the area of disagreement is so narrow that it is cheaper to compromise than to do battle. (2) Recognition, experience in bargaining, and the resulting maturity bring a sense of responsibility to labor unions. (3) Because collective bargaining replaces the weakness of the individual in bargaining and better enables employees to raise wages and improve labor standards, strikes to secure these objectives tend to be eliminated. (4) Collective bargaining substitutes what may be called industrial democracy—joint consensual determination of wages and other conditions of employment—for the unilateral and sometimes arbitrary power of the employer. Moreover, the collective agreement establishes a rule of law; it is the measure of both the employer's and employees' rights and obligations.

Although the Wagner Act was intended to provide a foundation for a comprehensive system of industrial relations, it was not a complete labor code. The sponsors dealt only with the labor problems which seemed most urgent in 1935, leaving others to state law or to the future. Three limitations are especially significant.

*First.* The Wagner Act was concerned primarily with the organizational phase of labor relations. The aim was to prevent practices which interfered with the growth of labor unions and the development of collective bargaining. Once the union was organized and the employer accorded it recognition as the representative of its employees, the function of the statute, as originally conceived, was completed. Even the duty to bargain with the majority representatives was imposed by Section 8(5) chiefly because the refusal to bargain was a method of destroying the union. (In this respect the development of the law has departed significantly from the original conception.)

*Second.* The Wagner Act was concerned exclusively with the activities of employers which were thought to violate the rights guaranteed by

Section 7. Unions were not beyond reproach, but most of them were so weak that their misconduct raised no serious national problems until the 1940's. Hence the original statute did not deal with their activities.

*Third.* The Wagner Act left substantive terms and conditions of employment entirely to private negotiation. The Act did not fix wages, hours or other conditions of employment. It did not authorize any administrative tribunal to fix them. When a dispute arose concerning substantive terms and conditions of employment, the Act provided no governmental machinery for its adjustment. The basic theory of the law in its original form, as today, was that the arrangement of substantive terms and conditions of employment was a private responsibility from which the government should stand apart. It was hoped that the processes of collective bargaining would result in a lessening of industrial strife, but no one supposed that strikes would not occur. In the end the force which makes management and labor agree is often an awareness of the costs of disagreement. The strike is the motive power which makes collective bargaining operate. Freedom to strike, the threat of a strike and possibly a number of actual strikes are, therefore, indispensable parts of a national labor policy based upon the establishment of wages, hours and other terms and conditions of employment by private collective bargaining.

The enactment of the Wagner Act was followed by an immediate constitutional challenge from major industries. The chief argument was that the Act, when applied to manufacturing establishments, went beyond the power of Congress under the commerce clause and invaded the powers reserved to the states by the Tenth Amendment. The NLRA gives the NLRB jurisdiction over unfair labor practices and questions of representation "affecting commerce." In the test cases which came before the Supreme Court the NLRB had applied the statute to an interstate bus line, the Associated Press, an integrated producer of basic steel, and a small clothing manufacturer who shipped and sold suits in interstate commerce.

The government was successful in all four cases. The Court's principal opinion was in NLRB v. Jones & Laughlin Steel Corp., 301 U.S. 1, 57 S.Ct. 615, 81 L.Ed. 893 (1937), in which the Court articulated an expansive view of Congress's power to regulate the manufacturing sector of the economy:

> * * * Although activities may be intrastate in character when separately considered, if they have such a close and substantial relation to interstate commerce that their control is essential or appropriate to protect that commerce from burdens and obstructions, Congress cannot be denied the power to exercise that control. * * *
>
> It is thus apparent that the fact that the employees here concerned were engaged in production is not determinative. The question remains as to the effect upon interstate commerce of the labor practice involved. * * * Giving full weight to respondent's contention with respect to a break in the complete continuity of the "stream of commerce" by reason of respondent's manufacturing operations, the fact remains that the stoppage of those opera-

tions by industrial strife would have a most serious effect upon interstate commerce. In view of respondent's far-flung activities, it is idle to say that the effect would be indirect or remote. It is obvious that it would be immediate and might be catastrophic. We are asked to shut our eyes to the plainest facts of our national life and to deal with the question of direct and indirect effects in an intellectual vacuum. Because there may be but indirect and remote effects upon interstate commerce in connection with a host of local enterprises throughout the country, it does not follow that other industrial activities do not have such a close and intimate relation to interstate commerce as to make the presence of industrial strife a matter of the most urgent national concern. When industries organize themselves on a national scale, making their relation to interstate commerce the dominant factor in their activities, how can it be maintained that their industrial labor relations constitute a forbidden field into which Congress may not enter when it is necessary to protect interstate commerce from the paralyzing consequences of industrial war? We have often said that interstate commerce itself is a practical conception. It is equally true that interferences with that commerce must be appraised by a judgment that does not ignore actual experience.

Experience has abundantly demonstrated that the recognition of the right of employees to self-organization and to have representatives of their own choosing for the purpose of collective bargaining is often an essential condition of industrial peace. Refusal to confer and negotiate has been one of the most prolific causes of strife. This is such an outstanding fact in the history of labor disturbances that it is a proper subject of judicial notice and requires no citation of instances. * * *

It is not necessary again to detail the facts as to respondent's enterprise. Instead of being beyond the pale, we think that it presents in a most striking way the close and intimate relation which a manufacturing industry may have to interstate commerce and we have no doubt that Congress had constitutional authority to safeguard the right of respondent's employees to self-organization and freedom in the choice of representatives for collective bargaining.

---

## THE CONGRESS OF INDUSTRIAL ORGANIZATIONS

Other than the enactment of the National Labor Relations Act, perhaps the most significant development in labor union history during the 1930s was the rise of the great industrial unions associated in the Congress of Industrial Organizations. The industrial unions organized the great mass production industries which had theretofore been scarcely touched by labor unions. Their power and the spread of unionism into these new areas brought about fundamental changes not only in the labor movement but also in the nature and processes of collective bargaining.

Early in the 1930s, it became apparent to John L. Lewis, Sidney Hillman, David Dubinsky and a number of others that the workers in the mass production industries could not be brought into the labor movement unless substantial changes were made in the structure and thinking of the American Federation of Labor. The principle of craft unionism was unsuited to industries, such as rubber and automobiles, where production engineering had broken skilled jobs down into simple repetitive movements which workers could easily learn to perform. Not only was it difficult, if not impossible, to fit these jobs into the structure of the established craft unions, but the workers lacked any feeling of craft solidarity which might furnish a basis for group action. A second difficulty was the adherence of many AFL leaders to the principle that organization must be voluntary and should not be imposed from outside. Since there was neither an active union movement nor any tradition of unionism in the mass production industries, and since they were the strongholds of anti-unionism, it seemed manifest to Lewis and his associates that organizers must be sent into the field without awaiting a spontaneous movement which could never arise. The AFL was not equipped for this task since it had never had the primary responsibility for spearheading an organizing campaign.

When these considerations and others like them were placed before the AFL by Lewis, Hillman and their associates, they encountered strong opposition. The crafts were unwilling to surrender jurisdiction to industrial organizations. Their motives were doubtless compounded of a desire to retain their power, reluctance to abandon a traditional and successful principle, and perhaps the recollection of the conflicts of interest between skilled craftsmen and unskilled workers competing for the same jobs. The matter was hotly debated at a number of annual conventions and meetings of the Executive Board and ultimately came to a head in the 1935 annual convention. The industrial unionists summoned an informal gathering to discuss methods of keeping industrial unionism alive, and shortly thereafter the officers of eight AFL international unions formed the Committee for Industrial Organization. Although they professed their desire to work within the AFL, their action challenged the principle of exclusive jurisdiction, which was deeply embedded in trade union philosophy. In the eyes of the old line AFL leaders the members of the Committee were plainly guilty of "dual unionism"—treason in the labor movement—and they ordered the committee to disband. When it refused, the unions which joined it were suspended from the AFL. In 1937 the Congress of Industrial Organizations was formally organized.

The organizational structure of the CIO closely followed the established AFL pattern. The CIO philosophy, however, contrasted sharply with the trade unions' historic ideals. As their names imply, the CIO International Unions embraced the workers in entire industries or groups of industries—United Automobile Workers of America, United Steelworkers of America, Textile Workers Union of America, etc. While the aims of AFL were influenced by its tendency to favor the skilled workers, the CIO was primarily a movement of the unskilled workers; in negotiating wage increases, for example, the CIO more often pressed for flat increases "across the board", thus raising the real wages of the unskilled workers more rapidly than those of the skilled. On the whole the CIO unions were probably less attached to existing institutions than the AFL and quicker to espouse political action. Thus, the CIO displayed an intense interest not only in traditional labor objectives, but in price control, low cost housing, improved educational opportunities, public health and foreign policy.

The emergence of the CIO had a profound influence on the administration of the Wagner Act. In particular, it vastly complicated the task of the National Labor Relations Board in determining the appropriate unit in which to conduct representation elections pursuant to Section 9 of the Act. The CIO, of course, was generally committed to the concept of industrial unionism and sought to represent all workers within the plants and companies of given industries. On the other hand, the AFL was founded on the principle of craft unionism with the result that AFL unions sought to represent particular groups of skilled workers within plants and companies. As a result, CIO and AFL unions vigorously pressed their respective claims before the NLRB, particularly in industries already organized by the CIO, where AFL unions sought to split off groups of craftsmen into separate units.

During the early 1950's, there was increased pressure within the AFL and CIO to reunite. In 1953, a no-raiding pact was drawn up and approved by sixty-five AFL affiliates and twenty-nine CIO affiliates, representing a total of ten million workers. Under its terms, the signatory unions agreed not to attempt to displace another union and raid its membership in any plant where an "established bargaining relationship" existed. Disputes involving the application of the agreement were referred to arbitration if the parties could not agree among themselves. Following the adoption of the no-raiding agreement, plans for total unification developed rapidly, and a draft constitution to this effect was prepared and ratified by the AFL and CIO in 1955.

# VI.  The Taft-Hartley Act[a]

From 1935 until 1947, the national labor policy was founded upon the Norris–LaGuardia and Wagner Acts supplemented by wartime emergency measures. The Norris–LaGuardia Act established the predicate that peace-

**a.** For comments on the Taft–Hartley amendments, see—in addition to the references supplied in the Bibliography on p. vii supra and those cited in the text of this section—Cox, Some Aspects of the Labor Management Relations Act, 1947, 61 Harv. L.Rev. 1, 274 (1947–48); Perkins, Basic Labor Law Issues Under the Taft–Hartley Act, 27 B.U.L.Rev. 371 (1947); Wollett, Collective Bargaining, Public Policy and the NLRA of 1947, 23 Wash.L.Rev. 205 (1948). See generally H. Millis & E. Brown, From the Wagner Act to Taft–Hartley (1950), and Taft–Hartley Symposium: The First Fifty Years, 47 Cath. U.L. Rev. 763–977 (1998).

ful, concerted activities—strikes, boycotts, or picketing—should not be enjoinable by law. The Wagner Act established the twin rights to organize and bargain collectively and made it government policy to encourage unionization and collective bargaining. Both statutes made permanent contributions to our national labor policy, but their fundamental assumptions were modified by the enactment of the Taft–Hartley Act in 1947. The Taft–Hartley bill was bitterly opposed by organized labor and most so-called "liberals." It was vetoed by President Truman and passed over his veto.

Between 1935 and 1947, labor unions grew and collective bargaining spread rapidly with the aid and encouragement of the federal government. In 1935, only three million workers belonged to labor unions; in 1947, there were nearly fifteen million union members. Two thirds of the workers in manufacturing were covered by union agreements and about one third in non-manufacturing industries outside of agriculture and the professions. In some industries, such as coal mining, construction, railroading, and trucking, over four fifths of the employees worked under collective bargaining agreements.

Although government policies scarcely explain this phenomenal development, they exerted important influence. One factor was the Wagner Act and the work of the NLRB. The bare legal protection curbed anti-union tactics. For the government to prosecute an employer for unfair labor practices gave psychological impetus to unionization. Furthermore the NLRB in both Washington and the regional offices was staffed by enthusiasts burning with zeal for organized labor.

A second factor was the federal government's wartime labor policy. The United States could not become the arsenal of democracy without the whole-hearted cooperation of organized labor, and the surest method of obtaining cooperation was to give unions a permanent role in directing the mobilization and allocation of our national resources. Prominent labor figures were given positions of leadership in major federal agencies, such as the Office of Defense Mobilization and the War Production Board, and President Roosevelt made it plain that high officials in the labor movement had quick access to the White House. Labor's role in government reached a peak in the organization of the War Labor Board, which was tripartite; the public, industry and organized labor were equally represented. After Pearl Harbor the country could not safely tolerate any interruption in the production and distribution of goods. Organized labor gave a pledge not to resort to strikes provided that all labor management controversies not resolved in collective bargaining were submitted to the War Labor Board for final decision.

The psychological impact of these measures was tremendous. The union organizer could plausibly argue "It is patriotic to join a union. The President wants you to become a union member." The role of unions in government and the high praise regularly heaped upon organized labor by government officials seemed to prove the point.

The third important factor was the policies of the War Labor Board. The public members of the War Labor Board and many of the employer members were staunch believers in strong unions and collective bargaining. Their policies and decisions gave it encouragement. Still more important, once a union had organized a plant War Labor Board policies encouraged the development of procedures confirming and strengthening the union's role in the plant—use of company bulletin boards, preferential seniority for shop stewards, strong grievance machinery controlled by the union, and arbitration of unsettled grievances.

By 1947, the labor movement had achieved great power. Sumner Slichter wrote, "The trade unions are the most powerful economic organizations in the community—in fact, they are the most powerful economic organizations which the community has ever seen." (Slichter, The Challenge of Industrial Relations (1947).) Yet it would be a mistake to suppose that power of labor unions was evenly distributed. In the South and in many agricultural states organized labor was weak indeed. Unions were much stronger, by and large, in manufacturing and mining than in wholesale and retail distribution or among office and clerical workers. The United Mine Workers could defy public opinion but most unions were still vulnerable to shifts in the wind of public sentiment.

The public was worried about the power of unions. Its worry was partly an irrational but widespread fear of "the labor bosses." John L. Lewis and the United Mine Workers had carried on two long strikes during wartime in defiance of the government ending only when the government granted substantial concessions. In 1946 there was a great wave of strikes which shut down the steel mills, automobile assembly plants, packinghouses, electrical products industry, the East and West Coast seaports and a few public utilities. Today it seems plain that this wave of strikes simply marked release from wartime restrictions. In 1947 there were many who saw the danger of nationwide stoppages as a threat to the social system.

But if some of the fear was irrational, there were also careful observers sympathetic to organized labor who perceived the need for measures halting a number of abuses of power by organized labor: (1) Too many strikes were called under circumstances threatening serious injury to the public health or safety (for example, in the coal mines and in public utilities); (2) some unions were primarily used as vehicles for racketeering; (3) strikes and picketing were too often marked by violence; (4) many building trades unions refused during the war to admit new members and charged them exorbitant fees for issuing working permits; (5) the construction industry was also hampered by strikes resulting from jurisdictional disputes between competing craft groups; (6) the secondary boycott had become an exceedingly powerful weapon in the hands of certain unions, for example the International Brotherhood of Teamsters (which could tie up any business dependent upon trucking for supplies or outgoing shipments) and the United Brotherhood of Carpenters (which could boycott at construction sites any materials produced by a firm on which it sought to impose economic pressure); and (7) a number of unions abused closed and union shop contracts, by limiting union membership (and thus jobs) to family members or by expulsion of members for improper reasons (such as criticizing union officials or testifying adversely to the union in an arbitration proceeding).

In analyzing the background of the Taft–Hartley Act one must also give a prominent place to anti-unionism. Many business concerns continued to make war on all unions despite the National Labor Relations Act. Others accepted the forms of collective bargaining under legal and economic compulsion hoping that the tide would turn and they might some day be free from "the union." The National Association of Manufacturers, for example, rejected the position of a minority seeking to eviscerate the Wagner Act. It sought, rather, for a law that would help management to keep unions out and would assist management, if unionized, "in keeping the upper hand." H. Harris, The Right to Manage: Industrial Relations Policies of American Business in the 1940s, 121 (1982).

The irreconcilables were strengthened by the changing frontiers of union organization. By the end of the war most of the big industrial concerns in the Northeast and Midwest had been organized as well as on the Pacific Coast. Union organizers were now seeking to enlist distributive and clerical workers many of whom were employed in small enterprises where they worked in close contact with the boss. People who genuinely sympathized with the plight of unorganized workers in mines, mills and factories doubted the need for unions in wholesale and retail trades or office buildings where the business itself was smaller and economically weaker than the union.

In sum, the Taft–Hartley Act was the product of diverse forces—the off-spring, a critic might say, of an unhappy union between the opponents of all collective bargaining and the critics of the unions' abuses of power. The former group was probably the more influential of the two in writing the Taft–Hartley amendments, for organized labor's unfortunate decision to oppose all legislation left its sympathetic critics in a dilemma.

In reflecting on the fifty years since its enactment, one might say that the Taft–Hartley Act has left these marks upon our labor laws.

*First,* the Taft–Hartley Act abandoned the notion that law has no role to play in the handling of labor disputes. The philosophy of the Norris–LaGuardia Act was qualified, if not rejected, and the labor injunction was revived in a modified and restricted form which eliminated many abuses. Section 8(b) outlaws the following concerted activities, among others:

(1) violence and intimidation;

(2) secondary boycotts; i.e. the refusal to work for employer *A* unless he ceases to do business with employer *B*, with whom the union has its real dispute;

(3) strikes to compel an employer to commit some unfair labor practice, such as discharging an employee for belonging (or not belonging) to a particular union, or bargaining with the striking union after the NLRB has certified a different representative;

(4) jurisdictional strikes over work assignments.

The weapons thus withheld, especially the secondary boycott, had been important to certain unions in the past. Nevertheless, the points at which the Taft–Hartley Act revives legal intervention into everyday disputes are trivial in comparison to those it leaves untouched. Also, the law intrudes only in areas where the overwhelming consensus of opinion condemns the unlawful conduct.

*Second,* the Taft–Hartley Act carried forward the fundamental rights to organize and bargain collectively, but it also ushered in a period of marked change in the government's attitude towards unionization. The amendments represent an abandonment of the policy of affirmatively encouraging the spread of union organization and collective bargaining. This appears most strikingly in Section 7, which now places the right to refrain from such activities on equal footing with the rights originally guaranteed, and in the provisions subjecting the organizational activities of labor unions to restrictions similar to those imposed on the activities of employers. The government, instead of aiding one side, now stands in the center. The change of policy appears to have been based on the belief that labor unions had become so strong that legislative action was required to redress the balance of power in the collective bargaining process. But it is not the unions with great economic power that feel the change; it is the unorganized employees and the weak, newly-organized locals.

*Third,* the Taft–Hartley Act ratified previous NLRB regulation of collective bargaining and even extended governmental regulation of the negotiation of collective bargaining agreements. Prior to 1947 the NLRB had gone a considerable distance in regulating both the subject matter of collective bargaining and the way in which negotiations should be conducted. Congress accepted this approach. By imposing a duty to bargain collectively upon labor unions it espoused the view that the public has an interest not only in the employer's dealing with the employees as a group but also in the way in which collective negotiations are carried on. This was underscored by the detail in which Section 8(d) regulates the renewal or reopening of collective bargaining agreements. In the Taft–Hartley Act Congress also undertook to regulate for the first time the substantive terms which might be included in a labor contract. Section 8(a)(3) outlaws the closed shop and permits only a limited form of union shop. Section 302 prescribes and limits the terms of pension and health and welfare trust funds.

*Fourth,* the Taft–Hartley Act marks a turning point at which law began to play a larger role in the administration of collective bargaining agreements. NLRA Section 301 provides that suits for violation of collective bargaining agreements in industries affecting commerce may be brought by or against a labor organization as an entity in any appropriate federal court. This has encouraged both unions and employers to seek legal sanctions in situations in which they might otherwise have relied upon persuasion or economic power. Since 1947 there has been rapid growth in the law pertaining to the interpretation and enforcement of labor contracts.

The longer term practical impact of Taft–Hartley has been assessed by one student of the period:

> [T]he Taft–Hartley Act helped restrict American industrial unionism to roughly the same social and regional terrain that it had won in the previous decade. The CIO effort to penetrate textile, furniture, food processing, and chemical plants in the South was severely hampered by Section 14b of the Taft–Hartley Act, which permitted individual states to outlaw the union shop. At the same time, the prohibition of secondary boycotts and mass picketing contained in the act made it much more difficult for strong unions to use their organizational muscle to aid the unionization effort of weaker groups in the retail and agricultural sectors, even in highly unionized regions of the North and West. Moreover, this containment of the union impulse also proved effective within already organized factories and offices. The Taft–Hartley Act defined as managers many supervisory workers who had been strongly attracted to unionism in the 1940s, and it prohibited their use of NLRB procedures when they sought union recognition. This legislative edict allowed employers to smash the promising foremen's organizations in the auto, steel, rubber, and shipbuilding industries and gave managers a powerful anti-union weapon in bureaucratically structured workplaces such as insurance and telephone offices, where a large number of supervisory personnel could be used as a bulwark against effective union organization.

N. Lichtenstein, Labor's War at Home: The CIO in World War II, 239–240 (1982).

## VII.   THE LANDRUM–GRIFFIN ACT[a]

Twelve years after the passage of the Taft–Hartley Act, Congress once again undertook to enact basic changes in the body of national labor legislation. At the outset, Congress sought to draft provisions to regulate the internal affairs of unions. Nevertheless, this effort was soon coupled with a quite separate undertaking designed to introduce amendments to the National Labor Relations Act governing the relations between unions and employers.

In general, the amendments to the NLRA were in keeping with the basic purposes that had underlain the Taft–Hartley amendments of 1947. Various loopholes in the secondary boycott provisions were closed; in particular, the exertion of secondary pressures through the use of "hot cargo" agreements was prohibited. Substantial limitations were also placed upon the power of unions to picket for the purpose of organizing workers or

---

**a.** See J. Bellace & A. Berkowitz, The Landrum–Griffin Act: Twenty Years of Federal Protection of Union Members' Rights (1979); D. McLaughlin & A. Schoomaker, The Landrum–Griffin Act and Union Democracy (1979).

obtaining recognition from an employer. These restrictions, however, simply represented an extension of the policy which Congress had adopted in 1947 to limit union activities which tended to coerce employees in deciding whether or not to join a union. As a "sweetener" for the labor unions, workers who had been replaced in the course of an economic strike were expressly given the right to vote in union elections. In this way, employers would be discouraged from provoking a strike in order to hire non-union replacements and thereby oust the incumbent labor organization.

Far more novel were the provisions regulating the internal affairs of labor organizations, for earlier legislation had scarcely touched upon this subject. For several years there had been growing concern about the relationship between the union and its members. The problem became prominent during the 1950s when hearings by a Select Committee of the Senate (the McClellan Committee) produced evidence of misconduct by the officials of a few unions ranging from embezzlement to the making of "sweetheart" contracts with employers. To cope with abuses of this sort, a wide variety of provisions were enacted by the Congress. Certain provisions required that elections be held periodically for local and national union officers and that union members be assured a right to vote, to run for union office, and to comment upon and nominate candidates. Every union member was given an equal right to attend membership meetings and to participate in the voting and deliberations at such meetings. Other provisions required the filing of extensive information bearing upon the financial affairs of unions and their officials. Still other sections of the Act flatly prohibited certain types of conduct such as the embezzlement of union funds or property and the making of loans by a union to its officials in excess of a stipulated amount.

A more detailed consideration of the Labor Management Reporting and Disclosure Act is reserved until Part Ten of the casebook.

## VIII.    JURISDICTION, ORGANIZATION AND PROCEDURE OF THE NLRB

----

## A.    NLRB JURISDICTION

The two most significant statutes which accord the rights of unionization and collective bargaining to American workers are the National Labor Relations Act of 1935, as amended in 1947 and 1959, and the Railway Labor Act of 1926, as amended in 1934, which covers employees of railroad and airline carriers. As broad as is the coverage of these statutes, it is important to note that large segments of the workforce are not covered by either; indeed, it is probable that not much more than half of the total labor force in the United States is covered by the NLRA or RLA.

The coverage of the National Labor Relations Act, while far broader than that of the Railway Labor Act, is by no means all-embracing in its coverage of American workers. Large numbers of "employees" fall into special categories which are specifically excluded by Section 2(3) of the NLRA, and many others work for "employers" who are excluded under Section 2(2). Still other workers are employed in enterprises which have too tenuous a connection with interstate commerce to be subject to the Labor Act.

In expressly wording the NLRA to cover enterprises "affecting commerce," Congress appeared to extend the Act to the full limit of its constitutional power. In Wickard v. Filburn, 317 U.S. 111, 63 S.Ct. 82, 87 L.Ed. 122 (1942), Congress was held to have authority under the commerce clause to regulate even the production of wheat consumed entirely at the farm on which it was grown because changes in the volume of such wheat could affect the supply and demand for grain sold across State boundaries. Since the *Wickard* case, the commerce power has been held to extend to used car dealers, grocery stores, newspapers selling but 1½% of their copies in other States, maintenance firms, and a host of other activities having but a slender relationship to interstate commerce. See, respectively, Liddon White Truck Co., 76 NLRB 1181 (1948); Providence Public Market Co., 79 NLRB 1482 (1948); Mabee v. White Plains Pub. Co., 327 U.S. 178, 66 S.Ct. 511, 90 L.Ed. 607 (1946); D.A. Schulte, Inc. v. Gangi, 326 U.S. 712, 66 S.Ct. 177, 90 L.Ed. 421 (1945). There would seem to be very few, if any, business enterprises whose activities have no discernible effect upon commerce between the States. Cf. NLRB v. Reliance Fuel Oil Corp., 297 F.2d 94 (2d Cir.1961), rev'd, 371 U.S. 224, 83 S.Ct. 312, 9 L.Ed.2d 279 (1963).

As a practical matter, it has not been necessary under the Act to determine the exact boundaries of the commerce power, for the National Labor Relations Board has not been given sufficient funds to enforce the law even with respect to all of the myriad enterprises that are plainly subject to the commerce clause. As a result, the Board has voluntarily refused to take cognizance of a great number of employers who, though technically within reach of the commerce power, are not considered to have a significant impact on commerce. The Board has declared that employers must engage directly or indirectly in interstate commerce to an extent exceeding certain prescribed dollar minima in order to be subject to its jurisdiction. The following is a list of some of the standards which the Board has established:

1. *Retail Concerns:* All such concerns doing $500,000 or more gross volume of business.

2. *Non-retail Firms:* All such firms with an annual outflow or inflow, direct or indirect, in excess of $50,000.

3. *Instrumentalities, Links and Channels of Interstate Commerce* (trucking companies, etc.): All such entities which derive $50,000 or more annually from the interstate (or linkage) portion of their operations, or from services performed for employers in commerce.

4. *Public Utilities:* All utilities which have at least $250,000 gross annual volume or qualify under the jurisdictional standard applicable to non-retail firms.

5. *Transit Systems* (other than taxicabs, which are governed by the standard for retail concerns): All such systems with an annual gross volume of $250,000 or more.

6. *Newspapers and Communications Systems:* Radio, television, telegraph and telephone systems: $100,000 gross volume. Newspapers: $200,000 gross volume.

7. *National Defense:* All firms having a "substantial impact on national defense."

8. *Proprietary and Nonprofit Hospitals:* All such institutions with gross annual revenue of at least $250,000.

9. *Law Firms and Legal Assistance Programs:* All such entities with gross annual revenue of at least $250,000.

Through the cumulative effect of the limits on the commerce power itself and the self-imposed restrictions of the Board, several million employees have been left outside the scope of the National Labor Relations Act.

Section 2(2) of the NLRA excludes several important categories of *employers*—the United States Government, wholly owned government corporations, Federal Reserve Banks, states and their political subdivisions, and railroads and airlines subject to the Railway Labor Act. To the excluded categories of employers specifically listed in the Act, the Supreme Court, in a 5–to–4 decision, has added secondary schools operated by the Roman Catholic Church. In NLRB v. CATHOLIC BISHOP OF CHICAGO, 440 U.S. 490, 99 S.Ct. 1313, 59 L.Ed.2d 533 (1979), the Court was confronted with the question whether the NLRB could properly assert jurisdiction to order bargaining between two groups of Catholic high schools and their lay teachers. The Court found that a construction of the NLRA so as to permit Board jurisdiction would raise a serious constitutional question under the First Amendment regarding the entanglement of the federal government in the operations of private religious schools. It therefore held that there was no clear congressional purpose to permit such jurisdiction and affirmed an order of the court of appeals denying enforcement of the Board order. See Note, NLRB Regulation of Parochial Schools: A Practical Free Exercise Accommodation, 97 Yale L.J. 135 (1987).

No doubt the most significant group of excluded employers are public employers—federal, state, county and municipal governments. Their exclusion results in the lack of coverage by the Labor Act for roughly 20 million American workers, some 15 percent of the workforce. Of these, roughly 3 million employees work for federal agencies (in civilian capacities in Washington, D.C. and throughout the country), and some 17 million state and local government employees work for police and fire departments, school boards, court systems, highway and sanitation departments, and the like. Most of these public employees are, however, accorded rights to unionize and to engage in collective bargaining (with the common exception of the right to strike) that are modeled upon those accorded to private-sector workers by the National Labor Relations Act.

The rights of employees in the federal service to organize and to bargain collectively were not formally protected until 1962, when President Kennedy promulgated Executive Order 10988. Now these rights are incorporated in the Civil Service Reform Act, 92 Stat. 1111, 5 U.S.C. §§ 7101–35. The statute creates a Federal Labor Relations Authority, patterned after the NLRB, with similar powers over representation elections and unfair labor practice cases. Federal-employee unions are forbidden "to call, or participate in, a strike, work stoppage, or slowdown, or picketing of an agency in a labor-management dispute if such picketing interferes with an agency's operations." The federal act also narrows the scope of collective bargaining subjects in comparison with the private sector, provides for consultation rights for certain minority unions when there is no majority representative, and requires unions to provide for "the maintenance of democratic procedures and practices."

The organizing and bargaining rights of state and local employees are accorded for the most part through state statutes modeled upon the NLRA. These statutes began to be widely enacted in the late 1960s; as such public-sector laws became widespread, so too did membership in public-sector unions. By 1980—and the percentages were not much different in the year 2000—roughly 38 percent of all government workers (federal and state, predominantly the latter) were members of labor unions and roughly 43 percent were employed in bargaining units that were represented by unions. These figures are approximately four times the equivalent figures in private-sector employment.

Section 2(3) adds to these employer exclusions a number of classes of excluded *employees*. One excluded employee class consists of agricultural laborers. The Board has interpreted this exclusion rather narrowly, holding that no worker can be considered agricultural unless his duties form an integral part of ordinary farming operations. Moreover, his work must ordinarily be of a sort performed before the products can be marketed through normal channels. Hence, employees primarily engaged in duties which merely serve to increase the value of already-marketable products do not fall within the exclusion unless their duties are merely an incident to the employer's normal farming operations. Under this interpretation, workers employed in slaughtering, packing, processing and refining and the like have been found to be subject to the NLRA. The Supreme Court has generally deferred to the Board's decisions on these jurisdictional matters. See Bayside Enterprises, Inc. v. NLRB, 429 U.S. 298, 97 S.Ct. 576, 50 L.Ed.2d 494 (1977); Holly Farms Corp. v. NLRB, 517 U.S. 392, 116 S.Ct. 1396, 134 L.Ed.2d 593 (1996). Nevertheless, as a result of the agricultural exemption, some 1½ million workers are removed from the Act's coverage.

The labor-management relations of agricultural workers are governed by the laws of the individual states. Most of these continue to develop their rules through common law decisions, with judges using the same uncertain criteria observed in judicial decisions at the turn of the century; but others apply "little" Wagner or Norris–LaGuardia Acts. See, e.g., Bravo v. Dolsen Cos., 125 Wn.2d 745, 888 P.2d 147 (1995). There are, however, four states—Arizona, California, Idaho, and Kansas—which in the early 1970s enacted legislation patterned for the most part after the NLRA; Agricultural Labor Relations Boards are created, organizing and bargaining rights are accorded to agricultural workers within the state, and provision is made for elections and unfair labor practice proceedings. See Babbitt v. United Farm Workers Nat'l. Union, 442 U.S. 289, 99 S.Ct. 2301, 60 L.Ed.2d 895 (1979); Agricultural Labor Relations Bd. v. Superior Court, 16 Cal.3d 392, 128 Cal.Rptr. 183, 546 P.2d 687 (1976), appeal dismissed, 429 U.S. 802, 97 S.Ct. 33, 50 L.Ed.2d 63 (1976).

Another significant category of workers explicitly excluded in Section 2(3) from the coverage of the NLRA is the "independent contractor." This exclusion, written in by Congress in the 1947 Taft–Hartley Act, has a particularly interesting background. In NLRB v. HEARST PUBLICATIONS, INC., 322 U.S. 111, 64 S.Ct. 851, 88 L.Ed. 1170 (1944), the Supreme Court had enforced a decision of the NLRB that the publishers of certain Los Angeles daily newspapers had a duty to bargain with a union representing "newsboys" who distributed their papers on the streets of that city; these workers (generally mature men) sold newspapers at established locations on a full-time basis and were dependent upon the proceeds of their sales for their livelihood. At the time of the Board and Court decisions Section 2(3) defined "employee," somewhat unhelpfully, as to "include any employee." The respondent companies argued that Congress intended by this language to import the distinction between "employees" and "independent contractors" in accordance with the common law *respondeat superior* test in cases of imputed tort liability.

The Supreme Court concluded that the so-called "right of control" test for purposes of *respondeat superior* was inapt in determining whether the newsboys were within the coverage of the National Labor Relations Act. It concluded that this test was vague in its application, was applied differently in different jurisdictions, and was, above all, irrelevant to the purposes of the Wagner Act, which "is federal legislation, administered by a national agency, intended to solve a national problem on a national scale." The Court concluded that "The mischief at which the Act is aimed and the remedies it offers are not confined exclusively to 'employees' within the traditional legal distinctions separating them from 'independent contractors.'"

Examining the purposes underlying the NLRA, the Court noted that "the particular workers in these cases are subject, as a matter of economic fact, to the evils the statute was designed to eradicate" (interruptions in commerce, economic helplessness, inequality of bargaining power) and that the remedies it affords (unionization and collective bargaining) "are appropriate for preventing them or curing their harmful effects in the special situation." The Court then propounded an "economic facts" test or "statutory purpose" test for construing the word "employee" in Section 2(3): "In short, when the particular situation of employment combines these characteristics, so that the economic facts of the relation make it more nearly one of employment than of independent business enterprise with respect to the ends sought to be accomplished by the legislation, those characteristics may outweigh technical legal classification for purposes unrelated to the statute's objectives and bring the relation within its protections." It concluded that the function of the court was limited when reviewing the Board's application of the broad statutory term to specific facts, and that the Board's determination regarding the Los Angeles newsboys had "warrant in the record" and "a reasonable basis in law," and should thus be enforced.

In amending the Labor Act in 1947 to exclude independent contractors, Congress flatly rejected the approach of the Supreme Court in the *Hearst* case. The text of the accompanying House Committee Report, H.R.Rep. No. 245, 80th Cong., 1st Sess. at 18 (1947), reprimanded the Board for having "expanded the definition of the term 'employee' beyond anything that it ever had included before," and reprimanded the Supreme Court in *Hearst* for relying upon the "theoretic expertness" of the Board. It can thus fairly be said that by excluding independent contractors from Section 2(3), Congress manifested an intention not only to narrow the scope of the Board's jurisdiction and the reach of the Act but also to curb the power of the Board in relation to that of the judiciary.

The Board has since applied the "right of control" test in determining whether, in particular cases, groups such as newsboys, taxicab drivers and insurance agents are to be treated as "employees" or as "independent contractors." Not surprisingly, a number of appeals courts subjected such Board findings to considerable scrutiny. This judicial assertiveness was, however, rejected by the Supreme Court in NLRB v. United Insurance Co., 390 U.S. 254, 88 S.Ct. 988, 19 L.Ed.2d 1083 (1968). There, the court of appeals overturned a Board determination that certain insurance agents—whose primary functions were to collect premiums from policyholders, to prevent the lapsing of policies, and to sell such new insurance as time allowed—were "employees." The Supreme Court observed: "On the one hand these debit agents perform their work primarily away from the company's offices and fix their own hours of work and work days; and clearly they are not as obviously employees as are production workers in a factory. On the other hand, however, they do not have the independence, nor are they allowed the initiative and decision-making authority, normally associated with an independent contractor." The Court acknowledged that the task for the Board was to apply common law principles of agency, that this "was not a purely factual finding by the Board, but involved the application of law to facts," and that "such a determination of pure agency law involved no special administrative expertise that a court does not possess." Nonetheless, the Court held that it was not proper for a reviewing court to assess the record de novo; "the Board's determination was a judgment made after a hearing with witnesses and oral argument had been held and on the basis of written briefs. Such a determination should not be set aside just because a court would, as an original matter, decide the case the other way. * * * Here the least that can be said for the Board's decision is that it made a choice between two fairly conflicting views, and under these circumstances the Court of Appeals should have enforced the Board's order."

The Commission on the Future of Worker–Management Relations (the eponymous "Dunlop Commission") took note in its 1994 Fact Finding Report of the growth of the "contingent workforce"—mostly part-time and often multiple job holders and temporary employees who are often paid less than full-time workers, are less likely to be covered by health or pension policies and are exempt from several labor protective laws. *See generally* Symposium on the Regulatory Future of Contingent Employment, 52 Washington and Lee L. Rev. 725–933 (1995). Included among these, however, are persons classified as "independent contractors"—some of whom are highly educated, highly paid consultants (and the like), and others of whom are treated as such to avoid employment benefits and the application of the Labor Act. The Commission's Final Report recommended the abandonment (by Congress) of the common law test:

> Workers who are economically dependent on the entity for whom they perform services generally should be treated as employees. Factors such as low wages, low skill levels, and having one or few employers should all militate against treatment as an independent contractor. A revised test based on the economic realities of the work relationship will eliminate the incentives to use the independent contractor form to evade the obligations of national workplace policy while leaving it fully available where its use is truly appropriate.

Another important excluded employee category consists of "supervisors." That term is defined in Section 2(11) to mean

> any individual having authority, in the interest of the employer, to hire, transfer, suspend, lay off, recall, promote, discharge, assign, reward, or discipline other employees, or responsibly to direct them, or to adjust their grievances, or effectively to recommend such action, if in connection with the foregoing the exercise of such authority is not of a merely routine or clerical nature, but requires the use of independent judgment.

Section 14(a) of the Labor Act makes it clear that there is no intention actually to prohibit supervisors from unionizing; it merely frees the employer from any obligation to deal with such supervisors "as employees for the purpose of any law, either national or local, relating to collective bargaining." Congress sought to guarantee the single-minded loyalty of supervisors and not, by giving them any right to organize and the employer a correlative duty to bargain, to encourage a conflict of economic interest between the employer and its own representatives. Moreover, any active participation in union affairs on the part of supervisors is likely to be construed as an interference by the employer in union activities, which constitutes a violation of Sections 8(a)(1) and (2) of the Labor Act; the effect of these provisions is to permit supervisors to enjoy only a nominal membership in a union which also represents rank-and-file employees. See generally Seitz, Legal, Legislative and Managerial Responses to the Organization of Supervisory Employees in the 1940s, 28 Am.J.Leg.Hist. 199 (1984).

Even as Congress excluded supervisors in 1947, it accorded professional employees presumptively separate bargaining units from non-professionals and defined them, in part, in terms of their exercise of independent judgment. It had been argued accordingly that the exclusion of one and the inclusion of the other created a degree of internal statutory tension which the NLRB was called upon to resolve; and that the question was a pressing one in view of the growth of professionals as a segment of the workforce. See generally Finkin, The Supervisory Status of Professional Employees, 45 FORD. L. REV. 809 (1977). This question was taken up by the United States Supreme Court in its application to four licensed practical nurses. NLRB v. HEALTH CARE & RETIREMENT CORP., 511 U.S. 571, 114 S.Ct. 1778, 128 L.Ed.2d 586 (1994). These were non-professional employees who, in addition to their duties in patient care, assigned work to nurses' aides and monitored their work to assure proper performance. The five-member majority opinion, written by Justice Kennedy, held them to be supervisors: It noted that the performance of any one of the disjunctively enumerated criteria under § 2(11) rendered the employee a supervisor; and it refused to read the authority "responsibly to direct" the work of others as excluding from its sweep a general category of responsible direction which is incident to the exercise of independent judgment in connection with patient care. In dictum, the majority rejected any distinction in the reach of that provision for professional employees, reiterating its analysis in the *Yeshiva* case (to be discussed presently). The dissent, written by Justice Ginsburg, stressed the degree to which the performance of ostensibly supervisory functions—especially "responsible direction"—is often an inextricable component of the performance of professional (and technical) work, independently of the employer's direct control. She opined that the majority's view was likely to result in the exclusion of a large number of professional (and technical) employees from the Act's protection.

The issue was revisited in NLRB v. Kentucky River Community Care, Inc., ___ U.S. ___, 121 S.Ct. 1861, ___ L.Ed.2d ___ (2001), concerning the status of six registered nurses. Justice Scalia, writing for the five-member majority, parsed the language of § 2(11) very closely. The Board was not free to exempt professionals from supervisory status because they exercise "independent judgment" only over the work of other less skilled workers, even if that direction is informed by their professional training or experience, while including as supervisors those professionals who exercise independent judgment over any of the remaining indicia of supervisory status, *e.g.* hire, fire, reward, *etcetera*. "[M]any professionals," the Labor Board argued, such as lawyers, doctors and nurses "customarily give judgment-based direction to the less-skilled employees with whom they work." To which Justice Scalia responded: "The problem with the argument is not the soundness of ... [the Board's] labor policy.... It is that the policy cannot be given effect through this statutory text." Justice Stevens, writing for the four dissenters, opined that the law's language was ambiguous and the Board's resolution of the statutory ambiguity was entitled to considerable deference, especially in view of the Act's separate treatment for professional employees." "[I]f," he opined, "the 'supervisor' is construed too broadly, without regard for the statutory context, then Congress' inclusion of professionals within the Act's protections is effectively nullified."

Although there is no express exclusion in the Labor Act for "managerial employees," such as company vice-presidents, they have been excluded by the "common law" of the Act. In spite of the fact that they are technically "employees" and that they may not directly "supervise" the work of others (but instead make company policy on sales, purchases or product lines), the United States Supreme Court, rejecting the Board's contrary view, concluded that Congress would not have intended to invite the conflict of interest that would flow were such managerial employees to organize and bargain with the employer; indeed, on a broader rationale, such managerial employees *are* "the employer." This Court-made exclusion for managerial employees (and the broader rationale) was adopted in NLRB v. BELL AEROSPACE CO., 416 U.S. 267, 94 S.Ct. 1757, 40 L.Ed.2d 134 (1974):

> The legislative history of the Taft–Hartley Act of 1947 may be summarized as follows. The House wanted to include certain persons within the definition of "supervisors," such as strawbosses, whom the Senate believed should be protected by the Act. As to these persons, the Senate's view prevailed. There were other persons, however, whom both the House and the Senate believed were plainly outside the Act. The House wanted to make the exclusion of certain of these persons explicit. In the conference agreement, representatives from both the House and the Senate agreed that a specific provision was unnecessary since the Board had long regarded such persons as outside the Act. Among those mentioned as impliedly excluded were persons working in "labor relations, personnel and employment departments," and "confidential employees." But assuredly this did not exhaust the universe of such excluded persons. The legislative history strongly suggests that there also were other employees, much higher in the managerial structure, who were likewise regarded as so clearly outside the Act that no specific exclusionary provision was thought necessary. For example, in its discussion of confidential employees, the House Report noted that "[M]ost of the people who would qualify as 'confidential employees' are *executives and are excluded from the Act in any event*." H.R.Rep. No. 245, at 23 (italics added). We think the inference is plain that "managerial employees" were paramount among this impliedly excluded group. * * *

The Board on remand, at 219 NLRB 384 (1975), formulated the definition of "managerial employees" as follows:

> [T]hose who formulate and effectuate management policies by expressing and making operative the decisions of their employer, and those who have discretion in the performance of their jobs independent of their employer's established policy * * *. [M]anagerial status is not conferred upon rank-and file workers, or upon those who perform routinely, but rather it is reserved for those in executive-type positions, those who are closely aligned with management as true representatives of management.

In a controversial decision, the Supreme Court divided five-to-four and held that the full-time faculty members at a large private university were all "managerial employees" and thus outside of the protections of the NLRA. In NLRB v. YESHIVA UNIV., 444 U.S. 672, 100 S.Ct. 856, 63 L.Ed.2d 115 (1980), the University administration refused to bargain with a faculty association which had been certified by the NLRB, and thus challenged the Board's policy, announced in 1970, of asserting jurisdiction over college and university faculty in the private sector. The Court majority, after examining the extent to which the faculty played a role on such matters as faculty appointments, curriculum, degree requirements and the like, concluded that they were in effect managers of the enterprise who were beyond the jurisdiction of the Board. The dissenting Justices stated that management of the institution was actually in the hands of the University administration, whose interests and decisions were sometimes in conflict with those of the faculty, and who commonly endorsed faculty decisions not because they were made in the interests of management but rather because the faculty were experienced professionals (and professional employees are clearly not excluded from the coverage of the NLRA).

The *Yeshiva* decision created considerable concern among proponents of labor-management cooperation. In 1989, the U.S. Department of Labor's project on Labor Law and the Future of Labor–Management Cooperation expressed the fear that employee participation in matters traditionally reserved to management would jeopardize the statutory employee status of workers, even non-professional blue-collar workers. This theme was reiterated somewhat more forcefully by the Dunlop Commission five years later. It called for a legislative narrowing of both the managerial exclusion in the wake of *Yeshiva*, and the supervisory exclusion in the wake of *Health Care & Retirement Corp.*:

> These Supreme Court cases fail to take into account the degree to which supervisory and managerial tasks have been diffused throughout the workforce in many American firms. As a result of the Court's interpretations, thousands of rank-and-file employees have lost or may lose their collective bargaining rights. The Commission believes the law can and should accommodate the desires of professionals and other employees to participate at work—whether they desire to do so via independent representation or otherwise.

Commission on the Future of Worker–Management Relations, Report and Recommendations 11 (1994).

To round out the Labor Board's engagement with higher education, after the Act was extended to non-profit health care facilities—in part after lobbying by the Committee of Residents and Interns—the Board held that medical residents and interns (house staff) were not statutory employees, but rather primarily students. Cedars–Sinai Medical Center, 223 NLRB 251 (1976). The Board reversed that ruling in Boston Medical Center, 330 NLRB No. 30 (1999). It has since extended the logic of that decision to hold that graduate assistants, who work as teachers or researchers while pursuing more advanced education, are also statutory employees. New York University, 332 NLRB No. 111 (2000).

A final category of employee that the Board has determined should be excluded from the coverage of the Act—despite no explicit congressional exclusion—is the so-called confidential employee. For some years, the Board was confronted with arguments that all employees having confidential business information should not be accorded full rights to organize and bargain collectively. The Board, however, determined that denial of such rights was appropriate only when the employee had access to confidential labor-relations information of the employer. In Ford Motor Co., 66 NLRB 1317 (1946), for example, the Board limited the term "confidential" so as to "embrace only those employees who assist and act in a confidential capacity to persons who exercise 'managerial' functions in the field of labor relations." Only these employees would have advance information of the employer's position on such matters as contract negotiations, the disposition of grievances, and other labor relations matters, and thus frustrate the normal operations of the collective bargaining process. This "labor nexus" standard for determining the exclusion of confidential employees was sustained by a divided Supreme Court in NLRB v. Hendricks County Rural Elec. Membership Corp., 454 U.S. 170, 102 S.Ct. 216, 70 L.Ed.2d 323 (1981). The Court concluded that the Board's longstanding practice was rooted in its understanding of the nature of the collective bargaining process, was in effect endorsed by Congress in the Taft–Hartley amendments, and had a "reasonable basis in law."

---

## PROBLEMS FOR DISCUSSION

**1.** Was the Supreme Court in the *Hearst* case deserving of congressional reprimand for not borrowing the common law agency test when determining who is an "employee" within the protection of the NLRA? Did the Court in fact give undue deference to the NLRB in giving content to the statutory definition?

**2.** Was the Supreme Court decision in the *United Insurance* case consistent with the congressional purpose reflected in the 1947 exclusion of "independent contractors" from Section 2(3)? Are the Court's reasons for judicial deference convincing? Is the application of the common law agency test outside the Board's expertise, as the Court suggests (at least as of 1969, when the case was decided, or today)?

**3.** Given the detailed itemization of excluded employers and employees in Section 2 of the NLRA, is it appropriate for the NLRB to fashion other implied exclusions, such as for managerial and confidential employees? Are such implied exclusions consistent with Section 14(c) of the Act?

---

## B.   NLRB ORGANIZATION AND PROCEDURE[c]

Although it is customary to speak of "the Board" as if the National Labor Relations Board and its large staff of employees thought and acted as a single person, this usage is highly misleading. In reality, the NLRB is composed of various categories of persons exercising quite different responsibilities. The adjudicative responsibilities of the agency are ultimately entrusted to the five Members of the Board, appointed by the President of the United States for five-year terms with the consent of the Senate. In the course of the Taft–Hartley amendments of 1947, the Congress also established the office of General Counsel, appointed to a four-year term by the President with the consent of the Senate. The General Counsel has authority to investigate charges of unfair labor practices, to decide whether complaints should be issued on the basis of these charges and to direct the prosecution of such complaints. The General Counsel also represents the Board in court proceedings to enforce or review Board decisions.

To assist the Board members and the General Counsel in discharging their responsibilities, a large staff has been created. Organizationally, the staff is divided between the Washington office and over fifty Regional, Subregional and Resident Offices. The Regional Offices are under the general supervision of the General Counsel. Each Regional Office is under the direction of a Regional Director aided by a Regional Attorney. Their staff consists principally of Field Examiners and Field Attorneys, who investigate charges, conduct elections, and prosecute complaints at hearings before Administrative Law Judges (called Trial Examiners prior to August 1972).

---

*UNFAIR LABOR PRACTICE CASES*

The General Counsel may issue a complaint only upon a formal charge that the employer or the union has engaged in an unfair labor practice. Such a charge may be filed by "any person," in the office for the region in which the alleged unfair labor practice occurred. (Copies of standard NLRB forms for filing unfair labor practice charges may be found in the Statutory Supplement to this casebook.) Section 10(b) of the Act requires that a

**c.** S. Straus & J. Higgins, Practice and Procedure Before the National Labor Relations Board (5th ed. 1996); E. Miller, An Administrative Appraisal of the NLRB (4th ed. 1999); L. Modjeska, NLRB Practice (1983); J. Norris & M. Shershin, How to Take a Case Before the NLRB (6th ed. 1992).

A particularly rich source of information about NLRB procedures is the Board's own Casehandling Manual and its Outline of Law and Procedure in Representation Cases. Both documents can be accessed at the NLRB website: http://www.nlrb.gov/manuals.html.

charge be filed and served upon the charged party within six months of the alleged unfair labor practice. When a charge is filed, the Regional Director normally requires the person making the charge to submit the supporting evidence in the form of affidavits, lists of witnesses, etc. The charged party (respondent) will then be asked to submit a reply and a Field Examiner or Attorney will make a thorough investigation of the facts and surrounding circumstances. For example, if a charge is filed against the employer, the NLRB staff member interviews the union officials and employees concerned, locates other witnesses, goes to the plant and may discuss the case with company officials.

If this preliminary investigation discloses that the charge is without foundation, the case is likely to be dropped forthwith. Otherwise, further investigation may ensue and there will commonly be an informal conference at the local office of the Board, attended by both the respondent and the charging party, at which the alleged unfair practices are thoroughly discussed and possible settlements considered. It is important to emphasize the informality of these investigations, conferences and settlements. Except for such steps as are required by sound administration, including the reduction to writing of any settlement agreement, the entire procedure up to this point is conducted with all possible informality and an eye to amicable adjustments.

The overwhelming preponderance of unfair labor practice cases have traditionally been disposed of in one way or another in the Regional Offices by these informal personal negotiations. In the fiscal year ending September 30, 1998 (the most recent year for which the Board has published figures), for example, of the 33,287 unfair labor practice charges that were "closed," 94 percent were closed by the NLRB Regional Offices prior to a formal hearing. (Within those cases, approximately 31 percent were disposed of by dismissing the charge, 31 percent by voluntary withdrawal of the charge, and 33 percent by settlement.)

If it is impossible to dispose of an unfair labor practice case in the Regional Office, formal proceedings are commenced by the filing of a complaint. The General Counsel has delegated to the Regional Directors authority to issue complaints except in cases "involving novel and complex issues." Should the Regional Director refuse to issue a complaint, the matter may be appealed to the General Counsel. If the General Counsel declines to issue a complaint, the charging party normally has no further recourse. NLRB v. United Food & Comm. Wkrs. Union, Local 23, 484 U.S. 112, 108 S.Ct. 413, 98 L.Ed.2d 429 (1987).

Upon the issuance of a complaint the Board may petition the district court, under Section 10(j) of the Act, for appropriate interlocutory relief preventing continuance of the unfair labor practice. Section 10(j) injunctions have been issued against unions as well as employers, the more common employer violations being discriminatory discharges, recognition of minority unions and bad faith or "surface" bargaining, and the more common union violations involving strike violence and hiring-hall discrimination.

When compared to the full range of unfair labor practice proceedings—some 30,000 charges filed each year and some 1,000 Board decisions—it is only rarely that Section 10(j) injunctions have been sought by the Board. This was particularly true prior to early 1994, at which time the General Counsel appointed by President Clinton embarked upon a vigorous campaign to have the Board authorize such injunction proceedings. In the 1980s, the Board typically authorized the General Counsel to seek some 35 to 50 such injunctions each year, and typically between 25 and 35 were ultimately sought (most of the others being settled prior to court action). In the fiscal year ending September 30, 1994, however, the comparable numbers were 83 Board authorizations and 62 petitions filed; and in the following year, 104 Board authorizations and 78 petitions filed. These numbers declined sharply in fiscal year 1998, however, when only 32 section 10(j) injunctions were sought. The "success rate" from 1980 to 1995, as measured by 10(j) injunctions actually issued by district courts, was generally some 90 percent. Although still utilized in a rather small proportion of the Board's cases, the 10(j) injunction has been a conspicuous part of the General Counsel's enforcement program under the Labor Act and has no doubt accounted for a great measure of additional informal compliance.

Once a decision is made within the Regional Office to issue a complaint, it is drafted by the Regional Attorney or a member of his or her staff; the complaint specifies the violations of the Act which the respondent is alleged to have committed and contains a notice of the time and place of hearing. The Act and the Board's rules give the respondent the right to answer a complaint. The answer is filed with the Regional Director, as are all motions made prior to the hearing.

The hearing is usually held in the city or town where the alleged violation occurred, before an Administrative Law Judge appointed from the Division of Administrative Law Judges in Washington (or from one of the geographically decentralized divisions which the Board has recently established). The case is prosecuted for the Board by an attorney from the Regional Office. The charging party is permitted to intervene, and its attorneys may take part in the proceedings. The respondent, of course, may and usually does appear by an attorney. Section 10(b) of the Act provides that unfair labor practice proceedings "shall, so far as practicable, be conducted in accordance with the rules of evidence applicable in the district courts" under the rules of civil procedure adopted by the Supreme Court. Evidence is introduced through witnesses and documents, just as in an ordinary civil trial. At the conclusion of the hearing both parties are entitled as a matter of right to argue orally before the Administrative Law Judge and file a written brief. In practice, however, it has not been customary for either party to make an oral argument.

After the hearing is completed, the Administrative Law Judge prepares a decision containing proposed findings of fact and recommendations for the disposition of the case. The Administrative Law Judge's decision is then filed with the Board, and a copy is served on the respondent and any other parties. Exceptions to the Administrative Law Judge's decision may then promptly be filed by counsel for any party, including the General Counsel. Permission to argue orally before the Board itself must be specially requested in writing, and it is granted only in unusual cases. If no exceptions are filed, the Board normally adopts the decision of the Administrative Law Judge.

In cases in which exceptions have been filed and briefs submitted, the Executive Secretary forwards the complete record to one of the five Board members, determined by rotation. Board members, through their legal staff of some twenty attorneys for each member, prepare a draft decision. In routine cases, a panel of three members will consider the case. When a draft opinion is sent to the other panel members, copies are also sent to members who are not on the panel so that they may consider whether the case is sufficiently important to warrant decision by the full Board; any member may ask to have a case referred to the full Board. Panel opinions may be approved by the participating members without any formal conference, but where there is a difference of opinion or an important issue is at stake a conference is held. In cases sufficiently important for decision by the full Board there is always a conference. Afterward, the opinion is prepared, approved by the members and issued by the Board.

The five members of the Board decide in this fashion more than one hundred unfair labor practice cases a month. It is obvious that in most of them the basic responsibility rests with the administrative law judge and the legal assistants who prepare draft decisions for the Board. Only a relatively small number of really important cases could receive full consideration from the members themselves, however conscientiously they attended to their duties.

The Rules and Regulations issued by the Board provide for handling a charge that a labor organization has violated Section 8(b) in the same manner that the Board handles charges against employers. In the case of strikes and other concerted activities alleged to violate Sections 8(b)(4), 8(b)(7), or 8(e), however, the Regional Office must give its investigation precedence over all other cases not of the same character. If there is reason to believe that the charge is true, the Regional Director is required by the Act to file a petition for "appropriate injunctive relief pending the final adjudication of the Board" (Section 10(*l*)). The proceeding before the Board is then expedited and upon the Board's final decision, any order of the district court expires. As already noted, the Regional Director may seek an injunction under Section 10(j)(if approved by the General Counsel and the Board itself) against union unfair labor practices defined under other subsections of Section 8(b).

Board orders carry no sanctions, although every Regional Office includes a compliance officer who determines whether Board orders are being complied with and endeavors to secure voluntary compliance. If the respondent does not comply with a Board order, the Board must secure enforcement by filing a petition in a federal court of appeals; this action is taken on behalf of the Board by its Enforcement Division (which is a part of the

Office of the General Counsel), and the enforcement petition is uniformly filed in the circuit in which the unfair labor practice was committed. The Board may in fact secure such an enforcement order even when there has been no refusal to comply. Similarly, if the respondent desires to have the Board's order reviewed and set aside, it may file a petition for that purpose since under Section 10(f) it is a "person aggrieved." That section gives such a person a choice of courts of appeals, for review may be sought where the unfair labor practice was committed, or where the person does business, or in the Court of Appeals for the District of Columbia. Respondents frequently avail themselves of the right to seek review without waiting for the Board to file a petition for enforcement, particularly since this will give the respondent the power to select the circuit for review, a choice sometimes thought to be significant in the ultimate outcome of the case. If the decision of the Board denies relief in whole or in part to the charging party, that party becomes a "person aggrieved" who may also seek appellate review. The Supreme Court has also held that a party who is not aggrieved by the Board's decision, and whose position is sustained by the Board, may nonetheless intervene to protect its interests in the event another party petitions for review or for enforcement. International Union, UAW, Local 283 v. Scofield, 382 U.S. 205, 86 S.Ct. 373, 15 L.Ed.2d 272 (1965).

Upon the filing of a petition for enforcement or for review by a court of appeals, the pleadings, testimony and transcript of proceedings before the Board are certified to the court, and the case is put on its ordinary appellate docket. No objection that has not been urged before the Board may be considered by the court, save in exceptional cases. In such proceedings, the court is authorized to enter a decree setting aside, enforcing, or modifying the order and enforcing it as so modified. Review of the decree of a court of appeals may be had in the Supreme Court upon the granting of a petition for a writ of certiorari in the same manner as other cases.

In reviewing an order issued by the NLRB, courts must accept the Board's findings of fact "if supported by substantial evidence on the record considered as a whole" (Section 10(f)). This general standard of review eludes precise definition. "Substantial evidence" requires more than a scintilla; taking account of the facts and inferences on both sides of the issue, there must be enough evidence to support the agency's conclusion in a reasonable and reasoning mind. In other words, the court must not freely substitute its judgment for the Board's, yet it need not approve findings that the judges consider unreasonable or unfair. The deference given to the Board's findings is based in part on the fact that the administrative law judge is in a position to observe the witnesses at first hand. It is also partly due to the fact that the Board is "one of those agencies presumably equipped or informed by experience to deal with a specialized field of knowledge, whose findings within that field carry the authority of an expertness which courts do not possess and therefore must respect." Universal Camera Corp. v. NLRB, 340 U.S. 474, 71 S.Ct. 456, 95 L.Ed. 456 (1951). The degree of deference which the courts will pay to the "expertness" of the Board tends to vary according to the nature of the question involved. In particular, if the issue is a highly technical one, far removed from the ordinary experience of the judge, the court will be less likely to disturb the Board's findings, particularly if the Board has set forth the basis for its findings with reasonable clarity and if its reasoning and conclusions do not appear inconsistent with its decisions in related cases.

When a federal court of appeals reviews a judgment of a trial court, it is second nature to distinguish between the lower court's findings of fact and its conclusions of law. The fact findings are to be upheld unless "clearly erroneous." The fact findings of the NLRB—and of all federal administrative agencies—are to be upheld if supported by "substantial evidence" on the whole record. These standards are both deferential; their differences and similarities will be explored later. When a federal court of appeals reviews a trial court's conclusions of "law," it is generally understood that review can be more vigorous. The lower court is to be upheld not simply because its conclusions are within a range of reasonableness; rather, the appellate court is free to assess whether, for example, the lower court's interpretation of a statute is right, i.e., whether the appellate court would have made the same interpretation in the first instance.

Judicial review of federal administrative agencies on matters of statutory interpretation is different, and is more deferential. The leading Supreme Court precedent on the matter is CHEVRON, U.S.A., INC. v. NATURAL RESOURCES DEFENSE COUNCIL, INC., 467 U.S. 837, 842–43, 104 S.Ct. 2778, 2781–82, 81 L.Ed.2d 694 (1984). Even though it is arguable that a court of appeals is at least as adept as the agency at construing federal statutory language (often involving an assessment of legislative history), and even though it is questionable whether the agency's familiarity with conditions in the economic sector it regulates gives it special insights into statutory interpretation, the Supreme Court in *Chevron* nonetheless endorsed substantial appellate deference to the agency, at least when the language of the controlling federal statute is less than precisely clear.

> When a court reviews an agency's construction of the statute which it administers, it is confronted with two questions. First, always, is the question whether Congress has directly spoken to the precise question at issue. If the intent of Congress is clear, that is the end of the matter; for the court, as well as the agency, must give effect to the unambiguously expressed intent of Congress. If, however, the court determines Congress has not directly addressed the precise question at issue, the court does not simply impose its own construction on the statute, as would be necessary in the absence of an administrative interpretation. Rather, if the statute is silent or ambiguous with respect to the specific issue, the question for the court is whether the agency's answer is based on a permissible construction of the statute.

> "The power of an administrative agency to administer a congressionally created ... program necessarily requires the formulation of policy and the making of rules to fill any gap left, implicitly or explicitly, by Congress." ... If Congress has explicitly left a gap for the agency to fill, there is an express delegation of

authority to the agency to elucidate a specific provision of the statute by regulation.... Sometimes the legislative delegation to an agency on a particular question is implicit rather than explicit. In such a case, a court may not substitute its own construction of a statutory provision for a reasonable interpretation made by the administrator of an agency.

*Chevron* may complicate the role of *stare decisis* in labor cases. See White, Time for a New Approach: Why the Judiciary Should Disregard the "Law of the Circuit" When Confronting Non–Acquiescence by the NLRB, 69 N.C.L.Rev. 639 (1991). Apart from that, the principles which guide appellate courts in reviewing questions of law and fact are plainly of a very general nature leaving much to the discretion of the judges involved. In exercising this discretion, courts will presumably be influenced to some degree by such other factors as the respect they hold for the capabilities and impartiality of the Board and the cogency and comprehensiveness of the arguments made by that agency in support of its conclusions. These factors are unavoidably subjective and may therefore cause considerable variation from one court to another concerning the nature of review. It is for this reason, perhaps, that there is often a significant disparity among circuit courts in their rates of affirmance of NLRB decisions. For example, among the circuit courts deciding more than a dozen Labor Board cases in the Board's 1998 fiscal year, 84.6 percent of its decisions reaching the Seventh Circuit court were affirmed in full there, while the District of Columbia Circuit court affirmed in full only 52 percent of the Board decisions it reviewed. (Examining the five-year period 1993–1997, significant disparities can also be observed, varying from a 52.3 percent full affirmance rate in the District of Columbia Circuit (of 68 cases) to 100 percent in the Eleventh Circuit (of 21 cases).) Statistics such as these suggest that the principles governing the scope and nature of judicial review should be taken as providing only the most general indication of the nature of review to be accorded by any given court in a particular case. See Brudney, A Famous Victory: Collective Bargaining Protections and the Statutory Aging Process, 74 N.C.L.Rev. 939 (1996).

Since the order made by the federal court of appeals in a proceeding under the Act is an equity decree, it may be enforced by proceedings for contempt. The Board has been held to have exclusive authority to prosecute civil contempts with the result that neither unions nor employers may petition the court for this purpose.

———

### REPRESENTATION CASES

In addition to the work that the Regional Office does in unfair labor practice cases, it also plays the most important day-to-day role in processing representation cases. Election petitions are filed in the Regional Office, and the bulk of these seek the holding of a representation election in order to determine the desires of the employees concerning the selection of a union for collective bargaining. (Other elections may be held to decertify a union already representing employees in bargaining.) Such representation petitions may be filed either by an employer upon whom a demand for recognition and bargaining has been made by a union, or by a union seeking to represent employees (and demonstrating that it has what is known as a "showing of interest" from thirty percent of the employees within the bargaining unit, generally evidenced by signed cards authorizing that union to be bargaining agent). A copy of the standard NLRB form of petition for representation election is set forth in the Statutory Supplement.

The regional staff investigates the petition, in order to determine such questions as whether the employer and the union are covered by the National Labor Relations Act and whether the group of employees within which the election is sought constitute "an appropriate bargaining unit." In most cases, these issues—along with questions as to the eligibility of particular voters, as well as the date of the election—are resolved through the consent of the parties, either on their own initiative or after an investigation and conference in the Regional Office. The parties can, in a consent-election agreement, vest in the Regional Director final authority to rule on any disputes that may arise concerning the conduct of the election and to issue his or her determination as to the result. Much more frequently used is an alternative form of agreement ("stipulation for consent"), which provides that the Board itself will have the final word with respect to these questions. (See the Stipulation for Consent form in the Statutory Supplement.)

If the above matters are contested, they will be made the subject of a hearing conducted by a hearing officer from the Regional Office. The transcript of the hearing is then transferred to the Regional Director, who makes decisions on such issues as the Board's jurisdiction, the appropriate bargaining unit, and the eligibility of voters. A formal Direction of Election is issued by the Regional Director—typically, about six weeks after the election petition was filed—and an election is ordered within a designated bargaining unit within a specified period, usually 25 to 30 days from the date of the election order.

The details of the election are arranged in the Regional Office. In general the procedure resembles any local election. A voting list is prepared, polling places and voting hours are designated, and notices are published in advance. Elections are almost invariably held at the employer's premises during working hours, to maximize voter turnout. The Board's agents supervise the election but employee observers may also be appointed and may challenge any ballot. The ballots are secret and in the first instance offer each employee an opportunity to vote for any union claiming the right to represent them or for "no union". At the close of the voting, the ballots are counted. Certain votes may be challenged, and if the challenges cannot be resolved informally the ballots will be set aside. If there are enough challenged votes to affect the outcome of the election, a ruling on the disputed ballots will be made by the Regional Director who will also pass upon any other objections which the parties may have taken to the election.

The decisions of the Regional Director—both before the election (e.g., appropriate bargaining unit) and after (e.g., objections)—are subject to review by the National Labor Relations Board, but the Board grants review only on the following grounds:

(1) Where a substantial question of law or policy is involved.

(2) Where the Regional Director's decision on a substantial factual issue is clearly and prejudicially erroneous.

(3) Where the conduct of the hearing in an election case or any ruling made in connection with the proceeding has resulted in prejudicial error.

(4) Where there are compelling reasons for reconsidering an important Board rule or policy.

Although most of the problems that arise in determining the eligibility of employees to vote are matters of detail (for example, whether a particular individual is a "supervisor" or is in some other bargaining unit), significant problems of eligibility may arise if an election takes place during the course of a strike, when the employer has kept the business going by hiring replacements for striking employees. In such cases, a determination must be made whether the strikers and/or their replacements are entitled to vote. If the strike has been precipitated or prolonged by the employer's unfair labor practices, it is well settled that the striking employees have the right to return to their jobs and to displace any replacements hired by the company subsequent to the commission of the unfair labor practice. Hence, in these situations, the strikers—but not the replacements—are eligible to vote. If, however, the strike is an "economic strike" rather than an "unfair labor practice strike," the employer does have the right to hire permanent replacements. Until recently, it had been long settled that replacements for economic strikers were indeed presumed to be permanent, so that they were allowed to vote. Pacific Tile & Porcelain Co., 137 NLRB 1358 (1962). But this rule was inconsistent with the Board's approach in unfair labor practice cases, in which economic-strike replacements are presumed to be temporary, with the burden resting upon the employer to show a mutual understanding between the employer and the replacements that they are permanent. In O.E. Butterfield, Inc., 319 NLRB 1004 (1995), the Board overruled *Pacific Tile* and held that the presumption of temporary status—and so of non-voting status—applied in representation cases as well as unfair labor practice cases.

The NLRB has formulated a number of principles to determine the eligibility of economic strikers and their permanent replacements. Unless strikers are found by the Board to be on strike over employer unfair labor practices, they will be presumed to be economic strikers and eligible to vote for up to one year. They will lose this status if, before the election, they obtain permanent employment elsewhere (a mere showing that they have accepted other work will not be sufficient, for this is often done merely to tide an employee through the strike); or if they are discharged or denied reinstatement for serious misconduct; or if they have their job eliminated for economic reasons. Similarly, replacements for economic strikers are presumed to be permanent employees and eligible to vote. They will lose this status if the party challenging that vote can prove that the replacement was not permanent. All issues as to voting eligibility of strikers and replacements are to be deferred until after the election for disposition by way of challenges. See Note, Equal Access in NLRB Elections: Determining the Voting Eligibility of Economic Strikers, 58 Geo.Wash.L.Rev. 549 (1990).

It is a well-settled rule that a labor organization will be certified as bargaining representative even though less than a majority of all of the employees in the unit cast ballots in its favor. It is enough that the union be designated by a majority of the valid ballots, even though only a small proportion of the eligible voters participate. In an election in which only one union is competing, a tie vote will thus result in the union's loss. What disposition should be made when two or more unions are involved, and there is no majority on the first ballot for any single union although the unions collectively have received a majority of the votes cast? Congress answered this question in 1947 when it enacted Section 9(c)(3), which provides that a run-off election shall be conducted in which the two highest choices on the first ballot (which may include "no union") shall appear on the run-off ballot.

Requests to set aside an election may be based on allegations of interference with the employees' freedom of choice. As will be discussed shortly (see pp. 147–48, infra), an election may be set aside and a new one ordered even though no unfair labor practices have occurred. Thus, although in the majority of cases in which elections have been set aside it has been because of coercive conduct by the employer or the union, there have been instances in which a new election has been ordered by virtue of misconduct either by employees (not authorized to act on behalf of the employer or the union) or by other persons in the community, P.D. Gwaltney, Jr., 74 NLRB 371 (1947)(community hysteria and terrorism), or even by agents of the NLRB itself, Athbro Precision Engineering Corp., 166 NLRB 966 (1967)(Board agent seen drinking beer with union representative during balloting day; "tends to destroy confidence in the Board's election process").

Decisions made by the NLRB in representation proceedings can normally not be challenged directly by judicial review. The Labor Act in its terms provides for judicial review, in the courts of appeals, only of final orders in unfair labor practice cases. If a person is aggrieved by a Board decision in a representation case, the appropriate manner for precipitating court action is for that person to commit an unfair labor practice, challenge within the unfair labor practice proceeding the decision made by the Board in the representation case (which the Board will normally reaffirm in the unfair labor practice case), and only then seek review in a court of appeals. Most commonly, this is done by an employer—seeking review, for example, of a Board appropriate-unit decision—by refusing to bargain with a union recently certified after a Board election. The purpose of this seemingly circuitous review mechanism, contemplated under Section 9(d) of the Act, is to prevent obstructive recourse to the courts at various stages of the representation proceeding and long delay in the determination of employee preferences on the matter of unionization. In certain extraordinary cases, however—to be explored further in the materials below (pp. 304–10)—a federal district court may have jurisdiction directly to enjoin the Board or a Regional Director from implementing a decision in the context of a representation proceeding.

In the fiscal year ending September 30, 1998, the NLRB conducted almost 3,800 representation elections—with over 250,000 eligible employee voters—in which a single union sought to be elected. The union won about 49 percent of those elections, an increase of 4 percent from 1994. (Elections involving competition between two or more unions were rather rare, numbering only 100.)

# PART TWO

# THE ESTABLISHMENT OF THE COLLECTIVE BARGAINING RELATIONSHIP

## I. PROTECTION OF THE RIGHT OF SELF-ORGANIZATION

### A. INTERFERENCE, RESTRAINT AND COERCION[a]

Section 8(a)(1) of the Act declares it to be an unfair labor practice to interfere with, restrain or coerce employees in the exercise of the right to self-organization, to form, join or assist labor organizations, to bargain collectively and to engage in concerted activities for the purpose of collective bargaining or other mutual aid or protection. Accordingly, it has been held that violations of sub-sections (2), (3), (4) and (5) are also violations of Section 8(a)(1). Nevertheless, it is convenient for purposes of analysis to distinguish the acts of interference, coercion and restraint which merely violate Section 8(a)(1) from those acts which also constitute violations of the other sections. Interference with employees' exercise of the right of self-organization may also be treated separately from the rather different problems raised by allegations of interference with other concerted activities.

In giving effect to Section 8(a)(1) to protect the right to join a union, the National Labor Relations Board has emphasized the need to preserve the employees' "free choice." The precise meaning of this term, however, is

---

**a.** See generally Bok, The Regulation of Campaign Tactics in Representation Elections Under the National Labor Relations Act, 78 Harv.L.Rev. 38 (1964); J. Getman, S. Goldberg & J. Herman, Union Representation Elections: Law and Reality (1976); R. Williams, NLRB Regulation of Election Conduct (2d ed. 1985).

not immediately clear. To be sure, one can readily deduce that employees must not be physically intimidated in deciding whether to support a union, for no choice made under these circumstances can be considered "free" in the ordinary sense of the word. But once one passes beyond a few obvious cases of this kind, further analysis is required to determine from what influences the employee is to be "free."

We may assume that having allowed the employees to decide for themselves whether or not to be represented by a union, Congress contemplated that they should be permitted to make a reasoned choice concerning this issue. Such a choice implies that employees should have access to relevant information, that they should use this data to estimate the probable consequences if the union is selected or rejected, and that they should appraise these consequences in the light of their own preferences and desires to determine whether a vote for the union promises to promote or impair their self-interest. This definition provides a key to the meaning of a free and unrestrained choice under the statute. Ideally, at least, the employees should be free from restrictions which unduly obstruct the flow of relevant information, from misrepresentations and threats which tend to distort their assessment of the consequences of unionization, and from acts of retribution which would penalize them for having exercised the choice guaranteed them under the Act.

The preceding discussion provides a framework for the materials that follow. The first group of cases takes up various rules imposed by the employer which limit employees or union organizers in communicating with one another on company property. The next series of cases has to do with the limitations which the Board may impose on the content of speeches and literature disseminated by the union and employer prior to an election under Section 9 of the NLRA. In particular, attention will be devoted to such problems as threats made by employers to discourage voting for the union; inflammatory speeches relating to racial policies of the union or the employer; and misrepresentations of material facts made by either side. The final group of cases will take up various forms of interference, other than speech, that may impair the employees' freedom of choice.

---

## 1.   RESTRICTIONS ON SOLICITATION AND DISTRIBUTION[b]

---

**b.** See Estlund, Labor, Property, and Sovereignty After Lechmere, 46 Stan. L. Rev. 305 (1994); Gorman, Union Access to Private Property: A Critical Assessment of Lechmere, Inc. v. NLRB, 9 Hofstra Lab. L.J. 1 (1991); Gould, The Question of Union Activity on Company Property, 18 Vand.L.Rev. 73 (1964); Hyde, Economic Labor Law v. Political Labor Relations: Dilemmas for Liberal Legalism, 60 Texas L.Rev. 1 (1981); Note, Property Rights and Job Security: Workplace Solicitation by Nonemployee Union Organizers, 94 Yale L.J. 374 (1984); Note, Still as Strangers: Nonemployee Union Organizers on Private Commercial Property, 62 Texas L.Rev. 111 (1983).

# Republic Aviation Corp. v. NLRB

324 U.S. 793, 65 S.Ct. 982, 89 L.Ed. 1372 (1945).

■ MR. JUSTICE REED delivered the opinion of the Court.

In the Republic Aviation Corporation case, the employer, a large and rapidly growing military aircraft manufacturer, adopted, well before any union activity at the plant, a general rule against soliciting which read as follows:

> "Soliciting of any type cannot be permitted in the factory or offices."

The Republic plant was located in a built-up section of Suffolk County, New York. An employee persisted after being warned of the rule in soliciting union membership in the plant by passing out application cards to employees on his own time during lunch periods. The employee was discharged for infraction of the rule and, as the National Labor Relations Board found, without discrimination on the part of the employer toward union activity.

Three other employees were discharged for wearing UAW–CIO union steward buttons in the plant after being requested to remove the insignia. The union was at that time active in seeking to organize the plant. The reason which the employer gave for the request was that as the union was not then the duly designated representative of the employees, the wearing of the steward buttons in the plant indicated an acknowledgment by the management of the authority of the stewards to represent the employees in dealing with the management and might impinge upon the employer's policy of strict neutrality in union matters and might interfere with the existing grievance system of the corporation.

The Board was of the view that wearing union steward buttons by employees did not carry any implication of recognition of that union by the employer where, as here, there was no competing labor organization in the plant. The discharges of the stewards, however, were found not to be motivated by opposition to the particular union, or we deduce, to unionism.

The Board determined that the promulgation and enforcement of the "no solicitation" rule violated Section 8(1) of the National Labor Relations Act as it interfered with, restrained and coerced employees in their rights under Section 7 and discriminated against the discharged employee under Section 8(3). It determined also that the discharge of the stewards violated Sections 8(1) and 8(3). As a consequence of its conclusions as to the solicitation and the wearing of the insignia, the Board entered the usual cease and desist order and directed the reinstatement of the discharged employee with back pay and also the rescission of "the rule against solicitation in so far as it prohibits union activity and solicitation on company property during the employees' own time." 51 N.L.R.B. 1186, 1189. The Circuit Court of Appeals for the Second Circuit affirmed, 142 F.2d 193, and we granted certiorari, 323 U.S. 688, 65 S.Ct. 55, because of conflict with the decisions of other circuits. * * * [We also granted certiorari in Le Tourneau Co. v. National Labor Relations Board, which raises the same issue.]

These cases bring here for review the action of the National Labor Relations Board in working out an adjustment between the undisputed right of self-organization assured to employees under the Wagner Act and the equally undisputed right of employers to maintain discipline in their establishments. Like so many others, these rights are not unlimited in the sense that they can be exercised without regard to any duty which the existence of rights in others may place upon employer or employee. Opportunity to organize and proper discipline are both essential elements in a balanced society.

The Wagner Act did not undertake the impossible task of specifying in precise and unmistakable language each incident which would constitute an unfair labor practice. On the contrary that Act left to the Board the work of applying the Act's general prohibitory language in the light of the infinite combinations of events which might be charged as violative of its terms. * * *

The gravamen of the objection of both Republic and Le Tourneau to the Board's orders is that they rest on a policy formulated without due administrative procedure. To be more specific it is that the Board cannot substitute its knowledge of industrial relations for substantive evidence. The contention is that there must be evidence before the Board to show that the rules and orders of the employers interfered with and discouraged union organization in the circumstances and situation of each company. Neither in the Republic nor the Le Tourneau cases can it properly be said that there was evidence or a finding that the plant's physical location made solicitation away from company property ineffective to reach prospective union members. Neither of these is like a mining or lumber camp where the employees pass their rest as well as their work time on the employer's premises, so that union organization must proceed upon the employer's premises or be seriously handicapped. * * *

[The Court then summarized the provisions of section 10(a), (b) and (c) which prescribe the procedure to be followed in unfair labor practice cases.]

Plainly this statutory plan for an adversary proceeding requires that the Board's orders on complaints of unfair labor practices be based upon evidence which is placed before the Board by witnesses who are subject to cross-examination by opposing parties. Such procedure strengthens assurance of fairness by requiring findings on known evidence. Ohio Bell Tel. Co. v. Public Utilities Comm. of Ohio, 301 U.S. 292, 302, 57 S.Ct. 724, 729, 81 L.Ed. 1093; United States v. Abilene & S. Ry. Co., 265 U.S. 274, 288, 44 S.Ct. 565, 569, 68 L.Ed. 1016. Such a requirement does not go beyond the necessity for the production of evidential facts, however, and compel evidence as to the results which may flow from such facts. Market St. R. Co. v. Railroad Comm. of California et al., 324 U.S. 548, 65 S.Ct. 770. An administrative agency with power after hearings to determine on the evidence in adversary proceedings whether violations of statutory commands have occurred may infer within the limits of the inquiry from the proven facts such conclusions as reasonably may be based upon the facts proven. One of the purposes which lead to the creation of such boards is to have decisions based upon evidential facts under the particular statute made by experienced officials with an adequate appreciation of the complexities of the subject which is entrusted to their administration. National Labor Relations Board v. Virginia Power Co., 314 U.S. 469, 479, 62 S.Ct. 344, 349, 86 L.Ed. 348; National Labor Relations Board v. Hearst Publications, 322 U.S. 111, 130, 64 S.Ct. 851, 860, 88 L.Ed. 1170.

In the Republic Aviation Corporation case the evidence showed that the petitioner was in early 1943 a non-urban manufacturing establishment for military production which employed thousands. It was growing rapidly. Trains and automobiles gathered daily many employees for the plant from an area on Long Island, certainly larger than walking distance. The rule against solicitation was introduced in evidence and the circumstances of its violation by the dismissed employee after warning was detailed.

As to the employees who were discharged for wearing the buttons of a union steward, the evidence showed in addition the discussion in regard to their right to wear the insignia when the union had not been recognized by the petitioner as the representative of the employees. * * *

No evidence was offered that any unusual conditions existed in labor relations, the plant location or otherwise to support any contention that conditions at this plant differed from those occurring normally at any other large establishment. * * *

These were the facts upon which the Board reached its conclusions as to unfair labor practices. The Intermediate Report in the Republic Aviation case, 51 NLRB at 1195, set out the reason why the rule against solicitation was considered inimical to the right of organization.[6] This was approved by the Board. Id., 1186. The Board's reasons for concluding that the petitioner's insistence that its employees refrain from wearing steward buttons appear at page 1187 of the report.[7] In the Le Tourneau Company case the discussion of the reasons underlying the findings was much more extended. * * * Furthermore, in both opinions of the Board full citation of authori-

**6.** 51 N.L.R.B. 1195: "Thus under the conditions obtaining in January 1943, the respondent's employees, working long hours in a plant engaged entirely in war production and expanding with extreme rapidity, were entirely deprived of their normal right to 'full freedom of association' in the plant on their own time, the very time and place uniquely appropriate and almost solely available to them therefor. The respondent's rule is therefore in clear derogation of the rights of its employees guaranteed by the Act."

**7.** We quote an illustrative portion. 51 N.L.R.B. 1187, 1188: "We do not believe that the wearing of a steward button is a representation that the employer either approves or recognizes the union in question as the representative of the employees, especially when, as here, there is no competing labor organization in the plant. Furthermore, there is no evidence in the record herein that the respondent's employees so understood the steward buttons or that the appearance of union stewards in the plant affected the normal operation of the respondent's grievance procedure. On the other hand, the right of employees to wear union insignia at work has long been recognized as a reasonable and legitimate form of union activity, and the respondent's curtailment of that right is clearly violative of the Act."

ties was given including Matter of Peyton Packing Company, 49 NLRB 828, 50 NLRB 355, hereinafter referred to.

The Board has fairly, we think, explicated in these cases the theory which moved it to its conclusions in these cases. The excerpts from its opinions just quoted show this. The reasons why it has decided as it has are sufficiently set forth. We cannot agree, as Republic urges, that in these present cases reviewing courts are left to "sheer acceptance" of the Board's conclusions or that its formulation of policy is "cryptic." See Eastern–Central Motor Carriers Ass'n v. United States, 321 U.S. 194, 209, 64 S.Ct. 499, 506, 88 L.Ed. 668.

Not only has the Board in these cases sufficiently expressed the theory upon which it concludes that rules against solicitation or prohibitions against the wearing of insignia must fall as interferences with union organization but in so far as rules against solicitation are concerned, it had theretofore succinctly expressed the requirements of proof which it considered appropriate to outweigh or overcome the presumption as to rules against solicitation. In the Peyton Packing Company case, 49 NLRB 828, at 843, hereinbefore referred to, the presumption adopted by the Board is set forth.[10]

Although this definite ruling appeared in the Board's decisions, no motion was made in the court by Republic or Le Tourneau after the Board's decisions for leave to introduce additional evidence to show unusual circumstances involving their plants or for other purposes. * * * We perceive no error in the Board's adoption of this presumption. The Board had previously considered similar rules in industrial establishments and the definitive form which the Peyton Packing Company decision gave to the presumption was the product of the Board's appraisal of normal conditions about industrial establishments. Like a statutory presumption or one established by regulation, the validity, perhaps in a varying degree, depends upon the rationality between what is proved and what is inferred.

In the Republic Aviation case, petitioner urges that irrespective of the validity of the rule against solicitation, its application in this instance did not violate Section 8(3), because the rule was not discriminatorily applied against union solicitation but was impartially enforced against all solicitors. It seems clear, however, that if a rule against solicitation is invalid as to

---

**10.** 49 N.L.R.B. at 843, 844: "The Act, of course, does not prevent an employer from making and enforcing reasonable rules covering the conduct of employees on company time. Working time is for work. It is therefore within the province of an employer to promulgate and enforce a rule prohibiting union solicitation during working hours. Such a rule must be presumed to be valid in the absence of evidence that it was adopted for a discriminatory purpose. It is no less true that time outside working hours, whether before or after work, or during luncheon or rest periods, is an employee's time to use as he wishes without unreasonable restraint, although the employee is on company property. It is therefore not within the province of an employer to promulgate and enforce a rule prohibiting union solicitation by an employee outside of working hours, although on company property. Such a rule must be presumed to be an unreasonable impediment to self-organization and therefore discriminatory in the absence of evidence that special circumstances make the rule necessary in order to maintain production or discipline."

union solicitation on the employer's premises during the employee's own time, a discharge because of violation of that rule discriminates within the meaning of Section 8(3) in that it discourages membership in a labor organization.

■ Mr. Justice Roberts dissents in each case.

---

Beth Israel Hosp. v. NLRB, 437 U.S. 483, 98 S.Ct. 2463, 57 L.Ed.2d 370 (1978). The Hospital had an explicit rule barring solicitation or distribution of literature by employees "in patient-care and all other work areas, and areas open to the public such as lobbies, cafeteria and coffee shop, corridors, elevators, gift shop, etc." When the Hospital's general director observed an employee distributing the union newsletter in the Hospital cafeteria to other employees, he ordered her to stop; the employee was also given a written notice threatening dismissal for further violation of the Hospital rule. (The newsletter, among other things, disparaged the Hospital's ability to provide adequate patient care, primarily because of understaffing.) The Board's finding of violations of Sections 8(a)(1)(for the no-solicitation rule) and 8(a)(3)(for the written notice), and its order requiring rescission of the rule as regards the cafeteria and coffee shop, were affirmed by the Supreme Court.

Although the Board generally requires employers to permit employee solicitation on union matters during nonworking time, it has tolerated hospital bans on such solicitation in working areas devoted strictly to patient care; but such solicitation must be permitted in other areas such as lounges and cafeterias open to visitors and even to patients "absent a showing that disruption to patient care would necessarily result if solicitation and distribution were permitted in those areas." Since Beth Israel Hospital produced no such evidence, the Board properly concluded that the possibility of disruption to patient care resulting from solicitation in the cafeteria (where a three-day survey revealed that 77% of the patrons were employees, 9% were visitors and 1.56% were patients) was remote.

The Court rejected the Hospital's argument that, because the potential disruption to patient care flowing from solicitation in a patient-access cafeteria was a medical judgment, the Board was inexpert on this matter and should not on judicial review be accorded the deference contemplated by *Republic Aviation.* "It is true that the Board is not expert in the delivery of health-care services, but neither is it in pharmacology, chemical manufacturing, lumbering, shipping or any of a host of varied and specialized business enterprises over which the Act confers its jurisdiction. But the Board is expert in federal national labor relations policy, and it is in the Board, not [the Hospital], that the 1974 amendments vested responsibility for developing that policy in the health-care industry. * * * The judicial role is narrow: The rule which the Board adopts is judicially reviewable for consistency with the Act, and for rationality," both of which requirements are satisfied in this case. The Court found that the Board's conclusion regarding lack of impact on patient care was supported by the record. Patient use of the cafeteria was voluntary, random and infrequent (and could be avoided by unusually sensitive patients), and the Hospital had itself permitted charitable solicitations there in the past. Even if the importance of the Hospital's mission was such as to warrant considering whether the union could effectively communicate with employees elsewhere on the premises, there was no such place at Beth Israel (the employee lockerrooms, where the Hospital did permit solicitation, being scattered, sex-segregated and available to only one-quarter of the workforce).

Two separate concurring opinions (speaking for a total of four Justices) emphasized that the cafeteria at Beth Israel was substantially comparable to an all-employee cafeteria, and that a different result might be warranted in other cases where the cafeteria was used principally by patients and their visitors.

NLRB v. MAGNAVOX CO., 415 U.S. 322, 94 S.Ct. 1099, 39 L.Ed.2d 358 (1974). The IUE had been bargaining representative of the Magnavox employees for nearly twenty years, during which time the labor contracts had authorized the company to issue rules for the "maintenance of orderly conditions on plant property" and had provided for bulletin boards for union notices. During that period, the company had prohibited employees from distributing literature on company property, including parking lots and other nonworking areas, even during nonworking time. When the company rejected a union proposal to change this no-solicitation rule, charges were filed with the NLRB under Section 8(a)(1). The Board held that, since the workplace was the natural and typically the only place where all employees could gather to discuss work matters including union-ization, the employer's ban was unlawful, with respect to both solicitation against the incumbent union and solicitation in support of that union. Although the court of appeals disagreed and found the contract provision to constitute a waiver of on-premises distribution, the Supreme Court reversed and gave its approval to the Board's decision.

The Court, in an opinion by Justice Douglas, endorsed *Republic Aviation* and the *Peyton Packing* presumptions, and noted that the employer had made no contention that its rule was necessary to promote production or discipline. It also held that the union did not have the power to waive the normally applicable solicitation and distribution rights of the employees. It is true that unions may waive the Section 7 right to strike, as a quid pro quo for grievance and arbitration provisions or other employer concessions; but such a waiver assumes that the union has been freely selected and is fairly representing employees in the bargaining unit. However, when the Section 7 right at stake is the exercise of a choice regarding unionization or a change in representative, "it is difficult to assume that the incumbent union has no self-interest of its own to serve by perpetuating itself as the bargaining representative." The union's access to a bulletin board is not a fair substitute, since it may be adequate to preserve the status quo but not to give the union's adversaries adequate access to co-workers. Although these arguments most clearly dictate the non-waiver of the distribution rights of employees opposed to the union, "employees supporting the union have as secure § 7 rights as those in opposition."

In a separate opinion, Justice Stewart (for himself and two other Justices) agreed that "the clear policy of federal labor law forbids either the union or the employer to freeze out another union or to entrench the incumbent union by infringing the § 7 rights of dissident employees." He saw no reason, however, why the incumbent union could not waive the literature-distribution rights of its own supporters, since the union was free to communicate through the bulletin board, union meetings and the force of its status as bargaining representative; for the Board now to restore these rights of union supporters would upset the "delicate balance achieved in the give and take of negotiations" and would give the union an undeserved windfall.

On the disputed issue, do you agree with Justice Douglas or with Justice Stewart? (See generally Note, The Contractual Waiver of Individual Rights Under the NLRA, 31 N.Y.L.S.L.Rev. 793 (1986).)

---

## PROBLEMS FOR DISCUSSION

**1.** The employers in the *Republic Aviation* case accused the National Labor Relations Board of resting its findings of "interference, restraint and coercion" not upon record evidence but rather upon unsupported inference based on its general knowledge of industrial affairs. How does the Supreme Court respond to this accusation? Is the response convincing? How large a role did the Board's "expertise" play in its decision?

**2.** You are counsel to a company at which a union has just begun an organizing campaign. You have been informed that there has been a significant increase in solicitation and discussion among employees on the shop floor during the working day, and that this has had an adverse impact on production. Although the company has never previously explicitly announced any rule against such solicitation, it asks you whether it may lawfully do so now. It also wishes to know precisely what language to use in such a no-solicitation rule, and in particular whether there is any material difference between declaring the rule applicable "during working hours" or "during working time." What advice would you give? See NLRB v. Roney Plaza Apts., 597 F.2d 1046 (5th Cir.1979); Our Way, Inc. v. International Brotherhood of Firemen, 268 NLRB 394 (1983).

**3.** The Company maintains three bulletin boards for its communication of matters of interest to employees. It has forbidden community groups to post notices, but it does allow employees to post items for sale or swap. The Union, which has commenced an organizing drive, has asked for permission to post notices of union meetings and been denied. Has the Company violated the NLRA? See Guardian Industries Corp. v. NLRB, 49 F.3d 317 (7th Cir.1995); Restaurant Corp. of America v. NLRB, 827 F.2d 799 (D.C.Cir.1987).

**4.** The food service workers have been attempting to organize the staff of Ristorante Beccho. The restaurant has a "no solicitation" rule that provides:

> No employee may solicit another employee to join or support any endeavor
> or project during his own work time anywhere on Company property; nor

may any employee solicit another employee during that employee's work time. This rule does not apply to non-work (free) time, such as breaks and meal breaks.

Nino Rotta, a waiter, told two other waiters of an upcoming union meeting while the three of them were picking up their orders from the chef. Rotta was given a written warning for violation of the policy. Rotta has pointed out that he had been allowed to sell hand-painted Christmas ornaments to both co-workers and customers while on duty and that another employee had sold raffle and theater tickets to co-workers while on duty. Has the company violated section 8(a)(1)? *See* 6 West Limited Corp. v. NLRB, 237 F.3d 767 (7th Cir.2001).

**5.** In June, some of the employees at the Restful Nursing Home began wearing blue union buttons about the size of a half-dollar with white print reading "Local 1199" in the middle and "Hospital Division AFL–CIO" around the border. The employer ordered the employees to remove the buttons, calling their attention to a longstanding rule barring the wearing of any buttons or insignia on uniforms. When one of the employees refused to remove the union button, he was given a formal disciplinary warning for insubordination and violation of working rules. Does the warning violate Section 8(a)(1)? See Malta Constr. Co. v. International Union of Operating Engineers, 276 NLRB 1494 (1985). *Compare* Meijer, Inc. v. NLRB, 130 F.3d 1209 (6th Cir.1997), *with* Eastern Omni Constructors, Inc. v. NLRB, 170 F.3d 418 (4th Cir.1999).

**6.** If an employer prohibits employee distribution of all printed materials in "work areas," but has its supervisors distribute anti-union literature in those areas, e.g. at the time clock, has the employer violated § 8(a)(1)? See Stoddard–Quirk Mfg. Co., 138 NLRB 615 (1962) and Beverly Enterprises–Hawaii, Inc., 326 NLRB 335 (1998).

**7.** Topdyne, Inc., maintains a companywide computer network that connects its employees, many of whom work at home, to the headquarters and to one another. Company rules prohibit any personal or nonbusiness use of the system; the Company retains the right to monitor employee use. On a Saturday night last month, Brenda Starr, a designer who works at home, used the Company's e-mail system to leave a message on the home computer of a co-worker suggesting they talk about seeking help from a union. She was discharged for violation of the computer-use policy. Has the Company committed an unfair labor practice? See Note, (Net)workers' Rights: The NLRA and Employee Electronic Communications, 105 Yale L.J. 1639 (1996).

Assume instead that Ms. Starr is part of a work group that transacts all of its business by e-mail with one another and that Starr's message was part of that group discourse at work. Would the Company have committed an unfair labor practice? *Compare* General Counsel Advice Memorandum in Pratt & Whitney, 1998 WL 1112978 (Feb. 23, 1998), *with* General Counsel Advice Memorandum in IRIS–USA, 2000 WL 257107 (Feb. 2, 2000).

-------

# Lechmere, Inc. v. National Labor Relations Board
502 U.S. 527, 112 S.Ct. 841, 117 L.Ed.2d 79 (1992).

■ JUSTICE THOMAS delivered the opinion of the Court.

This case requires us to clarify the relationship between the rights of employees under § 7 of the National Labor Relations Act, 49 Stat. 452, as amended, 29 U.S.C. § 157, and the property rights of their employers.

I

This case stems from the efforts of Local 919 of the United Food and Commercial Workers Union, AFL–CIO, to organize employees at a retail store in Newington, Connecticut, owned and operated by petitioner Lechmere, Inc. The store is located in the Lechmere Shopping Plaza, which occupies a roughly rectangular tract measuring approximately 880 feet from north to south and 740 feet from east to west. Lechmere's store is situated at the Plaza's south end, with the main parking lot to its north. A strip of 13 smaller "satellite stores" not owned by Lechmere runs along the west side of the Plaza, facing the parking lot. To the Plaza's east (where the main entrance is located) runs the Berlin Turnpike, a four-lane divided highway. The parking lot, however, does not abut the Turnpike; they are separated by a 46–foot–wide grassy strip, broken only by the Plaza's entrance. The parking lot is owned jointly by Lechmere and the developer of the satellite stores. The grassy strip is public property (except for a four-foot-wide band adjoining the parking lot, which belongs to Lechmere).

The union began its campaign to organize the store's 200 employees, none of whom was represented by a union, in June 1987. After a full-page advertisement in a local newspaper drew little response, nonemployee union organizers entered Lechmere's parking lot and began placing handbills on the windshields of cars parked in a corner of the lot used mostly by employees. Lechmere's manager immediately confronted the organizers, informed them that Lechmere prohibited solicitation or handbill distribution of any kind on its property,[1] and asked them to leave. They did so, and Lechmere personnel removed the handbills. The union organizers renewed this handbilling effort in the parking lot on several subsequent occasions; each time they were asked to leave and the handbills were removed. The organizers then relocated to the public grassy strip, from where they attempted to pass out handbills to cars entering the lot during hours (before opening and after closing) when the drivers were assumed to be primarily store employees. For one month, the union organizers returned daily to the grassy strip to picket Lechmere; after that, they picketed intermittently for another six months. They also recorded the license plate numbers of cars parked in the employee parking area; with the cooperation of the Connecticut Department of Motor Vehicles, they thus secured the names and addresses of some 41 nonsupervisory employees (roughly 20% of the store's total). The union sent four mailings to these employees; it also

---

1. Lechmere had established this policy several years prior to the union's organizing efforts. The store's official policy statement provided, in relevant part:

"Non-associates [i.e., nonemployees] are prohibited from soliciting and distributing literature at all times anywhere on Company property, including parking lots. Non-associates have no right of access to the non-working areas and only to the public and selling areas of the store in connection with its public use." Brief for Petitioner 7.

On each door to the store Lechmere had posted a 6 in. by 8 in. sign reading: "TO THE PUBLIC. No Soliciting, Canvassing, Distribution of Literature or Trespassing by Non–Employees in or on Premises." App. 115–116. Lechmere consistently enforced this policy inside the store as well as on the parking lot (against, among others, the Salvation Army and the Girl Scouts).

made some attempts to contact them by phone or home visits. These mailings and visits resulted in one signed union authorization card.

Alleging that Lechmere had violated the National Labor Relations Act by barring the nonemployee organizers from its property, the union filed an unfair labor practice charge with respondent National Labor Relations Board (Board). [The Board held, as had the administrative law judge, that Lechmere's exclusion of union representatives from its parking lot was unlawful, and a divided court of appeals enforced the Board's order.]

## II

### A

Section 7 of the NLRA provides in relevant part that "[e]mployees shall have the right to self-organization, to form, join, or assist labor organizations." 29 U.S.C. § 157. Section 8(a)(1) of the Act, in turn, makes it an unfair labor practice for an employer "to interfere with, restrain, or coerce employees in the exercise of rights guaranteed in [§ 7]." 29 U.S.C. § 158(a)(1). By its plain terms, thus, the NLRA confers rights only on *employees*, not on unions or their nonemployee organizers. In NLRB v. Babcock & Wilcox Co., 351 U.S. 105, 76 S.Ct. 679, 100 L.Ed. 975 (1956), however, we recognized that insofar as the employees' "right of self-organization depends in some measure on [their] ability * * * to learn the advantages of self-organization from others," id., at 113, 76 S.Ct., at 684, § 7 of the NLRA may, in certain limited circumstances, restrict an employer's right to exclude nonemployee union organizers from his property. It is the nature of those circumstances that we explore today.

*Babcock* arose out of union attempts to organize employees at a factory located on an isolated 100–acre tract. The company had a policy against solicitation and distribution of literature on its property, which it enforced against all groups. About 40% of the company's employees lived in a town of some 21,000 persons near the factory; the remainder were scattered over a 30–mile radius. Almost all employees drove to work in private cars and parked in a company lot that adjoined the fenced-in plant area. The parking lot could be reached only by a 100–yard–long driveway connecting it to a public highway. This driveway was mostly on company-owned land, except where it crossed a 31–foot–wide public right-of-way adjoining the highway. Union organizers attempted to distribute literature from this right-of-way. The union also secured the names and addresses of some 100 employees (20% of the total), and sent them three mailings. Still other employees were contacted by telephone or home visit.

The union successfully challenged the company's refusal to allow nonemployee organizers onto its property before the Board. While acknowledging that there were alternative, nontrespassory means whereby the union could communicate with employees, the Board held that contact at the workplace was preferable. *The Babcock & Wilcox Co.,* 109 N.L.R.B. 485, 493–494 (1954). "[T]he right to distribute is not absolute, but must be accommodated to the circumstances. Where it is impossible or unreasonably difficult for a union to distribute organizational literature to employees entirely off of the employer's premises, distribution on a nonworking area, such as the parking lot and the walkways between the parking lot and the gate, may be warranted." Id., at 493. Concluding that traffic on the highway made it unsafe for the union organizers to distribute leaflets from the right-of-way, and that contacts through the mails, on the streets, at employees' homes, and over the telephone would be ineffective, the Board ordered the company to allow the organizers to distribute literature on its parking lot and exterior walkways. Id., at 486–487.

The Court of Appeals for the Fifth Circuit refused to enforce the Board's order, NLRB v. Babcock & Wilcox Co., 222 F.2d 316 (1955), and this Court affirmed. While recognizing that "the Board has the responsibility of 'applying the Act's general prohibitory language in the light of the infinite combinations of events which might be charged as violative of its terms,'" 351 U.S., at 111–112, 76 S.Ct., at 683–684 (quoting NLRB v. Stowe Spinning Co., 336 U.S. 226, 231, 69 S.Ct. 541, 543, 93 L.Ed. 638 (1949)), we explained that the Board had erred by failing to make the critical distinction between the organizing activities of employees (to whom § 7 guarantees the right of self-organization) and nonemployees (to whom § 7 applies only derivatively). Thus, while "[n]o restriction may be placed on the employees' right to discuss self-organization among themselves, unless the employer can demonstrate that a restriction is necessary to maintain production or discipline," 351 U.S., at 113, 76 S.Ct., at 684 (emphasis added)(citing Republic Aviation Corp. v. NLRB, 324 U.S. 793, 803, 65 S.Ct. 982, 987, 89 L.Ed. 1372 (1945)), "no such obligation is owed nonemployee organizers," 351 U.S., at 113, 76 S.Ct., at 684. As a rule, then, an employer cannot be compelled to allow distribution of union literature by nonemployee organizers on his property. As with many other rules, however, we recognized an exception. Where "the location of a plant and the living quarters of the employees place the employees beyond the reach of reasonable union efforts to communicate with them," ibid., employers' property rights may be "required to yield to the extent needed to permit communication of information on the right to organize," id., at 112, 76 S.Ct., at 684.

Although we have not had occasion to apply Babcock's analysis in the ensuing decades, we have described it in cases arising in related contexts. Two such cases, Central Hardware Co. v. NLRB, 407 U.S. 539, 92 S.Ct. 2238, 33 L.Ed.2d 122 (1972), and Hudgens v. NLRB, 424 U.S. 507, 96 S.Ct. 1029, 47 L.Ed.2d 196 (1976), involved activity by union supporters on employer-owned property. The principal issue in both cases was whether, based upon Food Employees v. Logan Valley Plaza, Inc., 391 U.S. 308, 88 S.Ct. 1601, 20 L.Ed.2d 603 (1968), the First Amendment protected such activities. In both cases we rejected the First Amendment claims, and in Hudgens we made it clear that Logan Valley was overruled. Having decided the cases on constitutional grounds, we remanded them to the Board for consideration of the union supporters' § 7 claims under Babcock. In both cases, we quoted approvingly Babcock's admonition that accommodation between employees' § 7 rights and employers' property rights "must be obtained with as little destruction of the one as is consistent with the maintenance of the other," 351 U.S., at 112, 76 S.Ct., at 684. See *Central Hardware,* supra, at 544, 92 S.Ct., at 2241; *Hudgens,* supra, at 521, 522, 96 S.Ct., at 1037, 1038. There is no hint in *Hudgens* and *Central Hardware,* however, that our invocation of *Babcock*'s language of "accommodation" was intended to repudiate or modify *Babcock*'s holding that an employer need not accommodate nonemployee organizers unless the employees are otherwise inaccessible. Indeed, in *Central Hardware* we expressly noted that nonemployee organizers cannot claim even a limited right of access to a nonconsenting employer's property until "[a]fter the requisite need for access to the employer's property has been shown." 407 U.S., at 545, 92 S.Ct., at 2241.

[The Court also referred to its decision in Sears, Roebuck & Co. v. San Diego County Dist. Council of Carpenters, 436 U.S. 180 (1978), in which it had held that state trespass law as applied to nonemployee union organizers is not preempted by federal law under section 7 of the NLRA, in large part because the trespasses of such organizers are "far more likely to be unprotected than protected"; the burden on the union to show the lack of reasonable nontrespassory means of communicating its message to the employees "is a heavy one," rarely sustained in the NLRB decisions.]

### B

*Jean Country* [291 N.L.R.B. 11 (1988)] represents the Board's latest attempt to implement the rights guaranteed by § 7. It sets forth a three-factor balancing test:

"[I]n all access cases our essential concern will be [1] the degree of impairment of the Section 7 right if access should be denied, as it balances against [2] the degree of impairment of the private property right if access should be granted. We view the consideration of [3] the availability of reasonably effective alternative means as especially significant in this balancing process." 291 N.L.R.B., at 14.

The Board conceded that this analysis was unlikely to foster certainty and predictability in this corner of the law, but declared that "as with other legal questions involving multiple factors, the 'nature of the problem, as revealed by unfolding variant situations, inevitably involves an evolutionary process for its rational response, not a quick, definitive formula as a comprehensive answer.'" Ibid. (quoting Electrical Workers v. NLRB, 366 U.S. 667, 674, 81 S.Ct. 1285, 1289, 6 L.Ed.2d 592 (1961)).

Citing its role "as the agency with responsibility for implementing national labor policy," the Board maintains in this case that *Jean Country* is a reasonable interpretation of the NLRA entitled to judicial deference. Brief for Respondent 18, and n. 8; Tr. of Oral Arg. 22. It is certainly true, and we have long recognized, that the Board has the "special function of applying the general provisions of the Act to the complexities of industrial life." * * * Like other administrative agencies, the NLRB is entitled to judicial deference when it interprets an ambiguous provision of a statute that it administers. See, *e.g.,* NLRB v. Food & Commercial Workers, 484

U.S. 112, 123, 108 S.Ct. 413, 420, 98 L.Ed.2d 429 (1987); cf. Chevron U.S.A. Inc. v. Natural Resources Defense Council, Inc., 467 U.S. 837, 842–843, 104 S.Ct. 2778, 2781–2782, 81 L.Ed.2d 694 (1984).

Before we reach any issue of deference to the Board, however, we must first determine whether *Jean Country*—at least as applied to nonemployee organizational trespassing—is consistent with our past interpretation of § 7. "Once we have determined a statute's clear meaning, we adhere to that determination under the doctrine of *stare decisis,* and we judge an agency's later interpretation of the statute against our prior determination of the statute's meaning." Maislin Industries, U.S., Inc. v. Primary Steel, Inc., 497 U.S. 116, 131, 110 S.Ct. 2759, 2768, 111 L.Ed.2d 94 (1990).

In *Babcock,* as explained above, we held that the Act drew a distinction "of substance," 351 U.S., at 113, 76 S.Ct., at 684, between the union activities of employees and nonemployees. In cases involving *employee* activities, we noted with approval, the Board "balanced the conflicting interests of employees to receive information on self-organization on the company's property from fellow employees during nonworking time, with the employer's right to control the use of his property." Id., at 109–110, 76 S.Ct., at 682–683. In cases involving *nonemployee* activities (like those at issue in *Babcock* itself), however, the Board was not permitted to engage in that same balancing (and we reversed the Board for having done so). By reversing the Board's interpretation of the statute for failing to distinguish between the organizing activities of employees and nonemployees, we were saying, in *Chevron* terms, that § 7 speaks to the issue of nonemployee access to an employer's property. *Babcock*'s teaching is straightforward: § 7 simply does not protect nonemployee union organizers *except* in the rare case where "the inaccessibility of employees makes ineffective the reasonable attempts by nonemployees to communicate with them through the usual channels," 351 U.S., at 112, 76 S.Ct., at 684. Our reference to "reasonable" attempts was nothing more than a commonsense recognition that unions need not engage in extraordinary feats to communicate with inaccessible employees—*not* an endorsement of the view (which we expressly rejected) that the Act protects "reasonable" trespasses. Where reasonable alternative means of access exist, § 7's guarantees do not authorize trespasses by nonemployee organizers, *even* (as we noted in *Babcock,* id., at 112, 76 S.Ct., at 684) "under * * * reasonable regulations" established by the Board.

*Jean Country,* which applies broadly to "all access cases," 291 N.L.R.B., at 14, misapprehends this critical point. Its principal inspiration derives not from *Babcock,* but from the following sentence in *Hudgens:* "[T]he locus of th[e] accommodation [between § 7 rights and private property rights] may fall at differing points along the spectrum depending on the nature and strength of the respective § 7 rights and private property rights asserted in any given context." 424 U.S., at 522, 96 S.Ct., at 1037. From this sentence the Board concluded that it was appropriate to approach every case by balancing § 7 rights against property rights, with alternative means of access thrown in as nothing more than an "especially significant" consideration. As explained above, however, *Hudgens* did not purport to modify *Babcock,* much less to alter it fundamentally in the way *Jean Country* suggests. To say that our cases require accommodation between employees' and employers' rights is a true but incomplete statement, for the cases also go far in establishing the *locus* of that accommodation where nonemployee organizing is at issue. So long as nonemployee union organizers have reasonable access to employees outside an employer's property, the requisite accommodation has taken place. It is *only* where such access is infeasible that it becomes necessary and proper to take the accommodation inquiry to a second level, balancing the employees' and employers' rights as described in the *Hudgens* dictum. See *Sears,* 436 U.S., at 205, 98 S.Ct., at 1761; *Central Hardware,* 407 U.S., at 545, 92 S.Ct., at 2241. At least as applied to nonemployees, *Jean Country* impermissibly conflates these two stages of the inquiry—thereby significantly eroding *Babcock*'s general rule that "an employer may validly post his property against nonemployee distribution of union literature," 351 U.S., at 112, 76 S.Ct., at 684. We reaffirm that general rule today, and reject the Board's attempt to recast it as a multifactor balancing test.

### C

The threshold inquiry in this case, then, is whether the facts here justify application of *Babcock*'s inaccessibility exception. The ALJ below observed that "the facts herein convince me that reasonable alternative means [of communicating with Lechmere's employees] *were* available to the Union," 295 N.L.R.B., at 99 (emphasis added). Reviewing the ALJ's decision under *Jean Country,* however, the Board reached a different conclusion on this point, asserting that "there was no reasonable, effective alternative means available for the Union to communicate its message to [Lechmere's] employees." Id., at 93.

We cannot accept the Board's conclusion, because it "rest[s] on erroneous legal foundations," *Babcock,* 351 U.S., at 112, 76 S.Ct., at 684; see also NLRB v. Brown, 380 U.S. 278, 290–292, 85 S.Ct. 980, 987–988, 13 L.Ed.2d 839 (1965). As we have explained, the exception to *Babcock*'s rule is a narrow one. It does not apply wherever nontrespassory access to employees may be cumbersome or less-than-ideally effective, but only where "the *location of a plant and the living quarters of the employees* place the employees *beyond the reach* of reasonable union efforts to communicate with them," 351 U.S., at 113, 76 S.Ct., at 684 (emphasis added). Classic examples include logging camps, see NLRB v. Lake Superior Lumber Corp., 167 F.2d 147 (C.A.6 1948); mining camps, see *Alaska Barite Co.,* 197 N.L.R.B. 1023 (1972), enforced mem., 83 LRRM 2992 (CA9), cert. denied, 414 U.S. 1025, 94 S.Ct. 450, 38 L.Ed.2d 316 (1973); and mountain resort hotels, see NLRB v. S & H Grossinger's Inc., 372 F.2d 26 (C.A.2 1967). *Babcock*'s exception was crafted precisely to protect the § 7 rights of those employees who, by virtue of their employment, are isolated from the ordinary flow of information that characterizes our society. The union's burden of establishing such isolation is, as we have explained, "a heavy one," *Sears,* supra, 436 U.S., at 205, 98 S.Ct., at 1761, and one not satisfied by mere conjecture or the expression of doubts concerning the effectiveness of nontrespassory means of communication.

The Board's conclusion in this case that the union had no reasonable means short of trespass to make Lechmere's employees aware of its organizational efforts is based on a misunderstanding of the limited scope of this exception. Because the employees do not reside on Lechmere's property, they are presumptively not "beyond the reach," *Babcock,* 351 U.S., at 113, 76 S.Ct., at 684, of the union's message. Although the employees live in a large metropolitan area (Greater Hartford), that fact does not in itself render them "inaccessible" in the sense contemplated by *Babcock.* See *Monogram Models, Inc.,* 192 N.L.R.B. 705, 706 (1971). Their accessibility is suggested by the union's success in contacting a substantial percentage of them directly, via mailings, phone calls, and home visits. Such direct contact, of course, is not a necessary element of "reasonably effective" communication; signs or advertising also may suffice. In this case, the union tried advertising in local newspapers; the Board said that this was not reasonably effective because it was expensive and might not reach the employees. 295 N.L.R.B., at 93. Whatever the merits of that conclusion, other alternative means of communication were readily available. Thus, signs (displayed, for example, from the public grassy strip adjoining Lechmere's parking lot) would have informed the employees about the union's organizational efforts. (Indeed, union organizers picketed the shopping center's main entrance for months as employees came and went every day.) *Access* to employees, not *success* in winning them over, is the critical issue—although success, or lack thereof, may be relevant in determining whether reasonable access exists. Because the union in this case failed to establish the existence of any "unique obstacles," *Sears,* 436 U.S., at 205–206, n. 41, 98 S.Ct., at 1761–1762, n. 41, that frustrated access to Lechmere's employees, the Board erred in concluding that Lechmere committed an unfair labor practice by barring the nonemployee organizers from its property. * * *

The judgment of the First Circuit is therefore reversed, and enforcement of the Board's order denied.

■ Justice White, with whom Justice Blackmun joins, dissenting. * * *

In the case before us, the Court holds that *Babcock* itself stated the correct accommodation between property and organizational rights; it interprets that case as construing §§ 7 and 8(a)(1) of the National Labor Relations Act to contain a general rule forbidding third-party access, subject only to a limited exception where the union demonstrates that the location of the employer's place of business and the living quarters of the employees place the employees beyond the reach of reasonable efforts to communicate with them. * * *

For several reasons, the Court errs in this case. First, that *Babcock* stated that inaccessibility would be a reason to grant access does not indicate that there would be no other circumstance that would warrant entry to the employer's parking lot and would satisfy the Court's admonition that accommodation must be made with as little destruction of property rights as is consistent with the right of employees to learn the advantages of self-organization from others. Of course the union must show that its "reasonable efforts", without access, will not permit proper communication with employees. But I cannot believe that the Court in *Babcock* intended to confine the reach of such general considerations to the single circumstance that the Court now seizes upon. If the Court in *Babcock* indicated that nonemployee access to a logging camp would be required, it did not say that only in such situations could nonemployee access be permitted. Nor did *Babcock* require the Board to ignore the substantial difference between the entirely private parking lot of a secluded manufacturing plant and a shopping center lot which is open to the public without substantial limitation. Nor indeed did *Babcock* indicate that the Board could not consider the fact that employees' residences are scattered throughout a major metropolitan area; *Babcock* itself relied on the fact that the employees in that case lived in a compact area which made them easily accessible.

Moreover, the Court in *Babcock* recognized that actual communication with nonemployee organizers, not mere notice that an organizing campaign exists, is necessary to vindicate § 7 rights. 351 U.S., at 113, 76 S.Ct., at 684. If employees are entitled to learn from others the advantages of self-organization, ibid., it is singularly unpersuasive to suggest that the union has sufficient access for this purpose by being able to hold up signs from a public grassy strip adjacent to the highway leading to the parking lot.

Second, the Court's reading of *Babcock* is not the reading of that case reflected in later opinions of the Court. We have consistently declined to define the principle of *Babcock* as a general rule subject to narrow exceptions, and have instead repeatedly reaffirmed that the standard is a neutral and flexible rule of accommodation. In Central Hardware Co. v. NLRB, 407 U.S. 539, 544, 92 S.Ct. 2238, 2241, 33 L.Ed.2d 122 (1972), we explicitly stated that the "guiding principle" for adjusting conflicts between § 7 rights and property rights enunciated in *Babcock* is that contained in its neutral "accommodation" language. Hudgens v. NLRB, 424 U.S. 507, 96 S.Ct. 1029, 47 L.Ed.2d 196 (1976), gave this Court the occasion to provide direct guidance to the NLRB on this issue. In that case, we emphasized *Babcock*'s necessity-to-accommodate admonition, pointed out the differences between *Babcock* and *Hudgens,* and left the balance to be struck by the Board. "The locus of that accommodation * * * may fall at differing points along the spectrum depending on the nature and strength of the respective § 7 rights and private property rights asserted in any given context. In each generic situation, the primary responsibility for making this accommodation must rest with the Board in the first instance." 424 U.S., at 522, 96 S.Ct., at 1038. * * *

The majority today asserts that "[i]t is *only* where [reasonable alternative] access is infeasible that it becomes necessary and proper to take the accommodation inquiry to a second level, balancing the employees' and employers' rights." Ante, at 848. Our cases, however, are more consistent with the *Jean Country* view that reasonable alternatives are an important factor in finding the least destructive accommodation between § 7 and property rights. The majority's assertion to this effect notwithstanding, our cases do not require a prior showing regarding reasonable alternatives as a precondition to any inquiry balancing the two rights. The majority can hardly fault the Board for a decision which "conflates * * * two stages of the inquiry," ante, at 848, when no two-stage inquiry has been set forth by this Court.

Third, and more fundamentally, *Babcock* is at odds with modern concepts of deference to an administrative agency charged with administering a statute. See Chevron U.S.A. Inc. v. Natural Resources Defense Council, Inc., 467 U.S. 837, 104 S.Ct. 2778, 81 L.Ed.2d 694 (1984). When reviewing an agency's construction of a statute, we ask first whether Congress has spoken to the precise question at issue. *Chevron,* supra, at 842, 104 S.Ct., at 2781. If it has not, we do not simply impose our own construction on the statute; rather, we determine if the agency's view is based on a permissible construction of the statute. 467 U.S., at 843, 104 S.Ct., at 2781. *Babcock* did not ask if Congress had specifically spoken to the issue of access by third parties and did not purport to explain how the NLRA specifically dealt with what the access rule should be where third parties are concerned. * * * That being the case, the *Babcock* Court should have recognized that the Board's construction of the statute was a permissible one and deferred to its judgment. Instead, the Court simply announced that as far as access is concerned, third parties must be treated less favorably than employees. * * *

Had a case like *Babcock* been first presented for decision under the law governing in 1991, I am quite sure that we would have deferred to the Board, or at least attempted to find sounder ground for not doing so. Furthermore, had the Board ruled that third parties must be treated differently than employees and held them to the standard that the Court now says *Babcock* mandated, it is clear enough that we also would have accepted that construction of the statute. But it is also clear, at least to me, that if the Board later reworked that rule in the manner of *Jean Country,* we would also accept the Board's change of mind. See NLRB v. Curtin Matheson Scientific, Inc., 494 U.S., at 787, 110 S.Ct., at 1549; NLRB v. J. Weingarten, Inc., 420 U.S. 251, 265–266, 95 S.Ct. 959, 967–968, 43 L.Ed.2d 171 (1975).

As it is, the Court's decision fails to recognize that *Babcock* is at odds with the current law of deference to administrative agencies and compounds that error by adopting the substantive approach *Babcock* applied lock, stock, and barrel. And unnecessarily so, for, as indicated above, *Babcock* certainly does not require the reading the Court gives it today, and in any event later cases have put a gloss on *Babcock* that the Court should recognize.

Finally, the majority commits a concluding error in its application of the outdated standard of *Babcock* to review the Board's conclusion that there were no reasonable alternative means available to the union. * * * "The judicial role is narrow: * * * the Board's application of the rule, if supported by substantial evidence on the record as a whole, must be enforced." Ibid. The Board's conclusion as to reasonable alternatives in this case was supported by evidence in the record. Even if the majority cannot defer to that application, because of the depth of its objections to the rule applied by the NLRB, it should remand to the Board for a decision under the rule it arrives at today, rather than sitting in the place Congress has assigned to the Board.

The more basic legal error of the majority today, like that of the Court of Appeals in *Chevron,* is to adopt a static judicial construction of the statute when Congress has not commanded that construction. Cf. *Chevron,* supra, at 842, 104 S.Ct., at 2781. By leaving open the question of how § 7 and private property rights were to be accommodated under the NLRA, Congress delegated authority over that issue to the Board, and a court should not substitute its own judgment for a reasonable construction by the Board. * * *

It is evident, therefore, that, in my view, the Court should defer to the Board's decision in *Jean Country* and its application of *Jean Country* in this case. With all due respect, I dissent.

[The dissenting opinion of Justice Stevens is omitted.]

---

After the Supreme Court's decision in *Lechmere,* the court of appeals remanded to the NLRB to consider, in light of the Court's decision, the question whether the Lechmere Company had violated section 8(a)(1) by directing the non-employee union organizers to leave the grassy *public* area adjacent to the privately owned mall parking lot. The Board reaffirmed its previous ruling that Lechmere's action had indeed violated the Act: "The Supreme Court's vindication of the [employer's] private-property rights, if anything, elevates the gravity of [the employer's] attempt to bar union access to public property." 308 N.L.R.B. 1074 (1992).

---

## PROBLEMS FOR DISCUSSION

**1.** Section 2(3) of the NLRA defines a statutory "employee" as "any employee, and shall not be limited to the employees of a particular employer," in terms borrowed from the Norris–LaGuardia Act. Would it not suggest that Congress rejected the distinction between the expressive rights of persons who are employees of the particular (respondent) employer and those who are not? Cf. Marshall Field & Co. v. NLRB, 200 F.2d 375 (7th Cir.1952). (In defending this provision, Philip Levy, one of the draftsmen, proposed a further amendment that would have made clear that "union organizers" were covered within § 2(3). Memorandum of April 17, 1935 to Calvert Magruder. His proposal was not brought forward, apparently because it was thought not to be necessary.) *Babcock & Wilcox* and *Lechmere* decline to discuss § 2(3). Is it not essential to do so, however, in applying § 7?

**2.** Do you agree with the Supreme Court's application of the *Chevron* doctrine to the decision of the NLRB in the *Lechmere* case? When the Court concluded that the Board had improperly interpreted unambiguous language in the statute, did the Court act properly in deciding on its own (as the Court had earlier done in *Babcock*) whether there was sufficient proof of inadequate access by the union to the Lechmere workers?

**3.** After *Lechmere,* can the Board no longer interpret the "alternative access" test so as to allow union access to the property of an employer not in the category of the remote logging camp, mining camp or seagoing vessel? Does the NLRA compel such a narrow reading of the employees' section 7 rights? Is not the Board in a particularly good position to know whether a union can communicate its message through reasonable means away from company property, even when employees do not live on the company's premises?

**4.** How, after *Lechmere,* should the following cases be decided?

(a) A hospital has ejected a union organizer from a cafeteria that was open to members of the public. The organizer, who was initially allowed to sit in the cafeteria for hours at a time, chatting with employees, was ordered to leave only after hospital representatives learned that he was doing union business. See Oakwood Hospital v. NLRB, 983 F.2d 698 (6th Cir.1993).

(b) The union organizers can show that Lechmere, on the average of once or twice each month, allows the sale of Girl Scout cookies and charity raffles, and appeals by organizations like the Salvation Army, on its adjacent parking lot, after requests for permission to do so. *Compare* Sandusky Mall Co. v. NLRB, 242 F.3d 682 (6th Cir.2001), *with* Lucile Salter Packard Children's Hospital v. NLRB, 97 F.3d 583 (D.C.Cir.1996).

(c) A general contractor, building a privately situated condominium development, has terminated its unionized carpentry subcontractor and hired a non-union contractor to do the work. The union has commenced handbilling in front of the model unit, open to the public but on the private property, to protest the below-union wages and benefits paid by the developer. The developer has ordered them off the premises. Has it violated § 8(a)(1)? See Leslie Homes, Inc., 316 NLRB 123 (1995), review denied sub nom. Metropolitan Dist. Council of Phila. Bhd. of Carpenters v. NLRB, 68 F.3d 71 (3d Cir.1995); Oakland Mall, Ltd., 316 NLRB 1160 (1995).

(d) The employer has leased two stores. One lease includes the sidewalk adjacent to the store; one does not. The store's policy is to exclude all solicitation within 50 feet of its entrances. May it exclude union solicitors from the sidewalks that abut the store entrances? *Compare* O'Neil's Markets v. UFCW, Local 88, 95 F.3d 733 (8th Cir.1996), *with* Nicks, 326 NLRB 997 (1998). *See also* United Food and Commercial Workers v. NLRB, 222 F.3d 1030 (D.C.Cir.2000).

**5.** Given the property-based advantages to the union of having organizing done by persons classified as "employees," unions have since the *Lechmere* decision intensified their organizing efforts by having union-staff organizers apply for jobs with targeted companies. If hired, those persons do their assigned work for the company but also engage in organizing activities in their nonworking time on company property, as purportedly allowed under the *Republic Aviation* case; if their company wages are lower than the wages previously paid them by the union, the union makes up the difference. (This strategy has come to be known as "salting," and is used principally in the construction industry.) Some employers have argued that these "salts" are not to be considered as "employees" under the NLRA, because their loyalty is not to the employer but to the union, and they are obliged to carry out union orders to organize and even to quit their employment when their objectives are achieved. If not "employees," then it is not unlawful for the company intentionally to refuse to hire them or to discharge them once hired. The NLRB has treated these "salts" as "employees," and the courts of appeals are divided on the issue. How should the Supreme Court rule? See NLRB v. Town & Country Elec. Co., 516 U.S. 85, 116 S.Ct. 450, 133 L.Ed.2d 371 (1995).

May an employer refuse to hire a "salt" because of a blanket rule prohibiting any "moonlighting" by its employees? See Architectural Glass & Metal Co. v. NLRB, 107 F.3d 426 (6th Cir.1997). May it refuse to hire an applicant who writes "union organizer" on the application form contrary to the company's direction that no information be supplied on the form other than that which is expressly requested? See Tic–The Indus. Co. Southeast v. NLRB, 126 F.3d 334 (D.C.Cir.1997).

6.  Shamrock Refining Company operates a large chemical plant on three shifts. The Oil, Chemical and Atomic Workers (OCAW) seek to organize the employees there. One of the employees on the day shift (8 a.m. to 4 p.m.), Tom Williams, is one of the leaders in the unionization movement; he is bright, likeable, aggressive and articulate. His work exposes him to volatile chemicals, he works under arduous conditions, and his lunchtime is brief; he and his fellow workers must shower at the end of the work day, and most promptly head thereafter for their cars in the company parking lot, a short trip home, and a drink or two before dinner. The shift that works from 4 p.m. until midnight takes a dinner break from 7:30 until 8 p.m. Williams, anxious to gain entry to the company cafeteria at that time to engage in conversation and solicitation with the employees on the later shift, has driven his car into the company parking lot on three occasions and headed through the main entrance to the plant, but has each time been stopped by a guard. Williams has been told that, while he is free to solicit on his own mealtime on his own shift, he is not free to come onto company property when he is not at work there, and that continued attempts to do so may lead to discipline for insubordination.

You are counsel to the OCAW local which is seeking to organize Shamrock Refining. Inform the union whether there is any way that Williams can gain access on company property to the employees on the night shift. The union would prefer to have Williams meet with those employees inside the plant (in nonworking areas), but it also wants to know whether he can station himself on the company's parking lot and other privately owned approaches to the plant. See Automotive Plastic Technologies, Inc., 313 NLRB 462 (1993); Diamond Shamrock Co. v. NLRB, 443 F.2d 52 (3d Cir.1971).

---

## THE UNION'S QUEST FOR EQUAL ACCESS

By virtue of *Republic Aviation* and *Lechmere*, the union's access to employees on company property is quite limited. Essentially, employees may communicate information about the union only during their nonworking time, and paid union organizers have access only in the rarest circumstances (typically, when the employees live on company property). Not surprisingly, unions have found these strictures to be most confining, and they have attempted through the years to formulate legal strategies that would help establish channels of communication roughly comparable to those of the employer. In particular, unions have sought the right to address employees on the shop floor during the workday, as employers often do. Moreover, they have sought the right to be furnished with lists of employee names and addresses, in order to facilitate mailings, telephone calls and home visits.

An employer with a valid no-solicitation or no-distribution rule might on occasion wish to "violate" that rule, for example, by assembling its employees on company property during working hours for purposes of delivering an antiunion address. The rule may be concededly valid and the address concededly noncoercive and within the shelter of Section 8(c) of the Labor Act ("The expressing of any views, argument, or opinion, or the dissemination thereof, whether in written, printed, graphic, or visual form, shall not constitute or be evidence of an unfair labor practice under any of the provisions of this Act, if such expression contains no threat of reprisal or force or promise of benefit."). Yet the union may believe that it is put at a substantial disadvantage in the absence of a similar opportunity to address a "captive audience" for the purpose of communicating the union message. In Bonwit Teller, Inc. v. NLRB, 96 N.L.R.B. 608 (1951), remanded on other grounds, 197 F.2d 640 (2d Cir.1952), cert. denied, 345 U.S. 905, 73 S.Ct. 644, 97 L.Ed. 1342 (1953), the Board held the employer's denial of such a request to constitute an unfair labor practice. The employer was held to have interfered with the section 7 right of the employees "to hear both sides of the story under circumstances which reasonably approximate equality." Section 8(c) was thought no obstacle to such a conclusion since it was not the employer's speech that was treated as unlawful but rather its conduct in denying the union equal time. Two years later, in Livingston Shirt Co., 107 NLRB 400 (1953), the Board, with newly appointed members, departed from the *Bonwit Teller* rationale and concluded that Section 8(c) forbade the conditioning of the exercise of the employer's right to speak noncoercively upon its willingness to afford the union comparable time and setting. It stated that as a general matter there was a rough equality between the employer's use of its property to address its employees and the union's use of its property (the union hall) and of other solicitation methods (e.g., by employees on non-working time and by home visits). The Board held:

> We rule therefore that, in the absence of either an unlawful broad
> no-solicitation rule (prohibiting union access to company premises
> on other than working time) or a privileged no-solicitation rule
> (broad, but not unlawful because of the character of the business),
> an employer does not commit an unfair labor practice if he makes
> a preelection speech on company time and premises to his employ-
> ees and denies the union's request for an opportunity to reply.

In effect, the Board declared that it would require the employer to grant a union's request for equal time in, most typically, the retail and department-store trade (where employers could validly adopt a "broad but not unlaw-ful" rule barring solicitation even during nonworking time on the selling floor); but that there would be no such requirement for manufacturing and wholesale enterprises where valid no-solicitation rules obtained.

The United States Supreme Court was presented, in NLRB v. UNITED STEELWORKERS (NUTONE AND AVONDALE), 357 U.S. 357, 78 S.Ct. 1268, 2 L.Ed.2d 1383 (1958), with employer denials of union requests to depart from concededly valid no-solicitation rules subsequent to the employers' antiunion solicitation. The Court held that an employer's denial of such a request does not in itself constitute an unfair labor practice, stating that:

> [T]he Taft Hartley Act does not command that labor organizations
> as a matter of abstract law, under all circumstances, be protected
> in the use of every possible means of reaching the minds of
> individual workers, nor that they are entitled to use a medium of
> communication simply because the employer is using it.

The Court went on to state in dictum, however, that the result could be different if the no-solicitation rules "truly diminished the ability of the labor organizations involved to carry their message to the employees."

> If, by virtue of the location of the plant and of the facilities and
> resources available to the union, the opportunities for effectively
> reaching the employees with a pro-union message, in spite of a no-
> solicitation rule, are at least as great as the employer's ability to
> promote the legally authorized expression of his anti-union views,
> there is no basis for invalidating these "otherwise valid" rules.

The denial of "equal time" will thus ordinarily be presumed lawful (even, as in the *Avondale* case before the Court, when the employer's solicitation is in itself coercive and unlawful), and the burden will be upon the General Counsel to demonstrate that the union is seriously incapacitated from communicating with the employees by other means. (It is unclear, however, whether this burden is discharged simply upon a showing of "inequality" between the employer's "captive audience" speech and the union's alternative means, or by the more rigorous showing that objectively considered the union has no practicable means of communicating effectively with the employees.) The lack of alternative means will thus become an issue in these "equal time" cases, just as they are in cases of employer denials to nonemployees of access to its property for purposes of solicitation, but as they are not in cases of solicitation restrictions upon employees. The Court ignored the argument, although implicitly rejecting it, that apart from "alternative means" the employer's conduct should be held unlawful because, by "discriminatorily" applying the no-solicitation rule to the union but not to itself, the employer was conclusively demonstrating that the rule was designed to hamper the union rather than to effectuate any legitimate employer interest in plant safety, efficiency or discipline. See James Hotel Co., 142 NLRB 761 (1963)(employer's disregarding its own no-solicitation rule does not invalidate it, citing *Nutone*).

In a related area, NLRB remedies, the Board has, in cases involving aggravated employer unfair labor practices under Sections 8(a)(1) and (3), ordered that the charging union be given access by the employer to company property, either to solicit employees during nonworking time or to deliver a "captive audience" speech. United States Service Indus., Inc., 319 NLRB 231 (1995); Teamsters Local 115 v. NLRB (Haddon House Food

Prods., Inc.), 640 F.2d 392 (D.C.Cir.1981); United Steelworkers v. NLRB (Florida Steel Corp.), 646 F.2d 616 (D.C.Cir.1981)(an exhaustive treatment of the Board's "union access" remedies). See Note, "NLRB Orders Granting Unions Access to Company Property," 68 Cornell L.Rev. 895 (1983).

The Board has announced a firm rule outlawing "captive audience" speeches on company time within the 24–hour period prior to an election. PEERLESS PLYWOOD CO., 107 NLRB 427 (1953). The rule proscribes such addresses whether by company or union, in view of their "unwholesome and unsettling effect" so shortly before the election, and their tendency to "interfere with that sober and thoughtful choice which a free election is designed to reflect." To redress both the "mass psychology" created by the address and the unfair advantage it gives to the last speaker, violation of the *Peerless Plywood* rule will result in the setting aside of an election victory by the speaker and the ordering of a new election. By its terms, the decision does not impede noncoercive employer (or union) speeches before the 24–hour period, the dissemination of other forms of propaganda even during the 24–hour period, or the delivery during that period of campaign speeches on or off company property if employee attendance is voluntary and on the employee's own time.

––––––––

## PROBLEM  FOR  DISCUSSION

If a union places a sound truck alongside the plant on the day of the election to broadcast union songs which can be heard inside the plant throughout the workday, should the election, which the union won, be set aside? See Bro–Tech Corp. v. NLRB, 105 F.3d 890 (3d Cir.1997).

––––––––

## Excelsior Underwear Inc.

156 NLRB 1236 (1966).

[During an election campaign in which the employer had written to the employees, the union asked for a list of employee names and addresses in order to make a response, but the employer refused. The union lost the election, 206 to 35, and objected to the election for a number of reasons, one of which was the employer's refusal to furnish the list. When the regional director overruled these objections, the NLRB agreed to review the decision upon the union's petition, and consolidated another case raising similar issues. The Board determined that the cases presented questions of substantial importance and ordered oral argument, which is rarely done, and invited certain groups to file briefs amicus curiae and to participate in oral argument, among them the Chamber of Commerce of the United States, the AFL–CIO, the International Union of Electrical Workers, the United Auto Workers, the National Association of Manufacturers, the Retail Clerks Union, the Textile Workers Union, and the Teamsters.]

■ We are persuaded, for the reasons set out below, that higher standards of disclosure than we have heretofore imposed are necessary, and that prompt disclosure of the information here sought by the Petitioners should be required in all representation elections. Accordingly, we now establish a requirement that will be applied in all election cases. That is, within 7 days after the Regional Director has approved a consent-election agreement entered into by the parties pursuant to Section 102.62 of the National Labor Relations Board Rules and Regulations or after the Regional Director or the Board has directed an election pursuant to Section 102.62 of the National Labor Relations Board Rules and Regulations or after the Regional Director or the Board has directed an election pursuant to Sections 102.67, 102.69, or Section 102.85 thereof, the employer must file with the Regional Director an election eligibility list, containing the names and addresses of all the eligible voters. The Regional Director, in turn, shall make this information available to all parties in the case. Failure to comply with this requirement shall be grounds for setting aside the election whenever proper objections are filed.[5]

The considerations that impel us to adopt the foregoing rule are these: "The control of the election proceeding, and the determination of the steps necessary to conduct that election fairly [are] matters which Congress entrusted to the Board alone." In discharging that trust, we regard it as the Board's function to conduct elections in which employees have the opportunity to cast their ballots for or against representation under circumstances that are free not only from interference, restraint, or coercion violative of Act, but also from other elements that prevent or impede a free and reasoned choice. Among the factors that undoubtedly tend to impede such a choice is a lack of information with respect to one of the choices available. In other words, an employee who has had an effective opportunity to hear the arguments concerning representation is in a better position to make a more fully informed and reasoned choice. Accordingly, we think that it is appropriate for us to remove the impediment to communication to which our new rule is directed.

As a practical matter, an employer, through his possession of employee names and home addresses as well as his ability to communicate with employees on plant premises, is assured of the continuing opportunity to inform the entire electorate of his views with respect to union representation. On the other hand, without a list of employee names and addresses, a labor organization, whose organizers normally have no right of access to plant premises, has no method by which it can be certain of reaching all the employees with its arguments in favor of representation, and, as a result, employees are often completely unaware of that point of view. This is not, of course, to deny the existence of various means by which a party might be

---

**5.** However, the rule we have here announced is to be applied prospectively only. It will not apply in the instant cases but only in those elections that are directed, or consented to, subsequent to 30 days from the date of this Decision. We impose this brief period of delay to insure that all parties to forthcoming representation elections are fully aware of their rights and obligations as here stated.

able to communicate with a substantial portion of the electorate even without possessing their names and addresses. It is rather to say what seems to us obvious—that the access of all employees to such communications can be insured if all parties have the names and addresses of all the voters.[10] In other words, by providing all parties with employees' names and addresses, we maximize the likelihood that all the voters will be exposed to the arguments for, as well as against, union representation. * * *

While the rule we here announce is primarily predicated upon our belief that prompt disclosure of employee names and addresses is necessary to insure an informed electorate, there is yet another basis upon which we rest our decision. As noted [previously], an employer is presently under no obligation to supply an election eligibility list until shortly before the election. * * * With little time (and no home addresses) with which to satisfy itself as to eligibility of the "unknowns", the union is forced either to challenge all those who appear at the polls whom it does not know or risk having ineligible employees vote. The effect of putting the union to this choice, we have found, is to increase the number of challenges, as well as the likelihood that the challenges will be determinative of the election, thus requiring investigation and resolution by the Regional Director or the Board. Prompt disclosure of employee names as well as addresses will, we are convinced, eliminate the necessity for challenges based solely on lack of knowledge as to the voter's identity. * * *

The arguments against imposing a requirement of disclosure are of little force, especially when weighed against the benefits resulting therefrom. Initially, we are able to perceive no substantial infringement of employer interests that would flow from such a requirement. A list of employee names and addresses is not like a customer list, and an employer would appear to have no significant interest in keeping the names and addresses of his employees secret (other than a desire to prevent the union from communicating with his employees—an interest we see no reason to protect). Such legitimate interest in secrecy as an employer may have is, in any event, plainly outweighed by the substantial public interest in favor of disclosure where, as here, disclosure is a key factor in insuring a fair and free election. * * *

The argument is also made (by the Employer in the *Excelsior* case) that under the decisions of the Supreme Court in *NLRB v. Babcock & Wilcox,* and *NLRB v. United Steelworkers* (Nutone, Inc.), the Board may

---

**10.** A union that does not know the names or addresses of some of the voters may seek to communicate with them by distributing literature on sidewalks or street corners adjoining the employer's premises or by utilizing the mass media of communication. The likelihood that *all* employees will be reached by these methods is, however, problematical at best. See NLRB v. United Aircraft Corp., et al., 324 F.2d 128, 130 (C.A.2), cert. denied 376 U.S. 951. Personal solicitation on plant premises by employee supporters of the union, while vastly more satisfactory than the above methods, suffers from the limited periods of nonworking time available for solicitation (generally and legally forbidden during working time, Peyton Packing Company, Inc., 49 N.L.R.B. 828, 843) and, in a large plant, the sheer physical problems involved in communicating with fellow employees.

not require employer disclosure of employee names and addresses unless, in the particular case involved, the union would otherwise be unable to reach the employees with its message. * * *

Initially, as we read *Babcock* and *Nutone,* the existence of alternative channels of communication is relevant only when the opportunity to communicate made available by the Board would interfere with a significant employer interest—such as the employer's interest in controlling the use of property owned by him. Here, as we have shown, the employer has no significant interest in the secrecy of employee names and addresses. Hence, there is no necessity for the Board to consider the existence of alternative channels of communication before requiring disclosure of that information. Moreover, even assuming that there is some legitimate employer interest in non-disclosure, we think it relevant that the subordination of that interest which we here require is limited to a situation in which employee interests in self-organization are shown to be substantial. For, whenever an election is directed (the pre-condition to disclosure) the Regional Director has found that a real question concerning representation exists; when the employer consents to an election, he has impliedly admitted this fact. The opportunity to communicate on company premises sought in *Babcock* and *Nutone* was not limited to the situation in which employee organizational interests were substantial, i.e., in which an election had been directed; we think that on this ground also the cases are distinguishable. Finally, both *Babcock* and *Nutone* dealt with the circumstances under which the Board might find an employer to have committed an unfair labor practice in violation of Section 8 of the Act, whereas, the instant cases pose the substantially distinguishable issue of the circumstances under which the Board may set aside an election. * * *

* * * We do not limit the disclosure requirement to the situation in which the employer has mailed anti-union literature to employees' homes * * * because we believe that access to employee names and addresses is fundamental to a fair and free election regardless of whether the employer has sent campaign propaganda to employees' homes. We do not limit the requirement of disclosure to furnishing employee names and addresses to a mailing service * * * because this would create difficult practical problems and because we do not believe that the union should be limited to the use of the mails in its efforts to communicate with the entire electorate.

———

## PROBLEMS FOR DISCUSSION

**1.** The employers in *Excelsior* and the supporting amici curiae argued that the involuntary disclosure of employee names and addresses violated the employees' right under Section 7 to refrain from forming and joining labor organizations and also their right to have their privacy protected against harassment and coercion by the union in employee homes. The NLRB rejected these arguments. What do you suppose were the Board's reasons? Do you agree with them?

**2.** E–Gate, Inc., installs, services, and repairs computer systems nationwide. Its employees who perform computer installation, maintenance, and service work are called customer service representatives (CSRs). In its south-central region, covering Colorado, New Mexico, Oklahoma, Kansas, Missouri, Arkansas, and parts of Nebraska and Wyoming, the Company employs 236 CSRs. E–Gate's headquarters for the region is located in Englewood, Colorado, a Denver suburb. CSRs are geographically dispersed and do not report to work at any one location. Rather, they typically work out of their homes or vehicles and spend most of their time at customers' locations. The Union wishes to organize the CSRs. Must E–Gate supply it with a list of their names and addresses? Technology Service Solutions, 332 NLRB No. 100 (2000). If they communicate to their employer and to one another via a company e-mail system, must E–Gate give the Union access to the system? *See* Malin & Perritt, The National Labor Relations Act in Cyberspace: Union Organizing in Electronic Workplaces, 49 U. KAN. L. REV. 1 (2000).

---

In NLRB v. WYMAN–GORDON, 394 U.S. 759, 89 S.Ct. 1426, 22 L.Ed.2d 709 (1969), the Supreme Court confronted the question whether the names-and-addresses requirement set forth in the *Excelsior* decision was validly adopted by the National Labor Relations Board.[c] The Wyman–Gordon Company refused to provide the names and addresses of company employees after the Board ordered a representation election, and refused as well to comply with a subpoena issued by the Board for the names and addresses. The Court of Appeals for the First Circuit held that the *Excelsior* requirement was a "rule" as defined by the Administrative Procedure Act (i.e., "an agency statement of general or particular applicability and future effect") and that the Board had therefore not promulgated it through proper procedures when it formulated the "rule" in the context of an "adjudication" concerning the validity of the Excelsior election. Proper rulemaking proceedings under the APA would have entailed, among other things, publication in the Federal Register of notice of proposed rulemaking, a public hearing, and publication of the rule as adopted. The court of appeals also held that the invalidly adopted *Excelsior* "rule" could not be validly applied to the Wyman–Gordon Company.

Through a somewhat odd configuration of Supreme Court Justices, the Court reversed, and enforced the *Excelsior* requirement, even though six Justices concluded that the requirement was indeed a "rule" that was not validly adopted by the National Labor Relations Board.

Four Justices (in an opinion by Justice Fortas) concluded that the Board in *Excelsior* had announced a "rule" of general applicability (not applicable to the parties before it) without complying with the formalities or the substance of rulemaking. Nonetheless, these four Justices concluded that the direction to the Wyman–Gordon Company *was* a valid product of

**c.** Bernstein, The NLRB's Adjudication–Rulemaking Dilemma Under the Administrative Procedure Act, 79 Yale L.J. 571 (1970); Peck, The Atrophied Rule Making Powers of the National Labor Relations Board, 70 Yale L.J. 729 (1961); Peck, A Critique of the National Labor Relations Board Performance in Policy Formation: Adjudication and Rule Making, 117 U.Pa.L.Rev. 254 (1968); Shapiro, the Choice of Rule Making or Adjudication in the Development of Administrative Policy, 78 Harv.L.Rev. 921 (1965).

an adjudication and that the Board had the statutory power to issue a court-enforceable subpoena to turn over the list of employee names and addresses.

Three other Justices (in an opinion by Justice Black) concluded that the *Excelsior* requirement was a valid component of the "adjudication" of a specific case (i.e., a proceeding to rule upon objections to an election) in which the Board followed proper adjudicatory procedures (i.e., notice, pleadings, hearing and decision). These three Justices held that a federal administrative agency normally has the power to announce new doctrines either through rulemaking or through adjudication, and that the NLRA (section 6 in particular) and the APA should be read as conferring upon the Board the authority to decide, within its informed discretion, whether to formulate such doctrines in one type of proceeding or the other.

In separate dissents, Justices Douglas and Harlan concluded that the *Excelsior* requirement was an invalidly adopted "rule" that could not validly be applied to the Wyman–Gordon Company. Justice Douglas emphasized the Board's intention to apply the requirement to employers and unions generally, in all future cases. Rulemaking proceedings were required in such instances, because they would inform all parties of future regulation and provide an opportunity to be heard, and they would assure that legal principles would be clearly articulated and not easily circumvented by the agency. Justice Harlan emphasized the fact that the Board made the names-and-addresses requirement effective only thirty days after its decision, suggesting that the Board regarded the requirement as working a dramatic change in established patterns of conduct and thus as unfair in its application to the parties before it.

The broad view of the Board's authority expressed by Justice Black was ultimately endorsed by the full Court in NLRB v. BELL AEROSPACE CO., 416 U.S. 267, 94 S.Ct. 1757, 40 L.Ed.2d 134 (1974).

The Board in that case had narrowed its longstanding jurisdictional exclusion for "managerial employees" so as to exclude only those who would have a "conflict of interest in labor relations"; it therefore asserted jurisdiction over certain of the company's buyers. The court of appeals reversed, holding that such a change in Board doctrine—designed "to fit all cases at all times"—could be adopted only through rulemaking. The Supreme Court disagreed, holding that "the Board is not precluded from announcing new principles in an adjudicative proceeding and that the choice between rulemaking and adjudication lies in the first instance within the Board's discretion. Although there may be situations where the Board's reliance on adjudication would amount to an abuse of discretion or a violation of the Act, nothing in the present case would justify such a conclusion." The Court cited in support of its general principle the Fortas and Black opinions in *Wyman–Gordon*.

The *Bell Aerospace* decision ended with these further observations about the Board's choice of adjudicative proceedings in the context of that case.

The possible reliance of industry on the Board's past decisions with respect to buyers does not require a different result. It has not been shown that the adverse consequences ensuing from such reliance are so substantial that the Board should be precluded from reconsidering the issue in an adjudicative proceeding. Furthermore, this is not a case in which some new liability is sought to be imposed on individuals for past actions which were taken in good faith reliance on Board pronouncements. Nor are fines or damages involved here. In any event, concern about such consequences is largely speculative, for the Board has not yet finally determined whether these buyers are "managerial."

It is true, of course, that rulemaking would provide the Board with a forum for soliciting the informed views of those affected in industry and labor before embarking on a new course. But surely the Board has discretion to decide that the adjudicative procedures in this case may also produce the relevant information necessary to mature and fair consideration of the issues. Those most immediately affected, the buyers and the company in the particular case, are accorded a full opportunity to be heard before the Board makes its determination.

---

## 2. ELECTION PROPAGANDA[d]

### (a) Threats of Reprisal

One of the most difficult and controversial problems in the protection of freedom of self-organization is the degree of freedom of expression to be allowed employers. Company officials often wish to make speeches or distribute leaflets, bulletins and other publications in an effort to dissuade their employees from joining labor organizations. The character of these communications varies widely, running the gamut from a dignified letter to propaganda campaigns based essentially on base appeals to racial intolerance and to prejudice against the foreign-born.

**d.** See, in addition to the references at page 115, n. a: Aaron, Employer Free Speech: The Search for a Policy, in Public Policy and Collective Bargaining 28 (Shister et al., eds., 1962); Becker, Democracy in the Workplace: Union Representation Elections and Federal Labor Law, 77 Minn. L.Rev. 495 (1993); Christensen, Free Speech, Propaganda and the National Labor Relations Act, 38 N.Y.U.L.Rev. 243 (1963); Getman, Ruminations on Union Organizing in the Private Sector, 53 U.Chi.L.Rev. 45 (1986); Goldberg, Getman & Brett, Union Representation Elections: The Authors Respond to the Critics, 79 Mich.L.Rev. 564 (1981); Roomkin & Abrams, Using Behavioral Evidence in NLRB Regulation: A Proposal, 90 Harv.L.Rev. 1441 (1977); Shapiro, Why Do Voters Vote?, 86 Yale L.J. 1532 (1977); Symposium (Miller, Raskin, Eames, Flanagan), Four Perspectives on Union Representation Elections, 28 Stan.L.Rev. 1163 (1976).

The problem is difficult because it involves the pursuit of two inconsistent goals. We value freedom of expression so highly as to look askance at any restriction and forbid restraints not justified by the clearest necessity. Most of us also value full freedom for employees in forming, joining and assisting labor organizations of their own choosing—at least this is the national labor policy. To pursue either goal to its logical extreme necessarily causes some sacrifice of the other. Any argument which discloses the speaker's strong wishes is not wholly an appeal to reason if the listener is in the speaker's power. In a southern mill town where a textile concern is the only large employer and its owners dominate the whole community, even a dispassionate expression of the company's opinion will make the ordinary employee think twice about openly supporting a labor union distasteful to the employer. Judge Learned Hand described the situation very clearly in NLRB v. Federbush Co., 121 F.2d 954, 957 (2d Cir.1941):

> Words are not pebbles in alien juxtaposition; they have only a communal existence; and not only does the meaning of each interpenetrate the other, but all in their aggregate take their purport from the setting in which they are used of which the relation between the speaker and the hearer is perhaps the most important part. What to an outsider will be no more than the vigorous presentation of a conviction, to an employee may be the manifestation of a determination which it is not safe to thwart.

It is difficult to announce in general terms any principle that will in all cases fairly adjust the competing interests of free speech and uncoerced employee choice. The task of making that adjustment in particular cases is generally performed by the National Labor Relations Board subject to a review in the courts of appeals which is nominally rather circumscribed but which in fact can be rather vigorous. Where the line is to be drawn must unquestionably depend upon the values of the decisionmaker (particularly as to such matters as governmental regulation of private conduct and governmental fostering of unionization) and upon that person's appreciation of the dynamics of personal relations in an industrial setting. The Board presumably has a greater appreciation of these dynamics than do the courts. But there is a continuing debate concerning the extent to which the Board should interpose its "values" and, in any event, concerning whether on such matters the courts are any less competent than is the Board.

Under the Wagner Act the NLRB severely limited the employer's freedom of expression. The NLRB policy was to insist upon employers' observing rigid neutrality. The Board reasoned that the choice of a bargaining representative was the workers' exclusive concern, in which the employer had no more interest than the employees would have in participating in the choice of the company's board of directors. The rationale was never accepted by the courts without some qualification, and by 1941 the Supreme Court concluded, in NLRB v. Virginia Elec. & Power Co., 314 U.S. 469, 62 S.Ct. 344, 86 L.Ed. 348 (1941), that it was of dubious validity when tested against the First Amendment. The Court there essentially rejected the contention that all employer speeches or literature—whether criticizing a union or praising it—necessarily interfere with free employee choice and violate Section 8(a)(1). The Court did, however, authorize the Board to find coercion when the record in a particular case so justifies "under all of the circumstances." The Board still continued to regulate employer speech rather sharply, and Congress in 1947 enacted Section 8(c) of the Labor Act, which provides:

> The expressing of any views, argument, or opinion, or the dissemination thereof, whether in written, printed, graphic, or visual form, shall not constitute or be evidence of an unfair labor practice under any of the provisions of this Act, if such expression contains no threat of reprisal or force or promise of benefit.

As will be seen in the cases that follow, Section 8(c) has by no means resolved all problems in the accommodation of free speech and uncoerced employee choice or in the relationship between the Board and the appellate courts.

In 1948, in the noted case of GENERAL SHOE CORP., 77 NLRB 124, the Board—observing that Section 8(c) spoke only to the Board's use of speech and literature in unfair labor practice proceedings leading to a court-enforceable remedial order—held that that provision did not limit the Board's power in election cases. It therefore held that it had the power, as to elections that were won through communications or conduct which could not be held an unfair labor practice, to set aside the election results and order a new election. The Board majority reasoned as follows:

> When we are asked to invalidate elections held under our auspices, our only consideration derives from the Act which calls for freedom of choice by employees as to a collective bargaining representative. Conduct that creates an atmosphere which renders improbable a free choice will sometimes warrant invalidating an election, even though that conduct may not constitute an unfair labor practice. An election can serve its true purpose only if the surrounding conditions enable employees to register a free and untrammelled choice for or against a bargaining representative.
> * * *
>
> We do not subscribe to the view, apparently held by our two dissenting colleagues, that the criteria applied by the Board in a representation proceeding to determine whether certain alleged misconduct interfered with an election need necessarily be identical to those employed in testing whether an unfair labor practice was committed, although the result will ordinarily be the same. In election proceedings, it is the Board's function to provide a laboratory in which an experiment may be conducted, under conditions as nearly ideal as possible, to determine the uninhibited desires of the employees. It is our duty to establish those conditions; it is also our duty to determine whether they have been fulfilled. When, in the rare extreme case, the standard drops too low, because of our fault or that of others, the requisite laboratory conditions are not

present and the experiment must be conducted over again. That is the situation here.

After 1952, the Board began to give greater latitude to employer speech even in cases involving petitions to set aside elections. In "close cases," the Board tended to characterize the employer's remarks not as coercive but rather as the expression of the employer's legal position or its opinion or prediction. See, for example, Esquire, Inc., 107 NLRB 1238 (1954)(employer stated its disagreement with Board's bargaining-unit determination and its intention to litigate the issue, delaying bargaining for a year or two); Southwestern Co., 111 NLRB 805 (1955)(immigrant employees were warned of possible deportation if they joined the "Communist" union); Silver Knit Hosiery Mills, Inc., 99 NLRB 422 (1952)(company pointed out lost work and pay that would result from strikes and warned that any pay raise through unionization would result in lost customers and closing of the mill).

In 1961, with the advent of a new administration in the White House and the appointment of new members to the NLRB, the Board began to assert a greater role in regulating speech and literature in representation-election campaigns. Not only did the Board become more attentive to employee interests in determining whether speech was coercive and thus an unfair labor practice, but it also scrutinized campaign propaganda more vigorously for abuses short of coercion but sufficient to warrant setting aside a representation election.

A significant case in this development was DAL-TEX OPTICAL CO., 137 NLRB 1782 (1962). There, an election victory for the employer was set aside and Section 8(a)(1) violations found, based on the employer's threats and promises of benefit. Just before the re-run election was to take place, the employer's president delivered several speeches to employees in the plant. In one speech, he stated his belief that the first election was valid and his intention to litigate that matter through the courts if necessary; he pointed out that this could take years, that in the meantime the workers would be without a union, but that he would ultimately abide by the decisions of the courts. He then recounted a number of his employees' economic benefits and continued: "Do you want to gamble all of these things? If I am required by the Court to bargain with this Union, whenever that may be, I will bargain in good faith, but I will have to bargain on a cold-blooded business basis. You may come out with a lot less than you have now. * * * If I am required to bargain and I cannot agree there is no power on earth that can make me sign a contract with this Union, so what will probably happen is the Union will call a strike. I will go right along running this business and replace the strikers. * * * They will lose all of their benefits. Strikers will draw no wages, no unemployment compensation and be out of a job." These themes were reiterated in subsequent employer speeches.

The union lost the second election, 101–96, and filed objections which were sustained by the Board. It found that the employer's speeches contained illegal threats to impose economic loss and reprisals through the bargaining process; created a fear that if the union won the election there would be strikes that would necessarily cause a loss of employment and financial security; and conveyed the futility of designating the union as bargaining representative by emphasizing the delays of litigation and a determination not to bargain. The Board found these statements coercive, not protected by Section 8(c), and an unfair labor practice. A fortiori, they warranted setting aside an election, where the test for allowable conduct (i.e., the *General Shoe* "laboratory conditions" test) is stricter yet. Earlier decisions, in which the Board condoned implied threats couched in the guise of statements of legal position, were repudiated.

---

## NLRB v. Gissel Packing Co.

395 U.S. 575, 89 S.Ct. 1918, 23 L.Ed.2d 547 (1969).

[The Court considered four cases, all raising common issues of employer coercion during organizing campaigns and the authority of the Board to order the employer, as a remedy for such coercion, to bargain with a union which had demonstrated majority support through means other than a Board-supervised representation election. In one of the cases, the petitioner Sinclair Company operated two plants at which the Teamsters in 1965 had begun an organizing campaign, had obtained from 11 of 14 employees engaged in wire weaving signed cards authorizing the Teamsters to act as bargaining representative, and had made a request for recognition by the company, which the company refused. The Teamsters then petitioned for an election. In company communications to the employees, several references were made to a three-month strike in 1952, when the employees were represented by a different union; the strike had led to the union's loss of support among company employees. (Other portions of the Court's opinion are set forth at pages 312–24 infra.)]

■ When petitioner's president first learned of the Union's drive in July, he talked with all of his employees in an effort to dissuade them from joining a union. He particularly emphasized the results of the long 1952 strike, which he claimed "almost put our company out of business," and expressed worry that the employees were forgetting the "lessons of the past." He emphasized, secondly, that the Company was still on "thin ice" financially, that the Union's "only weapon is to strike," and that a strike "could lead to the closing of the plant," since the parent company had ample manufacturing facilities elsewhere. He noted, thirdly, that because of their age and the limited usefulness of their skills outside their craft, the employees might not be able to find re-employment if they lost their jobs as a result of a strike. Finally, he warned those who did not believe that the plant could go out of business to "look around Holyoke and see a lot of them out of business." The president sent letters to the same effect to the employees in early November, emphasizing that the parent company had no reason to stay in Massachusetts if profits went down.

During the two or three weeks immediately prior to the election on December 9, the president sent the employees a pamphlet captioned: "Do you want another 13–week strike?" stating, *inter alia,* that: "We have no doubt that the Teamsters Union can again close the Wire Weaving Department and the entire plant by a strike. We have no hopes that the Teamsters Union Bosses will not call a strike. * * * The Teamsters Union is a strike happy outfit." Similar communications followed in late November, including one stressing the Teamsters' "hoodlum control." Two days before the election, the Company sent out another pamphlet that was entitled: "Let's Look at the Record," and that purported to be an obituary of companies in the Holyoke–Springfield, Massachusetts, area that had allegedly gone out of business because of union demands, eliminating some 3,500 jobs; the first page carried a large cartoon showing the preparation of a grave for the Sinclair Company and other headstones containing the names of other plants allegedly victimized by the unions. Finally, on the day before the election, the president made another personal appeal to his employees to reject the Union. He repeated that the Company's financial condition was precarious; that a possible strike would jeopardize the continued operation of the plant; and that age and lack of education would make re-employment difficult. The Union lost the election 7–6, and then filed both objections to the election and unfair labor practice charges which were consolidated for hearing before the trial examiner.

\* \* \*

[The Board, finding that the president's communications were reasonably read by the employees in the circumstances to threaten loss of jobs if the union were to win the election, held that the employer had violated Section 8(a)(1) and that the election should be set aside. It also held that the employer violated Section 8(a)(5) by refusing to bargain in good faith with the Teamsters Union which at the time of its request for recognition demonstrated majority support through its authorization cards. The court of appeals sustained the conclusions of the Board, as well as its order that the employer bargain with the union on request. The Supreme Court, affirming the judgment of the court of appeals, considered Sinclair's claim that the Board and court had acted in violation of the First Amendment to the federal Constitution and Section 8(c) of the Labor Act.]

Any assessment of the precise scope of employer expression, of course, must be made in the context of its labor relations setting. Thus, an employer's rights cannot outweigh the equal rights of the employees to associate freely, as those rights are embodied in § 7 and protected by § 8(a)(1) and the proviso to § 8(c). And any balancing of those rights must take into account the economic dependence of the employees on their employers, and the necessary tendency of the former, because of that relationship, to pick up intended implications of the latter that might be more readily dismissed by a more disinterested ear. Stating these obvious principles is but another way of recognizing that what is basically at stake is the establishment of a nonpermanent, limited relationship between the employer, his economically dependent employee and his union agent, not the election of legislators or the enactment of legislation whereby that relationship is ultimately defined and where the independent voter may be freer to listen more objectively and employers as a class freer to talk. Cf. New York Times Co. v. Sullivan, 376 U.S. 254, 84 S.Ct. 710, 11 L.Ed.2d 686 (1964).

Within this framework, we must reject the Company's challenge to the decision below and the findings of the Board on which it was based. The standards used below for evaluating the impact of an employer's statements are not seriously questioned by petitioner and we see no need to tamper with them here. Thus, an employer is free to communicate to his employees any of his general views about unionism or any of his specific views about a particular union, so long as the communications do not contain a "threat of reprisal or force or promise of benefit." He may even make a prediction as to the precise effects he believes unionization will have on his company. In such a case, however, the prediction must be carefully phrased on the basis of objective fact to convey an employer's belief as to demonstrably probable consequences beyond his control or to convey a management decision already arrived at to close the plant in case of unionization. See Textile Workers v. Darlington Mfg. Co., 380 U.S. 263, 274, n. 20, 85 S.Ct. 994, 13 L.Ed.2d 827 (1965). If there is any implication that an employer may or may not take action solely on his own initiative for reasons unrelated to economic necessities and known only to him, the statement is no longer a reasonable prediction based on available facts but a threat of retaliation based on misrepresentation and coercion, and as such without the protection of the First Amendment. We therefore agree with the court below that "[c]onveyance of the employer's belief, even though sincere, that unionization will or may result in the closing of the plant is not a statement of fact unless, which is most improbable, the eventuality of closing is capable of proof." 397 F.2d 157, 160. As stated elsewhere, an employer is free only to tell "what he reasonably believes will be the likely economic consequences of unionization that are outside his control," and not "threats of economic reprisal to be taken solely on his own volition." NLRB v. River Togs, Inc., 382 F.2d 198, 202 (C.A.2d Cir.1967).

Equally valid was the finding by the court and the Board that petitioner's statements and communications were not cast as a prediction of "demonstrable 'economic consequences,' " 397 F.2d, at 160, but rather as a threat of retaliatory action. The Board found that petitioner's speeches, pamphlets, leaflets, and letters conveyed the following message: that the company was in a precarious financial condition; that the "strike-happy" union would in all likelihood have to obtain its potentially unreasonable demands by striking, the probable result of which would be a plant shutdown, as the past history of labor relations in the area indicated; and that the employees in such a case would have great difficulty finding employment elsewhere. In carrying out its duty to focus on the question: "[W]hat did the speaker intend and the listener understand?" (A. Cox, Law and the National Labor Policy 44 (1960)), the Board could reasonably conclude that the intended and understood import of that message was not to predict that unionization would inevitably cause the plant to close but to threaten to throw employees out of work regardless of the economic realities. In this connection, we need go no further than to point out (1) that petitioner had no support for its basic assumption that the union, which had not yet even presented any demands, would have to strike to be heard, and that it admitted at the hearing that it had no basis for attributing other plant closings in the area to unionism; and (2) that the Board has often found that employees, who are particularly sensitive to rumors of plant closings, take such hints as coercive threats rather than honest forecasts.

Petitioner argues that the line between so-called permitted predictions and proscribed threats is too vague to stand up under traditional First Amendment analysis and that the Board's discretion to curtail free speech rights is correspondingly too uncontrolled. It is true that a reviewing court must recognize the Board's competence in the first instance to judge the impact of utterances made in the context of the employer-employee relationship, see NLRB v. Virginia Electric & Power Co., 314 U.S. 469, 479, 62 S.Ct. 344, 349, 86 L.Ed. 348 (1941). But an employer, who has control over that relationship and therefore knows it best, cannot be heard to complain that he is without an adequate guide for his behavior. He can easily make his views known without engaging in " 'brinkmanship' " when it becomes all too easy to "overstep and tumble [over] the brink." Wausau Steel Corp. v. NLRB, 377 F.2d 369, 372 (7th Cir.1967). At the least he can avoid coercive speech simply by avoiding conscious overstatements he has reason to believe will mislead his employees. * * *

---

## PROBLEMS FOR DISCUSSION

**1.** During a vigorous campaign prior to a representation election, the president of the Ace Manufacturing Company makes a speech along the following lines: "I do not like unions, and I don't think you need one. I have always treated you well, and will continue to do so even without a union. Unions bring high initiation fees and monthly dues, which will come out of your pocket and reduce your earnings. Unions also bring hoodlumism, high prices and strikes, which neither you nor the Company can afford. Vote against the union, for the Company's benefit and for your own benefit." Has the Company violated Section 8(a)(1)?

**2.** Assume that the President of the Ace Manufacturing Company makes the speech set forth in Problem 1, and that three days later he discharges employee Smith, who has a poor work record and a leadership position in the Union. The Union has filed charges under Section 8(a)(3), alleging that the discharge was because of his union activities. At the unfair labor practice hearing, the General Counsel seeks to introduce evidence of the text of the President's speech, to prove anti-union animus. Counsel for the Company objects. How should the Administrative Law Judge rule?

**3.** Able Tool & Die Company, located in Westfield, Massachusetts, manufactures components of industrial machinery pursuant to orders from buyers in the New England states. It employs 42 workers engaged in production and maintenance work. The International Association of Machinists petitioned for an election among these employees, and the Regional Director of the NLRB set the election for January 30. On January 22, the Company President distributed to all employees, over his signature, the following leaflet:

### VOTE NO–UNION

The NLRB election will be held here at the plant on January 30. You will be asked to vote for the IAM or to vote for No–Union. I will abide by the results of the election, but it is important for you to know that while the Union has vigorously campaigned and said critical things about management, you stand to lose if you vote for the Union. A Union victory can result in SERIOUS HARM.

(1) Competing companies organized by the IAM in this region uniformly have a wage scale BELOW that which exists here at Able. If the Union wins the election, the Company will bargain with the Union as required by law, but the law gives the Company the right to bargain hard and to insist on the reduction of certain economic benefits which you now have.

(2) If tough bargaining takes place, the Union can extract concessions only by calling a strike. If you join the strike—and just you try not to!—you and your family will lose your earnings (which will not be replaced by unemployment benefits because you have chosen to leave work) and the law permits me to hire another worker to replace you permanently. You will lose all of the benefits that come with length of service with this Company.

(3) Should the Union insist that the Company take action which will result in higher prices, we have expressly been informed by our two principal customers that they will immediately cease buying from us. If they did this, just think how many jobs would be discontinued!

(4) Another way a union can harm our business is by striking. If we were struck, every account of any substance would desert us like a sinking ship. There would be a cutback in production, and perhaps a closing of our doors.

The choice on January 30 is yours and yours alone. Your future may depend on it. Vote to continue our happy working relationship. Vote NO–UNION.

On January 29, employees at Able received at their homes a mailing from the Westfield Chamber of Commerce which detailed the severe economic impact on the general business of Westfield in the event the Able plant were to close down. It also referred to prison terms served by two of the organizers sent to Westfield by the international office of the Machinists.

The election resulted in a 22–to–20 defeat for the Machinists.

A representative of the IAM has consulted you, and has asked what can be done to protect the interests of the Union. What is your response? See DTR Indus., Inc. v. NLRB, 39 F.3d 106 (6th Cir.1994); NLRB v. Village IX, Inc., 723 F.2d 1360 (7th Cir.1983); Larson Tool & Stamping Co., 296 NLRB 895 (1989); compare International Paper Co., 273 NLRB 615 (1984), with Oak Mfg. Co., 141 NLRB 1323 (1963); see Greensboro Hosiery Mills, Inc., 162 NLRB 1275 (1967), enf't denied, 398 F.2d 414 (4th Cir.1968); and *compare* Eagle Transp. Corp., 327 NLRB 1210 (1999), *with*

Blaser Tool & Mold Co. v. Assortment Sheet Metal Workers Union, 196 NLRB 374 (1972).

**4.** Assume that Able Tool & Die's management assembles its employees and reads to them the following corporate by-law the board of directors had adopted ten years earlier:

> *Section 2—Corporate Dissolution.* Able Tool & Die hereby expresses as a matter of corporate policy that operations will cease and the corporation will be dissolved in the event of unionization of its employees. As hereby authorized by the Board of Directors, this by-law may be announced to the employees of Able Tool & Die at any time deemed appropriate by the Board.

Has the Company committed an unfair labor practice? Wiljef Transp., Inc. v. NLRB, 946 F.2d 1308 (7th Cir.1991).

**5.** In Problem 3, supra, should Board action be affected had the Union loss been by a margin not of 22–to–20 but rather 36–to–6? Should the NLRB treat this wide disparity in votes as indicating a severe impact of the coercive statements, or rather as indicating that even a new and fully fair election would still result in an election victory for the Company? Can the Board answer such a question by resort to *a priori* reasoning?

Consider the results of a systematic empirical study in Getman, Goldberg & Herman, Union Representation Election: Law and Reality 150 n. 21 (1976): "The data indicate that no matter what type of speech employees are exposed to, the votes of approximately 80 percent are predictable on the basis of pre-campaign attitudes. Indeed, the data suggest that the actual number of employees influenced by the campaign is far less. Since no more than 20 percent, and probably far fewer, are subject to campaign influence, the Board would be on exceedingly safe ground if it were to refuse to entertain objections based on speech unless the margin of victory was less than 20 percent. By this rather simple change in its practice, the Board could eliminate a portion of its caseload of objections with little risk that employee rights of free choice were being injured."

**6.** You are counsel to Southern Textile Company, which has been alerted by the Textile Workers Union to an organizing campaign recently begun in one of your mills. The president of the company has expressed to you her deep concern about unionization, both as a matter of principle and as a matter of hard economics. She believes that Southern's capacity to compete in the market will be severely undermined by wage increases and by any serious interference with the right of management to direct the workforce. She has asked you to prepare a series of leaflets, to be distributed weekly to the employees and "to push my right to speak out against the union to the fullest extent the law allows, indeed maybe somewhat beyond, if that is likely to work."

(a) In dealing with the president's request, could you with confidence lift passages out of speeches or leaflets which the Board has ruled in past cases not to constitute unfair labor practices?

(b) Are you obliged to refuse your client's request, or to discourage her from taking such action, or to impose conditions on your willingness to honor her request? What is the appropriate response of the attorney in such a case?

**7.** Evaluate the following proposition: Because of (a) the possible infringement of First Amendment rights when Government bans arguably coercive speech; (b) the desirability of informing employees of the consequences of unionization; (c) the vagueness of any test requiring the finding of a coercive impact "under all of the circumstances" and the difficulties of administering such a standard (for the Regional Director, the Administrative Law Judge, the NLRB, the courts of appeals and, most important, the speakers at the plant level); (d) uncertainty regarding the validity of the Board's psychological assumptions; (e) the disrespect for law that is encouraged when "artful" draftsmanship is rewarded and post-election litigation is invited; (f) the frequent lack of an effective administrative remedy after the fact; and (g) the frequent possibility that opportunities for response by the other party to the election campaign will rectify any wrongdoing—the Board should not find speech coercive (either as an unfair labor practice or to set aside an election) unless it explicitly threatens conduct which would itself be unlawful.

———

## (b) Factual Misrepresentations[f]

Amid the robust exchanges that commonly characterize a representation-election campaign, there will frequently be inaccurate assertions about the motives, resources, and accomplishments and failures of the parties. Employers may make representations about the amount of union initiation fees and dues, or about the union's bargaining record at other companies, or about union strikes elsewhere, or about the company's financial plight or its comparative beneficence to its employees. The union, on the other hand, will tend to trumpet the number and extent of its negotiated gains at other companies, the poor benefits paid by the employer in comparison with its competitors, and the amount of company profits or assets that could better be diverted into personnel benefits. Misstatements about these matters may range from purposeful deceit on an important and hotly contested issue, uttered on the eve of the election, to inadvertent ambiguities on relatively insignificant matters uttered weeks before the election and lost in the welter of communication exchanges.

These statements may lack any threat of reprisal or coercion, and will thus be protected under section 8(c) against unfair labor practice sanctions. But they may nonetheless affect improperly the employees' assessment of the need for unionization and may therefore arguably warrant invalidation of election results. No issue has more sharply divided the National Labor Relations Board over the past forty years as much as the questions whether and in what manner to scrutinize election propaganda for factual misrepresentations.

On the one hand, the Board through its "laboratory conditions" standard is committed to assuring a fair and unfettered choice on the issue of collective bargaining. This would seem to contemplate an opportunity for employees, having full and accurate information, rationally to assess the merits of unionization. On the other hand, NLRB scrutiny of the content of campaign literature raises the spectre of government censorship and protracted litigation interfering with election finality, all in a context of

**f.** Note, A Look at the Revolving NLRB Policies Governing Union Representation     Election Campaigns, 19 Wake Forest L.Rev. 417 (1983).

uncertainty as to whether employees in fact give much attention and credence to the specific statements (as distinguished from the general themes) generated by employer and union. On the last point, a major empirical study—Getman, Goldberg & Herman, *Union Representation Elections: Law and Reality* (1976)—has raised serious doubts whether any significant number of votes in the typical labor election are at all influenced by the content of the parties' campaigns. The study concluded that by far the major determinants are the individuals' initial predisposition and general attitudes about working conditions and unions, and it recommended that for most purposes the NLRB should leave the election process and results unregulated. (A more detailed summary of the conclusions and recommendations of the Getman, Goldberg & Herman book is set out below at pp. 186–88. References are also made there to the rebuttals and other related literature that the book has spawned.)

Not surprisingly, the Board position on this issue has changed through the years, and not surprisingly these changes have tended to coincide with changes in Board membership reflecting changes in the White House. The Board's current approach to this issue (at least as of the date of publication of this book) is set forth in the following case.

------

## Midland National Life Insurance Co. v. Local 304A, United Food & Commercial Workers

263 NLRB 127 (1982).

[In a representation election held in April 1978, the union lost by a vote of 127 to 75, but the NLRB found that the employer had committed certain unfair labor practices and thus set aside the election. In May 1980, the Board's unfair labor practice order was enforced by the court of appeals. In the re-run election, held in October 1980, the vote was 107 in favor of the union and 107 against it; and the union once again filed objections. In January 1981, the hearing officer recommended that the challenges be sustained and that a third election be held. Reviewing that decision, in August 1982, the NLRB issued the following opinion, dealing with the union's claim that the employer had substantially misrepresented material facts during the election campaign.]

■ I.   * * * The facts are not complex. On the afternoon of October 15, 1980, the day before the election, the Employer distributed campaign literature to its employees with their paychecks. One of the distributions was a six-page document which included photographs and text depicting three local employers and their involvements with the Petitioner. The document also contained a reproduction of a portion of the Petitioner's 1979 financial report (hereinafter LMRDA report) submitted to the Department of Labor pursuant to the provisions of the Labor Management Reporting and Disclosure Act of 1959. The Petitioner learned of the document the next morning, 3½ hours before the polls were to open.

The first subject of the document, Meilman Food, Inc., was portrayed in "recent" pictures as a deserted facility, and was described in accompanying text as follows: "They too employed between 200 and 300 employees. This Local 304A struck this plant—violence ensued. *Now all of the workers are gone!* What did the Local 304A do for them? Where is the 304A union job security?" (Emphasis in original.) Jack Smith, the Petitioner's business representative, testified that Local 304A, the Petitioner, had been the representative of Meilman's employees, but that neither the Petitioner nor Meilman's employees had been on strike when the plant closed. He added that the employees had been working for at least 1½ years following the strike and prior to the closure of the facility.

The second and third employers pictured and discussed in the document were Luther Manor Nursing Home and Blue Cross/Blue Shield. The text accompanying the pictures of Luther Manor explained that:

"[a]lmost a year ago this same union that tells you they will 'make job security' (we believe you are the only ones who can do that) and will get you more pay, told the employees of LUTHER MANOR (again, here in Sioux Falls) * * * the union would get them a contract with job security and more money. Unfortunately Local 304A did not tell the Luther Manor employees what year or century they were talking about. Today the employees have no contract. Most of the union leaders left to work elsewhere. Their job security is the same (depends upon the individual as it always has). There has been no change or increase in wages or hours. The union has sent in three different sets of negotiators. Again, promises and performance are two different things. All wages, fringes, working conditions are remaining the same while negotiations continue."

The text accompanying the pictures of Blue Cross stated that "this same Local union won an election at Blue Cross/Blue Shield after promising less restrictive policies, better pay and more job security. Since the election a good percentage of its former employees are no longer working there. Ask them! The employees have been offered a wage increase—*next year* of 5% * * *." (Emphasis in original.)

Smith testified that the Petitioner took over negotiations at Luther Manor and at Blue Cross on or about July 1, 1980, after the Petitioner had merged with Retail Clerks, Local 1665, and that Retail Clerks, Local 1665, not the Petitioner, had conducted the prior negotiations and won the election at Blue Cross.

Assessing the statements concerning these local employers, the Hearing Officer concluded that, in its description of Meilman Food, the Employer intended to instill in the minds of its employees the false impression that the Petitioner had conducted a strike at Meilman, that violence had ensued, and that, as a direct result of the strike, all of the employees at Meilman were terminated. Evaluating the statements about Luther Manor and Blue Cross, the Hearing Officer found that the Employer had misrepresented the labor organization involved, and had implied that the Petitioner was an ineffectual and inefficient bargaining representative who would cause employees to suffer.

The Employer's distribution also included a portion of the Petitioner's 1979 LMRDA report which listed information concerning the Petitioner's assets, liabilities, and cash receipts and disbursements for the reporting period. Three entries on the reproduced page were underlined: total receipts, reported at $508,946; disbursements "On Behalf of Individual Members," reported at zero; and total disbursements, reported at $492,701. Other entries on the reproduced page showed disbursements of $93,185 to officers, and $22,662 to employees. The accompanying text stated that $141,000 of the Petitioner's funds went to "union officers and officials and those who worked for them," and that "NOTHING—according to the report they filed with the U.S. Government was spent 'on behalf of the individual members.' [sic]"

The Hearing Officer found that the report actually showed that the Petitioner disbursed only $115,847 to its officers and employees, a difference of $25,000 and that the Employer's statement attributed 19 percent more in income to the officials and employees than was actually received. He further found that, while the report showed that no sums had been spent "on behalf of the individual members," the instructions for the LMRDA report require that entry to reflect disbursements for "other than normal operating purposes," and that the Employer failed to include this fact in its distribution.

In accordance with his findings outlined above, the Hearing Officer concluded that the document distributed by the Employer contained numerous misrepresentations of fact of a substantial nature designed to portray the Petitioner as an organization staffed by highly paid officials and employees who were ineffectual as bargaining representatives, and that as a consequence employees would suffer with respect to job security and compensation. The Hearing Officer also determined that the document was distributed on the afternoon before the election, that the Petitioner did not become aware of it until approximately 10 a.m. election day, 2½ hours before the preelection conference and 3½ hours before the polls were to open, and that, owing to the nature of the misrepresentations, the Petitioner did not have sufficient time to respond effectively. Applying the standard found in General Knit of California, Inc.,[8] and Hollywood Ceramics Company, Inc.,[9] the Hearing Officer accordingly recommended that the objection be sustained and that a third election be directed.

We have decided to reject the Hearing Officer's recommendations and to certify the results of the election. We do so because, after painstaking evaluation and careful consideration, we have resolved to return to the sound rule announced in Shopping Kart Food Market, Inc.,[10] and to overrule General Knit and Hollywood Ceramics. Before discussing the controlling factors which underlie our decision, we believe it would be instructive to review briefly the Board's past treatment of this troublesome area.

---

**8.** 239 N.L.R.B. 619 (1978).      **10.** 228 N.L.R.B. 1311 (1977).

**9.** 140 N.L.R.B. 221 (1962).

II.  During the years under the Wagner Act, the Board made no attempt to regulate campaign propaganda, and concerned itself solely with conduct which might tend to coerce employees in their election choice. As the Board stated in Maywood Hosiery Mills, Inc., 64 NLRB 146, 150 (1945), "we cannot censor the information, misinformation, argument, gossip, and opinion which accompany all controversies of any importance and which, perceptively or otherwise, condition employees' desires and decisions; nor is it our function to do so." "[E]mployees," as the Board acknowledged even then, "undoubtedly recognize [campaign] propaganda for what it is, and discount it." Corn Products Refining Company, 58 NLRB 1441, 1442 (1944).

Following the enactment of the Taft–Hartley amendments, the Board continued to disregard issues concerning the truth or falsity of campaign propaganda.[11] N.P. Nelson Iron Works, Inc., 78 NLRB 1270, 1271 (1948); Carrollton Furniture Manufacturing Company, 75 NLRB 710, 712 (1948). Again relying on the ability of employees to recognize and assess campaign propaganda for what it is, the Board entrusted these matters to the "good sense" of the voters. Id. In an apparent effort to remove itself further from controversies of this nature, the Board also imposed a duty upon the parties to correct "inaccurate or untruthful statements by any of them." Id.

Even as it was refusing to consider the truth or falsity of campaign propaganda, the Board announced its "laboratory conditions" standard. General Shoe Corporation, 77 NLRB 124 (1948). Assessing certain conduct it characterized as "calculated to prevent a free and untrammeled choice by the employees," the Board noted that "[a]n election can serve its true purpose only if the surrounding circumstances enable employees to register [such a] choice for or against a bargaining representative." Id. at 126. * * * "In election proceedings, it is the Board's function to provide a laboratory in which an experiment may be conducted, under conditions as nearly ideal as possible, to determine the uninhibited desires of the employees." Id. at 127. However, as was subsequently explained in The Liberal Market, Inc., 108 NLRB 1481, 1482 (1954), the Board had a realistic recognition that elections did "not occur in a laboratory where controlled or artificial conditions may be established," and that, accordingly, the Board's goal was "to establish ideal conditions insofar as possible," and to assess "the actual facts in the light of realistic standards of human conduct." Id.

Exhibiting the understanding and realism espoused in Liberal Market, the Board recognized a limited exception to its general rule barring an examination of the effect of the truth or falsity of campaign propaganda upon the election results. Thus, where it appeared that employees were deceived as to the source of campaign propaganda by trickery or fraud, and that they could therefore neither recognize nor evaluate propaganda for

---

**11.** In considering the Taft–Hartley amendments to the Act, Congress expressed no disapproval of the Board's refusal to regulate such campaign propaganda, and in fact sought to reduce even further the Board's ability to restrict speech by enacting Sec. 8(c). See N.L.R.B. v. The Golub Corporation, et al., 388 F.2d 921 (2d Cir.1967).

what it was, the Board set aside the election. United Aircraft Corporation, 103 NLRB 102 (1953). See also The Timken–Detroit Axle Company, 98 NLRB 790 (1952). In those situations, the Board found that election standards had been "lowered * * * to a level which impaired the free and informed atmosphere requisite to an untrammeled expression of choice by the employees." United Aircraft Corporation, 103 NLRB at 105.

It was not until 20 years after the Board began establishing standards for elections that it deviated from its practice of refusing to consider the truth or falsity of campaign propaganda. In The Gummed Products Company, 112 NLRB 1092 (1955), the Board set aside an election where the union deliberately misrepresented wage rates it had negotiated with another employer. Recognizing that it "normally [would] not censor or police preelection propaganda by parties to elections, absent threats or acts of violence," the Board noted that "some limits" had been imposed. Id. at 1093. "Exaggerations, inaccuracies, partial truths, name-calling, and falsehoods, while not condoned, may be excused as legitimate propaganda, provided they are not so misleading as to prevent the exercise of free choice by employees in the election of their bargaining representative. The ultimate consideration is whether the challenged propaganda has lowered the standards of campaigning to the point where it may be said that the uninhibited desires of the employees cannot be determined in an election." Id. at 1093–94.

The Board refined this standard seven years later in Hollywood Ceramics Company, Inc., 140 NLRB 221 (1962). Overruling prior cases which indicated that intent to mislead was an element of the standard, the Board stated that "an election should be set aside only where there has been a misrepresentation or other similar campaign trickery, which involves a substantial departure from the truth, at a time which prevents the other party or parties from making an effective reply, so that the misrepresentation, whether deliberate or not, may reasonably be expected to have a significant impact on the election." Id. at 224.

In 1977, after 15 years of experience under this rule, a majority of the Board decided in Shopping Kart Food Market, Inc., 228 NLRB 1311 (1977), to overrule Hollywood Ceramics, and to return to Board practice which had preceded Gummed Products. Thus, the Board stated that it would "no longer probe into the truth or falsity of the parties' campaign statements," but would instead recognize and rely on employees "as mature individuals who are capable of recognizing campaign propaganda for what it is and discounting it." Id. at 1311, 1313. Consistent with this view, the majority also held that the Board would intervene "in instances where a party has engaged in such deceptive campaign practices as improperly involving the Board and its processes, or the use of forged documents which render the voters unable to recognize the propaganda for what it is." Id. at 1313.

A scant 20 months later, the Board reversed itself, overruled Shopping Kart, and reinstated the Hollywood Ceramics standard. General Knit of California, Inc., 239 NLRB 619 (1978). Finding that the rule propounded in Shopping Kart was "inconsistent with [the Board's] responsibility to insure fair elections," the Board stated that "there are certain circumstances where a particular misrepresentation * * * may materially affect an election," and that such an election should be set aside "in order to maintain the integrity of Board elections and thereby protect employee free choice." Id. at 620.

Many lessons and conclusions can be drawn from this summary of the Board's past practice regarding the role of misrepresentations in Board elections and, no doubt, many will be. However, one lesson which cannot be mistaken is that reasonable, informed individuals can differ, and indeed have differed, in their assessment of the effect of misrepresentations on voters and in their views of the Board's proper role in policing such misrepresentations. No one can or does dispute the ultimate purpose of this controversy, that is the necessity of Board procedures which insure the fair and free choice of a bargaining representative. The sole question facing us is how that "fair and free choice" is best assured.

III.   We begin with the recognition that Congress has entrusted a wide degree of discretion to the Board to establish the procedures necessary to insure the fair and free choice of bargaining representatives by employees. * * *

For numerous reasons, we find that the rule we announce today constitutes * * * a "justifiable and reasonable adjustment" of our democratic electoral processes. By returning to the sound principles espoused in Shopping Kart, not only do we alleviate the many difficulties attending the Hollywood Ceramics rule, but we also insure the certainty and finality of election results, and minimize unwarranted and dilatory claims attacking those results.

As was discussed earlier, an election would be set aside under Hollywood Ceramics

" * * * only where there has been a misrepresentation or other similar campaign trickery, which involves a substantial departure from the truth, at a time which prevents the other party * * * from making an effective reply, so that the misrepresentation, whether deliberate or not, may reasonably be expected to have a significant impact on the election."

As an initial matter, it is apparent that reasonable, informed individuals can differ on the multitude of subjective issues encompassed in this rule. When does a particular statement involve a "substantial" departure from the "truth"? Under what conditions has there been time for an "effective reply"? May the misrepresentation "reasonably be expected" to have a "significant impact" upon the election? As Professor Derek C. Bok concluded in his classic work on the Board's election procedures, restrictions on the content of campaign propaganda requiring truthful and accurate statements "resist every effort at a clear formulation and tend inexorably to give rise to vague and inconsistent rulings which baffle the parties and provoke litigation."[14]

---

**14.**  "The Regulation of Campaign Tactics in Representation Elections Under the National Labor Relations Act," 78 Harv. L.Rev. 38, 85 (1964).

The Board's experience under the Hollywood Ceramics rule bears this out. As was found in Shopping Kart, although the adoption of the Hollywood Ceramics rule "was premised on assuring employee free choice its administration has in fact tended to impede the attainment of that goal. The ill effects of the rule include extensive analysis of campaign propaganda, restriction of free speech, variance in application as between the Board and the courts, increasing litigation, and a resulting decrease in the finality of election results."

In sharp contrast to the Hollywood Ceramics standard, Shopping Kart "draws a clear line between what is and what is not objectionable." Thus, "elections will be set aside 'not on the basis of the *substance* of the representation, but the deceptive *manner* in which it was made.' * * * As long as the campaign material is what it purports to be, i.e., mere propaganda of a particular party, the Board would leave the task of evaluating its contents solely to the employees." Where, due to forgery, no voter could recognize the propaganda "for what it is," Board intervention is warranted. Further, unlike Hollywood Ceramics, the rule in Shopping Kart lends itself to definite results which are both predictable and speedy. The incentive for protracted litigation is greatly reduced, as is the possibility of disagreement between the Board and the courts. Because objections alleging false or inaccurate statements can be summarily rejected at the first stage of Board proceedings, the opportunity for delay is almost nonexistent.[18] Finally, the rule in Shopping Kart "furthers the goal of consistent and equitable adjudications" by applying uniformly to the objections of both unions and employers.

In addition to finding the Hollywood Ceramics rule to be unwieldy and counter-productive, we also consider it to have an unrealistic view of the ability of voters to assess misleading campaign propaganda. As is clear from an examination of our treatment of misrepresentations under the Wagner Act, the Board had long viewed employees as aware that parties to a campaign are seeking to achieve certain results and to promote their own goals. Employees, knowing these interests, could not help but greet the various claims made during a campaign with natural skepticism. The "protectionism" propounded by the Hollywood Ceramics rule is simply not warranted. On the contrary, as we found in Shopping Kart, "we believe that Board rules in this area must be based on a view of employees as mature individuals who are capable of recognizing campaign propaganda for what it is and discounting it."

---

**18.** The figures cited by our dissenting colleagues purporting to compare the "number of elections in which allegations of misleading statements were ruled upon" before and after Shopping Kart hardly establish that the policy change we enunciate today will not have the desired effects. That parties continued to file misrepresentation objections in 1978 simply demonstrated their acknowledgment of the reality that Shopping Kart could be overturned by a shift of one Board Member. In fact, that is what occurred when former Member Truesdale replaced former Member Walther on the Board. In any event, had our dissenting colleagues been more amenable to giving Shopping Kart a reasonable chance to take life, perhaps their point might have some merit.

This fact is apparently recognized to a certain extent even under Hollywood Ceramics. Thus, although the Board determined that a substantial misrepresentation had been made, the election would not be set aside if it also appeared that there had been ample time to respond. This result would obtain no matter how egregious the error or falsity, and regardless of whether in fact a response had been made.[21]

We appreciate that today's decision is likely to cause concern, just as did General Knit's quick retreat from Shopping Kart in 1978. Accordingly, we do not take this step lightly. We take it because of our emphatic belief that the rule in Shopping Kart is the most appropriate accommodation of all the interests here involved, and should be given a fair chance to succeed. Unlike its predecessor, it is a clear, realistic rule of easy application which lends itself to definite, predictable, and speedy results. It removes impediments to free speech by permitting parties to speak without fear that inadvertent errors will provide the basis for endless delay or overturned elections, and promotes uniformity in national labor law by minimizing the basis for disagreement between the Board and the courts of appeals. Weighing the benefits flowing from reinstatement of the Shopping Kart rule against the possibility that some voters may be misled by erroneous campaign propaganda, a result that even Hollywood Ceramics permits, we find that the balance unquestionably falls in favor of implementing the standard set forth in Shopping Kart.

In reaching this decision, we note that "[a]dministrative flexibility is * * * one of the principal reasons for the establishment of the regulatory agencies [because it] permits valuable experimentation and allows administrative policies to reflect changing policy views." Boyd Leedom, et al. v. International Brotherhood of Electrical Workers, Local Union No. 108, AFL–CIO, 278 F.2d 237, 243 (D.C.Cir.1960). As is obvious from today's decision, the policy views of the Board have changed. We cannot permit earlier decisions to endure forever if, in our view, their effects are deleterious and hinder the goals of the Act. The nature of administrative decision-making relies heavily upon the benefits of the cumulative experience of the decisionmakers. Such experience, in the words of the Supreme Court, "begets understanding and insight by which judgments * * * are validated or qualified or invalidated. The constant process of trial and error, on a wider and fuller scale than a single adversary litigation permits, differentiates perhaps more than anything else the administrative from the judicial process." N.L.R.B. v. J. Weingarten, Inc., 420 U.S. 251, 265–266 (1975).

Cumulative experience need not produce the same understanding and insight. Reasonable minds can and indeed have differed over the most appropriate resolution of this issue. That no one can dispute. However, we

---

**21.** See, *e.g.*, Illinois Central Community Hospital, 224 N.L.R.B. 632, 638 (1976). Despite our dissenting colleagues' professed concerns about the need to eliminate "lies, trickery, and fraud" from election propaganda, they focus only on misrepresentations occurring during the waning hours of campaigns that usually have been waged for several weeks.

again express our emphatic belief that on balance the rule in Shopping Kart best accommodates and serves the interests of all.

In sum, we rule today that we will no longer probe into the truth or falsity of the parties' campaign statements, and that we will not set elections aside on the basis of misleading campaign statements. We will, however, intervene in cases where a party has used forged documents which render the voters unable to recognize propaganda for what it is. Thus, we will set an election aside not because of the substance of the representation, but because of the deceptive manner in which it was made, a manner which renders employees unable to evaluate the forgery for what it is. As was the case in Shopping Kart, we will continue to protect against other campaign conduct, such as threats, promises, or the like, which interferes with employee free choice.

Accordingly, inasmuch as the Petitioner's objection alleges nothing more than misrepresentations, it is hereby overruled. Because the tally of ballots shows that the Petitioner failed to receive a majority of the valid ballots cast, we shall certify the results.

■ FANNING and JENKINS, Members, dissenting:

For the second time in five years, a bare majority of the Board has abandoned the flexible and balanced Hollywood Ceramics standard for determining when election campaign misrepresentations have overstepped the bounds of tolerability and substituted an ultra-permissive standard that places a premium on the well-timed use of deception, trickery, and fraud. In reestablishing the Shopping Kart rule, the present majority adds nothing to the debate that has accompanied the seesawing of Board doctrine in this area. Instead, the majority reiterates the familiar theme of the "unrealistic view of the ability of voters to assess misleading campaign propaganda" (which it attributes to Hollywood Ceramics) and the promise of elimination of delays caused by the processing of misrepresentation objections.

The considerations that went into Hollywood Ceramics, as the brief history set forth by the instant majority shows, represented the accumulated wisdom and experience of several generations of Board Members, from the General Shoe case in the 1940's, through Gummed Products in 1955 and Hollywood Ceramics in 1962. And the stated policies behind Hollywood Ceramics belie the majority's claim that it is based on an over-protectionist, condescending view of employees:

> "The basic policy underlying this rule, as well as the other rules in this election field, is to assure the employees full and complete freedom of choice in selecting a bargaining representative. The Board seeks to maintain, as closely as possible, laboratory conditions for the exercise of this basic right of the employees. One of the factors which may so disturb these conditions as to interfere with the expression of this free choice is gross misrepresentation about some material issue in the election. It is obvious that where employees cast their ballots upon the basis of a

material misrepresentation, such vote cannot reflect their uninhibited desires, and they have not exercised the kind of choice envisaged by the Act. * * *

"The Board has limited its intervention * * * because an election by secret ballot, conducted under Government auspices, should not be lightly set aside, and because we realize that additional elections upset the plant routine and prevent stable labor-management relations. We are also aware that absolute precision of statement and complete honesty are not always attainable in an election campaign, nor are they expected by the employees. Election campaigns are often hotly contested and feelings frequently run high. At such times a party may in its zeal, overstate its own virtues and the vices of the other without essentially impairing 'laboratory conditions.' Accordingly, in reaching its decision in cases where objections to elections have been filed alleging that one party misrepresented certain facts, the Board must balance the right of the employees to an untrammeled choice, and the right of the parties to wage a free and vigorous campaign with all the normal legitimate tools of electioneering."

What the majority does now is to give up, in the interest of possibly reducing litigation, a speculative thing at best, any attempt to balance the rights of the employees and the campaigners. However, their goal, which, as the Board noted in General Knit, must never take precedence over preservation of the integrity of the electoral process, seems to have eluded the Board's prior attempt under Shopping Kart. For, according to an internal audit conducted for the General Counsel, the number of elections in which allegations of misleading statements were ruled on increased from 327 in 1976, the year before Shopping Kart was decided, to 357 in 1978, the first full year after Shopping Kart was in effect, this despite a decrease (from 8,899 to 8,464) in the total number of elections conducted in those respective years.

In return for the illusory benefits of speed and a speculative lightening of its workload, the majority today errs in relinquishing the Board's obligation to put some limits on fraud and deceit as campaign tools. It is apparent that the system contemplated by Section 9 of the Act for representation elections has survived reasonably well during the decades in which the Board has taken a role in insuring the integrity of its elections. Indeed, the majority does not suggest deregulating the election process other than with respect to misrepresentations. In this connection, we are especially puzzled by the distinction the majority draws between forgery, which it will regulate, and other kinds of fraud, which it will not. The majority states that forgeries "render the voters unable to recognize the propaganda for what it is." Yet it is precisely the Board's traditional perception that there are some misrepresentations which employees can recognize "for what they are" and others which, in the Board's considered judgment, they cannot, that has made the Hollywood Ceramics doctrine so effective. In place of this approach, under which judgments take into account the facts of each case, the majority creates an irrebuttable presumption that employees can recognize all misrepresentations, however opaque and deceptive, except forgeries. Employees' free choice in elections, the only reason we run elections, must necessarily be inhibited, distorted, and frustrated by this new rule. To the majority, this is less important than the freedom to engage in lies, trickery, and fraud. Under the new rule, important election issues will be ignored in favor of irresponsible charges and deceit. Under Hollywood Ceramics, the Board did not attempt to sanitize elections completely but only to keep the campaign propaganda within reasonable bounds. Those bounds have now disappeared. Why?

Albeit today's American employees may be better educated, in the formal sense, than those of previous generations, and may be in certain respects more sophisticated, we do not honor them by abandoning them utterly to the mercies of unscrupulous campaigners, including the expert cadre of professional opinion molders who devise campaigns for many of our representation elections. In political campaigns, which are conducted over a much longer period of time and are subject to extensive media scrutiny, the voters have ready access to independent sources of information concerning the issues. In representation campaigns, they do not. Thus, it has been observed that: "Promises are often written on the wind, but statements of fact are the stuff upon which men and women make serious value judgments * * * [and] rank and file employees must largely depend upon the company and union to provide the data * * *." As we said in our dissent in Shopping Kart, the very high level of participation in Board elections as compared with political elections speaks well for the Board's role in insuring a measure of responsibility in campaigning. On the other hand, absent some external restraint, the campaigners will have little incentive to refrain from any last-minute deceptions that might work to their short-term advantage.

In sum, we are able to agree with the majority on very little. But one point of agreement is the majority's statement that, "The sole question facing us here is how [the fair and free choice of a bargaining representative] is best assured." For the reasons set forth above, and also for the reasons set forth in General Knit and our dissent in Shopping Kart, we find it impossible to answer that question by abandoning one of the most effective means the Board has yet devised for assuring that desired result.

Turning to the facts of the instant case, the Employer misrepresented to the employees that a strike called by the Union led directly to the closing of a large local employer and that the Union had bargained extensively with two other local employers without success. These were substantial misrepresentations concerning the central issue in the choice of a bargaining representative—its effectiveness. But the Employer did not limit itself to simple misrepresentations. It stepped beyond that and engaged in an elaborately conceived fraud when it presented and commented upon an excerpt from the Form LM–2 financial report the Union was required to file with the U.S. Department of Labor. Line 71 of the form, showing union disbursements "on behalf of individual members," appears to show that the Union made no such disbursements during the reporting year. The Employer both underlined that item and emphasized it in a separate notation. The Employer contrasted this negative disbursement figure with a figure which overstated by 19 percent the moneys paid to union officers and "those that worked for them." This contrast was designed, of course, to show that the hard-earned money collected from the Union's members benefited only union officials. What the excerpt and the Employer's notations concealed, however, was that the Labor Department's instructions for completing line 71 specifically exclude from disbursements "on behalf of individual members," all normal operating expenses. Thus, while a reader in possession of the instructions might realize that the Union's operating expenses, including salaries for the Union's staff, are incurred with the objective of benefiting all the members, the Employer carefully disguised this fact, egregiously distorted what the Union does with its members' money, and ingeniously made the Union itself appear to be the source of this misinformation. In addition, how many employees are going to read and understand this complicated form?

The Employer's fraudulent misstatement of the contents of this Government document is analogous to the mischaracterization of this Board's documents, and is at least equally objectionable. See Formco, Inc., 233 NLRB 61 (1977). Here, in sum, we have a fraudulent misrepresentation of a most serious and extreme nature, forming part of a series of material misrepresentations. Such conduct can hardly have failed to affect the election, especially since, with a tally of 107 to 107, the change of a single vote may have changed the outcome.

The majority through this decision is giving our election processes, possibly the most important part of installing a viable collective-bargaining relationship, over to the possible excesses of the participants and eliminating the Board from its statutory oversight responsibilities. Why? Accordingly, we must dissent.

[The Board's *Midland Life* decision, and the propriety of its constant policy changes in this area, have received judicial endorsement. See, e.g., NLRB v. Best Products Co., Inc., 765 F.2d 903 (9th Cir.1985). For a decision endorsing *Midland Life* but adding criteria much like those in *Hollywood Ceramics*, see NLRB v. St. Francis Healthcare Centre, 212 F.3d 945 (6th Cir.2000).]

----

## PROBLEMS FOR DISCUSSION

**1.** Did the Board overlook the fact that statements not too different from those made by the employer about the union's involvement in strikes and plant closings were treated by the Supreme Court in the *Gissel* case as potentially coercive, independent of their inaccuracy?

**2.** Does the Board's standard in *Shopping Kart* and *Midland National* invite the intentional use of last-minute misrepresentations in election campaigns? Should the Board, through either rulemaking or adjudication, declare that an election shall be set aside whenever the prevailing party has, within 24 hours before the opening of the polls, circulated a substantial misstatement of fact that bears upon a significant campaign issue and that is likely to have influenced the election outcome? (or, if that is thought to create problems of administrability, should the Board overturn an election on account of *any* day-before factual misrepresentation?) See AWB Metal, Inc., 306 NLRB 109 (1992), *enf'd*, 4 F.3d 993 (6th Cir.1993).

**3.** Would you as counsel to employer or union be prepared to draft untruthful campaign materials, now that the Board no longer chooses to scrutinize for factual accuracy? Are there any other disincentives to do so?

**4.** Given the history recounted in the *Midland* case, how much weight should a court reviewing the Board's recent policy give to that agency's "expertise"? Examine the closing paragraphs of the Board's decision in *Midland,* referring to its "cumulative experience." Is that simply a euphemism for constant change in policy views resulting from changes in politicized Board membership? Is such change truly objectionable, in view of the fact that the Board is purposely designed to be different from a judicial body and to change its composition with regularity through presidential appointments?

**5.** The empirical study published by Getman, Goldberg and Herman (referred to at page 156 supra) was featured prominently in all opinions in the *Shopping Kart* and *General Knit* cases. The Board members used the data uncovered in that study either to support the scholars' conclusions or, alternatively, to support the very opposite conclusions (i.e., that a significant number of employees were influenced by campaign communications and that a significant number of elections were affected thereby). The *General Knit* majority (who revived the *Hollywood Ceramics* principles) went further and discredited the study:

> The results of 43 years of conducting elections, investigating objections, and holding hearings at which employees testify concerning their recollection of campaign tactics convince us that employees are influenced by certain union and employer campaign statements.... Even if this particular study were clearly supportive of all of the authors' conclusions, however, we would still not find it an adequate ground for rejecting a rule which had been well established for 15 years. While we welcome research from the behavioral sciences, 1 study of only 31 elections in 1 area of the country—although it may provide food for thought—is simply not sufficient to disprove the assumptions upon which the Board has regulated election conduct, especially since, in our experience, statements made by either side can significantly affect voter preference.

Was the Board improperly disdainful of the empirical study? (Note that the study is not mentioned at all in the opinions in *Midland National Life Insurance.*)

**6.** A major bone of contention in the Board's decisions in this area is whether employees can be expected to evaluate on their own the credibility to be accorded to campaign rhetoric and representations. The *Hollywood* opponents condemned that decision as "patronizing," and made such statements as (in a dissenting opinion in *General Knit*): "If presidential elections were supervised by the Board's new majority here, democracy in the United States would be long dead or at least long denied." To what extent does the model of free-wheeling debate in political elections apply to the labor representation election?

Government scrutiny of political-campaign representations has been successfully challenged under the federal constitution. Should the same challenge be sustained to NLRB regulation? See Thomas v. Collins, 323 U.S. 516, 65 S.Ct. 315, 89

L.Ed. 430 (1945)(especially the concurring opinion of Justice Jackson); Bausch & Lomb, Inc. v. NLRB, 451 F.2d 873 (2d Cir.1971); Vanasco v. Schwartz, 401 F.Supp. 87 (E.D.N.Y.1975), aff'd by an equally divided Court, 423 U.S. 1041, 96 S.Ct. 763, 46 L.Ed.2d 630 (1976).

———

## (c) Inflammatory Appeals[g]

SEWELL MFG. CO., 138 NLRB 66 (1962). An election was held at the company's plants in two small Georgia towns, near the Alabama border. The Amalgamated Clothing Workers lost the election, 985–331, but the Board set it aside. During the preceding four months, the employer had circulated copies of Militant Truth, a four-page monthly which regularly had articles linking unions, blacks, racial integration, Communism and anti-Christianity. Two weeks before the election, the employer mailed to its employees a large picture of an unidentified black man dancing with an unidentified white woman and a newspaper article (from four years before, relating to a representation election in another state involving a different company and a different international union) with headlines referring to "race mixing" and with a photograph of a white man, identified as the president of the International Union of Electrical Workers, dancing with a black woman. Later, an article in a local newspaper cited financial contributions made by organized labor to the Congress of Racial Equality, and two days before the election the employer sent a letter to all employees in which he mentioned the fact that the union uses membership funds to support various civil rights groups.

The Board stated that, unlike a political election in which "the law permits wide latitude in the way of propaganda—truth and untruth, promises, threats, appeals to prejudice," the Board has the responsibility "to insure that the voters have the opportunity of exercising a reasoned, untrammeled choice" regarding unionization, and to conduct elections in which employees "cast their ballots for or against a labor organization in an atmosphere conducive to the sober and informed exercise of the franchise, free not only from interference, restraint, or coercion violative of the Act, but also from other elements which prevent or impede a reasoned choice." Although minor or isolated references to race might have to be tolerated, "prejudice based on color is a powerful emotional force" and "a deliberate appeal to such prejudice is not intended or calculated to encourage the reasoning faculty. * * * The Board does not intend to tolerate as 'electoral propaganda' appeals or arguments which can have no purpose except to inflame the racial feelings of voters in the election."

**g.** See Note, Labor Representation Elections and the Constitutional Right to Campaign Vigorously—The Use of Racial Propaganda, 23 So.Car.L.Q. 400 (1971); Pollitt, The National Labor Relations Board and Race Hate Progaganda in Union Organization Drives, 17 Stan.L.Rev. 373 (1965).

Some statements with racial overtones—such as the union's position on segregation or union financial contributions to civil rights groups—will be appropriate, but only if "temperate in tone, germane, and correct factually," because employees are entitled to have knowledge about these matters. But "the burden will be on the party making use of a racial message to establish that it was truthful and germane, and where there is doubt [it] will be resolved against him." In this case, the employer "calculatedly embarked on a campaign so to inflame racial prejudice of its employees that they would reject the [union] out of hand on racial grounds alone." The atmosphere was so inflamed that a reasoned decision by the employees was an impossibility. The "photographs and the news articles were not germane to any legitimate issue involved in the election and reinforce our conclusion that their purpose was to exacerbate racial prejudice and to create an emotional atmosphere of hostility" to the union.

---

## PROBLEMS FOR DISCUSSION

**1.** Do you believe that the justification for NLRB regulation in cases such as *Sewell* is more or less persuasive than the justification for regulation in cases such as *Dal–Tex* and *Gissel* on the one hand and *Hollywood Ceramics* and *General Knit* on the other? Stated another way, what is the order of priority for governmental regulation to assure dispassion, freedom from economic coercion, and accurate facts, in a labor election? Cf. YKK (U.S.A.) Inc. v. Collins, 269 NLRB 82 (1984). What weight, if any, should be given to the fact that race discrimination in employment is now outlawed by Title VII of the 1964 Civil Rights Act (passed after *Sewell* was decided)?

**2.** In 1974, the State of New York, as part of comprehensive legislation regulating state elections and campaigns, prohibited the use of literature or of the media to make "attacks on a candidate based on race, sex, religion or ethnic background." The legislation established a Board of Elections which promulgated a Fair Campaign Code (containing the same proscription) to be enforceable by fines and cease-and-desist orders. This legislative and administrative provision was held unconstitutional by a three-judge district court in Vanasco v. Schwartz, 401 F.Supp. 87 (E.D.N.Y.1975), aff'd by an equally divided Court, 423 U.S. 1041, 96 S.Ct. 763, 46 L.Ed.2d 630 (1976). The court stated that in political elections the First Amendment protects all speech except "fighting words" (whose very utterance inflicts injury or tends to incite an immediate breach of the peace) and "malicious" untruths (statements known to be false or with a reckless disregard of the truth). Neither exception applied here, where the state attempted to justify regulation simply on the grounds that attacks based on a candidate's race, sex, religion or ethnic background are unrelated to fitness for office. The court held: "Such an assumption is an exercise in self-delusion. The Supreme Court has recognized that [g]iven the realities of our political life, it is by no means easy to see what statements about a candidate might be altogether without relevance to his fitness for the office he seeks. * * * It would be a retreat from reality to hold that voters do not consider race, religion, sex or ethnic background when choosing political candidates. * * * New York's attempt to eliminate an entire segment of protected speech from the arena of public debate is clearly unconstitutional."

Earlier, in Thomas v. Collins, 323 U.S. 516, 65 S.Ct. 315, 89 L.Ed. 430 (1945), the Supreme Court had said: "[E]mployers' attempts to persuade to action with respect to joining or not joining unions are within the First Amendment's guaranty. * * * When to this persuasion other things are added which bring about coercion, or give it that character, the limit of the right has been passed. * * * But short of that limit the employer's freedom cannot be impaired."

Are the Board's decision, order and doctrine in *Sewell* constitutional?

**3.** On the day before a representation election at a Japanese-owned company outside Dayton, Ohio, the union circulated photocopies of a "letter to the editor" published in a popular magazine, and underlined parts of the letter. The letter was from a Japanese businessman, who had no connection to the company, critical of American workers. The underlined passages included such statements as, "I am appalled at the typical lazy, uneducated American workers I have to deal with in your country." The union won the election. Should the NLRB set it aside? See KI(USA) Corp. v. NLRB, 35 F.3d 256 (6th Cir.1994); Carrington South Health Care Center v. NLRB, 76 F.3d 802 (6th Cir.1996). Compare Catherine's, Inc., 316 NLRB 186 (1995), with Zartic, Inc., 315 NLRB 495 (1994).

────────

## 3. OTHER FORMS OF INTERFERENCE, RESTRAINT OR COERCION

# NLRB v. Lorben Corp.

345 F.2d 346 (2d Cir.1965).

■ MARSHALL, CIRCUIT JUDGE. * * * The basic facts are simple and undisputed. On April 1, 1963, Local 1922, International Brotherhood of Electrical Workers, AFL–CIO, began organizing respondent's plant and secured the adherence of four of the 25 or 26 employees. On April 4 the union held a meeting to decide what to do about the discharge of one of the employees believed to have been discharged for union activities. A strike was decided upon and picketing began the next day with placards reading: "Employees of Lorben Electronics Corporation on Strike—Please help us maintain decent working conditions." About two days later the discharged employee asked respondent's president whether he wanted to have any discussions with the union's officials and the president said he did not want to do so. Subsequently, respondent's president, on advice of counsel, prepared a paper with a question: "Do you wish Local 1922 of the Electrical Workers to represent you?" Under this were two columns, "yes" and "no." The plant superintendent handed the sheet to each employee explaining to each that each was free to sign or not sign. This was done throughout the plant. All of the employees signed in the "no" column. There is no evidence of any employee [sic] hostility to the union and the Trial Examiner found an absence of any "other unfair labor practices." However, the Examiner found that the respondent had violated the Act. While the Examiner mentioned the failure of respondent to advise the employees of the purpose of the interrogation and to assure them that no reprisals would follow, he based his decision primarily on his finding that the respondent had no legitimate purpose for the interrogation. The Board based its decision on the first two reasons and refused to rely on the third. We deny enforcement of the Board's order.

Employer interrogation of employees as to their desire to be represented by a particular union is not coercive or intimidating on its face. It is extremely difficult to determine how often and under what circumstances threats will be inferred by the employees. The resulting confusion from efforts to set up basic ground rules in this field is carefully explored by Prof. Derek C. Bok, The Regulation of Campaign Tactics in Representation Elections Under the National Labor Relations Act, 78 Harv.L.Rev. 38, 106 (1964).

The problem of delineating what is coercion by interrogation has resisted any set rules or specific limitations. The Board's original determination that interrogation by the employer was unlawful per se, Standard–Coosa–Thatcher Co., 85 N.L.R.B. 1358 (1949), was disapproved by the courts and the Board retreated to the position that interrogation would only be unlawful where it was found to be coercive in the light of all surrounding circumstances. As the Board stated in Blue Flash Express, Inc., 109 N.L.R.B. 591, 594 (1954): "We agree with and adopt the test laid down by the Court of Appeals for the Second Circuit in the Syracuse Color Press case [209 F.2d 596, cert. denied, 347 U.S. 966, 74 S.Ct. 777, 98 L.Ed. 1108 (1954) ]which we construe to be that the answer to whether particular interrogation interferes with, restrains, and coerces employees must be found in the record as a whole." In Bourne v. NLRB, 332 F.2d 47, 48 (2 Cir.1964), this Circuit reaffirmed this comprehensive approach and we attempted to suggest some of the many factors that must be considered anew in each case to determine whether a particular interrogation is coercive:

"(1) The background, i.e., is there a history of employer hostility and discrimination?

"(2) The nature of the information sought, e.g., did the interrogator appear to be seeking information on which to base taking action against individual employees?

"(3) The identity of the questioner, i.e., how high was he in the company hierarchy?

"(4) Place and method of interrogation, e.g., was employee called from work to the boss's office? Was there an atmosphere of 'unnatural formality'?"

\* \* \*

To enforce the Board's order which rests on this narrow ground alone, would be to depart from the line of decisions of this Circuit cited above, once approved by the Board, and we are not so inclined. While it is true that questioning can very well have a coercive effect where the purpose is not explained and there are no assurances against retaliation, cf. NLRB v. Camco, Inc., 340 F.2d 803 (5 Cir.1965), we hold that the absence of these two factors, without more and in the face of the undisputed facts in the record of this case, fails to show coercion within the meaning of section 8(a)(1). * * *

■ FRIENDLY, CIRCUIT JUDGE (dissenting):

The Board supported its conclusion that Lorben "violated 8(a)(1) of the Act in polling the employees" by saying that it relied "principally on the manner in which the poll was conducted, particularly the fact that Respondent did not explain the purpose of the poll to all of the employees, and did not offer or provide any assurance to the employees that their rights under the Act would not be infringed."

I fail to understand on what basis, in a case like this, we may properly reject the conditions to permissible interrogation which the Board has developed and here enforced. The Board's adoption, in Blue Flash Express, Inc., 109 N.L.R.B. 591, 594 (1954), of language used by this court in granting enforcement in NLRB v. Syracuse Color Press, Inc., 209 F.2d 596, 599 (2 Cir.), cert. denied, 347 U.S. 966, 74 S.Ct. 777, 98 L.Ed. 1108 (1954), did not prevent it from later concluding, in the light of experience, that proper administration demanded working rules for reconciling the employer's desire to know what was afoot and the employees' need to be free from harassment, which would provide a test more definite, and more readily applicable, than "whether, under all the circumstances, the interrogation reasonably tends to restrain or interfere with the employees in the exercise of rights guaranteed by the Act," 109 N.L.R.B. at 593. See NLRB v. A.P.W. Prods., Inc., 316 F.2d 899, 905–906 (2 Cir.1963); Dickinson, Administrative Justice and the Supremacy of Law in the United States 143, 205 (1927). An agency receiving over 14,000 unfair labor practice charges a year, see 28 NLRB Ann.Rep. 161 (1963), ought not be denied the right to establish standards, appropriate to the statutory purpose, that are readily understandable by employers, regional directors and trial examiners, and be forced to determine every instance of alleged unlawful interrogation by an inquiry covering an employer's entire union history and his behavior during the particular crisis and to render decisions having little or no precedential value since "the number of distinct fact situations is almost infinite." See Bok, [The Regulation of Campaign Tactics Under the National Labor Relations Act, 78 Harv.L.Rev. 38 (1964) ]at 111, and also at 64–65. The Board's power to rule that certain types of conduct constitute unfair labor practices without further proof of motivation or effect has been sustained in cases too numerous for anything more than illustrative citation. Republic Aviation Corp. v. NLRB, 324 U.S. 793, 65 S.Ct. 982, 89 L.Ed. 1372 (1945) (prohibition of union solicitation on company premises outside of working hours); Brooks v. NLRB, 348 U.S. 96, 75 S.Ct. 176, 99 L.Ed. 125 (1954) (one-year rule on duty to bargain); NLRB v. Katz, 369 U.S. 736, 82 S.Ct. 1107, 8 L.Ed.2d 230 (1962)(*per se* violations of duty to bargain); NLRB v. Marcus Trucking Co., 286 F.2d 583 (2 Cir.1961)(contract bar rule). * * *

* * * Strict rules may not suit the casual question privately put to a few employees. But when the employer sets in motion a formal tabulation

of this sort, it is not too much to ask that he provide some explanation and assure his employees against reprisal. Although my brothers condemn the Board's requirements, they do not explain why these rules are inappropriate or, more relevantly, why the Board may not reasonably think them so.
* * *

* * * [O]ne need not hold a doctoral degree in psychology to realize that the method of polling here utilized, in contrast to other methods of testing employee sentiment that were readily available, entailed serious risk that some employees would indicate a position quite different from that really held and would then feel obliged to adhere to it. Whether by design or by accident, the first workers to be questioned might be preponderantly against the union; the display of such votes would inevitably affect later voters who would be inclined to "follow the leader" and would see little use in bucking a trend; and all this could have a snowballing effect. I cannot believe that if the Board had utilized its rule-making power, under § 6 of the Act, see Peck, The Atrophied Rule–Making Powers of the National Labor Relations Board, 70 Yale L.J. 729 (1961), to prohibit such a means of ascertaining employee views as tending to "interfere with" rights guaranteed by § 7, and insisted on methods whereby each employee would indicate his sentiments without knowing those of others, any court would strike that down. I see no justification for a different result when the Board has followed the equally valid course of reaching its conclusion by the decision of a particular case. See NLRB v. A.P.W. Prods., Inc., supra, 316 F.2d at 905.

I would grant enforcement.

———

# International Union of Operating Engineers, Local 49 v. NLRB (Struksnes Construction Co.)

353 F.2d 852 (D.C.Cir.1965), on remand, 165 NLRB 1062 (1967).

[The respondent, Struksnes Construction Co., performed highway construction work in North Dakota. The union began to organize at one job site, and its representative, McPherson, requested recognition as bargaining agent; he asserted, in a letter of August 12, 1963, that the union represented twenty employees in what was a unit of twenty-six employees. Mr. Struksnes denied that the union had such support. He then proceeded to circulate among all of his employees a petition which was inscribed: "Do you want me to bargain with and sign a contract with Operating Engineers Local 49? Please sign your name and answer Yes or No." Struksnes personally solicited the signatures of employees at the end of one shift, and his two foremen secured signatures from the others. "I told them what was up here, and I asked them to sign yes or no, and it wouldn't make any difference." He did not, however, call a general meeting to explain his purpose for ascertaining the workers' desires regarding a union contract or to assure them of no reprisals. Twenty-four men signed the statement, nine voting yes, and fifteen voting no; the identity and the vote of each employee was known to Mr. Struksnes and his foremen. Apart from this incident there was no bias shown against union supporters and no interference with organizing efforts. The Board found the poll not to violate Section 8(a)(1), but the court of appeals set aside the Board's order.]

## OPINION OF THE COURT OF APPEALS

■ * * * We are by no means satisfied with the Board's ad hoc acquiescence in, if not approval of, the manner in which the Employer polled his men. * * * The Board here simply dismisses, *sub silentio*, the development of a permanent record of the votes of each employee set against his signature after interrogation had been conducted in personal approach by the employer and his foremen, and otherwise under the circumstances we outlined. Although a majority of the employees were members of the union, had they succumbed to coercion when they voted in the negative upon being queried as to whether or not they desired their employer to enter into a contract with their union? The Board's Decision and Order discloses no treatment of the possibly inherent restraint resulting from such contacts. * * *

In respect of the conclusion here reached by the Board, its reasoning seems to have applied and found satisfied the criteria suggested in *Blue Flash Express, Inc.* In our judgment, that is not enough * * *.

We think the Board should come to grips with this constantly recurring problem for the protection of the employees as to their section 7 rights and for that of an employer acting in good faith. It would seem that the Board could, in the exercise of its expertise, develop appropriate policy considerations[16] and outline at least minimal standards to govern the ascertainment of union status, or even in given permissible situations, the desire of the employees respecting a contract with the Union.[17]

We will set aside the Board's order and remand this case for further consideration not inconsistent with this opinion.

Reversed and remanded.

[The dissenting opinion of EDGERTON, C.J., has been omitted.]

## NLRB SUPPLEMENTAL DECISION AND ORDER

■ * * * A.  *Standards Applicable to Determining the Legality of Polls*

We have, in accord with the court's directive, reviewed Board and court decisions, as well as articles by scholars in this field, in order to establish

---

**16.** We agree with the views set forth in Judge Friendly's dissenting opinion in N.L.R.B. v. Lorben Corporation, * * *; and see Peck, The Atrophied Rule–Making Powers of the National Labor Relations Board, 70 Yale L.J. 729 (1961).

**17.** Rule-making in this area, it would seem, might have obviated the difficulty here as in many of the cases with which the Board says it has been "continually confronted." Certainly the Board has rule-making authority as the Act expressly provides. 29 U.S.C. § 156 (1964).

standards which may be used as guidelines to determine whether a poll is lawful.

In our view any attempt by an employer to ascertain employee views and sympathies regarding unionism generally tends to cause fear of reprisal in the mind of the employee if he replies in favor of unionism and, therefore, tends to impinge on his Section 7 rights. As we have pointed out, "An employer cannot discriminate against union adherents without first determining who they are." That such employee fear is not without foundation is demonstrated by the innumerable cases in which the prelude to discrimination was the employer's inquiries as to the union sympathies of his employees.

It was the Board's original view that an employer's poll of his employees was in and of itself coercive and therefore a *per se* violation of Section 8(a)(1).[8] Some courts disagreed with that view, and the Board in *Blue Flash* established the rule that whether a poll interferes with, restrains, or coerces employees "must be found in the record as a whole," and that the time, place, personnel involved, information sought, and the employer's known preference must be considered. The Board found the poll in *Blue Flash* lawful on the ground that (1) the employer's sole purpose was to ascertain whether the union demanding recognition actually represented a majority of the employees, (2) the employees were so informed, (3) assurances against reprisal were given, and (4) the questioning occurred in a background free from employer hostility to union organization.

Although the courts have not disapproved of the Board's *Blue Flash* rule, some of the courts have disagreed with the Board on the application of the rule in specific cases, and a few courts have adopted their own tests for determining whether a poll was lawful under *Blue Flash*. The result has been to create considerable uncertainty in this area of labor-management relations. Furthermore, our experience since *Blue Flash* indicates that that rule has not operated to discourage intimidation of employees by employer polls.

As recent Board decisions have emphasized, there are clearly uncoercive methods for an employer to verify a union's majority status. An employer faced with a union demand for recognition may normally refrain from according recognition; he may also request proof of majority status; or he may file a petition, or suggest that the union do so, and await the outcome of a Board election.

We have therefore determined, in the light of all the foregoing considerations, and in accord with the court's remand, to adopt the following revision of the *Blue Flash* criteria:

---

**8.** See cases to that effect cited in *Blue Flash Express, Inc.,* supra. It is well established that an employer, in questioning his employees as to their union sympathies, is not expressing views, argument, or opinion within the meaning of Section 8(c) of the Act, as the purpose of an inquiry is not to express views but to ascertain those of the person questioned. Martin Sprocket & Gear Co., Inc. v. N.L.R.B., 329 F.2d 417 (5th Cir.1964); N.L.R.B. v. Minnesota Mining & Mfg. Co., 179 F.2d 323 (8th Cir.1950).

Absent unusual circumstances, the polling of employees by an employer will be violative of Section 8(a)(1) of the Act unless the following safeguards are observed: (1) the purpose of the poll is to determine the truth of a union's claim of majority, (2) this purpose is communicated to the employees, (3) assurances against reprisal are given, (4) the employees are polled by secret ballot, and (5) the employer has not engaged in unfair labor practices or otherwise created a coercive atmosphere.

The purpose of the polling in these circumstances is clearly relevant to an issue raised by a union's claim for recognition and is therefore lawful. The requirement that the lawful purpose be communicated to the employees, along with assurances against reprisal, is designed to allay any fear of discrimination which might otherwise arise from the polling, and any tendency to interfere with employees' Section 7 rights. Secrecy of the ballot will give further assurance that reprisals cannot be taken against employees because the views of each individual will not be known. And the absence of employer unfair labor practices or other conduct creating a coercive atmosphere will serve as a further warranty to the employees that the poll does not have some unlawful object, contrary to the lawful purpose stated by the employer. In accord with presumptive rules applied by the Board with court approval in other situations, this rule is designed to effectuate the purposes of the Act by maintaining a reasonable balance between the protection of employee rights and legitimate interests of employers.

On the other hand, a poll taken while a petition for a Board election is pending does not, in our view, serve any legitimate interest of the employer that would not be better served by the forthcoming Board election. In accord with long-established Board policy, therefore, such polls will continue to be found violative of Section 8(a)(1) of the Act.

B.  *The Polling Issue in the Instant Case*

    \* \* \*

We have reviewed the circumstances of this poll in the light of the court's opinion and remand order and also of the rule established herein. In view of the failure of the Respondent to inform its employees of the purpose of the poll and the nonsecret manner in which the employees were polled, the Respondent's conduct would probably be found unlawful if this case were now before us for an initial determination under the new rule. We are satisfied, however, that in the special circumstances of this case no remedial order is warranted. Thus the poll previously was found lawful by the Board under the *Blue Flash* rule, which was in effect at the time the events herein occurred. Moreover, as the court noted in its opinion, the work at the jobsite where the poll was taken apparently was scheduled to be concluded within 3 months after these events took place, which was more than 3 years ago. All things considered, we find in these circumstances that effectuation of the purposes of the Act does not require a remedial order.

Accordingly, we shall reaffirm the Board's original Decision and Order dismissing the complaint in its entirety.

———

## PROBLEMS FOR DISCUSSION

**1.** What are the respective merits and disadvantages of the rather firm guidelines developed by the Board on remand in *Struksnes* and the more flexible guidelines mandated by the court of appeals in *Lorben*? In making that appraisal, you should consider such matters as the impact of these different guidelines upon the parties engaging in an organizing or election campaign, the Regional Director in issuing a complaint, the Administrative Law Judge and the Board in making their decision and the courts of appeals in reviewing that decision.

**2.** More particularly, would the *Struksnes* guidelines withstand judicial review? (As an initial matter, are they "rules" improperly adopted?) For example, assume that an employer, in an atmosphere free of coercion and discrimination, polls all of its employees to verify a union's majority claim, explains the reason to each employee and assures them all that no reprisals will follow; however, the poll is taken face-to-face on the shop floor by the department foreman. Will the Board find an unfair labor practice? If so, will this not simply be a rule barring all non-anonymous questioning as per se coercive? Will this likely be sustained on judicial review? Consider p. 187, item 8, infra.

**3.** Does a *union* violate Section 8(b)(1) of the NLRA by making home visits to employees and gathering authorization-card signatures there and on the shop floor? Are there material differences—either in the statutory language or in the dynamics of the situation—when the *employer* similarly asks employees to make their union attitudes known? See Louis–Allis Co. v. NLRB, 463 F.2d 512 (7th Cir.1972); Kusan Mfg. Co. v. District Lodge 155, 267 NLRB 740 (1983).

**4.** The Board distinguishes between cases involving an employer's comprehensive polling of large groups of workers, in which the *Struksnes* guidelines are applied, and cases involving the non-anonymous questioning, often spontaneous, of an individual employee about his or her union sympathies; in the latter situation, the Board asks whether the individual (or onlookers) would reasonably feel coerced "under all the circumstances."

Suppose the company wishes to make a video to show its workforce that their co-workers are satisfied and do not feel the need for union representation. To do so, it must secure permission from the employees to record them; and, to do that it must tell them the video will be used as part of an anti-union campaign. May it ask for that purpose? See Allegheny Ludlum Corp., 333 N.L.R.B. No. 109 (2000). May a union videotape *its* supporters? See Overnite Transp. Co. v. NLRB, 140 F.3d 259 (D.C.Cir.1998). May it videotape its supporters seeking signatures on a pro-union petition? *See* Randell Warehouse of Arizona, Inc. v. NLRB, 2001 WL 640644 (D.C.Cir. 2001).

**5.** Does the following conduct by an employer violate Section 8(a)(1)?

(a) After being informed of a union strike vote, the employer—a large, overcrowded hospital—submits questionnaires to all employees asking them whether, in the event of a strike, they intend to report to work. The employer's purpose is to plan by arranging for reassignments, overtime and replacements. See Preterm, Inc. v. District 1199, 240 NLRB 654 (1979).

(b) Learning that a union organizer has taken a room in a local motel, the employer plants an inconspicuous electronic surveillance device against the motel wall, enabling the company to learn which employees are sympathetic to the union; all persons in the motel room are unaware of the intrusion. See NLRB v. J.P. Stevens & Co., 563 F.2d 8 (2d Cir.1977), cert. denied, 434 U.S. 1064, 98 S.Ct. 1240, 55 L.Ed.2d 765 (1978); St. Mary's Hospital, 316 NLRB 947 (1995).

**6.** According to a 1999 survey, 38% of employers monitor their employees e-mail and internet use for a variety of business purposes: to protect trade secrets, to prevent sexual harassment, to assure work time is spent on work and the like. Some employers monitor internet chat-boards for remarks critical of the company. May a company monitor its system for "gripes"? Monitor websites for remarks critical of the Company or of its officers, managers or supervisors? Konop v. Hawaiian Airlines, Inc., 236 F.3d 1035 (9th Cir.2001).

———

# NLRB v. Exchange Parts Co.[h]

375 U.S. 405, 84 S.Ct. 457, 11 L.Ed.2d 435 (1964).

■ MR. JUSTICE HARLAN delivered the opinion of the Court.

This case presents a question concerning the limitations which § 8(a)(1) of the National Labor Relations Act, 49 Stat. 452 (1935), as amended, 29 U.S.C. § 158(a)(1), places on the right of an employer to confer economic benefits on his employees shortly before a representation election. The precise issue is whether that section prohibits the conferral of such benefits, without more, where the employer's purpose is to affect the outcome of the election. * * *

[On November 9, 1959, the Company was advised by the Boilermakers Union that a majority of employees had designated it as their bargaining representative. On November 16, the Union filed an election petition with the NLRB, and an election was ultimately ordered to be held on March 18, 1960. On March 4, the Company sent its employees a letter, accompanied by a detailed statement of the benefits granted by the Company since 1949; the letter made such statements as "The Union can't put any of those things in your envelope—*only the Company can do that.* * * * [I]t didn't take a Union to get any of those things and * * * it won't take a Union to get additional improvements in the future." Included in the statement of benefits for 1960 were a new system for computing overtime during holiday weeks which had the effect of increasing wages for those weeks, and a new vacation schedule which enabled employees to extend their vacations by sandwiching them between two weekends. This was the first general announcement of these changes to the employees. The Union lost the election.

**h.** See Jackson & Heller, Promises and     U.Pa.L.Rev. 1 (1982).
Grants of Benefits Under the NLRA, 131

[The Board found that the announcement and grant of the overtime and vacation benefits were arranged with the intention of inducing the employees to vote against the union, and held this to violate Section 8(a)(1). The court of appeals accepted the finding regarding the Company's intention but reversed the Board, noting that "the benefits were put into effect unconditionally on a permanent basis, and no one has suggested that there was any implication the benefits would be withdrawn, if the workers voted for the union." The Supreme Court reversed.]

The broad purpose of § 8(a)(1) is to establish "the right of employes to organize for mutual aid without employer interference." Republic Aviation Corp. v. N.L.R.B., 324 U.S. 793, 798, 65 S.Ct. 982, 985, 89 L.Ed. 1372. We have no doubt that it prohibits not only intrusive threats and promises but also conduct immediately favorable to employees which is undertaken with the express purpose of impinging upon their freedom of choice for or against unionization and is reasonably calculated to have that effect. In Medo Photo Supply Corp. v. N.L.R.B., 321 U.S. 678, 686, 64 S.Ct. 830, 834, 88 L.Ed. 1007, this Court said: "The action of employees with respect to the choice of their bargaining agents may be induced by favors bestowed by the employer as well as by his threats or domination." Although in that case there was already a designated bargaining agent and the offer of "favors" was in response to a suggestion of the employees that they would leave the union if favors were bestowed, the principles which dictated the result there are fully applicable here. The danger inherent in well-timed increases in benefits is the suggestion of a fist inside the velvet glove. Employees are not likely to miss the inference that the source of benefits now conferred is also the source from which future benefits must flow and which may dry up if it is not obliged.[3] The danger may be diminished if, as in this case, the benefits are conferred permanently and unconditionally. But the absence of conditions or threats pertaining to the particular benefits conferred would be of controlling significance only if it could be presumed that no question of additional benefits or renegotiation of existing benefits would arise in the future; and, of course, no such presumption is tenable.

Other Courts of Appeals have found a violation of § 8(a)(1) in the kind of conduct involved here. * * * It is true, as the court below pointed out, that in most cases of this kind the increase in benefits could be regarded as "one part of an overall program of interference and restraint by the employer," 304 F.2d, at 372, and that in this case the questioned conduct stood in isolation. Other unlawful conduct may often be an indication of the motive behind a grant of benefits while an election is pending, and to that

---

**3.** The inference was made almost explicit in Exchange Parts' letter to its employees of March 4, already quoted, which said: "The Union can't put any of those * * * [benefits] in your envelope—*only the Company can do that.*" (Original italics.) We place no reliance, however, on these or other words of the respondent dissociated from its con-

duct. Section 8(c) of the Act, 61 Stat. 142 (1947), 29 U.S.C. § 158(c), provides that the expression or dissemination of "any views, argument, or opinion" "shall not constitute or be evidence of an unfair labor practice under any of the provisions of this Act, if such expression contains no threat of reprisal or force or promise of benefit."

extent it is relevant to the legality of the grant; but when as here the motive is otherwise established, an employer is not free to violate § 8(a)(1) by conferring benefits simply because it refrains from other, more obvious violations. We cannot agree with the Court of Appeals that enforcement of the Board's order will have the "ironic" result of "discouraging benefits for labor." 304 F.2d, at 376. The beneficence of an employer is likely to be ephemeral if prompted by a threat of unionization which is subsequently removed. Insulating the right of collective organization from calculated good will of this sort deprives employees of little that has lasting value.

*Reversed.*

---

PROBLEMS FOR DISCUSSION

**1.** Why is a promise of benefit linked in Section 8(c) with a threat of reprisal, both being excluded from the protection of that section of the Act? When a union promises benefits contingent upon being elected bargaining representative, is there a violation of Section 8(b)(1)(or an exclusion from the protection of Section 8(c))?

**2.** When Justice Harlan in *Exchange Parts* considers an outright grant of a benefit, as distinguished from a promise to grant it if the union loses, how does he (and the other Justices) know that such a grant will be understood by employees to be an intrusive threat? If you were an employee and witnessed your employer granting an unprecedented benefit on the eve of a representation election, would you be intimidated?

**3.** Meshgear, Inc. has six plants; none is unionized. In the fall of 2001, in the wake of especially high absenteeism and quit-rates at its plant in Tennessee, it commissioned a study of working conditions by an outside consultant. He found the wage rates to be substantially below area standards and recommended a fifteen percent across-the-board increase. Meshgear had given wage increases in all its plants in 1993, 1996 and 1999. It had been considering a five percent increase in all of them to take effect in March 2002. The Machinists' Union started an organizing drive in the Tennessee plant just before the consultant's report was given to the Company. The Company has consulted you as counsel. It seeks your advice on what wage increases it can grant at any of its plants, including especially the Tennessee plant, and what it may say by letter or in a speech to the employees about their wage situation. What advice would you give? See Marshall Durbin Poultry Co. v. NLRB, 39 F.3d 1312 (5th Cir.1994); NLRB v. Circo Resorts, Inc., 646 F.2d 403 (9th Cir.1981).

**4.** The management of Acme Manufacturing Co. called ten meetings with employees in the one-month period prior to the date set for a Board-supervised representation election. Although attendance was voluntary, almost all of the employees attended these meetings. Meetings of this kind had not been held in the past and, with the exception of the plant manager, the management representatives at the meetings were not previously known to the employees. The president of Acme told the employees that the union organizing campaign had brought home to her the fact that employees might have some legitimate complaints. She refrained from specifically soliciting such complaints at these meetings, and in fact stated that while she had an open mind she was making no promises that action would be taken on any or all complaints. When the president opened up the meetings for questions and discussion, the employees inevitably began to air certain of their grievances, which led to further discourse (sometimes quite vigorous) between employees and management representatives. The union narrowly lost the election and, arguing that the meetings unlawfully interfered with employee rights, has sought a rerun election. How should the Board rule? Compare Raley's, Inc. v. Retail Clerks Union, 236 NLRB 971 (1978), enf'd mem., 608 F.2d 1374 (9th Cir.1979), with Clare Community Hospital v. Michigan Nurses Association, 273 NLRB 1755 (1985).

**5.** In Atlantic Limousine, Inc., 331 NLRB No. 134 (2000), the Board comprehensively reviewed its prior authority and announced a new policy barring employers and unions from holding raffles on the day of a representation election if,

> (1) eligibility to participate in the raffle or win prizes is in any way tied to voting in the election or being at the election site on election day or (2) the raffle is conducted at any time during a period beginning 24 hours before the scheduled opening of the polls and ending with the closing of the polls. The term "conducting a raffle" includes the following: (1) announcing a raffle; (2) distributing raffle tickets; (3) identifying the raffle winners; and (4) awarding the raffle prizes.

It announced that any violation would result in setting the election aside. Further, the Board said that it "will also look with disfavor on attempts to circumvent this rule by, for example, announcing a raffle more than 24 hours before the opening of the polls and then completing the raffle immediately after the closing of the polls." Is a raffle a "promise of benefit"?

---

## 4.  UNION MISCONDUCT AFFECTING SELF–ORGANIZATION

Most important of all the Taft–Hartley amendments affecting the establishment of collective bargaining relationships was the creation of a list of unfair labor practices by labor organizations. The heart of the original Wagner Act was contained in Section 7—

> "Employees shall have the right to self-organization, to form, join, or assist labor organizations, to bargain collectively through representatives of their own choosing, and to engage in concerted activities, for the purpose of collective bargaining or other mutual aid or protection."

In passing the original act Congress rejected the argument that mutuality required a grant of protection against interference, coercion and restraint by labor organizations as well as by employers; and although this decision was often defended on the ground that it would bring about federal intervention in matters better regulated by local police authorities, the true ground of objection was that such a measure would be inconsistent with the policy of encouraging union organization and collective bargaining.

The Taft–Hartley amendments remade Section 7 by guaranteeing employees, in addition to the right to form, join or assist labor organizations, "the right to refrain from any or all such activities". Moreover, Section 8(b)(1) declares it to be an unfair labor practice for a labor organization or its agents to restrain or coerce employees in the exercise of rights guaranteed by Section 7. Section 8(b)(4) prohibits various concerted activities to bring about unionization.

The psychological effect of this reversal of policy cut wide and deep into industrial relations. Since these amendments seem to declare the indifference of the government to the spread of organization, they remove one of the most effective arguments of the union organizer, who had theretofore been in a position to appeal to unorganized workers on the ground that in joining a labor union they would follow their government's desires. The practical impact of this group of amendments on techniques of organization is also important. For example, Section 8(b)(4) forbids the use of the secondary boycott to achieve recognition and also (as expanded in 1959 in Section 8(b)(7)) prohibits certain primary strikes and picketing by unions seeking immediate recognition and bargaining rights. These and related union violations in aid of organization are considered in detail in Part Four of this casebook.

Still other union organizational tactics are proscribed by Section 8(b)(1), also enacted in 1947. Its position and language, except for the omission of the words "interfere with," roughly parallel those of Section 8(a)(1), and its sponsors repeatedly explained that it would make it unfair for unions to engage in activities which were unfair when engaged in by employers.[i] But the scope of Section 8(b)(1) is very much narrower than that of Section 8(a)(1). One great difference is this: although an employer is forbidden to express the hope that it may be able to raise wages and improve working conditions if the union is defeated, an important argument made by labor organizations to secure union members, the legitimacy of which cannot be questioned, is that if enough employees join the union it will be able to obtain additional advantages whereas if they do not, it may be unable to prevent a reduction in wages. Many unions offer mutual insurance and similar benefits to their members in addition to what is obtained by collective bargaining. It cannot be the intent of Section 8(b)(1) to prohibit them from pointing out these advantages in seeking to enlist new members. Much the same is true of social pressures. While an employer may not segregate a union employee in order to hold him up to the ridicule of his fellows, it will scarcely be asserted that labor organizations are forbidden to ostracize nonmembers or to impose other social pressures upon them.

---

**i.** 93 Cong.Rec. 4136, 4500. In its original form the amendment, following the exact words of Section 8(a)(1), made it an unfair labor practice for a labor organization "to interfere with, restrain or coerce" employees in the exercise of the rights guaranteed by Section 7, Supplemental Views of Senator Taft and Others, S.Rep. 105, 80th Cong., 1st Sess., p. 50; 93 Cong.Rec. 4136. Senator Ives opposed this amendment as "definitely anti-labor". 93 Cong.Rec. 4139–4140. Five days later he stated that it would be acceptable if the words "interfere with" were struck out.

93 Cong.Rec. 4399. The deletion was made without objection on the basis of Senator Taft's statement that "elimination of the words 'Interfere with' would not, so far as they ['the attorneys'] know, have any effect on the court decisions. Elimination of those words would not make any substantial change in the meaning". 93 Cong.Rec. 4399. Moreover, as Senator Morse pointed out on the floor, the National Labor Relations Board appears never to have distinguished between interference and coercion or restraint. 93 Cong.Rec. 4557.

In many cases, however, especially those involving fraud or intimidation, the two sections operate alike. The NLRB Annual Report for the year ending June 30, 1950, gives a summary of typical cases under Section 8(b)(1)(A):

"Union conduct not connected with strikes was held violative of section 8(b)(1)(A) where it was found to have been reasonably calculated to coerce employees in maintaining or refraining from acquiring union membership. Thus, the Board * * * held coercive: a speech in front of an employer's store informing the audience that the union intended to organize the store and 'that wives and children of employees had better stay out of the way if they didn't want to get hurt'; a union president's warning to rival union supporters not to come to work, accompanied by such threats as that there would be 'trouble out there, guns, knives, and blackjacks'; assaults and batteries on nonunion employees during an organizational campaign; and a union official's remark to an employee, in the course of an organizational drive, that 'there may be trouble later' if the employees refused to sign a dues checkoff authorization."

It should be noted at this point that Section 8(b)(1)(A) serves two other important functions, typically outside the context of organizing activities. It protects workers who are already union members against disciplinary action taken by the union—such as expulsion, suspension or fines—for certain classes of protected employee activities. (See pp. 1140–67, infra.) It also provides a remedy before the NLRB for some forms of discrimination or oppression by a union representative against unpopular individuals or minority groups. (See pp. 1037–39, infra.)

The Labor Act also imposes some limits upon the extent to which a union may induce discrimination by the employer in aid of organization (see Section 8(b)(2) and pp. 1125–40, infra), and upon the extent to which a union may use promises of benefit.

The latter issue was explored by the Supreme Court in NLRB v. SAVAIR MFG. CO., 414 U.S. 270, 94 S.Ct. 495, 38 L.Ed.2d 495 (1973). There, in the course of an organizing campaign, a union solicited "recognition slips" from the employees; if they signed before the election, they would not have to pay any union initiation fee (sometimes referred to by the union as a "fine"), but those who did not sign were told they would have to pay the full fee if the union won the election. The union won the election, 22–20, but the employer refused to bargain, claiming that the election was invalidated by the union's "fee waiver" arrangement. The NLRB disagreed, finding that an employee induced by the fee waiver to sign a recognition slip in advance of the election (even though in fact opposing the union) would nonetheless feel completely free to vote against the union thereafter, particularly when a union loss would obviously mean that the employee would have no obligation to join the union or pay union dues. The Board therefore found that the fee waiver did not unfairly affect the election results. The Board also thought that the union had a legitimate interest in tendering such waivers, because many otherwise sympathetic employees could well be reluctant to pay money to the union before it had had an opportunity to do anything for the employees in return.

The Supreme Court disagreed. "By permitting the union to offer to waive an initiation fee for those employees signing a recognition slip prior to the election, the Board allows the union to buy endorsements and paint a false portrait of employee support during its election campaign." The Court found this to undermine the statutory policy of fair elections. Moreover, contrary to the Board's speculations, "certainly there may be some employees who would feel obliged to carry through on their stated intention to support the union" once having signed recognition slips, so that there would in fact be an incursion upon those employees' voting freedom. Referring to its decision in *Exchange Parts* regarding the coercive implications of employer benefits, the Court concluded: "The failure to sign a recognition slip may well seem ominous to nonunionists who fear that if they do not sign they will face a wrathful union regime, should the union win. That influence may well have had a decisive impact in this case where a change of one vote would have changed the result." (The Court refrained, however, from deciding whether the union's promise of a special benefit for promptly joining would constitute an unfair labor practice under section 8(b)(1).)

---

## PROBLEMS FOR DISCUSSION

**1.**  Re-examine the opinion of the Supreme Court in NLRB v. Exchange Parts Co., at page 179, supra. What would the Court's analysis have been had the *union* in the course of its organizing campaign promised employees increased overtime pay during holiday weeks and increased vacation pay, and the employer later sought to set aside a union election victory for that reason? See Smith Co., 192 NLRB 1098 (1971).

**2.**  The union promised to waive payment of dues and initiation fees until after a certification election and until it had negotiated an agreement with the employer. The union won the election 50–43. The employer refused to bargain, claiming that the union was able to "buy" employee-members before the election and portray a false picture of its employee support in violation of *Savair* and that therefore the election should be set aside. The Board, in a proceeding under Section 8(a)(5) for refusal to bargain, has rejected the employer's argument and issued a bargaining order. Should the Board's order be enforced on review? See NLRB v. Wabash Transformer Corp., 509 F.2d 647 (8th Cir.1975). During an election campaign, may a Union offer employees a free, all expense paid weekend in a city (Chicago) ostensibly to attend a union seminar to be held after the election? May it offer a "victory party" on the evening of the election? Comcast Cablevision–Taylor v. NLRB, 232 F.3d 490 (6th Cir.2000).

**3.**  At a rally on the eve of a representation election, attended by about a third of the employees involved, the Union announced that it had filed a class action lawsuit on behalf of the employees. The Union's lawyer explained the legal theory of the suit and that it would be "a long and difficult battle," but that if they were to prevail each employee might collect as much as $35,000. The Union won the election. Should the election be set aside? Assume that the argument for setting the election aside was that

> [O]nce the Union's attorney filed the . . . suit for the employees, the employees might vote for the Union because the employees hoped that the attorney would continue to pursue that particular suit, rather than because the Union's overall representation of the employees—at the negotiating table with the employer, with insurance companies, with legislators, and so forth—merited election.

*See* Nestle Ice Cream Co. v. NLRB, 46 F.3d 578 (6th Cir.1995), and Freund Baking Co. v. NLRB, 165 F.3d 928 (D.C.Cir.1999).

A number of commentators have considered the future role of labor unions vis-a-vis the large number of non-unionized employees. (The future of the Labor Act and of labor unions is considered in greater detail in Part IX, infra.) Some have argued for unions to assist the unrepresented in the vindication of their legal rights; this because the workplace is much more the subject of legal regulation today than at the time the Labor Act was passed, because the unrepresented may find it difficult to secure competent legal representation, and because the provision of such services might establish a beachhead for future representation under the Act. See Rabin, The Role of Unions in the Rights–Based Workplace, 25 U.S.F.L. Rev. 169 (1991); Gottesman, In Despair, Starting Over: Imagining a Labor Law for Unorganized Workers in The Legal Future of Employee Representation 57 (M. Finkin ed. 1994). If the election above is to be set aside, would the result impede the ability of unions to function as such service providers?

----

## 5.  AN EMPIRICAL POSTSCRIPT

As has already been mentioned, many of the Board's assumptions relating to the impact of election campaigns have been challenged as the result of a major empirical study, in Getman, Goldberg & Herman, *Union Representation Elections: Law and Reality* (1976). An attempt will be made here to summarize the findings and conclusions of those authors, although a full appreciation of their work will depend upon the student's examination of the complete book.

1.  Most workers are not unsophisticated about union organizing campaigns; a very substantial number have been union members elsewhere and a large number have voted in previous NLRB elections.

2.  Most workers have firm opinions about whether or not they want a union, even before the campaign has begun; these opinions are based on general attitudes about working conditions and unions. The votes of 81 percent of the employees could be predicted from their pre-campaign attitudes and intent.

3.  The amount of authorization cards signed by employees is a reasonably accurate predictor of their vote in a subsequent NLRB election. 72 percent of the employees who signed cards later voted for union representation. 79 percent of the employees who did not sign cards later voted against union representation.

4. Employees are not generally attentive to the campaign. The average employee in the study remembered fewer than 10 percent of the company campaign themes and 7 percent of the union themes. There is no evidence that specific issues of the employer's campaign were related to employee vote; initial union supporters who switched to the company were no more familiar with the company campaign than those who did not switch. Such a switch is not caused by greater information supplied by the company during the campaign or by employer coercion; rather, the employee's dissatisfaction with working conditions apparently lessens. Only the small percentage of employees who started as company supporters but ultimately vote for the union appear to fit the NLRB stereotype of the employee who is convinced by the campaign issues; such employees are significantly more familiar with the union campaign than company supporters who did not switch.

5. Although some 20 percent of the employees questioned reported employer threats of reprisals, or actual reprisals, against union supporters, this perception was unrelated to actual employer threats and reprisals. Even when employees are not reminded by the employer of its economic power and the ability to use it against union supporters, employees are aware of those facts. Lawful employer speech can just as effectively generate fears of reprisal, so that it is not surprising that employer campaigning viewed by the Board as potentially coercive and unlawful is not any more associated with a loss of union support than is "clean" campaigning. Indeed, persons starting out as union supporters are unaffected by threats or reprisals, as they have in effect anticipated these in making their initial decision to support the union; such employer action is regarded as confirmation of the need for protection by a union. Unions do not lose significantly more of their initial supporters in elections marked by very serious employer coercion than in elections in which there is no unlawful campaigning.

6. The promise or grant of benefits—even in conjunction with employer reprisals—does not increase the perception or fear of reprisals, in comparison to "clean" employer campaigns. Such promises or grants are regarded as untrustworthy or as inadequate compared to the expected benefits of unionization. Employees who reported promises and grants of benefit were actually more likely to vote for union representation than were other employees.

7. Any discharge of a union supporter during an organizing campaign is likely to be viewed by other union supporters as having been motivated by the employer's anti-union sentiments, whether or not that was in fact the case. That view does not, however, coerce such workers into voting against the union. In fact, employees reporting such a discriminatory discharge were more likely to vote for the union than employees not reporting such action.

8. Although illegal interrogation took place in some sixteen of the elections studied (involving more than 400 employees), and general interrogation was widespread in those elections, only 29 employees reported that

interrogation had taken place. Employees appear not to be sensitive to interrogation—indeed, some 43 percent of the union voters believed that the employer was fully aware of their position on unionization anyway—and it seems unlikely that interrogation is a substantial deterrent to union support.

9. In spite of the assumption in *Savair* that employees who are inclined to vote against the union will submerge that inclination once it is known that they have signed an authorization card, there is no empirical support for such an assumption. Nor does there appear to be any significant relationship between the proportion of authorization cards initially signed and a subsequent gain in union strength by the time of the election.

10. These and other conclusions induced the authors to make the following recommendations: (a) NLRB campaign regulations should not be based on Board assumptions about the impact of particular campaign practices. (b) As in a political campaign, labor elections should not be set aside (or unfair labor practices found) on account of written or oral campaign communications by employers or unions; the right of rebuttal, and voter intelligence, should be relied upon, rather than the government, to uncover invalid and irrelevant communications. (c) Express or implied threats and promises should not be unlawful and should not be a basis for invalidating an election; even discriminatory discharges should not justify invalidating an election, although there should of course be unfair labor practice redress for the discriminatee. (d) If an employer holds campaign meetings, or permits individual campaigning by supervisors, on company premises, it should be required to afford the union an equal opportunity. (e) Since flagrant retaliatory *acts* by an employer (as distinguished from speech) may have the effect of seriously chilling incipient union support, NLRB unfair labor practice remedies should be strengthened so as to include preliminary injunctive relief to obtain reinstatement of discharged employees, treble damages for lost earnings, and loss of government contracts.

A number of the most significant findings of the Getman, Goldberg & Herman study were confirmed in an election study by Professor Laura Cooper, in "Authorization Cards and Union Representation Election Outcome: An Empirical Assessment of the Assumption Underlying the Supreme Court's *Gissel* Decision," 79 Northwestern Univ.L.Rev. 87 (1984). Professor Cooper studied nearly 800 elections conducted over a three-year period in the Minneapolis Regional Office of the NLRB, and paid particular attention to the relationship between authorization cards gathered by the union and the ultimate election outcome. Contrary to the Board's usual assumption, the Cooper study found no reason to believe that the commission of employer unfair labor practices decreased union support. Indeed there was some reason to conclude that such illegal employer conduct actually contributed to union support; this was particularly the case in "close" elections (in which the union received between 45 and 55 percent of the votes).

In close elections, where unfair labor practices were committed, unions *gained* an average of 7.9% yet where no unfair labor practices were committed, unions *lost* an average of 8.1% of their support. Thus, in close elections, where the only statistically significant evidence of an impact of unfair labor practices on union support was found, the evidence is completely contrary to the Board's assumption that employer unfair labor practices cause unions to lose support. Of course, this study provided no means to ascertain why employer unfair labor practices tended to increase support for the union in these elections. Nevertheless, one can speculate that perhaps employees, rather than being intimidated out of voting for the union by the employer's actions, considered such actions further cause for seeking the protection of the union.

Other significant conclusions of the Cooper study can be summarized. Of the variables studied as a predictor of election outcome, authorization cards were the most reliable, but there is a significant drop-off from cards to pro-union votes: "Only when a union had cards from more than 60% of employees did it achieve at least an even chance of winning the election. * * * Unions with authorization cards from 90–100% of the employees * * * won only 65.7% of the time." Employee support for the union was not significantly eroded by the use of labor consultants (although the likelihood of discriminatory employer conduct did increase). Union support does decrease, however, the larger the turnout of the voters; "unions do worst in elections with extremely high turnouts, which comprise the vast majority of elections."

> The only additional factors that have a demonstrable, although smaller, impact on election results were bargaining unit size, length of time from card signing to election, and weekday on which the election was held. The larger the bargaining unit, the smaller was the union's chance of success. Delay between card signing and the election also decreased the union's chance of success. Holding elections on a Friday, rather than another day of the week, lessened the likelihood of a union victory. * * * Correlations presented here revealed no significant difference in election outcomes or in union vote loss between clean elections and elections with unfair labor practices. * * * [T]he Board, while retaining other remedies for specific employer unfair labor practices, need not automatically set aside the results of elections in which such conduct occurs. [I]f abandoning the remedy for employer unfair labor practices of setting elections aside decreases deterrence, the Board should be authorized to seek imposition of harsher penalties, including fines, upon employers.

The conclusions of the Getman–Goldberg–Herman study have not, however, gained unanimous endorsement. Critics of the study have pointed to both methodological and interpretive flaws. A number of commentators, for example, have questioned the soundness of drawing sample elections exclusively from "hotly contested cases," i.e., elections in which there was a high likelihood of vigorous and even illegal campaigning. See Eames, "An Analysis of the Union Voting Study from a Trade Unionist's Point of View," 28 Stan.L.Rev. 1181 (1976); Kochan, "Legal Nonsense, Empirical Examination and Policy Evaluation," 29 Stan.L.Rev. 1115 (1976); Roomkin, Book Review, 27 Case W.Res.L.Rev. 1056 (1977). This is thought to skew the survey in two respects. First, it did not provide a control group of a benign election atmosphere; "the study provides no data indicating how a group of voters act in the *absence* of threats" (Eames, supra, at 1182). Second, because the samples in the Getman–Goldberg–Herman study were selected because "something in the employers' history suggested that vigorous campaigns might take place," the pre-disposed employee attitudes uncovered in the study may have stemmed at least in part from previous employer behavior in the face of imminent unionization. (Kochan, supra, at 1119.)

Other critics focused on the fact that the Getman–Goldberg–Herman sample was drawn from only a small number of campaigns in one sector of the country (Phalen, "The Demise of *Hollywood Ceramics*: Fact and Fantasy," 46 U.Cinn.L.Rev. 450, 457–59 (1977)); or the fact that it covered only a nineteen-month period, during which peculiar economic conditions might have affected the results (Roomkin, supra, at 1061). Commentators also pointed out that each election in the Getman study was observed within an extremely limited time frame; the authors defined the campaign as beginning with the election order and did not conduct the initial wave of employee interviews until roughly three weeks before the election. It has thus been suggested that much of the campaign had in fact taken place before, when the organizing began, and that many employees had "already moved to the poles of their polarization before the study began" thus accounting for the very limited change of mind discovered in the Getman–Goldberg–Herman study. (Eames, supra, at 1185; Martin, "Employee Characteristics and Representation Election Outcomes," 38 Indus. & Lab. Rel. Rev. 365 (1985).)

Even if the methodological objections are overcome, continue some critics, the data derived from the Getman study do not support the authors' conclusions. Eames concluded that employee preference changes were more pronounced and that they varied to a greater degree than suggested in the study. Thus, in the "most successful company campaigns," the union lost 35% of its card signers by the time of the election, while in the "most successful union campaigns," the union gained 10% between signing and voting. Eames concluded that this variance "certainly indicates to me that the campaign makes a difference." (Eames, supra, at 1190.)

Other commentators, noting that many NLRB elections are decided by relatively small margins, have taken issue with the Getman–Goldberg–Herman conclusion that the number of voters swayed by the campaign was "statistically insignificant" and thus of no consequence. In Flanagan, "The Behavioral Foundations of Union Election Regulation," 28 Stan. L. Rev. 1195 (1976), the author points out that even assuming the reliability of the study's figures, at least 580 Board elections each year (of the 9000 conducted) are determined by campaign activity. Phalen, supra, notes that the "undecideds" discounted in the study provided the margin of victory in a full one-third of the elections surveyed. Freedman & Medoff, in their significant work, *What Do Unions Do?* (1984) (at pages 236–37), concluded: "[E]ven modest statistical effects on individual voters can cumulate to have powerful effects on the proportion of elections won by unions. Viewed from this perspective, the Getman–Goldberg–Herman data are consistent with, rather than inconsistent with" studies showing that employer campaigning is a major determinant of NLRB election results.

For responses to their critics, see Goldberg, Getman & Brett, "Union Representation Elections: Law and Reality: The Authors Respond to the Critics," 79 Mich. L. Rev. 564 (1981); and "The Relationship Between Free Choice and Labor Board Doctrine: Differing Empirical Approaches," 79 Northwestern U. L. Rev. 721 (1984).

---

## B.  Company Domination or Assistance[j]

In furtherance of the Act's purposes to protect the exercise of employee associational rights and to ensure to them freedom of choice concerning whether and by whom to be represented, Section 8(a)(2) forbids employers to dominate, assist or to interfere with the formation or administration of any labor organization. The purpose and rationale behind these statutory prohibitions can best be understood when considered in historical context.

As noted in Part I, the "labor question" was deeply vexing to reformers at the turn of the century. Progressive employers like Henry Dennison and the Filenes, reform-minded lawyers like Louis Brandeis, churchmen like Washington Gladden, as well as labor relations specialists, all struggled with a way to bring democracy to industry. As Woodrow Wilson observed in his Presidential Message of May 20, 1919:

> The object of all reform in this essential matter must be the genuine democratization of industry, based upon a full recognition of the right of those who work, in whatever rank, to participate in some organic way in every decision which directly affects their welfare and the part they are to play in industry. Some positive legislation is practicable.

58 Cong.Rev. 40 (1919). A student of the period has explained:

> The great variety of programs of industrial democracy were animated by a great variety of motives. Some advocates wanted a Christian capitalism, some wanted to fight off the trade unions, and others wanted a new social order. Fundamentally, these pro-

---

**j.** For useful background, *see* Note, New Standards for Domination and Support Under Section 8(a)(2), 82 Yale L.J. 510 (1973); Kohler, Models of Worker Partic- ipation: The Uncertain Significance of Sec- tion 8(a)(2), 27 Boston Col. L. Rev. 499 (1986). Some of the more salient recent liter- ature is noted in Part IX, infra.

grams were of two kinds: those which seemed to challenge the traditional source of authority in the factory and those which left it intact, and perhaps even strengthened it.

The most popular primer of the second group was John Leitch's *Man to Man*. Reading the book today, without the assumptions of 1919, one finds it difficult to understand how so many thoughtful men could have taken Leitch so seriously.... He transferred the apparatus of a modified American constitution to the factory. There was a "House of Representatives," usually elected by a meeting of all employees below the rank of foreman; a "Senate," consisting of superintendents and foreman; and a "Cabinet," composed of executive officers and presided over by the president.... Of course, this was closer to Alexander Hamilton's ideal government than to Brandeis'. Leitch wished to have the worker see his employer, and the employer see himself, as the executive of the workers' best interest.

S. Haber, Efficiency and Uplift 124–125 (1964).

Thus, well before the passage of the National Industrial Recovery Act in 1933 there was a flowering of interest in and experimentation with employee representation committees and works councils. See generally E. Burton, Employee Representation (1926), and C. French, The Shop Committee in the United States (1923). Some, like the plan instituted by John D. Rockefeller, Jr. at the Colorado Fuel and Iron Company (after the infamous "Ludlow Massacre" of 1914), were plainly intended to keep unions out. Others, such as the very extensive plan at the Filene store in Boston, were intended to involve employees in the enterprise and to give them the sense of having an interest in its success. See M. LaDamme, The Filene Store (1930). But whether a well-intentioned system of meaningful employee participation, or a device to create an employer-controlled sham of a labor union, both became fixed with the label of "company union."

Proponents of these arrangements offered them as a method of group dealing that would establish an atmosphere of mutual trust through improved communication with employees, thereby securing employee identity and cooperation with management's goals. Underlying these schemes was the premise that there are no fundamental conflicts of interest between management and workers; hence they were promoted as an alternative to the adversarial model of industrial relations collective bargaining represents. "Company unions" consisted essentially of two distinct types. Until the early 1930s, the prevailing form involved the use of joint committees on which both employee and management representatives served. Typically, management unilaterally promulgated and implemented the plan, often in response to an "outside" organizational effort. Generally consisting of equal numbers of employee and management representatives with equal voting power, these committees functioned primarily as a forum for discussion and consultation; final decisional authority over the committees' recommendations usually remained in management. Normally, employee representatives met only when management was present, and no provision was made for general meetings of workers with their representatives.

The passage of the National Industrial Recovery Act in 1933 prompted both a change in the form of company unions and their rapid adoption by many employers who had previously resisted any form of group dealings with their employees. The NIRA's Section 7(a) provided in part that "employees shall have the right to organize and bargain collectively through representatives of their own choosing," free of employer interference, coercion or restraint. This language, and the construction early given it, caused many existing representation plans to undergo a metamorphosis that resulted in their resembling trade unions in structure and operation. Similarly, many unorganized employers, fearful of being compelled to bargain with an outside organization (either by governmental order or as a result of a successful organizing effort) initiated a company union instead.

The prototype post-NIRA version of the company union—or employee committee, as they were also known—made provision for separate meetings of employee representatives, reserving meetings with management only for presentation of proposals and discussion. (This supposedly made the plans less subject to challenge on grounds of interference or restraint; nevertheless, it was customary for management representatives to be present at all meetings to give information and advice). Like the bodies after which they were patterned, the post-NIRA company unions had elected officers and representatives, a membership, by-laws, and other attributes of independent unions. Management, however, instigated the committee's formation, and usually framed its constitution and by-laws, presenting them to employees for ratification. Although employees usually elected their representatives, candidates were restricted to current company employees, and often minimum age and length-of-service requirements were imposed. Representatives' terms were normally of limited duration.

Although theoretically they were to act as bargaining representatives, few post-NIRA company unions concluded a written agreement that established wages, hours or other employment conditions. Furthermore, most committees' proposed undertakings were subject to management's approval. Membership was often an incident of employment, but because there were rarely any associated dues or fees, most company unions had no treasury and thus were unable to finance a strike, employ outside experts, or undertake other activities independent of the employer. Consequently, management normally supplied the committee with secretarial service, office space, and the like, and paid the employee representatives at their usual rate for time spent on committee business.

In terms of the numbers of employees covered, the company union was a highly successful alternative to collective bargaining. By 1935, company unions represented 2.5 million employees (about 60 percent of the number of trade union members) and they were growing at a faster rate than were the trade unions. Of the representation plans in existence in 1935, three-fifths had been organized since 1933. While representation plans did significantly stem the advance of independent union organizing efforts, they were generally instituted by relatively beneficent employers and they did provide many workers for the first time with a voice concerning their working conditions.

The prohibition of company unionism—that is, of employer domination or financial assistance—was one of the more hotly argued questions presented in the enactment of the Labor Act. Henry Dennison, of the company that bore his name and member of the then National Labor Board, testified before the Senate committee in opposition to the provision that would eventually become section 8(2):

MR. DENNISON. We have employee representation and have had since 1919. We have not called it a company union because we did not like the flavor of the word as it grew up shortly after the war.

THE CHAIRMAN. What form of company representation? How do they select their representatives?

MR. DENNISON. The employees' representatives constitute a council elected by them, set up by themselves independently, and dealing with management through joint committees or in any other way they may see fit on all the subjects that we have to deal with.

THE CHAIRMAN. How often do they meet?

MR. DENNISON. They meet regularly once every 2 weeks, the executive committee does, but there are meetings as often as circumstances require, as they think they need them.

THE CHAIRMAN. Is there any regular yearly or annual election?

MR. DENNISON. Yes; an annual election in December.

They are subdivided into divisional committees for detailed work and joined by an executive committee of eight, and the council as a whole acts on such matters as interest the whole plant.

\* \* \*

SENATOR BORAH. Your organization is really a company union, is it not?

MR. DENNISON. It is a company union, if that term—it is difficult to define it. They have no dues, for example; there are no requirements and never have been to join; there is really nothing to joining; you vote once a year if you wish to for this representative committee, and one does not know who votes and who does not. Usually a very large majority vote but it is really straining words to call it a union.

THE CHAIRMAN. Aren't there are bylaws?

MR. DENNISON. Yes; there is a structure, just the form of election and how committees should be related. It is a fairly simple set of bylaws.

\* \* \*

... As to the attitude and practices of many employers, I have no illusions. I have fought these practices too long for that. I can understand and appreciate Senator Wagner's natural desire, arising out of his inestimable service on the Labor Board, to use a scalpel on them. But by virtue of its task, that Board saw chiefly the bad and some of the worst cases. There are hundreds of companies in which a sound system of joint and mutual participation in management has developed or is developing. These had no quarrels to bring to a Labor Board.

For similar reasons union leaders get to know many more of the unsound and vicious cases than of the sound ones.

Even if few, these companies who have established a basis for wholesome mutual business relationships between management and workers should be cultivated as seeding ground or laboratories from which we may learn, not dug up with the tares by these two paragraphs [of the bill forbidding company domination or support].

I know that if these two paragraphs are stricken out there will remain more so-called "company unions" under the employer's thumb than if they are left in. But my firm conviction is that under today's conditions, this evil will be short-lived, whereas the evils of forcing the growth of outside unions beyond the rate at which capable leaders can be discovered and can gain experience will last a generation. In few if any plans can a hog-tied company union survive more than a year or two; they either evolve into true and independent employee representation or blow up and reform into stiff and often antagonistic unions controlled from without....

We must not forget, also, that the influences set up by this bill must apply themselves to the more than 90 percent of industrial establishments in this country which have less than 100 employees. To cramp all systematic contact in these plants, as this bill cramps it, is a proposal to be considered most carefully.

\* \* \*

I am equally deeply convinced that employee representation, so built as to afford the maximum of mutual contact and participation ... is invaluable as a supplement to outside unionism. I believe that out of their slowly freeing competition and the gradual comparison of the two forms we shall be able to develop modifications of each which will tend toward making possible the realization into actuality of the truth that any business organization which can knit itself into a single organism will prove superior as an institution of broad social value, to one which must exist in two somewhat stiffly cooperating and sometimes actively conflicting segments.

1 Legislative History of the National Labor Relations Act 435–438 (Commemorative Ed.)(1985).

---

## Report of the Senate Committee on Education and Labor on the Wagner Act

S.Rep. 573, 74th Cong., 1st Sess., pp. 9–11 (1935).

The second unfair labor practice deals with the so-called "company-union problem." It forbids an employer to dominate or interfere with the formation or administration of any labor organization or contribute financial or other support to it. * * *

This bill does nothing to outlaw free and independent organizations of workers who by their own choice limit their cooperative activities to the limits of one company. Nor does anything in the bill interfere with the freedom of employers to establish pension benefits, outing clubs, recreational societies, and the like, so long as such organizations do not extend their functions to the field of collective bargaining, and so long as they are not used as a covert means of discriminating against or in favor of membership in any labor organization. Such agencies, confined to their proper sphere, have promoted amicable relationships between employers and employees and the committee earnestly hopes that they will continue to function.

The so-called "company-union" features of the bill are designed to prevent interference by employers with organizations of their workers that serve or might serve as collective bargaining agencies. Such interferences exist when employers actively participate in framing the constitution or bylaws of labor organizations; or when, by provisions in the constitution or bylaws, changes in the structure of the organization cannot be made without the consent of the employer. It exists when they participate in the internal management or elections of a labor organization or when they supervise the agenda or procedure of meetings. It is impossible to catalog all the practices that might constitute interference, which may rest upon subtle but conscious economic pressure exerted by virtue of the employment relationship. The question is one of fact in each case. And where several of these interferences exist in combination, the employer may be said to dominate the labor organization by overriding the will of employees.

The committee feels justified, particularly in view of statutory precedents, in outlawing financial or other support as a form of unfair pressure. It seems clear that an organization or a representative or agent paid by the employer for representing employees cannot command, even if deserving it, the full confidence of such employees. And friendly labor relations depend

upon absolute confidence on the part of each side in those who represent it.
* * *

---

# Electromation, Inc.

309 NLRB 990 (1992), enf'd, 35 F.3d 1148 (7th Cir.1994).

[The NLRB decided this case after oral argument was heard and briefs filed by the parties as well as by a number of organizations serving as amicus curiae.]

■ This case presents the issue of whether "Action Committees" composed, in part, of the Respondent's employees constitute a labor organization within the meaning of Section 2(5) of the Act and whether the Respondent's conduct vis a vis the "Action Committees" violated Section 8(a)(2) and (1) of the Act. In the notice of hearing of May 14, 1991, the Board framed the pertinent issues as follows:

> (1) At what point does an employee committee lose its protection as a communication device and become a labor organization?

> (2) What conduct of an employer constitutes domination or interference with the employee committee?

For the reasons below, we find that the Action Committees were not simply "communication devices" but instead constituted a labor organization within the meaning of Section 2(5) of the Act and that the Respondent's conduct towards the Action Committees constituted domination and interference in violation of Section 8(a)(2) and (1). These findings rest on the totality of the record evidence, and they are not intended to suggest that employee committees formed under other circumstances for other purposes would necessarily be deemed "labor organizations" or that employer actions like some of those at issue here would necessarily be found, in isolation or in other contexts, to constitute unlawful support, interference, or domination.

## I.

The Respondent is engaged in the manufacture of electrical components and related products. It employs approximately 200 employees. These employees were not represented by any labor organization at the time of the events described herein.

[In response to financial difficulties, the employer-Respondent in late 1988 substituted a year-end payment for the anticipated 1989 wage increase, and made changes in its attendance bonus policy. This provoked a petition from the employees, and led to a meeting between the company President, John Howard, and several employees, at which there were discussions of several economic issues. Howard then met with company supervisors, and he and they decided that "it was very unlikely that further unilateral management action to resolve these problems was going to come anywhere near making everybody happy ... and we thought that the best course of action would be to involve the employees in coming up with solutions to these issues"; they decided that "action committees" would be a way to involve employees. Howard met once again with the employee group, and proposed the creation of action committees to deal with each of the five areas that he had identified as the subject of employee complaints; he stated that if these committees "came up with solutions that ... we believed were within budget concerns and they generally felt would be acceptable to the employees, that we would implement these suggestions or proposals." Although the reaction of the employee group was initially unfavorable, they ultimately endorsed the idea.]

On January 19, the Respondent posted a memorandum directed to all employees announcing the formation of five Action Committees and posted sign-up sheets for each Action Committee. The memorandum explained that each Action Committee would consist of six employees and one or two members of management, as well as the Respondent's Employees Benefits Manager, Loretta Dickey, who would coordinate all the Action Committees. The sign-up sheets explained the responsibilities and goals of each Committee. No employees were involved in the drafting of the policy goals expressed in the sign-up sheets. The Respondent determined the number of employees permitted to sign-up for the Action Committees. The Respondent informed two employees who had signed up for more than one committee that each would be limited to participation on one committee. After the Action Committees were organized, the Respondent posted a notice to all employees announcing the members of each Committee and the dates of the initial Committee meetings. The Action Committees were designated as (1) Absenteeism/Infractions, (2) No Smoking Policy, (3) Communication Network, (4) Pay Progression for Premium Positions, and (5) Attendance Bonus Program.

The Action Committees began meeting in late January and early February.[6] The Respondent's coordinator of the Action Committees, Dickey, testified that management expected that employee members on the Committees would "kind of talk back and forth" with the other employees in the plant, get their ideas, and that, indeed, the purpose of the Respondent's postings was to ensure that "anyone [who] wanted to know what was going on, they could go to these people" on the Action Committees. Other management representatives, as well as Dickey, participated in the Action Committees' meetings, which were scheduled to meet on a weekly basis in a conference room on the Respondent's premises. The Respondent paid employees for their time spent participating and supplied necessary materials. Dickey's role in the meetings was to facilitate the discussions.

On February 13, the Union made a demand to the Respondent for recognition. There is no evidence that the Respondent was aware of organizing efforts by the Union until this time. On about February 21, Howard informed Dickey of the recognition demand and, at the next

---

**6.** The no-smoking committee was never organized and held no meetings.

scheduled meeting of each Action Committee, Dickey informed the members that the Respondent could no longer participate but that the employees could continue to meet if they so desired. The Absenteeism/Infraction and the Communication Network Committees each decided to continue their meetings on company premises; the Pay Progression Committee disbanded; and the Attendance Bonus Committee decided to write up a proposal they had discussed previously and not to meet again. The Attendance Bonus Committee's proposal was one of two proposals that the employees had developed concerning attendance bonuses. The first one, developed at the committee's second or third meeting, was pronounced unacceptable by the Respondent's controller, a member of that committee, because it was too costly. Thereafter the employees devised a second proposal, which the controller deemed fiscally sound. The proposal was not presented to President Howard because the Union's campaign to secure recognition had intervened.

On March 15, Howard informed employees that "due to the Union's campaign, the Company would be unable to participate in the committee meetings and could not continue to work with the committees until after the election," which was to be held on March 31 * * *.

[The Administrative Law Judge held that the action committees were "labor organizations" within the NLRA definition, and that the company dominated and impermissibly assisted them.]

In its exceptions and brief, the Respondent contends that the Action Committees were not statutory labor organizations and did not interfere with employee free choice. It notes that no proposals from any committee were ever implemented, that the committees were formed in the absence of knowledge of any union activity, and that they followed a tradition of similar employer-employee meetings.

## II.

[The Board quoted the text of sections 2(5) and 8(a)(2) of the NLRA.]

* * * [We] seek guidance from the legislative history to discern what kind of activity Congress intended to prohibit when it made it an unfair labor practice for an employer to "dominate or interfere with the formation or administration of any labor organization" or to contribute support to it.[9]

---

**9.** A number of the amici have suggested that, even if the language and legislative history of the provisions at issue show a clear congressional intent to impose a broad prohibition extending to activities like those of the Respondent and the employee committees at issue in this case, and even if that understanding of congressional intent was expressed in an opinion of the Supreme Court, the Board is free to adjust the breadth of the prohibition in light of changing economic realities. In particular, the amici argue that, for the sake of American competitiveness in world markets, it is desirable to allow employers to create and support employee/management committees in the manner that the Respondent did with respect to the Action Committees here. While we agree that when the Board has the latitude to change a particular construction of the statute we may appropriately take into account changing industrial realities, we do not agree that we are free so to act either when congressional intent to the contrary is absolutely clear or the Supreme Court has decreed that a particular reading of the statute is required to reflect such an intent, or both * * *.

The legislative history reveals that the provisions outlawing company dominated labor organizations were a critical part of the Wagner Act's purpose of eliminating industrial strife through the encouragement of collective bargaining. Early in his opening remarks Senator Wagner stated:

Genuine collective bargaining is the only way to attain equality of bargaining power * * *. The greatest obstacles to collective bargaining are employer-dominated unions, which have multiplied with amazing rapidity since the enactment of [the National Industrial Recovery Act]. Such a union makes a sham of equal bargaining power * * *. (O)nly representatives who are not subservient to the employer with whom they deal can act freely in the interest of employees. For these reasons the very first step toward genuine collective bargaining is the abolition of the employer dominated union as an agency for dealing with grievances, labor disputes, wages, rates, or hours of employment.

* * * Congress concluded that ridding collective bargaining of employer-dominated organizations, the formation and administration of which had been fatally tainted by employer "domination" or "interference," would advance the Wagner Act's goal of eliminating industrial strife. That conclusion was based on the nation's experience under the NIRA, recounted by witnesses at the Senate hearings, that employer interference in setting up or running employee "representation" groups actually robbed employees of the freedom to choose their own representatives. Senator Wagner here made a distinction, important for this inquiry, between interference and minimal conduct—"merely suggesting to his employees that they organize a union or committee"—that the nation's experience had shown did not rob employees of their right to a representative of their own choosing. As Senator Wagner stated:

The question is entirely one of fact and turns upon whether or not the employee organization is entirely the agency of the workers * * *. The organization itself should be independent of the employer-employee relationship.

In sum, Congress brought within its definition of "labor organization" a broad range of employee groups, and it sought to ensure that such groups were free to act independently of employers in representing employee interests.

### III.

Before a finding of unlawful domination can be made under Section 8(a)(2) a finding of "labor organization" status under Section 2(5) is required. Under the statutory definition set forth in Section 2(5), the organization at issue is a labor organization if (1) employees participate, (2) the organization exists, at least in part, for the purpose of "dealing with" employers, and (3) these dealings concern "conditions of work" or concern other statutory subjects, such as grievances, labor disputes, wages, rates of pay, or hours of employment. Further, if the organization has as a purpose the representation of employees, it meets the statutory definition of "employee representation committee or plan" under Section 2(5) and will constitute a labor organization if it also meets the criteria of employee participation and dealing with conditions of work or other statutory subjects. Any group, including an employee representation committee, may meet the statutory definition of "labor organization" even if it lacks a formal structure, has no elected officers, constitution or bylaws, does not meet regularly, and does not require the payment of initiation fees or dues. Fire Alert Co., 182 NLRB 910, 912 fn. 12 (1970), enfd. 77 LRRM 2895 (10th Cir.1971); Armco, Inc., 271 NLRB 350 (1984). Thus, a group may be an "employee representation committee" within the meaning of Section 2(5) even if there is no formal framework for conducting meetings among the represented employees (i.e. those employees whose conditions of employment are the subject of committee dealings) or for otherwise eliciting the employees' views. * * *

In considering the interplay between Section 2(5) and Section 8(a)(2), we are guided by the Supreme Court's opinion in NLRB v. Cabot Carbon Co., 360 U.S. 203 (1959). In Cabot Carbon the Court held that the term "dealing with" in Section 2(5) is broader than the term "collective bargaining" and applies to situations that do not contemplate the negotiation of a collective bargaining agreement.[21] * * *

Notwithstanding that "dealing with" is broadly defined under Cabot Carbon, it is also true that an organization whose purpose is limited to performing essentially a managerial or adjudicative function is not a labor organization under Section 2(5). In those circumstances, it is irrelevant if the impetus behind the organization's creation emanates from the employer. See General Foods Corp., 231 NLRB 1232 (1977)(employer created job enrichment program composed of work crews of entire employee complement); Mercy–Memorial Hospital, 231 NLRB 1108 (1977)(committee decided validity of employees' complaints and did not discuss or deal with employer concerning the complaints); John Ascuaga's Nuggett, 230 NLRB 275, 276 (1977)(employees' organization resolved employees' grievances and did not interact with management).

Although Section 8(a)(2) does not define the specific acts that may constitute domination, a labor organization that is the creation of management, whose structure and function are essentially determined by management, * * * and whose continued existence depends on the fiat of manage-

---

**21.** As Member Devaney notes, witnesses cautioned the Senate committee that limiting "labor organization" to groups that engage in collective bargaining with an employer might fail to capture employer-dominated organizations, many of which never wrested a single concession, let alone a bargaining agreement, from the employer. Referring again to the abuses Congress meant to proscribe in enacting the Wagner Act, we view "dealing with" as a bilateral mechanism involving proposals from the employee committee concerning the subjects listed in Sec. 2(5), coupled with real or apparent consideration of those proposals by management. A unilateral mechanism, such as a "suggestion box," or "brainstorming" groups or meetings, or analogous information exchanges does not constitute "dealing with."

ment, is one whose formation or administration has been dominated under Section 8(a)(2). In such an instance, actual domination has been established by virtue of the employer's specific acts of creating the organization itself and determining its structure and function.[24] However, when the formulation and structure of the organization is determined by employees, domination is not established, even if the employer has the potential ability to influence the structure or effectiveness of the organization. See Duquesne University, 198 NLRB 891, 892–893 (1972). * * *

The Board's analysis of Section 2(5) and Section 8(a)(2) generally has met with judicial approval. * * *[25] The Board, however, has been less than successful in the Sixth Circuit. See, e.g., NLRB v. Scott & Fetzer Co., 691 F.2d 288 (6th Cir.1982); Airstream, Inc. v. NLRB, 877 F.2d 1291 (6th Cir.1989).

* * * As noted previously (fn. 24), Board precedent and decisions of the Supreme Court indicate that the presence of antiunion motive is not critical to finding an 8(a)(2) violation. We also see no basis in the statutory language, the legislative history, or decisions apart from Scott & Fetzer to require a finding that the employees believe their organization to be a labor union. * * *

Of course, Section 2(5) literally requires us to inquire into the "purpose" of the employee entity at issue because we must determine whether it exists "for the purpose of dealing" with conditions of employment. But "purpose" is different from motive; and the "purpose" to which the statute directs inquiry does not necessarily entail subjective hostility towards unions. Purpose is a matter of what the organization is set up to do, and that may be shown by what the organization actually does. If a purpose is to deal with an employer concerning conditions of employment, the Section 2(5) definition has been met regardless of whether the employer has created it, or fostered its creation, in order to avoid unionization or whether employees view that organization as equivalent to a union.[27]

---

**24.** Sec. 8(a)(2) does not require a finding of antiunion animus or a specific motive to interfere with Sec. 7 rights. In NLRB v. Newport News Shipbuilding Co., 308 U.S. 241 (1939), the Supreme Court found that an employer had dominated a statutory labor organization even though the "Committee" in question operated to the apparent satisfaction of the employees who had signified their desire for its continuance. The Court also noted that there was no evidence that the employer objected to its employees joining labor unions and that there had been no discrimination against them because of membership in outside unions. See also Garment Workers' Union (Bernhard–Altmann Texas Corp.) v. NLRB, 366 U.S. 731 (1961) (good-faith belief in union's majority status is no defense under Sec. 8(a)(2) to the grant of exclusive recognition to a union that does not have support of the majority of employees) * * *.

**25.** In NLRB v. Northeastern University, 601 F.2d 1208 (1st Cir.1979); Hertzka & Knowles v. NLRB, 503 F.2d 625 (9th Cir. 1974); and Chicago Rawhide Mfg. Co. v. NLRB, 221 F.2d 165 (7th Cir.1955), the courts denied enforcement in circumstances where the impetus behind the organizations emanated from the employees themselves. Without passing on the merits of the underlying Board decisions in those cases, we find those cases distinguishable from the cases cited in our discussion herein, and from the instant case.

**27.** In this we differ from Member Raudabaugh's view that employee perception of an employee committee is a significant ele-

## IV.

Applying these principles to the facts of this case, we find, in agreement with the judge, that the Action Committees constitute a labor organization within the meaning of Section 2(5) of the Act; and that the Respondent dominated it, and assisted it, i.e., contributed support, within the meaning of Section 8(a)(2).

First, there is no dispute that employees participated in the Action Committees. Second, we find that the activities of the committees constituted dealing with an employer. Third, we find that the subject matter of that dealing—which included the treatment of employee absenteeism and employee remuneration in the form of bonuses and other monetary incentives—concerned conditions of employment. Fourth, we find that the employees acted in a representational capacity within the meaning of Section 2(5). Taken as a whole, the evidence underlying these findings shows that the Action Committees were created for, and actually served, the purpose of dealing with the Respondent about conditions of employment.

* * * The evidence thus overwhelmingly demonstrates that a purpose of the Action Committees, indeed their only purpose, was to address employees' disaffection concerning conditions of employment through the creation of a bilateral process involving employees and management in order to reach bilateral solutions on the basis of employee-initiated proposals. This is the essence of "dealing with" within the meaning of Section 2(5).[28]

* * * [W]e find that employee-members of the Action Committees acted in a representational capacity and that the Action Committees were an "employee representation committee or plan" as set forth in Section 2(5).

There can also be no doubt that the Respondent's conduct vis a vis the Action Committees constituted "domination" in their formation and administration. It was the Respondent's idea to create the Action Committees. When it presented the idea to employees on January 18, the reaction, as the Respondent's President Howard admitted, was "not positive." Howard then informed employees that management would not "just unilaterally make changes" to satisfy employees' complaints. As a result, employees essentially were presented with the Hobson's choice of accepting the status quo, which they disliked, or undertaking a bilateral "exchange of ideas"

---

ment in evaluating its lawfulness. Much of the harm implicit in employer—dominated organizations is that, when they are successful, they appear to employees to be the result of an exercise of statutory freedoms, when in fact they are coercive by their very nature. Thus, we cannot agree that employee perceptions of the nature of an employee committee are significant indicators of their lawfulness.

**28.** We find no basis in this record to conclude that the purpose of the Action Committees was limited to achieving "quality" or "efficiency" or that they were designed to be a "communication device" to promote generally the interests of quality or efficiency. We, therefore, do not reach the question of whether any employer initiated programs that may exist for such purposes, as described by amici in this proceeding, may constitute labor organizations under Sec. 2(5). Cf. General Foods Corp., supra.

within the framework of the Action Committees, as presented by the Respondent. The Respondent drafted the written purposes and goals of the Action Committees which defined and limited the subject matter to be covered by each Committee, determined how many members would compose a committee and that an employee could serve on only one committee, and appointed management representatives to the Committees to facilitate discussions.[30] Finally, much of the evidence supporting the domination finding also supports a finding of unlawful contribution of support. In particular, the Respondent permitted the employees to carry out the committee activities on paid time within a structure that the Respondent itself created.[31]

On these facts, we find that the Action Committees were the creation of the Respondent and that the impetus for their continued existence rested with the Respondent and not with the employees. Accordingly, the Respondent dominated the Action Committees in their formation and administration and unlawfully supported them.

[Member Devaney concurred separately to stress how the challenged "action committees" were established by the Company for the purpose of bargaining with it over terms and conditions of employment, which usurped the employees' right to choose their own representation and placed the employer on both sides of the bargaining table.]

■ MEMBER OVIATT, concurring.

* * * I join in the majority opinion, but I do so as much for what the opinion does not condemn as an unfair labor practice as for what it does find to be a violation of Section 8(a)(2) and (1). Thus, I write separately to stress the wide range of lawful activities which I view as untouched by this decision.

In my view, the critical question in most cases of alleged violations of Section 8(a)(2) through domination or support of an entity that includes employees among its membership is whether the entity is created with any

**30.** As Member Devaney notes in his concurrence, the "bargaining" going on through the Action Committees was not between the employees and management. Rather, each committee contained supervisors or managers and the committee charged with compensation issues had its proposals evaluated by the Respondent's controller before they were presented to the Respondent. Thus, the situation here put the Respondent in the position of sitting on both sides of the bargaining table with an "employee committee" that it could dissolve as soon as its usefulness ended and to which it owed no duty to bargain in good faith.

**31.** We do not hold that paying employee members of a committee for their meeting time and giving that committee space to meet and supplies is per se a violation of Sec.

8(a)(2). Here, however, the Respondent's assistance was in furtherance of its unlawful domination of the Action Committees and cannot be separated from that domination. Because the Respondent's conduct in supplying materials and furnishing space to the Action Committees occurred in the context of the Respondent's domination of these groups, this case is distinguishable from instances where an employer confers such benefits in the context of an amicable, arm's-length relationship with a legitimate representative organization. See Duquesne University, 198 NLRB at 891. (Certain employer benefits resulting from "friendly cooperation" with a lawfully recognized labor organization do not constitute an 8(a)(2) violation (dictim).)

purpose to deal with "grievances, labor disputes, wages, rates of pay, hours of employment, or conditions of work" as set forth in the Section 2(5) definition of "labor organization." In this case, I have no doubt that the subject matter of the Action Committees falls comfortably within the definition. * * *

There is, however, an important area of industrial relations where committees and groups of employees and managerial personnel act together with the purpose of communicating, addressing and solving problems in the workplace that do not implicate the matters identified in Section 2(5). Among the employee-participation groups that may be established by management are so-called "quality circles" whose purpose is to use employee expertise by having the group examine certain operational problems such as labor efficiency and material waste. See, Beaver, Are Worker Participation Plans "Labor Organizations" Within the Meaning of Section 2(5)? A Proposed Framework of Analysis, Lab.L.J. 226 (1985). Other such committees have been dubbed "quality-of-work-life programs." These involve management's attempt to draw on the creativity of its employees by including them in decisions that affect their work lives. These decisions may go beyond improvements in productivity and efficiency to include issues involving worker self-fulfillment and self-enhancement. See, Fulmer and Coleman, Do Quality-of Work–Life Programs Violate Section 8(a)(2)?, 35 Lab.L.J. 675 (1984). Others of these programs stress joint problem-solving structures that engage management and employees in finding ways of improving operating functions. See, Lee, Collective Bargaining and Employee Participation: An Anomalous Interpretation of the National Labor Relations Act, 38 Lab.L.J. 206, 207 (1987). And then there are employee-management committees that are established by a company with the purpose of creating better communications between employer and employee by exploring employee attitudes, communicating certain information to employees, and making management more aware of employee problems. See, Beaver, supra.

Where there is a labor union on the scene, these employee-management cooperative programs may act as a complement to the union. They can not, however, lawfully usurp the traditional role of the Union in representing the employees in collective bargaining about grievances, wages, hours, and terms and conditions of work. Where no labor union represents the employees, these programs are often established to open lines of communication so that the operation may take advantage of employee technical knowledge and expertise. See, Note, New Standards For Domination and Support Under 8(a)(2), 82 Yale Law Journal 510, 511 (1973).

Certainly, I find nothing in today's decision that should be read as a condemnation of cooperative programs and committees of the type I have outlined above. The statute does not forbid direct communication between the employer and its employees to address and solve significant productivity and efficiency problems in the workplace. In my view, committees and groups dealing with these subjects alone plainly fall outside the Section 2(5) definition of "labor organization" since they are not concerned with grievances, labor disputes, wages, rates of pay, hours of employment or conditions of work. Indeed, in this age of increased global competition I consider it of critical importance that management and employees be able, indeed, are encouraged, to engage in cooperative endeavors to improve production methods and product quality.

It is with this understanding of the scope of the majority decision that I join in its reasoning and result.[5]

Member Raudabaugh also would give persuasive weight to the fact that an employer expressly assures employees that, notwithstanding the existence of an employee participatory program, they are free to "select traditional union representation * * *." No authority is cited for giving weight to this kind of a statement when the Board is adjudicating an 8(a)(2) case. Such an assurance would be hollow indeed if the employees have already been unlawfully influenced not to choose an outside organization by the establishment of an in-house committee in violation of 8(a)(2). Further, exactly what the Employer said, how he said it, and to whom and when it was said, could well be disputed, creating the potential for additional trial issues. Thus, Member Raudabaugh's test, however well-intentioned, provides a road map for increased litigation, not cooperation. In my view, today's Employer does not need to be confronted with the possibility of more litigation and the costs associated therewith, but should be free, within the limits of our Statute, to encourage problem solving through cooperation so as to better compete in the world marketplace.

Finally, as the majority opinion shows, Newport News Shipbuilding, supra, is still good law. That case, and Garment Workers Union (Bernhard Altmann), supra, wisely reject the employer good-faith-motive principle embraced by Member Raudabaugh. The employer's subjective intent in no way dissipates the impact on the employees of the presence of an employer-dominated, in-house committee that substitutes for a legitimate labor organization's collective bargaining function. Sec. 8(a)(2) addresses that impact, not the employer's intentions.

[In a concurring opinion, Member Raudabaugh acknowledged that employee participation programs (EPPs) are typically "labor organizations" under section 2(5) of the NLRA, because they involve the presentation of proposals or ideas to management, and management responses thereto. However, he concluded that section 8(a)(2) should be reinterpreted so as to reflect less the adversary concept of collective bargaining as contemplated by the Wagner Act and more the principles that he extracted from the later Taft–Hartley Act, i.e., employee free choice whether or not to be represent-

---

**5.** Like the majority, I reject Member Raudabaugh's efforts to rewrite Sec. 8(a)(2). In my view his 4–part test significantly erodes Congressional intent as understood by the Supreme Court. Thus, Member Raudabaugh would be guided in part by the extent to which the "employees do not view the committee" as a substitute for collective bargaining. Under Member Raudabaugh's approach the employees' perception must be "reasonable." This, however, simply encourages a separate contest over "reasonableness," a factor not contemplated by Congress or the statute.

ed through traditional labor unions and the encouragement of amicable and peaceful resolution of disputes. "My view is not a rejection of collective bargaining and the underlying adversarial model but a recognition of changed statutory language making room for a variety of choices for shaping workplace relations with employee free choice charting the course." Accordingly, in seeking an accommodation between labor-management cooperation and the section 7 rights of employees, Member Raudabaugh would examine the following factors in each case: "(1) the extent of the employer's involvement in the structure and operation of the committees; (2) whether the employees, from an objective standpoint, reasonably perceive the EPP as the substitute for full collective bargaining through a traditional union; (3) whether employees have been assured of their Section 7 right to choose to be represented by a traditional union under a system of full collective bargaining, and (4) the employer's motives in establishing the EPP.... No single factor would necessarily be dispositive." It would thus not automatically violate section 8(a)(2) for an employer to tell its employees it favors an EPP, or to have managers and supervisors as EPP members (without being given a dominant role), or to suggest the rules and policies of the EPP, or to provide it with meeting rooms, writing materials, secretarial assistance and meeting time during the workday. As to the second factor, the committee could not be set up by the employer in response to employee grievances and complaints but rather "to accomplish its own entrepreneurial interests, e.g., enhanced product quality and improved production efficiency," so as not to appear to be "a substitute for traditional union representation." Further, the employer's motive must not be, for example, to stifle an ongoing union campaign but "solely to enhance lawful entrepreneurial goals."]

————

As the Board's reference to the numerous amici appearing before it in *Electromation*, and the concurrences of Members Oviatt and Raudabaugh, make clear, the extent to which § 8(a)(2) is seen as an obstacle to systems of "employee participation" has assumed considerable significance. This will be returned to in Part IX, infra; but it should be noted here that the 1994 Report of the Commission on the Future of Worker–Management Relations recommended that Congress clarify section 8(a)(2) to insure that "employee participation programs" should not be outlawed simply because they involve the discussion of terms and conditions of employment "where such discussion is incidental to the broad purposes of these programs." Report and Recommendations 8 (1994) (member Douglas Fraser, former President of the United Auto Workers, dissenting). It also recommended that the right of employee participants to communicate their views and to seek outside expertise be protected under section 8(a)(1).

There is a large and growing industrial relations literature on "quality of work life" programs, self-directing work teams, and other forms of employee participation. Without prejudicing one's conclusions with respect to the role of labor organizations (or their absence) in effecting such systems, a sobering note of caution was sounded by a participant-observer of the introduction of an extensive system of worker participation at a non-unionized manufacturing plant. He concluded that, to a considerable extent, the experiment had not succeeded: "[M]eaningful democracy in an organization is not a minor adjustment of style and priority but requires a truly radical shift away from traditional norms of corporate organization." J. Witte, Democracy, Authority and Alienation in Work: Workers' Participation in an American Corporation 156 (1980). It is not a matter of employee expertise or even of managerial good will, but of power. Thus on issues of wages and employee grievances he observed (at pp. 90–91) that,

> In the vast majority of cases, participation in these issues on an ad hoc basis will eventually be subverted, forgotten, or shunted off to a group in which management domination is ensured. Without the job security and advancement guarantees afforded by a union, even the most active, hostile workers will eventually give up; while more timid workers, protecting their futures with the company, will subside much earlier....

> It was not that these employees lacked the capability to argue such questions, or that they were persuaded to accept management's point of view; it was simply that they lacked the formal mandate and the organizational power of a union—power necessary to provide a degree of security and a more equitable basis on which to resolve these conflicting issues.

------

## PROBLEMS FOR DISCUSSION

**1.** The nursing staff of Doctors' Hospital has for many years had a Nursing Services Organization ("NSO") supported initially by individual dues and later by a $500 annual contribution from the hospital. Delegates from the various nursing departments meet once a month; a general membership meeting is held twice a year. The hospital's Vice–President for Nursing serves on the NSO executive committee. The function of the NSO, according to the Vice–President for Nursing, is "as a means for active problem solving and decision making regarding nursing departments policies, practice issues, and projects (e.g. career paths, shared governance, clerical ladder, budget process)." There are no committees, but the membership meetings have been used as a means of announcing policies and to survey member reaction to proposed benefit changes by circulation of a questionnaire. Must the NSO be disestablished as a company dominated labor organization? See NLRB v. Peninsula General Hospital Medical Center, 36 F.3d 1262 (4th Cir.1994) and Polaroid Corp., 329 NLRB No. 47 (1999).

**2.** Professional employees—physicians, architects, university professors—often participate in the development of their employers' policies. Does the participation of such professional employees in autonomous "work teams" or decisionmaking groups (e.g., faculty committees effectively determining curriculum or personnel issues) make them supervisory employees under Section 2(11) of the Act, or managerial employees under the Board's implied exclusion from the Act's coverage? See NLRB v. Yeshiva University, 444 U.S. 672, 100 S.Ct. 856, 63 L.Ed.2d 115

(1980); FHP, Inc./Union of American Physicians and Dentists, 274 NLRB 1141 (1985). See also Rabban, "Can American Labor Law Accommodate Collective Bargaining by Professional Employees," 99 Yale L.J. 689 (1990).

**3.** To similar effect, would the participation of non-professional, blue-collar workers in work groups or teams that decide work assignment or scheduling among themselves also result in their exclusion from the coverage of the Act? See General Foods Corp. v. American Federation of Grain Millers, 231 NLRB 1232 (1977). See also Note, "Does Employer Implementation of Employee Production Teams Violate Section 8(a)(2) of the National Labor Relations Act?," 49 Ind. L.J. 516 (1974).

**4.** The Board in *Electromation* reiterates that employee committees to which actual "adjudicative" power over grievances has been given do not "deal with" the employer and so are not statutory labor organizations. When would such a body so "deal" as to become a labor organization? See Keeler Brass Automotive Group, 317 NLRB 1110 (1995). And if it is a labor organization, what constitutes impermissible domination or interference? Apropos that question, Chairman Gould, concurring in the above, observed:

> One factor favoring dismissal [of the complaint] is that the employer here did not create the committee in response to organizing efforts by a union or concerted action by the employees. There is no indication that the committee was created as a means to undercut independent action by employees. Instead, the employer simply wished to involve employees in the grievance procedure. Under my view, the creation of the committee in these circumstances, standing alone, does not support a violation finding. Other factors favoring dismissal are that participation on the committee was voluntary, employees were the only voting members of the committee, and all voting members were elected by employees. The committee, therefore, allowed some exercise of free choice and provided some scope for independence.
>
> There are many other aspects of the committee, however, that remain within the employer's control and, therefore, support a finding of domination. The employer set the time limit of terms for membership in the committee, established eligibility rules, established election procedures and conducted the election, announced the results of the election, dictated the number of employees who could serve on the committee, established the meeting days, and allowed special meetings (outside regular meeting days) to be held only with management approval. These elements of control indicate that the committee is not capable of action independent of the employer. Perhaps the most telling aspect of dependency is that the committee cannot even make a decision about when it will meet without prior approval from the employer.

**5.** The Nassau Contractors' Association negotiates on behalf of numerous construction companies with area construction unions. During negotiations between the Association and the Union of Operating Engineers, Clifford Smith and William Dean were members of the Union negotiating team and Milton Hendrickson, president of Hendrickson Brothers, one of the companies represented by the Association, was a member of the Association negotiating team. Both Smith and Dean are master mechanics and were employed by members of the Association at the time of the negotiations. The duties of a master mechanic are to make recommendations for the hiring of mechanics and to supervise the other mechanics to make sure that heavy equipment is kept in good working order. Smith is employed by Hendrickson, is responsible for the maintenance of over one million dollars worth of equipment, maintains a desk in the general offices of Hendrickson Bros., and has access to a company car at all times. Has the Association and/or Hendrickson Bros. violated Section 8(a)(2)? See Power Piping Co. v. Larry Jones, 291 NLRB 494 (1988).

Assume that employees Smith and Dean are not members of the union's negotiating team but are: (a) union vice-president and secretary-treasurer; or (b) representatives of the local union to the International's annual meeting; or (c) simply members of the local. Does their status in any of these cases raise a serious issue of violation under Section 8(a)(2)?

---

## International Ladies' Garment Workers v. NLRB (Bernhard–Altmann Texas Corp.)

366 U.S. 731, 81 S.Ct. 1603, 6 L.Ed.2d 762 (1961).

■ MR. JUSTICE CLARK delivered the opinion of the Court.

\* \* \*

In October 1956 the petitioner union initiated an organizational campaign at Bernhard–Altmann Texas Corporation's knitwear manufacturing plant in San Antonio, Texas. No other labor organization was similarly engaged at that time. During the course of that campaign, on July 29, 1957, certain of the Company's Topping Department employees went on strike in protest against a wage reduction. That dispute was in no way related to the union campaign, however, and the organizational efforts were continued during the strike. Some of the striking employees had signed authorization cards solicited by the union during its drive, and, while the strike was in progress, the union entered upon a course of negotiations with the employer. As a result of those negotiations, held in New York City where the home offices of both were located, on August 30, 1957, the employer and union signed a "memorandum of understanding." In that memorandum the company recognized the union as exclusive bargaining representative of "all production and shipping employees." The union representative asserted that the union's comparison of the employee authorization cards in its possession with the number of eligible employee representatives of the company furnished it indicated that the union had in fact secured such cards from a majority of employees in the unit. Neither employer nor union made any effort at that time to check the cards in the union's possession against the employee roll, or otherwise, to ascertain with any degree of certainty that the union's assertion, later found by the Board to be erroneous, was founded on fact rather than upon good-faith assumption. The agreement, containing no union security provisions, called for the ending of the strike and for certain improved wages and conditions of employment. It also provided that a "formal agreement containing these terms" would "be promptly drafted \* \* \* and signed by both parties within the next two weeks."

Thereafter, on October 10, 1957, a formal collective bargaining agreement, embodying the terms of the August 30 memorandum, was signed by the parties. The bargaining unit description set out in the formal contract, although more specific, conformed to that contained in the prior memorandum. It is not disputed that as of execution of the formal contract the union in fact represented a clear majority of employees in the appropriate unit. * * *

At the outset, we reject as without relevance to our decision the fact that, as of the execution date of the formal agreement on October 10, petitioner represented a majority of the employees. As the Court of Appeals indicated, the recognition of the minority union on August 30, 1957, was "a *fait accompli* depriving the majority of the employees of their guaranteed right to choose their own representative." 280 F.2d at page 621. It is, therefore, of no consequence that petitioner may have acquired by October 10 the necessary majority if, during the interim, it was acting unlawfully. Indeed, such acquisition of majority status itself might indicate that the recognition secured by the August 30 agreement afforded petitioner a deceptive cloak of authority with which to persuasively elicit additional employee support. * * *

In their selection of a bargaining representative, § 9(a) of the Wagner Act guarantees employees freedom of choice and majority rule. J.I. Case Co. v. National Labor Relations Board, 321 U.S. 332, 339, 64 S.Ct. 576, 581, 88 L.Ed. 762. In short, as we said in Brooks v. National Labor Relations Board, 348 U.S. 96, 103, 75 S.Ct. 176, 181, 99 L.Ed. 125, the Act placed "a nonconsenting minority under the bargaining responsibility of an agency selected by a majority of the workers." Here, however, the reverse has been shown to be the case. Bernhard–Altmann granted exclusive bargaining status to an agency selected by a minority of its employees, thereby impressing that agent upon the nonconsenting majority. There could be no clearer abridgment of § 7 of the Act, assuring employees the right "to bargain collectively through representatives of their own choosing" or "to refrain from" such activity. It follows, without need of further demonstration, that the employer activity found present here violated § 8(a)(1) of the Act which prohibits employer interference with, and restraint of, employee exercise of § 7 rights. Section 8(a)(2) of the Act makes it an unfair labor practice for an employer to "contribute * * * support" to a labor organization. The law has long been settled that a grant of exclusive recognition to a minority union constitutes unlawful support in violation of that section, because the union so favored is given "a marked advantage over any other in securing the adherence of employees." * * *

The petitioner, while taking no issue with the fact of its minority status on the critical date, maintains that both Bernhard–Altmann's and its own good-faith beliefs in petitioner's majority status are a complete defense. To countenance such an excuse would place in permissibly careless employer and union hands the power to completely frustrate employee realization of the premise of the Act—that its prohibitions will go far to assure freedom of choice and majority rule in employee selection of representatives. We find nothing in the statutory language prescribing *scienter* as an element of the unfair labor practices are involved. The act made unlawful by § 8(a)(2) is employer support of a minority union. Here that support is an accomplished fact. More need not be shown, for, even if mistakenly, the employees' rights have been invaded. It follows that prohibited conduct cannot be excused by a showing of good faith.

This conclusion, while giving the employee only the protection assured him by the Act, places no particular hardship on the employer or the union. It merely requires that recognition be withheld until the Board-conducted election results in majority selection of a representative. The Board's order here, as we might infer from the employer's failure to resist its enforcement, would apparently result in similarly slight hardship upon it. We do not share petitioner's apprehension that holding such conduct unlawful will somehow induce a breakdown, or seriously impede the progress of collective bargaining. If an employer takes reasonable steps to verify union claims, themselves advanced only after careful estimate—precisely what Bernhard–Altmann and petitioner failed to do here—he can readily ascertain their validity and obviate a Board election. We fail to see any onerous burden involved in requiring responsible negotiators to be careful, by cross-checking, for example, well-analyzed employer records with union listings or authorization cards. Individual and collective employee rights may not be trampled upon merely because it is inconvenient to avoid doing so. Moreover, no penalty is attached to the violation. Assuming that an employer in good faith accepts or rejects a union claim of majority status, the validity of his decision may be tested in an unfair labor practice proceeding. If he is found to have erred in extending or withholding recognition, he is subject only to a remedial order requiring him to conform his conduct to the norms set out in the Act, as was the case here. No further penalty results. * * *

[The partial dissent of JUSTICE DOUGLAS has been omitted.]

------

## PROBLEM FOR DISCUSSION

Assume that the union in the above case presented to the employer a list of its members, conceded that they constituted a minority of the bargaining unit, and asked the employer to enter into a full labor agreement (including wages and fringe benefits, grievance and arbitration procedures, but excluding any kind of union security provision) covering only the union's membership as constituted from time to time. Advise the employer whether it is obliged to enter into such a "members only" agreement. Advise the employer whether it is permitted to enter into such an agreement.

------

NOTE: It is ordinarily a violation of Section 8(a)(2) for a company to enter into a collective agreement with any union before that company has hired a substantial proportion of its full workforce. In 1959, Congress enacted Section 8(f) as part of the Landrum–Griffin Act. The Section authorizes, in the construction industry only, the execution of an agreement with a minority union (not otherwise illegally dominated or assisted) which requires membership in that union within seven days (instead of the usual thirty days under the proviso to Section 8(a)(3)) as a condition of employment. Such "pre-hire agreements" were authorized in the construction industry because of the short duration of many jobs in that industry and because of the common practice and need of employers to rely on union hiring halls to supply a pool of skilled labor. (See 1959 U.S.Code Cong. and Admin.News p. 2344). Section 8(f) expressly provides, however, that such pre-hire agreements will not serve as a contract bar to a representation or decertification election under Section 9. The NLRB has set forth comprehensive principles concerning the effect of section 8(f) upon the duty to deal with the signatory union and to adhere to the agreement, in Deklewa v. International Association of Bridge Workers, 282 NLRB 1375 (1987), enf'd sub nom. International Ass'n of Bridge Workers, Local 3 v. NLRB, 843 F.2d 770 (3d Cir.1988).

----

## Abraham Grossman d/b/a Bruckner Nursing Home[k]

262 NLRB 955 (1982).

The facts of the case are not in dispute and may be briefly summarized as follows:

In the spring of 1974, Local 144, Hotel, Hospital, Nursing Home & Allied Health Services Union, S.E.I.U., AFL–CIO (hereinafter referred to as Local 144) and Local 1115, Joint Board, Nursing Home and Hospital Employees Division (hereinafter referred to as Local 1115), began organizational activities at Respondent Employer's nursing home facility in New York, New York. In early September 1974, Local 144 notified the Employer that it possessed a majority of signed authorization cards, and a date was set for a card count. Shortly thereafter, Local 1115 sent a mailgram to the Employer which stated that it was engaged in organizational activity among the Employer's employees and that the Employer should not extend recognition to any other labor organization. On September 23, 1974, Local 1115 filed charges against the Employer and Local 144 alleging violations of Sections 8(a)(1) and 8(b)(1)(A) through interference with the employees' right to select a union of their choice.

The card count was conducted on September 27, 1974, by an extension specialist of the New York State School of Industrial and Labor Relations. Thereafter, the extension specialist informed the Employer that Local 144 represented a majority of its employees. Local 144 subsequently requested negotiations, but the Employer refused pending the outcome of the unfair labor practice charges filed by Local 1115.

----

**k.** See Estreicher & Telsey, A Recast *Midwest Piping* Doctrine: The Case for Judicial Acceptance, 36 Lab.L.J. 14 (1985); Getman, The *Midwest Piping* Doctrine, 31 U.Chi.L.Rev. 292 (1964).

On November 29, 1974, the unfair labor practice charges filed by Local 1115 were dismissed by the Regional Director. Negotiations between Local 144 and the Employer commenced shortly thereafter and culminated in the execution of a collective-bargaining agreement on December 18, 1974. Local 1115 then filed, on March 7, 1975, the charges at issue in this proceeding.

On September 27, 1974, the date of the card check, Respondent Employer had approximately 125 people in its employ. At that time, Local 1115 had two authorization cards, while Local 144 possessed signed authorization cards from approximately 80 to 90 percent of the Employer's employees. No representation petition was filed on behalf of either labor organization in this proceeding.

With respect to the foregoing facts, the Administrative Law Judge found that Local 1115 possessed a "colorable claim" to representation herein based on its continuous efforts to obtain employee support during the fall of 1974, and the fact that it had actually obtained a few authorization cards. The Administrative Law Judge concluded that the Employer "by executing a collective-bargaining agreement * * * in the face of a real question concerning representation which had not been settled [by] the special procedures of the Act" had rendered unlawful assistance to Local 144 in violation of Section 8(a)(2) of the Act. In what has become a standard remedy in this type of setting, the Administrative Law Judge ordered that the Employer cease giving effect to the collective-bargaining agreement with Local 144, and further ordered the Employer to withdraw and withhold recognition from Local 144 unless and until it has been certified in a Board-conducted election.

In this and a companion case, RCA del Caribe, Inc., 262 NLRB No. 116 (1982)(Chairman Van de Water and Member Jenkins dissenting), we undertake a reevaluation of what has come to be known as the *Midwest Piping*[1] doctrine, a rule which, in one form or another, has been part of Board law for over 35 years. In *RCA del Caribe*, we set forth a new policy with respect to the requirements of employer neutrality when an incumbent union is challenged by an "outside" union. In this case, we will focus our attention on initial organizing situations involving two or more rival labor organizations.

As originally formulated, the "*Midwest Piping* doctrine" was an attempt by the Board to insure that, in a rival union situation, an employer would not render "aid" to one of two or more unions competing for exclusive bargaining representative status through a grant of recognition in advance of a Board-conducted election. In *Midwest Piping* itself, the Board found that an employer gave unlawful assistance to a labor organization

---

**1.** Midwest Piping and Supply Co., Inc., 63 N.L.R.B. 1060 (1945). [Editors' Note: In that case the Board found "that the respondent, by executing a 'union shop' agreement with the Steamfitters in the face of the representation proceedings pending before the Board, indicated its approval of the Steamfitters, accorded it unwarranted prestige, encouraged membership therein, discouraged membership in the Steelworkers, and thereby rendered unlawful assistance to the Steamfitters, which interfered with, restrained, and coerced its employees in the exercise of rights guaranteed in Section 7 of the Act."]

when the employer recognized one of two competing labor organizations, both of which had filed representation petitions, and both of which had campaigned extensively for the mantle of exclusive bargaining representative. In the context of that case, we held that the employer had arrogated the resolution of the representation issue, and that a Board-conducted election was the "best" means of ascertaining the true desires of employees. We further stated that employers presented with rival claims from competing unions (in the form of representation petitions) should follow a course of strict neutrality with respect to the competing unions until such time as the "real question concerning representation" had been resolved through the mechanism of a Board-conducted election.

In cases that followed soon thereafter, we applied the principle that the duty of strict employer neutrality and the necessity of a Board-conducted election were operative only when a representation petition had been filed with the Board, and further noted that the "doctrine" should be "strictly construed" and "sparingly applied."

In subsequent decisions, the Board removed the requirement that a representation petition actually be filed, stating that a petition was not a prerequisite to the finding of a "real" or "genuine" question concerning representation. The removal of the prerequisite of a petition stemmed in part from the need to recognize the existence of a rival union contest even before formal invocation of the Board's election procedures so as to insure that those procedures would be available. If more than one union enjoyed at least some employee support, we perceived a Board-conducted election as the best way, often the only way, to guarantee employees a fair and free opportunity to make the final choice of a bargaining representative. Although often unstated, another reason for removing the petition requirement in a rival union setting was to preclude the serious possibility of employer abuse where no petition had been filed. Often we were faced with the scenario of a union presenting a substantial showing of majority support based on cards which the employer would reject while invariably professing a preference for the Board's election procedures. A short time thereafter, the employer would recognize another union and, typically, sign a contract in a remarkably accelerated bargaining process. This scenario was played once too often, so we determined that in order to protect the democratic right of employees to their own collective-bargaining representative, and to prevent employer abuse, we would require an election whenever there were two or more unions on the scene, and each had some support or organizational interest in the unit sought. We defined the "interest" that a union must have to trigger the operation of the *Midwest Piping* doctrine as a "colorable claim," a claim that was not "clearly unsupportable," or a claim that was not "naked." Thus, we held that the original *Midwest Piping* requirement of strict employer neutrality would be operative where a question concerning representation existed even though no petition had been filed unless and until a Board-conducted election had been held and the results certified.

Difficulties with this modification of the original *Midwest Piping* decision arose in defining precisely what was meant by the terms "naked claim," "clearly unsupportable claim," and "colorable claim." Inevitably we were called upon to make close judgments as to whether 8 cards in a unit of over 90 employees made a colorable claim, whether prior organizational activity constituted a clearly unsupportable claim, or whether an expressed interest in organizing a certain group of employees was simply a naked claim. While attempting to maintain flexibility and to decide these questions on a case-by-case basis, we were unable to provide employers, unions, and employees alike with clear standards that would enable them to discern the fine line between a colorable claim and a naked one.

Extending the *Midwest Piping* doctrine frequently allowed a minority union possessing a few cards to forestall the recognition of a majority union in an effort either to buy time to gather more support for itself or simply to frustrate its rivals. For instance, here, where one union enjoys overwhelming support and the other has but a few cards, collective bargaining would be delayed until the 8(a)(2) charge has been resolved and the results of a later Board-conducted election have been certified. This delay would occur simply because an employer has done what in the absence of a rival claimant it may (but by no means has to) do in recognizing a majority union based on authorization cards. Ironically, in this factual setting, invoking "employee free choice" to justify Board intervention would clearly impede and frustrate the expression of employee preference, as well as the collective-bargaining process. For here, where employees have made a free choice and the employer has recognized that choice, the ultimate aim of that choice—the establishment of a collective-bargaining relationship and the benefits flowing therefrom—could not be achieved because another union has a "colorable claim" to representation.

Meanwhile, circuit courts refused to enforce many of our decisions based on "modified" *Midwest Piping* violations. The courts took a distinctly different approach to the problems presented by the rival union situation. Whereas the Board viewed the matter in terms of protecting employee free choice and the integrity and efficacy of our election process, the courts took the view that the question concerning representation was resolved whenever an employer recognized a bona fide majority claimant and had not actually aided, in the traditional Section 8(a)(2) sense of that word, the recognized labor organization. At the point an unassisted majority union had been recognized, the courts considered the matter settled, and the question concerning representation resolved. However, reiterating its concern for the Section 7 rights of employees and employer manipulation of the recognition process, the Board held to the view that our election machinery was still the optimum means of resolving the rival union representation question. Just as often as the Board reaffirmed its adherence to the now "modified" *Midwest Piping* doctrine, however, the courts of appeals refused to enforce our decisions finding 8(a)(2) violations on this basis.

We have reviewed the Board's experience with *Midwest Piping* with a desire to accommodate the view of the courts of appeals in light of our statutory mandate to protect employees' freedom to select their bargaining representatives and in harmony with our statutory mandate to encourage collective bargaining. Having identified the difficult problems in this area, it is the Board's task to reconcile the various interests of policy and law involved in fashioning a rule which will give, as far as possible, equal consideration to each of those interests in the light of industrial reality. We have concluded that this task has not been accomplished through the modified *Midwest Piping* doctrine. Accordingly, we will no longer find 8(a)(2) violations in rival union, initial organizing situations when an employer recognizes a labor organization which represents an uncoerced, unassisted majority, before a valid petition for an election has been filed with the Board.[13] However, once notified of a valid petition, an employer must refrain from recognizing any of the rival unions. Of course, we will continue to process timely filed petitions and to conduct elections in the most expeditious manner possible, following our normal procedures with respect to intervention and placement of parties on the ballot.

Making the filing of a valid petition the operative event for the imposition of strict employer neutrality in rival union, initial organizing situations will establish a clearly defined rule of conduct and encourage both employee free choice and industrial stability. Where one of several rival labor organizations cannot command the support of even 30 percent of the unit, it will no longer be permitted to forestall an employer's recognition of another labor organization which represents an uncoerced majority of employees and thereby frustrate the establishment of a collective-bargaining relationship. Likewise, an employer will no longer have to guess whether a real question concerning representation has been raised but will be able to recognize a labor organization unless it has received notice of a properly filed petition.

On the other hand, where a labor organization has filed a petition, both the Act and our administrative experience dictate the need for resolution of the representation issue through a Board election rather than

---

**13.** Although an employer will no longer automatically violate Sec. 8(a)(2) by recognizing one of several rival unions before an election petition has been filed, we emphasize that an employer will still be found liable under Sec. 8(a)(2) for recognizing a labor organization which does not actually have majority employee support. International Ladies' Garment Workers' Union, AFL–CIO [Bernhard–Altmann Texas Corporation] v. NLRB, 366 U.S. 731 (1961). This longstanding principle applies in either a single or rival union organizational context and is unaffected by the revised *Midwest Piping* doctrine announced in this case. For instance, if an occasion arises where an employer is faced with recognition demands by two unions, both of which claim to possess valid authorization card majority support, the employer must beware the risk of violating Sec. 8(a)(2) by recognizing either union even though no petition has been filed. In such a situation, there is a possibility that the claimed majority support of the recognized union could in fact be nonexistent. Consequently, the safe course would be simply to refuse recognition, as clearly authorized under Linden Lumber Division, Summer & Co. v. NLRB, 419 U.S. 301 (1974). Either of the unions or the employer could then file a representation petition.

through employer recognition. When a union has demonstrated substantial support by filing a valid petition, an active contest exists for the employees' allegiance. This contest takes on special significance where rival unions are involved since there an employer's grant of recognition may unduly influence or effectively end a contest between labor organizations. As long ago as 1938, the Supreme Court noted that, in enacting Section 8(a)(2) and (1) of the Act, Congress had been influenced by "data showing that once an employer has conferred recognition on a particular organization it has a marked advantage over any other in securing the adherence of employees, and hence in preventing the recognition of any other." Without questioning the reliability of authorization cards or unduly exalting election procedure, we believe the proper balance will be struck by prohibiting an employer from recognizing any of the competing unions for the limited period during which a representation petition is in process even though one or more of the unions may present a valid card majority.

In addition to avoiding potential undue influence by an employer, our new approach provides a satisfactory answer to problems created by execution of dual authorization cards. It is our experience that employees confronted by solicitations from rival unions will frequently sign authorization cards for more than one union. Dual cards reflect the competing organizational campaigns. They may indicate shifting employee sentiments or employee desire to be represented by either of two rival unions. In this situation, authorization cards are less reliable as indications of employee preference. When a petition supported by a 30–percent showing of interest has been filed by one union, the reliability of a rival's expression of a card majority is sufficiently doubtful to require resolution of the competing claims through the Board's election process.

* * *

Applying the principles outlined above to the facts of the instant case, it is clear that no petition was filed by either of the rival unions and that the Employer recognized a clear majority claimant in extending recognition to Local 144. Accordingly, inasmuch as no petition was filed and recognition was granted to a labor organization with an uncoerced, unassisted majority, we shall dismiss the instant complaint in its entirety.

———

## PROBLEMS FOR DISCUSSION

**1.** Assume, in the above case, that Local 144 did indeed present signed authorization cards from 80 percent of the Company's employees, but that Local 1115 was able to secure signed cards from 30 percent of those employees. (What legitimate explanation might there be for such an overlap?) If Local 1115 petitions for a representation election in such circumstances, will the NLRB order an election? If the Board does order an election, how would you respond to the Company's question whether it may commence bargaining with Local 144? If the Board were to find that recognition of Local 144 as exclusive bargaining representative violates

Section 8(a)(2), would the Company have a plausible chance of securing a judicial reversal?

**2.** RCA has for a number of years negotiated successive labor agreements with the International Brotherhood of Electrical Workers (IBEW) covering all production and maintenance employees. The most recent two-year contract bore an expiration date of January 2 of this year. Negotiations for a new agreement continued past the January 2 termination, and on January 10, a valid election petition was filed by Independent Union, and copies of the petition were promptly served upon RCA and IBEW. IBEW insisted that RCA continue to negotiate toward a new agreement. It presented to the Company separate sheets from 150 of the 200 employees in the unit; the sheets had been signed by the employees within the preceding week, and stated the employees' support for IBEW as exclusive bargaining representative and also urged the NLRB to dismiss the Independent Union's election petition. The Company verified the signatures by comparing them with employee records. It therefore promptly resumed negotiations with IBEW, and the next day reached an agreement providing among other things for wage increases and improved insurance coverage.

Independent Union claims that RCA has violated Section 8(a)(2), relying on *Midwest Piping* and *Bruckner Nursing Home*. RCA and IBEW, however, contend that their situation is distinguishable by virtue of IBEW's status as an incumbent and long-recognized bargaining representative. How should the Board decide the case? See RCA del Caribe, Inc. v. Kuinlam, 262 NLRB 963 (1982).

———

## C.  DISCRIMINATION[10]

# Edward G. Budd Mfg. Co. v. NLRB

138 F.2d 86 (3d Cir.1943).

[In 1933, the employees of the company formed an association and elected representatives to confer with management on various matters of mutual concern. The association was initially suggested by management and was established pursuant to a plan drawn up by company officials. After its formation, management cooperated fully with the organization and treated its representatives with "extraordinary leniency." In 1941, however, the UAW sought unsuccessfully to organize the employees. Thereafter, the union filed charges alleging that the company had unlawfully

---

**10.** See Christensen & Svanoe, Motive and Intent in the Commission of Unfair Labor Practices: The Supreme Court and the Fictive Formality, 77 Yale L.J. 1269 (1968); Getman, Section 8(a)(3) of the NLRA and the Effort to Insulate Free Employee Choice, 32 U. Chi. L. Rev. 735 (1965); Note, Intent, Effect, Purpose, and Motive as Applicable Elements to § 8(a)(1) and § 8(a)(3) violations of the National Labor Relations Act, 7 Wake Forest L.Rev. 616 (1971); Oberer, The Scienter Factor in Sections 8(a)(1) and (3) of the Labor Act: of Balancing, Hostile Motive, Dogs and Tails, 52 Cornell L.Q. 491 (1967); White, Modern Discrimination Theory and the National Labor Relations Act, 39 Wm. & Mary L. Rev. 99 (1997).

supported and dominated the association and had discharged two employees, Milton Davis and Walter Weigand (a representative of the association), for supporting the union. Following a complaint, the Board issued a decision and order requiring the disestablishment of the association and the reinstatement of the two employees. On petition to review the Board's order, the court of appeals found sufficient evidence to uphold the conclusion that the association was employer-dominated in violation of section 8(2) and that Milton Davis had been discriminatorily discharged in violation of section 8(3). The court then considered the discharge of Walter Weigand.]

■ The case of Walter Weigand is extraordinary. If ever a workman deserved summary discharge it was he. He was under the influence of liquor while on duty. He came to work when he chose and he left the plant and his shift as he pleased. In fact, a foreman on one occasion was agreeably surprised to find Weigand at work and commented upon it. Weigand amiably stated that he was enjoying it.[6] He brought a woman (apparently generally known as the "Duchess") to the rear of the plant yard and introduced some of the employees to her. He took another employee to visit her and when this man got too drunk to be able to go home, punched his time-card for him and put him on the table in the representatives' meeting room in the plant in order to sleep off his intoxication. Weigand's immediate superiors demanded again and again that he be discharged, but each time higher officials intervened on Weigand's behalf because as was naively stated he was "a representative" [of the association]. In return for not working at the job for which he was hired, the petitioner gave him full pay and on five separate occasions raised his wages. One of these raises was general; that is to say, Weigand profited by a general wage increase throughout the plant, but the other four raises were given Weigand at times when other employees in the plant did not receive wage increases.

The petitioner contends that Weigand was discharged because of cumulative grievances against him. But about the time of the discharge it was suspected by some of the representatives that Weigand had joined the complaining CIO union. One of the representatives taxed him with this fact and Weigand offered to bet a hundred dollars that it could not be proved. On July 22, 1941 Weigand did disclose his union membership to the vice-chairman (Rattigan) of the Association and to another representative (Mullen) and apparently tried to persuade them to support the union. Weigand asserts that the next day he with Rattigan and Mullen, were seen talking to CIO organizer Reichwein on a street corner. The following day, according to Weigand's testimony, Mullen came to Weigand at the plant and stated that Weigand, Rattigan and himself had been seen talking to Reichwein and that he, Mullen, had just had an interview with Personnel Director McIlvain and Plant Manager Mahan. According to Weigand,

6. Weigand stated that he was carried on the payroll as a "rigger". He was asked what was a rigger. He replied: "I don't know; I am not a rigger."

Mullen said to him, "Maybe you didn't get me in a jam." And, "We were seen down there." The following day Weigand was discharged.

As this court stated in National Labor Relations Board v. Condenser Corp., supra, 3 Cir., 128 F.2d at page 75, an employer may discharge an employee for a good reason, a poor reason or no reason at all so long as the provisions of the National Labor Relations Act are not violated. It is, of course, a violation to discharge an employee because he has engaged in activities on behalf of a union. Conversely an employer may retain an employee for a good reason, a bad reason or no reason at all and the reason is not a concern of the Board. But it is certainly too great a strain on our credulity to assert, as does the petitioner, that Weigand was discharged for an accumulation of offenses. We think that he was discharged because his work on behalf of the CIO had become known to the plant manager. That ended his sinecure at the Budd plant. The Board found that he was discharged because of his activities on behalf of the union. The record shows that the Board's finding was based on sufficient evidence.

The order of the Board will be enforced.

---

# PROBLEMS FOR DISCUSSION

**1.** In the *Budd* case, was there not "just cause" for Weigand's discharge, solely on the basis of his work record? If the Board had found that the discharge was for work-related reasons, would its conclusion have been supported "by evidence," as was the standard for impregnability of Board fact-findings on judicial review under the Wagner Act of 1935? Would its conclusion have been supported "by substantial evidence on the record considered as a whole," the standard as amended by the Taft–Hartley Act in 1947?

**2.** What is the purpose of the remedy in the Section 8(a)(3) case? Was it proper, for example, for the Board to order that Weigand be reinstated? What was the purpose of the reinstatement order? A deterrent or punishment as to the Budd Company? Protection for Weigand and restoration for the wrong done him? A demonstration to other employees that the Government will not permit unionization to be jeopardized by employer reprisal?

**3.** In an action in a civil court for breach of an employment contract on the part of the employer, to what remedies will the wronged employee normally be entitled? Should any conventional limitations upon the remedial power of a court of law or equity similarly apply to the National Labor Relations Board? Does Section 10(c) offer any illumination?

**4.** Assume that, upon his reinstatement, Weigand continues to live a life of leisure and debauchery while on the job. What is the Company's recourse?

---

## The "discrimination" requirement

The *Budd* case and the *Mueller Brass* case which follows involve the discharge of an employee, with the employer claiming that the discharge was for a legitimate work-related reason, while the General Counsel claims that the employer's true motive was "discrimination," i.e., retaliation for being a union member or supporter. It is clear that if a discriminatory motive and a discouragement of union support can be shown, Section 8(a)(3) will be violated; such a discharge will violate Section 8(a)(1) as well.

Might there not be circumstances, however, in which a discharge will so chill union membership or other union activity, even without a hostile intent directed at the union, that an unfair labor practice might properly be found? Presumably, a violation would be found not under Section 8(a)(3) but rather under Section 8(a)(1)—which the student by now appreciates can be violated simply by proof that the impact on Section 7 rights outweighs any legitimate employer interest.

Suppose, for example, that the most active and effective union organizer on the company payroll is also the most junior employee and the most incompetent as well. In the midst of an organizing campaign, the employer—without knowledge that the worker in question is a union organizer—lays him off, or discharges him, as a result of a loss in volume of business. Empirical evidence suggests that many union supporters will view the layoff or discharge as motivated by hostility to the union; at the least, the momentum of the organizing campaign will be slowed by the worker's absence from the plant. Should the employer's action be deemed a violation of Section 8(a)(1) on the theory that although the business reason is substantial it is outweighed by the adverse impact on unionization? In fact, the NLRB endorses no such theory. Why not?

What should be the result if the disciplinary action is more directly related to the employee's union activities? Suppose, for example, that the union organizer is fired because he is engaged in organizing—but that he is doing so during working time when he is needed at his work station? Here, unlike the first example, it is arguable that the discharge was *because* of his union activity such that the adverse impact on Section 7 rights would be even greater. Nonetheless, we know that the discharge will be upheld, under *Republic Aviation Corp. v. NLRB*, p. 117, supra. If the discharge does not violate Section 8(a)(1), as the Court stated in unequivocal dictum, then presumably it would not violate Section 8(a)(3) either.

Consider, however, that in *Republic Aviation* the unlawful firing for lunchtime solicitation was based upon a company rule posted long before the advent of the union, and the Court was prepared to assume that the employer would have discharged any employee engaged in lunchtime solicitation whether or not on union business. Presumably, the discharge "discouraged union membership" (broadly understood to embrace union-supporting activities) within Section 8(a)(3). But was this effect brought about by "discrimination"? Notice how the Supreme Court, in its discussion of the discharge, effectively eliminates a separate motive requirement under Section 8(a)(3). Should the Court have instead found the discharge to violate Section 8(a)(1), with the adverse impact on Section 7 rights outweighing the employer's negligible interest in banning lunchtime solicitation? (Note also that the reinstatement and backpay might have been treated simply as a remedy for the underlying Section 8(a)(1) violation stemming from the ban on solicitation, rather than for an independent violation by virtue of the discharge.)

*Republic Aviation* was a fairly early Supreme Court decision, and the 8(a)(3) issue was a subsidiary one—so perhaps one ought not place too much weight on the Court's analysis of it. More recently, however, the Court was presented with a case in which two employee organizers were discharged by the employer in good faith, after he was informed (erroneously) that the employees threatened to use dynamite if necessary to secure union recognition. Should the employer's good faith, its lack of hostility to the union as such, and its lack of retaliatory motive provide a defense?—reasoning from first principles? reasoning under Section 8(a)(3)? under Section 8(a)(1)? See NLRB v. Burnup & Sims, 379 U.S. 21, 85 S.Ct. 171, 13 L.Ed.2d 1 (1964).

The great bulk of discharge cases brought to the National Labor Relations Board are framed under Section 8(a)(3), with the 8(a)(1) violation following derivatively. It is, in other words, generally required that there be proof that the discharge, or lesser discipline, was a product of anti-union animus. In some cases, the record will suggest that the business-related reason proffered by the employer for the discharge is in fact no more than a pretext, and that the sole reason for the discharge was in fact the employee's union activities. In other cases, the record will suggest that the business-related reason did in fact enter into the employer's decision but that the decision was also in part attributable to anti-union animus. (Would you characterize the *Budd Mfg.* case as a "pretext" case or a "dual motive" case?) In these cases, turning upon the often complex issue of subjective motivation, what are the proof burdens placed upon the General Counsel and the employer?

For many years, the answer to that question was unclear. The NLRB tended to find a violation of the Act if anti-union animus contributed in any part to the discipline, no matter how poor the employee's work record might have been. Many decisions in the courts of appeals, however, required that there be a finding that the anti-union motive was a "substantial" motive or the "predominant" motive or the "sole" motive for the discharge. (Do you believe that the Board's approach was consistent with the language and the spirit of the statute? Were there good reasons for the courts to require the more onerous showing? Consider these questions in the context of the *Budd* and *Mueller Brass* cases.)

The Board attempted to clarify its position, and to respond in some degree to appellate criticism, in Wright Line, 251 NLRB 1083 (1980), enf'd, 662 F.2d 899 (1st Cir.1981), cert. denied, 455 U.S. 989, 102 S.Ct. 1612, 71 L.Ed.2d 848 (1982). There, the Board adverted to Section 10(c) of the NLRA, which states that unfair labor practice violations must be based "upon the preponderance of the testimony" taken by the Board, and it held that the General Counsel had the burden of proving that the employee's conduct protected by Section 7 was a substantial or motivating factor in the discharge. Even if this was shown and the employer did not rebut that showing, the employer could avoid a finding of violation by proving by a preponderance of the evidence that the discharge was for job-related reasons such that the employee would have lost his or her job even in the absence of protected conduct. In effect, the employer's business justification was to be an affirmative defense, as to which the employer bore the burden not simply of initiating the introduction of evidence but also of persuading the fact-finder. In a pretext case, the affirmative defense of business justification would be wholly without merit; in a dual-motive case, the business reason would in fact have been given some weight by the employer in discharging the employee, and the employer would then have to prove that the discharge would have been carried out for that reason alone. If the employer failed to establish the affirmative defense, the General Counsel would prevail regardless of the degree of unlawful motivation involved.

The Supreme Court was confronted in NLRB v. TRANSPORTATION MANAGEMENT CORP., 462 U.S. 393, 103 S.Ct. 2469, 76 L.Ed.2d 667 (1983), with the question whether the *Wright Line* allocation of the burden of proof was consistent with the statement in Section 10(c) that the burden lay with the General Counsel to prove the case "upon a preponderance of the testimony." The Supreme Court upheld the Board's approach.

The Court noted that the Board properly placed upon the General Counsel the burden of persuasion on the question whether the employee was discharged at least in part because he or she engaged in protected activities. The Court then stated that it was reasonable and within the Board's power to base an unfair labor practice violation on that "partial" motivation alone. An employer's showing that the adverse disciplinary action would have occurred in any event could (if the Board wished) be held by the Board to go only to the question of permissible remedy; on that remedial issue, the burden of proof could surely have been placed on the employer. Instead, the Board has chosen to implement a rule yet more favorable to the employer—that the employer can use the fact that the employee would have in any event been discharged for business reasons as an affirmative defense to the claimed violation of Section 8(a)(3). "We are unprepared to hold that this is an impermissible construction of the Act. * * * The Board's allocation of the burden of proof is clearly reasonable in this context. * * * The employer is a wrongdoer; he has acted out of a motive that is declared illegitimate by the statute. It is fair that he bear the risk that the influence of legal and illegal motives cannot be separated, because he knowingly created the risk and because the risk was created not by innocent activity but by his own wrongdoing." On the facts of the particular case, the Court held that the Board had a reasonable evidentiary basis for concluding that the discharged employee would not have been discharged were it not for his efforts to establish a union, and for concluding that the employer had not carried the burden of persuasion to the contrary.

The Seventh Circuit glossed the meaning of these respective burdens in the context of a case where the employer alleged that the complainant, whom the Board's General Counsel alleged to have been discharged for union activity, had already been earmarked for discharge which the employee had not been told pending the hiring of his replacement. NLRB v. GATX Logistics, Inc., 160 F.3d 353 (7th Cir.1998). GATX argued that the General Counsel must first prove that the employee's protected activity contributed to his discharge "by a preponderance of the evidence" *before* the burden of going forward to satisfy the *Wright Line* test can be shifted to it. The court disagreed, *id.* n.2 at 356–357 (citations omitted):

> *Wright Line*'s reference to "a *prima facie* showing sufficient to support the *inference* that protected conduct was a 'motivating factor' in the employer's decision," 251 NLRB at 1089 (emphasis supplied), may have been intended simply as a measure of the quantum of evidence that the General Counsel must present at the hearing before the ALJ in order to survive the equivalent of a motion for judgment as a matter of law, and thus to require the employer to put on a case. Typically, such motions are resolved without regard to the weight of the evidence.... Whether the General Counsel has carried the burden of *persuasion* is necessarily a question addressed to the weight of the evidence, however, and for that reason it is one that will usually be addressed at the conclusion of the hearing. Indeed, Board precedent indicates that the answer to this question must be based on the record as a whole, including whatever evidence the employer has presented.

*See also* FES, 331 NLRB No. 20 (2000) (adopting guidelines on respective burdens of proof in refusal-to-hire cases under § 8(a)(3)).

---

## PROBLEMS FOR DISCUSSION

**1.** Is the issue decided in *Transportation Management* of great practical consequences? How often will the evidence as to job-related "cause" be so evenly and delicately balanced that the outcome of the case will turn on whether the employer or the General Counsel must "persuade" the NLRB? Was the evidence in the *Budd* case (or below in *Mueller Brass*) thus delicately balanced? Will the fact that the Board—with Supreme Court approval—now places the burden of persuasion regarding "cause" upon the employer likely induce the General Counsel not to develop the kind of evidence of illicit motive fully presented in those cases?

**2.** What if, in a Section 8(a)(3) case, the company proves that the charging party would have been discharged or laid off for cause anyway, and then the General Counsel proves that the union animus accelerated the severance by one month? Has an unfair labor practice been proven? If so, what is the remedy?

**3.** Could the NLRB now change its approach in cases like *Transportation Management,* and hold that Section 8(a)(3) is violated whenever anti-union animus is present in *any* degree when an employee is discharged, even if there would have been a discharge for "cause" anyway? Should the Board adopt such a principle? What are the competing considerations?

---

# Mueller Brass Co. v. NLRB

544 F.2d 815 (5th Cir.1977).

■ JAMES C. HILL, CIRCUIT JUDGE.

This case is before the court upon the petition of Mueller Brass Co. (the "Company") for review of, and upon cross-application for enforcement of, an order of the National Labor Relations Board (the "Board"). The issues presented are whether substantial evidence on the record as a whole supports the Board's findings that the Company violated Sections 8(a)(1) and (3) of the National Labor Relations Act (the "Act"), 29 U.S.C.A. §§ 158(a)(1) and (3), by discharging employees Hansford Stone and James Roy Rogers * * *.

The appropriate standard of review in this case is clear. We are to sustain the Board's determinations if they are supported by substantial evidence on the record considered as a whole. 29 U.S.C.A. § 160(e); NLRB v. Brown, 380 U.S. 278, 85 S.Ct. 980, 13 L.Ed.2d 839 (1965); Universal Camera Corp. v. NLRB, 340 U.S. 474, 71 S.Ct. 456, 95 L.Ed. 456 (1951); International Organization of Masters, Mates and Pilots v. NLRB, 539 F.2d 554 (5th Cir.1976). It is not our function to overturn the Board's choice between two equally plausible inferences from the facts if the choice is reasonable, even though we might reach a contrary result if deciding the case *de novo*. NLRB v. United Insurance Co., 390 U.S. 254, 88 S.Ct. 988, 19 L.Ed.2d 1083 (1968); NLRB v. Mueller Brass Co., 501 F.2d 680, 683–684 (5th Cir.1974); NLRB v. Standard Forge & Axle Co., 420 F.2d 508 (5th Cir.1969), cert. denied, 400 U.S. 903, 91 S.Ct. 140, 27 L.Ed.2d 140 (1970). However, even though our scope of review is thus limited, we should deny enforcement if, after a full review of the record, we are unable *conscientiously* to conclude that the evidence supporting the Board's determinations is substantial.[2] Universal Camera Corp. v. NLRB, supra; NLRB v. Mueller Brass Co., 509 F.2d 704, 707 (5th Cir.1975); NLRB v. O.A. Fuller Super Markets, Inc., 374 F.2d 197, 200 (5th Cir.1967).

The Company began production in 1971 in Fulton, Mississippi. The union conducted unsuccessful organizing campaigns in 1971 and 1973, and began its third campaign in early 1974. In NLRB v. Mueller Brass Co., 501 F.2d 680 (5th Cir.1974), this Court upheld the Board's findings that the Company violated §§ 8(a)(1) and (3) of the Act by discharging an employee, and by making threats and suggesting that union organizers were being blacklisted by employees [sic] in the area. Significantly, this court found that "[t]here is no question from the record that the Company was strongly anti-union." Id. at 685.

Later, in NLRB v. Mueller Brass Co., 509 F.2d 704 (5th Cir.1975), this court refused to enforce orders of the Board. This court found that "even

---

**2.** It is important to bear in mind that "[t]he substantiality of evidence must take into account whatever in the record fairly detracts from its weight." Universal Camera Corp. v. NLRB, 340 U.S. at 488, 71 S.Ct. at 464. See also Bowman Transportation, Inc. v. Arkansas–Best Freight System, Inc., 419 U.S. 281, 234 n. 2, 95 S.Ct. 438, 42 L.Ed.2d 447 (1974).

considered against the Company's prior anti-union sentiment," the unrefuted testimony did not constitute substantial evidence that the Company had created an impression of surveillance. In addition, this Court upheld the suspension of an employee involved in the case *sub judice,* finding no substantial evidence to indicate that the Company had treated him differently from other employees who falsified a report in violation of Company rules. With this background, we proceed to the case at bar.

Hansford Stone, Jr. went to work for the Company in March, 1972. Stone was given a verbal warning about absenteeism in February, 1974, and he received a written warning in April, 1974. Stone was specifically informed and warned about an automatic termination under Plant Rule 40.[4]

On April 25, 1974, Stone went to see his physician, Dr. Collum, who advised him that he should go to the hospital. Stone reported this to the Company and Glenn Grissom, the personnel representative, placed him on sick leave. Grissom advised Stone that he should contact the Company when he was able to return to work and that he should present his doctor's release at that time.

Stone was hospitalized from April 25 until May 4, but he did not return to work until May 14. He did not contact the Company between the date of his hospital release and the date of his return to work. Charles Henson, the Company's general foreman, received a report that Stone had been seen around town and, upon inquiry, the Company received a note on May 9 from Dr. Collum stating that Stone should have been able to return to work on May 6, 1974. Thus, on May 9, 1974, Stone was terminated pursuant to Plant Rule 40. Subsequently, the Company received an insurance report indicating that Stone had been discharged from the hospital and that no home confinement was required.

Stone presented himself for work on May 14, 1974. He presented a May 13th note from Dr. Collum stating that he should be able to return to work on May 14. Stone was shown Dr. Collum's May 9th note and asked why he did not report to work on May 6. Stone stated that he had contracted a sore throat. He then left and returned the same day with a third note from Dr. Collum attempting to void the preceding two notes. The Company refused to reinstate him.

The Administrative Law Judge (ALJ) found that Stone's unexcused absence from work in combination with his previous record of absenteeism and the report that he had been seen visiting around town were a sufficient basis for the Company's belief that he had deliberately overstayed his excused absence and then prevailed upon his doctor to contradict his earlier reports. Despite the Company's admitted opposition to the union and its knowledge of Stone's sympathies,[5] the ALJ concluded that Stone was

---

**4.** Company Rule 40 of the 1974 rules provided: An employee who is absent for three consecutive working days without permission will be considered a voluntary quit.

**5.** In fact, the ALJ had previously concluded that remarks made to Stone by Company officials violated Section 8(a)(1) of the Act. See infra.

terminated for violating the rule about unexcused absences. The Board disagreed and from its review of the record concluded that the discharge of Stone was motivated by the Company's opposition to the union and its desire to rid itself of a known union adherent.

The conduct of Stone *pales* in comparison to the actions which formed the basis for the discharge of James Roy Rogers. Rogers began his employment with the Company in February, 1972. Prior to his discharge in February, 1974, he worked the 11:00 p.m. to 7:00 a.m. shift at the plant. Rogers had been active in union organization for approximately one and one-half years and was well known as a union activist by Company officials. He was discharged for conduct which was characterized by the Administrative Law Judge as "vulgar and offensive" by "any standard of acceptable conduct."

In summary, on January 31, 1974, during the 5:00 a.m. break Rogers displayed a mechanized artificial male sex organ to a female employee at the plant. The female employee was embarrassed and turned away. The very next night Rogers, on a dare from a fellow employee, approached another female employee and made her an indecent and offensive proposition. She, too, was embarrassed and upset by the remark.

A few days later Frank Robinson, the Company's Industrial Relations Manager, received a report that there had been an incident in the plant the previous week which had upset the female employees. The person responsible for the incident was not identified. The next day Robinson began an inquiry into the matter and after an extensive investigation, Rogers was interviewed and admitted the incidents involved. Rogers was then discharged by the Company for violation of Plant Rule 22.[6]

With regard to the discharge of Rogers, the ALJ felt that, in light of the Company's opposition to the union, its knowledge of Rogers' union sympathies, its prior discrimination against him,[7] and its protracted investigation into his offenses, despite the absence of employee complaints, compared to its investigations into prior offenses toward female employees, the discharge of Rogers for his improper conduct was a pretext for finally getting rid of him. The Board agreed with the ALJ that the discharge of Rogers was pretextual.

In controversies involving employee discharges or suspensions, the motive of the employer is the controlling factor. NLRB v. Brown, 380 U.S. at 287, 85 S.Ct. at 986. Absent a showing of anti-union motivation, an employer may discharge an employee without running afoul of the fair labor laws for a good reason, a bad reason or no reason at all. *NLRB v. O.A. Fuller Super Markets, Inc.,* supra. The mere fact that a specific employee not only breaks a Company rule but also evinces a pro-union sentiment is

**6.**  Company Rule 22 provides:

An employee shall not engage in disorderly, immoral, indecent or illegal conduct.

**7.**  Rogers' name was prominent in 204 N.L.R.B. 617 (1973), *enforcement granted,* 501 F.2d 680 (5th Cir.1974), and he was suspended in 208 N.L.R.B. 534 (1974), *enforcement denied,* 509 F.2d 704 (5th Cir. 1975).

alone not sufficient to destroy the just cause for his discharge. NLRB v. Mueller Brass Co., 509 F.2d at 711; see NLRB v. Soft Water Laundry, Inc., 346 F.2d 930 (5th Cir.1965). The essence of discrimination in violation of Section 8(a)(3) of the Act is in treating like cases differently. Finally, the Board must sustain the burden of showing evidence on the record which establishes a reasonable inference of causal connection between the Company's antiunion animus and the employee's discharge.

In the case *sub judice*, the ALJ concluded that the Company's antiunion sentiment played no part in its decision to terminate Hansford Stone. In reversing, the Board overstepped its bounds. As we observed in NLRB v. McGahey, 233 F.2d 406, 412–13 (5th Cir.1956):

> The Board's error is the frequent one in which the existence of the reasons stated by the employer as the basis for the discharge is evaluated in terms of its reasonableness. If the discharge was excessively harsh, if lesser forms of discipline would have been adequate, if the discharged employee was more, or just as, capable as the one left to do the job, or the like then, the argument runs, the employer must not actually have been motivated by managerial considerations, and (here a full 180 degree swing is made) the stated reason thus dissipated as pretense, nought remains but antiunion purpose as the explanation. But as we have so often said: management is for management. Neither Board nor Court can second-guess it or give it gentle guidance by over-the-shoulder supervision. Management can discharge for good cause, or bad cause, or no cause at all. It has, as the master of its own business affairs, complete freedom with but one specific, definite qualification: it may not discharge when the real motivating purpose is to do that which Section 8(a)(3) forbids.

The Board cites two reasons for its decision to reverse the conclusion of the ALJ: the fact that the Company made no effort to contact Stone prior to discharging him and the Company's failure to credit the doctor's final note which attempted to void all previous notes. However unreasonable the Board may consider these actions on the part of the Company, there is no evidence in the record to indicate that the Company had ever conducted its business otherwise. We know of no requirement that it do so. We conclude that there is no substantial evidentiary basis in the record for the finding that the discharge of Stone was discriminatory and in violation of Section 8(a)(3) of the Act.

We are literally shocked by the conclusion of the Board that Rogers was discharged in violation of the Act and that he is entitled to be reinstated. Rogers' admitted conduct and statements were vulgar and offensive by any standard of decency. The Board was of the opinion that, in light of the prevailing mores in the plant and the treatment afforded to prior transgressors of decent moral standards, the termination of Rogers was pretextual. The answer to such an argument lies in Frosty Morn Meats, Inc. v. NLRB, 296 F.2d 617, 621 (5th Cir.1961):

* * * If, however, the misdeeds of the employee are so flagrant that he would almost certainly be fired anyway there is no room for discrimination to play a part. The employee will not have been harmed by the employer's union animus, and neither he nor any others will be discouraged from membership in a union, since all will understand that the employee would have been fired anyway. It must be remembered that the statute prohibits discrimination, and that the focus on dominant motivation is only a test to reveal whether discrimination has occurred. Discrimination consists in treating like cases differently. If an employer fires a union sympathizer or organizer, a finding of discrimination rests on the assumption that in the absence of the union activities he would have treated the employee differently.

When an employee gives his employer as much reason to fire him as Judkins did, by refusing to follow instructions and by giving not only his supervisors but also his fellow employees the impression that he was uncooperative, there is no basis for the conclusion that the employer has treated him differently than he would have treated a nonunion employee. As a speculative matter, it may or may not be true that union animus loomed larger in the employer's motivation than Judkins' shortcomings as a worker. But when the evidence of just cause for discharge is as great as it is here, the record as a whole does not support the conclusion that the discharged employee was deprived of any right because of union activities. The power of reinstatement is remedial. It is not punitive. It is not to penalize an employer for anti-unionism by forcing on the pay-roll an employee unfit to stay on the job.

Rogers was discharged for good and sufficient cause. Insofar as the Board's order requires reinstatement and back pay for him, enforcement is denied. * * *

■ GODBOLD, CIRCUIT JUDGE (dissenting):

The majority opinion departs from our proper role in reviewing NLRB orders and from the standards that guide us in this role.

(1) The discharge of Stone

The majority opinion is neither more nor less than a retrial of this aspect of the case.

Stone has a prior record of absenteeism and was warned about it. From April 25 to May 4 he was hospitalized. He did not report for work, and the company was told that he was being seen around town. Thereafter it received three notes from Stone's doctor. The first note, received May 9, stated that Stone should have been able to return to work May 6. That same day the company terminated him without discussion or notice, pursuant to a plant rule that one absent for three consecutive working days without permission would be considered a voluntary quit.

Stone showed up for work May 14 bringing the second note from his doctor, dated May 13. It said that he should be able to return to work May 14. Stone was not permitted to go to work, and he left the plant. The company then called the doctor and asked him what the May 13 note meant, and the doctor said that it referred to a sore throat that Stone had contracted. An hour later the doctor called back and asked the company to accept the May 13 note as a release for Stone's return to work and to destroy the May 9 note. Later the same day, May 14, Stone came back with the third note, in which the doctor said that he probably told Stone to take a week off after leaving the hospital on May 4, because of his back problems, but that he was well enough to work as of May 14, that all previous statements made by the doctor were "null and void" and no other notes would be forthcoming.

The ALJ drew from these events an inference that Stone had used his excused absence for sickness as an excuse to stay out after May 6 and had prevailed on the doctor to contradict his earlier reports. That was a permissible inference. The Board, however, drew a different inference. It noted the following elements of proof: (1) The company was hostile to the union and previously had been before the NLRB for commission of unfair labor practices. (2) The company knew of Stone's union sentiment and had actively sought to dissuade him from his union adherence. (3) The company made no effort to contact Stone to determine his condition. (4) On May 9, after determining Stone's release date from the hospital, the company summarily terminated him and gave him no notice that he had been terminated. (5) The company admitted it had no reason to doubt the authenticity of the third note from the doctor. From all of the evidence the Board drew inferences that the third note dissipated the suspicion that Stone had been malingering, and that the discharge was pretextual. Certainly it was entitled to draw these inferences from the evidence before it.

Language quoted by Judge Hill from NLRB v. McGahey, 233 F.2d 406 (C.A.5, 1956), does not change the standard of review that this court has followed in innumerable cases. Further on in the opinion the court specifically noted that:

> In the choice between lawful and unlawful motives, the record taken as a whole must present a substantial basis of believable evidence pointing toward the unlawful one.

Id. at 413. *McGahey* teaches us that reasonableness, or lack of it, may be circumstantial evidence of the employer's motive in a discharge case, but the Board's view of employer action is not to be treated as talismanic. In the present case the Board did not consider the employer's action in the context of reasonableness or unreasonableness. It accepted the third note as credible, found it was sufficient to dissipate the charge of malingering, and pointed out that the company admitted there was no reason to doubt the authenticity of the note. On this evidence the Board concluded that the discharge was pretextual. Similarly, if introduced, evidence that the company was not acting in accordance with its usual practices would have been part of the overall evidence to be considered. But it is quite different to hold that evidence of motive is insubstantial unless it includes evidence of behavior inconsistent with usual practices.

This is a substantial evidence case. The record fully supports the Board's inference of improper motive.

(2) The discharge of Rogers

This is a plain, everyday substantial evidence case except for two factors. First, the status of Rogers as a target for company action is recorded in two previous decisions of this court. Second, Rogers' conduct, which the Board found was the asserted basis for a pretextual discharge, was sexually oriented.[1]

In Mueller I, NLRB v. Mueller Brass Co., 501 F.2d 680 (C.A.5, 1974), we enforced a Board order finding Mueller guilty of § 8(a)(3) discharges and § 8(a)(1) coercion. One of the targets of the coercive company statements was Rogers. 501 F.2d at 686. In that same case the ALJ made this finding with respect to Rogers:

> * * * respondent's industrial relations manager, Gregory, told an employee in September 1972, that Rogers' name was on the desk of every employer in the area as a "union pusher" and that, if he lost his job with respondent, he would be unable to get another in that area.

This was quoted and relied upon in *Mueller II,* discussed below. See 509 F.2d at 708 n.5.[2] In Mueller II, NLRB v. Mueller Brass Co., 509 F.2d 704 (C.A.5, 1975), we declined to enforce a Board order making Rogers whole for a three-day suspension for falsifying excuses for absenteeism because there was no substantial evidence that he was treated differently than others committing like offenses. In the present case, *Mueller III,* the Board properly considered this background in reaching its conclusions that the discharge was pretextual.

I turn now to the factor strongly emphasized by the majority, the sexual content of Rogers' actions. The Board found that what Rogers did was not out of keeping with the general level of conduct in the plant, where bawdy sexual horseplay was commonplace, accepted, and not the subject of discipline. The evidence fully supports the Board's finding. Pornographic pictures were passed around by employees and pornographic books left in accessible places for employees and supervisors to examine. The use of strong language, including four-letter words, dirty jokes and suggestive remarks was common among employees and supervisors. One witness told

---

**1.** "In view of Respondent's opposition to the Union, its knowledge of Rogers' union sympathies, its prior discrimination against him, and the protracted investigation into Rogers' two offenses, despite the absence of any employee complaints, as compared with its complacency over complaints by women employees in similar situations, I am satisfied that Respondent relied on Rogers' improper conduct as a pretext for finally getting rid of him. I therefore find that Respondent violated Section 8(a)(3) in discharging Rogers."

Appendix p. 359.

**2.** Additionally, in *Mueller I,* this court found that there was "no question from the record that the Company was strongly anti-union." 501 F.2d at 685.

of means in the plant to order films, plainly referring to pornographic films. The general foreman on Rogers' 11 p.m. to 7 a.m. shift freely exchanged sex jokes with female employees and joined in the general appreciation of pornographic material which turned up around the plant. There is testimony that in one incident he invited two women to examine a book with pictures of men and women having intercourse and approved their suggestion that they take it into the ladies' room to look at it even though neither was scheduled for a break. This foreman was present when Rogers had the artificial sex organ, saw it and laughed at it, and did not say or do anything about its presence. The industrial relations manager of the plant was present, saw the organ and laughed at it. Another foreman saw it later the same evening and "just died laughing." Rogers displayed the device to a group of male and female employees. Only one gave any indication of offense. The rest laughed at it.

Of equal, if not greater significance, is the evidence of other specific incidents of sexually oriented evidence [sic] that did not subject the participants to discipline. Rule 22 was given as the basis for Rogers' discharge: "An employee shall not engage in disorderly, immoral, indecent or illegal conduct." No one other than Rogers has ever been discharged for violation of this rule. I have already described the conduct of Rogers' foreman and the industrial relations manager with respect to the very circumstances which cost Rogers his job. Also there is evidence of three specific incidents of sexually oriented conduct by male employees toward female employees. With respect to one incident, the husband and the father of the female victim complained to the plant manager and he promised to take action. There is no evidence that any action was ever taken, and the supervisor who was the alleged culprit was later promoted. More than a year later the female employee asked about the matter and was told that she ought to drop it since her complaint was so old.

In two other incidents female employees complained of offensive, sexually oriented remarks made to them by male employees. One of these occurred just a week before the hearing in this case. The male employees were not disciplined.

* * * [T]he discipline inflicted was the harshest available. This uncontroverted evidence of disparate treatment acquires even greater force when laid against the strong antiunion bias specifically manifested in the past by threats directed at Rogers. 509 F.2d at 708 n. 5. * * *

There are, of course, many cases in which employees have been fired for obscene language or conduct, and the discharges have been held not to violate the Act. The key to understanding is that the drawing of permissible inferences from consideration of what the employee did and said, the mores of the work place, the employee's union adherence, and the antiunion bias of the employer, is the province of the Board, not to be undone by judges. In this instance, the Board was entitled to conclude that, although Rogers' conduct was "bad" in the sense that it was coarse and vulgar, he would not have been discharged in the absence of antiunion bias. It then becomes our duty to enforce. We do not sit as monitors of the level of sexual horseplay permitted in industrial plants or as censors of conduct by a worker which from an Olympian level we think distasteful. Nor do we have any business substituting our judgments of good taste for the experience and expertise of the Board in day-to-day matters of industrial life. * * *

---

*Judicial review of Board fact-findings*

During the Taft–Hartley debates in 1946 and 1947, considerable dissatisfaction was expressed concerning the narrow scope of judicial review of NLRB findings. There were wide differences in this respect between the House and Senate bills, and the Conference Report, which made relevant changes in sections 10(b), (c) and (e), was a compromise. The Statement of the House Managers (H.R.Rep. No. 510, 80th Cong., 1st Sess. 55–56 (1947), 1 Leg.Hist.LMRA 559–60) explained that:

"Under the language of section 10(e) of the present act, findings of the Board, upon court review of Board orders, are conclusive 'if supported by evidence'. By reason of this language, the courts have, as one has put it, in effect 'abdicated' to the Board. * * * In many instances deference on the part of the courts to specialized knowledge that is supposed to inhere in administrative agencies has led the courts to acquiesce in decisions of the Board, even when the findings concerned mixed issues of law and of fact (N.L.R.B. v. Hearst Publications, Inc., 322 U.S. 111, 64 S.Ct. 851, 88 L.Ed. 1170; Packard Motor Car Co. v. N.L.R.B., 330 U.S. 485, 67 S.Ct. 789, 91 L.Ed. 1040, decided March 10, 1947), or when they rested only on inferences that were not, in turn, supported by facts in the record (Republic Aviation v. N.L.R.B., 324 U.S. 793, 65 S.Ct. 982, 89 L.Ed. 1372, 157 A.L.R. 1081; Le Tourneau Co. v. N.L.R.B., 324 U.S. 793, 65 S.Ct. 982, 89 L.Ed. 1372, 157 A.L.R. 1081).

"As previously stated in the discussion of amendments to section 10(b) and section 10(c), by reason of the new language concerning the rules of evidence and the preponderance of the evidence, presumed expertness on the part of the Board in its field can no longer be a factor in the Board's decisions. * * *

"The Senate amendment provided that the Board's findings with respect to questions of fact should be conclusive if supported by substantial evidence on the record considered as a whole. The provisions of section 10(b) of the conference agreement insure the Board's receiving only legal evidence, and section 10(c) insures its deciding in accordance with the preponderance of the evidence. These two statutory requirements in and of themselves give rise to questions of law which the courts will hereafter be called upon to determine—whether the requirements have been met. This, in conjunction with the language of the Senate amendment with respect to the Board's findings of fact—language which the conference agreement adopts—will very materially broaden the scope of the courts' reviewing power. This is not to say that the courts will be required to decide any case de novo, themselves weighing the evidence, but they will be under a duty to see that the Board observes the provisions of the earlier sections, that it does not infer facts that are not supported by evidence or that are not consistent with evidence in the record, and that it does not concentrate on one element of proof to the exclusion of others without adequate explanation of its reasons for disregarding or discrediting the evidence that is in conflict with its findings. The language also precludes the substitution of expertness for evidence in making decisions. It is believed that the provisions of the conference agreement relating to the courts' reviewing power will be adequate to preclude such decisions as those in [the] *Hearst, Republic Aviation,* and *Le Tourneau,* etc., cases, [see pp. 97, 117 of the Casebook, supra] without unduly burdening the courts. The conference agreement therefore carries the language of the Senate amendment into section 10(e) of the amended act."

In UNIVERSAL CAMERA CORP. v. NLRB, 340 U.S. 474, 490, 71 S.Ct. 456, 466, 95 L.Ed. 456 (1951), the Court held that under the amendment to Section 10(e) "courts must now assume more responsibility for the reasonableness and fairness of Labor Board decisions than some courts have shown in the past." On the other hand, the Court pointed out that Section 10(e) was not intended "to negative the function of the Labor Board as one of these agencies presumably equipped or informed by experience to deal with a specialized field of knowledge, whose findings within that field carry the authority of an expertness which courts do not possess and therefore must respect. Nor does it mean that even as to matters not requiring expertise a court may displace the Board's choice between two fairly conflicting views, even though the court would justifiably have made a different choice had the matter been before it *de novo.* Congress has merely made it clear that a reviewing court is not barred from setting aside a Board decision when it cannot conscientiously find that the evidence supporting that decision is substantial, when viewed in the light that the record in its entirety furnishes, including that body of evidence opposed to the Board's view." 340 U.S. 474, 488, 71 S.Ct. 456, 464–65, 95 L.Ed. 456 (1951).

———

## PROBLEMS FOR DISCUSSION

**1.** Is the passage quoted from the Supreme Court in *Universal Camera* consistent with the objectives articulated in the House Report? Is the majority decision in *Mueller Brass* consistent with the passage quoted from *Universal Camera?*

**2.** Consider the discharge of Stone, in *Mueller Brass,* for unexcused absenteeism. What evidence was likely before the Administrative Law Judge on the issue of Stone's ailments between May 4 and May 14? How free was the NLRB to disagree with the ALJ on this issue? How much weight should be given by the appeals court to the fact that the NLRB and the ALJ disagreed, when the court applies the test of "substantial evidence on the record considered as a whole"? Was the court correct in concluding that, at worst, the record sustained the inference that the company was merely acting "unreasonably" and not discriminatorily?

**3.** Consider the discharge of Rogers for indecent conduct. Given the facts set forth in the majority and dissenting opinions, is the only reasonable conclusion that Rogers was discharged "for cause"? (Consider the prevailing mores within the plant, and the apparent supervisory condonation.) If it is plausible to conclude that the indecent-conduct accusation was merely a pretext, must not the Board's order be enforced? What are the relative capabilities of the ALJ, the NLRB, and the appellate court in assessing the gravity of the employee's misdeeds and therefore the likely motive of the employer?

It should be noted that the maintenance of a racially or sexually hostile work atmosphere—of a pattern of racial slurs and unwanted sexual innuendo by co-workers—can subject an employer to liability under Title VII of the Civil Rights Act of 1964. See Meritor Savings Bank, FSB v. Vinson, 477 U.S. 57, 106 S.Ct. 2399, 91 L.Ed.2d 49 (1986). Such conduct may also be actionable at common law on a theory of infliction of emotional distress for which the employer might be liable under *respondeat superior*. Should the company's assertion of a concern for its legal liability, given the open and notorious course of conduct by both workers and supervisors, be a defense to the Labor Act claim? What if the employer acted both out of a concern to avoid liability, to send a signal to employees of how seriously it viewed sexual harassment, *and* to rid itself of a union activist?

**4.** Had the Board's conclusions regarding the company's motive in both discharges been reached by a federal trial judge, could a court of appeals have reversed them as "clearly erroneous"? Had they been made by a civil jury, could a trial court have properly overturned them on a motion for a judgment n.o.v. or for a new trial? Is the NLRB entitled to a greater or lesser measure of deference on appellate review of fact-findings than the trial judge or the jury?

**5.** Is it fair to say that the NLRB's decision reflects a belief that the policies of the NLRB might be too readily subverted if an anti-union employer could point to a minor contemporaneous delinquency by a union supporter as a justification for severe discipline? Is it fair to say that the opinion of the court majority reflects a belief that sound economic judgments by employers might be too readily subverted if a delinquent employee could point to contemporaneous union activity as a shield protecting incompetence or substandard behavior on the job? If this is an accurate statement of the conflict between the NLRB and the court of appeals, whose view should prevail? See generally Note, Deference to NLRB Adjudicatory Decisionmaking: Has Judicial Review Become Meaningless?, 58 U.Cinc.L.Rev. 653 (1989).

**6.** How does the court majority know that in the case of a discharged union supporter who has committed "flagrant misdeeds", onlooking employees will understand that their own jobs are not jeopardized by their union activities? Compare the findings in the Getman, Goldberg & Herman study, at pp. 186–88 supra.

---

# NLRB v. Adkins Transfer Co.

226 F.2d 324 (6th Cir.1955).

■ McALLISTER, CIRCUIT JUDGE.

The National Labor Relations Board filed a petition for enforcement of its order issued against respondent, Adkins Transfer Company, finding it guilty of violation of Section 8(a)(3) and (1) of the National Labor Relations Act * * *.

Respondent is a small truck line operator, carrying on its business between Chicago and Nashville, with the latter as the extreme southern point served. Its Nashville terminal utilized approximately eight trucks per day in transporting shipments to other cities, and four pick-up trucks for local work in Nashville. There is no evidence of any anti-union attitude on the part of the respondent, but, on the contrary, it has been on good terms with the local Teamsters Union, which is the charging party in the case. In fact, all of its road drivers are members of the Teamsters Union, and all of its local pick-up men and dock men are also members of the union. In addition, all extra employees engaged by respondent are procured by calling the local Teamsters union hall, whereupon the union sends such extra employees to respondent's place of business. This practice is followed in spite of the fact that there is in effect in the State of Tennessee the type of statute known as an open shop statute.

In November, 1953, respondent employed a mechanic and a helper whose duties were exclusively the maintenance and servicing of respondent's trucks. These are the employees involved in this case. In the same month that their employment commenced, the two employees joined the local Teamsters Union. Thereafter, the union demanded that respondent bargain with it for the purpose of entering into two contracts—one, a mechanic's contract for one of the employees, and the other, a service contract, for the other employee. At that time, one of the employees was paid at the rate of $1.25 per hour, and the other, 75 cents per hour. The union representative met with respondent's president and showed him copies of the union's uniform contracts covering mechanics and service men which were currently in effect between the union and other Nashville motor carriers. The various job classifications and the applicable wage rates specified in the contracts were discussed. As the union representative pointed out, under the contracts which he proposed that respondent adopt, one of the employees would receive $1.75 an hour, an increase of 50 cents over his current rate, and the other would receive between $1.25 and $1.40 per hour, an increase of between 50 and 65 cents over his current rate. There was no discussion as to whether a compromise could be reached on wage scales.

The first meeting between the union representative and respondent's president took place November 16. A second meeting occurred November 20. On the next day, the foreman came into the shop where the two employees were working, and stated that he had bad news for them—that the president was going to close the shop because he was not going to pay the union scale. At the direction of respondent's president, the foreman thereafter discharged the two employees. Respondent's president testified with regard to this incident, without contradiction or challenge, that it was "purely and simply a question of costs." Respondent's mechanical work since the discharge of the employees has been done on a job-by-job basis by local truck and automobile dealers, and the servicing has been done partly by its own operating employees and partly by independent business concerns. Respondent's president testified that he found this method of having the mechanical work done had resulted in even lower labor costs than those entailed by its former method of operation, under which respondent had paid $2.00 an hour for the combined services of the two employees. Respondent never replaced the two men, and its president testified on the hearing that it did not intend to.

A hearing was held before the trial examiner who, after listening to the witnesses, filed findings of fact, conclusions of law, and a recommendation. He set forth in his findings that respondent's president testified, credibly, that, based upon his experience in dealing with the union, he believed that if respondent had continued its maintenance department at Nashville without raising the wages of the two employees to meet the union scale, a strike would have ensued which would have effectively closed down respondent's entire business operations. The examiner stated that the accuracy of such opinion was substantiated by the statement of the union representative who testified, on the hearing, that he knew of no instance when the union permitted a contracting employer to pay union members different wage rates than were provided in the union's uniform industry agreement for the particular employee classification. He found that respondent's president, rather than capitulating to the union demands and increasing the wages of the two employees, which he considered economically disadvantageous to respondent, had discontinued the maintenance department and discharged the two maintenance employees. He further found that respondent's president testified that the fact that the two employees joined the union did not motivate their discharge. The trial examiner concluded his findings with the following statement: "This is not a case where an employer who is generally hostile towards unions and opposes employee organization seeks to defeat his employees' efforts to engage in collective bargaining by discontinuing a department in which a majority of the employees have selected a collective bargaining representative. * * * In this regard, it is significant that the complaint does not charge that the Respondent has refused to bargain in good faith with the Union. Here, the Respondent had only two practical choices, either to pay its maintenance employees the wage rates demanded by the Union, or discontinue its maintenance department. No area for bargaining with the Union existed." The examiner then went on to point out that the union representative had testified that, if respondent had kept the maintenance department open but had declined to sign the union contract, the union procedure would have been to call a strike, and that a strike in which the Teamsters Union controlled the over-the-road men and the dock men—as in this case— usually resulted in a 100% shutdown of the company. The examiner, therefore, found that respondent had committed no unfair labor practice by choosing to discontinue its maintenance department and to discharge the two maintenance employees, especially in the absence of evidence of other unfair labor practices or animus toward the union; and that, accordingly, respondent did not discharge the employees to encourage or discourage membership in the labor organization, in violation of Section 8(a)(1) and (3) of the Act. He concluded by recommending that the complaint be dismissed.

The Board, however, rejected the recommendations of the trial examiner and his conclusions as to the alleged unfair labor practices. It held that the discharges established a prima facie case that the dismissal was violative of Section 8(a)(3) and (1) of the Act for the reason that the employees would not have been so summarily dismissed if they had not joined the union, and had not sought, through the union, to exercise the rights incident to union membership. The Board further said that respondent had not sustained its burden of dispelling the inferences fairly to be drawn, and that its claim that the dismissals represented an attempt to resolve a difficult economic position was supported "by nothing more than its subjective anticipation of what the Union might do, rather than upon what the Union actually did do in its representation of these employees." It, therefore, held that the dismissal was violative of the Act and outlined the remedies already mentioned. * * *

We are of the view that the trial examiner was right and the Board was wrong in its decision and order. Only such discrimination as encourages or discourages membership in a labor organization is proscribed by the Act. * * * There was no such discrimination in the instant case. A company may suspend its operations or change its business methods so long as its change in operations is not motivated by the illegal intention to avoid its obligations under the Act. National Labor Relations Board v. Houston Chronicle Pub. Co., 5 Cir., 211 F.2d 848. An employer may discharge or refuse to reemploy one of his employees for any reason, just or unjust, except discrimination because of union activities and relationships, and the controlling and ultimate fact which determines an issue of the kind here presented is, what was the true reason back of the discharge. * * *

It is true that what might be termed the secondary reason for the discharge of the two employees was because they were members of the union, but the fact that they were members of the union was only incidental, and was not the real reason behind their discharge. The real reason was because the union wage scales were too high for respondent to operate profitably the department in question; and, since the employees were members of the union, respondent would be obliged to pay those rates, or close the department, or suffer a strike. It is plain that there was no interference or restraint or coercion of the employees in their rights to self-organization or collective bargaining, and there was no discrimination to encourage or discourage membership in a labor organization. Consequently, there was no violation of Section 8(a)(3) and (1) of the Act.

Respondent had no feeling against the labor union. All of his employees were already members of the union, and his relations with them and the union were friendly and cooperative. The only consideration that actuated respondent in dismissing the employees was, not that they were members of the union, but that the union wage scales were too high for this particular employment and that such services could be more cheaply performed by outside business concerns. All of these facts are indubitable from the evidence before us. It is our view that the trial examiner's finding and recommended disposition are both factually and legally correct, and that the Board's findings of fact to the contrary are not supported by substantial evidence on the record as a whole.

In accordance with the foregoing, a decree will be entered denying enforcement of the order of the Board.

————

## PROBLEMS FOR DISCUSSION

**1.** Is the court correct in concluding that the employer did not "discriminate" in a manner which "discourages" union membership? Would the mechanic and helper not have retained their jobs had they not sought union membership and representation? Does not their discharge for this reason clearly discriminate and discourage? *Who* is discouraged from union membership and activities?

**2.** Did the Board in *Adkins Transfer* disagree with the principle, endorsed by the appeals court, that an employer may transfer or subcontract work which the advent of the union makes it uneconomical to continue doing through one's own employees? What are the strongest arguments that the Board might make in rejecting such a principle? Are these arguments convincing?

**3.** Alternatively, was the Board in agreement with the court's principle just summarized, while merely holding that the facts in the record did not yet render that principle applicable? Phrased another way, would not the Board and court have both held that the subcontracting was lawful had the employer first signed the union's area agreement; and would they not both have found the subcontracting unlawful had it taken place when the two employees were first overheard speaking favorably about joining the Teamsters Union?

**4.** Under the principle adopted by the court, what must the employer show about the costs of meeting the union's wage demands, in order to validate the transfer or subcontracting of work away from unionized employees? (Is this a situation in which, under *Wright Line* and *Transportation Management,* the burden of proof will lie with the employer?) Is this another example of the law rewarding those who are best capable of retaining adroit attorneys and accountants?

————

An analogous problem to that presented in the principal case arises when an employer "because of the union" decides to close its plant and relocate elsewhere. There is general agreement that if the employer's move is motivated by hostility toward and a desire to escape the union, the action violates Section 8(a)(3). "It is * * * well settled that [the employer] may not transfer its situs to deprive his employees of rights protected by Section 7." Local 57, ILGWU v. NLRB (Garwin Corp.), 374 F.2d 295 (D.C.Cir. 1967), cert. denied 387 U.S. 942, 87 S.Ct. 2074, 18 L.Ed.2d 1328 (1967)(BURGER, J.). The relocation is said to be for "anti-union animus" and is labelled a "runaway shop." Over the years, however, there has been disagreement between the Board and the courts of appeals as to the legality of a relocation which is precipitated by wage increases, actual or impending, effected through unionization. As in *Adkins Transfer,* the courts have been generally more willing than the Board to countenance employer relocation triggered by a worsening economic picture to which the union substantially contributes. For example, in NLRB v. RAPID BINDERY, INC., 293

F.2d 170 (2d Cir.1961), the employer moved its bindery operation from cramped and outmoded quarters very shortly after a union was certified; the employer impressed the employees while the election was pending with the likelihood of such a move, and it failed to bargain with the union concerning the relocation after the union was certified. Although the Board found a violation of Section 8(a)(3), the court of appeals reversed, holding:

> "All of the evidence points to motivation for sound business reasons. Though there may have been animosity between Union and Rapid, animosity furnishes no basis for the inference that this was the preponderant motive for the move when convincing evidence was received demonstrating business necessity. The decided cases do not condemn an employer who considers his relationship with his plant's union as only one part of the broad economic picture he must survey when he is faced with determining the desirability of making changes in his operations."

In another case, NLRB v. LASSING, 284 F.2d 781 (6th Cir.1960), cert. den. 366 U.S. 909, 81 S.Ct. 1085, 6 L.Ed.2d 235 (1961), the court stated:

> "The advent of the Union was a new economic factor which necessarily had to be evaluated by the respondent as a part of the overall picture pertaining to costs of operation. It is completely unrealistic in the field of business to say that management is acting arbitrarily or unreasonably in changing its method of operations based on reasonably anticipated increased costs, instead of waiting until such increased costs actually materialize.
>
> " * * * Fundamentally, the change was made because of reasonably anticipated increased costs, regardless of whether this increased cost was caused by the advent of the Union or by some other factor entering into the picture."

Is it practical, or even possible, to authorize relocations or plant removals motivated by the anticipation of increased costs which a union will bring, but to hold illegal such action when motivated by "anti-union animus"? What is anti-union animus, if not a resistance to the union because of the economic burdens it will impose—in the form not only of increased financial benefits for the workers but also of restrictions upon the employer in governing the enterprise, which presumably can also be translated into economic burdens? Are not these added labor-related costs exactly what engenders employer antipathy toward the union? How often is it that the employer nurtures "anti-union animus" which is not economically based? If such is rare indeed, then what is left of Section 8(a)(3) in these kinds of cases?

These issues arise not only in cases of layoff and subcontracting, as in *Adkins Transfer,* and of plant relocation, but also in cases of the closing and termination of the business of a single plant of a multi-plant concern, or of the complete termination and liquidation of an enterprise. That is the scenario of the following case.

## PROBLEM FOR DISCUSSION

In February 1999, the Teamsters won an election to represent the Company's trucking workers. A few weeks later the Company, in retaliation, closed the department, sold its trucks, and contracted out the work. The regional director issued a complaint, and in March of 2000, the ALJ found a violation of § 8(a)(3) and recommended that the trucking department be restored and the employees reinstated there, finding no evidence of "undue hardship." In September 2001, the Board accepted the ALJ's recommended order. The case was then heard before the Court of Appeals. How should it rule? See Coronet Foods, Inc. v. NLRB, 158 F.3d 782 (4th Cir.1998).

---

## Textile Workers Union v. Darlington Mfg. Co.

380 U.S. 263, 85 S.Ct. 994, 13 L.Ed.2d 827 (1965).

■ Mr. Justice Harlan delivered the opinion of the Court.

* * *

Darlington Manufacturing Company was a South Carolina corporation operating one textile mill. A majority of Darlington's stock was held by Deering Milliken & Co., a New York "selling house" marketing textiles produced by others. Deering Milliken in turn was controlled by Roger Milliken, president of Darlington, and by other members of the Milliken family. The National Labor Relations Board found that the Milliken family, through Deering Milliken, operated 17 textile manufacturers, including Darlington, whose products, manufactured in 27 different mills, were marketed through Deering Milliken.

In March 1956 petitioner Textile Workers Union initiated an organizational campaign at Darlington which the company resisted vigorously in various ways, including threats to close the mill if the union won a representation election. On September 6, 1956, the union won an election by a narrow margin. When Roger Milliken was advised of the union victory, he decided to call a meeting of the Darlington board of directors to consider closing the mill. Mr. Milliken testified before the Labor Board:

> "I felt that as a result of the campaign that had been conducted and the promises and statements made in these letters that had been distributed [favoring unionization], that if before we had had some hope, possible hope of achieving competitive [costs] * * * by taking advantage of new machinery that was being put in, that this hope had diminished as a result of the election because a majority of the employees had voted in favor of the union * * *." (R. 457.)

The board of directors met on September 12 and voted to liquidate the corporation, action which was approved by the stockholders on October 17. The plant ceased operations entirely in November, and all plant machinery and equipment was sold piecemeal at auction in December.

The union filed charges with the Labor Board claiming that Darlington had violated §§ 8(a)(1) and 8(a)(3) of the National Labor Relations Act by closing its plant, and § 8(a)(5) by refusing to bargain with the union after the election. The Board, by a divided vote, found that Darlington had been closed because of the anti-union animus of Roger Milliken, and held that to be a violation of § 8(a)(3). The Board also found Darlington to be part of a single integrated employer group controlled by the Milliken family through Deering Milliken; therefore Deering Milliken could be held liable for the unfair labor practices of Darlington. Alternatively, since Darlington was a part of the Deering Milliken enterprise, Deering Milliken had violated the Act by closing part of its business for a discriminatory purpose. The Board ordered back pay for all Darlington employees until they obtained substantially equivalent work or were put on preferential hiring lists at the other Deering Milliken mills. Respondent Deering Milliken was ordered to bargain with the union in regard to details of compliance with the Board order. 139 N.L.R.B. 241.

On review, the Court of Appeals, sitting *en banc,* denied enforcement by a divided vote. 325 F.2d 682. The Court of Appeals held that even accepting *arguendo* the Board's determination that Deering Milliken had the status of a single employer, a company has the absolute right to close out a part or all of its business regardless of anti-union motives. The court therefore did not review the Board's finding that Deering Milliken was a single integrated employer. We granted certiorari * * * to consider the important questions involved. We hold that so far as the Labor Act is concerned, an employer has the absolute right to terminate his entire business for any reason he pleases, but disagree with the Court of Appeals that such right includes the ability to close part of a business no matter what the reason. We conclude that the case must be remanded to the Board for further proceedings.

Preliminarily it should be observed that both petitioners argue that the Darlington closing violated § 8(a)(1) as well as § 8(a)(3) of the Act. We think, however, that the Board was correct in treating the closing only under § 8(a)(3). Section 8(a)(1) provides that it is an unfair labor practice for an employer "to interfere with, restrain, or coerce employees in the exercise of" § 7 rights. Naturally, certain business decisions will, to some degree, interfere with concerted activities by employees. But it is only when the interference with § 7 rights outweighs the business justification for the employer's action that § 8(a)(1) is violated. See, *e.g.,* Labor Board v. Steelworkers, 357 U.S. 357, 78 S.Ct. 1268, 2 L.Ed.2d 1383; Republic Aviation Corp. v. Labor Board, 324 U.S. 793, 65 S.Ct. 982, 89 L.Ed.2d 1372. A violation of § 8(a)(1) alone therefore presupposes an act which is unlawful even absent a discriminatory motive. Whatever may be the limits of § 8(a)(1), some employer decisions are so peculiarly matters of management prerogative that they would never constitute violations of § 8(a)(1), whether or not they involved sound business judgment, unless they also violated § 8(a)(3). Thus it is not questioned in this case that an employer has the right to terminate his business, whatever the impact of such action on concerted activities, if the decision to close is motivated by other than discriminatory reasons. But such action, if discriminatorily motivated, is encompassed within the literal language of § 8(a)(3). We therefore deal with the Darlington closing under that section.

We consider first the argument, advanced by the petitioner union but not by the Board, and rejected by the Court of Appeals, that an employer may not go completely out of business without running afoul of the Labor Act if such action is prompted by a desire to avoid unionization. Given the Board's findings on the issue of motive, acceptance of this contention would carry the day for the Board's conclusion that the closing of this plant was an unfair labor practice, even on the assumption that Darlington is to be regarded as an independent unrelated employer. A proposition that a single businessman cannot choose to go out of business if he wants to would represent such a startling innovation that it should not be entertained without the clearest manifestation of legislative intent or unequivocal judicial precedent so construing the Labor Act. We find neither.

So far as legislative manifestation is concerned, it is sufficient to say that there is not the slightest indication in the history of the Wagner Act or of the Taft–Hartley Act that Congress envisaged any such result under either statute.

As for judicial precedent * * * the courts of appeals have generally assumed that a complete cessation of business will remove an employer from future coverage by the Act. Thus the Court of Appeals said in this case: The Act "does not compel a person to become or remain an employee. It does not compel one to become or remain an employer. Either may withdraw from that status with immunity, so long as the obligations of an employment contract have been met." 325 F.2d, at 685. * * *

The AFL–CIO suggests in its *amicus* brief that Darlington's action was similar to a discriminatory lockout, which is prohibited "because designed to frustrate organizational efforts, to destroy or undermine bargaining representation, or to evade the duty to bargain." One of the purposes of the Labor Act is to prohibit the discriminatory use of economic weapons in an effort to obtain future benefits. The discriminatory lockout designed to destroy a union, like a "runaway shop," is a lever which has been used to discourage collective employee activities in the future. But a complete liquidation of a business yields no such future benefit for the employer, if the termination is bona fide. It may be motivated more by spite against the union than by business reasons, but it is not the type of discrimination which is prohibited by the Act. The personal satisfaction that such an employer may derive from standing on his beliefs or the mere possibility that other employers will follow his example are surely too remote to be considered dangers at which the labor statutes were aimed. Although employees may be prohibited from engaging in a strike under certain conditions, no one would consider it a violation of the Act for the same employees to quit their employment *en masse,* even if motivated by a desire to ruin the employer. The very permanence of such action would negate any future economic benefit to the employees. The employer's right to go out of business is no different.

We are not presented here with the case of a "runaway shop," whereby Darlington would transfer its work to another plant or open a new plant in another locality to replace its closed plant. Nor are we concerned with a shutdown where the employees, by renouncing the union, could cause the plant to reopen. Such cases would involve discriminatory employer action for the purpose of obtaining some benefit in the future from the new employees. We hold here only that when an employer closes his entire business, even if the liquidation is motivated by vindictiveness towards the union, such action is not an unfair labor practice.[20]

While we thus agree with the Court of Appeals that viewing Darlington as an independent employer the liquidation of its business was not an unfair labor practice, we cannot accept the lower court's view that the same conclusion necessarily follows if Darlington is regarded as an integral part of the Deering Milliken enterprise.

The closing of an entire business, even though discriminatory, ends the employer-employee relationship; the force of such a closing is entirely spent as to that business when termination of the enterprise takes place. On the other hand, a discriminatory partial closing may have repercussions on what remains of the business, affording employer leverage for discouraging the free exercise of § 7 rights among remaining employees of much the same kind as that found to exist in the "runaway shop" and "temporary closing" cases. Moreover, a possible remedy open to the Board in such a case, like the remedies available in the "runaway shop" and "temporary closing" cases, is to order reinstatement of the discharged employees in the other parts of the business. No such remedy is available when an entire business has been terminated. By analogy to those cases involving a continuing enterprise we are constrained to hold, in disagreement with the Court of Appeals, that a partial closing is an unfair labor practice under § 8(a)(3) if motivated by a purpose to chill unionism in any of the remaining plants of the single employer and if the employer may reasonably have foreseen that such closing will likely have that effect.

While we have spoken in terms of a "partial closing" in the context of the Board's finding that Darlington was part of a larger single enterprise

---

**20.** Nothing we have said in this opinion would justify an employer interfering with employee organizational activities by threatening to close his plant, as distinguished from announcing a decision to close already reached by the board of directors or other management authority empowered to make such a decision. We recognize that this safeguard does not wholly remove the possibility that our holding may result in some deterrent effect on organizational activities independent of that arising from the closing itself. An employer may be encouraged to make a definitive decision to close on the theory that its mere announcement before a representation election will discourage the employees from voting for the union, and thus his decision may not have to be implemented. Such a possibility is not likely to occur, however, except in a marginal business; a solidly successful employer is not apt to hazard the possibility that the employees will call his bluff by voting to organize. We see no practical way of eliminating this possible consequence of our holding short of allowing the Board to order an employer who chooses so to gamble with his employees not to carry out his announced intention to close. We do not consider the matter of sufficient significance in the overall labor-management relations picture to require or justify a decision different from the one we have made.

controlled by the Milliken family, we do not mean to suggest that an organizational integration of plants or corporations is a necessary prerequisite to the establishment of such a violation of § 8(a)(3). If the persons exercising control over a plant that is being closed for anti-union reasons (1) have an interest in another business, whether or not affiliated with or engaged in the same line of commercial activity as the closed plant, of sufficient substantiality to give promise of their reaping a benefit from the discouragement of unionization in that business; (2) act to close their plant with the purpose of producing such a result; and (3) occupy a relationship to the other business which makes it realistically foreseeable that its employees will fear that such business will also be closed down if they persist in organizational activities, we think that an unfair labor practice has been made out.

Although the Board's single employer finding necessarily embraced findings as to Roger Milliken and the Milliken family which, if sustained by the Court of Appeals, would satisfy the elements of "interest" and "relationship" with respect to other parts of the Deering Milliken enterprise, that and the other Board findings fall short of establishing the factors of "purpose" and "effect" which are vital requisites of the general principles that govern a case of this kind.

Thus, the Board's findings as to the purpose and foreseeable effect of the Darlington closing pertained *only* to its impact on the Darlington employees. No findings were made as to the purpose and effect of the closing with respect to the employees in the other plants comprising the Deering Milliken group. It does not suffice to establish the unfair labor practice charged here to argue that the Darlington closing necessarily had an adverse impact upon unionization in such other plants. We have heretofore observed that employer action which has a foreseeable consequence of discouraging concerted activities generally does not amount to a violation of § 8(a)(3) in the absence of a showing of motivation which is aimed at achieving the prohibited effect. * * *

In these circumstances, we think the proper disposition of this case is to require that it be remanded to the Board so as to afford the Board the opportunity to make further findings on the issue of purpose and effect. * * *

■ MR. JUSTICE STEWART took no part in the decision of this case.

■ MR. JUSTICE GOLDBERG took no part in the consideration or decision of this case.

––––––

On remand, the Board reversed the Trial Examiner and found that the Millikens had closed the Darlington plant with the purpose of deterring union organization at other establishments in which they had dominant interests. The United States Court of Appeals for the Fourth Circuit enforced the ensuing order by a 5–2 vote. Darlington Mfg. Co. v. NLRB,

397 F.2d 760 (4th Cir.1968), cert. denied, 393 U.S. 1023, 89 S.Ct. 632, 21 L.Ed.2d 567 (1969). In response to the claim of Roger Milliken that the record demonstrated that the purpose of the Darlington closing was (if not for legitimate business reasons) to exact retribution against only the employees at that site, the court concluded: "[I]t was sufficient for the Board to find that the election of the union was a substantial cause of Darlington's closing and that the employer was actually motivated, at least in part, by a purpose to chill unionism in other Deering Milliken mills. The coexistence of this chilling purpose with an antiunion purpose directed against Darlington does not impair the Board's decision."

---

PROBLEMS FOR DISCUSSION

**1.** After observing that Section 8(a)(1) may be violated without proof of anti-union animus while such animus must be shown to violate Section 8(a)(3), Justice Harlan states that cases of plant closings must be treated under Section 8(a)(3). Why? Might not the problem illustrated by such cases as *Adkins Transfer* and *Darlington* be better analyzed in terms of Section 8(a)(1)?

**2.** Why should the fairness or unfairness of a business closing depend upon its effect upon the organizational freedom of other employees not directly affected by the closing? Why is the effect upon employees whose jobs are eliminated unimportant? Can they demonstrate that there has been "discrimination" which "discourages" union membership? Is the Court's requirement that there be an intention to discourage, and discouragement of, employees *other* than the dischargees also a requirement in the case of a discharge of a single employee?

**3.** Was Justice Harlan correct in asserting that there is no effective remedy for the discriminatory shutdown of an entire business?

**4.** George Lithograph Company until recently ran a complete printing operation, but it closed down its mailing department (which was being profitably operated) when the employees there were organized by the Lithographers and Photoengravers Union. That union, which intends to attempt to organize employees elsewhere within the George plant, filed a charge alleging that the closing of the department constituted a violation of Sections 8(a)(1) and (3) of the Labor Act. The Administrative Law Judge found that there was "not a scintilla of evidence from which it could be reasonably inferred that the closing of the mailing department had a chilling effect on the union activities of Respondent's remaining employees." The Union has filed exceptions with the Board to the report of the Administrative Law Judge. What arguments should the Union make? Should the Board reverse its Judge? See George Lithograph Co. v. San Francisco Oakland Mailers Local No. 18, 204 NLRB 431 (1973).

**5.** Assume that a New York manufacturer of women's clothing, recently organized, closes down its plant—avowedly to escape the union and to "show" the employees that unionization was unwise—and moves its equipment to a newly purchased plant building in Florida. Assume also that the cost of labor in Florida is somewhat cheaper than in New York, and that attempts at unionization in the relevant area in Florida have been over the years met with worker indifference if not hostility. Can the "runaway" employer successfully argue that, on such a record, *Darlington* compels the dismissal of a Section 8(a)(3) complaint? See Local 57, Intern. Ladies' Garment Workers' v. NLRB (Garwin Corp.), 374 F.2d 295 (D.C.Cir.1967).

———

### A NOTE ON SUPERVISORS

With the widespread growth in industrial unionism in the late 1930s and early 1940s, foremen, the first line of supervision, found themselves in an anomalous position. They were considered to be the first rung on the managerial ladder, but were not treated as managerial colleagues by higher authority. Much of their functional authority had been stripped away and given to centralized personnel departments; no longer could they secure the production for which they were responsible by unilaterally changing wage rates or summarily discharging workers. But they found themselves lacking the protection against unjust discharge for themselves that collective agreements gave the employees under their supervision; and, especially during the War, they found themselves in many cases making less than the employees they supervised, who were working heavy overtime schedules.

One response was the formation of the Foremen's Association of America, which sought to unionize foremen. Initially the NLRB denied foremen the right to unionize altogether. It then modified its position to prohibit discharge of foremen for union membership or activity. It next allowed foremen to organize, but only in separate and autonomous unions. Finally, it abandoned that requirement, and in Packard Motor Car Co. v. NLRB, 330 U.S. 485, 67 S.Ct. 789, 91 L.Ed. 1040 (1947), the Supreme Court endorsed that view.

Reversal of Packard Motor Car was high on management's list for legislative change. See generally H. Harris, The Right to Manage: Industrial Relations Policies of American Business in the 1940's, 74–89 (1982). In the words of one corporate manager of the time,

> Take away from us our foremen and we are lost; because they are the people ... that have got to be held responsible for production, for cost, for accident prevention, and for all the various phases of the business. They are the representatives of management out there on the firing line.

Id. at 85. Congress agreed and exempted supervisors from the definition of a statutory "employee" under section 2(3). It supplied a carefully crafted definition of a supervisor in section 2(11).

There are, however, situations where an employer may attempt to use supervisors as an instrument to effect unfair labor practices vis-a-vis rank and file workers. The NLRB therefore held that, even though supervisors do not enjoy statutory protection for organizing or seeking to engage in collective bargaining, they may not be disciplined: (1) for testifying before the Board or in processing an employee's grievance; (2) for refusing to commit an unfair labor practice; or (3) as a pretext for discharging a pro-union crew. Eventually the Board took the position that it violated the Act to discharge a supervisor as part of a "pattern of conduct" aimed at coercing employees in the exercise of their section 7 rights. But in Parker–Robb Chevrolet, Inc. v. Automobile Salesmen's Union, 262 NLRB 402, petition for review denied sub nom. Automobile Salesmen's Local 1095 v. NLRB, 711 F.2d 383 (D.C.Cir.1983), the Board abandoned that position. The discharge of a supervisor will violate the Act only if it "directly interferes" with an employee's exercise of section 7 rights. In that case Terry Doss, the crew chief of a group of employees scheduled to be discharged, arguably for engaging in union organization, protested the discharge on grounds that they were some of the best employees; he was then discharged, ostensibly for economic reasons. The Board applied this test and denied relief. The Court of Appeals for the District of Columbia Circuit sustained the Board, finding that its narrowing of the reach of Section 8(a)(1) in the protection of supervisors against discriminatory discipline "is consistent with the structure of the Act, has a reasonable basis in law, and is certainly defensible."

The court traced the course of the Board's decisions in this area, finding that the rationale behind the "pattern of conduct" cases had been that anti-union discipline directed against a supervisor "instilled fear in rank-and-file employees that their own protected union activities would subject them to a similar fate." Appellate courts had criticized this view, holding that to invalidate the discriminatory discharge of a supervisor because of the incidental or secondary effect on employees in effect brought supervisory employees under the protection of the NLRA, thus giving too little weight to the employer's right to demand loyalty from its supervisors. The Board's new approach—which requires proof that a supervisor's discharge "directly interferes" with the section 7 rights of statutorily protected employees—was, the court of appeals held, adopted openly, explained in full, and properly "takes into account the fact that a supervisor is not protected if he engages in union or concerted activity and that an employer may not commit unfair labor practices regardless of whether they are funnelled through a supervisor." See Bethel, "The NLRB and the Discharge of Supervisors: *Parker–Robb* Brings Questionable Reform," 54 U.Colo.L.Rev. 1 (1982). On the issue of remedies, see Kenrich Petrochemicals, Inc. v. NLRB, 907 F.2d 400 (3d Cir.)(en banc), cert. denied, 498 U.S. 981, 111 S.Ct. 509, 112 L.Ed.2d 522 (1990).

———

## PROBLEM FOR DISCUSSION

**1.** The Board in *Parker–Robb* stated: "It is irrelevant that an employer may have hoped, or even expected, that its decision to terminate a supervisor for his union or concerted activity would cause employees to reconsider, and perhaps abandon, their own concerted or union activity. No matter what the employer's subjective hope or expectation, that circumstance cannot change the character of its otherwise lawful conduct." Is such a conclusion consistent with the Supreme Court analysis in *Darlington*? Is it likely that the congressional exclusion of supervisors from the coverage of the NLRA was shaped by an intention to protect such employer conduct?

**2.**  Although supervisors are non-employees for the purposes of this statute, they are employees at common law, and as such would enjoy the statutory and common law protections against retaliatory discharge developed in areas other than the Labor Act. See the discussion in Part I, supra. Under the common law, as it is developing in a number of jurisdictions, for example, an employee cannot be dismissed for protesting to the employer a variety of illegal—or, in some jurisdictions, merely wrongful—acts. Should these developments, half a century after Taft–Hartley, place in question the strength of the policy of a supervisor's total duty of loyalty owed to management? *See* Benjamin Aaron and Matthew Finkin, The Law of Employee Loyalty in the United States, 20 COMP. LAB. L. & POL'Y J. 321 (1999).

----

## D.   REMEDIES FOR UNFAIR LABOR PRACTICES[m]

# Phelps Dodge Corp. v. NLRB

313 U.S. 177, 61 S.Ct. 845, 85 L.Ed. 1271 (1941).

■ MR. JUSTICE FRANKFURTER delivered the opinion of the Court.

The dominating question which this litigation brings here for the first time is whether an employer subject to the National Labor Relations Act may refuse to hire employees solely because of their affiliations with a labor union. Subsidiary questions grow out of this central issue relating to the means open to the Board to "effectuate the policies of this Act [chapter]," if it finds such discrimination in hiring an "unfair labor practice". Other questions touching the remedial powers of the Board are also involved. * * *

It is no longer disputed that workers cannot be dismissed from employment because of their union affiliations. Is the national interest in industrial peace less affected by discrimination against union activity when men are hired? The contrary is overwhelmingly attested by the long history of industrial conflicts, the diagnosis of their causes by official investigations, the conviction of public men, industrialists and scholars. * * * Such a policy is an inevitable corollary of the principle of freedom of organization. Discrimination against union labor in the hiring of men is a dam to self organization at the source of supply. The effect of such discrimination is not confined to the actual denial of employment; it inevitably operates

----

**m.**  For a comprehensive treatment of the Board's remedies for all unfair labor practices, see P. Walther, J.F. Hunsicker & J. Kane, NLRB Remedies for Unfair Labor Practices (2d ed. 1986). See also Note, J.P. Stevens: Searching for a Remedy to Fit the Wrong, 55 No.Car.L.Rev. 696 (1977); Schatz- ki, Some Observations About the Standards Applied to Labor Injunction Litigation Under Sections 10(j) and 10(*l*) of the NLRA, 59 Ind.L.J. 565 (1984); Siegel, Section 10(j) of the NLRA: Suggested Reforms for an Expanded Use, 13 B.C. Ind. & Comm.L.Rev. 457 (1972).

against the whole idea of the legitimacy of organization. In a word, it undermines the principle which, as we have seen, is recognized as basic to the attainment of industrial peace.

* * * [A]n embargo against employment of union labor was notoriously one of the chief obstructions to collective bargaining through self-organization. Indisputably the removal of such obstructions was the driving force behind the enactment of the National Labor Relations Act. The prohibition against "discrimination in regard to hire" must be applied as a means towards the accomplishment of the main object of the legislation. We are asked to read "hire" as meaning the wages paid to an employee so as to make the statute merely forbid discrimination in one of the terms of men who have secured employment. So to read the statute would do violence to a spontaneous textual reading of § 8(3) in that "hire" would serve no function because, in the sense which is urged upon us, it is included in the prohibition against "discrimination in regard to * * * any term or condition of employment". Contemporaneous legislative history, and, above all, the background of industrial experience forbid such textual mutilation. * * *

Since the refusal to hire Curtis and Daugherty solely because of their affiliation with the Union was an unfair labor practice under § 8(3), the remedial authority of the Board under § 10(c) became operative. Of course it could issue, as it did, an order "to cease and desist from such unfair labor practice" in the future. Did Congress also empower the Board to order the employer to undo the wrong by offering the men discriminated against the opportunity for employment which should not have been denied them?

Reinstatement is the conventional correction for discriminatory discharges. Experience having demonstrated that discrimination in hiring is twin to discrimination in firing, it would indeed be surprising if Congress gave a remedy for the one which it denied for the other. * * * [I]f § 10(c), had empowered the Board to "take such affirmative action * * * as will effectuate the policies of this Act [chapter]", the right to restore to a man employment which was wrongfully denied him could hardly be doubted. * * * Attainment of a great national policy through expert administration in collaboration with limited judicial review must not be confined within narrow canons for equitable relief deemed suitable by chancellors in ordinary private controversies. Compare Virginian R. Co. v. System Federation, 300 U.S. 515, 552, 57 S.Ct. 592, 601, 81 L.Ed. 789. To differentiate between discrimination in denying employment and in terminating it, would be a differentiation not only without substance but in defiance of that against which the prohibition of discrimination is directed. * * * To attribute such a function to the participial phrase [in section 10(c) ]introduced by "including" is to shrivel a versatile principle to an illustrative application. We find no justification whatever for attributing to Congress such a casuistic withdrawal of the authority which, but for the illustration, it clearly has given the Board. The word "including" does not lend itself to such destructive significance. * * *

* * * There remain for consideration the limitations upon the Board's power to undo the effects of discrimination. Specifically, we have the question of the Board's power to order employment in cases where the men discriminated against had obtained "substantially equivalent employment." * * *

Denial of the Board's power to order opportunities of employment in this situation derives wholly from an infiltration of a portion of § 2(3) into § 10(c). The argument runs thus: § 10(c) specifically refers to "reinstatement of employees"; the latter portion of § 2(3) refers to an "employee" as a person "who has not obtained any other regular and substantially equivalent employment"; therefore, there can be no reinstatement of an employee who has obtained such employment. The syllogism is perfect. But this is a bit of verbal logic from which the meaning of things has evaporated. * * *

To deny the Board power to neutralize discrimination merely because workers have obtained compensatory employment would confine the "policies of this Act" to the correction of private injuries. The Board was not devised for such a limited function. * * * To be sure, reinstatement is not needed to repair the economic loss of a worker who, after discrimination, has obtained an equally profitable job. But to limit the significance of discrimination merely to questions of monetary loss to workers would thwart the central purpose of the Act, directed as that is toward the achievement and maintenance of workers' self-organization. That there are factors other than loss of wages to a particular worker to be considered is suggested even by a meager knowledge of industrial affairs. Thus, to give only one illustration, if men were discharged who were leading efforts at organization in a plant having a low wage scale, they would not unnaturally be compelled by their economic circumstances to seek and obtain employment elsewhere at equivalent wages. In such a situation, to deny the Board power to wipe out the prior discrimination by ordering the employment of such workers would sanction a most effective way of defeating the right of self-organization.

Therefore, the mere fact that the victim of discrimination has obtained equivalent employment does not itself preclude the Board from undoing the discrimination and requiring employment. But neither does this remedy automatically flow from the Act itself when discrimination has been found. A statute expressive of such large public policy as that on which the National Labor Relations Board is based must be broadly phrased and necessarily carries with it the task of administrative application. There is an area plainly covered by the language of the Act and an area no less plainly without it. But in the nature of things Congress could not catalogue all the devices and stratagems for circumventing the policies of the Act. Nor could it define the whole gamut of remedies to effectuate these policies in an infinite variety of specific situations. Congress met these difficulties by leaving the adaptation of means to end to the empiric process of administration. The exercise of the process was committed to the Board, subject to limited judicial review. Because the relation of remedy to policy is peculiarly a matter for administrative competence, courts must not enter the allowable area of the Board's discretion and must guard against the danger of sliding unconsciously from the narrow confines of law into the more spacious domain of policy. On the other hand, the power with which Congress invested the Board implies responsibility—the responsibility of exercising its judgment in employing the statutory powers. * * *

[The Board had also ordered that the workers wrongfully denied employment should be compensated with backpay from the date of the discrimination to the date of their employment by the Company, less actual earnings. The Supreme Court, over Board assertions of burden and in-administrability, held that the Board ought in appropriate cases to deduct as well moneys which the worker could have earned during the backpay period but which he unjustifiably refused to earn.]

―――――

In ABF Freight System, Inc. v. NLRB, 510 U.S. 317, 114 S.Ct. 835, 127 L.Ed.2d 152 (1994), the United States Supreme Court held that the Board is not precluded from ordering the reinstatement with backpay of an employee who had been discharged in violation of § 8(a)(3) but who had lied under oath in the hearing before the Board's Administrative Law Judge. The Board had held that it could weigh the severity of this later employee delinquency against the severity of the employer's initial statutory violation in discharging for anti-union reasons, and that the former would not in all cases automatically outweigh the latter when fashioning a remedy to advance statutory policies. The Supreme Court relied heavily on its decision in Chevron U.S.A., Inc. v. Natural Resources Defense Council, Inc., 467 U.S. 837, 104 S.Ct. 2778, 81 L.Ed.2d 694 (1984), as requiring the "greatest deference" to the Board's remedial authority.

―――――

*REMEDIES FOR EMPLOYER COERCION AND DISCRIMINATION*

Any statutory system for the protection of employee rights will be only as effective as the remedies afforded. Broad declaration of such rights in the statute and in the decisions of the National Labor Relations Board will convince neither employers nor employees if the remedies are meager in impact and slow in coming. That fact perhaps best explains the passions raised by the so-called Labor Reform Act that passed the House of Representatives in 1977 but was the victim of a nineteen-day filibuster in the Senate. The bill would have made few changes in the "substantive" provisions of the NLRA but would have expedited the Board's election procedures and augmented its remedial powers. See H.R. 8410, 95th Cong., 1st Sess. (1977); S. 2467, 95th Cong., 2d Sess. (1978); B. Townley, Labor Law Reform in U.S. Industrial Relations (1986); and Rosen, Labor Law Reform: Dead or Alive?, 57 U.Det.J.Urb.L. 1 (1979).

Serious weaknesses have been identified—by scholars as well as by the Board itself—in the Board's traditional remedies in cases of employer coercion and discrimination under Sections 8(a)(1) and (3). A most telling summary of those weaknesses is set forth by Professor Weiler in his provocative article, "Promises to Keep: Securing Workers' Rights to Self–Organization Under the NLRA," 96 Harv.L.Rev. 1769, 1787–1803 (1983). The following passages (through page 259) are from that article.

———

It would seem logical * * * that a major aim of Board action should be the prevention of employer interference with the employees' collective right to self-organization. The remedial philosophy as it has evolved, however, is heavily oriented toward the repair of harm inflicted on individual victims of antiunion action by employers.

Consider, as an illustration of the difference between protecting a group right to self-organization and repairing the harms done to individuals, the case of an employee discharged in response to his union organizing activities. The law might repair the harm to this individual by restoring him to his job and making up the income that he has lost. If the employer's purpose had simply been to punish the worker for supporting the union, the fact that the law would effectively undo this damage at the employer's expense might discourage the use of the tactic in the future.

But the real purpose of such discharges is to break the momentum of the union's organizing campaign. By the time the discharged employee has been reinstated, much of the union's support may have melted away, and the election may thus have been lost. Unlike the discharged employee's loss of wages, this setback to the employees' quest for a collective voice in their workplace cannot easily be repaired. To protect the employees' group rights, the NLRA must rely on the preventive force of its sanctions. But the traditional remedies for discriminatory discharge—backpay and reinstatement[67]—simply are not effective deterrents to employers who are tempted to trample on their employees' rights.

*The Backpay Award.*—At first blush, the backpay award might seem to serve both remedial and deterrent functions. Although from the employees' point of view the award is merely compensation for what has been lost, from the employer's point of view it is a financial penalty: the employer is required to pay for services it has not received. The problem is that this "fine"—paid to the worker rather than the state—is far too small to be a

**67.** The NLRB may also issue a cease-and-desist order that must be posted somewhere in the plant. See D. McDowell & K. Huhn, NLRB Remedies for Unfair Labor Practices 19–78 (1976). This remedy, it might be argued, is primarily designed to prevent injury to the group right to a free choice about collective bargaining. I know of no one who claims that such an order by itself materially aids in the preservation of this right. The problem is that the damage has already been done, and the employees, observing the negligible consequences to their employer, may be understandably cynical about the law's ability to protect their rights in the future.

significant deterrent. * * * [T]he average backpay award in 1980 was only $2000. The small size of the average award is partly attributable to cases in which employers settle quickly and reinstate the employees to limit the monetary loss. But even in troublesome cases in which reinstatement is not forthcoming for months or years, the employer's potential liability is inherently limited. Early in the life of the Wagner Act, the principle was settled that the proper measure of the backpay award is not the wages the guilty employer failed to pay, but rather the net loss suffered by the employee after the deduction of any wages earned in the interim in another job.[69] Indeed, the law requires the employee to take all reasonable steps necessary to mitigate his loss by finding another job. If he fails to take such steps, his potential earnings may be deducted from the backpay award even if they are not actually earned.[70]

The combination of the net loss and mitigation doctrines is the most telling illustration of the supremacy of the reparative policy over the deterrent policy in American labor law. If the backpay remedy were designed to deter the employer's unlawful conduct, there would be no reason to deduct any wages that the employee earned, or could have earned, in another job. By minimizing the employer's potential liability, such a deduction removes most of the deterrent effect of the backpay award.

Because of the ineffectiveness of the current reparative remedies in containing the incidence of employer unfair labor practices, many critics and legislators have sought to reorient the remedial philosophy of the NLRA to emphasize prevention as an independent objective. Among such reformers there is little sentiment for using criminal sanctions for this purpose. Instead, a favorite proposal is a multiple damage award, such as those used in fair labor standards and antitrust law. One key provision of the Labor Reform Act would have directed the Board to award to employees who had been discriminatorily discharged during an organizational campaign double the wages they would have earned had they not been fired, with no setoff for wages earned elsewhere. Thus, for example, if an employer illegally fired two union supporters, each earning $20,000 a year, and refused to take them back until a decision was rendered by an

---

**69.** See Pennsylvania Greyhound Lines, 1 N.L.R.B. 1, 51 (1935). The net loss principle not only prevents the employee from collecting a "windfall profit" of double earnings following his illegal dismissal, but also precludes the Board from requiring the employer to reimburse the third-party source of those interim earnings. See, *e.g.*, Republic Steel Corp. v. NLRB, 311 U.S. 7, 12–13, 61 S.Ct. 77, 79–80, 85 L.Ed. 6 (1940)(holding that an employer could not be required to reimburse the WPA for payments made to an employee who had been unlawfully discharged). In *Republic Steel,* the Supreme Court held that no matter how broad the language of section

10(c), the Board did not have the authority to devise punitive measures designed to deter rather than to compensate. See id. at 10–12. The assumption of the law, then, is that prevention can only be the serendipitous by-product of remedies designed to redress injuries inflicted on employees.

**70.** The mitigation doctrine was borrowed from contract law, in which liability is not predicated on fault; ironically, the doctrine is applied under a labor statute that bases liability on a showing of subjective unlawful intent on the part of the employer. * * *

administrative law judge a year later, the employer's liability would total $80,000. This is a substantial sum for the kind of small firm that is the target of much union organizing activity.

One should not, however, overestimate the deterrent effect of even such an exemplary award. Suppose a firm has just twenty-five employees in a unit that is the target of a union organization drive, and suppose these employees receive an average of $20,000 per year in wages and benefits at a total annual cost to the employer of $500,000. Assuming an average union wage effect of 20%, the employer can predict that, if the union succeeds, the firm's wage bill for the first year alone will jump by $100,000, a sum exceeding the penalty for illegally firing two employees. To the extent that discriminatory discharges are effective in forestalling union organizing campaigns, the potential liability for a multiple backpay award (which itself would have to be discounted by the difficulty of proving the charge) may be a sensible investment in long-term labor cost containment.

Nevertheless, the double-backpay remedy with no mitigation requirement was too "punitive" to survive in Congress. The House amended the bill to provide for deduction of wages actually earned, and the Senate Committee went on to reduce the award to one-and-one half times backpay. The assumption that NLRB remedies should be reparative rather than punitive was so pervasive that even the Labor Reform Act's supporters defended the measure as a means of compensating discharged workers for actual harms suffered over and above lost pay.

*Reinstatement.*—What about reinstatement, the other standard form of relief? In principle, such an in-kind remedy seems nicely designed to play both a reparative and a preventive role. The dismissed employee gets his job back, and his fellow workers see the power of collective action and labor law protection. Not only is the employer deprived of the fruits of its illegal behavior, but it also suffers a serious erosion of its hitherto absolute sway within its own plant. The prospect of such a result would seem to be a major disincentive to flouting the law in the first place.

The reinstatement remedy, however, has proved to be far less effective in practice than in theory. It is one thing for the NLRB to calculate the amount of wages lost and see that this sum is paid to the discharged employee. It is quite another thing for an outside agency to try to reconstruct an enduring employment relationship. An employer that is sufficiently antiunion to break the law by firing a union supporter is also likely to feel quite vindictive when forced to take the employee back, and may well start looking for an excuse to get rid of him again. The employee, fully aware of this attitude, will often be reluctant to return, especially if returning means giving up another job that he has obtained in the interim.

There have been two systematic studies of the efficacy of the reinstatement remedy, one from New England in the early 1960's and the other from Texas in the early 1970's. Both studies reached remarkably similar conclusions. First, only about 40% of the employees for whom reinstatement was ordered actually took their jobs back. The major reason given by employees for declining reinstatement was fear of employer retaliation, a factor that may well also have affected some of those who said that they had simply found better jobs. The employees' fears were apparently well founded; of employees who did go back, nearly 80% were gone within a year or two, and most blamed their departure on vindictive treatment by the employer. If the reinstatement remedy is judged by its ability to reestablish an enduring employment relationship, the verdict is clear: this goal is achieved in only about 10% of the meritorious cases. Small wonder that the prospect of a reinstatement order does not loom large for the antiunion employer making a coldblooded assessment of the legal sanctions it faces.

Time is the crucial variable in reinstatement cases. If the Board can secure reinstatement quickly, the wrongfully discharged employee is likely to accept the offer. In time, however, the employee generally obtains another job, which he will be reluctant to leave for the bleak prospects at his old position. Thus, he becomes progressively less likely to assert his reinstatement rights. Only about 5% of reinstatement offers obtained after six months are in fact accepted.

The timing of reinstatement is even more significant insofar as this remedy is designed to undo the chilling effect of a discriminatory discharge on the group impulse toward collective bargaining. If the dismissed employee were returned to his job immediately, the employer's attempt at intimidation would likely backfire. The message the employees would receive instead would be a demonstration of how effective a trade union could be in asserting and defending employees' rights against oppressive management. But if that lesson is to be at all influential, reinstatement must come before the representation election is actually conducted—normally about two months after the union has filed its petition. Although delay is unfortunate for the individual worker, he usually finds another job and will eventually receive all his lost pay. But delay is fatal to the viability of a union organizing drive. If the law is to have any chance of vindicating the employees' group right to "bargain collectively through representatives of their own choosing," the reinstatement it promises must come quickly.

*The* Gissel *Bargaining Order.*—If either the union or the employer violates the legal standards governing the representation campaign, the Board may delay or even rerun the election to ensure that the outcome is untainted by illegal intimidation. If the employer has committed unfair labor practices so serious that they render a fair and free election impossible, the Board may order the employer to bargain with the union even though the union has not won a secret ballot election. Approved by the Supreme Court in *NLRB v. Gissel Packing Co.*,[90] the bargaining order is specifically designed to repair the harm done to the group rights promised by section 7 of the NLRA. At the same time, the prospect of such an order should be a significant deterrent to antiunion conduct, because an employer that violated the law in order to avoid unionization could end up with a union anyway, whereas an employer that campaigned vigorously within the law would stand a fair chance of winning the election and thereby exclud-

90.  395 U.S. 575, 89 S.Ct. 1918, 23 L.Ed.2d 547 (1969). [See page 312 infra.]

ing the union from its plant. *Gissel*-type orders, then, appear to promise the happiest of results: they would repair the damage done to the statutory rights of the employees while also providing a tangible disincentive to the type of behavior that produced the damage.

In practice, this promise has proved—and must inevitably prove—illusory. The vigorous debate about matters of high principle that still rages over the legitimacy of using bargaining orders in place of secret ballot elections is really beside the point. A bargaining order is an effort by an outside agency to construct a lasting collective bargaining relationship between a trade union and an employer whose antiunion behavior has been so egregious that the Board is prepared to bypass the normal secret ballot election. What can the union do with the bargaining order? Although the order requires the employer to sit down at the negotiating table and go through the motions of trying to reach an agreement, the governing principle of freedom of contract under the NLRA means that the employer is not required to consent to any significant changes in working conditions. The Board cannot direct the employer to make a reasonable contract offer.

If a decent employment package is to be extracted from a recalcitrant employer, it must come through the efforts of the workers themselves—that is, through the threat of strike action. Here lies the catch–22 of *Gissel*. The bargaining order has been issued because the employer's behavior is thought to have so thoroughly cowed the employees that they cannot express their true desires about collective bargaining even within the secrecy of the voting booth. But all the order can do is license the union to bring negotiations to the point at which its leadership must ask those same employees to put their jobs on the line by going on strike.

Again, timing is crucial. If a bargaining order is granted within a few weeks (or even months) of the organizing drive, while the attraction of collective bargaining remains strong among the employees, it might still be effective. But as time passes, employee interest wanes. Normal turnover will deprive the union of some key supporters, and to many of the replacements the union will seem a remote outsider that caused some trouble in the distant past. It is highly unlikely, therefore, that an order issued by the NLRB after protracted legal proceedings will actually produce a viable and enduring collective bargaining relationship.

*Delay Under the NLRA.*—We have seen that time is of the essence in implementing NLRB remedies. If either a reinstatement order or a *Gissel* bargaining order is to be effective, it must come quickly. The question that arises, then, is how long an employer can forestall an enforceable order in an unfair labor practice proceeding. The answer is distressing: nearly 1000 days as of 1980.

Table III sets out the various stages in the Board's process and gives the median time taken at each stage, as these figures fluctuated between 1960 and 1980. * * *

## TABLE III
### DELAY IN PROCESSING UNFAIR LABOR PRACTICE CHARGES, 1960–1980
(all times in days)

| Year | Filing to Complaint | Complaint to Close of Hearing | Close of Hearing to ALJ Decision | ALJ to Board Decision | Filing to Board Decision | Bd. Decis. to C.A. Opinion |
|------|------|------|------|------|------|------|
| 1960 | 52 | 66 | 88 | 149 | 426 | |
| 1965 | 59 | 67 | 123 | 122 | 390 | |
| 1970 | 57 | 58 | 84 | 124 | 348 | |
| 1975 | 54 | 55 | 72 | 134 | 332 | 359 |
| 1980 | 46 | 155 | 158 | 133 | 484 | 485 |

One should not assume that this lengthy route must be traveled in all cases. Most employers do not resist to the bitter end. In fact, the regional offices dispose of over 80% of the charges filed each year without issuing formal complaints. The vast majority of cases handled in this manner, however, are unfounded charges that are withdrawn or administratively dismissed. Nearly half of the "meritorious" charges—those that eventually secure some relief for the complainant by way of settlement or order—do enter the formal process through the issuance of a complaint. Even among these, however, the majority are settled before the ALJ hearing actually takes place. Only a tiny fraction of the caseload, 500 decisions each year, reaches the circuit courts. Such a small number of cases, it might be argued, does not warrant major surgery on the system.

That upbeat conclusion would, however, be misleading. Any informal settlement of the case requires the employer's consent. The fact that an enforceable order for relief will not be available for almost three years lurks in the background of the settlement negotiations and reduces the employee's bargaining power. An employer will be reluctant to settle a discriminatory discharge case if the result will be reinstatement of a key union supporter during the representation campaign. The prospect of long delay in prosecuting a formal charge increases the likelihood that the employer will be able to persuade the aggrieved employee to accept a cash payment and waive his right to reinstatement. When the effects of procedural delay on the dynamics of settlement in unfair labor practice cases are taken into account, the magnitude of the problem is clear. Delay is the Achilles heel of the regulatory approach to the representation process under the NLRA.

--------

The Board has not been insensitive to the issues raised in Professor Weiler's article, at least in cases involving particularly pervasive or continuing employer violations of the Labor Act. It has during the past twenty years developed a number of remedies requiring the employer more broadly and effectively to disseminate notice of its wrongdoings and of its obligations to cure them, as well as remedies that afford the union greater access to employees on company property. The Board's remedial inventiveness was, more than anything else, a response to the recidivist pattern of unfair labor practices on the part of J.P. Stevens & Co., a multi-plant textile concern in the South, which embarked upon a campaign of vigorous and pervasively illegal resistance to unionization.

This resistance was marked by threats of discharge and of plant closings, actual discharges and other discipline, coercive interrogation, surveillance, restrictions upon solicitation for the union, and the use of Company bulletin boards to publicize the names of union supporters. In a number of instances, the Board issued the following remedial orders (some of which were thought by some courts of appeals to go beyond the policies of the NLRA, but do you agree?) : (1) to post the usual notice not only in the individual Company plants in which the unfair labor practices had been committed but in all of its forty-three plants in North and South Carolina; (2) to mail a copy of the notice to each employee at the forty-three plants; (3) to convene all employees during working time and have a responsible Company official read them the notice; (4) to give the Union access to those plants for one year to use the Company bulletin boards where employee notices are posted; (5) to allow union organizers to have access to parking lots and other nonwork areas, including areas within the company's plants (such as cafeterias or canteens); (6) to afford an opportunity to a union representative to address groups of workers on the shop floor whenever company representatives make anti-union speeches; (7) to furnish the Union upon request a list of employee names and addresses in all of the Company's plants; and (8) to reimburse the NLRB for its litigation expenses, including the salary of its attorneys. (Ultimately, on October 19, 1980, an historic agreement was reached between J.P. Stevens and the Amalgamated Clothing and Textile Workers Union, in which the Company granted certain economic benefits to the unionized employees at one of its North Carolina plants and $3 million in backpay there as well, and agreed to abide in all of its plants by applicable judicial and NLRB orders and precedents in resisting future unionization efforts; in return, the Union agreed to end its world-wide boycott of J.P. Stevens products and its campaign to discredit company officials. See N.Y. Times, October 20, 1980.)

In more recent cases, involving other employer-respondents, the Board has imposed additional remedial requirements, such as placing the remedial notice in appropriate company publications, publishing it in all local newspapers for several weeks, having it read by the president of the company (and not merely by the president's designee or by an NLRB official), and giving the union for a two-year period the right to deliver a thirty-minute speech to employees on working time prior to any Board election in which the union participates.

All of these "notice" and "access" remedies have been tested numerous times on judicial review. Which of them do you believe to be the most subject to question? Do any of them fall outside the scope of the Board's remedial powers as articulated in the *Phelps Dodge* decision? The Court of Appeals for the District of Columbia Circuit has been particularly thoughtful in dealing with these issues on review. See Conair Corp. v. NLRB, 721 F.2d 1355 (D.C.Cir.1983); United Steelworkers v. NLRB (Florida Steel Corp.), 646 F.2d 616 (D.C.Cir.1981); Teamsters Local 115 v. NLRB (Haddon House Food Prods., Inc.), 640 F.2d 392 (D.C.Cir.1981). For a company-wide order in the context of illegal acts at dozens of locations, see Beverly Calif. Corp. v. NLRB, 227 F.3d 817 (7th Cir.2000).

No matter how creative the NLRB may be in fashioning remedies, it is almost inevitable that there will be a high degree of ineffectiveness for Board orders issued at the end of an unfair labor practice proceeding, many months after the critical events. Many charging parties would wish to have interim relief while an unfair labor practice proceeding makes its way through the Administrative Law Judge, the NLRB and the court of appeals.

Such relief is in fact available under Section 10(j) of the Act, which authorizes the Board to seek a temporary injunction in a federal district court to restrain either the union or the employer from engaging in unfair labor practices. The injunction may be sought after a complaint has been issued by the Regional Director and while an unfair labor practice hearing is pending before an Administrative Law Judge. The legislative history of Section 10(j) indicates that the purpose of this section was to prevent parties from "violating the Act to accomplish their unlawful objective before being placed under any legal restraint [thereby making it] impossible or not feasible to restore or preserve the status quo pending litigation." In light of this purpose, the section seems plainly suited to certain forms of unlawful behavior relating to organizational activity, as well as to various other types of unfair labor practices. For example, it seems well within the intendment of Section 10(j) to seek a temporary injunction to restrain violence occurring during an organizing campaign or to prevent an employer from frustrating the union's organizational efforts through flagrant unfair practices which would otherwise have to be contested during many months of litigation.

The General Counsel has traditionally been rather reluctant to seek the Board's authorization to petition for an injunction under section 10(j) of the Act, and the Board has traditionally been even more reluctant to grant it. In fiscal year 1990, for example, which was fairly representative of the period 1984 to 1993, the General Counsel sought authorization in 41 cases and the Board granted authorization in 39. With the appointment of both a new General Counsel and Labor Board under President Clinton, both the willingness to seek and to grant permission to petition increased: in fiscal year 1994, permission was sought in 85 cases and granted in 83; and in fiscal year 1995, permission was ought in 109 cases and granted by the Board in 104. (The majority of such cases are either settled or relief is granted in full or part.) The number of petitions sought declined sharply in 1997 and 1998. But even the doubling or near tripling of petitions sought must be placed in the context of the several thousand cases (typically, 3500 to 4000 each year) in which the Board issues a complaint, *i.e.* which it determines to have merit. The largest number of 10(j) proceedings are instituted for employer interference with organizing campaigns (either before or after the union had claimed majority support), undermining the bargaining representative (including withdrawal of recognition and/or subcontracting), and segregating of corporate assets (closing of an operation or liquidating of assets in order to evade potential backpay liability).

Although the Act authorizes the Board to seek section 10(j) relief whenever there is reasonable cause to believe the Act has been violated, the courts generally require more than that in order to warrant the issuance of equitable relief; indeed there is a highly nuanced division among the Circuits on the governing standards. This was addressed recently by the Ninth Circuit in Miller v. California Pacific Medical Center, 19 F.3d 449 (9th Cir.1994). It opined that in § 10(j) cases the public interest "is to insure that an unfair labor practice will not succeed because the Board takes too long to investigate and adjudicate the charge." The district court must take the likelihood of "irreparable injury" into account, which in this context is taken to overlap with proof of likely success on the merits. As the court explained:

> In assessing whether the Board has met its burden, it is necessary to factor in the district court's lack of jurisdiction over unfair labor practices, and the deference accorded to NLRB determinations by the courts of appeals.... While the district court is not required to defer to the Board in deciding whether interim relief is "just and proper," it should evaluate the probabilities of the complaining party prevailing in light of the fact that ultimately, the Board's determination on the merits will be given considerable deference. By the same token, because it is the Board and not the district court which has primary responsibility for declaring federal labor policy, we agree with Judge Friendly that "[e]ven on an issue of law, the district court should be hospitable to the views of the General Counsel, however novel." ... In short, the Board can make a threshold showing of likelihood of success by producing some evidence to support the unfair labor practice charge, together with an arguable legal theory.

> If the respondent concedes the substance of the unfair labor practice charge, or if the Board demonstrates that it is likely to prevail on the merits, we presume irreparable injury.... If the charge is disputed, or if the Board has only a fair chance of succeeding on the merits, the court must consider the possibility of irreparable injury.

> In this connection, as well as in considering the balance of hardships, the district court must take into account the probability that declining to issue the injunction will permit the allegedly unfair labor practice to reach fruition and thereby render meaningless the Board's remedial authority.... Where the Board and the respondent each make a showing of hardship, the district court must exercise its sound discretion to determine whether the balance tips in the Board's favor.

*Id.* at 460–461 (citations omitted).

Note that under section 10($l$) the seeking of an injunction is statutorily mandated when a complaint has been issued in certain cases of alleged union unfair labor practices. The General Counsel of the Board told the Commission on the Future of Labor–Management Relations that section 10($l$) cases take five days for the Board to process; but because the Board's permission must be sought in section 10(j) cases, these take about 65 days or more to secure Board approval. The Commission recommended that section 10($l$) be extended to all cases of employer discrimination against employees "from the beginning of an organizing effort to the signing of a first contract." Commission on the Future of Worker-Management Relations, Report and Recommendations 21 (1994). Do you agree?

## II. Selection of the Representative for the Purposes of Collective Bargaining[a]

To a considerable extent, the conduct of collective bargaining in American industry is initiated through voluntary employer recognition of a union as the freely chosen representative of a majority of employees, without the need for governmental intervention. To an extent that is far greater than in other industrialized nations, however, American labor relations have been characterized by employer resistance to unionization— resistance that has become much more pervasive in recent years. In such circumstances, a union will often have to resort to the procedures of the National Labor Relations Board. As has just been noted, the Board may order an employer to bargain as a remedy for seriously coercive or discriminatory unfair labor practices, even though the union has not won a formal Board-supervised certification election; the Board's authority is explored in greater detail at pp. 312 et seq., infra. But in the far greater number of cases, in which the employer has not acted illegally and its dispute with the union centers about such matters as a doubt about the union's claim of majority support, or disagreement about the unit of employees which the union is to represent, or where there is a conflict between two competing unions each claiming to be the majority choice, collective bargaining does not begin until the Board makes an authoritative determination as to such issues. It does so in its certification proceedings under Section 9 of the NLRA, in accordance with procedures outlined at pp. 110–14, supra.

Typically a proceeding under Section 9 is commenced by a union petition for investigation and certification filed in the appropriate regional office of the NLRB. Such a petition takes the form shown in the Statutory Supplement to this casebook, and sets forth the names of the employer and the petitioning union, the size and composition of the unit claimed to be appropriate, the name of any competing union and other relevant information. Through the years, the NLRA has announced an evolving policy

**a.** S. Strauss & J. Higgins, Jr., Practice & Procedure (Before the National Labor Relations Board (5th ed. 1996); L. Modjeska, NLRB Practice (1983).

toward petitions filed by *employers*. At first, no provision was made for an employer petition, for fear that an employer might too readily interfere with employee self-organization by filing for an election at opportune moments. Then the statute was amended to permit an employer petition as a shield against the crossfire of two competing unions presenting conflicting representation claims. In the Taft–Hartley amendments of 1947, Congress went further and authorized an employer to file whenever any person or labor organization presents a claim for recognition as the bargaining representative.

The Taft–Hartley Act also made a highly significant change in representation proceedings by introducing the petition for "decertification". Under Section 9(c)(1)(A)(ii) any employee or group of employees may file a petition alleging that a substantial number of employees assert that a majority in the bargaining unit do not wish to be represented by the collective bargaining representative currently certified (or informally recognized) by the employer. If the Board "finds that a question of representation exists", it is to conduct an election to determine the desires of the employees. Generally speaking the same rules govern proceedings on petitions for decertification as govern other proceedings under Section 9.

When a petition is filed under Section 9, regardless of who files it, three broad questions may arise: (A) whether to proceed with an investigation and certification; (B) what is the unit appropriate for the purposes of collective bargaining; and (C) how, and the extent to which, federal courts review NLRB decisions in representation proceedings. These questions are discussed in the following sections of this chapter.

––––––

## A.   Grounds for Not Proceeding to an Investigation and Certification

The most important grounds on which the Board may decline to proceed to an investigation or certification have been (1) the want of a substantial interest on the part of the petitioning union, (2) the commission of unremedied unfair labor practices, (3) a prior certification or the lapse of less than a year since the last previous election, and (4) the subsistence of a valid collective bargaining agreement.

A petitioning union, while it need not show a majority, must nevertheless make a preliminary showing of real strength among the employees before the Board will proceed to investigation and certification. The showing is usually made by submitting to the Regional Office cards recently signed by individual employees authorizing the union to act as their representative. A Board Agent checks the cards against the company payroll and when there is doubt may inquire into the currency and authenticity of the signatures. A showing of authorizations from 30 per cent of the employees in an appropriate bargaining unit is both necessary and sufficient. (A second union wishing to intervene in the representation proceeding, for example to block an election agreement or to introduce evidence bearing on the eligibility of voters or on the appropriate bargaining unit, may do so upon a showing of only 10 percent support; an incumbent union generally needs to make no such showing. All that is needed for a union to secure a place on the ballot is a single authorization card.) The employer has never been given the right, however, to challenge the evidence of the union's strength or to urge dismissal on the ground that a sufficient showing had not been made. The rule is an administrative expedient for avoiding expenditure of money and personnel in cases in which no certification is likely to result and the question is therefore regarded as one with which the employer has no legitimate concern. It has in fact been held that the Regional Director is not obligated to disclose authorization cards upon demand made under the Freedom of Information Act. Pacific Molasses Co. v. NLRB, 577 F.2d 1172 (5th Cir.1978).

For many years, it has been the Board's policy not to proceed with an election while substantial unfair labor practice charges are pending; a union will sometimes file a so-called blocking charge, which the Board will resolve before proceeding with the processing of an earlier-filed election petition. Whether or not an unfair labor practice charge has been filed, however, a union which believes that the employer has acted unlawfully during the organizing campaign may choose to proceed to an election and, if it loses, to seek a bargaining order on the basis of the prior events. If the election is set aside and the union shows that it had majority support prior to the unfair practices, the Board may order the employer to bargain with the union.

In order to impart as much stability to a collective bargaining relationship once established as is consistent with full freedom of choice, the Board has had a rule of long standing that the certification of a collective bargaining representative is a bar to another investigation within one year. It applies a correlative principle in its unfair labor practice cases: an employer must honor the Board's certification for a year and continue to bargain with the certified union despite changes in employee sentiment. (See pages 334–38, infra.) Congress extended this certification-bar principle to any case in which there has been a prior NLRB election, regardless whether a union is or is not certified as the winner. Section 9(c)(3), added to the Act in 1947, forbids holding an election within twelve months of a preceding valid election.

One of the most difficult problems in representation controversies has been to determine the effect to be given to a valid subsisting collective bargaining agreement when it is alleged that a majority of the employees in an appropriate bargaining unit wish to be represented by a different union than the union which negotiated the agreement with the employer.

One solution to the problem would be to hold that a collective bargaining agreement bars a new certification throughout its existence; but this would permit the contracting parties to insulate the union's position for an unreasonably long time, inconsistent with the statutory policy of assuring workers full freedom of choice as to union representation. But to exalt the latter policy would lead to a too frequent reassessment of employee prefer- ences, at the expense of the kind of industrial stability which flows from a freely negotiated collective bargaining agreement. The Board's solution— one which attempts to balance the conflicting policies of stability and self- determination—has been its so-called contract bar rules, which in their original incarnation forbade proceeding to a new election within one year of a contract's coming into existence. Today, the contract may bar (with some exceptions) an election for up to three years of its term.

If a collective agreement is to serve as a bar, it must be reduced to writing and be executed by all the contracting parties. The agreement must apply to the employees covered in the rival union's petition. It must encompass employees in an appropriate unit and it must grant recognition to the union as exclusive representative of all workers in that unit, union members and nonmembers alike. In addition, the contract must embody substantial terms and conditions of employment and not merely concern itself with wages alone or with provisions of an insubstantial or peripheral nature.[b] A collective bargaining agreement containing "a clearly unlawful union-security provision" is no bar to an election, but "contracts contain- ing ambiguous though not clearly unlawful union-security provisions will bar representation proceedings in the absence of a determination of illegali- ty as to the particular provision involved by this Board or a Federal court pursuant to an unfair labor practice proceeding."[c] In 1962, the Board took the further step of declaring that contracts would act as a bar even though they contain provisions in violation of Section 8(e);[d] but also ruled that contracts discriminating amongst employees on grounds of race would not bar an election.[e]

Once a contract is executed satisfying all the preceding requirements, it will immediately be deemed to operate as a bar (unless the agreement clearly specifies some condition precedent to its becoming binding in effect).[f] On the other hand, the agreement may later cease to be a bar for any one of several reasons. In the first place, a contract for a fixed term will bar a petition filed by a rival union for only the first three years of its life, even if the specified term is for a longer period and even though contracts of a greater duration are commonly used in the industry or area in question.[g] (A contract which fails to provide any fixed duration will not serve as a bar for any period whatsoever.)[h]

---

**b.** All of these requirements were set forth by the Board in Appalachian Shale Products Co., 121 NLRB 1160 (1958).

**c.** Paragon Products Corp., 134 NLRB 662 (1961).

**d.** Food Haulers, Inc., 136 NLRB 394 (1962).

**e.** Pioneer Bus Co., Inc., 140 NLRB 54 (1962).

**f.** Appalachian Shale Products Co., 121 NLRB 1160, 1162 (1958).

**g.** General Cable Corp., 139 NLRB 1123 (1962). If the agreement is for a longer term, it will still serve as a bar to the filing of an election petition by the signatory employ- er or union (unless the union was recognized without certification, in which case it can even during the contract term seek an elec- tion and certification).

**h.** Ibid.

Second, if the bargaining representative has become "defunct," the contract will not act as a bar to an election. A union is held to be defunct if it is unable or unwilling to represent the employees in the bargaining unit.[i] Inability or unwillingness may be evidenced, for example, by a failure for more than a brief period to hold meetings, elect officers or process grievances. A major case announcing the reasons behind the "defunctness" exception to the contract-bar rule is Container Corp., 61 NLRB 823 (1945), where the Board stated:

> Normally, a current agreement between an employer and a labor organization acting as the exclusive bargaining representative of employees in an appropriate unit is both means and proof of the achievement of that stability which is an objective of the statute, for such an agreement identifies the employees' recognized bargaining representative, settles questions pertaining to wages, hours, and working conditions, and betokens the successful operation of the collective bargaining process. * * * [In the instant case, the] contract is not being administered on behalf of the employees; it cannot be interpreted and enforced through the application of its grievance procedure, or altered to meet changing circumstances by the process of collective bargaining. To treat the instrument in these circumstances as a bar to an immediate determination of representatives would in no real sense stabilize industrial relations, but would, rather, negate the purposes of the Act.

Third, an existing labor contract will not bar a representation election if the bargaining representative is involved in a "schism." A schism exists when a local union votes in open meeting to disaffiliate from its parent because of a basic intra-union conflict over policy existing at the highest level of the parent union. Such a policy split becomes so serious as to disrupt intra-union relationships and so fractures the bargaining representative as to generate confusion and instability. The confusion can be eliminated and stability restored only by holding a new election. Hershey Chocolate Corp., 121 NLRB 901 (1958).

Finally, a contract may cease to operate as a bar when changes in circumstances have occurred due to expansion or changes in the employer's operations. Thus, if less than 30% of the existing staff were working for the employer when the contract in question was executed or if less than 50% of the present job classifications existed on the date of execution, the contract will have no barring effect. The same result will obtain following relocation of facilities or a merger of two or more operations provided that these changes either involve the hiring of substantially all new employees or create an entirely new operation with major changes in personnel. These principles were announced by the Board in General Extrusion Co., 121 NLRB 1165 (1958).

---

i. Hershey Chocolate Corp., 121 NLRB 901 (1958).

Ordinarily, contracts that constitute a bar to an election will cease to do so upon their termination.[j] Nevertheless, a rival union or a decertification petitioner must bear certain other requirements in mind in order for the petition to be considered by the Board. In particular, the rival union must file its petition not more than 90 days nor less than 60 days before the termination of the contract.[k] The purpose of these rules is to discourage election activity too far in advance of termination and to provide during the last 60 days an insulated period during which the parties to the old agreement can work out a new contract without being distracted by claims from rival unions. If a new contract is agreed upon and executed during this period, it too will serve as a bar provided that it satisfies the various requirements previously discussed, and provided, of course, that no petition was timely filed in the preceding "open" period of thirty days. If no such contract has been executed when the 60 days expire, however, a petition can be filed at any time prior to the execution of a new agreement. The principal case announcing these rules is DELUXE METAL FURNITURE Co., 121 NLRB 995 (1958).

AMERICAN SEATING Co., 106 NLRB 250 (1953). In September 1949, the United Automobile Workers, affiliated with the CIO, was certified by the NLRB as the bargaining representative for the employer's production and maintenance workers. A three-year contract was signed, effective July 1, 1950. Near the end of the second year of the contract, an election petition was filed by the Pattern Makers Association, affiliated with the AFL, seeking to sever a craft unit of pattern makers from the UAW unit. Over the opposition of the UAW and the company, the Board ordered an election; under the contract-bar rules prevailing at that time, a contract would bar an election for only two years absent proof that contracts for three years were customary in the industry. The Pattern Makers Association won the election within the severed craft unit, and were certified as bargaining representative.

When the Association approached the company in October 1952 with proposals for a comprehensive bargaining agreement, the company responded that the UAW contract—validly negotiated by the "agent" originally designated by the pattern makers as "principals"—was binding until its expiration date nine months later. In a proceeding under Section 8(a)(5) challenging the company's refusal to bargain, the General Counsel contended that the UAW contract was "inoperative" as to the pattern makers. The Board found an unfair labor practice, for the following reasons.

---

**j.** As mentioned above, a contract for a fixed term will not be considered to bar a rival petition after the elapse of three years. For the purpose of the following discussion, therefore, "termination" refers to the termination date specified in the contract *or* a date three years subsequent to the execution of the contract, whichever occurs sooner.

**k.** Leonard Wholesale Meats, Inc., 136 NLRB 1000 (1962). In health care institutions, brought within the Labor Act in 1974, the analogous "open" period is 90 to 120 days prior to contract termination. Trinity Lutheran Hosp. v. Operating Engineers, Local 6, 218 NLRB 199 (1975).

"The Respondent's principal-agent argument assumes that common law principles of agency control the relationship of exclusive bargaining representative to employees in an appropriate unit. We think that this assumption is unwarranted and overlooks the unique character of that relationship under the National Labor Relations Act. * * * A duly selected statutory representative is the representative of a shifting group of employees in an appropriate unit—which includes not only those employees who approve such relationship, but also those who disapprove and those who have never had an opportunity to express their choice. Under agency principles, a principal has the power to terminate the authority of his agent at any time. Not so in the case of a statutory bargaining representative. Thus, in its most important aspects the relationship of statutory bargaining representative to employees in an appropriate unit resembles a political rather than a private law relationship. In any event, because of the unique character of the statutory representative, a solution for the problem presented in this case must be sought in the light of that special relationship rather than by the device of pinning labels on the various parties involved and applying without change principles of law evolved to govern entirely different situations. * * *

"The purpose of the Board's rule holding a contract of unreasonable duration not a bar to a new determination of representatives is the democratic one of insuring to employees the right at reasonable intervals of reappraising and changing, if they so desire, their union representation. Bargaining representatives are thereby kept responsive to the needs and desires of their constituents; and employees dissatisfied with their representatives know that they will have the opportunity of changing them by peaceful means at an election conducted by an impartial government agency. Strikes for a change of representatives are thereby reduced and the effects of employee dissatisfaction with their representatives are mitigated. But, if a newly chosen representative is to be hobbled in the way proposed by the Respondent, a great part of the benefit to be derived from the no-bar rule will be dissipated. There is little point in selecting a new bargaining representative which is unable to negotiate new terms and conditions of employment for an extended period of time.

"We hold that, for the reason which led the Board to adopt the rule that a contract of unreasonable duration is not a bar to a new determination of representatives, such a contract may not bar full statutory collective bargaining, including the reduction to writing of any agreement reached, as to any group of employees in an appropriate unit covered by such contract, upon the certification of a new collective bargaining representative for them. Accordingly, we find that by refusing on and after October 16, 1952, to bargain with the Pattern Makers concerning wages, hours and other working conditions for employees in the unit of pattern makers, the Respondent violated Section 8(a)(5) and (1) of the Act."

## PROBLEMS FOR DISCUSSION

**1.** Suppose that the employer in the *American Seating* case had reduced the pattern makers' wages immediately after the NLRB certification to a rate lower than that fixed in the UAW contract. Would it be liable for breach of contract? If so, who should bring the action? Could UAW maintain an action? Compare U.S. Gypsum Co. v. United Steelworkers, 384 F.2d 38 (5th Cir.1967). Alternatively, would you support the argument that the labor contract merely serves as the status quo which the employer may change after bargaining to impasse, so that its conduct is regulated only by Section 8(a)(5) and not by the entire contract?

**2.** Assume that the UAW contract contained a clause providing that there should be no strikes during the term of the agreement. Assume further that American Seating Co. and Pattern Makers' League were unable to agree upon the terms of a new contract after good faith negotiations. Would it be a breach of contract for the pattern makers to strike?

**3.** Suppose that Pattern Makers negotiated a substantial wage increase, that other skilled employees began to talk of seeking craft representation and that UAW, before the expiration of its contract, demanded immediate wage increases for all employees. Would American have a duty to bargain? (Consult section 8(d) of the Labor Act.)

———

## B.  APPROPRIATE BARGAINING UNIT[j]

### 1.  SIGNIFICANCE

Section 9(a) of the federal Labor Act provides that a representative chosen by "the majority of the employees in a unit appropriate for such purposes" is to be the "exclusive" representative of all employees in that unit. As an incident to conducting a representation election, the Board must determine which group of jobs shall serve as the election constituency. That group of jobs is denoted the appropriate bargaining unit, and the persons employed in those jobs at the time of the election are entitled to vote whether they wish to continue to settle terms and conditions of employment on an individual basis—or, as some would have it, by "unilateral" act of the employer—or whether they wish to have one or another employee representative. Any such majority representative, the "exclusive" spokesman in dealing with the employer on these matters, is empowered and obliged to bargain not only for the employees who voted for it or who are its members, but for *all* employees in the bargaining unit. The model of majority rule within discretely bounded election units is obviously borrowed from the American political tradition.

**j.** See J. Abodeely, R. Hammer & A. Sandler, The NLRB and the Appropriate Bargaining Unit (1981); A. Weber, The Structure of Collective Bargaining (1961); Leslie, Labor Bargaining Units, 70 Va.L.Rev. 353 (1984).

Several important and sometimes misunderstood features of this statutory design should be noted. First, the unit is comprised of jobs or job classifications and not of the particular persons working at those jobs at any given time. The bargaining unit does not change simply because Machinist Jones retires and is replaced by Machinist Williams. Second, what is commonly known as the "appropriate bargaining unit" might more accurately be denoted the appropriate *election* unit since employees represented in different election units may choose to "re-group" as a single larger entity for purposes of conducting actual negotiations. The composition of the *negotiating* unit will thus frequently depend less upon the Board's unit determination than upon the structure of the employer and the union and upon alliances among employers or unions. Third, a determination of the appropriate bargaining unit by the National Labor Relations Board is not a prerequisite to bargaining; an employer and a union are in most instances free to agree informally upon an appropriate unit and upon the commencement of bargaining for the employees in that unit. Fourth, it is the task of the Board to delineate only "an" appropriate bargaining unit; it is not obliged to select only one which is the most appropriate or the optimal unit. The Board thus theoretically has a wide variety of choices. The employees in a single plant might be grouped as one unit or divided according to craft or department, or into larger classifications. If a single company has several plants they may constitute one unit or several units. Bargaining also takes place in multiemployer units on a city-wide, regional or even industry-wide basis.

While the Labor Act empowers the Board to make unit determinations, it gives the Board only the most modest guidance in doing so. Section 9(b) begins:

> The Board shall decide in each case whether, in order to assure to employees the fullest freedom in exercising the rights guaranteed by this Act, the unit appropriate for the purposes of collective bargaining shall be the employer unit, craft unit, plant unit, or subdivision thereof

and proceeds to add explicit limitations upon the Board's powers in three rather narrowly circumscribed situations. One of the limitations protects the right of craft employees to be represented separately, in spite of an earlier certification within a more all-encompassing bargaining unit. Another forbids the Board to group professional and nonprofessional employees within a single bargaining unit "unless a majority of the professional employees vote for inclusion in such unit." Section 2(12) defines a professional employee as one whose work is predominantly intellectual, requiring the constant exercise of discretion and judgment and knowledge of an advanced type acquired through prolonged, specialized and intellectual instruction (as opposed to the routine or physical work of a nonprofessional). Section 9(b) also unqualifiedly forbids the Board to include within a single unit both guards and non-guards, regardless of the preferences of the guards. Congress was primarily concerned with the conflict of loyalties which would confront the guards if they were expected to enforce the employer's security rules and protect its property against fellow unit members, especially during periods of economic confrontation. For these reasons, the statute goes beyond forbidding the grouping of guards and non-guards in the same bargaining unit and forbids the Board as well to certify any employee organization as a representative for a separate unit of guards if that organization "admits to membership, or is affiliated directly or indirectly with an organization which admits to membership, employees other than guards."

These limitations in Section 9(b), and several other pertinent restrictions upon the Board's authority in election cases (such as the election-bar rule) were not incorporated in the original Wagner Act of 1935 but were added in the Taft–Hartley Act of 1947 in the context of a Congressional call for greater legislative and judicial limitation of agency discretion. In spite of that, Board decisions on unit-determination matters typically invite a judgmental assessment of a number of relevant criteria and are typically shielded rather well against extensive judicial review. Judicial review is limited both because of the presumed expertise of the agency, stemming from its familiarity with the industrial context and, as noted above, the possible appropriateness of a number of different bargaining units in the same case. Moreover, as a matter of procedure, a unit determination can, except in the most extraordinary circumstances, be challenged only by the rather circuitous method of committing an unfair labor practice; this method is sufficiently exhausting and frequently technically obscure so as to serve as an additional obstacle to effective judicial supervision.

Although the jurisdiction of the Board to adjudicate unfair labor practice cases is perhaps the more dramatic, its jurisdiction to make unit determinations is at the heart of our system of collective bargaining and has a most pervasive impact upon industrial relations.

(1) A large unit, commonly favored by the employer, will typically be much more difficult for the union to organize than a small one. The size of the unit may thus determine whether there will be an election at all (since the union must first make a "showing of interest") and if so, whether collective bargaining will be instituted.

(2) A large unit may engross within it employees of differing skills, attitudes and interests. The more diversified the constituency, the more likely there will be conflicts of interest and strains upon the union's ability to represent all unit employees fairly in negotiating and administering the collective bargaining agreement.

(3) The size and composition of the unit will directly affect the structure and composition of the union representative, which not only must represent all in the unit but must also court all unit employees as a source of financial and bargaining power.

(4) The smaller and the more homogeneous the unit, the more likely it is that the individual worker will be effectively represented and will have his voice heard in a democratic manner within union councils; the larger

the unit, the more diluted the impact of any single employee on the shaping of union policy.

(5) The size of the unit will also shape the kinds of issues that will be addressed in collective bargaining and dealt with in the labor agreement.

(6) Fragmented units tend to bring economic headaches to the employer. Not only are they typically easier to organize, but they also involve the greater cost and disruption that come with frequent bargaining cycles and meetings; moreover, they expose the employer to "whipsaw" strikes by employees in one unit which inure, cumulatively, to the benefit of employees in other units.

(7) Fragmented units, represented by different unions, often bring with them disputes between those unions about the right to represent employees of uncertain representational status (*e.g.*, in newly created job titles) or the right of members of one union to oust from their jobs members of another (a work-assignment dispute).

(8) Larger units bring the danger of a more massive work-stoppage in the event of a bargaining dispute; smaller units may permit the employer to transfer work from one unit, shut down by a strike, to some other unit which is still in operation and subject to an existing labor contract (or which is not organized at all).

As can be noted, different unions and different employers may have differing preferences regarding the size of the bargaining unit, depending upon the nature of the industry and the structure and composition of the workforce. On the whole, however, it is likely that unions will favor the smaller unit, since it can be more readily organized. Since 1960, the Board has tended to echo this preference, since the smaller unit assures greater homogeneity of employee interest and maximizes employee self-determination.

In a very large proportion of the cases in which representation petitions are filed, the problem of defining the collective bargaining unit can be resolved without the necessity for formal proceedings. Either the parties' mutual consent, or the pattern of organization or Board precedents in the industry, will set at rest any possible question. In these cases, the Regional Director and the parties work out a stipulation defining the unit and there remains only the task of determining which union, if any, is the majority choice.

But where voluntary agreement on the unit cannot be achieved, formal proceedings are required. A hearing officer from the regional office will preside and—unlike the unfair labor practice hearing, at which the Board through its General Counsel functions as prosecutor—the leading role in the representation hearing will be played by the employer and union(s) concerned. The evidence gathered in the hearing is transmitted to the Regional Director, who determines the appropriate bargaining unit; that determination is then subject to review, but only on limited grounds, by the NLRB.

## 2. CRITERIA FOR UNIT DETERMINATIONS

The Board's unit determination generally takes the form of an endorsement or a (rare) veto of the unit requested by the petitioning party. (See the form of petition in the Supplement.) As noted above, the Board does not "comb the record" in the abstract to select the optimal unit. The Labor Act tells the Board very little about the criteria or standards which should be employed in making unit determinations. Section 9(b) enjoins the Board "to assure to employees the fullest freedom in exercising the rights guaranteed by this Act." Those rights, enumerated in Section 7, are the right to form and join a union, to bargain collectively and to engage in concerted activities to those ends—and the right to refrain from doing so. If the Board holds "appropriate" a very large unit covering, for example, many geographically dispersed plants staffed by employees of differing skills and working conditions, the exercise of Section 7 rights may be frustrated: effective communication by the union in organizing and in formulating and administering contract terms may be hampered, intensive interest in collective bargaining within one group of employees may be "cancelled out" by the votes of those elsewhere who oppose it, and negotiation and administration of the labor contract may be crippled by the conflicting interests of employees within the unit. Conversely, a unit which is "too small," and which excludes some employees with common skills, working conditions and economic interests, may curtail the bargaining power of the union representing only the unit employees, may generate (perhaps with the aid of the employer) divisions and in-fighting among employees in the plant or conversely may generate pressures to settle terms of employment for the non-unit employees along the lines negotiated for the unit employees (in spite of the possible desire of the non-unit employees to "refrain from" unionization and collective bargaining). For these reasons, the Board in making its unit determinations seeks an employee group which is united by *community of interest,* and which neither embraces employees having a substantial conflict of economic interest nor omits employees sharing a unity of economic interest with other employees in the election or bargaining constituency.

The Board draws upon this criterion of community of interest in order to determine whether, for example, employees with special craft skills and training should be separated out for purposes of voting and bargaining or whether they should be grouped along with semi-skilled and unskilled employees in an "industrial" unit; whether "production and maintenance" employees should be grouped in a single unit with "white-collar employees" doing technical or clerical work; whether the unit should comprise only employees working in a single plant, store or office of the employer or whether there should be a grouping of employees in several—or indeed all—of the employer's plants, stores or offices; and whether it is sound to go even beyond the employees of a single employer and to group those employees with persons employed by other employers in the same industry in the same competitive market. In making judgments about "community of interest" in these different settings, the Board will look to such factors as: (1) similarity in the scale and manner of determining earnings; (2) similarity in employment benefits, hours of work and other terms and conditions of employment; (3) similarity in the kind of work performed; (4) similarity in the qualifications, skills and training of the employees; (5) frequency of contact or interchange among the employees; (6) geographic proximity; (7) continuity or integration of production processes; (8) common supervision and determination of labor-relations policy; (9) history of collective bargaining; (10) desires of the affected employees; (11) extent of union organization. See NLRB v. Purnell's Pride, Inc., 609 F.2d 1153 (5th Cir.1980).

It can readily be seen that community of interest is a vague standard which does not lend itself to mechanical application. It is a multi-factor criterion, and it is rare in any given case that all of the factors point conveniently in the direction of the same size unit. As already noted, it is indeed possible that on the basis of community of interest, the Board may conclude that there are several units any one of which may be, in the language of the statute, "a unit appropriate" for collective bargaining.

Perhaps no issue regarding bargaining units and "community of interest" has been more difficult and divisive for the NLRB in recent years than the determination of appropriate units in hospital and other health-care institutions.[m]

In the Taft–Hartley Act of 1947, Congress amended the definition of "employer" in Section 2(2) so as to exclude private non-profit hospitals. Both before that and subsequently, the NLRB declined as a matter of discretion to assert jurisdiction over all private hospitals, whether non-profit or proprietary. Congress concluded by 1974 that there was no reason to deny employees of health-care institutions the protections of the National Labor Relations Act and that indeed the right to organize and bargain collectively would help to reduce serious labor disputes and disruptive work stoppages in this increasingly significant sector of the economy. The exclusion for non-profit hospitals was eliminated from the Act in 1974, and certain special provisions were inserted regarding notification and mediation relating to contract negotiations and strikes. See Sections 8(d) and (g). Although there was some concern reflected in the legislative history regarding the possible "proliferation" of bargaining units in health-care institutions, with attendant frequency of negotiations and work stoppages, Congress enacted no special provisions concerning health-care bargaining units.

Left to its own devices on this issue, the Board struggled and vacillated in a period of judicial criticism and rapid changes in Board membership. Through case-by-case adjudication, the Board initially declared what was in effect a presumption favoring seven different occupational groupings as the basis for bargaining unit determinations; but then, with a change in

**m.** Bumpass, Appropriate Bargaining Units in Health Care Institutions: An Analysis of Congressional Intent and its Implementation by the NLRB, 20 Boston Coll.L.Rev. 867 (1979); Comment, Labor Relations in the Health Care Industry, 54 Tul.L.Rev. 416 (1980); Note, The National Labor Relations Board's Proposed Rules on Health Care Bargaining Units, 76 Va.L.Rev. 115 (1990).

membership and a greater felt concern about undue "proliferation" of units, the Board in effect created a presumption for no more than two units (one for professionals and one for non-professionals). In 1987, however, the Board determined that the issue could be best resolved through rulemaking proceedings. It published proposed rules about health-care bargaining units and conducted extensive hearings, and it ultimately issued a rule—codified at 29 C.F.R. Pt. 103, 54 Fed. Reg. 16336 (1989)—which provides in pertinent part:

(a) Except in extraordinary circumstances and in circumstances in which there are existing nonconforming units, the following shall be appropriate units, and the only appropriate units, for petitions filed pursuant to section 9(c)(1)(A)(i) or 9(c)(1)(B) of the National Labor Relations Act, as amended, except that, if sought by labor organizations, various combinations of units may also be appropriate:

(1) All registered nurses. (2) All physicians. (3) All professionals except for registered nurses and physicians. (4) All technical employees. (5) All skilled maintenance employees. (6) All business office clerical employees. (7) All guards. (8) All nonprofessional employees except for technical employees, skilled maintenance employees, business office clerical employees, and guards. *Provided That* a unit of five or fewer employees shall constitute an extraordinary circumstance.

(b) Where extraordinary circumstances exist, the Board shall determine appropriate units by adjudication.

(c) Where there are existing non-conforming units in acute care hospitals and a petition for additional units is filed pursuant to sec. 9(c)(1)(A)(i) or 9(c)(1)(B), the Board shall find appropriate only units which comport, insofar as practicable, with the appropriate unit set forth in paragraph (a) of this section.

The NLRB's power to adopt the rule, and the rule itself, were sustained by the Supreme Court against a challenge by the American Hospital Association in the following case.

--------

## American Hospital Ass'n v. NLRB

499 U.S. 606, 111 S.Ct. 1539, 113 L.Ed.2d 675 (1991).

■ JUSTICE STEVENS delivered the opinion of the Court.

For the first time since the National Labor Relations Board was established in 1935, the Board has promulgated a substantive rule defining the employee units appropriate for collective bargaining in a particular line of commerce. The rule is applicable to acute care hospitals and provides, with three exceptions, that eight and only eight units shall be appropriate in any such hospital. The three exceptions are for cases that present extraordinary circumstances, cases in which nonconforming units already exist, and cases in which labor organizations seek to combine two or more of the eight specified units. The extraordinary circumstances exception applies automatically to hospitals in which the eight unit rule will produce a unit of five or fewer employees. See 29 CFR § 103.30 (1990).

Petitioner, American Hospital Association, brought this action challenging the facial validity of the rule on three grounds: First, petitioner argues that § 9(b) of the National Labor Relations Act requires the Board to make a separate bargaining unit determination "in each case" and therefore prohibits the Board from using general rules to define bargaining units; second, petitioner contends that the rule that the Board has formulated violates a congressional admonition to the Board to avoid the undue proliferation of bargaining units in the health care industry; and, finally, petitioner maintains that the rule is arbitrary and capricious.

The United States District Court for the Northern District of Illinois agreed with petitioner's second argument and enjoined enforcement of the rule. 718 F.Supp. 704 (1989). The Court of Appeals found no merit in any of the three arguments and reversed. 899 F.2d 651 (C.A.7 1990). Because of the importance of the case, we granted certiorari, 498 U.S. 894, 111 S.Ct. 242, 112 L.Ed.2d 201 (1990). We now affirm.

I

Petitioner's first argument is a general challenge to the Board's rulemaking authority in connection with bargaining unit determinations based on the terms of the National Labor Relations Act (NLRA), 49 Stat. 449, 29 U.S.C. § 151 et seq., as originally enacted in 1935. * * *

Sections 3, 4, and 5 of the Act created the Board and generally described its powers. §§ 153–155. Section 6 granted the Board the "authority from time to time to make, amend, and rescind * * * such rules and regulations as may be necessary to carry out the provisions" of the Act. § 156. This grant was unquestionably sufficient to authorize the rule at issue in this case unless limited by some other provision in the Act.

Petitioner argues that § 9(b) provides such a limitation because this section requires the Board to determine the appropriate bargaining unit "in each case." § 159(b). We are not persuaded. Petitioner would have us put more weight on these three words than they can reasonably carry.

* * * Section 9(b) provides:

> "The Board shall decide *in each case* whether, in order to insure to employees the full benefit of their right to self-organization and to collective bargaining, and otherwise to effectuate the policies of this Act, the unit appropriate for the purposes of collective bargaining shall be the employer unit, craft unit, plant unit, or subdivision thereof." (Emphasis added.)

Petitioner reads the emphasized phrase as a limitation on the Board's rulemaking powers. Although the contours of the restriction that petitioner ascribes to the phrase are murky, petitioner's reading of the language would prevent the Board from imposing any industry-wide rule delineating the appropriate bargaining units. We believe petitioner's reading is inconsistent with the natural meaning of the language read in the context of the statute as a whole.

The more natural reading of these three words is simply to indicate that whenever there is a disagreement about the appropriateness of a unit, the Board shall resolve the dispute. Under this reading, the words "in each case" are synonymous with "whenever necessary" or "in any case in which there is a dispute." Congress chose not to enact a general rule that would require plant unions, craft unions or industry-wide unions for every employer in every line of commerce, but also chose not to leave the decision up to employees or employers alone. Instead, the decision "in each case" in which a dispute arises is to be made by the Board.

In resolving such a dispute, the Board's decision is presumably to be guided not simply by the basic policy of the Act but also by the rules that the Board develops to circumscribe and to guide its discretion either in the process of case-by-case adjudication or by the exercise of its rulemaking authority. The requirement that the Board exercise its discretion in every disputed case cannot fairly or logically be read to command the Board to exercise standardless discretion in each case. As a noted scholar on administrative law has observed: "[T]he mandate to decide 'in each case' does not prevent the Board from supplanting the original discretionary chaos with some degree of order, and the principal instruments for regularizing the system of deciding 'in each case' are classifications, rules, principles, and precedents. Sensible men could not refuse to use such instruments and a sensible Congress would not expect them to." K. Davis, Administrative Law Text 145 (3d ed. 1972). * * *

[The petitioner acknowledged that the Board had announced general principles in earlier bargaining-unit cases, but that those had functioned merely as presumptions to be applied on a case-by-case basis.] Contrary to petitioner's contention, the Board's rule is not an irrebuttable presumption; instead, it contains an exception for "extraordinary circumstances." Even if the rule did establish an irrebuttable presumption, it would not differ significantly from the prior rules adopted by the Board. As with its prior rules, the Board must still apply the rule "in each case." For example, the Board must decide in each case, among a host of other issues, whether a given facility is properly classified as an acute care hospital and whether particular employees are properly placed in particular units.

Our understanding that the ordinary meaning of the statutory language cannot support petitioner's construction is reinforced by the structure and the policy of the NLRA. As a matter of statutory drafting, if Congress had intended to curtail in a particular area the broad rulemaking authority granted in § 6, we would have expected it to do so in language expressly describing an exception from that section or at least referring specifically to the section. And, in regard to the Act's underlying policy, the goal of facilitating the organization and recognition of unions is certainly served by rules that define in advance the portions of the work force in which organizing efforts may properly be conducted. * * *

In sum, we believe that the meaning of § 9(b)'s mandate that the Board decide the appropriate bargaining unit "in each case" is clear and contrary to the meaning advanced by petitioner. Even if we could find any ambiguity in § 9(b) after employing the traditional tools of statutory construction, we would still defer to the Board's reasonable interpretation of the statutory text. Chevron USA Inc. v. Natural Resources Defense Council, Inc., 467 U.S. 837, 842–843, 104 S.Ct. 2778, 2781–2782, 81 L.Ed.2d 694 (1984). We thus conclude that § 9(b) does not limit the Board's rulemaking authority under § 6.

## II

[In considering the petitioner's second argument, the Court traced the legislative history of the 1974 NLRA health-care amendments and noted in particular a statement in both the House and Senate Committee Reports that "Due consideration should be given by the Board to preventing proliferation of bargaining units in the health care industry."]

Petitioner also suggests that the admonition "is an authoritative statement of what Congress intended when it extended the Act's coverage to include nonproprietary hospitals." Brief for Petitioner 30. Even if we accepted this suggestion, we read the admonition as an expression by the Committees of their desire that the Board give "due consideration" to the special problems that "proliferation" might create in acute care hospitals. Examining the record of the Board's rulemaking proceeding, we find that it gave extensive consideration to this very issue. See App. 20, 78–84, 114, 122, 131, 140, 158–159, 191–194, 246–254.

In any event, we think that the admonition in the Committee Reports is best understood as a form of notice to the Board that if it did not give appropriate consideration to the problem of proliferation in this industry, Congress might respond with a legislative remedy. So read, the remedy for noncompliance with the admonition is in the hands of the body that issued it. * * * If Congress believes that the Board has not given "due consideration" to the issue, Congress may fashion an appropriate response.

## III

Petitioner's final argument is that the rule is arbitrary and capricious because "it ignores critical differences among the more than 4,000 acute-care hospitals in the United States, including differences in size, location, operations, and work-force organization." * * *

The Board responds to this argument by relying on the extensive record developed during the rulemaking proceedings, as well as its experience in the adjudication of health care cases during the 13–year period between the enactment of the health care amendments and its notice of proposed rulemaking. Based on that experience, the Board formed the "considered judgment" that "acute care hospitals do not differ in substantial, significant ways relating to the appropriateness of units." App. 188–

189. Moreover, the Board argues, the exception for "extraordinary circumstances" is adequate to take care of the unusual case in which a particular application of the rule might be arbitrary.

* * * Given the extensive notice and comment rulemaking conducted by the Board, its careful analysis of the comments that it received, and its well-reasoned justification for the new rule, we would not be troubled even if there were inconsistencies between the current rule and prior NLRB pronouncements. The statutory authorization "from time to time to make, amend, and rescind" rules and regulations expressly contemplates the possibility that the Board will reshape its policies on the basis of more information and experience in the administration of the Act. See 29 U.S.C. § 156. The question whether the Board has changed its view about certain issues or certain industries does not undermine the validity of a rule that is based on substantial evidence and supported by a "reasoned analysis." See Motor Vehicle Mfrs. Assn. v. State Farm Mutual Automobile Ins. Co., 463 U.S. 29, 42, 57, 103 S.Ct. 2856, 2866, 2874, 77 L.Ed.2d 443 (1983).

The Board's conclusion that, absent extraordinary circumstances, "acute care hospitals do not differ in substantial, significant ways relating to the appropriateness of units," App. 189, was based on a "reasoned analysis" of an extensive record. * * *

---

### 3.   SINGLE–LOCATION VERSUS MULTI–LOCATION UNIT[n]

Many companies carry on their operations in a variety of geographical locations. Manufacturing concerns may have several plants; retail enterprises may have a network of individual stores; insurance companies may have many separate offices. Where a union seeks to organize a company of this kind, it is possible to conceive of a unit comprising all the employees in the company, or all of the firm's employees within a given geographical region (state, municipality, etc.), or all the employees within a single plant, office or store, or, conceivably, only a particular class of employees within a single plant or branch, such as the cafeteria employees at a downtown department store.

The determinations of the Board in cases of this kind will often touch upon strong interests of the parties concerned. From the union's standpoint, a narrowly defined unit may markedly influence the success of an organizing drive, for it may be much easier to win elections in a few separate stores than to mount a successful campaign simultaneously in a number of plants or stores spread out over a substantial geographical area. Conversely, the employer may favor a broader unit not only because it will make the job of the union organizer more difficult but also because it may

---

**n.** Comment, Appropriate Bargaining Unit Determinations in the Retail Chain Industry, 14 B.C.Ind. & Comm.L.Rev. 94 (1972); Note, The Board and Section 9(c)(5): Multilocation and Single–Location Bargaining Units in the Insurance and Retail Industries, 79 Harv.L.Rev. 811 (1966).

be simpler administratively to deal with a single bargaining agent representing all of its places of business in a given area.

Faced with these conflicting interests the NLRB tended at one time to favor the union's claim for a smaller unit in order to encourage collective bargaining. May Department Stores, 50 NLRB 669 (1943), is a fair example. After failing to make a sufficient showing of membership in support of its petition for certification as representative of a store-wide unit of several thousand employees, a CIO union sought certification as the representative of the 28 workers in the men's busheling department. Both the company and AFL opposed the establishment of such a unit on the ground that the appropriate unit was store-wide, and pointed to the admitted purpose of CIO to organize the employees on that basis. Nevertheless, the Board set up the unit sought by CIO.

"Assuming, without deciding, that a store-wide unit will best effectuate the purposes of the Act, we note that no labor organization claims to represent the employees in such a unit. We believe that collective bargaining should be made an immediate possibility for the employees in the busheling rooms without requiring them to await the uncertain date when the employees may be organized in a larger unit. We find accordingly that the employees in the busheling rooms constitute an appropriate unit. However, our finding in this respect does not preclude a later determination at another stage of self-organization that a larger unit is appropriate."

Section 9(c)(5) was added by the Taft–Hartley Act as a result of the criticism of these decisions. In view of this Section, the Board has conceded that "extent of organization" (as exemplified by the *May Department Stores* decision) cannot be used as the *sole* reason for establishing a given unit. But the Board has maintained that extent of organization remains a relevant factor to be considered, and this position has been upheld by the Supreme Court, in NLRB v. Metropolitan Life Ins. Co., 380 U.S. 438, 85 S.Ct. 1061, 13 L.Ed.2d 951 (1965).

The weight given by the NLRB to the extent of organization has varied over the years. During the 1950's, the NLRB frequently required multi-store and multi-plant units, particularly where wages and personnel policies were centrally administered for the plants and stores in question. Commencing in 1962, however, the Board seemed more willing once again to establish smaller units of employees in order to facilitate collective bargaining. In Sav-on Drugs, Inc., 138 NLRB 1032 (1962), the Board reversed its policy of grouping together a company's retail stores in a metropolitan or similar area and held that a single store might constitute an appropriate unit. It recognized that several factors, such as the geographical separation of each store, favored a single store unit, and that its former policy frequently "operated to impede the exercise by employees in retail chain operations of their rights to self-organization." Two years later, the Board went yet further and held, in Frisch's Big Boy Ill-Mar, Inc., 147 NLRB 551 (1964), enf't denied, 356 F.2d 895 (7th Cir.1966), that a single store in a chain-store operation is "presumptively appropriate."

Unit determinations for multi-plant operations proceeded along a line parallel to the retail chain-store determinations. In DIXIE BELLE MILLS, INC., 139 NLRB 629 (1962), the Board announced what was in substance a presumption that one plant of a multi-plant industrial operation is an appropriate unit. In that case, in which the union petitioned for an election at a single textile plant, the Board found the employees at that plant to constitute an appropriate unit in spite of the fact that the same employer operated other mills and warehouses twenty miles away, and in spite of the finding of the Regional Director that the company's operations at the different locations were integrated. The Board emphasized the low degree of employee interchange and the autonomy of supervision at the individual-plant level on day-to-day business and labor relations decisions. The Board announced the following guidelines:

"A single plant unit, being one of the unit types listed in the statute as appropriate for bargaining purposes, is presumptively appropriate. * * * Moreover, even assuming that the unit urged by the Employer and found by the Regional Director here may be the most appropriate unit, this does not establish it as the only appropriate one. * * * [T]he crucial question in each case is whether the unit requested is appropriate."

This single-location presumption has been widely followed by the NLRB in multi-location industries. See, *e.g.*, Metropolitan Life Ins. Co., 156 NLRB 1408 (1966); Wyandotte Savings Bank v. Retail Store Employees Union, 245 NLRB 943 (1979).

On September 28, 1995, the NLRB published a proposed rule on the appropriateness of single-location bargaining units in all except the construction industries and the maritime trades on sea-going vessels. 60 Fed. Reg. 50146. It would declare single-location units to be appropriate "except in extraordinary circumstances" provided fifteen or more employees are at the location, that the employer does not have another location within a mile of the requested location, and that a supervisor is present at the location for a "regular and substantial period." The reason for adopting a rule was the reduction of litigation:

The Board currently considers a number of factors in single location cases to determine whether the presumptive appropriateness of a requested single location has been rebutted. Often, the parties seek to prove the existence or absence of various factors by introducing voluminous testimony and documentary evidence concerning a myriad of facts. The parties litigate the significance of each fact and factor, and then the Regional Director and, if a request for review is filed, the Board determines whether the various factors exist, and are significant. The parties and the public are left to their own devices to deduce which facts and factors may or may not be deemed most significant in a particular case, although * * * the result in the majority of cases is that the single facility unit requested is found appropriate.

Congress subsequently attached a rider to the Board's appropriation denying any funds for the pursuit of such a rule thereby compelling the NLRB to terminate that proceeding. If such a rule were to be adopted, would it curtail the number of cases presented to the Board and the courts? Consider that question in the context of the following case, in which a court of appeals reviews two NLRB single-location unit determinations announced through the Board's customary adjudicatory proceedings.

---

# NLRB v. Chicago Health & Tennis Clubs, Inc.

567 F.2d 331 (7th Cir.1977), cert. denied, 437 U.S. 904, 98 S.Ct. 3089, 57 L.Ed.2d 1133 (1978).

■ SWYGERT, CIRCUIT JUDGE.

In the two cases before us, the National Labor Relations Board ("the Board") petitions for enforcement of its orders directing each of the respondents to cease and desist from refusing to bargain collectively with the union which had been certified as the exclusive bargaining representative. These two cases have been consolidated for this opinion because they present the identical legal issue: whether the Board abused its discretion in certifying a single retail store as an appropriate unit for collective bargaining where such store constitutes only one of a chain of stores owned and operated by the company in the Chicago metropolitan area. For the reasons set forth, we grant the petition in *Chicago Health Clubs* and deny enforcement in *Saxon Paint*.

I

(A) *Parties*

No. 77–1227. Chicago Health & Tennis Clubs is an Illinois corporation engaged in the sale of club memberships and providing services of exercise training and weight loss counseling for its members. It operates sixteen clubs in the Chicago metropolitan area (Chicago and suburbs). Its central office is located in Chicago's central business district and all clubs are within a 28–mile radius of this office.

No. 77–1504. Saxon Paint & Home Care Centers is an Illinois corporation engaged in the retail sale of paint, wallpaper, and home decorating supplies. It owns and operates twenty-one stores in the Chicago metropolitan area (Cook County). In addition, Saxon has seven other stores in Illinois, Indiana, and Wisconsin. Although these seven stores are operated by separate corporate entities, they are owned in part by the same stockholders and are operated through a single managerial hierarchy. All of the Chicago metropolitan area stores are within a 30–mile radius of each other.

(B) *Procedural History*

[In each of the two cases, a local of the Retail Clerks Union petitioned for a representation election in a unit limited to the employees of a single store in the company's chain. The Regional Director found the single-store unit appropriate, and the Board denied review. The union won the election in both instances, but the employer refused to bargain, claiming the inappropriateness of the unit. The Board found refusals to bargain in violation of Sections 8(a)(1) and (5), and has petitioned for enforcement of its bargaining orders.]

## II

The primary responsibility for determining the appropriateness of a unit for collective bargaining rests with the Board. It is given broad discretion in determining bargaining units "to assure to employees the fullest freedom in exercising the rights guaranteed by [the Act]." 29 U.S.C. § 159(b). The Board is not required to select the most appropriate bargaining unit in a given factual situation; it need choose only an appropriate unit within the range of appropriate units. Wil–Kil Pest Control Co. v. NLRB, 440 F.2d 371, 375 (7th Cir.1971). It follows that Board unit determinations are rarely to be disturbed. South Prairie Construction Co. v. Local No. 627, International Union, 425 U.S. 800, 805, 96 S.Ct. 1842, 48 L.Ed.2d 382 (1976); Packard Motor Co. v. NLRB, 330 U.S. 485, 491, 67 S.Ct. 789, 91 L.Ed.2d 1040 (1947).

Although Board determinations are subject to limited review, they are not immune from judicial scrutiny. * * * [W]e have the responsibility of determining whether the Board's unit determinations were unreasonable, * * * arbitrarily or capriciously made, * * * or unsupported by substantial evidence. * * *

In making unit determinations, the Board must effect the policy of the Act to assure employees the fullest freedom in exercising their rights, yet at the same time "respect the interest of an integrated multi-unit employer in maintaining enterprise-wide labor relations." NLRB v. Solis Theatre Corp., 403 F.2d 381, 382 (2d Cir.1968). * * * In reaching its decision, the Board considers several criteria, no single factor alone being determinative. * * * These factors include: (a) geographic proximity of the stores in relation to each other * * *; (b) history of collective bargaining or unionization * * *; (c) extent of employee interchange between various stores * * *; (d) functional integration of operations * * *; and (e) centralization of management, particularly in regard to central control of personnel and labor relations. * * * As the geographic proximity of the stores in the two cases before us is almost identical, our decision whether to grant the petitions for enforcement must rest on an analysis of the other factors.

One further item deserves note before proceeding to a discussion of the individual cases. Although the Board has vascillated in deciding the proper scope of a bargaining unit in the retail chain industry, it has apparently now adopted the administrative policy that a single store is "presumptively an appropriate unit for bargaining." Haag Drug Corp., 169 N.L.R.B. 877–78 (1968). That presumption, however, is not conclusive and "may be overcome where factors are present in a particular case which would counter the appropriateness of a single store unit. . . ." Id. at 878.

We turn now to the two cases before us.

(A) *Saxon Paint, No. 77–1504*

Although the Board recognized that the Chicago area Saxon stores exhibited "a high degree of centralized administration," it nevertheless found a single store unit appropriate. In large part, the Board based its unit determination on the role of the local store manager, adopting the Regional Director's finding that "substantial responsibility is invested in the Employer's store managers." We believe that the Board exaggerated the control exercised by the store manager over labor and administrative matters and hold that the Board's finding that the store manager possesses autonomy and authority is not supported by substantial evidence.

The evidence in the record clearly establishes that Saxon is a highly integrated operation. Each Saxon store is similar in all respects to each of the other Saxon stores in Cook County. All of the stores are open on the same days and at the same times. They sell the same merchandise at the same price and the physical layout of each store is similar. Special sales and promotions are held at the same time in each store with the same sale prices being charged. Advertising covers the entire metropolitan area and is prepared by headquarters as are store signs and window displays. The stores are "as much alike in this respect as peas in a pod." NLRB v. Frisch's Big Boy Ill–Mar, Inc., 356 F.2d 895, 896 (7th Cir.1966).

Personnel and labor relations policies for the Saxon stores are also centrally administered, being formulated by the personnel director who maintains his office at corporate headquarters. Payrolls, accounts, personnel files, and other records are maintained at the general office. Employee job classifications are the same at each store, and employees within a particular classification perform the same duties and are required to have the same skills and experience. Employees within the same classification, experience, and seniority receive the same wages. A uniform fringe benefit program is maintained at each store, and store employees enjoy company-wide seniority.

The actual operations of the Cook County stores are also highly centralized. [The court sketched the important role of district managers, who frequently visited the stores within their territories and assured that they were operated in compliance with centralized policies and procedures.]

At the store level and below the district managers, the company employs fourteen store managers in all three districts. Seven of these managers are assigned to single stores, the remaining seven managers are each assigned to two stores. The evidence establishes that, contrary to the Board's conclusion, these store managers have limited involvement in the store's non-labor business activities. The individual store managers have no authority to commit the employer's credit, purchase or order merchandise and supplies, arrange for repair or maintenance work, change prices, or resolve customer complaints. At best it can be said that it is the responsibility of the store managers to implement the company's policies and procedures within the individual stores.

The store managers' involvement in labor relations and personnel matters is also severely limited. They have no authority to do any of the following: (a) hire new employees; (b) grant promotions, wage increases or changes in job classifications; (c) discharge or suspend employees for disciplinary reasons; (d) lay-off employees; (e) handle employee grievances; (f) grant requests for vacations or leaves of absence; (g) permanently or temporarily transfer employees between any of the stores; and (h) post the weekly work schedule without prior approval by the district manager. While the store manager may offer recommendations in certain of these areas, the record shows that these recommendations, even in such key areas as employee discharge, may not be followed. Furthermore, in certain areas such as promotion and wage increases, the store manager may not even be consulted before a decision is made. As the Second Circuit noted in NLRB v. Solis Theatre Corp., 403 F.2d 381, 383 (2d Cir.1968):

> It appears, therefore, that instead of being in a decision making position, the "manager" has little or no authority on labor policy but is subject to detailed instructions from the central office.

That Saxon is completely integrated functionally is best illustrated by its hiring and training practices. Hiring is done almost exclusively through the corporate offices. Job applications are taken and interviews are held at the personnel office. The store manager may interview an applicant only after the applicant has first interviewed with the personnel director and then the district manager. Applicants may be rejected and new employees hired, however, without prior consultation with or participation by the store manager.

Similarly, the training of new employees comes under the primary jurisdiction of the central personnel department. The company issues manuals to all new employees and provides them with formal training, lasting from one to two weeks, at its corporate headquarters. In sum, it is apparent that there is no local autonomy among the individual stores and that the store managers lack the authority to resolve issues which would be subject to collective bargaining. See Frisch's Big Boy, 356 F.2d at 897.

That Saxon's business is both centralized and integrated and that the individual stores lack meaningful identity as a self-contained unit is further supported by the numbers of employee transfers, both temporary and permanent, among the metropolitan area stores. During a thirteen month period and discounting employees not covered in the unit, eighteen percent of all employees were transferred permanently among the Chicago stores. Additional testimony showed that temporary transfers frequently occur, almost on a daily basis. While this alone may be insufficient to negate a single store unit, we cannot agree with the Board's finding that "the degree of employee interchange [was] too inconsequential and insubstantial to rebut the appropriateness of a single store unit," particularly when this factor is considered in light of all of the other factors.

That a single store is inappropriate here is further shown by the history of collective bargaining. The pattern of unionization both at stores in other regions and at stores within the Chicago metropolitan area has always been district wide. * * *

For the reasons herein stated, we conclude that the Board's determination that a single Saxon store was an appropriate bargaining unit is not supported by substantial evidence and therefore is arbitrary and unreasonable. Accordingly, the Board's order is set aside and enforcement is denied.

(B) *Chicago Health Clubs, No. 77–1227*

*Chicago Health Clubs* is, at first sight, quite similar factually to *Saxon Paint.* The company's sixteen stores (clubs) are in a similar geographic proximity to each other. Many of its operations and procedures are centralized.

Other similarities are readily apparent. Chicago Health Clubs has two area supervisors (similar to Saxon's district managers) who oversee its sixteen clubs. These supervisors visit their respective clubs two or three times a week and maintain frequent telephone contact. Despite these similarities, we conclude that substantial evidence supports the Board's finding that a single club is an appropriate bargaining unit.

Notably absent in this case is any prior history of collective bargaining. In addition, the extent of employee interchange among the various clubs is minimal. Furthermore, there are significant differences in the functional integration of the clubs, the extent to which the company is centralized, and the degree of autonomy of the local club managers.

Unlike the Saxon stores which are virtually identical with each other, Chicago Health Clubs operates at least three types of clubs. Some clubs exclusively serve women, others serve men on one day and women on another. Still others serve men and women on the same day. The clubs also differ in the type of facilities available. Some have handball courts, others have swimming pools. One has a tennis court.

Although many aspects of the company's operations and procedures are centralized, they are not as highly centralized as in *Saxon Paint.* For example, even though official personnel and payroll records are maintained at the central office, each club manager also maintains records detailing needed information about the club employees. Similarly, the central office controls the advertising for all sixteen clubs, but the advertising may be directed at only one geographical area or may be on behalf of only one of the clubs.

Also unlike the store managers in *Saxon Paint,* the club managers exercise a marked degree of control over personnel and labor relations matters. Applicants apply at the individual clubs and are interviewed by the club manager without further interview by the area supervisor. Part-time employees, a large number if not a majority of all employees, are hired and fired by the club manager without consultation with the area supervisor. Although full-time employees are hired with the approval of the area supervisor, the decision is based on the applicant's interview with the club manager. In hiring, the club manager sets the wage rate for new employees within the perimeters determined by the area supervisor.

Additionally, unlike the store managers in *Saxon Paint,* the club managers here exercise considerable disciplinary authority over rank-and-file employees. A club manager may reprimand employees without prior approval. Moreover, in extreme cases, the club manager has the authority to discharge or suspend employees without prior consultation with the area supervisor.

The club manager exercises control over the working conditions of employees in many other respects. For example, the club manager handles employee complaints and grievances about wages and hours, schedules vacations, grants or denies overtime, decides whether employees may take their lunch break on or off the premises, administers the local payroll system, and trains employees in exercise instruction and sales. Thus, unlike *Saxon Paint* and like *Walgreen,* much of the day-to-day employment activities are supervised directly by the local club manager "without significant interference" by the central corporate organization.

Based on the autonomy of the club manager, the insubstantial amount of employee interchange among the metropolitan clubs, and the absence of any collective bargaining history, we conclude that the Board's determination that a single store was an appropriate bargaining unit is reasonable in light of all the facts presented in this case. Since Chicago Health Clubs has admitted its refusal to bargain with the union representing this single club, we accordingly enforce the Board's order.

In summary, the Board's order in No. 77–1227 shall be enforced. Enforcement of the Board's order in No. 77–1504 is denied.

---

## PROBLEMS FOR DISCUSSION

**1.** How pertinent is it, in deciding the appropriate bargaining unit, that the store manager does or does not have significant decisionmaking authority on such non-personnel matters as pricing and advertising of merchandise, repairs to the store, or resolution of customer complaints? How pertinent is the centralization of such personnel matters as payroll records and personnel files?

**2.** In its decision upholding a single-location unit in the Chicago Health Club chain, the court emphasized the discretion of the store manager regarding a number of personnel issues, such as hiring, firing, discipline, and initial pay determination within the bounds determined by the area supervisor. When collective bargaining turns to such issues as pay scale, sick leave, medical insurance, vacations and holidays, life insurance, liability coverage, and the like, how likely is it that the single store manager will have effective decisionmaking authority at the bargaining table? If his or her authority is effectively encumbered by the need to comport with company-wide policies and practices on these major employment issues, should the single club be deemed an appropriate bargaining unit? If the union wins separate elections at separate clubs within the Chicago chain, will decisionmaking on the employer side of the bargaining table likely be made separately or centrally? Would section 9 of the NLRA be better understood if it referred not to a unit appropriate for "bargaining" but rather to an appropriate "election" unit?

---

## 4. MULTIEMPLOYER AND COORDINATED BARGAINING[o]

It is estimated that some 40 percent of American workers are covered by collective bargaining agreements that are negotiated on a multiemployer basis. A number of employers within a single area or industry may band together to bargain as a group with a single union which represents employees at all of the companies. This is a common if not dominant bargaining pattern in such industries as clothing, construction, longshore and maritime, trucking and warehousing, coal mining, and wholesale and retail trades. The multiemployer pattern may reflect the desire of several small employers who seek greater leverage in dealing with a single common union (*e.g.*, clothing, trucking, retail stores), or of unions representing employees whose work for any given employer is likely to be short-lived (*e.g.*, construction and maritime). Where multiemployer bargaining prevails, negotiations are usually carried on between the international union and an association of employers selling in the same market. A single master agreement is usually signed and thereafter subsidiary agreements dealing with the problems of individual companies may be worked out between the employers and the local unions concerned.

The perceived benefits of multiemployer bargaining are several. For both the employers and the union, it brings less expensive, less frequent and more informed negotiations than would obtain on an individual-employer basis. Both parties generally favor the full knowledge about and uniformity of the wage rates and working conditions obtaining among all employers in the area or industry. The wider the basis of discussion, the more likely that negotiations will be in the hands of experienced leaders who will bring to their aid staffs of experts with detailed industry data. It also makes possible the exploration of problems such as technological displacement on an industry-wide basis and thus facilitates economic arrangements that no company could undertake alone.

Workers desire industry-wide bargaining also because it may help the union to secure gains which no one employer can grant for fear of competitive disadvantage. It may also strengthen the union leaders' position of control, and makes it more difficult for disaffected workers or an insurgent union to mount an effective campaign for decertification within the larger bargaining unit. Many employers believe that they have greater bargaining power when they can face a potential strike as a group, unlike

**o.** See Benetar, Coalition Bargaining Under the NLRA, and Abramson, Coordinated Bargaining by Unions, N.Y.U. 20th Annual Conf. on Labor 219, 231 (1968); Goldberg, Coordinated Bargaining Tactics of Unions, 54 Cornell L.Rev. 897 (1969); Leslie, Multiemployer Bargaining Rules, 75 Va.L.Rev. 241 (1989); C. Rehmus, Multiemployer Bargaining (1965); Vetter, Commentary on "Multiemployer Bargaining Rules": Searching for the Right Questions, 75 Va.L.Rev. 285 (1989).

when the union bargains with competing companies one at a time threatening each with a strike while the others are filling the needs of their customers. Companies can be assured that their rivals will not enjoy competitive advantages based upon disparate labor costs and working practices. The national officers of a union are likely to have a better understanding of management problems than local leaders.

But for all these advantages there may be offsetting costs. Most serious perhaps is the scope of any strike resulting from a breakdown in industry-wide negotiations. The public importance of negotiations rises in rapid progression as proportionately larger segments of an industry become involved. It is also argued that multi-employer bargaining results in undue restraints upon competition. If all the companies selling in a single market are to grant identical wage increases, they may conclude that their selfish interests are served better by granting whatever increase is necessary to buy labor peace and then passing the cost on to the public than by attempting to hold down costs. The very existence of high labor costs in an industry may discourage the entry of new competitors or the migration of industry to different geographic areas; and this may be aggravated when a union uses multi-employer bargaining (with or without the consent of the employers) to establish embargoes on goods produced in other geographic areas, or to refuse to supply labor to any company not a member of the employers' association, or to escalate its wage demands to employers outside of the association in order to make it uneconomical for them to remain in business. Such agreements raise serious problems of legality under the federal antitrust laws, a subject considered in greater detail at pages 881–914, infra.

Although the existence of multi-employer bargaining therefore raises very broad questions of economic and social policy, the National Labor Relations Board has refrained from addressing those questions in determining whether a multi-employer unit is appropriate for the purposes of collective bargaining. The NLRA does not specifically authorize the Board to find multi-employer units appropriate, yet even in the early years of that Act bargaining on a multi-employer or industry-wide basis was not unusual and the Board interpreted the term "employer" in Section 2(2) to reflect this industrial fact. Shipowner's Ass'n of the Pacific Coast, 7 NLRB 1002 (1938). The term "employer" included any person acting in an employer's interest and that person, the Board reasoned, might be an association, so that the "employer" unit referred to in Section 9 of the NLRA could be a multi-employer association. (The Taft–Hartley amendments to Section 2(2) did not change the Board's reasoning. Associated Shoe Industries of Southeastern Mass., Inc., 81 NLRB 224 (1949)).

The Board cannot direct an election for an initial union representative in a multiemployer unit. Such a unit can only be established consensually, after a representative has been designated. In determining whether such a unit is in fact appropriate, the Board looks for an employer's participation for a substantial period of time in joint bargaining negotiations and its consistent adoption of the agreements resulting from such negotiations;

such a controlling bargaining history indicates a desire on the part of the participating employers to be bound by joint, rather than individual, action and warrants the establishment of the multi-employer unit. Neither the lack of a formal association of employers nor the fact that the results of joint negotiations have been incorporated in separate uniform contracts will be determinative. Conversely, the mere adoption by an employer of contracts negotiated by an employer group will not be held to require the inclusion of its employees in the multi-employer unit. Consistent with its principle that the multi-employer unit is a consensual unit, the Board will look also for the consent of the union having representative status.

Prior to 1952, once a multi-employer unit had been established it would control the structure of bargaining for all categories of workers employed by a participating company. Concern arose, however, that this policy impeded union organization because it forced all subsequent organization within a company to be on a multi-employer basis. In Joseph E. Seagram & Sons, 101 NLRB 101 (1952), the Board reversed its policy, so that an employer may be part of a multi-employer unit for one category of its employees but may function as a single-employer unit with regard to other groups of employees.

An employer decision to participate in multi-employer bargaining is not irrevocable. Changes in economic conditions may convince a company or a union that it would be wise to withdraw from multi-employer bargaining and to bargain on an individual basis. But to permit a party to withdraw at any time—particularly once bargaining has begun and the terms of a contract begin to take shape—would invite disruptive maneuvering and could unfairly upset the assumptions on which all parties have been relying in their dealings. Accordingly, the Board has imposed limitations, through the unfair labor practice provisions dealing with good-faith bargaining, upon the power of the parties to withdraw from multi-employer bargaining. Those limitations are discussed, and approved, in the following decision of the Supreme Court.

A characteristic of the contemporary labor market much commented on by labor economists and other social scientists has been the growth of "contingent" (or "non-standard") employment. One component of this weltered category consists of "leased workers"—persons "supplied" by and under contract with one employer, but who perform services for a second, "user" employer under contract with the supplier of labor services. In Greenhoot, Inc., 205 NLRB 250 (1973), the Board held that where a building management company supplied workers to a number of separate building owners and was a joint employer with each of them, a single unit of all the employees so supplied would be a multi-employer unit which the Board could not order in the absence of an agreement of all the employers. The Board later extended that logic in Lee Hospital, 300 NLRB 947 (1990), opining that if a company that contracted to operate a hospital's department of anesthesiology was a joint employer with the hospital of the personnel employed to do that work, those employees could not be included in a unit of the hospital's employees absent the contractor's consent, for such would also be a multi-employer unit. In M.B. Sturgis, 331 NLRB No. 173 (2000), four members of the Board abandoned that element of *Lee Hospital*. Five years after oral argument in three consolidated cases, the Board held that the jointly employed temporary workers could be included in a bargaining unit of the user's permanent employees, subject to the Board usual "community of interest" standards. Member Brame dissented. Of the dissent, the Board majority opined in pertinent part:

> Our colleague . . . contends that the jointly employed employees and the solely employed employees in each unit do not have the "same" employer as a matter of law and logic. Unlike true multiemployer bargaining, however, all the employees in fact share the same employer, i.e., the user employer. Separating "regular" employees—i.e., the solely employed—from the "temporaries" who may (as in the instant cases) share the same classifications, skills, duties, and supervision, creates an artificial division that is not required by the statute. We therefore overrule *Lee Hospital* and find no statutory requirement of employer consent to a unit combining solely and jointly employed employees of a single user employer. As we noted at the outset of this section, prior to *Lee Hospital* the Board applied the community of interest test to decide whether to include jointly employed employees in units with solely employed employees. See *Globe City Discount*, 209 NLRB 213 (1974). As we find no statutory obstacles to such units today, we will return to the application of this traditional test to determine the appropriateness of these units.

---

# Charles D. Bonanno Linen Service, Inc. v. NLRB

454 U.S. 404, 102 S.Ct. 720, 70 L.Ed.2d 656 (1982).

■ JUSTICE WHITE delivered the opinion of the Court.

The issue here is whether a bargaining impasse justifies an employer's unilateral withdrawal from a multiemployer bargaining unit. The National Labor Relations Board (Board) concluded that an employer attempting such a withdrawal commits an unfair labor practice in violation of §§ 8(a)(5) and 8(a)(1) of the National Labor Relations Act (Act), 29 U.S.C. §§ 158(a)(5) and 158(a)(1), by refusing to execute the collective-bargaining agreement later executed by the union and the multiemployer association. The Court of Appeals for the First Circuit enforced the Board's order. 630 F.2d 25 (1980). Both the Board and the Court of Appeals recognized that several other Courts of Appeals had previously rejected the Board's position on this issue. We granted certiorari, 450 U.S. 979, 101 S.Ct. 1512, 67 L.Ed.2d 813 (1981), to resolve the conflict among the Circuits on this important question of federal labor law. We affirm the judgment of the Court of Appeals.

I

The factual findings of the Administrative Law Judge were affirmed by the Board and are undisputed. Petitioner, Charles D. Bonanno Linen Service, Inc. (Bonanno), is a Massachusetts corporation engaged in laundering, renting, and distributing linens and uniforms. Teamsters Local No. 25 (Union) represents its drivers and helpers as well as those of other linen supply companies in the area. For several years, Bonanno has been a member of the New England Linen Supply Association (Association), a group of 10 employers formed to negotiate with the Union as a multiemployer unit and a signatory of the contracts negotiated between the Union and the Association. On February 19, 1975, Bonanno authorized the Association's negotiating committee to represent it in the anticipated negotiations for a new contract. Bonanno's president became a member of the committee.

The Union and the Association held 10 bargaining sessions during March and April. On April 30, the negotiators agreed upon a proposed contract, but four days later the Union members rejected it. By May 15, according to the stipulations of the parties, the Union and the Association had reached an impasse over the method of compensation: the Union demanded that the drivers be paid on commission, while the Association insisted on continuing payment at an hourly rate.

Several subsequent meetings failed to break the impasse. On June 23, the Union initiated a selective strike against Bonanno. In response, most of [sic] Association members locked out their drivers. Despite sporadic meetings, the stalemate continued throughout the summer. During this period two of the employers met secretly with the Union, presumably in an effort to reach a separate settlement. These meetings, however, never reached the level of negotiations.

Bonanno hired permanent replacements for all of its striking drivers. On November 21, it notified the Association by letter that it was "withdrawing from the Association with specific respect to negotiations at this time because of an ongoing impasse with Teamsters Local 25." Pet for Cert 58. Bonanno mailed a copy of its revocation letter to the Union and read the letter over the phone to a Union representative.

Soon after Bonanno's putative withdrawal, the Association ended the lockout. It told the Union that it wished to continue multiemployer negotiations. Several negotiating sessions took place between December and April, without Bonanno participating. In the middle of April, the Union abandoned its demand for payment on commission and accepted the Association's offer of a revised hourly wage rate. With this development, the parties quickly agreed on a new contract, dated April 23, 1976, and given retroactive effect to April 18, 1975.

Meanwhile, on April 9, 1976, the Union had filed the present action, alleging that Bonanno's purported withdrawal from the bargaining unit constituted an unfair labor practice. In a letter dated April 29, the Union informed Bonanno that because the Union had never consented to the withdrawal, it considered Bonanno to be bound by the settlement just reached. In a reply letter, Bonanno denied that it was bound by the contract.

An Administrative Law Judge concluded, after a hearing, that no unusual circumstances excused Bonanno's withdrawal from the multiemployer bargaining unit. The Board affirmed, ordering Bonanno to sign and implement the contract retroactively. In a supplemental decision, the Board explained the basis of its decision that Bonanno's attempt to withdraw from the multiemployer [unit] was untimely and ineffective. 243 N.L.R.B. 1093 (1979). The Court of Appeals enforced the Board's order. 630 F.2d 25 (1980).

## II

The standard for judicial review of the Board's decision in this case was established by Labor Board v. Truck Drivers, 353 U.S. 87, 77 S.Ct. 643, 1 L.Ed.2d 676 (1957) *(Buffalo Linen)*. There, the Union struck a single employer during negotiations with a multiemployer bargaining association. The other employers responded with a lockout. Negotiations continued, and an agreement was reached. The Union, claiming that the lockout violated its rights under §§ 7 and 8 of the Act, then filed charges with the Board. The Board rejected the claim, but the Court of Appeals held that the lockout was an unfair practice.

This Court in turn reversed. That the Act did not expressly authorize or deal with multiemployer units or with lockouts in that context was recognized. Nonetheless, multiemployer bargaining had "long antedated the Wagner Act" and had become more common as employers, in the course of complying with their duty to bargain under the Act, "sought through group bargaining to match increased union strength." 353 U.S., at 94–95, 77 S.Ct., at 646–647 (footnote omitted). Furthermore, at the time of the debates on the Taft–Hartley amendments, Congress had rejected a proposal to limit or outlaw multiemployer bargaining. The debates and their results offered "cogent evidence that in many industries the multiemployer bargaining basis was a vital factor in the effectuation of the national policy of promoting labor peace through strengthened collective bargaining." 353 U.S., at 95, 77 S.Ct., at 647.[3] Congress' refusal to

---

**3.** As the Court of Appeals explained in this case:

"Multiemployer bargaining offers advantages to both management and labor. It enables smaller employers to bargain 'on an equal basis with a large union' and avoid 'the competitive disadvantages resulting from nonuniform contractual terms.' NLRB v. Truck Drivers Local 449, 353 U.S. 87, 96, 77 S.Ct. 643, 647, 1 L.Ed.2d 676 * * * (1957). At the same time, it facilitates the development of industry-wide, worker benefit programs

that employers otherwise might be unable to provide."

"More generally, multiemployer bargaining encourages both sides to adopt a flexible attitude during negotiations; as the Board explains, employers can make concessions 'without fear that other employers will refuse to make similar concessions to achieve a competitive advantage,' and a union can act similarly 'without fear that the employees will be dissatisfied at not receiving the same benefits which the union might win from

intervene indicated that it intended to leave to the Board's specialized judgment the resolution of conflicts between union and employer rights that were bound to arise in multiemployer bargaining. In such situations, the Court said:

> "The ultimate problem is the balancing of the conflicting legitimate interests. The function of striking that balance to effectuate national labor policy is often a difficult and delicate responsibility, which the Congress committed primarily to the National Labor Relations Board, subject to limited judicial review." 353 U.S., at 96, 77 S.Ct., at 647.

Thus, the Court of Appeals' rejection of the Board's justification of the lockout as an acceptable effort to maintain the integrity of the multiemployer unit and its refusal to accept the lockout as a legitimate response to the whipsaw strike had too narrowly confined the exercise of the Board's discretion. 353 U.S., at 97, 77 S.Ct., at 648.

Multiemployer bargaining has continued to be the preferred bargaining mechanism in many industries,[4] and as *Buffalo Linen* predicted, it has raised a variety of problems requiring resolution. One critical question concerns the rights of the union and the employers to terminate the multiemployer bargaining arrangement. Until 1958, the Board permitted both employers and the union to abandon the unit even in the midst of bargaining. Bearing & Rim Supply Co., 107 N.L.R.B. 101, 102–103 (1953); Stamford Wallpaper, 92 N.L.R.B. 1173 (1951); Morand Bros. Beverage Co., 91 N.L.R.B. 409, 413, 416–418 (1950), enforced in part on other grounds, 190 F.2d 576, 581–582 (C.A.7 1951). But in Retail Associates, Inc., 120 N.L.R.B. 388 (1958), the Board announced guidelines for withdrawal from multiemployer units. These rules, which reflect an increasing emphasis on the stability of multiemployer units, permit any party to withdraw prior to the date set for negotiation of a new contract or the date on which negotiations actually begin, provided that adequate notice is given. Once negotiations for a new contract have commenced, however, withdrawal is permitted only if there is "mutual consent" or "unusual circumstances" exist. Id., at 395.

The Board's approach in *Retail Associates* has been accepted in the courts, as have its decisions that unusual circumstances will be found where an employer is subject to extreme financial pressures or where a bargaining unit has become substantially fragmented. But as yet there is

---

other employers.' Brief, at 10. Finally, by permitting the union and employers to concentrate their bargaining resources on the negotiation of a single contract, multiemployer bargaining enhances the efficiency and effectiveness of the collective bargaining process and thereby reduces industrial strife." 630 F.2d, at 28.

4. A recent survey of major collective-bargaining agreements (those covering 1,000 or more employees) found that of 1,536 major agreements, 648 (42%) were multiemployer agreements and that 3,238,400 employees were covered by these agreements. U.S. Bureau of Labor Statistics, Dept. of Labor, Bull. No. 2065, Characteristics of Major Collective Bargaining Agreements—January 1, 1978, at 12, table 1.8 (1980).

no consensus as to whether an impasse in bargaining in a multiemployer unit is an unusual circumstance justifying unilateral withdrawal by the Union or by an employer. After equivocating for a time, the Board squarely held that an impasse is not such an unusual circumstance. Hi–Way Billboards, Inc., 206 N.L.R.B. 22 (1973). * * * After again considering the question in this case, the Board issued its decision reaffirming its position that an impasse is not an unusual circumstance justifying withdrawal. Its decision was sustained and enforced by the Court of Appeals for the First Circuit.

## III

We agree with the Board and with the Court of Appeals. The Board has recognized the voluntary nature of multiemployer bargaining. It neither forces employers into multiemployer units nor erects barriers to withdrawal prior to bargaining. At the same time, it has sought to further the utility of multiemployer bargaining as an instrument of labor peace by limiting the circumstances under which any party may unilaterally withdraw during negotiations. Thus, it has reiterated the view expressed in Hi–Way Billboards that an impasse is not sufficiently destructive of group bargaining to justify unilateral withdrawal. As a recurring feature in the bargaining process, impasse is only a temporary deadlock or hiatus in negotiations "which in almost all cases is eventually broken, through either a change of mind or the application of economic force." Charles D. Bonanno Linen Service, 243 N.L.R.B. 1093, 1093–1094 (1979). Furthermore, an impasse may be "brought about intentionally by one or both parties as a device to further, rather than destroy, the bargaining process." Id., at 1094. Hence, "there is little warrant for regarding an impasse as a rupture of the bargaining relation which leaves the parties free to go their own ways." Ibid. As the Board sees it, permitting withdrawal at impasse would as a practical matter undermine the utility of multiemployer bargaining.

Of course, the ground rules for multiemployer bargaining have not come into being overnight. They have evolved and are still evolving, as the Board, employing its expertise in the light of experience, has sought to balance the "conflicting legitimate interests" in pursuit of the "national policy of promoting labor peace through strengthened collective bargaining." Buffalo Linen, supra, 353 U.S., at 96, 97, 77 S.Ct., at 647, 648. The Board might have struck a different balance from the one it has, and it may be that some or all of us would prefer that it had done so. But assessing the significance of impasse and the dynamics of collective bargaining is precisely the kind of judgment that Buffalo Linen ruled should be left to the Board. We cannot say that the Board's current resolution of the issue is arbitrary or contrary to law.

If the Board's refusal to accept an impasse, standing alone, as an unusual circumstance warranting withdrawal were the only issue in this case, we would affirm without more. But several Courts of Appeals have rejected Hi–Way Billboards on the grounds that impasse may precipitate a strike against one or all members of the unit and that upon impasse the

Board permits the union to execute interim agreements with individual employers. These Courts of Appeals consider the possibility of such events as sufficient grounds for any employer in the unit to withdraw.

In [NLRB v.] Beck Engraving Co., [522 F.2d 475 (1975),] for example, the Court of Appeals for the Third Circuit held that an impasse followed by a selective strike justified unilateral withdrawal from the bargaining unit. Because at that juncture labor relations law, as interpreted by the Board, would permit the union to execute an interim agreement with the struck employer, the Court of Appeals concluded that the union and the employer entering into such an agreement would be given unfair advantage against other employers if the latter were not permitted to withdraw from the unit. The Court of Appeals thought the employer's right to withdraw and the union's privilege of executing interim contracts should mature simultaneously. It concluded that the Board's approach too drastically upset the bargaining equilibrium to be justified in the name of maintaining the stability of the bargaining unit.

The Board's reasons for adhering to its *Hi–Way Billboards* position are telling. They are surely adequate to survive judicial review. First, it is said that strikes and interim agreements often occur in the course of negotiations prior to impasse and that neither tactic is necessarily associated with impasse. Second, it is "vital" to understand that the Board distinguishes "between interim agreements which contemplate adherence to a final unitwide contract and are thus not antithetical to group bargaining and individual agreements which are clearly inconsistent with, and destructive of, group bargaining." 243 N.L.R.B., at 1096. In Sangamo Construction Co., 188 N.L.R.B. 159 (1971), and Plumbers and Steamfitters Union No. 323 (P.H.C. Mechanical Contractors), 191 N.L.R.B. 592 (1971), the agreements arrived at with the struck employers were only temporary: both the union and the employer executing the interim agreement were bound by any settlement resulting from multiemployer bargaining. "[I]n both cases, since the early signers maintained a vested interest in the outcome of final union-association negotiations, the multiemployer unit was neither fragmented nor significantly weakened," 243 N.L.R.B. at 1096, and unilateral withdrawal was not justified.

On the other hand, where the union, not content with interim agreements that expire with the execution of a unit-wide contract, executes separate agreements that will survive unit negotiations, the union has so "effectively fragmented and destroyed the integrity of the bargaining unit," ibid., as to create an "unusual circumstance" under Retail Associates rules. * * *

The Board therefore emphatically rejects the proposition that the negotiation of truly interim, temporary agreements, as distinguished from separate, final contracts, is "inconsistent with the concept of multiemployer bargaining units." Charles D. Bonanno Linen Service, 243 N.L.R.B. 1093, 1096 (1979). Although interim agreements establish terms and conditions of employment for one or more employer members of the unit pending the outcome of renewed group bargaining, all employers, including those executing interim agreements, have an "equivalent stake" in the final outcome because the "resulting group agreement would then apply to all employers, including each signer of an interim agreement." Ibid. Such interim arrangements "preclude a finding that the early signers had withdrawn from the unit." Ibid. Although the Board concedes that interim agreements exert economic pressure on struck employers, this fact should no more warrant withdrawal than the refusal of one employer to join with others in a lockout. In any event, the Board's view is that interim agreements, on balance, tend to deter rather than promote unit fragmentation since they preserve a continuing mutual interest by all employer members in a final association-wide contract.

The Board also rests on this Court's admonition that the Board should balance "conflicting legitimate interests" rather than economic weapons and bargaining strength. Its conclusion is that the interest in unit stability, recognized as a major consideration by both *Buffalo Linen* and NLRB v. Brown, 380 U.S. 278, 85 S.Ct. 980, 13 L.Ed.2d 839 (1965), adequately justifies enforcement of the obligation to bargain despite the execution of a temporary agreement.

Of course, no interim or separate agreements were executed in this case. But neither did the impasse initiate any right to execute an agreement inconsistent with the duty to abide by the results of group bargaining. Some Courts of Appeals, taking a different view of the interests involved, question the legitimacy of enforcing the duty to bargain where impasse has occurred and interim agreements have been or may be executed. We think the Board has confined itself within the zone of discretion entrusted to it by Congress.

The balance it has struck is not inconsistent with the terms or purposes of the Act, and its decision should therefore be enforced.

## IV

The Chief Justice, in dissent, is quite right that this case turns in major part on the extent to which the courts should defer to the Board's judgment with respect to the critical factors involved. * * *

The Chief Justice, candidly accepting that the issue is one of balancing the legitimate interests involved, nonetheless disputes the Board's judgment regarding the underlying factors with respect to what would best serve the statutory goals. He rejects the Board's assessment of the significance of impasse and interim agreements in the multiemployer bargaining context and substitutes his own views. For example, he finds that the impasse in this case "was no 'temporary deadlock or hiatus in negotiations' as the Board claims; this was instead a complete breakdown in negotiations coupled with a prolonged strike and lock-out." Post, at 730. He also states, contrary to the Board's judgment, that when the parties have remained at impasse for a long period, "withdrawal of one or a few employers may facilitate rather than frustrate bargaining." Post, at 731. Thus, the Chief Justice avers, it would be "more consistent with [the goals of industrial peace] to permit withdrawal and allow negotiation of separate agreements than to force the parties into escalated economic warfare." Post, at 731.

The Chief Justice may be quite right. There is obviously room for differing judgments, however, as the conflicting judgments of the Courts of Appeals and the strong views of the Board on the issues now before us make clear. But the dissenting Justices would have us substitute our judgment for those of the Board with respect to the issues that Congress intended the Board should resolve. This we are unwilling to do. * * *

* * * [T]he Board in this case has developed a rule which, although it may deny an employer a particular economic weapon, does so in the interest of the proper and pre-eminent goal, maintaining the stability of the multiemployer unit. Because the Board has carefully considered the effect of its rule on that goal, we should defer to its judgment.

Affirmed.

[The concurring opinion of Justice Stevens, and the dissenting opinions of Chief Justice Burger (joined by Justice Rehnquist) and Justice O'Connor (joined by Justice Powell), are omitted.]

––––––––

## PROBLEM FOR DISCUSSION

For many years the Lumberworkers Union has bargained with an association of eighteen wood-products producers. The last collective bargaining agreement expired June 1998. The parties agreed to extend that contract until September 2000 while negotiations for a successor contract continued. No agreement was reached, and in September 2000 the union declared an impasse. In December 2000, the employer association implemented its last offer. There were no further negotiations thereafter, nor any strike, lockout or separate interim agreements. In March 2001, the union filed separate representation petitions for the employees of each of the eighteen companies. The companies have moved to dismiss the petition. How should the Regional Director rule? See El Cerrito Mill & Lumber Co., 316 NLRB 1005 (1995).

––––––––

In many of the industries in which multiemployer bargaining has developed, the employers are small and numerous and the union represents workers on an area-wide basis at a number of different companies. More recently, the converse structure has developed, with a single large company being confronted at the bargaining table by representatives of a number of different unions representing employees in different bargaining units within that company. The grouping of forces by the various unions has been called "coordinated" or "coalition" bargaining. As will be developed in greater detail below, see pages 444–45 infra, it is unlawful for a single union or groups of unions to insist upon, or to strike in support of demands for, the expansion of bargaining to units larger than those certified by the NLRB. At base, the rationale appears to be that bargaining about wages and other fundamental working conditions should not be frustrated by the use of economic weapons to modify the scope of bargaining units, when that issue has been (or can be) peacefully and expeditiously resolved by the Board. But union coordination in bargaining need not be directed at an improper expansion of the unit for bargaining. The function of coordinated or coalition bargaining has been considered in cases in which an employer has refused to bargain with a properly recognized or certified union which brings to the bargaining table representatives of other unions from other company bargaining units. The following case contains a full discussion of the dynamics of coalition or coordinated bargaining so that, although it arises in the context of what may be (at this point in the course) unfamiliar principles of law, it constitutes a useful introduction to this development in bargaining structure.

---

## General Electric Co. v. NLRB

412 F.2d 512 (2d Cir. 1969).

■ FEINBERG, CIRCUIT JUDGE: * * *

[General Electric, a manufacturer and seller of electrical equipment and related products, employs about 290,000 workers in over 60 plants and 400 other installations, such as service shops and warehouses. About half of its employees are represented by more than 80 unions in roughly 150 bargaining units; approximately 80,000 workers in some 90 of those units are represented by the International Union of Electrical, Radio and Machine Workers (IUE). The company, which does business in all 50 states, has traditionally bargained with the IUE International for a single national agreement covering all employees represented by the IUE and its locals; local issues are addressed in supplementary local contracts. During the term of the 1963–66 national agreement, the IUE and seven other international unions whose locals also had agreements with General Electric formed a Committee on Collective Bargaining (CCB). This was an outgrowth of the unions' dissatisfaction with the traditional separate negotiations between the company and the different unions, in which the unions believed that General Electric was playing off each union against the other. The avowed purposes of the members of the CCB were to coordinate bargaining in 1966 with GE and its chief competitor, Westinghouse, to formulate national goals and otherwise support one another.

[When the CCB attempted to persuade company representatives to meet for preliminary discussions prior to the October 1966 contract termination date, GE responded in March 1966 that it would meet with the IUE but would not participate in any "eight-union coalition discussions or in any other steps in the direction of industry-wide bargaining." When company representatives appeared for a meeting in early May, after receiving assurances of individual bargaining from IUE, they noted that the IUE negotiating committee had added seven members—one from each of the other seven unions comprising the CCB—and promptly refused to confer.

This refusal persisted even after GE was informed that the seven new members were not voting members of the IUE committee and were present solely to aid in IUE negotiations, not to represent their own unions. The IUE filed refusal-to-bargain charges under Section 8(a)(5) of the Labor Act, and an action was initiated by the Board for a preliminary injunction under Section 10(j) to compel GE to bargain with the "mixed" committee; amidst injunctions, reversals and stays, the company bargained in August 1966, sometime with the IUE alone and sometime with the "mixed" committee. It was not until October 1968 that the NLRB issued a decision finding GE to have violated Section 8(a)(5). The company petitioned for review of the Board's order, which required bargaining with the IUE through its committee, and the Board cross-petitioned for enforcement.]

The basic question before us is whether a union's inclusion of members of other unions on its bargaining committee justifies an employer's refusal to bargain. The Company contends that there is more to the case than that, claiming that the IUE was engaged in an illegal attempt to obliterate bargaining unit lines and was, as the Board put it, " 'locked in' to a conspiratorial understanding." We discuss that phase of the case below, but turn first to the crucial issue before us.

Section 7 of the National Labor Relations Act, 29 U.S.C. § 157, guarantees certain rights to employees, including the right to join together in labor organizations and "to bargain collectively through representatives of their own choosing." This right of employees and the corresponding right of employers, see section 8(b)(1)(B) of the Act, 29 U.S.C. § 158(b)(1)(B), to choose whomever they wish to represent them in formal labor negotiations is fundamental to the statutory scheme. In general, either side can choose as it sees fit and neither can control the other's selection, a proposition confirmed in a number of opinions, some of fairly ancient vintage. * * *

There have been exceptions to the general rule that either side can choose its bargaining representatives freely, but they have been rare and confined to situations so infected with ill-will, usually personal, or conflict of interest as to make good-faith bargaining impractical. See, e.g., NLRB v. ILGWU, 274 F.2d 376, 379 (3d Cir.1960)(ex-union official added to employer committee to "put one over on the union"); Bausch & Lomb Optical Co., 108 N.L.R.B. 1555 (1954)(union established company in direct competition with employer); NLRB v. Kentucky Utilities Co., 182 F.2d 810 (6th Cir.1950)(union negotiator had expressed great personal animosity towards employer). But cf. NLRB v. Signal Manufacturing Co., 351 F.2d 471 (1st Cir.1965)(*per curiam*), cert. denied 382 U.S. 985, 86 S.Ct. 562, 15 L.Ed.2d 474 (1966)(similar claim of animosity rejected). Thus, the freedom to select representatives is not absolute, but that does not detract from its significance. Rather the narrowness and infrequency of approved exceptions to the general rule emphasizes its importance. Thus, in arguing that employees may not select members of other unions as "representatives of their own choosing" on a negotiating committee, the Company clearly undertakes a considerable burden, characterized in an analogous situation in

NLRB v. David Buttrick Co., 399 F.2d 505, 507 (1st Cir.1968), as the showing of a "clear and present" danger to the collective bargaining process. * * *

Turning to specific policy reasons for inclusion of members of other unions on a negotiating committee, we are told that a union has an interest in using experts to bargain, whether the expertise be on technical, substantive matters or on the general art of negotiating. In filling that need, no good reason appears why it may not look to "outsiders," just as an employer is free to do. See Detroit Newspaper Publishers Ass'n v. NLRB, 372 F.2d 569, 572 (6th Cir.1967); NLRB v. Local 294, International Brotherhood of Teamsters, 284 F.2d 893 (2d Cir.1960). However, the heat generated by this controversy does not arise from that bland consideration. The Company has in the past made effective use of its own ability to plan centralized bargaining strategy in dealing with the various unions representing its employees while keeping the actual bargaining with each union separate. * * * IUE claims that having members of the other unions on its committee increases communications between all of them and to that extent reduces the ability of the Company to play one off against the other. In any event, the plain facts are that the IUE proposed negotiating technique is a response to the Company's past bargaining practices, that it is designed to strengthen the IUE's bargaining position, and that both sides know it.

The Board held that a mixed-union negotiating committee is not per se improper and that absent a showing of "substantial evidence of ulterior motive or bad faith" an employer commits an unfair labor practice unless it bargains with such a group. The Company and *amicus* attack the Board rule on a number of grounds. * * *

The claim that outside influences and alleged conflicts require an outright ban on mixed-union committees is not weighty in view of the cases discussed above * * *. Equally unpersuasive is the assertion that the Board made an improper effort to adjust economic power. The Board gave no such rationale for its decision. Of course, it would be nonsense to pretend that IUE's purpose was not to increase its bargaining strength, but that goal is a normal one for unions or employers. That Board application of an old policy to a new situation may have such an effect does not vitiate a rule if it is otherwise justified. The possibility that there will be improper attempts to ignore unit boundaries is, of course, real. The Company argues that different unions certified for separate units may not force an employer to bargain with them jointly as to all units on any subject, despite the implications of United States Pipe & Foundry Co. v. NLRB, 298 F.2d 873 (5th Cir.), cert. denied, 370 U.S. 919, 82 S.Ct. 1557, 8 L.Ed.2d 499 (1962), which approved an arrangement whereby three unions conditioned their agreements in separate but substantially simultaneous negotiations upon a joint demand for common contract expiration dates. The Board did not come to grips with this problem, and we similarly do not now consider the extent to which the law permits cooperation in bargaining among unions or employers. Compare Wagner, Multi–Union Bargaining: A Legal Analysis,

19 Lab.L.J. 731 (1968), and Note, Is Coalition Bargaining Legal?, 18 W.Res.L.Rev. 575 (1967), with Anker, Pattern Bargaining, Antitrust Laws and the National Labor Relations Act, 19 N.Y.U.Ann.Conf. on Labor 81 (1967). The point is that the chance that negotiators may improperly press impermissible subjects is inherent in the bargaining process, and therefore must be taken. As to the increased difficulty in determining motives of the other side, we agree that this may occur. However, although evidence that bargaining for other employees is being attempted may be difficult to obtain, the Board is certainly capable of making such a determination when a case comes before it. * * * In view of the overall policy of encouraging free selection of representatives, we agree with the Board's rejection of a per se rule which bans mixed-union committees.

In sum, we do not think that the Company has demonstrated the type of clear and present danger to the bargaining process that is required to overcome the burden on one who objects to the representatives selected by the other party. We hold that the IUE did have the right to include members of other unions on its negotiating committee, and the Company was not lawfully entitled to refuse to bargain with that committee so long as it sought to bargain solely on behalf of those employees represented by the IUE, a question we discuss further below.

[The court then went on to hold that, since General Electric was not obligated by its contract to commence formal bargaining until August 1966, its refusal to bargain with the mixed committee became unlawful only at that time and not as early as the informal and preliminary discussions sought by the IUE in May. The court also found that there was evidence to support the conclusion of the Board that the IUE was not "locked in" to joint bargaining with the other seven unions so as to relinquish its freedom of independent decisionmaking and that the IUE had no "ulterior motive" or bad faith in negotiating through its mixed committee; the committee at no time tried to bargain for any employees other than those represented by the IUE, and the court concluded that the company thus had an obligation at least to confer with the committee to put to the test the claim of the IUE that it was negotiating for itself alone.]

_____

## C. Review of Representation Proceedings[p]

The National Labor Relations Act has no provision for direct judicial review of Board determinations, such as the appropriate bargaining unit, made in the course of representation proceedings. While Section 10(f) does provide that a party may have judicial review if "aggrieved by a final

**p.** See Cox, The Major Labor Decisions of the Supreme Court, Proceedings of ABA Section of Lab. Rel. Law 23, 31–37 (1959)(discussing _Leedom v. Kyne_); Goldberg, District Court Review of NLRB Representation Proceedings, 42 Ind.L.J. 455 (1967); Harper, The Case for Limiting Judicial Review of Labor Board Certification Decisions, 55 Geo. Wash.L.Rev. 262 (1987); Note, Leedom v. Kyne and the Implementation of a National Labor Policy, 1981 Duke L.J. 853.

order" of the Board, decisions in representation proceedings are not "final orders." AFL v. NLRB, 308 U.S. 401, 60 S.Ct. 300, 84 L.Ed. 347 (1940). Since such orders issue only in unfair labor practice cases, an aggrieved party must commit an unfair labor practice in order to obtain judicial review. Section 9(d) provides that the record in the representation case is to become a part of the record which is certified to the federal court of appeals in the unfair labor practice case. Perhaps the most common example of this rather elaborate review machinery in action is the employer's refusal to bargain with a union certified by the Board as bargaining representative, when that certification is based upon a determination of a bargaining unit or of the validity of the union's election victory which the employer wishes to challenge on review. The reasons why Congress was reluctant to provide for direct judicial review of representation decisions are explored in the opinions in Leedom v. Kyne, immediately following.

Even when review can finally be secured in a court of appeals, it is difficult to secure a reversal on the merits of a Board representation decision. Such matters as the appropriateness of the bargaining unit and the impact of a party's speech or conduct upon the outcome of a labor election often raise complex or subtle issues meet for the exercise of an expert and experienced judgment by the administrative agency. Since Congress has provided so little guidance on these representation issues in the terms of the Labor Act, courts are loathe to overrule a Board decision in which the agency has taken care to scrutinize the record, to state its standards for decision and to articulate the reasons for its conclusion—even if the court might have been inclined to reach a different result had it decided the case in the first instance. While most courts of appeals accord a substantial measure of deference in representation cases, the decision in cases such as *Chicago Health Clubs,* at p. 283, supra, demonstrate that there are courts which seek vigorously to be assured that the Board is not masking arbitrary action with stock formulae and reliance on dubious precedents.

---

## Leedom v. Kyne

358 U.S. 184, 79 S.Ct. 180, 3 L.Ed.2d 210 (1958).

■ MR. JUSTICE WHITTAKER delivered the opinion of the Court.

* * * Buffalo Section, Westinghouse Engineers Association, Engineers and Scientists of America, a voluntary unincorporated labor organization, hereafter called the Association, was created for the purpose of promoting the economic and professional status of the nonsupervisory professional employees of Westinghouse Electric Corporation at its plant in Cheektowaga, New York, through collective bargaining with their employer. In October 1955, the Association petitioned the National Labor Relations Board for certification as the exclusive collective bargaining agent of all nonsupervisory professional employees, being then 238 in number, of the Westinghouse Company at its Cheektowaga plant, pursuant to the provisions of § 9 of the

Act, 29 U.S.C. § 159, 29 U.S.C.A. § 159. A hearing was held by the Board upon the petition. A competing labor organization was permitted by the Board to intervene. It asked the Board to expand the unit to include employees in five other categories who performed technical work and were thought by it to be "professional employees" within the meaning of § 2(12) of the Act, 29 U.S.C. § 152(12), 29 U.S.C.A. § 152(12). The Board found that they were not professional employees within the meaning of the Act. However, it found that nine employees in three of those categories should nevertheless be included in the unit because they "share a close community of employment interests with [the professional employees, and their inclusion would not] destroy the predominantly professional character of such a unit." The Board, after denying the Association's request to take a vote among the professional employees to determine whether a majority of them favored "inclusion in such unit," included the 233 professional employees and the nine nonprofessional employees in the unit and directed an election to determine whether they desired to be represented by the Association, by the other labor organization, or by neither. The Association moved the Board to stay the election and to amend its decision by excluding the nonprofessional employees from the unit. The Board denied that motion and went ahead with the election at which the Association received a majority of the valid votes cast and was thereafter certified by the Board as the collective bargaining agent for the unit.

Thereafter respondent, individually, and as president of the Association, brought this suit in the District Court against the members of the Board. * * * [The trial court] denied the Board's motion [for summary judgment] and granted the plaintiff's motion and entered judgment setting aside the Board's determination of the bargaining unit and also the election and the Board's certification. 148 F.Supp. 597.

On the Board's appeal it did not contest the trial court's conclusion that the Board, in commingling professional with nonprofessional employees in the unit, had acted in excess of its powers and had thereby worked injury to the statutory rights of the professional employees. Instead, it contended only that the District Court lacked jurisdiction to entertain the suit. The Court of Appeals held that the District Court did have jurisdiction and affirmed its judgment. 101 App.D.C. 398, 249 F.2d 490. Because of the importance of the question and the fact that it has been left open in our previous decisions, we granted certiorari, 355 U.S. 922, 78 S.Ct. 366, 2 L.Ed.2d 353.

Petitioners, members of the Board, concede here that the District Court had jurisdiction of the suit under § 24(8) of the Judicial Code, 28 U.S.C. § 1337, 28 U.S.C.A. § 1337, unless the review provisions of the National Labor Relations Act destroyed it. In American Federation of Labor v. National Labor Relations Board, 308 U.S. 401, 60 S.Ct. 300, 303, 84 L.Ed. 347, this Court held that a Board order in certification proceedings under § 9 is not "a final order" and therefore is not subject to judicial review except as it may be drawn in question by a petition for enforcement or review of an order, made under § 10(c) of the Act, restraining an unfair labor practice. But the court was at pains to point out in that case that "[t]he question [there presented was] distinct from * * * whether petitioners are precluded by the provisions of the Wagner Act from maintaining an independent suit in a district court to set aside the Board's action because contrary to the statute * * *." Id., 308 U.S. at page 404, 60 S.Ct. at page 302. * * *

The record in this case squarely presents the question found not to have been presented by the record in American Federation of Labor v. National Labor Relations Board, supra. This case, in its posture before us, involves "unlawful action of the Board [which] has inflicted an injury on the [respondent]." Does the law, "apart from the review provisions of the * * * Act," afford a remedy? We think the answer surely must be yes. This suit is not one to "review," in the sense of that term as used in the Act, a decision of the Board made within its jurisdiction. Rather it is one to strike down an order of the Board made in excess of its delegated powers and contrary to a specific prohibition in the Act. Section 9(b)(1) is clear and mandatory. It says that in determining the unit appropriate for the purposes of collective bargaining, "the Board *shall not* (1) decide that any unit is appropriate for such purposes if such unit includes both professional employees and employees who are not professional employees unless a majority of such professional employees vote for inclusion in such unit." (Emphasis added.) Yet the Board included in the unit employees whom it found were not professional employees, after refusing to determine whether a majority of the professional employees would "vote for inclusion in such unit." Plainly, this was an attempted exercise of power that had been specifically withheld. It deprived the professional employees of a "right" assured to them by Congress. Surely, in these circumstances, a Federal District Court has jurisdiction of an original suit to prevent deprivation of a right so given. * * *

In Switchmen's Union of North America v. National Mediation Board, 320 U.S. 297, 64 S.Ct. 95, 88 L.Ed. 61, this Court held that the District Court did not have jurisdiction of an original suit to review an order of the National Mediation Board determining that all yardmen of the rail lines operated by the New York Central system constituted an appropriate bargaining unit, because the Railway Labor Board had acted within its delegated powers. But in the course of that opinion the Court announced principles that are controlling here. "If the absence of jurisdiction of the federal courts meant a sacrifice or obliteration of a right which Congress had created, the inference would be strong that Congress intended the statutory provisions governing the general jurisdiction of those courts to control." * * *

Here, differently from the Switchmen's case, "absence of jurisdiction of the federal courts" would mean "a sacrifice or obliteration of a right which Congress" has given professional employees, for there is no other means, within their control (American Federation of Labor v. National Labor Relations Board, supra), to protect and enforce that right. And "the inference [is] strong that Congress intended the statutory provisions governing the general jurisdiction of those courts to control." 320 U.S. at page 300, 64 S.Ct. at page 97. This Court cannot lightly infer that Congress does not intend judicial protection of rights it confers against agency action taken in excess of delegated powers. * * *

The Court of Appeals was right in holding, in the circumstances of this case, that the District Court had jurisdiction of this suit, and its judgment is affirmed.

Affirmed.

■ Mr. Justice Brennan, whom Mr. Justice Frankfurter joins, dissenting.

The legislative history of the Wagner Act, and the Taft–Hartley amendments, shows a considered congressional purpose to restrict judicial review of National Labor Relations Board representation certifications to review in the Courts of Appeals in the circumstances specified in § 9(d), 29 U.S.C. § 159(d), 29 U.S.C.A. § 159(d). The question was extensively debated when both Acts were being considered, and on both occasions Congress concluded that, unless drastically limited, time-consuming court procedures would seriously threaten to frustrate the basic national policy of preventing industrial strife and achieving industrial peace by promoting collective bargaining.

The Congress had before it when considering the Wagner Act the concrete evidence that delays pending time-consuming judicial review could be a serious hindrance to the primary objective of the Act—bringing employers and employees together to resolve their differences through discussion. Congress was acutely aware of the experience of the predecessor of the present Labor Board under the National Industrial Recovery Act, which provided that investigations and certifications by the Board could be brought directly to the courts for review. Such direct review was determined by the Congress to be "productive of a large measure of industrial strife * * *," and was specifically eliminated in the Wagner Act. Although Congress recognized that it was necessary to determine employee representatives before collective bargaining could begin, Congress concluded that the chance for industrial peace increased correlatively to how quickly collective bargaining commenced. For this reason Congress ordained that the courts should not interfere with the prompt holding of representation elections or the commencement of collective bargaining once an employee representative has been chosen. Congress knew that if direct judicial review of the Board's investigation and certification of representatives was not barred, "the Government can be delayed indefinitely before it takes the first step toward industrial peace." Therefore, § 9(d) was written to provide "for review in the courts only after the election has been held and the Board has ordered the employer to do something predicated upon the results of the election." [79 Cong.Rec. 7658.] After the Wagner Act was passed, a proposed amendment to allow judicial review after an election but before an unfair labor practice order was specifically rejected. In short, Congress set itself firmly against direct judicial review of the investigation and certification of representatives, and required the prompt initiation of the collective-bargaining process after the Board's certification, because of the risk that time-consuming review might defeat the objectives of the national labor policy. See American Federation of Labor v. National Labor Relations Board, 308 U.S. 401, 409–411, 60 S.Ct. 300, 304–305, 84 L.Ed. 347; Madden v. Brotherhood and Union of Transit Employees, 4 Cir., 147 F.2d 439, 158 A.L.R. 1330.

When the Taft–Hartley amendments were under consideration, employers complained that because § 9(d) allowed judicial review to an employer only when unfair labor practice charges were based in whole or in part upon facts certified following an investigation of representatives, these "cumbersome proceedings" meant that the employer could have review only by committing an unfair labor practice "no matter how much in good faith he doubted the validity of the certification." A House amendment therefore provided for direct review in the Courts of Appeals of Board certifications on appeal of any person interested, as from a final order of the Board. Opponents revived the same arguments successfully employed in the Wagner Act debates: "Delay would be piled upon delay, during which time collective bargaining would be suspended pending determination of the status of the bargaining agent. Such delays can only result in industrial strife." Both sides recognized that the House amendment would produce a fundamental change in the law. The Senate rejected the House amendment; the amendments proposed by that body continued only the indirect and limited review provided in original § 9(d). In conference, the Senate view prevailed. Senator Taft reported:

> "Subsection 9(d) of the conference agreement conforms to the Senate amendment. The House bill contained a provision which would have permitted judicial review of certifications even before the entry of an unfair labor practice order. In receding on their insistence on this portion, the House yielded to the view of the Senate conferees that such provision would permit dilatory tactics in representation proceedings."

The Court today opens a gaping hole in this congressional wall against direct resort to the courts. * * *

There is nothing in the legislative history to indicate that the Congress intended any exception from the requirement that collective bargaining begin without awaiting judicial review of a Board certification or the investigation preceding it. Certainly nothing appears that an exception was intended where the attack upon the Board's action is based upon an alleged misinterpretation of the statute. The policy behind the limitation of judicial review applies just as clearly when the challenge is made on this ground. Plainly direct judicial review of a Board's interpretation of the statute is as likely to be as drawn out, and thus as frustrative of the national policy, as is review of any other type of Board decision. * * * I daresay that the ingenuity of counsel will, after today's decision, be entirely adequate to the task of finding some alleged "unlawful action," whether in statutory interpretation or otherwise, sufficient to get a foot in a District Court door under 28 U.S.C. § 1337, 28 U.S.C.A. § 1337. * * *

It is not support for the Court's decision that the respondent union may suffer hardship if review under 28 U.S.C. § 1337, 28 U.S.C.A. § 1337 is not open to it. The Congress was fully aware of the disadvantages and possible unfairness which could result from the limitation on judicial review enacted in § 9(d). The House proposal for direct review of Board certifications in the Taft–Hartley amendments was based in part upon the fact that, under the Wagner Act, the operation of § 9(d) was "unfair to * * * the union that loses, which has no appeal at all no matter how wrong the certification may be; [and to] the employees, who also have no appeal * * *." Congress nevertheless continued the limited judicial review provided by § 9(d) because Congress believed the disadvantages of broader review to be more serious that the difficulties which limited review posed for the parties. Furthermore, Congress felt that the Board procedures and the limited review provided in § 9(d) were adequate to protect the parties.

* * * The Board, in making the certification in dispute, has interpreted [§ 9(b) ]as requiring the approval of the professional employees of a mixed bargaining unit of professionals and nonprofessionals only when the professionals are a minority in the unit, since only in such a case would they need this protection against the ignoring of their particular interests. This interpretation is the basis of respondent union's complaint in its action under 28 U.S.C.A. § 1337 in the District Court. But an alleged error in statutory construction was also the basis of the District Court action in the *Switchmen's* case. Thus the two cases are perfectly parallel. And just as surely as in the case of the Mediation Board under the Railway Labor Act, the Congress has barred District Court review of National Labor Relations Board certifications under the Labor Management Relations Act. * * *

The Court seizes upon the language in Switchmen's, "If the absence of jurisdiction of the federal courts meant a sacrifice or obliteration of a right which Congress had created, the inference would be strong that Congress intended the statutory provisions governing the general jurisdiction of those courts to control." 320 U.S. at page 300, 64 S.Ct. at page 97. * * * The Court used the "sacrifice or obliteration" language solely to distinguish the situation where Congress created a "right" but no tribunal for its enforcement. * * *

But here, as the Congress provided the Mediation Board under the Railway Labor Act, the Congress has provided an agency, the NLRB, to protect the "right" it created under the National Labor Relations Act. Congress has in addition enacted "an appropriate safeguard and opportunity to be heard" in procedures to be followed by the Board. It has indeed gone further than in the Railway Labor Act. Whereas no judicial review of any kind was there provided, some, although limited, judicial review is provided under § 9(d). This was considered by Congress as "a complete guarantee against arbitrary action by the Board." Plainly we have here a situation where it may be said precisely as in Switchmen's that "Congress for reasons of its own decided upon the method for protection of the 'right' it created. It selected the precise machinery and fashioned the tool which it deemed suited to that end." * * *

I would reverse and remand the case to the District Court with instructions to dismiss the complaint for lack of jurisdiction of the subject matter.

———

BOIRE v. GREYHOUND CORP., 376 U.S. 473, 84 S.Ct. 894, 11 L.Ed.2d 849 (1964). A union filed a petition for an election among the porters, janitors and maids working at four Florida bus terminals operated by Greyhound. The petition designated Greyhound and Floors, Inc. as employers, Floors being a corporation engaged by Greyhound to provide cleaning, maintenance and related services for the four terminals. At the Board hearing on the petition, Greyhound claimed that Floors was the sole employer of the employees in question. But the Board found that although Floors hired, paid, disciplined, transferred, promoted and discharged the employees, Greyhound was also an employer since it took part in setting up work schedules, determined the number of employees needed, and helped direct the work performed. Greyhound then filed suit in a federal district court to enjoin the forthcoming election. The district court concluded that it had jurisdiction on the basis of Leedom v. Kyne and further found that the Board's findings were insufficient as a matter of law to establish a joint employer relationship. The court of appeals affirmed. On certiorari, *held*, the judgment should be reversed. "[W]hether Greyhound possessed sufficient indication of control to be an 'employer' is essentially a factual issue, unlike the question in Kyne, which depended solely upon construction of the statute. The Kyne exception is a narrow one, not to be extended to permit plenary District Court review of Board orders in certification proceedings whenever it can be said that an erroneous assessment of the particular facts before the Board has led it to a conclusion which does not comport with the law."

———

## PROBLEMS FOR DISCUSSION

**1.** After the filing of an election petition by the Ridgewood College Faculty Association, representatives of the College administration moved to dismiss on the ground that the College is an instrumentality of the state government and is therefore excluded from the definition of "employer" in the Labor Act. The College, although privately founded, has in recent years financed almost one-third of its annual budget with grants from the state legislature, and it has been agreed that one-third of its trustees are to be appointed by the state Board of Regents. After a hearing, the Regional Director concluded that the College is to be treated as a private rather than a public institution. The Regional Director has ordered that an election be held in thirty days, and the Board has refused to review this order.

Can the College secure a district court injunction against the holding of a representation election? Given the parties, the Board's action, and the timing of the injunction request, is the case more or less appropriate for injunctive relief than was Leedom v. Kyne? Cf. Physicians Nat. House Staff Ass'n v. Fanning, 642 F.2d 492 (D.C.Cir.1980), cert. denied, 450 U.S. 917, 101 S.Ct. 1360, 67 L.Ed.2d 342 (1981).

**2.** Assume that the faculty of Ridgewood College has no tenure and plays no role whatsoever even in an advisory capacity in matters of educational policy. The Faculty Association is elected and negotiates a collective agreement providing for a faculty senate and committee structure with jurisdiction for admissions, degree requirements and curriculum. At the conclusion of the contract, the administration filed a "unit clarification" petition with the Regional Director asking the Director to hold that the faculty are now rendered managerial employees because of their decisionmaking role. The Regional Director agrees and the Board has declined to review that decision. Can the Faculty Association do anything to secure judicial review of the decision? *See* College of Osteopathic Medicine & Surgery, 265 NLRB 295 (1982).

# III. Securing Bargaining Rights Through Unfair Labor Practice Proceedings

It is generally agreed that a Board-conducted election is the fairest way to determine the collective bargaining preference of employees: the secret-ballot procedure takes place after both sides have an opportunity to air their positions under "laboratory conditions." Proceedings under Section 9 of the Labor Act are not, however, the only way for a union to secure representative status. Resistance to unions may be on the increase since the early 1980s, but it is still true that many unions are voluntarily recognized without formal certification. This is, of course, lawful provided the union in fact has majority support in an appropriate bargaining unit. See pages 210–12, supra.

It is also possible for a union to seek bargaining status through unfair labor practice proceedings brought against the employer, typically upon claims that the employer improperly refused to bargain with the union pursuant to Section 8(a)(5). In spite of the apparent advantages of the more expeditious "laboratory" experiment under Section 9, the question remains whether Congress did contemplate that a union could compel the employer to grant or to continue bargaining status through other methods. This issue generally arises in one of three situations.

(1) The employer rejects the union's showing of majority support through authorization cards and then engages in coercive unfair labor practices designed to undermine that support. Under what circumstances may the Board, as a remedy for the employer unfair labor practices, order the employer to bargain with the union?

(2) The employer rejects the union's showing of majority support through authorization cards and, while engaging in no coercive conduct, insists that the union be certified after a Board-conducted election before it will recognize it as bargaining representative. May the Board order the employer to bargain with the union?

(3) A union has at some time in the past been extended bargaining rights, either after Board certification or after informal recognition, but the employer claims that it believes the union no longer has majority support and that it will therefore withdraw recognition. Under what circumstances

will the Board find this withdrawal to be unlawful and therefore order the employer to continue bargaining with the union?

These are the issues to be treated in the materials immediately following. All raise in common the question whether in particular circumstances a union should be required to demonstrate its representative status through a secret-ballot election rather than through unfair labor practice proceedings in which there is reliance upon authorization cards or earlier designations which now may be "stale" and inaccurate. Those who are generally sympathetic to the election procedures argue that a Board bargaining order, after a lengthy proceeding based on events long in the past, runs the serious risk of imposing an unwanted and unrepresentative union upon the employees in the bargaining unit. Those who are sympathetic to the bargaining order urge either that in many instances it will more accurately reflect employee wishes than will an election or that it will foster industrial stability in the face of disruptive and unnecessary demands for an election.

------

## NLRB v. Gissel Packing Co.[a]

395 U.S. 575, 89 S.Ct. 1918, 23 L.Ed.2d 547 (1969).

■ MR. CHIEF JUSTICE WARREN delivered the opinion of the Court.

These cases involve the extent of an employer's duty under the National Labor Relations Act to recognize a union that bases its claim to representative status solely on the possession of union authorization cards, and the steps an employer may take, particularly with regard to the scope and content of statements he may make, in legitimately resisting such card-based recognition. The specific questions facing us here are whether the duty to bargain can arise without a Board election under the Act; whether union authorization cards, if obtained from a majority of employees without misrepresentation or coercion, are reliable enough generally to provide a valid, alternate route to majority status; whether a bargaining order is an appropriate and authorized remedy where an employer rejects a card majority while at the same time committing unfair practices that tend to undermine the union's majority and make a fair election an unlikely possibility; and whether certain specific statements made by an employer to

a.  See Brudney, A Famous Victory: Collective Bargaining Protections and the Statutory Aging Process, 74 N.C.L.Rev. 939 (1996); Christensen & Christensen, Gissel Packing and "Good Faith Doubt": The Gestalt of Required Recognition of Unions Under the NLRA, 37 U.Chi.L.Rev. 411 (1970); Cooper, Authorization Cards and Union Representation Election Outcome: An Empirical Assessment of the Assumption Underlying the Supreme Court's Gissel Decision, 79 Nw. U.L.Rev. 87 (1984); Lankford, Nonmajority Bargaining Orders: A Study in Indecision, 46 Alb.L.J. 363 (1982); Note, The Propriety of Section 10(j) Bargaining Orders in Gissel Situations, 82 Mich.L.Rev. 112 (1983); Note, NLRB v. Gissel Packing Co.: Bargaining Orders and Employee Free Choice, 45 N.Y.U.L.Rev. 318 (1970); Note, "After All, Tomorrow is Another Day": Should Subsequent Events Affect the Validity of Bargaining Orders?, 31 Stanford L.Rev. 505 (1979).

his employees constituted such an election-voiding unfair labor practice and thus fell outside the protection of the First Amendment and § 8(c) of the Act, 49 Stat. 452, as amended, 29 U.S.C. § 158(c). For reasons given below, we answer each of these questions in the affirmative.

\* \* \*

Nos. 573 and 691.

In each of the cases from the Fourth Circuit, the course of action followed by the Union and the employer and the Board's response were similar. In each case, the union waged an organizational campaign, obtained authorization cards from a majority of employees in the appropriate bargaining unit, and then on the basis of the cards, demanded recognition by the employer. All three employers refused to bargain on the ground that authorization cards were inherently unreliable indicators of employee desires; and they either embarked on, or continued, vigorous antiunion campaigns that gave rise to numerous unfair labor practice charges. In *Gissel,* where the employer's campaign began almost at the outset of the Union's organizational drive, the Union (petitioner in No. 691), did not seek an election, but instead filed three unfair labor practice charges against the employer, for refusing to bargain in violation of § 8(a)(5), for coercion and intimidation of employees in violation of § 8(a)(1), and for discharge of union adherents in violation of § 8(a)(3). In *Heck's* an election sought by the Union was never held because of nearly identical unfair labor practice charges later filed by the Union as a result of the employer's antiunion campaign, initiated after the Union's recognition demand. And in *General Steel,* an election petitioned for by the Union and won by the employer was set aside by the Board because of the unfair labor practices committed by the employer in the pre-election period.

In each case, the Board's primary response was an order to bargain directed at the employers, despite the absence of an election in *Gissel* and *Heck's* and the employer's victory in *General Steel.* More specifically, the Board found in each case that (1) the union had obtained valid authorization cards[4] from a majority of the employees in the bargaining unit and was thus entitled to represent the employees for collective bargaining purposes; and (2) that the employers' refusal to bargain with the unions in violation of § 8(a)(5) was motivated not by a "good faith" doubt of the unions' majority status, but by a desire to gain time to dissipate that status. The Board based its conclusion as to the lack of good faith doubt on the fact

---

**4.** The cards used in all four campaigns in Nos. 573 and 691 and in the one drive in No. 585 unambiguously authorized the Union to represent the signing employee for collective bargaining purposes; there was no reference to elections. Typical of the cards was the one used in the Charleston campaign in *Hecks,* and it stated in relevant part:

"Desiring to become a member of the above Union of the International Brotherhood of Teamsters, Chauffeurs, Warehousemen and Helpers of America, I hereby make application for admission to membership. I hereby authorize you, or your agents or representatives to act for me as collective bargaining agent on all matters pertaining to rates of pay, hours or any other condition of employment."

that the employers had committed substantial unfair labor practices during their antiunion campaign efforts to resist recognition. Thus, the Board found that all three employers had engaged in restraint and coercion of employees in violation of § 8(a)(1)—in *Gissel,* for coercively interrogating employees about union activities, threatening them with discharge and promising them benefits; in *Heck's,* for coercively interrogating employees, threatening reprisals, creating the appearance of surveillance, and offering benefits for opposing the Union; and in *General Steel,* for coercive interrogation and threats of reprisals, including discharge. In addition, the Board found that the employers in *Gissel* and *Heck's* had wrongfully discharged employees for engaging in union activities in violation of § 8(a)(3). And, because the employers had rejected the card-based bargaining demand in bad faith, the Board found that all three had refused to recognize the unions in violation of § 8(a)(5).

Only in *General Steel* was there any objection by an employer to the validity of the cards and the manner in which they had been solicited, and the doubt raised by the evidence was resolved in the following manner. The customary approach of the Board in dealing with allegations of misrepresentation by the union and misunderstanding by the employees of the purpose for which the cards were being solicited has been set out in Cumberland Shoe Corp., 144 N.L.R.B. 1268 (1964), and reaffirmed in Levi Strauss & Co., 172 N.L.R.B. No. 57, 68 L.R.R.M. 1338 (1968). Under the *Cumberland Shoe* doctrine, if the card itself is unambiguous (i.e., states on its face that the signer authorizes the union to represent the employee for collective bargaining purposes and not to seek an election), it will be counted unless it is proved that the employee was told that the card was to be used *solely* for the purpose of obtaining an election. In *General Steel,* the trial examiner considered the allegations of misrepresentation at length and, applying the Board's customary analysis, rejected the claims with findings that were adopted by the Board and are reprinted in the margin.[5]

Consequently, the Board ordered the companies to cease and desist from their unfair labor practices, to offer reinstatement and back pay to the employees who had been discriminatorily discharged, to bargain with the Union on request, and to post the appropriate notices.

[The Court of Appeals for the Fourth Circuit rejected the Board's findings that the employers' refusal to bargain violated § 8(a)(5) and declined to enforce those portions of the Board's orders directing the

---

**5.** "Accordingly, I reject respondent's contention that if a man is told that his card will be secret, or will be shown only to the Labor Board for the purpose of obtaining election, that this is the absolute equivalent of telling him that it will be used 'only' for the purpose of obtaining an election.

"With respect to the 97 employees named in the attached Appendix B Respondent in its brief contends, in substance, that their cards should be rejected because each of

these employees was told *one or more* of the following: (1) that the card would be used to get an election (2) that he had the right to vote either way, even though he signed the card (3) that the card would be kept secret and not shown to anybody except to the Board in order to get an election. For reasons heretofore explicated, I conclude that these statements, singly or jointly, do not foreclose use of the cards for the purpose designated on their face."

respondent companies to bargain in good faith, holding that the 1947 Taft–Hartley amendments to the Act withdrew from the Board the authority to order an employer to bargain under § 8(a)(5) on the basis of cards, in the absence of NLRB certification, unless the employer knows independently of the cards that there is in fact no representation dispute. Thus, under these rulings a company could not be ordered to bargain unless (1) there was no question about a union's majority status (either because the employer agreed the cards were valid or had conducted its own poll so indicating), or (2) the employer's § 8(a)(1) and (3) unfair labor practices committed during the representation campaign were so extensive and pervasive that a bargaining order was the only available Board remedy irrespective of a card majority.

[In case 585, the Sinclair Company refused to recognize the Teamsters Union, which had obtained authorization cards from 11 of the Company's 14 employees. The Company did not assert any irregularities in the solicitation of the cards, but claimed that cards are inherently unreliable. The Union petitioned for a representation election, and the Company embarked upon a vigorous campaign of speeches, pamphlets, leaflets and letters attacking the Teamsters and unions in general. The Company stated that it was in an unsound financial state; that the Teamsters were a "strike-happy" union, run by hoodlums, which would make unreasonable demands; that a strike would probably cause the Company to close the plant; that many unionized plants in the area had closed and that a plant closing because of the Teamsters would lead to the workers' unemployment because of their age and limited skills. The Union lost the election 7 to 6 and filed both objections to the election and unfair labor practice charges. The Board found that the Company's statements violated Section 8(a)(1) and that its refusal to bargain was designed to gain time to dissipate the Teamsters' majority and thus violated Section 8(a)(5); it set aside the election, issued a cease-and-desist order, and ordered the Company to bargain, finding that its conduct had been so inherently coercive and pervasive that a bargaining order would be proper even in the absence of a card majority. The Court of Appeals for the First Circuit sustained the Board's findings and conclusions and enforced its order in full.]

## II.

In urging us to reverse the Fourth Circuit and to affirm the First Circuit, the National Labor Relations Board * * * asks us to approve its current practice, which is briefly as follows. When confronted by a recognition demand based on possession of cards allegedly signed by a majority of his employees, an employer need not grant recognition immediately, but may, unless he has knowledge independently of the cards that the union has a majority, decline the union's request and insist on an election, either by requesting the union to file an election petition or by filing such a petition himself under § 9(c)(1)(B). If, however, the employer commits independent and substantial unfair labor practices disruptive of election conditions, the Board may withhold the election or set it aside, and issue instead a bargaining order as a remedy for the various violations. * * *

\* \* \* [T]he Union, petitioner in No. 691, argues that we should accord a far greater role to cards in the bargaining area than the Board itself seeks in this litigation. In order to understand the differences between the Union and the Board, it is necessary to trace the evolution of the Board's approach to authorization cards from its early practice to the position it takes on oral argument before this Court. Such an analysis requires viewing the Board's treatment of authorization cards in three separate phases: (1) under the *Joy Silk* doctrine, (2) under the rules of the *Aaron Brothers* case, and (3) under the approach announced at oral argument before this Court.

The traditional approach utilized by the Board for many years has been known as the *Joy Silk* doctrine. Joy Silk Mills, Inc., 85 N.L.R.B. 1263 (1949), enforced 87 U.S.App.D.C. 360, 185 F.2d 732 (1950). Under that rule, an employer could lawfully refuse to bargain with a union claiming representative status through possession of authorization cards if he had a "good faith doubt" as to the union's majority status; instead of bargaining, he could insist that the union seek an election in order to test out his doubts. The Board, then, could find a lack of good faith doubt and enter a bargaining order in one of two ways. It could find (1) that the employer's independent unfair labor practices were evidence of bad faith, showing that the employer was seeking time to dissipate the union's majority. Or the Board could find (2) that the employer had come forward with no reasons for entertaining any doubt and therefore that he must have rejected the bargaining demand in bad faith. \* \* \*

The leading case codifying modifications to the *Joy Silk* doctrine was Aaron Brothers, 158 N.L.R.B. 1077 (1966). There the Board made it clear that it had shifted the burden to the General Counsel to show bad faith and that an employer "will not be held to have violated his bargaining obligation \* \* \* simply because he refuses to rely on cards, rather than an election, as the method for determining the union's majority." 158 N.L.R.B., at 1078. Two significant consequences were emphasized. The Board noted (1) that not every unfair labor practice would automatically result in a finding of bad faith and therefore a bargaining order; the Board implied that it would find bad faith only if the unfair labor practice was serious enough to have the tendency to dissipate the union's majority. The Board noted (2) that an employer no longer needed to come forward with reasons for rejecting a bargaining demand. The Board pointed out, however, that a bargaining order would issue if it could prove that an employer's "course of conduct" gave indications as to the employer's bad faith. \* \* \*

Although the Board's brief before this Court generally followed the approach as set out in *Aaron Brothers,* supra, the Board announced at oral argument that it had virtually abandoned the *Joy Silk* doctrine altogether. Under the Board's current practice, an employer's good faith doubt is largely irrelevant, and the key to the issuance of a bargaining order is the commission of serious unfair labor practices that interfere with the election processes and tend to preclude the holding of a fair election. Thus, an employer can insist that a union go to an election, regardless of his subjective motivation, so long as he is not guilty of misconduct; he need give no affirmative reasons for rejecting a recognition request, and he can demand an election with a simple "no comment" to the union. The Board pointed out, however, (1) that an employer could not refuse to bargain if he *knew*, through a personal poll for instance, that a majority of his employees supported the union, and (2) that an employer could not refuse recognition initially because of questions as to the appropriateness of the unit and then later claim, as an afterthought, that he doubted the union's strength. * * *

### III.

### A.

The first issue facing us is whether a union can establish a bargaining obligation by means other than a Board election and whether the validity of alternate routes to majority status, such as cards, was affected by the 1947 Taft–Hartley amendments. The most commonly traveled route for a union to obtain recognition as the exclusive bargaining representative of an unorganized group of employees is through the Board's election and certification procedures under § 9(c) of the Act (29 U.S.C. § 159(c)(1964 ed.)); it is also, from the Board's point of view, the preferred route. A union is not limited to a Board election, however, for, in addition to § 9, the present Act provides in § 8(a)(5)(29 U.S.C. § 158(a)(5)(1964 ed.)), as did the Wagner Act in § 8(5), that "it shall be an unfair labor practice for an employer * * * to refuse to bargain collectively with the representatives of his employees, subject to the provisions of section 9(a)." Since § 9(a), in both the Wagner Act and the present Act, refers to the representative as the one "designated or selected" by a majority of the employees without specifying precisely how that representative is to be chosen, it was early recognized that an employer had a duty to bargain whenever the union representative presented "convincing evidence of majority support." Almost from the inception of the Act, then, it was recognized that a union did not have to be certified as the winner of a Board election to invoke a bargaining obligation; it could establish majority status by other means under the unfair labor practice provision of § 8(a)(5)—by showing convincing support, for instance, by a union-called strike or strike vote, or, as here, by possession of cards signed by a majority of the employees authorizing the union to represent them for collective bargaining purposes.

We have consistently accepted this interpretation of the Wagner Act and the present Act, particularly as to the use of authorization cards. See, *e.g.*, NLRB v. Bradford Dyeing Assn., 310 U.S. 318, 339–340, 60 S.Ct. 918, 929, 84 L.Ed. 1226 (1940); Franks Bros. Co. v. NLRB, 321 U.S. 702, 64 S.Ct. 817, 88 L.Ed. 1020 (1944); United Mine Workers v. Arkansas Flooring Co., 351 U.S. 62, 76 S.Ct. 559, 100 L.Ed. 941 (1956). * * * we find unpersuasive the Fourth Circuit's view that the 1947 Taft–Hartley amendments, enacted some nine years before our decision in *United Mine Workers,* supra, require us to disregard that case. * * * An early version of the bill in the House would have amended § 8(5) of the Wagner Act to permit the Board to find a refusal to bargain violation only where an employer had failed to bargain with a union "currently recognized by the employer or certified as such [through an election] under section 9." Section 8(a)(5) of H.R. 3020, 80th Cong., 1st Sess. (1947). The proposed change, which would have eliminated the use of cards, was rejected in Conference (H.R.Conf. Rep.No. 510, 80th Cong., 1st Sess., 41 (1947)), however, and we cannot make a similar change in the Act simply because, as the employers assert, Congress did not expressly approve the use of cards in rejecting the House amendment. Nor can we accept the Fourth Circuit's conclusion that the change was wrought when Congress amended § 9(c) to make election the sole basis for *certification* by eliminating the phrase "any other suitable method to ascertain such representatives," under which the Board had occasionally used cards as a certification basis. A certified union has the benefit of numerous special privileges which are not accorded unions recognized voluntarily or under a bargaining order[14] and which, Congress could determine, should not be dispensed unless a union has survived the crucible of a secret ballot election.

The employers rely finally on the addition to § 9(c) of subparagraph (B), which allows an employer to petition for an election whenever "one or more individuals or labor organizations have presented to him a claim to be recognized as the representative defined in section 9(a)." That provision was not added, as the employers assert, to give them an absolute right to an election at any time; rather, it was intended, as the legislative history indicates, to allow them, after being asked to bargain, to test out their doubts as to a union's majority in a secret election which they would then presumably not cause to be set aside by illegal antiunion activity.[16] We agree with the Board's assertion here that there is no suggestion that Congress intended § 9(c)(1)(B) to relieve any employer of his § 8(a)(5) bargaining obligation where, without good faith, he engaged in unfair labor practices disruptive of the Board's election machinery. And we agree that the policies reflected in § 9(c)(1)(B) fully support the Board's present administration of the Act; for an employer can insist on a secret ballot election, unless, in the words of the Board, he engages "in contemporane-

---

**14.** E.g., protection against the filing of new election petitions by rival unions or employees seeking decertification for 12 months (§ 9(c)(3)), protection for a reasonable period, usually one year, against any disruption of the bargaining relationship because of claims that the union no longer represents a majority (see Brooks v. NLRB, 348 U.S. 96, 75 S.Ct. 176, 99 L.Ed. 125 (1954)), protection against recognitional picketing by rival unions (§ 8(b)(4)(C)), and freedom from the restrictions placed in work assignments disputes by § 8(b)(4)(D), and on recognitional and organizational picketing by § 8(b)(7).

**16.** The Senate report stated that the "present Board rules * * * discriminate against employers who have reasonable grounds for believing that labor organizations claiming to represent the employees are really not the choice of the majority." S.Rep. No. 105, 80th Cong., 1st Sess., 10–11 (1947). Senator Taft stated during the debates:

"Today an employer is faced with this situation. A man comes into his office and says, 'I represent your employees. Sign this agreement or we strike tomorrow.' * * * The employer has no way in which to determine whether this man really does represent his employees or does not. The bill gives him the right to go to the Board * * * and say, 'I want an election. I want to know who is the bargaining agent for my employees.'" 93 Cong.Rec. 3954 (1947).

ous unfair labor practices likely to destroy the union's majority and seriously impede the election." Brief for Petitioner 36.

\* \* \*

## B.

We next consider whether authorization cards are such inherently unreliable indicators of employee desires that whatever the validity of other alternate routes to representative status, the cards themselves may never be used to determine a union's majority and to support an order to bargain. In this context, the employers urge us to take the step the 1947 amendments and their legislative history indicate Congress did not take, namely, to rule out completely the use of cards in the bargaining arena. Even if we do not unhesitatingly accept the Fourth Circuit's view in the matter, the employers argue, at the very least we should overrule the *Cumberland Shoe* doctrine and establish stricter controls over the solicitation of the cards by union representatives.

The objections to the use of cards voiced by the employers and the Fourth Circuit boil down to two contentions: (1) that, as contrasted with the election procedure, the cards cannot accurately reflect an employee's wishes, either because an employer has not had a chance to present his views and thus a chance to insure that the employee choice was an informed one, or because the choice was the result of group pressures and not individual decision made in the privacy of a voting booth; and (2) that quite apart from the election comparison, the cards are too often obtained through misrepresentation and coercion which compound the cards' inherent inferiority to the election process. Neither contention is persuasive, and each proves too much. The Board itself has recognized, and continues to do so here, that secret elections are generally the most satisfactory—indeed the preferred—method of ascertaining whether a union has majority support. The acknowledged superiority of the election process, however, does not mean that cards are thereby rendered totally invalid, for where an employer engages in conduct disruptive of the election process, cards may be the most effective—perhaps the only—way of assuring employee choice. As for misrepresentation, in any specific case of alleged irregularity in the solicitation of the cards, the proper course is to apply the Board's customary standards (to be discussed more fully below) and rule there was no majority if the standards were not satisfied. It does not follow that because there are some instances of irregularity, the cards can never be used; otherwise, an employer could put off his bargaining obligation indefinitely through continuing interference with elections.

That the cards, though admittedly inferior to the election process, can adequately reflect employee sentiment when that process has been impeded, needs no extended discussion, for the employers' contentions cannot withstand close examination. The employers argue that their employees cannot make an informed choice because the card drive will be over before the employer has had a chance to present his side of the unionization issues. Normally, however, the union will inform the employer of its organization drive early in order to subject the employer to the unfair labor practice provisions of the Act; the union must be able to show the employer's awareness of the drive in order to prove that his contemporaneous conduct constituted unfair labor practices on which a bargaining order can be based if the drive is ultimately successful. * * *

Further, the employers argue that without a secret ballot an employee may, in a card drive, succumb to group pressures or sign simply to get the union "off his back" and then be unable to change his mind as he would be free to do once inside a voting booth. But the same pressures are likely to be equally present in an election, for election cases arise most often with small bargaining units where virtually every voter's sentiments can be carefully and individually canvassed. And no voter, of course, can change his mind after casting a ballot in an election even though he may think better of his choice shortly thereafter.

The employers' second complaint, that the cards are too often obtained through misrepresentation and coercion, must be rejected also in view of the Board's present rules for controlling card solicitation, which we view as adequate to the task where the cards involved state their purpose clearly and unambiguously on their face. We would be closing our eyes to obvious difficulties, of course, if we did not recognize that there have been abuses, primarily arising out of misrepresentations by union organizers as to whether the effect of signing a card was to designate the union to represent the employee for collective bargaining purposes or merely to authorize it to seek an election to determine that issue. And we would be equally blind if we did not recognize that various courts of appeals and commentators have differed significantly as to the effectiveness of the Board's *Cumberland Shoe* doctrine to cure such abuses.

* * *

We need make no decision as to the conflicting approaches used with regard to dual-purpose cards, for in each of the five organization campaigns in the four cases before us the cards used were single-purpose cards, stating clearly and unambiguously on their face that the signer designated the union as his representative. * * *

In resolving the conflict among the circuits in favor of approving the Board's *Cumberland* rule, we think it sufficient to point out that employees should be bound by the clear language of what they sign unless that language is deliberately and clearly canceled by a union adherent with words calculated to direct the signer to disregard and forget the language above his signature. There is nothing inconsistent in handing an employee a card that says the signer authorizes the union to represent him and then telling him that the card will probably be used first to get an election. * * *

We agree, however, with the Board's own warnings in Levi Strauss, 172 N.L.R.B.No. 57, 68 L.R.R.M. 1338, 1341, and n. 7 (1968), that in hearing testimony concerning a card challenge, trial examiners should not neglect their obligation to ensure employee free choice by a too easy mechanical application of the *Cumberland* rule.[27] We also accept the observation that employees are more likely than not, many months after a card drive and in response to questions by company counsel, to give testimony damaging to the union, particularly where company officials have previously threatened reprisals for union activity in violation of § 8(a)(1). We therefore reject any rule that requires a probe of an employee's subjective motivations as involving an endless and unreliable inquiry. We nevertheless feel that the trial examiner's findings in *General Steel* (see n. 5, supra) represent the limits of the *Cumberland* rule's application. We emphasize that the Board should be careful to guard against an approach any more rigid than that in *General Steel*. And we reiterate that nothing we say here indicates our approval of the *Cumberland Shoe* rule when applied to ambiguous, dual-purpose cards. * * *

## C.

Remaining before us is the propriety of a bargaining order as a remedy for a § 8(a)(5) refusal to bargain where an employer has committed independent unfair labor practices which have made the holding of a fair election unlikely or which have in fact undermined a union's majority and caused an election to be set aside. We have long held that the Board is not limited to a cease-and-desist order in such cases, but has the authority to issue a bargaining order without first requiring the union to show that it has been able to maintain its majority status. See NLRB v. Katz, 369 U.S. 736, 748, n. 16, 82 S.Ct. 1107, 1114, 8 L.Ed.2d 230 (1962); NLRB v. P. Lorillard Co., 314 U.S. 512, 62 S.Ct. 397, 86 L.Ed. 380 (1942). And we have held that the Board has the same authority even where it is clear that the union, which once had possession of cards from a majority of the employees, represents only a minority when the bargaining order is entered. Franks Bros. Co. v. NLRB, 321 U.S. 702, 64 S.Ct. 817, 88 L.Ed. 1020 (1944). We see no reason now to withdraw this authority from the Board. If the Board could enter only a cease-and-desist order and direct an election

---

**27.** In explaining and reaffirming the *Cumberland Shoe* doctrine in the context of unambiguous cards, the Board stated:

"Thus the fact that employees are told in the course of solicitation that an election is contemplated, or that a purpose of the card is to make an election possible, provides in our view *insufficient* basis in itself for vitiating unambiguously worded authorization cards on the theory of misrepresentation. A different situation is presented, of course, where union organizers solicit cards on the explicit or indirectly expressed representation that they will use such cards *only* for an election and subsequently seek to use them for a different purpose...."

The Board stated further in a footnote:

"The foregoing does not of course imply that a finding of misrepresentation is confined to situations where employees are expressly told in *haec verba* that the 'sole' or 'only' purpose of the cards is to obtain an election. The Board has never suggested such a mechanistic application of the foregoing principles, as some have contended. The Board looks to substance rather than to form. It is not the use or nonuse of certain key or 'magic' words that is controlling but, whether or not the totality of circumstances surrounding the card solicitation is such, as to add up to an assurance to the card signer that his card will be used for no purpose other than to help get an election." 172 N.L.R.B. No. 57, 68 L.R.R.M. 1338, 1341, and n. 7.

or a rerun, it would in effect be rewarding the employer and allowing him "to profit from [his] own wrongful refusal to bargain," Franks Bros., supra, at 704, while at the same time severely curtailing the employees' right freely to determine whether they desire a representative. The employer could continue to delay or disrupt the election processes and put off indefinitely his obligation to bargain; and any election held under these circumstances would not be likely to demonstrate the employees' true, undistorted desires.[31]

The employers argue that the Board has ample remedies, over and above the cease-and-desist order, to control employer misconduct. The Board can, they assert, direct the companies to mail notices to employees, to read notices to employees during plant time and to give the union access to employees during working time at the plant, or it can seek a court injunctive order under § 10(j)(29 U.S.C. § 160(j)) as a last resort. In view of the Board's power, they conclude, the bargaining order is an unnecessarily harsh remedy that needlessly prejudices employees' § 7 rights solely for the purpose of punishing or restraining an employer. Such an argument ignores that a bargaining order is designed as much to remedy past election damage[32] as it is to deter future misconduct. If an employer has succeeded in undermining a union's strength and destroying the laboratory conditions necessary for a fair election, he may see no need to violate a cease-and-desist order by further unlawful activity. The damage will have been done, and perhaps the only fair way to effectuate employee rights is to re-

---

**31.** A study of 20,153 elections held between 1960 and 1962 shows that in over two-thirds of the cases, the party who caused the election to be set aside [i.e., the "wrongdoer" who won the first election] won in the rerun election. See D. Pollitt, NLRB ReRun Elections: A Study, 41 N.C.L.Rev. 209, 212 (1963). The study shows further that certain unfair labor practices are more effective to destroy election conditions for a longer period of time than others. For instance, in cases involving threats to close or transfer plant operations, the union won the rerun only 29% of the time, while threats to eliminate benefits or refuse to deal with the union if elected seemed less irremediable with the union winning the rerun 75% of the time. Id., at 215–216. Finally, time appears to be a factor. The figures suggest that if a rerun is held too soon after the election before the effects of the unfair labor practices have worn off, or too long after the election when interest in the union may have waned, the chances for a changed result occurring are not as good as they are if the rerun is held sometime in between those periods. Thus, the study showed that if the rerun is held within 30 days of the election or over nine months after, the chances that a different result will

occur are only one in five; when the rerun is held within 30–60 days after the election, the chances for a changed result are two in five. Id., at 221.

**32.** The employers argue that the Fourth Circuit correctly observed that, "in the great majority of cases, a cease and desist order with the posting of appropriate notices will eliminate any undue influences upon employees voting in the security of anonymity." NLRB v. S.S. Logan Packing Co., 386 F.2d, at 570. It is for the Board and not the courts, however, to make that determination, based on its expert estimate as to the effects on the election process of unfair labor practices of varying intensity. In fashioning its remedies under the broad provisions of § 10(c) of the Act (29 U.S.C.A. 160(c)), the Board draws on a fund of knowledge and expertise all its own, and its choice of remedy must therefore be given special respect by reviewing courts. See Fibreboard Paper Products Corp. v. NLRB, 379 U.S. 203, 85 S.Ct. 398, 13 L.Ed.2d 233 (1964). "[I]t is usually better to minimize the opportunity for reviewing courts to substitute their discretion for that of the agency." Consolo v. FMC, 383 U.S. 607, 621, 86 S.Ct. 1018, 1027, 16 L.Ed.2d 131 (1966).

establish the conditions as they existed before the employer's unlawful campaign. There is, after all, nothing permanent in a bargaining order, and if, after the effects of the employer's acts have worn off, the employees clearly desire to disavow the union, they can do so by filing a representation petition. * * *

* * * While refusing to validate the general use of a bargaining order in reliance on cards, the Fourth Circuit nevertheless left open the possibility of imposing a bargaining order, without need of inquiry into majority status on the basis of cards or otherwise, in "exceptional" cases marked by "outrageous" and "pervasive" unfair labor practices. Such an order would be an appropriate remedy for those practices, the court noted, if they are of "such a nature that their coercive effects cannot be eliminated by the application of traditional remedies, with the result that a fair and reliable election cannot be had." NLRB v. S.S. Logan Packing Co., 386 F.2d 562, 570 (C.A.4th Cir.1967); see also NLRB v. Heck's, Inc., 398 F.2d 337, 338. The Board itself, we should add, has long had a similar policy of issuing a bargaining order, in the absence of a § 8(a)(5) violation or even a bargaining demand, when that was the only available, effective remedy for substantial unfair labor practices. See, *e.g.,* United Steelworkers of America v. NLRB, 126 U.S.App.D.C. 215, 376 F.2d 770 (1967); J.C. Penney Co., Inc. v. NLRB, 384 F.2d 479, 485–486 (C.A.10th Cir.1967).

The only effect of our holding here is to approve the Board's use of the bargaining order in less extraordinary cases marked by less pervasive practices which nonetheless still have the tendency to undermine majority strength and impede the election processes. The Board's authority to issue such an order on a lesser showing of employer misconduct is appropriate, we should reemphasize, where there is also a showing that at one point the union had a majority; in such a case, of course, effectuating ascertainable employee free choice becomes as important a goal as deterring employer misbehaviour. In fashioning a remedy in the exercise of its discretion, then, the Board can properly take into consideration the extensiveness of an employer's unfair practices in terms of their past effect on election conditions and the likelihood of their recurrence in the future. If the Board finds that the possibility of erasing the effects of past practices and of ensuring a fair election (or a fair rerun) by the use of traditional remedies, though present, is slight and that employee sentiment once expressed through cards would, on balance, be better protected by a bargaining order, then such an order should issue.

We emphasize that under the Board's remedial power there is still a third category of minor or less extensive unfair labor practices, which, because of their minimal impact on the election machinery, will not sustain a bargaining order. There is, the Board says, no *per se* rule that the commission of any unfair practice will automatically result in a § 8(a)(5) violation and the issuance of an order to bargain. See Aaron Brothers, supra.

With these considerations in mind, we turn to an examination of the orders in these cases. In *Sinclair,* No. 585, the Board made a finding, left undisturbed by the First Circuit, that the employer's threats of reprisal were so coercive that, even in the absence of a § 8(a)(5) violation, a bargaining order would have been necessary to repair the unlawful effect of those threats. The Board therefore did not have to make the determination called for in the intermediate situation above that the risks that a fair rerun election might not be possible were too great to disregard the desires of the employees already expressed through the cards. The employer argues, however, that his communications to his employees were protected by the First Amendment and § 8(c) of the Act (29 U.S.C. § 158(c)(1964 ed.)), whatever the effect of those communications on the union's majority or the Board's ability to ensure a fair election; it is to that contention that we shall direct our final attention in the next section.

In the three cases in Nos. 573 and 691 from the Fourth Circuit, on the other hand, the Board did not make a similar finding that a bargaining order would have been necessary in the absence of an unlawful refusal to bargain. Nor did it make a finding that, even though traditional remedies might be able to ensure a fair election, there was insufficient indication that an election (or a rerun in *General Steel*) would definitely be a more reliable test of the employees' desires than the card count taken before the unfair labor practices occurred. * * * [W]e therefore remand these cases to the Board for proper findings.

> \* \* \*

---

## PROBLEMS FOR DISCUSSION

**1.** Under the *Joy Silk Mills* doctrine, what did the Board infer from the fact that the employer had engaged in coercive and discriminatory conduct after its refusal to bargain? For what violation of the Act was the bargaining order a remedy? What are the answers to these two questions after the Supreme Court's decision in *Gissel*? Although the *Gissel* Court states, at the outset of part IIIC of its opinion, that the bargaining order is designed to cure the employer's refusal to bargain in violation of Section 8(a)(5), is that consistent with the Court's own analysis, or with the position taken by the Board on oral argument, or with the Court's decision five years later in *Linden Lumber* (immediately below)?

**2.** Assume that a union gathers a majority of cards, but never shows them to the employer or demands recognition. The employer thereafter commits serious violations of Sections 8(a)(1) and (3). May the Board order the employer to bargain with the union? See NLRB v. Marsellus Vault & Sales, Inc., 431 F.2d 933 (2d Cir.1970).

**3.** The *Gissel* decision approves the issuance of a bargaining order when the Board concludes that the employer's unlawful conduct has made a fair election unlikely (and that the earlier-gathered cards better reflect uncoerced employee preferences). At what precise time should the possible fairness of an election be determined: (a) at the time of the employer's unlawful conduct? (b) at the time of the issuance by the Regional Director of a complaint? (c) at the time of the decision of the Administrative Law Judge? (d) at the time of the Board's decision? (e) at the time of the appeal, if there is one? (f) at the time of remand to the NLRB, should the court conclude that the Board's decision is for some reason defective? See generally NLRB

v. Cell Agric. Mfg. Co., 41 F.3d 389 (8th Cir.1994); see also America's Best Quality Coatings Corp. v. NLRB, 44 F.3d 516 (7th Cir.), cert. denied, 515 U.S. 1158, 115 S.Ct. 2609, 132 L.Ed.2d 853 (1995).

---

In most cases decided since *Gissel,* the Board has simply recounted the employer violations and made a conclusory finding on the question whether they were severe enough to preclude a fair election. For example, in General Stencils, Inc., 178 NLRB 108 (1969), the Board issued a bargaining order in a case in which a union, which had demonstrated a majority by authorization cards, had not petitioned for an election. A bargaining order was found necessary because the employer's threats of plant closings and loss of jobs were "widespread," "tended to destroy the employee' free choice," and "were of such a nature as to have a lingering effect and make a fair * * * election quite dubious if not impossible."

The Court of Appeals upheld most—but not all—of the Board's findings of specific violations. NLRB v. General Stencils, Inc., 438 F.2d 894 (2d Cir.1971). The court then found itself unsure whether a bargaining order was still warranted. The court noted widespread inconsistencies in past Board decisions and criticized the Board for failing to establish any criteria defining when employer violations were serious enough to warrant a bargaining order. The Board was urged to employ one of three methods (in descending order of desirability) to articulate its position on bargaining orders. The best course would be for the Board to use the rulemaking procedure to hold hearings and formulate general principles defining the kinds of employer coercion most likely to lead to bargaining orders and those curable by milder remedies. Alternatively, the full Board could announce such general principles in a particular case. Third, the Board could explain fully in each case "just what it considers to have precluded a fair election and why, and in what respects the case differs from others where it has reached an opposite conclusion." The court remanded the case to the Board for a new determination whether a bargaining order was warranted.

On remand, a three-member panel declined to formulate any general principles. General Stencils, Inc. v. International Union of District 50, 195 NLRB 1109 (1972). Rather, it affirmed the bargaining order on the ground that threats of job closings and job loss were "serious" threats which would interfere with employee freedom and would not otherwise be curable. Chairman Miller, in a dissenting opinion, did attempt to formulate a rough set of principles. He agreed with his colleagues that the great variety of situations faced by the Board made it extremely difficult to arrive at such a formulation. But he found at least two situations in which a bargaining order would be warranted in nearly all cases. One was the case of significant benefits granted during an organizing campaign, and the other was the case of repeated discriminatory acts in violation of Section 8(a)(3). The Board's remedies in both cases—in the former merely a cease-and-desist order, and in the latter a make-whole remedy that typically comes far too late—are generally unable to erase the coercive effects of the employer's conduct. Moreover, in these cases the employer is not merely speaking coercively but "demonstrates *by his actions* that he will oppose the union by unlawful means and that employees who support it do so at their grave peril." When employer threats are the basis for the unfair labor practice finding, Chairman Miller would have the Board consider what threats were made (the most serious being loss of jobs or plant closing); whether they were likely under all the circumstances to be seriously regarded (giving weight to the individual who made the threat, whether it was made informally or in printed literature, and its specificity); and the extent of dissemination among employees.

The Court of Appeals, commending Chairman Miller's attempt to establish general rules, again refused to enforce the bargaining order on the ground that the Board's conclusion was not "supported by substantial evidence on the record considered as a whole." NLRB v. General Stencils, Inc., 472 F.2d 170 (2d Cir.1972). The court did not agree that the record supported the conclusion that the employer's violations were serious. Dissenting Judge Hays urged enforcement, pointing to language in *Gissel* which indicated that the Board has almost total discretion, because of its expertise, to decide when a bargaining order is appropriate. The same Court of Appeals has more recently reiterated its disaffection with the Board in bargaining-order cases, and has explicitly adopted and elaborated upon Chairman Miller's guidelines for what the court refers to as "hallmark" violations warranting a bargaining order. NLRB v. Jamaica Towing, Inc., 632 F.2d 208 (2d Cir.1980). Almost every other circuit has joined in the criticism. E.g., NLRB v. Appletree Chevrolet, Inc., 608 F.2d 988 (4th Cir.1979); Montgomery Ward & Co. v. NLRB, 904 F.2d 1156 (7th Cir.1990); *compare* Traction Wholesale Center Co. v. NLRB, 216 F.3d 92 (D.C.Cir. 2000), *with* Vincent Indus. Plastics, Inc. v. NLRB, 209 F.3d 727 (D.C.Cir. 2000). See generally Bethel and Melfi, Judicial Enforcement of NLRB Bargaining Orders: What Influences the Courts?, 22 U.C. Davis L.Rev. 139 (1988).

Is it not illusory for the courts to expect the Board to differentiate between the impact of "egregious" unfair labor practices and the impact of "technical" unfair labor practices, when there is significant empirical evidence that employee preferences for the union are not really affected differentially by lawful employer conduct and unlawful employer conduct? See pages 184–88, supra. The General Counsel has issued a memorandum (GC 99–8 (Nov. 10, 1999)) setting forth guidelines for NLRB personnel considering requests for *Gissel* remedial bargaining orders; this memorandum deals with the factual issues to be addressed in issuing such orders, explores the question whether such orders are properly issued in cases involving only section 8(a)(1) violations, and urges consideration of injunctions under section 10(j) in such cases. (The text of GC 99–8 can be found on the NLRB website at <http://www.nlrb.gov/gcmemo/gc99–8.html>.)

––––––––

GOURMET FOODS, INC. v. WAREHOUSE EMPLOYEES OF ST. PAUL, 270 NLRB 578 (1984). In this case, the Board considered the question whether it has the power, when the employer commits serious and repeated violations of the Act, to order that employer to bargain with a union that has never in the past demonstrated majority support among employees in an appropriate bargaining unit. In a 1979 decision in *United Dairy Farmers,* the Board declined to issue such a "nonmajority bargaining order," but the Court of Appeals for the Third Circuit ruled that the Board had such power under the Act, and on remand the Board issued such an order. United Dairy Farmers Cooperative Ass'n v. NLRB, 633 F.2d 1054 (3d Cir.1980), on remand, 257 NLRB 772 (1981) (*United Dairy II*). The Board reiterated that it could issue a nonmajority bargaining order in the *Conair* decision in 1982, but the Court of Appeals for the District of Columbia Circuit disagreed and denied enforcement. Conair Corp. v. NLRB, 721 F.2d 1355 (D.C.Cir.1983). In the *Gourmet Foods* decision, rendered the following year by the Board after the appointment of a new member, the Board embraced the view of the District of Columbia Circuit, concluded that the majority-rule principle of the Act rendered a nonmajority bargaining order beyond the Board's power, and overruled its decision in *Conair;* one member dissented.

The Board stated that proponents of the nonmajority bargaining order regarded it as the only effective remedy for "pervasive and outrageous" unfair labor practices (denominated Category I cases by virtue of the Supreme Court's analysis in the *Gissel* decision). The Board concluded, however:

> Our own review of the statute, its legislative history, Board and court precedent, and legal commentary have convinced us that the majority rule principle is such an integral part of the Act's current substance and procedure that it must be adhered to in fashioning a remedy, even in the most "exceptional" cases. We view the principle as a direct limitation on the Board's existing statutory remedial authority as well as policy that would render improper exercise of any remedial authority to grant nonmajority bargaining orders which the Board might possess.

The Board majority believed that such an order would constitute an improper imposition by the Board of its own choice of exclusive representative upon the majority of employees. This would be true even were an attempt made to limit the remedy only to situations in which a "reasonable possibility" or "reasonable basis" existed for concluding that the union would have enjoyed majority support but for the employer's unfair labor practices; this would substitute unreliable guesswork and speculation for objective evidence (such as a majority of authorization cards). The Supreme Court's discussion of Category I cases in *Gissel* did not imply that the Board had the power to issue a bargaining order in the absence of a showing of past majority support, but simply "left open the issue." Even if the Board had the power to issue an order it should not do so as a matter of policy, in view of "the negative impact of such imposition on the public's perception of the Board as an impartial agency" that protects employee right to choose under Section 7 and does not make the choice for them.

The dissenting member asserted that the nonmajority bargaining order was the only remedy that could effectively protect employees against employers whose unlawful acts "are so coercive as to prevent majority support from ever developing." The Supreme Court discussion of Category I cases in *Gissel,* although dictum, strongly suggests the Court's endorsement of the nonmajority bargaining order. The statutory context and legislative history of the Act's majority-rule principle shows that it was adopted in order to protect employee free choice and self-organization from employer and union coercion, "not as an absolute limitation on the Board's ability to remedy such coercion when it occurs." In any event, the Board has with judicial approval often dispensed with a requirement of absolute majority support in order to promote other statutory policies—as evidenced by presumptions regarding majority status after certification or voluntary recognition, bargaining orders after majority status has been lost as a result of employer unfair labor practices, and the certification of a union after an election in which fewer than 50 percent of eligible unit employees have voted. The nonmajority bargaining order is within the Board's remedial powers under Section 10(c) of the Act, as it makes whole the employee victims of outrageous and pervasive unfair labor practices, and deters such conduct. Any risks of imposing a minority union on even an interim basis will be minimized by reserving the nonmajority bargaining order for only exceptional cases, giving great weight to whether the union would have secured majority support but for the employer's wrongdoing. This risk "is greatly outweighed by the risk that, without a bargaining order, all employees would be indefinitely denied their statutory right to make a fair determination whether they desire union representation. * * * [T]he bargaining order is temporary, designed to insure only a reasonable period of good-faith bargaining and to dissipate the lingering effects of the employer's unfair labor practices. It is not intended to guarantee a prolonged collective-bargaining relationship, only the right of employees freely to choose or reject this relationship."

---

## PROBLEMS FOR DISCUSSION

**1.** Which position—that of the NLRB majority in *Gourmet Foods* (and the D.C. Circuit) or the dissenting member (and the Third Circuit)—will better effectuate the Section 7 policy of protecting the free choice of employees in the selection of their bargaining representative? Which is more firmly supported by the pertinent passages in the Supreme Court *Gissel* opinion? See Note, Nonmajority Bargaining Orders, 20 U. of Mich.J.L. Reform 617 (1987).

**2.** If, contrary to the assumptions of the Board majority, it could reasonably be determined that a union would have secured majority support but for the employer's outrageous and pervasive violations, would the majority support a bargaining order? Would such a determination necessarily rest upon unreliable speculation? Consider the following situation: a union within a short time secures signed authorization cards from 40 percent of the employees in the plant and petitions the NLRB for a certification election; the employer immediately discharges the union leaders, threatens further firings and even the closing of the plant; it coercively interrogates employees about their support for the union, and grants an unprecedented bonus; and the union loses the election, 42 to 40.

3. Empirical studies make it clear that, although signed authorization cards are perhaps that the best indicator of how employees will vote in a fair secret-ballot election, there is nonetheless a significant expectable diminution in union support between card-signing and vote (even absent employer unfair labor practices). Professor Cooper's study of nearly 800 recent elections led her to the following conclusions:

> [I]n elections in which the union had authorization cards from a bare majority of the electorate—situations in which the Board would find the cards sufficient to permit a bargaining order under *Gissel*—unions won only 40.9% of the time. Only when a union had cards from more than 60% of employees did it achieve at least an even chance of winning the election. Another interesting finding ... is that an increase in the proportion of authorization cards collected over 70% did not substantially increase the union's chance of success. Unions with authorization cards from 90–100% of the employees still won only 65.7% of the time. * * * Thus, permitting a union with authorization card support from only a bare majority of employees to become the employees' exclusive bargaining representative fails to effectuate the sentiments of those employees about unionization that they probably would express if they were allowed to participate in a secret ballot election. If the Board indeed is interested in issuing bargaining orders in cases in which unions would have won the election, then the Board might require authorization cards from substantially more than a majority of the employees—perhaps the 62.5% figure found here—to better gauge when a union has at least an even chance of winning.

In view of the very strong emphasis placed in *Gourmet Foods* upon avoiding the imposition on the bargaining unit of a union likely lacking in majority support, ought not the Board adopt Professor Cooper's suggestion and refrain from issuing a *Gissel* bargaining order on anything much less than a two-thirds card showing? (Indeed, because even unions with a near–100% card showing will likely lose one election in three, ought not the present Board disregard cards altogether as a reliable indicator of the propriety of bargaining orders?) See Cooper, "Authorization Cards and Union Representation Election Outcome: An Empirical Assessment of the Assumption Underlying the Supreme Court's *Gissel* Decision," 79 Northwestern U.L.Rev. 87 (1984); NLRB v. Village IX, Inc., 723 F.2d 1360 (7th Cir.1983).

4. Several employees at a New York City swimsuit manufacturer recently expressed their interest in being represented by the Garment Workers Union. The company immediately embarked upon a campaign of threats, coercive interrogations, and the firing of union leaders. Nonetheless, the union won a representation election by a substantial margin. Promptly, the company announced that it was closing and moving the operation to Florida. The day the union filed unfair labor practice charges, the company declared its lease in New York at an end, transferred all of its sewing equipment to a truck, and moved it to Florida, where it opened a similar business and hired new local workers.

The Board found that the company had committed serious violations of Sections 8(a)(1) and (3). It stated that it had the power to order the employer to return to New York and re-hire the former employees there, but it concluded that it ought not order the employer to do so. (Do you agree?) The Board, however, ordered the company to offer reinstatement in the Florida location to its New York employees and payment of their moving expenses. Realizing that none of the New York workers (almost all of whom were married women) would likely take advantage of the company's mandated offer, the Board concluded that the only way to remove the consequences of the unfair labor practices that would benefit the company was to order the company to bargain for one year in Florida with the union that had won the New York election, irrespective of whether that union had majority status among the Florida employees. The Board concluded that no other feasible remedy would redress the serious employer violations, and that it was proper temporarily to subordinate the interest of the Florida workers.

Is this a more or less appealing case for a bargaining order than *Gourmet Foods?* Should the Board's order be enforced on judicial review? See Local 57, Intern. Ladies' Garment Workers v. NLRB (Garwin Corp.), 374 F.2d 295 (D.C.Cir. 1967).

---

## Linden Lumber Div., Summer & Co. v. NLRB

419 U.S. 301, 95 S.Ct. 429, 42 L.Ed.2d 465 (1974).

[The Supreme Court here confronted the issues it explicitly left open in its *Gissel* decision—whether an employer (absent the commission of unfair labor practices) may decline to bargain with a union having a card majority and whether the employer must accompany any such refusal with a petition for a representation election. The Court was presented with two cases (*Linden* and *Wilder*) in which employers had refused to extend recognition to unions with majority-card showings. In both the Board had concluded that it was not unlawful to refuse to accept evidence of majority status other than the results of a Board election, such as authorization cards or participation in a union-called strike; the Board did not deem it relevant to inquire into whether the employers had good or bad reasons for their refusal. A divided Supreme Court (5 to 4) approved the Board's conclusions, in an opinion by Justice Douglas.]

■ To take the Board's position is not to say that authorization cards are wholly unreliable as an indication of employee support of the union. An employer concededly may have valid objections to recognizing a union on that basis. His objection to cards may, of course, mask his opposition to unions. On the other hand he may have rational, good-faith grounds for distrusting authorization cards in a given situation. He may be convinced that the fact that a majority of the employees strike and picket does not necessarily establish that they desire the particular union as their representative. Fear may indeed prevent some from crossing a picket line; or sympathy for strikers, not the desire to have the particular union in the saddle, may influence others. These factors make difficult an examination of the employer's motive to ascertain whether it was in good faith. To enter that domain is to reject the approval by *Gissel* of the retreat which the Board took from its "good faith" inquiries.

The union which is faced with an unwilling employer has two alternative remedies under the Board's decision in the instant case. It can file for an election; or it can press unfair labor practices against the employer under *Gissel*. The latter alternative promises to consume much time. In *Linden* the time between filing the charge and the Board's ruling was about 4½ years; in *Wilder*, about 6½ years. The Board's experience indicates that the median time in a contested case is 388 days. *Gissel*, 395 U.S., at 611 n. 30, 89 S.Ct., at 1938. On the other hand the median time between the filing of the petition for an election and the decision of the regional director is about 45 days. In terms of getting on with the problems of inaugurating regimes of industrial peace, the policy of encouraging secret elections under the Act is favored. The question remains—should the burden be on the union to ask for an election or should it be the responsibility of the employer?

The Court of Appeals concluded that since Congress in 1947 authorized employers to file their own representation petitions by enacting § 9(c)(1)(B) the burden was on them. But the history of that provision indicates it was aimed at eliminating the discrimination against employers which had previously existed under the Board's prior rules, permitting employers to petition for an election only when confronted with claims by two or more unions. There is no suggestion that Congress wanted to place the burden of getting a secret election on the employer. * * *

The Board has at least some expertise in these matters and its judgment is that an employer's petition for an election, though permissible, is not the required course. It points out in its brief here that an employer wanting to gain delay can draw a petition to elicit protests by the union, and the thought that an employer petition would obviate litigation over the sufficiency of the union's showing of interest is in its purview apparently not well taken. A union petition to be sure must be backed by a 30% showing of employee interest. But the sufficiency of such a showing is not litigable by the parties.

In light of the statutory scheme and the practical administrative procedural questions involved, we cannot say that the Board's decision that the union should go forward and ask for an election on the employer's refusal to recognize the authorization cards was arbitrary and capricious or an abuse of discretion.

In sum, we sustain the Board in holding that, unless an employer has engaged in an unfair labor practice that impairs the electoral process,[10] a union with authorization cards purporting to represent a majority of the employees, which is refused recognition, has the burden of taking the next step in invoking the Board's election procedure.

Reversed.

■ Mr. Justice Stewart, with whom Mr. Justice White, Mr. Justice Marshall, and Mr. Justice Powell join, dissenting. * * *

---

**10.** We do not reach the question whether the same result obtains if the employer breaches its agreement to permit majority status to be determined by means other than a Board election. See Snow & Sons, 134 N.L.R.B. 709 (1961), enf'd, 308 F.2d 687 (C.A.9 1962). * * *

Section 9(a) expressly provides that the employees' exclusive bargaining representative shall be the union "designated or selected" by a majority of the employees in an appropriate unit. Neither § 9(a) nor § 8(a)(5), which makes it an unfair labor practice for an employer to refuse to bargain with the representative of his employees, specifies how that representative is to be chosen. The language of the Act thus seems purposefully designed to impose a duty upon an employer to bargain whenever the union representative presents convincing evidence of majority support, regardless of the method by which that support is demonstrated. And both the Board and this Court have in the past consistently interpreted §§ 8(a)(5) and 9(a) to mean exactly that. * * *

As the Court recognized in *Gissel,* the 1947 Taft–Hartley amendments strengthen this interpretation of the Act. One early version of the House bill would have amended the Act to permit the Board to find an employer unfair labor practice for refusing to bargain with a union only if the union was "currently recognized by the employer or certified as such [through an election] under section 9." Section 8(a)(5) of H.R. 3020, 80th Cong., 1st Sess. The proposed change, which would have eliminated any method of requiring employer recognition of a union other than a Board-supervised election, was rejected in Conference. H.R.Conf.Rep. No. 510, 80th Cong., 1st Sess., 41. After rejection of the proposed House amendment, the House Conference Report explicitly stated that § 8(a)(5) was intended to follow the provisions of "existing law." Ibid. And "existing law" unequivocally recognized that a union could establish majority status and thereby impose a bargaining obligation on an unwilling employer by means other than petitioning for and winning a Board-supervised election. NLRB v. Gissel Packing Co., supra, at 596–598, 89 S.Ct. 1918, 1930–1932.

[The NLRB] may define "convincing evidence of majority support" solely by reference to objective criteria—for example, by reference to "a union-called strike or strike vote, or, as here, by possession of cards signed by a majority of the employees * * *." Id., at 597, 89 S.Ct. at 1931.

Even with adoption of such an objective standard for measuring "convincing evidence of majority support," the employer's "subjective" doubts would be adequately safeguarded by § 9(c)(1)(B)'s assurance of the right to file his own petition for an election. * * *

* * * When an employer is confronted with "convincing evidence of majority support," he has the *option* of petitioning for an election or consenting to an expedited union-petitioned election. As the Court explains, § 9(c)(1)(B) does not require the employer to exercise this option. If he does not, however, and if he does not voluntarily recognize the union, he must take the risk that his conduct will be found by the Board to constitute a violation of his § 8(a)(5) duty to bargain. In short, petitioning for an election is not an employer obligation; it is a device created by Congress for the employer's self-protection, much as Congress gave unions the right to petition for elections to establish their majority status but deliberately chose not to require a union to seek an election before it could impose a

bargaining obligation on an unwilling employer. NLRB v. Gissel Packing Co., 395 U.S., at 598–599, 89 S.Ct., at 1932–1933. * * *

———

## PROBLEMS FOR DISCUSSION

**1.** In explaining the Court's preference for NLRB-supervised representation elections over Section 8(a)(5) unfair labor practice proceedings as a method for establishing bargaining rights, Justice Douglas stated little more than that elections are significantly shorter. Can you think of additional reasons that he might have offered?

**2.** In its *Gissel* decision, the Court conjectured that most employers know when a union is organizing and gathering authorization cards, so that employees are generally as likely to learn of the employer's arguments against unionization then as they are when there is a full campaign leading to a certification election. (This proposition also bears upon the issue in *Linden Lumber,* does it not?) Are you in agreement with the Court's methodology or its conclusion?

Consider the conclusions of Professors Getman, Goldberg & Herman, in Union Representation Elections: Law and Reality 134–35 (1976). Their empirical study of NLRB elections led them to conclude that in most elections the employer does *not* know about the card-signing drive in time to respond before a majority of the cards have been signed. They also conclude, however, that even had the employer been initially aware and had conducted a counter-campaign, relatively few workers who were inclined to sign an authorization card would have been convinced by the employer to do otherwise. "In sum, the voting decision, made after hearing the employer's arguments, is not substantially more informed than the card-signing decision. * * * The fact that most employees sign cards before having heard the employer's arguments ought not prevent the issuance of a bargaining order based on cards." (The authors nonetheless endorse the *Linden Lumber* decision. Ibid. at 153.)

**3.** Should the *Linden Lumber* decision be legislatively overruled? The Commission on the Future of Worker–Management Relations found the average period between the filing of a petition and the holding of an election—of between seven to eight weeks—to be too long. The time elapsed allows (if not encourages) a heated campaign that heightens the adversarial quality of the relationship and makes the achievement of a collective agreement (should the union win) more difficult. The Commission recommended that the election be held as promptly as possible—within two weeks—and that any contested issues be heard later, a power the Board once exercised but currently lacks as a result of the Taft–Hartley Act. See Angelica Healthcare Services Group, 315 NLRB 1320 (1995). Alternatively, Professor Paul Weiler has recommended, based on the Canadian experience, that the NLRA should be amended to authorize the Board to certify a union on the basis of authorization cards from a majority of the employees, a power the Board exercised until 1939. He contends that employers have no more right to participate in employee representation elections than does the Canadian government have a right to participate in an American presidential campaign simply because the election outcome will significantly affect Canadian interests. See Weiler, Promises to Keep: Securing Workers' Rights to Self–Organization Under the NLRA, 96 Harv. L. Rev. 1979 (1983). Do you agree? Is the argument to employer non-intervention persuasive? See Becker,

Democracy in the Workplace: Union Representation Elections and Federal Labor Law, 77 Minn. L. Rev. 495 (1993).

--------

## Brooks v. NLRB[b]

348 U.S. 96, 75 S.Ct. 176, 99 L.Ed. 125 (1954).

■ MR. JUSTICE FRANKFURTER delivered the opinion of the Court.

The National Labor Relations Board conducted a representation election in petitioner's Chrysler–Plymouth agency on April 12, 1951. District Lodge No. 727, International Association of Machinists, won by a vote of eight to five, and the Labor Board certified it as the exclusive bargaining representative on April 20. A week after the election and the day before the certification, petitioner received a handwritten letter signed by 9 of the 13 employees in the bargaining unit stating: "We, the undersigned majority of the employees * * * are not in favor of being represented by Union Local No. 727 as a bargaining agent."

Relying on this letter and the decision of the Court of Appeals for the Sixth Circuit in National Labor Relations Board v. Vulcan Forging Co., 188 F.2d 927, petitioner refused to bargain with the union. The Labor Board found, 98 N.L.R.B. 976, that petitioner had thereby committed an unfair labor practice in violation of §§ 8(a)(1) and 8(a)(5) of the amended National Labor Relations Act, 61 Stat. 140–141, 29 U.S.C. § 158(a)(1), (a)(5), 29 U.S.C.A. § 158(a)(1, 5), and the Court of Appeals for the Ninth Circuit enforced the Board's order to bargain, 204 F.2d 899. In view of the conflict between the Circuits, we granted certiorari, 347 U.S. 916, 74 S.Ct. 517.

The issue before us is the duty of an employer toward a duly certified bargaining agent if, shortly after the election which resulted in the certification, the union has lost, without the employer's fault, a majority of the employees from its membership.

Under the original Wagner Act, the Labor Board was given the power to certify a union as the exclusive representative of the employees in a bargaining unit when it had determined by election or "any other suitable method", that the union commanded majority support. § 9(c), 49 Stat. 453. In exercising this authority the Board evolved a number of working rules, of which the following are relevant to our purpose:

(a) A certification, if based on a Board-conducted election, must be honored for a "reasonable" period, ordinarily "one year," in the absence of "unusual circumstances."

(b) "Unusual circumstances" were found in at least three situations: (1) the certified union dissolved or became defunct; (2) as a result of a schism, substantially all the members and officers of the certified union

**b.** See Comment, "Application of the Good–Faith–Doubt Test to the Presumption of Continued Majority Status of Incumbent Unions," 1981 Duke L.J. 718.

transferred their affiliation to a new local or international; (3) the size of the bargaining unit fluctuated radically within a short time.

(c) Loss of majority support after the "reasonable" period could be questioned in two ways: (1) employer's refusal to bargain, or (2) petition by a rival union for a new election.

(d) If the initial election resulted in a majority for "no union," the election—unlike a certification—did not bar a second election within a year.

The Board uniformly found an unfair labor practice where, during the so-called "certification year," an employer refused to bargain on the ground that the certified union no longer possessed a majority. While the courts in the main enforced the Board's decisions, they did not commit themselves to one year as the determinate content of reasonableness. The Board and the courts proceeded along this line of reasoning:

(a) In the political and business spheres, the choice of the voters in an election binds them for a fixed time. This promotes a sense of responsibility in the electorate and needed coherence in administration. These considerations are equally relevant to healthy labor relations.

(b) Since an election is a solemn and costly occasion, conducted under safeguards to voluntary choice, revocation of authority should occur by a procedure no less solemn than that of the initial designation. A petition or a public meeting—in which those voting for and against unionism are disclosed to management, and in which the influences of mass psychology are present—is not comparable to the privacy and independence of the voting booth.

(c) A union should be given ample time for carrying out its mandate on behalf of its members, and should not be under exigent pressure to produce hothouse results or be turned out.

(d) It is scarcely conducive to bargaining in good faith for an employer to know that, if he dillydallies or subtly undermines, union strength may erode and thereby relieve him of his statutory duties at any time, while if he works conscientiously toward agreement, the rank and file may, at the last moment, repudiate their agent.

(e) In situations, not wholly rare, where unions are competing, raiding and strife will be minimized if elections are not at the hazard of informal and short-term recall.

Certain aspects of the Labor Board's representation procedures came under scrutiny in the Congress that enacted the Taft–Hartley Act in 1947, 61 Stat. 136. Congress was mindful that, once employees had chosen a union, they could not vote to revoke its authority and refrain from union activities, while if they voted against having a union in the first place, the union could begin at once to agitate for a new election. The National Labor Relations Act was amended to provide that (a) employees could petition the Board for a decertification election, at which they would have an opportunity to choose no longer to be represented by a union, 61 Stat. 144, 29 U.S.C. § 159(c)(1)(A)(ii), 29 U.S.C.A. § 159(c)(1)(A)(ii); (b) an employer, if in doubt as to the majority claimed by a union without formal election or beset by the conflicting claims of rival unions, could likewise petition the Board for an election, 61 Stat. 144, 29 U.S.C. § 159(c)(1)(B), 29 U.S.C.A. § 159(c)(1)(B); (c) after a valid certification or decertification election had been conducted, the Board could not hold a second election in the same bargaining unit until a year had elapsed, 61 Stat. 144, 29 U.S.C. § 159(c)(3), 29 U.S.C.A. § 159(c)(3); (d) Board certification could only be granted as the result of an election, 61 Stat. 144, 29 U.S.C. § 159(c)(1), 29 U.S.C.A. § 159(c)(1), though an employer would presumably still be under a duty to bargain with an uncertified union that had a clear majority, see National Labor Relations Board v. Kobritz, 1 Cir., 193 F.2d 8.

The Board continued to apply its "one-year certification" rule after the Taft–Hartley Act came into force, except that even "unusual circumstances" no longer left the Board free to order an election where one had taken place within the preceding 12 months. * * * The issue is open here. * * *

Petitioner contends that whenever an employer is presented with evidence that his employees have deserted their certified union, he may forthwith refuse to bargain. In effect, he seeks to vindicate the rights of his employees to select their bargaining representative. * * * The underlying purpose of this statute is industrial peace. To allow employers to rely on employees' rights in refusing to bargain with the formally designated union is not conducive to that end, it is inimical to it. Congress has devised a formal mode for selection and rejection of bargaining agents and has fixed the spacing of elections, with a view of furthering industrial stability and with due regard to administrative prudence.

We find wanting the arguments against these controlling considerations. * * *

To be sure, what we have said has special pertinence only to the period during which a second election is impossible. * * * [T]he Board has ruled that one year after certification the employer can ask for an election or, if he has fair doubts about the union's continuing majority, he may refuse to bargain further with it. This, too, is a matter appropriately determined by the Board's administrative authority.

We conclude that the judgment of the Court of Appeals enforcing the Board's order must be affirmed.

———

Upon the expiration of the "certification year," the presumption of majority status continues, but it becomes rebuttable. There is also a presumption of continued majority status following the expiration of a collective bargaining agreement. The applicable principles were reviewed by the Board in BARTENDERS ASS'N v. LOCAL 510, 213 N.L.R.B. 651 (1974). There, the union and the employers' association had a long history of collective bargaining. Following the expiration of a labor contract in June 1973, the union and the association continued to negotiate. In August, the employers notified the union that they doubted the union's continued majority and would not bargain until the union demonstrated that it had majority support. The Board endorsed the following statement:

"It is well settled that a certified union, upon expiration of the first year following its certification, enjoys a rebuttable presumption that its majority representative status continues. This presumption is designed to promote stability in collective-bargaining relationships, without impairing the free choice of employees. Accordingly, once the presumption is shown to be operative, a *prima facie* case is established that an employer is obligated to bargain and that its refusal to do so would be unlawful. The *prima facie* case may be rebutted if the employer affirmatively establishes either (1) that at the time of the refusal the union in fact no longer enjoyed majority representative status; or (2) that the employer's refusal was predicated on a good-faith and reasonably grounded doubt of the union's continued majority status. As to the second of these, i.e., 'good faith doubt,' two prerequisites for sustaining the defense are that the asserted doubt must be based on objective considerations and it must not have been advanced for the purpose of gaining time in which to undermine the union. [This second point means, in effect, the assertion of doubt must be raised 'in a context free of unfair labor practices.']"

The Board held that the rebuttable presumption favoring the incumbent union operates in the same manner if the union's majority status was initially established without the benefit of Board certification. The employer association attempted to establish an objective basis for a good faith doubt by pointing out that only about one-third of the employees in the appropriate unit had authorized dues checkoffs under the expired contract and that fewer than half were union members. The Board, however, observed that employees could be union supporters without wishing to incur the obligations of union membership; moreover, the number of employees authorizing dues checkoffs was a particularly unreliable indication of union support, since some employees might pay dues directly to the union. The employer association was therefore ordered to bargain.

The principles of presumptive majority support for the incumbent union can on occasion place the employer in a most difficult legal position, for pointing in the other direction are the principles embraced in the so-called *Midwest Piping* doctrine. In Midwest Piping & Supply Co., 63 NLRB 1060 (1945)(see pp. 213–18, supra), the Board held that an employer must refrain from recognizing either of two unions which are presenting conflicting recognition claims in an NLRB election proceeding; favoring one union unfairly accords it prestige and induces employees to support it. The Board has vacillated on the question whether an employer must take a similarly neutral position when it is engaged in bargaining for a successor labor agreement with an incumbent union, and an insurgent union makes a majority claim or petitions for an election (supported by a thirty percent showing of interest). Would you advise an employer that the incumbent union is presumed to have continued majority support, and the employer must continue to bargain, up until the time the insurgent union makes a colorable claim of majority support? or up until the time that it petitions for an election? or up until the time the insurgent wins the election, and not before then? See RCA del Caribe, Inc. v. Kuinlam, 262 NLRB 963 (1982); Signal Transformer Co. v. Local 431, 265 NLRB 272 (1982).

An employer is generally free to test a union's continuing majority upon the expiration of a contract either by refraining from recognizing and bargaining with the union, thus precipitating an unfair labor practice charge under Section 8(a)(5), or by petitioning for a representation election. At one time the Board held that the employer had to demonstrate in the refusal-to-bargain case that it had a good faith doubt of the union's continuing majority, in order to make out a defense, but that no such showing had to be made to warrant the employer's securing an election. Recognizing the anomaly, the Board changed this rule in United States Gypsum Co., 157 NLRB 652 (1966), and now requires that an employer, in order to secure a representation election to test the status of an incumbent union, must also demonstrate objective grounds for doubting the union's majority support.

————

## PROBLEMS FOR DISCUSSION

**1.** Are not the principles articulated in the *Brooks* decision unconvincing from the perspective of both the employer and the union? Thus, consider the employer's argument: "When the contract term ends, why should the union be presumed to have continued majority support? *Gissel* and *Linden Lumber* assume that elections are the preferred method for assessing employee support for the union, and that lesser showings (such as presumptions anchored in an employee referendum years before) run the risk of imposing an unwanted union on a majority of the workers. What is unfair about making the union justify its incumbency in all cases through a prompt election?" Compare Daisy's Originals, Inc. v. NLRB, 468 F.2d 493 (5th Cir.1972), with NLRB v. Frick Co., 423 F.2d 1327 (3d Cir.1970). See also NLRB v. Tahoe Nugget, Inc., 584 F.2d 293 (9th Cir.1978).

The union, on the other hand, argues: "Why should an employer be able to challenge the union's incumbency, when the contract expires, for *any* reason—even a 'good faith doubt' that its majority status continues? The statute is designed to protect *employee* rights, and employees are fully protected in their own right to challenge their union's status through a decertification election under Section 9(c)(1)(A)(ii). If the employees do not petition to oust their union, why should an employer—in good faith or otherwise—be able to do so?"

Which position is soundest—the employer's, the union's, or the Supreme Court's in *Brooks*?

**2.** When United Shoe Workers presented evidence that 390 of 560 employees had become members, Sof'-Shoe, Inc. granted recognition and commenced collective bargaining. Negotiations have gone on for four months. Some points of agreement have been reached but not on such major issues as wages, seniority, union security, and arbitration. Sof'-Shoe is convinced (1) that all except 60 or 70 employees have already lost interest in United Shoe Workers and (2) that, if it were to withdraw recognition and grant an immediate, long-overdue wage increase, union sentiment would disappear entirely. What would be your advice? See NLRB v. San Clemente Pub. Corp., 408 F.2d 367 (9th Cir.1969); Brennan's Cadillac, Inc., 231 NLRB 225 (1977).

--------

## NLRB v. Curtin Matheson Scientific, Inc.[c]

494 U.S. 775, 110 S.Ct. 1542, 108 L.Ed.2d 801 (1990).

■ Justice Marshall delivered the opinion of the Court.

This case presents the question whether the National Labor Relations Board, in evaluating an employer's claim that it had a reasonable basis for doubting a union's majority support, *must* presume that striker replacements oppose the union. We hold that the Board acted within its discretion in refusing to adopt a presumption of replacement opposition to the union and therefore reverse the judgment of the Court of Appeals.

I

Upon certification by the NLRB as the exclusive bargaining agent for a unit of employees, a union enjoys an irrebuttable presumption of majority support for one year. Fall River Dyeing & Finishing Corp. v. NLRB, 482 U.S. 27, 37, 107 S.Ct. 2225, 2232, 96 L.Ed.2d 22 (1987). During that time, an employer's refusal to bargain with the union is *per se* an unfair labor practice under §§ 8(a)(1) and 8(a)(5) of the National Labor Relations Act, 49 Stat. 452, as amended, 29 U.S.C. §§ 158(a)(1), 158(a)(5) (1982 ed.). See Celanese Corp. of America, 95 N.L.R.B. 664, 672 (1951); R. Gorman, Labor Law, Unionization and Collective Bargaining 109 (1976). After the first year, the presumption continues but is rebuttable. *Fall River,* supra, at 38, 107 S.Ct., at 2233. Under the Board's longstanding approach, an employer may rebut that presumption by showing that, at the time of the refusal to bargain, either (1) the union did not *in fact* enjoy majority support, or (2) the employer had a "good faith" doubt, founded on a sufficient objective basis, of the union's majority support. Station KKHI, 284 N.L.R.B. 1339 (1987), enf'd, 891 F.2d 230 (C.A.9 1989). The question presented in this case is whether the Board must, in determining whether an employer has presented sufficient objective evidence of a good-faith doubt, presume that striker replacements oppose the union.

The Board has long presumed that new employees hired in nonstrike circumstances support the incumbent union in the same proportion as the employees they replace. See, *e.g.,* National Plastic Products Co., 78 N.L.R.B. 699, 706 (1948). The Board's approach to evaluating the union

c.   See Flynn, The Economic Strike Bar: Looking Beyond the "Union Sentiments" of Permanent Replacements, 61 Temple L.Rev. 691 (1988); LeRoy, Strike Crossovers and Strike Replacements: An Empirical Test of the NLRB's No Presumption Policy, 33 Ariz. L.Rev. 291 (1991).

sentiments of employees hired to replace strikers, however, has not been so consistent. Initially, the Board appeared to assume that replacements did not support the union. See, *e.g.*, Stoner Rubber Co., 123 N.L.R.B. 1440, 1444 (1959) (stating that it was not "unreasonable [for the employer] to assume that none of the ... permanent replacements were union adherents") * * * *

[I]n Cutten Supermarket, 220 N.L.R.B. 507 (1975), the Board reversed course completely, stating that striker replacements, like new employees generally, are presumed to *support* the union in the same ratio as the strikers they replaced. Id., at 509. The Board's initial adherence to this new approach, however, was equivocal. * * * Nevertheless, in Windham Community Memorial Hospital, 230 N.L.R.B. 1070 (1977), enf'd, 577 F.2d 805 (C.A.2 1978), the Board explicitly reaffirmed Cutten Supermarket, stating that "[t]he general rule ... is that new employees, including striker replacements, are presumed to support the union in the same ratio as those whom they have replaced." 230 N.L.R.B., at 1070. * * * Finally, in 1980, the Board reiterated that the presumption that new employees support the union applies equally to striker replacements. Pennco, Inc., 250 N.L.R.B. 716, 717–718 (1980), enf'd, 684 F.2d 340 (CA6), cert. denied, 459 U.S. 994, 103 S.Ct. 355, 74 L.Ed.2d 392 (1982).

In 1987, after several Courts of Appeals rejected the Board's approach, the Board determined that no universal generalizations could be made about replacements' union sentiments that would justify a presumption either of support for or of opposition to the union. Station KKHI, 284 N.L.R.B. 1339 (1987). On the one hand, the Board found that the prounion presumption lacked empirical foundation because "incumbent unions and strikers sometimes have shown hostility toward the permanent replacements" and "replacements are typically aware of the union's primary concern for the striker's welfare, rather than that of the replacements." Id., at 1344. On the other hand, the Board found that an anti-union presumption was "equally unsupportable" factually. Ibid. The Board observed that a striker replacement "may be forced to work for financial reasons, or may disapprove of the strike in question but still desire union representation and would support other union initiatives." Ibid. Moreover, the Board found as a matter of policy that adoption of an antiunion presumption would "substantially impair the employees' right to strike by adding to the risk of replacement the risk of loss of the bargaining representative as soon as replacements equal in number to the strikers are willing to cross the picket line." Ibid. See also Pennco, Inc., 250 N.L.R.B., at 717. Accordingly, the Board held that it would not apply any presumption regarding striker replacements' union sentiments, but would determine their views on a case-by-case basis. 284 N.L.R.B., at ___.

## II

We now turn to the Board's application of its *Station KKHI* no-presumption approach in this case. Respondent Curtin Matheson Scientific, Inc., buys and sells laboratory instruments and supplies. In 1970, the Board certified Teamsters Local 968, General Drivers, Warehousemen and Helpers as the collective-bargaining agent for respondent's production and maintenance employees. On May 21, 1979, the most recent bargaining agreement between respondent and the Union expired. Respondent made its final offer for a new agreement on May 25, but the Union rejected that offer. Respondent then locked out the 27 bargaining-unit employees. On June 12, respondent renewed its May 25 offer, but the Union again rejected it. The Union then commenced an economic strike. The record contains no evidence of any strike-related violence or threats of violence.

Five employees immediately crossed the picket line and reported for work. On June 25, while the strike was still in effect, respondent hired 29 permanent replacement employees to replace the 22 strikers. The Union ended its strike on July 16, offering to accept unconditionally respondent's May 25 contract offer. On July 20, respondent informed the Union that the May 25 offer was no longer available. In addition, respondent withdrew recognition from the Union and refused to bargain further, stating that it doubted that the Union was supported by a majority of the employees in the unit. Respondent subsequently refused to provide the Union with information it had requested concerning the total number of bargaining-unit employees on the payroll, and the job classification and seniority of each employee. As of July 20, the bargaining unit consisted of 19 strikers, 25 permanent replacements, and the 5 employees who had crossed the picket line at the strike's inception.

On July 30, the Union filed an unfair labor practice charge with the Board [under sections 8(a)(1) and 8(a)(5). The Board held] that respondent lacked sufficient objective basis to doubt the Union's majority support. 287 N.L.R.B. No. 35 (1987). * * *

* * * [R]egarding respondent's hiring of striker replacements, the Board stated that, in accordance with the *Station KKHI* approach, it would "not use any presumptions with respect to [the replacements'] union sentiments," but would instead "take a case-by-case approach [and] require additional evidence of a lack of union support on the replacements' part in evaluating the significance of this factor in the employer's showing of good-faith doubt." 287 N.L.R.B., at ___ (slip op., at 8–9). The Board noted that respondent's only evidence of the replacements' attitudes toward the Union was its employee relations director's account of a conversation with one of the replacements. The replacement employee reportedly told her that he had worked in union and nonunion workplaces and did not see any need for a union as long as the company treated him well; in addition, he said that he did not think the Union in this case represented the employees. Id., at ___; see n. 4, supra. The Board did not determine whether this statement indicated the replacement employee's repudiation of the Union, but found that the statement was, in any event, an insufficient basis for "inferring the union sentiments of the replacement employees as a group." 287 N.L.R.B., at ___ (slip op., at 9).

The Board therefore concluded that "the evidence [was] insufficient to rebut the presumption of the Union's continuing majority status." Id., at

___ (slip op., at 10). Accordingly, the Board held that respondent had violated §§ 8(a)(1) and 8(a)(5) by withdrawing recognition from the Union, failing to furnish the requested information, and refusing to execute a contract embodying the terms respondent had offered on May 25, 1979. The Board ordered respondent to bargain with the Union on request, provide the requisite information, execute an agreement, and make the bargaining-unit employees whole for whatever losses they had suffered from respondent's failure to execute a contract.

The Court of Appeals, in a divided opinion, refused to enforce the Board's order, holding that respondent was justified in doubting the Union's majority support. 859 F.2d 362 (C.A.5 1988). Specifically, the court rejected the Board's decision not to apply any presumption in evaluating striker replacements' union sentiments and endorsed the so-called "Gorman presumption" that striker replacements oppose the union.[6] We granted certiorari, 492 U.S. 905, 109 S.Ct. 3212, 106 L.Ed.2d 563 (1989), to resolve a circuit split on the question whether the Board must presume that striker replacements oppose the union.

### III

### A

This Court has emphasized often that the NLRB has the primary responsibility for developing and applying national labor policy. * * *

This Court therefore has accorded Board rules considerable deference. See Fall River Dyeing & Finishing Corp. v. NLRB, 482 U.S. 27, 42, 107 S.Ct. 2225, 2235, 96 L.Ed.2d 22 (1987); NLRB v. Iron Workers, 434 U.S. 335, 350, 98 S.Ct. 651, 660, 54 L.Ed.2d 586 (1978). We will uphold a Board rule as long as it is rational and consistent with the Act * * * *

### B

Before assessing the Board's justification for rejecting the antiunion presumption, we will make clear precisely how that presumption would differ in operation from the Board's current approach. As noted above, * * *, the starting point for the Board's analysis is the basic presumption that the union is supported by a majority of bargaining-unit employees. The employer bears the burden of rebutting that presumption, after the certification year, either by showing that the union in fact lacks majority support or by demonstrating a sufficient objective basis for doubting the union's majority status. Respondent here urges that in evaluating an employer's claim of a good-faith doubt, the Board must adopt a second,

---

**6.** The "Gorman presumption" derives its name from Professor Robert Gorman's statement in his labor law treatise that "if a new hire agrees to serve as a replacement for a striker (in union parlance, as a strikebreaker, or worse), it is generally assumed that he does not support the union and that he ought not be counted toward a union majority." R. Gorman, Labor Law, Unionization and Collective Bargaining 112 (1976). In context, however, this statement does not appear to endorse a presumption, but seems merely to describe the Board's former approach to evaluating replacements' union sentiments. Id., at 112–113 (citing Titan Metal Mfg. Co., 135 N.L.R.B. 196 (1962)).

subsidiary presumption—that replacement employees oppose the union. Under this approach, if a majority of employees in the bargaining unit were striker replacements, the employer would not need to offer *any* objective evidence of the employees' union sentiments to rebut the presumption of the union's continuing majority status. The presumption of the replacements' opposition to the union would, in effect, override the presumption of continuing majority status. In contrast, under its no-presumption approach the Board "take[s] into account the particular circumstances surrounding each strike and the hiring of replacements, while retaining the long-standing requirement that the employer must come forth with some objective evidence to substantiate his doubt of continuing majority status." 859 F.2d, at 370 (Williams, J., dissenting).

## C

We find the Board's no-presumption approach rational as an empirical matter. Presumptions normally arise when proof of one fact renders the existence of another fact "so probable that it is sensible and timesaving to assume the truth of [the inferred] fact . . . until the adversary disproves it." E. Cleary, McCormick on Evidence § 343, p. 969 (3d ed. 1984). Although replacements often may not favor the incumbent union, the Board reasonably concluded, in light of its long experience in addressing these issues, that replacements may in some circumstances desire union representation despite their willingness to cross the picket line. Economic concerns, for instance, may force a replacement employee to work for a struck employer even though he otherwise supports the union and wants the benefits of union representation. In this sense the replacement worker is no different from a striker who, feeling the financial heat of the strike on herself and her family, is forced to abandon the picket line and go back to work. Cf. Lyng v. Automobile Workers, 485 U.S. 360, 371, 108 S.Ct. 1184, 1192, 99 L.Ed.2d 380 (1988)(recognizing that "a striking individual faces an immediate and often total drop in income during a strike"). In addition, a replacement, like a nonstriker or a strike crossover, may disagree with the purpose or strategy of the particular strike and refuse to support that strike, while still wanting that union's representation at the bargaining table.

Respondent insists that the interests of strikers and replacements are diametrically opposed and that unions inevitably side with the strikers. For instance, respondent argues, picket-line violence often stems directly from the hiring of replacements. Furthermore, unions often negotiate with employers for strike settlements that would return the strikers to their jobs, thereby displacing some or all of the replacements. See Belknap, Inc. v. Hale, 463 U.S. 491, 513–514, 103 S.Ct. 3172, 3184–3185, 77 L.Ed.2d 798 (1983)(BLACKMUN, J., concurring in judgment). Respondent asserts that replacements, aware of the union's loyalty to the strikers, most likely would not support the union. * * *

These arguments do not persuade us that the Board's position is irrational. Unions do not inevitably demand displacement of all strike replacements. * * *

The extent to which a union demands displacement of permanent replacement workers logically will depend on the union's bargaining power. * * * If, for example, the jobs at issue do not require highly trained workers and the replacements perform as well as the strikers did, the employer will have little incentive to hire back the strikers and fire the replacements; consequently, the union will have little bargaining power. Consumers' reaction to a strike will also determine the union's bargaining position. If the employer's customers have no reluctance to cross the picket line and deal with the employer, the union will be in a poor position to bargain for a favorable settlement. Thus, a union's demands will inevitably turn on the strength of the union's hand in negotiations. A union with little bargaining leverage is unlikely to press the employer—at least not very forcefully or for very long—to discharge the replacements and reinstate all the strikers. Cognizant of the union's weak position, many if not all of the replacements justifiably may not fear that they will lose their jobs at the end of the strike. They may still want that union's representation after the strike, though, despite the union's lack of bargaining strength during the strike, because of the union's role in processing grievances, monitoring the employer's actions, and performing other non-strike roles. Because the circumstances of each strike and the leverage of each union will vary greatly, it was not irrational for the Board to reject the antiunion presumption and adopt a case-by-case approach in determining replacements' union sentiments.[9] * * *

Furthermore, the Board has not deemed picket-line violence or a union's demand that replacements be terminated irrelevant to its evaluation of replacements' attitudes toward the union. The Board's position, rather, is that "the hiring of permanent replacements who cross a picket line, *in itself,* does not support an inference that the replacements repudiate the union as collective-bargaining representative." Station KKHI, 284 N.L.R.B., at 1344 (emphasis added). In both Station KKHI and this case, the Board noted that the picket line was peaceful, id., at ___; Curtin Matheson Scientific, 287 N.L.R.B., at ___; and in neither case did the employer present evidence that the union was actively negotiating for ouster of the replacements. * * * *

In sum, the Board recognized that the circumstances surrounding each strike and replacements' reasons for crossing a picket line vary greatly. Even if replacements often do not support the union, then, it was not irrational for the Board to conclude that the probability of replacement opposition to the union is insufficient to justify an antiunion presumption.

---

**9.** Justice Scalia characterizes this view as "embarrassingly wide of the mark" and asserts, without any factual support, that unions "almost certain[ly]" demand displacement of striker replacements. Post, at 1560 (Scalia, J., dissenting). We are confident that the Board, with its vast reservoir of experience in resolving labor disputes, is better situated than members of this Court to determine the frequency with which unions demand displacement of striker replacements.

Furthermore, the facts of this case belie Justice Scalia's sweeping characterization of the inevitability of such demands, as the Union did not negotiate for the discharge of replacements as a condition for settling the strike. * * *

## D

The Board's refusal to adopt an antiunion presumption is also consistent with the Act's "overriding policy" of achieving " 'industrial peace.' " *Fall River,* 482 U.S., at 38, 107 S.Ct., at 2233 (quoting Brooks v. NLRB, 348 U.S. 96, 103, 75 S.Ct. 176, 181, 99 L.Ed. 125 (1954)). In *Fall River,* the Court held that the presumption of continuing majority support for a union "further[s] this policy by 'promot[ing] stability in collective-bargaining relationships, without impairing the free choice of employees.' " * * *

The Board's approach to determining the union views of strike replacements is directed at this same goal because it limits employers' ability to oust a union without adducing any evidence of the employees' union sentiments and encourages negotiated solutions to strikes. It was reasonable for the Board to conclude that the antiunion presumption, in contrast, could allow an employer to eliminate the union merely by hiring a sufficient number of replacement employees. That rule thus might encourage the employer to avoid good-faith bargaining over a strike settlement, and instead to use the strike as a means of removing the union altogether. * * * Restricting an employer's ability to use a strike as a means of terminating the bargaining relationship serves the policies of promoting industrial stability and negotiated settlements. * * *

Furthermore, it was reasonable for the Board to decide that the antiunion presumption might chill employees' exercise of their statutory right to engage in "concerted activities," including the right to strike. See 49 Stat. 452, as amended, 29 U.S.C. § 157 (1982 ed.)("Employees shall have the right ... to engage in ... concerted activities for the purpose of collective bargaining or other mutual aid or protection"). If an employer could remove a union merely by hiring a sufficient number of replacements, employees considering a strike would face not only the prospect of being permanently replaced, but also a greater risk that they would lose their bargaining representative, thereby diminishing their chance of obtaining reinstatement through a strike settlement. It was rational for the Board to conclude, then, that adoption of the antiunion presumption could chill employees' exercise of their right to strike.[13]

Although the Board generally may not act "as an arbiter of the sort of economic weapons the parties can use," NLRB v. Insurance Agents', 361 U.S. 477, 497, 80 S.Ct. 419, 431, 4 L.Ed.2d 454 (1960), it may adopt rules

---

**13.** Justice Scalia entirely ignores the Board's policy considerations, apparently on the rationale that policy is an illegitimate factor in the Board's decision. See post, at 1562–1563 (Scalia, J., dissenting). This argument is founded on the premise that the issue before us is the factual question whether substantial evidence supports the Board's finding that respondent lacked a good-faith doubt. As stated earlier, however, * * *, the real question is whether the Board must, in assessing the objective reasonableness of an employer's doubt, adopt a particular presumption. Certainly the Board is entitled to consider *both* whether the presumption is factually justified *and* whether that presumption would disserve the Act's policies. See Baptist Hospital, 442 U.S., at 787, 99 S.Ct., at 2606. We need not determine whether the Board's policy considerations *alone* would justify its refusal to adopt the presumption urged by respondent because we find the Board's decision not irrational as a factual matter. See supra, at 1550–1553.

restricting conduct that threatens to destroy the collective-bargaining relationship or that may impair employees' right to engage in concerted activity. * * * We therefore find, in light of the considerable deference we accord Board rules, see supra, at 1548–1549, that the Board's approach is consistent with the Act.

■ Chief JUSTICE REHNQUIST, concurring.

The Board's "no-presumption" rule seems to me to press to the limit the deference to which the Board is entitled in assessing industrial reality, but for the reasons stated in the opinion of the Court I agree that limit is not exceeded. * * *

[The dissenting opinion of Justice Blackmun is omitted.]

■ JUSTICE SCALIA, with whom JUSTICE O'CONNOR and JUSTICE KENNEDY join, dissenting.

The Court makes heavy weather out of what is, under well-established principles of administrative law, a straightforward case. * * * Since the principal employment-related interest of strike replacements (to retain their jobs) is almost invariably opposed to the principal interest of the striking union (to replace them with its striking members) it seems to me impossible to conclude on this record that the employer did not have a reasonable, good-faith doubt regarding the union's majority status. The Board's factual finding being unsupported by substantial evidence, it cannot stand. I therefore dissent from the judgment reversing the Fifth Circuit's refusal to enforce the Board's order.

* * * As the Board's cases have explained:

"Strike replacements can reasonably foresee that, if the union is successful, the strikers will return to work and the strike replacements will be out of a job. It is understandable that unions do not look with favor on persons who cross their picket lines and perform the work of strikers." Leveld Wholesale, Inc., 218 N.L.R.B. 1344, 1350 (1975).

"The Union had been bargaining agent for those discharged employees and there can be no question that the Union's loyalty lay with these employees. The interests of the discharged employees were diametrically opposed to those of the strike replacements. If the discharged employees returned to work, the strike replacements would lose their jobs." Beacon Upholstery Co., 226 N.L.R.B. 1360, 1368 (1976) (footnote omitted).

* * * There was, moreover, not a shred of affirmative evidence that any strike replacement supported, or had reason to support, the union. On those facts, any reasonable factfinder must conclude that the respondent possessed, not necessarily a certainty, but at least a reasonable, good-faith doubt, that the union did not have majority support. At least three Circuit Courts of Appeals have effectively agreed with this assessment, considering

strike replacements as opposed to the union in reversing Board findings of no reasonable, good-faith doubt. * * *

---

## PROBLEM FOR DISCUSSION

Ironwork, Inc. and the Ironworkers' Union have been negotiating over the terms of a new collective bargaining agreement after the previous one expired on October 1. On October 15, the Company made its final offer and the Union struck. Starting October 28, picketing employees began to return to work and to express dissatisfaction with being represented by the Union. About two-thirds had done so by November 14. On November 24, the Union telegrammed the Company its acceptance of the October 15 offer and made an unconditional offer for the remaining strikers to return to work. On November 25, the Company telegrammed the Union that it "now has reason to believe that the Union no longer represents a majority of the employees in the appropriate unit and therefore disavows any obligation to carry on any further negotiations." Has the Company violated section 8(a)(5)? What should be the remedy? See Auciello Iron Works, Inc. v. NLRB, 517 U.S. 781, 116 S.Ct. 1754, 135 L.Ed.2d 64 (1996).

---

## Allentown Mack Sales and Service, Inc. v. NLRB

522 U.S. 359, 118 S.Ct. 818, 139 L.Ed.2d 797 (1998).

■ SCALIA, J., delivered the opinion for a unanimous Court with respect to Part I, the opinion of the Court with respect to Part II, in which STEVENS, SOUTER, GINSBURG, and BREYER, JJ., joined, and the opinion of the Court with respect to Parts III and IV, in which REHNQUIST, C.J., and O'CONNOR, KENNEDY, and THOMAS, JJ., joined. REHNQUIST, C.J., filed an opinion concurring in part and dissenting in part, in which O'CONNOR, KENNEDY, and THOMAS, JJ., joined. BREYER, J., filed an opinion concurring in part and dissenting in part, in which STEVENS, SOUTER, and GINSBURG, JJ., joined.

■ JUSTICE SCALIA delivered the opinion of the Court.

Under longstanding precedent of the National Labor Relations Board, an employer who believes that an incumbent union no longer enjoys the support of a majority of its employees has three options: to request a formal, Board-supervised election, to withdraw recognition from the union and refuse to bargain, or to conduct an internal poll of employee support for the union. The Board has held that the latter two are unfair labor practices unless the employer can show that it had a "good faith reasonable doubt" about the union's majority support. We must decide whether the Board's standard for employer polling is rational and consistent with the National Labor Relations Act, and whether the Board's factual determinations in this case are supported by substantial evidence in the record.

I

Mack Trucks, Inc., had a factory branch in Allentown, Pennsylvania, whose service and parts employees were represented by Local Lodge 724 of the International Association of Machinists and Aerospace Workers, AFL–CIO. Mack notified its Allentown managers in May of 1990 that it intended to sell the branch, and several of those managers formed Allentown Mack Sales, Inc., the petitioner here, which purchased the assets of the business on December 20, 1990, and began to operate it as an independent dealership. From December 21, 1990, to January 1, 1991, Allentown hired 32 of the original 45 Mack employees.

During the period before and immediately after the sale, a number of Mack employees made statements to the prospective owners of Allentown Mack Sales suggesting that the incumbent union had lost support among employees in the bargaining unit. In job interviews, eight employees made statements indicating, or at least arguably indicating, that they personally no longer supported the union. In addition, Ron Mohr, a member of the union's bargaining committee and shop steward for the Mack Trucks service department, told an Allentown manager that it was his feeling that the employees did not want a union, and that "with a new company, if a vote was taken, the Union would lose." 316 N.L.R.B. 1199, 1207, 1995 WL 221136 (1995). And Kermit Bloch, who worked for Mack Trucks as a mechanic on the night shift, told a manager that the entire night shift (then 5 or 6 employees) did not want the union.

On January 2, 1991, Local Lodge 724 asked Allentown Mack Sales to recognize it as the employees' collective-bargaining representative, and to begin negotiations for a contract. The new employer rejected that request by letter dated January 25, claiming a "good faith doubt as to support of the Union among the employees." Id., at 1205. The letter also announced that Allentown had "arranged for an independent poll by secret ballot of its hourly employees to be conducted under guidelines prescribed by the National Labor Relations Board." Ibid. The poll, supervised by a Roman Catholic priest, was conducted on February 8, 1991; the union lost 19 to 13. Shortly thereafter, the union filed an unfair-labor-practice charge with the Board.

The Administrative Law Judge (ALJ) concluded that Allentown was a "successor" employer to Mack Trucks, Inc., and therefore inherited Mack's bargaining obligation and a presumption of continuing majority support for the union. Id., at 1203. The ALJ held that Allentown's poll was conducted in compliance with the procedural standards enunciated by the Board in Struksnes Construction Co., 165 N.L.R.B. 1062 (1967), but that it violated ss 8(a)(1) and 8(a)(5) of the National Labor Relations Act (Act), 49 Stat. 452, as amended, 29 U.S.C. ss 158(a)(1) and 158(a)(5), because Allentown did not have an "objective reasonable doubt" about the majority status of the union. The Board adopted the ALJ's findings and agreed with his conclusion that Allentown "had not demonstrated that it harbored a reasonable doubt, based on objective considerations, as to the incumbent Union's continued majority status after the transition." 316 N.L.R.B., at

1199. The Board ordered Allentown to recognize and bargain with Local 724.

On review in the Court of Appeals for the District of Columbia Circuit, Allentown challenged both the facial rationality of the Board's test for employer polling and the Board's application of that standard to the facts of this case. The court enforced the Board's bargaining order, over a vigorous dissent. 83 F.3d 1483 (1996). We granted certiorari. 520 U.S. 1103, 117 S.Ct. 1105, 137 L.Ed.2d 307 (1997).

## II

... Courts must defer to the requirements imposed by the Board if they are "rational and consistent with the Act," Fall River Dyeing & Finishing Corp. v. NLRB, 482 U.S. 27, 42, 107 S.Ct. 2225, 2235, 96 L.Ed.2d 22 (1987), and if the Board's "explication is not adequate, irrational or arbitrary," NLRB v. Erie Resistor Corp., 373 U.S. 221, 236, 83 S.Ct. 1139, 1149, 10 L.Ed.2d 308 (1963). Allentown argues that it is irrational to require the same factual showing to justify a poll as to justify an outright withdrawal of recognition, because that leaves the employer with no legal incentive to poll. Under the Board's framework, the results of a poll can never supply an otherwise lacking "good faith reasonable doubt" necessary to justify a withdrawal of recognition, since the employer must already have that same reasonable doubt before he is permitted to conduct a poll. ...

While the Board's adoption of a unitary standard for polling, RM [Representation management, or employer-initiated] elections, and withdrawals of recognition is in some respects a puzzling policy, we do not find it so irrational as to be "arbitrary [or] capricious" within the meaning of the Administrative Procedure Act, 5 U.S.C. § 706. The Board believes that employer polling is potentially "disruptive" to established bargaining relationships and "unsettling" to employees, and so has chosen to limit severely the circumstances under which it may be conducted. Texas Petrochemicals Corp., 296 N.L.R.B. 1057, 1061, 1989 WL 224426 (1989), enf'd as modified, 923 F.2d 398 (C.A.5 1991). The unitary standard reflects the Board's apparent conclusion that polling should be tolerated only when the employer might otherwise simply withdraw recognition and refuse to bargain.

It is true enough that this makes polling useless as a means of insulating a contemplated withdrawal of recognition against an unfair-labor-practice charge—but there is more to life (and even to business) than escaping unfair-labor-practice findings. An employer concerned with good employee relations might recognize that abrupt withdrawal of recognition—even from a union that no longer has majority support—will certainly antagonize union supporters, and perhaps even alienate employees who are on the fence. Preceding that action with a careful, unbiased poll can prevent these consequences. The "polls are useless" argument falsely assumes, moreover, that every employer will *want* to withdraw recognition as soon as he has enough evidence of lack of union support to defend against an unfair-labor-practice charge. It seems to us that an employer whose evidence met the "good-faith reasonable doubt" standard might nonetheless want to withdraw recognition only if he had conclusive evidence that the union *in fact* lacked majority support, lest he go through the time and expense of an (ultimately victorious) unfair-labor-practice suit for a benefit that will only last until the next election. See Texas Petrochemicals, supra, at 1063. And finally, it is probably the case that, though the standard for conviction of an unfair labor practice with regard to polling is identical to the standard with regard to withdrawal of recognition, the chance that a charge will be filed is significantly less with regard to the polling, particularly if the union wins.

It must be acknowledged that the Board's avowed preference for RM elections over polls fits uncomfortably with its unitary standard; as the Court of Appeals pointed out, that preference should logically produce a more rigorous standard for polling. 83 F.3d, at 1487. But there are other reasons why the standard for polling ought to be *less* rigorous than the standard for Board elections. For one thing, the consequences of an election are more severe: if the union loses an employer poll it can still request a Board election, but if the union loses a formal election it is barred from seeking another for a year. See 29 U.S.C. § 159(c)(3). If it would be rational for the Board to set the polling standard either higher or lower than the threshold for an RM election, then surely it is not irrational for the Board to split the difference.

## III

The Board held Allentown guilty of an unfair labor practice in its conduct of the polling because it "ha[d] not demonstrated that it held a reasonable doubt, based on objective considerations, that the Union continued to enjoy the support of a majority of the bargaining unit employees." 316 N.L.R.B., at 1199. We must decide whether that conclusion is supported by substantial evidence on the record as a whole. Fall River Dyeing, 482 U.S., at 42, 107 S.Ct., at 2235; Universal Camera Corp. v. NLRB, 340 U.S. 474, 71 S.Ct. 456, 95 L.Ed. 456 (1951). Put differently, we must decide whether on this record it would have been possible for a reasonable jury to reach the Board's conclusion. See, e.g., NLRB v. Columbian Enameling & Stamping Co., 306 U.S. 292, 300, 59 S.Ct. 501, 505, 83 L.Ed. 660 (1939); Consolidated Edison Co. v. NLRB, 305 U.S. 197, 229, 59 S.Ct. 206, 216–217, 83 L.Ed. 126 (1938).

Before turning to that issue, we must clear up some semantic confusion. The Board asserted at argument that the word "doubt" may mean either "uncertainty" or "disbelief," and that its polling standard uses the word only in the latter sense. We cannot accept that linguistic revisionism. "Doubt" is precisely that sort of "disbelief" (failure to believe) which consists of an uncertainty rather than a belief in the opposite. If the subject at issue were the existence of God, for example, "doubt" would be the disbelief of the agnostic, not of the atheist. A doubt is an uncertain, tentative, or provisional disbelief. See, e.g., Webster's New International

Dictionary 776 (2d ed.1949) (def. 1: "A fluctuation of mind arising from defect of knowledge or evidence; uncertainty of judgment or mind; unsettled state of opinion concerning the reality of an event, or the truth of an assertion, etc."); 1 The New Shorter Oxford English Dictionary 734 (1993) (def. 1: "Uncertainty as to the truth or reality of something or as to the wisdom of a course of action; occasion or room for uncertainty"); American Heritage Dictionary 555 (3d ed.1992) (def. 1: "A lack of certainty that often leads to irresolution").

The question presented for review, therefore, is whether, on the evidence presented to the Board, a reasonable jury could have found that Allentown lacked a genuine, reasonable uncertainty about whether Local 724 enjoyed the continuing support of a majority of unit employees. In our view, the answer is no. The Board's finding to the contrary rests on a refusal to credit probative circumstantial evidence, and on evidentiary demands that go beyond the substantive standard the Board purports to apply.

The Board adopted the ALJ's finding that 6 of Allentown's 32 employees had made "statements which could be used as objective considerations supporting a good-faith reasonable doubt as to continued majority status by the Union." 316 N.L.R.B., at 1207. (These included, for example, the statement of Rusty Hoffman that "he did not want to work in a union shop," and "would try to find another job if he had to work with the Union." Id., at 1206.) The Board seemingly also accepted (though this is not essential to our analysis) the ALJ's willingness to assume that the statement of a seventh employee (to the effect that he "did not feel comfortable with the Union and thought it was a waste of $35 a month," ibid.) supported good-faith reasonable doubt of his support for the union—as in our view it unquestionably does. And it presumably accepted the ALJ's assessment that "7 of 32, or roughly 20 percent of the involved employees" was not alone sufficient to create "an objective reasonable doubt of union majority support," id., at 1207. The Board did not specify how many express disavowals would have been enough to establish reasonable doubt, but the number must presumably be less than 16 (half of the bargaining unit), since that would establish reasonable *certainty*. Still, we would not say that 20% first-hand-confirmed opposition (even with no countering evidence of union support) is alone enough to require a conclusion of reasonable doubt. But there was much more.

For one thing, the ALJ and the Board totally disregarded the effect upon Allentown of the statement of an eighth employee, Dennis Marsh, who said that "he was not being represented for the $35 he was paying." Ibid. The ALJ, whose findings were adopted by the Board, said that this statement "seems more an expression of a desire for better representation than one for no representation at all." Ibid. It seems to us that it is, more accurately, simply an expression of dissatisfaction with the union's performance—which *could* reflect the speaker's desire that the union represent him more effectively, but *could also* reflect the speaker's desire to save his $35 and get rid of the union. The statement would assuredly engender an *uncertainty* whether the speaker supported the union, and so could not be entirely ignored.

But the most significant evidence excluded from consideration by the Board consisted of statements of two employees regarding not merely their own support of the union, but support among the work force in general. Kermit Bloch, who worked on the night shift, told an Allentown manager "that the entire night shift did not want the Union." Ibid. The ALJ refused to credit this, because "Bloch did not testify and thus could not explain how he formed his opinion about the views of his fellow employees." Ibid. Unsubstantiated assertions that other employees do not support the union certainly do not establish *the fact of that disfavor* with the degree of reliability ordinarily demanded in legal proceedings. But under the Board's enunciated test for polling, it is not the fact of disfavor that is at issue (the poll itself is meant to establish that), but rather the existence of a reasonable uncertainty on the part of the employer regarding that fact. On that issue, absent some reason for the employer to know that Bloch had no basis for his information, or that Bloch was lying, reason demands that the statement be given considerable weight.

Another employee who gave information concerning overall support for the union was Ron Mohr, who told Allentown managers that "if a vote was taken, the Union would lose" and that "it was his feeling that the employees did not want a union." Ibid. The ALJ again objected irrelevantly that "there is no evidence with respect to how he gained this knowledge." Id., at 1208. In addition, the Board held that Allentown "could not legitimately rely on [the statement] as a basis for doubting the Union's majority status," id., at 1200, because Mohr was "referring to Mack's existing employee complement, not to the individuals who were later hired by [Allentown]," ibid. This basis for disregarding Mohr's statements is wholly irrational. Local 724 had never won an election, or even an informal poll, within the actual unit of 32 Allentown employees. Its claim to represent them rested entirely on the Board's presumption that the work force of a successor company has the same disposition regarding the union as did the work force of the predecessor company, if the majority of the new work force came from the old one. See id., at 1197, n. 3; Fall River Dyeing, 482 U.S., at 43, 46–52, 107 S.Ct., at 2236, 2237–41. The Board cannot rationally adopt that presumption for purposes of imposing the duty to bargain, and adopt precisely the opposite presumption (i.e., contend that there is no relationship between the sentiments of the two work forces) for purposes of determining what evidence tends to establish a reasonable doubt regarding union support. Such irrationality is impermissible even if, as Justice Breyer's dissent suggests, it would further the Board's political objectives.

It must be borne in mind that the issue here is not whether Mohr's statement clearly establishes a majority in opposition to the union, but whether it contributes to a reasonable uncertainty whether a majority in favor of the union existed. We think it surely does. Allentown would reasonably have given great credence to Mohr's assertion of lack of union support, since he was not hostile to the union, and was in a good position to assess antiunion sentiment. Mohr was a union shop steward for the service department, and a member of the union's bargaining committee; according to the ALJ, he "did not indicate personal dissatisfaction with the Union." 316 N.L.R.B., at 1208. It seems to us that Mohr's statement has undeniable and substantial probative value on the issue of "reasonable doubt."

Accepting the Board's apparent (and in our view inescapable) concession that Allentown received reliable information that 7 of the bargaining-unit employees did not support the union, the remaining 25 would have had to support the union by a margin of 17 to 8—a ratio of more than 2 to 1—if the union commanded majority support. The statements of Bloch and Mohr would cause anyone to doubt that degree of support, and neither the Board nor the ALJ discussed any evidence that Allentown should have weighed on the other side. The most pro-union statement cited in the ALJ's opinion was Ron Mohr's comment that he personally "could work with or without the Union," and "was there to do his job." Id., at 1207. The Board cannot covertly transform its presumption of continuing majority support into a working assumption that *all* of a successor's employees support the union until proved otherwise. Giving fair weight to Allentown's circumstantial evidence, we think it quite impossible for a rational factfinder to avoid the conclusion that Allentown had reasonable, good-faith grounds to doubt—to be *uncertain about*—the union's retention of majority support.

### IV

That conclusion would make this a fairly straightforward administrative-law case, except for the contention that the Board's factfinding here was not an aberration. Allentown asserts that, although "the Board continues to cite the words of the good faith doubt branch of its withdrawal of recognition standard," a systematic review of the Board's decisions will reveal that "it has in practice eliminated the good faith doubt branch in favor of a strict head count." Brief for Petitioner 10. The Board denies (not too persuasively) that it has insisted upon a strict head count, but does defend its factfinding in this case by saying that it has regularly rejected similarly persuasive demonstrations of reasonable good-faith doubt in prior decisions. . . .

It is certainly conceivable that an adjudicating agency might consistently require a particular substantive standard to be established by a quantity or character of evidence so far beyond what reason and logic would require as to make it apparent that the *announced* standard is not *really* the effective one. And it is conceivable that in certain categories of cases an adjudicating agency which purports to be applying a preponderance standard of proof might so consistently demand in fact more than a preponderance, that all should be on notice from its case law that the genuine burden of proof is more than a preponderance. The question arises, then, whether, if that should be the situation that obtains here, we ought to measure the evidentiary support for the Board's decision against the standards consistently applied rather than the standards recited. As a theoretical matter (and leaving aside the question of legal authority), the Board could certainly have raised the bar for employer polling or withdrawal of recognition by imposing a more stringent requirement than the reasonable-doubt test, or by adopting a formal requirement that employers establish their reasonable doubt by more than a preponderance of the evidence. Would it make any difference if the Board achieved precisely the same result by formally leaving in place the reasonable-doubt and preponderance standards, but consistently applying them as though they meant something other than what they say? We think it would.

The Administrative Procedure Act, which governs the proceedings of administrative agencies and related judicial review, establishes a scheme of "reasoned decisionmaking." Motor Vehicle Mfrs. Assn. of United States, Inc. v. State Farm Mut. Automobile Ins. Co., 463 U.S. 29, 52, 103 S.Ct. 2856, 2871, 77 L.Ed.2d 443 (1983). Not only must an agency's decreed result be within the scope of its lawful authority, but the process by which it reaches that result must be logical and rational. . . . It is hard to imagine a more violent breach of that requirement than applying a rule of primary conduct or a standard of proof which is in fact different from the rule or standard formally announced. And the consistent repetition of that breach can hardly mend it. . . .

The Board can, of course, forthrightly and explicitly adopt counter-factual evidentiary presumptions (which are in effect substantive rules of law) as a way of furthering particular legal or policy goals—for example, the Board's irrebuttable presumption of majority support for the union during the year following certification, see, e.g., Station KKHI, 284 N.L.R.B. 1339, 1340, 1987 WL 89811 (1987), enf'd, 891 F.2d 230 (C.A.9 1989). The Board might also be justified in forthrightly and explicitly adopting a rule of evidence that categorically excludes certain testimony on policy grounds, without reference to its inherent probative value. (Such clearly announced rules of law or of evidentiary exclusion would of course be subject to judicial review for their reasonableness and their compatibility with the Act.) . . . When the Board purports to be engaged in simple factfinding, unconstrained by substantive presumptions or evidentiary rules of exclusion, it is not free to prescribe what inferences from the evidence it will accept and reject, but must draw all those inferences that the evidence fairly demands. "Substantial evidence" review exists precisely to ensure that the Board achieves minimal compliance with this obligation, which is the foundation of all honest and legitimate adjudication.

. . . Of course the Board is entitled to be skeptical about the employer's claimed reliance on second-hand reports when the reporter has little basis for knowledge, or has some incentive to mislead. But that is a matter of logic and sound inference from all the circumstances, not an arbitrary rule of disregard to be extracted from prior Board decisions.

The same is true of the Board precedents holding that "an employee's statements of dissatisfaction with the quality of union representation may not be treated as opposition to union representation," and that "an employer may not rely on an employee's anti-union sentiments, expressed during a job interview in which the employer has indicated that there will be no union." 83 F.3d, at 1488, citing Destileria Serralles, Inc., 289 N.L.R.B. 51, 1988 WL 214114 (1988), enf'd, 882 F.2d 19 (C.A.1 1989), and Middleboro Fire Apparatus, Inc., 234 N.L.R.B. 888, 894, 1978 WL 7283, enf'd, 590 F.2d 4 (C.A.1 1978). It is of course true that such statements are not clear evidence of an employee's opinion about the union—and if the Board's substantive standard required clear proof of employee disaffection, it might be proper to ignore such statements altogether. But that is not the standard, and, depending on the circumstances, the statements can unquestionably be probative to some degree of the employer's good-faith reasonable doubt.

    \* \* \*

We conclude that the Board's "reasonable doubt" test for employer polls is facially rational and consistent with the Act. But the Board's factual finding that Allentown Mack Sales lacked such a doubt is not supported by substantial evidence on the record as a whole. The judgment of the Court of Appeals for the D.C. Circuit is therefore reversed, and the case is remanded with instructions to deny enforcement.

■ Chief Justice Rehnquist, with whom Justice O'Connor, Justice Kennedy, and Justice Thomas join, concurring in part and dissenting in part.

I concur in the judgment of the Court and in Parts I, III, and IV. However, I disagree that the Board's standard is rational and consistent with the National Labor Relations Act, and I therefore dissent as to Part II. . . .

I think the Board's reasoning comes up short on two counts. First, there is no support in the language of the Act for its treatment of polling, and second, its treatment of polling even apart from the statute is irrational.

The Act does not address employer polling. The Board's authority to regulate employer polling at all must therefore rest on its power to prohibit any practices that "interfere with, restrain, or coerce employees in the exercise" of their right to bargain collectively under s 8(a)(1), 29 U.S.C. s 158(a)(1). The Board fails to demonstrate how employer polling, conducted in accord with procedural safeguards and with no overt coercion or threats of reprisal, violates the terms of the Act. . . .

A poll conducted in accord with the Board's substantial procedural safeguards would not coerce employees in the exercise of their rights. In Struksnes Constr. Co., 165 N.L.R.B. 1062, 1063 (1967), the Board, in addressing the validity of an employer poll during a union's organizing drive, held that polling does not violate the Act if "(1) the purpose of the poll is to determine the truth of the union's claim to majority, (2) this purpose is communicated to employees, (3) assurances against reprisal are given, (4) the employees are polled by secret ballot, and (5) the employer has not engaged in unfair labor practices or otherwise created a coercive atmosphere." In Texas Petrochemicals, 296 N.L.R.B., at 1063–64, the Board imposed an additional requirement of advance notice of the time and place of the poll. These substantial safeguards make coercion or restraint of employees highly unlikely.

Additionally, the Board's rationale gives short shrift to the Act's goal of protecting employee choice. Auciello Iron Works, 517 U.S., at 790–791, 116 S.Ct., at 1760. By ascertaining employee support for the union, a poll indirectly promotes this goal. Employees are not properly represented by a union lacking majority support. Employers also have a legitimate, recognized interest in not bargaining with a union lacking majority support. Texas Petrochemicals, supra, at 1062. The ability to poll employees thus provides the employer (and the employees) with a neutral and effective manner of obtaining information relevant to determining the employees' proper representative and the employer's bargaining obligations.... I conclude that the Board's standard restricts polling in the absence of coercion or restraint of employee rights and therefore is contrary to the Act.

Quite apart from the lack of statutory authority for the Board's treatment of polling, I think this treatment irrationally equates employer polls, RM elections, and unilateral withdrawals of recognition. The Board argues that having the same standard for polls and unilateral withdrawals is reasonable because the employer can still use polls to confirm a loss of majority support. As a practical matter, this leaves little room for polling.... But even conceding some remaining value to polling, the Board's rationale fails to address the basic inconsistency of imposing the same standard on two actions having dramatically different effects. Surely a unilateral withdrawal of recognition creates a greater disruption of the bargaining relationship and greater "doubts" in the minds of employees than does a poll. Consistent with the Board's reliance on such disruption to justify its polling standard, the standard for unilateral withdrawals should surely be higher.

The Board also asserts that having the same standard for RM elections and employer polls is justified by common practical and legal consequences, i.e., the risk of the union's loss of its position as bargaining representative. But this argument fails as a factual matter. As the Board admits, a RM election is binding on a losing union for one year, 29 U.S.C. s 159(c)(3), while a union losing a poll may petition for a Board election at any time. Brief for Respondent 40, n. 12. These differing consequences suggest the standard for polling should be lower.... The Board thus irrationally equates the standard for polling with the standards for both unilateral withdrawals of recognition and RM elections.

The conclusion that the Board's standard is both irrational and without support in the Act is reinforced by long-standing decisions from this Court. Under [the reasoning in NLRB v. Gissel Packing Co., 395 U.S. 575 (1969),] employer solicitation of employee views is protected speech, although such solicitation can constitutionally be prohibited where it amounts to coercion or threats of reprisal. There is no logical basis for a distinction between soliciting views, as in the instant case, and communicating views. Our decisions have concluded that First Amendment protection extends equally to the right to receive information, ... and to the right to solicit information or responses.... In my view, ... the Board must allow polling where it does not tend to coerce or restrain employees....

■ Justice Breyer, with whom Justice Stevens, Justice Souter, and Justice Ginsburg join, concurring in part and dissenting in part.

I concur in Parts I and II and dissent from Parts III and IV of the Court's opinion....

The majority opinion begins by properly stating the Board's conclusion, namely that the employer, Allentown, did not demonstrate that it "held a reasonable doubt, *based on objective considerations*, that the Union continued to enjoy the support of a majority of the bargaining unit employees." Ante, at 823 (emphasis added). The opinion, however, then omits the words I have italicized and transforms this conclusion, rephrasing it as: "Allentown lacked a genuine, reasonable uncertainty about whether Local 724 enjoyed the continuing support of a majority of unit employees." Ante, at 823. Key words of a technical sort that the Board has used in hundreds of opinions written over several decades to express what the Administrative Law Judge (ALJ) here called *"objective* reasonable doubt" have suddenly disappeared, leaving in their place what looks like an ordinary jury standard that might reflect, not an agency's specialized knowledge of the workplace, but a court's common understanding of human psychology. The only authority cited for the transformation, the dictionary, in fact offers no support, for the majority has looked up the wrong word, namely "doubt," instead of the right word, "objective." In any event, the majority's interpretation departs from settled principles permitting agencies broad leeway to interpret their own rules....

.... The majority [takes] issue with the ALJ's decision not to count in Allentown's favor three ... statements, made by employees Marsh, Bloch, and Mohr. Id., at 1206–1207. The majority says that these statements required the ALJ and the Board to find for Allentown. I cannot agree.

Consider Marsh's statement. Marsh said, as the majority opinion notes, that " 'he was not being represented for the $35 he was paying.' " Ante, at 824; 316 N.L.R.B., at 1207. The majority says that the ALJ was wrong not to count this statement in the employer's favor. Ante, at 824. But the majority fails to mention that Marsh made this statement to an Allentown manager while the manager was interviewing Marsh to determine whether he would, or would not, be one of the 32 employees whom Allentown would re-employ. The ALJ, when evaluating all the employee statements, wrote that statements made to the Allentown managers during the job interviews were "somewhat tainted as it is likely that a job applicant will say whatever he believes the prospective employer wants to hear." 316 N.L.R.B., at 1206. In so stating, the ALJ was reiterating the Board's own normative general finding that employers should not "rely in asserting a good-faith doubt" upon "[s]tatements made by employees during the course of an interview with a prospective employer." Middleboro Fire Apparatus, Inc., 234 N.L.R.B. 888, 894, 1978 WL 7283, enf'd, 590 F.2d 4 (C.A.5 1978). The Board also has found that " '[e]mployee statements of dissatisfaction with a union are not deemed the equivalent of withdrawal of support for the union.'" Torch Operating Co., 322 N.L.R.B. 939, 943, 1997 WL 34911 (1997) (quoting Briggs Plumbingware, Inc. v. NLRB, 877 F.2d 1282, 1288 (C.A.6 1989)); see also Destileria Serralles, Inc., 289 N.L.R.B. 51, 1988 WL 214114 (1988), 882 F.2d 19 (C.A.1 1989). Either of these general Board findings (presumably known to employers advised by the labor bar), applied by the ALJ in this particular case, provides more than adequate support for the ALJ's conclusion that the employer could not properly rely upon Marsh's statement as help in creating an "objective" employer doubt.

.... That Board conclusion represents an exercise of the kind of discretionary authority that Congress placed squarely within the Board's administrative and fact-finding powers and responsibilities....

Consider next Bloch's statement, made during his job interview with Worth, that those on the night shift (five or six employees) "did not want the Union.".... The majority says that "reason demands" that Bloch's statement "be given considerable weight." Ante, at 824. But why? The Board, drawing upon both reason and experience, has said it will "view with suspicion and caution" one employee's statements "purporting to represent the views of other employees." ...

How is it unreasonable for the Board to provide this kind of guidance, about what kinds of evidence are more likely, and what kinds are less likely, to support an "objective reasonable doubt" (thereby helping an employer understand just when he may refuse to bargain with an established employee representative, in the absence of an employee-generated union decertification petition)? Why is it unreasonable for an ALJ to disregard a highly general conclusory statement such as Bloch's, a statement that names no names, is unsupported by any other concrete testimony, and was made during a job interview by an interviewer who foresees a nonunionized workforce? To put the matter more directly, how can the majority substitute its own judgment for that of the Board and the ALJ in respect to such detailed workplace-related matters, particularly on the basis of this record, where the question of whether we should set aside this kind of Board rule has not even been argued?

Finally, consider the Allentown manager's statement that Mohr told him that "if a vote was taken, the Union would lose."....

One can find reflected in the majority opinion some of the reasons the ALJ gave for discounting the significance of Mohr's statement. The majority says of the ALJ's first reason (namely that "there is no evidence with respect to how" Mohr "gained this knowledge") that this reason is "irrelevan[t]." Ante, at ___. But why so? The lack of any specifics provides some support for the possibility that Mohr was overstating a conclusion, say, in a job-preserving effort to curry favor with Mack's new managers. More importantly, since the absence of detail or support brings Mohr's statement well within the Board's pre-existing cautionary evidentiary principle (about employee statements regarding the views of other employees), it diminishes the reasonableness of any employer reliance....

The majority fails to mention [another reason given by the ALJ] for discounting Mohr's statement, namely, that Mohr did not indicate "whether he was speaking about a large majority of the service employees being dissatisfied with the Union or a small majority." 316 N.L.R.B., at 1208. It fails to mention the ALJ's belief that the statement was "almost off-the-cuff." Ibid. It fails to mention the ALJ's reference to the "Board's historical treatment of unverified assertions by an employee about other employees' sentiments" (which, by itself, would justify a considerable discount). Ibid. And, most importantly, it leaves out the ALJ's conclusion. The ALJ did not conclude that Mohr's statement lacked evidentiary significance. Rather, the ALJ concluded that the statement did not provide "*sufficient* basis, even when considered with other employee statements relied upon, to meet the Board's objective reasonable doubt standard." Ibid. (emphasis added).

.... That conclusion is well within the Board's authority to make findings and to reach conclusions on the basis of record evidence, which authority Congress has granted, and this Court's many precedents have confirmed. See, e.g., Beth Israel Hospital v. NLRB, 437 U.S. at 504, 98 S.Ct. at 2475....

---

Levitz Furniture Co., 333 N.L.R.B. No. 105 (2001). A majority of the Board concluded that, consistent with *Allentown Mack*, it would adopt a different and more demanding standard for an employer's withdrawal of recognition of an incumbent union than for the filing of an employer petition (a so-called RM petition) for a representation election directed at such a union. (It left for a later determination whether the current standard of "uncertainty" as developed by the Supreme Court in *Allentown Mack* should continue to govern the employer's ability to conduct a poll of its employees.)

With respect to a withdrawal of recognition, the Board overruled its "good faith doubt" standard that it had applied for 50 years, under Celanese Corp., 95 N.L.R.B. 664 (1951). The Board found that "there are compelling legal and policy reasons why employers should not be allowed to withdraw recognition merely because they harbor uncertainty or even disbelief concerning unions' majority status." Instead, "an employer may unilaterally withdraw recognition from an incumbent union only where the union has actually lost the support of the majority of the bargaining unit employees," with the burden of proof resting with the employer (to counter the presumption of continuing majority support). The Board reasoned that an employer's good faith belief that the union has lost majority support should no more be a defense to a claim of violation of § 8(a)(5) than is the employer's good faith belief that the union actually has a majority a defense to a claimed violation of § 8(a)(2). Thus, the employer who in good faith relies on "objective evidence" of loss of support, e.g., a petition from a majority of the workers (as was presented in the *Levitz* case, followed by the union's counter-petition), withdraws recognition at the peril of a finding of an unfair labor practice under § 8(a)(5).

With respect, however, to an employer's filing of an RM petition challenging a union's continuing majority support, the Board adopted the "lower" standard of good faith employer "uncertainty." This conclusion was buttressed by the Board's preference for elections to decide representation status (rather than unilateral withdrawal of recognition) when employers are presented with conflicting evidence of majority support. "Thus, by liberalizing the standard for holding RM elections, we are promoting both employee free choice (by making it easier to ascertain employee support for unions via Board elections) and stability in collective-bargaining relationships (which remain intact during representation proceedings)"—because the union continues to enjoy its representation status during the pendency of an RM petition.

Turning to the evidence required to establish an employer's reasonable "uncertainty," the Board stated that, clearly, anti-union petitions and firsthand statements by employees concerning personal opposition to an incumbent union could contribute to employer uncertainty. In the past, the Board did not consider employees' unverified statements regarding other employees' anti-union sentiments, or employee statements expressing dissatisfaction with the union's bargaining performance, as reliable to establish good faith doubt (in the sense of "disbelief"). Now, however, these kinds of statements—in view of *Allentown Mack*—may be considered to satistfy the lower standard of good faith uncertainty, for the filing of an RM petition. The Board stressed that such evidence needs to be reliable, not speculative.

---

## PROBLEMS FOR DISCUSSION

**1.** Did the *Allentown Mack* majority act properly when it interpreted the Board's own formulation—"reasonable doubt" of majority support—by referring to dictionary definitions while rejecting as untenable the interpretation utilized by the Board itself for decades? Given the fact that the NLRA is altogether silent on this matter, does the standard of review set forth in the Supreme Court's *Chevron* decision permit the Court to substitute "uncertainty" for "disbelief" in the Board's formulation of the applicable employer defense?

**2.** Once the Court majority held that "uncertainty" was the touchstone for applying the employer's "reasonable doubt" defense, should the Court not have remanded to the Board to review the record facts with the proper standard in mind? Did it? Why? In applying the proper "uncertainty" standard itself, did the Court too readily allow the employer to mount a defense based on altogether unsubstantiated and unexplained statements by one employee about how groups of other employees felt about the union?

**3.** Review the Supreme Court decisions in *Curtin Matheson* and *Allentown Mack*, and the NLRB decision in *Levitz*. Assume you represent a unionized employer which has been struck during contract negotiations and which has hired strikebreakers in substantial numbers. You have been asked whether the employer may withdraw recognition, or petition for an election, or take a poll among the employees. What advice can you give?

**4.** Assume that an employer which has withdrawn recognition from an incumbent union has in fact miscalculated, and the NLRB finds a violation of § 8(a)(5). Can the Board issue a meaningful remedy, or is it effectively limited to an order to cease and desist, and to resume bargaining?

# PART THREE

# Negotiation of the Collective Bargaining Agreement

Prior to the enactment of the Railway Labor Act and the National Labor Relations Act, it was economic force which ultimately determined whether an employer would recognize a union for purposes of collective bargaining, what subjects would be discussed at the bargaining table, what kinds of bargaining techniques and substantive proposals would be presented, and what pressure tactics would be brought to bear outside the bargaining room. To what extent has the law—particularly the NLRA—altered this picture of voluntarism fueled by threats of and resort to economic combat?

Of course, even the strongest and most adamant employer may no longer refuse to recognize the bargaining representative designated or selected by a majority of its employees in an appropriate bargaining unit. Sections 8(a)(5) and 9(a) unequivocally impose that obligation. The law also appears to some extent to limit the kinds of bargaining techniques used and proposals made, for Section 8(d) requires that both parties "confer in good faith." The law has also to a considerable extent taken from the unfettered control of the parties the substantive agenda to be discussed at the bargaining table, for it mandates that both parties have a duty to bargain about "wages, hours, and other terms and conditions of employment." The law also, obviously, forbids resort to such economic weapons as discriminatory discharges and secondary boycotts as means of extracting bargaining concessions, but other weapons not expressly outlawed elsewhere in the statute may be proscribed under Sections 8(a)(5) and 8(b)(3).

In sum, Congress has to a considerable degree replaced a bargaining structure based on voluntarism and economic force with one based on legal compulsion. This policy is reinforced by a host of federal (and state) statutes that limit managerial control and promulgate substantive rules regarding the workplace. Employers are broadly forbidden to discriminate in the hiring, firing, and on-the-job treatment of employees on the basis of race, sex, religion, national origin, age, disability, and of course union activities. Employers are required by state and federal law to furnish a safe work environment. The minimum wage law, combined with laws requiring premium pay for excessive daily and weekly work, shape pay structures and working hours throughout private industry. Returning veterans of the armed forces must be accorded certain job privileges. Workers who are injured on the job, or temporarily or indefinitely denied work opportunities, are entitled to workmen's compensation or unemployment compensation from funds to which the employer must contribute. Federal social security laws also protect disabled or retired workers and their survivors. Comprehensive federal labor and tax laws protect the pension rights, contributions and funds provided for retiring workers. Companies working on government projects are subjected to elaborate mandates regarding wages, discrimination and other forms of employee treatment.

What, then, remains of "free" collective bargaining? As to the substantive content of the employer-employee relationship, there is a great deal. The regulations recited above, while important and comprehensive, effectively set only minimum standards, leaving for individual or collective negotiations the establishment of yet more protective workplace rules. Not only can arrangements be negotiated for higher than minimum pay and greater than required pension-vesting rights, but there remains a vast range of areas to which these legal rules do not speak at all—such as nondiscriminatory criteria (e.g., seniority or skill) for layoffs and promotions, the establishment of grievance and arbitration procedures to resolve disputes, and a wide range of benefits such as health insurance, leaves of absence and the like. Even a quick glance at the sample collective bargaining agreement in the Statutory Supplement to this casebook will demonstrate that legally mandated workplace rules hardly have preempted the field.

At least as pertinently, American labor policy reflects the belief that the process by which workplace rules are set is to be essentially a free one, without government dictating what proposals and counterproposals can be made, how they are to be timed, when and how economic pressure is to be applied, and the like. But this policy of laissez faire must of necessity be accommodated to the above-described policy of mandated recognition and mandated bargaining "in good faith."

These are the issues explored in this chapter.

(1) How far does the designation of a union as the "exclusive representative of all the employees in such unit for the purposes of collective bargaining" exclude other methods of dealing with wages and conditions of employment, such as discussions with individual employees or another union, unilateral employer action or concerted action by independent groups of employees within the bargaining unit?

(2) What does the duty to bargain collectively about clearly-bargainable subjects require of the employer and the union in their relations with each other? Section 8(d) provides that the duty includes "to meet at reasonable times and confer in good faith." What is the meaning of "good faith"? How may the absence of good faith be demonstrated?

(3) Over what topics must the employer and the union bargain collectively? In other words, what content should be given to the statutory phrase "wages, hours, and other terms and conditions of employment" contained in Section 8(d)?

(4) What is the role of the strike in the collective bargaining process and what steps have been taken, by Government and by private parties, to minimize recourse to the strike? How are the rights and obligations of the parties affected during the period of a strike?

# I.   EXCLUSIVE REPRESENTATION AND MAJORITY RULE[a]

## J.I. Case Co. v. National Labor Relations Board

321 U.S. 332, 64 S.Ct. 576, 88 L.Ed. 762 (1944).

■ MR. JUSTICE JACKSON delivered the opinion of the Court.

This case was heard by the National Labor Relations Board on stipulated facts which so far as concern present issues are as follows:

The petitioner, J.I. Case Company, at its Rock Island, Illinois, plant, from 1937 offered each employee an individual contract of employment. The contracts were uniform and for a term of one year. The Company agreed to furnish employment as steadily as conditions permitted, to pay a specified rate, which the Company might redetermine if the job changed, and to maintain certain hospital facilities. The employee agreed to accept the provisions, to serve faithfully and honestly for the term, to comply with factory rules, and that defective work should not be paid for. About 75% of the employees accepted and worked under these agreements.

According to the Board's stipulation and finding, the execution of the contracts was not a condition of employment, nor was the status of individual employees affected by reason of signing or failing to sign the contracts. It is not found or contended that the agreements were coerced,

---

**a.** See Schatzki, Majority Rule, Exclusive Representation, and the Interests of Individual Workers: Should Exclusivity be Abolished?, 123 U.Pa.L.Rev. 897 (1975); Smith, Evolution of the "Duty to Bargain" Concept in American Law, 39 Mich.L.Rev. 1065 (1941); Weyand, Majority Rule in Collective Bargaining, 45 Col.L.Rev. 556 (1945). For an examination of similar issues from the perspective of comparative law, see Bok, Reflections on the Distinctive Character of American Labor Laws, 84 Harv.L.Rev. 1394 (1971).

obtained by any unfair labor practice, or that they were not valid under the circumstances in which they were made.

While the individual contracts executed August 1, 1941 were in effect, a C.I.O. union petitioned the Board for certification as the exclusive bargaining representative of the production and maintenance employees. On December 17, 1941 a hearing was held, at which the Company urged the individual contracts as a bar to representation proceedings. The Board, however, directed an election, which was won by the union. The union was thereupon certified as the exclusive bargaining representative of the employees in question in respect to wages, hours, and other conditions of employment.

The union then asked the Company to bargain. It refused, declaring that it could not deal with the union in any manner affecting rights and obligations under the individual contracts while they remained in effect. It offered to negotiate on matters which did not affect rights under the individual contracts, and said that upon the expiration of the contracts it would bargain as to all matters. Twice the Company sent circulars to its employees asserting the validity of the individual contracts and stating the position that it took before the Board in reference to them.

The Board held that the Company had refused to bargain collectively, in violation of § 8(5) of the National Labor Relations Act, 29 U.S.C.A. § 158(5); and that the contracts had been utilized, by means of the circulars, to impede employees in the exercise of rights guaranteed by § 7 of the Act, 29 U.S.C.A. § 157, with the result that the Company had engaged in unfair labor practices within the meaning of § 8(1) of the Act. It ordered the Company to cease and desist from giving effect to the contracts, from extending them or entering into new ones, from refusing to bargain and from interfering with the employees; and it required the Company to give notice accordingly and to bargain upon request. * * *

Contract in labor law is a term the implications of which must be determined from the connection in which it appears. Collective bargaining between employer and the representatives of a unit, usually a union, results in an accord as to terms which will govern hiring and work and pay in that unit. The result is not, however, a contract of employment except in rare cases; no one has a job by reason of it and no obligation to any individual ordinarily comes into existence from it alone. The negotiations between union and management result in what often has been called a trade agreement, rather than in a contract of employment. Without pushing the analogy too far, the agreement may be likened to the tariffs established by a carrier, to standard provisions prescribed by supervising authorities for insurance policies, or to utility schedules of rates and rules for service, which do not of themselves establish any relationships but which do govern the terms of the shipper or insurer or customer relationship whenever and with whomever it may be established. Indeed, in some European countries, contrary to American practice, the terms of a collectively negotiated trade agreement are submitted to a government department and if approved become a governmental regulation ruling employment in the unit.

After the collective trade agreement is made, the individuals who shall benefit by it are identified by individual hirings. The employer, except as restricted by the collective agreement itself and except that he must engage in no unfair labor practice or discrimination, is free to select those he will employ or discharge. But the terms of the employment already have been traded out. There is little left to individual agreement except the act of hiring. This hiring may be by writing or by word of mouth or may be implied from conduct. In the sense of contracts of hiring, individual contracts between the employer and employee are not forbidden, but indeed are necessitated by the collective bargaining procedure.

But, however engaged, an employee becomes entitled by virtue of the Labor Relations Act somewhat as a third party beneficiary to all benefits of the collective trade agreement, even if on his own he would yield to less favorable terms. The individual hiring contract is subsidiary to the terms of the trade agreement and may not waive any of its benefits, any more than a shipper can contract away the benefit of filed tariffs, the insurer the benefit of standard provisions, or the utility customer the benefit of legally established rates.

Concurrent existence of these two types of agreement raises problems as to which the National Labor Relations Act makes no express provision. * * *

Individual contracts, no matter what the circumstances that justify their execution or what their terms, may not be availed of to defeat or delay the procedures prescribed by the National Labor Relations Act looking to collective bargaining, nor to exclude the contracting employee from a duly ascertained bargaining unit; nor may they be used to forestall bargaining or to limit or condition the terms of the collective agreement. "The Board asserts a public right vested in it as a public body, charged in the public interest with the duty of preventing unfair labor practices." National Licorice Co. v. National Labor Relations Board, 309 U.S. 350, 364, 60 S.Ct. 569, 577, 84 L.Ed. 799. Wherever private contracts conflict with its functions, they obviously must yield or the Act would be reduced to a futility.

It is equally clear since the collective trade agreement is to serve the purpose contemplated by the Act, the individual contract cannot be effective as a waiver of any benefit to which the employee otherwise would be entitled under the trade agreement. The very purpose of providing by statute for the collective agreement is to supersede the terms of separate agreements of employees with terms which reflect the strength and bargaining power and serve the welfare of the group. Its benefits and advantages are open to every employee of the represented unit, whatever the type or terms of his pre-existing contract of employment.

But it is urged that some employees may lose by the collective agreement, that an individual workman may sometimes have, or be capable of getting, better terms than those obtainable by the group and that his freedom of contract must be respected on that account. We are not called upon to say that under no circumstances can an individual enforce an agreement more advantageous than a collective agreement, but we find the mere possibility that such agreements might be made no ground for holding generally that individual contracts may survive or surmount collective ones. The practice and philosophy of collective bargaining looks with suspicion on such individual advantages. Of course, where there is great variation in circumstances of employment or capacity of employees, it is possible for the collective bargain to prescribe only minimum rates or maximum hours or expressly to leave certain areas open to individual bargaining. But except as so provided, advantages to individuals may prove as disruptive of industrial peace as disadvantages. They are a fruitful way of interfering with organization and choice of representatives; increased compensation, if individually deserved, is often earned at the cost of breaking down some other standard thought to be for the welfare of the group, and always creates the suspicion of being paid at the long-range expense of the group as a whole. Such discriminations not infrequently amount to unfair labor practices. The workman is free, if he values his own bargaining position more than that of the group, to vote against representation; but the majority rules, and if it collectivizes the employment bargain, individual advantages or favors will generally in practice go in as a contribution to the collective result. We cannot except individual contracts generally from the operation of collective ones because some may be more individually advantageous. Individual contracts cannot subtract from collective ones, and whether under some circumstances they may add to them in matters covered by the collective bargain, we leave to be determined by appropriate forums under the laws of contracts applicable, and to the Labor Board if they constitute unfair labor practices. * * *

As so modified [in details not here material] the decree is

Affirmed.

————

## PROBLEMS FOR DISCUSSION

**1.** Under Public Resolution 44 (H.J.Res. 375, 48 Stat. 1183, 73d Cong., 2d Sess.), Congress in 1934—acting pursuant to the short-lived National Industrial Recovery Act—created the "old" National Labor Relations Board with modest authority to enforce the statutory "right of employees to organize and to select their representatives for the purpose of collective bargaining." Neither the Act nor the Resolution, however, specifically provided for or defined the duty to bargain collectively. If the NLRA had been similarly designed, so that there was in substance a Section 7 but no Section 9(a), would the objectives of the former Section be fostered—or frustrated—by *implying* a principle of exclusive representation by the majority representative? Does not free collective bargaining under Section 7 invite a pluralistic scheme of representation, with each labor organization bargaining only on behalf of its own supporters (and non-union workers continuing to bargain individually)? See Houde Engineering Corp., 1 N.L.R.B. (old series) 35 (1934).

**2.** Jones runs a small machine shop in a locality in which there is strong demand for skilled machinists. International Association of Machinists has been certified by the NLRB as the bargaining representative of Jones' employees. Jones has three skilled machinists, older men not connected with the union, who he fears may leave his employ. Jones wishes to offer them a wage increase, a special bonus, or perhaps a secret promise of a pension upon retirement, without discussing the matter with IAM. Jones has consulted your senior partner as his lawyer about the advisability of this step. Your senior seeks your recommendation. What advice would you give?

**3.** You represent a company which is currently negotiating for its third successive labor agreement, and is in the midst of a strike. Negotiations have deadlocked over several issues, particularly the assignment of overtime (the company demanding that overtime be assigned among all employees by rotation and the union demanding that it be assigned by seniority). The company believes that if its position can be explained to the striking employees, they will be prepared to return to work. Provide answers to the following questions. May the company send leaflets to and undertake individual discussions with employees in order to explain its position? May the company invite employees to attend a meeting for this purpose on company property (preferably without a union representative present)? May the company distribute ballots to employees asking them to indicate their support for, or opposition to, the company's last offer? Compare United Technologies Corp. v. International Association of Machinists, 274 NLRB 609 (1985), with Obie Pacific, Inc. v. Seattle Local 49, 196 NLRB 458 (1972).

You might also want to address the question put to you by the company president, in frustration: "Isn't there anything in the United States Constitution or the labor laws that gives me the right to speak freely to my own workers?!"

---

# Emporium Capwell Co. v. Western Addition Community Organization[b]

420 U.S. 50, 95 S.Ct. 977, 43 L.Ed.2d 12 (1975).

■ Opinion of the Court by MR. JUSTICE MARSHALL * * *.

This case presents the question whether, in light of the national policy against racial discrimination in employment, the National Labor Relations Act protects concerted activity by a group of minority employees to bargain with their employer over issues of employment discrimination. The National Labor Relations Board held that the employees could not circumvent their elected representative to engage in such bargaining. The Court of Appeals for the District of Columbia Circuit reversed and remanded, holding that in certain circumstances the activity would be protected. 485

**b.** See Atleson, Work Group Behavior and Wildcat Strikes: The Causes and Functions of Industrial Disobedience, 34 Ohio St. L.Rev. 751 (1973); Cantor, Dissident Worker Action, After *The Emporium*, 29 Rutgers L.Rev. 35 (1975); Gould, The Status of Unauthorized and "Wildcat" Strikes Under the National Labor Relations Act, 52 Cornell L.Q. 672 (1967); Lynd, The Right to Engage in Concerted Activity After Union Recognition: A Study of Legislative History, 50 Indiana L.J. 720 (1975); Silverstein, Union Decisions on Collective Bargaining Goals: A Proposal for Interest Group Participation, 77 Mich. L.Rev. 1485 (1979).

F.2d 917. Because of the importance of the issue to the administration of the Act, we granted certiorari. 415 U.S. 913, 94 S.Ct. 1407, 39 L.Ed.2d 466. We now reverse.

## I.

[The Emporium Capwell Company and the Department Store Employees Union were parties to a collective bargaining agreement which contained a no-strike no-lockout clause, grievance and arbitration machinery, and a prohibition of employment discrimination by reason of race, color, creed, national origin, age, sex, or union activity. In response to employee complaints that the company was discriminating on the basis of race in making assignments and promotions, the Union's secretary-treasurer, Walter Johnson, prepared a report which he submitted to the Company; the report referred to "the possibility of racial discrimination" as a matter of central concern and one which if not corrected might be potentially explosive. At a meeting of Company employees convened by the Union (to which representatives of the California Fair Employment Practices Committee were invited), testimony about Company practices was taken down by a court reporter and Johnson stated that he had concluded the Company was discriminating and that the Union would process every discrimination grievance to arbitration if necessary. Although some of the Company's employees at the meeting stated that contract procedures were inadequate to handle such a systemic grievance and that the Union should instead picket the Company, Johnson explained that the labor contract forbade that and stated that successful individual grievants would be helping all other employees who were victims of discrimination.

[The Union then demanded that the Company convene the joint union-management Adjustment Board provided for in the contract, but when the Adjustment Board met, four of the vocal employees—James Hollins, Tom Hawkins and two others—refused to participate; Hollins read a statement objecting to reliance on individual grievances and demanding that the president of the Company meet with the four protestants to work out a broader agreement for dealing with the discrimination issue. Hollins later unsuccessfully attempted to have discussions with the Company president, and soon after, he and Hawkins and several other dissident employees held a press conference at which they denounced the Company's policy as racist, reiterated their desire to deal directly with "the top management," and announced their intention to picket and institute a boycott of the store.

[Some ten days later, Hollins, Hawkins and at least two other employees picketed the store throughout the day and distributed at the entrance handbills urging consumers not to patronize the store.[2] First Johnson and

---

**2.** The full text of the handbill read:

" * * BEWARE * * * * * BEWARE * *
 * * BEWARE * *
"EMPORIUM SHOPPERS
" 'Boycott Is On' 'Boycott Is On'
'Boycott Is On'

"For years at The Emporium black, brown, yellow and red people have worked at the lowest jobs, at the lowest levels. Time and time again we have seen intelligent, hard working brothers and sisters denied promotions and respect.

then the Company warned these employees that they might be discharged if their activities continued, and when Hollins and Hawkins repeated their conduct they were terminated. After the filing of a Section 8(a)(1) charge by the Western Addition Community Organization, a local civil rights association to which Hollins and Hawkins belonged, an NLRB trial examiner found that they had resorted to concerted activity in the good-faith belief that the Company was discriminating against minority employees; he concluded, however, that their activity was not protected by Section 7 and that their discharges thus did not violate Section 8(a)(1).]

The Board, after oral argument, adopted the findings and conclusions of its Trial Examiner and dismissed the complaint. 192 NLRB 173. Among the findings adopted by the Board was that the discharged employees' course of conduct

> "was no mere presentation of a grievance, but nothing short of a demand that the [Company] bargain with the picketing employees for the entire group of minority employees."[5]

The Board concluded that protection of such an attempt to bargain would undermine the statutory system of bargaining through an exclusive, elected representative, impede elected unions' efforts at bettering the working conditions of minority employees "and place on the Employer an unreasonable burden of attempting to placate self-designated representatives of minority groups while abiding by the terms of a valid bargaining agreement and attempting in good faith to meet whatever demands the bargaining representative put forth under that agreement."[6]

"The Emporium is a 20th Century colonial plantation. The brothers and sisters are being treated the same way as our brothers are being treated in the slave mines of Africa.

"Whenever the racist pig at The Emporium injures or harms a black sister or brother, they injure and insult all black people. THE EMPORIUM MUST PAY FOR THESE INSULTS. Therefore, we encourage all of our people to take their money out of this racist store, until black people have full employment and are promoted justly through out The Emporium.

"We welcome the support of our brothers and sisters from the churches, unions, sororities, fraternities, social clubs, Afro–American Institute, Black Panther Party, WACO and the Poor Peoples Institute."

**5.** 192 N.L.R.B., at 185. The evidence marshaled in support of this finding consisted of Hollins' meeting with the Company president in which he said that he wanted to discuss the problem perceived by minority employees; his statement that the picketers would not desist until the president treated with them; Hawkins' testimony that their purpose in picketing was to "talk to the top management to get better conditions"; and his statement that they wanted to achieve their purpose through "group talk and through the president if we could talk to him," as opposed to use of the grievance-arbitration machinery.

**6.** The Board considered but stopped short of resolving the question of whether the employees' invective and call for a boycott of the Company bespoke so malicious an attempt to harm their employer as to deprive them of the protection of the Act. The Board decision is therefore grounded squarely on the view that a minority group member may not bypass the Union and bargain directly over matters affecting minority employees, and not at all on the tactics used in this particular attempt to obtain such bargaining.

Member Jenkins dissented on the ground that the employees' activity was protected by § 7 because it concerned the terms and conditions of their employment. Member Brown agreed but expressly relied upon his view that the facts revealed no attempt to bargain

On respondent's petition for review the Court of Appeals reversed and remanded. The court was of the view that concerted activity directed against racial discrimination enjoys a "unique status" by virtue of the national labor policy against discrimination, as expressed in both the NLRA, see United Packinghouse Workers Union v. NLRB, 135 U.S.App. D.C. 111, 416 F.2d 1126, cert. den. 396 U.S. 903, 90 S.Ct. 216, 24 L.Ed.2d 179 (1969), and in Title VII of the Civil Rights Act of 1964, 42 U.S.C. § 2000e et seq. [42 U.S.C.A. § 2000e et seq.], and that the Board had not adequately taken account of the necessity to accommodate the exclusive bargaining principle of the NLRA to the national policy of protecting action taken in opposition to discrimination from employer retaliation.[7] The court recognized that protection of the minority group concerted activity involved in this case would interfere to some extent with the orderly collective-bargaining process, but it considered the disruptive effect on that process to be outweighed where protection of minority activity is necessary to full and immediate realization of the policy against discrimination. In formulating a standard for distinguishing between protected and unprotected activity, the majority held that the "Board should inquire, in cases such as this, whether the union was actually remedying the discrimination to the *fullest extent possible by the most expedient and efficacious means.* Where the union's efforts fall short of this high standard, the minority group's concerted activity cannot lose its section 7 protection." Accordingly, the court remanded the case for the Board to make this determination and, if it found in favor of the employees, to consider whether their particular tactics were so disloyal to their employer as to deprive them of § 7 protection under our decision in NLRB v. Local Union No. 1229, 346 U.S. 464, 74 S.Ct. 172, 98 L.Ed. 195 (1953).

## II

Before turning to the central questions of labor policy raised by this case, it is important to have firmly in mind the character of the underlying conduct to which we apply them. As stated, the Trial Examiner and the Board found that the employees were discharged for attempting to bargain with the Company over the terms and conditions of employment as they affected racial minorities. Although the Court of Appeals expressly declined to set aside this finding, respondent has devoted considerable effort to

"but simply to urge [the Company] to take action to correct conditions of racial discrimination which the employees reasonably believed existed at The Emporium." 192 N.L.R.B., at 179.

7.  Section 704(a) of Title VII, 42 U.S.C. § 2000e–3(a) [42 U.S.C.A. § 2000e–3(a)] provides:

"It shall be an unlawful employment practice for an employer to discriminate against any of his employees or applicants for employment, for an employment agency, or joint labor-management committee control-ling apprenticeship or other training or retraining, including on-the-job training programs, to discriminate against any individual, or for a labor organization to discriminate against any member thereof or applicant for membership, because he has opposed any practice made an unlawful employment practice by this subchapter, or because he has made a charge, testified, assisted, or participated in any manner in an investigation, proceeding, or hearing under this subchapter."

attacking it in this Court, on the theory that the employees were attempting only to present a grievance to their employer within the meaning of the first proviso to § 9(a).[12] We see no occasion to disturb the finding of the Board. Universal Camera Corp. v. NLRB, 340 U.S. 474, 491, 71 S.Ct. 456, 95 L.Ed. 456 (1951). The issue, then, is whether such attempts to engage in separate bargaining are protected by § 7 of the Act or proscribed by § 9(a).

## A

\* \* \* Central to the policy of fostering collective bargaining, where the employees elect that course, is the principle of majority rule. See NLRB v. Jones & Laughlin Steel Corp., 301 U.S. 1, 57 S.Ct. 615, 81 L.Ed. 893 (1937). If the majority of a unit chooses union representation, the NLRA permits them to bargain with their employer to make union membership a condition of employment, thereby imposing their choice upon the minority. 29 U.S.C. §§ 157, 158(a)(3) [29 U.S.C.A. §§ 157, 158(a)(3)]. In establishing a regime of majority rule, Congress sought to secure to all members of the unit the benefits of their collective strength and bargaining power, in full awareness that the superior strength of some individuals or groups might be subordinated to the interest of the majority. Vaca v. Sipes, 386 U.S. 171, 182, 87 S.Ct. 903, 17 L.Ed.2d 842 (1967); J.I. Case Co. v. NLRB, 321 U.S. 332, 338–339, 88 L.Ed. 762, 64 S.Ct. 576 (1944); H.R.Rep. No. 972, 74th Cong., 1st Sess., 18, II Leg.Hist. of the NLRA 2974 (1935). As a result, "[t]he complete satisfaction of all who are represented is hardly to be expected." Ford Motor Co. v. Huffman, 345 U.S. 330, 338, 73 S.Ct. 681, 97 L.Ed. 1048 (1953).

\* \* \*

In vesting the representatives of the majority with this broad power Congress did not, of course, authorize a tyranny of the majority over minority interests. First, it confined the exercise of these powers to the context of a "unit appropriate for the purposes of collective bargaining,"

---

**12.**  That proviso states:

"That any individual employee or a group of employees shall have the right at any time to present grievances to their employer and to have such grievances adjusted, without the intervention of the bargaining representative, as long as the adjustment is not inconsistent with the terms of a collective-bargaining contract or agreement then in effect \* \* \*."

Respondent clearly misapprehends the nature of the "right" conferred by this section. The intendment of the proviso is to permit employees to present grievances and to authorize the employer to entertain them without opening itself to liability for dealing directly with employees in derogation of the duty to bargain only with the exclusive bargaining representative, a violation of § 8(a)(5). H.R.Rep. No. 245, 80th Cong., 1st Sess., p. 7 (1947); H.R.Rep. No. 510, 80th Cong., 1st Sess., p. 46 (1947)(Conference Comm). The Act nowhere protects this "right" by making it an unfair labor practice for an employer to refuse to entertain such a presentation, nor can it be read to authorize resort to economic coercion. This matter is fully explicated in Black–Clawson Co. v. Machinists, 313 F.2d 179 (C.A.2 1962). See also Republic Steel v. Maddox, 379 U.S. 650, 85 S.Ct. 614, 13 L.Ed.2d 580 (1965). If the employees' activity in the present case is to be deemed protected, therefore, it must be so by reason of the reading given to the main part of § 9(a), in light of Title VII and the national policy against employment discrimination, and not by burdening the proviso to that section with a load it was not meant to carry.

i.e., a group of employees with a sufficient commonality of circumstances to ensure against the submergence of a minority with distinctively different interests in the terms and conditions of their employment. See Allied Chemical Workers v. Pittsburgh Plate Glass Co., 404 U.S. 157, 171, 92 S.Ct. 383, 393, 30 L.Ed.2d 341 (1971). Second, it undertook in the 1959 Landrum–Griffin amendments, 73 Stat. 519, to assure that minority voices are heard as they are in the functioning of a democratic institution. Third, we have held, by the very nature of the exclusive bargaining representative's status as representative of all unit employees, Congress implicitly imposed upon it a duty fairly and in good faith to represent the interests of minorities within the unit. Vaca v. Sipes, supra; Wallace Corp. v. NLRB, 323 U.S. 248, 65 S.Ct. 238, 89 L.Ed. 216 (1944); cf. Steele v. Louisville & N.R. Co., 323 U.S. 192, 65 S.Ct. 226, 89 L.Ed. 173 (1944). And the Board has taken the position that a union's refusal to process grievances against racial discrimination, in violation of that duty, is an unfair labor practice. Hughes Tool Co., 147 N.L.R.B. 1573 (1964); see Miranda Fuel Co., 140 NLRB 181 (1962), enforcement denied 326 F.2d 172 (C.A.2 1963). Indeed, the Board has ordered a union implicated by a collective-bargaining agreement in discrimination with an employer to propose specific contractual provisions to prohibit racial discrimination. See Local Union No. 12, United Rubber Workers of America v. NLRB, 368 F.2d 12 (C.A.5 1966)(enforcement granted).

### B

Against this background of long and consistent adherence to the principle of exclusive representation tempered by safeguards for the protection of minority interests, respondent urges this Court to fashion a limited exception to that principle: employees who seek to bargain separately with their employer as to the elimination of racially discriminatory employment practices peculiarly affecting them, should be free from the constraints of the exclusivity principle of § 9(a). Essentially because established procedures under Title VII or, as in this case, a grievance machinery, are too time-consuming, the national labor policy against discrimination requires this exception, respondent argues, and its adoption would not unduly compromise the legitimate interests of either unions or employers.

Plainly, national labor policy embodies the principles of nondiscrimination as a matter of highest priority, Alexander v. Gardner–Denver Co., 415 U.S. 36, 47, 94 S.Ct. 1011, 39 L.Ed.2d 147 (1974), and it is a commonplace that we must construe the NLRA in light of the broad national labor policy of which it is a part. See Textile Workers v. Lincoln Mills, 353 U.S. 448, 456–458, 77 S.Ct. 912, 1 L.Ed.2d 972 (1957). These general principles do not aid respondent, however, as it is far from clear that separate bargaining is necessary to help eliminate discrimination. Indeed, as the facts of this case demonstrate, the proposed remedy might have just the opposite effect. The collective-bargaining agreement in this case prohibited without qualification all manner of invidious discrimination and made any claimed violation a grievable issue. The grievance procedure is directed precisely at determining whether discrimination has occurred. That orderly determination, if affirmative, could lead to an arbitral award enforceable in court. Nor is there any reason to believe that the processing of grievances is inherently limited to the correction of individual cases of discrimination. Quite apart from the essentially contractual question of whether the Union could grieve against a "pattern or practice" it deems inconsistent with the nondiscrimination clause of the contract, one would hardly expect an employer to continue in effect an employment practice that routinely results in adverse arbitral decisions.

The decision by a handful of employees to bypass the grievance procedure in favor of attempting to bargain with their employer, by contrast, may or may not be predicated upon the actual existence of discrimination. An employer confronted with bargaining demands from each of several minority groups would not necessarily, or even probably, be able to agree to remedial steps satisfactory to all at once. Competing claims on the employer's ability to accommodate each group's demands, e.g., for reassignments and promotions to a limited number of positions, could only set one group against the other even if it is not the employer's intention to divide and overcome them. Having divided themselves, the minority employees will not be in position to advance their cause unless it be by recourse *seriatim* to economic coercion, which can only have the effect of further dividing them along racial or other lines. Nor is the situation materially different where, as apparently happened here, self-designated representatives purport to speak for all groups that might consider themselves to be victims of discrimination. Even if in actual bargaining the various groups did not perceive their interests as divergent and further subdivide themselves, the employer would be bound to bargain with them in a field largely preempted by the current collective-bargaining agreement with the elected bargaining representative. * * *

What has been said here in evaluating respondent's claim that the policy against discrimination requires § 7 protection for concerted efforts at minority bargaining has obvious implications for the related claim that legitimate employer and union interests would not be unduly compromised thereby. The court below minimized the impact on the Union in this case by noting that it was not working at cross-purposes with the dissidents, and that indeed it could not do so consistent with its duty of fair representation and perhaps its obligations under Title VII. As to the Company, its obligations under Title VII are cited for the proposition that it could have no legitimate objection to bargaining with the dissidents in order to achieve full compliance with that law.

This argument confuses the employees' substantive right to be free of racial discrimination with the procedures available under the NLRA for securing these rights. Whether they are thought to depend upon Title VII or have an independent source in the NLRA, they cannot be pursued at the expense of the orderly collective-bargaining process contemplated by the NLRA. The elimination of discrimination and its vestiges is an appropriate subject of bargaining, and an employer may have no objection to incorporating into a collective agreement the substance of his obligation not to discriminate in personnel decisions; the Company here has done as much, making any claimed dereliction a matter subject to the grievance-arbitration machinery as well as to the processes of Title VII. But that does not mean that he may not have strong and legitimate objections to bargaining on several fronts over the implementation of the right to be free of discrimination for some of the reasons set forth above. Similarly, while a union cannot lawfully bargain for the establishment or continuation of discriminatory practices, see Steele v. Louisville & N.R. Co., supra, 42 U.S.C. § 2000–2(c)(3) [42 U.S.C.A. § 2000–2(c)(3)], it has a legitimate interest in presenting a united front on this as on other issues and in not seeing its strength dissipated and its stature denigrated by subgroups within the unit separately pursuing what they see as separate interests. When union and employer are not responsive to their legal obligations, the bargain they have struck must yield pro tanto to the law, whether by means of conciliation through the offices of the EEOC, or by means of federal court enforcement at the instance of either that agency or the party claiming to be aggrieved.

Accordingly, we think neither aspect of respondent's contention in support of a right to short-circuit orderly, established processes for eliminating discrimination in employment is well-founded. The policy of industrial self-determination as expressed in § 7 does not require fragmentation of the bargaining unit along racial or other lines in order to consist with the national labor policy against discrimination. And in the face of such fragmentation, whatever its effect on discriminatory practices, the bargaining process that the principle of exclusive representation is meant to lubricate could not endure unhampered.

[In Part III of its opinion, the Court considered whether the exclusive-representation policies of the NLRA were to be subordinated to the very specific protection accorded by Title VII against employer reprisals for employee efforts to oppose unlawful discrimination. See note 7 supra. The Court, assuming arguendo that Section 704(a) protects employee picketing and the institution of a consumer boycott of an employer, held nonetheless that violations of that section were to be challenged under the procedures set forth in Title VII. To the employees' claim that NLRB unfair labor practice proceedings are more expeditious and effective than remedies involving the EEOC, the Court responded that this argument "is properly addressed to the Congress and not to this Court or the NLRB."]

■ Mr. Justice Douglas, dissenting.

The Court's opinion makes these union members—and others similarly situated—prisoners of the union. The law, I think, was designed to prevent that tragic consequence. Hence, I dissent.

Petitioners, who are black and were members of a union through which they obtained employment by the Emporium, would seem to have suffered rank discrimination because of their race. They theoretically had a cause of action against their union for breach of its duty of fair representation spelled out in Steele v. Louisville R. Co., 323 U.S. 192, 65 S.Ct. 226, 89 L.Ed. 173. But as the law on that phase of the problem has evolved it would seem that the burden on the employee is heavy. See Vaca v. Sipes, 386 U.S. 171, 190, 87 S.Ct. 903, 17 L.Ed.2d 842, where it was held that the union action must be "arbitrary, discriminatory, and in bad faith."

The employees might also have sought relief under Title VII of the Civil Rights Act of 1964, which forbids discrimination in employment on the basis of "race, color, religion, sex or national origin." * * *

In this case, the employees took neither of the foregoing courses, each fraught with obstacles, but picketed to protest Emporium's practices. I believe these were "concerted activities" protected under § 7 of the National Labor Relations Act. The employees were engaged in a traditional form of labor protest, directed at matters which are unquestionably a proper subject of employee concern. * * *

The Board has held that the employees were unprotected because they sought to confront the employer outside the grievance process, which was under union control. The Court upholds the Board, on the view that this result is commanded by the principle of "exclusive representation" embodied in § 9 of the NLRA. But in the area of racial discrimination the union is hardly in a position to demand exclusive control, for the employee's right to nondiscriminatory treatment does not depend upon union demand but is based on the law. * * *

The law should facilitate the involvement of unions in the quest for racial equality in employment, but it should not make the individual a prisoner of the union. While employees may reasonably be required to approach the union first, as a kind of "exhaustion" requirement before resorting to economic protest, cf NLRB v. Tanner Motor Livery, 419 F.2d 216 (CA9), they should not be under continued inhibition when it becomes apparent that the union response is inadequate. The Court of Appeals held that the employees should be protected from discharge unless the Board found on remand that the union had been prosecuting their complaints "to the fullest extent possible, by the most expeditious means." I would not disturb this standard. Union conduct can be oppressive even if not made in bad faith. The inertia of weak-kneed, docile union leadership can be as devastating to the cause of racial equality as aggressive subversion. Continued submission by employees to such a regime should not be demanded.

I would affirm the judgment below.

————

## PROBLEMS FOR DISCUSSION

**1.** Had there been no union and no collective bargaining agreement at the Emporium store, would not Hollins and Hawkins have been clearly engaging in "concerted activity for mutual aid or protection" protected by Section 7? (Put aside the question whether their abusive terminology might warrant forfeiting this protection.) Does the fact that there *is* a designated union—which Hollins and Hawkins earnestly believe to be inadequately representing the interests of a substantial number of employees—make their peaceful concerted activity any less within the language, and the spirit, of Section 7? (As with the *J.I. Case* decision, is not Section 9(a) taking back important individual and group rights which Section 7 appears clearly to grant?)

**2.** Might the Court have given weight to the fact that the ultimate object of the protesters was one that the majority union endorsed? Would it be appropriate, in other words, to protect "wildcat" activity that promotes a position that the union supports while holding unprotected such activity the object of which is not endorsed by the bargaining representative? Compare East Chicago Rehab. Center v. NLRB, 710 F.2d 397 (7th Cir.1983), with AAL, Inc. v. United Food Workers, 275 NLRB 84 (1985).

**3.** Although the Board and the Supreme Court make much of the finding that Hollins and Hawkins had demanded to "bargain" with the company president, would the case have been decided any differently had it been found that this was not their purpose? What exactly was it about their activity which led to the conclusion that they sought to "bargain"?

**4.** Assume that Smith, an African–American employee of the Emporium Capwell Co., was passed over for a promotion which he claims was due him under the terms of the collective bargaining agreement. Believing that he can present his grievance more aggressively and effectively than can the union, Smith has written to the Company president to demand an interview and to demand that the promotion be given to him; his letter also asserts that if the labor contract as presently written does provide for the promotion of another in preference to him, the contract ought to be promptly changed. Smith states that he is willing to meet alone with the Company president, but that he would much prefer to have along with him employees Jones and Williams (who are also officers in the Western Addition Community Organization). You are counsel for the Company, and the president has consulted you as to the response he should give to Smith's letter. What issues do you see and what advice would you give your client? See Landers v. National R.R. Passengers Corp., 485 U.S. 652, 108 S.Ct. 1440, 99 L.Ed.2d 745 (1988).

———

*THE LIMITS OF MAJORITY RULE*

As *J.I. Case* and *Emporium Capwell* make clear, the interests and wishes of individuals and minority groups within the bargaining unit must be subordinated to the exclusive-bargaining status of the majority labor organization. It is inevitable that, on occasion, certain groups or individuals will believe that the bargaining representative is ignoring their interests. Does the law provide any recourse?

(1) In defining the *appropriate bargaining unit,* the Board will attempt to exclude groups of workers who have a conflict of interests, or who lack a community of interests, with the unit in which the election will be held. The excluded group will then be able to select their own majority representative, or no representative at all.

(2) Employees have the periodic right to vote out the union in a *decertification election,* whether the union was initially recognized informally or was the victor in an NLRB representation election. The frequency of such elections is, of course, limited by the election-bar and certification-bar rules and particularly by the contract-bar rule, by which the incumbent

union can insulate itself against a decertification election for up to three years.

(3) The Landrum–Griffin Act of 1959 provides for what is known as a *bill of rights for union members*. Its purpose is to guarantee a substantial measure of democratic rights and procedures within the internal affairs of the union, so that minority groups within the union have the opportunity to modify union policies. Members are given the right to speak on all matters at union meetings, to vote for candidates for union office, and to be eligible to stand for election to union office (subject to "reasonable" union rules).

(4) A worker who is in the bargaining unit for which the majority union speaks *does not automatically have to become a member* of that union. A unit member must become a union "member" only if the employer and the union negotiate a collective bargaining provision making membership a condition of continued employment; this is known as a union-shop provision, and Congress has chosen to permit this one exception to the mandates of Section 8(a)(3) through the provisos to that section. The "membership" that the employer and the union may agree to require is no more than the obligation to pay to the union an amount equivalent to union dues; the theory is that all employees in the unit receive the benefits of the union's activities as bargaining representative and grievance processor, so that it is reasonable to require all employees to pay a "fee" for such services. Section 14(b) of the NLRA empowers states to enact "right to work" laws which make such union-shop provisions unlawful and unenforceable (an unusual deference to state policy in the midst of a comprehensive scheme of federal regulation).

(5) On matters other than "wages, hours, and other terms or conditions of employment"—that is, on so-called *nonmandatory subjects*—there is no duty to bargain exclusively with the majority representative, and on these matters individual or minority-group bargaining can lawfully be carried on.

(6) As already noted in connection with *Emporium Capwell,* the proviso to Section 9(a) explicitly preserves to individual employees the right to *present and to process grievances*.

All of these limitations on majority rule are explored in greater detail elsewhere in this book.

(7) Among the most significant limitations upon the union's power to accommodate interests within the bargaining unit is the *duty of fair representation.* This duty was initially inferred by the Supreme Court under the Railway Labor Act in the famous *Steele* decision, which follows; soon after, it was extended to unions in industries covered by the National Labor Relations Act. The Court concluded that this duty is enforceable by civil actions in the federal (and state) courts, and the National Labor Relations Board has more recently held, with judicial approval, that a breach of the duty is also an unfair labor practice. The duty of fair representation is

treated in greater detail below, but it is useful at this time to examine the source and basics of the doctrine.

_____

## Steele v. Louisville & Nashville R. Co.<sup></sup><sup></sup>ᶜ

323 U.S. 192, 65 S.Ct. 226, 89 L.Ed. 173 (1944).

■ MR. CHIEF JUSTICE STONE delivered the opinion of the Court.

The question is whether the Railway Labor Act, 48 Stat. 1185, 45 U.S.C. § 151 et seq., 45 U.S.C.A. § 151 et seq., imposes on a labor organization, acting by authority of the statute as the exclusive bargaining representative of a craft or class of railway employees, the duty to represent all the employees in the craft without discrimination because of their race, and, if so, whether the courts have jurisdiction to protect the minority of the craft or class from the violation of such obligation.

* * * Petitioner, a Negro, is a locomotive fireman in the employ of respondent railroad, suing on his own behalf and that of his fellow employees who, like petitioner, are Negro firemen employed by the Railroad. Respondent Brotherhood, a labor organization, is, as provided under § 2, Fourth of the Railway Labor Act, the exclusive bargaining representative of the craft of firemen employed by the Railroad and is recognized as such by it and the members of the craft. The majority of the firemen employed by the Railroad are white and are members of the Brotherhood, but a substantial minority are Negroes who, by the constitution and ritual of the Brotherhood, are excluded from its membership. As the membership of the Brotherhood constitutes a majority of all firemen employed on respondent Railroad, and as under § 2, Fourth, the members because they are the majority have the right to choose and have chosen the Brotherhood to represent the craft, petitioner and other Negro firemen on the road have been required to accept the Brotherhood as their representative for the purposes of the Act.

On March 28, 1940, the Brotherhood, purporting to act as representative of the entire craft of firemen, without informing the Negro firemen or

_____

c. See T. Boyce & R. Turner, Fair Representation, the NLRB and the Courts (rev. ed. 1984); Clark, The Duty of Fair Representation: A Theoretical Structure, 51 Texas L.Rev. 1119 (1973); Cox, The Duty of Fair Representation, 2 Vill.L.Rev. 151 (1957); Finkin, The Limits of Majority Rule in Collective Bargaining, 64 Minn.L.Rev. 183 (1980); Goldberg, The Duty of Fair Representation: What the Courts Do In Fact, 34 Buff.L.Rev. 89 (1985); Harper & Lupu, Fair Representation as Equal Protection, 98 Harv.L.Rev. 1211 (1985); Klare, The Quest for Industrial Democracy and the Struggle Against Racism: Perspectives from Labor Law and Civil Rights Law, 61 Ore.L.Rev. 157 (1982); J. McKelvey (ed.), The Changing Law of Fair Representation (1985); Murphy, The Duty of Fair Representation Under Taft–Hartley, 30 Mo.L.Rev. 373 (1965); Sherman, Union's Duty of Fair Representation and the Civil Rights Act of 1964, 49 Minn.L.Rev. 771 (1965); Sovern, The National Labor Relations Act and Racial Discrimination, 62 Colum.L.Rev. 563 (1962); Wellington, Union Democracy and Fair Representation: Federal Responsibility in a Federal System, 67 Yale L.J. 1327 (1958). For additional articles, see p. 1013 infra.

giving them opportunity to be heard, served a notice on respondent Railroad and on twenty other railroads operating principally in the southeastern part of the United States. The notice announced the Brotherhood's desire to amend the existing collective bargaining agreement in such manner as ultimately to exclude all Negro firemen from the service. By established practice on the several railroads so notified only white firemen can be promoted to serve as engineers, and the notice proposed that only "promotable", i.e., white, men should be employed as firemen or assigned to new runs or jobs or permanent vacancies in established runs or jobs.

On February 18, 1941, the railroads and the Brotherhood, as representative of the craft, entered into a new agreement which provided that not more than 50% of the firemen in each class of service in each seniority district of a carrier should be Negroes; that until such percentage should be reached all new runs and all vacancies should be filled by white men; and that the agreement did not sanction the employment of Negroes in any seniority district in which they were not working. The agreement reserved the right of the Brotherhood to negotiate for further restrictions on the employment of Negro firemen on the individual railroads. On May 12, 1941, the Brotherhood entered into a supplemental agreement with respondent Railroad further controlling the seniority rights of Negro firemen and restricting their employment. The Negro firemen were not given notice or opportunity to be heard with respect to either of these agreements, which were put into effect before their existence was disclosed to the Negro firemen.

Until April 8, 1941, petitioner was in a "passenger pool", to which one white and five Negro firemen were assigned. These jobs were highly desirable in point of wages, hours and other considerations. Petitioner had performed and was performing his work satisfactorily. Following a reduction in the mileage covered by the pool, all jobs in the pool were, about April 1, 1941, declared vacant. The Brotherhood and the Railroad, acting under the agreement, disqualified all the Negro firemen and replaced them with four white men, members of the Brotherhood, all junior in seniority to petitioner and no more competent or worthy. As a consequence petitioner was deprived of employment for sixteen days and then was assigned to more arduous, longer, and less remunerative work in local freight service. In conformity to the agreement, he was later replaced by a Brotherhood member junior to him, and assigned work on a switch engine, which was still harder and less remunerative, until January 3, 1942. On that date, after the bill of complaint in the present suit had been filed, he was reassigned to passenger service. * * *

[The complaint sought, among other things, an injunction against enforcement of the labor agreements between the Railroad and the Brotherhood and damages against the Brotherhood. The Supreme Court of Alabama concluded that the complaint stated no cause of action. It held that the Railroad was obligated by statute to bargain with the Brotherhood as the majority representative of the craft, and that the Brotherhood had the statutory power both to create and to destroy the plaintiff's seniority rights. It construed the Railway Labor Act as imposing no duty on the Brotherhood to protect the rights of minorities from discrimination or unfair treatment, however gross.]

If, as the state court has held, the Act confers this power on the bargaining representative of a craft or class of employees without any commensurate statutory duty toward its members, constitutional questions arise. For the representative is clothed with power not unlike that of a legislature which is subject to constitutional limitations on its power to deny, restrict, destroy or discriminate against the rights of those for whom it legislates and which is also under an affirmative constitutional duty equally to protect those rights. If the Railway Labor Act purports to impose on petitioner and the other Negro members of the craft the legal duty to comply with the terms of a contract whereby the representative has discriminatorily restricted their employment for the benefit and advantage of the Brotherhood's own members, we must decide the constitutional questions which petitioner raises in his pleading.

But we think that Congress, in enacting the Railway Labor Act and authorizing a labor union, chosen by a majority of a craft, to represent the craft, did not intend to confer plenary power upon the union to sacrifice, for the benefit of its members, rights of the minority of the craft, without imposing on it any duty to protect the minority. Since petitioner and the other Negro members of the craft are not members of the Brotherhood or eligible for membership, the authority to act for them is derived not from their action or consent but wholly from the command of the Act. Section 2, Fourth, provides: "Employees shall have the right to organize and bargain collectively through representatives of their own choosing. The majority of any craft or class of employees shall have the right to determine who shall be the representative of the craft or class for the purposes of this Act * * *." * * *

Section 2, Second, requiring carriers to bargain with the representative so chosen, operates to exclude any other from representing a craft. Virginian R. Co. v. System Federation, supra, 300 U.S. 545, 57 S.Ct. 598, 81 L.Ed. 789. The minority members of a craft are thus deprived by the statute of the right, which they would otherwise possess, to choose a representative of their own, and its members cannot bargain individually on behalf of themselves as to matters which are properly the subject of collective bargaining. Order of Railroad Telegraphers v. Railway Express Agency, 321 U.S. 342, 64 S.Ct. 582, and see under the like provisions of the National Labor Relations Act, J.I. Case Co. v. National Labor Relations Board, 321 U.S. 332, 64 S.Ct. 576, and Medo Photo Supply Corp. v. National Labor Relations Board, 321 U.S. 678, 64 S.Ct. 830. * * *

Unless the labor union representing a craft owes some duty to represent non-union members of the craft, at least to the extent of not discriminating against them as such in the contracts which it makes as their representative, the minority would be left with no means of protecting their interests, or indeed, their right to earn a livelihood by pursuing the occupation in which they are employed. While the majority of the craft chooses the bargaining representative, when chosen it represents, as the Act by its term makes plain, the craft or class, and not the majority. The fair interpretation of the statutory language is that the organization chosen to represent a craft is to represent all its members, the majority as well as the minority, and it is to act for and not against those whom it represents. It is a principle of general application that the exercise of a granted power to act in behalf of others involves the assumption toward them of a duty to exercise the power in their interest and behalf, and that such a grant of power will not be deemed to dispense with all duty toward those for whom it is exercised unless so expressed.

We think that the Railway Labor Act imposes upon the statutory representative of a craft at least as exacting a duty to protect equally the interests of the members of the craft as the Constitution imposes upon a legislature to give equal protection to the interests of those for whom it legislates. Congress has seen fit to clothe the bargaining representative with powers comparable to those possessed by a legislative body both to create and restrict the rights of those whom it represents, cf. J.I. Case Co. v. National Labor Relations Board, supra, 321 U.S. 335, 64 S.Ct. 579, but it has also imposed on the representative a corresponding duty. We hold that the language of the Act to which we have referred, read in the light of the purposes of the Act, expresses the aim of Congress to impose on the bargaining representative of a craft or class of employees the duty to exercise fairly the power conferred upon it in behalf of all those for whom it acts, without hostile discrimination against them.

This does not mean that the statutory representative of a craft is barred from making contracts which may have unfavorable effects on some of the members of the craft represented. Variations in the terms of the contract based on differences relevant to the authorized purposes of the contract in conditions to which they are to be applied, such as differences in seniority, the type of work performed, the competence and skill with which it is performed, are within the scope of the bargaining representation of a craft, all of whose members are not identical in their interest or merit. [Citations omitted.] Without attempting to mark the allowable limits of differences in the terms of contracts based on differences of conditions to which they apply, it is enough for present purposes to say that the statutory power to represent a craft and to make contracts as to wages, hours and working conditions does not include the authority to make among members of the craft discriminations not based on such relevant differences. Here the discriminations based on race alone are obviously irrelevant and invidious. Congress plainly did not undertake to authorize the bargaining representative to make such discriminations. [Citations omitted.]

The representative which thus discriminates may be enjoined from so doing, and its members may be enjoined from taking the benefit of such discriminatory action. No more is the Railroad bound by or entitled to take the benefit of a contract which the bargaining representative is prohibited by the statute from making. In both cases the right asserted, which is derived from the duty imposed by the statute on the bargaining representative, is a federal right implied from the statute and the policy which it has adopted. It is the federal statute which condemns as unlawful the Brotherhood's conduct. "The extent and nature of the legal consequences of this condemnation, though left by the statute to judicial determination, are nevertheless to be derived from it and the federal policy which it has adopted." Deitrick v. Greaney, 309 U.S. 190, 200, 201, 60 S.Ct. 480, 485, 84 L.Ed. 694. [Other citations omitted.]

So long as a labor union assumes to act as the statutory representative of a craft, it cannot rightly refuse to perform the duty, which is inseparable from the power of representation conferred upon it, to represent the entire membership of the craft. While the statute does not deny to such a bargaining labor organization the right to determine eligibility to its membership, it does require the union, in collective bargaining and in making contracts with the carrier, to represent non-union or minority union members of the craft without hostile discrimination, fairly, impartially, and in good faith. Wherever necessary to that end, the union is required to consider requests of nonunion members of the craft and expressions of their views with respect to collective bargaining with the employer and to give to them notice of and opportunity for hearing upon its proposed action. * * *

In the absence of any available administrative remedy, the right here asserted, to a remedy for breach of the statutory duty of the bargaining representative to represent and act for the members of a craft, is of judicial cognizance. That right would be sacrificed or obliterated if it were without the remedy which courts can give for breach of such a duty or obligation and which it is their duty to give in cases in which they have jurisdiction. * * *

We conclude that the statute contemplates resort to the usual judicial remedies of injunction and award of damages when appropriate for breach of that duty.

The judgment is accordingly reversed and remanded for further proceedings not inconsistent with this opinion.

Reversed.

■ Mr. Justice Black concurs in the result. [The concurring opinion of Mr. Justice Murphy is omitted.]

———

Ford Motor Co. v. Huffman, 345 U.S. 330, 73 S.Ct. 681, 97 L.Ed. 1048 (1953). Plaintiff sued to have certain provisions of a collective bargaining agreement declared invalid. In their contract, the company and the United Automobile Workers agreed to give seniority credit for military service to employees who completed a probationary period of six months with Ford, even though they had not worked for Ford before the war. This went beyond the requirement of a federal statute that seniority continue to accrue for persons whose service for Ford was interrupted by military duty. The effect of this pre-employment seniority credit was to give greater seniority to certain employees who were first employed by Ford at a time subsequent to plaintiff's employment but who were credited with seniority based on their prior military service. The plaintiff asserted that the union had violated its duty of fair representation by discriminating on the basis of a factor not ordinarily considered directly relevant to wages and working conditions. The Supreme Court *held* that the disputed provisions did not evidence a breach of the union's duty of fair representation. It stressed the discretion of the union to make reasonable distinctions among employees and concluded that the seniority credit was "within the reasonable bounds of relevancy." The Court observed:

> "Inevitably differences arise in the manner and degree to which the terms of any negotiated agreement affect individual employees and classes of employees. The mere existence of such differences does not make them invalid. The complete satisfaction of all who are represented is hardly to be expected. A wide range of reasonableness must be allowed a statutory bargaining representative in serving the unit it represents, subject always to complete good faith and honesty of purpose in the exercise of its discretion. * * * Seniority rules governing promotions, transfers, layoffs and similar matters may, in the first instance, revolve around length of competent service. Variations acceptable in the discretion of bargaining representatives, however, may well include differences based upon such matters as the unit within which seniority is to be computed, the privileges to which it shall relate, the nature of the work, the time at which it is done, the fitness, ability or age of the employees, their family responsibilities, injuries received in course of service, and time or labor devoted to related public service, whether civil or military, voluntary or involuntary."

---

## PROBLEMS FOR DISCUSSION

**1.** Is it a violation of the duty of fair representation if a union flatly declines to process meritorious grievances raised by black or female workers in the bargaining unit? Do the language and logic of the *Steele* case extend to contract administration and grievance processing, as distinguished from contract negotiation? Is the first proviso in Section 9(a) of the NLRA relevant to this issue?

**2.** Section 8(b)(2) has since 1947 made it unlawful for a union to give priority to union members in negotiating benefits or in grievance processing. Does a union also violate Section 8(b)(2) when it negotiates greater benefits for white workers than it does for black workers? Does such an agreement induce the employer to "discriminate" so as to "encourage union membership"?

**3.** If the NLRB is indeed an alternative forum for enforcing the duty of fair representation, why would an aggrieved employee ever resort to a court proceeding to enforce the duty?

**4.** Does it violate the duty of fair representation for a union to deny membership, or membership benefits (such as low-cost life insurance policies or travel programs), to particular workers whom the union leadership "does not like"? Can an effective argument be made that an incident of the duty of fair representation is also non-discriminatory admission to union membership for all workers in the bargaining unit?

**5.** Could the union—consistent with its duty of fair representation—negotiate a contract provision requiring preferential hiring of male job *applicants?* (That would, except in the rarest of instances, be a violation of Title VII of the Civil Rights Act of 1964. But would it violate the duty of fair representation?) Would it be a violation of that duty for the union to agree to reduce drastically medical insurance coverage for retired workers formerly employed by the company in order to increase the number of paid holidays for currently employed workers? Cf. Karo v. San Diego Symphony Orch. Ass'n, 762 F.2d 819 (9th Cir.1985).

**6.** Was the Court in the *Huffman* case correct in stating that the union could negotiate seniority preferences (beyond what was required by statute) for veterans of the armed forces hired by the Ford Motor Company? Consider the language in the *Steele* decision in which the Court gives examples of "differences relevant to the authorized purposes of the contract."

---

## II.   THE DUTY TO BARGAIN IN GOOD FAITH[a]

In 1947, Congress defined what it meant for an employer or labor organization to be obligated to "bargain collectively," as required by Sections 8(a)(5) and 8(b)(3), respectively. Section 8(d) provides that

> "to bargain collectively is the performance of the mutual obligation of the employer and the representative of the employees to meet at reasonable times and confer in good faith with respect to wages, hours, and other terms and conditions of employment, or the negotiation of an agreement, or any question arising thereunder, and the execution of a written contract incorporating any agreement reached if requested by either party, but such obligation does not compel either party to agree to a proposal or require the making of a concession."

Clearly, the statute requires that certain conduct be objectively manifested. The parties must "meet at reasonable times and confer" and must if requested execute a writing that incorporates any agreement reached. As starkly clear as these directives seem, they are not free of ambiguity. How long an interval between meetings is "unreasonable"? Are there any circumstances under which the employer (or union) may be excused from meeting at all? It is, for example, generally understood that the parties are not obliged to continue meeting once they have in good faith bargained to a deadlock or "impasse" and it appears that further discussions would be

---

**a.** See Cox, The Duty to Bargain in Good Faith, 71 Harv.L.Rev. 1401 (1958); Duvin, The Duty to Bargain: Law in Search of Policy, 64 Col.L.Rev. 248 (1964); Fleming, The Obligation to Bargain in Good Faith, 47 Va.L.Rev. 988 (1961); Gross, Cullen & Han-slowe, Good Faith in Labor Negotiations: Tests and Remedies, 53 Cornell L.Rev. 1009 (1968); Smith, Evolution of the "Duty to Bargain" Concept in American Law, 39 Mich. L.Rev. 1065 (1941).

fruitless; until circumstances change sufficiently to break the impasse (most obviously, if one party modifies its demands and requests a meeting), the duty to bargain is satisfied without "meeting." The court in dictum in General Electric Co. v. NLRB, p. 300 supra, stated that in some rare instances a party could refuse to meet for negotiations if the composition of the bargaining team across the table was purposely selected in order to be disruptive and offensive. Even less clear than the duty to "meet" is the duty to "confer." Most of the Problems for Discussion which follow this Note invite analysis of that statutory requirement.

The duty to bargain prescribed by Section 8(d) encompasses not only the obligation to meet and confer with respect to wages, hours and terms and conditions of employment. It includes the obligation to bargain "in good faith." The reasons for this requirement have been described as follows in Cox, The Duty to Bargain in Good Faith, 71 Harv.L.Rev. 1401, 1412–13 (1958):

> "It was not enough for the law to compel the parties to meet and treat without passing judgment upon the quality of the negotiations. The bargaining status of a union can be destroyed by going through the motions of negotiating almost as easily as by bluntly withholding recognition. The NLRB reports are filled with cases in which a union won an election but lacked the economic power to use the strike as a weapon for compelling the employer to grant it real participation in industrial government. As long as there are unions weak enough to be talked to death, there will be employers who are tempted to engage in the forms of bargaining without the substance. The concept of 'good faith' was brought into the law of collective bargaining as a solution to this problem."

The duty to bargain "in good faith" has been defined in general terms on many occasions. A typical formulation is that of the Court of Appeals for the Ninth Circuit in N.L.R.B. v. Montgomery Ward & Co., 133 F.2d 676 (9th Cir.1943), where the court described the duty as "an obligation * * * to participate actively in the deliberations so as to indicate a present intention to find a basis for agreement." Not only must the employer have "an open mind and a sincere desire to reach an agreement" but "a sincere effort must be made to reach a common ground." Is this a useful formulation? How literally can its application be made the basis of decision? In reading the following cases, see if you can develop any preferable formulation.

Although bad faith may occasionally be demonstrated by the declarations of the party in question, proof must ordinarily be derived by drawing inferences from external conduct. In some cases, an argument may be made that bad faith can be inferred from the nature of the substantive proposals which the respondent has made during the negotiations. The *A–1 Sandwiches* decision, infra, is illustrative. More often, an effort is made to determine bad faith from the tactics or procedures employed by the respondent in bargaining with the other party. In certain cases, the Board has sought to single out particular tactics used by the respondent as *per se* violations of the duty to bargain in good faith. See the *Insurance Agents, Katz* and *Truitt Mfg.* cases, infra. In other proceedings, a finding of bad faith has been based upon the totality of the bargaining tactics employed.

------

## PROBLEMS FOR DISCUSSION

**1.** Because of past disputes, during the term of several contracts, about the intended meaning of contract provisions and about oral assurances given at past negotiation sessions, the company wishes to know whether it may condition bargaining in the future upon the presence in the bargaining room of a certified court stenographer who is to prepare a verbatim transcript of the proceedings. The union has already stated that it regards the presence of a stenographer in negotiations as an insult, that it objects to the practice, and that it is prepared to challenge it by filing a charge under Section 8(a)(5). Advise the company concerning the legality (and the wisdom) of its position. See Latrobe Steel Co. v. NLRB, 630 F.2d 171 (3d Cir.1980); Pennsylvania Tel. Guild v. Bell Telephone, 277 NLRB 501 (1985). (Can the company lawfully "get the upper hand" simply by bringing in the stenographer as part of the company's bargaining team, or simply by turning on a tape recorder when negotiations begin?)

**2.** Immediately after its certification as collective bargaining representative of employees of the Ames Cotton Company, the Union presented a proposed contract and asked for a conference with Ames's executives. At the conference the Union explained its proposals and gave supporting reasons. Ames asked a good many questions about their meaning and effect and at the end of the conference its president said, "I am sure we understand your position, although we would be glad to meet again if you think there is anything which requires further clarification. However, we cannot agree to any of your demands. If there is no further business, we may as well adjourn." Has Ames committed an unfair labor practice?

**3.** Carolina Cotton Company engaged in collective bargaining with Union Local 53, the certified representative of its employees, and a tentative agreement was reached on nearly all the terms of a collective agreement including wages. Several times during the negotiations Local 53 broached the subject of union security and asked the company to agree to put a union shop clause into the contract. On the first occasion Andrews, the vice president in charge of industrial relations, replied, "We will not sign a union shop contract. Our minds are made up. Let's not waste time arguing about it. I know all the arguments, and you know that I know them. I made them all and suggested every conceivable compromise during the ten years I was a federal conciliator. Now let's get back to business." Whenever the union came back to this subject, Andrews left the room saying, "You're just wasting time." Has the company violated Section 8(a)(5)?

**4.** The Union represents employees at a number of supermarkets in the metropolitan area, and recently won a representation election at the Ace Supermarket. At the first scheduled bargaining session, the Union representative handed over to the Ace negotiating team a copy of a collective bargaining agreement, which was said to be "the same contract that is signed by every market we represent; we can't make any changes with you, or else every other market in the area will expect to get the same changes, and we are not prepared to renegotiate with everybody else. We'll be glad to explain what the reasons are for each of these provisions, but you'll have to sign it as is." Has the Union violated Section 8(b)(3)?

———

# NLRB v. A–1 King Size Sandwiches, Inc.

732 F.2d 872 (11th Cir.), cert. denied, 469 U.S. 1035, 105 S.Ct. 508, 83 L.Ed.2d 399 (1984).

■ Dyer, Senior Circuit Judge:

This case is before us upon the application of the National Labor Relations Board pursuant to Section 10(e) of the National Labor Relations Act, 29 U.S.C. §§ 151, 160(e)(1982), for enforcement of its order issued against A–1 King Size Sandwiches, Inc.

The Hotel, Motel, Restaurant Employees & Bartenders Union, Local No. 737, filed an unfair labor practice charge against the Company, alleging that the Company failed to bargain in good faith, and, instead, engaged in surface bargaining. In due course the administrative law judge issued a decision finding that the Company had violated Section 8(a)(1) and (5) of the Act, 29 U.S.C. §§ 158(a)(1), (5)(1982), by engaging in surface bargaining with no intention of entering into a collective bargaining agreement. The Board affirmed the administrative law judge's rulings, findings and conclusions.

The Company argues that its proposals were not so unusually harsh, vindictive or unreasonable that they were predictably unacceptable, and its bargaining was therefore in good faith. We disagree and enforce.

The Company produces sandwiches and pies on an assembly line. It sells, distributes and delivers these products to convenience stores. After a Board certification of the Union, as the exclusive bargaining representative for a unit of the Company's production and maintenance employees, shuttle truck drivers, and shipping helpers, including between fifty and sixty employees, A–1 unsuccessfully challenged certification by refusing to bargain. The Board's bargaining order was enforced by the United States Court of Appeals, Fifth Circuit.

There were eighteen bargaining sessions at agreed times and places during an eleven-month period. The negotiations did not result in a contract. The parties reached agreement on a recognition clause; plant visitation by Union representatives; the number, rights and duties of Union stewards; the Union's use of a bulletin board; pay for jury duty; leaves of absence; and a procedure for processing grievances and conducting arbitrations with respect to matters of interpretation or application of express provisions of the contract. As to all other subjects no agreement was reached. The administrative law judge properly found that the Company met at reasonable times and places, and that the Company bore no animus toward the Union. There is no evidence that the Company engaged in any conduct away from the bargaining table that might tend to show it would not conclude an agreement with the Union.

The well-settled principles bearing upon the issues here presented are easily stated but not so easily applied. Section 8(a)(5) of the Act, 29 U.S.C. § 158(a)(5)(1982), makes it an unfair labor practice for an employer to refuse to bargain collectively with the employees' representative. The Supreme Court, in establishing the parameters to be applied under the Act, has said, "the Act does not compel any agreement whatsoever between employees and employers." NLRB v. American Nat'l Ins., 343 U.S. 395, 402, 72 S.Ct. 824, 828, 96 L.Ed. 1027 (1952)(citing Labor Board v. Jones & Laughlin Steel, 301 U.S. 1, 45, 57 S.Ct. 615, 628, 81 L.Ed. 893 (1937)). "And it is equally clear that [under section 8(d) of the Act] the Board may not, either directly or indirectly, compel concessions or otherwise sit in judgment upon the substantive terms of collective bargaining agreements." *American Nat'l Ins.*, 343 U.S. at 404, 72 S.Ct. at 829. However, "[e]nforcement of the obligation to bargain collectively is crucial to the statutory scheme. And, as has long been recognized, performance of the duty to bargain requires more than a willingness to enter upon a sterile discussion of union-management differences." 343 U.S. at 402, 72 S.Ct. at 828. Moreover,

> In evaluating the parties' good faith, the Board is not precluded from examining the substantive proposals put forth. Indeed * * * if the Board is not to be blinded by empty talk and by mere surface motions of collective bargaining, it must take some cognizance of the reasonableness of the positions taken by the employer in the course of bargaining negotiations.

NLRB v. F. Strauss & Son, Inc., 536 F.2d 60, 64 (5th Cir.1976)(quoting NLRB v. Reed & Prince Mfg. Co., 205 F.2d 131, 134 (1st Cir.1953), cert. denied, 346 U.S. 887, 74 S.Ct. 139, 98 L.Ed. 391 (1953)); see also Huck Mfg. v. NLRB, 693 F.2d 1176, 1188 (5th Cir.1982). And "[s]ometimes, especially if the parties are sophisticated, the only indicia of bad faith may be the proposals advanced and adhered to," NLRB v. Wright Motors, Inc., 603 F.2d 604, 609 (7th Cir.1979).

In Chevron Oil Company, Standard Oil Company of Texas Division v. NLRB, 442 F.2d 1067, 1074 (5th Cir.1971), the Court was careful to iterate what it had said on previous occasions, "We do not hold that under no possible circumstances can the mere content of various proposals and counter proposals of management and union be sufficient evidence of a want of good faith to justify a holding to that effect." Id. at 1074 (quoting NLRB v. Cummer–Graham Co., 279 F.2d 757, 761 (5th Cir.1960) and White v. NLRB, 255 F.2d 564, 569 (5th Cir.1958)).

The question to be decided is a narrow one: Whether the content of the Company's bargaining proposals together with the positions taken by the Company are sufficient to establish that it entered into bargaining with no real intention of concluding a collective bargaining agreement. We defer to the Board to make the initial determination, but we are required to review the proposals to determine whether the Board's findings are supported by substantial evidence on the record as a whole. See *Huck Mfg.*, 693 F.2d at 1187; *F. Strauss & Son, Inc.*, supra, 536 F.2d at 65.

## WAGES

The Company's proposal on wages retained its historic method of paying each employee. Wage increases were to be determined solely on the basis of semi-annual merit wage reviews in which the Union would be given notice of each separate review and could participate in the process, but the Company would make the final decision as to any increases. Under the wage proposal the Company was barred from reducing the wages of any employee whose wages had once risen above that level. The Union proposed a specific wage schedule but the Company adhered to its original wage proposal.

The Company insisted that it remain in total control over wages. Its proposal to continue granting wage increases on the basis of semi-annual wage reviews, in which the Company would make the final decision, coupled with the Company's Management Rights clause, infra, under which it had the exclusive right to evaluate, reward, promote and demote employees, left the Union's "participation" in the process meaningless. The Union was foreclosed from introducing factors other than merit into the equation. It had no contractual remedies since the granting or withholding of merit increases would not be arbitrable. The Union could not strike and, in fact, it had no leverage to require its views to be taken into account. Moreover, once an employee's wage rate increased above the level of the rate existing at the time of the contract, the Company could unilaterally reduce that which had been given in a previous merit increase and the Union could not grieve such action. It could not strike, and under the Zipper Clause, infra, it could not even discuss the matter with the Company. Thus, the Company's unalterable position was that it remain in total control of this mandatory subject of bargaining.

## MANAGEMENT RIGHTS

The Company submitted a management rights clause which initially provided that the Company retained exclusively all of its normal inherent rights and exempted the Company's decisions concerning these rights from the grievance procedure. Later the Company proposed a new management rights clause, which was much broader than the first proposal, and which reserved exclusively to the Company all authority customarily exercised by Management and "each and every right, power and privilege that it had ever enjoyed, whether exercised or not, except insofar as [the Company] has, by express and specific terms of the agreement, agreed to limitations." It further provided that the Company was authorized to:

1. Determine the qualifications and select its employees.

2. Determine the size and composition of its work forces.

3. Determine work schedules and all methods of production.

4. Assign overtime work.

5. Determine the number and types of equipment.

6. Hire, retire, promote, demote, evaluate, transfer, suspend, assign, direct, lay off and recall employees.

7. Reward, reprimand, discharge or otherwise discipline employees.

8. Determine job content and minimum training qualifications for job classifications and the amounts and types of work to be performed by employees.

9. Establish and change working rules and regulations.

10. Establish new jobs and abolish or change existing jobs.

11. Increase or decrease the number of jobs or employees.

12. Determine whether and to what extent the work required in its operations should be performed by employees.

13. Have supervisors or other non-union employees perform work of the kind performed by employees of the Union.

14. Determine assignments of work.

15. Discontinue, transfer or assign all or any part of its functions, services or production or other operations.

16. Subcontract any part of the Company's work.

17. Expand, reduce, alter, combine, transfer, assign, cease or create any job, job classification, department or operation for business purposes.

18. Alter or vary practices.

19. Otherwise generally manage the business, direct the work force and establish terms and conditions of employment.

The new proposal further expanded the original by providing that the Company could exercise all of its reserved rights without advising the Union of any such proposed action, change or modification, and exempted the Company from any requirement to negotiate over the decision, or its effects on employees except as altered by the Agreement. The substituted proposal no longer contained a clause expressly excluding the Company's decisions from the grievance and arbitration procedure.

This proposal gave the Company the absolute right to subcontract work, assign it to supervisors, abolish jobs, and transfer, discontinue or assign any or all of its operations. It also required the Union to relinquish the employees' statutory right to notice and bargaining over such actions and their effects. Finally, the grievance and arbitration procedure was largely illusory because actions taken under this clause were subject to that procedure only if the right was limited by express contractual provision, and there was no such limitation.

## ZIPPER CLAUSE

The Company proposed a "zipper" clause under which "the parties [waived the] right to bargain during the life of the agreement regarding any subject or any matter referred to or covered in the agreement or any other subject matter which could be considered a mandatory or permissive subject of bargaining under existing law." The Union offered to agree to the clause if the latter portion waiving the right to bargain over any other mandatory or permissive bargaining subject was deleted. The Company refused.

## NO STRIKE CLAUSE

The Company proposed a no strike clause that prohibited both the Union and employees from calling, encouraging, ratifying, participating in or engaging in any primary or sympathy strike, slow down, boycott, picketing or any other work interruption for any reason, including but not limited to alleged or actual unfair labor practices, alleged or actual unfair employment practices under any anti-discrimination law, alleged or actual breaches of contract, and showing support or sympathy for other employees or Union or their activities. The Union, although conceding that any contract would contain a no-strike clause, objected to waiving employees' right to strike over unfair labor practices or unfair employment practices. The Company declined to change the proposal. This extremely broad "no strike" clause clearly prohibited any strike for any reason.

## DISCHARGE AND DISCIPLINE

The Union proposed that the company have the right to discipline an employee for any just or sufficient cause. The Company, citing meritless discrimination charges filed against it, refused the proposal because it would subject all of the discipline and discharge actions to grievance-arbitration. This is a common non-controversial clause. When considered with the rights expressly reserved in the management rights clause, to suspend, reprimand, discharge, or otherwise discipline employees, the Company retained unfettered control over discharges and discipline.

## LAYOFF AND RECALL

With respect to layoff and recall, the Company proposed that the layoff of employees would be at the Company's sole discretion. Company-wide seniority would be considered but not controlling. Selection for layoff would not be the subject of grievance or arbitration. Recall from layoff was to be at the discretion of the Company and it was not required to consider seniority. The Company insisted on the clause as presented because it wanted to make the decisions on the basis of productivity and not seniority and not make the ability question subject to grievance and arbitration.

This clause gave the Company absolute control over the selection of employees for layoff and recall and freed it from its statutory obligation to bargain over these subjects.

## DUES CHECK–OFF

The Union proposed a dues check-off clause which the Company rejected as being nothing more than a Union security device and because it made employees' earnings appear lower.

## NON–DISCRIMINATION CLAUSE

The Union proposed a non-discrimination clause. The Company rejected this proposal saying that it merely restated existing law. Further, the Company considered the Union trigger-happy about filing complaints and did not want such complaints to be arbitrable.

The Union finally proposed a "swap off." The Union would agree to some type of management rights, no strike and zipper clauses if the Company would agree to a just cause for discipline and discharge provision, and seniority for layoff and recall provision. The Company refused.

Deciding when a party has reached the "point when hard bargaining ends and obstructionist intransigence begins," NLRB v. Big Three Industries, 497 F.2d 43, 47 (5th Cir.1974), is "an inescapably elusive inquiry." Id. at 46. But it is clear from our extended recital of the proposals made over a ten-month period that the Company insisted on unilateral control over virtually all significant terms and conditions of employment, including discharge, discipline, layoff, recall, subcontracting and assignment of unit work to supervisors.

Its efforts were focused on requiring the employees to surrender statutory rights to bargain, or strike, without offering any real incentive for a surrender of such rights.

The Company refused to give the Union any voice whatsoever concerning employee work and safety rules, time studies, production quotas, overtime assignments, transfers, retirement, demotions and employee qualifications—all mandatory subjects of bargaining. Elimination of unit work, discipline or discharge of employees, layoff and recall were all exempted from the grievance and arbitration procedure.

The Company's rejection of the Union's dues check-off provision was not based on any legitimate business reason and does not satisfy the statutory obligation to bargain in good faith. See NLRB v. J.P. Stevens & Co., Gulistan Div., 538 F.2d 1152, 1165 (5th Cir.1976). Furthermore, we are unimpressed with the Company's rejection of a non-discriminatory clause because the Union "was trigger-happy" about filing complaints. The clause did no more than require the Company to abide by federal law to avoid discrimination against its employees on account of race, sex, age, national origin or union affiliation.

Finally, it is worthy of note that the Company responded to the Union's objections to the breadth of its original management rights and zipper clauses by submitting new proposals that were even broader. Such bargaining is clearly an indicia [sic] that the Company had little desire to work towards agreement of a contract.

The Board correctly inferred bad faith from the Company's insistence on proposals that are so unusually harsh and unreasonable that they are predictably unworkable. See NLRB v. Wright Motors, 603 F.2d at 610. They would have left the Union and the employees with substantially fewer rights and less protection than they would have had if they had relied solely upon the Union's certification. See NLRB v. Johnson Mfg. Co. of Lubbock, 458 F.2d 453 (5th Cir.1972). The Board in *Johnson* found that:

> the Company insisted on retaining unilateral control of matters which are traditionally bargainable subjects; that is, wages, hours, suspensions, disciplinary actions, discharges, and other conditions of employment, while at the same time insisting that the Union forfeit its primary defense to employer abuse of control. Moreover, the Respondents' insistence that the Union give up its right to bargain about, or to arbitrate, labor disputes in return for an agreement which merely incorporated existing company practices, and merely providing the Union with the right to strike in protest of alleged violations of the contract during its term, was an unfair demand of the Union. . . . The Company was unwilling to offer any provisions which would give its employees or the Union anything more than they would have with no contract at all. As pointed out, the Company insisted as a price for any contract, that its employees give up their statutory rights to be properly represented by a union and contemporaneously insisted that the Union's hands be tied in the effective processing and settling of employee grievances. . . .

NLRB v. Johnson, 458 F.2d at 455.

The *Johnson* court enforced the Board's order "because these findings clearly demonstrated surface bargaining used as a cloak to conceal the employer's bad faith." Id. at 455 (citations omitted). Here we are faced with proposals that go further than those in *Johnson,* i.e., the management rights and zipper clauses are broader, and the Company's demand for a no-strike clause without any concessions was not present in *Johnson.*

\* \* \*

Finally, NLRB v. Crockett–Bradley, 598 F.2d 971 (5th Cir.1979) and Chevron Oil Co., Standard Oil Co. of Texas Division v. NLRB, 442 F.2d 1067 (5th Cir.1971) relied on by the Company are readily distinguishable. In *Crockett–Bradley* the employees were not barred from striking or grieving employer actions concerning significant terms and conditions of employment, and in *Chevron* the employer did not demand unilateral control over every significant term and condition of employment.

ENFORCED.

---

NLRB v. CUMMER-GRAHAM CO., 279 F.2d 757 (5th Cir.1960). The employer insisted upon a no-strike clause but would not grant the union's request for an arbitration clause. The court of appeals reversed the Board's finding of a refusal to bargain in good faith. It conceded that in practice no-strike clauses were commonly accompanied by arbitration clauses; and that "if we were entitled to an opinion, which we are not," arbitration would be a desirable adjunct. But the court concluded that a party could lawfully insist on one without the other, and that "These are matters for management and labor to resolve, if they can, at the bargaining table. If they cannot there be decided, then neither Board nor Court can compel an agreement or require a concession."

NLRB v. HERMAN SAUSAGE CO., 275 F.2d 229 (5th Cir.1960): "If the insistence is genuinely and sincerely held, if it is not mere window dressing, it may be maintained forever though it produce a stalemate. Deep conviction, firmly held and from which no withdrawal will be made, may be more than the traditional opening gambit of a labor controversy. It may be both the right of the citizen and essential to our economic legal system * * * of free collective bargaining. The Government, through the Board, may not subject the parties to direction either by compulsory arbitration or the more subtle means of determining that the position is inherently unreasonable, or unfair, or impracticable, or unsound."

CHEVRON OIL CO. v. NLRB, 442 F.2d 1067 (5th Cir.1971). The court reversed the Board's finding of bad faith which had been based principally on the employer's position regarding management rights as well as a no-strike no-arbitration clause. The court held that the employer, which consistently refused to adopt a number of union counterproposals on these matters, was simply utilizing its economic strength to engage in hard bargaining with a weaker union. "In our opinion the matter at hand resolves itself into purely a question of hard bargaining between two parties who were possessed of disparate economic power: A relatively weak Union encountered a relatively strong Company. The Company naturally desired to use its advantage to retain as many rights as possible. We do not believe, however, that that desire is inconsistent with good faith bargaining."

ATLAS METAL PARTS CO. v. NLRB, 660 F.2d 304 (7th Cir.1981). The union and the company had had a bargaining relationship since 1956. Bargaining on a new agreement began in 1978 with the union making 24 proposed changes and the company countering with 36. Two months later the only issues separating the parties were union security and dues checkoff. The company wished to eliminate provisions, which had been in their collective agreements for twenty years, and replace them with provisions giving employees freedom of choice. The union struck for 13 weeks during which period the union increased its economic demands and the company reintroduced some of the initial proposals it had receded from during the prior bargaining. The NLRB found a lack of good faith bargaining, focusing largely upon the Company's demand for an alteration in the union security provision. The Court of Appeals disagreed. "An employer is entitled to advance a position sincerely held, notwithstanding the employer's having taken a different position at an earlier time.... '[A] party ... is entitled to stand firm on a position if he reasonably believes ... that he has sufficient bargaining strength to force agreement by the other party.'" Id. at 308.

> During the strike, Union increased its demands on wages and accident/sickness benefits, and Atlas responded by reintroducing several original proposals. The board condemned only the action of Atlas, ignored the conduct of Union, and disregarded the effect on

the parties' relative economic strengths of Atlas' successful weathering of the strike. It is not illegal for a party to take advantage of a shift in economic strength in a bona fide attempt to obtain agreement on original proposals seen as furthering its best interest. Here, after the strike, it was not illegal for Atlas to use its dominant bargaining position in seeking contract terms most favorable to it.

Id. at 309.

-----

## PROBLEMS FOR DISCUSSION

**1.** In September, after negotiations had almost been concluded for an initial contract, the employer insisted that the contract provide for a termination date of January 12 of the following year, the anniversary date of the union's certification by the NLRB. Is insistence upon such a short term an unfair labor practice or merely "hard bargaining"? If objectionable, is that because it evinces an unlawful state of mind, or because it is contrary to a legislative policy of industrial stability, or for some other reason? See Solo Cup Co. v. NLRB, 332 F.2d 447 (4th Cir.1964); Star Expansion Indus. Corp., 164 NLRB 563 (1967). How should a similar case be analyzed when the employer insists upon a contract term of five years?

**2.** In response to union requests for a "checkoff" provision, pursuant to which the employer would deduct from the paycheck of all employees so authorizing periodic union dues and remit them directly to the union, the employer has consistently replied that such a provision will under no circumstances be incorporated in the agreement. At various times, the employer has given one or more of these reasons: The checkoff involves costly bookkeeping procedures; it is not the company's policy to aid the union in dues collection, which is the union's job; there is an undesirable "psychological" factor when the employees receive their pay already reduced by the amount of union dues. (In fact, the checkoff would add no measurable amount to the employer's bookkeeping expenses, and it is already making payroll deductions for federal and state income taxes, health insurance premiums and charitable contributions.) Is the employer's persistent refusal to grant the checkoff a refusal to bargain in good faith? Need the employer, provided that it is bargaining in good faith on all other matters under discussion, give *any* reason for its refusal to grant the checkoff provision? See Alba–Waldensian, Inc., 167 NLRB 695 (1967); Farmers Co–operative Gin Ass'n, 161 NLRB 887 (1966).

If the employer is held to have bargained in bad faith, what remedy should the board issue? See H.K. Porter Co. v. NLRB, 397 U.S. 99, 90 S.Ct. 821, 25 L.Ed.2d 146 (1970).

**3.** Assume that a company puts together a set of bargaining proposals, including a reduction of wages below their current levels, that it believes the union will reject. With that likelihood in prospect, it also develops a "contingency plan," providing for beefed-up security and the hiring of permanent replacements. Has the company engaged in permissible "hard bargaining" or impermissible "surface bargaining"? See ConAgra, Inc. v. NLRB, 117 F.3d 1435 (D.C.Cir.1997).

**4.** After several months of bargaining over the company's proposal which, in its last revision, it termed its "final offer," the company developed an "alternative proposal" that was considerably worse for the employees than its "final offer," entailing a loss of seniority and a reduction in wage levels. It told the union that if impasse were reached on the final offer, it would implement the alternative. In the penultimate bargaining session, the union rejected the final offer whereupon the company stated that the alternative was "now on the table for discussion." The union voted to strike and the company has implemented the alternative. Has the company violated § 8(a)(5) by engaging in this "regressive bargaining"? See Telescope Casual Furniture, 326 NLRB 588 (1998); Oklahoma Fixture Co., 331 NLRB No. 145 (2000).

----

*THE DUTY TO DISCLOSE INFORMATION*[b]

In NLRB v. TRUITT MFG. CO., 351 U.S. 149, 76 S.Ct. 753, 100 L.Ed. 1027 (1956), the Supreme Court was presented for the first time with the question whether the duty to bargain in good faith under Section 8(a)(5) requires an employer to turn over to the union upon demand information in the possession of the company which the union claims is important to informed bargaining. In that case, the employer had offered a 2½-cent-an-hour wage increase in the course of bargaining for a new labor contract, and contended that it "would break the company" to pay the 10–cent-an-hour increase sought by the union. When the union requested permission to have a certified public accountant examine the company's financial records to ascertain the merit of the claim of financial inability, the company refused, asserting both that the average wage at the company was higher than that of competing companies and that "confidential financial information concerning the affairs of this Company is not a matter of bargaining or discussing with the Union." The NLRB found a violation of Section 8(a)(5), stating that "it is settled law, that when an employer seeks to justify the refusal of a wage increase upon an economic basis, * * * good-faith bargaining under the Act requires that upon request the employer attempt to substantiate its economic position by reasonable proof." The Board ordered the employer to turn over the requested information.

The Court of Appeals for the Sixth Circuit refused enforcement. It concluded: "The statute requires good faith bargaining with respect to wages and other matters affecting the terms and conditions of employment, not with respect to matters which lie within the province of management, such as the financial condition of the company, its manufacturing costs or the payment of dividends. * * * To bargain in good faith does not mean that the bargainor must substantiate by proof statements made by him in the course of the bargaining. It means merely that he bargain with a sincere desire to reach an agreement. There can be no question but that

---

**b.** See Bartosic & Hartley, The Employer's Duty to Supply Information to the Union, 58 Cornell L.Rev. 23 (1972); Bloch, The Disclosure of Profits in the Normal Course of Collective Bargaining: All Relevant Information Should Be on the Table, 2 Lab.Law. 47 (1986); Miller, Employer's Duty to Furnish Economic Data to Unions—Revisited, 17 Lab. L.J. 272 (1966); Shedlin, Regulation of Disclosure of Economic and Financial Data and the Impact on the American System of Labor–Management Relations, 41 Ohio St. L.J. 441 (1980).

the company here was bargaining in that spirit." The court distinguished an earlier decision in which the employer was ordered to furnish information about employee wages, a subject which was within the scope of mandatory bargaining and about which the Truitt Company had in fact offered information. The court also concluded that the Board's decision would require any company which resists a wage increase on economic grounds to open its books, a "concession" which Section 8(d) expressly provides shall not be necessary in bargaining.

The Supreme Court reversed and directed that the Board's order be enforced. Observing that both parties treated the company's ability to pay increased wages as highly relevant, the Court majority concluded that the Board "has a right to consider an employer's refusal to give information about its financial status. * * * Good-faith bargaining necessarily requires that claims made by either bargainer should be honest claims. This is true about an asserted inability to pay an increase in wages. If such an argument is important enough to present in the give and take of bargaining, it is important enough to require some sort of proof of its accuracy. And it would certainly not be farfetched for a trier of fact to reach the conclusion that bargaining lacks good faith when an employer mechanically repeats a claim of inability to pay without making the slightest effort to substantiate the claim. * * * We do not hold, however, that in every case in which economic inability is raised as an argument against increased wages it automatically follows that the employees are entitled to substantiating evidence. Each case must turn upon its particular facts. The inquiry must always be whether or not under the circumstances of the particular case the statutory obligation to bargain in good faith has been met."

In a separate opinion, Justice Frankfurter stated that Sections 8(a)(5) and 8(d) require "an honest effort to come to terms"; good faith means more than "merely going through the motions of negotiating; it is inconsistent with a predetermined resolve not to budge from an initial position. But it is not necessarily incompatible with stubbornness or even with what to an outsider may seem unreasonableness." Contending that a want of good faith must be found by examining the history of dealings and the full negotiations between the parties, Justice Frankfurter criticized the Board for creating a *per se* rule and making only one fact dispositive—the company's failure to substantiate by proof its claim of financial inability to pay a wage increase.

The Court later held that the duty to disclose "unquestionably extends beyond the period of contract negotiations and applies to labor-management relations during the term of an agreement." NLRB v. ACME INDUSTRIAL Co., 385 U.S. 432, 87 S.Ct. 565, 17 L.Ed.2d 495 (1967). In the *Acme* case, the union during the term of its labor contract inferred from the employer's removal of certain machinery from the plant that the employer was committing a breach of the contract, which had provisions dealing with subcontracting and with the removal of plant equipment. The union filed grievances and requested that the company supply it with information concerning the removal of plant equipment. The company's denial was found by the Board and ultimately by the Supreme Court to violate the duty to bargain, which the Court held to continue during the process of grievance settlement under an existing labor contract. The Court also held that the union need not wait to press its claim for information in an arbitration proceeding and that the Board was properly "acting upon the probability that the desired information was relevant, and that it would be of use to the union in carrying out its statutory duties and responsibilities" of administering the collective bargaining agreement.

---

## PROBLEMS FOR DISCUSSION

**1.** Was the Supreme Court in *Truitt* endorsing a test for "good faith bargaining" which turns upon the subjective state of mind of the parties, or upon their objective conduct at the bargaining table? (Or both?) What particular circumstances were present in that case to show a bad faith refusal to open the company's books which would not be present in every case in which the employer refuses to meet a union's wage demands partly for financial reasons?

**2.** The current collective bargaining agreement between the Health Care Workers Union at a single facility of Nurturcare, Inc. has an interest arbitration provision, i.e., in the event of impasse an arbitrator will decide the terms of the future contract. The agreement is about to expire and in an initial meeting with the union, Nurturcare's representative made a half-hour presentation on the company's financial situation, especially that its stock had fallen, that several of its facilities were up for sale, that it had serious cash flow problems, and that "while we're not going under, we're having trouble staying afloat." The company proposed a wage freeze in the next contract. The union has demanded monthly cash flow, income, and balance sheets since the date of the current contract to the present for this and all other Nurturcare facilities in the state. Must Nurturcare provide that information? See Torrington Extend-A-Care Employee Ass'n v. NLRB, 17 F.3d 580 (2d Cir.1994). See also ConAgra, Inc. v. NLRB, 117 F.3d 1435 (D.C.Cir.1997), and Stroehmann Bakeries, Inc. v. NLRB, 95 F.3d 218 (2d Cir.1996).

**3.** The Insurance Agents Union has been bargaining representative for all of the district agents of the Prudential Insurance Company for some twenty years. There are some 17,000 agents working for the Company in thirty-four states, in 478 administrative districts. The turnover rate of unit members is roughly 25 percent per year. During the most recent negotiations, the Union has asked Prudential to supply it with a list of names and addresses of all employees in the unit, urging that such information was "necessary and relevant to the Union's performance and fulfillment of its statutory functions and duties as collective bargaining representative of all these employees." Prudential has refused to furnish the list, asserting that its policy is not to disclose this information to any organization for any purpose and that the true motive of the Union is to use this list not for purposes of collective bargaining but rather to increase its membership and facilitate its dues collection. Must Prudential disclose the list to the Union? See Prudential Ins. Co. v. NLRB, 412 F.2d 77 (2d Cir.1969), cert. denied, 396 U.S. 928, 90 S.Ct. 263, 24 L.Ed.2d 226 (1969); Utica Observer–Dispatch v. NLRB, 229 F.2d 575 (2d Cir.1956).

---

# Detroit Edison Co. v. NLRB

440 U.S. 301, 99 S.Ct. 1123, 59 L.Ed.2d 333 (1979).

■ Mr. Justice Stewart delivered the opinion of the Court.

The duty to bargain collectively imposed upon an employer by § 8(a)(5) of the National Labor Relations Act, includes a duty to provide relevant information needed by a labor union for the proper performance of its duties as the employees' bargaining representative. NLRB v. Truitt Mfg. Co., 351 U.S. 149, 76 S.Ct. 753, 100 L.Ed. 1027; NLRB v. Acme Industrial Co., 385 U.S. 432, 87 S.Ct. 565, 17 L.Ed.2d 495. In this case an employer was brought before the Board to answer a complaint that it had violated this statutory duty when it refused to disclose certain information about employee aptitude tests requested by a union in order to prepare for arbitration of a grievance. The employer supplied the union with much of the information requested, but refused to disclose three items: the actual test questions, the actual employee answer sheets, and the scores linked with the names of the employees who received them. The Board, concluding that all the items requested were relevant to the grievance and would be useful to the union in processing it, ordered the employer to turn over all of the materials directly to the union, subject to certain restrictions on the union's use of the information. 218 N.L.R.B. 1024 (1975). A divided Court of Appeals for the Sixth Circuit ordered enforcement of the Board's order without modification. 560 F.2d 722 (1977).

We granted certiorari to consider an important question of federal labor law. * * *

[The Company had for many years used aptitude tests to predict job performance. Shortly before the Union was designated bargaining representative for operating and maintenance employees, the company's industrial psychologists revalidated the tests, which were administered to employees and applicants under assurances that scores would be kept confidential; the psychologists deemed themselves ethically bound not to reveal the test questions or actual scores to either management or employee representatives. The labor agreement provided that promotions were to be based on seniority whenever the qualifications and abilities of the employee applicants were not significantly different. When six Instrument Man B positions came open, ten unit employees bid but none received a passing score on the test, and the Company filled the jobs with applicants from outside the unit. The Union filed a grievance challenging the fairness of the test and the bypassing of senior unit employees, and requested various materials relating to the Instrument Man B testing program. The Company turned over copies of the test-validation study, but not the actual test papers or scores; it invoked the need to assure the integrity of future tests and the privacy interests of the examinees.

[The Union filed unfair labor practice charges, claiming that the requested information was relevant and necessary to the arbitration. The arbitration proceeded (with the Union reserving the right to reopen should it win its unfair labor practice case) on the basis of some information supplied by the Company, and the grievance was denied. In the later unfair labor practice proceeding, the Board ordered the Company to turn over the test questions, the answer sheets, and the individual scores directly to the Union (and not merely to an expert intermediary); the court of appeals enforced the Board order.]

* * * They [the Board and the court] concluded that the Union should be able to determine for itself whether it needed a psychologist to interpret the test battery and answer sheets. Both recognized the Company's interest in maintaining the security of the tests, but both reasoned that appropriate restrictions on the Union's use of the materials would protect this interest.[9] Neither was receptive to the Company's claim that employee privacy and the professional obligations of the Company's industrial psychologists should outweigh the Union request for the employee-linked scores.

## II

Because of the procedural posture of this case, the questions that have been preserved for our review are relatively narrow. * * * The first concerns the Board's choice of a remedy for the Company's failure to disclose copies of the test battery and answer sheets. The second, and related, question concerns the propriety of the Board's conclusion that the Company committed an unfair labor practice when it refused to disclose, without a written consent from the individual employees, the test scores linked with the employee names.

## A

We turn first to the question whether the Board abused its remedial discretion when it ordered the Company to deliver directly to the Union the copies of the test battery and answer sheets. The Company's position, stripped of the argument that it had no duty at all to disclose these materials, is as follows: It urges that disclosure directly to the Union would carry with it a substantial risk that the test questions would be disseminated. Since it spent considerable time and money validating the Instrument Man B tests and since its tests depend for reliability upon the examinee's lack of advance preparation, it contends that the harm of dissemination would not be trivial. The future validity of the tests is tied to secrecy, and disclosure to employees would not only threaten the Company's investment but would also leave the Company with no valid means of measuring

---

**9.** The Board, although it ordered the Company to supply the tests and answer sheets directly to the Union, incorporated by reference the Administrative Law Judge's restrictions on the Union's use of the materials. Under those restrictions, the Union was given the right "to use the tests and the information contained therein to the extent necessary to process and arbitrate the grievances, but not to copy the tests, or otherwise use them, for the purpose of disclosing the tests or the questions to employees who have in the past, or who may in the future take these tests, or to anyone (other than the arbitrator) who may advise the employees of the contents of the tests." After the conclusion of the arbitration, the Union was required to return "all copies of the battery of tests" to the Company. The Court of Appeals, in enforcing the Board's order, stated that the "restrictions on use of the materials and obligation to return them to Detroit Edison are part of the decision and order which we enforce." 560 F.2d 722, 726.

employee aptitude. The Company also maintains that its interest in preserving the security of its tests is consistent with the federal policy favoring the use of validated, standardized and nondiscriminatory employee selection procedures reflected in the Civil Rights Act of 1964. * * *

A union's bare assertion that it needs information to process a grievance does not automatically oblige the employer to supply all the information in the manner requested. The duty to supply information under § 8(a)(5) turns upon "the circumstances of the particular case," NLRB v. Truitt Mfg. Co., 351 U.S., at 153, 76 S.Ct., at 756, and much the same may be said for the type of disclosure that will satisfy that duty. See, e.g., American Cyanamid Co., 129 N.L.R.B. 683, 684 (1960). Throughout this proceeding, the reasonableness of the Company's concern for test secrecy has been essentially conceded. The finding by the Board that this concern did not outweigh the Union's interest in exploring the fairness of the Company's criteria for promotion did not carry with it any suggestion that the concern itself was not legitimate and substantial. Indeed, on this record—which has established the Company's freedom under the collective contract to use aptitude tests as a criterion for promotion, the empirical validity of the tests, and the relationship between secrecy and test validity—the strength of the company's concern has been abundantly demonstrated. The Board has cited no principle of national labor policy to warrant a remedy that would unnecessarily disserve this interest, and we are unable to identify one.

It is obvious that the remedy selected by the Board does not adequately protect the security of the tests. The restrictions barring the Union from taking any action that might cause the tests to fall into the hands of employees who have taken or are likely to take them are only as effective as the sanctions available to enforce them. In this instance, there is substantial doubt whether the Union would be subject to a contempt citation were it to ignore the restrictions. * * * Moreover, the Union clearly would not be accountable in either contempt or unfair labor practice proceedings for the most realistic vice inherent in the Board's remedy—the danger of inadvertent leaks.

* * * [T]he rule of deference to the Board's choice of remedy does not constitute a blank check for arbitrary action. The role that Congress in § 10(e) has entrusted to the courts in reviewing the Board's petitions for enforcement of its orders is not that of passive conduit. See Fibreboard Corp. v. NLRB, supra, 379 U.S., at 216, 85 S.Ct., at 405. The Board in this case having identified no justification for a remedy granting such scant protection to the Company's undisputed and important interests in test secrecy, we hold that the Board abused its discretion in ordering the Company to turn over the test battery and answer sheets directly to the Union.

### B

The dispute over Union access to the actual scores received by named employees is in a somewhat different procedural posture, since the Company did on this issue preserve its objections to the basic finding that it had violated its duty under § 8(a)(5) when it refused disclosure. The Company argues that even if the scores were relevant to the Union's grievance (which it vigorously disputes), the Union's need for the information was not sufficiently weighty to require breach of the promise of confidentiality to the examinees, breach of its industrial psychologists' code of professional ethics, and potential embarrassment and harassment of at least some of the examinees. The Board responds that this information does satisfy the appropriate standard of "relevance," see NLRB v. Acme Industrial Inc., 385 U.S. 432, 87 S.Ct. 565, 17 L.Ed.2d 495, and that the Company, having "unilaterally" chosen to make a promise of confidentiality to the examinees, cannot rely on that promise to defend against a request for relevant information. The professional obligations of the Company's psychologists, it argues, must give way to paramount federal law. Finally, it dismisses as speculative the contention that employees with low scores might be embarrassed or harassed.

We may accept for the sake of this discussion the finding that the employee scores were of potential relevance to the Union's grievance, as well as the position of the Board that the federal statutory duty to disclose relevant information cannot be defeated by the ethical standards of a private group. Cf. Nash v. Florida Industrial Comm'n, 389 U.S. 235, 239, 88 S.Ct. 362, 366, 19 L.Ed.2d 438. Nevertheless we agree with the Company that its willingness to disclose these scores only upon receipt of consents from the examinees satisfied its statutory obligations under § 8(a)(5).

The Board's position appears to rest on the proposition that union interests in arguably relevant information must always predominate over all other interests, however legitimate. But such an absolute rule has never been established,[14] and we decline to adopt such a rule here. There are situations in which an employer's conditional offer to disclose may be warranted. This we believe is one.

The sensitivity of any human being to disclosure of information that may be taken to bear on his or her basic competence is sufficiently well known to be an appropriate subject of judicial notice. There is nothing in this record to suggest that the Company promised the examinees that their scores would remain confidential in order to further parochial concerns or to frustrate subsequent union attempts to process employee grievances. And it has not been suggested at any point in this proceeding that the

---

**14.** See Emeryville Research Center, Shell Development Co. v. NLRB, 441 F.2d 880 (C.A.9 1971)(refusal to supply relevant salary information in precise form demanded did not constitute violation of § 8(a)(5) when company's proposed alternatives were responsive to union's need); Shell Oil Co. v. NLRB, 457 F.2d 615 (C.A.9 1972)(refusal to supply employee names without employee consent not unlawful when company had well-founded fear that nonstriking employees would be harassed); cf. Kroger Co. v. NLRB, 399 F.2d 455 (C.A.6 1968)(no disclosure of operating ratio data when, under circumstances, interests of employer predominated); United Aircraft Corp., 192 NLRB 382, 390 (employer acted reasonably in refusing to honor generalized request for employee medical records without employee's permission), modified on other grounds, Lodges 743 and 1746 v. United Aircraft Corp., 534 F.2d 422 (C.A.2 1975).

Company's unilateral promise of confidentiality was in itself violative of the terms of the collective-bargaining agreement. Indeed, the Company presented evidence that disclosure of individual scores had in the past resulted in the harassment of some lower scoring examinees who had, as a result, left the Company.

Under these circumstances, any possible impairment of the function of the Union in processing the grievances of employees is more than justified by the interests served in conditioning the disclosure of the test scores upon the consent of the very employees whose grievance is being processed. The burden on the Union in this instance is minimal. The Company's interest in preserving employee confidence in the testing program is well founded.

* * * Accordingly, we hold that the order requiring the Company unconditionally to disclose the employee scores to the Union was erroneous.

The judgment is vacated and the case remanded to the Court of Appeals for the Sixth Circuit for further proceedings consistent with this opinion.

It is so ordered.

[Justice White wrote a dissenting opinion for himself and for Justices Brennan and Marshall. As to the company's failure to disclose the test questions and answer sheets, there was no dispute that this was an unfair labor practice, and the only issue was the Board's remedial authority to order that they be turned over directly to the union. Remedial matters are within the Board's broad discretionary authority and should not be disturbed "unless it can be shown that the order is a patent attempt to achieve ends other than those which can fairly be said to effectuate the policies of the Act." The Board had ordered release of the questions and answers only on condition that the union preserve their secrecy, and it was convinced that the union was likely to take care not to disclose them either intentionally or inadvertently; the dissenters concluded that "this Court is ill equipped to fault the Board on a matter so plainly summoning the Board's keen familiarity with industrial behavior." Moreover, the Court's tacit endorsement of the company's proposal to turn over the test questions not to the union but to a psychologist "is fundamentally at odds with the basic structure of the bargaining process," for it interjects a third party "as a partner, if not primary actor, in promotion-related grievance proceedings" and thus undermines the statutory status accorded to the union.

[The dissenting Justices also faulted the majority for concluding, contrary to the Board, that the company acted lawfully in declining to disclose the examinees' test scores absent their consent. The ALJ had concluded that there was no probative evidence that the employees' sensitivities would likely be abused by such disclosure. The dissenters therefore concluded that the company had failed to satisfy its burden of establishing a justification for nondisclosure. The dissenters continued:

Moreover, there is no basis in the governing statute or regulations for attributing ascendant importance to the employees' confidentiality interests. Whether confidentiality considerations should prevail in the circumstances of this case is, as the Company and majority agree, principally a matter of policy. But it cannot be gainsaid that the Board is the body charged in the first instance with the task of discerning and effectuating congressional policies in the labor-management area. Its judgments in that regard should not be lightly overturned. Yet the Court strikes its own balance according decisive weight to concerns having no asserted or apparent foundation in the statute it purports to construe or in other applicable legislation.

The Court lightly dismisses the Union's interest in receipt of the examinees' identified scores, with or without consent, by declaring the burdens involved as "minimal." * * * Were individual examinees to withhold consent, and thus prevent the Union from scrutinizing their scores in light of their demographic and occupational characteristics, the Union might be inhibited in its efforts to discern patterns or anomalies indicating bias in the operation of the tests. Thus, the Board directed divulgence of the scores to the employees' statutory bargaining representative to enable it effectively to fulfill its vital statutory functions. Such a limited intrusion, * * * for the purpose of vindicating grave statutory policies, hardly signals an occasion for judicial intervention.

[In a separate opinion, Justice Stevens—noting that "this is a close case on both issues"—dissented along with Justice White regarding the Board's remedial order to turn over the test questions and answers, but concurred with the majority "that the Union should not be permitted to invade the individual employees' interest in the confidentiality of their test scores without their consent."]

------

## PROBLEMS FOR DISCUSSION

**1.** In the course of negotiations for a new contract, the Union negotiator, in support of his claim for higher wages, exclaims: "As things are now, 15 percent of our members are on food stamps." The Company negotiator responds: "I can't believe that's true. But if it is, then maybe we ought to reconsider the Company's wage proposals. Tell me who those 15 percent are." The Union negotiator has refused. Has the Union committed an unfair labor practice? (An initial question, of course, is whether a union has any duty to provide information in negotiations.) See Local 13, Detroit Newspaper Printing & Graphic Communications Union v. NLRB (Oakland Press Co.), 598 F.2d 267 (D.C.Cir.1979).

**2.** The Oil, Chemical & Atomic Workers Union (OCAW) represents the production employees of the Minnesota Mining and Manufacturing Company at its Chemolite Plant in Minnesota. OCAW has requested that the Company furnish various health and safety data, among them: (1) mortality statistics on all past employees; (2) results of clinical studies of employees undertaken by the Company; (3) illness and accident data derived from insurance programs and workmen's compensation claims; (4) the generic names of all substances used and produced at the Chemolite

Plant; (5) radiation sources in the plant and a listing of radiation incidents requiring notification of state and federal agencies; and (6) a listing of contaminants monitored by the Company. The Company contends that it cannot comply with the first three requests because that would require disclosure of personal information sheltered by the doctor-patient privilege; and that it cannot comply with the last three requests because that would require the disclosure of its trade secrets. OCAW has filed charges of refusal to bargain in violation of Section 8(a)(5).

If the NLRB determines that the health and safety data are relevant to OCAW's responsibilities as bargaining representative, must the Company automatically furnish the data? Conversely, if—in spite of the relevance of the data—the Company can demonstrate that disclosure would undermine significant interests in personal privacy or commercial secrecy, will the Company have a full defense? To the extent the NLRB is inclined to sustain the positions of both OCAW and the Company, might it leave the degree and form of disclosure to be negotiated in good faith between the parties? See Hercules, Inc. v. NLRB, 833 F.2d 426 (2d Cir.1987); Oil, Chemical & Atomic Workers Local No. 6–418 v. NLRB (Minn. Mining & Mfg. Co.), 711 F.2d 348 (D.C.Cir.1983). *Cf.* Roseburg Forest Prods. Co., 331 NLRB No. 124 (2000)(Americans with Disabilities Act).

**3.** The Company utilizes a large high-powered fan installed in a large roof cubicle for the purpose of ventilating the plant. The design of the fan is such that employees working nearby are affected by the extremely high noise and vibration; they claim that it causes headaches, fatigue and anxiety. The bargaining representative has asked the employer to permit an industrial hygienist employed by the union to come onto plant premises to inspect and to run some tests on the fan. The employer has refused. The union argues that access is for the purpose of securing information that bears directly upon its responsibilities to bargain about employment conditions. The Company contends that it has an absolute right to exclude such a "stranger" from plant property or, alternatively, that the union can secure access only upon demonstration that the information it seeks is unobtainable any other way. How should the dispute be resolved? See Hercules, Inc. v. NLRB, 833 F.2d 426 (2d Cir.1987); NLRB v. Holyoke Water Power Co., 778 F.2d 49 (1st Cir.1985).

**4.** Two cocktail waitresses at a gambling casino were discharged as a result of complaints by two customers, and the union has challenged the discharge via the grievance procedure in the collective bargaining agreement. It has requested the names, addresses, and telephone numbers of the complaining customers. The casino has offered to contact the customers and to release their names if they so authorize. The union has rejected the offer and filed a charge of a violation of § 8(a)(5). Should a complaint issue? See Resorts Int'l Hotel Casino v. NLRB, 996 F.2d 1553 (3d Cir.1993).

---

# NLRB v. Insurance Agents' International Union

361 U.S. 477, 80 S.Ct. 419, 4 L.Ed.2d 454 (1960).

■ Mr. Justice Brennan delivered the opinion of the Court.

This case presents an important issue of the scope of the National Labor Relations Board's authority under § 8(b)(3) of the National Labor Relations Act, which provides that "It shall be an unfair labor practice for a labor organization or its agents * * * to refuse to bargain collectively with an employer, provided it is the representative of his employees * * *." The precise question is whether the Board may find that a union, which confers with an employer with the desire of reaching agreement on contract terms, has nevertheless refused to bargain collectively, thus violating that provision, solely and simply because during the negotiations it seeks to put economic pressure on the employer to yield to its bargaining demands by sponsoring on-the-job conduct designed to interfere with the carrying on of the employer's business.

Since 1949 the respondent Insurance Agents' International Union and the Prudential Insurance Company of America have negotiated collective bargaining agreements covering district agents employed by Prudential in 35 States and the District of Columbia. * * *

In January 1956 Prudential and the union began the negotiation of a new contract to replace an agreement expiring in the following March. Bargaining was carried on continuously for six months before the terms of the new contract were agreed upon on July 17, 1956. It is not questioned that, if it stood alone, the record of negotiations would establish that the union conferred in good faith for the purpose and with the desire of reaching agreement with Prudential on a contract.

However, in April 1956, Prudential filed a § 8(b)(3) charge of refusal to bargain collectively against the union. The charge was based upon actions of the union and its members outside the conference room, occurring after the old contract expired in March. The union had announced in February that if agreement on the terms of the new contract was not reached when the old contract expired, the union members would then participate in a "Work Without a Contract" program—which meant that they would engage in certain planned, concerted on-the-job activities designed to harass the company.

A complaint of violation of § 8(b)(3) issued on the charge and hearings began before the bargaining was concluded. It was developed in the evidence that the union's harassing tactics involved activities by the member agents such as these: refusal for a time to solicit new business, and refusal (after the writing of new business was resumed) to comply with the company's reporting procedures; refusal to participate in the company's "May Policyholders' Month Campaign"; reporting late at district offices the days the agents were scheduled to attend them, and refusing to perform customary duties at the offices, instead engaging there in "sit-in-mornings," "doing what comes naturally" and leaving at noon as a group; absenting themselves from special business conferences arranged by the company; picketing and distributing leaflets outside the various offices of the company on specified days and hours as directed by the union; distributing leaflets each day to policyholders and others and soliciting policyholders' signatures on petitions directed to the company; and presenting the signed policyholders' petitions to the company at its home office while simultaneously engaging in mass demonstrations there.

The hearing examiner found that there was nothing in the record, apart from the mentioned activities of the union during the negotiations, that could be relied upon to support an inference that the union had not fulfilled its statutory duty; in fact nothing else was relied upon by the Board's General Counsel in prosecuting the complaint. The hearing examiner's analysis of the congressional design in enacting the statutory duty to bargain led him to conclude that the Board was not authorized to find that such economically harassing activities constituted a § 8(b)(3) violation. The Board's opinion answers flatly "We do not agree" and proceeds to say " * * * the Respondent's reliance upon harassing tactics during the course of negotiations for the avowed purpose of compelling the Company to capitulate to its terms is the antithesis of reasoned discussion it was duty-bound to follow. Indeed, it clearly revealed an unwillingness to submit its demands to the consideration of the bargaining table where argument, persuasion, and the free interchange of views could take place. In such circumstances, the fact that the Respondent continued to confer with the Company and was desirous of concluding an agreement does not *alone* establish that it fulfilled its obligation to bargain in good faith * * *." 119 N.L.R.B., at 769, 770–771. Thus the Board's view is that irrespective of the union's good faith in conferring with the employer at the bargaining table for the purpose and with the desire of reaching agreement on contract terms, its tactics during the course of the negotiations constituted *per se* a violation of § 8(b)(3). Accordingly, as is said in the Board's brief, "The issue here * * * comes down to whether the Board is authorized under the Act to hold that such tactics, which the Act does not specifically forbid but Section 7 does not protect, support a finding of a failure to bargain in good faith as required by Section 8(b)(3)."

*First.* * * * [T]he nature of the duty to bargain in good faith * * * imposed upon employers by § 8(5) of the original Act was not sweepingly conceived. The Chairman of the Senate Committee declared: "When the employees have chosen their organization, when they have selected their representatives, all the bill proposes to do is to escort them to the door of their employer and say, 'Here they are, the legal representatives of your employees.' What happens behind those doors is not inquired into, and the bill does not seek to inquire into it."

The limitation implied by the last sentence has not been in practice maintained—practically, it could hardly have been—but the underlying purpose of the remark has remained the most basic purpose of the statutory provision. That purpose is the making effective of the duty of management to extend recognition to the union; the duty of management to bargain in good faith is essentially a corollary of its duty to recognize the union. * * * Collective bargaining, then, is not simply an occasion for purely formal meetings between management and labor, while each maintains an attitude of "take it or leave it"; it presupposes a desire to reach ultimate agreement, to enter into a collective bargaining contract. See Heinz Co. v. National Labor Relations Board, 311 U.S. 514, 61 S.Ct. 320, 85 L.Ed. 309. This was the sort of recognition that Congress, in the Wagner Act, wanted extended to labor unions; recognition as the bargaining agent of the employees in a process that looked to the ordering of the parties' industrial relationship through the formation of a contract. See Local 24,

International Brotherhood of Teamsters Union v. Oliver, 358 U.S. 283, 295, 79 S.Ct. 297, 304, 3 L.Ed.2d 312.

But at the same time, Congress was generally not concerned with the substantive terms on which the parties contracted. Cf. Terminal Railroad Ass'n v. Brotherhood of Railroad Trainmen, 318 U.S. 1, 6, 63 S.Ct. 420, 423, 87 L.Ed. 571. Obviously there is tension between the principle that the parties need not contract on any specific terms and a practical enforcement of the principle that they are bound to deal with each other in a serious attempt to resolve differences and reach a common ground. And in fact criticism of the Board's application of the "good-faith" test arose from the belief that it was forcing employers to yield to union demands if they were to avoid a successful charge of unfair labor practice. Thus, in 1947 in Congress the fear was expressed that the Board had "gone very far, in the guise of determining whether or not employers had bargained in good faith, in setting itself up as the judge of what concessions an employer must make and of the proposals and counterproposals that he may or may not make." H.R.Rep. No. 245, 80th Cong., 1st Sess., p. 19. Since the Board was not viewed by Congress as an agency which should exercise its powers to arbitrate the parties' substantive solutions of the issues in their bargaining, a check on this apprehended trend was provided by writing the good-faith test of bargaining into § 8(d) of the Act. * * *

*Second.* At the same time as it was statutorily defining the duty to bargain collectively, Congress, by adding § 8(b)(3) of the Act through the Taft–Hartley amendments, imposed that duty on labor organizations. Unions obviously are formed for the very purpose of bargaining collectively; but the legislative history makes it plain that Congress was wary of the position of some unions, and wanted to ensure that they would approach the bargaining table with the same attitude of willingness to reach an agreement as had been enjoined on management earlier. It intended to prevent employee representatives from putting forth the same "take it or leave it" attitude that had been condemned in management. 93 Cong.Rec. 4135, 4363, 5005.

*Third.* It is apparent from the legislative history of the whole Act that the policy of Congress is to impose a mutual duty upon the parties to confer in good faith with a desire to reach agreement, in the belief that such an approach from both sides of the table promotes the over-all design of achieving industrial peace. See National Labor Relations Board v. Jones & Laughlin Steel Corp., 301 U.S. 1, 45, 57 S.Ct. 615, 628, 81 L.Ed. 893. Discussion conducted under that standard of good faith may narrow the issues, making the real demands of the parties clearer to each other, and perhaps to themselves, and may encourage an attitude of settlement through give and take. The mainstream of cases before the Board and in the courts reviewing its orders, under the provisions fixing the duty to bargain collectively, is concerned with insuring that the parties approach the bargaining table with this attitude. But apart from this essential standard of conduct, Congress intended that the parties should have wide latitude in their negotiations, unrestricted by any governmental power to regulate the substantive solution of their differences. See Local 24, International Brotherhood of Teamsters Union v. Oliver, supra, 358 U.S. at page 295, 79 S.Ct. at page 304.

We believe that the Board's approach in this case—unless it can be defended, in terms of § 8(b)(3), as resting on some unique character of the union tactics involved here—must be taken as proceeding from an erroneous view of collective bargaining. It must be realized that collective bargaining, under a system where the Government does not attempt to control the results of negotiations, cannot be equated with an academic collective search for truth—or even with what might be thought to be the ideal of one. The parties—even granting the modification of views that may come from a realization of economic interdependence—still proceed from contrary and to an extent antagonistic viewpoints and concepts of self-interest. The system has not reached the ideal of the philosophic notion that perfect understanding among people would lead to perfect agreement among them on values. The presence of economic weapons in reserve, and their actual exercise on occasion by the parties, is part and parcel of the system that the Wagner and Taft–Hartley Acts have recognized. Abstract logical analysis might find inconsistency between the command of the statute to negotiate toward an agreement in good faith and the legitimacy of the use of economic weapons, frequently having the most serious effect upon individual workers and productive enterprises, to induce one party to come to the terms desired by the other. But the truth of the matter is that at the present statutory stage of our national labor relations policy, the two factors—necessity for good-faith bargaining between parties, and the availability of economic pressure devices to each to make the other party incline to agree on one's terms—exist side by side. One writer recognizes this by describing economic force as "a prime motive power for agreements in free collective bargaining." Doubtless one factor influences the other; there may be less need to apply economic pressure if the areas of controversy have been defined through discussion; and at the same time, negotiation positions are apt to be weak or strong in accordance with the degree of economic power the parties possess. A close student of our national labor relations laws writes: "Collective bargaining is curiously ambivalent even today. In one aspect collective bargaining is a brute contest of economic power somewhat masked by polite manners and voluminous statistics. As the relation matures, Lilliputian bonds control the opposing concentrations of economic power; they lack legal sanctions but are nonetheless effective to contain the use of power. Initially it may be only fear of the economic consequences of disagreement that turns the parties to facts, reason, a sense of responsibility, a responsiveness to government and public opinion, and moral principle; but in time these forces generate their own compulsions, and negotiating a contract approaches the ideal of informed persuasion." Cox, The Duty to Bargain in Good Faith, 71 Harv.L.Rev. 1401, 1409.

For similar reasons, we think the Board's approach involves an intrusion into the substantive aspects of the bargaining process—again, unless there is some specific warrant for its condemnation of the precise tactics involved here. The scope of § 8(b)(3) and the limitations on Board power which were the design of § 8(d) are exceeded, we hold, by inferring a lack of good faith not from any deficiencies of the union's performance at the bargaining table by reason of its attempted use of economic pressure, but solely and simply because tactics designed to exert economic pressure were employed during the course of the good-faith negotiations. Thus the Board in the guise of determining good or bad faith in negotiations could regulate what economic weapons a party might summon to its aid. And if the Board could regulate the choice of economic weapons that may be used as part of collective bargaining, it would be in a position to exercise considerable influence upon the substantive terms on which the parties contract. As the parties' own devices became more limited, the Government might have to enter even more directly into the negotiation of collective agreements. Our labor policy is not presently erected on a foundation of government control of the results of negotiations. See S.Rep. No. 105, 80th Cong., 1st Sess., p. 2. Nor does it contain a charter for the National Labor Relations Board to act at large in equalizing disparities of bargaining power between employer and union.

*Fourth.* The use of economic pressure, as we have indicated, is of itself not at all inconsistent with the duty of bargaining in good faith. * * * The Board freely (and we think correctly) conceded here that a "total" strike called by the union would not have subjected it to sanctions under § 8(b)(3), at least if it were called after the old contract, with its no-strike clause, had expired. Cf. United Mine Workers, supra. The Board's opinion in the instant case is not so unequivocal as this concession (and therefore perhaps more logical). But in the light of it and the principles we have enunciated, we must evaluate the claim of the Board to power, under § 8(b)(3), to distinguish among various economic pressure tactics and brand the ones at bar inconsistent with good-faith collective bargaining. We conclude its claim is without foundation.

(a) The Board contends that the distinction between a total strike and the conduct at bar is that a total strike is a concerted activity protected against employer interference by §§ 7 and 8(a)(1) of the Act, while the activity at bar is not a protected concerted activity. We may agree *arguendo* with the Board that this Court's decision in the Briggs–Stratton case, International Union, U.A.W., A.F. of L., Local 232 v. Wisconsin Employment Relations Board, 336 U.S. 245, 69 S.Ct. 516, 93 L.Ed. 651, establishes that the employee conduct here was not a protected concerted activity. On this assumption the employer could have discharged or taken other appropriate disciplinary action against the employees participating in these "slow-down," "sit-in," and arguably unprotected disloyal tactics. See National Labor Relations Board v. Fansteel Metallurgical Corp., 306 U.S. 240, 59 S.Ct. 490, 83 L.Ed. 627; National Labor Relations Board v. Local No. 1229, Intern. B. of Electrical Workers, 346 U.S. 464, 74 S.Ct. 172, 98 L.Ed. 195. But surely that a union activity is not protected against disciplinary action does not mean that it constitutes a refusal to bargain in good faith. The reason why the ordinary economic strike is not evidence of a failure to bargain in good faith is not that it constitutes a protected activity but that, as we have developed, there is simply no inconsistency between the application of economic pressure and good-faith collective bargaining. The Board suggests that since (on the assumption we make) the union members' activities here were unprotected, and they could have been discharged, the activities should also be deemed unfair labor practices, since thus the remedy of a cease-and-desist order, milder than mass discharges of personnel and less disruptive of commerce, would be available. The argument is not persuasive. There is little logic in assuming that because Congress was willing to allow employers to use self-help against union tactics, if they were willing to face the economic consequences of its use, it also impliedly declared these tactics unlawful as a matter of federal law. Our problem remains that of construing § 8(b)(3)'s terms, and we do not see how the availability of self-help to the employer has anything to do with the matter.

(b) The Board contends that because an orthodox "total" strike is "traditional" its use must be taken as being consistent with § 8(b)(3); but since the tactics here are not "traditional" or "normal," they need not be so viewed. Further, the Board cites what it conceives to be the public's moral condemnation of the sort of employee tactics involved here. But again we cannot see how these distinctions can be made under a statute which simply enjoins a duty to bargain in good faith. Again, these are relevant arguments when the question is the scope of the concerted activities given affirmative protection by the Act. But as we have developed, the use of economic pressure by the parties to a labor dispute is not a grudging exception to some policy of completely academic discussion enjoined by the Act; it is part and parcel of the process of collective bargaining. On this basis, we fail to see the relevance of whether the practice in question is time-honored or whether its exercise is generally supported by public opinion. It may be that the tactics used here deserve condemnation, but this would not justify attempting to pour that condemnation into a vessel not designed to hold it. The same may be said for the Board's contention that these activities, as opposed to a "normal" strike, are inconsistent with § 8(b)(3) because they offer maximum pressure on the employer at minimum economic cost to the union. One may doubt whether this was so here, but the matter does not turn on that. Surely it cannot be said that the only economic weapons consistent with good-faith bargaining are those which minimize the pressure on the other party or maximize the disadvantage to the party using them. The catalog of union and employer weapons that might thus fall under ban would be most extensive.

*Fifth.* These distinctions essayed by the Board here, and the lack of relationship to the statutory standard inherent in them, confirm us in our conclusion that the judgment of the Court of Appeals, setting aside the order of the Board, must be affirmed. For they make clear to us that when the Board moves in this area, with only § 8(b)(3) for support, it is functioning as an arbiter of the sort of economic weapons the parties can use in seeking to gain acceptance of their bargaining demands. It has sought to introduce some standard of properly "balanced" bargaining power, or some new distinction of justifiable and unjustifiable, proper and "abusive" economic weapons into the collective bargaining duty imposed by the Act. The Board's assertion of power under § 8(b)(3) allows it to sit in judgment upon every economic weapon the parties to a labor contract negotiation employ, judging it on the very general standard of that section, not drafted with reference to specific forms of economic pressure. We have expressed our belief that this amounts to the Board's entrance into the substantive aspects of the bargaining process to an extent Congress has not countenanced.

* * * Congress has been rather specific when it has come to outlaw particular economic weapons on the part of unions. [The Court here cited Sections 8(b)(4) and 8(b)(7).] * * * [I]t is clear to us that the Board needs a more specific charter than § 8(b)(3) before it can add to the Act's prohibitions here. * * * Congress might be of opinion that greater stress should be put on the role of "pure" negotiation in settling labor disputes, to the extent of eliminating more and more economic weapons from the parties' grasp, and perhaps it might start with the ones involved here; or in consideration of the alternatives, it might shrink from such an undertaking. But Congress' policy has not yet moved to this point, and with only § 8(b)(3) to lean on, we do not see how the Board can do so on its own.

Affirmed.

■ [MR. JUSTICE FRANKFURTER, joined by MR. JUSTICE HARLAN and MR. JUSTICE WHITTAKER, filed a separate opinion.]

---

## PROBLEMS FOR DISCUSSION

**1.** Are the *Truitt* and *Insurance Agents* cases consistent in their premises and reasoning? If they are inconsistent, which decision offers the preferable approach?

**2.** The Business Agent of International Brotherhood of Teamsters called at the office of the President of Quincy Lumber Co., and told him, "Your employees have designated Teamsters as their bargaining agent. Here is the contract we sign with lumber yards. Sign on page 9." Quincy agreed to recognize Teamsters and bargain collectively, knowing that majority of the employees had joined the union. However, Quincy expressed a desire to discuss the terms of the contract. The Business Agent replied, "This is the same contract we sign with all lumber yards. We'll discuss it if you wish, but there's a car full of pickets across the street who'll shut the yard down if you don't sign now." If Quincy refused to sign could it obtain legal relief against the picketing?

---

## NLRB v. Katz[c]

369 U.S. 736, 82 S.Ct. 1107, 8 L.Ed.2d 230 (1962).

■ MR. JUSTICE BRENNAN delivered the opinion of the Court.

Is it a violation of the duty "to bargain collectively" imposed by § 8(a)(5) of the National Labor Relations Act for an employer, without

**c.** See Dannin & Wagar, Lawless Law? The Subversion of the National Labor Relations Act, 34 Loy. L.A. L. Rev. 197 (2000); Earle, The Impasse Doctrine, 64 Chi.-Kent L.Rev. 407 (1988); Schatzki, The Employer's Unilateral Act—A Per Se Violation—Some-

first consulting a union with which it is carrying on bona fide contract negotiations, to institute changes regarding matters which are subjects of mandatory bargaining under § 8(d) and which are in fact under discussion? The National Labor Relations Board answered the question affirmatively in this case, in a decision which expressly disclaimed any finding that the totality of the respondents' conduct manifested bad faith in the pending negotiations. 126 N.L.R.B. 288. A divided panel of the Court of Appeals for the Second Circuit denied enforcement of the Board's cease-and-desist order, finding in our decision in Labor Board v. Insurance Agents' Union, 361 U.S. 477, 80 S.Ct. 419, 4 L.Ed.2d 454, a broad rule that the statutory duty to bargain cannot be held to be violated, when bargaining is in fact being carried on, without a finding of the respondent's subjective bad faith in negotiating. 2 Cir., 289 F.2d 700. * * *

We find nothing in the Board's decision inconsistent with *Insurance Agents* and hold that the Court of Appeals erred in refusing to enforce the Board's order.

The respondents are partners engaged in steel fabricating under the firm name of Williamsburg Steel Products Company. * * * The first meeting between the company and the union took place on August 30, 1956. * * * It is undisputed that the subject of merit increases was raised at the August 30, 1956, meeting although there is an unresolved conflict as to whether an agreement was reached on joint participation by the company and the union in merit reviews, or whether the subject was simply mentioned and put off for discussion at a later date. It is also clear that proposals concerning sick leave were made. Several meetings were held during October and one in November, at which merit raises and sick leave were each discussed on at least two occasions. It appears, however, that little progress was made. * * *

Meanwhile, on April 16, 1957, the union had filed the charge upon which the General Counsel's complaint later issued. As amended and amplified at the hearing and construed by the Board, the complaint's charge of unfair labor practices particularly referred to three acts by the company: unilaterally granting numerous merit increases in October 1956 and January 1957; unilaterally announcing a change in sick-leave policy in March 1957; and unilaterally instituting a new system of automatic wage increases during April 1957. * * *

The [company's] defense was that the Board could not hinge a conclusion that § 8(a)(5) had been violated on unilateral actions alone, without making a finding of the employer's subjective bad faith at the bargaining table; and that the unilateral actions were merely evidence relevant to the

times, 44 Texas L.Rev. 470 (1966); Stewart & Engeman, Impasse, Collective Bargaining and Action, 39 U.Cinn.L.Rev. 233 (1970).

issue of subjective good faith. This argument prevailed in the Court of Appeals. * * *

The duty "to bargain collectively" enjoined by § 8(a)(5) is defined by § 8(d) as the duty to "meet * * * and confer in good faith with respect to wages, hours, and other terms and conditions of employment." Clearly, the duty thus defined may be violated without a general failure of subjective good faith; for there is no occasion to consider the issue of good faith if a party has refused even to negotiate *in fact*—"to meet * * * and confer"—about any of the mandatory subjects. A refusal to negotiate *in fact* as to any subject which is within § 8(d), and about which the union seeks to negotiate, violates § 8(a)(5) though the employer has every desire to reach agreement with the union upon an over-all collective agreement and earnestly and in all good faith bargains to that end. We hold that an employer's unilateral change in conditions of employment under negotiation is similarly a violation of § 8(a)(5), for it is a circumvention of the duty to negotiate which frustrates the objectives of § 8(a)(5) much as does a flat refusal.

The unilateral actions of the respondent illustrate the policy and practical considerations which support our conclusion.

We consider first the matter of sick leave. A sick-leave plan had been in effect since May 1956, under which employees were allowed ten paid sick-leave days annually and could accumulate half the unused days, or up to five days each year. Changes in the plan were sought and proposals and counter-proposals had come up at three bargaining conferences. In March 1957, the company, without first notifying or consulting the union, announced changes in the plan, which reduced from ten to five the number of paid sick-leave days per year, but allowed accumulation of twice the unused days, thus increasing to ten the number of days which might be carried over. This action plainly frustrated the statutory objective of establishing working conditions through bargaining. Some employees might view the change to be a diminution of benefits. Others, more interested in accumulating sick-leave days, might regard the change as an improvement. If one view or the other clearly prevailed among the employees, the unilateral action might well mean that the employer had either uselessly dissipated trading material or aggravated the sick-leave issue. On the other hand, if the employees were more evenly divided on the merits of the company's changes, the union negotiators, beset by conflicting factions, might be led to adopt a protective vagueness on the issue of sick leave, which also would inhibit the useful discussion contemplated by Congress in imposing the specific obligation to bargain collectively.

Other considerations appear from consideration of the respondents' unilateral action in increasing wages. At the April 4, 1957 meeting, the employers offered, and the union rejected, a three-year contract with an immediate across-the-board increase of $7.50 per week, to be followed at the end of the first year and again at the end of the second by further increases of $5 for employees earning less than $90 at those times. Shortly thereafter, without having advised or consulted with the union, the company announced a new system of automatic wage increases whereby there would be an increase of $5 every three months up to $74.99 per week; an increase of $5 every six months between $75 and $90 per week; and a merit review every six months for employees earning over $90 per week. It is clear at a glance that the automatic wage increase system which was instituted unilaterally was considerably more generous than that which had shortly theretofore been offered to and rejected by the union. Such action conclusively manifested bad faith in the negotiations, Labor Board v. Crompton–Highland Mills, 337 U.S. 217, 69 S.Ct. 960, 93 L.Ed. 1320, and so would have violated § 8(a)(5) even on the Court of Appeals' interpretation, though no additional evidence of bad faith appeared. An employer is not required to lead with his best offer; he is free to bargain. But even after an impasse is reached he has no license to grant wage increases greater than any he has ever offered the union at the bargaining table, for such action is necessarily inconsistent with a sincere desire to conclude an agreement with the union.[12]

The respondents' third unilateral action related to merit increases, which are also a subject of mandatory bargaining. Labor Board v. Allison & Co., 6 Cir., 165 F.2d 766. The matter of merit increases had been raised at three of the conferences during 1956 but no final understanding had been reached. In January 1957, the company, without notice to the union, granted merit increases to 20 employees out of the approximately 50 in the unit, the increases ranging between $2 and $10. This action too must be viewed as tantamount to an outright refusal to negotiate on that subject, and therefore as a violation of § 8(a)(5), unless the fact that the January raises were in line with the company's long-standing practice of granting quarterly or semiannual merit reviews—in effect, were a mere continuation of the status quo—differentiates them from the wage increases and the changes in the sick-leave plan. We do not think it does. Whatever might be the case as to so-called "merit raises" which are in fact simply automatic increases to which the employer has already committed himself, the raises here in question were in no sense automatic, but were informed by a large measure of discretion. There simply is no way in such case for a union to know whether or not there has been a substantial departure from past practice, and therefore the union may properly insist that the company negotiate as to the procedures and criteria for determining such increases.

It is apparent from what we have said why we see nothing in Insurance Agents contrary to the Board's decision. The union in that case had not in any way whatever foreclosed discussion of any issue, by unilateral actions or otherwise. The conduct complained of consisted of partial-strike tactics designed to put pressure on the employer to come to terms with the union negotiators. We held that Congress had not, in § 8(b)(3), the counterpart of

**12.** Of course, there is no resemblance between this situation and one wherein an employer, after notice and consultation, "unilaterally" institutes a wage increase identical with one which the union has rejected as too low. See National Labor Relations Board v. Bradley Washfountain Co., 192 F.2d 144, 150–152; National Labor Relations Board v. Landis Tool Co., 193 F.2d 279.

§ 8(a)(5), empowered the Board to pass judgment on the legitimacy of any particular economic weapon used in support of genuine negotiations. But the Board *is* authorized to order the cessation of behavior which is in effect a refusal to negotiate, or which directly obstructs or inhibits the actual process of discussion, or which reflects a cast of mind against reaching agreement. Unilateral action by an employer without prior discussion with the union does amount to a refusal to negotiate about the affected conditions of employment under negotiation, and must of necessity obstruct bargaining, contrary to the congressional policy. It will often disclose an unwillingness to agree with the union. It will rarely be justified by any reason of substance. It follows that the Board may hold such unilateral action to be an unfair labor practice in violation of § 8(a)(5), without also finding the employer guilty of overall subjective bad faith. While we do not foreclose the possibility that there might be circumstances which the Board could or should accept as excusing or justifying unilateral action, no such case is presented here.

The judgment of the Court of Appeals is reversed and the case is remanded with direction to the court to enforce the Board's order.

It is so ordered.

■ MR. JUSTICE FRANKFURTER took no part in the decision of this case.

■ MR. JUSTICE WHITE took no part in the consideration or decision of this case.

---

## PROBLEMS FOR DISCUSSION

**1.** Assume that the employer is obligated under the collective bargaining agreement to provide full pay for certain holidays and to contribute 60% of the cost of the employees' group insurance. Suppose further that the contract has expired, that negotiations over a new agreement have not yet reached an impasse, and that the employer has suddenly announced, without prior notification to the union, that it has discontinued holiday pay and the insurance contributions. What arguments would you make on behalf of the employer, and what disposition should the Board make in the event of a complaint charging the employer with violating Section 8(a)(5)? See Daily News of Los Angeles v. NLRB, 73 F.3d 406 (D.C.Cir.1996); Local 155, Molders v. NLRB, 442 F.2d 742 (D.C.Cir.1971).

**2.** The employer, a painting contractor, and the Painters' Union have a collective bargaining agreement which provides that employees within the unit are to work seven hours a day, five days a week. Although the contract makes no mention of any production quota, it has been the tradition, known to all parties, that journeymen painters complete an average of 11.5 rooms per week. On May 7, at a special meeting of the Union, a resolution was adopted to the effect that no journeyman was to paint more than ten rooms per week, given the desire of the membership to safeguard the health and safety of the painters and to improve the quality of their work. (Violations of this work rule were to be punishable by fine.) The resolution was implemented, and the employer has asked whether the Union's action constitutes an unlawful refusal to bargain in good faith. Does it? New York Dist. Council

No. 9, Painters v. NLRB, 453 F.2d 783 (2d Cir.1971), cert. denied, 408 U.S. 930, 92 S.Ct. 2491, 33 L.Ed.2d 343 (1972).

———

Duffy Tool & Stamping, L.L.C. v. NLRB, 233 F.3d 995 (7th Cir.2000). In the course of bargaining after the union had won a representation election, the employer put forward a proposal for a "no fault" attendance policy under which a tardy worker would get a certain number of points for every incident of tardiness, regardless whether he or she was at fault, and after accumulating a specified number of points, the employee could be discharged. The company's existing attendance policy was more lenient. Upon the union's firm expression of opposition to the no-fault proposal, the employer put it into effect in the midst of bargaining; it later discharged some workers who might not have been discharged under the old policy. The NLRB found that the employer violated section 8(a)(5), because although the parties may have been deadlocked over the no-fault policy, they were not yet deadlocked on all of the mandatory bargaining issues then under negotiation and so had not reached an "overall impasse."

The court of appeals began by reviewing the prevailing principles that in narrow circumstances allow an employer in the course of bargaining "to operate his business as he did before bargaining began and therefore [to] alter the terms and conditions of the workers' employment." Such unilateral action can be taken "if the parties deadlock" or "if the union takes steps to delay or avoid bargaining" or if there is an "exigency requiring immediate change in the terms or conditions of employment to stave off disaster." The issue to be decided here was whether, as the company contended, the privilege to implement a proffered bargaining proposal is activated when there is a deadlock on that proposal alone, even if bargaining continues on other mandatory subjects.

The court (noting a division among the courts of appeals, with most siding with the NLRB) ruled against the employer. It held that, "The employer's position would empty the duty to bargain of meaning, and this in two respects." First, "by removing issues from the bargaining agenda early in the bargaining process, it would make it less likely for the parties to find common ground" on the totality of the contract; "a negotiation is more likely to be successful when there are several issues to be resolved ... rather than just one, because it is easier in the former case to strike a deal that will make both parties feel they are getting more from peace than from war." Second, "if by deadlocking on a particular issue the employer is free to implement his proposal with regard to that issue, he signals to the workers that the union is a paper tiger" and this "would embolden him to hold out for a deal so unfavorable to the union as to preclude agreement." In both respects, the employer would impede the overall objective of the NLRA, which is to achieve labor peace through good faith negotiations. The court continued:

> There is a further and we think conclusive objection to Duffy's position. There really is no such animal as a deadlock on a single issue in a multifaceted negotiation; or if there is it is vanishing

rare, a truly endangered species. Nothing is more common during a negotiation than for one or both parties to make nonnegotiable demands. Usually this is bluffing, since if the negotiation is truly multifaceted, there is generally a price at which the parties will surrender these demands. * * * It is inconceivable that the employer is so wedded to a "no fault" attendance policy—an idea that first occurred to it during the negotiation—that it would not abandon the policy in exchange for a suitable concession in some other term of the collective bargaining agreement. * * * [T]he employer might be able to extract generous concessions in exchange for backing down from his demand. An unreasonable refusal to even consider backing down from a demand plainly not central to the employer's business or labor relations would itself be a sign of bad faith. * * *

---

## McClatchy Newspapers, Inc. v. NLRB

131 F.3d 1026 (D.C.Cir.1997).

■ SILBERMAN, CIRCUIT JUDGE:

This dispute encompasses two cases, one involving McClatchy's Sacramento newspaper and the other its Modesto newspaper. In both cases, the National Labor Relations Board found that McClatchy committed an unfair labor practice by unilaterally implementing a discretionary merit pay proposal, even though McClatchy had bargained to impasse over the proposal with the union.... McClatchy petitions for review of the orders, and the Board cross-petitions for enforcement. We enforce [both orders].

I.

At the Sacramento Bee, the Northern California Newspaper Guild, Local 52 represents editorial, advertising, and telephone switchboard employees. McClatchy's most recent collective bargaining agreement with the union, which expired in 1986, set pay through a combination of wage scales and discretionary merit raises. The agreement defined 28 job classifications, each setting a minimum salary that automatically increased with each year of experience. Once an employee reached the maximum salary for his or her classification, raises were based solely on merit, as determined by the company. McClatchy retained full discretion over the timing and amount of these merit raises, and its decisions were excluded from the contractual grievance and arbitration procedure. Within 10 days of performing a merit evaluation, McClatchy would notify the union of the result, and the union then could make nonbinding comments and participate in the appeals process at the employee's request.

When the 1986 agreement expired, McClatchy and the union each proposed a new wage system. From the outset, their proposals were diametrically opposed: McClatchy wanted to move to a system based entirely on its determination of merit; the union wanted to eliminate the merit system altogether. McClatchy's final offer proposed to grandfather current employees earning less than their classification's maximum, but this plan only superficially preserved the old wage scales. Ninety percent of the employees were already at the top salary step in their class, so the offer kept most raises in McClatchy's complete discretion. And, since the 1986 scales were out of step with the cost of living, salaries for the remaining 10% would effectively be determined by the publisher's discretion as well. The parties bargained in good faith, but ultimately deadlocked over wage terms for the new agreement. Following impasse, McClatchy asserted that it was implementing its final offer and began granting increases to employees without consulting the union. Under the terms of McClatchy's proposal—as was true under the 1986 agreement—the union's role was restricted to making nonbinding comments and participating in the appeal process only if asked by the employee. The union filed an unfair labor practice charge against McClatchy, alleging that implementing "merit" increases without the union's consent violated McClatchy's duty to bargain with the union over wages.

Before the Board resolved the union's Sacramento complaint, petitioner reached an impasse with the union over a similar discretionary pay proposal for its Modesto Bee editorial staff. The only difference in the Modesto proposal was that it fixed the timing of merit increases. At the Sacramento Bee, McClatchy could consider employees for increases as frequently or infrequently as it wished, but at the Modesto Bee, increases were tied to the annual review process. As it had in Sacramento, petitioner implemented its final offer after impasse and gave raises to some employees. The union filed a second unfair labor practice charge against McClatchy. . . .

The Board considered the Sacramento case first. The General Counsel argued that because McClatchy had a statutory obligation to bargain over "wages, hours, and terms of employment," granting individual raises without consulting the union violated the National Labor Relations Act. McClatchy maintained that it had satisfied that duty by bargaining to impasse over the discretionary pay proposal. Once it had exhausted the bargaining process by reaching impasse, McClatchy asserted, it was privileged to implement its "last, best, and final offer" over the union's objection. Relying on its decision in *Colorado-Ute Electric Association*, 295 N.L.R.B. No. 67 (1989), enf. denied, 939 F.2d 1392 (10th Cir.1991), the Board rejected McClatchy's defense. [The Board reasoned that the employer had unilaterally insisted that the union waive its statutory right to be consulted about the mandatory issue of wage changes. A three-judge panel of this court of appeals remanded, with the Board's "waiver" theory getting the tentative support of only one judge; Chief Judge Edwards suggested that the Board consider a limited exception to the impasse doctrine, in which the employer's bypassing the union in setting wage rates could be seen as a kind of "de-collectivization" of bargaining. On remand, the Board indeed fashioned an exception to the "implementation after impasse" doctrine, based on the notion that such implementation is legitimate "only as a method for breaking the impasse."]

... In other words, the Board grounded its new "narrow exception" on the impact that implementation would have on the collective bargaining process:

> Were we to allow the Respondent here to implement its merit wage increase proposal and thereafter expect the parties to resume negotiations for a new collective-bargaining agreement, it is apparent that during the subsequent negotiations the Guild would be unable to bargain knowledgeably and thus have any impact on the present determination of unit employee wage rates. The Guild also would be unable to explain to its represented employees how any intervening changes in wages were formulated, given the Respondent's retention of discretion over all aspects of these increases. Further, the Respondent's implementation of this proposal would not create any fixed, objective status quo as to the level of wage rates, because the Respondent's proposal for a standardless practice of granting raises would allow recurring, unpredictable alterations of wages [sic] rates and would allow the Respondent to initially set and repeatedly change the standards, criteria, and timing of these increases. The frequency, extent, and basis for these wage changes would be governed only by the Respondent's exercise of its discretion.

Id. at 6. Echoing Chief Judge Edwards' de-collectivization remark, the decision noted that petitioner's "ongoing ability to exercise its economic force in setting wage increases [without the Guild's participation] ... would simultaneously disparage the Guild by showing ... its incapacity to act as the employees' representative in setting terms and conditions of employment." Id. The Board took pains to emphasize that its holding was limited to a case where an employer refused to state any "definable objective procedures and criteria" for determining merit. Id. It decided the Modesto case by the same reasoning. . . .

## II.

Although the parties agree the case is one in which petitioner unilaterally implemented the terms of its final offers, it does seem somewhat anomalous to refer to the institution of the new wage regime as an "implementation of terms." Essentially, these wage proposals—particularly the one for the Sacramento Bee—have no terms. Indeed, the Board's opinion expresses the tentative view that under NLRB v. Katz, 369 U.S. 736, 82 S.Ct. 1107, 8 L.Ed.2d 230 (1962), "a wholly discretionary merit wage policy (i.e., without identifiable procedures and criteria) does not itself 'establish' terms and conditions of employment at any point prior to the actual exercise of this discretion in setting discrete wage rates for unit employees." *McClatchy II* at 6 n. 24 (emphasis added). In other words, the Board questioned whether the impasse doctrine should even apply to the employer's action. We think there is something to this query, but since it is not the Board's holding, we obviously cannot rely on it in reviewing the Board's decision.

Although petitioner's argument is somewhat diffuse, we detect three lines of attack against the Board's order. The first is that the NLRA—or at least its "settled doctrine"—contemplates that an employer will be able to implement its last offer to the union after impasse; thus, the argument goes, the Board either lacked authority to craft the "narrow exception" applied in this case or was arbitrary and capricious in doing so. Second, petitioner claims that the Board implicitly treats its merit pay proposal as a permissive bargaining subject, despite the Supreme Court's recognition that comparable management discretion clauses are mandatory subjects of bargaining. Finally, the Board is accused of inadequately setting forth the boundaries of the exception it has crafted and insufficiently reconciling its own precedent.

\* \* \*

The NLRA is wholly silent on the question whether an employer may implement its final offer after impasse. To be sure, the general language of the Act, including § 8(a)(5) and § 8(d), have been authoritatively interpreted by the Supreme Court, and the Board is not free under *Chevron* to alter any of those interpretations even if they otherwise would be permissible readings of the Act. See Lechmere, Inc. v. NLRB, 502 U.S. 527, 536–37, 112 S.Ct. 841, 847–48, 117 L.Ed.2d 79 (1992); Maislin Indus. v. Primary Steel, Inc., 497 U.S. 116, 131, 110 S.Ct. 2759, 2768–69, 111 L.Ed.2d 94 (1990). But the Supreme Court, while it has recognized the Board's doctrine, has never held that an employer has the *right* under the statute to implement its final offer, let alone considered whether the Board is entitled to craft exceptions to this supposed right. Indeed, not even the Board has ever held that the NLRA requires this rule.

. . . . Even if the Board has never before determined that an exception to its doctrine was warranted, however, it is not clear that the statute prevents it from doing so in this case. Petitioner argues that this exception is inconsistent with NLRB v. Insurance Agents' International Union, AFL–CIO, 361 U.S. 477, 80 S.Ct. 419, 4 L.Ed.2d 454 (1960), which forbids the Board to act "as an arbiter of the sort of economic weapons the parties can use in seeking to gain acceptance of their bargaining demands." Id. at 497, 80 S.Ct. at 431. But the Supreme Court, in Charles D. Bonanno Linen Service v. NLRB, 454 U.S. 404, 102 S.Ct. 720, 70 L.Ed.2d 656 (1982), has also emphasized that the Board has wide latitude to monitor the bargaining process. [In that case, the Supreme Court agreed with the NLRB that an impasse in multiemployer bargaining could not in itself entitle a single employer unilaterally to withdraw from the larger unit, lest stability of multiemployer bargaining be generally jeopardized.]

Thus it is true, as petitioner stresses, that *Insurance Agents* prohibited the Board from "act[ing] at large in equalizing disparities of bargaining power between employer and union." *Insurance Agents,* 361 U.S. at 490, 80 S.Ct. at 428. But it is also true, as *Bonanno Linen* makes apparent, that regulating the process of collective bargaining may involve the Board in making determinations that necessarily implicate—if they do not rest directly on—the Board's appraisal of conditions that will affect the parties' bargaining power. Although the line between economic neutrality and authority over process is exceedingly difficult to draw, we think that this case is marginally closer to *Bonanno Linen* than to *Insurance Agents*. Here, as in *Bonanno Linen*, the Board has denied the employer a particular economic tactic for the sake of preserving the stability of the collective bargaining process. The post-impasse rule itself regulates process through power. The Board has told us that its rationale for permitting an employer to unilaterally implement its final offer after impasse is that such an action breaks the impasse and therefore encourages future collective bargaining. The theory might well be thought somewhat strained, for it does not explain why the Board decided to handle impasse with this rule instead of another. The Board could have adopted, for example, a rule requiring the status quo to remain in effect until either the union or the employer was willing to resume negotiations. Stagnancy might pressure both the employer and the union to bend. But the rule it did choose—allowing the employer to implement its final offer—moves the process forward by giving one party, the employer, economic leverage. And in this case, where the employer has advanced no substantive criteria for its merit pay proposal, the Board has decided that the economic power it has granted would go too far. Rather than merely pressuring the union, implementation might well irreparably undermine its ability to bargain. Since the union could not know what criteria, if any, petitioner was using to award individual salary increases, it could not bargain against those standards; instead, it faced a discretionary cloud. As the Board put it, "the present case represents a blueprint for how an employer might effectively undermine the bargaining process while at the same time claiming that it was not acting to circumvent its statutory bargaining obligation." *McClatchy II* at 6. We think that it is within the Board's authority to prevent this development:

> [T]he Board, employing its expertise in the light of experience, has sought to balance the "conflicting legitimate interests" in pursuit of the "national policy of promoting labor peace through strengthened collective bargaining." The Board might have struck a different balance from the one it has, and it may be that some or all of us would prefer that it had done so. *But assessing the significance of impasse and the dynamics of collective bargaining is precisely the kind of judgment that Buffalo Linen ruled should be left to the Board.*

*Bonanno Linen*, 454 U.S. at 413, 102 S.Ct. at 725 (emphasis added) (citations omitted). Of course, if relative bargaining strength were not a matter that the Board could consider in determining whether petitioner's action furthered the collective bargaining process, the Board's reasoning would be vulnerable. But that is not how we read *Bonanno Linen*.

Not only does an employer's implementation of a proposal such as petitioner's deprive the union of "purchase" in pursuing future negotiations, the Board also concluded that by excluding the union from the process by which individual rates of pay are set petitioner "simultaneously disparag[ed] the Guild by showing ... its incapacity to act as the employees' representative in setting terms and conditions of employment." *McClatchy II* at 6. It knew no specifics about the merit raises, therefore it had no information to relay. In that regard, the Board echoed concerns expressed in Chief Judge Edwards' prior concurring opinion that petitioner's implementation of its proposal could be seen as seeking de-collectivization of bargaining. The Board concluded that petitioner's action was "so *inherently* destructive of the fundamental principles of collective bargaining that it could not be sanctioned as part of a doctrine created to break impasse and restore active collective bargaining." *McClatchy II* at 6 (citations omitted). Petitioner particularly objects to this passage, arguing that the phrase "inherently destructive"—which, as the Board acknowledges, comes from NLRB v. Great Dane Trailers, 388 U.S. 26, 87 S.Ct. 1792, 18 L.Ed.2d 1027 (1967)—applies only to employer behavior that is claimed to violate § 8(a)(3), the anti-discrimination provision of the Act. But the Board explained that it was using the term only to show that, as in *Great Dane*, the employer's action will have "foreseeable consequences" notwithstanding its motive. We do not see why that observation is independently objectionable.

\* \* \*

Nevertheless, petitioner contends that the Board's logic is inconsistent with NLRB v. American National Insurance, 343 U.S. 395, 72 S.Ct. 824, 96 L.Ed. 1027 (1952), which held that a clause giving an employer discretion over "management functions" such as promotions, discipline and work scheduling is a mandatory subject of bargaining—i.e., one on which an employer is entitled to insist to the point of impasse. The Court there said that the Board is not entitled to "sit in judgment upon the substantive terms of collective bargaining agreements," id. at 404, 72 S.Ct. at 829, and petitioner asserts that the Board is doing just that in this case. The Board, petitioner argues, has really based its entire reasoning on its judgment about the substance of petitioner's pay proposal.

It seems to us that petitioner may well overread *American National Insurance*. The Court there dealt with a management functions clause that was traditional in the insurance industry. Can one imagine employee's pay—in *any* industry—being described as a subject of a *management functions* clause? And the Court held only that "[a]ny fears the Board may entertain that use of management functions clauses will lead to *evasion* of an employer's duty to bargain collectively as to 'rates of pay, wages, hours, and conditions of employment' do not justify condemning all bargaining for management functions clauses concerning any 'condition of employment'.... " Id. at 409, 72 S.Ct. at 832 (emphasis added). We rather doubt that *American National Insurance* means that no employer proposal could be condemned as a *per se* indication of bad faith bargaining. Suppose, for instance, an employer proposed that all working conditions, including wages and hours, were to be determined in accordance with the employer's total discretion. The offered agreement would have just three clauses: (1)

union recognition, (2) the employer's discretion over all terms, and (3) a no-strike clause. That would seem to be the paradigm management functions clause "evading" the employer's collective bargaining duty.

In any event, the Board did not hold, as it did in *American National Insurance*, that petitioner's insistence on its pay proposal was a permissive subject of bargaining; petitioner was therefore entitled to insist on it to impasse. Petitioner claims, however, that by declaring its "implementation" after impasse illegal the Board has done indirectly what it could not do directly. If an employer cannot implement its proposal then the union has a permanent "veto," see Colorado–Ute Elec. Ass'n v. NLRB, 939 F.2d 1392, 1404 (10th Cir.1991), which, it is argued, is simply another way for the Board to treat an employer's insistence on the proposal as illegal. Petitioner's argument has a good deal of force, but it does not quite carry the day. As the Board's counsel pointed out, the two steps of bargaining to impasse and implementing after impasse are not practically equivalent and therefore can be judged according to different standards. If a party can force an impasse over a subject, its authority to do so gives it significant leverage over all other matters. That ability is not lost—at least not totally—by the Board's holding that the same proposal may not be unilaterally implemented after impasse.

.... It is important to recognize ... that the Board's decision does not prevent an employer from implementing a merit pay proposal post-impasse—so long as the proposal defines "merit" with objective criteria.

The Board's conclusion that petitioner may not unilaterally implement its proposal certainly draws from the substance of that proposal. But that is not unprecedented. To some degree, the Board often considers substance when regulating process. The Board must look to the content of a proposal to decide whether a subject is mandatory or permissive under § 8(d). See NLRB v. Wooster Div. of Borg–Warner Corp., 356 U.S. 342, 78 S.Ct. 718, 2 L.Ed.2d 823 (1958). As petitioner itself concedes, the Board may consider the content of a proposal when making a determination whether the employer is engaged in "surface bargaining." See, e.g., NLRB v. Pacific Grinding Wheel Co., 572 F.2d 1343, 1348 (9th Cir.1978). Here, as in those instances, the Board's reliance on substance is not the same as "compelling McClatchy to agree to a proposal." See 29 U.S.C. § 158(d).

\* \* \*

Finally, petitioner argues that the Board has not explained adequately why it is making an exception for a proposal that affords an employer complete discretion over the grounds for and timing of wage increases. Petitioner asks, why are wages to be thought different than hours or other working conditions the statute also treats as mandatory subjects of bargaining? The Board explained that wages are "a key term and condition of employment and a primary basis of negotiations," *McClatchy II* at 6. That proposition, drawn perforce from the Board's expertise, seems hard to challenge in a reviewing court.... We think the Board is free to draw on its expertise to determine that wages are typically of paramount importance in collective bargaining and to suggest that wages, unlike scheduling or a host of other decisions generally thought closely tied to management operations, are expected to be set bilaterally in a collective bargaining relationship.[8] . . .

---

## PROBLEM FOR DISCUSSION

One of Homeware, Inc.'s bargaining proposals with the union representing its sales clerks ("associates") concerns the scope of the arbitration provision. The Company would have the collective agreement provide:

> All previously unasserted Associate claims arising under federal, state or local statutory or common law shall be subject to arbitration. Merely by way of example, these claims include, but are not limited to, claims arising under the Age Discrimination in Employment Act (ADEA), Title VII of the Civil Rights Act of 1964, as amended, including the amendments of the Civil Rights Act of 1991, the Americans with Disabilities Act (ADA), the Fair Labor Standards Act (FLSA), 42 U.S.C. § 1981, as amended, . . . state discrimination statutes, state statutes and/or common law regulating employment termination, the law of contract or the law of tort; including, but not limited to, claims for malicious prosecution, wrongful discharge, wrongful arrest/wrongful imprisonment, intentional/negligent infliction of emotional distress or defamation.

The Union has rejected this proposal, among others. After a bargaining impasse was reached, the Company announced that it was implementing its final proposals, including the above, save that, in the absence of union agreement, the individual employee rather than the Union would have recourse to arbitration. Has Homeware, Inc. committed an unfair labor practice?

---

*"BOULWARISM": A FINAL PROBLEM FOR DISCUSSION*[d]

In NLRB v. GENERAL ELECTRIC CO., 418 F.2d 736 (2d Cir.1969), the Board and the Court of Appeals were presented with a vexing problem arising from the General Electric bargaining strategy known as Boulwarism (named after a vice president for personnel relations). As negotiations for the 1960 contract approached, the Company used its local management personnel to help determine the desires of the workforce on the type and level of economic benefits. These were translated by the Company into specific proposals, whose cost and effectiveness were researched in order to

---

**8.** We think the Board also has the authority to decide that having fixed standards as well as fixed timing for considering raises is necessary if an employer wishes to implement its proposal. Thus we find no fault with the Board's decision to treat the Modesto and Sacramento proposals identically, even though Modesto had fixed timing.

**d.** See Cooper, Boulwarism and the Duty to Bargain in Good Faith, 20 Rutgers L.Rev. 653 (1966); Gross, Cullen & Hanslowe, Good Faith in Labor Negotiations: Tests and Remedies, 53 Cornell L.Rev. 1009 (1968); H. Northrup, Boulwarism (1964); Note, Boulwarism: Legality and Effect, 76 Harv.L.Rev. 807 (1963).

determine an attractive bargaining offer within the Company's means. The Company then attempted to "sell" its proposals to its employees and the general public through a publicity campaign in plant newspapers, bulletins, letters, television and radio announcements and personal contacts. At the bargaining table, the Company announced that it rejected the usual "horse-trading" approach to bargaining, with each side eventually compromising initial unreasonable positions; it advertised its initial proposals as "fair and firm." Though willing to accept Union suggestions based on facts it might have overlooked, General Electric refused to change its position simply because the Union disagreed with it. After a number of other actions by GE that were later found clearly to be unfair labor practices—including a refusal to turn over information and offering proposals first to local unions rather than to the designated committee bargaining on their behalf—the Union ultimately signed an agreement with the Company.

In the Section 8(a)(5) proceeding initiated by the Union, the attention of the Board and the court focused primarily upon the legality of the Company's technique of making an opening "fair and firm" offer and its communications campaign designed to convince the workers that the Company was best able to discern their interests and that the Company was firm in its bargaining proposals.

Among the contentions made to support the General Counsel's case were these: (1) The announcement of an initial offer that is "fair and firm" reflects a closed mind and a "take it or leave it" attitude that is in substance a refusal to bargain and per se unlawful. (2) The Company's communications campaign designed to convince the employees that the Company was more sensitive to their best interests than was the Union unlawfully denigrated the bargaining representative and effectively constituted direct dealing with the employees. (3) The emphasis in the Company's communications campaign upon the firmness of its proposals as a central element in its bargaining strategy placed the Company in a position where it would be humiliated to make any concessions and thus unlawfully made compromise and adjustment impracticable. (4) The fact that the Company might have been prepared to sign *some* agreement—provided it embodied only the Company's proposals—cannot be sufficient to satisfy the duty to bargain in good faith.

Among the contentions made to support the Company's case were these: (1) To make out a violation of Section 8(a)(5), the circumstances must show an unwillingness to reach an agreement with the Union; the General Counsel conceded that GE had no such subjective purpose, and in fact GE did sign an agreement. (2) It is not unlawful for a party to reject the other party's proposals out of confidence that it has superior bargaining power. A union does not violate Section 8(b)(3) when it insists on imposing area standards in the face of the employer's claim of inability to pay, or when it is firm in its demands because it knows the employer cannot stand a strike. Neither should the Company violate Section 8(a)(5) in comparable circumstances. (3) For the Board or court to condemn the Company for its technique of making a "fair and firm" offer is improperly to intrude and sit in judgment upon the reasonableness of the parties' substantive proposals, and is also improperly to erect a single model of bargaining—the "horse trading" model—as the only acceptable and lawful model of collective bargaining in the United States. (4) To condemn an employer for communicating to its employees its belief in the desirability of its proposals, as well as its intention to adhere to them for that reason, would contravene the letter and spirit of Section 8(c) of the National Labor Relations Act.

How would you decide this case if you were a member of the Court of Appeals?

## III. Subjects of Collective Bargaining[a]

The cases set forth as part of the historical introduction to this book illustrate the longstanding concern of workers for improved wages, shorter working hours, and enhanced job security. The drafters of the Wagner Act obviously intended—through Sections 8(a)(5) and 9(a)—to require the employer to bargain in good faith about these matters with the majority union. That union was to be accepted as an interested partner in regulating these core workplace issues.

Unions and employees have also had interests in participating in entrepreneurial decisions that go beyond this core. Many significant decisions about the scope and direction of the enterprise can affect the job security of the workers and the strength and influence of the union as an institution. This is true of such decisions as contracting out bargaining-unit work to another company, or replacing unit employees with computerized machinery, or relocating or closing down a facility. Recent experiments have involved the workers in structuring the very processes by which they manufacture their company's products and participating in the company's managing board.

Whether the workers will be entitled by law to participate effectively in the shaping of these major business and investment decisions has been one of the most hotly contested issues in American labor law. Management contends that sound economic policy demands that these decisions be made on the basis of the efficient utilization of resources, and that those who invest in the company and those who manage it are best equipped to make such decisions. Workers argue not only that they are able to contribute to informed decisionmaking on such matters, but also that they too have "invested" time and energy in the enterprise so that it is proper to afford

a. See J. Atleson, Values and Assumptions in American Labor Law, Chap. 7 (1983); Cox and Dunlop, Regulation of Collective Bargaining by the National Labor Relations Board, 63 Harv.L.Rev. 389, 427 (1950); P. Miscimarra, The NLRB and Managerial Discretion: Plant Closings, Relocations, Subcontracting and Automation (1983); Modjeska, Guess Who's Coming to the Bargaining Table?, 39 Ohio St.L.J. 415 (1978); Note, Subjects of Bargaining Under the NLRA and the Limits of Liberal Political Imagination, 97 Harv.L.Rev. 475 (1983); Oldham, Organized Labor, the Environment and the Taft–Hartley Act, 71 Mich.L.Rev. 936 (1973).

them a significant participatory role. The basic question for the law student to consider is: What role does and should the law play in allocating decisionmaking functions between labor and management?

The language of Sections 8(d) and 9(a) can easily be read as a command to bargain upon each and every subject embraced within the critical phrase, rates of pay, wages, hours, and other conditions of employment, but the words are scarcely compelling. Probably, neither Congress nor the public had any notion when the Wagner Act was adopted in 1935 that the law was undertaking to define the scope of collective bargaining. Senator Walsh, the Chairman of the Senate Labor Committee, had explained (79 Cong.Rec. 7660 (1935)):

> When the employees have chosen their organization, when they have selected their representatives, all the bill proposed to do is to escort them to the door of their employer and say "Here they are, the legal representatives of your employees." What happens behind those doors is not inquired into and the bill does not seek to inquire into it.

> As an original question, therefore, it seems quite possible that the law might have come to be that a union and an employer who genuinely accepts the union as the employees' representative will be left to work out and, if necessary, to fight out between themselves whether any particular subject (such as pensions, merit increases or subcontracting) will be included in their negotiations and covered by their contract.

But the law has taken a different course. Two rules seem quite settled. *First*, the duty to bargain extends to each and every subject embraced within the statutory phrase, so that it is an unfair labor practice for either the employer or union to refuse to bargain about such a subject upon the request of the other. See NLRB v. Katz, 369 U.S. 736, 82 S.Ct. 1107, 8 L.Ed.2d 230 (1962), at p. 402 supra. *Second*, there are other subjects which fall outside the phrase, wages, hours and other terms and conditions of employment, and which, therefore, are not statutory. There is no duty to bargain about these topics. Under some circumstances, insisting upon bargaining to agreement on a non-statutory subject may be a *per se* violation of either Section 8(a)(5) or 8(b)(3). NLRB v. Wooster Div. of Borg–Warner Corp., see p. 419 infra.

The materials that follow focus upon two questions: (1) What are the statutory subjects and what are the principles according to which they are to be identified? and (2) What are the consequences that flow from treating an issue as a mandatory (or nonmandatory) subject of bargaining? The two questions are interrelated because one cannot intelligently consider whether a particular topic—subcontracting of maintenance work, for example— should be a mandatory subject of collective bargaining without understanding what are the legal as well as the practical consequences of that decision. The task of classifying bargaining subjects as mandatory has arisen in at least three settings: (a) The union requests that the employer bargain about the subject, but the employer refuses; if the subject is within the statutory categories, the employer's refusal obviously constitutes a violation of Section 8(a)(5), but if the subject is non-statutory, there is no duty to bargain and the employer's refusal is privileged. (b) The employer without consulting with the union on the subject, implements a change in its operations; such a "unilateral" change will violate the Act if it relates to a mandatory subject but not otherwise. (c) The employer during negotiations takes a position on a subject, and demands that the union concede on that subject as a condition of reaching an agreement. Conversely, the union might take an adamant stand on an issue, and back its insistence with a strike.

All of the major cases that follow deal with the problem of characterizing a subject (sometimes during formal contract negotiations and sometimes not) as "mandatory" or "permissive." (A third category, an "illegal" contract provision, would surely be non-mandatory and would indeed not even be regarded as permissible for inclusion in the labor agreement.) In the *Fibreboard, First National Maintenance,* and *Pittsburgh Plate Glass* decisions—which were cases which combined the elements just described in fact-settings (a) and (b)—once the disputed subject was characterized, the legal consequences flowed readily. In the *American National Insurance* and *Borg–Warner* cases, which involved the employer's insistence on its position at the bargaining table, the Supreme Court had to decide not only how the subject matter should be characterized but also whether insistence was consistent with the statutory obligation to bargain in good faith. The answer to that latter question determines the relative spheres of collective-bargaining responsibility between government and private parties; or, to put it another way, it determines the extent to which private economic force can be used in support of bargaining demands and thus ultimately the substantive content of the labor contract. (The duty to bargain about a particular subject is often affected by any collective bargaining agreement which is in existence at the time. Although the issue of the duty to bargain during the contract term is considered in some degree in the *Pittsburgh Plate Glass* case, a more detailed discussion is reserved for a later point in this case book; see pp. 848–67, infra.)

## Cox and Dunlop, Regulation of Collective Bargaining by the National Labor Relations Board

63 Harv.L.Rev. 389 (1950).

The [decided cases] * * * appear to commit the NLRB to defining the scope of collective bargaining. But it is uncertain whether the rulings represent an administrative determination that such matters fall within the area of joint responsibility, or merely mark out the range of topics about which management and union are to negotiate, leaving their classification among the three categories [for management to decide, for the union to decide, or for both to decide jointly] to the bargaining process.

To make the problem concrete we may refer again to the *Inland Steel* litigation. Inland announced the categorical position that there was no statutory duty to bargain with the Steelworkers about retirements and pensions and then refused to engage in further discussions. The NLRB held that the refusal violated section 8(a)(5). Let us suppose, however, that Inland had given the Steelworkers this answer:

"We recognize your authority to speak for the employees about pensions or any other subject and we are glad to discuss the matter with you. Our position is that the union should agree to give the company exclusive responsibility over pensions and retirements. The subjects are linked with corporate tax and financial policies and involve complex statistical inquiries. Moreover, our employees are represented in different units by 23 unions of which you are only one. It would be intolerable to bargain about a company pension plan each year with each of 23 unions. We will be glad to hear your views and to explain our thinking on the subject and if you convince us that we are wrong, we will of course go on to consider whether a new pension fund should be established and what its terms should be."

Would this position violate section 8(a)(5)?

The same question arises with respect to other subjects on which the NLRB has held employers must bargain. Does the NLRB's declaration that an employer must negotiate with the bargaining representative about the subcontracting of work mean that the union must be allowed to share in each decision as to what work may be let out and what work will be kept in the shop? Or may the employer bargain for a provision in the collective agreement either recognizing that this aspect of planning the work will be the exclusive function of management or calling for him to talk the matter over with the union but reserving the right to make the decision? The NLRB has also said that an employer is required to bargain about the scheduling of shifts. When the scheduling of shifts requires the careful synchronization of complicated processes, must management agree to fix the starting time of each shift by the give-and-take of bargaining or may it assert that the resolution of technological problems should be made the exclusive function of management by the terms of the collective bargaining agreement?

*A priori* the bare words of section 8(a)(5) are open to two conflicting interpretations, which may be stated somewhat argumentatively as follows: *First.* Section 8(a)(5) makes it an unfair labor practice "to refuse to bargain collectively" with the representative designated by a majority of the employees. Section 9(a) plainly declares that the representative's authority extends to "rates of pay, wages, hours of employment, or other conditions of employment." Therefore, the employer must bargain with respect to each such subject and, as in the *Inland Steel* case, a refusal to discuss a subject covered by the quoted phrase is an unfair labor practice. Nor can this duty be satisfied by going through the forms of bargaining; the employer must have an open mind and sincere desire to reach an agreement. But although an employer must discuss every subject embraced within section 9(a), he complies with the duty to bargain if he negotiates in

good faith any question as to whether a specific term or condition of employment (1) should be established by the collective agreement; or (2) should be fixed periodically by joint management-union determination within the framework of the contract; or (3) should be left to management's discretion or individual bargaining without the intervention of the bargaining agent.

*Second.* Under sections 8(a)(5) and 9(a) an employer must bargain collectively with respect to each subject embraced within the quoted phrase. The essential policy of the statute is that industrial peace can be achieved by taking from management exclusive control over wages, hours, and the other aspects of the employment relationship defined by section 9(a). For that reason the Supreme Court and courts of appeals have repeatedly held that section 8(a)(5) makes unilateral action by an employer an unfair labor practice. The employer who insists upon unilateral control of any "condition of employment" is therefore guilty of an unfair labor practice even though he backs his position by argument and negotiates in good faith.

The choice between these interpretations will determine how the line is to be drawn between the area of exclusive management functions on the one side and the sphere of joint management-union responsibility on the other. Similar questions will have to be decided in drawing a line between the sphere of joint responsibility and the union's internal affairs. Under the first interpretation the lines would be drawn by managements and unions in the course of their annual contract negotiations and, if they could not agree, by recourse to economic weapons. Under the second interpretation the line would be drawn by the NLRB and the courts. Since pensions and merit increases are held to be covered by section 9(a), management could not bargain for exclusive responsibility without running afoul of section 8(a)(5); decisions with respect to them would have to be joint decisions. Similarly the Board and courts would decide as issues of statutory construction whether letting subcontracts and scheduling shifts are management's functions or problems requiring joint determination.

　　* * *

Collective bargaining has developed a variety of procedures to deal with * * * merit increases. At one end of the spectrum are those methods by which the parties have entirely or largely removed questions of increases above the scale from the area of joint determination by agreements vesting in management exclusive authority over such increases. At the other end are contracts giving the union sole responsibility for their distribution. Between the extremes lie the contracts placing such matters in the area of joint determination. The following contract provisions are illustrative of agreed assignment to management control:

"Where voluntary increases are given to employees on account of special skill, superior workmanship, or for other reasons, the Union shall be notified; such action on the part of the Employer shall be final and no other employee shall have the right to demand similar treatment." * * *

"Employees shall receive not less than the job rates for the work performed. * * *" (Agreement between Standard Oil Co. of Cal. and Oil Workers Int'l Union, Local 547, CIO, effective November 3, 1948).

There are many contracts which treat merit increases as falling within the area of joint control. For example:

"No increase shall be granted to any employee unless consented to by the union." * * *

The above reference to specific agreements indicates that collective bargaining has elected in numerous instances to exclude merit increases from the area of joint determination. These decisions have been made by aggressive unions, mature in collective bargaining, generally in situations where individual workers may have considerable individual bargaining power, or where qualitative factors of skill or personality are not readily standardized. It would indeed be a strange result of a law designed to "encourage collective bargaining" to preclude an employer in bargaining from taking a position on merit increases which had been accepted and incorporated in agreements between unions and many other employers, including his competitors.

* * *

---

## NLRB v. American National Insurance Co.[b]
343 U.S. 395, 72 S.Ct. 824, 96 L.Ed. 1027 (1952).

■ MR. CHIEF JUSTICE VINSON delivered the opinion of the Court.

This case arises out of a complaint that respondent refused to bargain collectively with the representatives of its employees as required under the National Labor Relations Act, as amended.

The Office Employees' International Union A.F. of L., Local No. 27, certified by the National Labor Relations Board as the exclusive bargaining representative of respondent's office employees, requested a meeting with respondent for the purpose of negotiating an agreement governing employment relations. At the first meetings, beginning on November 30, 1948, the Union submitted a proposed contract covering wages, hours, promotions, vacations and other provisions commonly found in collective bargaining agreements, including a clause establishing a procedure for settling grievances arising under the contract by successive appeals to management with ultimate resort to an arbitrator.

On January 10, 1949 following a recess for study of the Union's contract proposals, respondent objected to the provisions calling for unlim-

---

**b.** For a most thoughtful and fully developed colloquy regarding the allocation of authority in the workplace under the NLRA, see Klare, Judicial Deradicalization of the Wagner Act and the Origins of Modern Legal Consciousness, 1937–41, 62 Minn.L.Rev. 265 (1978), and Comment, The Radical Potential of the Wagner Act: The Duty to Bargain Collectively, 129 U.Pa.L.Rev. 1392 (1981).

ited arbitration. To meet this objection, respondent proposed a so-called management functions clause listing matters such as promotions, discipline and work scheduling as the responsibility of management and excluding such matters from arbitration. The Union's representative took the position "as soon as [he] heard [the proposed clause]" that the Union would not agree to such a clause so long as it covered matters subject to the duty to bargain collectively under the Labor Act.

Several further bargaining sessions were held without reaching agreement on the Union's proposal or respondent's counterproposal to unlimited arbitration. As a result, the management functions clause was "by-passed" for bargaining on other terms of the Union's contract proposal. On January 17, 1949, respondent stated in writing its agreement with some of the terms proposed by the Union and, where there was disagreement, respondent offered counterproposals, including a clause entitled "Functions and Prerogatives of Management" along the lines suggested at the meeting of January 10th. The Union objected to the portion of the clause providing:

> "The right to select and hire, to promote to a better position, to discharge, demote or discipline for cause, and to maintain discipline and efficiency of employees and to determine the schedules of work is recognized by both union and company as the proper responsibility and prerogative of management to be held and exercised by the company, and while it is agreed that an employee feeling himself to have been aggrieved by any decision of the company in respect to such matters, or the union in his behalf, shall have the right to have such decision reviewed by top management officials of the company under the grievance machinery hereinafter set forth, it is further agreed that the final decision of the company made by such top management officials shall not be further reviewable by arbitration."

At this stage of the negotiations, the National Labor Relations Board filed a complaint against respondent based on the Union's charge that respondent had refused to bargain as required by the Labor Act and was thereby guilty of interfering with the rights of its employees guaranteed by Section 7 of the Act and of unfair labor practices under Sections 8(a)(1) and 8(a)(5) of the Act. While the proceeding was pending, negotiations between the Union and respondent continued with the management functions clause remaining an obstacle to agreement. * * * Finally, on January 13, 1950, after the Trial Examiner had issued his report but before decision by the Board, an agreement between the Union and respondent was signed. The agreement contained a management functions clause that rendered nonarbitrable matters of discipline, work schedules and other matters covered by the clause. The subject of promotions and demotions was deleted from the clause and made the subject of a special clause establishing a union-management committee to pass upon promotion matters. * * *

The Board agreed with the Trial Examiner that respondent had not bargained in a good faith effort to reach an agreement with the Union [based on all of the circumstances, including a unilateral change in working conditions during bargaining]. But the Board rejected the Examiner's views on an employer's right to bargain for a management functions clause and held that respondent's action in bargaining for inclusion of any such clause "constituted, quite [apart from] Respondent's demonstrated bad faith, per se violations of Section 8(a)(5) and (1)." Accordingly, the Board not only ordered respondent in general terms to bargain collectively with the Union (par. 2(a)), but also included in its order a paragraph designed to prohibit bargaining for any management functions clause covering a condition of employment. (Par. 1(a)). 89 N.L.R.B. 185. * * *

*First.* The National Labor Relations Act is designed to promote industrial peace by encouraging the making of voluntary agreements governing relations between unions and employers. The Act does not compel any agreement whatsoever between employees and employers. Nor does the Act regulate the substantive terms governing wages, hours and working conditions which are incorporated in an agreement.[8] The theory of the Act is that the making of voluntary labor agreements is encouraged by protecting employees' rights to organize for collective bargaining and by imposing on labor and management the mutual obligation to bargain collectively. * * *

In 1947, the fear was expressed in Congress that the Board "has gone very far, in the guise of determining whether or not employers had bargained in good faith, in setting itself up as the judge of what concessions an employer must make and of the proposals and counterproposals that he may or may not make." Accordingly, the Hartley Bill, passed by the House, eliminated the good faith test and expressly provided that the duty to bargain collectively did not require submission of counterproposals. As amended in the Senate and passed as the Taft–Hartley Act, the good faith test of bargaining was retained and written into Section 8(d) of the National Labor Relations Act. That Section contains the express provision that the obligation to bargain collectively does not compel either party to agree to a proposal or require the making of a concession.

Thus it is now apparent from the statute itself that the Act does not encourage a party to engage in fruitless marathon discussions at the expense of frank statement and support of his position. And it is equally clear that the Board may not, either directly or indirectly, compel concessions or otherwise sit in judgment upon the substantive terms of collective bargaining agreements.

*Second.* The Board offers in support of the portion of its order before this Court a theory quite apart from the test of good faith bargaining

---

**8.** Terminal Railroad Ass'n of St. Louis v. Trainmen, 318 U.S. 1, 6, 63 S.Ct. 420, 423, 87 L.Ed. 571:

"The Railway Labor Act, like the National Labor Relations Act, does not undertake governmental regulation of wages, hours, or working conditions. Instead it seeks to provide a means by which agreement may be reached with respect to them. The national interest expressed by those Acts is not primarily in the working conditions as such. So far as the Act itself is concerned these conditions may be as bad as the employees will tolerate or be made as good as they can bargain for. The Act does not fix and does not authorize anyone to fix generally applicable standards for working conditions. * * *"

prescribed in Section 8(d) of the Act, a theory that respondent's bargaining for a management functions clause as a counterproposal to the Union's demand for unlimited arbitration was, *"per se,"* a violation of the Act.

Counsel for the Board do not contend that a management functions clause covering some condition of employment is an illegal contract term. As a matter of fact, a review of typical contract clauses collected for convenience in drafting labor agreements shows that management functions clauses similar in essential detail to the clause proposed by respondent have been included in contracts negotiated by national unions with many employers.[16] The National War Labor Board, empowered during the last war "[t]o decide the dispute, and provide by order the wages and hours and all other terms and conditions (customarily included in collective-bargaining agreements)," ordered management functions clauses included in a number of agreements. Several such clauses ordered by the War Labor Board provided for arbitration in case of union dissatisfaction with the exercise of management functions, while others, as in the clause proposed by respondent in this case, provided that management decisions would be final. Without intimating any opinion as to the form of management functions clause proposed by respondent in this case or the desirability of including any such clause in a labor agreement, it is manifest that bargaining for management functions clauses is common collective bargaining practice.

If the Board is correct, an employer violates the Act by bargaining for a management functions clause touching any condition of employment without regard to the traditions of bargaining in the particular industry or such other evidence of good faith as the fact in this case that respondent's clause was offered as a counterproposal to the Union's demand for unlimited arbitration. The Board's argument is a technical one for it is conceded that respondent would not be guilty of an unfair labor practice if, instead of proposing a clause that removed some matters from arbitration, it simply refused in good faith to agree to the Union proposal for unlimited arbitration. The argument starts with a finding, not challenged by the court below or by respondent, that at least some of the matters covered by the management functions clause proposed by respondent are "conditions of employment" which are appropriate subjects of collective bargaining under Sections 8(a)(5), 8(d) and 9(a) of the Act. The Board considers that employer bargaining for a clause under which management retains initial responsibility for work scheduling, a "condition of employment," for the duration of the contract is an unfair labor practice because it is "in derogation of" employees' statutory rights to bargain collectively as to conditions of employment.[22]

---

**16.** Writers advocating inclusion of detailed management functions clauses in collective bargaining agreements urge the desirability of defining the respective functions of management and labor in matters such as work scheduling consistent with the needs of the particular industry. See Cox and Dunlop, Regulation of Collective Bargaining by the National Labor Relations Board, 63 Harv. L.Rev. 389 (1950) * * *.

**22.** The Board's argument would seem to prevent an employer from bargaining for a "no-strike" clause, commonly found in labor

Conceding that there is nothing unlawful in including a management functions clause in a labor agreement, the Board would permit an employer to "propose" such a clause. But the Board would forbid bargaining for any such clause when the Union declines to accept the proposal, even where the clause is offered as a counterproposal to a Union demand for unlimited arbitration. Ignoring the nature of the Union's demand in this case, the Board takes the position that employers subject to the Act must agree to include in any labor agreement provisions establishing fixed standards for work schedules or any other condition of employment. An employer would be permitted to bargain as to the content of the standard so long as he agrees to freeze a standard into a contract. Bargaining for more flexible treatment of such matters would be denied employers even though the result may be contrary to common collective bargaining practice in the industry. The Board was not empowered so to disrupt collective bargaining practices. On the contrary, the term "bargain collectively" as used in the Act "has been considered to absorb and give statutory approval to the philosophy of bargaining as worked out in the labor movement in the United States." Order of Railroad Telegraphers v. Railway Express Agency, 1944, 321 U.S. 342, 346, 64 S.Ct. 582, 585, 88 L.Ed. 788.

Congress provided expressly that the Board should not pass upon the desirability of the substantive terms of labor agreements. Whether a contract should contain a clause fixing standards for such matters as work scheduling or should provide for more flexible treatment of such matters is an issue for determination across the bargaining table, not by the Board. If the latter approach is agreed upon, the extent of union and management participation in the administration of such matters is itself a condition of employment to be settled by bargaining.

Accordingly, we reject the Board's holding that bargaining for the management functions clause proposed by respondent was, *per se,* an unfair labor practice. Any fears the Board may entertain that use of management functions clauses will lead to evasion of an employer's duty to bargain collectively as to "rates of pay, wages, hours and conditions of employment" do not justify condemning all bargaining for management functions clauses covering any "condition of employment" as *per se* violations of the Act. The duty to bargain collectively is to be enforced by application of the good faith bargaining standards of Section 8(d) to the facts of each case rather than by prohibiting all employers in every industry from bargaining for management functions clauses altogether.

*Third.* * * * Accepting as we do the finding of the court below that respondent bargained in good faith for the management functions clause proposed by it, we hold that respondent was not in that respect guilty of refusing to bargain collectively as required by the National Labor Relations

agreements, requiring a union to forego for the duration of the contract the right to strike expressly granted by Section 7 of the Act. However, the Board has permitted an employer to bargain in good faith for such a clause. Shell Oil Co., 77 N.L.R.B. 1306 (1948). This result is explained by referring to the "salutary objective" of such a clause. Bethlehem Steel Co., 89 N.L.R.B. 341, 345 (1950).

Act. Accordingly, enforcement of paragraph 1(a) of the Board's order was properly denied.

■ MR. JUSTICE MINTON, with whom MR. JUSTICE BLACK and MR. JUSTICE DOUGLAS join, dissenting:

\* \* \* This case is one where the employer came into the bargaining room with a demand that certain topics upon which it had a duty to bargain were to be removed from the agenda—that was the price the Union had to pay to gain a contract. There is all the difference between the hypothetical "management functions" clauses envisioned by the majority and this "management functions" clause as there is between waiver and coercion. No one suggests that an employer is guilty of an unfair labor practice when it proposes that it be given unilateral control over certain working conditions and the union accepts the proposal in return for various other benefits. But where, as here, the employer tells the union that the only way to obtain a contract as to wages is to agree not to bargain about certain other working conditions, the employer has refused to bargain about those other working conditions. \* \* \*

An employer may not stake out an area which is a proper subject for bargaining and say, "As to this we will not bargain." To do so is a plain refusal to bargain in violation of § 8(a)(5) of the Act. If employees' bargaining rights can be cut away so easily, they are indeed illusory. I would reverse.

----

## PROBLEMS FOR DISCUSSION

**1.** The Court in *American National Insurance* appears to hold that it is unlawful for an employer to come to the bargaining table and state "Decisions about promotions and demotions are none of the union's business and I will not discuss the matter"; but that it is lawful for the employer to state "I will discuss with you today the matter of control over promotions and demotions, but it is my firm position that they are none of the union's business and that I will not discuss them with the union during the term of the contract." Is this a sensible distinction? Is it an administrable one?

**2.** What does the Court mean in *American National Insurance* when it states that the adoption of the Board's position would give the Board too great a measure of control over the substantive terms of the labor contract? Had the Board's position been adopted, would it be illegal for the employer to insist upon a merit-pay provision reposing in the employer exclusive power to award merit increases for high-quality work? To insist upon employer power to award such increases after "meeting and conferring" (but not bargaining to impasse) with the union? To insist upon a provision establishing an employer-union committee with the power to award such increases? To insist upon employer power to award such increases subject to review by a neutral arbitrator for discrimination or arbitrariness? Compare the power of the Board to disapprove employer insistence on such clauses under the principles ultimately adopted by the Supreme Court.

----

# NLRB v. Wooster Division of Borg–Warner Corp.

356 U.S. 342, 78 S.Ct. 718, 2 L.Ed.2d 823 (1958).

■ MR. JUSTICE BURTON delivered the opinion of the Court.

In these cases an employer insisted that its collective-bargaining contract with certain of its employees include: (1) a "ballot" clause calling for a pre-strike secret vote of those employees (union and non-union) as to the employer's last offer, and (2) a "recognition" clause which excluded, as a party to the contract, the International Union which had been certified by the National Labor Relations Board as the employees' exclusive bargaining agent, and substituted for it the agent's uncertified local affiliate. The Board held that the employer's insistence upon either of such clauses amounted to a refusal to bargain, in violation of § 8(a)(5) of the National Labor Relations Act, as amended. The issue turns on whether either of these clauses comes within the scope of mandatory collective bargaining as defined in § 8(d) of the Act. For the reasons hereafter stated, we agree with the Board that neither clause comes within that definition. Therefore, we sustain the Board's order directing the employer to cease insisting upon either clause as a condition precedent to accepting any collective-bargaining contract.

Late in 1952, the International Union, United Automobile, Aircraft and Agricultural Implement Workers of America, CIO (here called International) was certified by the Board to the Wooster (Ohio) Division of the Borg–Warner Corporation (here called the company) as the elected representative of an appropriate unit of the company's employees. Shortly thereafter, International chartered Local No. 1239, UAW–CIO (here called the Local). Together the unions presented the company with a comprehensive collective-bargaining agreement. In the "recognition" clause, the unions described themselves as both the "International Union, United Automobile, Aircraft and Agricultural Implement Workers of America and its Local Union No. 1239, U.A.W.–C.I.O. * * *."

The company submitted a counter-proposal which recognized as the sole representative of the employees "Local Union 1239, affiliated with the International Union, United Automobile, Aircraft and Agricultural Implement Workers of America (UAW–CIO)." The unions' negotiators objected because such a clause disregarded the Board's certification of International as the employees' representative. The negotiators declared that the employees would accept no agreement which excluded International as a party.

The company's counterproposal also contained the "ballot" clause, * * *. In summary, this clause provided that, as to all nonarbitrable issues (which eventually included modification, amendment or termination of the contract), there would be a 30–day negotiation period after which, before the union could strike, there would have to be a secret ballot taken among all employees in the unit (union and non-union) on the company's last offer. In the event a majority of the employees rejected the company's last offer, the company would have an opportunity, within 72 hours, of making a new proposal and having a vote on it prior to any strike. The unions' negotiators announced they would not accept this clause "under any conditions."

From the time that the company first proposed these clauses, the employees' representatives thus made it clear that each was wholly unacceptable. The company's representatives made it equally clear that no agreement would be entered into by it unless the agreement contained both clauses. In view of this impasse, there was little further discussion of the clauses, although the parties continued to bargain as to other matters. The company submitted a "package" proposal covering economic issues but made the offer contingent upon the satisfactory settlement of "all other issues * * *." The "package" included both of the controversial clauses. On March 15, 1953, the unions rejected that proposal and the membership voted to strike on March 20 unless a settlement were reached by then. None was reached and the unions struck. Negotiations, nevertheless, continued. On April 21, the unions asked the company whether the latter would withdraw its demand for the "ballot" and "recognition" clauses if the unions accepted all other pending requirements of the company. The company declined and again insisted upon acceptance of its "package," including both clauses. Finally, on May 5, the Local, upon the recommendation of International, gave in and entered into an agreement containing both controversial clauses.

In the meantime, International had filed charges with the Board claiming that the company, by the above conduct, was guilty of an unfair labor practice within the meaning of § 8(a)(5) of the Act. * * * [The Board found a violation, and the Court of Appeals enforced the Board's order as to the "recognition" clause but refused enforcement as to the "ballot" clause.]

Read together, [Section 8(a)(5) and Section 8(d)] establish the obligation of the employer and the representative of its employees to bargain with each other in good faith with respect to "wages, hours, and other terms and conditions of employment * * *." The duty is limited to those subjects, and within that area neither party is legally obligated to yield. National Labor Relations Board v. American Insurance Co., 343 U.S. 395, 72 S.Ct. 824, 96 L.Ed. 1027. As to other matters, however, each party is free to bargain or not to bargain, and to agree or not to agree.

The company's good faith has met the requirements of the statute as to the subjects of mandatory bargaining. But that good faith does not license the employer to refuse to enter into agreements on the ground that they do not include some proposal which is not a mandatory subject of bargaining. We agree with the Board that such conduct is, in substance, a refusal to bargain about the subjects that are within the scope of mandatory bargaining. This does not mean that bargaining is to be confined to the statutory subjects. Each of the two controversial clauses is lawful in itself. Each would be enforceable if agreed to by the unions. But it does not follow that, because the company may propose these clauses, it can lawfully insist upon them as a condition to any agreement.

Since it is lawful to insist upon matters within the scope of mandatory bargaining and unlawful to insist upon matters without, the issue here is whether either the "ballot" or the "recognition" clause is a subject within the phrase "wages, hours, and other terms and conditions of employment" which defines mandatory bargaining. The "ballot" clause is not within that definition. It relates only to the procedure to be followed by the employees among themselves before their representative may call a strike or refuse a final offer. It settles no term or condition of employment—it merely calls for an advisory vote of the employees. It is not a partial "no-strike" clause. A "no-strike" clause prohibits the employees from striking during the life of the contract. It regulates the relations between the employer and the employees. See National Labor Relations Board v. American Insurance Co., supra, 343 U.S. at page 408, n. 22, 72 S.Ct. at page 831, 96 L.Ed. 1027. The "ballot" clause, on the other hand, deals only with relations between the employees and their unions. It substantially modifies the collective-bargaining system provided for in the statute by weakening the independence of the "representative" chosen by the employees. It enables the employer, in effect, to deal with its employees rather than with their statutory representative. Cf. Medo Photo Corp. v. National Labor Relations Board, 321 U.S. 678, 64 S.Ct. 830, 88 L.Ed. 1007.

The "recognition" clause likewise does not come within the definition of mandatory bargaining. The statute requires the company to bargain with the certified representative of its employees. It is an evasion of that duty to insist that the certified agent not be a party to the collective-bargaining contract. The Act does not prohibit the voluntary addition of a party, but that does not authorize the employer to exclude the certified representative from the contract. * * *

■ Mr. Justice Frankfurter joins this opinion insofar as it holds that insistence by the company on the "recognition" clause, in conflict with the provisions of the Act requiring an employer to bargain with the representative of his employees, constituted an unfair labor practice. He agrees with the views of Mr. Justice Harlan regarding the "ballot" clause. The subject matter of that clause is not so clearly outside the reasonable range of industrial bargaining as to establish a refusal to bargain in good faith, and is not prohibited simply because not deemed to be within the rather vague scope of the obligatory provisions of § 8(d).

■ Mr. Justice Harlan, whom Mr. Justice Clark and Mr. Justice Whittaker join, concurring in part and dissenting in part.

I agree that the company's insistence on the "recognition" clause constituted an unfair labor practice, but reach that conclusion by a different route from that taken by the Court. However, in light of the finding below that the company bargained in "good faith," I dissent from the view that its insistence on the "ballot" clause can support the charge of an unfair labor practice. * * *

Preliminarily, I must state that I am unable to grasp a concept of "bargaining" which enables one to "propose" a particular point, but not to "insist" on it as a condition to agreement. The right to bargain becomes illusory if one is not free to press a proposal in good faith to the point of insistence. Surely adoption of so inherently vague and fluid a standard is apt to inhibit the entire bargaining process because of a party's fear that strenuous argument might shade into forbidden insistence and thereby produce a charge of an unfair labor practice. This watered-down notion of "bargaining" which the Court imports into the Act with reference to matters not within the scope of § 8(d) appears as foreign to the labor field as it would be to the commercial world. To me all of this adds up to saying that the Act limits *effective* "bargaining" to subjects within the three fields referred to in § 8(d), that is "wages, hours, and other terms and conditions of employment," even though the Court expressly disclaims so holding.

I shall discuss my difficulties with the Court's opinion in terms of the "ballot" clause. The "recognition" clause is subject in my view to different considerations.

## I.

At the start, I question the Court's conclusion that the "ballot" clause does not come within the "other terms and conditions of employment" provision of § 8(d). The phrase is inherently vague and prior to this decision has been accorded by the Board and courts an expansive rather than a grudging interpretation. Many matters which might have been thought to be the sole concern of management are now dealt with as compulsory bargaining topics. E.g. National Labor Relations Board v. J.H. Allison & Co., 6 Cir., 165 F.2d 766, 3 A.L.R.2d 990 (merit increases). And since a "no-strike" clause is something about which an employer can concededly bargain to the point of insistence, see Shell Oil Co., 77 N.L.R.B. 1306, I find it difficult to understand even under the Court's analysis of this problem why the "ballot" clause should not be considered within the area of bargaining described in § 8(d). It affects the employer-employee relationship in much the same way, in that it may determine the timing of strikes or even whether a strike will occur by requiring a vote to ascertain the employees' sentiment prior to the union's decision.

Nonetheless I shall accept the Court's holding that this clause is not a condition of employment, for even though the union would accordingly not be *obliged* under § 8(d) to bargain over it, in my view it does not follow that the company was *prohibited* from insisting on its inclusion in the collective bargaining agreement. In other words, I think the clause was a permissible, even if not an obligatory, subject of good faith bargaining.

The legislative history behind the Wagner and Taft–Hartley Acts persuasively indicates that the Board was never intended to have power to prevent good faith bargaining as to any subject not violative of the provisions or policies of those Acts. * * *

The decision of this Court in 1952 in National Labor Relations Board v. American National Insurance Co., supra, was fully in accord with this legislative background in holding that the Board lacked power to order an employer to cease bargaining over a particular clause because such bargaining under the Board's view, entirely apart from a showing of bad faith, constituted *per se* an unfair labor practice. * * *

The most cursory view of decisions of the Board and the circuit courts under the National Labor Relations Act reveals the unsettled and evolving character of collective bargaining agreements. Provisions which two decades ago might have been thought to be the exclusive concern of labor or management are today commonplace in such agreements. The bargaining process should be left fluid, free from intervention of the Board leading to premature crystallization of labor agreements into any one pattern of contract provisions, so that these agreements can be adapted through collective bargaining to the changing needs of our society and to the changing concepts of the responsibilities of labor and management. What the Court does today may impede this evolutionary process. * * * I do not deny that there may be instances where unyielding insistence on a particular item may be a relevant consideration in the over-all picture in determining "good faith," for the demands of a party might in the context of a particular industry be so extreme as to constitute some evidence of an unwillingness to bargain. But no such situation is presented in this instance by the "ballot" clause. "No-strike" clauses, and other provisions analogous to the "ballot" clause limiting the right to strike, are hardly novel to labor agreements. And in any event the uncontested finding of "good faith" by the Trial Examiner forecloses that issue here.

Of course an employer or union cannot insist upon a clause which would be illegal under the Act's provisions, National Labor Relations Board v. National Maritime Union, 2 Cir., 175 F.2d 686, or conduct itself so as to contravene specific requirements of the Act. Medo Photo Supply Corp. v. Labor Board, 321 U.S. 678, 64 S.Ct. 830, 88 L.Ed. 1007. But here the Court recognizes, as it must, that the clause is lawful under the Act, and I think it clear that the company's insistence upon it violated no statutory duty to which it was subject. * * *

## II.

The company's insistence on the "recognition" clause, which had the effect of excluding the International Union as a party signatory to agreement and making Local 1239 the sole contracting party on the union side, presents a different problem. In my opinion the company's action in this regard did constitute an unfair labor practice since it contravened specific requirements of the Act.

* * * The employer's duty to bargain with the representatives includes not merely the obligation to confer in good faith, but also " * * * the execution of a written contract incorporating any agreement reached if requested * * * " by the employees' representatives. § 8(d). I think it hardly debatable that this language must be read to require the company, if so requested, to sign any agreement reached with the same representative with which it is required to bargain. By conditioning agreement upon a

change in signatory from the certified exclusive bargaining representative, the company here in effect violated this duty.

I would affirm the judgment of the Court of Appeals in both cases and require the Board to modify its cease and desist order so as to allow the company to bargain over the ballot clause.

———

# PROBLEMS FOR DISCUSSION

**1.** A principal reason given for the Court's decision is that insistence upon a nonmandatory subject "is, in substance, a refusal to bargain about the subjects that are within the scope of mandatory bargaining." Do you agree? (Is this not also true of insistence upon one mandatory subject as a condition to agreeing upon other mandatory subjects?) Could the Court have articulated a more tenable rationale for barring insistence upon nonmandatory subjects in general, or for barring insistence upon the "ballot" and "recognition" clauses in *Borg–Warner*?

**2.** If you are attorney for a party which is very intent, in its labor negotiations, upon securing a concession from the other party on a matter which is not clearly a mandatory subject, what advice must you give, based on *Borg–Warner*? Consider explaining: (a) how the Board and courts will likely go about deciding whether the issue is mandatory or permissive; (b) how assertive your client may be at the bargaining table; and (c) the wisdom and legality (and morality) of feigning insistence on an actually inconsequential mandatory subject, while "signaling" that the insistence will be dropped if the other party concedes on the matter that is strongly desired.

**3.** On the question of the "ballot clause," do you agree more with the opinion of Mr. Justice Burton or that of Mr. Justice Harlan? Why is a no-strike clause a "mandatory" subject, and how materially different is the ballot clause? Is the ballot clause contrary to federal labor policy? Compare Sections 203(c) and 209(b) of the Labor Act.

**4.** Can management lawfully insist to the point of impasse on a contract clause prohibiting either party from taking action to "interfere with, restrain or coerce by discipline, discharge, fine or otherwise" any employee who chooses to engage in or refrain from a strike? See U.O.P. Norplex v. NLRB, 445 F.2d 155 (7th Cir.1971). Can the union lawfully insist upon such a provision?

**5.** If the contract already has a union-shop provision, requiring all employees to join the union and pay dues, may the employer insist upon a provision that the union may not increase membership dues without the employer's consent? See North Bay Dev. Disabilities Serv., Inc. v. NLRB, 905 F.2d 476 (D.C.Cir.1990), cert. denied, 498 U.S. 1082, 111 S.Ct. 952, 112 L.Ed.2d 1041 (1991).

**6.** May a union lawfully insist, as a condition of signing a labor agreement, that it contain a provision for a three-member arbitration panel as the final step in the grievance procedure (rather than the unreviewable determination of the employer's vice-president for labor relations)?

———

*THE MANDATORY-PERMISSIVE DISTINCTION*[c]

As the law has developed since *Borg–Warner,* bargaining subjects are divided into three categories: mandatory, permissive, and illegal. All of the Justices in *Borg–Warner* expressly or impliedly endorsed the proposition that it is an unfair labor practice to insist upon the inclusion in the contract of an illegal provision or to use economic force in support of such a demand. Even a voluntarily negotiated illegal provision is unenforceable and void. See Penello v. International Union, United Mine Workers, 88 F.Supp. 935 (D.D.C.1950)(Section 10(j) injunction against union insistence that labor contract include a provision for a closed shop and for a welfare and retirement fund with benefits limited to union members). The mandatory-permissive distinction is made in order to determine: whether a party must bargain in good faith if requested; whether pertinent information must be disclosed; whether unilateral action may be taken without bargaining to impasse; and whether insistence backed by economic force is lawful.

Is it wise to categorize a particular issue as inherently either mandatory or permissive, given these diverse purposes for which the categorization is made? For example, assume that a company is planning to close its plant in New Jersey and to relocate to North Carolina. The law could very well be construed to permit the employer to make that move without discussing the issue with the union or even without giving the union any advance notice. Does it follow, however, if the union learns of the employer's plans, regards the matter as of great moment to the employees in the bargaining unit, and insists that the employer reconsider/retract that decision—and institutes a work stoppage in protest—that Section 8(b)(3) would make the union's conduct illegal? That is essentially the issue put by Justice Harlan in his separate opinion in *Borg–Warner.* Could not the interests of both management and labor be accorded weight by permitting the union to be firm in asserting its position and its concern, while permitting the employer to be equally firm in declining even to discuss the issue? Does not the law as articulated in *Borg–Warner* impede the serious exploration at the bargaining table of issues that are of moment to one or another party—and thus do a disservice to collective bargaining?

In any event, *Borg–Warner* holds a firm place in our labor jurisprudence, and reinforces the need to draw the line between mandatory and permissive subjects. The following cases exemplify the process of categorization.

DOUDS v. INTERNATIONAL LONGSHOREMEN'S ASS'N, 241 F.2d 278 (2d Cir. 1957). In August, 1956, ILA and the New York Shipping Ass'n began to

**c.** See Note, Major Operational Decisions and Free Collective Bargaining: Eliminating the Mandatory/Permissive Distinction, 102 Harv.L.Rev. 1971 (1989); Note, The Viability of Distinguishing Between Mandatory and Permissive Subjects of Bargaining in a Cooperative Setting, 41 Vand.L.Rev. 577 (1988). For a useful treatment of the different purposes for which the mandatory-permissive distinction is made, see Feller & Finkin, "Legislative Issues in Faculty Collective Bargaining," in Faculty Bargaining in Public Higher Education, 73, at 117–21 (Carnegie Council on Policy Studies in Higher Education 1977).

negotiate a contract to replace an expiring agreement covering longshoremen in the port of Greater New York. ILA demanded that the contract be expanded to cover the East and Gulf Coasts. During the bargaining, the NLRB conducted a representation proceeding in the course of which it confined the scope of the bargaining unit to the port of Greater New York and conducted an election in that unit which was won by ILA. After certification as the representative for employees in the port of Greater New York, ILA continued to demand an agreement covering the East and Gulf Coasts and when the Association refused, a strike was called to enforce the demand. Upon a charge filed by the Association, the NLRB issued a complaint and sought a temporary injunction under Section 10(j) enjoining ILA from insisting upon a change in the bargaining unit. Upon appeal from an order granting the injunction, *held* that ILA was violating Section 8(b)(3). "This distinction between private bargaining over conditions of employment and the administrative determination of the unit appropriate for bargaining is clear. The parties cannot bargain meaningfully about wages or hours or conditions of employment unless they know the unit of bargaining. That question is for the Board to decide on a petition under Section 9(c) of the Act, and its decision is conclusive on the parties * * * although the decision may subsequently be changed."

"The machinery for initial decision and subsequent change is provided in the statute * * *. The process of change not permitted by the Act is one that denies the Board this ultimate control of the bargaining unit and disrupts the bargaining process itself. This is precisely what occurs when, after the Board has decided what the appropriate bargaining unit is, one party over the objection of the other demands a change in that unit. Such a demand interferes with the required bargaining 'with respect to rates of pay, wages, hours and conditions of employment' in a manner excluded by the Act. It is thus a refusal to bargain in good faith within the meaning of Section 8(b)(3)."

NLRB v. DETROIT RESILIENT FLOOR DECORATORS LOCAL UNION NO. 2265, 317 F.2d 269 (6th Cir.1963). After obtaining recognition from the employer, the union proposed that a contract be signed incorporating a provision which obligated the employer to contribute to a fund, already supported by a number of employers, which was devoted exclusively to "promoting, publicizing, and advancing the interests of the floor covering industry." Although the employer was a member of this industry, he resisted making such contributions. After prolonged discussion, however, the employer signed the agreement, subject to a reservation allowing him to contest the right of the union to insist upon the provision. The Board ruled that the provision was not a mandatory subject of bargaining. "An industry promotion fund seems to us to be outside of the employment relationship. It concerns itself rather with the relationship of employers to one another or, like advertising, with the relationship of an employer to the consuming public. The ability of an employer or an industry to meet changing conditions may, as the respondent argues, affect employees' opportunities in the long run, and labor organizations are understandably concerned with the future of the industries from which their members derive their livelihood. Such long-range prospects may also be affected by conditions and events of even more general applicability such as developments on the economic or political scene, legislation, taxation, and foreign competition. Nothing prevents an employer and a union from joining voluntarily in a mutual effort to attempt to influence their industry's course of development, provided, of course, that other legislative enactments do not prohibit such activities. To hold, however, under this Act, that one party must bargain at the behest of another on any matter which might conceivably enhance the prospects of the industry would transform bargaining over the compensation, hours, and employment conditions of employees into a debate over policy objectives." On petition to enforce the Board's order, *held,* enforcement granted.

FORD MOTOR CO. (CHICAGO STAMPING PLANT) v. NLRB, 441 U.S. 488, 99 S.Ct. 1842, 60 L.Ed.2d 420 (1979). For many years, Ford provided in-plant food services, particularly cafeterias and vending machines, to its employees in its Chicago Heights plant; these facilities were operated by ARA Services, Inc. (with Ford having the right to review and approve the quality, quantity, and price of the food served). Labor contracts since 1967 expressly dealt with such matters as cafeteria supervision, the restocking of vending machines, and menu variety; but Ford always refused to bargain about in-plant food and beverage prices. In February 1976, Ford informed the Union that cafeteria and vending-machine prices would be increased, and rejected the Union's request to bargain over both price and services and to supply information relevant to Ford's involvement in food services.

The Board found this conduct to violate Section 8(a)(5) and ordered the Company to bargain and to provide the requested information. The court of appeals—although sharing the prevailing view in the courts that in-plant food prices were not a subject of mandatory bargaining—enforced the Board's order on the facts of the case, giving considerable weight to the fact that the length of the lunch period and the distance of restaurants made it impracticable for the employees to eat away from the plant (so that the in-plant food "can be viewed as a physical dimension of one's working environment").

The Supreme Court affirmed (making no special mention of the lack of reasonable eating alternatives). It observed that the Board has special expertise in classifying bargaining subjects as "terms or conditions of employment" and that "if its construction of the statute is reasonably defensible, it should not be rejected merely because the courts might prefer another view of the statute." The Court held that "the Board's consistent view that in-plant food prices and services are mandatory bargaining subjects is not an unreasonable or unprincipled construction of the statute and that it should be accepted and enforced."

Since employees must eat at some point during the workday "the availability of food during working hours and the conditions under which it is to be consumed are matters of deep concern to workers." When management in its own interest provides in-plant feeding facilities, food prices and service "may reasonably be considered" a bargainable subject, for they are germane to the working environment. To require the employer to bargain will not "permit the Union to usurp managerial decisionmaking" and will serve the ends of the NLRA by funneling into collective bargaining (rather than strikes and other forms of economic warfare) substantial disputes which can arise over the pricing of in-plant food and beverages. The Court also observed that many contract provisions concerning in-plant food services have been negotiated, and that non-price aspects of such services had been in the Ford agreement at this plant for many years. (It then set forth statistics on the percentage of companies providing in-plant food services, but no statistics on how many of those companies treated such matters in their labor contracts.)

To Ford's argument that food prices and service are too trivial to be made mandatory subjects of bargaining, the Court stated that the employees in this case were sufficiently upset about the matter, and that even minor increases in the cost of meals can amount over time to a substantial sum of money. To Ford's argument that it would be disruptive to secure approval in advance of every minor change in price or service, the Court responded: "[I]t is sufficient compliance with the statutory mandate if management honors a specific union request for bargaining about changes that have been made or are to be made." Moreover, problems arising from frequent changes can be anticipated in the collective bargaining agreement.

JOHNSON-BATEMAN CO. v. INTERNATIONAL ASSOCIATION OF MACHINISTS, 295 NLRB 180 (1989). Since 1960, the company had had successive collective bargaining agreements covering its production and maintenance employees. Without objection from the union, the company periodically (and unilaterally) announced work rules regarding a number of issues. Among these was a rule declaring drinking or possession of alcoholic beverages on company premises or company time, and reporting for work under the influence of alcohol or drugs, to be cause for discharge or discipline. In December 1986, the company without notifying or bargaining with the union posted a notice to the effect that "any injuries requiring treatment will now be accompanied by a drug/alcohol test." The union objected to the new policy and to the employer's refusal to negotiate about it, but the company insisted on implementing it, and the union filed charges under section 8(a)(5) of the NLRA. The Board held that the new test requirement was a mandatory subject of bargaining.

Invoking the *Ford Motor* decision of the Supreme Court, the Board first considered whether the testing requirement was "germane to the working environment." The Board noted the similarity between the requirement and company-imposed physical examinations and polygraph testing, both of which it had held to be mandatory subjects of bargaining. In Medicenter v. Hotel & Restaurant Employees, 221 NLRB 670 (1975), the Board had held that there was a duty to bargain about the institution of polygraph testing designed to determine responsibility for certain acts of vandalism on company property; such testing "substantially varied both the mode of investigation and the character of proof on which an employee's job security might depend," and thus altered the "terms and conditions of employment." The drug/alcohol testing in the instant case had been implemented because of an increasingly high number of workplace accidents, resulting in sharply increasing insurance rates; the company suspected that drug use was the cause. The test is thus a "condition" of employment "because it has the potential to affect the continued employment of employees who become subject to it." Similar to *Medicenter,* the employer's action—which would introduce sophisticated testing technology—would substantially vary both the mode of investigation and character of proof regarding the dischargeable behavior of drug and alcohol use.

Not only was the testing requirement "germane to the working environment," but it was also held by the Board not to be "among those managerial decisions that lie at the core of entrepreneurial control" (a standard articulated first by Justice Stewart in his concurring opinion in the *Fibreboard* case, immediately below). The testing requirement is "not entrepreneurial in character, is not fundamental to the basic direction of the enterprise, and does not impinge only indirectly upon employment security"; rather it is "a change in an important facet of the workaday life of employees," "a more limited decision directed toward reducing workplace accidents and attendant insurance rates."

The Board concluded—after rejecting a number of employer arguments that the union had "waived" its right to mandatory bargaining on the issue—that the company's unilateral implementation of its testing requirement was a violation of section 8(a)(5).

---

## PROBLEMS FOR DISCUSSION

**1.** How many unconvincing propositions can you detect in the Supreme Court's *Ford Motor* decision? For example, should NLRB determinations about the scope of mandatory bargaining (a "question of law," is it not?) be judicially reversed only if "unprincipled" or not "reasonably defensible"? Should all matters of "deep concern" to employees be, by virtue of that fact, classified as mandatory subjects? Is it pertinent that many employers furnish cafeteria facilities (as distinguished from their bargaining about it)? Will classifying in-plant food prices as mandatory subjects limit resort to strikes and other forms of economic warfare? Will a unilateral change in food prices at the Ford plant be lawful, absent subsequent demand for bargaining about it and refusal by the Company? (Whatever happened to the *Katz* case?)

**2.** Since 1985, the Ryder Technical Institute had paid its employees an annual Christmas bonus. The bonus for each employee was calculated according to a complex formula based on the employee's position and length of service, and recommendations from supervisors. In August of last year, the Teamsters Union was certified as bargaining agent for all of Ryder's employees. A collective bargaining agreement was executed in October which made no mention of the Christmas bonuses. That December, the employer, without consulting with the Union, failed to give any Christmas bonuses. The Union filed a Section 8(a)(5) charge, claiming that Ryder had unilaterally changed wages without bargaining. The employer argued that the bonus was not a part of wages but rather a gift given at its discretion. How should the Administrative Law Judge rule? Compare Radio Television Tech. School, Inc. v. NLRB, 488 F.2d 457 (3d Cir.1973), with Benchmark Industries, Inc. v. Amalgamated Clothing and Textile Workers Union, 270 NLRB 22 (1984). See also Bonnell/Tredegar Indus., Inc. v. NLRB, 46 F.3d 339 (4th Cir.1995).

**3.** Employees of the Silver Bell Mine are represented by the United Mine Workers. Seventy percent of the employees live in the town of Silver Bell, which is owned by the mining company, and nearly all of the residents of Silver Bell are employees of the mining company. The nearest concentration of housing not owned by the company is twenty-five miles from the mine. Rent for the company-owned housing was unchanged for fifteen years until last month, when the company, without bargaining with Union, raised all rents twenty-five percent. Has the mining company violated Section 8(a)(5)? See American Smelting and Refining Co. v. NLRB, 406 F.2d 552 (9th Cir.1969), cert. denied, 395 U.S. 935, 89 S.Ct. 1998, 23 L.Ed.2d 450 (1969).

Assume, instead, that a unionized company engaged in manufacturing has set aside a large room on the first floor of its headquarters to serve as a child-care center for children of its employees; the rates for use of the center are comparable to child-care rates elsewhere in the community. In order to make room for computer equipment, the company has decided that it must close down the center and use that space. It wishes to know whether it must bargain with the union regarding the closing of the center. What advice would you give?

**4.** Locals 1, 2 and 3 of the Chemical Workers Union have been selected as majority representative, respectively, at the Company's plants in Atlanta, Baltimore and Chicago. The locals formed a single coordinated bargaining committee, believing that basic wages and working conditions should be uniform at all three locations. The Company, however, refused to deal with the committee and insisted on separate negotiations. When representatives of the three locals met with the employer for separate negotiations at the different locations, the Company was presented with identical proposals; each local was particularly insistent upon the termination of its agreement on June 30 three years thereafter. Each local proved to be firm in its bargaining position, the Atlanta local recently initiated a strike, and strike votes have been passed by the members of the other two locals. The Company has filed charges of violations of Section 8(b)(3) at each Regional Office. Should the Regional Director issue complaints and seek Section 10(j) injunctions? See AFL–CIO Joint Negotiating Committee (Phelps Dodge Corp.) v. NLRB, 459 F.2d 374 (3d Cir.1972), cert. denied, 409 U.S. 1059, 93 S.Ct. 553, 34 L.Ed.2d 511 (1972). *See also* Don Lee Distrib., Inc. v. NLRB, 145 F.3d 834 (6th Cir.1998) (comparable coordination by employers).

**5.** Are the installation of hidden video surveillance equipment, the period of retention of the tapes, access to the tapes, and the use or uses to which the tapes may be put, mandatory bargaining subjects? See Colgate–Palmolive Co., 323 NLRB 515 (1997).

———

## Fibreboard Paper Products Corp. v. NLRB[d]

379 U.S. 203, 85 S.Ct. 398, 13 L.Ed.2d 233 (1964).

■ MR. CHIEF JUSTICE WARREN delivered the opinion of the Court.

This case involves the obligation of an employer and the representative of his employees under §§ 8(a)(5), 8(d) and 9(a) of the National Labor Relations Act to "confer in good faith with respect to wages, hours, and other terms and conditions of employment." The primary issue is whether the "contracting out" of work being performed by employees in the bargaining unit is a statutory subject of collective bargaining under those sections.

[A local of the Steelworkers Union had represented the maintenance employees of Fibreboard Paper Products Corporation for more than twenty years when in May 1959 the Union notified the Company of its desire to renegotiate the agreement about to expire on July 31. The Company postponed meeting with the Union until July 27, at which time it announced that, upon the basis of a recent study of possible cost savings in its maintenance operations, it intended to contract out that work to a third party. At another meeting on July 30, the Company announced that it had selected Fluor Maintenance, Inc. to do the maintenance work. Fluor had assured the Company that costs could be curtailed by reducing the work force, decreasing fringe benefits and overtime payments, and preplanning and rescheduling services. Fluor was to be paid its costs of operation plus a fixed fee of $2250 per month. The Company distributed a letter stating that bargaining for a successor contract would be pointless in view of the imminent termination of bargaining-unit employees. On July 31, the employment of Fibreboard's maintenance workers was terminated and Fluor employees took over; the Union promptly set up a picket line at the plant.]

The Union filed unfair labor practice charges against the Company, alleging violations of §§ 8(a)(1), 8(a)(3) and 8(a)(5). [T]he Board adhered to the Trial Examiner's finding that the Company's motive in contracting out its maintenance work was economic rather than anti-union but found nonetheless that the Company's "failure to negotiate with * * * [the Union] concerning its decision to subcontract its maintenance work constituted a violation of Section 8(a)(5) of the Act."[2] * * *

The Board ordered the Company to reinstitute the maintenance operation previously performed by the employees represented by the Union, to reinstate the employees to their former or substantially equivalent positions with back pay computed from the date of the Board's supplemental decision, and to fulfill its statutory obligation to bargain.

---

**d.** See Rabin, *Fibreboard* and the Termination of Bargaining Unit Work: The Search for Standards in Defining the Scope of the Duty to Bargain, 71 Colum.L.Rev. 803 (1971); Rabin, The Decline and Fall of *Fibreboard*, N.Y.U. 24th Annual Conf. on Labor 237 (1972).

**2.** The Board did not disturb [the] holding that the Company had not violated §§ 8(a)(1) or 8(a)(3), or [the] holding that the Company had satisfied its obligation to bargain about termination pay.

On appeal, the Court of Appeals for the District of Columbia Circuit granted the Board's petition for enforcement. * * * Because of the limited grant of certiorari, we are concerned here only with whether the subject upon which the employer allegedly refused to bargain—contracting out of plant maintenance work previously performed by employees in the bargaining unit, which the employees were capable of continuing to perform—is covered by the phrase "terms and conditions of employment" within the meaning of § 8(d).

The subject matter of the present dispute is well within the literal meaning of the phrase "terms and conditions of employment." See Order of Railroad Telegraphers v. Chicago & N.W. R. Co., 362 U.S. 330, 80 S.Ct. 761, 4 L.Ed.2d 774. A stipulation with respect to the contracting out of work performed by members of the bargaining unit might appropriately be called a "condition of employment." The words even more plainly cover termination of employment which, as the facts of this case indicate, necessarily results from the contracting out of work performed by members of the established bargaining unit.

The inclusion of "contracting out" within the statutory scope of collective bargaining also seems well designed to effectuate the purposes of the National Labor Relations Act. One of the primary purposes of the Act is to promote the peaceful settlement of industrial disputes by subjecting labor-management controversies to the mediatory influence of negotiation. The Act was framed with an awareness that refusals to confer and negotiate had been one of the most prolific causes of industrial strife. Labor Board v. Jones & Laughlin Steel Corp., 301 U.S. 1, 42–43, 57 S.Ct. 615, 626–627, 81 L.Ed. 893. To hold, as the Board has done, that contracting out is a mandatory subject of collective bargaining would promote the fundamental purpose of the Act by bringing a problem of vital concern to labor and management within the framework established by Congress as most conducive to industrial peace.

The conclusion that "contracting out" is a statutory subject of collective bargaining is further reinforced by industrial practices in this country. While not determinative, it is appropriate to look to industrial bargaining practices in appraising the propriety of including a particular subject within the scope of mandatory bargaining. National Labor Relations Board v. American Nat. Ins. Co., 343 U.S. 395, 408, 72 S.Ct. 824, 831, 96 L.Ed. 1027. Industrial experience is not only reflective of the interests of labor and management in the subject matter but is also indicative of the amenability of such subjects to the collective bargaining process. Experience illustrates that contracting out in one form or another has been brought, widely and successfully, within the collective bargaining framework. Provisions relating to contracting out exist in numerous collective bargaining agreements, and "contracting out work is the basis of many grievances; and that type of claim is grist in the mills of the arbitrators." United Steelworkers of America v. Warrior & Gulf Nav. Co., 363 U.S. 574, 584, 80 S.Ct. 1347, 1354, 4 L.Ed.2d 1409. * * *

The facts of the present case illustrate the propriety of submitting the dispute to collective negotiation. The Company's decision to contract out the maintenance work did not alter the Company's basic operation. The maintenance work still had to be performed in the plant. No capital investment was contemplated; the Company merely replaced existing employees with those of an independent contractor to do the same work under similar conditions of employment. Therefore, to require the employer to bargain about the matter would not significantly abridge his freedom to manage the business.

The Company was concerned with the high cost of its maintenance operation. It was induced to contract out the work by assurances from independent contractors that economies could be derived by reducing the work force, decreasing fringe benefits, and eliminating overtime payments. These have long been regarded as matters peculiarly suitable for resolution within the collective bargaining framework, and industrial experience demonstrates that collective negotiation has been highly successful in achieving peaceful accommodation of the conflicting interests. Yet, it is contended that when an employer can effect cost savings in these respects by contracting the work out, there is no need to attempt to achieve similar economies through negotiation with existing employees or to provide them with an opportunity to negotiate a mutually acceptable alternative. The short answer is that, although it is not possible to say whether a satisfactory solution could be reached, national labor policy is founded upon the congressional determination that the chances are good enough to warrant subjecting such issues to the process of collective negotiation. * * * While "the Act does not encourage a party to engage in fruitless marathon discussions at the expense of frank statement and support of his position," National Labor Relations Board v. American Nat. Ins. Co., 343 U.S. 395, 404, 72 S.Ct. 824, 829, it at least demands that the issue be submitted to the mediatory influence of collective negotiations. As the Court of Appeals pointed out, "it is not necessary that it be likely or probable that the union will yield or supply a feasible solution but rather that the union be afforded an opportunity to meet management's legitimate complaints that its maintenance was unduly costly."

We are thus not expanding the scope of mandatory bargaining to hold, as we do now, that the type of "contracting out" involved in this case—the replacement of employees in the existing bargaining unit with those of an independent contractor to do the same work under similar conditions of employment—is a statutory subject of collective bargaining under § 8(d). Our decision need not and does not encompass other forms of "contracting out" or "subcontracting" which arise daily in our complex economy.

The only question remaining is whether, upon a finding that the Company had refused to bargain about a matter which is a statutory subject of collective bargaining, the Board was empowered to order the resumption of maintenance operations and reinstatement with back pay. We believe that it was so empowered. * * * There has been no showing that the Board's order restoring the *status quo ante* to insure meaningful bargaining is not well designed to promote the policies of the Act. Nor is there evidence which would justify disturbing the Board's conclusion that the order would not impose an undue or unfair burden on the Company.[10]

It is argued, nonetheless, that the award exceeds the Board's powers under § 10(c) in that it infringes the provision that "no order of the Board shall require the reinstatement of any individual as an employee who has been suspended or discharged, or the payment to him of any back pay, if such individual was suspended or discharged for cause * * *." The legislative history of the provision indicates that it was designed to preclude the Board from reinstating an individual who had been discharged because of misconduct. There is no indication, however, that it was designed to curtail the Board's power in fashioning remedies when the loss of employment stems directly from an unfair labor practice as in the case at hand.

The judgment of the Court of Appeals is affirmed.

|MR. JUSTICE GOLDBERG took no part in the consideration or decision of this case.]

■ MR. JUSTICE STEWART, with whom MR. JUSTICE DOUGLAS and MR. JUSTICE HARLAN join, concurring.

Viewed broadly, the question before us stirs large issues. The Court purports to limit its decision to "the facts of this case." But the Court's opinion radiates implications of such disturbing breadth that I am persuaded to file this separate statement of my own views.

* * * The Court most assuredly does not decide that every managerial decision which necessarily terminates an individual's employment is subject to the duty to bargain. Nor does the Court decide that subcontracting decisions are as a general matter subject to that duty. The Court holds no more than that this employer's decision to subcontract this work, involving "the replacement of employees in the existing bargaining unit with those of an independent contractor to do the same work under similar conditions of employment" is subject to the duty to bargain collectively. Within the narrow limitations implicit in the specific facts of this case, I agree with the Court's decision. * * *

The basic question is whether the employer failed to "confer in good faith with respect to * * * terms and conditions of employment" in unilaterally deciding to subcontract this work. This question goes to the scope of the employer's duty in the absence of a collective bargaining agreement.[2] * * *

---

**10.** The Board stated: "We do not believe that requirement [restoring the *status quo ante*] imposes an undue or unfair burden on Respondent. The record shows that the maintenance operation is still being performed in much the same manner as it was prior to the subcontracting arrangement. Respondent has a continuing need for the services of maintenance employees; and Respon-

dent's subcontract is terminable at any time upon 60 days' notice." 138 N.L.R.B., at 555, n. 19.

**2.** There was a time when one might have taken the view that the National Labor Relations Act gave the Board and the courts no power to determine the subjects about which the parties must bargain—a view expressed by Senator Walsh when he said that

It is important to note that the words of the statute are words of limitation. The National Labor Relations Act does not say that the employer and employees are bound to confer upon any subject which interests either of them; the specification of wages, hours, and other terms and conditions of employment defines a limited category of issues subject to compulsory bargaining. The limiting purpose of the statute's language is made clear by the legislative history of the present Act. As originally passed, the Wagner Act contained no definition of the duty to bargain collectively. In the 1947 revision of the Act, the House bill contained a detailed but limited list of subjects of the duty to bargain, excluding all others. In conference the present language was substituted for the House's detailed specification. While the language thus incorporated in the 1947 legislation as enacted is not so stringent as that contained in the House bill, it nonetheless adopts the same basic approach in seeking to define a limited class of bargainable issues.

* * * [T]he Court's opinion seems to imply that any issue which may reasonably divide an employer and his employees must be the subject of compulsory collective bargaining.[6]

Only a narrower concept of "conditions of employment" will serve the statutory purpose of delineating a limited category of issues which are subject to the duty to bargain collectively. Seeking to effect this purpose, at least seven circuits have interpreted the statutory language to exclude various kinds of management decisions from the scope of the duty to bargain. In common parlance, the conditions of a person's employment are most obviously the various physical dimensions of his working environment. What one's hours are to be, what amount of work is expected during those hours, what periods of relief are available, what safety practices are observed, would all seem conditions of one's employment. There are other less tangible but no less important characteristics of a person's employment which might also be deemed "conditions"—most prominently the characteristic involved in this case, the security of one's employment. On one view of the matter, it can be argued that the question whether there is to be a job is not a condition of employment; the question is not one of imposing conditions on employment, but the more fundamental question whether there is to be employment at all. However, it is clear that the Board and the courts have on numerous occasions recognized that union demands for provisions limiting an employer's power to discharge employees are manda-

public concern ends at the bargaining room door. 79 Cong.Rec. 7659 (1939). See Cox and Dunlop, Regulation of Collective Bargaining by the NLRB, 63 Harv.L.Rev. 389. But too much law has been built upon a contrary assumption for this view any longer to prevail, and I question neither the power of the Court to decide this issue nor the propriety of its doing so.

**6.** The opinion of the Court seems to assume that the only alternative to compulsory collective bargaining is unremitting eco-

nomic warfare. But to exclude subjects from the ambit of compulsory collective bargaining does not preclude the parties from seeking negotiations about them on a permissive basis. And there are limitations upon the use of economic force to compel concession upon subjects which are only permissively bargainable. National Labor Relations Board v. Wooster Div. of Borg–Warner Corp., 356 U.S. 342, 78 S.Ct. 718, 2 L.Ed.2d 823.

torily bargainable. Thus, freedom from discriminatory discharge, seniority rights, the imposition of a compulsory retirement age, have been recognized as subjects upon which an employer must bargain, although all of these concern the very existence of the employment itself.

While employment security has thus properly been recognized in various circumstances as a condition of employment, it surely does not follow that every decision which may affect job security is a subject of compulsory, collective bargaining. Many decisions made by management affect the job security of employees. Decisions concerning the volume and kind of advertising expenditures, product design, the manner of financing, and of sales, all may bear upon the security of the workers' jobs. Yet it is hardly conceivable that such decisions so involve "conditions of employment" that they must be negotiated with the employees' bargaining representative.

In many of these areas the impact of a particular management decision upon job security may be extremely indirect and uncertain, and this alone may be sufficient reason to conclude that such decisions are not "with respect to * * * conditions of employment." Yet there are other areas where decisions by management may quite clearly imperil job security, or indeed terminate employment entirely. An enterprise may decide to invest in labor-saving machinery. Another may resolve to liquidate its assets and go out of business. Nothing the Court holds today should be understood as imposing a duty to bargain collectively regarding such managerial decisions, which lie at the core of entrepreneurial control. Decisions concerning the commitment of investment capital and the basic scope of the enterprise are not in themselves primarily about conditions of employment, though the effect of the decision may be necessarily to terminate employment. If, as I think clear, the purpose of § 8(d) is to describe a limited area subject to the duty of collective bargaining, those management decisions which are fundamental to the basic direction of a corporate enterprise or which impinge only indirectly upon employment security should be excluded from that area.

Applying these concepts to the case at hand, I do not believe that an employer's subcontracting practices are, as a general matter, in themselves conditions of employment. Upon any definition of the statutory terms short of the most expansive, such practices are not conditions—tangible or intangible—of any person's employment. The question remains whether this particular kind of subcontracting decision comes within the employer's duty to bargain. On the facts of this case, I join the Court's judgment, because all that is involved is the substitution of one group of workers for another to perform the same task in the same plant under the ultimate control of the same employer. The question whether the employer may discharge one group of workers and substitute another for them is closely analogous to many other situations within the traditional framework of collective bargaining. Compulsory retirement, layoffs according to seniority, assignment of work among potentially eligible groups within the plant—all involve similar questions of discharge and work assignment, and all have been recognized as subjects of compulsory collective bargaining.

\* \* \* [H]ad the employer in this case chosen to bargain with the union about the proposed subcontract, negotiations would have inevitably turned to the underlying questions of cost, which prompted the subcontracting. Insofar as the employer frustrated collective bargaining with respect to these concededly bargaining issues by its unilateral act of subcontracting this work, it can properly be found to have violated its statutory duty under § 8(a)(5).

This kind of subcontracting falls short of such larger entrepreneurial questions as what shall be produced, how capital shall be invested in fixed assets, or what the basic scope of the enterprise shall be. In my view, the Court's decision in this case has nothing to do with whether any aspects of those larger issues could under any circumstances be considered subjects of compulsory collective bargaining under the present law.

I am fully aware that in this era of automation and onrushing technological change, no problems in the domestic economy are of greater concern than those involving job security and employment stability. Because of the potentially cruel impact upon the lives and fortunes of the working men and women of the Nation, these problems have understandably engaged the solicitous attention of government, of responsible private business, and particularly of organized labor. It is possible that in meeting these problems Congress may eventually decide to give organized labor or government a far heavier hand in controlling what until now have been considered the prerogatives of private business management. That path would mark a sharp departure from the traditional principles of a free enterprise economy. Whether we should follow it is, within constitutional limitations, for Congress to choose. But it is a path which Congress certainly did not choose when it enacted the Taft–Hartley Act.

———

## PROBLEM FOR DISCUSSION

The facts of *Fibreboard*—in particular, the picketing initiated by the Steelworkers local—suggest yet another reason why it may be important to distinguish mandatory from permissive subjects. Assume that the Fibreboard employees in the neighboring production unit had engaged in a work stoppage and that the Fibreboard company discharged them. If the subcontracting were held to be a matter of mandatory bargaining, then the company would have committed an unfair labor practice by refusing to bargain, the strike would have been a protected "unfair labor practice strike," the discharges of the strikers would be unlawful, and the company would be required to reinstate the strikers with full backpay. If, however, the subcontracting were held to be only permissive, then the strike instigated by the union would violate Section 8(b)(3), and the strikers' activity would not be sheltered against discharge. (These matters will be explored in greater detail at pages 535–38, infra.) Is it sound legal policy to make such greatly significant liabilities (backpay in the case of the employer, and job loss in the case of the employees) turn upon elusive characterization of the subjects of bargaining—often definitively made many months, and sometimes years, after the event?

———————

*"WAIVER" BY CONTRACT OR PAST PRACTICE*

It should be emphasized that a holding by the Board or a court that subcontracting is a "term or condition of employment" does not necessarily mean that the employer must first bargain with the union to impasse before implementing a decision to subcontract. The decision of the Fibreboard Company, for example, was effected at a time when no contract was in existence between it and the union. Had there been a contract, there may have been some provision which gave to the Company—perhaps in a "management rights" clause—the power to subcontract work. Such a clear provision might be deemed a "waiver" by the union of its statutory right to require the employer to bargain, and disputes over the meaning of such a provision would ordinarily be tested before an arbitrator. The duty to bargain during the contract term, the relationship between that duty and contract arbitration, and the details of the "waiver" principle are considered in greater detail at Part Five, sec. IV, infra.

Not only was there no contract provision on which the Fibreboard Company could rely, but its decision to subcontract worked a change in the status quo; it had apparently never subcontracted this kind of work before. When, however, an employer's decision to subcontract is consistent with past practice, it is that practice which will be treated as the status quo, and the employer is free to continue "unilaterally" to subcontract consistent with that status quo and need bargain only regarding a departure therefrom. The Board will also not likely find a duty to bargain when the subcontracting has a minimal or no impact on job security of workers in the bargaining unit. These principles were articulated by the Board in WESTINGHOUSE ELEC. CORP., 150 NLRB 1574 (1965). The employer in that case had for almost twenty-five years entered into thousands of subcontracts covering its maintenance operations as well as the manufacture of various components, tools and dies, and parts. Most of the maintenance jobs could have been done by the company's employees and many of the parts and components and the like could have been manufactured by the company itself. (In addition, the union had bargained unsuccessfully in three separate contract negotiations to obtain some limitation on management's power to subcontract.) The union filed a charge with the NLRB under Section 8(a)(5), claiming that these subcontracts constituted refusals to bargain in good faith. The Board concluded that, while the employer was obligated to bargain about its subcontracting practices should the union raise the issue at general contract negotiations, the employer was free to continue to make such subcontracting decisions as before without notice to or consultation with the union:

> In sum—bearing in mind particularly that the recurrent contracting out of work here in question was motivated solely by

economic considerations; that it comported with the traditional methods by which the Respondent conducted its business operations; that it did not during the period here in question vary significantly in kind or degree from what had been customary under past established practice; that it had no demonstrable adverse impact on employees in the unit; and that the Union had the opportunity to bargain about changes in existing subcontracting practices at general negotiating meetings—for all these reasons cumulatively, we conclude that Respondent did not violate its statutory bargaining obligation by failing to invite union participation in individual subcontracting decisions.

---

# First National Maintenance Corp. v. NLRB[e]

452 U.S. 666, 101 S.Ct. 2573, 69 L.Ed.2d 318 (1981).

■ Justice Blackmun delivered the opinion of the Court.

Must an employer, under its duty to bargain in good faith "with respect to wages, hours, and other terms and conditions of employment," §§ 8(d) and 8(a)(5) of the National Labor Relations Act, as amended (the Act), 29 U.S.C. §§ 158(d) and 158(a)(5), negotiate with the certified representative of its employees over its decision to close a part of its business? In this case, the National Labor Relations Board (the Board) imposed such a duty on petitioner with respect to its decision to terminate a contract with a customer, and the United States Court of Appeals, although differing over the appropriate rationale, enforced its order.

## I

Petitioner, First National Maintenance Corporation (FNM), is a New York corporation engaged in the business of providing housekeeping, cleaning, maintenance, and related services for commercial customers in the New York City area. It supplies each of its customers, at the customer's

---

e. See J. Atleson, Values and Assumptions in American Labor Law, Chap. 7 (1983); George, To Bargain or Not to Bargain: A New Chapter in Work Relocation Decisions, 69 Minn.L.Rev. 667 (1985); H. Northrup & P. Miscimarra, Government Protection of Employees Involved in Mergers and Acquisitions (1989); Note, Automating the Workplace: Mandatory Bargaining Under *Otis II*, 1989 U.Ill.L.Rev. 435; Note, Decision Bargaining and the National Labor Relations Act—A Plea for the Resurrection of *First National Maintenance Corp.*, 68 Texas L.Rev. 625 (1990); Note, the Viability of Distinguishing Between Mandatory and Permissive Subjects of Bargaining in a Cooperative Setting: In Search of Industrial Peace, 41 Vand.L.Rev. 577 (1988); Wachter & Cohen, The Law and Economics of Collective Bargaining: An Introduction and Application to the Problems of Subcontracting, Partial Closure, and Relocation, 136 U.Pa.L.Rev. 1349 (1988); Harper, Leveling the Road from *Borg–Warner* to *First National Maintenance*: The Scope of Mandatory Bargaining, 68 Va.L.Rev. 1447 (1982); Kohler, Distinctions Without Differences: Effects Bargaining in Light of *First National Maintenance*, 5 Indus.Rel.L.J. 402 (1983); P. Miscimarra, The NLRB and Managerial Discretion: Plant Closings, Relocations, Subcontracting and Automation (1983); Note, Mandatory Bargaining and the Disposition of Closed Plants, 95 Harv.L.Rev. 1896 (1982).

premises, contracted-for labor force and supervision in return for reimbursement of its labor costs (gross salaries, FICA and FUTA taxes, and insurance) and payment of a set fee. It contracts for and hires personnel separately for each customer, and it does not transfer employees between locations.[1]

During the Spring of 1977, petitioner was performing maintenance work for the Greenpark Care Center, a nursing home in Brooklyn. Its written agreement dated April 28, 1976, with Greenpark specified that Greenpark "shall furnish all tools, equipment [sic], materials, and supplies," and would pay petitioner weekly "the sum of five hundred dollars plus the gross weekly payroll and fringe benefits." App. in No. 79–4167 (CA2), pp. 43, 44. Its weekly fee, however, had been reduced to $250 effective November 1, 1976. Id., at 46. The contract prohibited Greenpark from hiring any of petitioner's employees during the term of the contract and for 90 days thereafter. Id., at 44. Petitioner employed approximately 35 workers in its Greenpark operation.

Petitioner's business relationship with Greenpark, seemingly, was not very remunerative or smooth. In March 1977, Greenpark gave petitioner the 30 days' written notice of cancellation specified by the contract, because of "lack of efficiency." Id., at 52. This cancellation did not become effective, for FNM's work continued after the expiration of that 30–day period. Petitioner, however, became aware that it was losing money at Greenpark. On June 30, by telephone, it asked that its weekly fee be restored at the $500 figure and, on July 6, it informed Greenpark in writing that it would discontinue its operations there on August 1 unless the increase were granted. Id., at 47. By telegram on July 25, petitioner gave final notice of termination. Id., at 48.

While FNM was experiencing these difficulties, District 1199, National Union of Hospital and Health Care Employees, Retail, Wholesale and Department Store Union, AFL–CIO (the union), was conducting an organization campaign among petitioner's Greenpark employees. On March 31, 1977, at a Board-conducted election, a majority of the employees selected the union as their bargaining agent. On July 12, the union's vice president, Edward Wecker, wrote petitioner, notifying it of the certification and of the union's right to bargain, and stating: "We look forward to meeting with you or your representative for that purpose. Please advise when it will be convenient." Id., at 49. Petitioner neither responded nor sought to consult with the union.

On July 28, petitioner notified its Greenpark employees that they would be discharged 3 days later. Wecker immediately telephoned petitioner's secretary-treasurer, Leonard Marsh, to request a delay for the purpose

---

1. The record does not show the precise dimension of petitioner's business. See 242 N.L.R.B. 462, 464 (1979). One of the owners testified that petitioner at that time had "between two and four" other nursing homes as customers. Ibid. The administrative law judge hypothesized, however: "This is a large Company. For all I know, the 35 men at this particular home were only a small part of its total business in the New York area." Id., at 465.

of bargaining. Marsh refused the offer to bargain and told Wecker that the termination of the Greenpark operation was purely a matter of money, and final, and that the 30–days' notice provision of the Greenpark contract made staying on beyond August 1 prohibitively expensive. Id., at 79–81, 83, 85–86, 94. Wecker discussed the matter with Greenpark's management that same day, but was unable to obtain a waiver of the notice provision. Id., at 91–93, 98–99. Greenpark also was unwilling itself to hire the FNM employees because of the contract's 90–day limitation on hiring. Id., at 100–101, 106–107. With nothing but perfunctory further discussion, petitioner on July 31 discontinued its Greenpark operation and discharged the employees. Id., at 110–116.

The union filed an unfair labor practice charge against petitioner, alleging violations of the Act's §§ 8(a)(1) and (5). After a hearing held upon the Regional Director's complaint, the administrative law judge made findings in the union's favor. Relying on Ozark Trailers, Inc., 161 N.L.R.B. 561 (1966), he ruled that petitioner had failed to satisfy its duty to bargain concerning both the decision to terminate the Greenpark contract and the effect of that change upon the unit employees. * * * The National Labor Relations Board adopted the administrative law judge's findings without further analysis * * *.

The United States Court of Appeals for the Second Circuit, with one judge dissenting in part, enforced the Board's order, although it adopted an analysis different from that espoused by the Board. 627 F.2d 596 (1980). The Court of Appeals reasoned that no *per se* rule could be formulated to govern an employer's decision to close part of its business. Rather, the court said, § 8(d) creates a *presumption* in favor of mandatory bargaining over such a decision, a presumption that is rebuttable "by showing that the purposes of the statute would not be furthered by imposition of a duty to bargain," for example, by demonstrating that "bargaining over the decision would be futile," or that the decision was due to "emergency financial circumstances," or that the "custom of the industry, shown by the absence of such an obligation from typical collective bargaining agreements, is not to bargain over such decisions." Id., at 601–602.

The Court of Appeal's decision in this case appears to be at odds with decisions of other Courts of Appeals, some of which decline to require bargaining over any management decision involving "a major commitment of capital investment" or a "basic operational change" in the scope or direction of an enterprise, and some of which indicate that bargaining is not mandated unless a violation of § 8(a)(3)(a partial closing motivated by antiunion animus) is involved. The Court of Appeals for the Fifth Circuit has imposed a duty to bargain over partial closing decisions. See NLRB v. Winn–Dixie Stores, Inc., 361 F.2d 512, cert. denied, 385 U.S. 935, 87 S.Ct. 295, 17 L.Ed.2d 215 (1966). The Board itself has not been fully consistent in its rulings applicable to this type of management decision.

Because of the importance of the issue and the continuing disagreement between and among the Board and the Courts of Appeals, we granted certiorari. 449 U.S. 1076, 101 S.Ct. 854, 66 L.Ed.2d 798 (1981).

## II

\* \* \* Although parties are free to bargain about any legal subject, Congress has limited the mandate or duty to bargain to matters of "wages, hours, and other terms and conditions of employment." \* \* \* Congress deliberately left the words "wages, hours, and other terms and conditions of employment" without further definition, for it did not intend to deprive the Board of the power further to define those terms in light of specific industrial practices.[14]

Nonetheless, in establishing what issues must be submitted to the process of bargaining, Congress had no expectation that the elected union representative would become an equal partner in the running of the business enterprise in which the union's members are employed. Despite the deliberate open-endedness of the statutory language, there is an undeniable limit to the subjects about which bargaining must take place:

> "Section 8(d) of the Act, of course, does not immutably fix a list of subjects for mandatory bargaining. \* \* \* But it does establish a limitation against which proposed topics must be measured. In general terms, the limitation includes only issues that settle an aspect of the relationship between the employer and the employees." Chemical & Alkali Workers v. Pittsburgh Plate Glass Co., 404 U.S. 157, 178, 92 S.Ct. 383, 397, 30 L.Ed.2d 341 (1971).

See also Ford Motor Co. v. NLRB, 441 U.S. 488, 99 S.Ct. 1842, 60 L.Ed.2d 420 (1979); Fibreboard Paper Products Corp. v. NLRB, 379 U.S. 203, 85 S.Ct. 398, 13 L.Ed.2d 233 (1964); Teamsters v. Oliver, 358 U.S. 283, 79 S.Ct. 297, 3 L.Ed.2d 312 (1959).

---

**14.** In enacting the Labor Management Relations Act, 1947, Congress rejected a proposal in the House to limit the subjects of bargaining to

"(i) [w]age rates, hours of employment, and work requirements; (ii) procedures and practices relating to discharge, suspension, lay-off, recall, seniority, and discipline, or to promotion, demotion, transfer and assignment within the bargaining unit; (iii) conditions, procedures, and practices governing safety, sanitation, and protection of health at the place of employment; (iv) vacations and leaves of absence; and (v) administrative and procedural provisions relating to the foregoing subjects." H.R. 3020 § 2(11), 80th Cong., 1st Sess. (1947).

The adoption, instead, of the general phrase now part of § 8(d) was clearly meant to preserve future interpretation by the Board. See H.R.Rep. No. 245, 80th Cong., 1st Sess., 71 (1947)(minority report) ("The appropriate scope of collective bargaining cannot be determined by a formula; it will inevitably depend upon the traditions of an industry, the social and political climate at any given time, the needs of employers and employees, and many related factors. What are proper subject matters for collective bargaining should be left in the first instance to employers and trade-unions, and in the second place, to any administrative agency skilled in the field and competent to devote the necessary time to a study of industrial practices and traditions in each industry or area of the country, subject to review by the courts. It cannot and should not be strait-jacketed by legislative enactment."); H.R.Conf.Rep. No. 510, 80th Cong., 1st Sess., 34–35 (1947). U.S.Code Cong.Serv. 1947 p. 1135. Specific references in the legislative history to plant closings, however, are inconclusive. See 79 Cong.Rec. 7673, 9682 (1935)(comments of Sen. Walsh and Rep. Griswold).

Some management decisions, such as choice of advertising and promotion, product type and design, and financing arrangements, have only an indirect and attenuated impact on the employment relationship. See *Fibreboard,* 379 U.S., at 223, 85 S.Ct., at 409 (Stewart, J., concurring). Other management decisions, such as the order of succession of layoffs and recalls, production quotas, and work rules, are almost exclusively "an aspect of the relationship" between employer and employee. *Chemical Workers,* 404 U.S., at 178, 92 S.Ct., at 397. The present case concerns a third type of management decision, one that had a direct impact on employment, since jobs were inexorably eliminated by the termination, but had as its focus only the economic profitability of the contract with Greenpark, a concern under these facts wholly apart from the employment relationship. This decision, involving a change in the scope and direction of the enterprise, is akin to the decision whether to be in business at all, "not in [itself] primarily about conditions of employment, though the effect of the decision may be necessarily to terminate employment." *Fibreboard,* 379 U.S., at 223, 85 S.Ct., at 409 (Stewart, J., concurring). Cf. Textile Workers v. Darlington Co., 380 U.S. 263, 268, 85 S.Ct. 994, 998, 13 L.Ed.2d 827 (1965)("an employer has the absolute right to terminate his entire business for any reason he pleases"). At the same time, this decision touches on a matter of central and pressing concern to the union and its member employees: the possibility of continued employment and the retention of the employees' very jobs. See Brockway Motor Trucks, Etc. v. NLRB, 582 F.2d 720, 735–736 (C.A.3 1978); Ozark Trailers, Inc., 161 N.L.R.B. 561, 566–568 (1966).

Petitioner contends it had no duty to bargain about its decision to terminate its operations at Greenpark. This contention requires that we determine whether the decision itself should be considered part of petitioner's retained freedom to manage its affairs unrelated to employment.[15] The aim of labeling a matter a mandatory subject of bargaining, rather than simply permitting, but not requiring, bargaining, is to "promote the fundamental purpose of the Act by bringing a problem of vital concern to labor and management within the framework established by Congress as most conducive to industrial peace," *Fibreboard,* 379 U.S., at 211, 85 S.Ct., at 403. The concept of mandatory bargaining is premised on the belief that collective discussions backed by the parties' economic weapons will result in decisions that are better for both management and labor and for society as a whole. *Ford Motor Co.,* 441 U.S., at 500–501, 99 S.Ct., at 1851; *Borg–Warner,* 356 U.S., at 350, 78 S.Ct., at 723 (condemning employer's proposal of "ballot" clause as weakening the collective-bargaining process). This will be true, however, only if the subject proposed for discussion is amenable to resolution through the bargaining process. Management must be free from

**15.** There is no doubt that petitioner was under a duty to bargain about the results or effects of its decision to stop the work at Greenpark, or that it violated that duty. Petitioner consented to enforcement of the Board's order concerning bargaining over the effects of the closing and has reached agreement with the union on severance pay. App. to No. 79–4167 (CA2), at 21–22.

the constraints of the bargaining process[17] to the extent essential for the running of a profitable business. It also must have some degree of certainty beforehand as to when it may proceed to reach decisions without fear of later evaluations labeling its conduct an unfair labor practice. Congress did not explicitly state what issues of mutual concern to union and management it intended to exclude from mandatory bargaining. Nonetheless, in view of an employer's need for unencumbered decision-making, bargaining over management decisions that have a substantial impact on the continued availability of employment should be required only if the benefit, for labor-management relations and the collective bargaining process, outweighs the burden placed on the conduct of the business.

The Court in *Fibreboard* implicitly engaged in this analysis with regard to a decision to subcontract for maintenance work previously done by unit employees. Holding the employer's decision a subject of mandatory bargaining, the Court relied not only on the "literal meaning" of the statutory words, but also reasoned:

> "The Company's decision to contract out the maintenance work did not alter the Company's basic operation. The maintenance work still had to be performed in the plant. No capital investment was contemplated; the Company merely replaced existing employees with those of an independent contractor to do the same work under similar conditions of employment. Therefore, to require the employer to bargain about the matter would not significantly abridge his freedom to manage the business." 379 U.S., at 213, 85 S.Ct., at 404.

The Court also emphasized that a desire to reduce labor costs, which it considered a matter "peculiarly suitable for resolution within the collective bargaining framework," id., at 214, 85 S.Ct., at 404, was at the base of the employer's decision to subcontract * * * The prevalence of bargaining over "contracting out" as a matter of industrial practice generally was taken as further proof of the "amenability of such subjects to the collective bargaining process." Id., at 211, 85 S.Ct., at 403.

With this approach in mind, we turn to the specific issue at hand: an economically-motivated decision to shut down part of a business.

### III

### A

Both union and management regard control of the decision to shut down an operation with the utmost seriousness. As has been noted, however, the Act is not intended to serve either party's individual interest,

---

17.  The employer has no obligation to abandon its intentions or to agree with union proposals. On proper subjects, it must meet with the union, provide information necessary to the union's understanding of the problem, and in good faith consider any proposals the union advances. In concluding to reject a union's position as to a mandatory subject, however, it must face the union's possible use of strike power. See generally Fleming, The Obligation to Bargain in Good Faith, 47 Va.L.Rev. 988 (1961).

but to foster in a neutral manner a system in which the conflict between these interests may be resolved. It seems particularly important, therefore, to consider whether requiring bargaining over this sort of decision will advance the neutral purposes of the Act.

A union's interest in participating in the decision to close a particular facility or part of an employer's operations springs from its legitimate concern over job security. The Court has observed: "The words of [§ 8(d)] * * * plainly cover termination of employment which * * * necessarily results" from closing an operation. *Fibreboard,* 379 U.S., at 210, 85 S.Ct., at 402. The union's practical purpose in participating, however, will be largely uniform: it will seek to delay or halt the closing. No doubt it will be impelled, in seeking these ends, to offer concessions, information, and alternatives that might be helpful to management or forestall or prevent the termination of jobs.[19] It is unlikely, however, that requiring bargaining over the decision itself, as well as its effects, will augment this flow of information and suggestions. There is no dispute that the union must be given a significant opportunity to bargain about these matters of job security as part of the "effects" bargaining mandated by § 8(a)(5). See, *e.g.,* NLRB v. Royal Plating & Polishing Co., 350 F.2d 191, 196 (C.A.3 1965); NLRB v. Adams Dairy, Inc., 350 F.2d 108 (C.A.8 1965), cert. denied, 382 U.S. 1011, 86 S.Ct. 619, 15 L.Ed.2d 526 (1966). And, under § 8(a)(5), bargaining over the effects of a decision must be conducted in a meaningful manner and at a meaningful time, and the Board may impose sanctions to insure its adequacy. A union, by pursuing such bargaining rights, may achieve valuable concessions from an employer engaged in a partial closing. It also may secure in contract negotiations provisions implementing rights to notice, information, and fair bargaining. See BNA, Basic Patterns in Union Contracts 62–64 (9th ed., 1979).

Moreover, the union's legitimate interest in fair dealing is protected by § 8(a)(3), which prohibits partial closings motivated by anti-union animus, when done to gain an unfair advantage. Textile Workers v. Darlington Co., 380 U.S. 263, 85 S.Ct. 994, 13 L.Ed.2d 827 (1965). Under § 8(a)(3) the Board may inquire into the motivations behind a partial closing. An employer may not simply shut down part of its business and mask its desire to weaken and circumvent the union by labeling its decision "purely economic."

---

**19.** We are aware of past instances where unions have aided employers in saving failing businesses by lending technical assistance, reducing wages and benefits or increasing production, and even loaning part of earned wages to forestall closures. See S. Slichter, J. Healy & E. Livernash, The Impact of Collective Bargaining on Management 845–851 (1960); C. Golden & H. Rutenberg. The Dynamics of Industrial Democracy 263–291 (1942). See also United States Steel Workers, Etc. v. U.S. Steel Corp., 492 F.Supp. 1 (N.D.Ohio), aff'd in part and vacated in part, 631 F.2d 1264 (C.A.6 1980)(union sought to purchase failing plant); 104 Lab. Rel.Rep. 239 (1980)(employee ownership plan instituted to save company); *id.,* at 267–268 (union accepted pay cuts to reduce plant's financial problems). These have come about without the intervention of the Board enforcing a statutory requirement to bargain.

Thus, although the union has a natural concern that a partial closing decision not be hastily or unnecessarily entered into, it has some control over the effects of the decision and indirectly may ensure that the decision itself is deliberately considered. It also has direct protection against a partial closing decision that is motivated by an intent to harm a union.

Management's interest in whether it should discuss a decision of this kind is much more complex and varies with the particular circumstances. If labor costs are an important factor in a failing operation and the decision to close, management will have an incentive to confer voluntarily with the union to seek concessions that may make continuing the business profitable. Cf. U.S. News & World Report, Feb. 9, 1981, p. 74; BNA, Labor Relations Yearbook–1979, p. 5 (UAW agreement with Chrysler Corp. to make concessions on wages and fringe benefits). At other times, management may have great need for speed, flexibility, and secrecy in meeting business opportunities and exigencies. It may face significant tax or securities consequences that hinge on confidentiality, the timing of a plant closing, or a reorganization of the corporate structure. The publicity incident to the normal process of bargaining may injure the possibility of a successful transition or increase the economic damage to the business. The employer also may have no feasible alternative to the closing, and even good-faith bargaining over it may be both futile and cause the employer additional loss.

There is an important difference, also, between permitted bargaining and mandated bargaining. Labeling this type of decision mandatory could afford a union a powerful tool for achieving delay, a power that might be used to thwart management's intentions in a manner unrelated to any feasible solution the union might propose. * * *

While evidence of current labor practice is only an indication of what is feasible through collective bargaining, and not a binding guide, see *Chemical Workers,* 404 U.S., at 176, 92 S.Ct., at 396, that evidence supports the apparent imbalance weighing against mandatory bargaining. We note that provisions giving unions a right to participate in the decisionmaking process concerning alteration of the scope of an enterprise appear to be relatively rare. Provisions concerning notice and "effects" bargaining are more prevalent. * * *

Further, the presumption analysis adopted by the Court of Appeals seems ill suited to advance harmonious relations between employer and employee. An employer would have difficulty determining beforehand whether it was faced with a situation requiring bargaining or one that involved economic necessity sufficiently compelling to obviate the duty to bargain. If it should decide to risk not bargaining, it might be faced ultimately with harsh remedies forcing it to pay large amounts of backpay to employees who likely would have been discharged regardless of bargaining, or even to consider reopening a failing operation. * * * Also, labor costs may not be a crucial circumstance in a particular economically-based partial termination. See, *e.g.,* NLRB v. International Harvester Co., 618 F.2d 85 (C.A.9 1980)(change in marketing structure); NLRB v. Thompson

Transport Co., 406 F.2d 698 (C.A.10 1969)(loss of major customer). And in those cases, the Board's traditional remedies may well be futile. See ABC Trans–National Transport, Inc. v. NLRB, 642 F.2d 675 (C.A.3 1981) (although employer violated its "duty" to bargain about freight terminal closing, court refused to enforce order to bargain). If the employer intended to try to fulfill a court's direction to bargain, it would have difficulty determining exactly at what stage of its deliberations the duty to bargain would arise and what amount of bargaining would suffice before it could implement its decision. Compare Burns Ford, Inc., 182 N.L.R.B. 753 (1970)(one week's notice of layoffs sufficient), and *Hartmann Luggage Co.,* 145 N.L.R.B. 1572 (1964) (entering into executory subcontracting agreement before notifying union not a violation since contract not yet final), with Royal Plating & Polishing Co., 148 N.L.R.B. 545, 555 (1964), enf. denied, 350 F.2d 191 (C.A.3 1965)(two weeks' notice before final closing of plant inadequate). If an employer engaged in some discussion, but did not yield to the union's demands, the Board might conclude that the employer had engaged in "surface bargaining," a violation of its good faith. See NLRB v. Reed & Prince Mfg. Co., 205 F.2d 131 (CA1), cert. denied, 346 U.S. 887, 74 S.Ct. 139, 98 L.Ed. 391 (1953). A union, too, would have difficulty determining the limits of its prerogatives, whether and when it could use its economic powers to try to alter an employer's decision, or whether, in doing so, it would trigger sanctions from the Board. * * *

We conclude that the harm likely to be done to an employer's need to operate freely in deciding whether to shut down part of its business purely for economic reasons outweighs the incremental benefit that might be gained through the union's participation in making the decision;[22] and we hold that the decision itself is *not* part of § 8(d)'s "terms and conditions," over which Congress has mandated bargaining.[23]

---

**22.** In this opinion we of course intimate no view as to other types of management decisions, such as plant relocations, sales, other kinds of subcontracting, automation, etc., which are to be considered on their particular facts. See, *e.g.,* International Ladies' Garment Workers Union v. NLRB, 150 U.S.App.D.C. 71, 463 F.2d 907 (1972)(plant relocation predominantly due to labor costs); Weltronic Co. v. NLRB, 419 F.2d 1120 (C.A.6 1969), cert. denied, 398 U.S. 938, 90 S.Ct. 1841, 26 L.Ed.2d 270 (1970)(decision to move plant three miles); Dan Dee West Virginia Corp., 180 N.L.R.B. 534 (1970)(decision to change method of distribution, under which employee-drivers became independent contractors); Young Motor Truck Service, Inc., 156 N.L.R.B. 661 (1966)(decision to sell major portion of business). See also Schwarz, Plant Relocation or Partial Termination— The Duty to Decision–Bargain, 39 Ford. L.Rev. 81, 100–102 (1970).

**23.** Despite the contentions of *amicus* AFL–CIO our decision in Order of Railroad Telegraphers v. Chicago & N.W.R. Co., 362 U.S. 330, 80 S.Ct. 761, 4 L.Ed.2d 774 (1960), does not require that we find bargaining over this partial closing decision mandatory. In that case, a union certified as bargaining agent for certain railroad employees requested that the railroad bargain over its decision to close down certain stations thereby eliminating a number of jobs. When the union threatened to strike over the railroad's refusal to bargain on this issue, the railroad sought an injunction in federal court. Construing the scope of bargaining required by § 2, First, of the Railway Labor Act, 45 U.S.C. § 152, the Court held that the union's effort to negotiate was not "an unlawful bargaining demand," 362 U.S., at 341, 80 S.Ct., at 767, and that the District Court was precluded from enjoining the threatened strike by § 4 of the Norris–LaGuardia Act, 29

B

In order to illustrate the limits of our holding, we turn again to the specific facts of this case. First, we note that when petitioner decided to terminate its Greenpark contract, it had no intention to replace the discharged employees or to move that operation elsewhere. Petitioner's sole purpose was to reduce its economic loss, and the union made no claim of anti-union animus. In addition, petitioner's dispute with Greenpark was solely over the size of the management fee Greenpark was willing to pay. The union had no control or authority over that fee. The most that the union could have offered would have been advice and concessions that Greenpark, the third party upon whom rested the success or failure of the contract, had no duty even to consider. These facts in particular distinguish this case from the subcontracting issue presented in *Fibreboard*. Further, the union was not selected as the bargaining representative or certified until well after petitioner's economic difficulties at Greenpark had begun. We thus are not faced with an employer's abrogation of ongoing negotiations or an existing bargaining agreement. Finally, while petitioner's business enterprise did not involve the investment of large amounts of capital in single locations, we do not believe that the absence of "significant investment or withdrawal of capital," *General Motors Corp., GMC Truck & Coach Div.*, 191 N.L.R.B., at 952, is crucial. The decision to halt work at this specific location represented a significant change in petitioner's operations, a change not unlike opening a new line of business or going out of business entirely.

The judgment of the Court of Appeals, accordingly, is reversed and the case is remanded to that court for further proceedings consistent with this opinion.

It is so ordered.

U.S.C. § 104, which deprives federal courts of "jurisdiction to issue any restraining order or temporary or permanent injunction in any case involving or growing out of any labor dispute to prohibit any person or persons participating or interested in such dispute * * * from * * * [c]easing or refusing to perform any work * * *." Although the Court in part relied on an expansive interpretation of § 2, First, which requires railroads to "exert every reasonable effort to make and maintain agreements concerning rates of pay, rules, and working conditions," and § 13(c) of the Norris–LaGuardia Act, 29 U.S.C. § 13(c), defining "labor dispute" as "any controversy concerning terms or conditions of employment," its decision also rested on the particular aims of the Railway Labor Act and national transportation policy. See 362 U.S., at 336–338, 80 S.Ct., at 764–765. The manda-

tory scope of bargaining under the Railway Labor Act and the extent of the prohibition against injunctive relief contained in Norris–LaGuardia are not coextensive with the National Labor Relations Act and the Board's jurisdiction over unfair labor practices. See Chicago & N.W.R. Co. v. Transportation Union, 402 U.S. 570, 579, n. 11, 91 S.Ct. 1731, 1736, n. 11, 29 L.Ed.2d 187 (1971) ("parallels between the duty to bargain in good faith and duty to exert every reasonable effort, like all parallels between the NLRA and the Railway Labor Act, should be drawn with the utmost care and with full awareness of the differences between the statutory schemes"). Cf. Boys Markets, Inc. v. Retail Clerks, 398 U.S. 235, 90 S.Ct. 1583, 26 L.Ed.2d 199 (1970); Buffalo Forge Co. v. United Steelworkers of America, 428 U.S. 397, 96 S.Ct. 3141, 49 L.Ed.2d 1022 (1976).

■ JUSTICE BRENNAN, with whom JUSTICE MARSHALL joins, dissenting. * * *

As this Court has noted, the words "terms and conditions of employment" plainly cover termination of employment resulting from a management decision to close an operation. Fibreboard Paper Products Corp. v. NLRB, 379 U.S. 203, 210, 85 S.Ct. 398, 402, 13 L.Ed.2d 233 (1964). As the Court today admits, the decision to close an operation "touches on a matter of central and pressing concern to the union and its member employees." Moreover, as the Court today further concedes, Congress deliberately left the words "terms and conditions of employment" indefinite, so that the NLRB would be able to give content to those terms in light of changing industrial conditions. In the exercise of its congressionally-delegated authority and accumulated expertise, the Board has determined that an employer's decision to close part of its operations affects the "terms and conditions of employment" within the meaning of the Act, and is thus a mandatory subject for collective bargaining. Ozark Trailers, Inc., 161 N.L.R.B. 561 (1966). Nonetheless, the Court today declines to defer to the Board's decision on this sensitive question of industrial relations, and on the basis of pure speculation reverses the judgment of the Board and of the Court of Appeals. I respectfully dissent.

The Court bases its decision on a balancing test. It states that "bargaining over management decisions that have a substantial impact on the continued availability of employment should be required only if the benefit, for labor-management relations and the collective-bargaining process, outweighs the burden placed on the conduct of the business." I cannot agree with this test, because it takes into account only the interests of *management;* it fails to consider the legitimate employment interests of the workers and their Union. Cf. Brockway Motor Trucks v. NLRB, 582 F.2d 720, 734–740 (3d Cir.1978)(balancing of interests of workers in retaining their jobs against interests of employers in maintaining unhindered control over corporate direction). This one-sided approach hardly serves "to foster in a neutral manner" a system for resolution of these serious, two-sided controversies.

Even if the Court's statement of the test were accurate, I could not join in its application, which is based solely on speculation. Apparently, the Court concludes that the benefit to labor-management relations and the collective-bargaining process from negotiation over partial closings is minimal, but it provides no evidence to that effect. The Court acknowledges that the Union might be able to offer concessions, information, and alternatives that might obviate or forestall the closing, but it then asserts that "[i]t is unlikely, however, that requiring bargaining over the decision * * * will augment this flow of information and suggestions." Recent experience, however, suggests the contrary. Most conspicuous, perhaps, were the negotiations between Chrysler Corporation and the United Auto Workers, which led to significant adjustments in compensation and benefits, contributing to Chrysler's ability to remain afloat. See Wall St. Journal, Oct. 26, 1979, at 3, col. 1. Even where labor costs are not the direct cause of a company's financial difficulties, employee concessions can often enable the company to continue in operation—if the employees have the opportunity to offer such concessions.*

The Court further presumes that management's need for "speed, flexibility, and secrecy" in making partial closing decisions would be frustrated by a requirement to bargain. In some cases the Court might be correct. In others, however, the decision will be made openly and deliberately, and considerations of "speed, flexibility, and secrecy" will be inapposite. Indeed, in view of management's admitted duty to bargain over the effects of a closing, it is difficult to understand why additional bargaining over the closing itself would necessarily unduly delay or publicize the decision.

I am not in a position to judge whether mandatory bargaining over partial closings *in all cases* is consistent with our national labor policy, and neither is the Court. The primary responsibility to determine the scope of the statutory duty to bargain has been entrusted to the NLRB, which should not be reversed by the courts merely because they might prefer another view of the statute. Ford Motor Co. v. NLRB, 441 U.S. 488, 495–497, 99 S.Ct. 1842, 1848–1849, 60 L.Ed.2d 420 (1979); see NLRB v. Erie Resistor Corp., 373 U.S. 221, 236, 83 S.Ct. 1139, 1149, 10 L.Ed.2d 308 (1963). I therefore agree with the Court of Appeals that employers presumptively have a duty to bargain over a decision to close an operation, and that this presumption can be rebutted by a showing that bargaining would be futile, that the closing was due to emergency financial circumstances, or that, for some other reason, bargaining would not further the purposes of the National Labor Relations Act. * * *

---

PROBLEMS FOR DISCUSSION

**1.** How convincing are the following reasons offered by Justice Blackmun to support the Court's conclusion that the "partial closing" decision was not a mandatory subject of bargaining?

(a) Unions are able to secure protection and achieve concessions through "effects" bargaining.

(b) Employees are protected against discriminatory closings by Section 8(a)(3).

(c) If labor costs are at the root of the employer's decision, there will be a natural incentive to bargain with the union on a permissive basis.

(d) Companies generally need speed, flexibility and secrecy in closing facilities.

---

* Indeed, in this case, the Court of Appeals found: "On the record, * * * there is sufficient reason to believe that, given the opportunity, the union might have made concessions, by accepting a reduction in wages or benefits (take-backs) or a reduction in the work force, which would in part or in whole have enabled Greenpark to give FNM an increased management fee. At least, if FNM had bargained over its decision to close, that possibility would have been tested, and management would still have been free to close the Greenpark operation if bargaining did not produce a solution." 627 F.2d 596, 602 (C.A.2 1980).

(e) Unions otherwise would be able unfairly to stall management's implementation of its decision.

(f) Standard labor agreements deal with effects of closings but do not restrict the decision itself.

(g) Employers might not know whether they have bargained sufficiently to satisfy their statutory duty, or whether they have a legitimate "compelling" defense.

(h) Unions too would be uncertain whether they can be adamant and strike or picket.

**2.** How convincing is the Court's assessment that the underlying issue in the "partial closing" decision by First National Maintenance was so unrelated to labor costs that discussions with the union could not likely be pertinent or fruitful? (Did FNM have *any* operating expenses other than labor costs?) Did the Court give too little weight to the absence of "significant investment or withdrawal of capital"?

**3.** Considering the fact that the National Labor Relations Act is designed to empower employees to protect their economic interests through collective bargaining, and that the Act says little or nothing about protecting managerial interests, how is one to justify the "balancing" analysis articulated by the Court?

**4.** Consider the Court's extended footnote 23, in which it purports to distinguish its earlier decision in the *Railroad Telegraphers* case under the Railway Labor Act. As stated, that case involved the question whether the Norris–LaGuardia Act forbade the issuance of a federal-court injunction against a strike in protest of the railroad's decision to close down certain stations and terminate the workers there. The Court found that Act to govern, because there was a "controversy concerning terms or conditions of employment." It stated: "The employment of many of these station agents hangs on the number of railroad stations that will either be completely abandoned or consolidated with other stations. * * * We cannot agree with the Court of Appeals that the union's effort to negotiate about the job security of its members 'represents an attempt to usurp legitimate managerial prerogative in the exercise of business judgment with respect to the most economical and efficient conduct of its operations.' It is too late now to argue that employees can have no collective voice to influence railroads to act in a way that will preserve the interests of the employees as well as the interests of the railroad and the public at large." Are you persuaded by the Court's distinguishing of this case in *First National Maintenance?*

-----

# United Food & Commercial Workers, Local 150–A v. NLRB (Dubuque Packing Co.)

1 F.3d 24 (D.C.Cir.1993), cert. denied, 511 U.S. 1138, 114 S.Ct. 2157, 128 L.Ed.2d 882 (1994).

■ BUCKLEY, CIRCUIT JUDGE:

Dubuque Packing Company petitions for review of a National Labor Relations Board order holding that it committed unfair labor practices by breaching its duty to bargain with its union regarding the relocation of its "hog kill and cut" operations. We hold that the new standard adopted by the Board for evaluating such claims is an acceptable reading of the National Labor Relations Act and Supreme Court precedents; that the

Board's finding that Dubuque owed a duty to bargain was supported by substantial evidence; and that the Board properly applied its new test retroactively to the facts of this case. Hence, we deny Dubuque's petition and enforce the Board's remedial order. * * *

I.  Background

A.  Facts and Procedural History

The facts of this case were set forth at length in our earlier opinion, United Food & Commercial Workers Int'l Union, Local 150–A v. NLRB, 880 F.2d 1422, 1423–27 (D.C.Cir.1989)("UFCW I''); in relevant part, they are these. Beginning about 1977, the Dubuque Packing Company, a processor and packager of beef and pork, began losing money at its Dubuque, Iowa, home plant. In 1978, Dubuque won an agreement from the plant's workers, who were represented by the United Food and Commercial Workers International Union ("UFCW"), requiring the workers to produce at higher rates in return for a one-time cash payment. In August 1980, Dubuque extracted concessions worth approximately $5 million per annum in return for a pledge that it would not ask for further concessions before the September 1, 1982, expiration of the union contract then in effect. In March 1981, however, it again requested concessions, this time in the form of additional productivity increases in its hog kill department.

On March 30, 1981, the events at issue here began to unfold. On that date, Dubuque gave six-months' notice, as required by its labor contract, of its intention to close its hog kill and cut operations at Dubuque. Various maneuvers between the company and the UFCW ensued, culminating in the union's rejection of a wage freeze aimed at keeping the Dubuque hog kill and cut operation open. The following day, June 10, 1981, the company announced that it was considering relocating—rather than closing—its hog kill and cut department, and that it was also considering relocating up to 900 Dubuque plant pork processing jobs. The UFCW responded by requesting detailed financial information from Dubuque, which the company refused to provide. Dubuque then advised its employees in writing that they could save their jobs by approving its wage freeze proposal. On June 28, 1981, the wage freeze was resubmitted to the workers for a vote, accompanied by the union leadership's recommendation that it be rejected until Dubuque opened its books. The workers voted overwhelmingly with their union and against the company. Three days later, Dubuque informed the union that its decision to close the hog kill and cut department was "irrevocable."

Over the next few months, Dubuque and the UFCW continued to negotiate over Dubuque's proposed relocation of its pork processing operations. On October 1, 1981, Dubuque opened a hog kill and cut operation at its newly acquired Rochelle, Illinois, plant and, two days later, eliminated approximately 530 hog kill and cut jobs at the Dubuque plant. On October 19, 1981, an agreement was signed granting wage concessions for the remaining workers at the Dubuque plant in return for the company's agreement to keep the 900 pork processing jobs in Dubuque and to extend the current labor agreement. By early 1982, however, the company's hope of obtaining new financing had collapsed, taking with it Dubuque's prospects for remaining in business at Dubuque and Rochelle. Both plants were closed and sold on October 15, 1982.

On June 26, 1981, and August 7, 1981, the UFCW filed unfair labor practice complaints with the Board. It claimed that Dubuque had refused to bargain in good faith as to both the consummated relocation and the proposed one, objecting especially to the company's alleged duplicity and its refusal to disclose financial data. On June 17, 1985, an administrative law judge ("ALJ") rendered a decision on these complaints. Dubuque Packing Co., Nos. 33–CA–5524, 33–CA–5588 (ALJ June 15, 1985)("ALJ Decision"), appended to Dubuque Packing Co., 287 N.L.R.B. 499 (1987). The ALJ suggested that Dubuque's conduct may indeed have fallen below the standards of good-faith bargaining, ALJ Decision, 287 N.L.R.B. at 538, 540 n. 132, but he nevertheless held that Dubuque committed no unfair labor practice, id. at 543, because it was under no duty to negotiate over its decision to relocate. Id. at 540. Over two years later, the NLRB summarily affirmed the ALJ, adopting his findings and opinion. Dubuque Packing Co., 287 N.L.R.B. 499 (1987).

On review of the Board's decision, we remanded the case, declaring that the Board's opinion had been inadequately explained. UFCW I, 880 F.2d at 1439. * * *

On remand, the Board unanimously approved a new test [which it applied] to the relocation of the Dubuque hog kill and cut operation and found that a duty to bargain had existed and had been breached. Id. at 398. As a remedy, it ordered Dubuque to pay back wages to all employees terminated as a result of the relocation, from the date of their termination to October 15, 1982, the date operations ceased at Dubuque and Rochelle. * * *

[Dubuque] petitioned for review of the Board ruling * * * while the NLRB cross-petitioned for the enforcement of its order. * * *

B. Legal Framework

The critical question in this litigation is whether Dubuque's relocation of its hog kill and cut operation constitutes a mandatory subject of bargaining under the National Labor Relations Act ("NLRA" or "Act") * * * [i.e.,] whether a plant relocation such as the one executed by Dubuque constitutes a "term[ ][or] condition[ ]of employment" under section 8(d) of Act; if it does, then Dubuque's failure to bargain in good faith over the relocation constitutes an unfair labor practice under section 8(a)(5). The two critical Supreme Court decisions interpreting "terms and conditions of employment" for these purposes are First National Maintenance Corp. v. NLRB, 452 U.S. 666, 101 S.Ct. 2573, 69 L.Ed.2d 318 (1981), which held that an employer's decision to close a part of its business is not a mandatory subject of bargaining, and Fibreboard Paper Products Corp. v. NLRB, 379 U.S. 203, 85 S.Ct. 398, 13 L.Ed.2d 233 (1964), which held that the replacement of union labor with subcontracted workers is.

II.   Discussion

A.   Dubuque's Petition

Dubuque argues that the Board's new test improperly interprets Supreme Court precedent, that it was improperly applied to these facts, and that the Board erred by retroactively applying its new test to this case. We disagree on all counts.

### 1.   *The Legality of the Board's New Test*

Dubuque claims the Board erred in finding that its relocation involved a "term[ ][or] condition[ ]of employment" subject to mandatory bargaining under the NLRA. In particular, it argues that the Board's new test represents an impermissible reading of the Supreme Court's decision in *First National Maintenance*. In reviewing such claims, we will respect the Board's "policy choices," so long as "its interpretation of what the Act requires is reasonable, in light of the purposes of the Act and the controlling precedent of the Supreme Court." UFCW I, 880 F.2d at 1429. * * *

In these proceedings, the Board set out to enunciate a new legal test "guided by the principles set forth in *First National Maintenance*." Dubuque Packing, 303 N.L.R.B. at 390. It adopted the following standard for determining whether "a decision to relocate [bargaining] unit work," id., is a mandatory subject of bargaining: Initially, the burden is on the [NLRB] General Counsel to establish that the employer's decision involved a relocation of unit work unaccompanied by a basic change in the nature of the employer's operation. If the General Counsel successfully carries his burden in this regard, he will have established prima facie that the employer's relocation decision is a mandatory subject of bargaining. At this juncture, the employer may produce evidence rebutting the prima facie case by establishing that the work performed at the new location varies significantly from the work performed at the former plant, establishing that the work performed at the former plant is to be discontinued entirely and not moved to the new location, or establishing that the employer's decision involves a change in the scope and direction of the enterprise. Alternatively, the employer may proffer a defense to show by a preponderance of the evidence: (1) that labor costs (direct and/or indirect) were not a factor in the decision, or (2) that even if labor costs were a factor in the decision, the union could not have offered labor cost concessions that could have changed the employer's decision to relocate. Id. at 391. * * *

The Board's test involves three distinct layers of analysis. First, the test recognizes a category of decisions lying "at the core of entrepreneurial control," Fibreboard, 379 U.S. at 223, 85 S.Ct. at 409 (Stewart, J., concurring), in which employers may unilaterally take action. Specifically, the test exempts from the duty to bargain relocations involving (1) "a basic change in the nature of the employer's operation," (2) "a change in the scope and direction of the enterprise," (3) situations in which "the work performed at the new location varies significantly from the work performed at the former plant," or (4) situations in which "the work performed at the former plant is to be discontinued entirely and not moved to the new location." Dubuque Packing, 303 N.L.R.B. at 391.

This language would appear broad enough to cover key entrepreneurial decisions such as setting the scale (e.g., the quantity of product produced) and scope (e.g., the type of product produced) of the employer's operations, and determining the basic method of production. Moreover, as to these issues, the Board's test requires an analysis based on the objective differences between the employer's old and new operations. It asks whether various types of "basic change," "change," "vari[ance]," or "discontinu[ance]" were involved in the relocation. Where such objective differences appear, an entrepreneurial decision is deemed to have been taken, and the employer is permitted to relocate without negotiating.

The second layer of the Board's analysis is a subjective one. Cf. Dubuque Packing, 303 N.L.R.B. at 392 (referring to the employer's "motivation for the relocation decision"). Under this heading, the relevant question is whether "labor costs (direct and/or indirect) were . . . a factor" in the employer's relocation decision. Id. at 391. As illustrated by the Board, this analysis will distinguish relocations motivated by labor costs from those motivated by other perceived advantages of the new location. Compare id. at 390 n. 9 (collecting cases in which the relocation was motivated by labor costs) with id. at 390 n. 10 (collecting cases in which the decision was motivated by other factors).

The third layer includes a futility provision. As we shall see below, the Board permits an employer to relocate without negotiating where its union either would not or could not offer sufficient concessions to change its decision. See Dubuque Packing, 303 N.L.R.B. at 391. Also, the Board has pledged to consider circumstances such as the need to implement a relocation "expeditiously" in determining whether bargaining over a relocation has reached "a bona fide impasse," id. at 392; that is, the point at which a party may act unilaterally.

Dubuque objects that the Board's test is inconsistent with *First National Maintenance*. Its argument tends toward the proposition that a *per se* rule exempting relocation decisions from the duty to bargain is implicit in *First National Maintenance*'s reasoning, if not its holding. Dubuque's general objection is that the Board's test is insufficiently protective of management prerogatives, both on its face and because it is not capable of certainty in application. Dubuque pointedly reminds us that *First National Maintenance* held that employers "must have some degree of certainty beforehand" as to which decisions are and are not subject to a bargaining duty. See First National Maintenance, 452 U.S. at 679, 101 S.Ct. at 2581. More specifically, Dubuque argues that relocation decisions must be exempt from the duty to bargain because they involve the reallocation of capital, observing that allocations of capital are "core managerial decisions." See Brief for Dubuque at 38.

We pause to emphasize that our analysis of the Board's test is premised on our resolution of an important ambiguity in the Board's statement of its second affirmative defense. As stated by the Board, that defense requires an employer to establish that "the union *could not* have offered labor cost concessions that could have changed the employer's decision to relocate." Dubuque Packing, 303 N.L.R.B. at 391 (emphasis added). On its face, this language might be read as an impossibility exception—a provision allowing an employer to eschew negotiations only if its union could not possibly have changed the relocation decision no matter how accommodating the union might have been at the bargaining table. This reading is strengthened by the Board's illustration of the defense, which involves a case in which an employer "would not remain at the present plant because ... the costs for modernization of equipment or environmental controls were greater than [the value of] any labor cost concessions the union *could* offer." Id. (emphasis added).

Despite this evidence, we think this defense was intended to cover situations in which bargaining would be futile, as well as ones in which it would be impossible for the union to persuade the employer to rescind its relocation decision. Immediately after setting forth its test and the above illustration, the Board stated that under the second affirmative defense, "an employer would have a bargaining obligation *if the union could and would* offer concessions that approximate, meet, or exceed the anticipated costs or benefits that prompted the relocation decision." Dubuque Packing Co., 303 N.L.R.B. at 391 (emphasis added). * * * As we read it, the Board's test holds that no duty to bargain exists where bargaining would be futile—either because the union was unable to offer sufficient concessions, or because it was unwilling to do so.

Viewing the Board's test through the lens of this interpretation, we find it sufficiently protective of an employer's prerogative to manage its business. Under *First National Maintenance*, employers may be required to negotiate management decisions where "the benefit, for labor-management relations and the collective-bargaining process, outweighs the burden placed on the conduct of the business." First National Maintenance, 452 U.S. at 679, 101 S.Ct. at 2581. The Board's test exempts from the duty to negotiate relocations that, viewed objectively, are entrepreneurial in nature. It exempts decisions that, viewed subjectively, were motivated by something other than labor costs. And it explicitly excuses employers from attempting to negotiate when doing so would be futile or impossible. What is left are relocations that leave the firm occupying much the same entrepreneurial position as previously, that were taken because of the cost of labor, and that offer a realistic hope for a negotiated settlement. The Board's determination that bargaining over such decisions promises benefits outweighing the "burden[s] placed on the conduct of [an employer's] business" was in no way unreasonable.

Similarly, the Board was also justified in finding that its test accords with Supreme Court precedent. A relocation satisfying the three layers of the Board's test will resemble the subcontracting decision held subject to a mandatory bargaining duty in *Fibreboard* in three distinct ways: Because of the new test's objective component, such a relocation will not "alter the Company's basic operation," Fibreboard, 379 U.S. at 213, 85 S.Ct. at 404, in a way that implicates the employer's "core of entrepreneurial control," id. at 223, 85 S.Ct. at 409 (Stewart, J., concurring); because of the new test's subjective component, "a desire to reduce labor costs" will lie "at the base of the employer's decision," see First National Maintenance, 452 U.S. at 680, 101 S.Ct. at 2581 (discussing *Fibreboard*); and because of the new test's exclusion of situations in which bargaining would be futile, there will be some prospect of resolving the relocation dispute "within the collective bargaining framework." Fibreboard, 379 U.S. at 213–14, 85 S.Ct. at 404. Like its balancing of burdens and benefits, the Board's finding that its test accords with precedent is fully defensible.

Dubuque counters that relocation decisions should not be treated the same as the subcontract considered in *Fibreboard* because they will differ from that arrangement on a crucial point—relocations involve the expenditure of capital. Cf. Fibreboard, 379 U.S. at 225, 85 S.Ct. at 410 (Stewart, J., concurring)("larger entrepreneurial questions [such] as * * * *how capital shall be invested in fixed assets* "not governed by *Fibreboard*'s holding)(emphasis added); id. at 213, 85 S.Ct. at 404 (noting that "[n]o capital investment was contemplated" in connection with the subcontract). Furthermore, as Dubuque points out, key portions of the *First National Maintenance* opinion relied on Justice Stewart's concurrence in *Fibreboard*, which was particularly solicitous of management prerogatives over capital expenditure. See, e.g., First National Maintenance, 452 U.S. at 676–77, 101 S.Ct. at 2579–80 (citing Fibreboard, 379 U.S. at 223, 85 S.Ct. at 409 (Stewart, J., concurring)).

For several reasons, we remain unconvinced. First, the Board's test exempts from the duty to bargain relocations in which "the work performed at the new location varies significantly from the work performed at the former plant." Dubuque Packing, 303 N.L.R.B. at 391. Under this standard, relocations involving a sufficiently altered pattern of fixed-capital use (such as a shift from a labor-intensive production line to a fully automated factory) would appear exempt from the bargaining duty. Cf. Local 777, Democratic Union Org. Comm., Seafarers Int'l Union v. NLRB, 603 F.2d 862, 884 (D.C.Cir.1978)("*Local 777*")(stating that "major shifts in the capital investment or corporate strategy of a company are not mandatory bargaining subjects"). Second, many "terms and conditions of employment" over which employers are plainly bound to bargain involve the expenditure of "capital." Unless management rights are impermissibly invaded every time a union bargains for a breakroom water-cooler or shop-floor safety equipment, the realm of mandatory bargaining must include at least some decisions involving capital expenditures. Third, while *First National Maintenance* did reflect the influence of Justice Stewart's *Fibreboard* opinion, it did not reiterate that opinion's specific concerns with management's prerogative over the expenditure of capital, or otherwise indicate that a line protecting all decisions to expend capital must be drawn. Given this, and the deference owed the Board's policy choices, see UFCW I, 880 F.2d at 1429, we find that the Board's test does not impermissibly fail to protect management's prerogatives over capital investment. The dicta Dubuque cites are too thin to bear the weight placed on them.

Dubuque's final contention is that the test is so imprecise that employers are denied the degree of certainty or guidance that it believes the Supreme Court mandated in *First National Maintenance*. See 452 U.S. at 679, 101 S.Ct. at 2581. While we can agree that *First National Maintenance* affirms management's need for "*some* degree of certainty" so that it "may proceed to reach decisions without fear of later evaluations labeling its conduct an unfair labor practice," id. (emphasis added), this does not require that the Board establish standards devoid of ambiguity at the margins. The test announced in *Dubuque Packing* provides more than the "some" degree of certainty required by the Supreme Court. It establishes rules on which management may plan with a large degree of confidence; and while the test undoubtedly leaves areas of uncertainty between relocation decisions that are clearly within the exclusive prerogatives of management and those that are equally clearly subject to negotiation, these will in time be narrowed through future adjudications. We therefore conclude that the standard adopted by the Board was a reasonable policy choice and that its decision to proceed by adjudication, not rulemaking, was also within its discretion. See NLRB v. Bell Aerospace Co., 416 U.S. 267, 294, 94 S.Ct. 1757, 1772, 40 L.Ed.2d 134 (1974)(upholding a decision to proceed by adjudication where the relevant facts "vary widely depending on the company or industry"); see also Bechtel v. FCC, 957 F.2d 873, 881 (D.C.Cir.1992)(affirming that an agency may "choose to make new policy through either rulemaking or adjudication").

Finally, we find no fatal uncertainty in the Board's test as it applies to these facts. As we explain below, the Board's ruling easily survives Dubuque's contention that the test's requirements were not met in regard to its particular relocation. Employers should have no trouble understanding that actions such as Dubuque's run afoul of the Board's newly articulated standard.

## 2. *The Application of the Board's Test to Dubuque*

Dubuque next contends that the Board improperly applied its test to the facts of this case and that under the new standard, properly applied, its actions did not give rise to a bargaining duty. In addressing this contention, we are required by statute to uphold "the findings of the Board with respect to questions of fact if supported by substantial evidence on the record considered as a whole." 29 U.S.C. § 160(f).

Dubuque objects, first, to the Board's finding that its relocation did not constitute a change in the scope and direction of its business. It relies for support on the ALJ's finding that the Rochelle plant was a "smaller, newer, more modern ..., better laid out" facility and his conclusion "that [Dubuque's] relocation of the hog kill and cut to Rochelle clearly turned on a fundamental change in the scope, nature, and direction of [its] business of which labor costs were but a single important factor." ALJ Decision, 287 N.L.R.B. at 538. The Board rejected this conclusion, stating that "[t]here is no evidence that the relocation decision was accompanied by a basic change in the nature of the employer's operation." Dubuque Packing, 303 N.L.R.B. at 393.

The Board's position enjoys ample support in the record. In fact, its rejection of the ALJ's conclusion is specifically supported by the ALJ's findings. The ALJ stated that Dubuque

> used the Rochelle facility to substantially replace the Dubuque facility. As production in Rochelle increased, there was a corresponding reduction at Dubuque until the hog kill and cut processing departments and related operations there were completely phased out. Larry J. Tangeman, general plant superintendent at Dubuque, became superintendent of the Rochelle facility and about 13 members of Dubuque management also were transferred to Rochelle, as was certain production equipment. The purposes of the Rochelle plant, to slaughter hogs, dress carcasses, and to process pork into hams, bacon, and sausage, were the same as at the Dubuque plant.

ALJ Decision, 287 N.L.R.B. at 529. Indeed, in view of these facts, the ALJ felt it necessary to "find" on the record that "the transfer . . . did not constitute subcontracting." Id. at 529 n. 82. Aside from the ALJ's conclusory statement, Dubuque points to nothing indicating that the Dubuque and Rochelle operations were objectively dissimilar enough (in scale of operations for example) for the relocation to constitute a "basic change in the nature of the employer's operation" as that phrase is used in the test. See Dubuque Packing, 303 N.L.R.B. at 391. Viewed as a whole, the record offers substantial support for the Board's position.

Dubuque's second contention is that because "the record . . . is very clear that the union 'would not' offer labor concessions," bargaining would have been futile; hence it was not required. * * *

While we agree that our precedent, like the Board's test, relieves employers from any duty to bargain in the face of a union's adamantine intransigence, that principle has no bearing here. As counsel for the UFCW pointed out at oral argument, the UFCW "could, would, and did" accept concessions—in 1978, in August 1980, and again in October 1981—all in a vain attempt to keep the Dubuque facility open. Indeed, the vote that led to Dubuque's "irrevocable" decision to relocate was not a vote to categorically refuse Dubuque's overtures, but a vote to insist on financial disclosure as a prelude to bargaining. The Board's finding that good-faith bargaining between Dubuque and the UFCW might not have been futile was substantially supported by the record.

### 3. *Retroactivity*

Finally, Dubuque argues that the Board erred by "retroactively" employing its new test in this case. Again, we disagree.

Our formulation of the standard for evaluating challenges to the retroactive application of a ruling from an agency adjudication has varied.

\* \* \* What has not varied is our consistent willingness to approve the retroactive application of rulings that do not represent an "abrupt break with well-settled policy" but merely "attempt to fill a void in an unsettled area of the law." \* \* \* As a practical matter, where an agency ruling seeks only to clarify the contours of established doctrine, we will almost *per force* allow its retroactive application.

In this case, the Board's test merely clarifies the line between relocation decisions that, because they are analogous to subcontracting arrangements, are subject to a duty to bargain and those that, because they are analogous to partial closings, are not. At the time Dubuque announced its "irrevocable" decision to relocate, the question of whether relocation decisions must be negotiated was an old one and the existence of this legal "interstice" was apparent. \* \* \* Thus, the Board's test does not "create a new rule, either by overruling past precedents relied upon by the parties or because it was an issue of first impression," District Lodge 64, 949 F.2d at 447; rather it "fill[s] a void" in the law. \* \* \*Because we find on these facts no special inequity in allowing this interstitial ruling to apply retroactively, we affirm the Board's application of its new test to the present case.

III. Conclusion

For the foregoing reasons, we deny Dubuque's petition for review [and] enforce the Board's remedial order against Dubuque \* \* \*. So ordered.

———

# PROBLEMS FOR DISCUSSION

**1.** It was the apparent purpose of the members of the NLRB to: (a) achieve unanimity on this complex issue; (b) to adhere to the teaching of the Supreme Court in *First National Maintenance;* (c) to assure more clearly the rights of employees in major corporate decisions less "drastic" than the closing of part or all of a business; (d) to provide clear guidelines to companies and unions seeking to know their bargaining rights and duties; and (e) to provide clear guidelines for the parties in litigation before the Board. Did the Board achieve these objectives with *Dubuque Packing?*

**2.** Does the Board give too great weight to employer interests when it holds that there is no duty to bargain about the decision to relocate whenever there is a "basic change in the nature" of the company's business? (What does that mean? Why should that matter?) Does the Board give too great weight to employee interests when it holds that there *is* a duty to bargain about the decision to relocate whenever labor costs are "a factor" in the decision? (How often will that *not* be the case?)

**3.** Would it be feasible, and wise, for the NLRB to extrapolate from the guidelines announced in *Dubuque Packing* so as to have them apply to *all* major corporate decisions, such as automation, subcontracting and even partial closings? Would such an extension be consistent with *First National Maintenance* and with *Fibreboard?* See Mid–State Ready Mix, a Torrington Indus., 307 NLRB 809 (1992). For example, should the Board hold that a decision to subcontract bargaining-unit work is a mandatory subject of bargaining even when it is made to increase production in the face of a labor shortage, the high cost of expansion, freight costs, and the cyclical nature of demand–i.e., concerns not based on labor costs? See Dorsey Trailers, Inc. v. NLRB, 134 F.3d 125 (3d Cir.1998).

———

DORSEY TRAILERS, INC. v. NLRB, 233 F.3d 831 (4th Cir. 2000). The company closed one of its four facilities and transferred the work done there to a remaining facility in the south. The Board held that the company violated section 8(a)(5) in doing so unilaterally, in view of the conclusion that the relocation was in part because of labor costs and so was a mandatory subject of bargaining. The court of appeals reversed. It held that under the Supreme Court decision in *First National Maintenance*, the fact that the relocation involved a decision about the withdrawal and location of capital resources, and thus required corporate flexibility, rendered it beyond the scope of mandatory bargaining. The court drew no distinction between partial closings and relocations, and it repudiated the Board's decision in *Dubuque Packing* and the premise there that some relocations are based altogether on factors other than labor costs.

———

On August 4, 1988, the Plant Closings Bill—the "Worker Adjustment and Retraining Notification Act," 29 U.S.C. §§ 2101–08—became law without the President's signature. It affects employers with 100 or more employees and deals with "plant closings," i.e., a permanent or temporary shutdown of a single site that results in a loss of employment for 50 or more employees during any 30–day period, and "mass layoffs," i.e., a reduction in force of 33% of the employees or at least 50 employees during any thirty day period. In either case, sixty days notice must be given to the union, if the employees are represented under the NLRA, or to the employees individually if they are not so represented. The Act may be enforced by a suit in federal district court brought by the union or by the aggrieved employees. See United Food & Commercial Wkrs. v. Brown Group, Inc., 517 U.S. 544, 116 S.Ct. 1529, 134 L.Ed.2d 758 (1996).

The employer is not liable for failure to give notice, however, if it was "actively seeking capital or business which, if obtained, would have enabled the employer to avoid or postpone the shutdown and the employer reasonably and in good faith believed that giving the notice required would have precluded the employer from obtaining the needed capital or business," or if the closing or layoff is caused by "business circumstances that were not reasonably foreseeable as of the time that notice would have been required." The Act exempts from coverage strikes, lockouts, and the hiring of permanent replacements for economic strikers; that is, in the latter case, notice need not be given to strikers if the hiring of permanent replacements would otherwise work a "mass layoff" within the meaning of the Act. The Secretary of Labor in April 1989 promulgated regulations implementing the Act. 20 C.F.R. §§ 639.1–639.10. (The full text of the WARN Act is set forth in the Statutory Supplement to this casebook.) However, a study comparing employer notice before and after WARN concluded that the Act had had scant practical impact. Addison & Blackburn, The Worker Adjustment and Retraining Notification Act: Effects on Notice Provision, 47 Indus. & Lab. Rel. Rev. 650 (1994).

———

## Allied Chemical and Alkali Workers v. Pittsburgh Plate Glass Co.

404 U.S. 157, 92 S.Ct. 383, 30 L.Ed.2d 341 (1971).

■ MR. JUSTICE BRENNAN delivered the opinion of the Court.

Under the National Labor Relations Act, as amended, mandatory subjects of collective bargaining include pension and insurance benefits for active employees, and an employer's mid-term unilateral modification of such benefits constitutes an unfair labor practice. This cause presents the question whether a mid-term unilateral modification that concerns, not the benefits of active employees, but the benefits of already retired employees also constitutes an unfair labor practice. The National Labor Relations Board, one member dissenting, held that changes in retired employees' retirement benefits are embraced by the bargaining obligation and that an employer's unilateral modification of them constitutes an unfair labor practice in violation of §§ 8(a)(5) and (1) of the Act. 177 N.L.R.B. 911 (1969). The Court of Appeals for the Sixth Circuit disagreed and refused to enforce the Board's cease-and-desist order, 427 F.2d 936 (1970). We granted certiorari, 401 U.S. 907, 91 S.Ct. 867, 27 L.Ed.2d 804 (1971). We affirm the judgment of the Court of Appeals.

I

Since 1949, Local 1, Allied Chemical and Alkali Workers of America, has been the exclusive bargaining representative for the employees "working" on hourly rates of pay at the Barberton, Ohio, facilities of respondent Pittsburgh Plate Glass Co. In 1950, the Union and the Company negotiated an employee group health insurance plan, in which, it was orally agreed, retired employees could participate by contributing the required premiums, to be deducted from their pension benefits. * * *

[In negotiations for the 1962 and 1964 contracts, the Company agreed to make monthly contributions of two dollars and four dollars respectively toward the cost of medical insurance premiums for persons retiring after 1962. Medicare, a national health program, was enacted in November 1965 and shortly after, the Company announced its intention to cancel the negotiated health plan for retirees and to substitute supplemental Medicare coverage toward which it would pay three dollars per month. After the Union protested, the Company stated that it had reconsidered and had decided instead to write each retired employee, offering to pay the supplemental Medicare premium if the employee would withdraw from the negotiated plan. Over the Union's objections, the Company wrote to its 190 retirees, fifteen of whom elected to withdraw from the negotiated plan. The Union filed charges under Section 8(a)(5).]

[T]he Company was ordered to cease and desist from refusing to bargain collectively about retirement benefits and from making unilateral adjustments in health insurance plans for retired employees without first negotiating in good faith with the Union. The Company was also required to rescind, at the Union's request, any adjustment it had unilaterally instituted and to mail and post appropriate notices.

## II

\* \* \*

Together, [Sections 1, 8(a)(5), 8(d) and 9(a)] establish the obligation of the employer to bargain collectively, "with respect to wages, hours, and other terms and conditions of employment," with "the representatives of his employees" designated or selected by the majority "in a unit appropriate for such purposes." This obligation extends only to the "terms and conditions of employment" of the employer's "employees" in the "unit appropriate for such purposes" that the union represents. \* \* \*

*First.* \* \* \* We have repeatedly affirmed that the task of determining the contours of the term "employee" [in Section 2(3) of the NLRA] "has been assigned primarily to the agency created by Congress to administer the Act." NLRB v. Hearst Publications, 322 U.S. 111, 130, 64 S.Ct. 851, 860, 88 L.Ed. 1170 (1944). See also Iron Workers v. Perko, 373 U.S. 701, 706, 83 S.Ct. 1429, 1432, 10 L.Ed.2d 646 (1963); NLRB v. Atkins & Co., 331 U.S. 398, 67 S.Ct. 1265, 91 L.Ed. 1563 (1947). But we have never immunized Board judgments from judicial review in this respect. "[T]he Board's determination that specified persons are 'employees' under this Act is to be accepted if it has 'warrant in the record' and a reasonable basis in law." NLRB v. Hearst Publications, supra, 322 U.S., at 131, 64 S.Ct., at 861.

In this cause we hold that the Board's decision is not supported by the law. The Act, after all, as § 1 makes clear, is concerned with the disruption to commerce that arises from interference with the organization and collective-bargaining rights of "workers"—not those who have retired from the work force. The inequality of bargaining power that Congress sought to remedy was that of the "working" man, and the labor disputes that it ordered to be subjected to collective bargaining were those of employers and their active employees. Nowhere in the history of the National Labor Relations Act is there any evidence that retired workers are to be considered as within the ambit of the collective-bargaining obligations of the statute.

To the contrary, the legislative history of § 2(3) itself indicates that the term "employee" is not to be stretched beyond its plain meaning embracing only those who work for another for hire. \* \* \* The ordinary meaning of "employee" does not include retired workers; retired employees have ceased to work for another for hire.

The decisions on which the Board relied in construing § 2(3) to the contrary are wide of the mark. The Board enumerated "unfair labor practice situations where the statute has been applied to persons who have not been initially hired by an employer or whose employment has terminated. Illustrative are cases in which the Board has held that applicants for employment and registrants at hiring halls—who have never been hired in the first place—as well as persons who have quit or whose employers have gone out of business are 'employees' embraced by the policies of the Act." 177 N.L.R.B., at 913 (citations omitted). Yet all of these cases involved people who, unlike the pensioners here, were members of the active work force available for hire and at least in that sense could be identified as "employees." No decision under the Act is cited, and none to our knowledge exists, in which an individual who has ceased work without expectation of further employment has been held to be an "employee." * * *

*Second.* Section 9(a) of the Labor Relations Act accords representative status only to the labor organization selected or designated by the majority of employees in a "unit appropriate" "for the purposes of collective bargaining." * * *

In this cause, in addition to holding that pensioners are not "employees" within the meaning of the collective-bargaining obligations of the Act, we hold that they were not and could not be "employees" included in the bargaining unit. The unit determined by the Board to be appropriate was composed of "employees of the Employer's plant * * * working on hourly rates, including group leaders who work on hourly rates of pay * * *." Apart from whether retirees could be considered "employees" within this language, they obviously were not employees "working" or "who work" on hourly rates of pay. Although those terms may include persons on temporary or limited absence from work, such as employees on military duty, it would utterly destroy the function of language to read them as embracing those whose work has ceased with no expectation of return. * * *

Here, even if, as the Board found, active and retired employees have a common concern in assuring that the latter's benefits remain adequate, they plainly do not share a community of interests broad enough to justify inclusion of the retirees in the bargaining unit. Pensioners' interests extend only to retirement benefits, to the exclusion of wage rates, hours, working conditions, and all other terms of active employment. Incorporation of such a limited-purpose constituency in the bargaining unit would create the potential for severe internal conflicts that would impair the unit's ability to function and would disrupt the processes of collective bargaining. Moreover, the risk cannot be overlooked that union representatives on occasion might see fit to bargain for improved wages or other conditions favoring active employees at the expense of retirees' benefits. * * *

*Third.* The Board found that bargaining over pensioners' rights has become an established industrial practice. But industrial practice cannot alter the conclusions that retirees are neither "employees" nor bargaining unit members. The parties dispute whether a practice of bargaining over pensioners' benefits exists and, if so, whether it reflects the views of labor and management that the subject is not merely a convenient but a mandatory topic of negotiation. But even if industry commonly regards retirees' benefits as a statutory subject of bargaining, that would at most, as we suggested in Fibreboard Corp. v. NLRB, 379 U.S. 203, 211, 85 S.Ct. 398, 403, 13 L.Ed.2d 233 (1964), reflect the interests of employers and employees in the subject matter as well as its amenability to the collective-bargaining process; it would not be determinative. Common practice cannot change the law and make into bargaining unit "employees" those who are not.

## III

Even if pensioners are not bargaining unit "employees," are their benefits, nonetheless, a mandatory subject of collective bargaining as "terms and conditions of employment" of active employees who remain in the unit? The Board held, alternatively, that they are, on the ground that they "vitally" affect the "terms and conditions of employment" of active employees principally by influencing the value of both their current and future benefits. 177 N.L.R.B., at 915.[17] * * *

Section 8(d) of the Act, of course, does not immutably fix a list of subjects for mandatory bargaining. See, e.g., Fibreboard Corp. v. N.L.R.B., supra, 379 U.S., at 220–221, 85 S.Ct., at 407–408 (Stewart, J., concurring); Richfield Oil Corp. v. NLRB, 97 U.S.App.D.C. 383, 389–390, 231 F.2d 717, 723–724 (1956). But it does establish a limitation against which proposed topics must be measured. In general terms, the limitation includes only issues that settle an aspect of the relationship between the employer and employees. See, e.g., NLRB v. Borg–Warner Corp., 356 U.S. 342, 78 S.Ct. 718, 2 L.Ed.2d 823 (1958). Although normally matters involving individuals outside the employment relationship do not fall within that category, they are not wholly excluded. In Teamsters Union v. Oliver, 358 U.S. 283, 79 S.Ct. 297, 3 L.Ed.2d 312 (1959), for example, an agreement had been negotiated in the trucking industry, establishing a minimum rental that carriers would pay to truck owners who drove their own vehicles in the carriers' service in place of the latter's employees. Without determining whether the owner-drivers were themselves "employees," we held that the minimum rental was a mandatory subject of bargaining, and hence immune from state antitrust laws, because the term "was integral to the establish-

---

**17.** The Board also noted "that changes in retirement benefits for retired employees affect the availability of employer funds for active employees." 177 N.L.R.B., at 915. That, again, is quite true. But countless other employer expenditures that concededly are not subjects of mandatory bargaining, such as supervisors' salaries and dividends, have a similar impact. The principle that underlies the Board's argument sweeps with far too broad a brush. The Board does suggest in its brief that pensioners' benefits are different from other employer expenses because they are normally regarded as part of labor costs. The employer's method of accounting, however, hardly provides a suitable basis for distinction. In any case, the impact on active employees' compensation from changes in pensioners' benefits is, like the effect discussed in the text of including retirees under the same health insurance plan as active employees, too insubstantial to bring those changes within the collective-bargaining obligation.

ment of a stable wage structure for clearly covered employee-drivers." United States v. Drum, 368 U.S. 370, 382–383, n. 26, 82 S.Ct. 408, 414, 7 L.Ed.2d 360 (1962). Similarly, in Fibreboard Corp. v. NLRB, supra, at 215, we held that "the type of 'contracting out' involved in this case—the replacement of employees in the existing bargaining unit with those of an independent contractor to do the same work under similar conditions of employment—is a statutory subject of collective bargaining * * *." * * * We agree with the Board that the principle of *Oliver* and *Fibreboard* is relevant here; in each case the question is not whether the third-party concern is antagonistic to or compatible with the interests of bargaining-unit employees, but whether it vitally affects the "terms and conditions" of their employment. But we disagree with the Board's assessment of the significance of a change in retirees' benefits to the "terms and conditions of employment" of active employees.

The benefits that active workers may reap by including retired employees under the same health insurance contract are speculative and insubstantial at best. As the Board itself acknowledges in its brief, the relationship between the inclusion of retirees and the overall insurance rate is uncertain. Adding individuals increases the group experience and thereby generally tends to lower the rate, but including pensioners, who are likely to have higher medical expenses, may more than offset that effect. In any event, the impact one way or the other on the "terms and conditions of employment" of active employees is hardly comparable to the loss of jobs threatened in *Oliver* and *Fibreboard*. * * *

The mitigation of future uncertainty and the facilitation of agreement on active employees' retirement plans, that the Board said would follow from the union's representation of pensioners, are equally problematical. * * * By advancing pensioners' interests now, active employees * * * have no assurance that they will be the beneficiaries of similar representation when they retire. * * *

We recognize that "classification of bargaining subjects as 'terms [and] conditions of employment' is a matter concerning which the Board has special expertise." Meat Cutters v. Jewel Tea, 381 U.S. 676, 685–686, 85 S.Ct. 1596, 1600, 14 L.Ed.2d 640 (1965). The Board's holding in this cause, however, depends on the application of law to facts, and the legal standard to be applied is ultimately for the courts to decide and enforce. We think that in holding the "terms and conditions of employment" of active employees to be *vitally* affected by pensioners' benefits, the Board here simply neglected to give the adverb its ordinary meaning. Cf. NLRB v. Brown, 380 U.S. 278, 292, 85 S.Ct. 980, 988, 13 L.Ed.2d 839 (1965).

IV

The question remains whether the Company committed an unfair labor practice by offering retirees an exchange for their withdrawal from the already negotiated health insurance plan. * * * We need not resolve, however, whether there was a "modification" within the meaning of § 8(d), because we hold that even if there was, a "modification" is a prohibited unfair labor practice only when it changes a term that is a mandatory rather than a permissive subject of bargaining.

Paragraph (4) of § 8(d), of course, requires that a party proposing a modification continue "in full force and effect * * * all the terms and conditions of the existing contract" until its expiration. * * * The provision begins by defining "to bargain collectively" as meeting and conferring "with respect to wages, hours, and other terms and conditions of employment." It then goes on to state that "the duty to bargain collectively shall also mean" that mid-term unilateral modifications and terminations are prohibited. Although this part of the section is introduced by a "proviso" clause, * * * it quite plainly is to be construed *in pari materia* with the preceding definition. Accordingly, just as § 8(d) defines the obligation to bargain to be with respect to mandatory terms alone, so it prescribes the duty to maintain only mandatory terms without unilateral modification for the duration of the collective-bargaining agreement. * * *

The structure and language of § 8(d) point to a more specialized purpose than merely promoting general contract compliance. The conditions for a modification or termination set out in paragraphs (1) through (4) plainly are designed to regulate modifications and terminations so as to facilitate agreement in place of economic warfare. * * * When a proposed modification is to a permissive term, therefore, the purpose of facilitating accord on the proposal is not at all in point, since the parties are not required under the statute to bargain with respect to it. The irrelevance of the purpose is demonstrated by the irrelevance of the procedures themselves of § 8(d). Paragraph (2), for example, requires an offer "to meet and confer with the other party for the purpose of negotiating a new contract or a contract containing the proposed modifications." But such an offer is meaningless if a party is statutorily free to refuse to negotiate on the proposed change to the permissive term. The notification to mediation and conciliation services referred to in paragraph (3) would be equally meaningless, if required at all.[23] We think it would be no less beside the point to read paragraph (4) of § 8(d) as requiring continued adherence to permissive as well as mandatory terms. The remedy for a unilateral mid-term modification to a permissive term lies in an action for breach of contract, * * * not in an unfair-labor-practice proceeding.

As a unilateral mid-term modification of a permissive term such as retirees' benefits does not, therefore, violate § 8(d), the judgment of the Court of Appeals is

Affirmed.

---

**23.**  The notification required by paragraph (3) is "of the existence of a dispute." Section 2(9) of the Act defines "labor dispute" to include "any controversy concerning terms, tenure or conditions of employment, or concerning the association or representation of persons in negotiating, fixing, maintaining, changing, or seeking to arrange terms or conditions of employment * * *." 49 Stat. 450, as amended, 29 U.S.C. § 152(9). Since controversies over permissive terms are excluded from the definition, a paragraph (3) notice might not be required in the case of a proposed modification to such a term even if § 8(d) applied.

Mr. Justice Douglas dissents.

---

PROBLEMS FOR DISCUSSION

**1.** Improvements in retirement benefits for current retirees are a common subject of collective bargaining. See 2 Collective Bargaining Negotiations and Contracts secs. 48.53–48.54 (BNA 1990). If so, what is the purpose or effect of categorizing it as a non-mandatory bargaining subject?

**2.** Must the employer bargain with respect to the following provisions proposed by the union in the current negotiations? (a) The employer shall not discriminate on the basis of race or sex in hiring. (b) The employer shall not hire any job applicant other than one referred from the union hiring hall. (c) The employer shall discontinue the administration of lie-detector and drug-and-alcohol tests for job applicants? See Star Tribune v. Newspaper Guild, 295 NLRB 543 (1989).

**3.** Is the Supreme Court consistent in the standard it uses in reviewing NLRB determinations whether a subject is mandatory or permissive? Compare the justification for the Court's reversal in *Allied Chemical*, where the Board purported to apply the "vitally affects" test developed in earlier judicial and Board decisions, with the Court's deference to the Board in applying a statutory definition in the *Ford Motor* case at page 446 supra. How much deference *should* the Board be given on this matter?

**4.** The Rubber Workers Union represents the production and maintenance employees of the Triple–R Company (Run–Right–Retreads), a mid-sized manufacturer of retread tires in Smalltown, Pennsylvania. Triple–R is the only significant company in town, employing almost two-thirds of the eligible workforce. Emissions from the plant have been polluting the air and water of the community; the plant itself, however, is fully ventilated. The Union seeks to add the following provision to the collective bargaining agreement: "Pollution Control—The Company shall not operate at any time without an emission-control system installed and operating. If the plant is closed because of an alleged violation of this provision, all employees covered by this agreement shall receive full compensation at their regular rate of pay for all time lost." The Union wishes to know whether it may only propose this provision, or may be adamant about it. What is your advice? See Oldham, "Organized Labor, the Environment and the Taft–Hartley Act," 71 Mich.L.Rev. 936 (1973).

---

# IV.  The Role of the Strike and Third–Party Impasse Resolution

At the center of most discussions concerning collective bargaining is a debate about the necessity and utility of the strike. This debate has become particularly heated in recent years, with the increase in work stoppages among public employees, but it has been with us for decades in the private sector, particularly in industries (such as transportation, communications, steel, defense) which are generally regarded as vital to the national welfare. Although the peaceful work stoppage is one of the activities protected under the Labor Act by Section 7, a protection which is underlined in

Section 13, it has also been the expressed desire of Congress to have disagreements at the bargaining table resolved without recourse to economic weapons.

This section of the casebook will consider: First, the premises underlying the American system of collective bargaining in the private sector, and the role of the strike in that system; second, the machinery that is available to resolve negotiating disputes by means short of a work stoppage, most particularly by mediation and other third-party procedures; and third, the impact of the strike upon the duty of the parties under Section 8 of the Labor Act to bargain in good faith.

---

## 1.   THE PREMISES OF COLLECTIVE BARGAINING AND THE ROLE OF THE STRIKE

Collective bargaining is a part of an economy founded on private enterprise. Wages and other terms and conditions of employment are determined not by the government but by the people concerned. Of course, the aggregation of large amounts in capital in corporations and somewhat later the combination of large numbers of workers into unions has made private negotiation of wages something quite different from what it was a hundred years ago. Also, government policies have undoubted effects on wage levels. But even when allowances are made for those forces, it remains essentially true that collective bargaining is a system for fixing the price of labor without government regulation of the whole structure of wages and prices. Moreover, most of the organized labor movement would not have it otherwise. Since the eighteen-eighties one of the strongest characteristics of the American labor movement has been its dedication to practical objectives which it has sought to obtain by private economic action within our existing society rather than by political reforms aimed at remaking our social and economic institutions. In this respect the American labor movement has been almost unique.

How, then, does collective bargaining work? Why do management and union ever get together? The answers appear to be two. In the first place the long negotiations over the terms of a collective bargaining contract themselves tend to bring about agreement, or at least to narrow the area of disagreement. But the second factor that makes collective bargaining work is the strike. Everyone who has been in a tough wage negotiation where the stakes were high knows that the bargain is never struck until one minute before midnight when there is no place else to go, nothing left to do, no possible escape from choosing between a strike and a compromise. In the final analysis collective bargaining works as a method of fixing terms and conditions of employment only because there comes a time when both sides conclude that the risks of losses through a strike are so great that compromise is cheaper than economic battle. And when one side or both miscalculate and conclude that the risks are worth running and a strike occurs, it is settled only when each side is convinced that continuing the struggle will cost more than acceptance of the terms the other offers. To put it in a phrase, the strike or the fear of a strike is the motive power that makes collective bargaining operate.

In most industries we are ready enough to accept this way of fixing employees' wages. It works pretty well on the whole and such economic waste as results from strikes is more than offset by the advantages of leaving industry and labor free to work out their own agreements. The trouble comes in those industries where a strike becomes intolerable to the public long before the strike can serve its function of making the parties— management and labor—agree on a voluntary settlement of their differences. In such instances, we are confronted with a dilemma. So long as our labor policy is predicated on collective bargaining, we cannot wholly eliminate the risk of strikes. Nor can we discard collective bargaining without substituting for the private negotiation of wages a high degree of government regulation. We must pay for our freedom.

---

## 2. FACILITATION OF VOLUNTARY AGREEMENTS

Although this dilemma is most stark in vital industries, it exists in all. Congress has attempted to preserve the right to strike as a last resort but to encourage the parties first to exhaust all attempts at direct negotiation as well as third-party intervention in order to reach a settlement which will reflect the private interests of the parties.

*Notification and the "Cooling Off" Period.* Section 8(d) provides elaborate procedural requirements designed to help settle labor disputes and, in particular, to avert hasty and ill-considered strikes. Section 8(d)(1) requires that any party desiring to terminate or modify an existing collective bargaining agreement must serve written notice on the other party at least sixty days prior to the expiration date of the contract or, if the contract provides no such date, sixty days prior to the time when the termination or modification is to be made. Section 8(d)(3) stipulates that within thirty days of submitting the written notice required by 8(d)(1), the moving party must inform the Federal Mediation and Conciliation Service together with any State or Territorial agency which is designed and empowered to mediate or conciliate the dispute. Finally, Section 8(d)(4) demands that the party continue

> in full force and effect without resorting to strike or lock-out, all the terms and conditions of the existing contract for a period of sixty days after such notice is given or until the expiration date of such contract, whichever occurs later * * *.

> A failure to comply with these provisions constitutes an unlawful refusal to bargain within the meaning of Section 8(a)(5) or Section 8(b)(3). In addition, Section 8(d)(4) provides that any employee who strikes within any notice period prescribed in Section 8(d) will lose his status as an employee of the employer concerned for the

purposes of Sections 8, 9 and 10 of the Act unless and until he is reemployed by that employer.

In 1974, Congress eliminated from the Labor Act an exclusion for private nonprofit hospitals which had been a part of the Act since 1947. (Public Law 93–360 (July 26, 1974).) It also expressed a concern for the peculiar need in health care institutions for the uninterrupted rendition of services to the public and took a number of steps to facilitate the settlement of contract negotiation disputes beyond those already set forth in Section 8(d). Requirements for giving notice to federal and/or state mediation agencies are expanded in connection with contract negotiations, and are for the first time imposed (under Section 8(g)) in connection with "any strike, picketing or other concerted refusal to work at any health care institution." The Federal Mediation and Conciliation Service is directed (rather than merely authorized) to intervene to effect a settlement in health-care negotiations; and the Service is empowered to appoint an impartial Board of Inquiry to investigate any dispute and make settlement recommendations.

*Conciliation and Mediation.* When a conciliation or mediation agency becomes involved in an unresolved labor negotiation, its purpose is to bring the parties to agreement on the terms of a contract through the use of informed and creative persuasion. By holding joint conferences and shuttling between individual conferences with each party, the mediator (the term conciliator has come to be used interchangeably) gains the parties' confidence, ascertains the parties' true priorities, and induces them to analyze the obstacles to settlement as well as the feasible concessions. The mediator can dispel misunderstandings about the other party's position, or about practices elsewhere, or about pertinent laws or administrative rulings. He or she can also facilitate bargaining by conveying a belief that one or another of the parties "means business" when the adversary believes it merely to be engaging in rhetoric (*e.g.*, the union threatening a strike or the company pleading incapacity).

*Fact-Finding Boards.* Reliance has sometimes been placed on fact finding to supplement normal conciliation and mediation services. In the railway labor field this has become an integral part of the collective bargaining process, and that experience—along with more recent experiences under state public-sector bargaining legislation—was incorporated in the NLRA in the 1974 amendments dealing with private health care institutions. Under the Railway Labor Act, the National Mediation Board may enter into a negotiation after either party gives notice of an intended change in rates of pay, rules or working conditions, and if mediation fails, the President may—if the dispute threatens to deprive any section of the country of essential transportation service—appoint under Section 10 of the Act an Emergency Board to investigate the pertinent facts and report them to the President. Throughout the period of mediation and investigation, neither party may make any change in the conditions out of which the dispute arose, but thereafter there may be lawful resort to economic weapons.

A similar, but more condensed, time-table is set forth in Section 213 of the National Labor Relations Act, relating to the role of the Federal Mediation Service in health care disputes. The Director of the Service—if he or she is of the opinion that "a threatened or actual strike or lockout affecting a health care institution will, if permitted to occur or to continue, substantially interrupt the delivery of health care in the locality concerned"—may appoint an impartial board of inquiry to investigate the dispute and actually to make recommendations for its settlement. Throughout the pertinent period, the parties must maintain the status quo and must refrain from striking, locking out, or changing working conditions.

*National Emergencies.* Sections 206 through 210 of the Labor–Management Relations Act of 1947 set forth detailed procedures to govern strikes which are deemed to constitute a national emergency. The statute provides that if the President believes that an actual or threatened strike will imperil the national health or safety, he may impanel a board of inquiry. This board is expressly forbidden to make recommendations for the settlement of the dispute but is directed to investigate the causes and circumstances of the controversy. Having received the report of the board, the President may conclude that the strike is a threat to national health or safety whereupon he can direct the Attorney General to petition any appropriate district court for an injunction. If the district court finds that a strike affects all or a substantial part of an industry engaged in interstate commerce or in the production of goods for commerce and that the continuation of the strike will imperil the national health or safety, the Court shall have jurisdiction to enjoin the strike. Thereafter, bargaining between the parties continues with the aid of the Federal Mediation and Conciliation Service. Sixty days after the issuing of the injunction, the board of inquiry must submit a further report setting forth the current status of the dispute and the employer's last offer of settlement. Within the next fifteen days, a vote must be taken among the employees to determine whether they will agree to accept the last offer of the employer. Whether or not the foregoing measures have resulted in a settlement between the parties, the injunction must be dissolved after it has been in force for eighty days.

In 1959, these procedures were tested in the courts as a result of a strike by more than half a million steelworkers against some 97 steel companies. When stockpiles had dwindled and an estimated 250,000 workers had been laid off in dependent industries, the President, having received a report from a board of inquiry, ordered the Attorney General to seek an injunction. After an injunction had been granted by the district court and affirmed by the Court of Appeals, the case was taken on certiorari to the Supreme Court. The union argued to the Court that the statute permitted injunctions only where the physical well-being of the citizenry was in jeopardy and where the judge in his discretion had determined that other techniques for averting the crisis were unavailing. These arguments were rejected by the Court in a per curiam decision which limited the role of the courts under the national emergency provisions to a determination of whether the national health or safety is imperiled by the strike. On the basis of the affidavits by experts and government officials, the Court concluded that critical defense needs were involved which constituted a threat to the national safety. UNITED STEELWORKERS V. UNITED STATES, 361 U.S. 39, 80 S.Ct. 1, 4 L.Ed.2d 12 (1959). The national emergency provisions have been invoked in a number of other industries, including coal, atomic energy, maritime, and telecommunications.

---

### 3.   THE EFFECT OF A STRIKE UPON THE DUTY TO BARGAIN

The use of the strike is "part and parcel" of the process of collective bargaining in the United States. The underlying theory, developed at pages 468–69 supra, is reflected in such decisions as NLRB v. Insurance Agents Int'l Union, at p. 405 supra. That case holds that, barring specific congressional outlawry, a union's resort during negotiations to a peaceful work stoppage—even if regarded as unconventional, peculiarly disruptive and indeed obnoxious by common standards—does not in itself violate the duty to bargain in good faith. (It may be, however, that such stoppages render the employees susceptible to discharge.) The question remains whether such union activity in some way modifies the duty of the employer so to bargain. Although it has been argued that a conventional peaceful strike is so disruptive of amicable relations between union and employer that it ought to relieve the employer of the duty to continue dealing at the bargaining table, that argument has been clearly and consistently rejected. As the court held in NLRB v. J.H. Rutter–Rex Mfg. Co., 245 F.2d 594 (5th Cir.1957):

> "The duty to bargain did not terminate with the calling or execution of the strike. The strike, or threat of it, so carefully recognized as a right in the Act, Section 13, 29 U.S.C.A. § 163, is a means of self-help allowed to a union as pressure in the bargaining process. How or why the strike is called, or how conducted, may well have significant effect upon the right of strikers for reinstatement or reemployment or in other respects not necessary to indicate. But the mere fact that a Union has without justification precipitated a strike does not make the union or the employees for whom it is the bargaining representative outlaws so that they forfeit all of the benefits of the Act. The calling of such a strike does not infect all that thereafter occurs with the virus of that action. A strike does not in and of itself suspend the bargaining obligation."

The strike in the *Rutter–Rex* case was a protected economic strike. Is the duty to bargain suspended when the union or employees engage in activities which are unprotected or unlawful? In Phelps Dodge Copper Prods. Corp., 101 NLRB 360 (1952), the employer was held not to have violated the Act when it refused to continue contract negotiations while the union engaged in an unprotected slowdown. The Board held that the slowdown "negates the existence of honest and sincere dealing in the

Union's contemporaneous request to negotiate in these circumstances. The Respondent was not required to indulge in the futile gesture of honoring the Union's request." Are there sound reasons for thus suspending the employer's duty to bargain? Can this holding survive the Supreme Court decision in *Insurance Agents?* See NLRB v. Katz, 369 U.S. 736, 741 n. 7, 82 S.Ct. 1107, 1111 n. 7, 8 L.Ed.2d 230 (1962). See generally C. Perry, A. Kramer & T. Schneider, Operating During Strikes: Company Experience, NLRB Policies, and Governmental Regulations (1982).

As will be developed in materials below, at p. 548, the employer during the strike is entitled by law to hire temporary or even permanent replacements for the strikers in order to keep its business going. Appeals directly to employees to break ranks with the union, and appeals to strike replacements, raise questions of individual bargaining and the bypassing of the majority representative. Such appeals might also hold out inducements which exceed those currently being offered to the union at the bargaining table, and may thus indicate that the employer is not using its best efforts to reach a settlement with the union. NLRB v. Katz, p. 412 supra. But it is sometimes difficult to tell whether the employer has offered such unlawfully extravagant terms to strikebreakers. Thus, in Pacific Gamble Robinson Co. v. NLRB, 186 F.2d 106 (6th Cir.1950), the most recent wage offer to the union during a strike was a ten-cent increase to 87 cents an hour for starting employees and 98 cents an hour for workers employed for a year or more. The employer hired four nonunion replacements (who presumably did not satisfy the one-year requirement) at the rate of 98 cents an hour. The court of appeals reversed the finding of the Board that this action violated Section 8(a)(5):

> "The finding that the offer of 98 cents made to replacements after the strike was higher than that made to the union on August 15, and repeated on September 8, ignores the fact that the flat 98 cent rate which was all that was offered the replacements included no right of seniority or vacation with pay, no provision as to the length of the work week, as to overtime, arbitration, and none of the other valuable features of the contract. On the conceded facts the offer made to the union was much more advantageous than that made to the replacements."

There is, however, no duty to bargain with the union over the terms on which replacements are hired:

> To compel bargaining by a struck employer subject to the obligation imposed by Section 8(a)(5) of the Act is necessarily to impose the concomitant obligation on the striking representative under Section 8(b)(3) of the Act. Both will be obliged to bargain "to reach ultimate agreement," ... but in this instance for an agreement on the terms under which strike replacements can be employed. Yet, such a rule places the striking representative in a true "Catch–22" situation: If it bargains in the manner required by the Act, then it undermines its own strike objective by allowing the struck employer to continue operations with replacements

working under terms formulated as a result of its own negotiations; but, if it bargains in a manner consistent with its strike
objective of curtailing the struck employer's operations, then it
likely will be bargaining in a manner to avoid reaching agreement
on employment terms for replacements, to impede their being
hired, and, thus, in a manner that violates the Act.

Service Electric Co. v. International Brotherhood of Electrical Workers, 281
NLRB 633, 639 (1986).

---

# Land Air Delivery, Inc. v. NLRB

862 F.2d 354 (D.C.Cir.1988).

■ SILBERMAN, CIRCUIT JUDGE:

## I.

Land Air Delivery, Inc. is an air freight motor carrier that engages in
the pickup and delivery of small packages for overnight carriers. In 1973,
the Board certified Teamsters Local 41 as the exclusive bargaining agent of
"[a]ll truck drivers and warehousemen" employed by Land Air. In 1975,
the Board clarified the bargaining unit by excluding independent contractors who transported freight for Land Air. At the time of the strike that led
to this litigation, Land Air employed 13 bargaining unit truckdrivers and
used an additional group of independent contractor drivers.

\* \* \*

In November 1984, the union notified the company that the union had
authorized a strike, pursuant to the terms of the NMFA ["National Master
Freight Agreement"], to protest both the company's failure to comply with
certain grievance awards and its refusal to take a deadlocked grievance to
the next step of the grievance procedure. All 13 unit employees struck, and
Land Air immediately hired replacement workers. To continue its business
during the strike in Kansas City, Land Air used a mix of employees from
other locations, its contractors and contractor drivers, newly-hired employees, and its own staff and supervisors. The company hired eight new
employees in November and December 1984; three of these employees were
terminated in December 1984, and five were terminated on March 28,
1985. Thus, as of March 28, 1985, Land Air had terminated all of its
replacement employees.

The company also signed agreements with 12 independent contractors
between February 20 and March 1, 1985. Five of these persons had not
been contractors before the strike, and all 12 contractors continued to work
for Land Air after the end of the strike. Although the exact timing is not
clear from the record, the combination of subcontracting on February 20

and March 1 and termination of replacement employees on March 28 resulted in the elimination of all bargaining unit positions by March 1985.

\* \* \*

The strike ended on April 9, 1985, when the union members offered orally to return to work unconditionally. At that time, the general manager of Land Air informed the former strikers that there was no work for them. On April 11, the union's business agent communicated the same unconditional offer to Land Air by mail. Land Air took no action to reinstate the striking employees, and the union filed a charge against the company alleging that it had committed an unfair labor practice by refusing to reinstate the strikers. The Board's regional director dismissed the charge, finding that "the subject strike was an economic strike giving the employees the right to reinstatement only at such time when positions become available." Because Land Air had not hired any new employees since the unconditional offer of April 9, the regional director concluded that the company's refusal to reinstate the strikers was not a violation of the Act. \* \* \* On February 20, 1986, the union filed an amended charge alleging violations of sections 8(a)(1), (3), and (5), and specifying:

> On or about February 1, 1985, [Land Air] by its officers, agents and representatives subcontracted out bargaining unit work without notice to or bargaining with the Union.

> On or about April 9, 1985, [Land Air] by its officers, agents and representatives failed and refused to reinstate striking employees who had made an unconditional offer to return to work.

The administrative law judge found that Land Air had violated sections 8(a)(1), (3), and (5) of the Act by permanently subcontracting unit work without prior bargaining. He determined that by March 1985, petitioner had contracted out all bargaining unit positions. He ordered the company to reinstate nine strikers and directed that they receive backpay from Land Air (four of the striking employees were not ordered reinstated because of specific instances of employee misconduct).... The Board affirmed the ALJ's findings on these issues, and Land Air petitions this court for review.

## II.

Petitioner contends that as a matter of law an employer is entitled to replace economic strikers permanently with subcontractors *at any time* during the strike without bargaining with the union over that decision.[2] The Board, on the other hand, appears to maintain that an employer is *never* (even during an economic strike) permitted to subcontract permanently, without bargaining over the decision.[3] We reject petitioner's conten-

---

**2.** Although neither petitioner nor the Board in their briefs is entirely clear as to what is meant by *permanent* subcontracting, we take the term to mean subcontracting for an indefinite future period not to terminate at the expiration of the strike.

**3.** The Board urged that an employer has two options when faced with an economic strike: (1) it can hire permanent employee replacements or (2) it can contract out the work on a temporary basis. But cf. *Elliott River Tours, Inc.*, 246 N.L.R.B. 935

tion, and do not find it necessary, in order to resolve this case, to pass on the Board's proposition. Even if pressing "business necessity" would justify permanently contracting out unit work, Land Air has not shown such necessity here.

Long settled is the rule that an employer—at least absent an economic strike—is obliged to bargain with his union before he decides to subcontract. The basis for this requirement is that subcontracting erodes the bargaining unit and is an "appropriate" subject for collective bargaining. Fibreboard Paper Products Corp. v. NLRB, 379 U.S. 203, 85 S.Ct. 398, 13 L.Ed.2d 233 (1964). Also long settled, however, is the principle that an employer faced with an economic strike is entitled to replace strikers permanently with new employees. NLRB v. Mackay Radio, 304 U.S. 333, 58 S.Ct. 904, 82 L.Ed. 1381 (1938). Land Air claims that Mackay Radio in effect "trumps" Fibreboard, because there is no meaningful distinction between replacing strikers with permanent employees and replacing them with permanent subcontractors. We see at least a theoretical distinction, however, and that difference probably has practical consequences.

A permanent subcontract diminishes the bargaining unit by the scope of the subcontract. See International Union, UAW v. NLRB, 381 F.2d 265, 266 (D.C.Cir.), cert. denied, 389 U.S. 857, 88 S.Ct. 82, 19 L.Ed.2d 122 (1967). Contracting out all bargaining unit work, as occurred in this case, completely destroys the bargaining unit. Although as a practical matter it may be true that total replacement of strikers by new permanent employees will often result in a decertification of the union, there is a legal difference between the employer unilaterally dissolving the unit by contracting out its work and the employees in the unit themselves decertifying the union. Until decertification, the employer is obliged to bargain with the striking union over all terms and conditions of employment in the bargaining unit, and his obligation would be lessened if a portion of the work of the unit were permanently subcontracted. Bringing on permanent replacements, moreover, does not necessarily lead to the extinction of the bargaining unit. A striking union might be able to gain the allegiance of at least some of the replacement employees who, combined with strikers, could provide the union with continued majority support. We think, therefore, that the Board is within its authority to treat permanent subcontracting during a strike differently from the use of permanent employee replacements for purposes of section 8(a)(5) of the Act.

Despite our conclusion that permanent subcontracting is not legally equivalent to the use of permanent replacements, we still must confront the question whether permanent subcontracting violated the NLRA under the circumstances of this case. Petitioner relies for support primarily on the

(1979)(Board countenanced contracting out for two years, which exceeded the duration of the strike, because subcontractor demanded long term as condition for taking on the work). In view of *Elliott River Tours,* we do not take the Board's current position to preclude argument that at least long-term subcontracting is available in special circumstances, i.e., when permanent replacements or temporary subcontractors are not viable options.

decision of the Ninth Circuit in Hawaii Meat Company v. NLRB, 321 F.2d 397 (9th Cir.1963), where the court held that an employer's unilateral decision to subcontract work permanently during an economic strike did not violate section 8(a)(5). But cf. American Cyanamid v. NLRB, 592 F.2d 356, 360 n. 7 (7th Cir.1979)(reading Hawaii Meat as compatible with distinction between generally permissible temporary subcontracting in face of strike and generally impermissible permanent subcontracting); see also Soule Glass & Glazing Co. v. NLRB, 652 F.2d 1055, 1088–89 (1st Cir.1981); NLRB v. King Radio Corp., 416 F.2d 569, 572 (10th Cir.1969) (distinguishing between permanent and temporary subcontracting). Judge Duniway's opinion in *Hawaii Meat,* however, was carefully drawn to deal with the exigencies of the particular situation presented, and to exclude from the decision's compass cases like the instant one. In *Hawaii Meat,* the employer determined before the strike to subcontract permanently its hauling operations in the event of a strike, and it notified the union of its plans just before the strike. It was undisputed that the employer's purpose in subcontracting was totally defensive—to keep its plant operating during the strike. Id. at 399. The court rejected the Board's finding of a violation of section 8(a)(5), because to require an employer to bargain to impasse over a subcontracting decision under those exigent circumstances would be to give the union a practical veto over the decision. As the court observed, the union could easily delay an impasse and thereby prevent the employer from continuing business during the strike. See id. at 400. We read *Hawaii Meat,* then, to stand for no more than the proposition that an employer may not be obliged to bargain with a union about permanent subcontracting during a strike when that subcontracting is necessary to the business purpose of keeping the plant continuously in operation and time of decision is of the essence.

Although the Board has permitted unilateral subcontracting that extends beyond the end of a strike in a case where the subcontractor insisted on such an arrangement, see Elliott River Tours, 246 N.L.R.B. 935 (1979)(two year subcontract), it does not appear to have accepted even our narrow reading of *Hawaii Meat* that permanent subcontracting may be undertaken without first bargaining when needed to continue operations. See supra note 3. It is unnecessary for us to pass on the Board's reluctance to endorse *Hawaii Meat,* however, because it is clear to us that the ALJ was amply supported in his finding that petitioner's decision was not motivated by business necessity.[6]

---

**6.** In its line of cases concerning temporary subcontracting during an economic strike, the Board uses the phrase "business necessity" to refer to decisions motivated by the desire to maintain business operations during the course of a strike. See Elliott River Tours, 246 N.L.R.B. at 935; Empire Terminal, 151 N.L.R.B. 1359, 1364–65 (1965), aff'd sub nom. Dallas General Drivers, Local No. 745 v. NLRB, 355 F.2d 842 (D.C.Cir.1966); Shell Oil Co., 149 N.L.R.B. 283, 285 (1964). It is not clear from the Board's decisions where the burden of proof lies on that issue, nor has the Board enunciated a standard of proof. As far as we can tell, for example, it has never held that an employer must meet the burden of demonstrating that defensive measures taken were its only option or that they were the option

The subcontracting at issue in this case took place more than three months after the strike started, and Land Air had successfully operated during that entire period with a mixture of employees from other locations, pre-strike contractors, new employees, and office staff and supervisors. * * *

In the context of the past years of dispute between petitioner and the union over the degree of subcontracting, Land Air's decision to subcontract all of its driving work during the union's ineffective strike hardly looks motivated by business necessity. Rather, it appears that petitioner seized the opportunity it thought legally available to fashion a final solution to the dispute over the use of independent contractors. There is no reason to believe that negotiation with the union over that issue was any more inappropriate or anomalous in March 1985 than it had been in previous years. See American Cyanamid Co. v. NLRB, 592 F.2d 356, 361 (7th Cir.1979)("There has been no showing that this company would have been harmed by negotiating with the union [during a strike] prior to contracting out the maintenance work permanently."). The union could not have at that point, as it could have in *Hawaii Meat,* used manipulative bargaining to stymie Land Air's efforts to maintain operations.

So, we see no need to consider what circumstances would justify an employer's unilateral decision permanently to subcontract bargaining unit work to withstand a strike. Whatever those circumstances arguably might be, they do not exist in this case. Land Air was able to operate at the onset of the strike without permanently contracting out unit work, and there is no evidence that it was unable to continuing [sic] doing so.[8]

* * *

For the foregoing reasons, the petition for review is

Denied.

---

## PROBLEMS FOR DISCUSSION

**1.** Assume that on February 1 the company had approached the union with a demand permanently to subcontract the unit work. What demand or counter-offer would the union be in a position to make? Was the subject "amenable to bargaining" in *Fibreboard* terms?

**2.** Are you persuaded by the distinction between permanent replacement and permanent subcontracting? Was the bargaining unit "destroyed" by thirty-day renewable contracts made with individual drivers characterized as independent contractors, which is what happened in *Land Air Delivery*? Could the union have demanded that thirty-days notice be given to the independent contractors and the

that would have the least adverse effect on the bargaining unit.

**8.** Because the company's unilateral decision to use contractors was illegal under section 8(a)(5), it follows that the use of contractors cannot justify the company's refusal to reinstate the employees. Thus, the Board also was correct to find a violation of section 8(a)(3).

work reallocated to the strikers? In Belknap, Inc. v. Hale, 463 U.S. 491, 103 S.Ct. 3172, 77 L.Ed.2d 798 (1983), the Supreme Court held that the federal Labor Act did not preempt state court actions by displaced "permanent" replacements on theories of breach of contract—the promise not to be displaced in a strike settlement—or fraud. As a result, it may be very costly for an employer to agree to supplant "permanent replacements" with reinstated strikers. Should there be a duty to bargain over permanent replacement?

**3.** If an employer locks out its workforce, may it then permanently subcontract their work after bargaining with the union or can the Board reasonably view this as "inherently destructive" of employee statutory rights? See International Paper Co. v. NLRB, 115 F.3d 1045 (D.C.Cir.1997).

---

# V.  Bargaining Remedies[a]

## H. K. Porter Co. v. NLRB

397 U.S. 99, 90 S.Ct. 821, 25 L.Ed.2d 146 (1970).

■ Mr. Justice Black delivered the opinion of the Court.

After an election respondent United Steelworkers Union was, on October 5, 1961, certified by the National Labor Relations Board as the bargaining agent for certain employees at the Danville, Virginia, plant of the petitioner, H.K. Porter Co. Thereafter negotiations commenced for a collective-bargaining agreement. Since that time the controversy has see-sawed between the Board, the Court of Appeals for the District of Columbia Circuit, and this Court. This delay of over eight years is not because the case is exceedingly complex, but appears to have occurred chiefly because of the skill of the company's negotiators in taking advantage of every opportunity for delay in an act more noticeable for its generality than for its precise prescriptions. The entire lengthy dispute mainly revolves around the union's desire to have the company agree to "check off" the dues owed to the union by its members, that is, to deduct those dues periodically from the company's wage payments to the employees. The record shows, as the Board found, that the company's objection to a checkoff was not due to any general principle or policy against making deductions from employees' wages. The company does deduct charges for things like insurance, taxes, and contributions to charities, and at some other plants it has a checkoff

---

**a.** See J.F. Hunsicker, J. Kane & P. Walther, NLRB Remedies for Unfair Labor Practices (2d ed. 1986); Gross, Cullen & Hanslowe, Good Faith in Labor Negotiations: Tests and Remedies, 53 Cornell L.Rev. 1009 (1968); McCulloch, Past, Present and Future Remedies Under Section 8(a)(5) of the NLRA, 19 Lab.L.J. 131 (1968); D. McDowell & K. Huhn, NLRB Remedies for Unfair Labor Practices (1976); Note, The Use of Section 10(j) of the Labor–Management Relations Act in Employer Refusal-to-Bargain Cases, 1976 U.Ill.L.F. 845 (1976); Morris, The Role of the NLRB and the Courts in the Collective Bargaining Process: A Fresh Look at the Conventional Wisdom and Unconventional Remedies, 30 Vand.L.Rev. 661 (1977); St. Antoine, A Touchstone for Labor Board Remedies, 14 Wayne L.Rev. 1039 (1968).

arrangement for union dues. The evidence shows, and the court below found, that the company's objection was not because of inconvenience, but solely on the ground that the company was "not going to aid and comfort the union." Efforts by the union to obtain some kind of compromise on the checkoff request were all met with the same staccato response to the effect that the collection of union dues was the "union's business" and the company was not going to provide any assistance. Based on this and other evidence the Board found, and the Court of Appeals approved the finding, that the refusal of the company to bargain about the checkoff was not made in good faith, but was done solely to frustrate the making of any collective-bargaining agreement. * * *

[After further negotiations, and proceedings before the Board and the Court of Appeals, the Board ultimately] issued a supplemental order requiring the petitioner to "[g]rant to the Union a contract clause providing for the checkoff of union dues." 172 N.L.R.B. No. 72, 68 L.R.R.M. 1337. The Court of Appeals affirmed this order, H. K. Porter Co. v. NLRB, 134 U.S.App.D.C. 227, 414 F.2d 1123 (1969). We granted certiorari to consider whether the Board in these circumstances has the power to remedy the unfair labor practice by requiring the company to agree to check off the dues of the workers. 396 U.S. 817, 90 S.Ct. 79, 24 L.Ed.2d 68. For reasons to be stated we hold that while the Board does have power under the National Labor Relations Act, 61 Stat. 136, as amended, to require employers and employees to negotiate, it is without power to compel a company or a union to agree to any substantive contractual provision of a collective-bargaining agreement.

* * *

The object of this Act was not to allow governmental regulation of the terms and conditions of employment, but rather to ensure that employers and their employees could work together to establish mutually satisfactory conditions. The basic theme of the Act was that through collective bargaining the passions, arguments, and struggles of prior years would be channeled into constructive, open discussions leading, it was hoped, to mutual agreement. But it was recognized from the beginning that agreement might in some cases be impossible, and it was never intended that the Government would in such cases step in, become a party to the negotiations and impose its own views of a desirable settlement. * * *

In discussing the effect of [the addition of Section 8(d) in 1947], this Court said it is "clear that the Board may not, either directly or indirectly, compel concessions or otherwise sit in judgment upon the substantive terms of collective bargaining agreements." NLRB v. American Ins. Co., 343 U.S. 395, 404, 72 S.Ct. 824, 829, 96 L.Ed. 1027 (1952). Later this Court affirmed that view stating that "it remains clear that § 8(d) was an attempt by Congress to prevent the Board from controlling the settling of the terms of collective bargaining agreements." NLRB v. Insurance Agents', 361 U.S. 477, 487, 80 S.Ct. 419, 4 L.Ed.2d 454 (1960). The parties to the instant case are agreed that this is the first time in the 35–year history of the Act that the Board has ordered either an employer or a union to agree to a substantive term of a collective-bargaining agreement.

Recognizing the fundamental principle "that the National Labor Relations Act is grounded on the premise of freedom of contract," 128 U.S.App. D.C., at 349, 389 F.2d, at 300, the Court of Appeals in this case concluded that nevertheless in the circumstances presented here the Board could properly compel the employer to agree to a proposed checkoff clause. The Board had found that the refusal was based on a desire to frustrate agreement and not on any legitimate business reason. On the basis of that finding the Court of Appeals approved the further finding that the employer had not bargained in good faith, and the validity of that finding is not now before us. Where the record thus revealed repeated refusals by the employer to bargain in good faith on this issue, the Court of Appeals concluded that ordering agreement to the checkoff clause "may be the only means of assuring the Board, and the court, that [the employer] no longer harbors an illegal intent." 128 U.S.App.D.C., at 348, 389 F.2d at 299.

In reaching this conclusion the Court of Appeals held that § 8(d) did not forbid the Board from compelling agreement. That court felt that "[s]ection 8(d) defines collective bargaining and relates to a determination of whether a * * * violation has occurred and not to the scope of the remedy which may be necessary to cure violations which have already occurred." 128 U.S.App.D.C., at 348, 389 F.2d, at 299. We may agree with the Court of Appeals that as a matter of strict, literal interpretation that section refers only to deciding when a violation has occurred, but we do not agree that that observation justifies the conclusion that the remedial powers of the Board are not also limited by the same considerations that led Congress to enact § 8(d). It is implicit in the entire structure of the Act that the Board acts to oversee and referee the process of collective bargaining, leaving the results of the contest to the bargaining strengths of the parties. It would be anomalous indeed to hold that while § 8(d) prohibits the Board from relying on a refusal to agree as the sole evidence of bad-faith bargaining, the Act permits the Board to compel agreement in that same dispute. The Board's remedial powers under § 10 of the Act are broad, but they are limited to carrying out the policies of the Act itself. One of these fundamental policies is freedom of contract. While the parties' freedom of contract is not absolute under the Act, allowing the Board to compel agreement when the parties themselves are unable to agree would violate the fundamental premise on which the Act is based—private bargaining under governmental supervision of the procedure alone, without any official compulsion over the actual terms of the contract.

* * * It may well be true, as the Court of Appeals felt, that the present remedial powers of the Board are insufficiently broad to cope with important labor problems. But it is the job of Congress, not the Board or the courts, to decide when and if it is necessary to allow governmental review of proposals for collective-bargaining agreements and compulsory submission to one side's demands. The present Act does not envision such a process.

The judgment is reversed and the case is remanded to the Court of Appeals for further action consistent with this opinion.

Reversed and remanded.

Mr. Justice White took no part in the decision of this case.

Mr. Justice Marshall took no part in the consideration or decision of this case.

Mr. Justice Harlan, concurring. * * *

■ Mr. Justice Douglas, with whom Mr. Justice Stewart concurs, dissenting: * * *

[T]he Board has the power, where one party does not bargain in good faith, "to take such affirmative action * * * as will effectuate the policies" of the Act. * * *

Here the employer did not refuse the checkoff for any business reason, whether cost, inconvenience, or what not. Nor did the employer refuse the checkoff as a factor in its bargaining strategy, hoping that delay and denial might bring it in exchange favorable terms and conditions. Its reason was a resolve to avoid reaching any agreement with the union.

In those narrow and specialized circumstances, I see no answer to the power of the Board in its discretion to impose the checkoff as "affirmative action" necessary to remedy the flagrant refusal of the employer to bargain in good faith.

The case is rare, if not unique, and will seldom arise. * * *

---

## PROBLEMS FOR DISCUSSION

**1.** Was the employer well advised not to challenge the Board's finding that it had bargained in bad faith? Was that finding consistent with the federal policy most strongly emphasized by the Supreme Court, that is, the policy of non-interference by the federal government in setting the substantive terms of the labor contract? Is it an unfair labor practice for either party to insist on a position for which it has no "need"? Need *any* reason be adduced for a bargaining position if the proponent is simply strong enough to back that position with economic strength?

**2.** With the refusal-to-bargain finding now sustained in the *Porter* case, and the checkoff order overturned, what order *is* to issue against the Porter Company? Whatever the order is to be, would not a refusal by the Company to incorporate a checkoff provision be a violation of the order, so that the same issue of Board power would arise once more?

**3.** The Company and the Union reached tentative agreement on a package of Company proposals. The Company then withdrew these proposals which withdrawal the Labor Board finds to constitute bargaining in bad faith. May the Board order the Company to implement the proposals retroactive to a date when it concludes an agreement would have been made? See TNT USA, Inc. v. NLRB, 208 F.3d 362 (2d Cir.2000).

**4.** After an election among the over-the-road drivers employed by the American Manufacturing Company of Texas, the Teamsters were certified as the bargaining representative. Within the week, the company posted a notice that it had negotiated an agreement of sale of its trucks, that henceforth the company's products would be transported by an independent trucking firm, and that all of its drivers were immediately laid off. The Board sustained the union's charge of a Section 8(a)(5) violation, and ordered not only that the employer cease and desist from refusing to bargain and that it bargain with the union, but also that it resume trucking operations and offer reinstatement and backpay to all of the drivers laid off. American Manufacturing is a small firm, and the evidence indicates that it would cost the Company $250,000 to purchase a new fleet of trucks. It also appears that the Company has found it more economical to hire the outside firm than to transport its own products. Should the court enforce the order of reinstitution, reinstatement and backpay? *Compare* Naperville Ready Mix, Inc. v. NLRB, 242 F.3d 744 (7th Cir.2001), *with* NLRB v. American Mfg. Co., 351 F.2d 74 (5th Cir.1965). Would your analysis differ if American had not sold the trucks but had instead leased them to an independent hauler and laid off its own drivers? *Cf.* Kronenberger d/b/a American Needle & Novelty Co. v. Cap Makers Union, 206 NLRB 534 (1973).

Is your analysis of the Board's remedial order different from what it would be had the Company's termination of its drivers been for discriminatory reasons, in retaliation for their having selected a union?

---

# Ex–Cell–O Corporation[b]

185 NLRB 107 (1970).

[The United Automobile Workers requested recognition on August 3, 1964, but the Ex–Cell–O Corporation refused the request and the union petitioned for an election, which was held on October 22. The union won the election, but the company filed objections (regarding alleged union misrepresentations) which were overruled by the Acting Regional Director. The Board granted the company's request for review of that decision, which was ultimately affirmed by the Board on October 28, 1965, and the union was certified. The company informed the union that it would not bargain, as a means of securing court review of the Board's action, and a hearing on the union's charge under Sections 8(a)(1) and (5) was commenced on June 1, 1966. After an unsuccessful company attempt to secure an injunction against the Regional Director and the Trial Examiner, the latter closed the hearing on December 21, 1966 and issued his decision on March 2, 1967. The Trial Examiner found a refusal to bargain and recommended that a cease-and-desist order issue and that the company be directed to make its employees whole for any monetary losses suffered on account of the company's unlawful refusal. The Board granted the company's request for

**b.** See McGuiness, Is the Award of Damages for Refusals to Bargain Consistent With National Labor Policy?, 14 Wayne L.Rev. 1086 (1968); Schlossberg & Silard, The Need for a Compensatory Remedy in Refusal-to-Bargain Cases, 14 Wayne L.Rev. 1059 (1968).

review as well as for oral argument, consolidated the *Ex–Cell–O* case with three cases raising similar issues, and invited briefs *amicus curiae* and participation in oral argument (in July 1967) by such organizations as the Chamber of Commerce of the United States, the National Association of Manufacturers, the AFL–CIO, the Teamsters and the NAACP Legal Defense Fund. The Board rendered its decision on August 25, 1970, in which it adopted the findings, conclusions and recommendations of the Trial Examiner as significantly modified in the opinion below.]

■ It is not disputed that Respondent refused to bargain with the Union, and we hereby affirm the Trial Examiner's conclusion that Respondent thereby violated Section 8(a)(1) and (5) of the Act. The compensatory remedy which he recommends, however, raises important issues concerning the Board's powers and duties to fashion appropriate remedies in its efforts to effectuate the policies of the National Labor Relations Act.

It is argued that such a remedy exceeds the Board's general statutory powers. In addition, it is contended that it cannot be granted because the amount of employee loss, if any, is so speculative that an order to make employees whole would amount to the imposition of a penalty. And the position is advanced that the adoption of this remedy would amount to the writing of a contract for the parties, which is prohibited by Section 8(d).

We have given most serious consideration to the Trial Examiner's recommended financial reparations Order, and are in complete agreement with his finding that current remedies of the Board designed to cure violations of Section 8(a)(5) are inadequate. A mere affirmative order that an employer bargain upon request does not eradicate the effects of an unlawful delay of 2 or more years in the fulfillment of a statutory bargaining obligation. It does not put the employees in the position of bargaining strength they would have enjoyed if their employer had immediately recognized and bargained with their chosen representative. It does not dissolve the inevitable employee frustration or protect the Union from the loss of employee support attributable to such delay. The inadequacy of the remedy is all the more egregious where, as in the recent N.L.R.B. v. Tiidee Products, Inc., case, the court found that the employer had raised "frivolous" issues in order to postpone or avoid its lawful obligation to bargain. We have weighed these considerations most carefully. For the reasons stated below, however, we have reluctantly concluded that we cannot approve the Trial Examiner's Recommended Order that Respondent compensate its employees for monetary losses incurred as a consequence of Respondent's determination to refuse to bargain until it had tested in court the validity of the Board's certification.

Section 10(c) of the Act directs the Board to order a person found to have committed an unfair labor practice to cease and desist and "to take such affirmative action including reinstatement of employees with or without back pay, as will effectuate the policies of this Act." This authority, as our colleagues note with full documentation, is extremely broad and was so intended by Congress. It is not so broad, however, as to permit the punishment of a particular respondent or a class of respondents. Nor is the statutory direction to the Board so compelling that the Board is without discretion in exercising the full sweep of its power, for it would defeat the purposes of the Act if the Board imposed an otherwise proper remedy that resulted in irreparable harm to a particular respondent and hampered rather than promoted meaningful collective bargaining. Moreover, as the Supreme Court recently emphasized, the Board's grant of power does not extend to compelling agreement. (H.K. Porter Co., Inc. v. N.L.R.B., 397 U.S. 99.) It is with respect to these three limitations upon the Board's power to remedy a violation of Section 8(a)(5) that we examine the UAW's requested remedy in this case.

The Trial Examiner concluded that the proposed remedy was not punitive, that it merely made the employees partially whole for losses occasioned by the Respondent's refusal to bargain, and was much less harsh than a backpay order for discharged employees, which might require the Respondent to pay wages to these employees as well as their replacements. Viewed solely in the context of an assumption of employee monetary losses resulting directly from the Respondent's violation of Section 8(a)(5), as finally determined in court, the Trial Examiner's conclusion appears reasonable. There are, however, other factors in this case which provide counterweights to that rationale. In the first place, there is no contention that this Respondent acted in a manner flagrantly in defiance of the statutory policy. On the contrary, the record indicates that this Respondent responsibly fulfills [sic] its legally established collective-bargaining obligations. It is clear that Respondent merely sought judicial affirmance of the Board's decision that the election of October 22, 1964, should not be set aside on the Respondent's objections. In the past, whenever an employer has sought court intervention in a representation proceeding the Board has argued forcefully that court intervention would be premature, that the employer had an unquestioned right under the statute to seek court review of any Board order before its bargaining obligation became final. Should this procedural right in 8(a)(5) cases be tempered by a large monetary liability in the event the employer's position in the representation case is ultimately found to be without merit? Of course, an employer or a union which engages in conduct later found in violation of the Act, does so at the peril of ultimate conviction and responsibility for a make-whole remedy. But the validity of a particular Board election tried in an unfair labor practice case is not, in our opinion, an issue on the same plane as the discharge of employees for union activity or other conduct in flagrant disregard of employee rights. There are wrongdoers and wrongdoers. Where the wrong in refusing to bargain is, at most, a debatable question, though ultimately found a wrong, the imposition of a large financial obligation on such a respondent may come close to a form of punishment for having elected to pursue a representation question beyond the Board and to the courts. * * *

In *Tiidee Products* the court suggested that the Board need not follow a uniform policy in the application of a compensatory remedy in 8(a)(5) cases. Indeed, the court noted that such uniformity in this area of the law would be unfair when applied "to unlike cases." The court was of the opinion that the remedy was proper where the employer had engaged in a "manifestly unjustifiable refusal to bargain" and where its position was "palpably without merit."[7] * * * [T]he court in *Tiidee Products* distinguished those cases in which the employer's failure to bargain rested on a "debatable question." With due respect for the opinion of the Court of Appeals for the District of Columbia, we cannot agree that the application of a compensatory remedy in 8(a)(5) cases can be fashioned on the subjective determination that the position of one respondent is "debatable" while that of another is "frivolous." What is debatable to the Board may appear frivolous to a court, and vice versa. Thus, the debatability of the employer's position in an 8(a)(5) case would itself become a matter of intense litigation. * * *

It is argued that the instant case is distinguishable from *H.K. Porter* in that here the requested remedy merely would require an employer to compensate employees for losses they incurred as a consequence of their employer's *failure to agree* to a contract he *would* have agreed to *if* he had bargained in good faith. In our view, the distinction is more illusory than real. The remedy in *H.K. Porter* operates prospectively to bind an employer to a specific contractual term. The remedy in the instant case operates retroactively to impose financial liability upon an employer flowing from a *presumed* contractual agreement. The Board infers that the latter contract, though it never existed and does not and need not exist, was *denied* existence by the employer because of his refusal to bargain. In either case the employer has not agreed to the contractual provision for which he must accept full responsibility *as though he had agreed to it*. Our colleagues contend that a compensatory remedy is not the "writing of a contract" because it does not "specify new or continuing terms of employment and does not prohibit changes in existing terms and conditions." But there is no basis for such a remedy unless the Board finds, as a matter of fact, that a contract would have resulted from bargaining. The fact that the contract, so to speak, is "written in the air" does not diminish its financial impact upon the recalcitrant employer who, willy-nilly, is forced to accede to terms never mutually established by the parties. Despite the admonition of the Supreme Court that Section 8(d) was intended to mean what it says, i.e., that the obligation to bargain "does not compel either party to agree to a proposal or require the making of a concession," one of the parties under this remedy is forced by the Government to submit to the other side's demands. It does not help to argue that the remedy could not be applied unless there was substantial evidence that the employer would have yielded to these demands during bargaining negotiations. Who is to say in a specific case how much an employer is prepared to give and how much a union is willing to take? Who is to say that a favorable contract would, in any event, result from the negotiations? And it is only the employer of such good will as to whom the Board might conclude that he, at least, would have given

---

**7.** In these cases, at least, it would seem incumbent on the Board to utilize to the fullest extent its authority under Sec. 10(j) and (e) of the Act, thereby minimizing the pernicious delay in collective bargaining and consequent loss of benefits to the employees affected. See also Justice Harlan's concurrence in *H.K. Porter,* supra.

his employees a fair increase, who can be made subject to a financial reparations order; should such an employer be singled out for the imposition of such an order? To answer these questions the Board would be required to engage in the most general, if not entirely speculative, inferences, to reach the conclusion that employees were deprived of specific benefits as a consequence of their employer's refusal to bargain.

Much as we appreciate the need for more adequate remedies in 8(a)(5) cases, we believe that, as the law now stands, the proposed remedy is a matter for Congress, not the Board. In our opinion, however, substantial relief may be obtained immediately through procedural reform, giving the highest possible priority to 8(a)(5) cases combined with full resort to the injunctive relief provisions of Section 10(j) and (e) of the Act.

\* \* \*

■ Members McCulloch and Brown, dissenting in part:

Although concurring in all other respects in the Decision and Order of the Board, we part company with our colleagues on the majority in that we would grant the compensatory remedy recommended by the Trial Examiner. Unlike our colleagues, we believe that the Board has the statutory authority to direct such relief and that it would effectuate the policies of the Act to do so in this case. \* \* \*

The Board has already recognized in certain refusal-to-bargain situations that the usual bargaining order is not sufficient to expunge the effects of an employer's unlawful and protracted denial of its employees' right to bargain. Though the bargaining order serves to remedy the loss of legal right and protect its exercise in the future, it does not remedy the financial injury which may also have been suffered. In a number of situations the Board has ordered the employer who unlawfully refused to bargain to compensate its employees for their resultant financial losses. Thus, some employers unlawfully refuse to sign after an agreement. The Board has in these cases ordered the employer to execute the agreement previously reached and, according to its terms, to make whole the employees for the monetary losses suffered because of the unlawful delay in its effectuation.

Similarly, in *American Fire Apparatus Co.*, the employer violated Section 8(a)(5) by unilaterally discontinuing payment of Christmas bonuses, and the Board concluded that only by requiring the bonuses to be paid could the violation be fully remedied.

\* \* \* And in *Fibreboard Paper Products Corp.*, the employer unilaterally contracted out its maintenance operations in violation of Section 8(a)(5). The Board concluded that an order to bargain about this decision could not, by itself, adequately remedy the effects of the violation. It further ordered the employer to reinstate the employees and to make them whole for any loss of earnings suffered on account of the unlawful conduct. The Supreme Court upheld the compensatory remedy, and stated that "There has been no showing that the Board's order restoring the *status quo ante* to insure meaningful bargaining is not well designed to promote the policies of the Act." \* \* \*

The present case is but another example of a situation where a bargaining order by itself is not really adequate to remedy the effects of an unlawful refusal to bargain. The Union herein requested recognition on August 3, 1964, and proved that it represented a majority of employees 2½ months later in a Board-conducted election. Nonetheless, since October 1965 the employer, by unlawfully refusing to bargain with the Union, has deprived its employees of their legal right to collective bargaining through their certified bargaining representative.[50] While a bargaining order at this time, operating prospectively, may insure the exercise of that right in the future, it clearly does not repair the injury to the employees here, caused by the Respondent's denial of their rights during the past 5 years.

In these refusal-to-bargain cases there is at least a legal injury. Potential employee losses incurred by an employer's refusal to bargain in violation of the Act are not limited to financial matters such as wages. Thus, it is often the case that the most important employee gains arrived at through collective bargaining involve such benefits as seniority, improved physical facilities, a better grievance procedure, or a right to arbitration. Therefore, even the remedy we would direct herein is not complete, limited as it is to only some of the monetary losses which may be measured or estimated. The employees would not be made whole for all the losses incurred through the employer's unfair labor practice. But, where the legal

---

**50.** We find no merit in the Respondent's contention in the present case that, at least in a "technical" refusal-to-bargain situation, a compensatory remedy would penalize it for obtaining judicial review of the Board's representation proceedings. In Consolo v. Federal Maritime Commission, supra at 624–625, the Court rejected the same contention. Relying on a case involving the Board (NLRB v. Electric Vacuum Cleaner Company, Inc., 315 U.S. 685), the Court concluded that "At any rate it has never been the law that a litigant is absolved from liability for that time during which his litigation is pending" (Id. at 624–625) and noted (at 625) that the time of appeal allowed the respondent to continue its unlawful conduct [and] thus in turn [to] continue to injure the petitioner. That such a remedy would include the entire amount lost by the wronged party, instead of being reduced by the amount accruing while the violator was contesting the issue, no more makes the remedy penal in character under this Act than it does elsewhere. "The litigant must pay for his experience, like others who have tried and lost." Life & Casualty Ins. Co. v. McCray, 291 U.S. 566, 575.

There is no question of the right of an employer to test the legal propriety of a Board certification or to test its legal position respecting any issue of law or fact upon which a Board bargaining order is predicated: but it should not thereby realize benefits not usually flowing from such a proceeding. In other words, should an employer choose to await court action, and if its legal position be sustained, it would not only be absolved of the duty to bargain, but also of any monetary remedy arising out of the order contemplated herein; if, on the other hand, an employer be found to have rested its refusal to bargain on an erroneous view of law or fact, any loss to employees incurred by its continued adherence to that error should be borne by that employer and not by its employees. That is the risk taken by all litigants.

The employer's argument for tolling the compensatory period during the time he contests the violation is contrary to the policy of the Act in fostering the prompt commencement of collective bargaining, a policy shown explicitly in the denial of judicial review of the Board's representation proceedings. To allow the employer to avoid making his employees whole for the period bargaining was delayed by his litigating a mistaken view of the law would encourage such delay in the areas in which Congress particularly deemed speed to be essential.

injury is accompanied by financial loss, the employees should be compensated for it. * * *

This type of compensatory remedy is in no way forbidden by Section 8(d).[54] It would be designed to compensate employees for injuries incurred by them by virtue of the unfair labor practices and would not require the employer to accept the measure of compensation as a term of any contract which might result from subsequent collective bargaining. The remedy contemplated in no way "writes a contract" between the employer and the union, for it would not specify new or continuing terms of employment and would not prohibit changes in existing terms and conditions. All of these would be left to the outcome of bargaining, the commencement of which would terminate Respondent's liability.

Furthermore, this compensatory remedy is not a punitive measure. It would be designed to do no more than reimburse the employees for the loss occasioned by the deprivation of their right to be represented by their collective-bargaining agent during the period of the violation. The amount to be awarded would be only that which would reasonably reflect and be measured by the loss caused by the unlawful denial of the opportunity for collective bargaining. * * * Accordingly, as the reimbursement order sought herein is meant to enforce public policy, the Board's exercise of its discretion in ordering such a remedy would not be strictly confined to the same considerations which govern comparable awards in either equity courts or damage awards in legal actions. In the first place, it is well established that, where the defendant's wrongful act prevents exact determination of the amount of damage, he cannot plead such uncertainty in order to deny relief to the injured person, but rather must bear the risk of the uncertainty which was created by his own wrong. The Board is often faced with the task of determining the precise amount of a make-whole order where the criteria are less than ideal, and has successfully resolved the questions presented.[62]

---

**54.** The provision in Sec. 8(d) that neither party is required to agree to a proposal or make a concession appears to have been designed not for the situation before us, but to preclude the Board from evaluating "the merits of the provisions of the parties" as a factor in determining whether bargaining was in good faith. House Conference Report, Legislative History, p. 538.

**62.** The problem most frequently arises when we must determine the amount of backpay due to unlawfully discharged employees. As we recently stated in connection with this issue (The Buncher Company, 164 NLRB 340, enfd. 405 F.2d 787 (C.A.3)):

In solving many of the problems which arise in backpay cases, the Board occasionally is required to adopt formulas which result in backpay determinations that are close approximations because no better basis exists for determining the exact amount due. However, the fact that the exact amount due is incalculable is no justification for permitting the Respondent to escape completely his legal obligation to compensate the victims of his discriminatory actions for the loss of earnings which they suffered. In general, courts have acknowledged that in solving such backpay problems, the Board is vested with wide discretion in devising procedures and methods which will effectuate the purposes of the Act and has generally limited its review to whether a method selected was "arbitrary or unreasonable in the circumstances involved," or whether in determining the amount, a "rational basis" was utilized.

But even if a reimbursement order were judged by legal or equitable principles regarding damages, the remedy would not be speculative. It is well established that the rule which precludes recovery of "uncertain damages" refers to uncertainty as to the fact of injury, rather than to the amount. Where, as here, the employer has deprived its employees of a statutory right, there is by definition a legal injury suffered by them, and any uncertainty concerns only the amount of the accompanying reimbursable financial loss. * * *

Accordingly, uncertainty as to the amount of loss does not preclude a make-whole order proposed here, and some reasonable method or basis of computation can be worked out as part of the compliance procedure. These cannot be defined in advance, but there are many methods for determining the measurable financial gain which the employees might reasonably have expected to achieve, had the Respondent fulfilled its statutory obligation to bargain collectively. The criteria which prove valid in each case must be determined by what is pertinent to the facts. Nevertheless, the following methods for measuring such loss do appear to be available, although these are neither exhaustive nor exclusive. Thus, if the particular employer and union involved have contracts covering other plants of the employer, possibly in the same or a relevant area, the terms of such agreements may serve to show what the employees could probably have obtained by bargaining. The parties could also make comparisons with compensation patterns achieved through collective bargaining by other employees in the same geographic area and industry. Or the parties might employ the national average percentage changes in straight time hourly wages computed by the Bureau of Labor Statistics. * * *

In the instant case, as noted above, a *prima facie* showing of loss can readily be made out by measuring the wage and benefit increments that were negotiated for employees at Respondent's other organized plants against those given employees in this bargaining unit during the period of Respondent's unlawful refusal to bargain. Granted that the task of determining loss may be more difficult in other cases where no similar basis for comparison exists, this is not reason enough for the Board to shirk its statutory responsibilities, and no reason at all for it to do so in a case such as this where that difficulty is not present. * * *

---

Following the Board's *Ex-Cell-O* decision, the UAW petitioned the Court of Appeals for the District of Columbia Circuit for review of the Board's decision not to award monetary compensation. In International Union, UAW v. NLRB, 449 F.2d 1046 (D.C.Cir.1971), the court reproved the Board for rejecting that court's decision in *Tiidee Products*. The court remanded the case to the Board for "express determinations whether Ex-Cell-O's objections to the certification were frivolous or fairly debatable, and whether 'make-whole' compensation or some other special remedy is appropriate." The court rejected the Board's argument that the Board and the courts would be unable to agree on what was "frivolous" litigation, and stated that "courts should accord the usual latitude to the Board" in determining whether litigation was as a matter of fact frivolous. However, before the Board had an opportunity to decide *Ex–Cell–O* on remand, the court of appeals issued a separate decision on the employer's petition for review of the Board's bargaining order. Ex–Cell–O Corp. v. NLRB, 449 F.2d 1058 (D.C.Cir.1971). Enforcing the Board's order, the court conducted an independent evaluation of the record and concluded that the employer's objections were, in fact, "fairly debatable" and that therefore a compensatory award was inappropriate. Thus, six and one-half years after the election, the court enforced the Board's order that the employer bargain with the union that won that election.

Meanwhile, the Board wrestled with the *Tiidee* case on remand. It acknowledged that the decision of the court of appeals was the law of the case but concluded that it could not construct from the evidence the contract to which the parties would have agreed had the employer promptly bargained. Thus, it was impossible to calculate a compensatory award. Instead, the Board, noting the flagrant employer violations of the Act, ordered the employer to pay to the Board and the union the costs of litigation, to mail a copy of the Board-ordered notice to each employee, to give the union access to company bulletin boards, and to supply the union with an up-to-date list of employee names and addresses. TIIDEE PRODS., INC., 194 NLRB 1234 (1972). The Court of Appeals granted enforcement (except for reimbursement of the Board's litigation expenses), finding that the Board's inability to calculate a make-whole remedy was an adequate reason for not doing so. The court also found that the Board had used its expert and informed discretion to balance the difficulties of computation against the "relative ease and certainty" of calculating the costs of litigation. International Union of Elec., Radio and Mach. Workers AFL–CIO v. NLRB, 502 F.2d 349 (D.C.Cir.1974), cert. denied, Tiidee Products, Inc. v. NLRB, 421 U.S. 991, 95 S.Ct. 1997, 44 L.Ed.2d 481 (1975).

---

# PROBLEMS FOR DISCUSSION

**1.** Do you agree with the views of the majority of the Board or the dissenting members in the *Ex-Cell-O* case? In appraising those views, consider how you would reconstruct the agreement that the parties would have reached had the Company promptly bargained after the certification. The chart on the following page compares the terms and conditions obtaining at the Ex–Cell–O plant in Elwood, Indiana, at which the refusal-to-bargain occurred, and those obtaining under labor contracts at other Ex–Cell–O plants. (Interestingly, California's Agricultural Labor Relations Act expressly provides for "make whole" relief in refusal-to-bargain cases. See generally George Arakelian Farms, Inc. v. ALRB, 49 Cal.3d 1279, 265 Cal.Rptr. 162, 783 P.2d 749 (1989).)

**2.** The Court of Appeals for the District of Columbia was willing to limit the "make-whole" order to the case of the "flagrant" refusal to bargain (as opposed to the case of the employer seeking to secure judicial review of "debatable" challenges to the union's status). Is this distinction a sound one?

**3.**  If a company, that had engaged in a pattern of unfair labor practices, increases the wages of its non-union workforce by 5.5%, but bargains with its unionized workforce for no more than a 4.5% increase, may the Board order a 1% wage increase as a remedy? *See* Fieldcrest Cannon, Inc. v. NLRB, 97 F.3d 65 (4th Cir.1996).

| | ELWOOD, INDIANA Employee Handbook (Revised 5-63) | BLUFFTON, OHIO 4-3-65 Agreement | LIMA, OHIO 4-1-65 Agreement | FOSTORIA, OHIO 4-1-65 Agreement | TRAVERSE CITY, MICH. 5-8-65 Agreement | DETROIT, MICH. 4-1-55 Agreement |
|---|---|---|---|---|---|---|
| Shift Premium | Afternoon $.12 Midnight $.16 | Same | Same | Same | Afternoon $.15 Midnight $.20 | Afternoon $.16 Midnight $.20 |
| Overtime | Daily, time and one half up to 10 hrs. and up to 8 hrs. on Saturdays. Double time for the excess and for Sundays and Holidays. | Same | Same | Same | Same | Same |
| Holidays | 7 (8 in 1965 or 1966 (Tr. 181)) | 9 | 9 | 9 | 8 (9 in 1966) | 8 (9 in 1966) |
| Vacations | Year's Serv. / Hrs. Pay / Days off<br>1 / 40 / 5<br>3 / 60 / 7<br>5 / 80 / 10<br>10 / 100 / 12 | Year's Serv. / Pay / Days off<br>1 / 2%** / 5<br>3 / 2.8% / 7<br>5 / 4% / 10<br>10 / 5% / 12 | Same as Bluffton | Year's Serv. / Hrs. Pay / Days off<br>1 / 40 / 5<br>3 / 60 / 7<br>5 / 80 / 10<br>10 / 100 / 12<br>15 / 120 / 15 | Year's Serv. / Pay / Days off<br>1 / 2.5% / 5<br>3 / 3.5% / 5<br>5 / 5.5% / 10<br>10 / 6% / 12<br>15 / 7% / 15 | Same as Fostoria |
| Deferred Pay Plan | Additional $.05 per hour, payable on layoff, leave of absence, termination or retirement. | None | None | None | None | None |
| Hospital & Surgical Insurance | Co. pays 75%*** | Co. pays all, incl. after retirement. | Same | Same | Same | Same |
| Group Life Insurance | $4500 | $6000 | Same | Same | $6500 | $7000 |
| Accidental Death | 2250 | 3000 | Same | Same | 3250 | 3500 |
| Sickness & Accident Benefit | $40.25–45.50 per week | $60.00 per week | $50–65 per week | $50–65 per week | $65 per week | $70 per week |
| Bereavement Pay | No mention | Yes | Same | Same | Same | Same |
| Automatic Cost-of-living Adjustment | No mention | Yes | Same | Same | Same | Same |
| Supplemental Unemployment Benefits | No (TR. 182) | Yes | Same | Same | Same | Same |

\* Same as in column to the left.
\*\* Percent of past year's earnings.
\*\*\* Co. subsequently absorbed a cost increase.

# PART FOUR

# Strikes, Picketing and Boycotts

As already noted in the historical materials, supra, peaceful strikes, picketing and boycotts were commonly outlawed in the state courts through judicially developed principles of tort, and to a significant degree by federal courts under the antitrust laws. A gradual appreciation by state courts and legislatures, and by Congress, of the interests of workers led to a retreat from legal intervention in the 1920s and 1930s. Peaceful concerted activity was sheltered against antitrust remedies, principally through enactment and hospitable construction of the Norris–LaGuardia Act of 1932. Shelter against employer coercion and discrimination was provided by the Wagner Act of 1935. The 1940 decision of the Supreme Court in Thornhill v. Alabama, at page 73, supra, appeared to give constitutionally protected status to peaceful picketing as a form of free speech.

By 1947, however, Congress concluded that certain peaceful union pressure had been used abusively and should be outlawed through the Taft–Hartley Act itemizing a number of union unfair labor practices. The Supreme Court retreated from the broadest ramifications of *Thornhill,* so that much federal and state regulation of union activities was now immune from constitutional attack under the First and Fourteenth Amendments. The 1959 Landrum–Griffin Act expanded the congressional limits on those activities.

In sum, the federal Labor Act reflects an elaborate regulatory policy— in part protecting peaceful concerted activity against governmental restrictions or employer retaliation, in part outlawing it, and in part leaving both union and employer to rely upon economic force and counter-force. How the law should regulate the economic weapons of the parties is an issue of major significance in our jurisprudence. At one level, the availability or outlawry of economic force determines in large measure the substantive outcome of a labor-management dispute. At a more general level, it enhances or restricts the amount of individual and group freedom to promote one's economic interests, the kind of freedom that our society often elevates to constitutionally protected status.

The materials that follow deal with three major issues: (1) The limitations imposed by the NLRA upon the employer's right to discipline or otherwise interfere with employees who engage in concerted activities; (2) the constitutional limitations, if any, on the power of the state and federal governments to regulate strikes, picketing and boycotts; and (3) the legality of these concerted activities under the Act.

## I.   Rights of Employee Protesters Under the NLRA

### A.   Protected and Unprotected Concerted Activity[a]

Although, as will be seen below, certain union-inspired group pressures are outlawed, there is a wide range of forms of worker protest that are neither union-inspired nor violations of Section 8(b). In such cases, employees are less concerned with Board remedies than they are with the employer's own remedies of self-help, the most serious being discharge from employment. Although the Wagner Act was primarily aimed at guaranteeing employees the rights to form, join and assist labor organizations and to bargain collectively through representatives of their own choosing, Section 7 also guarantees "the right to engage in other concerted activities for the purpose of collective bargaining or other mutual aid or protection * * *." Section 8(a)(1) prohibits employer action which coerces, restrains or interferes with the exercise of this right. Section 8(a)(3) also outlaws employer discouragement of union membership—which has been broadly construed to encompass concerted activity protected by Section 7 in support of a labor organization—which is accomplished by "discrimination."

When employees engage in concerted activity and the employer takes some responsive action, two sorts of questions arise: First, what kinds of activities in which employees engage are protected by Section 7? Second, given employee action which is protected concerted activity, does Section 8(a)(1) or (3) make any employer act which discourages it unfair and unlawful, or only those acts which interfere "unduly" or "unreasonably" or

---

**a.**   See J. Atleson, Values and Assumptions in American Labor Law, chaps. 3 and 5 (1983); Cantor, Dissident Worker Action, After *The Emporium*, 29 Rutgers L.Rev. 35 (1975); Cox, The Right to Engage in Concerted Activities, 26 Ind.L.J. 319 (1951); Estlund, What Do Workers Want? Employee Interests, Public Interests, and Freedom of Expression Under the National Labor Relations Act, 140 U. Pa. L.Rev. 921 (1992); Finkin, Labor Law by Boz—A Theory of *Meyers Industries, Inc., Sears, Roebuck & Co.*, and *Bird Engineering*, 71 Iowa L.Rev. 155 (1985); Getman, The Protection of Economic Pressure by Section 7 of the National Labor Relations Act, 115 U.Pa. L.Rev. 1195 (1967); Schatzki, Some Observations and Suggestions Concerning a Misnomer—"Protected" Concerted Activities, 47 Texas L.Rev. 378 (1969).

"without justification"? If the latter, is it for the Board or the courts to strike the balance? These two questions will be considered in order in this and the following section of the casebook.

As the language of Section 7 makes rather clear on its face, it is not necessary to have a union sponsoring concerted activity, or anywhere on the scene, in order that such activity be protected as "concerted activities for * * * mutual aid or protection." In NLRB v. WASHINGTON ALUMINUM CO., 370 U.S. 9, 82 S.Ct. 1099, 8 L.Ed.2d 298 (1962), the Supreme Court held that employees who had staged a spontaneous walkout because they believed it was too cold to continue to work had engaged in protected activity, even though they were not unionized or seeking to unionize and they had not presented any specific demand to their employer. The Court therefore found their discharge to violate Section 8(a)(1). Nonetheless, activity to be protected against discharge must be "concerted" and must be designed to advance the employees' "mutual aid or protection." What do these terms mean? Are they meant to confine the protections afforded by the statute, as well as to expand them?

----

## NLRB v. City Disposal Systems, Inc.[b]

465 U.S. 822, 104 S.Ct. 1505, 79 L.Ed.2d 839 (1984).

■ JUSTICE BRENNAN delivered the opinion of the Court.

James Brown, a truck driver employed by respondent, was discharged when he refused to drive a truck that he honestly and reasonably believed to be unsafe because of faulty brakes. Article XXI of the collective-bargaining agreement between respondent and Local 247 of the International Brotherhood of Teamsters, Chauffeurs, Warehousemen and Helpers of America, which covered Brown, provides:

> "[t]he Employer shall not require employees to take out on the streets or highways any vehicle that is not in safe operating condition or equipped with safety appliances prescribed by law. It shall not be a violation of the Agreement where employees refuse to operate such equipment unless such refusal is unjustified."

The question to be decided is whether Brown's honest and reasonable assertion of his right to be free of the obligation to drive unsafe trucks

---

**b.** See Bethel, Constructive Concerted Activity Under the NLRA: Conflicting Signals from the Court and the Board, 59 Indiana L.J. 582 (1984); Dolin, The *Interboro* Doctrine and the Courts, 31 Am.U.L.Rev. 551 (1982); Fischl, Self, Others, and Section 7: Mutualism and Protected Protest Activities Under the NLRA, 89 Colum.L.Rev. 789; George, Divided We Stand: Concerted Activi- ty and the Maturing of the NLRA, 56 Geo. Wash.L.Rev. 509 (1988); Gorman & Finkin, The Individual and the Requirement of "Concert" Under the National Labor Relations Act, 130 U.Pa.L.Rev. 286 (1981); Note, Protection of Individual Action as "Concerted Activity" Under the NLRA, 68 Cornell L.Rev. 369 (1983).

constituted "concerted activit[y]" within the meaning of § 7 of the National Labor Relations Act (NLRA or Act), 29 U.S.C. § 157. * * *

## I

The facts are not in dispute in the current posture of this case. Respondent, City Disposal System, Inc. (City Disposal), hauls garbage for the City of Detroit. Under the collective-bargaining agreement with Local Union No. 247, respondent's truck drivers haul garbage from Detroit to a land fill about 37 miles away. Each driver is assigned to operate a particular truck, which he or she operates each day of work, unless that truck is in disrepair.

James Brown was assigned to truck No. 245. On Saturday, May 12, 1979, Brown observed that a fellow driver had difficulty with the brakes of another truck, truck No. 244. As a result of the brake problem, truck No. 244 nearly collided with Brown's truck. After unloading their garbage at the land fill, Brown and the driver of truck No. 244 brought No. 244 to respondent's truck-repair facility, where they were told that the brakes would be repaired either over the weekend or in the morning of Monday, May 14.

Early in the morning of Monday, May 14, while transporting a load of garbage to the land fill, Brown experienced difficulty with one of the wheels of his own truck—No. 245—and brought that truck in for repair. At the repair facility, Brown was told that, because of a backlog at the facility, No. 245 could not be repaired that day. Brown reported the situation to his supervisor, Otto Jasmund, who ordered Brown to punch out and go home. Before Brown could leave, however, Jasmund changed his mind and asked Brown to drive truck No. 244 instead. Brown refused, explaining that "there's something wrong with that truck. . . . [S]omething was wrong with the brakes . . . there was a grease seal or something leaking causing it to be affecting the brakes." Brown did not, however, explicitly refer to Article XXI of the collective-bargaining agreement or to the agreement in general. In response to Brown's refusal to drive truck No. 244, Jasmund angrily told Brown to go home. At that point, an argument ensued and Robert Madary, another supervisor, intervened, repeating Jasmund's request that Brown drive truck No. 244. Again, Brown refused, explaining that No. 244 "has got problems and I don't want to drive it." Madary replied that half the trucks had problems and that if respondent tried to fix all of them it would be unable to do business. He went on to tell Brown that "[w]e've got all this garbage out here to haul and you tell me about you don't want to drive." Brown responded, "Bob, what you going to do, put the garbage ahead of the safety of the men?" Finally, Madary went to his office and Brown went home. Later that day, Brown received word that he had been discharged. He immediately returned to work in an attempt to gain reinstatement but was unsuccessful.

[Brown promptly filed a grievance challenging the company's direction to him to drive the truck, and challenging his discharge; the union, however, found no merit in the grievance and declined to process it. Brown then filed an unfair labor practice charge, and the Administrative Law Judge found a violation of Section 8(a)(1), concluding that Brown had engaged in "concerted activity" within Section 7: "[W]hen an employee makes complaints concerning safety matters which are embodied in a contract, he is acting not only in his own interest, but is attempting to enforce such contract provisions in the interest of all the employees covered under the contract." The NLRB agreed, and ordered Brown's reinstatement with backpay. The court of appeals, however, refused to enforce, concluding that Brown's refusal to drive truck No. 244 was not "concerted activity" because done solely on his own behalf; to be protected, an individual complaint "must be made on behalf of other employees or at least be made with the object of inducing or preparing for group action and have some arguable basis in the collective bargaining agreement." The Supreme Court granted certiorari to resolve a conflict within the circuits on this issue of "constructive concerted activity," and reversed (5 to 4) the court of appeals.]

## II

Section 7 of the NLRA provides that "[e]mployees shall have the right to * * * join or assist labor organizations, to bargain collectively through representatives of their own choosing, and to engage in other concerted activities for the purpose of collective bargaining or other mutual aid or protection." 29 U.S.C. § 157 (emphasis added). The NLRB's decision in this case applied the Board's longstanding "Interboro doctrine," under which an individual's assertion of a right grounded in a collective-bargaining agreement is recognized as "concerted activit[y]" and therefore accorded the protection of § 7.[6] See Interboro Contractors, Inc., 157 N.L.R.B. 1295, 1298 (1966), enforced, 388 F.2d 495 (C.A.2 1967); Bunney Bros. Construction Co., 139 N.L.R.B. 1516, 1519 (1962). The Board has relied on two justifications for the doctrine: First, the assertion of a right contained in a collective-bargaining agreement is an extension of the concerted action that produced the agreement, Bunney Bros. Construction, supra, at 1519; and second, the assertion of such a right affects the rights of all employees covered by the collective-bargaining agreement. Interboro Contractors, supra, at 1298.

We have often reaffirmed that the task of defining the scope of § 7 "is for the Board to perform in the first instance as it considers the wide variety of cases that come before it," Eastex, Inc. v. NLRB, 437 U.S. 556, 568, 98 S.Ct. 2505, 57 L.Ed.2d 428 (1978), and, on an issue that implicates its expertise in labor relations, a reasonable construction by the Board is entitled to considerable deference, NLRB v. Iron Workers, 434 U.S. 335, 350, 98 S.Ct. 651, 54 L.Ed.2d 586 (1978) NLRB v. Hearst Publications, Inc.,

---

**6.** The NLRB has recently held that, where a group of employees are not unionized and there is no collective-bargaining agreement, an employee's assertion of a right that can only be presumed to be of interest to other employees is not concerted activity. Meyers Industries, 268 N.L.R.B. No. 73 (1984). The Board, however, distinguished that case from the cases involving the Interboro doctrine, which is based on the existence of a collective-bargaining agreement. The Meyers case is thus of no relevance here.

322 U.S. 111, 130–131, 64 S.Ct. 851, 88 L.Ed. 1170 (1944). The question for decision today is thus narrowed to whether the Board's application of § 7 to Brown's refusal to drive truck No. 244 is reasonable.[7] Several reasons persuade us that it is.

A

Neither the Court of Appeals nor respondent appears to question that an employee's invocation of a right derived from a collective-bargaining agreement meets § 7's requirement that an employee's action be taken "for purposes of collective bargaining or other mutual aid or protection." As the Board first explained in the Interboro case, a single employee's invocation of such rights affects all the employees that are covered by the collective-bargaining agreement. Interboro Contractors, Inc., supra, at 1298. This type of generalized effect, as our cases have demonstrated, is sufficient to bring the actions of an individual employee within the "mutual aid or protection" standard, regardless of whether the employee has his own interests most immediately in mind. See, e.g., NLRB v. J. Weingarten, Inc., 420 U.S. 251, 260–261, 95 S.Ct. 959, 43 L.Ed.2d 171 (1975).

The term "concerted activit[y]" is not defined in the Act but it clearly enough embraces the activities of employees who have joined together in order to achieve common goals. See, e.g., Meyers Industries, 268 N.L.R.B. No. 73, at 3 (1984). What is not self-evident from the language of the Act, however, and what we must elucidate, is the precise manner in which particular actions of an individual employee must be linked to the actions of fellow employees in order to permit it to be said that the individual is engaged in concerted activity. We now turn to consider the Board's analysis of that question as expressed in the Interboro doctrine.

Although one could interpret the phrase, "to engage in concerted activities," to refer to a situation in which two or more employees are working together at the same time and the same place toward a common goal, the language of § 7 does not confine itself to such a narrow meaning. In fact, § 7 itself defines both joining and assisting labor organizations— activities in which a single employee can engage—as concerted activities.[8] Indeed, even the courts that have rejected the Interboro doctrine recognize the possibility that an individual employee may be engaged in concerted

---

**7.** Respondent argues that because "the scope of the 'concerted activities' clause in Section 7 is essentially a jurisdictional or legal question concerning the coverage of the Act," we need not defer to the expertise of the Board. Brief for Respondent 13. We have never, however, held that such an exception exists to the normal standard of review of Board interpretations of the Act; indeed, we have not hesitated to defer to the Board's interpretation of the Act in the context of issues substantially similar to that presented here. *E.g.* NLRB v. J. Weingarten, Inc., 420

U.S. 251, 266–267, 95 S.Ct. 959, 43 L.Ed.2d 171 (1975)(right under § 7 to have union representative present at investigatory interview of employee). See also Bayside Enterprises, Inc. v. NLRB, 429 U.S. 298, 302–303, 97 S.Ct. 576, 50 L.Ed.2d 494 (1977) (definition of agricultural workers).

**8.** Section 7 lists these and other activities initially and concludes the list with the phrase "*other* concerted activities," thereby indicating that the enumerated activities are deemed to be "concerted." * * *

activity when he acts alone. They have limited their recognition of this type of concerted activity, however, to two situations: (1) that in which the lone employee intends to induce group activity, and (2) that in which the employee acts as a representative of at least one other employee. See, e.g., Aro, Inc. v. NLRB, 596 F.2d, at 713, 717 (CA6 1979); NLRB v. Northern Metal Co. 440 F.2d 881, 884 (C.A.3 1971). The disagreement over the Interboro doctrine, therefore, merely reflects differing views regarding the nature of the relationship that must exist between the action of the individual employee and the actions of the group in order for § 7 to apply. We cannot say that the Board's view of that relationship, as applied in the Interboro doctrine, is unreasonable.

The invocation of a right rooted in a collective-bargaining agreement is unquestionably an integral part of the process that gave rise to the agreement. That process—beginning with the organization of a union, continuing into the negotiation of a collective-bargaining agreement, and extending through the enforcement of the agreement—is a single, collective activity. Obviously, an employee could not invoke a right grounded in a collective-bargaining agreement were it not for the prior negotiating activities of his fellow employees. Nor would it make sense for a union to negotiate a collective-bargaining agreement if individual employees could not invoke the rights thereby created against their employer. Moreover, when an employee invokes a right grounded in the collective-bargaining agreement, he does not stand alone. Instead, he brings to bear on his employer the power and resolve of all his fellow employees. When, for instance, James Brown refused to drive a truck he believed to be unsafe, he was in effect reminding his employer that he and his fellow employees, at the time their collective-bargaining agreement was signed, had extracted a promise from City Disposal that they would not be asked to drive unsafe trucks. He was also reminding his employer that if it persisted in ordering him to drive an unsafe truck, he could reharness the power of that group to ensure the enforcement of that promise. It was just as though James Brown was reassembling his fellow union members to reenact their decision not to drive unsafe trucks. A lone employee's invocation of a right grounded in his collective-bargaining agreement is, therefore, a concerted activity in a very real sense. * * *[10]

10.  Of course, at some point an individual employee's actions may become so remotely related to the activities of fellow employees that it cannot reasonably be said that the employee is engaged in concerted activity. For instance, the Board has held that if an employer were to discharge an employee for purely personal "griping," the employee could not claim the protection of § 7. See, e.g., Capitol Ornamental Concrete Specialties, Inc., 248 N.L.R.B. 851 (1980).

In addition, although the Board relies entirely on its interpretation of § 7 as support of the Interboro doctrine, it bears noting that under § 8(a)(1), an employer commits an unfair labor practice if he or she "interfere[s] with, [or] restrain[s]" concerted activity. It is possible, therefore, for an employer to commit an unfair labor practice by discharging an employee who is not himself involved in concerted activity, but whose actions are related to other employees' concerted activities in such a manner as to render his discharge an interference or restraint on those activities. In the context of the Interboro doctrine, for instance, even if an individual's invocation of rights provided for in a collective-bargaining agreement, for some reason,

The Interboro doctrine is also entirely consistent with the purposes of the Act, which explicitly include the encouragement of collective bargaining and other "practices fundamental to the friendly adjustment of industrial disputes arising out of differences as to wages, hours, or other working conditions." 29 U.S.C. § 151. Although, as we have said, there is nothing in the legislative history of § 7 that specifically expresses the understanding of Congress in enacting the "concerted activities" language, the general history of § 7 reveals no inconsistency between the Interboro doctrine and congressional intent. That history begins in the early days of the labor movement, when employers invoked the common law doctrines of criminal conspiracy and restraint of trade to thwart workers' attempts to unionize. See Automobile Workers, Local 232 v. Wisconsin Employment Relations Board (Briggs & Stratton), 336 U.S. 245, 257–258, 69 S.Ct. 516, 93 L.Ed. 651 (1949). As this Court recognized in NLRB v. Jones & Laughlin Steel Corp., 301 U.S. 1, 33, 57 S.Ct. 615, 81 L.Ed. 893 (1937), a single employee at that time "was helpless in dealing with an employer; * * * he was dependent ordinarily on his daily wage for the maintenance of himself and his family; * * * if the employer refused to pay him the wages that he thought fair, he was nevertheless unable to leave the employ and resist arbitrary and unfair treatment; * * * union was essential to give laborers opportunity to deal on an equality with their employer."

Congress's first attempt to equalize the bargaining power of management and labor, and its first use of the term "concert" in this context, came in 1914 with the enactment of §§ 6 and 20 of the Clayton Act, which exempted from the antitrust laws certain types of peaceful union activities. 15 U.S.C. § 17; 29 U.S.C. § 52.[11] There followed, in 1932, the Norris–LaGuardia Act, which declared that "the individual * * * worker shall be free from the interference, restraint, or coercion, of employers * * * in self-organization or in *other concerted activities for the purpose of collective bargaining or other mutual aid or protection.*" 29 U.S.C. 102 (emphasis added). This was the source of the language enacted in § 7. It was adopted first in § 7(a) of the National Industrial Recovery Act and then, in 1935, in § 7 of the NLRA. See generally Gorman & Finkin, The Individual and the Requirement of "Concert" Under the National Labor Relations Act, 130 U.Pa.L.Rev. 286, 331–346 (1981).

Against this background, it is evident that, in enacting § 7 of the NLRA, Congress sought generally to equalize the bargaining power of the employee with that of his employer by allowing employees to band together in confronting an employer regarding the terms and conditions of their employment. There is no indication that Congress intended to limit this protection to situations in which an employee's activity and that of his fellow employees combine with one another in any particular way. Nor,

---

were not concerted activity, the discharge of that individual would still be an unfair labor practice if the result were to restrain or interfere with the concerted activity of negotiating or enforcing a collective-bargaining agreement.

**11.** In § 20 of the Clayton Act, Congress provided that "no * * * injunction shall prohibit any person or persons, whether singly or *in concert*, from * * * ceasing to perform any work [or other specified activities]." 29 U.S.C. § 52 (emphasis added).

more specifically, does it appear that Congress intended to have this general protection withdrawn in situations in which a single employee, acting alone, participates in an integral aspect of a collective process. Instead, what emerges from the general background of § 7—and what is consistent with the Act's statement of purpose—is a congressional intent to create an equality in bargaining power between the employee and the employer throughout the entire process of labor organizing, collective bargaining, and enforcement of collective-bargaining agreements.

The Board's Interboro doctrine, based on a recognition that the potential inequality in the relationship between the employee and the employer continues beyond the point at which a collective-bargaining agreement is signed, mitigates that inequality throughout the duration of the employment relationship, and is, therefore, fully consistent with congressional intent. Moreover, by applying § 7 to the actions of individual employees invoking their rights under a collective-bargaining agreement, the Interboro doctrine preserves the integrity of the entire collective-bargaining process; for by invoking a right grounded in a collective-bargaining agreement, the employee makes that right a reality, and breathes life, not only into the promises contained in the collective-bargaining agreement, but also into the entire process envisioned by Congress as the means by which to achieve industrial peace.

To be sure, the principal tool by which an employee invokes the rights granted him in a collective-bargaining agreement is the processing of a grievance according to whatever procedures his collective-bargaining agreement establishes. No one doubts that the processing of a grievance in such a manner is concerted activity within the meaning of § 7. See, *e.g.,* NLRB v. Ford Motor Co. 683 F.2d 156, 159 (C.A.6 1982); Crown Central Petroleum Corp. v. NLRB, 430 F.2d 724, 729 (C.A.5 1970). Indeed, it would make little sense for § 7 to cover an employee's conduct while negotiating a collective-bargaining agreement, including a grievance mechanism by which to protect the rights created by the agreement, but not to cover an employee's attempt to utilize that mechanism to enforce the agreement.

In practice, however, there is unlikely to be a bright-line distinction between an incipient grievance, a complaint to an employer, and perhaps even an employee's initial refusal to perform a certain job that he believes he has no duty to perform. It is reasonable to expect that an employee's first response to a situation that he believes violates his collective-bargaining agreement will be a protest to his employer. Whether he files a grievance will depend in part on his employer's reaction and in part upon the nature of the right at issue. In addition, certain rights might not be susceptible of enforcement by the filing of a grievance. In such a case, the collective-bargaining agreement might provide for an alternative method of enforcement, as did the agreement involved in this case, see supra, at 1507, or the agreement might be silent on the matter. Thus, for a variety of reasons, an employee's initial statement to an employer to the effect that he believes a collectively bargained right is being violated, or the employee's initial refusal to do that which he believes he is not obligated to do, might serve as both a natural prelude to, and an efficient substitute for, the filing of a formal grievance. As long as the employee's statement or action is based on a reasonable and honest belief that he is being, or has been, asked to perform a task that he is not required to perform under his collective-bargaining agreement, and the statement or action is reasonably directed toward the enforcement of a collectively bargained right, there is no justification for overturning the Board's judgment that the employee is engaged in concerted activity, just as he would have been had he filed a formal grievance.

The fact that an activity is concerted, however, does not necessarily mean that an employee can engage in the activity with impunity. An employee may engage in concerted activity in such an abusive manner that he loses the protection of § 7. See, e.g., Crown Central Petroleum Corp. v. NLRB, 430 F.2d 724, 729 (C.A.5 1970); Yellow Freight System, Inc. 247 N.L.R.B. 177, 181 (1980). Cf. Eastex, Inc. v. NLRB, 437 U.S. 556, 98 S.Ct. 2505, 57 L.Ed.2d 428 (1978); NLRB v. Babcock & Wilcox Co., 351 U.S. 105, 76 S.Ct. 679, 100 L.Ed. 975 (1956). Furthermore, if an employer does not wish to tolerate certain methods by which employees invoke their collectively bargained rights, he is free to negotiate a provision in his collective-bargaining agreement that limits the availability of such methods. No-strike provisions, for instance, are a common mechanism by which employers and employees agree that the latter will not invoke their rights by refusing to work. In general, if an employee violates such a provision, his activity is unprotected even though it may be concerted. Mastro Plastics Corp. v. NLRB, 350 U.S. 270, 76 S.Ct. 349, 100 L.Ed. 309 (1956). Whether Brown's action in this case was unprotected, however, is not before us.

* * *

## III

* * *

Respondent argues that Brown's action was not concerted because he did not explicitly refer to the collective-bargaining agreement as a basis for his refusal to drive the truck. Brief of Respondent 21–22. The Board, however, has never held that an employee must make such an explicit reference for his actions to be covered by the Interboro doctrine, and we find that position reasonable. We have often recognized the importance of "the Board's special function of applying the general provisions of the Act to the complexities of industrial life." NLRB v. Erie Resistor Corp., 373 U.S. 221, 236, 83 S.Ct. 1139, 10 L.Ed.2d 308 (1963). As long as the nature of the employee's complaint is reasonably clear to the person to whom it is communicated, and the complaint does, in fact, refer to a reasonably perceived violation of the collective-bargaining agreement, the complaining employee is engaged in the process of enforcing that agreement. In the context of a workplace dispute, where the participants are likely to be unsophisticated in collective-bargaining matters, a requirement that the employee explicitly refer to the collective-bargaining agreement is likely to serve as nothing more than a trap for the unwary. * * *

In this case, because Brown reasonably and honestly invoked his right to avoid driving unsafe trucks, his action was concerted. It may be that the collective-bargaining agreement prohibits an employee from refusing to drive a truck that he reasonably believes to be unsafe, but that is, in fact, perfectly safe. If so, Brown's action was concerted but unprotected. As stated above, however, the only issue before this Court and the only issue passed upon by the Board or the Court of Appeals is whether Brown's action was concerted, not whether it was protected.

\* \* \* We therefore reverse the judgment of the Court of Appeals and remand the case for further proceedings consistent with this opinion, including an inquiry into whether respondent may continue to defend this action on the theory that Brown's refusal to drive truck No. 244 was unprotected, even if concerted.

It is so ordered.

■ JUSTICE O'CONNOR, with whom The CHIEF JUSTICE, JUSTICE POWELL and JUSTICE REHNQUIST join, dissenting.

\* \* \* Although the concepts of individual action for personal gain and "concerted activity" are intuitively incompatible,[2] the Court today defers to the Board's judgment that the Interboro doctrine is necessary to safeguard the exercise of rights previously won in the collective bargaining process. Since I consider the Interboro doctrine to be an exercise in undelegated legislative power by the Board, I respectfully dissent.

In my view, the fact that the right the employee asserts ultimately can be grounded in the collective bargaining agreement is not enough to make the individual's self-interested action concerted. If it could, then *every* contract claim could be the basis for an unfair labor practice complaint. But the law is clear that an employer's alleged violation of a collective agreement cannot, by itself, provide the basis for an unfair labor practice complaint. See NLRB v. C & C Plywood, 385 U.S. 421, 427–428, 87 S.Ct. 559, 17 L.Ed.2d 486 (1967); Dowd Box Co. v. Courtney, 368 U.S. 502, 509–513, 82 S.Ct. 519, 7 L.Ed.2d 483 (1962). Congress once considered a proposal that would have given the Board "general jurisdiction over all alleged violations of collective bargaining agreements." NLRB v. C & C Plywood, supra, at 427, 87 S.Ct., at 563. But it realized that "[t]o have conferred upon the National Labor Relations Board generalized power to determine the rights of parties under all collective agreements would have been a step toward governmental regulation of the terms of those agreements." Ibid. Thus, Congress expressly decided that, "[o]nce [the] parties have made a collective bargaining contract[,] the enforcement of that contract should be left to the usual processes of the law and not to the . . . Board." H.R.Conf.Rep. No. 510, 80th Cong., 1st Sess., 42 (1946). By basing

---

**2.** The Court and the Board agree that the Act cannot be read to cover, or to give the Board jurisdiction over, purely personal, though work-related, claims of individual employees. See ante, at n 10; Brief for the National Labor Relations Board 16, and n 9. They also agree that the mere fact that an asserted right can be presumed to be of interest to other employees is not a sufficient basis for labeling it "concerted." See ante, at n 6; Meyers Industries, 268 N.L.R.B. 493 (1984).

the determination whether activity is "concerted" on the assertion's ultimate grounding in the collective bargaining agreement, the Interboro doctrine's extension of the concerted activity proviso transfers the final authority for interpreting all contracts and for resolving all contract disputes back to the Board. This arrogation of power violates Congress' decision to the contrary. * * *

This Court has previously recognized that the labor laws were designed to encourage employees to act together. See, e.g., NLRB v. Weingarten, Inc., 420 U.S. 251, 260–264, 95 S.Ct. 959, 43 L.Ed.2d 171 (1975). Even a single employee acting in good faith and asserting a right contained in the collective bargaining agreement may be too fearful, inarticulate, or lacking in skill to relate accurately either the event being investigated or the relevant extenuating factors. Other disinterested employees, especially knowledgeable union stewards, can assist the employee and the employer in eliciting the relevant facts and in preventing misunderstandings and hard feelings. * * * The fact that two employees receive coverage where one acting alone does not is therefore entirely consistent with the labor laws' emphasis on collective action. See NLRB v. Allis–Chalmers Mfg. Co., 388 U.S. 175, 180, 87 S.Ct. 2001, 18 L.Ed.2d 1123 (1967); Republic Steel Corp. v. Maddox, 379 U.S. 650, 653, 85 S.Ct. 614, 13 L.Ed.2d 580 (1965).

* * * When employees act together in expressing a mutual concern, contractual or otherwise, their action is "concerted" and the statute authorizes them to seek vindication through the Board's administrative processes. In contrast, when an employee acts alone in expressing a personal concern, contractual or otherwise, his action is not "concerted;" in such cases, the statute instructs him to seek vindication through his union, and where necessary, through the courts. * * *

The Interboro doctrine is therefore against Congress' judgment as to how contract rights are best vindicated.

Finally, the Interboro doctrine makes little sense when applied to the facts of this case. There is no evidence that employee James Brown discussed the truck's alleged safety problem with other employees, sought their support in remedying the problem, or requested their or his union's assistance in protesting to his employer. He did not seek to warn others of the problem or even initially to file a grievance through his union. He simply asserted that the truck was not safe enough for *him* to drive. James Brown was not engaging in "concerted activity" in any reasonable sense of the term, and therefore his employer could not have violated § 8(a)(1) of the Act when it discharged him. The fact that the right asserted can be found in the collective bargaining agreement may be relevant to whether activity of that type should be "protected," but not to whether it is "concerted." The Interboro doctrine is, in my view, unreasonable in concluding otherwise.

I do not mean to imply by this dissent that conduct should not be considered "concerted" because it is engaged in by only a single employee. The crucial issue is, as the Court notes, the precise nature of the relationship that must exist between the action of an individual employee and the actions of the group. * * * An employee certainly engages in "concerted activity" when he acts with or expressly on behalf of one or more of the other employees. And, as several of the courts of appeals have concluded, the statutory language can even be stretched to cover an individual who takes action with the proven object of inducing, initiating, or preparing for group action. See, e.g., Aro, Inc. v. NLRB, 596 F.2d 713, 717 (C.A.6 1979); NLRB v. Northern Metal Co., 440 F.2d 881, 884 (C.A.3 1971); see also Kohls v. NLRB, 629 F.2d 173, 176–177 (C.A.D.C.1980). But it stretches the language past its snapping point to cover an employee's action that is taken solely for personal benefit.

Accordingly, I respectfully dissent.

--------

# PROBLEMS FOR DISCUSSION

**1.** Examine again the legislative history set forth by the Court. Given the strong congressional emphasis upon protecting the individual employee, who lacks bargaining power comparable to that of the employer, how can it reasonably be argued that an individual who peaceably complains about his working conditions may be summarily discharged for doing so? Does not the congressional use of the term "concerted activities," given its roots in criminal-conspiracy doctrine, suggest that Congress meant to shelter group protest and individual protest comparably—rather than that it meant to exalt only the one and afford lesser protection for the other? See Gorman & Finkin, "The Individual and the Requirement of 'Concert' Under the National Labor Relations Act," 130 U.Pa.L.Rev. 286 (1981).

**2.** Does not the legislative history, and the thrust of the Court's logic, suggest that there should be protection against discharge for individual protesters even absent a union and absent a collective bargaining agreement? (After all, is not the Court merely reaching its result by piling fiction upon fiction: the employee's protest renews group action, when in fact there is none; the refusal to follow the employer's work order is essentially a compliance with the contractual grievance procedure, when in fact it is not; the grievance refers to the contract, when in fact the employee makes no mention of the contract provision and may be totally unaware of it?)

Why did the Court stop short of such a conclusion? Why should doing exactly what Brown did, but in a non-union company, not be sheltered by Section 7 against discharge? Might the Court have been fearful of injecting the NLRB, without clear congressional authorization, into an unmanageable array of employer-worker disputes in the vast non-union sector of the American economy? Would every arguably insubordinate employee who is disciplined therefor—from a one-day suspension to summary discharge—then have recourse to the Board under Section 8(a)(1)? Is that protection not currently available, however, to *two* allegedly insubordinate workers acting together?

**3.** In Meyers Industries, Inc., 268 NLRB 493 (1984), mentioned by the Supreme Court, it was alleged that truckdriver Prill—employed by a non-union company— could not lawfully be discharged for refusing to drive an unsafe truck and for reporting the situation to two state safety agencies (resulting in a number of citations against the employer for violation of state regulations). The Board had previously held, in Alleluia Cushion Co., 221 NLRB 999 (1975), that an individual's filing of a claim under a statute governing workplace safety was to be treated as protected "concerted" activity in view of the presumption that fellow workers were also concerned about the protested conditions and consented to the individual's protest. In *Meyers,* the Board overruled *Alleluia* and other similar cases.

Might "concert" be found in such statutory-claim cases under the rationale of *City Disposal*? Or did the Supreme Court reject that conclusion? (Compare footnote 6 of the majority with footnote 2 of the dissent.) See the Board's reformulation of its rationale in Meyers Indus., Inc., 281 NLRB 882 (1986)(Meyers II), and the court's enforcement in Prill v. NLRB, 835 F.2d 1481 (D.C.Cir.1987)(Prill II). In Myth, Inc., 326 NLRB No. 28 (1998), the Board declined the General Counsel's invitation to restore the theory of *Alleluia Cushion* and to hold unlawful an employer's reprisal against a single employee for filing a wage claim with the appropriate state agency.

**4.** Assume that the following situations arise in a non-union company. Are the employees engaging in protected "concerted" activity?

(a) Two truckdrivers share the truck cab and take turns driving; both refuse to drive what they regard as an unsafe truck and so inform their employer.

(b) Two truckdrivers are assigned to drive a specific truck, but alone and in separate six-hour shifts. Without discussing the matter with each other, each separately concludes that the truck is unsafe, and each informs the company of his own refusal to drive. (Compare Brown and his fellow driver of truck 244 in *City Disposal.*)

(c) One truckdriver refuses to drive what he regards as an unsafe truck, stating to a co-worker, "I'm taking your truck. I'm not driving mine. I smell fumes." *See* NLRB v. Portland Airport Limousine Co., 163 F.3d 662 (1st Cir.1998).

Do these hypotheticals suggest that the prevailing definition of "concerted" activities is, in the words of the Court, a "trap for the unwary"?

**5.** Acting on rumors that the employer had inadequate funds in its checking account to cover the paychecks just issued to them, three employees during their lunch hour drove to the employer's bank and one of them, Amy Able, went inside to inquire of the bank manager regarding the employer's account balance. At a cocktail party that night, the bank manager informed the company president of Ms. Able's inquiry, and the next morning, Ms. Able was told by the president (who was unaware of the involvement of the other two employees) to "punch the time clock for the last time, and never show your face around here again!" Advise Ms. Able on her rights under the Labor Act to get back her job. See Air Surrey Corp. v. NLRB, 601 F.2d 256 (6th Cir.1979).

---

The phrase "concerted activities * * * for mutual aid or protection" was given a generous interpretation by the Supreme Court in NLRB v. J. WEINGARTEN, INC., 420 U.S. 251, 95 S.Ct. 959, 43 L.Ed.2d 171 (1975). There, an employee was suspected of being responsible for cash shortages and was called to an interview with the store manager; the manager interrogated her in the presence of a security specialist and refused her requests to call in the union steward or some other union representative. The Board held that the employer's exertion of pressure on the employee to submit to the interview, which she had reasonable fear would result in her discipline, constituted coercion of the employee in the exercise of "concerted activities

* * * for mutual aid or protection." The Court began its analysis by noting that the employee's request for assistance by the union representative was within the literal coverage of the statutory phrase. It then continued: "This is true even though the employee alone may have an immediate stake in the outcome; he seeks 'aid or protection' against a perceived threat to his employment security. The union representative whose participation he seeks is however safeguarding not only the particular employee's interest, but also the interests of the entire bargaining unit by exercising vigilance to make certain that the employer does not initiate or continue a practice of imposing punishment unjustly. The representative's presence is an assurance to other employees in the bargaining unit that they too can obtain his aid and protection if called upon to attend a like interview." Concerted activity for mutual aid or protection is therefore as present here as it was held to be in NLRB v. Peter Cailler Kohler Swiss Chocolates Co., 130 F.2d 503, 505–506 (2d Cir.1942), cited with approval by this Court in Houston Insulation Contractors Ass'n v. NLRB, 386 U.S. 664, 668–669, 87 S.Ct. 1278, 1280–1281, 18 L.Ed.2d 389 (1967):

> "When all the other workmen in a shop make common cause with a fellow workman over his separate grievance, and go out on strike in his support, they engage in a 'concerted activity' for 'mutual aid or protection,' although the aggrieved workman is the only one of them who has any immediate stake in the outcome. The rest know that by their action each of them assures himself, in case his turn ever comes, of the support of the one whom they are all then helping; and the solidarity so established is 'mutual aid' in the most literal sense, as nobody doubts."

"The Board's construction plainly effectuates the most fundamental purposes of the Act. In § 1, 29 U.S.C. § 151 [29 U.S.C.A. § 151], the Act declares that it is a goal of national labor policy to protect 'the exercise by workers of full freedom of association, self-organization, and designation of representatives of their own choosing, for the purpose of * * * mutual aid or protection.' To that end the Act is designed to eliminate the 'inequality of bargaining power between employees * * * and employers.' Ibid. Requiring a lone employee to attend an investigatory interview which he reasonably believes may result in the imposition of discipline perpetuates the inequality the Act was designed to eliminate and bars recourse to the safeguards the Act provided 'to redress the perceived imbalance of economic power between labor and management.' American Ship Building Co. v. NLRB, 380 U.S. 300, 316, 85 S.Ct. 955, 13 L.Ed.2d 855 (1965). * * * The Board's construction also gives recognition to the right when it is most useful to both employee and employer. A single employee confronted by an employer investigating whether certain conduct deserves discipline may be too fearful or inarticulate to relate accurately the incident being investigated, or too ignorant to raise extenuating factors. A knowledgeable union representative could assist the employer by eliciting favorable facts * * *."

For similar reasons, the Court held that a union representative who seeks upon request to accompany the employee to a so-called investigatory interview may not be disciplined for such conduct. International Ladies' Garment Workers' Union v. Quality Mfg. Co., 420 U.S. 276, 95 S.Ct. 972, 43 L.Ed.2d 189 (1975).

---

## PROBLEMS FOR DISCUSSION

**1.** Inasmuch as *Weingarten* was predicated in part on a concern for the lone, fearful, "ignorant" employee, should the employer be required to inform the employee of his or her *Weingarten* rights before the interrogation may proceed? See Montgomery Ward & Co., 269 NLRB 904 (1984). See also Silard, Rights of the Accused Employee in Company Disciplinary Investigations, Proceedings of New York University Twenty–Second Annual Conference on Labor 217 (T. Christensen & A. Christensen eds. 1970).

**2.** Does Section 7 protect the right of an employee in a *non-union* company, confronted with an employer demand to appear for an interview concerning the distribution of narcotics on company property, to insist upon the presence and assistance of a co-worker (a first-year law student) at the interview? See E.I. DuPont & Co., 289 NLRB 627 (1988), review denied sub nom. Slaughter v. NLRB, 876 F.2d 11 (3d Cir.1989), and Epilepsy Foundation of Northeast Ohio, 331 NLRB No. 92 (2000), overruling Sears, Roebuck & Co., 274 NLRB 230 (1985). *See also* Note, Extending *Weingarten* Rights to Nonunion Employees, 1986 Colum.L.Rev. 618; Note, Limiting the *Weingarten* Right in the Nonunion Setting: The Implications of *Sears Roebuck & Co.,* 35 Cath. U. L. Rev. 1033 (1986).

**3.** Does Section 7 protect the right of an employee in a unionized company to insist upon the presence of the shop steward at a meeting in which the plant manager is to inform the employee of a final decision to terminate him because of his use of drugs on company property? See NLRB v. Certified Grocers of California, Ltd., 587 F.2d 449 (9th Cir.1978).

**4.** Karl Klepto worked for the Ace Precious Metal Company for several years. Some months ago, he was suspected of secretly carrying company property away from the plant; supervisors had noticed materials missing from his workplace and had also noticed surreptitious movements on his way out of the plant each day. When Klepto's supervisor called him into her office for an interview, Klepto asked to have a union representative present. When none could be found, the supervisor pressed Klepto with a number of questions and got him to confess. He was immediately fired. The Union has filed a charge against the Company under Section 8(a)(1), and has asked that Klepto be reinstated and awarded backpay. You are the Administrative Law Judge. Assuming you find a violation of the NLRA, what remedy should be recommended? See Communication Workers, Local 5008 v. NLRB, 784 F.2d 847 (7th Cir.1986); Taracorp Industries, 273 NLRB 221 (1984).

**5.** Assume that in the preceding problem, the Company and Union have a collective bargaining agreement providing that "The employer may interview any employee in connection with any disciplinable offense without the presence of a Union representative." Assume that the Company relied on that provision, denied Klepto an opportunity for Union representation, extracted the confession, and discharged him. Klepto files a charge with the NLRB, asserting that his "Weingarten rights" are not subject to "waiver" by the union. Should the Regional Director issue a Section 8(a)(1) complaint? See Prudential Ins. Co. v. Marie Spencer, 275 NLRB 208 (1985).

---

## Eastex, Inc. v. NLRB

437 U.S. 556, 98 S.Ct. 2505, 57 L.Ed.2d 428 (1978).

■ MR. JUSTICE POWELL delivered the opinion of the Court.

Employees of petitioner sought to distribute a union newsletter in nonworking areas of petitioner's property during nonworking time urging employees to support the union and discussing a proposal to incorporate the state "right-to-work" statute into the state constitution and a presidential veto of an increase in the federal minimum wage. The newsletter also called on employees to take action to protect their interests as employees with respect to these two issues. The question presented is whether petitioner's refusal to allow the distribution violated § 8(a)(1) of the National Labor Relations Act * * *

[In March and April 1974, certain employees of the Company and officers of Local 801 of the United Paperworkers International Union (the collective bargaining representative of the Company's production employees) sought to distribute a union newsletter in nonworking areas of the plant. The first and fourth sections of the newsletter urged employees to support the Union and extolled the benefits of union solidarity. The second section encouraged employees to write their state legislators to oppose incorporating the state "right to work" law (which bans union shop agreements) into a revised state constitution; the newsletter warned that such incorporation could weaken unions. The third section of the newsletter, after noting the President's veto of a bill increasing the federal minimum wage and comparing the increase in prices and profits in the oil industry, urged the employees to register to vote in federal elections and to support candidates sympathetic to labor. Company officials refused all requests to circulate the newsletter in nonworking areas of the plant, and the Union filed an unfair labor practice charge.

[The Board and the court of appeals concluded that the employer violated Section 8(a)(1). They rejected the Company's claim that, because the newsletter was not directed at conditions in the workplace over which the employer had control, its distribution was not for the "mutual aid and protection" of the employees. They also concluded that the Company had shown no "special circumstances" which would justify a ban upon employees' solicitation in nonworking areas of the plant on nonworking time.]

## II

Two distinct questions are presented. The first is whether, apart from the location of the activity, distribution of the newsletter is the kind of concerted activity that is protected from employer interference by §§ 7 and 8(a)(1) of the National Labor Relations Act. If it is, then the second question is whether the fact that the activity takes place on petitioner's property gives rise to a countervailing interest that outweighs the exercise of § 7 rights in that location. * * *

### A

Section 7 provides that "[e]mployees shall have the right * * * to engage in * * * concerted activities for the purpose of collective bargaining or other mutual aid or protection * * *." Petitioner contends that the activity here is not within the "mutual aid or protection" language because it does not relate to a "specific dispute" between employees and their own employer "over an issue which the employer has the right or power to affect." * * * Petitioner rejects the idea that § 7 might protect any activity that could be characterized as "political," and suggests that the discharge of an employee who engages in any such activity would not violate the Act.

We believe that petitioner misconceives the reach of the "mutual aid or protection" clause. The "employees" who may engage in concerted activities for "mutual aid or protection" are defined by § 2(3) of the Act, 29 U.S.C.A. § 152(3), to "include any employee, and shall not be limited to the employees of a particular employer, unless the Act explicitly states otherwise * * *." This definition was intended to protect employees when they engage in otherwise proper concerted activities in support of employees of employers other than their own. In recognition of its intent, the Board and the courts long have held that the "mutual aid or protection" clause encompasses such activity.[13] Petitioner's argument on this point ignores the language of the Act and its settled construction.

We also find no warrant for petitioner's view that employees lose their protection under the "mutual aid or protection" clause when they seek to improve terms and conditions of employment or otherwise improve their lot as employees through channels outside the immediate employee-employer relationship. The 74th Congress knew well enough that labor's cause often is advanced on fronts other than collective bargaining and grievance settlement within the immediate employment context. It recognized this fact by choosing, as the language of § 7 makes clear, to protect concerted activities for the somewhat broader purpose of "mutual aid or protection"

---

**13.** E.g., Fort Wayne Corrugated Paper Co. v. NLRB, 111 F.2d 869, 874 (C.A.7 1940), enforcing 11 N.L.R.B. 1, 5–6 (1939)(right to assist in organizing another employer's employees); NLRB v. J.G. Boswell Co., 136 F.2d 585, 595 (C.A.9 1943), enforcing 35 N.L.R.B. 968 (1941)(right to express sympathy for striking employees of another employer); Redwing Carriers, Inc., 137 N.L.R.B. 1545, 1546–1547 (1962), enforced sub nom. Teamster Local 79 v. NLRB, 117 U.S.App.D.C. 84, 325 F.2d 1011 (1963), cert. denied, 377 U.S. 905, 84 S.Ct. 1165, 12 L.Ed.2d 176 (1964)(right to honor picket line of another employer's employees); NLRB v. Alamo Ex-press Co., 430 F.2d 1032, 1036 (C.A.5 1970), cert. denied, 400 U.S. 1021, 91 S.Ct. 584, 27 L.Ed.2d 633 (1971), enforcing 170 N.L.R.B. 315 (1968)(accord); Washington State Service Employees State Council No. 18, 188 N.L.R.B. 957, 959 (1971)(right to demonstrate in support of another employer's employees); Yellow Cab, Inc., 210 N.L.R.B. 568, 569 (1974)(right to distribute literature in support of another employer's employees). We express no opinion, however, as to the correctness of the particular balance struck between employees' exercise of § 7 rights and employers' legitimate interests in any of the above-cited cases.

as well as for the narrower purposes of "self-organization" and "collective bargaining." Thus, it has been held that the "mutual aid or protection" clause protects employees from retaliation by their employers when they seek to improve working conditions through resort to administrative and judicial forums, and that employees' appeals to legislators to protect their interests as employees are within the scope of this clause. To hold that activity of this nature is entirely unprotected—irrespective of location or the means employed—would leave employees open to retaliation for much legitimate activity that could improve their lot as employees. As this could "frustrate the policy of the Act to protect the right of workers to act together to better their working conditions," NLRB v. Washington Aluminum Co., 370 U.S. 9, 14, 82 S.Ct. 1099, 1102, 8 L.Ed.2d 298 (1962), we do not think that Congress could have intended the protection of § 7 to be as narrow as petitioner insists.[17]

It is true, of course, that some concerted activity bears a less immediate relationship to employees' interests as employees than other such activity. We may assume that at some point the relationship becomes so attenuated that an activity cannot fairly be deemed to come within the "mutual aid or protection" clause. It is neither necessary nor appropriate, however, for us to attempt to delineate precisely the boundaries of the "mutual aid or protection" clause. That task is for the Board to perform in the first instance as it considers the wide variety of cases that come before it.[18] Republic Aviation Corp. v. NLRB, 324 U.S. 793, 798, 65 S.Ct. 982, 985,

---

**17.** Petitioner relies upon several cases said to construe § 7 more narrowly than do we. NLRB v. Leslie Metal Arts Co., 509 F.2d 811 (C.A.6 1975), and Shelly & Anderson Furniture Mfg. Co. v. NLRB, 497 F.2d 1200 (C.A.9 1974), both quote the same treatise for the proposition that to be protected under § 7, concerted activity must seek "a specific remedy" for a "work-related complaint or grievance." 509 F.2d, at 813, and 497 F.2d, at 1202–1203, quoting 18B Business Organizations, T. Kheel, Labor Law § 10.02[3], at 10–21 (1973). It was unnecessary in those cases to decide whether the protection of § 7 went beyond the treatise's formulation, for the activity in both cases was held to be protected. Moreover, in stating its "rule," the treatise relied upon takes no note of the cases cited in nn. 13, 15, and 16, supra. Compare R. Gorman, Labor Law 296–302 (1976). The Courts of Appeals for the Sixth and Ninth Circuits themselves have taken a broader view of the "mutual aid or protection" clause than the reference to the treatise in the above-cited cases would seem to suggest. See, e.g., Kellogg Co. v. NLRB, 457 F.2d 519, 522–523 (C.A.6 1972), and cases there cited; Kaiser Engineers v. NLRB, 538 F.2d 1379, 1384–1385 (C.A.9 1976). * * *

This leaves only G & W Electric Specialty Co. v. NLRB, 360 F.2d 873 (C.A.7 1966), which refused to enforce a Board order because the concerted activity there—circulation of a petition concerning management of an employee-run credit union—"involved no request for any action upon the part of the Company and did not concern a matter over which the Company had any control." Id., at 876. *G & W Electric* cites no authority for its narrowing of § 7, and it ignores a substantial weight of authority to the contrary, including the Seventh Circuit's own prior holding in Fort Wayne Corrugated Paper Co. v. NLRB, 111 F.2d 869, 874 (1940). See n. 13, supra. We therefore do not view any of these cases as persuasive authority for petitioner's position.

**18.** In addition, even when concerted activity comes within the scope of the "mutual aid or protection" clause, the forms such activity permissibly may take may well depend on the object of the activity. "The argument that the employer's lack of interest or control affords a legitimate basis for holding that a subject does not come within 'mutual aid or protection' is unconvincing. The argument that economic pressure should be un-

89 L.Ed. 1372 (1945); Phelps Dodge Corp. v. NLRB, 313 U.S. 177, 194, 61 S.Ct. 845, 852, 85 L.Ed. 1271 (1941). To decide this case, it is enough to determine whether the Board erred in holding that distribution of the second and third sections of the newsletter is for the purpose of "mutual aid or protection."

The Board determined that distribution of the second section, urging employees to write their legislators to oppose incorporation of the state "right-to-work" statute into a revised state constitution, was protected because union security is "central to the union concept of strength through solidarity" and "a mandatory subject of bargaining in other than right-to-work states." 215 N.L.R.B., at 274. The newsletter warned that incorporation could affect employees adversely "by weakening Unions and improving the edge business has at the bargaining table." The fact that Texas already has a "right-to-work" statute does not render employees' interest in this matter any less strong, for, as the Court of Appeals noted, it is "one thing to face a legislative scheme which is open to legislative modification or repeal" and "quite another thing to face the prospect that such a scheme will be frozen in a concrete constitutional mandate." 550 F.2d, at 205. We cannot say that the Board erred in holding that this section of the newsletter bears such a relation to employees' interests as to come within the guarantee of the "mutual aid or protection" clause. * * *

The Board held that distribution of the third section, criticizing a presidential veto of an increase in the federal minimum wage and urging employees to register to vote to "defeat our enemies and elect our friends," was protected despite the fact that petitioner's employees were paid more than the vetoed minimum wage. It reasoned that the "minimum wage inevitably influences wage levels derived from collective bargaining, even those far above the minimum," and that "concern by [petitioner's] employees for the plight of other employees might gain support for them at some future time when they might have a dispute with their employer." 215 N.L.R.B., at 274 (internal quotation marks omitted). We think that the Board acted within the range of its discretion in so holding. Few topics are of such immediate concern to employees as the level of their wages. The Board was entitled to note the widely recognized impact that a rise in the minimum wage may have on the level of negotiated wages generally, a phenomenon that would not have been lost on petitioner's employees. The union's call, in the circumstances of this case, for these employees to back persons who support an increase in the minimum wage, and to oppose those who oppose it, fairly is characterized as concerted activity for the "mutual aid or protection" of petitioner's employees and of employees generally.

In sum, we hold that distribution of both the second and the third sections of the newsletter is protected under the "mutual aid or protection" clause of § 7.

---

protected in such cases is more convincing." Getman, The Protection of Economic Pressure By Section 7 of the National Labor Relations Act, 115 U.Pa.L.Rev. 1195, 1221 (1967).

## B

The question that remains is whether the Board erred in holding that petitioner's employees may distribute the newsletter in nonworking areas of petitioner's property during nonworking time. Consideration of this issue must begin with the Court's decisions in Republic Aviation Corp. v. NLRB, 324 U.S. 793, 65 S.Ct. 982, 89 L.Ed. 1372 (1945), and NLRB v. Babcock & Wilcox Co., 351 U.S. 105, 76 S.Ct. 679, 100 L.Ed. 975 (1956). * * *

It is apparent that the instant case resembles *Republic Aviation* rather closely. * * * The only possible ground of distinction is that part of the newsletter in this case does not address purely organizational matters, but rather concerns other activity protected by § 7. The question, then, is whether this difference required the Board to apply a different rule here than it applied in *Republic Aviation*.

* * * It is apparent that the complexity of the Board's rules and the difficulty of the Board's task might be compounded greatly if it were required to distinguish not only between literature that is within and without the protection of § 7, but also among subcategories of literature within that protection. * * *

We need not go so far in this case, however, as to hold that the *Republic Aviation* rule properly is applied to every in-plant distribution of literature that falls within the protective ambit of § 7. This is a new area for the Board and the courts which has not yet received mature consideration. * * * For this reason, we confine our holding to the facts of this case.

Petitioner concedes that its employees were entitled to distribute a substantial portion of this newsletter on its property. In addition, as we have held above, the sections to which petitioner objected concern activity which petitioner, in the absence of a countervailing interest of its own, is not entitled to suppress. Yet petitioner made no attempt to show that its management interests would be prejudiced in any manner by distribution of these sections, and in our view any incremental intrusion on petitioner's property rights from their distribution together with the other sections would be minimal. Moreover, it is undisputed that the Union undertook the distribution in order to boost its support and improve its bargaining position in upcoming contract negotiations with petitioner. Thus, viewed in context, the distribution was closely tied to vital concerns of the Act. In these circumstances, we hold that the Board did not err in applying the *Republic Aviation* rule to the facts of this case. The judgment of the Court of Appeals therefore is

Affirmed.

[In a dissenting opinion joined by the Chief Justice, Justice Rehnquist formulated the question before the Court as "whether Congress has authorized the Board to displace an employer's right to prevent the distribution on his property of political material concerning matters over which he has no control." He criticized the Court for deferring to the NLRB's imposition of a substantial burden on the property rights of the employer, absent any

Court precedent and absent an "unmistakable expression" of congressional approval.]

---

## PROBLEMS FOR DISCUSSION

**1.** The Glitz Casino has an employee stock ownership plan (ESOP) that holds one percent of the Casino's stock. A baccarat dealer named Wally Winn has devised a detailed proposal for a change in the ESOP that would give the employees 50 percent ownership of the company. Under Winn's plan, the ESOP would borrow $300 million to purchase 50 percent of the outstanding shares of stock in the Casino and would assume $400 million of the Casino's debt (a so-called leveraged buyout); the $700 million total debt would be paid over time from the 50% Casino profits that would be claimable by the ESOP. The tax benefits to be derived would mean, Winn argued, that the proposal could be implemented at no cost to the shareholders or to the employees. Winn discussed the proposal with his co-workers, and after getting some support, he distributed leaflets that described the proposal, that pointed out that employees could thereby effectively control the management of the Casino, and that stated that they would benefit through increased job stability, pay and retirement benefits, as well as from enhanced morale, productivity and profitability through "participatory management." The Casino ordered Winn to stop circulating the leaflets, and henceforth to refrain from distributing any materials about his ESOP proposal unless the Casino pre-approved them. Winn filed a charge under section 8(a)(1).

The NLRB found for the Casino. In its opinion, it stated:

"The thrust of the proposal was to cast employees in the role of owners with ultimate corporate control, and thus fundamentally to change how and by whom the corporation would be managed. The current employees would not enjoy any of the envisioned benefits unless and until they, through the ESOP, effectively controlled the corporation. Although Winn presented his proposal within the employee-employer relationship, it was designed to change that relationship. The test of whether an employee's activity is protected is not whether it relates to employees' interests generally but whether it relates to 'the interests of employees qua employees'. Here, the proposal advances employees' interests not as employees but as entrepreneurs, owners and managers. The complaint must be dismissed."

The case has been taken to a court of appeals, on which you sit. How would you decide it? See Harrah's Lake Tahoe Resort Casino, 307 NLRB 182 (1992).

**2.** A non-unionized Company's introduction of a random drug testing policy has proved highly controversial among employees. Many of them have joined a local civic organization seeking a city ordinance to ban such employment policies and seeking as well the election of a city council member committed to that effort. Employees have sought to solicit membership and support for the organization, in non-work areas on non-work time, but the Company has prohibited that solicitation. Has any unfair labor practice been committed? See NLRB v. Motorola, Inc., 991 F.2d 278 (5th Cir.1993).

**3.** Big K Cement Co. is seeking regulatory approval to burn hazardous waste at its cement kiln. This effort is opposed by the Cement Workers Union, which represents Big K's workers and which fears for the health of employees exposed to the heavy metals involved in the process. The Union has participated in the regulatory proceedings and has sought the support of various community groups. Steve Greene, a clerk-typist at Big K, is the founder and leader of the Earth Concerns Organization (ECO) and is an ardent environmentalist. The Union has appointed him as its local environmental officer. Greene's supervisor at Big K observed him photocopying an ECO article on "sham recycling" dealing with the heavy metals issue. Big K discharged Greene for unauthorized use of company equipment and materials on paid time. Has the company violated the NLRA? See Blue Circle Cement Co. v. NLRB, 41 F.3d 203 (5th Cir.1994).

---

### *"Unprotected" concerted activity*[c]

Even assuming that employees are engaged in "concerted" activity for "mutual aid or protection" it does not necessarily follow that such activity is immune from discipline. The broad language of Section 7 has never been read without qualification, for it could not seriously be argued that industrial sabotage (e.g., destroying company equipment or products) even in the cause of unionization or improvement in working conditions ought to be sheltered by the Labor Act against immediate dismissal. With no legislative guidelines thus to distinguish between "protected" and "unprotected" concerted activity, the Board and courts have assumed the task of drawing that distinction. Although the decisions have been informed by the knowledge that classification one way or the other will render the employees either immune from or susceptible to discharge, they offer very little by way of analysis or even by way of a realization that the Board is engaging in a lawmaking enterprise of major dimensions. The cases rather assume that employees ought not be protected from employer self-help when their conduct is either in violation of law or is so fundamentally contrary to the dictates of the employment relationship as to warrant characterization as "indefensible," or "reprehensible" or "disloyal." See, e.g., Aroostook County Regional Ophthalmology Center v. NLRB, 81 F.3d 209 (D.C.Cir.1996) (medical employees complaining about working conditions while treating patients).

Thus, concerted activity—even for mutual aid and protection—will be held to fall without the protection of Section 7 if its objective is contrary to the terms or spirit of the National Labor Relations Act or allied federal legislation. For example, if the object of the striking employees is to induce the employer to discharge a worker because he is a dissident voice within the union, the union commits an unfair labor practice by seeking to compel the employer to violate Section 8(a)(3), and the participating employees are deemed to be unprotected against summary discharge. It has also been held lawful for an employer to discharge workers who have engaged in a work stoppage the object of which is to force the employer to grant an immediate

---

**c.** In addition to the materials cited at page 514 supra, see A. Thieblot, Jr. & T. Haggard, Union Violence: The Record and Response by Courts, Legislatures, and the NLRB (1983).

wage increase at a time when federal regulations barred such an increase without the prior authorization of a wage-stabilization agency. American News Co., 55 NLRB 1302 (1944).

As earlier materials in this book have demonstrated, a union's use of economic pressure in support of demands falling outside the scope of mandatory bargaining (i.e., "wages, hours and other terms or conditions of employment") will constitute a refusal to bargain in good faith. Employees participating in such concerted activity are thus engaging in unprotected activity and are liable to immediate discharge. A number of cases have dealt with the issue whether the termination or replacement of a particular supervisor constitutes a mandatory subject or a permissive subject (within the prerogative of the employer), the characterization ultimately determining not so much the outlawry of the union's activity but rather the legality of the employer's resort to discipline against striking employees. *E.g.,* Dobbs Houses, Inc. v. NLRB, 325 F.2d 531 (5th Cir.1963). Also unprotected is strike activity, at or near the end of the term of a labor contract, which is directed at the modification of contract terms but which has not been preceded by the formal notification of the other party and of state and federal mediation agencies, and the cooling-off periods, mandated by Section 8(d) of the Labor Act. Section 8(d) is (along with a companion Section 8(g) governing concerted activities in health care institutions) unique in that it shows Congress explicitly declaring that employees who engage in such a premature strike are amenable to immediate discharge; Congress relieved the Board of drawing such an implication from the Act, by clearly divesting such strikers of their status as "employees" within the unfair labor practice and representation sections of the Act.

More common than the cases in which activity is deemed unprotected because of the employees' objective are cases in which activity is held to fall without Section 7 because of the method of protest utilized by the employees. If that method is in direct violation of federal law—for example, it is a secondary boycott in violation of Section 8(b)(4) or is a shipboard work stoppage contrary to the mutiny provisions of the federal Criminal Code— the employees may be discharged. See Southern S.S. Co. v. NLRB, 316 U.S. 31, 62 S.Ct. 886, 86 L.Ed. 1246 (1942). (*Held,* NLRB abuses its discretion under Section 10(c) by reinstating mutineers. "It is sufficient for this case to observe that the Board has not been commissioned to effectuate the policies of the Labor Relations Act so single-mindedly that it may wholly ignore other and equally important Congressional objectives.")

The use of methods deemed contrary to the "spirit" although not the terms of the federal Labor Act will be regarded as unprotected. Perhaps the major decision on this point is that of the Supreme Court in Emporium Capwell Co. v. Western Addition Community Organization, 420 U.S. 50, 95 S.Ct. 977, 43 L.Ed.2d 12 (1975), at p. 367, supra. In that case—which could be usefully restudied at this point—the Court held that the employer was not forbidden by the Labor Act to discharge two employees who (without the endorsement of the incumbent union) engaged in peaceful picketing and leafletting designed to induce the employer to bargain with them with a view toward altering its policies on the hiring and promotion of minority-group workers. Even the laudable objective of eliminating race discrimination in employment was held not to supersede the exclusive-representation principles of the Labor Act, and the peaceful concerted activity was held unprotected against discharge. In effect, the Court held that the employees in the bargaining unit, by electing a majority representative, had waived the immunity from discharge that the NLRA would accord them when engaging in peaceful group protests about working conditions.

An even more specific example of such a "waiver" is the no-strike clause in a collective bargaining agreement. Although a strike in breach of such a provision is not prohibited by the Labor Act, it is unprotected and may be met with employer discipline. It is therefore often necessary for the Board to construe a contractual no-strike clause in order to determine its breadth. For example, does a typical promise not to strike during the term of the labor agreement relinquish the otherwise available Section 7 right to engage in a "sympathy strike" that takes the form of refusing to cross a picket line set up by co-workers who are negotiating a new contract in a different bargaining unit? (The Board's position on this issue has hardly been constant. See Indianapolis Power & Light Co., 273 NLRB 1715 (1985); U.S. Steel Corp. v. NLRB, 711 F.2d 772 (7th Cir.1983).) Does the no-strike promise also embrace work stoppages designed to protest an employer unfair labor practice, as distinguished from an "economic strike" to secure demands at the bargaining table?

The latter issue was presented to the Supreme Court in Mastro Plastics Corp. v. NLRB, 350 U.S. 270, 76 S.Ct. 349, 100 L.Ed. 309 (1956). There, the labor agreement contained a union promise that "there shall be no interference of any kind with the operations of the Employers, or any interruptions or slackening of production of work by any of its members. The Union further agrees to refrain from engaging in any strike or work stoppage during the term of this agreement." As the contract neared its expiration date, the employer discharged one of the union's supporters and rendered unlawful assistance to an insurgent union seeking to oust the incumbent. The incumbent union called a strike, which was found by the Board not to be in support of contract demands but rather to be a protest against and an attempt to remedy the employer's unfair labor practices. When the unfair labor practice strikers later offered to return to work, the employer refused reinstatement and discharged them.

The Supreme Court noted the policy favoring enforcement of no-strike promises. It concluded, however, that the contract provision in the case before it should properly be construed to apply only to strikes seeking to "change existing economic terms" or strikes over the "meaning and application of various contractual provisions." It should not be understood to waive the right to strike over employer attempts to oust the bargaining representative. "Whatever may be said of the legality of such a waiver when explicitly stated, there is no adequate basis for implying its existence without a more compelling expression of it than appears in * * * this contract." Accordingly, the strike was protected, and the employees were unlawfully discharged. Compare, however, Arlan's Department Store, 133 N.L.R.B. 802 (1961), and Dow Chem. Co. v. NLRB, 636 F.2d 1352 (3d Cir.1980)(a general no-strike clause does waive the right to strike over "non-serious" employer unfair labor practices which can also be redressed as contract breaches through the grievance and arbitration procedures).

If strikers engage in concerted activities which violate the criminal and tort laws of the state, that too will render their conduct unprotected. Perhaps the most famous illustration is NLRB v. Fansteel Metallurgical Corp., 306 U.S. 240, 59 S.Ct. 490, 83 L.Ed. 627 (1939), in which employees, in violation of a state-court injunction, engaged in a prolonged sitdown strike, forcible seizure of the plant, and destruction of the employer's property. The Supreme Court upheld the discharge of the strikers. The same will be true when the strikers engage in actual and threatened violence on the picket line or at the homes of fellow workers. *E.g.*, NLRB v. Thayer Co., 213 F.2d 748 (1st Cir.1954), see p. 565, infra. There will be some point, however, at which conduct on the picket line will be sufficiently "tolerable" when tested by the norms of industrial confrontation such that the policies inherent in Section 7 must supersede even those of state criminal and tort law. As the NLRB has observed: "[T]he emotional tension of a strike almost inevitably gives rise to a certain amount of disorder and * * * conduct on a picket line cannot be expected to approach the etiquette of the drawing room or breakfast table." Republic Creosoting Co., 19 NLRB 267 (1940). Analogous issues will be raised when employees make accusations or comments concerning the employer which in other contexts might be regarded as defamatory, or when they engage in their activity on company property in a manner which in other contexts would be deemed trespassory. It is initially the task of the Board to draw the line between conduct sheltered by Section 7 and conduct which should be deemed unprotected because of its closeness to assault, slander or trespass. The Board or a court will sometimes explain its result in such instances simply by labeling the conduct as "indefensible" or "reprehensible" or "irresponsible."

This label has also been appended to employee protests which are timed to create an uncommon risk of injury to the employer's plant or equipment, or of spoilage to the company's goods or to goods of others which the company is processing. For example, the court in NLRB v. Marshall Car Wheel & Foundry Co., 218 F.2d 409 (5th Cir.1955), called the employees' conduct "irresponsible" and hence unprotected when they walked out of the plant at a time when molten iron was being held in a cupola which would be subjected to costly damage were the iron retained there for a long period of time.

The Supreme Court decision in the *Jefferson Standard* case, which follows, finds the Court dealing with concerted activities which raise a number of the issues outlined in this Note. Does the Court illuminate the standards by which such activity is to be judged as protected or unprotected against discharge?

———

# NLRB v. Local 1229, IBEW (Jefferson Standard Broadcasting Co.)

346 U.S. 464, 74 S.Ct. 172, 98 L.Ed. 195 (1953).

■ Mr. Justice Burton delivered the opinion of the Court.

The issue before us is whether the discharge of certain employees by their employer constituted an unfair labor practice, within the meaning of §§ 8(a)(1) and 7 of the Taft–Hartley Act, justifying their reinstatement by the National Labor Relations Board. For the reason that their discharge was "for cause" within the meaning of § 10(c) of that Act, we sustain the Board in not requiring their reinstatement.

In 1949, the Jefferson Standard Broadcasting Company (here called the company) was a North Carolina corporation engaged in interstate commerce. Under a license from the Federal Communications Commission, it operated, at Charlotte, North Carolina, a 50,000–watt radio station, with call letters WBT. It broadcasts 10 to 12 hours daily by radio and television. The television service, which it started July 14, 1949, representing an investment of about $500,000, was the only such service in the area. Less than 50% of the station's programs originated in Charlotte. The others were piped in over leased wires, generally from New York, California or Illinois from several different networks. Its annual gross revenue from broadcasting operations exceeded $100,000 but its television enterprise caused it a monthly loss of about $10,000 during the first four months of that operation, including the period here involved. Its rates for television advertising were geared to the number of receiving sets in the area. Local dealers had large inventories of such sets ready to meet anticipated demands.

The company employed 22 technicians. In December 1948, negotiations to settle the terms of their employment after January 31, 1949, were begun between representatives of the company and of the respondent Local Union No. 1229, International Brotherhood of Electrical Workers, American Federation of Labor (here called the union). The negotiations reached an impasse in January 1949, and the existing contract of employment expired January 31. The technicians, nevertheless, continued to work for the company and their collective-bargaining negotiations were resumed in July, only to break down again July 8. The main point of disagreement arose from the union's demand for the renewal of a provision that all discharges from employment be subject to arbitration and the company's counterproposal that such arbitration be limited to the facts material to each discharge, leaving it to the company to determine whether those facts gave adequate cause for discharge.

July 9, 1949, the union began daily peaceful picketing of the company's station. Placards and handbills on the picket line charged the company with unfairness to its technicians and emphasized the company's refusal to renew the provision for arbitration of discharges. The placards and handbills named the union as the representative of the WBT technicians. The employees did not strike. They confined their respective tours of picketing to their off-duty hours and continued to draw full pay. There was no violence or threat of violence and no one has taken exception to any of the above conduct.

But on August 24, 1949, a new procedure made its appearance. Without warning, several of its technicians launched a vitriolic attack on the quality of the company's television broadcasts. Five thousand handbills were printed over the designation "WBT Technicians." These were distributed on the picket line, on the public square two or three blocks from the company's premises, in barber shops, restaurants and busses. Some were mailed to local businessmen. The handbills made no reference to the union, to a labor controversy or to collective bargaining. They read:

"Is Charlotte A Second–Class City?

"You might think so from the kind of Television programs being presented by the Jefferson Standard Broadcasting Co. over WBTV. Have you seen one of their television programs lately? Did you know that all the programs presented over WBTV are on film and may be from one day to five years old. There are no local programs presented by WBTV. You cannot receive the local baseball games, football games or other local events because WBTV does not have the proper equipment to make these pickups. Cities like New York, Boston, Philadelphia, Washington receive such programs nightly. Why doesn't the Jefferson Standard Broadcasting Company purchase the needed equipment to bring you the same type of programs enjoyed by other leading American cities? Could it be that they consider Charlotte a second-class community and only entitled to the pictures now being presented to them?

"WBT Technicians"

This attack continued until September 3, 1949, when the company discharged ten of its technicians, whom it charged with sponsoring or distributing these handbills. The company's letter discharging them tells its side of the story.[5]

5.   "Dear Mr. * * *,

"When you and some of our other technicians commenced early in July to picket against this Company, we felt that your action was very ill-considered. We were paying you a salary of * * * per week, to say nothing of other benefits which you receive as an employee of our Company, such as time-and-a-half pay for all work beyond eight hours in any one day, three weeks vacation each year with full pay, unlimited sick leave with full pay, liberal life insurance and hospitalization, for you and your family, and retirement and pension benefits unexcelled anywhere. Yet when we were unable to agree upon the terms of a contract with your Union, you began to denounce us publicly as 'unfair.'

"And ever since early July while you have been walking up and down the street with placards and literature attacking us, you have continued to hold your job and receive your pay and all the other benefits referred to above.

"Even when you began to put out propaganda which contained many untruths about our Company and great deal of personal abuse and slander, we still continued to treat you exactly as before. For it has been our understanding that under our labor laws, you have a very great latitude in trying to make the public believe that your employer is unfair to you.

"Now, however, you have turned from trying to persuade the public that we are unfair *to*

September 4, the union's picketing resumed its original tenor and, September 13, the union filed with the Board a charge that the company, by discharging the above-mentioned ten technicians, had engaged in an unfair labor practice. The General Counsel for the Board filed a complaint based on those charges and, after hearing, a trial examiner made detailed findings and a recommendation that all of those discharged be reinstated with back pay. 94 N.L.R.B. 1507, 1527. The Board found that one of the discharged men had neither sponsored nor distributed the "Second–Class City" handbill and ordered his reinstatement with back pay. It then found that the other nine had sponsored or distributed the handbill and held that the company, by discharging them for such conduct, had not engaged in an unfair labor practice. The Board, accordingly, did not order their reinstatement. One member dissented. Id., at 1507 et seq. Under § 10(f) of the Taft–Hartley Act, the union petitioned the Court of Appeals for the District of Columbia Circuit for a review of the Board's order and for such a modification of it as would reinstate all ten of the discharged technicians with back pay. That court remanded the cause to the Board for further consideration and for a finding as to the "unlawfulness" of the conduct of the employees which had led to their discharge. 91 U.S.App.D.C. 333, 202 F.2d 186.[7] We granted certiorari because of the importance of the case in the administration of the Taft–Hartley Act. 345 U.S. 947, 73 S.Ct. 865.

In its essence, the issue is simple. It is whether these employees, whose contracts of employment had expired, were discharged "for cause." * * *

The company's letter shows that it interpreted the handbill as a demonstration of such detrimental disloyalty as to provide "cause" for its refusal to continue in its employ the perpetrators of the attack. We agree.

*you* and are trying to persuade the public that we give inferior service *to them.* While we are struggling to expand into and develop a new field, and incidentally losing large sums of money in the process, you are busy trying to turn customers and the public against us in every possible way, even handing out leaflets on the public street advertising that our operations are 'second-class,' and endeavoring in various ways to hamper and totally destroy our business. Certainly we are not required by law or common sense to keep you in our employment and pay you a substantial salary while you thus do your best to tear down and bankrupt our business.

"You are hereby discharged from our employment. Although there is nothing requiring us to do so, and the circumstances certainly do not call for our doing so, we are enclosing a check payable to your order for two weeks advance or severance pay.

"Very truly yours,

"Jefferson Standard Broadcasting

Company

"By: Charles H. Crutchfield

*"Vice President*

"Enclosure"

**7.** The Court of Appeals said:

"Protection under § 7 of the Act * * * is withdrawn only from those concerted activities which contravene either (a) specific provisions or basic policies of the Act or of related federal statutes, or (b) specific rules of other federal or local law that is not incompatible with the Board's governing statute. * * *

"We think the Board failed to make the finding essential to its conclusion that the concerted activity was unprotected. Sound practice in judicial review of administrative orders precludes this court from determining 'unlawfulness' without a prior consideration and finding by the Board." * * *

Section 10(c) of the Taft–Hartley Act expressly provides that "No order of the Board shall require the reinstatement of any individual as an employee who has been suspended or discharged, or the payment to him of any back pay, if such individual was suspended or discharged for cause." There is no more elemental cause for discharge of an employee than disloyalty to his employer. It is equally elemental that the Taft–Hartley Act seeks to strengthen, rather than to weaken, that cooperation, continuity of service and cordial contractual relation between employer and employee that is born of loyalty to their common enterprise.

Congress, while safeguarding, in § 7, the right of employees to engage in "concerted activities for the purpose of collective bargaining or other mutual aid or protection," did not weaken the underlying contractual bonds and loyalties of employer and employee. The conference report that led to the enactment of the law said:

"[T]he courts have firmly established the rule that under the existing provisions of section 7 of the National Labor Relations Act, employees are not given any right to engage in unlawful or other improper conduct.

" * * * Furthermore, in section 10(c) of the amended act, as proposed in the conference agreement, it is specifically provided that no order of the Board shall require the reinstatement of any individual or the payment to him of any back pay if such individual was suspended or discharged for cause, and this, of course, applies with equal force whether or not the acts constituting the cause for discharge were committed in connection with a concerted activity." H.R.Rep. No. 510, 80th Cong., 1st Sess. 38–39.

This has been clear since the early days of the Wagner Act. [Citations omitted.] The above cases illustrate the responsibility that falls upon the Board to find the facts material to such decisions. The legal principle that insubordination, disobedience or disloyalty is adequate cause for discharge is plain enough. The difficulty arises in determining whether, in fact, the discharges are made because of such a separable cause or because of some other concerted activities engaged in for the purpose of collective bargaining or other mutual aid or protection which may not be adequate cause for discharge. Cf. National Labor Relations Board v. Peter Cailler Kohler Swiss Chocolates Co., 2 Cir., 130 F.2d 503.

In the instant case the Board found that the company's discharge of the nine offenders resulted from their sponsoring and distributing the "Second–Class City" handbills of August 24—September 3, issued in their name as the "WBT Technicians." Assuming that there had been no pending labor controversy, the conduct of the "WBT Technicians" from August 24 through September 3 unquestionably would have provided adequate cause for their disciplinary discharge within the meaning of § 10(c). Their attack related itself to no labor practice of the company. It made no reference to wages, hours or working conditions. The policies attacked were those of finance and public relations for which management, not technicians, must be responsible. The attack asked for no public sympathy or support. It was a continuing attack, initiated while off duty, upon the very interests which the attackers were being paid to conserve and develop. Nothing could be further from the purpose of the Act than to require an employer to finance such activities. Nothing would contribute less to the Act's declared purpose of promoting industrial peace and stability.

The fortuity of the coexistence of a labor dispute affords these technicians no substantial defense. While they were also union men and leaders in the labor controversy, they took pains to separate those categories. In contrast to their claims on the picket line as to the labor controversy, their handbill of August 24 omitted all reference to it. The handbill diverted attention from the labor controversy. It attacked public policies of the company which had no discernible relation to that controversy. The only connection between the handbill and the labor controversy was an ultimate and undisclosed purpose or motive on the part of some of the sponsors that, by the hoped-for financial pressure, the attack might extract from the company some future concession. A disclosure of that motive might have lost more public support for the employees than it would have gained, for it would have given the handbill more the character of coercion than of collective bargaining. Referring to the attack, the Board said "In our judgment, these tactics, in the circumstances of this case, were hardly less 'indefensible' than acts of physical sabotage." 94 N.L.R.B., at 1511. In any event, the findings of the Board effectively separate the attack from the labor controversy and treat it solely as one made by the company's technical experts upon the quality of the company's product. As such, it was as adequate a cause for the discharge of its sponsors as if the labor controversy had not been pending. The technicians, themselves, so handled their attack as thus to bring their discharge under § 10(c).

The Board stated "We * * * do not decide whether the disparagement of product involved here would have justified the employer in discharging the employees responsible for it, had it been uttered in the context of a conventional appeal for support of the union in the labor dispute." Id., at 1512, n. 18. This underscored the Board's factual conclusion that the attack of August 24 was not part of an appeal for support in the pending dispute. It was a concerted separable attack purporting to be made in the interest of the public rather than in that of the employees.

We find no occasion to remand this cause to the Board for further specificity of findings. Even if the attack were to be treated, as the Board has not treated it, as a concerted activity wholly or partly within the scope of those mentioned in § 7, the means used by the technicians in conducting the attack have deprived the attackers of the protection of that section, when read in the light and context of the purpose of the Act.

Accordingly, the order of the Court of Appeals remanding the cause to the National Labor Relations Board is set aside, and the cause is remanded to the Court of Appeals with instructions to dismiss respondent's petition to modify the order of the Board. It is so ordered.

Order set aside and cause remanded with instructions.

■ MR. JUSTICE FRANKFURTER, whom MR. JUSTICE BLACK and MR. JUSTICE DOUGLAS join, dissenting. * * * On this central issue—whether the Court of Appeals rightly or wrongly found that the Board applied an improper criterion—this Court is silent. It does not support the Board in using "indefensible" as the legal litmus nor does it reject the Court of Appeals' rejection of that test. This Court presumably does not disagree with the assumption of the Court of Appeals that conduct may be "indefensible" in the colloquial meaning of that loose adjective, and yet be within the protection of § 7.

Instead, the Court, relying on § 10(c) which permits discharges "for cause," points to the "disloyalty" of the employees and finds sufficient "cause" regardless of whether the handbill was a "concerted activity" within § 7. Section 10(c) does not speak of discharge "for disloyalty." If Congress had so written that section, it would have overturned much of the law that had been developed by the Board and the courts in the twelve years preceding the Taft–Hartley Act. The legislative history makes clear that Congress had no such purpose but was rather expressing approval of the construction of "concerted activities" adopted by the Board and the courts. Many of the legally recognized tactics and weapons of labor would readily be condemned for "disloyalty" were they employed between man and man in friendly personal relations. In this connection it is significant that the ground now taken by the Court, insofar as it is derived from the provision of § 10(c) relating to discharge "for cause," was not invoked by the Board in justification of its order.

To suggest that all actions which in the absence of a labor controversy might be "cause"—or, to use the words commonly found in labor agreements, "just cause"—for discharge should be unprotected, even when such actions were undertaken as "concerted activities for the purpose of collective bargaining", is to misconstrue legislation designed to put labor on a fair footing with management. Furthermore, it would disregard the rough and tumble of strikes, in the course of which loose and even reckless language is properly discounted.

"Concerted activities" by employees and dismissal "for cause" by employers are not disassociated legal criteria under the Act. They are like the two halves of a pair of shears. Of course, as the Conference Report on the Taft–Hartley Act said, men on strike may be guilty of conduct "in connection with a concerted activity" which properly constitutes "cause" for dismissal and bars reinstatement. But § 10(c) does not obviate the necessity for a determination whether the distribution of the handbill here was a legitimate tool in the labor dispute or was so "improper," as the Conference Report put it, as to be denied the protection of § 7 and to constitute a discharge "for cause." It is for the Board, in the first instance, to make these evaluations, and a court of appeals does not travel beyond its proper bounds in asking the Board for greater explicitness in light of the correct legal standards for judgment.

The Board and the courts of appeals will hardly find guidance for future cases from this Court's reversal of the Court of Appeals, beyond that which the specific facts of this case may afford. More than that, to float such imprecise notions as "discipline" and "loyalty" in the context of labor controversies, as the basis of the right to discharge, is to open the door wide to individual judgment by Board members and judges. One may anticipate that the Court's opinion will needlessly stimulate litigation. * * *

---

ELK LUMBER CO., 91 NLRB 333 (1950).[d] As a result of certain physical improvements in the plant, the non-union company unilaterally changed the rate of pay of carloaders to $1.52½ cents per hour (compared to an average of $2.71 previously earned on an incentive basis). This induced several carloaders to reduce their pace of work so as to load only one car a day; they made it clear that they would increase their pace if their pay were increased. After about a month of engaging in this slowdown, five workers were discharged. Although the slowdown was the result of an agreement among the workers, the Board found it to be unprotected activity.

The Board formulated the issue for decision as "whether the particular activity involved is so indefensible as to warrant the employer in discharging the participating employees. Either an unlawful objective or the adoption of improper means of achieving it may deprive employees engaged in concerted activities of the protection of the Act." The Board concluded that "the plan of decreasing their production to the amount they considered adequate for the pay they were then receiving * * * constituted a refusal on their part to accept the terms of employment set by their employer without engaging in a stoppage, but to continue rather to work on their own terms." Employees have no right to "prescribe all conditions and regulations affecting their employment." It was therefore held that the discharge was lawful.

The Board relied upon NLRB v. Montgomery Ward & Co., 157 F.2d 486 (8th Cir.1946), in which employees at one of the employer's plants refused to process orders from another plant where a strike was in progress. The court found the employees' refusal, while they remained at work, to be outside the protection of Section 7:

> It was implied in the contract of hiring that these employees would do the work assigned to them in a careful and workmanlike manner; that they would comply with all reasonable orders and conduct themselves so as not to work injury to the employer's business; that they would serve faithfully and be regardful of the interests of the employer during the term of their service, and carefully discharge their duties to the extent reasonably required. * * * Any employee may, of course, be lawfully discharged for disobedience of the employer's directions in breach of his contract.

**d.** See J. Atleson, Values and Assumptions in American Labor Law, ch. 3 (1983); Finkin, Labor Law by Boz—A Theory of *Meyers Indus., Inc., Sears, Roebuck & Co.* and *Bird Engineering,* 71 Iowa L.Rev. 155, 188–94 (1985); Getman, The Protection of Economic Pressure by Section 7 of the NLRA, 115 U.Pa.L.Rev. 1195 (1967); compare Getman, The Protected Status of Partial Strikes After *Lodge 76:* A Comment, 29 Stan.L.Rev. 205 (1977), with Lopatka, A Reply to Professor Getman, 29 Stan.L.Rev. 1181 (1977).

\* \* \* While these employees had the undoubted right to go on a strike and quit their employment, they could not continue to work and remain at their positions, accept the wages paid to them, and at the same time select what part of their allotted tasks they cared to perform of their own volition, or refuse openly or secretly, to the employer's damage, to do other work.

--------

## PROBLEMS FOR DISCUSSION

**1.** After negotiations for a new contract had failed, the employees of the Patterson–Sargent Company struck. The Company, a paint manufacturer, continued to operate by using its supervisors on production jobs, whereupon various employees distributed circulars which were entitled "Beware Paint Substitute." The circulars warned customers that Patterson–Sargent paints were not being made by "the well-trained experienced employees who have made the paint you have always bought" and that the paint might peel, crack, blister or scale. The final sentence pointed out to customers that they would be informed when they could again buy Patterson–Sargent paint made by the regular employees. The Company discharged those employees who had distributed the circulars and refused to reinstate them when the strike was over. Has the Company violated Section 8(a)(3)? See Patterson–Sargent Company, 115 NLRB 1627 (1956); Sierra Pub. Co. v. NLRB, 889 F.2d 210 (9th Cir.1989).

**2.** Maxine Lomax was a low-level supervisor directly in charge of the work of a number of employees in the men's and women's clothing department of the Thriftee Department Store. Ms. Lomax was discharged by Thriftee after a dispute about her working hours. She was well-liked by many of the employees, who frequently turned to her for assistance in her capacity as supervisor; she would often relieve employees at their counter and floor positions, and would help them out when they were unusually busy or when they were temporarily called away from the store on urgent business. Her presence was clearly a boost to employee morale. On the day that Ms. Lomax was discharged, some twenty employees appealed to the management of Thriftee to reconsider the discharge and to rehire Ms. Lomax, but when management refused, the employees walked out. Thriftee promptly announced that the employees were discharged and refused to process their applications for reinstatement, submitted several days later. Has Thriftee violated Section 8(a)(1)? See Plastilite Corp., 153 NLRB 180 (1965), mdf'd on other grounds, 375 F.2d 343 (8th Cir.1967).

Are there any circumstances in which the group writing of a letter, or the staging of a protest, regarding the identity or conduct of a company *president* could be regarded as activity to be protected against discipline? See NLRB v. Oakes Mach. Corp., 897 F.2d 84 (2d Cir.1990).

Or, *per contra*, were an employee to protest (on behalf of a group) the promotion of an especially disliked coworker to a managerial position, could he be discharged for it? See Atlantic–Pacific Constr. Co. v. NLRB, 52 F.3d 260 (9th Cir.1995).

**3.** Assume that in Problem 2, after being informed by Thriftee that Ms. Lomax would not be rehired, the employees secretly decided to stage their walkout several days later, the date of the storewide Labor Day sale, in order to have the maximum effect on Thriftee's business. The employees reported for work as usual, including the morning of the Labor Day sale, but walked out in a group at 11 a.m. that day, announcing their intention not to return until Ms. Lomax was rehired. Thriftee was not able to service the customers, and the doors were closed at noon. Thriftee immediately informed the striking employees of their discharge, citing the irreparable harm to customer relations by the work stoppage at such a busy time. Does that affect the determination of the legality of the discharges? *See* Bob Evans Farms, Inc. v. NLRB, 163 F.3d 1012 (7th Cir.1998). *See also* NLRB v. Federal Security, Inc., 154 F.3d 751 (7th Cir.1998).

**4.** Why is a peaceful concerted work slowdown not protected under Section 7? Are the employees really trying by their slowdown unilaterally to alter working conditions? If their slowdown is regarded as an improper and insubordinate refusal to do assigned work, why is that not truer yet of a total work stoppage (clearly protected under Section 7)? Is the reason simply because the Board believes that the partial or "quickie" strike gives employees too great leverage over the employer?

**5.** Assume, in the *Elk Lumber* case, that the carloaders—rather than slowing the pace of their work—chose to return late from lunch and to leave early at the end of the day. The company then immediately discharged them. Does their right to reinstatement depend upon whether they intended their group protest as a first step in a full-fledged continuing walkout, rather than one step in a campaign of intermittent and unannounced stoppages? Would this be a practicable standard? Should the jobs of workers—particularly unorganized workers reacting spontaneously and without professional advice—depend upon this distinction? See Polytech, Inc., 195 NLRB 695 (1972); First Nat. Bank of Omaha, 171 NLRB 1145 (1968), enf'd, 413 F.2d 921 (8th Cir.1969).

**6.** Fibers, Inc., a non-unionized firm, has announced that for two days free ice cream cones would be given to employees in the lunchroom to celebrate a "sole supplier" agreement with a major customer. In response, two employees wrote and posted a letter which provided in part:

> The employees of Fibers, Inc. would like to express their great appreciation of the 52 flavors of left over ice cream from the closed Meadow Gold Plant. It has boosted moral [sic] tremendously. Several employees were heard to say they were going to work harder together, and do better so we could have some more old ice cream.

> We realize what a tremendous sacrifice this has been for the management and will be long remembered. We hope this has not cut into computer expenses.

They were dismissed for action "disruptive to the workforce * * * undermining to management and fellow workers." Has Fibers, Inc. violated the Act? Compare New River Industries, Inc. v. NLRB, 945 F.2d 1290 (4th Cir.1991), with Reef Industries, Inc. v. NLRB, 952 F.2d 830 (5th Cir.1991), reh'g denied, publication granted, 952 F.2d 839 (5th Cir.1992).

**7.** Graduate students at Ivy University devote several hours each week to working as teaching fellows in aid of professors teaching undergraduates. These so-called TAs are seeking to organize a union that will, among other things, advocate their interests on matters of wages and health insurance. In an effort to gain members and to rally support from the university community, the TAs have refused to submit student grades for the fall semester and have refused to return the undergraduates' bluebooks to the course professors. However, they have performed their other duties such as meeting with students, proctoring examinations, and preparing for the following semester's classes. The University, which concedes that the TAs are "employees" and covered by the NLRA, has threatened to dismiss them for engaging in a partial strike and an improper "misappropriation" of the employer's property akin to a sit-down strike. The teaching fellows have filed charges under section 8(a)(1). How should the case be decided? *See* Yale University, 330 NLRB No. 28 (1999).

**8.** Libby Borden is a service representative for E–Serv which provides communications service—including the resolution of technical problems—for Yo–Yo Dyne, Inc. Ms. Borden dispatches service requests to technicians with whom she interacts by e-mail. Much of the service work requires interaction with the telephone company and trouble-shooting at the phone company on Yo–Yo Dyne's problems. Ms. Borden has learned that the phone company employees might soon go out on strike. She has e-mailed E–Serv's technicians telling them that a strike was impending at the phone company and urging their "support" for that effort. She e-mailed them a second time urging them to refuse to cross any picket line set up at the phone company and not to refer service requests to the phone company. She has been discharged. Has Yo–Yo Dyne violated the Act? *See* Electronic Data Systems Corp., 331 NLRB No. 52 (2000).

---------

## B. EMPLOYER RESPONSES TO CONCERTED ACTIVITIES[e]

## NLRB v. Mackay Radio & Telegraph Co.

304 U.S. 333, 58 S.Ct. 904, 82 L.Ed. 1381 (1938).

■ MR. JUSTICE ROBERTS delivered the opinion of the Court.

[Respondent, a California corporation engaged in the transmission of foreign and interstate communications, maintains an office at San Francisco where it employs upwards of sixty supervisors, operators and clerks, many of whom are members of Local 3 of the American Radio Telegraphists, a national labor organization; respondent's parent company, whose headquarters were in New York, deals with representatives of the national organization. In September, 1935, in view of the unsatisfactory state of negotiations for a new collective bargaining agreement, the national officers

---

**e.** See J. Atleson, Values and Assumptions in American Labor Law, chaps. 1 and 8 (1983); Barron, A Theory of Protected Employer Rights: A Revisionist Analysis of the Supreme Court's Interpretation of the NLRA, 59 Texas L.Rev. 421 (1981); Christensen & Svanoe, Motive and Intent in the Commission of Unfair Labor Practices: The Supreme Court and the Fictive Formality, 77 Yale L.J. 1269 (1968); P. Cox, Reexamination of the Role of Employer Motive Under Sections 8(a)(1) and 8(a)(3) of the NLRA, 5 U. Puget Sound L.Rev. 161 (1982); Estreicher, Strikers and Replacements, 3 Lab.Law. 897 (1987); Getman, Section 8(a)(3) of the NLRA and the Effort to Insulate Free Employee Choice, 32 U.Chi.L.Rev. 735 (1965); Janofsky, New Concepts in Interference and Discrimination Under the NLRA—The Legacy of *American Ship Building & Great Dane Trailers*, 70 Colum.L.Rev. 81 (1970); Note, Equal Access in NLRB Elections: Determining the Voting Eligibility of Economic Strikers, 58 Geo. Wash.L.Rev. 549 (1990); C. Perry, A. Kramer & T. Schneider, Operating During Strikes (1984); Weiler, Striking a New Balance: Freedom of Contract and the Prospects for Union Representation, 98 Harv.L.Rev. 351 (1984).

called a strike which took effect at midnight on October 4 (and which ultimately lasted only three days). Respondent, in order to maintain service, brought employees from other offices to fill the places of the San Francisco strikers. When the strike proved unsuccessful in other parts of the country, a number of San Francisco employees became convinced that they should return to work before their places were filled by new workers. Respondent informed them that they might return to work in a body but that since it had promised eleven workers brought to San Francisco an opportunity to remain there if they desired, the return of the strikers would have to be handled in such a way as not to displace the eleven. Later one of respondent's officials gave the striking employees a list on which the names of eleven strikers were checked off as ineligible for reinstatement until their applications were approved by the New York office. When it turned out that only five of the new employees wished to stay in San Francisco, six of the eleven checked off resumed their work without challenge. The remaining five, who were prominent in the activities of the union and in connection with the strike, were not reinstated in the course of the next three weeks. Local 3 thereupon filed charges with the Board.

[The Board concluded that respondent by refusing to reinstate the five workers in question, "thereby discharging said employees," discriminated in regard to tenure of employment in violation of section 8(1) and (3). Accordingly the Board ordered their reinstatement with back pay. The Circuit Court of Appeals set aside the order of the Board, but the Supreme Court reversed and sustained the Board's order. In the opening sections of its opinion, the Court held that the strike took place in connection with a current labor dispute as defined in Section 2(9), and therefore that the strikers retained their status as "employees" under Section 2(3) and were thus protected against employer unfair labor practices.]

*Fourth.* It is contended that the Board lacked jurisdiction because respondent was at no time guilty of any unfair labor practice. * * * There is no evidence and no finding that the respondent was guilty of any unfair labor practice in connection with the negotiations in New York. On the contrary, it affirmatively appears that the respondent was negotiating with the authorized representatives of the union. Nor was it an unfair labor practice to replace the striking employees with others in an effort to carry on the business. Although section 13 of the act, 29 U.S.C.A. § 163, provides, "Nothing in this Act [chapter] shall be construed so as to interfere with or impede or diminish in any way the right to strike," it does not follow that an employer, guilty of no act denounced by the statute, has lost the right to protect and continue his business by supplying places left vacant by strikers. And he is not bound to discharge those hired to fill the places of strikers, upon the election of the latter to resume their employment, in order to create places for them. The assurance by respondent to those who accepted employment during the strike that if they so desired their places might be permanent was not an unfair labor practice, nor was it such to reinstate only so many of the strikers as there were vacant places to be filled. But the claim put forward [by the Board] is that the unfair labor practice indulged by the respondent was discrimination in reinstating striking employees by keeping out certain of them for the sole reason that they had been active in the union. As we have said, the strikers retained, under the act, the status of employees. Any such discrimination in putting them back to work is, therefore, prohibited by section 8.

*Fifth.* The Board's findings as to discrimination are supported by evidence. * * * The Board found, and we cannot say that its finding is unsupported, that, in taking back six of the eleven men and excluding five who were active union men, the respondent's officials discriminated against the latter on account of their union activities and that the excuse given that they did not apply until after the quota was full was an afterthought and not the true reason for the discrimination against them.

As we have said, the respondent was not bound to displace men hired to take the strikers' places in order to provide positions for them. It might have refused reinstatement on the grounds of skill or ability, but the Board found that it did not do so. It might have resorted to any one of a number of methods of determining which of its striking employees would have to wait because five men had taken permanent positions during the strike, but it is found that the preparation and use of the list, and the action taken by respondent, was with the purpose to discriminate against those most active in the union. There is evidence to support these findings. * * *

*Seventh.* The affirmative relief ordered by the Board was within its powers and its order was not arbitrary or capricious. * * *

■ Mr. Justice Cardozo and Mr. Justice Reed took no part in the consideration or decision of this case.

———

## PROBLEMS FOR DISCUSSION

**1.** Does not the permanent replacement of strikers (and the retention of non-strikers) constitute the clearest conceivable "discrimination in regard to hire or tenure of employment" which discourages union membership and activities? How, then, can the Court conclude that such replacement does not violate the Act? Is there any support for an exception in the text of the Act? In its purposes?

Could the General Counsel have prevailed on this issue if he had demonstrated that the employer could have kept the business going with merely temporary replacements? (How protracted was the strike?) That the employer was really motivated by a desire to break the union?

**2.** Notice that this case involves the replacement of "economic" strikers—that is, strikers who are using the stoppage as a means of extracting some bargaining concession from the employer. Can this case be used as a precedent when an economic striker, rather than being permanently replaced, is discharged outright? See NLRB v. Browning–Ferris Indus., 700 F.2d 385 (7th Cir.1983).

Can this case be used as a precedent when the employee being permanently replaced is not an economic striker but is rather an "unfair labor practice striker," i.e., where the stoppage is a protest against an unfair labor practice committed by the employer? What arguments can be made to permit the unfair labor practice striker to be reinstated after an attempted permanent replacement (and thus to "bump" the replacement)? On the other hand, what arguments can be made for treating the economic striker *more* favorably than the unfair labor practice striker?

––––––––

In July, 1991, the House of Representatives (then controlled by the Democratic Party) passed H.R. 5, the Workplace Fairness Act, which would have amended the National Labor Relations Act and the Railway Labor Act to prohibit the hiring of permanent replacements in most strike situations. The Senate failed to enact a companion bill, and efforts to do so came to a final defeat when in July 1994 S. 55 was dropped, in the face of a threatened filibuster. The election of the Republican-controlled House and Senate in November 1994 removed the striker-replacement bills from the congressional agenda.

President Clinton, however, utilizing his power to issue executive orders relating to the procurement operations of the federal government, promulgated in March 1995 Executive Order No. 12,954, 60 Fed. Reg. 13,023, which authorized the Secretary of Labor to terminate federal contracts (and to bar future contracts) with any companies that had, essentially anywhere in its business, permanently replaced economic strikers. The rationale was to promote governmental efficiency through the retention of experienced workers and the reduced length of strikes. Although congressional leaders criticized the executive order as an improper circumvention of legislative authority, no congressional action was taken to overturn it.

Instead, a lawsuit was brought by several business associations, and the Executive Order was struck down in CHAMBER OF COMMERCE OF THE U.S. v. REICH, 74 F.3d 1322 (D.C.Cir.1996). The court held that, despite the usual powers of the President under the so-called Procurement Act (40 U.S.C. § 471 et seq.) "to ensure the economical and efficient administration and completion of Federal Government contracts," he was impliedly forbidden by the policies of the NLRA to deny to employers an economic weapon allowed as a countermeasure (since the *Mackay* decision) against the employees' right to strike. The court noted that the Executive Order announced "a broad policy governing the behavior of thousands of American companies" (6.5% of the gross domestic product) and "affecting millions of American workers" (26 million workers, or 22% of the U.S. labor force). An earlier court decision upholding a presidential executive order requiring an affirmative-action covenant in federally assisted construction contracts was distinguished, as not involving any conflict with a preemptive federal statute such as the NLRA—preemptive with respect to both state and federal executive authority.

––––––––

# NLRB v. Erie Resistor Corp.
373 U.S. 221, 83 S.Ct. 1139, 10 L.Ed.2d 308 (1963).

■ MR. JUSTICE WHITE delivered the opinion of the Court.

[During a strike over the terms of a new collective bargaining agreement the company, which was under intense competitive pressure, continued production with the aid of non-strikers. Later, the company hired replacements to whom it promised some form of super-seniority at the end of the strike. Later but still during the strike, the company announced that the super-seniority would take the form of adding twenty years to the length of a worker's actual service for purposes of future layoffs and recalls (but not for other employee benefits based on seniority). The offer was extended to strikers who would return to work. In a short time, a substantial number of the strikers went back to work, and the union capitulated and signed a new contract and a settlement agreement (which left the company's super-seniority plan in effect pending the final disposition of unfair labor practice charges). The company then reinstated those strikers whose jobs had not been filled, and at about the same time the union received some 173 resignations from membership (out of an initial unit of 478 employees). Although within a few weeks the company's workforce had returned to nearly its pre-strike size, some nine months later it had slipped back to nearly half that size; many employees laid off during this cutback were reinstated strikers who had not been credited with super-seniority.

[The union filed charges challenging both the super-seniority plan and the later layoffs. The NLRB held that specific evidence of the Respondent's discriminatory motivation is not required to establish the alleged violations of the Act, and that the employer's argument (accepted by the Trial Examiner) that its overriding purpose in granting super-seniority was to keep its plant open and that business necessity justified its conduct was unacceptable since "to excuse such conduct would greatly diminish, if not destroy, the right to strike guaranteed by the Act, and would run directly counter to the guarantees of Sections 8(a)(1) and (3) that employees shall not be discriminated against for engaging in protected concerted activities." Accordingly, the Board declined to make findings as to the specific motivation of the plan or its business necessity in the circumstances here. The Court of Appeals rejected as unsupportable the rationale of the Board that a preferential seniority policy is illegal however motivated.

["We are of the opinion that inherent in the right of an employer to replace strikers during a strike is the concomitant right to adopt a preferential seniority policy which will assure the replacements some form of tenure, provided the policy is adopted *solely* to protect and continue the business of the employer. We find nothing in the Act which proscribes such a policy. Whether the policy adopted by the Company in the instant case was illegally motivated we do not decide. The question is one of fact for decision by the Board." 303 F.2d, at 364.

[It consequently denied the Board's petition for enforcement and remanded the case for further findings.]

We think the Court of Appeals erred in holding that, in the absence of a finding of specific illegal intent, a legitimate business purpose is always a defense to an unfair labor practice charge. Cases in this Court dealing with unfair labor practices have recognized the relevance and importance of showing the employer's intent or motive to discriminate or to interfere with union rights. But specific evidence of such subjective intent is "not an indispensable element of proof of violation." Radio Officers' Union of Commercial Telegraphers Union, A.F.L. v. National Labor Relations Board, 347 U.S. 17, 44, 74 S.Ct. 323, 98 L.Ed. 455. "Some conduct may by its very nature contain the implications of the required intent; the natural foreseeable consequences of certain action may warrant the inference. * * * The existence of discrimination may at times be inferred by the Board, for 'it is permissible to draw on experience in factual inquiries.' " Local 357, International Brotherhood of Teamsters, Chauffeurs, Warehousemen and Helpers of America v. National Labor Relations Board, 365 U.S. 667, 675, 81 S.Ct. 835, 839, 6 L.Ed.2d 11.

Though the intent necessary for an unfair labor practice may be shown in different ways, proving it in one manner may have far different weight and far different consequences than proving it in another. When specific evidence of a subjective intent to discriminate or to encourage or discourage union membership is shown, and found, many otherwise innocent or ambiguous actions which are normally incident to the conduct of a business may, without more, be converted into unfair labor practices. [The Court cited cases involving hiring, discharge, subcontracting, and plant removal.] Such proof itself is normally sufficient to destroy the employer's claim of a legitimate business purpose, if one is made, and provides strong support to a finding that there is interference with union rights or that union membership will be discouraged. Conduct which on its face appears to serve legitimate business ends in these cases is wholly impeached by the showing of an intent to encroach upon protected rights. The employer's claim of legitimacy is totally dispelled.

The outcome may well be the same when intent is founded upon the inherently discriminatory or destructive nature of the conduct itself. The employer in such cases must be held to intend the very consequences which foreseeably and inescapably flow from his actions and if he fails to explain away, to justify or to characterize his actions as something different than they appear on their face, an unfair labor practice charge is made out. Radio Officers Union of Commercial Telegraphers Union, A.F.L. v. National Labor Relations Board, supra. But as often happens, the employer may counter by claiming that his actions were taken in the pursuit of legitimate business ends and that his dominant purpose was not to discriminate or to invade union rights but to accomplish business objectives acceptable under the Act. Nevertheless his conduct *does* speak for itself—it *is* discriminatory and it *does* discourage union membership and whatever the claimed overriding justification may be, it carries with it unavoidable consequences which the employer not only foresaw but which he must have intended. As is not uncommon in human experience, such situations present a complex of motives and preferring one motive to another is in reality the far more delicate task, reflected in part in decisions of this Court of weighing the interests of employees in concerted activity against the interest of the employer in operating his business in a particular manner and of balancing in the light of the Act and its policy the intended consequences upon employee rights against the business ends to be served by the employer's conduct. This essentially is the teaching of the Court's prior cases dealing with this problem and, in our view, the Board did not depart from it.

The Board made a detailed assessment of super-seniority and, to its experienced eye, such a plan had the following characteristics:

(1) Super-seniority affects the tenure of all strikers whereas permanent replacement, proper under Mackay, affects only those who are, in actuality, replaced. It is one thing to say that a striker is subject to loss of his job at the strike's end but quite another to hold that in addition to the threat of replacement, all strikers will at best return to their jobs with seniority inferior to that of the replacements and of those who left the strike.

(2) A super-seniority award necessarily operates to the detriment of those who participated in the strike as compared to non-strikers.

(3) Super-seniority made available to striking bargaining unit employees as well as to new employees is in effect offering individual benefits to the strikers to induce them to abandon the strike.

(4) Extending the benefits of super-seniority to striking bargaining unit employees as well as to new replacements deals a crippling blow to the strike effort. At one stroke, those with low seniority have the opportunity to obtain the job security which ordinarily only long years of service can bring, while conversely, the accumulated seniority of older employees is seriously diluted. This combination of threat and promise could be expected to undermine the strikers' mutual interest and place the entire strike effort in jeopardy. The history of this strike and its virtual collapse following the announcement of the plan emphasize the grave repercussions of super-seniority.

(5) Super-seniority renders future bargaining difficult, if not impossible, for the collective bargaining representative. Unlike the replacement granted in Mackay which ceases to be an issue once the strike is over, the plan here creates a cleavage in the plant continuing long after the strike is ended. Employees are henceforth divided into two camps: those who stayed with the union and those who returned before the end of the strike and thereby gained extra seniority. This breach is reemphasized with each subsequent layoff and stands as an ever-present reminder of the dangers connected with striking and with union activities in general.

In the light of this analysis, super-seniority by its very terms operates to discriminate between strikers and non-strikers, both during and after a strike, and its destructive impact upon the strike and union activity cannot be doubted. The origin of the plan, as respondent insists, may have been to keep production going and it may have been necessary to offer super-seniority to attract replacements and induce union members to leave the strike. But if this is true, accomplishment of respondent's business purpose inexorably was contingent upon attracting sufficient replacements and strikers by offering preferential inducements to those who worked as opposed to those who struck. We think the Board was entitled to treat this case as involving conduct which carried its own indicia of intent and which is barred by the Act unless saved from illegality by an overriding business purpose justifying the invasion of union rights. \* \* \*

\* \* \* In view of the deference paid the strike weapon by the federal labor laws and the devastating consequences upon it which the Board found was and would be precipitated by respondent's inherently discriminatory super-seniority plan, we cannot say the Board erred in the balance which it struck here. Although the Board's decisions are by no means immune from attack in the courts as cases in the Court amply illustrate, e.g., National Labor Relations Board v. Babcock & Wilcox Co., 351 U.S. 105, 76 S.Ct. 679, 100 L.Ed. 975; National Labor Relations Board v. United Steelworkers, 357 U.S. 357, 78 S.Ct. 1268, 2 L.Ed.2d 1383; National Labor Relations Board v. Insurance Agents, 361 U.S. 477, 80 S.Ct. 419, 4 L.Ed.2d 454, its findings here are supported by substantial evidence, Universal Camera Corp. v. National Labor Relations Board, 340 U.S. 474, 71 S.Ct. 456, 95 L.Ed. 456, its explication is not inadequate, irrational or arbitrary, compare Phelps Dodge Corp. v. National Labor Relations Board, 313 U.S. 177, 196–197, 61 S.Ct. 845, 853–854, 85 L.Ed. 1271; National Labor Relations Board v. United Steelworkers, supra, and it did not exceed its powers or venture into an area barred by the statute. Compare National Labor Relations Board v. Insurance Agents, supra. \* \* \*

--------

## PROBLEMS FOR DISCUSSION

**1.** Are you convinced by the conclusion that super-seniority for returning strikers is so much more devastating than permanent replacement of strikers?

**2.** Is it fair to capsulize the Court's decision in *Erie Resistor* as follows: (a) Intention to discriminate against union members, or to deprive employees of statutory rights, is not necessary to a violation of Sections 8(a)(1) and (3); (b) the NLRA permits the Board to weigh the severity of different employer responses to union activity and to outlaw those which have too devastating an impact on that activity, regardless of the absence of an employer's discriminatory motive; and (c) the federal courts are to give great deference to the Board's exercise of judgment in this weighing process? Do any of these propositions survive the decision of the Court in *American Ship Building,* page 557 infra?

--------

In NLRB v. TRUCK DRIVERS LOCAL UNION No. 449 (BUFFALO LINEN), 353 U.S. 87, 77 S.Ct. 643, 1 L.Ed.2d 676 (1957), the Court had, before *Erie Resistor,* deferred to the expertise of the Board in adjusting the interests of employers and their workers in the use of economic weapons. There, a number of laundry concerns were joined in a multi-employer association, which bargained with a single union for a comprehensive labor agreement for the employees at all of the companies. During negotiations, the union called a strike at only one of the companies, hoping to secure a favorable settlement with that company while all other competing companies remained in business and then to utilize this "whipsaw" technique on each company in turn. Upon the strike at the one company, however, the other members of the employer association locked out their employees, and the union claimed that the lockout was in violation of Sections 8(a)(1) and (3) of the Labor Act. The Board had in prior cases authorized a lockout only when reasonably believed necessary by the employer to anticipate a strike which would otherwise have been timed to cause undue harm to the employer's equipment or business. To these so-called defensive lockouts, the Board in this case added the multi-employer lockout as a legitimate employer response to union concerted activity, and the Supreme Court upheld the decision of the Board. It stated:

"Although the Act protects the right of the employees to strike in support of their demands, this protection is not so absolute as to deny self-help by employers when legitimate interests of employees and employers collide. Conflict may arise, for example, between the right to strike and the interest of small employers in preserving multi-employer bargaining as a means of bargaining on an equal basis with a large union and avoiding the competitive disadvantages resulting from nonuniform contractual terms. The ultimate problem is the balancing of the conflicting legitimate interests. The function of striking that balance to effectuate national labor policy is often a difficult and delicate responsibility, which the Congress committed primarily to the National Labor Relations Board, subject to limited judicial review.

"The Court of Appeals recognized that the National Labor Relations Board has legitimately balanced conflicting interests by permitting lockouts where economic hardship was shown. The court erred, however, in too narrowly confining the exercise of Board discretion to the cases of economic hardship. We hold that in the circumstances of this case the Board correctly balanced the conflicting interests in deciding that a temporary lockout to preserve the multi-employer bargaining basis from the disintegration threatened by the Union's strike action was lawful."

# American Ship Building Co. v. NLRB[f]

380 U.S. 300, 85 S.Ct. 955, 13 L.Ed.2d 855 (1965).

■ Mr. Justice Stewart delivered the opinion of the Court.

The American Shipbuilding company operates four shipyards on the Great Lakes—at Chicago, at Buffalo, and at Toledo and Lorain, Ohio. The company is primarily engaged in the repairing of ships, a highly seasonal business concentrated in the winter months when the freezing of the Great Lakes renders shipping impossible. What limited business is obtained during the shipping season is frequently such that speed of execution is of the utmost importance to minimize immobilization of the ships.

Since 1952 the employer has engaged in collective bargaining with a group of eight unions. Prior to the negotiations here in question, the employer had contracted with the unions on five occasions, each agreement having been preceded by a strike. The particular chapter of the collective bargaining history with which we are concerned opened shortly before May 1, 1961, when the unions notified the company of their intention to seek modification of the current contract, due to expire on August 1. * * *

[O]n August 9, after extended negotiations, the parties separated without having resolved substantial differences on the central issues dividing them and without having specific plans for further attempts to resolve them—a situation which the trial examiner found was an impasse. Throughout the negotiations, the employer displayed anxiety as to the unions' strike plans, fearing that the unions would call a strike as soon as a ship entered the Chicago yard or delay negotiations into the winter to increase strike leverage. The union negotiator consistently insisted that it was his intention to reach an agreement without calling a strike; however, he did concede incomplete control over the workers—a fact borne out by the occurrence of a wildcat strike in February 1961. Because of the danger of an unauthorized strike and the consistent and deliberate use of strikes in prior negotiations, the employer remained apprehensive of the possibility of a work stoppage.

In light of the failure to reach an agreement and the lack of available work, the employer decided to lay off certain of his workers. On August 11 the employees received a notice which read: "Because of the labor dispute which has been unresolved since August 1, 1961, you are laid off until further notice." The Chicago yard was completely shut down and all but two employees laid off at the Toledo yard. A large force was retained at Lorain to complete a major piece of work there and the employees in the Buffalo yard were gradually laid off as miscellaneous tasks were completed. Negotiations were resumed shortly after these layoffs and continued for the

---

**f.**  See Baird, Lockout Law: The Supreme Court and the NLRB, 38 Geo. Wash.L.Rev. 396 (1970); Bernhardt, Lockouts: An Analysis of Board and Court Decisions Since Brown and American Ship, 57 Corn.L.Rev. 211 (1972); Feldesman & Koretz, Lockouts, 46 B.U.L.Rev. 329 (1966); Meltzer, Lockouts Under the LMRA: New Shadows on an Old Terrain, 28 U.Chi.L.Rev. 614 (1961); Oberer, Lockouts and the Law: The Importance of America Shipbuilding and Brown Food, 51 Cornell L.Q. 193 (1966).

following two months until a two-year contract was agreed upon on October 27. The employees were recalled the following day.

[After the usual unfair labor practice proceedings the Board concluded, 3–2 that the employer "by curtailing its operations at the South Chicago yard with the consequent layoff of the employees coerced employees in the exercise of their bargaining rights in violation of Section 8(a)(1) of the Act, and discriminated against its employees within the meaning of Section 8(a)(3) of the Act."[5] The decision followed established Board precedent.] "The Board has held that, absent special circumstances, an employer may not during bargaining negotiations either threaten to lock out or lock out his employees in aid of his bargaining position. Such conduct the Board has held presumptively infringes upon collective bargaining rights of employees in violation of Section 8(a)(1), and the lockout, with its consequent layoff, amounts to a discrimination within the meaning of Section 8(a)(3). In addition, the Board has held that such conduct subjects the Union and employees it represents to unwarranted and illegal pressure and creates an atmosphere in which the free opportunity for negotiation contemplated by Section 8(a)(5) does not exist." Quaker State Oil Refining Co., 121 N.L.R.B. 334, 337.

In analyzing the status of the bargaining lockout under §§ 8(a)(1) and 8(a)(3) of the National Labor Relations Act, it is important that the practice with which we are here concerned be distinguished from other forms of temporary separation from employment. No one would deny that an employer is free to shut down his enterprise temporarily for reasons of renovation or lack of profitable work unrelated to his collective bargaining situation. Similarly, we put to one side cases where the Board has concluded on the basis of substantial evidence that the employer has used a lockout as a means to injure a labor organization or to evade his duty to bargain collectively. Hopwood Retinning Co., 104 F.2d 302, 4 N.L.R.B. 922; Scott Paper Box Co., 195 Ark. 1105, 115 S.W.2d 839, 81 N.L.R.B. 535. What we are here concerned with is the use of a temporary layoff of employees solely as a means to bring economic pressure to bear in support of the employer's bargaining position, after an impasse has been reached. This is the only issue before us, and all that we decide.

To establish that this practice is a violation of § 8(a)(1), it must be shown that the employer has interfered with, restrained, or coerced employees in the exercise of some right protected by § 7 of the Act. The Board's position is premised on the view that the lockout interferes with two of the rights guaranteed by § 7: the right to bargain collectively and the right to strike. In the Board's view, the use of the lockout "punishes" employees for the presentation of and adherence to demands made by their

---

**5.** Although the complaint stated a violation of § 8(a)(5) as well, the Board made no findings as to this claim, believing that there would have been no point in entering a bargaining order because the parties had long since executed an agreement. The passage quoted in the text of this opinion below from NLRB v. Insurance Agents' Int'l Union, 361 U.S. 477, 80 S.Ct. 419, 4 L.Ed.2d 454 (1960), infra, has even more direct application to the § 8(a)(5) question. * * *

bargaining representatives and so coerces them in the exercise of their right to bargain collectively. It is important to note that there is here no allegation that the employer used the lockout in the service of designs inimical to the process of collective bargaining. There was no evidence and no finding that the employer was hostile to his employees banding together for collective bargaining or that the lockout was designed to discipline them for doing so. It is therefore inaccurate to say that the employer's intention was to destroy or frustrate the process of collective bargaining. What can be said is that he intended to resist the demands made of him in the negotiations and to secure modification of these demands. We cannot see that this intention is in any way inconsistent with the employees' rights to bargain collectively.

Moreover, there is no indication, either as a general matter or in this specific case, that the lockout will necessarily destroy the unions' capacity for effective and responsible representation. The unions here involved have vigorously represented the employees since 1952, and there is nothing to show that their ability to do so has been impaired by the lockout. Nor is the lockout one of those acts which is demonstrably so destructive of collective bargaining that the Board need not inquire into employer motivation, as might be the case, for example, if an employer permanently discharged his unionized staff and replaced them with employees known to be possessed of a violent antiunion animus. Cf. Labor Board v. Erie Resistor Corp., 373 U.S. 221, 83 S.Ct. 1139, 10 L.Ed.2d 308. The lockout may well dissuade employees from adhering to the position which they initially adopted in the bargaining, but the right to bargain collectively does not entail any "right" to insist on one's position free from economic disadvantage. Proper analysis of the problem demands that the simple intention to support the employer's bargaining position as to compensation and the like be distinguished from a hostility to the process of collective bargaining which could suffice to render a lockout unlawful. See Labor Board v. Brown, 380 U.S. 278, 85 S.Ct. 980.

The Board has taken the complementary view that the lockout interferes with the right to strike protected under §§ 7 and 13 of the Act in that it allows the employer to pre-empt the possibility of a strike and thus leave the union with "nothing to strike against." Insofar as this means that once employees are locked out, they are deprived of their right to call a strike against the employer because he is already shut down, the argument is wholly specious, for the work stoppage which would have been the object of the strike has in fact occurred. It is true that recognition of the lockout deprives the union of exclusive control of the timing and duration of work stoppages calculated to influence the result of collective bargaining negotiations, but there is nothing in the statute which would imply that the right to strike "carries with it" the right exclusively to determine the timing and duration of all work stoppages. The right to strike as commonly understood is the right to cease work—nothing more. No doubt a union's bargaining power would be enhanced if it possessed not only the simple right to strike but also the power exclusively to determine when work stoppages shall occur, but the Act's provisions are not indefinitely elastic, content-free forms to be shaped in whatever manner the Board might think best conforms to the proper balance of bargaining power.

Thus, we cannot see that the employer's use of a lockout solely in support of a legitimate bargaining position is in any way inconsistent with the right to bargain collectively or with the right to strike. Accordingly, we conclude that on the basis of the findings made by the Board in this case, there has been no violation of § 8(a)(1).

Section 8(a)(3) prohibits discrimination in regard to tenure or other conditions of employment to discourage union membership. Under the words of the statute there must be both discrimination and a resulting discouragement of union membership. It has long been established that a finding of violation under this section will normally turn on the employer's motivation. See Labor Board v. Brown, 380 U.S. 278, 85 S.Ct. 980; Radio Officers' Union v. Labor Board, 347 U.S. 17, 43, 74 S.Ct. 323, 337, 98 L.Ed. 455; Labor Board v. Jones & Laughlin Steel Corp., 301 U.S. 1, 46, 57 S.Ct. 615, 628, 81 L.Ed. 893. Thus when the employer discharges a union leader who has broken shop rules, the problem posed is to determine whether the employer has acted purely in disinterested defense of shop discipline or has sought to damage employee organization. It is likely that the discharge will naturally tend to discourage union membership in both cases, because of the loss of union leadership and the employees' suspicion of the employer's true intention. But we have consistently construed the section to leave unscathed a wide range of employer actions taken to serve legitimate business interests in some significant fashion, even though the act committed may tend to discourage union membership. See, e.g., Labor Board v. Mackay Radio & Telegraph Co., 304 U.S. 333, 347, 58 S.Ct. 904, 911, 82 L.Ed. 1381. Such a construction of § 8(a)(3) is essential if due protection is to be accorded the employer's right to manage his enterprise. See Textile Workers v. Darlington Mfg. Co., 380 U.S. 263, 85 S.Ct. 994.

This is not to deny that there are some practices which are inherently so prejudicial to union interests and so devoid of significant economic justification that no specific evidence of intent to discourage union membership or other antiunion animus is required. In some cases, it may be that the employer's conduct carries with it an inference of unlawful intention so compelling that it is justifiable to disbelieve the employer's protestations of innocent purpose. Radio Officers' Union v. Labor Board, supra, 347 U.S., at 44–45, 74 S.Ct. at 337–338; Labor Board v. Erie Resistor Corp., supra. Thus where many have broken a shop rule, but only union leaders have been discharged, the Board need not listen too long to the plea that shop discipline was simply being enforced. In other situations, we have described the process as the "far more delicate task * * * of weighing the interests of employees in concerted activity against the interest of the employer in operating his business in a particular manner * * *." Labor Board v. Erie Resistor Corp., supra, 373 U.S. at 229, 83 S.Ct. at 1145.

But this lockout does not fall into that category of cases arising under § 8(a)(3) in which the Board may truncate its inquiry into employer motivation. As this case well shows, use of the lockout does not carry with it any necessary implication that the employer acted to discourage union membership or otherwise discriminate against union members as such. The purpose and effect of the lockout was only to bring pressure upon the union to modify its demands. Similarly, it does not appear that the natural tendency of the lockout is severely to discourage union membership while serving no significant employer interest. In fact, it is difficult to understand what tendency to discourage union membership or otherwise discriminate against union members was perceived by the Board. There is no claim that the employer locked out only union members, or locked out any employee simply because he was a union member; nor is it alleged that the employer conditioned rehiring upon resignation from the union. * * *

To find a violation of § 8(a)(3) then, the Board must find that the employer acted for a proscribed purpose. Indeed, the Board itself has always recognized that certain "operative" or "economic" purposes would justify a lockout. But the Board has erred in ruling that only these purposes will remove a lockout from the ambit of § 8(a)(3), for that section requires an intention to discourage union membership or otherwise discriminate against the union. There was not the slightest evidence and there was no finding, that the employer was actuated by a desire to discourage membership in the union as distinguished from a desire to affect the outcome of the particular negotiations in which he was involved. We recognize that the "union membership" which is not to be discouraged refers to more than the payment of dues and that measures taken to discourage participation in protected union activities may be found to come within the proscription. Radio Officers' Union v. Labor Board, supra, 347 U.S., at 39–40, 74 S.Ct., at 335. However, there is nothing in the Act which gives employees the right to insist on their contract demands, free from the sort of economic disadvantage which frequently attends bargaining disputes. Therefore, we conclude that where the intention proven is merely to bring about a settlement of a labor dispute on favorable terms, no violation of § 8(a)(3) is shown.

The conclusions which we draw from analysis of §§ 8(a)(1) and 8(a)(3) are consonant with what little of relevance can be drawn from the balance of the statute and its legislative history. In the original version of the Act, the predecessor of § 8(a)(1) declared it an unfair labor practice "[t]o attempt, by interference, influence, restraint, favor, coercion, or lockout, or by any other means, to impair the right of employees guaranteed in section 4." * * * [It is clear that the Senate] Committee was concerned with the status of the lockout and that the bill, as reported and as finally enacted, contained no prohibition on the use of the lockout as such.

Although neither § 8(a)(1) nor § 8(a)(3) refers specifically to the lockout, various other provisions of the Labor Management Relations Act do refer to the lockout, and these references can be interpreted as a recognition of the legitimacy of the device as a means of applying economic pressure in support of bargaining positions. Thus 29 U.S.C.A. § 158(d)(4) prohibits the use of strike or lockout unless requisite notice procedures have been complied with; 29 U.S.C.A. § 173(c) directs the Federal Mediation and Conciliation Service to seek voluntary resolution of labor disputes without resort to strikes or lockouts; and 29 U.S.C.A. §§ 176, 178, authorize procedures whereby the President can institute a board of inquiry to forestall certain strikes or lockouts. The correlative use of the terms "strike" and "lockout" in these sections contemplates that lockouts will be used in the bargaining process in some fashion. This is not to say that these provisions serve to define the permissible scope of a lockout by an employer. That, in the context of the present case, is a question ultimately to be resolved by analysis of §§ 8(a)(1) and 8(a)(3).

The Board has justified its ruling in this case and its general approach to the legality of lockouts on the basis of its special competence to weigh the competing interests of employers and employees and to accommodate these interests according to its expert judgment. "The Board has reasonably concluded that the availability of such a weapon would so substantially tip the scales in the employer's favor as to defeat the Congressional purpose of placing employees on a par with their adversaries at the bargaining table." To buttress its decision as to the balance struck in this particular case, the Board points out that the employer has been given other weapons to counterbalance the employees' power of strike. The employer may permanently replace workers who have gone out on strike, or by stockpiling and subcontracting, maintain his commercial operations while the strikers bear the economic brunt of the work stoppage. Similarly, the employer can institute unilaterally the working conditions which he desires once his contract with the union has expired. Given these economic weapons, it is argued, the employer has been adequately equipped with tools of economic self-help.

There is of course no question that the Board is entitled to the greatest deference in recognition of its special competence in dealing with labor problems. In many areas its evaluation of the competing interests of employer and employee should unquestionably be given conclusive effect in determining the application of §§ 8(a)(1), (a)(3), and (a)(5). However, we think that the Board construes its functions too expansively when it claims general authority to define national labor policy by balancing the competing interests of labor and management.

While a primary purpose of the National Labor Relations Act was to redress the perceived imbalance of economic power between labor and management, it sought to accomplish that result by conferring certain affirmative rights on employees and by placing certain enumerated restrictions on the activities of employers. The Act prohibited acts which interfered with, restrained, or coerced employees in the exercise of their rights to organize a union, to bargain collectively, and to strike; it proscribed discrimination in regard to tenure and other conditions of employment to discourage membership in any labor organization. The central purpose of these provisions was to protect employee self-organization and the process of collective bargaining from disruptive interferences by employers. Having protected employee organization in countervailance to the employers' bargaining power, and having established a system of collective bargaining whereby the newly coequal adversaries might resolve their disputes, the Act also contemplated resort to economic weapons should more peaceful measures not avail. Sections 8(a)(1) and 8(a)(3) do not give the Board a general authority to assess the relative economic power of the adversaries in the bargaining process and to deny weapons to one party or the other because of its assessment of that party's bargaining power. Labor Board v. Brown, 380 U.S. 278, 85 S.Ct. 980. In this case the Board has, in essence, denied the use of the bargaining lockout to the employer because of its conviction that use of this device would give the employer "too much power." In so doing, the Board has stretched §§ 8(a)(1) and 8(a)(3) far beyond their functions of protecting the rights of employee organization and collective bargaining. What we have recently said in a closely related context is equally applicable here:

> "[W]hen the Board moves in this area * * * it is functioning as an arbiter of the sort of economic weapons the parties can use in seeking to gain acceptance of their bargaining demands. It has sought to introduce some standard of properly 'balanced' bargaining power, or some new distinction of justifiable and unjustifiable, proper and 'abusive' economic weapons into * * * the Act. * * * We have expressed our belief that this amounts to the Board's entrance into the substantive aspect of the bargaining process to an extent Congress has not countenanced." Labor Board v. Insurance Agents' International Union, 361 U.S. 477, 497–498, 80 S.Ct. 419, 431.

We are unable to find that any fair construction of the provisions relied on by the Board in this case can support its finding of an unfair labor practice. Indeed, the role assumed by the Board in this area is fundamentally inconsistent with the structure of the Act and the function of the sections relied upon. The deference owed to an expert tribunal cannot be allowed to slip into a judicial inertia which results in the unauthorized assumption by an agency of major policy decisions properly made by Congress. Accordingly, we hold that an employer violates neither § 8(a)(1) nor § 8(a)(3) when, after a bargaining impasse has been reached, he temporarily shuts down his plant and lays off his employees for the sole purpose of bringing economic pressure to bear in support of his legitimate bargaining position.

Reversed.

[Mr. Justice White concurred in the reversal, but only because the record required the conclusion that the employer's purpose was not to exert economic pressure against the union but rather to avoid a strike which it reasonably feared would occur at a particularly disadvantageous time. He criticized the Court for unnecessarily passing upon the legality of the bargaining lockout and for overturning the Board's conclusion that the value of the bargaining lockout to the employer was here outweighed by its damaging consequences for the employees' right to bargain and to strike. Justice White rejected the conclusion of the majority that discriminatory motive was necessary to make out a violation, and said that even though the employer's conduct may have been in the pursuit of legitimate business ends, it unavoidably and foreseeably discouraged protected activity. "The balance and accommodation of 'conflicting legitimate interests' in labor relations does not admit of a simple solution and a myopic focus on the true intent or motive of the employer has not been the determinative standard of the Board or this Court. * * * The test is clearly one of choosing among several motivations or purposes and weighing the respective interests of employers and employees. And I think that is the standard the Court applies to the bargaining lockout in this case, but without heeding the fact the balance is for the Board to strike in the first instance."

[Mr. Justice Goldberg, joined by the Chief Justice, also concurred in the result and also on the theory that this was a defensive lockout, designed to anticipate a threatened strike so as to avoid "economic injury over and beyond the loss of business normally incident to a strike upon the termination of the collective bargaining agreement." The Justice pointed out that bargaining lockouts can arise under many different circumstances and that it was unwise to suggest that they were always per se lawful; earlier NLRB decisions "properly take into account, in determining the legality of lockouts under the labor statutes, such factors as the length, character and history of the collective bargaining relation between the union and the employer, as well as whether a bargaining impasse has been reached." Here, the employer had a long history of collective bargaining, was confronted with a history of past strikes, had locked out only after bargaining in good faith to impasse, and reasonably feared a strike at an unusually harmful time. The test to apply in these cases was not that announced by the majority—whether employer conduct not actually motivated by antiunion bias is "demonstrably so destructive of collective bargaining" or "so prejudicial to union interests and so devoid of significant economic justification"—but rather "whether the legitimate economic interests of the employer justify his interference with the rights of his employees—a test involving 'the balancing of the conflicting legitimate interests,' " and one which is "committed primarily to the National Labor Relations Board, subject to limited judicial review."]

---

PROBLEMS FOR DISCUSSION

**1.** Would the result in *American Ship Building* be the same if the employer locked out the employees prior to an impasse? See Darling & Co., 171 NLRB 801 (1968), enf'd sub nom. Lane v. NLRB, 418 F.2d 1208 (D.C.Cir.1969).

**2.** After the Union voted to reject the employer's "final offer," it decided that instead of striking it would authorize an "inside game." Under this strategy, the workers refuse to work voluntary overtime and generally "work-to-rule"—*i.e.*, adhere strictly to all company safety and other rules; do exactly and only what they are told; report to work precisely on time and park work trucks at company facilities at day's end (thus precluding employees from responding to after-hours emergencies); present all grievances as a group; advise non-employees to report unsafe conditions; and, advise customers of their right to more frequent service checks. The Union continued to negotiate while carrying out this strategy. Three weeks later the Company instituted a lockout. The Union filed charges of violation of §§ 8(a)(1), (3) and (5). Has the Company violated any of these provisions? Local 702, IBEW v. NLRB, 215 F.3d 11 (D.C.Cir.2000).

**3.** The labor contract between the Ottawa Silica Company and the union was due to expire on May 31. Prior to that time, the union and the company met several times to try to reach a settlement on a contract, and sent various written proposals and counterproposals to each other. These efforts, however, were to no avail and it was clear that either a strike or lockout would occur. On May 31, the company gave the union its final proposals. Before a vote could be taken, the company announced a lockout to commence on June 1. The lockout remained in effect for five days, during which time the company continued normal operations by temporarily replacing the employees with sales, supervisory, and management personnel. On June 5, the union agreed to the contract terms offered by the employer, and promptly filed unfair labor practice charges. Did Ottawa Silica violate Sections 8(a)(1) and/or 8(a)(3) by staging the lockout and using temporary replacements during the period of the lockout? See International Broth. of Boilermakers, Local 88 v. NLRB, 858 F.2d 756 (D.C.Cir.1988).

---

# NLRB v. Great Dane Trailers, Inc.

388 U.S. 26, 87 S.Ct. 1792, 18 L.Ed.2d 1027 (1967).

■ Mr. Chief Justice Warren delivered the opinion of the Court.

* * * The respondent company and the union entered into a collective bargaining agreement which was effective by its terms until March 31, 1963. The agreement contained a commitment by the company to pay vacation benefits to employees who met certain enumerated qualifications. In essence, the company agreed to pay specified vacation benefits to employees who, during the preceding year, had worked at least 1,525 hours. It was also provided that, in the case of a "lay-off, termination or quitting," employees who had served more than 60 days during the year would be entitled to pro-rata shares of their vacation benefits. Benefits were to be paid on the Friday nearest July 1 of each year.

The agreement was temporarily extended beyond its termination date, but on April 30, 1963, the union gave the required 15 days' notice of intention to strike over issues which remained unsettled at the bargaining table. Accordingly, on May 16, 1963, approximately 350 of the company's 400 employees commenced a strike which lasted until December 26, 1963. The company continued to operate during the strike, using nonstrikers, persons hired as replacements for strikers, and some original strikers who had later abandoned the strike and returned to work. On July 12, 1963, a number of the strikers demanded their accrued vacation pay from the company. The company rejected this demand, basing its response on the assertion that all contractual obligations had been terminated by the strike and, therefore, none of the company's employees had a right to vacation pay. Shortly thereafter, however, the company announced that it would grant vacation pay—in the amounts and subject to the conditions set out in the expired agreement—to all employees who had reported for work on July 1, 1963. The company denied that these payments were founded on the agreement and stated that they merely reflected a new "policy" which had been unilaterally adopted. * * * Violations of § 8(a)(3) and (1) were charged. A hearing was held before a trial examiner who found that the company's action in regard to vacation pay constituted a discrimination in terms and conditions of employment which would discourage union membership, as well as an unlawful interference with protected activity. He held that the company had violated § 8(a)(3) and (1) and recommended that it be ordered to cease and desist from its unfair labor practice and to pay the accrued vacation benefits to strikers. The Board, after reviewing the record, adopted the Trial Examiner's conclusions and remedy. * * *

The Court of Appeals held that, although discrimination between striking and nonstriking employees had been proved, the Board's conclusion that the company had committed an unfair labor practice was not well-founded inasmuch as there had been no affirmative showing of an unlawful motivation to discourage union membership or to interfere with the exercise of protected rights. Despite the fact that the company itself had not introduced evidence of a legitimate business purpose underlying its discriminatory action, the Court of Appeals speculated that it might have been motivated by a desire "(1) to reduce expenses; (2) to encourage longer tenure among present employees; or (3) to discourage early leaves immediately before vacation periods."

* * *

The unfair labor practice charged here is grounded primarily in § 8(a)(3) which requires specifically that the Board find a discrimination and a resulting discouragement of union membership. American Ship Building Co. v. National Labor Relations Board, 380 U.S. 300, 311, 85 S.Ct. 955, 963, 13 L.Ed.2d 855 (1965). There is little question but that the result of the company's refusal to pay vacation benefits to strikers was discrimination in its simplest form. Compare Republic Aviation Corp. v. National Labor Relations Board, 324 U.S. 793, 65 S.Ct. 982, 89 L.Ed. 1372 (1945), with Local 357, Intern. Broth. of Teamsters, Chauffeurs, Warehousemen and Helpers of America v. National Labor Relations Board, 365 U.S. 667, 81 S.Ct. 835, 6 L.Ed.2d 11 (1961). Some employees who met the conditions specified in the expired collective bargaining agreement were paid accrued vacation benefits in the amounts set forth in that agreement, while other employees who also met the conditions but who had engaged in protected concerted activity were denied such benefits. Similarly, there can be no doubt but that the discrimination was capable of discouraging membership in a labor organization within the meaning of the statute. Discouraging membership in a labor organization "includes discouraging participation in concerted activities * * * such as a legitimate strike." National Labor Relations Board v. Erie Resistor Corp., 373 U.S. 221, 233, 83 S.Ct. 1139, 1148, 10 L.Ed.2d 308 (1963). The act of paying accrued benefits to one group of employees while announcing the extinction of the same benefits for another group of employees who are distinguishable only by their participation in protected concerted activity surely may have a discouraging effect on either present or future concerted activity.

But inquiry under § 8(a)(3) does not usually stop at this point. The statutory language "discrimination * * * to * * * discourage" means that the finding of a violation normally turns on whether the discriminatory conduct was motivated by an anti-union purpose. American Ship Building Co. v. National Labor Relations Board, 380 U.S. 300, 85 S.Ct. 955 (1965). It was upon the motivation element that the Court of Appeals based its decision not to grant enforcement, and it is to that element which we now turn. In three recent opinions we considered employer motivation in the context of asserted § 8(a)(3) violations. American Ship Building Co. v. National Labor Relations Board, supra; National Labor Relations Board v. Brown, 380 U.S. 278, 85 S.Ct. 980, 13 L.Ed.2d 839 (1965); and National Labor Relations Board v. Erie Resistor Corp., supra. * * *

From this review of our recent decisions, several principles of controlling importance here can be distilled. First, if it can reasonably be concluded that the employer's discriminatory conduct was "inherently destructive" of important employee rights, no proof of antiunion motivation is needed and the Board can find an unfair labor practice even if the employer introduces evidence that the conduct was motivated by business considerations. Second, if the adverse effect of the discriminatory conduct on employee rights is "comparatively slight," an antiunion motivation must be proved to sustain the charge *if* the employer has come forward with evidence of legitimate and substantial business justifications for the conduct. Thus, in either situation, once it has been proved that the employer engaged in discriminatory conduct which could have adversely affected employee rights to *some* extent, the burden is upon the employer to establish that it was motivated by legitimate objectives since proof of motivation is most accessible to him.

Applying the principles to this case then, it is not necessary for us to decide the degree to which the challenged conduct might have affected employee rights. As the Court of Appeals correctly noted, the company came forward with no evidence of legitimate motives for its discriminatory conduct. 363 F.2d at 134. The company simply did not meet the burden of proof, and the Court of Appeals misconstrued the function of judicial review when it proceeded nonetheless to speculate upon what *might have* motivated the company. Since discriminatory conduct carrying a potential for adverse effect upon employee rights was proved and no evidence of a proper motivation appeared in the record, the Board's conclusions were supported by substantial evidence. Universal Camera Corp. v. National Labor Relations Board, 340 U.S. 474, 71 S.Ct. 456, 95 L.Ed. 456 (1951) and should have been sustained.

\* \* \*

■ Mr. Justice Harlan, whom Mr. Justice Stewart joins, dissenting.

\* \* \*

The "legitimate and substantial business justification" test may be interpreted as requiring only that the employer come forward with a nonfrivolous business purpose in order to make operative the usual requirement of proof of antiunion motive. If this is the result of today's decision, then the Court has merely penalized Great Dane for not anticipating this requirement when arguing before the Board. * * *

On the other hand, the use of the word "substantial" in the burden of proof formulation may give the Board a power which it formerly had only in § 8(a)(3) cases like *Erie Resistor,* supra. The Board may seize upon that term to evaluate the merits of the employer's business purposes and weigh them against the harm that befalls the union's interests as a result of the employer's action. If this is the Court's meaning, it may well impinge upon the accepted principle that "the right to bargain collectively does not entail any 'right' to insist on one's position free from economic disadvantage." American Ship Building Co. v. National Labor Relations Board, supra, at 309, 85 S.Ct. at 962. Employers have always been free to take reasonable measures which discourage a strike by pressuring the economic interests of employees, including the extreme measure of hiring permanent replacements, without having the Board inquire into the "substantiality" of their business justifications. National Labor Relations Board v. McKay Radio & Telegraph Co., 304 U.S. 333, 58 S.Ct. 904, 82 L.Ed. 1381. If the Court means to change this rule, though I assume it does not, it surely should not do so without argument of the point by the parties and without careful discussion. * * *

## PROBLEMS FOR DISCUSSION

**1.** Would the result be different if the employer had testified that it did not give vacation pay to strikers in order to reduce its costs of production?

**2.** A two-year collective bargaining agreement between the United States Pipe and Foundry Company and the union was due to expire on November 30. The employer and the union met at various times throughout October and November without reaching an agreement. However, the employees continued to work after the contract had expired on the basis of the last contract proposals by the Company. Since an impasse had been reached, the Company announced that certain changes would be made, effective December 19. These changes included a cancellation of a wage increase put into effect at the expiration of the prior contract and the cancellation of some employee benefits such as paid holidays and vacation pay. The employees nevertheless continued to work until the employer instituted a total lockout the following January. Five months later, a new agreement was signed and the lockout was ended. Did the Company violate the Labor Act by its withdrawal of benefits on December 19? If it did, will the ensuing total lockout in January also be a violation of the Act? Compare United States Pipe and Foundry Co., 180 NLRB 325 (1969), enf'd sub nom. Local 155, Molders v. NLRB, 143 U.S.App.D.C. 20, 442 F.2d 742 (D.C.Cir.1971), with NLRB v. Great Falls Employers' Council, Inc., 277 F.2d 772 (9th Cir.1960).

**3.** The Pittsburgh–Des Moines Steel Company had a practice of giving annual Christmas bonuses to its employees. These bonuses were based on a five-factor formula: (1) overall results, (2) overall productivity, (3) results at each individual plant (the company had five plants), (4) productivity at each individual plant, and (5) continuity of work effort at each individual plant. Last year, the maintenance unit at one of the company's plants engaged in an economic strike for 57 days. Consequently, the productivity at their plant was lower than normal. All employees in the company's five plants received Christmas bonuses except for the one unit which went out on strike. Has the company violated the Labor Act? See Pittsburgh–Des Moines Steel Co. v. NLRB, 284 F.2d 74 (9th Cir.1960).

———

# Laidlaw Corp.[g]

171 NLRB 1366 (1968).

[The Union on January 10, 1966 voted to reject the Company's wage offer and notified the Company of its intention to strike on January 12. On January 11, the plant manager announced that any striking employees who were replaced would "lose forever your right to employment by this company." The strike began on January 12, and on January 14 one Massey, a striker, applied for reinstatement but was told that his job had been filled and that even if he were reemployed he would be paid not at the wage rate obtaining at the time of the strike but rather at the rate paid a new hire. On January 18, Massey was informed of an opening in his job classification and was asked to return, but with treatment as a new employee; Massey refused to return on that basis and continued to strike. At a union meeting on February 10, many of the strikers voted to return to work, and they made unconditional application to do so on February 11; other strikers submitted such applications soon after. The Company announced that it had hired replacements for most of the strikers and that those strikers were not entitled to reinstatement. Although the Company did hire a number of the striker-applicants for vacancies existing at the time of their application, reinstatement applications were considered only on the date of application, and if there were excess vacancies on any later date they were filled by new hires, no check being made of the earlier reinstatement applications of February 11. Beginning on February 16, the Company notified the strikers (except those reinstated or declining reinstatement) of their termination as of the date of their written applications. It continued, however, to advertise for permanent help and a number of new employees were hired due to turnover, created in part by the departure of some permanent replacements. At a union meeting of February 20, a group of strikers protested the termination notices and the failure to reinstate most of the strikers, and decided to renew their strike effort on February 21 in protest against the Company's alleged unfair labor practice.

**g.** See Finkin, The Truncation of *Laid-law* Rights by Collective Agreements, 3 Ind.   Rel.L.J. 591 (1979).

[The Trial Examiner found that Massey was not entitled to reinstatement on January 14 when his job was filled by a permanent replacement, but that he remained an employee within Section 2(3) of the Labor Act and was thus entitled to full reinstatement when he reapplied at a time when the position was vacant. The Trial Examiner also concluded that the termination of the other strikers also violated Sections 8(a)(1) and (3), since they remained employees under the Act, their applications for reinstatement were continuous, they were entitled to full reinstatement when vacancies in their jobs later arose, and they were discriminated against when the Company hired new employees rather than offer positions to the strikers. It was also held that the failure to reinstate strikers as of February 11 converted the strike as of that date from an economic strike to an unfair labor practice strike.]

■ We concur in the conclusions of the Trial Examiner and in the relief granted Respondent's employees. In so doing we rely particularly on the principles set forth in N.L.R.B. v. Fleetwood Trailer Co., [389 U.S. 375 (1967)] in which the Supreme Court discussed the rights of economic strikers to reinstatement and the responsibility of employers to fully reinstate economic strikers, absent "legitimate and substantial business justifications," in a situation where production increased and more jobs were reestablished.

In *Fleetwood*, the employer was held to have violated the Act by failing to reinstate strikers and by hiring new employees for jobs which were reestablished when the employer resumed full production some 2 months after the strikers applied for reinstatement. In so finding, the Court pointed out that by virtue of Section 2(3) of the Act, an individual whose work ceases due to a labor dispute remains an employee if he has not obtained other regular or substantially equivalent employment, and that an employer refusing to reinstate strikers must show that the action was due to legitimate and substantial business justification. The Court further held that the burden of proving such justification was on the employer and also pointed out that the primary responsibility for striking a proper balance between the asserted business justifications and the invasion of employee rights rests with the Board rather than the courts. The Court also noted that an act so destructive of employee rights, without legitimate business justification, is an unfair labor practice without reference to intent or improper motivation. Furthermore, the Court explicitly rejected the argument, asserted by the employer in *Fleetwood* (389 U.S. at 380–381) and relied upon by the Respondent in the instant case, that reinstatement rights are determined at the time of initial application.

It was clearly error to hold that the right of the strikers to reinstatement expired on August 20, when they first applied. *This basic right to jobs cannot depend on job availability as of the moment when applications are filed.* The right to reinstatement does not depend upon technicalities relating to application. On the contrary, *the status of the striker as an employee continues until he has obtained "other regular and substantially equivalent employment."* [Emphasis supplied.]

Application of these principles to the case before us makes it evident that the results reached by the Trial Examiner were correct, even though he did not have the benefit of the Supreme Court's *Fleetwood* decision, which issued subsequently.

Thus, in the case of Massey, he remained an employee when he rejoined the strike after his first effort to be reinstated was rejected even though at that particular moment he had been replaced. The right to reinstatement did not expire when the original application was made. When the position again became vacant, Massey, an economic striker who was still an employee, was available and entitled to full reinstatement unless there were legitimate and substantial business justifications for the failure to offer complete reinstatement. However, it is evidence that no such justifications existed, for in fact Respondent needed and desired Massey's services, and it was Respondent who sought out Massey when the vacancy occurred. But its offer of employment as a new employee or as an employee with less than rights accorded by full reinstatement (such as denial of seniority) was wholly unrelated to any of its economic needs, could only penalize Massey for engaging in concerted activity, was inherently destructive of employee interests, and thus was unresponsive to the requirements of the statute, N.L.R.B. v. Erie Resistor Corp. In these circumstances there was no valid reason why Massey should not have been offered complete reinstatement, and Respondent's failure to do so was in violation of Section 8(a)(3) and (1) of the Act.

[The Board also held that Massey's fellow strikers were also treated unlawfully when they were not reinstated after February 11, pursuant to their request, as job openings arose. This was true if the strike after that date was converted into an unfair labor practice strike or even if it remained an economic strike (in which case their right to reinstatement would be precisely the same as Massey's).]

\* \* \* As Respondent brought forward no evidence of business justification for refusing to reinstate these experienced employees while continuing to advertise for and hire new unskilled employees, we find such conduct was inherently destructive of employee rights. This right of reinstatement continued to exist so long as the strikers had not abandoned the employ of Respondent for other substantial and equivalent employment. Moreover, having signified their intent to return by their unconditional application for reinstatement and by their continuing presence, it was incumbent on Respondent to seek them out as positions were vacated. Having failed to fulfill its obligation to reinstate the employees to their jobs as vacancies arose, the Respondent thereby violated Section 8(a)(3) and (1) of the Act.
\* \* \*[14]

---

**14.** See also NLRB v. Erie Resistor Corp., supra.

The decision of the Board was upheld in LAIDLAW CORP. v. NLRB, 414 F.2d 99 (7th Cir.1969), cert. denied, 397 U.S. 920, 90 S.Ct. 928, 25 L.Ed.2d 100 (1970), and has since been endorsed by other courts of appeals. On review, the Laidlaw Corporation argued that even if the Board was correct in finding that its refusal to grant reinstatement was unlawful it was an abuse of the Board's discretion to apply that newly declared principle of law to Laidlaw and to impose a substantial backpay award against the company in spite of the fact that its conduct was lawful at the time it was performed. The company relied on a number of cases which held that in certain situations the Board's adoption of a new rule or policy may not be applied retroactively where its practical effect is to create a hardship on the employer disproportionate to the public ends to be accomplished. The court, however, disagreed: "In the case before us, we believe that the importance of protecting the statutory rights of Laidlaw's employees outweighs the fact that the company may have relied on a prior Board rule or policy. We are in agreement with the statement made by the General Counsel in his brief: 'Unless the disadvantaged strikers are compensated, they will have been penalized for exercising statutorily protected rights and the effect of discouraging future such exercises will not be completely dissipated. In these circumstances, it was not arbitrary or capricious for the Board to conclude that complete vindication of employee rights should take precedence over the employer's reliance on prior Board law.'"

In TRANS WORLD AIRLINES v. INDEPENDENT FEDERATION OF FLIGHT ATTEND-ANTS, 489 U.S. 426, 109 S.Ct. 1225, 103 L.Ed.2d 456 (1989), the Court held that an employer was not required at the cessation of a strike to restore strikers with greater seniority to positions held by junior employees who chose not to honor the strike. In an opinion grounded in the Railway Labor Act, but equally applicable to the NLRA, the Court declined to "expand" *Erie Resistor*. The employer policy of retaining junior "cross-overs," in the Court's view, merely put pressure on the strikers as a group to abandon the strike, and so was in effect indistinguishable from the hiring of permanent replacements. Further, the workplace cleavage perpetuated by the award of super-seniority was not present, inasmuch as any striker who later re-turned to the unit would do so with full seniority over junior cross-overs. Thus, the consequence to the strikers was an "inevitable effect of an employer's use of economic weapons available during a period of self-help." Moreover, to require the employer to oust the cross-over employee while (under *Mackay*) keeping the permanent replacement at work after the strike would "penalize" those who decided not to strike in order to benefit those who did.

Justices Brennan and Marshall dissented as did Justice Blackmun. The former two dissenters read *Erie Resistor* as denying employers the ability to offer cross-overs positions that would otherwise require years of seniority

Even if a finding of antiunion motivation is necessary, the employer's preference for strangers over tested and competent employ-ees is sufficient basis for inferring such mo-tive, and we, in agreement with the Trial Examiner, would do so if we considered mo-tive material.

to acquire, because of the effect it would have on the exercise of the right to strike. Justice Blackmun grounded his dissent in his reading of the Railway Labor Act to preclude offers of permanence to replacements and cross-overs absent a showing of business necessity.

––––––––

## PROBLEMS FOR DISCUSSION

**1.** Were the *Mackay* issue—the employer's right to hire permanent replacements for economic strikers—to arise afresh today, what would be the analytical approach and the likely decision, given the decision of the Supreme Court in *Great Dane Trailers* and that of the Board in *Laidlaw*?

**2.** Is it lawful for an employer on the eve of a strike to state to its employees, as did the Laidlaw Corporation, that strikers will be permanently replaced and forever lose their employment status with the company?

**3.** A majority of the employees at Magnar Research Co. went out on strike on February 1 over new contract terms. The company hired permanent replacements for most of the strikers, and on July 1 most of the strikers applied unconditionally for reinstatement. The company informed them that no jobs were available because of the replacements but that they would be placed on a preferential hiring list. On July 1 a year later, however, the company informed the many former strikers who had not yet been returned to work that their preferential hiring status was terminated and that henceforth they would be considered for job openings in competition with new applicants; the company stated that one year had passed since their application for reinstatement, and that it was too burdensome to keep records for any longer period or to attempt to contact former employees thereafter, given the usual changes in addresses and telephone numbers. Does this announced termination of preferential hiring rights violate Sections 8(a)(1) and (3)?

Assume that, in terminating the preferential hiring rights of former strikers, the company relied upon a clause in the then expired (and since renewed) labor contract which provided that an employee who was laid off would lose his seniority rights for purposes of recall one year after the date of layoff. Would this modify the analysis under Sections 8(a)(1) and (3)? See Brooks Research & Mfg., Inc., 202 NLRB 634 (1973).

**4.** At the conclusion of an economic strike, the employer's workforce consisted of 94 employees: 69 permanent strike replacements and 25 former strikers who had abandoned the strike. In a subsequent economic downturn, the employer laid off 15 employees, of whom 14 were strike replacements. They were told the layoff was indefinite and that they should seek other work. Three months later, the employer began to recall employees from layoff, most of whom were strike replacements; it did not consider recalling unreinstated strikers because no "vacancy" existed for them. The ALJ held that action to violate § 8(a)(3), on the ground that the layoff of replacements for an indefinite period per se creates a vacancy that triggers *Laidlaw* rights. The Board agreed with the result, but not the theory:

> [W]e find that this analysis fails to satisfactorily take into account the employer's right to permanently replace economic strikers and to assure the replacements of the permanency of their positions. *NLRB v. Mackay Radio & Telegraph Co.,* 304 U.S. 333, 58 S.Ct. 904, 82 L.Ed. 1381 (1938). A replacement could hardly be called "permanent" were we to find that every

layoff for an indefinite period creates a vacancy which activates a striker's reinstatement rights. See *Giddings & Lewis, Inc. v. NLRB*, 675 F.2d 926 (7th Cir.1982), denying enf. of 255 NLRB No. 93 (1981).

On the other hand, a strike also does not terminate the employment relationship of a striker.... Thus, the key question presented in cases involving the layoff of permanent replacements is whether the layoff in fact signified the departure of the replacements under *Laidlaw* with the consequent creation of a vacancy which triggers the strikers' rights to reinstatement when the vacated position again opens up. This issue appears to be an open question which we resolve today in the following manner.

... When it is alleged that an employer has violated Section 8(a)(3) by recalling laid-off permanent replacements ahead of unreinstated strikers, we shall require the General Counsel to first establish a prima facie case that the layoff truly signified the departure of the replacements under *Laidlaw* and thus created vacancies to which the unreinstated strikers were entitled to be recalled. In this regard, the General Counsel will be required to show that a strike has occurred; that the strikers have made an unconditional offer to return to work; that a layoff of permanent striker replacements has occurred; that the replacements were recalled from layoff instead of the former strikers; and that, based on objective factors, the laid-off permanent replacements had no reasonable expectancy of recall. Cf. *Bancroft Cap Co.*, 245 NLRB 547 fn. 1. The objective factors relevant to the replacements' reasonable expectancy of recall would include, inter alia, evidence concerning the employer's past business experience, the employer's future plans, the length of the layoff, the circumstances of the layoff, and what the employee was told regarding the likelihood of recall. See, e.g., *Atlas Metal Spinning Co.*, 266 NLRB 180 (1983); *Bancroft Cap*, supra. Once the General Counsel has established a prima facie case that a *Laidlaw* vacancy exists to which the striker is entitled, the burden shall shift to the employer to show that in fact no such *Laidlaw* vacancy occurred or that its failure to recall the striker was otherwise based on legitimate and substantial business justifications, such as those identified in *Fleetwood Trailer....*

Aqua–Chem, Inc., 288 NLRB 1108 (1988), enf'd, 910 F.2d 1487 (7th Cir.1990), cert. denied, 501 U.S. 1238, 111 S.Ct. 2871, 115 L.Ed.2d 1037 (1991).

How does this differ from allowing the award of super-seniority to strikebreakers? Is there a principled basis for a rule that says an employer which expands its workforce after a strike and so reinstates strikers, cannot give an assurance of preference to replacements in subsequent contraction; but an employer that contracts its workforce following a strike may give a preference to replacements in a subsequent expansion?

**5.** In many strike situations in which an employer offers permanent positions to strikebreakers, the conclusion of the strike is accompanied by an agreement between the employer and the union to reinstate the strikers to their original positions and to displace the replacements. In Belknap, Inc. v. Hale, 463 U.S. 491, 103 S.Ct. 3172, 77 L.Ed.2d 798 (1983), the Supreme Court held that the federal labor act did not preempt state-court actions by the displaced "permanent" replacements on theories of tortious misrepresentation or breach of their employment contract. Does the Court's decision make it more likely that employers will "hedge" their offers of permanent positions for strikebreakers (so that the offers will in truth be for less than a permanent position)? Does it make it more likely, on the contrary, that employers will resist strike-settlement agreements whereby strikers will be returned to work?

**6.** After an unsuccessful economic strike at Urbana Steel, the union was decertified and the strikers made an unconditional offer to return to work. Shortly thereafter, Urbana contracted with a temporary employment agency to supply a number of workers for work previously performed by strikers. The company pays a fee to the agency which, in turn, pays wages and benefits to the employees doing the work. Urbana's labor costs are 40% less than it would be had it reinstated the strikers. Has it violated the Labor Act? Cf. NLRB v. Oregon Steel Mills, 47 F.3d 1536 (9th Cir.1995).

---

*EMPLOYEE REFUSALS TO CROSS PICKET LINES*

A particularly vexing problem in determining the reach of protection under Sections 8(a)(1) and (3) has been the treatment of employees who refuse to cross a picket line. If the picket line is at his own company, the employee who honors it and refuses to report to work will be deemed—if the picket line is the product of a lawful strike or picketing—to be a participant in that same activity and to be protected against discipline under Section 8(a)(1). If, however, the picket line is illegal—for example, it is incident to a secondary boycott in violation of Section 8(b)(4)—the employee making common cause with the picketers will himself be engaging in unprotected activity and will be amenable to discharge. The more difficult problem arises when the employee respects a lawful picket line (whether or not sponsored by his own union) at another company. While it has been generally agreed that his decision to honor that picket line, even though made "as an individual," is "concerted" activity, for a considerable period there had been less agreement as to whether it should be deemed "for mutual aid or protection" and, even if so, whether to permit discipline by the employer. (Of course, the Board might find any statutory right to have been "waived" by the union by contract. See, e.g., Local Union 1395, IBEW v. NLRB (Indianapolis Power & Light Co.), 797 F.2d 1027 (D.C.Cir. 1986) (Board may presume a general no-strike clause to waive right to engage in a sympathy strike).) See generally Fischl, Self, Others and Section 7: Mutualism and Protected Protest Activities Under the NLRA, 89 Colum.L.Rev. 789; Note, The Contractual Waiver of Individual Rights Under the NLRA, 31 N.Y.L.S. L.Rev. 793 (1986). One would have had to dig rather deeply in the reported cases to find fully articulated reasons on either side of the issue.

Reasons for protecting the refusal to cross a lawful picket line established elsewhere are that the refusal represents a showing of support for others in the labor movement who may some day be called upon to give comparable support when the now "lone" employee is himself a participant in lawful concerted activity; this conduct has also been made the special object of congressional concern in a proviso to Section 8(b)(4), declaring that it shall not be illegal (somewhat different from declaring that it shall be protected) to honor a picket line established at another company by the bargaining representative there; and, finally, to respect a picket line at another company is not designed to exert continuing and hurtful economic pressure on one's employer to make concessions in bargaining. Those who argue that respecting the picket line elsewhere should be treated as unprotected activity can point out that it smacks of the secondary boycott, with the employer of the refusing employee suffering pro tanto a work stoppage as a result of a labor dispute to which it is not a party and over which it has no control. Moreover, the refusal to cross the picket line can be treated as a breach of the employment contract, with the employee violating his employer's directions to work, instead picking and choosing the work that he wishes to do while remaining on the company payroll. NLRB v. L.G. Everist, Inc., 334 F.2d 312 (8th Cir.1964).

The prevailing view is that an employee's refusal to cross a picket line at another company is concerted activity, is for mutual aid or protection, and is protected under section 7 of the NLRA. That does not, however, mean that the employer is forbidden to take responsive measures in the interest of pursuing its business. Rather, the respective rights of the employee and employer are—essentially like the situation of the economic striker—to be determined by a balancing process, in which the interest of the employee in honoring the picket line is weighed against the business justification of the employer in replacing the employee or taking other self-protective measures. For excellent discussions of the meandering movement of the law in this area, and examples of the balancing process, see NLRB v. Browning–Ferris Indus., 700 F.2d 385 (7th Cir.1983)(Posner, J.), and Business Services by Manpower, Inc. v. NLRB, 784 F.2d 442 (2d Cir.1986)(Friendly, J.).

Rather consistently, the NLRB has found the employee's section 7 right to be sufficiently weighty so as to outbalance the employer's need to replace the employee permanently, and certainly discharge has been regarded as unjustifiable. See, e.g., Western Stress, Inc., 290 NLRB 678 (1988). The courts, however, have been just as consistently inclined to give more weight to the employer's interest in avoiding the delay and ill will that result from the failure of its employees to cross a stranger picket line, and have therefore sustained permanent replacement and even, under unusual circumstances, discharge. See *Browning–Ferris* and *Business Services by Manpower*, supra. In reviewing the Board decisions, the courts of appeals have not been reluctant to make an independent assessment of the particular facts of the case and an independent weighing of the respective interests of employer and employee.

––––––––

## PROBLEMS FOR DISCUSSION

**1.** Overnite Transportation Company is engaged in interstate freight transportation from its central terminal. Its employees are assigned no particular route but rather deliver freight according to assignments at the terminal and respond to radio calls in their trucks to make additional pickups at various locations. Last week, employee Styles received a radio call to pick up freight at the Warren Company, but when Styles arrived at the Warren plant and saw a picket line there, he drove past and made other pickups and deliveries at other locations. In the afternoon, Styles returned to the Warren plant to see whether conditions there had changed, but when he saw that they had not, he radioed in to the terminal and told the dispatcher that he could not in good conscience make the assigned pickup through the picket line. When the dispatcher promptly relayed this message to the terminal manager, the manager just as promptly informed Styles over his truck radio that he could not tolerate employees deciding which pickups and deliveries to make and which routes to drive, and that he should return to the terminal immediately and collect a final paycheck. Is it legal for the company thus to terminate Styles' employment? Are there any other facts necessary to make an informed conclusion? See NLRB v. Browning–Ferris Indus., 700 F.2d 385 (7th Cir.1983).

**2.** During a strike at Montgomery Ward's Chicago mail order house, orders were rerouted from Chicago to the Kansas City house, where the employees are represented by the same union as at Chicago. Three employees at the Kansas City location refused to process mail orders which they believed were being routed from Chicago, and they were discharged for doing so. Are the discharges illegal? See NLRB v. Montgomery Ward & Co., 157 F.2d 486 (8th Cir.1946).

———

# Metropolitan Edison Co. v. NLRB[h]

460 U.S. 693, 103 S.Ct. 1467, 75 L.Ed.2d 387 (1983).

■ JUSTICE POWELL delivered the opinion of the Court.

The issue is whether an employer may discipline union officials more severely than other union employees for participating in an unlawful work stoppage.

I

Metropolitan Edison Company began construction of a two-unit nuclear generating station at Three Mile Island in 1968. Over half of its employees were represented by the International Brotherhood of Electrical Workers. Article XI of the collective-bargaining agreement between the company and the union provided:

> "The Brotherhood and its members agree that during the term of this agreement there shall be no strikes or walkouts by the Brotherhood or its members, and the Company agrees that there shall be no lockouts of the Brotherhood or its members, it being the desire of both parties to provide uninterrupted and continuous service to the public." App. to Pet. for Cert. A–32.

Despite this no-strike clause, union members participated in four unlawful work stoppages between 1970 and 1974. On each occasion the company disciplined the local union officials more severely than the other partici-

---

**h.** See Note, Selective Discipline of Union Officials After *Metropolitan Edison v.* *NLRB,* 63 B.U.L.Rev. 473 (1983).

pants. Twice the union filed a grievance because of the disparate treatment accorded its officials, and in both cases the arbitrators upheld the company's actions.[2] They found that union officials have an affirmative duty to uphold the bargaining agreement. The breach of that duty justified the company's imposition of more severe sanctions.

On August 30, 1977, an unrelated union, the Operating Engineers, set up an informational picket line at the entrance to the Three Mile Island construction site. When members of the Electrical Workers union refused to cross the picket line, company officials spoke to David Lang, the local union president. They told him that he had a duty as a union official to ensure that the Electrical Workers' members complied with the no-strike clause. It was the company's view that Lang could fulfill this duty only by crossing the picket line and thereby inducing other employees to follow.

Although instructed repeatedly to cross the line, Lang declined to do so. He was aware that the other employees were unlikely to follow him and sought instead to learn the cause of the picket line. On being told that the line would not be removed unless the Operating Engineers' business agent ordered it, Lang attempted to reach him. He also directed Gene Light, the Electrical Workers' vice-president, to continue his efforts to persuade the pickets to remove their line. After approximately four hours, Light and Lang were able to negotiate a settlement between the Operating Engineers and Metropolitan Edison. The settlement required the company to establish a separate entrance to the construction site. When this was done, the picket line came down and the union's members returned to work.

Metropolitan Edison disciplined all of its employees who refused to cross the picket line by imposing 5-to 10-day suspensions. Light and Lang, however, each received 25-day suspensions and were warned that future participation in any unlawful work stoppage would result in their immediate discharge. The company explained that the additional penalty was imposed because of their failure as union officials to make "every bona fide effort to prevent the unlawful work stoppage," specifically their failure to attempt to end the strike by crossing the picket line.

[The Board held that selective discipline of union officials violated §§ 8(a)(1) and (3), and the court of appeals agreed. The Supreme Court affirmed.]

---

**2.** In 1972, Metropolitan Edison disciplined union officials more severely than the other employees for not instructing striking employees to return to work. The company's actions were upheld by the arbitrator, who found "that Union officials have an *affirmative duty* to protect the authority of the Union leadership from illegitimate action on the part of employees, and to uphold the sanctity of the Agreement and its established grievance procedures." App. to Pet. for Cert. A–60 (emphasis in original).

Two years later the company again determined that a senior shop steward was not taking sufficient corrective action during an unlawful work stoppage and imposed a greater penalty on him than on the other participants. This action also was upheld on arbitration. See id., at A–62, 71.

Once in 1970 and again in 1973, the company imposed a more severe penalty on union officials who participated in an unlawful work stoppage. The officials were suspended for 1 and 5 days respectively, but the union chose not to take these cases to arbitration. See App. 29, 32.

## II

This case does not present the question whether an employer may impose stricter penalties on union officials who take a leadership role in an unlawful strike. The Administrative Law Judge found that neither Light nor Lang acted as a strike leader.[6] Nor does this case question the employer's right to discipline union officials who engage in unprotected activity. Neither the union nor the Board has argued that union officials who fail to honor a no-strike clause are immunized from being disciplined in the same manner as other strike participants. The narrow question presented is whether an employer unilaterally may define the actions a union official is required to take to enforce a no-strike clause and penalize him for his failure to comply.

Metropolitan Edison advances two arguments to justify the additional sanctions it imposed on Light and Lang. It contends first that its actions did not violate § 8(a)(3) because a union official has a duty to ensure compliance with the terms of the collective bargaining agreement. Breach of this duty justifies the imposition of an additional penalty on union officials. Alternatively, the company contends that a union in effect may waive any statutory protection that otherwise would be accorded its officials by agreeing that they will undertake specific action to assure compliance with the no-strike clause. In this case, the arbitration awards and the union's acquiescence in the harsher sanctions imposed on its officials are sufficient to establish a clear contractual duty. We examine these arguments in turn.

### A

[The Court set forth the analysis of Section 8(a)(3) as developed in such cases as *American Ship Building, Erie Resistor,* and *Great Dane Trailers.*]

### B

The Board has found that disciplining union officials more severely than other employees for participating in an unlawful work stoppage "is contrary to the plain meaning of Section 8(a)(3) and would frustrate the policies of the Act if allowed to stand." Precision Castings Co., 233 N.L.R.B., at 184. This conduct, in the Board's view, is "inherently destruc-

---

**6.** The Board has held that employees who instigate or provide leadership for unprotected strikes may be subject to more severe discipline than other employees. See Midwest Precision Castings Co., 244 N.L.R.B. 597, 598 (1979); Chrysler Corp., 232 N.L.R.B. 466, 474 (1977). In making this factual determination the Board has recognized that a remark made by a union official may have greater significance than one made by a rank-and-file member. See *Midwest Precision Castings, supra,* at 599.

In this case the Board accepted the Administrative Law Judge's finding that Light and Lang were not strike leaders, and the Court of Appeals affirmed that finding. See 663 F.2d 478, 484 (1981). We note also that the disciplinary notices issued to both Light and Lang made clear that the additional penalties imposed on them were not based on any perceived leadership role in initiating or maintaining the strike.

tive" of protected individual rights because it discriminates solely on the basis of union status. * * *

We defer to the Board's conclusion that conduct such as Metropolitan Edison's adversely affects protected employee interests. Section 8(a)(3) not only proscribes discrimination that affects union membership, it also makes unlawful discrimination against employees who participate in concerted activities protected by § 7 of the Act. See Radio Officers' Union v. NLRB, 347 U.S. 17, 39–40, 74 S.Ct. 323, 335, 98 L.Ed. 455 (1954). Holding union office clearly falls within the activities protected by § 7, see General Motors Corp., 218 N.L.R.B. 472, 477 (1975), and there can be little doubt that an employer's unilateral imposition of discipline on union officials inhibits qualified employees from holding office, see Szewczuga v. NLRB, 686 F.2d 962, 973 (C.A.D.C.1982).

Determining that such conduct adversely affects protected employee interests does not conclude the inquiry. If the employer comes forward with a legitimate explanation for its conduct, the Board must "strike the proper balance between the asserted business justifications and the invasion of employee rights." NLRB v. Great Dane Trailers, Inc., 388 U.S., at 33–34, 87 S.Ct. at 1797. In this case the company has argued that its actions were justified because there is an implied duty on the part of the union officials to uphold the terms of the collective-bargaining agreement. Unquestionably there is support for the proposition that union officials, as leaders of the rank and file, have a legal obligation to support the terms of the contract and to set a responsible example for their members. * * * But it does not follow that an employer may assume that a union official is required to attempt to enforce a no-strike clause by complying with the employer's directions and impose a penalty on the official for declining to comply. As the Board has concluded, the imposition of such a penalty would violate § 8(a)(3).

We think the Board's view is consistent with the policies served by the Act. "The entire process of collective bargaining is structured and regulated on the assumption that '[t]he parties * * * proceed from contrary and to an extent antagonistic viewpoints and concepts of self-interest.'" General Building Contractors Association v. Pennsylvania, 458 U.S. 375, 102 S.Ct. 3141, 73 L.Ed.2d 835 (1982)(quoting NLRB v. Insurance Agents, 361 U.S. 477, 488, 80 S.Ct. 419, 426, 4 L.Ed.2d 454 (1960)). Congress has sought to ensure the integrity of this process by preventing both management and labor's representatives from being coerced in the performance of their official duties. See Florida Power & Light Co. v. Electrical Workers, 417 U.S. 790, 810–811, 94 S.Ct. 2737, 2747–48, 41 L.Ed.2d 477 (1974); id., at 814, 94 S.Ct., at 2749 (White, J., dissenting). Cf. 29 U.S.C. § 158(a)(2)(specifying employer domination of unions as an unfair labor practice). If, as the company urges, an employer could define unilaterally the actions that a union official is required to take, it would give the employer considerable leverage over the manner in which the official performs his union duties. Failure to comply with the employer's directions would place the official's job in jeopardy. But compliance might cause him to take actions that would diminish the respect and authority necessary to perform his job as a union official. This is the dilemma Congress sought to avoid. We believe the Board's decision furthers these policies and uphold its determination.

## III

The company argues that even if § 8(a)(3) would prohibit it from imposing a more severe penalty on union officials than on other employees, the union in effect has waived the protection afforded by the statute. The substance of this contention is that, in this case, the prior arbitration awards and the union's acquiescence in the harsher sanctions imposed on its officials are sufficient to establish a corresponding contractual duty. We are met at the outset, however, by the union's response that the statutory right to be free from discrimination may never be waived. We examine first the union's argument.

## A

This Court long has recognized that a union may waive a member's statutorily protected rights, including "his right to strike during the contract term, and his right to refuse to cross a lawful picket line." NLRB v. Allis–Chalmers Manufacturing Co., 388 U.S. 175, 180, 87 S.Ct. 2001, 2006, 18 L.Ed.2d 1123 (1967)(footnotes omitted). Such waivers are valid because they "rest on 'the premise of fair representation' and presuppose that the selection of the bargaining representative 'remains free.'" NLRB v. Magnavox Co., 415 U.S. 322 (1974) * * *.

We think a union's decision to bind its officials to take affirmative steps to end an unlawful work stoppage is consistent with "the premise of fair representation." Such a waiver imposes no constraints on the employees' ability to choose which union will represent them. Imposition of this duty is more closely related to the economic decision a union makes when it waives its members' right to strike. It merely requires union officials to take steps that are ancillary to the union's promise not to strike and provides the employer with an additional means of enforcing this promise. * * * A union and an employer reasonably could choose to secure the integrity of a no-strike clause by requiring union officials to take affirmative steps to end unlawful work stoppages. Indeed, a union could choose to bargain away this statutory protection to secure gains it considers of more value to its members. Its decision to undertake such contractual obligations promotes labor peace and clearly falls within the range of reasonableness accorded bargaining representatives.

## B

We consider finally whether the union waived its officials' rights. In *Mastro Plastics Corp.*, supra, the question was whether a general no-strike provision waived the specific right to strike over an unfair labor practice. While reserving the question whether a union might waive this right if it were "explicitly stated," the Court determined that "there is no adequate basis for implying [the] existence [of waiver] without a more compelling expression of it than appears in * * * this contract." 350 U.S., at 283, 76 S.Ct., at 358. Thus, we will not infer from a general contractual provision that the parties intended to waive a statutorily protected right unless the undertaking is "explicitly stated." More succinctly, the waiver must be clear and unmistakable.

In this case, Metropolitan Edison does not contend that the general no-strike clause included in the bargaining agreement imposed any explicit duty on the union officials. Rather it argues that the union's failure to change the relevant contractual language in the face of two prior arbitration decisions constitutes an implicit contractual waiver. * * * [W]e do not doubt that prior arbitration decisions may be relevant—both to other arbitrators and to the Board—in interpreting bargaining agreements. But to waive a statutory right the duty must be established clearly and unmistakably. Where prior arbitration decisions have been inconsistent, sporadic, or ambiguous, there would be little basis for determining that the parties intended to incorporate them in subsequent agreements. Assessing the clarity with which a party's duties have been defined of course will require consideration of the specific circumstances of each case. * * *

* * * During the history of collective bargaining between these two parties, however, there were only two arbitration decisions that imposed a higher duty on union officials. We do not think that two arbitration awards establish a pattern of decisions clear enough to convert the union's silence into binding waiver. This is especially so in light of the provision in the bargaining agreement that "[a] decision [by an arbitrator] shall be binding * * * for the term of *this* agreement." * * * We conclude that there is no showing that the parties intended to incorporate the two prior arbitration decisions into the subsequent agreement.

### IV

We accept the Board's conclusion that the imposition of more severe sanctions on union officials for participating in an unlawful work stoppage violates § 8(a)(3). While a union may waive this protection by clearly imposing contractual duties on its officials to ensure the integrity of no-strike clauses, we find that no waiver occurred here. Accordingly, the judgment of the Court of Appeals is affirmed.

----

### PROBLEMS FOR DISCUSSION

**1.** The Court made much of the fact that the employer punished Lang for declining to take specific steps, "unilaterally defined" by the employer, to stop the work stoppage. Is that the limit of the Court's holding? For example, had there been no unilateral direction by the Company to Lang, but he had been a leading instigator of the walkout, would the Supreme Court uphold more severe discipline for him than for those who merely followed along? Assume (again in the absence of directions from the employer) that Lang and two others had instigated the walkout and the Company imposed a longer disciplinary suspension on Lang than on the other two instigators, on the theory that he was a union officer and they were not, so that he had a greater obligation to promote enforcement of the labor agreement; would such disparate discipline violate Section 8(a)(3)?

**2.**   Was the Court correct in holding that the earlier arbitration decisions sustaining the imposition of greater discipline on union officials were not to be regarded as effectively controlling under the current labor contract? How many more times would the Court have wanted the very same issue to be submitted to arbitration before it would be prepared to conclude that there was a controlling "pattern of decisions"? Did the Court properly construe the contract provision concerning the binding effect of arbitration decisions? Compare West Penn Power Co., 274 NLRB 1160 (1985).

---

*Unfair labor practice strikes*[i]

In many cases coming before the Board, such as *Laidlaw Corp.,* p. 569, supra, it has been plain that the employer's unfair labor practices caused the employees to initiate or prolong a strike, and in such cases the Board has quite uniformly ordered the employer to reinstate the striking employees to their former positions, discharging if necessary replacements hired during the strike. In Matter of Brown Shoe Co., 1 NLRB 803 (1936), for example, the Board found that the respondent's arbitrary termination of a seniority agreement with the union in violation of section 8(1) was responsible for the strike at its plant on October 14, 1935: "An order requiring the respondent to cease and desist from such conduct will not wholly restore the union to at least the position it occupied in the Salem plant on the day of the strike. We, shall, therefore, in order to restore the status quo, order the respondent to offer reinstatement to those employees at the Salem plant who went out on strike on October 14, and to that end, if necessary, to displace employees hired since October 14 to take the places of strikers." In effect, the Board treats more favorably employees striking to protest conduct for which the NLRA provides a peaceful administrative remedy than employees who have no comparable means to better their terms of employment. Do you think that this is wise or unwise administrative policy?

Unfair labor practice strikers have also been treated somewhat more favorably than economic strikers concerning their rights to vote in representation elections held during the strike. Both economic and unfair labor practice strikers may vote, but the privilege of the economic striker expires if the election is held more than twelve months from the commencement of the strike. W. Wilton Wood, Inc., 127 NLRB 1675 (1960). And, since economic strikers are not entitled to "bump" their permanent replacements, such replacements may vote (in addition to the strikers), Rudolph Wurlitzer Co., 32 NLRB 163 (1941); but replacements for unfair labor

---

**i.**   See Note, Strike Misconduct: An Illusory Bar to Reinstatement, 72 Yale L.J. 182 (1962); Note, The Unfair Labor Practice Strike: A Critique and a Proposal for Change, 46 N.Y.U.L.Rev. 988 (1971).

practice strikers may not, Tampa Sand & Material Co., 137 NLRB 1549 (1962). The latter principle prevents the employer from committing an unfair labor practice and precipitating a strike, hiring replacements unsympathetic to the union and having them vote out the union in a representation election.

These distinctions in voting and reinstatement rights of economic and unfair labor practice strikers make it important on occasion to determine the "cause" of a strike. This issue is often complicated when a strike is initiated over bargaining demands or demands for recognition but, during the course of the strike, the employer commits unfair labor practices, e.g., refusing to bargain with a certified union or discriminatorily discharging a union supporter. Such an employer unfair labor practice will be held to "convert" the strike if it can be determined that the employer's action prolonged the strike beyond the date it would have terminated in due course as an economic strike. The *Laidlaw Corp.* case, at p. 569, supra, shows the Board applying the "conversion" doctrine, and finding that what had begun as a strike over bargaining demands became an unfair labor practice strike when it was prolonged by the union's vote to protest the employer's outright termination of strikers seeking reinstatement. The Board applied the usual rule that strikers who are permanently replaced during the economic phase of the strike are not entitled to immediate reinstatement, while strikers replaced after the date of conversion are.

The characterization of a strike as an unfair labor practice strike may also be important in determining whether there must be compliance with the notification and cooling-off requirements of Section 8(d) of the Labor Act or whether a strike violates a no-strike promise in a collective bargaining agreement. These issues were addressed by the Supreme Court in MASTRO PLASTICS CORP. v. NLRB, 350 U.S. 270, 76 S.Ct. 349, 100 L.Ed. 309 (1956). In that case, an incumbent union had notified the employer of its intention to modify their labor contract; this notice was given in compliance with Section 8(d) which provides for a sixty-day waiting period for striking subsequent to a notice requesting "termination or modification" of a contract. One month after the notice was given, the employer discharged an employee for union activity, and the union called a strike to protest the discharge. The employer then discharged the strikers, arguing that their strike during the sixty-day cooling off period caused them to forfeit their status as "employees" under the Act (as stipulated by Section 8(d)) so that they were liable to immediate discharge; and that the strike was in breach of the contract's no-strike clause, and was thus also unprotected activity for which they could be discharged. The Court rejected both these arguments, resting on the Board's finding that the strike was precipitated by the unlawful discharge. Its object was thus not "termination or modification" of the contract within Section 8(d), so that compliance with the sixty-day waiting period was not necessary and participation in the strike did not expose the strikers to the loss-of-status provision of that Section. The Court also held that the conventional no-strike clause in a labor contract should be read to bar only economic strikes and not unfair labor practice strikes. The strikers were ordered reinstated with backpay.

The distinctions noted above between economic strikers and unfair labor practice strikers assume that the strikers have engaged in no conduct which falls beyond the protection of Section 7. When strikers do engage in such unprotected conduct, there is yet another distinction that has for many years been made in the law, once again in favor of the unfair labor practice striker and his right to reinstatement. It has been held that—although the economic striker who engages in unprotected activity and is discharged cannot secure reinstatement—the Board does have the power to reinstate a striker discharged for unprotected activity when the striker was participating in an unfair labor practice strike.

The Court of Appeals for the First Circuit rested this distinction on close statutory analysis, in NLRB v. Thayer Co., 213 F.2d 748 (1st Cir.1954):

> [S]ince the power of the Board to order reinstatement under § 10(c) is dependent upon its finding that an unfair labor practice has been committed, and since by hypothesis the economic strike was not caused by an unfair labor practice, it becomes crucial to the question of reinstatement of an economic striker to inquire whether the strike as conducted constituted concerted activity within the protection of § 7.

> When the discharged employee was, however, engaged in a strike protesting an employer unfair labor practice, the Board—even if the discharge itself is not unlawful because of the striker's unprotected conduct—can order reinstatement as a remedy for the underlying statutory violation by the employer. In such cases, the power of the Board to order reinstatement is not necessarily dependent upon a determination that the strike activity was a "concerted activity" within the protection of § 7. Even if it was not, the National Labor Relations Board has power under § 10(c) to order reinstatement if the discharges were not "for cause" and if such an order would effectuate the policies of the Act. Of course the discharge of strikers engaged in non-Section 7 activities often may be for cause, or their reinstatement may not effectuate the policies of the Act, but in certain circumstances it may.

> * * * It ordinarily may be assumed that the Board, as a part of the process of determining whether reinstatement would effectuate the policies of the Act, will balance the severity of the employer's unfair labor practice which provoked the industrial disturbance against whatever employee misconduct may have occurred in the course of the strike.

The court observed that certain of the discharged strikers had engaged in mass picketing and some acts of violence and destruction of property. It concluded, however, that the trial examiner acted properly in recommending reinstatement in light of the fact that the strike resulted from the employer's "flagrant" unfair labor practices.

This position has been endorsed by other courts. *E.g.*, Local 833, UAW v. NLRB (Kohler Co.), 300 F.2d 699 (D.C.Cir.1962), cert. denied, 370 U.S.

911, 82 S.Ct. 1258, 8 L.Ed.2d 405 (1962): "To hold that employee 'misconduct' automatically precludes compulsory reinstatement ignores two considerations which we think important. First, the employer's antecedent unfair labor practices may have been so blatant that they provoked employees to resort to unprotected action. Second, reinstatement is the only sanction which prevents an employer from benefiting from his unfair labor practices through discharges which may weaken or destroy a union."

The NLRB had for many years declined to follow the *Thayer-Kohler* approach, but it ultimately acquiesced the year after the *Kohler* decision, in Blades Mfg. Corp., 144 NLRB 561 (1963).

In a more recent decision, however, the Board appears once again to have reverted to its prior position of refusing reinstatement to unfair labor practice strikers who engage in violence or other unprotected activity. In CLEAR PINE MOULDINGS, INC., 268 NLRB 1044 (1984), enf'd, 765 F.2d 148 (9th Cir.1985), cert. denied, 474 U.S. 1105, 106 S.Ct. 893, 88 L.Ed.2d 926 (1986), two strikers protesting what were ultimately found to be violations of Sections 8(a)(1), (3) and (5) were discharged; they had engaged in abusively threatening behavior at and away from the picket line. As an initial matter, the Board abandoned its prevailing rule that verbal threats by strikers unaccompanied by any intimidating physical acts or gestures did not amount to sufficiently serious misconduct warranting discharge or refusal to reinstate. It adopted instead an objective test to govern threats: "whether the misconduct is such that, under the circumstances existing, it may reasonably tend to coerce or intimidate employees in the exercise of rights protected under the Act." The Board found that the two strikers had manifestly engaged in such behavior, and the two-member Board plurality concluded that this was alone sufficient to deny reinstatement, even though the perpetrators were unfair labor practice strikers.

In deciding whether reinstatement should be ordered after an unfair labor practice strike, the Board has in the past balanced the severity of the employer's unfair labor practices that provoked the strike against the gravity of the striker's misconduct. We do not agree with this test. There is nothing in the statute to support the notion that striking employees are free to engage in or escalate violence or misconduct in proportion to their individual estimates of the degree of seriousness of an employer's unfair labor practices. Rather, it is for the Board to fashion remedies and policies which will discourage unfair labor practices and the resort to violence and unlawful coercion by employers and employees alike. In cases of picket line and strike misconduct, we will do this by denying reinstatement and backpay to employees who exceed the bounds of peaceful and reasoned conduct.[25]

---

[25]. Balancing the misconduct of strikers against the seriousness of the employer's unfair labor practice is inappropriate because it condones misconduct on the part of employees as a response to the employer's unfair labor practice and indeed makes it part of the remedy protected by the Act. Retaliation breeds retaliation and, in the emotion-charged strike atmosphere, retaliation will likely initiate an escalation of mis-

In a separate opinion, the other two members of the Board declined to endorse expressly the rejection of the Board's "balancing" test regarding unfair labor practice strikers. One of those members, however, counseled that the new standard for finding verbal threats to be intimidating should be applied cautiously: "[T]he Board must take care not to condemn statements which are not reasonably likely to instill fear of physical harm. * * * [P]icket line actions often include tense, angry, and hostile confrontations in which emotions run high and threats are hurled that cannot reasonably be interpreted as auguries of violence. The Board must take care not to impose on industrial disputes a code of ethics alien to the realities of confrontational strikes and picket lines and contrary to our national tradition of free speech."

## II. CONSTITUTIONAL LIMITATIONS ON GOVERNMENT REGULATION[a]

At least two constitutional doctrines affect the power of the federal or State governments to restrict the use of concerted action to enforce the demands of a labor union against an employer, or other employees, or a competing labor organization: (1) the concept of "due process" developed under the Fifth and Fourteenth Amendments, and (2) the freedom of communication protected against undue federal restriction by the First Amendment and, through the Fourteenth Amendment, against unwarranted curtailment by a State.

———

### A. FIFTH AND FOURTEENTH AMENDMENTS

The Fifth and Fourteenth Amendments guarantee that no one shall be deprived of "life, liberty or property without due process of law." There has been little litigation concerning the application of these provisions to strike action as distinguished from picketing. Perhaps the leading Supreme Court decision on the question—rendered in a rather unusual factual context—is

conduct culminating in the violent coercive actions we condemn. It would be virtually impossible for all practical purposes for employees to know what is expected of them during a strike because balancing remains illusive and would be applied only long after the operative events have occurred. Likewise we believe that the unclear and permissive standards previously employed by the Board have failed to adequately protect employee rights. Rather, it is our purpose to discourage any belief that misconduct is ever a proper element of labor relations. Only in this way can we honor the Act's commitment to the peaceful settlement of labor disputes without resort to coercion, intimidation, and violence. Therefore, we refuse to adopt a standard which will allow the illegal acts of one party to justify the wrongful acts of another.

**a.** See Cox, Strikes, Picketing and the Constitution, 4 Vanderbilt L.Rev. 574 (1951); Gregory, Constitutional Limitations on the Regulation of Union and Employer Conduct, 49 Mich.L.Rev. 191 (1950); Kohler, Setting the Conditions for Self–Rule: Unions, Associations, Our First Amendment Discourse and the Problem of *DeBartolo*, 1990 Wisc.L.Rev. 149.

Dorchy v. Kansas, 272 U.S. 306, 47 S.Ct. 86, 71 L.Ed. 248 (1926), in which Mr. Justice Brandeis delivered a unanimous opinion for the Court. There, a Kansas statute, while reserving to individual employees the right to quit at any time, made it a crime "to induce others to quit their employment for the purpose and with the intent to hinder, delay, limit or suspend the operation of" mining. Dorchy, as vice-president of a local of the United Mine Workers, was convicted, and sentenced to fine and imprisonment, for calling a strike designed to compel a mine company to pay a two-year-old disputed claim to an individual no longer employed by the company. Dorchy attacked the statute as in violation of the Fourteenth Amendment, claiming that the strike was a "liberty" protected by the Constitution. The Court upheld the statute as applied:

> The right to carry on business—be it called liberty or property—has value. To interfere with this right without just cause is unlawful. The fact that the injury was inflicted by a strike is sometimes a justification. But a strike may be illegal because of its purpose, however orderly the manner in which it is conducted. To collect a stale claim due to a fellow member of the union who was formerly employed in the business is not a permissible purpose. In the absence of a valid agreement to the contrary, each party to a disputed claim may insist that it be determined only by a court. * * * To enforce payment by a strike is clearly coercion. The Legislature may make such action punishable criminally, as extortion or otherwise. * * * And it may subject to punishment him who uses the power or influence incident to his office in a union to order the strike. Neither the common law, nor the Fourteenth Amendment confers the absolute right to strike.

The Court has since cited *Dorchy* approvingly (see International Union, UAW v. Wisconsin Employment Rel. Bd., 336 U.S. 245, 69 S.Ct. 516, 93 L.Ed. 651 (1949)), and there is little question—especially in light of the Court's decisions on picketing, to be discussed shortly, where there is the further constitutional concern for freedom of speech—that there is no absolute right to strike. The State courts have sustained numerous restrictions.

None of the cases, however, clearly examines in detail the interest of the employees, in order to determine whether their interest in striking for the purpose of securing better terms and conditions of employment is entitled to some degree of constitutional protection. On principle it would seem that the interest of employees in freedom to strike is cognizable under the Fifth and Fourteenth Amendments. Recourse to a strike involves the withholding of personal service and the association of individuals into a group. Withholding personal service is surely an exercise of "liberty" in the constitutional sense; and so too, recent Supreme Court cases have held, is the freedom to associate in labor organizations. The fact that the strike is a weapon—a form of self-help—used to advance the workers' interest in wages, hours and other terms and conditions of employment does not militate against the claim to some degree of constitutional protection. A constitution which assures the owner of property an opportunity to obtain a reasonable return on his capital surely must recognize the worker's interest in the conditions under which he labors and the price he receives for his work.

If it is correct to conclude that a restriction upon strikes is invalid under the Fifth or Fourteenth Amendment unless the requirements of substantive "due process" are satisfied, the constitutionality of each individual restriction can be determined only after analyzing in detail the needs which gave rise to the challenged legislation in order to determine whether they reasonably justify such a restriction. Unionization and collective bargaining in the public sector cannot be treated in detail in this casebook, but it should be noted here that there have been a number of court tests of the constitutionality of the very common legislative ban upon strikes by public employees. Such absolute strike prohibitions have consistently been sustained against constitutional attack. Greatest emphasis is placed upon the unique (and monopolistic) position of government in the rendition of essential services and upon the serious societal disruption that would result were governmental services to be interrupted by work stoppages.

A thorough discussion of the claim of constitutional protection for public-employee strikes may be found in UNITED FEDERATION OF POSTAL CLERKS v. BLOUNT, 325 F.Supp. 879 (D.D.C.1971), aff'd mem., 404 U.S. 802, 92 S.Ct. 80, 30 L.Ed.2d 38 (1971), in which a three-judge panel upheld a blanket statutory ban upon strikes by federal employees. The majority, noting that the right to strike in the private sector was given not by the Constitution but by federal legislation, observed that the denial of the strike to public employees was rooted in public interest and in long historical tradition. This denial—even taken alongside the statutory protection for private employees—was held not to be arbitrary or irrationally discriminatory, given the interest in assuring "the continuing functioning of the Government without interruption, to protect public health and safety or for other reasons." The majority did, however, assume that public employees had a constitutional right to organize in labor organizations. The concurring judge found this fundamental right to be so intertwined with the right to strike as to raise a serious question whether the latter right was not also constitutionally sanctioned:

> "A union that never strikes, or which can make no credible threat to strike may wither away in ineffectiveness. * * * I do not suggest that the right to strike is co-equal with the right to form labor organizations. * * * But I do believe that the right to strike is, at least, within constitutional concern and should not be discriminatorily abridged without substantial or 'compelling' justification."

> Although he believed that the right to strike under the Constitution should turn not on whether the employer was a private employer or a governmental agency but rather upon the essentiality of the services rendered, the concurring judge acknowledged that this was an extremely difficult line to draw (particularly for a

court) and that both history and judicial precedent compelled at least as an expedient that the distinction between public and private employees be regarded as crucial.

A more recent assessment of the constitutional status of public-employee strikes is that of the California Supreme Court in dicta, and the concurring opinions, in COUNTY SANITATION DIST. NO. 2 v. LOS ANGELES COUNTY EMPLOYEES ASS'N., 38 Cal.3d 564, 214 Cal.Rptr. 424, 699 P.2d 835 (1985). There, the court found arbitrary the longstanding per se prohibition on public-employee strikes under the common law of the state of California, and concluded that the state's highest court had the power to—and should—overturn that ban without waiting for legislative action. In very strong dicta, the court indicated that the right of all workers to withhold their labor, whether in the public sector or the private sector, may well be incident to the right of free association found within the federal and state constitutions, such that it cannot be abridged absent a substantial or compelling justification. The court concluded that public-employee strikes would henceforth be prohibited in California only if it could be demonstrated in the particular case that the strike posed an "imminent threat to public health or safety." An exhaustive and indeed exuberant defense of the constitutionally sanctioned status of the right to strike can be found in the concurring opinion of Chief Justice Bird.

---

## B.   PICKETING AND FREEDOM OF COMMUNICATION[b]

The student should at this time review the Supreme Court decision in *Thornhill v. Alabama*, at page 73 supra, and the questions that follow it. As the following cases show, the wide-ranging constitutional protection for picketing that was potentially available under *Thornhill* was narrowed soon after. Picketing is no longer assimilated to "pure" political speech, and the communicational element is found justifiably curbed if the state (or federal) government can invoke a significant social justification for doing so. *Thornhill*, of course, held that the state's interest in curbing merely economic injury to the picketed employer is not sufficiently weighty. Do the cases that mark the retreat from *Thornhill* satisfactorily explain why picketing cannot be treated as speech? Do they satisfactorily explain why it is that certain governmental concerns are regarded as sufficiently weighty as to justify barring picketing? What is left of the *Thornhill* decision?

---

## International Broth. of Teamsters, Local 695 v. Vogt, Inc.

354 U.S. 284, 77 S.Ct. 1166, 1 L.Ed.2d 1347 (1957).

■ MR. JUSTICE FRANKFURTER delivered the opinion of the Court.

This is one more in the long series of cases in which this Court has been required to consider the limits imposed by the Fourteenth Amend-

---

**b.**   See the articles cited at pp. 73, 587, supra.

ment on the power of a State to enjoin picketing. The case was heard below on the pleadings and affidavits, the parties stipulating that the record contained "all of the facts and evidence that would be adduced upon a trial on the merits * * *." Respondent owns and operates a gravel pit in Oconomowoc, Wisconsin, where it employs 15 to 20 men. Petitioner unions sought unsuccessfully to induce some of respondent's employees to join the unions and commenced to picket the entrance to respondent's business with signs reading, "The men on this job are not 100% affiliated with the A.F.L." "In consequence," drivers of several trucking companies refused to deliver and haul goods to and from respondent's plant, causing substantial damage to respondent. Respondent thereupon sought an injunction to restrain the picketing. * * *

[The State Supreme Court, in affirming the grant of the injunction against the picketing,] held that "One would be credulous indeed to believe under the circumstances that the Union had no thought of coercing the employer to interfere with its employees in their right to join or refuse to join the defendant Union." Such picketing, the court held, was for "an unlawful purpose," since Wis.Stat. § 111.06(2)(b) made it an unfair labor practice for an employee individually or in concert with others to "coerce, intimidate or induce any employer to interfere with any of his employes in the enjoyment of their legal rights * * * or to engage in any practice with regard to his employes which would constitute an unfair labor practice if undertaken by him on his own initiative." * * *

* * * It is not too surprising that the response of States—legislative and judicial—to use of the injunction in labor controversies should have given rise to a series of adjudications in this Court relating to the limitations on state action contained in the provisions of the Due Process Clause of the Fourteenth Amendment. It is also not too surprising that examination of these adjudications should disclose an evolving, not a static, course of decision.

The series begins with Truax v. Corrigan, 257 U.S. 312, 42 S.Ct. 124, 66 L.Ed. 254, in which a closely divided Court found it to be violative of the Equal Protection Clause—not of the Due Process Clause—for a State to deny use of the injunction in the special class of cases arising out of labor conflicts. The considerations that underlay that case soon had to yield, through legislation and later through litigation, to the persuasiveness of undermining facts. Thus, to remedy the abusive use of the injunction in the federal courts, see Frankfurter and Greene, The Labor Injunction, the Norris–LaGuardia Act, 47 Stat. 70, 29 U.S.C. § 101, 29 U.S.C.A. § 101, withdrew, subject to qualifications, jurisdiction from the federal courts to issue injunctions in labor disputes to prohibit certain acts. Its example was widely followed by state enactments.

Apart from remedying the abuses of the injunction in this general type of litigation, legislatures and courts began to find in one of the aims of picketing an aspect of communication. This view came to the fore in Senn

v. Tile Layers Union, 301 U.S. 468, 57 S.Ct. 857, 81 L.Ed. 1229, where the Court held that the Fourteenth Amendment did not prohibit Wisconsin from authorizing peaceful stranger picketing by a union that was attempting to unionize a shop and to induce an employer to refrain from working in his business as a laborer.

Although the Court had been closely divided in the Senn case, three years later, in passing on a restrictive instead of permissive state statute, the Court made sweeping pronouncements about the right to picket in holding unconstitutional a statute that had been applied to ban all picketing, with "no exceptions based upon either the number of persons engaged in the proscribed activity, the peaceful character of their demeanor, the nature of their dispute with an employer, or the restrained character and the accurateness of the terminology used in notifying the public of the facts of the dispute." Thornhill v. Alabama, 310 U.S. 88, 99, 60 S.Ct. 736, 743, 84 L.Ed. 1093. As the statute dealt at large with all picketing, so the Court broadly assimilated peaceful picketing in general to freedom of speech, and as such protected against abridgment by the Fourteenth Amendment.

These principles were applied by the Court in A.F.L. v. Swing, 312 U.S. 321, 61 S.Ct. 568, 85 L.Ed. 855, to hold unconstitutional an injunction against peaceful picketing, based on a State's common-law policy against picketing when there was no immediate dispute between employer and employee. On the same day, however, the Court upheld a generalized injunction against picketing where there had been violence because "it could justifiably be concluded that the momentum of fear generated by past violence would survive even though future picketing might be wholly peaceful." Milk Wagon Drivers Union v. Meadowmoor Dairies, 312 U.S. 287, 294, 61 S.Ct. 552, 555, 85 L.Ed. 836.

Soon, however, the Court came to realize that the broad pronouncements, but not the specific holding, of Thornhill had to yield "to the impact of facts unforeseen," or at least not sufficiently appreciated. Cf. People v. Charles Schweinler Press, 214 N.Y. 395, 108 N.E. 639, L.R.A.1918A, 1124; 28 Harv.L.Rev. 790. Cases reached the Court in which a State had designed a remedy to meet a specific situation or to accomplish a particular social policy. These cases made manifest that picketing, even though "peaceful," involved more than just communication of ideas and could not be immune from all state regulation. "Picketing by an organized group is more than free speech, since it involves patrol of a particular locality and since the very presence of a picket line may induce action of one kind or another, quite irrespective of the nature of the ideas which are being disseminated." Bakery and Pastry Drivers Local v. Wohl, 315 U.S. 769, 776, 62 S.Ct. 816, 819, 86 L.Ed. 1178 (concurring opinion); see Carpenters and Joiners Union, etc. v. Ritter's Cafe, 315 U.S. 722, 725–728, 62 S.Ct. 807, 808–810, 86 L.Ed. 1143.

These latter two cases required the Court to review a choice made by two States between the competing interests of unions, employers, their employees, and the public at large. In the Ritter's Cafe case, Texas had enjoined as a violation of its antitrust law picketing of a restaurant by unions to bring pressure on its owner with respect to the use of nonunion labor by a contractor of the restaurant owner in the construction of a building having nothing to do with the restaurant. The Court held that Texas could, consistent with the Fourteenth Amendment, insulate from the dispute a neutral establishment that industrially had no connection with it. This type of picketing certainly involved little, if any, "communication." * * *

The implied reassessments of the broad language of the Thornhill case were finally generalized in a series of cases sustaining injunctions against peaceful picketing, even when arising in the course of a labor controversy, when such picketing was counter to valid state policy in a domain open to state regulation. The decisive reconsideration came in Giboney v. Empire Storage & Ice Co., 336 U.S. 490, 69 S.Ct. 684, 93 L.Ed. 834. A union, seeking to organize peddlers, picketed a wholesale dealer [Empire] to induce it to refrain from selling to nonunion peddlers. The state courts, finding that such an agreement would constitute a conspiracy in restraint of trade in violation of the state antitrust laws, enjoined the picketing. This Court affirmed unanimously. * * * [We] concluded that it was "clear that appellants were doing more than exercising a right of free speech or press. * * * They were exercising their economic power together with that of their allies to compel Empire to abide by union rather than by state regulation of trade." Id., 336 U.S. at page 503, 69 S.Ct. at page 691.

The following Term, the Court decided * * * Building Service Emp. Intern. Union v. Gazzam, 339 U.S. 532 * * *. Following an unsuccessful attempt at unionization of a small hotel and refusal by the owner to sign a contract with the union as bargaining agent, the union began to picket the hotel with signs stating that the owner was unfair to organized labor. The State, finding that the object of the picketing was in violation of its statutory policy against employer coercion of employees' choice of bargaining representative, enjoined picketing for such purpose. This Court affirmed, rejecting the argument that "the Swing case, supra, is controlling. * * * In that case this Court struck down the State's restraint of picketing based solely on the absence of an employer-employee relationship. An adequate basis for the instant decree is the unlawful objective of the picketing, namely, coercion by the employer of the employees' selection of a bargaining representative. Peaceful picketing for any lawful purpose is not prohibited by the decree under review." Id., 339 U.S. at page 539, 70 S.Ct. at page 788.

A similar problem was involved in Local Union No. 10, United Ass'n of Journeymen, Plumbers and Steamfitters, etc. v. Graham, 345 U.S. 192, 73 S.Ct. 585, 587, 97 L.Ed. 946, where a state court had enjoined, as a violation of its "Right to Work" law, picketing that advertised that nonunion men were being employed on a building job. This Court found that there was evidence in the record supporting a conclusion that a substantial purpose of the picketing was to put pressure on the general contractor to eliminate nonunion men from the job and, on the reasoning of the cases that we have just discussed, held that the injunction was not in conflict with the Fourteenth Amendment.

This series of cases, then, established a broad field in which a State, in enforcing some public policy, whether of its criminal or its civil law, and whether announced by its legislature or its courts, could constitutionally enjoin peaceful picketing aimed at preventing effectuation of that policy.

\* \* \*

Of course, the mere fact that there is "picketing" does not automatically justify its restraint without an investigation into its conduct and purposes. State courts, no more than state legislatures, can enact blanket prohibitions against picketing. Thornhill v. Alabama and A.F.L. v. Swing, supra. The series of cases following Thornhill and Swing demonstrate that the policy of Wisconsin enforced by the prohibition of this picketing is a valid one. In this case, the circumstances set forth in the opinion of the Wisconsin Supreme Court afford a rational basis for the inference it drew concerning the purpose of the picketing. \* \* \*

Affirmed.

■ Mr. Justice Whittaker took no part in the consideration or decision of this case.

■ Mr. Justice Douglas, with whom The Chief Justice and Mr. Justice Black concur, dissenting.

The Court has now come full circle. In Thornhill v. Alabama, 310 U.S. 88, 102, 60 S.Ct. 736, 744, 84 L.Ed. 1093, we struck down a state ban on picketing on the ground that "the dissemination of information concerning the facts of a labor dispute must be regarded as within that area of free discussion that is guaranteed by the Constitution." Less than one year later, we held that the First Amendment protected organizational picketing on a factual record which cannot be distinguished from the one now before us. A.F.L. v. Swing, 312 U.S. 321, 61 S.Ct. 568, 85 L.Ed. 855. Of course, we have always recognized that picketing has aspects which make it more than speech. Bakery and Pastry Drivers Local v. Wohl, 315 U.S. 769, 776–777, 62 S.Ct. 816, 819, 820, 86 L.Ed. 1178 (concurring opinion). That difference underlies our decision in Giboney v. Empire Storage & Ice Co., 336 U.S. 490, 69 S.Ct. 684, 93 L.Ed. 834. There, picketing was an essential part of "a single and integrated course of conduct, which was in violation of Missouri's valid law." \* \* \*

But where, as here, there is no rioting, no mass picketing, no violence, no disorder, no fisticuffs, no coercion—indeed nothing but speech—the principles announced in Thornhill and Swing should give the advocacy of one side of a dispute First Amendment protection.

The retreat began when, in International Brotherhood of Teamsters Union v. Hanke, 339 U.S. 470, 70 S.Ct. 773, 94 L.Ed. 995, four members of the Court announced that all picketing could be prohibited if a state court decided that that picketing violated the State's public policy. \* \* \*

Today, the Court signs the formal surrender. State courts and state legislatures cannot fashion blanket prohibitions on all picketing. But, for practical purposes, the situation now is as it was when Senn v. Tile Layers Union, 301 U.S. 468, 57 S.Ct. 857, 81 L.Ed. 1229, was decided. State courts and state legislatures are free to decide whether to permit or suppress any particular picket line for any reason other than a blanket policy against all picketing. I would adhere to the principle announced in Thornhill. I would adhere to the result reached in Swing. I would return to the test enunciated in Giboney—that this form of expression can be regulated only to the extent that it forms an essential part of a course of conduct which the State can regulate or prohibit. I would reverse the judgment below.

————

INTERNATIONAL LONGSHOREMEN'S ASS'N v. ALLIED INTERNATIONAL, INC., 456 U.S. 212, 102 S.Ct. 1656, 72 L.Ed.2d 21 (1982). In January 1980, the President of the ILA—as a protest against the Russian invasion of Afghanistan—ordered union members to stop handling cargoes arriving from or destined for the Soviet Union. Longshoremen along the East and Gulf Coasts promptly refused to service ships carrying Russian cargoes. Allied, an American Company, imports Russian wood products for resale, and does so on ships operated by Waterman Steamship Lines. Waterman in turn employs Clark, a stevedoring company, to unload its ships docking in Boston. Clark—under a labor agreement with ILA Local 799—obtains longshoring employees through the union hiring hall. The ILA boycott of Russian goods disrupted Allied's shipments, forcing it to reduce its purchases and jeopardizing its ability to supply its customers. Allied claimed that the ILA had engaged in a secondary boycott, and it filed charges with the NLRB under Section 8(b)(4) and brought an action for damages under Section 303 of the Labor Act in the federal district court. The court dismissed the complaint, finding that the boycott was purely political and was a primary boycott of Russian goods. The court of appeals reversed, holding that the ILA boycott was an illegal secondary boycott. The Supreme Court affirmed.

For the Court's discussion of the secondary-boycott issue, see pages 633–34 infra. The ILA also contended that a federal ban upon its picketing would violate the First Amendment. The Court's complete discussion of that issue follows.

Application of § 8(b)(4) to the ILA's activity in this case will not infringe upon the First Amendment rights of the ILA and its members. We have consistently rejected the claim that secondary picketing by labor unions in violation of § 8(b)(4) is protected activity under the First Amendment. * * *[25] It would seem even

**25.** In International Broth. of Electrical Workers v. NLRB, 341 U.S. 694, 705, 71 S.Ct. 954, 960, 95 L.Ed. 1299 (1951) the Court held that "[t]he prohibition of inducement or encouragement of secondary pressure by § 8(b)(4)(A) carries no unconstitutional abridgement of free speech. The inducement or encouragement in the instant case took the form of picketing * * *. [W]e recently have recognized the constitutional right of states to proscribe picketing in furtherance of comparably unlawful objectives. There is no

clearer that conduct designed not to communicate but to coerce merits still less consideration under the First Amendment.[26] The labor laws reflect a careful balancing of interests. * * * There are many ways in which a union and its individual members may express their opposition to Russian foreign policy without infringing upon the rights of others.

-------

## PROBLEMS FOR DISCUSSION

**1.** In the *Vogt* case, Justice Frankfurter, discussing the earlier decision in *Ritter's Cafe,* stated that the secondary picketing there "certainly involved little, if any, 'communication.' " In the *Soviet Boycott* case, the Court characterized the union's conduct as "designed not to communicate but to coerce." Putting aside the fact that these characterizations are merely conclusory, are they accurate on the facts of the two cases? Are they any more accurate than a similar judicial characterization in *Vegelahn v. Guntner,* page 17 supra?

**2.** Examine the final sentence of the *Soviet Boycott* decision. Should picketing be subject to federal or state proscription because there are other less intrusive means by which union members may make their views known? Is that not true of *all* kinds of labor picketing?

**3.** Does the "political" character of the ILA protest give it more or less of a claim to constitutional protection, compared with a "strictly labor-related" protest? Do you agree with the Supreme Court's apparent answer to this question? How, for example, would the constitutional analysis be affected if the ILA picketed a dock adjacent to a Liberian cargo ship, protesting substandard wages paid foreign seamen and urging shippers to patronize only American vessels? See American Radio Ass'n. v. Mobile S.S. Ass'n., 419 U.S. 215, 95 S.Ct. 409, 42 L.Ed.2d 399 (1974).

-------

## Edward J. DeBartolo Corp. v. Florida Gulf Coast Bldg. & Constr. Trades Council

485 U.S. 568, 108 S.Ct. 1392, 99 L.Ed.2d 645 (1988).

■ JUSTICE WHITE delivered the opinion of the Court.

This case centers around the respondent union's peaceful handbilling of the businesses operating in a shopping mall in Tampa, Florida, owned by

reason why Congress may not do likewise." (footnote omitted).

**26.** Cf. NLRB v. Retail Store, 447 U.S. 607, 619, 100 S.Ct. 2372, 2379, 65 L.Ed.2d 377 (1980)("The statutory ban in this case affects only that aspect of the union's efforts to communicate its views that calls for an automatic response to a signal, rather than a reasoned response to an idea.") (Stevens, J.,

concurring); United States v. O'Brien, 391 U.S. 367, 376, 88 S.Ct. 1673, 1678, 20 L.Ed.2d 672 (1968)("This Court has held that when 'speech' and 'nonspeech' elements are combined in the same course of conduct, a sufficiently important governmental interest in regulating the non-speech element can justify incidental limitations on First Amendment freedoms.").

petitioner, the Edward J. DeBartolo Corporation (DeBartolo). The union's primary labor dispute was with H.J. High Construction Company (High) over alleged substandard wages and fringe benefits. High was retained by the H.J. Wilson Company (Wilson) to construct a department store in the mall, and neither DeBartolo nor any of the other 85 or so mall tenants had any contractual right to influence the selection of contractors.

The union, however, sought to obtain their influence upon Wilson and High by distributing handbills asking mall customers not to shop at any of the stores in the mall "until the Mall's owner publicly promises that all construction at the Mall will be done using contractors who pay their employees fair wages and fringe benefits."[1] The handbills' message was that "[t]he payment of substandard wages not only diminishes the working person's ability to purchase with earned, rather than borrowed, dollars, but it also undercuts the wage standard of the entire community." The handbills made clear that the union was seeking only a consumer boycott against the other mall tenants, not a secondary strike by their employees. At all four entrances to the mall for about three weeks in December 1979, the union peacefully distributed the handbills without any accompanying picketing or patrolling.

After DeBartolo failed to convince the union to alter the language of the handbills to state that its dispute did not involve DeBartolo or the mall lessees other than Wilson and to limit its distribution to the immediate vicinity of Wilson's construction site, it filed a complaint with the National Labor Relations Board (Board), charging the union with engaging in unfair

---

1.  The Handbill read:

"PLEASE *DON'T SHOP AT EAST LAKE SQUARE MALL* PLEASE

"The FLA. GULF COAST BUILDING TRADES COUNCIL, AFL–CIO, is requesting that you do not shop at the stores in the East Lake Square Mall because of The Mall ownership's contribution to substandard wages.

"The Wilson's Department Store under construction on these premises is being built by contractors who pay substandard wages and fringe benefits. In the past, the Mall's owner, The Edward J. DeBartolo Corporation, has supported labor and our local economy by insuring that the Mall and its stores be built by contractors who pay fair wages and fringe benefits. Now, however, and for no apparent reason, the Mall owners have taken a giant step backwards by permitting our standards to be torn down. The payment of substandard wages not only diminishes the working person's ability to purchase with earned, rather than borrowed, dollars, but it also undercuts the wage standard of the entire community. Since low construction

wages at this time of inflation means decreased purchasing power, do the owners of East Lake Mall intend to compensate for the decreased purchasing power of workers of the community by encouraging the stores in East Lake Mall to cut their prices and lower their profits?

"CUT–RATE WAGES ARE NOT FAIR UNLESS MERCHANDISE PRICES ARE ALSO CUT–RATE.

"We ask for your support in our protest against substandard wages. Please do not patronize the stores in the East Lake Square Mall until the Mall's owner publicly promises that all construction at the Mall will be done using contractors who pay their employees fair wages and fringe benefits.

"IF YOU MUST ENTER THE MALL TO DO BUSINESS, please express to the store managers your concern over substandard wages and your support of our efforts.

"We are appealing only to the public— the consumer. We are not seeking to induce any person to cease work or to refuse to make deliveries."

labor practices under § 8(b)(4) of the National Labor Relations Act (NLRA)
* * *.

[Section 8(b)(4)(B) of the National Labor Relations Act, as amended in
1959, outlaws the secondary boycott that takes the form of inducing
employees of a neutral or secondary employer to engage in a work stoppage.
It also forbids a union "to threaten, coerce, or restrain any person" who is
a neutral or secondary employer, and the Supreme Court had interpreted
the latter language to ban picketing at a secondary site directed to
customers there. A proviso to the section, however, shelters "publicity,
other than picketing, for the purpose of truthfully advising the public,
including consumers ... that a product or products are produced by an
employer with whom the labor organization has a primary dispute and are
distributed by another employer." In an earlier phase of this case, the
NLRB, without deciding whether the handbilling at the mall constituted a
"threat, coercion or restraint" within the meaning of Section 8(b)(4)(B),
held that it was in any event protected by the so-called publicity proviso.
The Supreme Court disagreed, however, finding that DeBartolo and the
other mall tenants could not be said to be "distributing products" of the
primary company, High. The Court therefore remanded to the NLRB the
questions whether the handbilling fell within the prohibition of the section
and, if so, whether it was protected by the First Amendment.]

On remand, the Board held that the union's handbilling was proscribed
by § 8(b)(4)(ii)(B). 273 N.L.R.B. 1431 (1985). It stated that under its prior
cases "handbilling and other activity urging a consumer boycott constituted
coercion." ...

The Court of Appeals for the Eleventh Circuit denied enforcement of
the Board's order [and construed] the section as not prohibiting consumer
publicity; DeBartolo petitioned for certiorari. Because this case presents
important questions of federal constitutional and labor law, we granted the
petition, 482 U.S. 913, 107 S.Ct. 3182, 96 L.Ed.2d 671 (1987), and now
affirm.

... [T]he Board has construed § 8(b)(4) of the Act to cover handbilling
at a mall entrance urging potential customers not to trade with any
retailers in the mall, in order to exert pressure on the proprietor of the
mall to influence a particular mall tenant not to do business with a
nonunion construction contractor. That statutory interpretation by the
Board would normally be entitled to deference unless that construction
were clearly contrary to the intent of Congress. Chevron U.S.A. Inc. v.
[Natural] Resources Defense Council, Inc., 467 U.S. 837, 842–843, and n. 9,
104 S.Ct. 2778, 2781–2782, and n. 9, 81 L.Ed.2d 694 (1984).

Another rule of statutory construction, however, is pertinent here:
where an otherwise acceptable construction of a statute would raise serious
constitutional problems, the Court will construe the statute to avoid such
problems unless such construction is plainly contrary to the intent of
Congress. [NLRB v. Catholic Bishop of Chicago, 440 U.S. 490, 99 S.Ct.
1313, 59 L.Ed.2d 533 (1979).] ... This approach not only reflects the
prudential concern that constitutional issues not be needlessly confronted,

but also recognizes that Congress, like this Court, is bound by and swears an oath to uphold the Constitution. The courts will therefore not lightly assume that Congress intended to infringe constitutionally protected liberties or usurp power constitutionally forbidden it. See Grenada County Supervisors v. Brogden, 112 U.S. 261, 269, 5 S.Ct. 125, 129, 28 L.Ed. 704 (1884).

We agree with the Court of Appeals and respondents that this case calls for the invocation of the *Catholic Bishop* rule, for the Board's construction of the statute, as applied in this case, poses serious questions of the validity of § 8(b)(4) under the First Amendment. The handbills involved here truthfully revealed the existence of a labor dispute and urged potential customers of the mall to follow a wholly legal course of action, namely, not to patronize the retailers doing business in the mall. The handbilling was peaceful. No picketing or patrolling was involved. On its face, this was expressive activity arguing that substandard wages should be opposed by abstaining from shopping in a mall where such wages were paid. Had the union simply been leafletting the public generally, including those entering every shopping mall in town, pursuant to an annual educational effort against substandard pay, there is little doubt that legislative proscription of such leaflets would pose a substantial issue of validity under the First Amendment. The same may well be true in this case, although here the handbills called attention to a specific situation in the mall allegedly involving the payment of unacceptably low wages by a construction contractor.

That a labor union is the leafletter and that a labor dispute was involved does not foreclose this analysis. We do not suggest that communications by labor unions are never of the commercial speech variety and thereby entitled to a lesser degree of constitutional protection. The handbills involved here, however, do not appear to be typical commercial speech such as advertising the price of a product or arguing its merits, for they pressed the benefits of unionism to the community and the dangers of inadequate wages to the economy and the standard of living of the populace. Of course, commercial speech itself is protected by the First Amendment, Virginia Pharmacy Bd. v. Virginia Citizens Consumer Council, Inc., 425 U.S. 748, 762, 96 S.Ct. 1817, 1826, 48 L.Ed.2d 346 (1976), and however these handbills are to be classified, the Court of Appeals was plainly correct in holding that the Board's construction would require deciding serious constitutional issues....

The Board was urged to construe the statute in light of the asserted constitutional considerations, but thought that it was constrained by its own prior authority and cases in the courts of appeals, as well as by the express language of the Act, to hold that § 8(b)(4) must be construed to forbid the handbilling involved here. Even if this construction of the Act were thought to be a permissible one, we are quite sure that in light of the traditional rule followed in *Catholic Bishop,* we must independently inquire whether there is another interpretation, not raising these serious constitutional concerns, that may fairly be ascribed to § 8(b)(4)(ii). This the Court has done in several cases.

... We follow this course here and conclude, as did the Court of Appeals, that the section is open to a construction that obviates deciding whether a congressional prohibition of handbilling on the facts of this case would violate the First Amendment.

The case turns on whether handbilling such as involved here must be held to "threaten, coerce, or restrain any person" to cease doing business with another, within the meaning of § 8(b)(4)(ii)(B). We note first that "induc[ing] or encourag[ing]" employees of the secondary employer to strike is proscribed by § 8(b)(4)(i). But more than mere persuasion is necessary to prove a violation of § 8(b)(4)(ii): that section requires a showing of threats, coercion, or restraints. Those words, we have said, are "nonspecific, indeed vague," and should be interpreted with "caution" and not given a "broad sweep," Drivers, supra, 362 U.S., at 290, 80 S.Ct., at 715; and in applying § 8(b)(1)(A) they were not to be construed to reach peaceful recognitional picketing. Neither is there any necessity to construe such language to reach the handbills involved in this case. There is no suggestion that the leaflets had any coercive effect on customers of the mall. There was no violence, picketing, or patrolling and only an attempt to persuade customers not to shop in the mall.

\* \* \*

NLRB v. Retail Store Employees, 447 U.S. 607, 100 S.Ct. 2372, 65 L.Ed.2d 377 (1980)(*Safeco*), ... held that consumer picketing urging a general boycott of a secondary employer aimed at causing him to sever relations with the union's real antagonist was coercive and forbidden by § 8(b)(4). It is urged that *Safeco* rules this case because the union sought a general boycott of all tenants in the mall. But "picketing is qualitatively 'different from other modes of communication,'" Babbitt v. Farm Workers, 442 U.S. 289, 311, n. 17, 99 S.Ct. 2301, 2315, n. 17, 60 L.Ed.2d 895 (1979)(quoting Hughes v. Superior Court, 339 U.S. 460, 465, 70 S.Ct. 718, 721, 94 L.Ed. 985 (1950)), and *Safeco* noted that the picketing there actually threatened the neutral with ruin or substantial loss. As Justice Stevens pointed out in his concurrence in *Safeco*, supra, 447 U.S., at 619, 100 S.Ct., at 2379, picketing is "a mixture of conduct and communication" and the conduct element "often provides the most persuasive deterrent to third persons about to enter a business establishment." Handbills containing the same message, he observed, are "much less effective than labor picketing" because they "depend entirely on the persuasive force of the idea." Ibid. Similarly, the Court stated in Hughes v. Superior Court, supra, 339 U.S., at 465, 70 S.Ct., at 721:

> "Publication in a newspaper, or by distribution of circulars, may convey the same information or make the same charge as do those patrolling a picket line. But the very purpose of a picket line is to exert influences, and it produces consequences, different from other modes of communication."

... [There is little] reason to find in the language of § 8(b)(4)(ii), standing alone, any clear indication that handbilling, without picketing, "coerces" secondary employers. The loss of customers because they read a handbill urging them not to patronize a business, and not because they are intimidated by a line of picketers, is the result of mere persuasion, and the neutral who reacts is doing no more than what its customers honestly want it to do. . . .

It is nevertheless argued that the second proviso to § 8(b)(4) makes clear that that section, as amended in 1959, was intended to proscribe nonpicketing appeals such as handbilling urging a consumer boycott of a neutral employer. That proviso reads as follows:

> "*Provided further,* That for the purposes of this paragraph (4) only, nothing contained in such paragraph shall be construed to prohibit publicity, other than picketing, for the purpose of truthfully advising the public, including consumers and members of a labor organization, that a product or products are produced by an employer with whom the labor organization has a primary dispute and are distributed by another employer, as long as such publicity does not have an effect of inducing any individual employed by any person other than the primary employer in the course of his employment to refuse to pick up, deliver, or transport any goods, or not to perform any services, at the establishment of the employer engaged in such distribution."

By its terms, the proviso protects nonpicketing communications directed at customers of a distributor of goods produced by an employer with whom the union has a labor dispute. Because handbilling and other consumer appeals not involving such a distributor are not within the proviso, the argument goes, those appeals must be considered coercive within the meaning of § 8(b)(4)(ii). Otherwise, it is said, the proviso is meaningless, for if handbilling and like communications are never coercive and within the reach of the section, there would have been no need whatsoever for the proviso.

This approach treats the proviso as establishing an exception to a prohibition that would otherwise reach the conduct excepted. But this proviso has a different ring to it. It states that § 8(b)(4) "shall not be construed" to forbid certain described nonpicketing publicity. That language need not be read as an exception. It may indicate only that without the proviso, the particular nonpicketing communication the proviso protects might have been considered to be coercive, even if other forms of publicity would not be. Section 8(b)(4), with its proviso, may thus be read as not covering nonpicketing publicity, including appeals to customers of a retailer as they approach the store, urging a complete boycott of the retailer because he handles products produced by nonunion shops.

The Board's reading of § 8(b)(4) would make an unfair labor practice out of any kind of publicity or communication to the public urging a consumer boycott of employers other than those the proviso specifically deals with. On the facts of this case, newspaper, radio, and television appeals not to patronize the mall would be prohibited; and it would be an unfair labor practice for unions in their own meetings to urge their members not to shop in the mall. Nor could a union's handbills simply urge not shopping at a department store because it is using a nonunion contractor, although the union could safely ask the store's customers not to buy there because it is selling mattresses not carrying the union label. It is difficult, to say the least, to fathom why Congress would consider appeals urging a boycott of a distributor of a nonunion product to be more deserving of protection than nonpicketing persuasion of customers of other neutral employers such as that involved in this case.

Neither do we find any clear indication in the relevant legislative history that Congress intended § 8(b)(4)(ii) to proscribe peaceful handbilling, unaccompanied by picketing, urging a consumer boycott of a neutral employer....

[A]mong the concerns of the proponents of the provision barring threats, coercion, or restraints aimed at secondary employers was consumer boycotts of neutral employers carried out by picketing. At no time did they suggest that merely handbilling the customers of the neutral employer was one of the evils at which their proposals were aimed.

... § 8(b)(4)(ii) was one of the amendments agreed upon by a House–Senate Conference on the House's Landrum–Griffin bill and the Senate's Kennedy–Ervin bill.... Senator Kennedy, the Chairman of the Conference Committee, in presenting the Conference Report on the Senate floor, 105 Cong.Rec. 17898–17899, 2 Leg.Hist. 1431–1432, stated that under the amendments as reported by the Conference Committee, a "union can hand out handbills at the shop, can place advertisements in newspapers, can make announcements over the radio, and can carry on all publicity short of having ambulatory picketing in front of a secondary site." ...

In our view, interpreting § 8(b)(4) as not reaching the handbilling involved in this case is not foreclosed either by the language of the section or its legislative history. That construction makes unnecessary passing on the serious constitutional questions that would be raised by the Board's understanding of the statute. Accordingly, the judgment of the Court of Appeals is

*Affirmed.*

---

## PROBLEMS FOR DISCUSSION

**1.** Suppose that, in the *Vogt* case, supra, the Wisconsin statute had been written or construed so as to outlaw not merely picketing with the purpose of having the employer pressure employees to join a union, but also handbilling consumers with that ultimate purpose. Would such a state statute be constitutional under the Fourteenth Amendment?

**2.** In determining the constitutionality of government limits on labor activity, how important is it that the appeals are directed at employees of the targeted company as well as employees of suppliers, and are aimed at causing a work stoppage, or rather are directed at individual consumers and are aimed at inducing them to withhold their patronage?

**3.** The Supreme Court treats handbilling at a secondary site as more akin to newspaper, radio and television appeals than to picketing appeals. Is that comparison warranted? Assume that a union, attempting to organize a small restaurant (outside of the discretionary jurisdiction of the NLRB), refrains from picketing but instead places the restaurant on the local labor council's "Do Not Patronize List" which is widely disseminated through union newspapers and similar channels. Could a state court enjoin such publication? If so, how ought the injunction be worded? See NLRB v. International Ass'n of Machinists, Lodge 942, 263 F.2d 796 (9th Cir.1959).

**4.** Given the fact that the definition of "picketing" is unclear (recall footnote 18 of the *Thornhill* opinion, p. 73 supra) and is not provided in the NLRA, what advice could you confidently give to persons about to engage in handbilling regarding how they should limit their physical activities? Can they take their handbills and "stand in front of or near entrances, walk around entrance areas and nearby parking lots, approach customers and have brief conversations with them?" See Storer Communications, Inc. v. National Ass'n of Broadcast Employees, 854 F.2d 144 (6th Cir.1988).

---

# Hudgens v. NLRB[c]

424 U.S. 507, 96 S.Ct. 1029, 47 L.Ed.2d 196 (1976).

■ Mr. Justice Stewart delivered the opinion of the Court.

A group of labor union members who engaged in peaceful primary picketing within the confines of a privately owned shopping center were threatened by an agent of the owner with arrest for criminal trespass if they did not depart. The question presented is whether this threat violated the National Labor Relations Act, as amended 61 Stat. 136, 29 U.S.C. § 151 et seq. The National Labor Relations Board concluded that it did, 205 N.L.R.B. 628, and the Court of Appeals for the Fifth Circuit agreed. 501 F.2d 161. We granted certiorari because of the seemingly important questions of federal law presented. 420 U.S. 971, 95 S.Ct. 1391, 43 L.Ed.2d 651.

I

The petitioner, Scott Hudgens, is the owner of the North DeKalb Shopping Center, located in suburban Atlanta, Ga. The center consists of a single large building with an enclosed mall. Surrounding the building is a parking area which can accommodate 2,640 automobiles. The shopping center houses 60 retail stores leased to various businesses. One of the lessees is the Butler Shoe Company. Most of the stores, including Butler's, can be entered only from the interior mall.

**c.** See Note, Shopping Center Picketing: The Impact of *Hudgens v. NLRB*, 45 Geo.Wash.L.Rev. 812 (1977).

In January 1971, warehouse employees of the Butler Shoe Company went on strike to protest the company's failure to agree to demands made by their union in contract negotiations. The strikers decided to picket not only Butler's warehouse but its nine retail stores in the Atlanta area as well, including the store in the North DeKalb Shopping Center. On January 22, 1971, four of the striking warehouse employees entered the center's enclosed mall carrying placards which read, "Butler Shoe Warehouse on Strike, AFL–CIO, Local 315." The general manager of the shopping center informed the employees that they could not picket within the mall or on the parking lot and threatened them with arrest if they did not leave. The employees departed but returned a short time later and began picketing in an area of the mall immediately adjacent to the entrances of the Butler store. After the picketing had continued for approximately 30 minutes, the shopping center manager again informed the picketers that if they did not leave they would be arrested for trespassing. The picketers departed. * * *

[Upon charges filed by the union, the NLRB held that Hudgens had violated Section 8(a)(1), and the Board's order was enforced by the court of appeals. In the decisions of the administrative law judge, the Board and the court of appeals—as well as in the arguments of counsel at each stage—there was considerable ambiguity as to whether the rights of the picketers were to rest solely upon Section 7 of the Labor Act or more broadly upon a constitutional right, sustained in earlier Court decisions, to enter upon "private" property (including shopping center property) having certain attributes of "public" property.] * * *[3]

* * * In the present posture of the case the most basic question is whether the respective rights and liabilities of the parties are to be decided under the criteria of the National Labor Relations Act alone, under a First Amendment standard, or under some combination of the two. It is to that question, accordingly, that we now turn.

It is, of course, a commonplace that the constitutional guarantee of free speech is a guarantee only against abridgment by government, federal or state. * * * But even truisms are not always unexceptionably true, and an exception to this one was recognized almost 30 years ago in the case Marsh v. Alabama, 326 U.S. 501, 66 S.Ct. 276, 90 L.Ed. 265. In *Marsh*, a Jehovah's Witness who had distributed literature without a license on a sidewalk in Chickasaw, Ala., was convicted of criminal trespass. Chickasaw was a so-called company town, wholly owned by the Gulf Shipbuilding Corporation. It was described in the Court's opinion as follows: " * * * the town and its shopping district are accessible to and freely used by the public in general and there is nothing to distinguish them from any other

---

**3.** Section 8(a)(1) makes it an unfair labor practice for "an employer" to "restrain, or coerce employees" in the exercise of their § 7 rights. While Hudgens was not the employer of the employees involved in this case, it seems to be undisputed that he was an employer engaged in commerce within the meaning of § 2(6) and (7) of the Act, 29 U.S.C. § 152(6) and (7). The Board has held that a statutory "employer" may violate § 8(a)(1) with respect to employees other than his own. See Austin Co., 101 N.L.R.B. 1257, 1258–1259. See also § 2(13) of the Act, 29 U.S.C. § 152(13).

town and shopping center except the fact that the title to the property belongs to a private corporation."

The Court pointed out that if the "title" to Chickasaw had "belonged not to a private but to a municipal corporation and had appellant been arrested for violating a municipal ordinance rather than a ruling by those appointed by the corporation to manage a company town it would have been clear that appellant's conviction must be reversed." 326 U.S., at 504, 66 S.Ct., at 277. Concluding that Gulf's "property interests" should not be allowed to lead to a different result in Chickasaw, which did "not function differently from any other town," 326 U.S., at 506–508, 66 S.Ct., at 279, the Court invoked the First and Fourteenth Amendments to reverse the appellant's conviction.

It was the *Marsh* case that in 1968 provided the foundation for the Court's decision in Amalgamated Food Employees Union Local 590 v. Logan Valley Plaza, Inc., 391 U.S. 308, 88 S.Ct. 1601, 20 L.Ed.2d 603. That case involved peaceful picketing within a large shopping center near Altoona, Pa. One of the tenants of the shopping center was a retail store that employed a wholly nonunion staff. Members of a local union picketed the store, carrying signs proclaiming that it was nonunion and that its employees were not receiving union wages or other union benefits. The picketing took place on the shopping center's property in the immediate vicinity of the store. A Pennsylvania court issued an injunction that required all picketing to be confined to public areas outside the shopping center, and the Supreme Court of Pennsylvania affirmed the issuance of this injunction. This Court held that the doctrine of the *Marsh* case required reversal of that judgment.

The Court's opinion pointed out that the First and Fourteenth Amendments would clearly have protected the picketing if it had taken place on a public sidewalk * * *. The Court's opinion then reviewed the *Marsh* case in detail, emphasized the similarities between the business block in Chickasaw, Ala., and the Logan Valley shopping center and unambiguously concluded:

> "The shopping center here is clearly the functional equivalent of the business district of Chickasaw involved in *Marsh*." 391 U.S., at 318, 88 S.Ct., at 1608.

Upon the basis of that conclusion, the Court held that the First and Fourteenth Amendments required reversal of the judgment of the Pennsylvania Supreme Court.

There were three dissenting opinions in the *Logan Valley* case, one of them by the author of the Court's opinion in *Marsh,* Mr. Justice Black. His disagreement with the Court's reasoning was total: * * *

> "The question is, Under what circumstances can private property be treated as though it were public? The answer that *Marsh* gives is when that property has taken on *all* the attributes of a town, i.e., 'residential buildings, streets, a system of sewers, a sewage disposal plant and a "business block" on which business places are

situated.' 326 U.S., at 502, 66 S.Ct., at 277. I can find nothing in *Marsh* which indicates that if one of these features is present, e.g., a business district, this is sufficient for the Court to confiscate a part of an owner's private property and give its use to people who want to picket on it." * * *

Four years later the Court had occasion to reconsider the *Logan Valley* doctrine in Lloyd Corp. v. Tanner, 407 U.S. 551, 92 S.Ct. 2219, 33 L.Ed.2d 131. That case involved a shopping center covering some 50 acres in downtown Portland, Ore. On a November day in 1968 five young people entered the mall of the shopping center and distributed handbills protesting the then ongoing American military operations in Vietnam. Security guards told them to leave, and they did so, "to avoid arrest." 407 U.S., at 556, 92 S.Ct., at 2223. They subsequently brought suit in a federal district court, seeking declaratory and injunctive relief. The trial court ruled in their favor, holding that the distribution of handbills on the shopping center's property was protected by the First and Fourteenth Amendments. The Court of Appeals for the Ninth Circuit affirmed the judgment, 446 F.2d 545, expressly relying on this Court's *Marsh* and *Logan Valley* decisions. This Court reversed the judgment of the Court of Appeals.

* * * [W]e make clear now, if it was not clear before, that the rationale of *Logan Valley* did not survive the Court's decision in the *Lloyd* case. Not only did the *Lloyd* opinion incorporate lengthy excerpts from two of the dissenting opinions in *Logan Valley,* 407 U.S., at 562–563, 565, 92 S.Ct., at 2225–2226, 2227; the ultimate holding in *Lloyd* amounted to a total rejection of the holding in *Logan Valley:*

"* * * Respondents contend * * * that the property of a large shopping center is 'open to the public,' serves the same purposes as a 'business district' of a municipality, and therefore has been dedicated to certain types of public use. The argument is that such a center has sidewalks, streets, and parking areas which are functionally similar to facilities customarily provided by municipalities. It is then asserted that all members of the public, whether invited as customers or not, have the same right of free speech as they would have on the similar public facilities in the streets of a city or town.

"The argument reaches too far. The Constitution by no means requires such an attenuated doctrine of dedication of private property to public use. The closest decision in theory, Marsh v. Alabama, supra, involved the assumption by a private enterprise of all of the attributes of a state-created municipality and the exercise by that enterprise of semi-official municipal functions as a delegate of the State. In effect, the owner of the company town was performing the full spectrum of municipal powers and stood in the shoes of the State. In the instant case there is no comparable assumption or exercise of municipal functions or power." 407 U.S., at 568–569, 92 S.Ct., at 2229 (footnote omitted).

* * *

"We hold that there has been no such dedication of Lloyd's privately owned and operated shopping center to public use as to entitle respondents to exercise therein the asserted First Amendment rights. * * * " 407 U.S., at 570, 92 S.Ct., at 2229.

If a large self-contained shopping center *is* the functional equivalent of a municipality, as *Logan Valley* held, then the First and Fourteenth Amendments would not permit control of speech within such a center to depend upon the speech's content. * * * "[A]bove all else, the First Amendment means that government has no power to restrict expression because of its message, its ideas, its subject matter, or its content." Police Department of Chicago v. Mosley, 408 U.S. 92, 95, 92 S.Ct. 2286, 2290, 33 L.Ed.2d 212. It conversely follows, therefore, that if the respondents in the *Lloyd* case did not have a First Amendment right to enter that shopping center to distribute handbills concerning Vietnam, then the respondents in the present case did not have a First Amendment right to enter this shopping center for the purpose of advertising their strike against the Butler Shoe Company.

We conclude, in short, that under the present state of the law the constitutional guarantee of free expression has no part to play in a case such as this.

### III

From what has been said it follows that the rights and liabilities of the parties in this case are dependent exclusively upon the National Labor Relations Act. Under the Act the task of the Board, subject to review by the courts, is to resolve conflicts between § 7 rights and private property rights, "and to seek a proper accommodation between the two." Central Hardware Co. v. NLRB, 407 U.S. 539, 543, 92 S.Ct. 2238, 2241, 33 L.Ed.2d 122. What is "a proper accommodation" in any situation may largely depend upon the content and the context of the § 7 rights being asserted. The task of the Board and the reviewing courts under the Act, therefore, stands in conspicuous contrast to the duty of a court in applying the standards of the First Amendment, which requires "above all else" that expression must not be restricted by government "because of its message, its ideas, its subject matter, or its content."

In the *Central Hardware* case, and earlier in the case of NLRB v. Babcock & Wilcox Co., 351 U.S. 105, 76 S.Ct. 679, 100 L.Ed. 975, the Court considered the nature of the Board's task in this area under the Act. Accommodation between employees' § 7 rights and employers' property rights, the Court said in *Babcock & Wilcox,* "must be obtained with as little destruction of one as is consistent with the maintenance of the other." 351 U.S., at 112, 76 S.Ct., at 684.

Both *Central Hardware* and *Babcock & Wilcox* involved organizational activity carried on by nonemployees on the employers' property.[10] The

---

**10.** A wholly different balance was struck when the organizational activity was carried on by employees already rightfully on the employer's property, since the employer's

context of the § 7 activity in the present case was different in several respects which may or may not be relevant in striking the proper balance. First, it involved lawful economic strike activity rather than organizational activity. * * * Second, the § 7 activity here was carried on by Butler's employees (albeit not employees of its shopping center store), not by outsiders. See NLRB v. Babcock & Wilcox Co., 351 U.S., at 111–113, 76 S.Ct., at 683–685. Third, the property interests impinged upon in this case were not those of the employer against whom the § 7 activity was directed, but of another.

The *Babcock & Wilcox* opinion established the basic objective under the Act: accommodation of § 7 rights and private property rights "with as little destruction of one as is consistent with the maintenance of the other." The locus of that accommodation, however, may fall at differing points along the spectrum depending on the nature and strength of the respective § 7 rights and private property rights asserted in any given context. In each generic situation, the primary responsibility for making this accommodation must rest with the Board in the first instance. * * *

For the reasons stated in this opinion, the judgment is vacated and the case is remanded to the Court of Appeals with directions to remand to the National Labor Relations Board, so that the case may be there considered under the statutory criteria of the National Labor Relations Act alone.

It is so ordered.

Vacated and remanded.

[Justices Powell and White wrote separate concurring opinions.]

■ MR. JUSTICE MARSHALL, with whom MR. JUSTICE BRENNAN joins, dissenting.

* * * [The dissenting opinion first criticized the opinion of the Court for reaching out to decide a constitutional question and to overrule *Logan Valley* when the decisions of the Board and the court of appeals had clearly rested on a construction of Section 7 of the Labor Act so that the Supreme Court could have disposed of the case on purely statutory grounds. The two dissenting Justices, in construing the statute, employed the test of *Babcock & Wilcox* and would have affirmed the conclusion of the court of appeals that the picketers could not effectively communicate with the patrons of the Butler Shoe Store in Hudgens' mall through advertising in newspapers, radio, television, mail, handbills or billboards or by picketing on public rights-of-way adjoining the shopping center. They then turned to the constitutional issue which had been addressed by the Court.]

The Court adopts the view that *Marsh* has no bearing on this case because the privately owned property in *Marsh* involved all the characteristics of a typical town. But there is nothing in *Marsh* to suggest that its general approach was limited to the particular facts of that case. The underlying concern in *Marsh* was that traditional public channels of

management interests rather than his property interests were there involved. Republic Aviation Corp. v. NLRB, 324 U.S. 793, 65 S.Ct. 982, 89 L.Ed. 1372. This difference is "one of substance." NLRB v. Babcock & Wilcox Co., 351 U.S., at 113, 76 S.Ct., at 685.

communication remain free, regardless of the incidence of ownership. Given that concern, the crucial fact in *Marsh* was that the company owned the traditional forums essential for effective communication; it was immaterial that the company also owned a sewer system and that its property in other respects resembled a town.

In *Logan Valley* we recognized what the Court today refuses to recognize—that the owner of the modern shopping center complex, by dedicating his property to public use as a business district, to some extent displaces the "State" from control of historical First Amendment forums, and may acquire a virtual monopoly of places suitable for effective communication. The roadways, parking lots and walkways of the modern shopping center may be as essential for effective speech as the streets and sidewalks in the municipal or company-owned town. I simply cannot reconcile the Court's denial of any role for the First Amendment in the shopping center with *Marsh's* recognition of a full role for the First Amendment on the streets and sidewalks of the company-owned town. * * *

In *Marsh,* the private entity had displaced the "state" from control of all the places to which the public had historically enjoyed access for First Amendment purposes, and the First Amendment was accordingly held fully applicable to the private entity's conduct. The shopping center owner, on the other hand, controls only a portion of such places, leaving other traditional public forums available to the citizen. But the shopping center owner may nevertheless control all places essential for the effective undertaking of some speech-related activities—namely, those related to the activities of the shopping center. As for those activities, then, the First Amendment ought to have application under the reasoning of *Marsh,* and that was precisely the state of the law after *Lloyd.* * * *

———

On remand, 230 N.L.R.B. 414 (1977), the NLRB held that Hudgens—by threatening through its agent to cause the arrest of Butler's warehouse employees engaged in picketing Butler's retail outlet in Hudgens' Mall—violated Section 8(a)(1). The Board considered the three differences between the instant fact situation and the situations in *Babcock & Wilcox* and *Central Hardware.*

(1) Although the case involved economic strike activity rather than organizational activity, the Board held the former to deserve "at least equal deference" by virtue of also being protected under Section 7 of the NLRA.

(2) As company employees, the picketers were entitled to at least as much protection as the nonemployee union organizers in *Babcock.* Also important was the audience for the picketing—not only the Butler employees but the store's potential customers, an undefined group. The Board found that it was not reasonable to require the union, in a dispute with a single store in the mall, to use television, radio and newspaper advertising. Nor would it be reasonable to require the union to use nearby public areas (500 feet away from the store), where the message of the pickets would be

"too greatly diluted to be meaningful"; moreover, the fact that "safety considerations, the likelihood of enmeshing neutral employers, and the fact that many people become members of the pickets' intended audience on impulse all weigh against requiring the pickets to remove to public property, or even to the sidewalks surrounding the Mall."

(3) As to the third factor in the Board's analysis—the ownership of the mall property—the Board pointed out that the privately owned property was open to the public and that the owner (who was not the union's targeted employer) was not a "neutral bystander" but had a financial interest in the success of its lessees, and acted as their agent in maintaining cleanliness and security. The Board concluded that, in finding that Hudgens' property rights must yield to the pickets' rights under Section 7, "we are simply subjecting the businesses on the Mall to the same risk of Section 7 activity as similar businesses fronting on public sidewalks now endure.... A contrary holding would enable employers to insulate themselves from Section 7 activities by simply moving their operations to leased locations on private malls, and would thereby render Section 7 meaningless as to their employees."

---

The NLRB struggled with the task given it by *Hudgens* to accommodate § 7 rights and property rights " 'with as little destruction of one as is consistent with the maintenance of the other.' " It essayed one approach in Fairmont Hotel, 282 NLRB 139 (1986), and shortly thereafter charted a different approach in Jean Country, 291 NLRB 11 (1988). *Jean Country* concerned organizational picketing in front of a store that was located in a private shopping center. The Board adopted a three-pronged test weighing the strength of the § 7 interest, the strength of the property interest, and the availability of alternative means to communicate the union's message to the intended audience. Insofar as access to private property by "nonemployee" union messengers is concerned, the *Jean Country* test was repudiated by the United States Supreme Court in *Lechmere, Inc. v. NLRB*, at p. 124 supra. Does *Jean Country* nevertheless retain any vitality when it comes to determining the basis of permissible protest by employees of the employer?

---

## PROBLEM FOR DISCUSSION

The Office Workers Union is in the midst of negotiating a new agreement with Digital Service Inc. (DSI). DSI has a workforce of some 60 employees, and is covered by the National Labor Relations Act. Its office is on the fifteenth floor of a 60–story building; two other business tenants occupy office space on that floor. DSI employees are now on strike, and are picketing and leafletting at the main ground-floor entrance to the office building. Obviously, most of the persons coming and going at that entrance are doing business with companies other than DSI. Union representatives wish to know whether they may station a small number of strikers, carrying signs and handbills, on the fifteenth floor. What advice would you give the Union? Compare Seattle–First Nat. Bank v. NLRB, 651 F.2d 1272 (9th Cir.1980), with Silverman v. 40–41 Realty Assocs., 668 F.2d 678 (2d Cir.1982).

## III. The National Labor Relations Act

### A. Organizational and Recognition Picketing[a]

Throughout the history of the labor movement, unions have often resorted to work stoppages and picketing as a means of pressuring employees to join and employers to bargain. The strike by the Baltimore unionists in *Plant v. Woods,* page 23 supra, was designed to secure a closed shop, i.e., to induce all company employees to become union members, and to induce the employer to hire only union members and to bargain exclusively with the Baltimore union. As did Massachusetts in that case, many states at and after the turn of the century treated such pressures as tortious and enjoinable; even after state courts came to allow peaceful picketing and strikes for "justifiable" objectives, many treated the union's quest for recognition as too indirectly related to the betterment of wages and other working conditions.

This view was changing by the 1930s and 1940s, when more state courts came to endorse the approach taken by Justice Holmes in the *Plant* case. An example is C.S. Smith Metropolitan Market Co. v. Lyons, 16 Cal.2d 389, 106 P.2d 414 (1940). There, members of the Amalgamated Meat Cutters Union picketed at the Long Beach stores of Smith Market. The union already had negotiated closed-shop agreements with other Long Beach supermarkets and butcher shops; Smith was non-union and—although it offered to pay the initiation fees of any employee who joined the union—none wished to join. Smith paid its butchers more than union scale and had hours of employment less than the union schedule elsewhere in Long Beach. The picketing resulted in a loss of business and induced other companies and their employees to refrain from selling or delivering merchandise. Although the state trial court enjoined the picketing, the California Supreme Court reversed.

The court held that laborers—as much as businessmen—are free, in the absence of legislation, "to inflict damage in the struggle of competition

---

**a.** For a general discussion of organizational picketing see Lauritzen, Organizational Picket Line—Coercion, 3 Stanford L.Rev. 413 (1951); Tobriner, Organizational Picket Line—Lawful Economic Pressure, 3 id. 423 (1951). For discussions concerning the effects of Section 8(b)(7), see Comment, Picketing for Area Standards: An Exception to Section 8(b)(7), 1968 Duke L.J. 767; Dunau, Some Aspects of the Current Interpretation of Section 8(b)(7), 52 Geo.L.J. 220 (1964); Meltzer, Organizational Picketing and the NLRB: Five on a Seesaw, 30 U.Chi.L.Rev. 78 (1962); Modjeska, Recognition Picketing Under the NLRA, 35 U.Fla.L.Rev. 633 (1983); Shawe, Federal Regulation of Recognition Picketing, 52 Geo.L.J. 248 (1964).

so long as they abstain from violence, fraud or other unlawful conduct." Work stoppages, picketing and boycotts may cause economic loss, but they are lawful if "inflicted in pursuit of a legally justifiable object." The court found these principles based upon a "widespread belief in competition, free enterprise, and equality of opportunity," and it found in a number of California statutes protecting workers a recognition of the "inequality of bargaining power between employer and employee."

> [C]ombination and organization are permissible on both sides, and the determination of terms and conditions of employment is to be left to bargaining and competition by these organizations in a free and unrestricted market.

> * * * [T]he determinative issue is whether the workmen are demanding something which is reasonably related to employment and to the purposes of collective bargaining. More specifically, the propriety of lawful concerted action depends upon whether the workmen have such an interest in the employment relationship that the attainment of their object will benefit them directly or will enhance their bargaining power.

> The members of a labor organization may have a substantial interest in the employment relations of an employer although none of them is or ever has been employed by him. The reason for this is that the employment relations of every employer affect the working conditions and bargaining power of employees throughout the industry in which he competes. Hence, where union and nonunion employees are engaged in a similar occupation and their respective employers are engaged in trade competition one with another, the efforts of the union to extend its membership to the employments in which it has no foothold is not an unreasonable aim.

> Modern industry is not organized on a single shop basis, and it is a logical corollary of the collective bargaining principle that independent labor organizations should be permitted to grow and extend their bargaining power beyond the single shop. The market for a product may be so competitive that one producer cannot maintain higher labor standards resulting in higher costs than those maintained by his nonunion competitors.

> Nor is the interest of the union in extending its organization any less substantial where the labor standards of the nonunion shop are on an equality with those of its union competitors. Under these circumstances it may reasonably be believed vital to union interests to organize such a shop, for there can be no doubt that the receipt by other workmen of equivalent benefits without suffering correlative union responsibility serves to create intra-union unrest and disaffections.

The court concluded that "the members of the butchers' union have a substantial interest in the employment relations of the market company."

A number of the companies that had labor agreements with the union had declined to adhere to union standards until competitors were organized; and Smith employees worked on Sundays and nights, when unionized stores were closed. "[I]t is clear that the continued operation of the [Smith] shops under nonunion conditions had an immediate effect upon both the working conditions and bargaining power of all the union butchers employed in Long Beach. The [union was], therefore, privileged to direct against the market company any peaceful form of concerted activity within their control."

Three judges filed a strong dissent. They regarded all workers as having the individual right "to ally himself with a group of his own seeking, and to select a representative for negotiations with his employer in whom he has faith and confidence. To have forced upon him membership in an association to which he is antagonistic, and to have imposed upon him as a representative, an agency which he does not desire, is so violative of his freedom of action and his liberty as an individual as to need no apology for the defense of these rights." The dissenters referred to the recently enacted National Labor Relations Act (which covered Smith Market) and pointed out that the statute forbade an employer's interference with the union affiliations of its employees. To permit the union to continue picketing would pressure the company to force its employees to join the union or else to discharge them. "If the company refuses to accede to the demand of the picketing union to violate the federal law it must suffer the loss of its business. If the company violates that law, as demanded by the picketing union, it is punishable thereunder." The picketing was thus for an unlawful purpose and should be enjoined.

The opinions in *Smith Metropolitan Market* suggest the very elaborate set of interests of all of the parties involved, some reinforcing and some conflicting. The employer seeks to avoid interruption of its business and to maintain a union-free environment. The employees have an interest in hearing the union's message, but also in making an uncoerced decision regarding unionization and in uninterrupted employment; some, of course, may support the union as a step toward improved working conditions. The public has an interest in learning the facts of the labor dispute, but also in the continued operation of the business. The picketing union seeks to secure members and to achieve bargaining status; this enhances its power and prestige, improves its financial base, and protects its negotiating gains at competing companies. It also has an interest in communicating its protest and its objectives to company employees, to other companies doing business with it, and to the public generally.

Is a common law court, without statutory guidance, able to "balance" or to establish priorities among these interests, in order to decide whether to outlaw the picketing? Even after the legislature speaks, it may be difficult to determine whether it has "intended" to forbid such organizational or recognition picketing. Does the Wagner Act as originally written give greater support to the union or to the employer in *Smith Metropolitan Market*? (Hindsight makes it clear that because the picketing by the Meat

Cutters Union was within the regulatory concerns of Congress, the state labor laws of California should have been preempted and the case dismissed. Although this would no doubt be the result today, preemption theory had not really begun to develop as early as 1940, so that the court's assertion of jurisdiction would not have been regarded as unusual.)

The network of interests involved in a recognition dispute becomes even more elaborate when there is a freely selected incumbent union on the scene, and an insurgent union is engaged in recognition picketing. Does that enhance the likelihood of a state-court injunction (in 1940)? What if Smith Market had a labor agreement with the Retail Clerks Union, and the Meat Cutters were picketing for the purpose of forcing the company to withdraw recognition, breach the contract, and recognize the Meat Cutters? (At first blush, the answer might seem clear. But what if it has been several years since the Retail Clerks Union was designated the bargaining representative? What if the Meat Cutters claim to have majority support? What if it claims that the Retail Clerks were an illegally supported union? What if it claims that it wants only to represent a small number of butchers working in the back of the supermarket? Could a state court be expected to deal with these subsidiary questions—even assuming that the NLRA did not inferentially bar it from doing so?)

Since the 1940s, it has indeed been the federal Labor Act that has determined the rights of unions and workers in picketing for an organizational or recognitional object. But the federal policy has undergone several distinct changes.

In passing the original Wagner Act Congress rejected the argument that mutuality required a grant of protection against interference, coercion and restraint by labor organizations as well as by employers; and although this decision was often defended on the ground that limitation of union activities would bring about federal intervention in matters better regulated by local police authorities, the true ground of objection was that such a measure would be inconsistent with the policy of encouraging union organization and collective bargaining.

> This erroneously conceived mutuality argument that since employers are to be prohibited from interfering with organization of workers, employees and labor organizations should be no more active than employers in the organization of employees is untenable; *this would defeat the very object of the bill.* [S.Rep. 573, 74th Cong., 1st Sess., p. 16.]

It soon became apparent, however, that the law could not in good conscience compel an employer to bargain with one union as the certified representative of its employees and at the same time protect the right of another union to picket in order to compel the employer to recognize it as the bargaining representative of the same employees. Hence, in passing the Taft–Hartley amendments of 1947, Congress included a provision, Section 8(b)(4)(C), which made it unlawful for a union to engage in a strike or picketing for recognition in defiance of the certification of another union as the bargaining representative of the employees in question.

In addition to Section 8(b)(4)(C), Congress in 1947 amended Section 7 to guarantee to employees not only the preexisting right to form, join or assist labor organizations, but also "the right to refrain from any or all such activities." Moreover, Section 8(b)(1) was inserted making it an unfair labor practice for a labor organization or its agents to restrain or coerce employees in the exercise of rights guaranteed by Section 7.

For many years it seemed possible that Section 8(b)(1) might prohibit a minority union from picketing for recognition regardless of whether any other union had already been certified. After having rejected this view during the earlier years of the Taft–Hartley Act, the National Labor Relations Board reversed its position in 1957 and declared that picketing under these circumstances restrained and coerced employees in the exercise of their rights under Section 7. Drivers Local 639 (Curtis Bros.), 119 NLRB 232 (1957). When the issue reached the Supreme Court, however, the Board was reversed, with the Court emphasizing the protection given to the right to strike in Section 13 of the NLRA and cautioning against an "expansive reading" of general provisions in such a way as to limit that right. The Court viewed the legislative history of Section 8(b)(1) as reflecting a congressional purpose to outlaw labor violence and not peaceful picketing pressures. The Court also thought that the 1947 Congress could not have written Section 8(b)(4)(C) to target recognition picketing in a very narrow set of circumstances while at the same time contemplating that Section 8(b)(1) would be used to ban such picketing far more broadly. Finally, the Court pointed out that in 1959—the year before the case reached the Court—Congress had once again specifically addressed the question of recognition picketing by adding Section 8(b)(7) to the Labor Act; that section deals precisely with situations (such as that in *Curtis Bros.*) where there is no incumbent certified union. Obviously, Congress believed that Section 8(b)(1) did not reach such picketing. NLRB v. Drivers Local No. 639, 362 U.S. 274, 80 S.Ct. 706, 4 L.Ed.2d 710 (1960).

The student should at this point examine Section 8(b)(7) with special care. It is exhaustively scrutinized by the Board in the following case.

---

## Hod Carriers Local 840 (Blinne Construction Co.)

135 NLRB 1153 (1962).

[In 1961, the Board held that the respondent union had violated Section 8(b)(7)(C), but—after the composition of the Board changed, as a result of new appointments by President Kennedy—the Board later granted the motion of the union to reconsider the case.]

■ Before proceeding to determine the application of Section 8(b)(7)(C) to the facts of the instant case, it is essential to note the interplay of the several sections of Section 8(b)(7), of which subparagraph (C) is only a constituent part.

The Section as a whole, as is apparent from its opening phrases, prescribes limitations only on picketing for an object of "recognition" or "bargaining" (both of which terms will hereinafter be subsumed under the single term "recognition") or for an object of organization. Picketing for other objects is not proscribed by this Section. Moreover, not all picketing for recognition or organization is proscribed. A "currently certified" union may picket for recognition or organization of employees for whom it is certified. And even a union which is not certified is barred from recognition or organizational picketing only in three general areas. The first area, defined in subparagraph (A) of Section 8(b)(7), relates to situations where another union has been lawfully recognized and a question concerning representation cannot appropriately be raised. The second area, defined in subparagraph (B), relates to situations where, within the preceding twelve months a "valid election" has been held.

The intent of subparagraphs (A) and (B) is fairly clear. Congress concluded that where a union has been lawfully recognized and a question concerning representation cannot appropriately be raised, or where the employees within the preceding twelve months have made known their views concerning representation, both the employer and the employees are entitled to immunity from recognition or organization picketing for prescribed periods.

Congress did not stop there, however. Deeply concerned with other abuses, most particularly "blackmail" picketing, Congress concluded that it would be salutary to impose even further limitations on picketing for recognition or organization. Accordingly, subparagraph (C) provides that even where such picketing is not barred by the provisions of (A) or (B) so that picketing for recognition or organization would otherwise be permissible, such picketing is limited to a reasonable period not to exceed thirty days unless a representation petition is filed prior to the expiration of that period. Absent the filing of such a timely petition, continuation of the picketing beyond the reasonable period becomes an unfair labor practice. On the other hand, the filing of a timely petition stays the limitation and picketing may continue pending the processing of the petition. Even here, however, Congress by the addition of the first proviso to subparagraph (C) made it possible to foreshorten the period of permissible picketing by directing the holding of an expedited election pursuant to the representation petition.

The expedited election procedure is applicable, of course, only in a Section 8(b)(7)(C) proceeding, i.e., where a Section 8(b)(7)(C) unfair labor practice charge has been filed. Congress rejected efforts to amend the provisions of Section 9(c) of the Act so as to dispense generally with pre-election hearings. Thus, in the absence of a Section 8(b)(7)(C) unfair labor practice charge, a union will not be enabled to obtain an expedited election by the mere device of engaging in recognition or organizational picketing and filing a representation petition.[10] And on the other hand, a picketing

---

**10.** Congress plainly did not intend such a result. See Congressman Barden's statement (105 Daily Cong.Rec., A. 8062, September 2, 1959; 2 L.H.1813). And

union which files a representation petition pursuant to the mandate of Section 8(b)(7)(C) and to avoid its sanctions will not be propelled into an expedited election, which it may not desire, merely because it has filed such a petition. In both the above situations, the normal representation procedures are applicable; the showing of a substantial interest will be required, and the preelection hearing directed in Section 9(c)(1) will be held.

This, in our considered judgment, puts the expedited election procedure prescribed in the first proviso to subparagraph C in its proper and intended focus. That procedure was devised to shield aggrieved employers and employees from the adverse effects of prolonged recognition or organizational picketing. Absent such a grievance, it was not designed either to benefit or to handicap picketing activity. As District Judge Thornton aptly stated in *Reed v. Roumell,* 185 F.Supp. 4 (E.D.Mich.1960), "If [the first proviso] were intended to confer a primary or independent right to an expedited election entirely separated from the statutory scheme, it would seem that such intention would have manifested itself in a more forthright manner, rather than in the shy seclusion of Section 8(b)(7)(C)."

Subparagraphs (B) and (C) serve different purposes. But it is especially significant to note their interrelationship. Congress was particularly concerned, even where picketing for recognition or organization was otherwise permissible, that the question concerning representation which gave rise to the picketing be resolved as quickly as possible. It was for this reason that it provided for the filing of a petition pursuant to which the Board could direct an expedited election in which the employees could freely indicate their desires as to representation. If, in the free exercise of their choice, they designate the picketing union as their bargaining representative, that union will be certified and it will by the express terms of Section 8(b)(7) be exonerated from the strictures of that Section. If, conversely, the employees reject the picketing union, that union will be barred from picketing for twelve months thereafter under the provisions of subparagraph (B).

The scheme which Congress thus devised represents what that legislative body deemed a practical accommodation between the right of a union to engage in legitimate picketing for recognition or organization and abuse of that right. One caveat must be noted in that regard. The Congressional scheme is, perforce, based on the premise that the election to be conducted under the first proviso to subparagraph (C) represents the free and uncoerced choice of the employee electorate. Absent such a free and uncoerced choice, the underlying question concerning representation is not resolved and, more particularly, subparagraph (B) which turns on the holding of a "valid election" does not become operative.

There remains to be considered only the second proviso to subparagraph (C). In sum, that proviso removes the time limitation imposed upon, and preserves the legality of, recognition or organizational picketing falling

---

the Board has ruled further that a charge filed by a picketing union or a person "fronting" for it may not be utilized to invoke an expedited election. *Claussen Baking Company,* 11–RC–1329, May 5, 1960. See also *Reed v. Roumell,* cited infra.

within the ambit of subparagraph (C), where that picketing merely advises the public that an employer does not employ members of, or have a contract with, a union unless an effect of such picketing is to halt pickups or deliveries, or the performance of services. Needless to add, picketing which meets the requirements of the proviso also renders the expedited election procedure inapplicable.

Except for the final clause in Section 8(b)(7) which provides that nothing in that Section shall be construed to permit any act otherwise proscribed under Section 8(b) of the Act, the foregoing sums up the limitations imposed upon recognition or organizational picketing by the Landrum–Griffin amendments. However, at the risk of laboring the obvious, it is important to note that structurally, as well as grammatically, subparagraphs (A), (B), and (C) are subordinate to and controlled by the opening phrases of Section 8(b)(7). In other words, the thrust of all the Section 8(b)(7) provisions is only upon picketing for an object of recognition or organization, and not upon picketing for other objects. Similarly, both structurally and grammatically, the two provisos in subparagraph (C) appertain only to the situation defined in the principal clause of that subparagraph.

Having outlined, in concededly broad strokes, the statutory framework of Section 8(b)(7) and particularly subparagraph (C) thereof, we may appropriately turn to a consideration of the instant case which presents issues going to the heart of that legislation.

The relevant facts may be briefly stated. On February 2, 1960, all three common laborers employed by Blinne at the Fort Leonard Wood job site signed cards designating the Union to represent them for purposes of collective bargaining. The next day the Union demanded that Blinne recognize the Union as the bargaining agent for the three laborers. Blinne not only refused recognition but told the Union it would transfer one of the laborers, Wann, in order to destroy the Union's majority.[13] Blinne carried out this threat and transferred Wann five days later, on February 8. Following this refusal to recognize the Union and the transfer of Wann the Union started picketing at Fort Wood. The picketing, which began on February 8, immediately following the discharge of Wann, had three announced objectives: (1) recognition of the Union; (2) payment of the Davis–Bacon scale of wages; and (3) protest against Blinne's unfair labor practices in refusing to recognize the Union and in threatening to transfer and transferring Wann.

The picketing continued, with interruptions due to bad weather, until at least March 11, 1960, a period of more than thirty days from the date the picketing commenced. The picketing was peaceful, only one picket was on duty, and the picket sign he carried read "C. A. Blinne Construction Company, unfair." The three laborers on the job (one was the replacement for Wann) struck when the picketing started.

---

**13.** Blinne's assumption that this transfer would destroy the Union's majority was in error. However, that error has no significance in this case.

The Union, of course, was not the certified bargaining representative of the employees. Moreover, no representation petition was filed during the more than thirty days in which picketing was taking place. On March 1, however, about three weeks after the picketing commenced and well within the statutory thirty-day period, the Union filed unfair labor practice charges against Blinne, alleging violations of Section 8(a)(1), (2), (3) and (5). On March 22, the Regional Director dismissed the Section 8(a)(2) and (5) charges, whereupon the Union forthwith filed a representation petition under Section 9(c) of the Act. Subsequently, on April 20, the Regional Director approved a unilateral settlement agreement with Blinne with respect to the Section 8(a)(1) and (3) charges which had not been dismissed. In the settlement agreement, Blinne neither admitted nor denied that it had committed unfair labor practices.[17]

General Counsel argues that a violation of Section 8(b)(7)(C) has occurred within the literal terms of that provision because (1) the Union's picketing was concededly for an object of obtaining recognition; (2) the Union was not currently certified as the representative of the employees involved; and (3) no petition for representation was filed within 30 days of the commencement of the picketing. Inasmuch as the Union made no contention that its recognition picketing was "informational" within the meaning of the second proviso to subparagraph (C) or that it otherwise comported with the strictures of that proviso, General Counsel contends that a finding of unfair labor practice is required.

* * * Respondent advances two major contentions. The first is that Section 8(b)(7)(C) does not apply to picketing by a majority union in an appropriate unit; the second is that employer unfair labor practices are a defense to a charge of a Section 8(b)(7) violation. We deal with the contentions in that order.

Respondent, urging the self-evident proposition that a statute should be read as a whole, argues that Section 8(b)(7)(C) was not designed to prohibit picketing for recognition by a union enjoying majority status in an appropriate unit. Such picketing is for a lawful purpose inasmuch as Sections 8(a)(5) and 9(a) of the Act specifically impose upon an employer the duty to recognize and bargain with a union which enjoys that status. Accordingly, Respondent contends, absent express language requiring such a result, Section 8(b)(7)(C) should not be read in derogation of the duty so imposed.

There is grave doubt that the argument here made is apposite in this case.[18] But, assuming its relevance, we find it to be without merit. To be

**17.** Although the transcript in these proceedings for obvious reasons makes no reference to the disposition of the representation petition filed by the Union on March 22, it is a matter of public record and known to the parties that the petition was dismissed on April 26, 1960, for the reason that, "the unit sought appears to be inappropriate and is also expected to go out of existence within about four months."

**18.** The argument here is based, as it must be, on the premise that Respondent not only represented a majority of the employees but that this majority status was in an appropriate unit. The latter proposition is by no means established. The Trial Examiner "assure, the legislative history is replete with references that Congress in framing the 1959 amendments was primarily concerned with "blackmail" picketing where the picketing union represented none or few of the employees whose allegiance it sought. Legislative references susceptible to an interpretation that Congress was concerned with the evils of majority picketing are sparse. Yet it cannot be gainsaid that Section 8(b)(7) by its explicit language exempts only "currently certified" unions from its proscriptions. Cautious as we should be to avoid a mechanical reading of statutory terms in involved legislative enactments, it is difficult to avoid giving the quoted words, essentially words of art, their natural construction. Moreover, such a construction is consonant with the underlying statutory scheme which is to resolve disputed issues of majority status, whenever possible, by the machinery of a Board election. Absent unfair labor practices or pre-election misconduct warranting the setting aside of the election, majority unions will presumably not be prejudiced by such resolution. On the other hand, the admitted difficulties of determining majority status without such an election are obviated by this construction.

Congress was presumably aware of these considerations. In any event, there would seem to be here no valid considerations, requiring that Congress be assumed to have intended a broader exemption than the one it actually afforded.

We turn now to the second issue, namely, whether employer unfair labor practices are a defense to a Section 8(b)(7)(C) violation. As set forth in the original Decision and Order, the Union argues that Blinne was engaged in unfair labor practices within the meaning of Section 8(a)(1) and (3) of the Act; that it filed appropriate unfair labor practice charges against Blinne within a reasonable period of time after the commencement of the picketing; that it filed a representation petition as soon as the Section 8(a)(2) and 8(a)(5) allegations of the charges were dismissed; that the Section 8(a)(1) and (3) allegations were in effect sustained and a settlement agreement was subsequently entered into with the approval of the Board; and that, therefore, this sequence of events should satisfy the requirements of Section 8(b)(7)(C).

The majority of the Board in the original Decision and Order rejected this argument. Pointing out that the representation petition was concededly filed more than thirty days after the commencement of the picketing, the majority concluded that the clear terms of Section 8(b)(7)(C) had been violated.

* * * It seems fair to say that Congress was unwilling to write an exemption into Section 8(b)(7)(C) dispensing with the necessity for filing a representation petition wherever employer unfair labor practices were alleged. The fact that the bill as ultimately enacted by the Congress did not contain the amendment to Section 10(*l*) which the Senate had adopted in S.

---

sumed" the existence of an appropriate unit for purposes of his analysis. The dismissal of the Section 8(a)(5) charge and, particularly, the subsequent dismissal of the representation petition and the reason given therefor tend to invalidate his assumption.

1555 [which would have made any Section 8(a) unfair labor practice, and not just a violation of Section 8(a)(2), a defense under Section 8(b)(7) ]cogently establishes that this reluctance was not due to oversight. On the other hand, it strains credulity to believe that Congress proposed to make the rights of unions and employees turn upon the results of an election which, because of the existence of unremedied unfair labor practices, is unlikely to reflect the true wishes of the employees.

We do not find ourselves impaled on the horns of this dilemma. Upon careful reappraisal of the statutory scheme we are satisfied that Congress meant to require, and did require, in a Section 8(b)(7)(C) situation, that a representation petition be filed within a reasonable period, not to exceed thirty days. By this device machinery can quickly be set in motion to resolve by a free and fair election the underlying question concerning representation out of which the picketing arises. This is the normal situation, and the situation which the statute is basically designed to serve.

There is legitimate concern, however, with the abnormal situation, that is, the situation where because of unremedied unfair labor practices a free and fair election cannot be held. We believe Congress anticipated this contingency also. Thus, we find no mandate in the legislative scheme to compel the holding of an election pursuant to a representation petition where, because of unremedied unfair labor practices or for other valid reason, a free and uncoerced election cannot be held. On the contrary, the interrelated provisions of subparagraphs (B) and (C), by their respective references to a "valid election" and to a "certif[ication of ]results" presuppose that Congress contemplated only a fair and free election. Only after such an election could the Board certify the results and only after such an election could the salutary provisions of subparagraph (B) become operative.

In our view, therefore, Congress intended that, except to the limited extent set forth in the first proviso,[23] the Board in Section 8(b)(7)(C) cases follow the tried and familiar procedures it typically follows in representation cases where unfair labor practice charges are filed. That procedure, as already set forth, is to hold the representation case in abeyance and refrain from holding an election pending the resolution of the unfair labor practice charges. Thus, the fears that the statutory requirement for filing a timely petition will compel a union which has been the victim of unfair labor practices to undergo a coerced election are groundless. No action will be taken on that petition while unfair labor practice charges are pending, and until a valid election is held pursuant to that petition, the union's right to picket under the statutory scheme, is unimpaired.

On the other side of the coin, it may safely be assumed that groundless unfair labor practice charges in this area, because of the statutory priority accorded Section 8(b)(7) violations, will be quickly dismissed. Following

---

**23.** As already noted, that proviso enables the Board to dispense with the preelection hearing prescribed in Section 9(c)(1), and to dispense also with the requirement of a showing of substantial interest.

such dismissal an election can be directed forthwith upon the subsisting petition, thereby effectuating the Congressional purpose. Moreover, the fact that a timely petition is on file will protect the innocent union, which through mistake of fact or law has filed a groundless unfair labor practice charge, from a finding of a Section 8(b)(7)(C) violation. Thus, the policy of the entire Act is effectuated and all rights guaranteed by its several provisions are appropriately safeguarded. See Mastro Plastics Corp. v. N. L. R. B., 350 U.S. 270, 285, 76 S.Ct. 349, 359.

The facts of the instant case may be utilized to demonstrate the practical operation of the legislative scheme. Here the union had filed unfair labor practice charges alleging violations by the employer of Section 8(a)(1), (2), (3) and (5) of the Act. General Counsel found the allegations of Section 8(a)(2) and (5) violations groundless. Hence had these allegations stood alone and had a timely petition been on file, an election could have been directed forthwith and the underlying question concerning representation out of which the picketing arose could have been resolved pursuant to the statutory scheme. The failure to file a timely petition frustrated that scheme.[24]

On the other hand, the Section 8(a)(1) and (3) charges were found meritorious. Under these circumstances, and again consistent with uniform practice, no election would have been directed notwithstanding the currency of a timely petition; the petition would be held in abeyance pending a satisfactory resolution of the unfair labor practice charges.[25] The aggrieved union's right to picket would not be abated in the interim and the sole prejudice to the employer would be the delay engendered by its own unfair labor practices. The absence of a timely petition, however, precludes disposition of the underlying question concerning representation which thus remains unresolved even after the Section 8(a)(1) and (3) charges are satisfactorily disposed of. Accordingly, to condone the refusal to file a timely petition in such situations would be to condone the flouting of a legislative judgment. Moreover, and most important, to impose a lesser requirement would fly in the face of the public interest which prompted that judgment.

---

**24.** We would, however, have had a much different case here if the Section 8(a)(5) charge had been found meritorious so as to warrant issuance of a complaint. A representation petition assumes an unresolved question concerning representation. A Section 8(a)(5) charge, on the other hand, presupposes that no such question exists and that the employer is wrongfully refusing to recognize or bargain with a statutory bargaining representative. Because of this basic inconsistency, the Board has over the years uniformly refused to entertain representation petitions where a meritorious charge of refusal to bargain has been filed and, indeed, has dismissed any representation petition which may already have been on file. The same considerations apply where a meritorious Section 8(a)(5) charge is filed in a Section 8(b)(7)(C) context. * * * So here, if a meritorious Section 8(a)(5) charge had been filed, a petition for representation would not have been required. * * *

**25.** The Board's practice of declining to entertain, or dismissing, representation petitions does not apply to situations involving unlawful interference or unlawful discrimination. The inconsistency latent in the refusal to bargain situation is not present in the latter situations and uniform practice has been merely to hold such petitions in abeyance.

Because we read Section 8(b)(7)(C) as requiring in the instant case the filing of a timely petition and because such a petition was admittedly not filed until more than thirty days after the commencement of the picketing, we find that Respondent violated Section 8(b)(7)(C) of the Act. As previously noted, it is undisputed that "an object" of the picketing was for recognition.[28] It affords Respondent no comfort that its picketing was also in protest against the discriminatory transfer of an employee and against payment of wages at a rate lower than that prescribed by law. Had Respondent confined its picketing to these objectives rather than, as it did, include a demand for recognition, we believe none of the provisions of Section 8(b)(7) would be applicable.[29] Under the circumstances here, however, Section 8(b)(7)(C) is applicable.

Accordingly, having concluded as in the original decision herein that a violation of Section 8(b)(7)(C) has occurred, albeit for differing reasons, we reaffirm the Order entered therein.

**28.** The counterpart provision of Section 8(b)(7) as passed by the Senate in S. 1555 limited its impact to situations where recognition was "the object" of picketing. See 1 L.H. 583. The bill as enacted, however, follows the pattern of Section 8(b)(4) and broadens the proscription to conduct which has "an object" which is forbidden. See NLRB v. Denver Building and Construction Trades Council, 341 U.S. 675, 688, 689, 71 S.Ct. 943, 951 (1951).

**29.** As noted at the outset, Section 8(b)(7) is directed only at recognition and organizational picketing and not at picketing for other objects including so-called protest picketing against unfair labor practices. There is ample legislative history to substantiate the proposition that Congress did not intend to outlaw picketing against unfair labor practices as such.

See, for example, 105 Daily Cong.Rec. 5756, 5766, 15121, 15907, 16400, 16541; 2 L.H. 1361, 1384, 1429, 1714. Absent other evidence (such as is present in this case) of an organizational, recognition or bargaining objective it is clear that Congress did not consider picketing against unfair labor practices as such to be also for proscribed objectives and, hence, outlawed. Parenthetically it follows that a cease-and-desist order issued against picketing in violation of Section 8(b)(7) will enjoin only picketing for recognition, bargaining, or organization and will not be a bar to protest picketing against unfair labor practices.

We are aware that this analysis runs counter to what the majority of the Board had held in Lewis Food Company, 115 N.L.R.B. 890, namely, that a strike to compel reinstatement of a discharged employee was necessarily a strike to force or require the employer "to recognize and bargain" with the union as to such matter. Implicit in that holding was the broader proposition that any strike or picketing in support of a demand which could be made through the process of collective bargaining was a strike or picketing for recognition or bargaining. Included in this category, presumably, would be picketing against standard wages or working conditions in a competing plant, or a strike in support of an economic demand at a bargaining table where neither recognition nor willingness to bargain are really in issue but only the reluctance of the employer to grant the particular economic demand. * * * We might well concede that in the long view all union activity, including strikes and picketing, has the ultimate economic objective of organization and bargaining. But we deal here not with abstract economic ideology. Congress itself has drawn a sharp distinction between recognition and organizational picketing and other forms of picketing, thereby recognizing, as we recognize, that a real distinction does exist. See Cox, op. cit., supra, 266. The Lewis Food issue and its ramifications are not crucial in this case. Moreover, the Lewis Food case itself has now been reversed in any event. Fanelli Ford Sales, 133 N.L.R.B. No. 163; see also Miratti's Inc., 132 N.L.R.B. No. 48, and Andes Candies, Inc., 133 N.L.R.B. No. 65.

[PHILIP RAY RODGERS and BOYD LEEDOM, MEMBERS, wrote separate opinions reaffirming the majority opinion originally rendered in this case. 130 N.L.R.B. 587 (1961). MEMBER FANNING concurred in part and dissented in part.]

---

## PROBLEMS FOR DISCUSSION

**1.** Assume that a representative of the Hotel and Restaurant Employees Union nails a sign to a telephone pole next to the entrance to the Jones Cafeteria and sits nearby, speaking to customers only if spoken to and simply observing those who enter and leave the cafeteria. The sign states that the cafeteria is "Unfair" and "Refuses to Recognize" the union. Assuming that the union lost a valid election two weeks ago, does this conduct by the union representative constitute an unfair labor practice?

**2.** The Hotel and Restaurant Employees Union has placed a solitary representative outside the entrance to Jones Cafeteria, who passes out leaflets to prospective patrons urging them not to enter the cafeteria because Jones is "unfair" and "pays substandard wages." An election was conducted by the NLRB two weeks ago in which a majority of Jones' employees voted against having the Hotel and Restaurant Employees represent them. Can Jones succeed in preventing the union from posting such a representative outside his cafeteria?

**3.** In September, after a period of picketing for recognition, the union lost a representation election by a substantial margin. The day after the election results were certified, the company discharged employees Arthur and Bemis, who had been active union supporters. The union promptly protested the discharges in a telephone call to the company, asserting that they were caused by hostility to the union and that they were otherwise arbitrary and without just cause. Just as promptly, the union filed a charge under Section 8(a)(3) and resumed picketing; its new picket signs read "Company Unfair. Discriminates Against Union Workers." After an investigation of the Section 8(a)(3) charge by the Regional Office, the Regional Director in November determined that Arthur and Bemis were discharged for reasons other than union activity and declined to issue a complaint. The union nonetheless continued to picket. May it do so without violating Section 8(b)(7)(B)? See Waiters Local 500 (Mission Valley Inn), 140 NLRB 433 (1963).

**4.** Giant Markets opened a new store in April and immediately recognized the Retail Clerks Union as bargaining representative for all of its employees. A contract was negotiated and was signed in September. In October, members of the Meat Cutters Union began picketing the Giant store, carrying signs stating "Giant Store Unfair to Meat–Counter Employees. Does Not Meet Area Standards." Since the meat counter employees were included within the bargaining unit and were subject to the contract with the Retail Clerks Union, Giant filed a charge under Section 8(b)(7)(A) and the Regional Director issued a complaint. The following facts were stipulated at the hearing before the Administrative Law Judge. Counsel for Giant conferred with counsel for the Meat Cutters in order to inquire what the area standards were that Giant was expected to meet. He was told that the Meat Cutters expected Giant to pay its meat counter employees the prevailing wage rates under Meat Cutter labor contracts and to meet the prevailing benefits regarding health, welfare and pension plans. Counsel for the Meat Cutters also produced an illustrative area contract, from which recognition and union-shop clauses had been stricken; provisions dealing with grievance-processing and arbitration were left unstricken. Counsel for the Meat Cutters reiterated that Giant was not being required to agree to the contract but only to "meet its standards," at which point the picketing would cease. The Meat Cutters frequently circulated letters in trade publications explaining that the picketing was aimed only at forcing the store to meet area standards.

Should the Judge find that the picketing violates the Labor Act? (Has Giant Markets violated the Labor Act?) Cf. NLRB v. Retail Clerks Local 899 (State–Mart, Inc.), 166 NLRB 818 (1967), enf'd, 404 F.2d 855 (9th Cir.1968).

**5.**  Martin's Shoe Factory has never bargained with a union, and no union election has ever been conducted among its employees. The Leather Workers Union began to solicit among the Martin employees and soon supplemented a demand for recognition by picketing, which continued for a week. When the picketing failed to turn away many of the factory workers, tempers flared on the picket line, and a pattern of serious threats and violence emerged; several workers were physically assaulted by picketers, and damage was done to employee automobiles in the adjacent lot. This violence continued throughout the second week of picketing, at which time the company filed a charge under Section 8(b)(7)(C). Should the Regional Director issue a complaint and seek a district court injunction pursuant to Section 10(*l*)?

Assume that upon the employer's statement of intention to file an unfair labor practice charge, the union withdraws its pickets. One month later, however, picketing resumes (accompanied by a request for recognition) and continues peacefully for two more weeks. Can the company secure relief against the picketing at this time?

———

The rather convoluted language of section 8(b)(7)(C) is capped by two provisos, one dealing with the expedited election (discussed in the *Blinne* case) and the other with informational picketing. The placement of the second proviso—which relates only to picketing under subsection (C)—has given rise to questions concerning its relationship to the principal ban of section 8(b)(7). One such question, considered by the Board soon after the 1959 amendments, is whether picketing, in order to be sheltered by the proviso, must be "purely" informational and free of any recognitional object or whether even recognition picketing may be validated if the requirements of the proviso are otherwise satisfied. In the so-called *Crown Cafeteria* case, the Board in 1961 initially held that the proviso sheltered only "purely" informational picketing which lacked an object of recognition or organization, but it reversed itself in a supplemental decision in 1962, after a change in Board membership. LOCAL JT. EXEC. BD. OF HOTEL EMPLOYEES, 130 NLRB 570 (1961), supplemental decision, 135 NLRB 1183 (1962). In that case, the employer rebuffed the union's demands for recognition and for hiring through the union's hiring hall, and the union picketed the public entrance to the cafeteria; the picket signs were addressed to "members of organized labor and their friends" and stated that the cafeteria was nonunion and that the cafeteria should not be patronized. The Trial Examiner concluded that the picketing, which went on for more than a reasonable period of time, was nonetheless lawful because it did not have the effect of inducing any stoppage of goods or services. A divided Board at first reversed the Trial Examiner. The Board majority held:

"We regard the Trial Examiner's and our dissenting colleagues' construction of the Act as undermining the carefully worked out program established by Congress in Section 8(b)(7). We cannot believe that Congress meant to permit recognition picketing merely because the picketing also takes the form of truthfully advising the public that the employer is nonunion, or does not have a union contract. Rather, we believe that Congress was careful to state that picketing will be permitted only if it is for 'the' purpose of so advising the public. Indeed the ban against picketing is particularly applicable in the present situation, where the Union did not represent the majority of the employees, and the only lawful course for Crown to follow was to refuse to recognize the Union, as it did. * * *

"We are satisfied that Congress added the proviso only to make clear that purely informational picketing, which publicizes the lack of a union contract or the lack of union organization, and which has no present object of recognition, should not be curtailed ' * * * unless an effect of such picketing is to induce any individual employed by any other person in the course of his employment, not to pick up, deliver or transport any goods or not to perform any services.' But that is not the situation in this case. As the Trial Examiner found, apart from the picketing, the Union was in fact demanding present recognition from Crown. * * *

"Consideration of the result of the Trial Examiner's, and our dissenting colleagues', contrary construction of the proviso convinces us of their error. They would permit present recognition picketing whenever the labor organization is careful to indicate by its picket signs only an ostensible purpose of advising the public. However, this would render meaningless, at the whim of a picketing union, the stated objective of Section 8(b)(7). The resulting nullification of the whole of Section 8(b)(7)(C) would most certainly result in an absurd situation. * * *."

The two dissenting Board members would have affirmed the decision of the Trial Examiner upholding the picketing, and a Board majority ultimately did so on reconsideration by adopting what had been the dissenting opinion. (The Board's supplemental decision and order were affirmed in SMITLEY v. NLRB, 327 F.2d 351 (9th Cir.1964).) Excerpts from that opinion follow.

        * * *

"Section 8(b)(7)(C), in its present form, was proposed in conference as a compromise to the House version of the bill in this area of legislation. That version was substantially as enacted, but *without* the proviso. From the structure of the section as it emerged from conference, it seems clear that Congress intended to permit a kind of picketing which, but for the proviso, would have come within the prohibition of the section. It logically follows that the intent was to exclude from the ban picketing which, while it embraced the proscribed object of recognition or organization, was nonetheless permitted because it met two specific conditions. The first condition was, as already stated, 'of truthfully advising the public (including consumers) that an employer does not employ members of, or have a contract with, a labor organization.' The second condition was added immediately after the first, i.e., 'unless an effect of such picketing is to induce any individual employed by any other person in the course of his employment not to pick up, deliver or transport any goods or not to perform any services.' In other words, Congress, by way of compromise, excluded from its prohibition recognition or organization picketing that met these two conditions. * * *

"To read the proviso the way our colleagues do would, it seems to us, have the patent effect of creating a new unfair labor practice not within the contemplation of Congress. For, if it is an unfair labor practice when a union does *not* engage in recognition or organization picketing if 'an effect of such picketing is to induce any individual employed by any other person in the course of his employment not to pick up, deliver or transport any goods or not to perform any services,' the prohibition obviously embraces an area wholly *outside* the statutory intendment. Even a casual reading of Section 8(b)(7) and its legislative history makes it abundantly clear that Congress was dealing solely with recognition and organization picketing. It could have dealt with other forms of picketing in that section, but did not. To hold that a work stoppage would convert non-recognition and non-organization picketing into an unfair labor practice under Section 8(b)(7)(C) is to write into the 1959 amendments an additional unfair labor practice. This, we feel is evident, Congress clearly did not do. * * * *"

---

## NLRB v. Local 3, International Broth. of Electrical Workers

317 F.2d 193 (2d Cir.1963).

■ ANDERSON, DISTRICT JUDGE.

   * * *

[The General Services Administration awarded a contract to one Picoult to renovate the Federal Post Office Building in Brooklyn. Local 3 protested the award of this work to Picoult, which chose to deal with a different union. Local 3 instituted picketing of the building, including side and rear delivery areas which were not traversed by the general public. On two occasions, deliveries to Picoult by employees of other companies were turned away by the picket line. The union claimed that its object was to have the subcontract let to a company which recognized it as bargaining representative and, failing that, simply to oust Picoult. The Board found the picketing to violate Section 8(b)(7)(C) and sought court enforcement of its order.]

One of the principal difficulties in construing and applying subparagraph (C) is that Section 8(b)(7) contains the partially synonymous words, "object" and "purpose", used in two distinct contexts but to which much of the same evidence is relevant. These are: "where an object thereof is forcing or requiring an employer to recognize or bargain * * *" and "for the purpose of truthfully advising the public * * *." It does not necessarily follow that, where an object of the picketing is forcing or requiring an employer to recognize or bargain, the purpose of the picketing, in the context of the second proviso, is not truthfully to advise the public, etc. The union may legitimately have a long range or strategic objective of getting the employer to bargain with or recognize the union and still the picketing may be permissive. This proviso gives the union freedom to appeal to the unorganized public for spontaneous popular pressure upon an employer; it is intended, however, to exclude the invocation of pressure by organized labor groups or members of unions, as such.

The permissible picketing is, therefore, that which through the dissemination of certain allowed representations, is designed to influence members of the unorganized public, as individuals, because the impact upon the employer by way of such individuals is weaker, more indirect and less coercive.

In this connection what is meant by "advising the public," as used in the second proviso, is highly pertinent. Congress expressly provided that the word "public" should not be so narrowly construed as to exclude consumers, but the whole context of the phrase in which it appears makes it clear that it was not intended to be so broadly defined as to include organized labor groups which, at a word or signal from the picketeers, would impose economic sanctions upon the employer; otherwise Section 8(b)(7) would be, in effect, almost entirely emasculated. By this latest amendment to the Taft–Hartley Act Congress sought to circumscribe a kind of picketing which, by its nature, could in most cases bring an employer to his knees by threatening the destruction of his business and which, because of the attendant loss of employment, had a material tendency to coerce employees in their freedom to accept or reject union membership or freely select the union they wanted to represent them.

Professor Cox of Harvard, now Solicitor General, who worked with the Senate Labor Committee Chairman on the Section 8(b)(7) amendment to the Taft–Hartley Act, has said,

> "Picketing before a union election is divided by section 8(b)(7) into two categories: (1) picketing which halts pick-ups or deliveries by independent trucking concerns or the rendition of services by the employees of other employers, and (2) picketing which appeals only to employees in the establishment and members of the public. * * * The theory is that the former class of picketing is essentially a signal to organized economic action backed by group discipline. Such economic pressure, if continued, causes heavy loss and increases the likelihood of the employer's coercing the employees to join the union. In the second type of picketing, the elements of communication predominate. If the employer loses patronage, it is chiefly because of the impact of the picket's message upon mem-

bers of the public acting as individuals * * *." The Landrum–Griffin Amendments to the National Labor Relations Act, 44 Minnesota Law Review 257.

Although the two categories are described by him in terms of the *effect* of each, the express language of the second proviso uses the words "for the purpose of" and it is difficult to see how they can be ignored. Nevertheless, the description of the two categories is helpful in gaining insight to the second proviso. The concepts of "signal" picketing and "publicity" picketing should be used in characterizing the union's tactical purpose rather than in describing the picketing's effect. Yet purpose can be determined only through what is said and done under certain circumstances; and the effect of the picketing is one of the circumstances considered in determining in any case what the purpose was in so far as it is the natural and logical consequence of what the picketeers are saying and doing.

The effect might fall short of "inducing any individual employed by any other person in the course of his employment, not to pick up, deliver or transport any goods or not to perform any services" and still be evidence of non-permissive purpose, such as display of qualifying signs accompanied by hostile gestures; or speech directed to persons unconnected with organized labor and not employees of secondary employers, such as a casual passer-by; or, for example, by forming a shoulder to shoulder picket line across an entrance which affected only members of the unorganized public who were not employees of a secondary employer.

Under the second proviso it is the difference in purpose which determines which is permissible picketing and which is not. In its context the second proviso means in terms of "signal" and "publicity" picketing that while most picketing with a "signaling" purpose is proscribed, most picketing for publicity is protected; the exceptions are that signal picketing is permissible when an object thereof is not forcing or requiring an employer to recognize or bargain, and publicity picketing is proscribed when it communicates more than the limited information expressly permitted by the second proviso or when it is apparently the purpose to advise organized labor groups or their members as shown by signal effects, unless there is persuasive proof that those effects are inspired by the employer who is seeking thereby to prevent legitimate second-proviso picketing by the union.

The Board must, therefore, approach its conclusion as to whether or not the picketing was "for the purpose of truthfully advising the public" by way of a finding of whether or not the union's tactical purpose was to signal economic action, backed by organized group discipline.

Accordingly the case is remanded.

———

## PROBLEMS FOR DISCUSSION

The following problems arise from the recent dispute between Widgets, Inc. and the International Union of Widgeteers (IUW). The union has been seeking to organize and represent the employees of Widgets.

(1) IUW stations pickets at both consumer entrances and delivery entrances, the signs reading: "FRIENDS OF THE LABOR MOVEMENT—WIDGETS, INC. UNFAIR, REFUSES TO RECOGNIZE IUW. DO NOT PATRONIZE. DO NOT CROSS THIS PICKET LINE." Throughout the first two weeks of picketing the Teamsters refuse to make deliveries. Widgets, Inc. thereupon files a charge under § 8(b)(7)(C). Evaluate the likelihood of success. (What *can* the Company do to end the picketing as promptly as possible?)

(2) IUW pickets patrol only the consumer entrances, having been told by the Union leaders to stay away from delivery entrances. The picket signs read: "THIS IS TO INFORM PUBLIC THAT WIDGETS, INC. DOES NOT HAVE A CON- TRACT WITH IUW. PLEASE DO NOT PATRONIZE." IUW leaders have informed the Teamsters to continue deliveries. They have also placed advertisements in local newspapers, stating that the purpose of the picketing is solely to inform the public that Widgets, Inc. does not employ Union labor. The picketing continues for two months. Can Widgets, Inc. secure relief under § 8(b)(7)?

(3) Same facts as in Problem 2, except that over the two-month period in which the picketing takes place, three truck drivers refuse to make deliveries, and one window washer refuses to enter the plant building to do his job. Is there a violation of § 8(b)(7)(C)?

(4) The IUW has just lost an election at Widgets. One week after certification of the results, the union begins picketing the customer entrance to the Widgets store. Two union organizers walk back and forth carrying signs stating: "WIDG- ETS, INC. DOES NOT HAVE A CONTRACT WITH THE IUW, AFL–CIO. DO NOT PATRONIZE." There is a separate entrance for employees and deliveries, which is not picketed. No deliveries are interrupted, and no one is threatened or physically prevented from entering the store. Nevertheless, business is sharply curtailed, and Mr. Widgets files a charge with the Regional Director alleging a violation of Section 8(b)(7). Should a complaint issue? Are there any constitutional obstacles to the Board's finding that the picketing violates the Labor Act and issuing a cease-and-desist order?

———

## B.  SECONDARY PRESSURE

### 1.  UNDER THE TAFT–HARTLEY ACT[b]

The provisions of the National Labor Relations Act prohibiting the secondary boycott were first inserted as part of the Taft–Hartley amend- ments of 1947. The core of the prohibition was contained in Section

**b.**  See R. Dereshinsky, A. Berkowitz & P. Miscimarra, The NLRB and Secondary Boycotts (rev. ed. 1981); Goetz, Secondary Boycotts and the LMRA: A Path Through the Swamp, 19 U.Kan.L.Rev. 651 (1971); Koretz, Federal Regulation of Secondary Picketing, 59 Col.L.Rev. 125 (1959); Lesnick, The Gra- vamen of the Secondary Boycott, 62 Co- lum.L.Rev. 1363 (1962); St. Antoine, What Makes Secondary Boycotts Secondary?, Southwestern Legal Foundation, 11th Ann. Inst. on Labor Law 5 (1965); Weiler, Striking a New Balance: Freedom of Contract and the Prospects for Union Representation, 98 Harv. L.Rev. 351 (1984).

8(b)(4)(A), which during the further amendment of the Labor Act in 1959 was carried forward with minor changes to become what is now Section 8(b)(4)(B). (In many of the cases that follow, the reference to Section 8(b)(4)(A) is to the 1947 text rather than to the section presently so labeled.) The outlawry of the secondary boycott was not, however, new to the law. Most states at common law treated the secondary boycott as an illegal exercise of coercion against a person who was "uninvolved" in the labor dispute of another company. E.g., Bricklayers' International Union v. Seymour Ruff & Sons, 160 Md. 483, 154 A. 52 (1931). The secondary boycott which affected the delivery or receipt of goods in interstate commerce was also consistently held to contravene the Sherman Antitrust Act and not to be saved by the labor-exempting provisions of the Clayton Act. Duplex Printing Press Co. v. Deering, 254 U.S. 443, 41 S.Ct. 172, 65 L.Ed. 349 (1921). The United States Supreme Court, however, in 1941 read the Norris–LaGuardia Act to shelter the secondary boycott from antitrust liability, both civil and criminal. United States v. Hutcheson, 312 U.S. 219, 61 S.Ct. 463, 85 L.Ed. 788 (1941). After granting a short-lived exemption from the antitrust laws—and indeed arguable affirmative endorsement in Section 7 of the Wagner Act of 1935—Congress came full circle in 1947 and declared the secondary boycott an unfair labor practice. Not only can the Board issue a cease-and-desist order, but even in advance of a Board hearing on the merits the Regional Director is to secure an injunction against probable violations of Section 8(b)(4)(B), pursuant to Section 10(*l*) of the Labor Act; Congress went so far as to declare the secondary boycott a federal tort remediable by an action for compensatory damages under Section 303.

Although Congress did not use the term "secondary boycott" in Section 8(b)(4) but attempted rather to spell out in detail certain proscribed conduct, the legislative history leaves no doubt that it was seeking to outlaw what had become known at common law (and in industrial parlance) as the secondary boycott. At its core, the secondary boycott is the application of economic pressure upon a person with whom the union has no dispute regarding its own terms of employment in order to induce that person to cease doing business with another employer with whom the union does have such a dispute. Thus, a union may seek to organize the employees at Company P, or may seek to extract economic concessions during a collective bargaining negotiation with Company P. An inducement of P's employees to engage in a work stoppage would be treated as "primary" concerted activity, and a request to Company S which buys the product of Company P to refrain from doing so would be a "primary" product boycott. In either situation the object is to cut off P's business and thereby to force an earlier capitulation to the union's demands. But if the request to Company S is unsuccessful, and the union attempts to coerce in turn that company to cease buying from (or supplying) Company P—and that coercion takes the form of appealing to S's employees to engage in a work stoppage or to S's customers to boycott S's product—the union's pressure becomes "secondary." The attempted withdrawal of services or patronage from S (generically referred to as a "boycott") pressures a person with whom the union has no underlying quarrel and whose employment relations it does not seek to alter. The object, just as in the primary boycott, is to fracture the ongoing business relationship between Company P and its suppliers or purchasers in order to make it increasingly costly for that company to resist the union's demands.

The reader should consider, at this point, why it is that there has for so long been a deeply ingrained opposition in law to the secondary boycott. In our social and economic system, we place a high value upon the freedom of individuals and groups to use peaceful methods to exert pressure on others to take lawful action, such as the withdrawal of patronage. Especially sympathetic is the case where the peaceful method used has as a substantial component the communication of pertinent information. Of course, there is sympathy for the "uninvolved" or "neutral" secondary employer, in at least as great a degree as there is for the primary employer who is "responsible" for the workers' grievances. But what factors induce a court or a legislature to conclude that direct picketing pressure on the former is to be curbed through the sanctions of our legal system? As a general matter, is the secondary boycott used by "strong" unions or "weak" unions? Does the decision to outlaw the secondary boycott commend itself to our sense of justice or utility as readily as does the decision (under Sections 8(a)(1) and 8(b)(1)) to outlaw, for example, physical or economic coercion of individual employees for the purpose of affecting their allegiance to a union?

Although it is generally rather clear whether a picketed company is a primary or secondary employer, there are some situations which give rise to close questions of characterization. Assume, for example, that employees working for a carpentry subcontractor on a construction site wish to secure for themselves the work of preparing doors for installation by trimming door edges and by carving out areas to receive hardware. When their employer brings "prefitted doors" to the jobsite for installation, the carpenters refuse to handle or install them. This is surely a work stoppage designed to pressure the carpentry subcontractor to boycott the manufacturer of the pre-fitted doors. Is this an illegal secondary boycott? As a starting point for analysis, the student should ask which company is the one whose personnel policy is being challenged by the union. Should the labelling of one or the other company as Company P or Company S turn upon whether the carpenters have traditionally done this work at the jobsite, or are seeking to acquire this work for the first time? Should it turn upon whether the carpentry subcontractor is free to purchase doors that are not prefitted, or is rather obligated by the specifications in its agreement with the general contractor to purchase pre-fitted doors? These issues are explored in greater detail below, at pages 672–87.

Confidence in identifying the secondary boycott also breaks down when the union's inducement of a boycott takes place neither completely at the location of Company P (the primary situs) through an appeal to P's employees or customers nor completely at the location of Company S (the secondary situs) through an appeal to S's employees or customers. It is quite common, for example, that picketing conducted at the primary situs and directed to primary employees will also turn away deliveries or pickups to be made by employees of secondary companies. Although to that extent the picketing may induce a brief work stoppage of secondary employees and an interruption in the business of the secondary employer, these effects have commonly been accepted as an "incident" of lawful primary picketing. Cf. N.L.R.B. v. International Rice Milling Co., 341 U.S. 665, 71 S.Ct. 961, 95 L.Ed. 1277 (1951). But picketing appeals even in the vicinity of primary employees may have a proliferating impact upon secondary employees and employers when the primary employees are working alongside employees of other companies at property owned by those other companies or by third persons. For example, as in the *Denver Building* case, infra, picketing against one subcontractor at a construction site may induce a work stoppage among employees of other subcontractors and interrupt deliveries of materials to the entire jobsite. Even picketing at the primary plant may be thought to exert undue pressure upon employees of independent contractors rendering services there, as was the issue in the *General Electric* case, p. 626 infra.

The statute contains little or nothing in its own terms to aid in the identification of the secondary boycott in such close cases. Even the central policy behind outlawing the secondary boycott—to shield "neutral" employers from pressures arising from labor disputes "not their own"—stops short of offering a clear answer. At base, the drawing of the line between primary and secondary activity in these borderline cases will be informed by the values and attitudes of the line-drawer, particularly that person's concern on the one hand for minimizing economic combat or on the other hand for maximizing the access of workers to peaceful measures for the furtherance of employee or union interests.

INTERNATIONAL LONGSHOREMEN'S ASS'N v. ALLIED INTERNATIONAL, INC., 456 U.S. 212, 102 S.Ct. 1656, 72 L.Ed.2d 21 (1982). The facts of this case, arising from an ILA boycott of Soviet goods after the invasion of Afghanistan, are set forth at page 595 supra. Allied, in its action for damages under Section 303, alleged that the ILA boycott was designed to force Allied (the importer), Waterman (the ship operator), and Clark (the stevedoring company) "to cease doing business" with one another and "to cease using, selling, handling, transporting, or otherwise dealing in" Russian products.

By its terms the statutory prohibition applies to the undisputed facts of this case. The ILA has no dispute with Allied, Waterman, or Clark. It does not seek any labor objective from these employers. Its sole complaint is with the foreign and military policy of the Soviet Union. As understandable and even commendable as the ILA's ultimate objectives may be, the certain effect of its action is to impose a heavy burden on neutral employers. And it is just such a burden, as well as widening of industrial strife, that the secondary boycott provisions were designed to prevent. As the

NLRB explained in ruling upon the regional director's complaint against the ILA:

"It is difficult to imagine a situation that falls more squarely within the scope of Section 8(b)(4) than the one before us today. Here, the Union's sole dispute is with the USSR over its invasion of Afghanistan. Allied, Waterman, and Clark have nothing to do with this dispute. Yet the Union's actions in furtherance of its disagreement with Soviet foreign policy have brought direct economic pressure on all three parties and have resulted in a substantial cessation of business. Thus, the conduct alleged in this case is precisely the type of conduct Congress intended the National Labor Relations Act to regulate." 257 N.L.R.B. No. 151, at 14 (footnotes omitted).

The ILA contended that its purpose was not to halt business among Allied, Waterman and Clark, but was rather to free its members from the morally repugnant duty of handling Russian goods. Nonetheless, concluded the Court, substantial economic loss to neutral parties was foreseeable and must be regarded as one of the objects of the boycott lest the statutory prohibition be rendered meaningless. Neither was it a defense that the reason for the boycott was not a labor dispute with a primary employer but was rather a political dispute with a foreign nation. The Court found no exclusion in the text of Section 8(b)(4) for political disputes, and no such intention manifested in the legislative history.

> We would create a large and undefinable exception to the statute if we accepted the argument that "political" boycotts are exempt from the secondary boycott provision. The distinction between labor and political objectives would be difficult to draw in many cases. In the absence of any limiting language in the statute or legislative history, we find no reason to conclude that Congress intended such a potentially expansive exception to a statutory provision purposefully drafted in broadest terms.

> We agree with the Court of Appeals that it is "more rather than less objectionable that a national labor union has chosen to marshal against neutral parties the considerable powers derived by its locals and itself under the federal labor laws in aid of a random political objective far removed from what has traditionally been thought to be the realm of legitimate union activity." 640 F.2d, at 1378. In light of the statutory language and purpose, we decline to create a far-reaching exemption from the statutory provision for "political" secondary boycotts.

---

## NLRB v. Denver Bldg. & Const. Trades Council

341 U.S. 675, 71 S.Ct. 943, 95 L.Ed. 1284 (1951).

■ MR. JUSTICE BURTON delivered the opinion of the Court.

The principal question here is whether a labor organization committed an unfair labor practice, within the meaning of § 8(b)(4)(A) of the National Labor Relations Act, 49 Stat. 449, 29 U.S.C. § 151, 29 U.S.C.A. § 151, as amended by the Labor Management Relations Act, 1947, by engaging in a strike, an object of which was to force the general contractor on a construction project to terminate its contract with a certain subcontractor on that project. For the reasons hereafter stated, we hold that such an unfair labor practice was committed.

[Doose & Lintner, a general contractor on a construction site, awarded the electrical subcontract (in the amount of $2,300) to Gould & Preisner, which proved to be the only nonunion subcontractor at that site. Representatives of the craft unions whose members worked at the site, and of the Denver Building and Construction Trades Council with which those unions were affiliated, informed Doose & Lintner that continued use of Gould & Preisner would result in picketing of the site and a refusal to work alongside such nonunion labor. After a single picket had patrolled for two weeks (carrying a placard stating "This Job Unfair to Denver Building and Construction Trades Council") and had turned away all of the workers except those of Gould & Preisner, Doose & Lintner finally ordered its electrical subcontractor off the job. Immediately thereafter, the picket was removed and all union employees resumed work. Gould & Preisner filed charges against the respondent Council and unions, alleging their inducement of a strike by the employees of the general contractor and other subcontractors, an object of which was to force Doose & Lintner to cease doing business with Gould & Preisner. The NLRB held the respondents' activity to be secondary, but the court of appeals found it to be primary and refused to enforce the Board's cease-and-desist order.]

While § 8(b)(4) does not expressly mention "primary" or "secondary" disputes, strikes or boycotts, that section often is referred to in the Act's legislative history as one of the Act's "secondary boycott sections." The other is § 303, 61 Stat. 158, 29 U.S.C. (Supp. III) § 187, 29 U.S.C.A. § 187, which uses the same language in defining the basis for private actions for damages caused by these proscribed activities.

Senator Taft, who was the sponsor of the bill in the Senate and was the Chairman of the Senate Committee on Labor and Public Welfare in charge of the bill, said, in discussing this section: " * * * under the provisions of the Norris–LaGuardia Act [29 U.S.C.A. § 101 et seq.], it became impossible to stop a secondary boycott or any other kind of a strike, no matter how unlawful it may have been at common law. All this provision of the bill does is to reverse the effect of the law as to secondary boycotts. It has been set forth that there are good secondary boycotts and bad secondary boycotts. Our committee heard evidence for weeks and never succeeded in having anyone tell us any difference between different kinds of secondary boycotts. So we have so broadened the provision dealing with secondary boycotts as to make them an unfair labor practice." 93 Cong.Rec. 4198. * * *

At the same time that §§ 7 and 13 safeguard collective bargaining, concerted activities and strikes between the primary parties to a labor dispute, § 8(b)(4) restricts a labor organization and its agents in the use of economic pressure where an object of it is to force an employer or other person to boycott someone else.

A.  We must first determine whether the strike in this case had a proscribed object. The conduct which the Board here condemned is readily distinguishable from that which it declined to condemn in the Rice Milling case, 341 U.S. 665, 71 S.Ct. 961. There the accused union sought merely to obtain its own recognition by the operator of a mill, and the union's pickets near the mill sought to influence two employees of a customer of the mill not to cross the picket line. In that case we supported the Board in its conclusion that such conduct was no more than was traditional and permissible in a primary strike. The union did not engage in a strike against the customer. It did not encourage concerted action by the customer's employees to force the customer to boycott the mill. It did not commit any unfair labor practice proscribed by § 8(b)(4).

In the background of the instant case there was a long-standing labor dispute between the Council and Gould & Preisner due to the latter's practice of employing nonunion workmen on construction jobs in Denver. The respondent labor organizations contend that they engaged in a primary dispute with Doose & Lintner alone, and that they sought simply to force Doose & Lintner to make the project an all-union job. If there had been no contract between Doose & Lintner and Gould & Preisner there might be substance in their contention that the dispute involved no boycott. If, for example, Doose & Lintner had been doing all the electrical work on this project through its own nonunion employees, it could have replaced them with union men and thus disposed of the dispute. However, the existence of the Gould & Preisner subcontract presented a materially different situation. The nonunion employees were employees of Gould & Preisner. The only way that respondents could attain their purpose was to force Gould & Preisner itself off the job. This, in turn, could be done only through Doose & Lintner's termination of Gould & Preisner's subcontract. The result is that the Council's strike, in order to attain its ultimate purpose, must have included among its objects that of forcing Doose & Lintner to terminate that subcontract. On that point, the Board adopted the following finding: "That *an* object, if not the only object, of what transpired with respect to * * * Doose & Lintner was to force or require them to cease doing business with Gould & Preisner seems scarcely open to question, in view of all of the facts. And it is clear at least as to Doose & Lintner, that that purpose was achieved." (Emphasis supplied.) 82 N.L.R.B. at 1212.

We accept this crucial finding. It was an object of the strike to force the contractor to terminate Gould & Preisner's subcontract.

B.  We hold also that a strike with such an object was an unfair labor practice within the meaning of § 8(b)(4)(A).

It is not necessary to find that the *sole* object of the strike was that of forcing the contractor to terminate the subcontractor's contract. This is emphasized in the legislative history of the section. See also, National Labor Relations Board v. Wine, Liquor & Distillery Workers Union, 2 Cir., 178 F.2d 584, 586, 16 A.L.R.2d 762.

We agree with the Board also in its conclusion that the fact that the contractor and subcontractor were engaged on the same construction project, and that the contractor had some supervision over the subcontractor's work, did not eliminate the status of each as an independent contractor or make the employees of one the employees of the other. The business relationship between independent contractors is too well established in the law to be overridden without clear language doing so. The Board found that the relationship between Doose & Lintner and Gould & Preisner was one of "doing business" and we find no adequate reason for upsetting that conclusion.

Finally, § 8(c) safeguarding freedom of speech has no significant application to the picket's placard in this case. Section 8(c) does not apply to a mere signal by a labor organization to its members, or to the members of its affiliates, to engage in an unfair labor practice such as a strike proscribed by § 8(b)(4)(A). That the placard was merely such a signal, tantamount to a direction to strike, was found by the Board. " * * * the issues in this case turn upon acts by labor organizations which are tantamount to directions and instructions to their members to engage in strike action. The protection afforded by Section 8(c) of the Act to the expression of 'any views, argument or opinion' does not pertain where, as here, the issues raised under Section 8(b)(4)(A) turn on official directions or instructions to a union's own members." 82 N.L.R.B. at 1213.

* * * The judgment of the Court of Appeals accordingly is reversed and the case is remanded to it for procedure not inconsistent with this opinion.

■ MR. JUSTICE JACKSON would affirm the judgment of the Court of Appeals.

■ MR. JUSTICE DOUGLAS, with whom MR. JUSTICE REED joins, dissenting.

The employment of union and nonunion men on the same job is a basic protest in trade union history. That was the protest here. The union was not out to destroy the contractor because of his antiunion attitude. The union was not pursuing the contractor to other jobs. All the union asked was that union men not be compelled to work alongside nonunion men on the same job. As Judge Rifkind stated in an analogous case, "the union was not extending its activity to a front remote from the immediate dispute but to one intimately and indeed inextricably united to it."

The picketing would undoubtedly have been legal if there had been no subcontractor involved—if the general contractor had put nonunion men on the job. The presence of a subcontractor does not alter one whit the realities of the situation; the protest of the union is precisely the same. In each the union was trying to protect the job on which union men were employed. If that is forbidden, the Taft–Hartley Act makes the right to strike, guaranteed by § 13, dependent on fortuitous business arrangements that have no significance so far as the evils of the secondary boycott are concerned. I would give scope to both § 8(b)(4) and § 13 by reading the restrictions of § 8(b)(4) to reach the case where an industrial dispute spreads from the job to another front.

---

## PROBLEMS FOR DISCUSSION

**1.** Although it is true that the general contractor that was picketed by the construction craft unions was not technically the "primary" employer, can it accurately be said that it was "neutral" and "uninvolved" in the labor dispute concerning the electrical subcontractor? Is there not a functional integration and interdependence among companies at a construction site akin to that of a single encompassing enterprise, such that applying secondary-boycott law in a case like *Denver Building* places construction unions at a disadvantage, when compared to workers in manufacturing industries, in the use of economic pressure?

These arguments were at the heart of legislation passed by both Houses of Congress in 1975 (see H.R. 5900, 94th Cong., 1st Sess.), which would have amended Section 8(b)(4) so as to permit construction-site work stoppages "directed at any of several employers who are in the construction industry and are jointly engaged as joint venturers or in the relationship of contractors and subcontractor in ... construction, alteration, painting, or repair" at the site. The avowed purpose (in the accompanying legislative reports) was to overrule *Denver Building* and to endorse the analysis of Justice Douglas in dissent. President Ford vetoed the legislation, condemning it as highly controversial and likely to lead to continued inflation in the construction industry. Would you have voted to override the veto?

**2.** Employees of Acme Supermarket are represented by the Retail Clerks Union and are on strike for increased contract benefits. The union has established a picket line at the consumer entrances, employee entrances and at the pickup and loading platforms at the rear of the store. Deliverymen from Bond Bakers, approaching the rear platform to make deliveries of bread and cake, refuse to cross the picket line or to complete deliveries. Is the union violating Section 8(b)(4)(B)?

**3.** Assume instead that the Acme employees picket not only the Acme site but also at the Bond Bakery, labelling Bond "Unfair" for continuing attempts to sell its merchandise at Acme Supermarket. Is the union violating Section 8(b)(4)(B)?

**4.** Employees of Acme Supermarket are on strike, and have set up a picket line at the Acme store. The object of the strike is to force Acme to stop purchasing bread and cakes from Bond and instead to assign such baking work to a group of Acme employees now working in a modest back-of-the-store baking operation; and also to force Acme to stop purchasing from Bond while Bond remains non-union (the Clerks Union is trying to organize the Bond employees). Is the union violating Section 8(b)(4)(B)?

**5.** The Retail Clerks Union represents all of the Acme employees in a single bargaining unit which excludes four employees working at a bakery counter, who bake, wrap, and otherwise prepare baked goods for sale at that counter and on the store's regular merchandise shelves. The Bakers Union has demanded that Acme recognize it as representative of the four employees, but Acme has refused. The bakery employees, and other representatives of the Bakers Union, are picketing Acme and turning away employees represented by the Retail Clerks, as well as customers. Is the Bakers Union violating Section 8(b)(4)(B)?

**6.** The scenario is the same as in problem (5), except that the bakery counter is run not by Acme but by Bond Bread, as a separate concession, with the four workers employed by Bond. The Bakers Union pickets for recognition and turns away Acme employees and customers. Is the Bakers Union violating Section 8(b)(4)(B)?

---

## Sailors Union of the Pacific (Moore Dry Dock Co.)

92 NLRB 547 (1950).

[A certain contract to transport gypsum had been withdrawn from an American ship, which employed members of the Sailors' Union of the Pacific, and given to the *S.S. Phopho,* a Panamanian flagship owned by the corporation Samsoc. The *Phopho* was tied at the Moore Dry Dock to be converted to enable it to carry gypsum. By February 16, 1950, a substantial portion of the crew had been hired, none of the crew being members of the Sailors' Union. The wages they had contracted for were less than half of the union scale. This crew began work, training, cleaning the ship, and preparing the ship for departure. On February 16, the union demanded that Samsoc recognize it as bargaining agent for the crew of the *Phopho,* which Samsoc refused to do. The next day, pickets arrived at the entrance to Moore Dry Dock, carrying signs declaring the *Phopho* to be unfair. The union requested permission to picket on Moore property adjacent to the ship, but permission was denied.

[The picketing had no effect on members of the crew of the *Phopho,* since they were quartered on the ship, and their shipping articles provided for resolution of all labor disputes by Panamanian officials. The effect on Moore employees, however, was marked. The Sailors' Union sent letters to the unions representing Moore employees, explaining the nature of the dispute and requesting that no work be done on the *Phopho.* Both the picket signs and the letters emphasized that the dispute was with Samsoc and limited to the *Phopho.* By February 21, all work on the *Phopho* by Moore employees had ceased. Moore employees did continue to work on other ships at the Moore dock. Moore then filed Section 8(b)(4) charges.]

■ Section 8(b)(4)(A) is aimed at secondary boycotts and secondary strike activities. It was not intended to proscribe primary action by a union having a legitimate labor dispute with an employer. Picketing at the premises of a primary employer is traditionally recognized as primary action even though it is "necessarily designed to induce and encourage third persons to cease doing business with the picketed employer." * * * Hence, if Samsoc, the owner of the *S.S. Phopho,* had had a dock of its own in California to which the *Phopho* had been tied up while undergoing conversion by Moore Dry Dock employees, picketing by the Respondent at the dock site would unquestionably have constituted *primary* action, even though the Respondent might have expected that the picketing would be more effective in persuading Moore employees not to work on the ship than to persuade the seamen aboard the *Phopho* to quit that vessel. The difficulty in the present case arises therefore, not because of any difference in picketing objectives, but from the fact that the *Phopho* was not tied up at its own dock, but at that of Moore, while the picketing was going on in front of the Moore premises.

In the usual case, the *situs* of a labor dispute is the premises of the primary employer. Picketing of the premises is also picketing of the *situs* * * *. But in some cases the *situs* of the dispute may not be limited to a fixed location; it may be ambulatory. * * * [W]e hold in the present case that, as the *Phopho* was the place of employment of the seamen, it was the *situs* of the dispute between Samsoc and the Respondent over working conditions aboard that vessel.

When the *situs* is ambulatory, it may come to rest temporarily at the premises of another employer. The perplexing question is: Does the right to picket follow the *situs* while it is stationed at the premises of a secondary employer, when the only way to picket that *situs* is in front of the secondary employer's premises? Admittedly, no easy answer is possible. Essentially the problem is one of balancing the right of a union to picket at the site of its dispute as against the right of a secondary employer to be free from picketing in a controversy in which it is not directly involved.

When a secondary employer is harboring the *situs* of a dispute between a union and a primary employer, the right of neither the union to picket nor of the secondary employer to be free from picketing can be absolute. The enmeshing of premises and *situs* qualifies both rights. In the kind of situation that exists in this case, we believe that picketing of the premises of a secondary employer is primary if it meets the following conditions: (a) The picketing is strictly limited to times when the *situs* of dispute is located on the secondary employer's premises; (b) at the time of the picketing the primary employer is engaged in its normal business at the *situs;* (c) the picketing is limited to places reasonably close to the location of the *situs;* and (d) the picketing discloses clearly that the dispute is with the primary employer. All these conditions were met in the present case. * * *

[In explaining how the second of these four conditions was satisfied, the Board observed: "The multitudinous steps of preparation, including hiring and training a crew and putting stores aboard, are as much a part of the normal business of a ship as the voyage itself."]

We believe that our dissenting colleagues' expressions of alarm are based on a misunderstanding of our decision. We are not holding, as the dissenters seem to think, that a union which has a dispute with a shipowner over working conditions of seamen aboard a ship may lawfully picket the premises of an independent shipyard to which the shipowner has delivered his vessel for overhaul and repair. We are only holding that, if a shipyard permits the owner of a vessel to use its dock for the purpose of readying the ship for its regular voyage by hiring and training a crew and putting stores aboard ship, a union representing seamen may then, within the careful limitations laid down in this decision, lawfully picket in front of the shipyard premises to advertise its dispute with the shipowner. * * *

Under the circumstances of this case, we therefore find that the picketing practice followed by the Respondent was primary and not secondary and therefore did not violate Section 8(b)(4)(A) of the Act.

[The dissenting opinion of MEMBERS REYNOLDS and MURDOCH is omitted.]

---

## PROBLEMS FOR DISCUSSION

**1.** Acme Supermarket employees are on strike for increased contract benefits. Acme gets its bread and cakes from Bond Bakers by pickups from Bond made by an Acme employee driving an Acme truck. The Acme driver reports to work each morning at 6:00 A.M. to assist unloading shipments of frozen vegetables. At 8:00 A.M. as he begins his daily drive to the Bond Bakery, the driver has been accompanied by a car transporting two Acme strikers, who alight from their car and picket around the Acme truck while it is taking on baked goods at the Bond loading platform. The picketing ceases when the bread has been loaded, and the truck returns to Acme with the strikers following. After the bread is unloaded, the truck returns to Bond to make another pickup, with the strikers continuing to follow. At 1:00 P.M. the truckdriver returns to Acme, and spends the next two hours servicing the truck and cleaning the garage and loading platform. Is the union representing the strikers violating Section 8(b)(4)(B)?

**2.** A struck employer has contracted with a labor contractor to supply it with replacement workers. The labor contractor has booked rooms for the replacements at a local motel. The union picketed in the parking lot of the motel at 4:30 a.m. The picket signs stated that the dispute is solely with the labor contractor and the replacement workers. The motel manager approached the strikers, and was asked why he would rent to "scabs." He assured the union they would be gone. Has the union violated § 8(b)(4)(ii)(B)? See District 29, United Mine Workers v. NLRB, 977 F.2d 1470 (D.C.Cir.1992).

---

# Douds v. Metropolitan Federation of Architects[c]

75 F.Supp. 672 (S.D.N.Y.1948).

■ RIFKIND, DISTRICT JUDGE. This is a petition brought by Charles T. Douds, Regional Director of the Second Region of the National Labor Relations Board to enjoin the respondent, Metropolitan Federation of Architects, Engineers, Chemists and Technicians, Local 231, United Office & Professional Workers of America, C.I.O., from engaging in certain activities alleged to be in violation of Section 8(b)(4)(A) of the National Labor Relations Act, as amended by § 101 of the Labor Management Relations

---

**c.** See Asher, Secondary Boycott—Allied, Neutral and Single Employers, 52 Geo. L.J. 406 (1964); Irving, Struck Work Ally Doctrine: Some Issues and Answers, 9 Ga. L.Rev. 303 (1976); Levin, "Wholly Unconcerned": The Scope and Meaning of the Ally Doctrine Under Section 8(b)(4) of the NLRA, 119 U.Pa.L.Rev. 283 (1970); Comment, Unions, Conglomerates, and Secondary Activity Under the NLRA, 129 U.Pa.L.Rev. 221 (1980).

Act of 1947, Public Law 101, 80th Congress, popularly known as the Taft–Hartley Act, 29 U.S.C.A. § 158(b)(4)(A). * * *

The testimony offered by the petitioner, the respondent, and the charging party at the hearings established the following facts:

Ebasco Services, Inc. is a corporation engaged, since 1905, in the business of supplying engineering services, such as planning and designing and drafting plans, for industrial and public utility installations. During the year ending September 1, 1947, the respondent union was the bargaining agent for Ebasco's employees. On that day the agreement between Ebasco and the union expired. A new agreement was not reached and a strike against Ebasco was commenced on September 5, 1947.

James P. O'Donnell and Guy M. Barbolini in 1946 organized a partnership, styled Project Engineering Company, herein called "Project". Its business is identical with Ebasco's—planning and designing and drafting plans for industrial installations although they seem to have specialized in chemical and petroleum plants. The partnership had an inception completely independent of Ebasco or its influence. There is no common ownership of any kind. It was through Project's solicitations that Ebasco first employed the partnership. An open contract dated December 19, 1946 marked the beginning of their business relations.

Prior to August, 1946, Ebasco never subcontracted any of its work. Subsequent to that date it subcontracted some of its work. At the time the strike was called, part of Ebasco's work had been let out to Project. An appreciable percentage of Project's business for some months antedating the strike consisted of work secured from Ebasco. After the strike had begun, an even greater percentage—about 75%—of its work was Ebasco's. Some work, which had been begun by Ebasco's workers, was transferred, after the commencement of the strike, in an unfinished condition to Project for completion.

In a brochure printed and distributed by Ebasco before the strike to its prospective customers, Ebasco represented itself as having available the services of a number of draftsmen and designers, which included the personnel of Project and of other subcontractors. The contract price of all the work done by Project for Ebasco was computed by adding to the compensation of the men engaged on Ebasco work a factor for overhead and profits. In their business relationship it was the practice of Project to furnish Ebasco with time sheets, showing the number of hours each of the former's employees spent on Ebasco work. Ebasco's statements to its customers contained the time spent by technicians, with no distinction made between the work done by Ebasco employees and subcontractors' employees.

Ebasco supervisory personnel made regular visits to Project to oversee the work on the subcontracts. After the strike was called and the work subcontracted increased, these visits increased in frequency and numbers of personnel involved. Ebasco supervisory personnel, whose subordinates were on strike, continued to supervise their "jobs", at Project's plant, where such work had been transferred. The working hours of Project employees were increased after the commencement of the Ebasco strike.

Delegations representing the respondent union approached the charging party on more than one occasion and asked, among other things, that it refuse to accept work which had come "off the boards" of Ebasco.

On October 28, 1947, respondent union ordered Project picketed and such picketing has continued since that day. The pickets carry signs which denominate Project a scab shop for Ebasco. A number of resignations at Project are attributable to the picketing.

The number of pickets has usually been reasonable and the picketing was ordinarily unaccompanied by violence. * * * Project continues to do engineering work for Ebasco—the kind of work which Ebasco employees themselves would be doing if they were not striking. * * *

One of the prohibitions of Section 8(b)(4)(A) of the Act is: "It shall be an unfair labor practice for a labor organization * * * to * * * encourage the employees of any employer to engage in, a strike * * * where an object thereof is * * * requiring * * * any * * * person * * * to cease doing business with any other person."

Is Project "doing business" with Ebasco within the meaning of the Act? The term is not defined in the Act itself. Section 2, 29 U.S.C.A. § 152, contains thirteen definitions, but none of doing business. * * * To find the limitations to which "doing business" must be confined recourse may be had to the legislative history to discover the mischief which Congress intended to remedy. In describing the "necessity for legislation" the House Committee on Education and Labor reported, Report No. 245, pp. 4–5:

"The employers' plight has likewise not been happy. * * *

"His business on occasions has been virtually brought to a standstill by disputes to which he himself was not a party and in which he himself had no interest." * * *

During the Congressional debates on the Bill, Senator Pepper objected to the provisions relating to the secondary boycott and stated an illustration in which he thought it would be unjust to apply them. Senator Taft, in reply, said: "I do not quite understand the case which the Senator has put. This provision makes it unlawful to resort to a secondary boycott to injure the business of a third person who is wholly unconcerned in the disagreement between an employer and his employees." (April 29, 1947, p. 4323 of the Congressional Record, Vol. 93.)

Examination of these expositions of Congressional purpose indicates that the provision was understood to outlaw what was theretofore known as a secondary boycott. It is to the history of the secondary boycott, therefore, that attention should be directed and it is in the light of that history that the term "doing business" should be evaluated. See Hellerstein, Secondary Boycotts in Labor Disputes, 1938, 47 Yale Law J. 341; Gromfine, Labor's Use of Secondary Boycotts, 1947, 15 Geo. Washington Law Rev. 327.

When the term is read with the aid of the glossary provided by the law of secondary boycott it becomes quite clear that Project cannot claim to be a victim of that weapon in labor's arsenal. To suggest that Project had no interest in the dispute between Ebasco and its employees is to look at the form and remain blind to substance. In every meaningful sense it had made itself party to the contest. Manifestly it was not an innocent bystander, nor a neutral. It was firmly allied to Ebasco and it was its conduct as ally of Ebasco which directly provoked the union's action.

Significant is the unique character of the contract between Ebasco and Project. Ebasco did not buy any articles of commerce from Project. Ebasco did not retain the professional services of Project. Ebasco "bought" from Project, in the words of the basic contract, "services of your designers and draftsmen * * * to work under the direction and supervision of the Purchaser." The purchase price consisted of the actual wages paid by Project plus a factor for overhead and profit. In practice the terms and implications of the agreement were fully spelled out. Ebasco supplied both direction and supervision of a detailed and pervasive character. It established the maximum wage rates for which it would be charged. Invoices were in terms of manhours, employee by employee. Daily tally was taken of the number of men at work on Ebasco assignments and communicated to Ebasco. The final product, the plans and drawings, were placed upon forms supplied by Ebasco, bearing its name, and were thus delivered to Ebasco's clients as Ebasco's work. In advertising its services to the industries which it served Ebasco held itself out as "having available" a number of designers and draftsmen which included those employed by Project.

True enough, the contract prescribes that "all employees furnished by the seller shall at all times be and remain employees of the seller". I do not, however, draw therefrom the inference advocated by the petitioner and the charging party. The very need for such a provision emphasizes the realization of the parties that they were doing business on terms which cast a shadow of doubt upon the identity of the employer. Without question, Ebasco and Project were free to contract who, as between themselves, should be subject to the burden and possessed of the privileges that attach to the employer of those on Project's payroll. But the law is not foreclosed by such agreements to examine the reality relevant to the purposes of a particular statute. Cf. Rutherford Food Corp. v. McComb, 1947, 331 U.S. 722, 67 S.Ct. 1473; N.L.R.B. v. Hearst Publications, Inc., 1944, 322 U.S. 111, 64 S.Ct. 851, 88 L.Ed. 1170.

I am unable to hold that corporate ownership or insulation of legal interests between two businesses can be conclusive as to neutrality or disinterestedness in a labor dispute.

The evidence is abundant that Project's employees did work, which, but for the strike of Ebasco's employees, would have been done by Ebasco. The economic effect upon Ebasco's employees was precisely that which would flow from Ebasco's hiring strikebreakers to work on its own premises. The conduct of the union in inducing Project's employees to strike is not different in kind from its conduct in inducing Ebasco's employees to strike.

If the latter is not amenable to judicial restraint, neither is the former. In encouraging a strike at Project the union was not extending its activity to a front remote from the immediate dispute but to one intimately and indeed inextricably united to it. See Bakery Drivers Local v. Wohl, 1942, 315 U.S. 769, 62 S.Ct. 816, 86 L.Ed. 1178; cf. Carpenters Union v. Ritter's Cafe, 1942, 315 U.S. 722, 62 S.Ct. 807, 86 L.Ed. 1143.

\* \* \* It must be apparent that a construction of the Act which outlaws the kind of union activity here involved would almost certainly cast grave doubts upon its constitutionality. It is preferable to interpret the disputed section so as to restrain only that kind of union activity which does not enjoy constitutional immunity.

The case at bar is not an instance of a secondary boycott.

For these reasons it is clear that there has been no violation of Section 8(b)(4)(A) and the court is therefore without power to grant the requested relief. \* \* \*

---

## PROBLEMS FOR DISCUSSION

**1.** Employees doing repair work for Cyber Computer Company are on strike for higher wages. Cyber Computers are sold with a one-year warranty. The usual duties of the strikers are to repair computers under warranty and also to repair computers leased from Cyber. During the strike, Cyber instructs customers needing repairs to have the repairs performed by another company of the customer's choice. The customers are told to send the repair bills to Cyber, which in turn agrees to pay the company performing the repairs. Accordingly, one of Cyber's major customers, Vick Chemical Co., arranges to have extensive repairs performed by Gates Computer Co., for which Cyber agrees to pay in installments. While such repair work is being performed, Cyber employees picket both Vick and Gates, seeking to force Gates to stop performing Cyber repairs. Does the picketing of Gates violate § 8(b)(4)(B)? Does the picketing of Vick? See NLRB v. Business Mach. & Office Appliance Mechanics Conference Bd. (Royal Typewriter Co.), 228 F.2d 553 (2d Cir.1955).

Suppose Cyber agreed with Vick that Vick would pay Gates for the repair work and that Cyber would then reimburse Vick. Gates Computer has no dealings with Cyber and is unaware of the strike. Could Gates then be lawfully picketed by the Cyber employees?

**2.** Members of the American Federation of Television and Radio Artists (AFTRA) are on strike against WBAL–TV, Baltimore, which is owned by the Hearst Corporation. AFTRA pickets the Baltimore News American, a newspaper owned by Hearst. The publisher of the News American files a Section 8(b)(4)(B) charge and the Regional Director issues a complaint. The Administrative Law Judge determines the following facts regarding the structure of the Hearst Corporation.

Hearst has its headquarters in New York and comprises twenty divisions, which are not separately incorporated. The News American and WBAL are controlled by different divisions. No member of the management of either division sits on the board of directors of Hearst and there is no overlap between the management of the two divisions. The management of each division has substantially complete control of the day-to-day operation of the division. Hearst does not influence the editorial policies of either the newspaper or the television station, although it does make certain news services and columns available to both. Both the television station and the newspaper employ their own news-gathering staffs. When one division advertises on the other's medium, it pays the going commercial rate. Both divisions employ the same labor lawyer, but they pursue separate labor relations policies without interference from New York. Each division controls its own budget, but must obtain approval from Hearst for capital expenditures in excess of $10,000.

(a) Is AFTRA violating Section 8(b)(4)(B) by picketing the News American? See AFTRA v. NLRB, 462 F.2d 887 (D.C.Cir.1972).

(b) Would your analysis differ materially if the Hearst Corporation operated the newspaper and television station not through divisions but rather through separately incorporated, wholly-owned subsidiaries?

(c) In the event you conclude that the picketing violates the Labor Act, what remedies are available to the injured parties? Under each of the remedies you can contemplate, who will determine whether the News American is an "ally" of the struck television station?

**3.** Since 1980 or thereabouts, certain unionized construction companies have chosen to become "double-breasted." The company creates a separate entity, with ownership by essentially the same persons, and opens business on a non-union basis; this allows for lower wages and other labor costs at the new company, and allows that company to bid for construction contracts at non-union sites. The work done by the two companies is the same; in some cases, supervisors or construction equipment from the original company are "lent" to the affiliated non-union company. Typically, day-to-day management is carried out by different persons at the two companies, as is the formulation and implementation of terms of employment. At one such company, Eltra Electric Service, Inc., the bargaining representative has demanded that the company dissolve, or sell its ownership interest in, the non-union Eltra–Two Company, but it has refused and the union has struck and is picketing at Eltra. Is the union's activity an illegal secondary boycott? Compare Sheet Metal Wkrs., Local 91 v. NLRB, 905 F.2d 417 (D.C.Cir.1990), with Becker Elec. Co. v. IBEW, Local 212, 927 F.2d 895 (6th Cir.1991). See generally South Prairie Constr. Co. v. Operating Eng'rs Local 627, 425 U.S. 800, 96 S.Ct. 1842, 48 L.Ed.2d 382 (1976).

---

# Local 761, International Union of Electrical, Radio and Mach. Workers v. NLRB[d]

366 U.S. 667, 81 S.Ct. 1285, 6 L.Ed.2d 592 (1961).

■ Mr. Justice Frankfurter delivered the opinion of the Court.

Local 761 of the International Union of Electrical, Radio and Machine Workers, AFL–CIO was charged with a violation of § 8(b)(4)(A) of the Taft–Hartley Act, 61 Stat. 136, 141, upon the following facts.

**d.** See Cantor, Separate Gates, Related Work, and Secondary Boycotts, 27 Rutgers L.Rev. 613 (1974); Zimmerman, Secondary Picketing and the Reserved Gate: The *General Electric* Doctrine, 47 Va.L.Rev. 1164 (1961).

General Electric Corporation operates a plant outside of Louisville, Kentucky, where it manufactures washers, dryers, and other electrical household appliances. The square-shaped, thousand-acre, unfenced plant is known as Appliance Park. A large drainage ditch makes ingress and egress impossible except over five roadways across culverts, designated as gates.

Since 1954, General Electric sought to confine the employees of independent contractors, described hereafter, who work on the premises of the Park, to the use of Gate 3–A and confine its use to them. The undisputed reason for doing so was to insulate General Electric employees from the frequent labor disputes in which the contractors were involved. Gate 3–A is 550 feet away from the nearest entrance available for General Electric employees, suppliers, and deliverymen. Although anyone can pass the gate without challenge, the roadway leads to a guardhouse where identification must be presented. Vehicle stickers of various shapes and colors enable a guard to check on sight whether a vehicle is authorized to use Gate 3–A. Since January 1958, a prominent sign has been posted at the gate which states: "GATE 3–A FOR EMPLOYEES OF CONTRACTORS ONLY—G.E. EMPLOYEES USE OTHER GATES." On rare occasions, it appears, a General Electric employee was allowed to pass the guardhouse, but such occurrence was in violation of company instructions. There was no proof of any unauthorized attempts to pass the gate during the strike in question.

The independent contractors are utilized for a great variety of tasks on the Appliance Park premises. Some do construction work on new buildings; some install and repair ventilation and heating equipment; some engage in retooling and rearranging operations necessary to the manufacture of new models; others do "general maintenance work." These services are contracted to outside employers either because the company's employees lack the necessary skill or manpower, or because the work can be done more economically by independent contractors. The latter reason determined the contracting of maintenance work for which the Central Maintenance department of the company bid competitively with the contractors. While some of the work done by these contractors had on occasion been previously performed by Central Maintenance, the findings do not disclose the number of employees of independent contractors who were performing these routine maintenance services, as compared with those who were doing specialized work of a capital-improvement nature.

The Union, petitioner here, is the certified bargaining representative for the production and maintenance workers who constitute approximately 7,600 of the 10,500 employees of General Electric at Appliance Park. On July 27, 1958, the Union called a strike because of 24 unsettled grievances with the company. Picketing occurred at all the gates, including Gate 3–A, and continued until August 9 when an injunction was issued by a Federal District Court. The signs carried by the pickets at all gates read: "LOCAL 761 ON STRIKE G.E. UNFAIR." Because of the picketing, almost all of the employees of independent contractors refused to enter the company premises.

Neither the legality of the strike or of the picketing at any of the gates except 3–A is in dispute, nor that the picketing was other than peaceful in nature. The sole claim was that the picketing before the gate exclusively used by employees of independent contractors was conduct proscribed by § 8(b)(4)(A).

The Trial Examiner recommended that the Board dismiss the complaint. He concluded that the limitations on picketing which the Board had prescribed in so-called "common situs" cases were not applicable to the situation before him, in that the picketing at Gate 3–A represented traditional primary action which necessarily had a secondary effect of inconveniencing those who did business with the struck employer. He reasoned that if a primary employer could limit the area of picketing around his own premises by constructing a separate gate for employees of independent contractors, such a device could also be used to isolate employees of his suppliers and customers, and that such action could not relevantly be distinguished from oral appeals made to secondary employees not to cross a picket line where only a single gate existed.

The Board rejected the Trial Examiner's conclusion, 123 N.L.R.B. 1547. It held that since only the employees of the independent contractors were allowed to use Gate 3–A, the Union's object in picketing there was "to enmesh these employees of the neutral employers in its dispute with the Company" thereby constituting a violation of § 8(b)(4)(A) because the independent employees were encouraged to engage in a concerted refusal to work "with an object of forcing the independent contractors to cease doing business with the Company."

The Court of Appeals for the District of Columbia granted enforcement of the Board's order * * *.

## I.

Section 8(b)(4)(A) of the National Labor Relations Act provides that it shall be an unfair labor practice for a labor organization

> " * * * to engage in, or to induce or encourage the employees of any employer to engage in a strike or a concerted refusal in the course of their employment to use, manufacture, process, transport, or otherwise handle or work on any goods, articles, materials, or commodities or to perform any services, where an object thereof is: (A) forcing or requiring * * * any employer or other person * * * to cease doing business with any other person * * *."

This provision could not be literally construed; otherwise it would ban most strikes historically considered to be lawful, so-called primary activity. "While § 8(b)(4) does not expressly mention 'primary' or 'secondary' disputes, strikes or boycotts, that section often is referred to in the Act's legislative history as one of the Act's 'secondary boycott sections.' " Labor Board v. Denver Building Council, 341 U.S. 675, 686, 71 S.Ct. 943, 950, 95 L.Ed. 1284. "Congress did not seek, by § 8(b)(4), to interfere with the ordinary strike * * *." Labor Board v. International Rice Milling Co., 341

U.S. 665, 672, 71 S.Ct. 961, 965, 95 L.Ed. 1277. The impact of the section was directed toward what is known as the secondary boycott whose "sanctions bear, not upon the employer who alone is a party to the dispute, but upon some third party who has no concern in it." International Brotherhood of Electrical Workers v. Labor Board, 181 F.2d 34, 37. Thus the section "left a striking labor organization free to use persuasion, including picketing, not only on the primary employer and his employees but on numerous others. Among these were secondary employers who were customers or suppliers of the primary employer and persons dealing with them * * * and even employees of secondary employers so long as the labor organization did not * * * 'induce or encourage the employees of any employer to engage in a strike or a concerted refusal in the course of their employment' * * *." Labor Board v. Local 294, International Brotherhood of Teamsters, 2 Cir., 284 F.2d 887, 889. * * *

Important as is the distinction between legitimate "primary activity" and banned "secondary activity," it does not present a glaringly bright line. The objectives of any picketing include a desire to influence others from withholding from the employer their services or trade. See Sailors' Union of the Pacific (Moore Dry Dock), 92 N.L.R.B. 547. "[I]ntended or not, sought for or not, aimed for or not, employees of neutral employers do take action sympathetic with strikers and do put pressure on their own employers." Seafarers International Union v. Labor Board, 105 U.S.App.D.C. 211, 265 F.2d 585, 590. "It is clear that, when a union pickets an employer with whom it has a dispute, it hopes, even if it does not intend, that all persons will honor the picket line, and that hope encompasses the employees of neutral employers who may in the course of their employment (delivery-men and the like) have to enter the premises." Id., at 591. "Almost all picketing, even at the situs of the primary employer and surely at that of the secondary, hopes to achieve the forbidden objective, whatever other motives there may be and however small the chances of success." Local 294, supra, at 890. But picketing which induces secondary employees to respect a picket line is not the equivalent of picketing which has an object of inducing those employees to engage in concerted conduct against their employer in order to force him to refuse to deal with the struck employer. Labor Board v. International Rice Milling, supra.

However difficult the drawing of lines more nice than obvious, the statute compels the task. * * * The nature of the problem, as revealed by unfolding variant situations, inevitably involves an evolutionary process for its rational response, not a quick, definitive formula as a comprehensive answer. And so, it is not surprising that the Board has more or less felt its way during the fourteen years in which it has had to apply § 8(b)(4)(A), and has modified and reformed its standards on the basis of accumulating experience. "One of the purposes which lead to the creation of such boards is to have decisions based upon evidential facts under the particular statute made by experienced officials with an adequate appreciation of the complexities of the subject which is entrusted to their administration." Republic Aviation Corp. v. Labor Board, 324 U.S. 793, 800, 65 S.Ct. 982, 986, 89 L.Ed. 1372.

## II.

The early decisions of the Board following the Taft–Hartley amendments involved activity which took place around the secondary employer's premises. For example in Wadsworth Building Co., supra, the union set up a picket line around the situs of a builder who had contracted to purchase prefabricated houses from the primary employer. The Board found this to be illegal secondary activity. See also Printing Specialties Union (Sealbright Pacific), 82 N.L.R.B. 271. In contrast, when picketing took place around the premises of the primary employer the Board regarded this as valid primary activity. In Oil Workers International Union (Pure Oil Co.), 84 N.L.R.B. 315, Pure had used Standard's dock and employees for loading its oil onto ships. The companies had contracted that, in case of a strike against Standard, Pure employees would take over the loading of Pure oil. The union struck against Standard and picketed the dock, and Pure employees refused to cross the picket line. The Board held this to be a primary activity, although the union's action induced the Pure employees to engage in a concerted refusal to handle Pure products at the dock. The fact that the picketing was confined to the vicinity of the Standard premises influenced the Board not to find that an object of the activity was to force Pure to cease doing business with Standard, even if such was a secondary effect.

> "A strike, by its very nature, inconveniences those who customarily do business with the struck employer. Moreover, any accompanying picketing of the employer's premises is necessarily designed to induce and encourage third persons to cease doing business with the picketed employer. It does not follow, however, that such picketing is therefore proscribed by Section 8(b)(4)(A) of the Act." 84 N.L.R.B., at 318. * * *

In United Electrical Workers (Ryan Construction Corp.), 85 N.L.R.B. 417, Ryan had contracted to perform construction work on a building adjacent to the Bucyrus plant and inside its fence. A separate gate was cut through the fence for Ryan's employees which no employee of Bucyrus ever used. The Board concluded that the union—on strike against Bucyrus—could picket the Ryan gate, even though an object of the picketing was to enlist the aid of Ryan employees, since Congress did not intend to outlaw primary picketing.

> "When picketing is wholly at the premises of the employer with whom the union is engaged in a labor dispute, it cannot be called 'secondary' even though, as is virtually always the case, an object of the picketing is to dissuade all persons from entering such premises for business reasons. It makes no difference whether 1 or 100 other employees wish to enter the premises. It follows in this case that the picketing of Bucyrus premises, which was primary because in support of a labor dispute *with Bucyrus,* did not lose its character and become 'secondary' at the so-called Ryan gate because Ryan employees were the only persons regularly entering Bucyrus premises at that gate." 85 N.L.R.B., at 418. See also General Teamsters (Crump, Inc.), 112 N.L.R.B. 311.

Thus, the Board eliminated picketing which took place around the situs of the primary employer—regardless of the special circumstances involved—from being held invalid secondary activity under § 8(b)(4)(A).

However, the impact of the new situations made the Board conscious of the complexity of the problem by reason of the protean forms in which it appeared. This became clear in the "common situs" cases—situations where two employers were performing separate tasks on common premises. The Moore Dry Dock case, supra, laid out the Board's new standards in this area. There, the union picketed outside an entrance to a dock where a ship, owned by the struck employer, was being trained and outfitted. Although the premises picketed were those of the secondary employer, they constituted the only place where picketing could take place; furthermore, the objectives of the picketing were no more aimed at the employees of the secondary employer—the dock owner—than they had been in the Pure Oil and Ryan cases. The Board concluded, however, that when the situs of the primary employer was "ambulatory" there must be a balance between the union's right to picket and the interest of the secondary employer in being free from picketing. It set out four standards for picketing in such situations which would be presumptive of valid primary activity: (1) that the picketing be limited to times when the situs of dispute was located on the secondary premises, (2) that the primary employer be engaged in his normal business at the situs, (3) that the picketing take place reasonably close to the situs, and (4) that the picketing clearly disclose that the dispute was only with the primary employer. These tests were widely accepted by reviewing federal courts. * * *

In Local 55 (PBM), 108 N.L.R.B. 363, the Board for the first time applied the Dry Dock test although the picketing occurred at premises owned by the primary employer. There, an insurance company owned a tract of land that it was developing, and also served as the general contractor. A neutral subcontractor was also doing work at the site. The union, engaged in a strike against the insurance company, picketed the entire premises, characterizing the entire job as unfair, and the employees of the subcontractor walked off. The Court of Appeals for the Tenth Circuit enforced the Board's order which found the picketing to be illegal on the ground that the picket signs did not measure up to the Dry Dock standard that they clearly disclose that the picketing was directed against the struck employer only. 218 F.2d 226.

The Board's application of the Dry Dock standards to picketing at the premises of the struck employer was made more explicit in Retail Fruit & Vegetable Clerks (Crystal Palace Market), 116 N.L.R.B. 856. The owner of a large common market operated some of the shops within, and leased out others to independent sellers. The union, although given permission to picket the owner's individual stands, chose to picket outside the entire market. The Board held that this action was violative of § 8(b)(4)(A) in that the union did not attempt to minimize the effect of its picketing, as required in a common-situs case, on the operations of the neutral employers utilizing the market. "We believe * * * that the foregoing principles should apply to all common situs picketing, including cases where, as here, the picketed premises are owned by the primary employer." 116 N.L.R.B., at 859. The Ryan case, supra, was overruled to the extent it implied the contrary. The Court of Appeals for the Ninth Circuit, in enforcing the Board's order, specifically approved its disavowance of an ownership test. 249 F.2d 591. The Board made clear that its decision did not affect situations where picketing which had effects on neutral third parties who dealt with the employer occurred at premises occupied solely by him. "In such cases, we adhere to the rule established by the Board * * * that more latitude be given to picketing at such separate primary premises than at premises occupied in part (or entirely) by secondary employers." 116 N.L.R.B., at 860, n. 10.

In rejecting the ownership test in situations where two employers were performing work upon a common site, the Board was naturally guided by this Court's opinion in Rice Milling, in which we indicated that the location of the picketing at the primary employer's premises was "not necessarily conclusive" of its legality. 341 U.S., at 671. Where the work done by the secondary employees is unrelated to the normal operations of the primary employer, it is difficult to perceive how the pressure of picketing the entire situs is any less on the neutral employer merely because the picketing takes place at property owned by the struck employer. The application of the Dry Dock tests to limit the picketing effects to the employees of the employer against whom the dispute is directed carries out the "dual congressional objectives of preserving the right of labor organizations to bring pressure to bear on offending employers in primary labor disputes and of shielding unoffending employers and others from pressures in controversies not their own." Labor Board v. Denver Building Council, supra, at 692.

### III.

From this necessary survey of the course of the Board's treatment of our problem, the precise nature of the issue before us emerges. With due regard to the relation between the Board's function and the scope of judicial review of its rulings, the question is whether the Board may apply the Dry Dock criteria so as to make unlawful picketing at a gate utilized exclusively by employees of independent contractors who work on the struck employers' premises. The effect of such a holding would not bar the union from picketing at all gates used by the employees, suppliers, and customers of the struck employer. Of course an employer may not, by removing all his employees from the situs of the strike, bar the union from publicizing its cause, see Local 618 v. Labor Board, 8 Cir., 249 F.2d 332. The basis of the Board's decision in this case would not remotely have that effect, nor any such tendency for the future.

The Union claims that if the Board's ruling is upheld, employers will be free to erect separate gates for deliveries, customers, and replacement workers which will be immunized from picketing. This fear is baseless. The key to the problem is found in the type of work that is being performed by those who use the separate gate. It is significant that the Board has since applied its rationale, first stated in the present case, only to situations where the independent workers were performing tasks unconnected to the normal operations of the struck employer—usually construction work on his buildings. In such situations, the indicated limitations on picketing activity respect the balance of competing interests that Congress has required the Board to enforce. On the other hand, if a separate gate were devised for regular plant deliveries, the barring of picketing at that location would make a clear invasion on traditional primary activity of appealing to neutral employees whose tasks aid the employer's everyday operations. The 1959 Amendments to the National Labor Relations Act, which removed the word "concerted" from the boycott provisions, included a proviso that "nothing contained in this clause (B) shall be construed to make unlawful, where not otherwise unlawful, any primary strike or primary picketing." 29 U.S.C.A. (Sup. I, 1959) § 158(b)(4)(B). The proviso was directed against the fear that the removal of "concerted" from the statute might be interpreted so that "the picketing at the factory violates section 8(b)(4)(A) because the pickets induce the truck drivers employed by the trucker not to perform their usual services where an object is to compel the trucking firm not to do business with the * * * manufacturer during the strike." Analysis of the bill prepared by Senator Kennedy and Representative Thompson, 105 Cong.Rec. 16589.

In a case similar to the one now before us, the Court of Appeals for the Second Circuit sustained the Board in its application of § 8(b)(4)(A) to a separate-gate situation. "There must be a separate gate, marked and set apart from other gates; the work done by the men who use the gate must be unrelated to the normal operations of the employer, and the work must be of a kind that would not, if done when the plant were engaged in its regular operations, necessitate curtailing those operations." United Steelworkers v. Labor Board, Doc. No. 26252, decided May 3, 1961. These seem to us controlling considerations.

## IV.

The foregoing course of reasoning would require that the judgment below sustaining the Board's order be affirmed but for one consideration, even though this consideration may turn out not to affect the result. The legal path by which the Board and the Court of Appeals reached their decisions did not take into account that if Gate 3–A was in fact used by employees of independent contractors who performed conventional maintenance work necessary to the normal operations of General Electric, the use of the gate would have been a mingled one outside the bar of § 8(b)(4)(A). In short, such mixed use of this portion of the struck employer's premises would not bar picketing rights of the striking employees. While the record shows some such mingled use, it sheds no light on its extent. It may well turn out to be that the instances of these maintenance tasks were so insubstantial as to be treated by the Board as *de minimis*. We cannot here guess at the quantitative aspect of this problem. It calls for Board determination. For determination of the questions thus raised, the case must be remanded by the Court of Appeals to the Board.

Reversed.

[THE CHIEF JUSTICE and MR. JUSTICE BLACK concurred in the result, and MR. JUSTICE DOUGLAS, dissented.]

---

# PROBLEMS FOR DISCUSSION

**1.** The Retail Clerks Union at the Acme Supermarket has called a strike for increased contract benefits, but the market is continuing in operation through the use of supervisory personnel. In an effort to separate deliverymen from the picketing Acme employees, Acme constructs a delivery platform at the edge of its parking lot and erects signs directing deliverymen to the platform through an unused driveway which is at all points considerably distant from the store and from customer and employee entrances. Nonetheless, a group of picketers station themselves at the driveway entrance, where no Acme employees are located, and turn away Bond Bakery delivery trucks. Is the Union violating Section 8(b)(4)(B)?

**2.** The scenario is the same as in problem 1, except that the driveway is reserved exclusively for employees of Concreet Construction Company, which is building for Acme (at the rear of its parking lot) a quick-food-service stand which will dispense sandwiches and hot snacks at lunch and dinner hours. The Concreet employees are turned away by the Acme picket line. Is the Union violating Section 8(b)(4)(B)?

**3.** The scenario is the same, except that Acme closes its market because of the serious curtailment of business caused by the picketing. A week later, the employees of Fashion Interiors appear at the driveway; they intend to occupy the supermarket building for a week, replacing linoleum with carpeting, installing new lighting fixtures, and repainting. The picketing by the Retail Clerks continues, both at the supermarket building and at the driveway, at a time when no other employees or customers are there, and the employees of Fashion Interiors are turned away and refuse to return to work. Is the Union violating Section 8(b)(4)(B)?

**4.** Burham Oil has a refinery in Burham, Texas, where it also produces petroleum coke in its coking unit (CU). It has contracted with Coker Cookers, Inc., to bundle and load the coke. Coker Cookers' employees operate the CU; they process the product, store it and load it on to trucks and rail cars. Purchasers of coke who wish it to be shipped via rail contract the Burlington Northern R.R. which bills them for the shipping costs. Burham maintains a reserved gate system: Gate 6 is reserved for Coker Cookers. Gate 7 is reserved for independent truckers who haul the coke. Gate 8 is reserved for use of the Burlington Northern R.R. which makes deliveries to and carries freight from the facility apart from its coking operation. The Oil and Chemical Workers Union has a labor dispute with Coker Cookers. It has picketed with signs directed at "Coker Cookers Unfair" at gates 6, 7 and 8. Is any of that picketing impermissible? *See* Oil, Chemical & Atomic Workers, Local 1–591 (Burlington Northern R.R.), 325 NLRB 324 (1998).

**5.** Assume that a union wishes to engage in "area standards" picketing of a non-union general contractor engaged in renovating an office building. The building has a large front entrance, open to the public, and a small rear entrance that opens on an alley. May the building owner designate the front entrance for use of all employees, visitors and suppliers except those of the contractor, and reserve the rear entrance for the exclusive use of the contractor? See Carpenters Local No. 33 v. NLRB, 873 F.2d 316 (D.C.Cir.1989).

--------

## 2. THE 1959 AMENDMENTS: CONSUMER APPEALS[e]

The 1959 amendments to Section 8(b)(4) were designed to close certain loopholes in the Taft–Hartley secondary boycott provisions. As enacted in 1947, those provisions made it an unfair labor practice for a labor organization to "encourage the employees of any employer" to engage in a strike or a "concerted refusal" to process, transport or otherwise handle goods where an object was to force one person to cease doing business with another. It had been held that the use of the terms "employees" and "employer" as defined in Section 2 of the Labor Act permitted a union to induce a secondary work stoppage by minor supervisors, farm workers, governmental and railway employees, and workers at nonprofit private hospitals. Congress closed this loophole in 1959 by banning a union inducement of a secondary work stoppage by "any individual employed by any person engaged in commerce or in an industry affecting commerce." Congress also in 1959 struck the word "concerted" from what had been Section 8(b)(4)(A) of the Taft–Hartley Act, and thus brought within the secondary boycott ban a union inducement of a single individual (*e.g.*, one truck driver) to refrain from transporting or handling goods produced by or destined for the primary employer. By a more significant amendment, Congress added a second proscribed method for effecting a secondary boycott; in addition to the inducement of a work stoppage, Congress now forbade a union "to threaten, coerce, or restrain any person engaged in commerce or in an industry affecting commerce" where the union's objective was secondary. This was incorporated in the newly numbered Section 8(b)(4)(B) as subsection (ii), while the work-stoppage ban was carried forward as subsection (i).

The prohibitions of the 1959 amendments were narrowly construed by the Supreme Court in NLRB v. SERVETTE, INC., 377 U.S. 46, 84 S.Ct. 1098, 12 L.Ed.2d 121 (1964). This case involved a strike against Servette, a wholesale distributor to retail supermarket chains. Representatives of the striking union sought to support the strike by requesting supermarket manag-

---

e. See Comment, Secondary Boycotts and the First Amendment, 51 U.Chi.L.Rev. 811 (1984); Engel, Secondary Consumer Picketing—Following the Struck Product, 52 Va. L.Rev. 189 (1966); Kohler, Setting the Conditions for Self–Rule: Unions, Associations, Our First Amendment Discourse and the Problem of *DeBartolo*, 1990 Wisc.L.Rev. 149; Lewis, Consumer Picketing and the Court—The Questionable Yield of *Tree Fruits,* 49 Minn. L.Rev. 479 (1965); Minch, Consumer Picketing: Reassessing the Concept of Employer Neutrality, 65 Calif.L.Rev. 172 (1977); Modjeska, The *Tree Fruits* Consumer Picketing Case—A Retrospective Analysis, 53 U.Cinn.L.Rev. 1005 (1984); Note, Picketing and Publicity Under Section 8(b)(4) of the LMRA, 73 Yale L.J. 1265 (1964); St. Antoine, Free Speech or Economic Weapon? The Persisting Problem of Picketing, 16 Suffolk L.Rev. 883 (1982); Shalov, The Landrum–Griffin Amendments: Labor's Use of the Secondary Boycott, 45 Corn.L.Q. 724 (1960).

ers to stop stocking Servette products. These requests were backed by a warning that handbills, urging customers not to purchase Servette products, would be distributed in front of stores selling Servette products. In some instances, such handbills were distributed. Servette filed a Section 8(b)(4) charge, but the Board dismissed the complaint. It held that subsection (i) was not violated because supermarket managers were not "individuals" within the meaning of that subsection and thus that inducements aimed at managers were not proscribed. The "threat" of handbilling and the actual handbilling were held not prohibited by subsection (ii) because handbilling was protected by the publicity proviso added to the Act in the 1959 amendments. The court of appeals reversed, finding violations in both the requests to the managers and the handbilling. The Supreme Court reinstated the Board's order dismissing the complaint, but for different reasons from those relied on by the Board.

The Supreme Court agreed with the court of appeals that the word "individual" included supermarket managers. But the Court found no illegal inducement. Section 8(b)(4)(i) was held to prohibit only encouraging someone to refuse to perform his duties. The managers were not being encouraged to withhold their services but rather to make a managerial decision within their authority. Encouraging or inducing someone to make such a decision was held not to violate subsection (i). The Court found support for this interpretation in the legislative history of the 1959 statute, which evidenced no congressional intention to expand the type of conduct outlawed under subsection (i), and also in the structure of the statute; if subsection (i) had been intended to prohibit appeals to managers making managerial decisions, then subsection (ii) prohibiting threats to managers making decisions would have been superfluous.

The Court also agreed with the Board that the proviso protected the union's distribution of handbills. The court of appeals had concluded that the proviso did not protect the handbilling because the proviso in terms protects only publicity concerning "products * * produced by an employer with whom the labor organization has a primary dispute * * *." Servette was a distributor and had not "produced" any goods. The Supreme Court, however, referring to the legislative purpose, gave a broad reading to the word "produced" in the proviso so as to encompass distribution:

> "The proviso was the outgrowth of a profound Senate concern that the unions' freedom to appeal to the public for support of their case be adequately safeguarded. * * * It would fall far short of achieving this basic purpose if the proviso applied only in situations where the union's labor dispute is with the manufacturer or processor. Moreover, a primary target of the 1959 amendments was the secondary boycotts conducted by the Teamsters Union, which ordinarily represents employees not of manufacturers, but of motor carriers. There is nothing in the legislative history which suggests that the protection of the proviso was intended to be any narrower in coverage than the prohibition to which it is an

exception, and we see no basis for attributing such an incongruous purpose to Congress."

The "threat" of handbilling was thus not prohibited by subsection (ii) because the "statutory protection for the distribution of handbills would be undermined if a threat to engage in protected conduct were not itself protected."

The Court reemphasized the broad scope of the "producer" proviso to Section 8(b)(4)(ii)(B)—but even so found it inapplicable—in EDWARD J. DEBARTOLO CORP. v. NLRB, 463 U.S. 147, 103 S.Ct. 2926, 77 L.Ed.2d 535 (1983). There, the Wilson Company contracted with High, a builder, to construct a department store in a Florida shopping center. The center was owned and operated by DeBartolo Company, and contained other retail stores. The local building trades council, contending that High was paying its construction workers substandard wages, distributed handbills at all shopping center entrances to all shopping center patrons while the Wilson store was under construction. The handbills asked the readers not to patronize any of the stores in the mall until DeBartolo promised that all construction there would be done by contractors who paid fair wages and fringe benefits. The handbills explicitly disclaimed any purpose to induce a stoppage of work or deliveries. DeBartolo filed unfair labor practice charges, and a complaint issued alleging that the object of the handbilling was to force retail-store tenants to cease doing business with DeBartolo, in order to force DeBartolo and/or Wilson not to do business with High. Both the NLRB and the reviewing court of appeals treated High as a "producer" (i.e., of store construction) and held that the publicity proviso applied and protected the handbilling.

The Supreme Court reversed, unanimously. The Court (relying on the Board's findings) agreed with the building trades council contention that it was making an appeal other than by picketing, that the appeal was truthful, and that it induced no stoppage of work or deliveries by employees of secondary employers. The Court also agreed, invoking *Servette*, that the "producer" requirement of the proviso should be read broadly:

> In this case, DeBartolo is willing to concede that Wilson distributes products that are "produced" by High within the meaning of the statute. This would mean that construction workers, like truck drivers, may perform services that are essential to the production and distribution of consumer goods. We may therefore assume in this case that High, the primary employer, is a producer within the meaning of the proviso. Indeed, we may assume here that the proviso's "coverage"—the types of primary disputes it allows to be publicized—is broad enough to include almost any primary dispute that might result in prohibited secondary activity.

The Court endorsed the view that "there is no suggestion either in the statute itself or in the legislative history that Congress intended the words 'product' and 'produced' to be words of special limitation."

Although, therefore, the relationship of High and Wilson was apparently conceded to fall within the "producer-distributor" relationship contemplated by the proviso, the Court held that the proviso could not be stretched so far as to shelter handbilling directed as well against DeBartolo and all of the other business tenants of the shopping mall. To treat DeBartolo and the cotenants as vulnerable to the handbilling because they all "symbiotically" derived benefit from High's construction work "would almost strip the distribution requirement of its limiting effect. * * * [T]he handbills at issue in this case did not merely call for a boycott of Wilson's products; they also called for a boycott of the products being sold by Wilson's cotenants. Neither DeBartolo nor any of the cotenants has any business relationship with High. Nor do they sell any products whose chain of production can reasonably be said to include High. Since there is no justification for treating the products that the cotenants distribute to the public as products produced by High, the Board erred in concluding that the handbills came within the protection of the publicity proviso."

[For a later phase of this case, see page 609, supra.]

---

## PROBLEM FOR DISCUSSION

The Warehouse Workers Union represents the employees of Unibooze, a beer distributor. Unibooze has insisted, in bargaining with the union, that retailers should be allowed to pick up directly at its warehouse rather than to have deliveries made by Unibooze employees. The union organized a demonstration at The Watering Whole, the area's largest beer retailer. Approximately 60–80 union members lined up to purchase small items—chips, single cans of beer, lottery tickets—with $20 bills. As soon as one purchase was made, the purchaser returned to the end of the line to make another small purchase. This tactic kept the store continuously occupied from 5:15 to 5:45 p.m., ordinarily the store's busiest hour. Unibooze—but not The Watering Whole—has filed a charge of violation of section 8(b)(4)(ii)(B) and the Regional Director has issued a complaint and sought an injunction under section 10(*l*). How should the court rule? See Pye v. Teamsters Local 122, 875 F.Supp. 921 (D.Mass.), aff'd, 61 F.3d 1013 (1st Cir.1995).

---

## NLRB v. Fruit & Vegetable Packers & Warehousemen, Local 760 [Tree Fruits]

377 U.S. 58, 84 S.Ct. 1063, 12 L.Ed.2d 129 (1964).

■ Mr. Justice Brennan delivered the opinion of the Court.

* * * The question in this case is whether the respondent unions violated [Section 8(b)(4)(ii)(B) of the NLRB as amended] when they limited their secondary picketing of retail stores to an appeal to the customers of the stores not to buy the products of certain firms against which one of the respondents was on strike.

Respondent Local 760 called a strike against fruit packers and warehousemen doing business in Yakima, Washington.[2] The struck firms sold Washington State apples to the Safeway chain of retail stores in and about Seattle, Washington. Local 760, aided by respondent Joint Council, instituted a consumer boycott against the apples in support of the strike. They placed pickets who walked back and forth before the customers' entrances of 46 Safeway stores in Seattle. The pickets—two at each of 45 stores and three at the 46th store—wore placards and distributed handbills which appealed to Safeway customers, and to the public generally, to refrain from buying Washington State apples, which were only one of numerous food products sold in the stores. Before the pickets appeared at any store, a letter was delivered to the store manager informing him that the picketing was only an appeal to his customers not to buy Washington State apples, and that the pickets were being expressly instructed "to patrol peacefully in front of the consumer entrances of the store, to stay away from the delivery entrances and not to interfere with the work of your employees, or with deliveries to or pickups from your store." A copy of written instructions to the pickets—which included the explicit statement that "you are also forbidden to request that the customers not patronize the store"—was enclosed with the letter. Since it was desired to assure Safeway employees that they were not to cease work, and to avoid any interference with pickups or deliveries, the pickets appeared after the stores opened for business and departed before the stores closed. At all times during the picketing, the store employees continued to work, and no deliveries or pickups were obstructed. Washington State apples were handled in normal course by both Safeway employees and the employees of other employers involved. Ingress and egress by customers and others was not interfered with in any manner.

[The NLRB found the union's conduct to violate § 8(b)(4), which the Board read to bar all consumer picketing in front of a secondary establishment. The Court of Appeals set aside the Board's order, holding that Safeway could not be "coerced" unless the picketing had a substantial economic impact on its business.]

The Board's reading of the statute—that the legislative history and the phrase "other than picketing" in the proviso reveal a congressional purpose to outlaw all picketing directed at customers at a secondary site—necessarily rested on the finding that Congress determined that such picketing always threatens, coerces or restrains the secondary employer. We therefore have a special responsibility to examine the legislative history for confirmation that Congress made that determination. Throughout the history of federal regulation of labor relations, Congress has consistently refused to prohibit peaceful picketing except where it is used as a means to achieve specific ends which experience has shown are undesirable. "In the

---

**2.** The firms, 24 in number, are members of the Tree Fruits Labor Relations Committee, Inc., which acts as the members' agent in labor disputes and in collective bargaining with unions which represent employees of the members. The strike was called in a dispute over terms of the renewal of a collective bargaining agreement.

sensitive area of peaceful picketing Congress has dealt explicitly with isolated evils which experience has established flow from such picketing." National Labor Relations Board v. Drivers etc. Local Union, 362 U.S. 274, 284, 80 S.Ct. 706, 712, 4 L.Ed.2d 710. We have recognized this congressional practice and have not ascribed to Congress a purpose to outlaw peaceful picketing unless "there is the clearest indication in the legislative history," ibid., that Congress intended to do so as regards the particular ends of the picketing under review. Both the congressional policy and our adherence to this principle of interpretation reflect concern that a broad ban against peaceful picketing might collide with the guarantees of the First Amendment.

We have examined the legislative history of the amendments to § 8(b)(4), and conclude that it does not reflect with the requisite clarity a congressional plan to proscribe all peaceful consumer picketing at secondary sites, and, particularly, any concern with peaceful picketing when it is limited, as here, to persuading Safeway customers not to buy Washington State apples when they traded in the Safeway stores. All that the legislative history shows in the way of an "isolated evil" believed to require proscription of peaceful consumer picketing at secondary sites was its use to persuade the customers of the secondary employer to cease trading with him in order to force him to cease dealing with, or to put pressure upon, the primary employer. This narrow focus reflects the difference between such conduct, and peaceful picketing at the secondary site directed only at the struck product. In the latter case, the union's appeal to the public is confined to its dispute with the primary employer, since the public is not asked to withhold its patronage from the secondary employer, but only to boycott the primary employer's goods. On the other hand, a union appeal to the public at the secondary site not to trade at all with the secondary employer goes beyond the goods of the primary employer, and seeks the public's assistance in forcing the secondary employer to cooperate with the union in its primary dispute.[7] This is not to say that this distinction was expressly alluded to in the debates. It is to say, however, that the consumer picketing carried on in this case is not attended by the abuses at which the statute was directed.

The story of the 1959 amendments, which we have detailed at greater length in our opinion filed today in National Labor Relations Board v.

---

**7.** The distinction between picketing a secondary employer merely to "follow the struck goods," and picketing designed to result in a generalized loss of patronage, was well established in the state cases by 1940. The distinction was sometimes justified on the ground that the secondary employer, who was presumed to receive a competitive benefit from the primary employer's nonunion, and hence lower, wage scales, was in "unity of interest" with the primary employer, Goldfinger v. Feintuch, 276 N.Y. 281, 286, 11 N.E.2d 910, 116 A.L.R. 477; Newark Ladder & Bracket Sales Co. v. Furniture Workers Union Local 66, 125 N.J.Eq. 99, 4 A.2d 49; Johnson v. Milk Drivers & Dairy Employees Union, Local 854, 195 So. 791 (Ct.App.La.), and sometimes on the ground that picketing restricted to the primary employer's product is "a primary boycott against the merchandise." Chiate v. United Cannery Agricultural Packing and Allied Workers of America, 2 CCH Lab.Cas. 125, 126 (Cal.Super.Ct.). See I Teller, Labor Disputes and Collective Bargaining § 123 (1940).

Servette, Inc., 377 U.S. 46, 84 S.Ct. 1098, 12 L.Ed.2d 121, begins with the original § 8(b)(4) of the Taft–Hartley Act. Its prohibition, in pertinent part, was confined to the inducing or encouraging of "the employees of any employer to engage in, a strike or a concerted refusal * * * [to] handle * * * any goods * * * " of a primary employer. This proved to be inept language. Three major loopholes were revealed. Since only inducement of "employees" was proscribed, direct inducement of a supervisor or the secondary employer by threats of labor trouble was not prohibited. Since only a "strike or concerted refusal" was prohibited, pressure upon a single employee was not forbidden. Finally, railroads, airlines and municipalities were not "employers" under the Act and therefore inducement or encouragement of their employees was not unlawful. * * *

[Justice Brennan examined the history of the 1959 legislation in the Senate. He observed that the bills which did pass the Senate in prior years contained no amendments to Section 8(b)(4), and that the proposals of certain individual Senators were not designed to curb consumer picketing.]

The House history * * * confirms our conclusion. From the outset the House legislation included provisions concerning secondary boycotts. The Landrum–Griffin bill, which was ultimately passed by the House, embodied the Eisenhower Administration's proposals as to secondary boycotts. The initial statement of Congressman Griffin in introducing the bill which bears his name, contains no reference to consumer picketing in the list of abuses which he thought required the secondary boycott amendments. Later in the House debates he did discuss consumer picketing, but only in the context of its abuse when directed against shutting off the patronage of a secondary employer.

In the debates before passage of the House bill he stated that the amendments applied to consumer picketing of customer entrances to retail stores selling goods manufactured by a concern under strike, if the picketing were designed to "coerce or to restrain the employer of [the] second establishment, to get him not to do business with the manufacturer * * *," and further that, "of course, this bill and any other bill is limited by the constitutional right of free speech. If the purpose of the picketing is to *coerce the retailer not to do business* with the manufacturer—then such a boycott could be stopped." (Italics supplied.)

* * * There is thus nothing in the legislative history prior to the convening of the Conference Committee which shows any congressional concern with consumer picketing beyond that with the "isolated evil" of its use to cut off the business of a secondary employer as a means of forcing him to stop doing business with the primary employer. When Congress meant to bar picketing *per se,* it made its meaning clear; for example, § 8(b)(7) makes it an unfair labor practice, "to picket or cause to be picketed * * * any employer * * *." In contrast, the prohibition of § 8(b)(4) is keyed to the coercive nature of the conduct, whether it be picketing or otherwise.

Senator Kennedy presided over the Conference Committee. He and Congressman Thompson prepared a joint analysis of the Senate and House bills. This analysis pointed up the First Amendment implications of the broad language in the House revisions of § 8(b)(4) stating,

> "The prohibition [of the House bill] reaches not only picketing but leaflets, radio broadcasts and newspaper advertisements, thereby interfering with freedom of speech.

> "* * * one of the apparent purposes of the amendment is to prevent unions from appealing to the general public as consumers for assistance in a labor dispute. This is a basic infringement upon freedom of expression."

This analysis was the first step in the development of the publicity proviso, but nothing in the legislative history of the proviso alters our conclusion that Congress did not clearly express an intention that amended § 8(b)(4) should prohibit all consumer picketing. Because of the sweeping language of the House bill, and its implications for freedom of speech, the Senate conferees refused to accede to the House proposal without safeguards for the right of unions to appeal to the public, even by some conduct which might be "coercive." The result was the addition of the proviso. But it does not follow from the fact that some coercive conduct was protected by the proviso, that the exception "other than picketing" indicates that Congress had determined that all consumer picketing was coercive.

No Conference Report was before the Senate when it passed the compromise bill, and it had the benefit only of Senator Kennedy's statement of the purpose of the proviso. He said that the proviso preserved "the right to appeal to consumers by methods other than picketing asking them to refrain from buying goods made by nonunion labor *and* to refrain from trading with a retailer who sells such goods. * * * We were not able to persuade the House conferees to permit picketing in front of that secondary shop, but were able to persuade them to agree that the unions shall be free to conduct informational activity short of picketing. In other words, the union can hand out handbills at the shop * * * and can carry on all publicity short of having ambulatory picketing * * *." (Italics supplied.) This explanation does not compel the conclusion that the Conference Agreement contemplated prohibiting any consumer picketing at a secondary site beyond that which urges the public, in Senator Kennedy's words, to "refrain from trading with a retailer who sells such goods." To read into the Conference Agreement, on the basis of a single statement, an intention to prohibit all consumer picketing at a secondary site would depart from our practice of respecting the congressional policy not to prohibit peaceful picketing except to curb "isolated evils" spelled out by the Congress itself.

Peaceful consumer picketing to shut off all trade with the secondary employer unless he aids the union in its dispute with the primary employer, is poles apart from such picketing which only persuades his customers not to buy the struck product. The proviso indicates no more than that the Senate conferees' constitutional doubts led Congress to authorize publicity other than picketing which persuades the customers of a secondary employer to stop all trading with him, but not such publicity which has the effect of cutting off his deliveries or inducing his employees to cease work. On the other hand, picketing which persuades the customers of a secondary employer to stop all trading with him was also to be barred. * * *

We come then to the question whether the picketing in this case, confined as it was to persuading customers to cease buying the product of the primary employer, falls within the area of secondary consumer picketing which Congress did clearly indicate its intention to prohibit under § 8(b)(4)(ii). We hold that it did not fall within that area, and therefore did not "threaten, coerce, or restrain" Safeway. While any diminution in Safeway's purchases of apples due to a drop in consumer demand might be said to be a result which causes respondents' picketing to fall literally within the statutory prohibition, "it is a familiar rule that a thing may be within the letter of the statute and yet not within the statute, because not within its spirit nor within the intention of the makers." Holy Trinity Church v. United States, 143 U.S. 457, 459, 12 S.Ct. 511, 512, 36 L.Ed. 226. See United States v. American Trucking Ass'ns, 310 U.S. 534, 543–544, 60 S.Ct. 1059, 1063–1064, 84 L.Ed. 1345. When consumer picketing is employed only to persuade customers not to buy the struck product, the union's appeal is closely confined to the primary dispute. The site of the appeal is expanded to include the premises of the secondary employer, but if the appeal succeeds, the secondary employers' purchases from the struck firms are decreased only because the public has diminished its purchases of the struck product. On the other hand, when consumer picketing is employed to persuade customers not to trade at all with the secondary employer, the latter stops buying the struck product, not because of a falling demand, but in response to pressure designed to inflict injury on his business generally. In such case, the union does more than merely follow the struck product; it creates a separate dispute with the secondary employer.

We disagree therefore with the Court of Appeals that the test of "to threaten, coerce, or restrain" for the purposes of this case is whether Safeway suffered or was likely to suffer economic loss. A violation of § 8(b)(4)(ii)(B) would not be established, merely because respondents' picketing was effective to reduce Safeway's sales of Washington State apples, even if this led or might lead Safeway to drop the item as a poor seller.

The judgment of the Court of Appeals is vacated and the case is remanded with direction to enter judgment setting aside the Board's order. It is so ordered.

■ Mr. Justice Douglas took no part in the consideration or decision of this case.

■ Mr. Justice Black, concurring.

Because of the language of § 8(b)(4)(ii)(B) of the National Labor Relations Act and the legislative history set out in the opinions of the Court and of my Brother Harlan, I feel impelled to hold that Congress, in passing this section of the Act, intended to forbid the striking employees of one business to picket the premises of a neutral business where the purpose of the picketing is to persuade customers of the neutral business not to buy goods supplied by the struck employer. Construed in this way, as I agree with Brother Harlan that it must be, I believe, contrary to his view, that the section abridges freedom of speech and press in violation of the First Amendment. * * *

In short, we have neither a case in which picketing is banned because the picketers are asking others to do something unlawful nor a case in which *all* picketing is, for reasons of public order, banned. Instead, we have a case in which picketing, otherwise lawful, is banned only when the picketers express particular views. The result is an abridgment of the freedom of these picketers to tell a part of the public their side of a labor controversy, a subject the free discussion of which is protected by the First Amendment.

I cannot accept my Brother Harlan's view that the abridgment of speech and press here does not violate the First Amendment because other methods of communication are left open. This reason for abridgment strikes me as being on a par with holding that governmental suppression of a newspaper in a city would not violate the First Amendment because there continue to be radio and television stations. First Amendment freedoms can no more validly be taken away by degrees than by one fell swoop.

■ Mr. Justice Harlan, whom Mr. Justice Stewart joins, dissenting. * * *

Nothing in the statute lends support to the fine distinction which the Court draws between general and limited product picketing. The enactment speaks pervasively of "threatening, coercing, or restraining any person"; the proviso differentiates only between modes of expression, not between types of secondary consumer picketing. For me, the Court's argument to the contrary is very unconvincing.

The difference to which the Court points between a secondary employer merely lowering his purchases of the struck product to the degree of decreased consumer demand and such an employer ceasing to purchase one product because of consumer refusal to buy any products, is surely too refined in the context of reality. It can hardly be supposed that in all, or even most, instances the result of the type of picketing involved here will be simply that suggested by the Court. Because of the very nature of picketing there may be numbers of persons who will refuse to buy at all from a picketed store, either out of economic or social conviction or because they prefer to shop where they need not brave a picket line. Moreover, the public can hardly be expected always to know or ascertain the precise scope of a particular picketing operation. Thus in cases like this, the effect on the secondary employer may not always be limited to a decrease in his sales of the struck product. And even when that is the effect, the employer may, rather than simply reducing purchases from the primary employer, deem it more expedient to turn to another producer whose product is approved by the union.

The distinction drawn by the majority becomes even more tenuous if a picketed retailer depends largely or entirely on sales of the struck product.

If, for example, an independent gas station owner sells gasoline purchased from a struck gasoline company, one would not suppose he would feel less threatened, coerced, or restrained by picket signs which said "Do not buy X gasoline" than by signs which said "Do not patronize this gas station." To be sure Safeway is a multiple article seller, but it cannot well be gainsaid that the rule laid down by the Court would be unworkable if its applicability turned on a calculation of the relation between total income of the secondary employer and income from the struck product.

The Court informs us that "Peaceful consumer picketing to shut off all trade with the secondary employer unless he aids the union in its dispute with the primary employer, is poles apart from such picketing which only persuades his customers not to buy the struck product." The difference was, it is stated, "well established in the state cases by 1940," that is before the present federal enactment. In light of these assertions, it is indeed remarkable that the Court not only substantially acknowledges that the statutory language does not itself support this distinction but cites no report of Congress, no statement of a legislator, not even the view of any of the many commentators in the area, in any way casting doubt on the applicability of § 8(b)(4)(ii)(B) to picketing of the kind involved here.

The Court's distinction fares no better when the legislative history of § 8(b)(4)(ii)(B) is examined. Even though there is no Senate, House, or Conference Report which sheds light on the matter, that hardly excuses the Court blinding itself to what the legislative and other background materials do show. Fairly assessed they, in my opinion, belie Congress' having made the distinction upon which the Court's thesis rests. Nor can the Court find comfort in the generalization that " 'In the sensitive area of peaceful picketing Congress has dealt explicitly with isolated evils which experience has established flow from such picketing';" in enacting the provisions in question Congress *was* addressing itself to a particular facet of secondary boycotting not dealt with in prior legislation, namely, peaceful secondary consumer picketing. I now turn to the materials which illuminate what Congress had in mind.

It is clear that consumer picketing in connection with secondary boycotting was at the forefront of the problems which led to the amending of the Taft–Hartley Act by the Labor–Management Reporting and Disclosure Act of 1959. * * *

Reporting on the compromise reached by the Conference Committee on the Kennedy–Ervin and Landrum–Griffin bills, Senator Kennedy, who chaired the Conference Committee, stated:

> "[T]he House bill prohibited the union from carrying on any kind of activity to disseminate informational material to secondary sites. They could not say that there was a strike in a primary plant. * * * Under the language of the conference [ultimately resulting in present § 8(b)(4)(ii)(B) ]we agreed there would not be picketing at a secondary site. What was permitted was the giving out of handbills or information through the radio, and so forth." 105 Cong.Rec. 17720, II Leg.Hist. 1389. * * *

Senator Kennedy spoke further on the Conference bill and particularized the union rights protected by the Senate conferees:

"(c) The right to appeal to consumers by methods other than picketing asking them to refrain from buying goods made by nonunion labor and to refrain from trading with a retailer who sells such goods.

"Under the Landrum–Griffin bill it would have been impossible for a union to inform the customers of a secondary employer that that employer or store was selling goods which were made under racket conditions or sweatshop conditions, or in a plant where an economic strike was in progress. We were not able to persuade the House conferees to permit picketing in front of that secondary shop, but we were able to persuade them to agree that the union shall be free to conduct informational activity short of picketing. In other words, the union can hand out handbills at the shop, can place advertisements in newspapers, can make announcements over the radio, and can carry on all publicity short of having ambulatory picketing in front of a secondary site." 105 Cong.Rec. 17898–17899, II Leg.Hist. 1432.

The Court does not consider itself compelled by these remarks to conclude that the Conference Committee meant to prohibit *all* secondary consumer picketing. A fair reading of these comments, however, can hardly leave one seriously in doubt that Senator Kennedy believed this to be precisely what the Committee had done; the Court's added emphasis on the word "and" is, I submit, simply grasping at straws, if indeed the phrase relied on does not equally well lend itself to a disjunctive reading. * * *

Under my view of the statute the constitutional issue is therefore reached. Since the Court does not discuss it, I am content simply to state in summary form my reasons for believing that the prohibitions of § 8(b)(4)(ii)(B), as applied here, do not run afoul of constitutional limitations. This Court has long recognized that picketing is "inseparably something more [than] and different" from simple communication. Hughes v. Superior Court, 339 U.S. 460, 464, 70 S.Ct. 718, 721, 94 L.Ed. 985; see, e.g., Building Service Employees v. Gazzam, 339 U.S. 532, 537, 70 S.Ct. 784, 787, 94 L.Ed. 1045; Bakery Drivers v. Wohl, 315 U.S. 769, 776, 62 S.Ct. 816, 819, 86 L.Ed. 1178 (concurring opinion of DOUGLAS, J.). Congress has given careful and continued consideration to the problems of labor-management relations, and its attempts to effect an accommodation between the right of unions to publicize their position and the social desirability of limiting a form of communication likely to have effects caused by something apart from the message communicated, are entitled to great deference. The decision of Congress to prohibit secondary consumer picketing during labor disputes is, I believe, not inconsistent with the protections of the First Amendment, particularly when, as here, other methods of communication are left open.

Contrary to my BROTHER BLACK, I think the fact that Congress in prohibiting secondary consumer picketing has acted with a discriminating eye is the very thing that renders this provision invulnerable to constitutional attack. That Congress has permitted other picketing which is likely to have effects beyond those resulting from the "communicative" aspect of picketing does not, of course, in any way lend itself to the conclusion that Congress here has aimed to "prevent dissemination of information about the facts of a labor dispute." Even on the highly dubious assumption that the "non-speech" aspect of picketing is always the same whatever the particular context, the social consequences of the "non-communicative" aspect of picketing may certainly be thought desirable in the case of "primary" picketing and undesirable in the case of "secondary" picketing, a judgment Congress has indeed made in prohibiting secondary but not primary picketing.

I would enforce the Board's order.

––––––

# PROBLEM FOR DISCUSSION

Employees of Bond Bakery, represented by the Bakers Union, are on strike for higher wages. A representative of the Union approaches the manager of Acme Supermarket and requests that he cease stocking Bond Bread. The representative informs the manager that if he does not comply, the Union will distribute handbills in front of Acme to Acme customers. He shows the manager a sample handbill which reads: "Acme sells Bond Bread. Bond employees on strike. Do not patronize Acme Supermarket." The manager refuses to comply. The Union responds by distributing handbills only at customer entrances and by taking out a full-page advertisement in the local newspaper. This activity turns away customers and induces two deliverymen not to complete deliveries to Acme. Do any of the Union's activities violate Section 8(b)(4)(B)?

––––––

In NLRB v. Retail Store Employees Union, Local No. 1001 (Safeco Title Ins. Co.), 447 U.S. 607, 100 S.Ct. 2372, 65 L.Ed.2d 377 (1980), the Supreme Court retreated somewhat from the broad permission given in *Tree Fruits* to product picketing at the secondary site. Safeco Title Insurance Company did business with five small title companies, which searched land titles, performed escrow services and sold title insurance; over 90 percent of their gross incomes derived from the sale of Safeco insurance. When contract negotiations between Safeco and the Union reached an impasse, the employees went on strike and picketed not only at Safeco's office in Seattle but also at each of the five local title companies. Handbills (the legality of which was not contested) were distributed asking consumers to cancel their Safeco policies; the picket signs, which were challenged through charges under Section 8(b)(4)(ii)(B), declared that Safeco had no contract with the Union. The Board held that since the Safeco insurance policies accounted for substantially all of the title companies' business, the picketing was calculated to induce customers not to patronize the neutral title companies at all. The court of appeals, en banc, refused to enforce the

Board's order, holding that picketing appeals limited to the primary product were lawful, regardless of the severity of the consequences to the neutral. A divided Supreme Court reversed and remanded for enforcement of the Board's order.

The Court noted the distinction in *Tree Fruits* between picketing which shuts off all trade with the secondary employer unless that employer aids the union in its dispute with the primary employer, and picketing which merely persuades the customers of the secondary employer not to buy the struck product; the former is unlawful, but the latter is not. The Court observed, however, that in many instances the effects of product picketing and of a total secondary boycott may be the same; it gave the illustration of picketing appeals at a housing subdivision (the neutral) urging prospective purchasers not to buy the houses built by the primary employer, a general contractor. The Court concluded that in the clash of interests between the neutral employer and a union seeking to picket at a "one-product secondary site," Congress decided that the former should prevail. Unlike *Tree Fruits,* where the picketing was directed against one item of many being sold by the neutral retailer, and where the union's success would result in declining sales of only the boycotted product, "secondary picketing against consumption of the primary product [purveyed by the title companies, i.e., the Safeco insurance] leaves responsive consumers no realistic option other than to boycott the title companies altogether"; the title companies stop using Safeco insurance "not because of a falling demand, but in response to pressure designed to inflict injury on [their] business generally."

The Court majority therefore concluded: "Product picketing that reasonably can be expected to threaten neutral parties with ruin or substantial loss simply does not square with the language or the purpose of § 8(b)(4)(ii)(B). Since successful secondary picketing would put the title companies to a choice between their survival and the severance of their ties with Safeco, the picketing plainly violates the statutory ban on the coercion of neutrals" with the object of forcing them to cease doing business with the primary employer. The Court also concluded that such a statutory ban upon the total boycott of a neutral "imposes no impermissible restrictions upon constitutionally protected speech."

In a particularly significant footnote, the Court majority speculated on how its newly announced rule would be applied: "If secondary picketing were directed against a product representing a major portion of a neutral's business, but significantly less than that represented by a single dominant product, neither *Tree Fruits* nor today's decision necessarily would control. The critical question would be whether, by encouraging customers to reject the struck product, the secondary appeal is reasonably likely to threaten the neutral party with ruin or substantial loss. Resolution of the question in each case will be entrusted to the Board's expertise."

In separate concurring opinions, Justices Blackmun and Stevens, criticizing the perfunctory manner in which the Court majority had rejected the constitutional challenge, set forth more detailed reasons for so holding.

Justice Blackmun believed that Congress had given effect to substantial governmental interests by striking a "delicate balance between union freedom of expression and the ability of neutral employers, employees, and consumers to remain free from coerced participation in industrial strife." Justice Stevens emphasized the greater governmental freedom in regulating picketing than, for example, handbilling; the former depends more on the persuasiveness of the picket's physical presence and "calls for an automatic response to a signal, rather than a reasoned response to an idea." The Congressional ban sustained in this case is, moreover, limited in geographical scope and is "sufficiently justified by the purpose to avoid embroiling neutrals in a third party's labor dispute."

Justice Brennan dissented, for himself and Justices White and Marshall. He believed the product picketing at the title companies to have been lawful under *Tree Fruits,* since the appeal did not attempt to induce a boycott of any product originating from nonprimary sources. "The *Tree Fruits* test reflects the distinction between economic damage sustained by the secondary firm solely by virtue of its dependence upon the primary employer's goods, and injuries inflicted upon interests of the secondary firm that are unrelated to the primary dispute—injuries that are calculated to influence the secondary retailer's conduct with respect to the primary dispute." The latter pressure places the economic interests of the secondary employer in jeopardy beyond the extent of the risk it has assumed by handling the primary employer's product, and spreads the disruptive impact of the primary dispute even to other businesses which sell nonprimary products to the secondary retailer. Justice Brennan attempted to point out other failings in the Court's analysis: the extent of harm to the neutral's business, and hence the coercion to cease dealing with the primary, is not necessarily congruent with the percentage of the secondary firm's business made up by the primary product; a single-product retailer will be badly harmed economically by a successful primary boycott, even when there is no appeal at the neutral site at all; whatever the percentage of its business constituted by the primary product, the neutral "necessarily assumes the risks of interrupted supply or declining sales" flowing from the manufacturer's labor problems; and the vague standard announced by the Court leaves a union uncertain, at least without access to the neutral's balance sheets, whether its product boycott will be lawful.

---

## PROBLEMS FOR DISCUSSION

**1.** Is the Court's reasoning in *Safeco* intelligible? Why should it be unlawful to employ product picketing to inflict economic injury on the neutral retailer precisely comparable to that which would flow from a successful strike at the primary company? In any event, why aren't the local title companies "allies" of Safeco and thereby just as lawfully vulnerable to picketing as Safeco is? See pp. 641–45, *supra.*

**2.** Is the Court's standard in *Safeco* for lawful product picketing (absence of "ruin or substantial loss" for the neutral retailer) intelligible? What facts must be available to the union's counsel in order that he or she may provide sound advice on whether product picketing may be carried out at the secondary site? (Will those facts likely be available?) Considering that peaceful product picketing which is found unlawful under *Safeco* may be enjoined, and may lead to substantial compensatory damage awards under Section 303, is the vagueness of the Court's standard subject to serious challenge under the First Amendment to the Federal Constitution (an issue not directly addressed by the Court)?

**3.**   Examining the constitutional question from another angle, is it so clearly constitutional for the federal government to bar truthful informational picketing directed at business customers in a situation like Safeco's? Is there a difference for constitutional purposes when the issue relates not to a labor dispute but to a matter of political or social justice? See Comment, Secondary Boycotts and the First Amendment, 51 U.Chi.L.Rev. 811 (1984); Harper, The Consumer's Emerging Right to Boycott: *NAACP v. Claiborne Hardware* and its Implications for American Labor Law, 93 Yale L.J. 409 (1984); Note, Labor Picketing and Commercial Speech: Free Enterprise Values in the Doctrine of Free Speech, 91 Yale L.J. 938 (1982); St. Antoine, Free Speech or Economic Weapon?, The Persisting Problem of Picketing, 16 Suffolk U.L.Rev. 883 (1982).

**4.**   The United Steelworkers are on strike against the Bay Refining Division of Dow Chemical Co., which produces Bay Gasoline. The Steelworkers picket three gasoline stations which sell Bay Gas, carrying signs which read: "BOYCOTT BAY GAS" and "BAY GAS MADE BY SCABS." The three stations are owned by Central Michigan Petroleum, Inc., Rupp Oil Co., and Alexander, Inc., respectively. Dow does not own any interest in or exert any control over any of the three stations. The Central Michigan station earns 98% of its revenues from the sale of Bay Gas and other Dow products. The Rupp station is also a General Tire dealership and earns 85% of its revenues from the sale of Dow products. The Alexander station is also a General Tire dealership and in addition sells another brand of fuel; 60% of its revenues are earned from the sale of gas, and 75% of gas sales are sales of Bay Gas. Does the picketing of any or all of these stations violate Section 8(b)(4)(B)? See Local 14055, United Steelworkers v. NLRB (Dow Chemical Co.), 524 F.2d 853 (D.C.Cir.1975), vacated and remanded, 429 U.S. 807, 97 S.Ct. 42, 50 L.Ed.2d 68 (1976), complaint dismissed, 229 NLRB 302 (1977).

**5.**   Could a union engaged in a dispute with a refrigeration company lawfully picket in front of the customer entrances of a supermarket, if the supermarket utilizes the services of the company to install and repair refrigeration facilities? See Local 142, Plumbers Union, 133 NLRB 307 (1961).

Would it be legal for that supermarket to be picketed by striking employees of the company which supplies the supermarket with paper bags? How should the picket signs be worded to maximize the union's chances for success? See Kroger Co. v. NLRB, 647 F.2d 634 (6th Cir.1980).

Would it be lawful for that supermarket to be picketed by employees who are on strike against a meat processing company, and whose picket signs state that "scab meat" is part of the hamburgers and sausages being sold in the supermarket meat department? (Could those pickets also station themselves in front of several McDonald's fast-food stores?) Compare Amalgamated Packinghouse Workers (Packerland Packing Co.), 218 NLRB 853 (1975), with Local 248, Meat Cutters (Milwaukee Meat Packers Ass'n), 230 NLRB 189 (1977).

# Edward J. DeBartolo Corp. v. Florida Gulf Coast Bldg. & Constr. Trades Council

485 U.S. 568, 108 S.Ct. 1392, 99 L.Ed.2d 645 (1988).

[The Court applied its decisions in *Tree Fruits* and *Safeco* and, because of constitutional concerns, narrowly construed section 8(b)(4)(ii)(B) so as not to bar customer *handbilling* at a secondary site. The text of the Court's opinion is set forth at pages 596 et seq. supra.]

---

## PROBLEMS FOR DISCUSSION

**1.** The Court in *DeBartolo* read the publicity proviso to Section 8(b)(4)(B) to be merely explanatory of the reach of the secondary-boycott ban in the area of consumer appeals; the proviso essentially reiterated a permission for handbilling that would have been elicited from an informed reading of the ban itself. Is that the usual, and natural, function that is served by a statutory proviso? Compare it to the publicity proviso to Section 8(b)(7) on recognition picketing, as significantly interpreted by the Board in the so-called *Crown Cafeteria* case, at page 625 supra. There, the Board interpreted the proviso to shelter conduct that would, in the absence of the proviso, have fallen within the ban of the basic language of the section; the proviso, in other words, was not merely explanatory but played the important substantive function of immunizing otherwise proscribed conduct. Should the approach to statutory analysis of the Supreme Court in *DeBartolo* be understood to discredit the Board's analysis in *Crown Cafeteria?*

**2.** It is obvious from the legislative history of the 1959 amendments to Section 8(b)(4) that union appeals to consumers at secondary sites were targeted by Congress for significant limitations. Now, after *Tree Fruits* and *DeBartolo,* such proscribed appeals appear to be limited to those carried out by picketing urging a total ban on business with the secondary employer; product-specific picketing appeals, and all other forms of communication at the secondary site (even urging a total boycott there), have been found not to fall within the statutory ban (so that even the publicity proviso is essentially unnecessary to achieve this objective). Does the Court's reading of the Act thus leave in the hands of unions such a wide variety of secondary consumer appeals as effectively to render the 1959 consumer amendments impotent?

---

## 3. HOT CARGO CLAUSES[f]

Suppose that the Teamsters Union succeeded in persuading all the trucking concerns in a given area to agree that they would not require their

---

f. See Carney & Florsheim, Treatment of Refusals to Cross Picket Lines: "By-Paths and Crookt Ways," 55 Cornell L.Q. 940 (1970); Feldacker, Subcontracting Restrictions and the Scope of Sections 8(b)(4)(A) and (B) and of 8(e) of the National Labor Relations Act, 17 Lab.L.J. 170 (1966); Hickey, Subcontracting Clauses Under Section 8(e) of the NLRA, 40 Notre Dame Lawyer 377 (1965); Lesnick, Job Security and Secondary Boycotts: The Reach of NLRA §§ 8(b)(4) and 8(e), 113 U.Pa.L.Rev. 1000 (1965); Note, A

employees to handle the goods of any employer who became involved in a labor dispute. If a labor dispute arose involving the ABC Furniture Store, would it be an unfair labor practice for the Teamsters to induce the trucking employees to refuse to handle ABC furniture in view of the agreements signed with their employers? For six or seven years, these "hot cargo" agreements were held to legitimize the secondary boycott, but in 1957 the Supreme Court held that such clauses could not serve as a valid defense in a case such as the one just described. LOCAL 1976, UNITED BROTH. OF CARPENTERS & JOINERS v. NLRB (SAND DOOR & PLYWOOD CO.), 357 U.S. 93, 78 S.Ct. 1011, 2 L.Ed.2d 1186 (1958). On the other hand, said the Court, if the truckers were to abide by their agreements voluntarily, without the Teamsters having to induce their employees not to work, there would be only a primary boycott rather than a violation of the Taft–Hartley Act.

Many observers felt that this was an impractical distinction. The effect upon the furniture company was the same whether or not the union induced the employees of the truckers not to handle the goods. Furthermore, one might wonder how voluntary was the truckers' participation in the primary boycott. Would a "hot cargo" agreement have been signed in the first place except under pressure from the Teamsters, and if a trucker should abide by the agreement when the occasion arose, was this not so because it feared that if it did not comply the Teamsters would be more demanding in the next negotiations or might remind the trucker of its failure to perform its part of the contract whenever it asked the union to help put a stop to a wildcat strike? The only way to deal with such pressures was to nip them in the bud by prohibiting the agreements themselves. This was the theory upon which the Senate voted to outlaw "hot cargo" contracts in the trucking industry during the deliberations preceding the 1959 amendments to the NLRA. In the House the prohibition was extended to all agreements by which an employer agrees with a labor organization not to handle or use the goods of another person. Eventually, a decision was reached to enact what is now Section 8(e) of the National Labor Relations Act.

---

## National Woodwork Mfr's Ass'n v. NLRB

386 U.S. 612, 87 S.Ct. 1250, 18 L.Ed.2d 357 (1967).

■ MR. JUSTICE BRENNAN delivered the opinion of the Court.

* * *

Rational Approach to Secondary Boycotts and Work Preservation, 57 Va.L.Rev. 1280 (1971); Note, Clarifying the Work Preservation/Work Acquisition Dichotomy Under Sections 8(b)(4)(B) and 8(e) of the NLRA, 35 Cath. U.L.Rev. 1061 (1986); St. Antoine, Secondary Boycotts and Hot Cargo: A Study in Balance of Power, 40 U.Det.L.J. 189 (1962); Shalov, The Landrum–Griffin Amendments: Labor's Use of the Secondary Boycott, 45 Corn.L.Q. 724 (1960).

Frouge Corporation, a Bridgeport, Connecticut concern, was the general contractor on a housing project in Philadelphia. Frouge had a collective bargaining agreement with the Carpenters' International Union under which Frouge agreed to be bound by the rules and regulations agreed upon by local unions with contractors in areas in which Frouge had jobs. Frouge was therefore subject to the provision of a collective bargaining agreement between the Union and an organization of Philadelphia contractors, the General Building Contractors Association, Inc. A sentence in a provision of that agreement entitled Rule 17 provides that " * * * no member of the District Council will handle * * * any doors * * * which have been fitted prior to being furnished on the job. * * * "Frouge's Philadelphia project called for 3,600 doors. Customarily, before the doors could be hung on such projects, "blank" or "blind" doors would be mortised for the knob, routed for the hinges, and beveled to make them fit between jambs. These are tasks traditionally performed in the Philadelphia area by the carpenters employed on the jobsite. However, precut and prefitted doors ready to hang may be purchased from door manufacturers. Although Frouge's contract and job specifications did not call for premachined doors, and "blank" or "blind" doors could have been ordered, Frouge contracted for the purchase of premachined doors from a Pennsylvania door manufacturer which is a member of the National Woodwork Manufacturers Association, petitioner in No. 110 and respondent in No. 111. The Union ordered its carpenter members not to hang the doors when they arrived at the jobsite. Frouge thereupon withdrew the prefabricated doors and substituted "blank" doors which were fitted and cut by his carpenters on the job-site.

The National Woodwork Manufacturers Association and another filed charges with the National Labor Relations Board against the Union alleging that by including the "will not handle" sentence of Rule 17 in the collective bargaining agreement the Union committed the unfair labor practice under § 8(e) of entering into an "agreement * * * whereby * * * [the] * * * employer * * * agrees to cease or refrain from handling * * * any of the products of any other employer * * *," and alleging further that in enforcing the sentence against Frouge, the Union committed the unfair labor practice under § 8(b)(4)(B) of "forcing or requiring any person to cease using * * * the products of any other * * * manufacturer * * *." The National Labor Relations Board dismissed the charges, 149 N.L.R.B. 646. The Board adopted the findings of the Trial Examiner that the "will not handle" sentence in Rule 17 was language used by the parties to protect and preserve cutting out and fitting as unit work to be performed by the jobsite carpenters. * * * The Court of Appeals for the Seventh Circuit reversed the Board. * * * We granted certiorari. * * *

## I.

Even on the doubtful premise that the words of § 8(e) unambiguously embrace the sentence of Rule 17, this does not end inquiry into Congress' purpose in enacting the section. It is a "familiar rule, that a thing may be within the letter of the statute and yet not within the statute, because not within its spirit nor within the intention of its makers." Holy Trinity

Church v. United States, 143 U.S. 457, 459, 12 S.Ct. 511, 512, 36 L.Ed. 226.
* * *

Strongly held opposing views have invariably marked controversy over labor's use of the boycott to further its aims by involving an employer in disputes not his own. But congressional action to deal with such conduct has stopped short of proscribing identical activity having the object of pressuring the employer for agreements regulating relations between him and his own employees. That Congress meant §§ 8(e) and 8(b)(4)(B) to prohibit only "secondary" objectives clearly appears from an examination of the history of congressional action on the subject; we may, by such an examination, "reconstitute the gamut of values current at the time when the words were uttered."

[The Court then traced the outlawry of the secondary boycott under the Sherman Act, its protection under the Norris–LaGuardia Act, and its outlawry once again under what is now Section 8(b)(4)(B); it emphasized that the latter section was directed at the secondary boycott as conventionally defined, that is, union pressure on a "neutral" employer to induce it to cease doing business with a "primary" employer with whom the union has its dispute.]

Despite this virtually overwhelming support for the limited reading of § 8(b)(4)(A), the Woodwork Manufacturers Association relies on Allen–Bradley Co. v. Local Union No. 3, etc., Electrical Workers, 325 U.S. 797, 65 S.Ct. 1533, as requiring that the successor section, § 8(b)(4)(B), be read as proscribing the District Council's conduct in enforcing the "will not handle" sentence of Rule 17 against Frouge. The Association points to the references to *Allen–Bradley* in the legislative debates leading to the enactment of the predecessor § 8(b)(4)(A). We think that this is an erroneous reading of the legislative history. *Allen–Bradley* held violative of the antitrust laws a combination between Local 3 of the International Brotherhood of Electrical Workers and both electrical contractors and manufacturers of electrical fixtures in New York City to restrain the bringing in of such equipment from outside the city. The contractors obligated themselves to confine their purchases to local manufacturers, who in turn obligated themselves to confine their New York City sales to contractors employing members of the local, this scheme supported by threat of boycott by the contractors' employees. While recognizing that the union might have had an immunity for its contribution to the trade boycott had it acted alone, citing *Hutcheson*, supra, the Court held immunity was not intended by the Clayton or Norris–LaGuardia Acts in cases in which the union's activity was part of a larger conspiracy to abet contractors and manufacturers to create a monopoly.

The argument that the references to *Allen–Bradley* in the debates over § 8(b)(4)(A) have broader significance in the determination of the reach of that section is that there was no intent on Local 3's part to influence the internal labor policies of the boycotted out-of-state manufacturers of electrical equipment. There are three answers to this argument: *First,* the boycott of out-of-state electrical equipment by the electrical contractors' employees was not in pursuance of any objective relating to pressuring their employers in the matter of *their* wages, hours, and working conditions; there was no work preservation or other primary objective related to the union employees' relations with their contractor employers. On the contrary, the object of the boycott was to secure benefits for the New York City electrical manufacturers and their employees. "This is a secondary object because the cessation of business was being used tactically, with an eye to its effect on conditions elsewhere." *Second,* and of even greater significance on the question of the inferences to be drawn from the references to *Allen–Bradley,* Senator Taft regarded the Local 3 boycott as in effect saying, "We will not permit any material made by any other union or by any non-union workers to come into New York City and be put into any building in New York City." 93 Cong.Rec. 4199, II 1947 Leg.Hist. 1107. This clearly shows that the Senator viewed the pressures applied by Local 3 on the employers of its members as having solely a secondary objective. The Senate Committee Report echoes the same view:

> "[It is] an unfair labor practice for a union to engage in the type of secondary boycott that has been conducted in New York City by local No. 3 of the IBEW, whereby electricians have refused to install electrical products of manufacturers employing electricians who are members of *some other labor organization other than local No. 3.*" S.Rep. No. 105, 80th Cong., 1st Sess., 22, I 1947 Leg.Hist. 428. (Emphasis supplied.)

Other statements on the floor of Congress repeat the same refrain. *Third,* even on the premise that Congress meant to prohibit boycotts such as that in *Allen–Bradley* without regard to whether they were carried on to affect labor conditions elsewhere, the fact is that the boycott in *Allen–Bradley* was carried on not as a shield to preserve the jobs of Local 3 members, traditionally a primary labor activity, but as a sword, to reach out and monopolize all the manufacturing job tasks for Local 3 members. It is arguable that Congress may have viewed the use of the boycott as a sword as different from labor's traditional concerns with wages, hours, and working conditions. But the boycott in the present case was not used as a sword; it was a shield carried solely to preserve the members' jobs. We therefore have no occasion today to decide the questions which might arise where the workers carry on a boycott to reach out to monopolize jobs or acquire new job tasks when their own jobs are not threatened by the boycotted product. * * *

In effect Congress, in enacting § 8(b)(4)(A) of the Taft–Hartley Act, returned to the regime of *Duplex Printing Press Co.* and *Bedford Stone Cutters,* supra, and barred as a secondary boycott union activity directed against a neutral employer, including the immediate employer when in fact the activity directed against him was carried on for its effect elsewhere.

Indeed, Congress in rewriting § 8(b)(4)(A) as § 8(b)(4)(B) took pains to confirm the limited application of the section to such "secondary" conduct. The word "concerted" in former § 8(b)(4)(A) was deleted to reach secondary conduct directed to only one individual. This was in response to the

Court's holding in National Labor Relations Board v. International Rice Milling Co., 341 U.S. 665, 71 S.Ct. 961, that "concerted" required proof of inducement of two or more employees. But to make clear that the deletion was not to be read as supporting a construction of the statute as prohibiting the incidental effects of traditional primary activity, Congress added the proviso that nothing in the amended section "shall be construed to make unlawful, where not otherwise unlawful, any primary strike or primary picketing." Many statements and examples proffered in the 1959 debates confirm this congressional acceptance of the distinction between primary and secondary activity.

## II.

The Landrum–Griffin Act amendments in 1959 were adopted only to close various loopholes in the application of § 8(b)(4)(A) which had been exposed in Board and court decisions. * * *

Section 8(e) simply closed still another loophole. In Local 1976, United Brotherhood of Carpenters, etc. v. National Labor Relations Board (Sand Door), 357 U.S. 93, 78 S.Ct. 1011, the Court held that it was no defense to an unfair labor practice charge under § 8(b)(4)(A) that the struck employer had agreed, in a contract with the union, not to handle nonunion material. However, the Court emphasized that the mere execution of such a contract provision (known as a "hot cargo" clause because of its prevalence in Teamsters Union contracts), or its voluntary observance by the employer, was not unlawful under § 8(b)(4)(A). Section 8(e) was designed to plug this gap in the legislation by making the "hot cargo" clause itself unlawful. The *Sand Door* decision was believed by Congress not only to create the possibility of damage actions against employers for breaches of "hot cargo" clauses, but also to create a situation in which such clauses might be employed to exert subtle pressures upon employers to engage in "voluntary" boycotts. Hearings in late 1958 before the Senate Select Committee explored seven cases of "hot cargo" clauses in Teamster union contracts, the use of which the Committee found conscripted neutral employers in Teamster organizational campaigns.

This loophole closing measure likewise did not expand the type of conduct which § 8(b)(4)(A) condemned. Although the language of § 8(e) is sweeping, it closely tracks that of § 8(b)(4)(A), and just as the latter and its successor § 8(b)(4)(B) did not reach employees' activity to pressure their employer to preserve for themselves work traditionally done by them, § 8(e) does not prohibit agreements made and maintained for that purpose.

The legislative history of § 8(e) confirms this conclusion. The Kennedy–Ervin bill as originally reported proposed no remedy for abuses of the "hot cargo" clauses revealed at the hearings of the Select Committee. Senators Goldwater and Dirksen filed a minority report urging that a prohibition against "hot cargo" clauses should be enacted to close that loophole. Their statement expressly acknowledged their acceptance of the reading of § 8(b)(4)(A) as applicable only "to protect genuinely neutral employers and their employees, not themselves involved in a labor dispute, against economic coercion designed to give a labor union victory in a dispute with some other employer." They argued that a prohibition against "hot cargo" clauses was necessary to further that objective. They were joined by Senator McClellan, Chairman of the Select Committee, in their proposal to add such a provision. Their statements in support consistently defined the evil to be prevented in terms of agreements which obligated neutral employers not to do business with other employers involved in labor disputes with the union. Senator Gore initially proposed, and the Senate first passed, a "hot cargo" amendment to the Kennedy–Ervin bill which outlawed such agreements only for "common carriers subject to Part II of the Interstate Commerce Act." This reflected the testimony at the Select Committee hearings which attributed abuses of such clauses primarily to the Teamsters Union. Significantly, such alleged abuses by the Teamsters invariably involved uses of the clause to pressure neutral trucking employers not to handle goods of other employers involved in disputes with the Teamsters Union.

The House Labor Committee first reported out a bill containing a provision substantially identical to the Gore amendment. The House Report expressly noted that since that proposal tracked the language of § 8(b)(4)(A) "it preserved the established distinction between primary activities and secondary boycotts." The substitute Landrum–Griffin bill, however, expanded the proposal to cover all industry and not common carriers alone. * * * An analysis of the substitute bill submitted by Representative Griffin referred to the need to plug the various loopholes in the "secondary boycott" provisions, one of which is the "hot cargo" agreement. In Conference Committee, the Landrum–Griffin application to all industry, and not just to common carriers, was adopted. * * *

In addition to all else, "the silence of the sponsors of [the] Amendments is pregnant with significance * * *." National Labor Relations Board v. Fruit & Vegetable Packers, etc., supra, 377 U.S. at 66, 84 S.Ct. at 1068. Before we may say that Congress meant to strike from workers' hands the economic weapons traditionally used against their employers' efforts to abolish their jobs, that meaning should plainly appear. "[I]n this era of automation and onrushing technological change, no problems in the domestic economy are of greater concern than those involving job security and employment stability. Because of the potentially cruel impact upon the lives and fortunes of the working men and women of the Nation, these problems have understandably engaged the solicitous attention of government, of responsible private business, and particularly of organized labor." Fibreboard Paper Prods. Corp. v. National Labor Relations Board, 379 U.S. 203, 225, 85 S.Ct. 398, 411, 13 L.Ed.2d 233 (concurring opinion of Stewart, J.). We would expect that legislation curtailing the ability of management and labor voluntarily to negotiate for solutions to these significant and difficult problems would be preceded by extensive congressional study and debate, and consideration of voluminous economic, scientific, and statistical data. The silence regarding such matters in the Eighty-sixth Congress is itself evidence that Congress, in enacting § 8(e), had no thought of prohibiting agreements directed to work preservation * * *.

Moreover, our decision in *Fibreboard Paper Prods. Corp.,* supra implicitly recognizes the legitimacy of work preservation clauses like that involved here. Indeed, in the circumstances presented in *Fibreboard,* we held that bargaining on the subject was made mandatory by § 8(a)(5) of the Act, concerning as it does "terms and conditions of employment." *Fibreboard* involved an alleged refusal to bargain with respect to the contracting-out of plant maintenance work previously performed by employees in the bargaining unit. * * * It would therefore be incongruous to interpret § 8(e) to invalidate clauses over which the parties may be mandated to bargain and which have been successfully incorporated through collective bargaining in many of this Nation's major labor agreements.

Finally, important parts of the historic accommodation by Congress of the powers of labor and management are §§ 7 and 13 of the National Labor Relations Act. * * * Section 13 preserves the right to strike, of which the boycott is a form, except as specifically provided in the Act. In the absence of clear indicia of congressional intent to the contrary, these provisions caution against reading statutory prohibitions as embracing employee activities to pressure their own employers into improving the employees' wages, hours, and working conditions. * * *

The Woodwork Manufacturers Association and *amici* who support its position advance several reasons, grounded in economic and technological factors, why "will not handle" clauses should be invalid in all circumstances. Those arguments are addressed to the wrong branch of government. * * *

### III.

The determination whether the "will not handle" sentence of Rule 17 and its enforcement violated § 8(e) and § 8(b)(4)(B) cannot be made without an inquiry into whether, under all the surrounding circumstances, the Union's objective was preservation of work for Frouge's employees, or whether the agreements and boycott were tactically calculated to satisfy union objectives elsewhere. Were the latter the case, Frouge, the boycotting employer, would be a neutral bystander, and the agreement or boycott would, within the intent of Congress, become secondary. There need not be an actual dispute with the boycotted employer, here the door manufacturer, for the activity to fall within this category, so long as the tactical object of the agreement and its maintenance is that employer, or benefits to other than the boycotting employees or other employees of the primary employer thus making the agreement or boycott secondary in its aim. The touchstone is whether the agreement or its maintenance is addressed to the labor relations of the contracting employer *vis-a-vis* his own employees. This will not always be a simple test to apply. But "[h]owever difficult the drawing lines more nice than obvious, the statute compels the task." Local 761, Inter. Union of Electrical, etc., Workers v. National Labor Relations Board, 366 U.S. 667, 674, 81 S.Ct. 1285, 1290.

That the "will not handle" provision was not an unfair labor practice in this case is clear. The finding of the Trial Examiner, adopted by the

Board, was that the objective of the sentence was preservation of work traditionally performed by the job-site carpenters. This finding is supported by substantial evidence, and therefore the Union's making of the "will not handle" agreement was not a violation of § 8(e).

Similarly, the Union's maintenance of the provision was not a violation of § 8(b)(4)(B). The Union refused to hang prefabricated doors whether or not they bore a union label, and even refused to install prefabricated doors manufactured off the jobsite by members of the Union. This and other substantial evidence supported the finding that the conduct of the Union on the Frouge jobsite related solely to preservation of the traditional tasks of the jobsite carpenters. * * *

[The concurring opinion of MR. JUSTICE HARLAN has been omitted.]

■ MR. JUSTICE STEWART, whom MR. JUSTICE BLACK, MR. JUSTICE DOUGLAS, and MR. JUSTICE CLARK join, dissenting. * * *

The Court concludes that the Union's conduct in this case falls outside the ambit of § 8(b)(4) because it had an ultimate purpose that it characterizes as "primary" in nature—the preservation of work for union members. But § 8(b)(4) is not limited to boycotts that have as their only purpose the forcing of any person to cease using the products of another; it is sufficient if that result is "an object" of the boycott. Legitimate union objectives may not be accomplished through means proscribed by the statute. See National Labor Relations Board v. Denver Bldg. & Const. Trades Council, 341 U.S. 675, 688–689, 71 S.Ct. 943, 951, 95 L.Ed. 1284. Without question, preventing Frouge from using Mohawk's pre–fitted doors was "an object" of the Union's conduct here.

It is, of course, true that courts have distinguished "primary" and "secondary" activities, and have found the former permitted despite the literal applicability of the statutory language. See Local 761, Intern. Union of Electrical, etc., Workers v. National Labor Relations Board, 366 U.S. 667, 81 S.Ct. 1285. But the Court errs in concluding that the product boycott conducted by the Union in this case was protected primary activity. As the Court points out, a typical form of secondary boycott is the visitation of sanctions on Employer A, with whom the union has no dispute, in order to force him to cease doing business with Employer B, with whom the union does have a dispute. But this is not the only form of secondary boycott that § 8(b)(4) was intended to reach. The Court overlooks the fact that a product boycott for work preservation purposes has consistently been regarded by the courts, and by the Congress that passed the Taft–Hartley Act, as a proscribed "secondary boycott."

  * * *

A proper understanding of the purpose of Congress in enacting § 8(b)(4) in that year requires an appreciation of the impact of this Court's 1945 decision in Allen Bradley Co. v. Local Union No. 3, IBEW, 325 U.S. 797, 65 S.Ct. 1533. * * * Just as in the case before us, the union enforced the product boycott to protect the work opportunities of its members. The Court found the antitrust laws applicable to the union's role in the scheme, but solely on the ground that the union had conspired with the manufacturers and contractors. Significantly for present purposes, the Court stated that "had there been no union-contractor-manufacturer combination the union's actions here * * * would not have been violations of the Sherman Act." 325 U.S., at 807, 65 S.Ct., at 1539. The Court further indicated that, by itself, a bargaining agreement authorizing the product boycott in question would not transgress the antitrust laws. 325 U.S., at 809, 65 S.Ct., at 1539. In conclusion, the Court recognized that allowing unions to effect product boycotts might offend sound public policy, but indicated that the remedy lay in the hands of the legislature * * *

Congress responded when it enacted the Taft–Hartley Act. * * * Two years after the *Allen Bradley* decision, the 80th Congress prohibited such product boycotts, but did so through the Taft–Hartley Act rather than by changing the antitrust laws. * * * It is entirely understandable that Congress should have sought to prohibit product boycotts having a work preservation purpose. Unlike most strikes and boycotts, which are temporary tactical maneuvers in a particular labor dispute, work preservation product boycotts are likely to be permanent, and the restraint on the free flow of goods in commerce is direct and pervasive, not limited to goods manufactured by a particular employer with whom the union may have a given dispute. * * *

The Court seeks to avoid the thrust of this legislative history stemming from *Allen Bradley* by suggesting that in the present case, the product boycott was used to preserve work opportunities traditionally performed by the Union, whereas in *Allen Bradley* the boycott was originally designed to create new job opportunities. But it is misleading to state that the union in *Allen Bradley* used the product boycott as a "sword." The record in that case establishes that the boycott was undertaken for the defensive purpose of restoring job opportunities lost in the depression. Moreover, the Court is unable to cite anything in *Allen Bradley,* or in the Taft–Hartley Act and its legislative history, to support a distinction in the applicability of § 8(b)(4) based on the origin of the job opportunities sought to be preserved by a product boycott. The Court creates its sword and shield distinction out of thin air; nothing could more clearly indicate that the Court is simply substituting its own concepts of desirable labor policy for the scheme enacted by Congress. * * *

In 1959 Congress enacted § 8(e) to ensure that § 8(b)(4)'s ban on boycotts would not be circumvented by unions that obtained management's agreement to practices which would give rise to a § 8(b)(4) violation if the union attempted unilaterally to enforce their observance. * * * Since, as has been shown, the product boycott enforced by the union in the case before us violates § 8(b)(4)(B), it follows that Rule 17, the provision in the collective bargaining agreement applied to authorize this same boycott by agreement, equally violates § 8(e). * * *

Finally, the Court's reliance on Fibreboard Paper Products Corp. v. National Labor Relations Board, 379 U.S. 203, 85 S.Ct. 398, 13 L.Ed.2d 233, is wholly misplaced. * * * [Unlike *Fibreboard,* which was limited to an employer's decision to contract out maintenance work within the plant,] an employer's decision as to the products he wishes to buy presents entirely different issues. That decision has traditionally been regarded as one within management's discretion, and *Fibreboard* does not indicate that it is a mandatory subject of collective bargaining, much less a permissible basis for a product boycott made illegal by federal labor law.

The relevant legislative history confirms and reinforces the plain meaning of the statute and establishes that the Union's product boycott in this case and the agreement authorizing it were both unfair labor practices. In deciding to the contrary, the Court has substituted its own notions of sound labor policy for the word of Congress. There may be social and economic arguments for changing the law of product boycotts established in § 8, but those changes are not for this Court to make.

I respectfully dissent.

———

NLRB v. Enterprise Ass'n of Steam and General Pipefitters, Local No. 638 (Austin Co.), 429 U.S. 507, 97 S.Ct. 891, 51 L.Ed.2d 1 (1977).[g] The Pipefitters Union signed a collective bargaining agreement with a heating and air-conditioning contractor (Hudik), providing that the threading and cutting of internal piping in climate-control units installed by Hudik would be performed at the jobsite by Hudik's employees covered by the contract; this was work traditionally performed by those employees. Hudik was then awarded a subcontract by Austin, the general contractor on a construction project known as the Norwegian Home for the Aged. Austin's job specifications, incorporated in the subcontract, provided for the installation of prefabricated climate-control units with internal piping already cut and threaded at the factory by the employees of the manufacturer, Slant/Fin. When these units arrived at the jobsite, Hudik's employees refused to install them; the union representative claimed that the use of those units was in violation of the labor contract. Austin, the general contractor, filed charges with the NLRB for violation of Section 8(b)(4)(B).

The Supreme Court (6-to-3) endorsed the Board's conclusion that, although the labor-contract provision was lawful, the refusal to handle was an unlawful secondary boycott. The Court (through Mr. Justice White) concluded that the jobsite work-preservation clause was lawful, but that the contract could not render lawful a work stoppage which was itself secondary and unlawful. "Regardless of whether an agreement is valid under § 8(e), it may not be enforced by means that would violate § 8(b)(4)." (The dissenting Justices agreed with this proposition, but disagreed with the majority's conclusion that the stoppage was a secondary boycott.)

The key issue was whether the product boycott was addressed to Hudik's labor relations among its own employees, or whether the union's

**g.**  See Leslie, Right to Control: A Study in Secondary Boycotts and Labor Antitrust, 89 Harv.L.Rev. 904 (1976).

conduct was "tactically calculated to satisfy [its] objectives elsewhere" (quoting from *National Woodwork*). The Board properly followed *National Woodwork* by looking to "the totality of the circumstances" to determine whether the union's objective was exclusively that of work preservation, giving weight (albeit not conclusive weight) to the fact that Hudik lacked the "right of control" over the use of pre–threaded piping at the time the union applied its pressure. Thus, Austin must be regarded as the primary employer, with the power to assign internal piping work. "There is ample support in the record for the Board's resolution of this question. * * * It is uncontrovertible that the work at this site could not be secured by pressure on Hudik alone and that the union's work objectives could not be obtained without exerting pressure on Austin as well. That the union may also have been seeking to enforce its contract and to convince Hudik that it should bid on no more jobs where pre–piped units were specified does not alter the fact that the union refused to install the Slant/Fin units and asserted that the piping work on the Norwegian Home job belonged to its members. It was not error for the Board to conclude that the union's objectives were not confined to the employment relationship with Hudik but included the object of influencing Austin in a manner prohibited by § 8(b)(4)(B)."

The dissenting Justices read *National Woodwork* to establish the principles that "If the purpose of a contract provision, or of economic pressure on an employer, is to secure benefits for that employer's own employees, it is primary; if the object is to affect the policies of some other employer toward his employees, the contract or its enforcement is secondary." But the majority disagreed: "The distinction between primary and secondary activity does not always turn on which group of employees the union seeks to benefit. There are circumstances under which the union's conduct is secondary when one of its purposes is to influence directly the conduct of an employer other than the struck employer. In these situations, a union's efforts to influence the conduct of the nonstruck employer are not rendered primary simply because it seeks to benefit the employees of the struck employer. *National Woodwork* itself embraced the view that the union's conduct would be secondary if its tactical object was to influence another employer."

The dissenters relied upon the Board's own finding that the object of the Pipefitters Union was to preserve the work traditionally done by the Hudik employees, and contended that Hudik was by no means a "neutral." After making an agreement with its employees to satisfy their concern about work preservation, it defied those obligations by voluntarily accepting a subcontract which it knew disabled it from keeping its bargain with the union. Even after entering into the subcontract, Hudik was not a "neutral" because it was in a position to negotiate with the union about such substitutes for compliance as premium pay to replace the lost work. "In short, the agreement in this case, as the Board found, was for a primary purpose; pressure brought to compel Hudik to agree to it would have been primary; and pressure brought to enforce it when Hudik breached it, whether by ordering prefabricated units himself, as in *National*

*Woodwork,* or by entering a contract that required him to breach it, was no less primary."

---

PROBLEM FOR DISCUSSION

Which, if any, of the following courses of action would be available to the Pipefitters Union to achieve their objectives in the labor contract with Hudik?

(a) File a grievance and take the case to arbitration under the appropriate provisions of the labor contract?

(b) Demand that Hudik discuss the payment of premium rates for the installation of each climate-control unit with prethreaded piping?

(c) Refuse to handle such units until Hudik agrees to incorporate such a premium-pay provision in the contract? See Carpenters Local 742 (J.L. Simmons Co.), 237 NLRB 564 (1978).

(d) Picket the general contractor Austin, or the entire construction site, until the general contractor altered the specifications for the climate-control units? (i.e., Should Austin exult in its victory, and in the apparent holding of the Supreme Court that it rather than Hudik is the primary employer?)

---

## Meat & Highway Drivers, Local Union No. 710 v. NLRB
335 F.2d 709 (D.C.Cir.1964).

■ WRIGHT, CIRCUIT JUDGE. The National Labor Relations Board has found that certain subcontracting clauses of petitioner's bargaining agreements and proposals are void under § 8(e) of the Labor Act, and that economic action to obtain their provisions violated § 8(b)(4)(i)(ii)(A) and (B). The subcontracting clauses involved will be referred to as the work allocation clause,[3] the union standards clause,[4] and the union signatory clauses.[5] By votes of 3–2, 4–1, and 5–0, respectively, the Board found these clauses to be secondary, and thus unlawful. The union petitions to review and set aside the Board's decision and the Board cross-petitions for enforcement.

The union here represents truck drivers employed by Wilson, Armour, Swift, and other Chicago packing companies who deliver meat and meat products in the Chicago area. The factual background of the dispute, as to

---

**3.** This clause provides, in pertinent part, that truck shipments by each meat packer to its customers within Chicago be made from a Chicago distribution facility of the employer "by employees covered by this agreement." * * *

**4.** This clause provides, in pertinent part, that in the event the packer does not have sufficient equipment to make all local deliveries itself, "it may contract with any cartage company whose truckdrivers enjoy the same or greater wages and other benefits as provided in this agreement for the making of such deliveries."

**5.** One such union signatory clause required that both shipments into Chicago, and local overflow work, be made only by carriers "party to the Central States or other Over-The-Road Teamster Motor Freight Agreement." The union acquiesces in the Board's finding that this clause violates § 8(e). * * *

which there is general agreement, is well stated in the separate opinion of Chairman McCulloch of the Board:

"For at least 20 years, meat packers in Chicago have agreed with [the union] that deliveries of meat products by truck within the Chicago area would be made directly by the packers, using their own equipment driven by employees represented by [the union]. During most of this period, deliveries to customers in the Chicago area originated from the packers' plant in Chicago. Toward the end of the last decade, extensive changes in the distribution of meat products were effected as the major packers moved much of their slaughtering and processing operations outside of Chicago. The relocation of Swift, Armour, and Wilson, the three major packers, caused a sharp reduction in employment both of inside plant workers and of local drivers. Of about 330 truckdrivers employed by Swift, Armour, and Wilson at the beginning of the prior contract term in May 1958, only 80 were still employed 3 years later when negotiations began for a new agreement. Drivers employed by the packers continued to make deliveries from the remaining plant facilities in Chicago to customers within a 50 mile radius, but deliveries to customers within the same area were increasingly being made by over-the-road drivers whose runs originated from the packers' facilities outside the Chicago area. It was to the problem of recovering the jobs lost by the local drivers in the Chicago area and retaining those still performed there that the Union addressed itself in the 1961 negotiations."

The Union proposals for the bargaining agreement, which were found by the Board to violate § 8(e), include the work allocation clause which requires that all deliveries in Chicago, whether from within the city or from out of state, be made by local employees covered by the agreement. Under this provision the packing companies would be required to divide into two stages their shipments from out of state to Chicago consignees, terminating the interstate segment at the Chicago terminal.

The Board found that the delivery of out-of-state shipments to Chicago consignees was work historically performed, not by local drivers who were members of the bargaining unit, but by over-the-road drivers employed by interstate carrier. Thus, according to the Board, since such deliveries were not bargaining unit work, they could not be the subject of a clause which would allocate that work to the bargaining unit; to do so would require the packers to cease doing business, at least in part, with the interstate carriers, violating § 8(e). In short, the Board says that the work allocation clause here provides for "work acquisition," not "work preservation," and consequently it is secondary in nature, falling outside the ambit of the cases declaring certain subcontracting clauses primary.

Resolution of the difficult issue of primary *versus* secondary activity, as it relates to this case, involves consideration of two factors: (1) jobs fairly claimable by the bargaining unit, and (2) preservation of those jobs for the bargaining unit. If the jobs are fairly claimable by the unit, they may, without violating either § 8(e) or § 8(b)(4)(A) or (B), be protected by provision for, and implementation of, no-subcontracting or union standards clauses in the bargaining agreements. Activity and agreements which directly protect fairly claimable jobs are primary under the Act. Incidental secondary effects of such activity and agreement do not render them illegal. Thus the "cease doing business" language in § 8(e) cannot be read literally because inherent in all subcontracting clauses, even those admittedly primary, is refusal to deal with at least some contractors.

Applying these principles to the work allocation clause here, we find that delivery in the Chicago area, irrespective of origin of the shipment, is work fairly claimable by the union. It has been said "that a union has always been free to bargain for the expansion of the employment opportunities within the bargaining unit." Comment, 62 Mich.L.Rev. 1176, 1190 (1964). The work here claimed is of a type which the men in the bargaining unit have the skills and experience to do. It would be difficult to deny that "[a] clause covering non-traditional work may be just as consecrated to the primary objective of bettering the lot of the bargaining unit employees and just as foreign to the congressional purpose for section 8(e) as those clauses involving only the work traditionally done within the bargaining unit." Id. at 1189.

Moreover, in the case before us, we have not work acquisition but work recapture. * * * Most of the packing houses have been moved out of Chicago, so that now most of the shipments for the area are out-of-state shipments. It is understandable, therefore, that the union, in bargaining for a new agreement, turned its attention to these out-of-state shipments in an effort to require that the last leg thereof be made by local drivers. Thus the union, under its new proposal, is attempting not only to retain jobs for local drivers, but to recapture some of the work lost by the movement of packing houses out of Chicago. Unquestionably, this work is fairly claimable by the local drivers, and their union's efforts in their behalf in that direction fall easily within the legitimate area of collective bargaining. We agree with Chairman McCulloch, joined by Member Brown, in dissenting from the opinion of the Board on this point:

"Deliveries to consignees in the Chicago area, regardless of origin, can justifiably be considered to be work of the employees within [the union's] unit. Even if it had never been customarily performed by unit members when it was part of an interstate haul, it is nevertheless so closely allied— and is in part identical—to the local deliveries previously recognized for almost 20 years to be unit work as to make bargaining about it mandatory. To hold otherwise is to say that a union may not seek to bargain with an employer either about the quantum of work, or the qualifications of its members to perform closely related work, whenever technological changes or mere changes in methods of distribution are to be effected."

Since we view this attempt on the part of the union to maintain and regain the local delivery jobs for members of the bargaining unit as a typical primary activity, we hold the work allocation clause valid under § 8(e), and economic activity to obtain it lawful under § 8(b)(4).

The union proposal also contained a union standards subcontracting clause which read:

"In the event that the Employer does not have sufficient equipment at any given time to deliver his then current sales or consignments within the Chicago city limits, it may contract with any cartage company whose truckdrivers enjoy the same or greater wages and other benefits as provided in this agreement for the making of such deliveries."[15]

The Board's basic reason for finding the subcontracting clause illegal is its view that a work standards clause accords "the Union a veto over the decision as to who may receive the signatory employer's subcontracts" by defining "the persons with whom the signatory employer may and may not do business." This view, given primary place in the Board's decision and utilized as the major argument in its brief on this point, follows the distinction that clauses which regulate "who" may receive subcontracting work are secondary, while only clauses which regulate "when" subcontracting occurs are primary. This court has rejected that distinction in a line of cases cited in the margin.[16] We have considered the matter once more and readopt the principles of these cases. * * *

To protect unit work by partially deterring such employer conduct, this clause would at least remove from the employer the temptation of cheap labor through substandard contractors. This is a usual function of a standards clause, as discussed in our prior opinions. We need not assume that an employer would use such a tactic as here discussed; it is enough that the union could fear it, and seek such a clause to prevent it. * * *

---

**15.** We take it that the phrase "same or greater wages and other benefits" requires only that total cost to the employer be the same or greater. Thus the temptation of cheap labor is removed without requiring details identical with the union contract.

**16.** Member Brown of the Board, who relied on Retail Clerks Union Local 770 v. N.L.R.B., dissented from the Board's decision that the provision here involved violated § 8(e). He said:

"In thus limiting the class of persons to whom the assigned work of the contract unit may be subcontracted, the Union's purpose, so far as this record reveals, is not to limit the employer in the persons with whom he does business in order to further a dispute at another employer's establishment, or to protest objectionable conditions at another employer's establishment, or to protest objectionable conditions at another employer's establishment, or to improve the conditions of the employees of another employer. Rather, the Union's objective was to accommodate the business needs of the employer while at the same time protecting the welfare of employees in the packer bargaining unit it represents.

"* * * [This clause] recognizes realistically that situations sometimes do arise when the packer may have drivers of his own available but insufficient equipment to carry out his operations. In such situations, the [clause] would permit the packer to contract with a cartage company; but only when the cartage company maintains the same or better labor standards. The [clause] thus discourages the packer's use of a cartage company as a device for undermining the work and standards which the packer had agreed to maintain for his employees. Accordingly, the [clause] serves both the packer's interest in flexibility and the Union's interest in preventing that flexibility from undercutting the job security of the packer's own employees through subcontracting their work for performance under substandard conditions.

"* * * [A]s noted previously, my colleagues would agree that a no-subcontracting agreement to preserve the work of the bargaining unit employees is lawful even though it absolutely precludes subcontracting of the work to other employers. Reason would dictate a similar result here in view of the similar object of the clause under consideration and where incidental effects are even less restrictive. * * *"

Certain contracts long in force between the union and some of the Chicago packers contain the following union signatory clause:

"Livestock, meat and meat products for delivery by truck to a distance not exceeding 50 miles from the Chicago Stock Yards, whether to final destination or point of transfer, shall be delivered by the Company in their own equipment except when there is a lack of equipment at individual plants or branches, *and then all effort will be made to contract a cartage company who employs members of Local No. 710.* * * * " (Emphasis supplied.)

While the work allocation features of this paragraph are valid, the provision requiring or encouraging a boycott of cartage companies who do not have union contracts is a violation of § 8(e). To make the selection of subcontractors turn upon union approval bears only a tenuous relation to the legitimate economic concerns of the employees in the unit, and enables the union to use secondary pressure in its dispute with the subcontractors. We therefore hold this provision void under § 8(e).

With reference to this union signatory clause, the union raises the issue of the scope of the ban. The Board found objectionable only the provision "and then all effort will be made to contract a cartage company who employs members of Local No. 710." Nevertheless, its order ran against the entire clause. The union argues that the objectionable portion should be excised, leaving the remainder of the clause intact as a viable promise capable of enforcement in keeping with the sense of the contract. Excision of the objectionable language would give the employers greater latitude under the contract. Thus excision should be acceptable to them. And the union, certainly, would rather see the language deleted than lose the benefit of the remainder of the clause. Deletion, then would leave the total collective bargaining agreement in a state close to the actual agreement of the parties. And deletion would satisfy totally the requirements of § 8(e). Accordingly, we hold that the Board should not invalidate more of the contract than is unlawful, "where the excess may be severed and separately condemned as it can here." Labor Board v. Rockaway News Co., 345 U.S. 71, 79, 73 S.Ct. 519, 31 LRRM 2432 (1953). * * *

---

## PROBLEMS FOR DISCUSSION

**1.** Consider the legality of each of the following labor-contract provisions, and whether it is necessary to have further information in particular cases. (You may assume that none of the provisions is sheltered by the clothing-industry and construction-industry provisos to Section 8(e).) See Truck Drivers Union Local No. 413 v. NLRB, 334 F.2d 539 (D.C.Cir.1964), cert. denied, 379 U.S. 916, 85 S.Ct. 264, 13 L.Ed.2d 186 (1964).

(a) Employer shall refrain from using piping which is trimmed by any other company prior to shipment to the jobsite.

(b) Employer shall refrain from using piping which is trimmed by any other company so long as there are unit employees who are on layoff and who are competent to perform such trimming work at the jobsite.

(c) Employer shall refrain from using piping which is trimmed by any company whose employees do not enjoy the same or greater wages and other benefits as provided in this agreement for the performance of such trimming work.

(d) It shall not be a violation of this agreement or a cause for discipline if employees refuse to work on, install or handle piping which has been manufactured by any company which does not employ members of this Union.

(e) No employee shall be required to perform any service on goods received at the jobsite which service would, but for the existence of a labor dispute involving any other company, be performed by the employees of such other company.

(f) No employee shall be required to perform any service or work on goods which have been shipped to the jobsite from or by any other company currently involved in a labor dispute.

(g) Employer shall not require any employee to cross or work behind any lawful picket line, whether at this Employer or any other employer and whether the picket line is of this Union or of any other union.

**2.** In *Enterprise Association,* page 681 supra, the Court majority placed great weight on the distinction between work preservation and work acquisition. "[U]nder the theory of the dissent, * * * striking workers may legally demand that their employer cease doing business with another company even if the union's object is to obtain new work so long as that work is for the benefit of the striking employees." The majority disagreed, and held that (apart from the "right of control" issue) it would have been illegal had the union in that case forced Hudik "to cease doing business with Austin, not to preserve, but to aggrandize, its own position and that of its members. Such activity is squarely within the statute." The Court has more recently reiterated this position. See NLRB v. International Longshoremen's Ass'n., 473 U.S. 61, 105 S.Ct. 3045, 87 L.Ed.2d 47 (1985)(holding Containerization Rules, negotiated by marine shipping companies and the ILA, to be lawful because preserving longshore work previously done within the unit).

Given the purpose of the secondary boycott provisions of the NLRA, is this distinction at all tenable? It traces its roots to the "sword-shield" distinction in *National Woodwork;* reexamine the pertinent passage there and determine whether the subsequent cases have not made too much of what was a rather casual makeweight. How tenable today is the suggestion of the court of appeals in the *Meat & Highway Drivers* case that work-acquisition provisions are primary and lawful if the work in question is "fairly claimable" by the members of the signatory union?

**3.** The Retail Clerks Union has a contract with Hughes Market which contains a clause that provides that Hughes "agrees that any employees performing bargaining unit work set forth in this Agreement, within its establishments, including employees of lessees, shall be members of [the bargaining unit of Hughes employees represented by the Retail Clerks]."

During the term of the contract, Hughes leases a portion of its premises to Saba Drugs, a prescription-writing pharmacy. Saba is completely walled off and is an entirely separate operation from Hughes, selling different products. Saba is a nonunion store. The Retail Clerks Union demands that Hughes terminate the lease with Saba unless the Saba employees join the bargaining unit represented by the

Union. Hughes responds that the contract provision does not cover this situation, and that if it does it is illegal under Section 8(e).

The Union also demands that Hughes cease permitting employees of Canada Dry Corp. to stock soda in the market. During the twenty years that Hughes has been open, Canada Dry employees have always stocked their own soda when making deliveries, while Hughes employees have stocked Coca–Cola and other brand sodas. The employer concedes that this work is covered by the contract clause, but maintains that the clause violates Section 8(e).

Assume that the case comes before the NLRB on charges filed by Hughes. Should the Board sustain the validity of the contract provision as it relates to the work done by the Saba employees? (Would it be important to know whether the labor contract contains an arbitration provision?) Should the Board sustain the validity of the provision as it relates to the work done by the Canada Dry employees? Must the provision be "rewritten" in order to be valid, and ought the Board do so? See Canada Dry Corp. v. NLRB, 421 F.2d 907 (6th Cir.1970); Retail Clerks Local 770 (Hughes Market, Inc.), 218 NLRB 680 (1975).

**4.** As discussed more fully below, at pp. 698–99, "double breasted" employers (operating through both unionized and non-union entities) have become a serious issue in the construction industry. In one approach to deal with the problem, the Sheet Metal Workers secured provisions of its collective agreements that: (1) declare as a "bad-faith employer" one that itself or through others under its control has an ownership interest in a business that engages in sheet metal work using employees whose wage package is inferior to the union's; (2) subjects the employer to a per diem fine for failure to notify the union that it is a "bad-faith employer"; and, (3) permits the union to rescind the collective agreement with any "bad-faith employer." This "integrity clause" has been challenged as violative of §§ 8(b)(4)(ii)(A) and 8(e). Is it? See Sheet Metal Workers, Local Union No. 91 v. NLRB, 905 F.2d 417 (D.C.Cir.1990).

**5.** Mead is the general contractor on a project for which Vining Electric and Short Elevator are both subcontractors. Vining has a dispute with the Electrical Workers Union over wages. Mead has set up a gate, the West Gate, exclusively reserved for Vining Electric's use and picketing by the Electric Workers is taking place there. Another gate, the East Gate, is reserved for all other contractors, deliverymen, etc. No picketing is occurring there. Short Elevator has a collective agreement with Elevator Workers Union that contains a no-strike clause, but declares that "work stoppages brought about by lawful picketing or strikes" by unions affiliated with the Building Trades Council shall not constitute a strike. Roy Reitz, an elevator worker, after entering the worksite through the East Gate for three days, decided as a matter of conscience that he could not report to a workplace that was being picketed. Short Elevator has filed charges that the unions have violated §§ 8(b)(4)(ii)(A) and 8(e) of the Act. Have they? See NLRB v. International Union of Elevator Constructors, 902 F.2d 1297 (8th Cir.1990).

---

*THE CLOTHING–INDUSTRY AND CONSTRUCTION–INDUSTRY PROVISOS*

Section 8(e) excludes from its ban hot cargo clauses of two kinds: agreements by jobbers or manufacturers in the clothing industry not to subcontract work to nonunion contractors, and agreements by construction employers not to subcontract jobsite work to nonunion contractors. These two provisos in Section 8(e) have somewhat different origins and reach.

In the clothing industry in the first decades of this century, manufacturers would frequently, in order to avoid unionization and higher wages, subcontract the work of cutting and sewing the fabric to ''outside'' contractors, whose operations were mobile, short-lived and difficult to unionize; ''jobbers'' also emerged, having no employees of their own but being primarily in the business of assigning work to contractors. The only practicable way for the clothing unions to improve the working conditions of the great preponderance of workers in the industry (some eighty percent worked for the contractors) was to secure agreements from the manufacturers and jobbers not to contract out work to nonunion shops. See Greenstein v. National Skirt & Sportswear Ass'n, Inc., 178 F.Supp. 681 (S.D.N.Y.1959). In realization of this economic reality, and of the integrated business relationship of the subcontractor and the manufacturer or jobber, Congress authorized hot cargo clauses in the clothing industry. Indeed, it went further and in Section 8(e) eliminated the clothing industry from the reach even of Section 8(b)(4)(B) and the totality of secondary boycott prohibitions. Thus, not only is it lawful in that industry to enter into an agreement not to contract work to nonunion shops, but it is also lawful for a union to induce a work stoppage to secure such an agreement (which would, if the agreement were illegal, otherwise violate Section 8(b)(4)(A)) and to induce a work stoppage the object of which is actually to force the manufacturer or jobber to cease doing business that it is presently doing with a nonunion contractor (which would, were it not for the expansive proviso, otherwise violate Section 8(b)(4)(B)).

Largely because of the frictions traditionally created by the presence in the construction industry of union and nonunion employees working side-by-side at the jobsite, Section 8(e) expressly exempts from its ban hot cargo provisions ''relating to the contracting or subcontracting of work to be done at the site of the construction.'' If, however, the construction employer agrees to refrain from accepting at the jobsite materials made elsewhere by a nonunion company, such an agreement is not sheltered by the proviso and will be held to violate Section 8(e). Since a work stoppage to obtain an unlawful hot cargo agreement violates Section 8(b)(4)(A), a strike to obtain a hot cargo clause relating to jobsite work is lawful, while a strike to obtain a hot cargo clause relating to work done elsewhere will violate Section 8(b)(4)(A) and may be the subject of an action for damages under Section 303 of the Labor Act. In contrast to the clothing industry, there is no explicit proviso in Section 8(e) which removes altogether the construction industry from the reach of Section 8(b)(4). The significance is that a strike which is designed not to secure a hot cargo clause but to enforce it—and thus to sever immediately the business relationship between the employer and a nonunion contractor—will be banned by Section 8(b)(4)(B). This will be true even if the nonunion employer is performing work at the jobsite; the strike to compel a cessation is unlawful, but an employer agreement is lawful, as is a lawsuit or a demand for arbitration, or any other measure short of a work stoppage or threats or coercion generated by the union.

NORTHEASTERN INDIANA BLDG. & CONSTR. TRADES COUNCIL, 148 NLRB 854 (1964), enf't denied on other grounds, 352 F.2d 696 (D.C.Cir.1965).

––––––

CONNELL CONSTR. CO. v. PLUMBERS AND STEAMFITTERS LOCAL UNION NO. 100, 421 U.S. 616, 95 S.Ct. 1830, 44 L.Ed.2d 418 (1975). Plumbers Local 100, seeking to organize plumbing and mechanical subcontractors in the Dallas, Texas area, picketed at a major construction project under the supervision of general contractor Connell, until it secured an agreement that Connell would use only mechanical subcontractors whose employees were represented by Local 100. The union had no interest in organizing any of Connell's own employees and had no conventional collective bargaining agreement with Connell. Connell brought an action, under federal and state antitrust laws, to enjoin the enforcement of the hot cargo agreement and any future union picketing aimed at enforcement. The Supreme Court, although it held that state antitrust regulation was ousted by federal labor law, held that the agreement was not exempt from the federal antitrust laws since it may have eliminated competition among mechanical subcontractors on bases other than wages and conditions of employment.

The Court rejected the union's argument that the hot cargo agreement, which was expressly limited to subcontracted mechanical work to be performed at the jobsite, was within the construction-industry proviso to Section 8(e) and therefore "permitted" under the federal labor law. Turning to the legislative history of Section 8(e) and the objective of Congress to authorize hot cargo agreements designed to eliminate the need of union members to work alongside nonunion employees at the jobsite, the Court concluded that the agreement between Local 100 and the "stranger" general contractor did not fall within the shelter of the proviso. The union represented no employees of Connell who would be discomfited by working alongside nonunion mechanical employees; the agreement, while designed to assure that mechanical work would be performed only by members of Local 100, would not assure that these members would avoid working alongside other nonunion crafts at the jobsite; and the object of the agreement was not even to organize subcontractor employees at a particular jobsite but was more generally to unionize mechanical subcontractors in the Dallas area. The Court doubted that Congress intended to shelter hot cargo agreements with contractors who were "strangers" to the union, thereby giving construction unions "an almost unlimited organizational weapon" in achieving "top-down" organizing against the wishes of employees. It concluded that the authorization given by the proviso to Section 8(e) "extends only to agreements in the context of collective-bargaining relationships and * * * possibly to common-situs relationships on particular jobsites as well."

WOELKE & ROMERO FRAMING, INC. v. NLRB, 456 U.S. 645, 102 S.Ct. 2071, 72 L.Ed.2d 398 (1982). In the two cases before the Court, construction unions in a collective bargaining relationship with certain subcontractors sought to negotiate a provision taking essentially this form: "The employer shall not subcontract any work to be done at the site of the construction, alteration, painting or repair of a building, structure, or other work to any person, firm or company who does not have an existing labor agreement with the union signatory to this agreement." In one case, such a provision was incorporated in the agreement; in the other, the employer would not agree to the provision and the union picketed and caused work stoppages. The employers claimed that the union-signatory clause violated Section 8(e) and that it was not sheltered by the construction-industry proviso because (drawing inspiration from the *Connell* decision) the clause was not limited in application to particular jobsites at which both union and nonunion workers are employed. The employers contended that the purpose of the statutory proviso was to permit construction unions to negotiate construction-site hot-cargo clauses in order to avoid the friction that would result from unionized employees working alongside nonunion employees. The Supreme Court concluded that the purpose of the proviso was not this narrow, and upheld the validity of the contract provisions sought by the unions.

The Court held that a construction-site union-signatory provision is lawful provided it is negotiated within the context of a collective bargaining relationship—even though the union might not be able to demonstrate that at a particular jobsite it represents workers who will be discomfited by the presence of any nonunion workers the employer might want to hire. The Court examined the legislative history of the proviso, and concluded that Congress was aware of union-signatory provisions such as those challenged and that Congress intended to preserve their validity. In the pertinent congressional discussions, jobsite friction received relatively little emphasis, and much more attention was given to the close community of interests of various subcontractors and the impact of the wages and working conditions of one set of employees upon another. Although the employers before the Court argued (again, drawing inspiration from *Connell*) that a broad reading of the proviso would permit top-down organizing pressure, the Court responded: "Such pressure is implicit in the construction industry proviso. * * * [W]e believe that Congress endorsed subcontracting agreements obtained in the context of a collective-bargaining relationship—and decided to accept whatever top-down pressure such clauses might entail. Congress concluded that the community of interests on the construction jobsite justified the top-down organizational consequences that might attend the protection of legitimate collective-bargaining objectives."

[Does the *Woelke & Romero* decision significantly undermine the narrowing interpretation given the construction-industry proviso by the Court in *Connell*?]

---

## PROBLEMS FOR DISCUSSION

**1.** Re-examine the *Denver Building* case, at page 634 supra, in which a union sought to picket the general contractor at the entire jobsite in order to oust the nonunion electrical subcontractor. Do the 1959 hot cargo amendments—and in particular the construction-industry proviso—shelter such picketing today? Would such picketing be sheltered by virtue of the Supreme Court decision in *Woelke & Romero*?

**2.** Would a contract provision between the general contractor at the Denver Building construction site and the electricians' union, in which the employer promised not to subcontract electrical work to any company employing nonunion workers, be lawful? Could the union strike to enforce such a clause? Could it demand arbitration or bring a lawsuit in the event the general contractor violated it? Could the union strike to secure such a provision in the first instance? Can the *Denver Building* decision thus be readily circumvented?

---

## C.  WORK ASSIGNMENT DISPUTES[h]

---

## NLRB v. Radio and Television Broadcast Engineers Union, Local 1212

364 U.S. 573, 81 S.Ct. 330, 5 L.Ed.2d 302 (1961).

■ MR. JUSTICE BLACK delivered the opinion of the Court.

This case, in which the Court of Appeals refused to enforce a cease-and-desist order of the National Labor Relations Board, grew out of a "jurisdictional dispute" over work assignments between the respondent union composed of television "technicians," and another union [Local 1, International Alliance of Theatrical Stage Employees], composed of "stage employees." Both of these unions were certified bargaining agents for their respective Columbia Broadcasting System employee members and had collective bargaining agreements in force with that company, but neither the certifications nor the agreements clearly apportioned between the employees represented by the two unions the work of providing electric lighting for television shows. This led to constant disputes, extending over a number of years, as to the proper assignment of this work, disputes that were particularly acrimonious with reference to "remote lighting," that is, lighting for telecasts away from the home studio. Each union repeatedly urged Columbia to amend its bargaining agreement so as specifically to allocate remote lighting to its members rather than to members of the other union. But, as the Board found, Columbia refused to make such an

---

**h.** See Atleson, The NLRB and Jurisdictional Disputes: The Aftermath of CBS, 53 Geo.L.J. 93 (1964); Cohen, The NLRB and Section 10(k): A Study of the Reluctant Dragon, 14 Lab.L.J. 905 (1963); Farmer & Powers, The Role of the National Labor Relations Board in Resolving Jurisdictional Disputes, 46 Va.L.Rev. 660 (1960); F. Henry, Work Assignment Disputes Under the National Labor Relations Act (1985); Leslie, The Role of the NLRB and the Courts in Resolving Union Jurisdictional Disputes, 75 Colum.L.Rev. 1470 (1975); O'Donoghue, Jurisdictional Disputes in the Construction Industry Since *CBS*, 52 Geo.L.J. 314 (1964); Player, Work Assignment Disputes Under Section 10(k): Putting the Substantive Cart Before the Procedural Horse, 52 Texas L.Rev. 417 (1974); Sussman, Section 10(k): Mandate for Change?, 47 B.U.L.Rev. 201 (1967).

agreement with either union because "the rival locals had failed to agree on the resolution of this jurisdictional dispute over remote lighting." Thus feeling itself caught "between the devil and the deep blue," Columbia chose to divide the disputed work between the two unions according to criteria improvised apparently for the sole purpose of maintaining peace between the two. But, in trying to satisfy both of the unions, Columbia has apparently not succeeded in satisfying either. During recent years, it has been forced to contend with work stoppages by each of the two unions when a particular assignment was made in favor of the other.

The precise occasion for the present controversy was the decision of Columbia to assign the lighting work for a major telecast from the Waldorf–Astoria Hotel in New York City to the stage employees. When the technicians' protest of this assignment proved unavailing, they refused to operate the cameras for the program and thus forced its cancellation. This caused Columbia to file the unfair labor practice charge which started these proceedings, claiming a violation of § 8(b)(4)(D) of the Taft–Hartley Act. That section clearly makes it an unfair labor practice for a labor union to induce a strike or a concerted refusal to work in order to compel an employer to assign particular work to employees represented by it rather than to employees represented by another union, unless the employer's assignment is in violation of "an order or certification of the Board determining the bargaining representative for employees performing such work * * *." Obviously, if § 8(b)(4)(D) stood alone, what this union did in the absence of a Board order or certification entitling its members to be assigned to these particular jobs would be enough to support a finding of an unfair labor practice in a normal proceeding under § 10(c) of the Act. But when Congress created this new type of unfair labor practice by enacting § 8(b)(4)(D) as part of the Taft–Hartley Act in 1947, it also added § 10(k) to the Act. Section 10(k), set out below, quite plainly emphasizes the belief of Congress that it is more important to industrial peace that jurisdictional disputes be settled permanently than it is that unfair labor practice sanctions for jurisdictional strikes be imposed upon unions. Accordingly, § 10(k) offers strong inducements to quarrelling unions to settle their differences by directing dismissal of unfair labor practice charges upon voluntary adjustment of jurisdictional disputes. And even where no voluntary adjustment is made, "the Board is empowered and directed," by § 10(k), "to hear and determine the dispute out of which such unfair labor practice shall have arisen," and upon compliance by the disputants with the Board's decision the unfair labor practice charges must be dismissed.

In this case respondent failed to reach a voluntary agreement with the stage employees union so the Board held the § 10(k) hearing as required to "determine the dispute." The result of this hearing was a decision that the respondent union was not entitled to have the work assigned to its members because it had no right to it under either an outstanding Board order or certification, as provided in § 8(b)(4)(D), or a collective bargaining agreement.[12] The Board refused to consider other criteria, such as the

---

**12.** This latter consideration was made necessary because the Board has adopted the position that jurisdictional strikes in support of contract rights do not constitute violations

employer's prior practices and the custom of the industry, and also refused to make an affirmative award of the work between the employees represented by the two competing unions. The respondent union refused to comply with this decision, contending that the Board's conception of its duty "to determine the dispute" was too narrow in that this duty is not at all limited, as the Board would have it, to strictly legal considerations growing out of prior Board orders, certifications or collective bargaining agreements. It urged, instead, that the Board's duty was to make a final determination, binding on both unions, as to which of the two union's employees was entitled to do the remote lighting work, basing its determination on factors deemed important in arbitration proceedings, such as the nature of the work, the practices and customs of this and other companies and of these and other unions, and upon other factors deemed relevant by the Board in the light of its experience in the field of labor relations. On the basis of its decision in the § 10(k) proceeding and the union's challenge to the validity of that decision, the Board issued an order under § 10(c) directing the union to cease and desist from striking to compel Columbia to assign remote lighting work to its members. The Court of Appeals for the Second Circuit refused to enforce the cease-and-desist order, accepting the respondent's contention that the Board had failed to make the kind of determination that § 10(k) requires. The Third and Seventh Circuits have construed § 10(k) the same way, while the Fifth Circuit has agreed with the Board's narrower conception of its duties. Because of this conflict and the importance of this problem, we granted certiorari.

We agree with the Second, Third and Seventh Circuits that § 10(k) requires the Board to decide jurisdictional disputes on their merits and conclude that in this case that requirement means that the Board should affirmatively have decided whether the technicians or the stage employees were entitled to the disputed work. The language of § 10(k), supplementing § 8(b)(4)(D) as it does, sets up a method adopted by Congress to try to get jurisdictional disputes settled. The words "hear and determine the dispute" convey not only the idea of hearing but also the idea of deciding a controversy. And the clause "the dispute out of which such unfair labor practice shall have arisen" can have no other meaning except a jurisdictional dispute under § 8(b)(4)(D) which is a dispute between two or more groups of employees over which is entitled to do certain work for an employer. To determine or settle the dispute as between them would normally require a decision that one or the other is entitled to do the work in dispute. Any decision short of that would obviously not be conducive to

of § 8(b)(4)(D) despite the fact that the language of that section contains no provision for special treatment of such strikes. See Local 26, International Fur Workers, 90 N.L.R.B. 1379. The Board has explained this position as resting upon the principle that "to fail to hold as controlling * * * the contractual preemption of the work in dispute would be to encourage disregard for observance of binding obligations under collective-bargaining agreements and invite the very jurisdictional disputes Section 8(b)(4)(D) is intended to prevent." National Association of Broadcast Engineers, supra, n. 46, at page 364.

quieting a quarrel between two groups which, here as in most instances, is of so little interest to the employer that he seems perfectly willing to assign work to either if the other will just let him alone. This language also indicates a congressional purpose to have the Board do something more than merely look at prior Board orders and certifications or a collective bargaining contract to determine whether one or the other union has a clearly defined statutory or contractual right to have the employees it represents perform certain work tasks. For, in the vast majority of cases, such a narrow determination would leave the broader problem of work assignments in the hands of the employer, exactly where it was before the enactment of § 10(k)—with the same old basic jurisdictional dispute likely continuing to vex him, and the rival unions, short of striking, would still be free to adopt other forms of pressure upon the employer. The § 10(k) hearing would therefore accomplish little but a restoration of the preexisting situation, a situation already found intolerable by Congress and by all parties concerned. If this newly granted Board power to hear and determine jurisdictional disputes had meant no more than that, Congress certainly would have achieved very little to solve the knotty problem of wasteful work stoppages due to such disputes. * * *

The Taft–Hartley Act as originally offered contained only a section making jurisdictional strikes an unfair labor practice. Section 10(k) came into the measure as the result of an amendment offered by Senator Morse which, in its original form, proposed to supplement this blanket proscription by empowering and directing the Board either "to hear and determine the dispute out of which such unfair labor practice shall have arisen or to appoint an arbitrator to hear and determine such dispute * * *." That the purpose of this amendment was to set up machinery by which the underlying jurisdictional dispute would be settled is clear and, indeed, even the Board concedes this much. The authority to appoint an arbitrator passed the Senate but was eliminated in conference, leaving it to the Board alone "to hear and determine" the underlying jurisdictional dispute. * * *

The Board contends, however, that this interpretation of § 10(k) should be rejected, despite the language and history of that section. In support of this contention, it first points out that § 10(k) sets forth no standards to guide it in determining jurisdictional disputes on their merits. * * * But administrative agencies are frequently given rather loosely defined powers to cope with problems as difficult as those posed by jurisdictional disputes and strikes. It might have been better, as some persuasively argued in Congress, to intrust this matter to arbitrators. But Congress, after discussion and consideration, decided to intrust this decision to the Board. It has had long experience in hearing and disposing of similar labor problems. With this experience and a knowledge of the standards generally used by arbitrators, unions, employers, joint boards and others in wrestling with this problem, we are confident that the Board need not disclaim the power given it for lack of standards. Experience and common sense will supply the grounds for the performance of this job which Congress has assigned the Board. * * *

We conclude therefore that the Board's interpretation of its duty under § 10(k) is wrong and that under that section it is the Board's responsibility and duty to decide which of two or more employee groups claiming the right to perform certain work tasks is right and then specifically to award such tasks in accordance with its decision. Having failed to meet that responsibility in this case, the Board could not properly proceed under § 10(c) to adjudicate the unfair labor practice charge. The Court of Appeals was therefore correct in refusing to enforce the order which resulted from that proceeding.

Affirmed.

————

PROBLEM FOR DISCUSSION

Consider the following situations and determine whether any of them would involve jurisdictional strikes within the meaning of 8(b)(4)(D):

a.  A union pickets to secure the reemployment of strikers whom the employer has replaced.

b.  A union strikes to induce the employer to sign a new collective bargaining contract which includes a clause carried over from the old agreement recognizing the union's right to perform certain types of jobs.

c.  A union strikes to compel the employer to allow his own drivers to load his trucks instead of continuing to have this work done by employees of the independent warehouses from which he obtains his supplies.

————

In its first major decision on work-assignment disputes after the *CBS* case, MACHINISTS LOCAL 1743 (J. A. JONES CONSTR. CO.), 135 NLRB 1402 (1962), the Board enumerated some of the criteria it would utilize in resolving such disputes and indicated how it conceived of the decisional process:

"At this beginning stage in making jurisdictional awards as required by the Court, the Board cannot and will not formulate general rules for making them. Each case will have to be decided on its own facts. The Board will consider all relevant factors in determining who is entitled to the work in dispute, e.g., the skills and work involved, certifications by the Board, company and industry practice, agreements between unions and between employers and unions, awards of arbitrators, joint boards, and the AFL–CIO in the same or related cases, the assignment made by the employer, and the efficient operation of the employer's business. This list of factors is not meant to be exclusive, but is by way of illustration. The Board cannot at this time establish the weight to be given the various factors. Every decision will have to be an act of judgment based on common sense and experience rather

> than on precedent. It may be that later, with more experience in
> concrete cases, a measure of weight can be accorded the earlier
> decisions."

In that case, a contractor had assigned the operation of electrically driven
cranes to electricians represented by the IBEW, over the claim of the
Machinists' Union that the cranes should be operated by employees in the
machine shop whom that union represented. Testing the respective union
claims against its newly announced criteria, the Board found that the
electricians rather than the machinists were entitled to operate the cranes.
The Board was cautious in the wording of its award, presumably because
an award formulated in terms of union membership might have raised
problems of union discrimination under Section 8(a)(3); the Board concluded, "In making this determination, we are assigning the disputed work to
electricians, who are represented by the IBEW, but not to the IBEW or its
members."

---

### THE ENFORCEMENT OF WORK–ASSIGNMENT AWARDS

Assume that in the Jones Construction case just above the Board had
awarded the disputed work to the *machinists,* but that the employer
continued to insist on giving the work to electricians. What action may the
Machinists Union take in order to induce the employer to comply with the
Board's award? Has either the company or the IBEW committed an unfair
labor practice which the NLRB can remedy by ordering the reassignment of
work? Would either be in contempt? Could the Machinists Union lawfully
picket to pressure the employer to reassign the work to its members? The
Supreme Court has spoken to these matters in NLRB v. PLASTERERS' LOCAL
UNION No. 79, 404 U.S. 116, 92 S.Ct. 360, 30 L.Ed.2d 312 (1971): "[T]he
§ 10(k) decision standing alone, binds no one. No cease-and-desist order
against either union or employer results from such a proceeding; the
impact of the § 10(k) decision is felt in the § 8(b)(4)(D) hearing because for
all practical purposes the Board's award determines who will prevail in the
unfair labor practice proceeding. If the picketing union persists in its
conduct despite a § 10(k) decision against it, a § 8(b)(4)(D) complaint
issues and the union will likely be found guilty of an unfair labor practice
and be ordered to cease and desist. On the other hand, if that union wins
the § 10(k) decision and the employer does not comply, the employer's
§ 8(b)(4)(D) case evaporates and the charges he filed against the picketing
union will be dismissed. Neither the employer nor the employees to whom
he has assigned the work are legally bound to observe the § 10(k) decision,
but both will lose their § 8(b)(4)(D) protection against the picketing which
may, as it did here, shut down the job. The employer will be under intense
pressure, practically, to conform to the Board's decision. This is the design
of the Act; Congress provided no other way to implement the Board's
§ 10(k) decision." [Read Section 8(b)(4)(D) carefully to see why it is that

the case under that section "evaporates" against continued picketing by the union which prevails in the Section 10(k) proceeding.]

Assume instead that in the Jones hypothetical, the Board in its 10(k) hearing awards the work to the machinists and the company in fact reassigns the work to them. IBEW believes that the Board has committed reversible error—but can it secure judicial review of the award, and if so when? It has been clearly held that Section 10(k) awards are not final orders and that they are therefore not directly reviewable by the federal courts. IBEW must precipitate a Section 8(b)(4)(D) proceeding by striking or picketing, and then must seek judicial review of the Board's cease-and-desist order in that proceeding. NLRB v. International Longshoremen's and Warehousemen's Union, Local No. 50, 504 F.2d 1209 (9th Cir.1974), cert. denied, 420 U.S. 973, 95 S.Ct. 1393, 43 L.Ed.2d 652 (1975). [Examine Section 10(*l*) of the Act to see whether the Regional Director could seek a district court injunction against IBEW for its picketing. This would provide another avenue for judicial review of the Board's 10(k) award, would it not?]

In the Ninth Circuit case just cited, the court took the very unusual step of declining to endorse the Board's work-assignment award. The court noted that very few appeals from such awards reach the courts, and that in all earlier cases the Board had been sustained. It also pointed out that the Board's awards have generally rested (as in bargaining-unit determination cases) upon the weighing of a number of factors, and that the Board's work assignment is to be judicially approved unless it is arbitrary or capricious. It nonetheless criticized the Board for having "moved almost aimlessly from factor to factor without making explicit how much weight a particular factor was given or in some instances even which union the factor favored." The court also noted the Board's apparent departure from earlier cases in the weight given to certain factors. The court concluded:

> The time has come * * * for the Board to accord a measure of weight to its past decisions and to establish some rational principles governing the weight that it gives to the various factors it considers in § 10(k) hearings. * * * [I]t will not suffice for the Board again to merely list the relevant factors and then come to a conclusion without explaining why it comes to that conclusion. * * * [W]hen the Board decides that certain factors take precedence over others, it must explain why and reconcile its decisions with its past judgments. Otherwise, § 10(k) will not bring the desired stability to the process by which jurisdictional disputes are resolved, and the courts will be unable to determine whether or not the Board's decisions are arbitrary and capricious.

On remand, 223 NLRB 1034 (1976), the Board explained its decision in greater detail, but it made no effort to generalize about, or to give weighted priority to the various factors it considered in making its work assignment. Was the court of appeals reasonable in expecting the Board to do so?

*CONGRESSIONAL PREFERENCE FOR PRIVATE RESOLUTION*

Congress in Section 10(k) contemplated governmental resolution of the work-assignment dispute only as a last resort in the event private resolution failed. Thus, that section provides that the hearing will not proceed at all if, within ten days of receiving notice of the filing of the Section 8(b)(4)(D) charge, "the parties to such dispute submit to the Board satisfactory evidence that they have adjusted, or agreed upon methods for the voluntary adjustment of, the dispute." Who are "the parties to such dispute"? The two competing unions?

The Supreme Court held in NLRB v. PLASTERERS' LOCAL UNION NO. 79, 404 U.S. 116, 92 S.Ct. 360, 30 L.Ed.2d 312 (1971), that the employer's participation in the adjustment process also had to be assured before the Board was authorized to stay its hand. There, the employer—a construction contractor engaged in installing tile—used members of the Tile Setters Union to lay tile and also to apply mortar on floors, walls and ceilings to receive tile. The Plasterers Union also claimed the latter work. It submitted its claim to the National Joint Board for the Settlement of Jurisdictional Disputes, a labor-management arbitration panel established in the construction industry in 1948. Both the Plasterers and Tile Setters were bound by such awards—and the Joint Board awarded the disputed work to the Plasterers. The employer did not participate in the proceedings of the Joint Board and was not bound by its decisions; it refused to take the mortaring work away from the Tile Setters. The Plasterers began to picket, and Section 8(b)(4)(D) and 10(k) proceedings were brought before the Board, which awarded the work to the Tile Setters. The Plasterers contended before the Supreme Court that the "parties" to the dispute were the two unions and that because they had "adjusted" their dispute before the construction industry's Joint Board, the NLRB could no longer properly hear the dispute.

The Supreme Court disagreed, and held that the employer in a work-assignment dispute is also a "party" whose participation in "voluntary adjustment" is necessary before the NLRB is required to stay its hand in the 10(k) case. Here, the employer was not disinterested—it had a labor agreement giving this work to the Tile Setters (and no such contract with the Plasterers), it believed it would lose plastering work to plastering contractors if that work were awarded to the Plasterers Union, and it thought it more efficient, less costly, and more consistent with industry practice to use the same craft to apply the adhesive as applied the tile. The Court stated that although in some cases employers have no stake in how a jurisdictional dispute is settled (just as long as it is settled promptly), in other cases employers are not neutral and have significant economic interests in the outcome of the 10(k) proceeding. The assignment may affect wages and other conditions of employment, costs, efficiency and work quality. "The usual focus of the legislative debates [relating to Sections 8(b)(4)(D) and 10(k) ]was on ways of protecting the employer from the economic havoc of jurisdictional strikes. But it does not follow from statements condemning the economically deleterious effects of inter-union strife that Congress intended an employer to have no say in a decision that may, practically, affect his business in a radical way."

----

## PROBLEM FOR DISCUSSION

May a court order all three parties to arbitrate a work-allocation dispute between two unions absent their mutual consent? *See* Emery Air Freight Corp. v. Teamsters, Local 295, 185 F.3d 85 (2d Cir.1999).

----

## D.  FEATHERBEDDING AND MAKE-WORK ARRANGEMENTS[i]

"Featherbedding" is the name given to employee practices which create or spread employment by "unnecessarily" maintaining or increasing the number of employees used, or the amount of time consumed, to work on a particular job. It may take the form of minimum-crew regulations on the railroad, make-work rules such as the setting and prompt destruction of unneeded "bogus" type in the newspaper industry, stand-by pay for musicians when a radio station broadcasts music from phonograph records, or production ceilings for work on the assembly line or at the construction site. Most of these practices stem from a desire on the part of employees for job security in the face of technological improvements or, as in the case of painters going over with a dry brush pipe already painted prior to delivery to the worksite, in the face of employer subcontracting. In addition to job security, employees often justify such practices as required by minimum standards of health and safety (*e.g.,* minimum-crew and production-ceiling limitations). These practices are "enforced" against uncooperative employees by union fines or, when there is no union on the scene, by social ostracism; and against uncooperative employers by contract remedies if the practices have been incorporated in a collective bargaining agreement and also by the use of concerted activities, such as the strike, picketing and boycott.

In spite of employee assertions that these so-called featherbedding practices are directly related to job security, health and safety, most courts at common law found these practices to be economically wasteful and without any legitimate employee justification. *E.g.,* Austin v. Painters' Dist. Council No. 22, 339 Mich. 462, 64 N.W.2d 550 (1954), cert. denied, 348 U.S. 979, 75 S.Ct. 571, 99 L.Ed. 762 (1955)(injunction granted against refusal to work with paint rollers, found not dangerous to employee health or safety); Opera on Tour v. Weber, 285 N.Y. 348, 34 N.E.2d 349 (1941), cert. denied, 314 U.S. 615, 62 S.Ct. 96, 86 L.Ed. 495 (1941)(injunction granted against strike induced by musicians in protest against use by traveling opera

----

**i.** See Aaron, Governmental Restraints on Featherbedding, 5 Stan.L.Rev. 680 (1953); Note, Drafting Problems and the Regulation of Featherbedding—an Imagined Dilemma, 73 Yale L.J. 812 (1964).

company of phonograph records rather than live orchestra). It was, indeed, not until 1942 that it was definitely held that such practices and supportive concerted activities were immune against federal antitrust proceedings under the Sherman Act; the union was held to be engaged in peaceful concerted activities in a dispute relating to conditions of employment and thus protected by the Norris–LaGuardia Act and by Section 20 of the Clayton Act. United States v. American Fed'n of Musicians, 47 F.Supp. 304 (N.D.Ill.1942), aff'd per curiam, 318 U.S. 741, 63 S.Ct. 665, 87 L.Ed. 1120 (1943).

At about the same time, however, Congress—in protest against certain particularly serious abuses committed by the musicians' union in the broadcasting industry—amended the Communications Act of 1934 by the Lea Act of 1946 (or anti-Petrillo Act, named in dubious honor of the then-president of the union), 47 U.S.C. § 506. The Act provides for fine and imprisonment for imposing restrictions on the recording of phonograph records for broadcast and, more relevantly, for inducing radio broadcasters to employ "any persons in excess of the number of employees needed * * * to perform actual services" or to pay more than once for services performed or to pay "for services * * * which are not to be performed." Another federal statute (the Hobbs Act) makes criminal the use or attempted use of extortion of money—by "actual or threatened force, violence, or fear"— which "obstructs, delays, or affects commerce" (18 U.S.C. § 1951, an amendment to the Federal Anti–Racketeering Act of 1934); it has been held by the Supreme Court to outlaw threats of union force or violence designed to induce an employer to pay for unwanted services of a particular class of laborers on a construction site. United States v. Green, 350 U.S. 415, 76 S.Ct. 522, 100 L.Ed. 494 (1956). Both the Lea Act and the Hobbs Act have lain dormant for more than twenty years, unused as weapons against featherbedding. This might be said to demonstrate both the difficulty of drafting legislation which bars the use of all featherbedding practices thought generally to be objectionable, and the unwisdom of criminalizing union activities which may be separated only slightly from peaceful pressure designed to promote the job security or safety of employees.

With at least some of these concerns in mind, Congress enacted Section 8(b)(6) as part of the Taft–Hartley amendments. That Section requires that a distinction be drawn between the employment of an unnecessary number of workers, all of whom perform actual services, and the payment of compensation to stand-bys. The House bill proscribed both practices: Section 12(a)(3) declared it to be unlawful to call or engage in a strike an object of which was to compel an employer to engage in a "featherbedding practice"; the latter term was defined to include requiring an employer either (a) to employ any person "in excess of the number of employees reasonably required by such employer to perform actual services," or (b) to pay "any money or other thing of value for services * * * which are not to be performed." (H.R.Rep.No.245, 80th Cong., 1st Sess. 25, 50, 61 (1947).) The Senate conferees objected to the first of these two clauses on the ground that "it was almost impossible for the courts to determine the exact number of men required in hundreds of industries and all kinds of functions." (93 Cong.Rec. 6601, 6603 (June 5, 1947).) Apparently the objection prevailed, for only the second clause was carried forward into the conference agreement. Thus, the legislative history makes it clear that labor unions remain free to press for make-work devices and to oppose the introduction of labor-saving machinery, but it would be an unfair labor practice to take action to establish stand-by arrangements or otherwise secure payments for which no work is required.

---

## NLRB v. Gamble Enterprises, Inc.

345 U.S. 117, 73 S.Ct. 560, 97 L.Ed. 864 (1953).

■ Mr. Justice Burton delivered the opinion of the Court.

\* \* \* For generations professional musicians have faced a shortage in the local employment needed to yield them a livelihood. They have been confronted with the competition of military bands, traveling bands, foreign musicians on tour, local amateur organizations and, more recently, technological developments in reproduction and broadcasting. To help them conserve local sources of employment, they developed local protective societies. Since 1896, they also have organized and maintained on a national scale the American Federation of Musicians, affiliated with the American Federation of Labor. By 1943, practically all professional instrumental performers and conductors in the United States had joined the Federation, establishing a membership of over 200,000, with 10,000 more in Canada.

The Federation uses its nationwide control of professional talent to help individual members and local unions. It insists that traveling band contracts be subject to its rules, laws and regulations. Article 18, § 4, of its By–Laws provides: "Traveling members cannot, without the consent of a Local, play any presentation performances in its jurisdiction unless a local house orchestra is also employed."

From this background we turn to the instant case. For more than 12 years the Palace Theater in Akron, Ohio, has been one of an interstate chain of theaters managed by respondent, Gamble Enterprises, Inc., which is a Washington corporation with its principal office in New York. Before the decline of vaudeville and until about 1940, respondent employed a local orchestra of nine union musicians to play for stage acts at that theater. When a traveling band occupied the stage, the local orchestra played from the pit for the vaudeville acts and, at times augmented the performance of the traveling band.

Since 1940, respondent has used the Palace for showing motion pictures with occasional appearances of traveling bands. Between 1940 and 1947, the local musicians, no longer employed on a regular basis, held periodic rehearsals at the theater and were available when required. When a traveling band appeared there, respondent paid the members of the local orchestra a sum equal to the minimum union wages for a similar engagement but they played no music.

The Taft–Hartley Act, containing § 8(b)(6), was passed, over the President's veto, June 23, 1947, and took effect August 22. Between July 2 and November 12, seven performances of traveling bands were presented on the Palace stage. Local musicians were neither used nor paid on those occasions. They raised no objections and made no demands for "stand-by" payments. However, in October, 1947, the American Federation of Musicians, Local No. 24 of Akron, Ohio, here called the union, opened negotiations with respondent for the latter's employment of a pit orchestra of local musicians whenever a traveling band performed on the stage. The pit orchestra was to play overtures, "intermissions" and "chasers" (the latter while patrons were leaving the theater). The union required acceptance of this proposal as a condition of its consent to local appearances of traveling bands. Respondent declined the offer and a traveling band scheduled to appear November 20 cancelled its engagement on learning that the union had withheld its consent. * * * [The union continued to block the appearance of traveling bands throughout the latter half of 1949, when no agreement could be reached on the union's demand that Gamble Enterprises employ a local orchestra for some number of engagements correlated to the number of traveling band appearances.]

In 1949, respondent filed charges with the National Labor Relations Board asserting that the union was engaging in the unfair labor practice defined in § 8(b)(6). [After the usual proceedings the Board dismissed the complaint, but the court of appeals reversed, holding that the union had violated Section 8(b)(6).]

We accept the finding of the Board, made upon the entire record, that the union was seeking actual employment for its members and not mere "stand-by" pay. The Board recognized that, formerly, before § 8(b)(6) had taken effect, the union had received "stand-by" payments in connection with traveling band appearances. Since then, the union has requested no such payments and has received none. It has, however, requested and consistently negotiated for actual employment in connection with traveling band and vaudeville appearances. It has suggested various ways in which a local orchestra could earn pay for performing competent work and, upon those terms, it has offered to consent to the appearance of traveling bands which are Federation-controlled. Respondent, with equal consistency, has declined these offers as it had a right to do.

Since we and the Board treat the union's proposals as in good faith contemplating the performance of actual services, we agree that the union has not, on this record, engaged in a practice proscribed by § 8(b)(6). It has remained for respondent to accept or reject the union's offers on their merits in the light of all material circumstances. We do not find it necessary to determine also whether such offers were "in the nature of an exaction." We are not dealing here with offers of mere "token" or nominal services. The proposals before us were appropriately treated by the Board as offers in good faith of substantial performances by competent musicians.

There is no reason to think that sham can be substituted for substance under § 8(b)(6) any more than under any other statute. Payments for "standing-by," or for the substantial equivalent of "standing-by," are not payments for services performed, but when an employer receives a bona fide offer of competent performance of relevant services, it remains for the employer, through free and fair negotiation, to determine whether such offer shall be accepted and what compensation shall be paid for the work done.

The judgment of the Court of Appeals, accordingly, is reversed and the cause is remanded to it.

■ JACKSON, J., dissenting:

* * * [T]he Court holds that so long as some exertion is performed or offered by the employees, no matter how useless or unwanted, it can never be said that there is an exaction "for services which are not performed or not to be performed." This language undoubtedly presents difficulties of interpretation, but I am not persuaded that it is so meaningless and empty in practice as the Court would make it. Congress surely did not enact a prohibition whose practical application would be restricted to those without sufficient imagination to invent some "work."

Before this Act, the union was compelling the theatre to pay for no work. When this was forbidden, it sought to accomplish the same result by compelling it to pay for useless and unwanted work. * * * Such subterfuge should not be condoned.

––––––

AMERICAN NEWSPAPER PUBLISHERS ASSOCIATION v. NLRB, 345 U.S. 100, 73 S.Ct. 552, 97 L.Ed. 852 (1953). This case involved a claim by newspaper publishers that the International Typographical Union was violating Section 8(b)(6). The union insisted on the inclusion in all collective bargaining agreements of a provision for the setting of "bogus" type—that is, the setting of type and then the prompt destruction of that type in the melting box—for standard advertisements supplied to the newspapers in a form ready for direct use.

As in the *Gamble* case, the Court read the proscriptions of Section 8(b)(6) narrowly in concluding that the Union was not in violation of the Act. The Court noted that the setting of bogus type was a longstanding practice, dating back to the nineteenth century, instituted to provide job security for union members. This work was to be performed only in slack periods so that it did not interfere with other work performed by union members. The Court traced the history of the statute and concluded that the statute was aimed only at prohibiting the "exaction" of payment when no services at all were performed. Noting that Congress intended to relieve the Board and the courts of the task of determining whether workers were "reasonably required," the Court held that "Section 8(b)(6) leaves to collective bargaining the determination of what, if any, work, including bona fide 'made work,' shall be included as compensable services and what rate of compensation shall be paid for it."

––––––

## PROBLEMS FOR DISCUSSION

**1.** During contract negotiations, Bond Bakers and the Bakers' Union have reached agreement on all contract provisions except those covering severance pay, vacation pay, and call-in pay. (Production at Bond fluctuates from day-to-day depending on the number of orders Bond receives from its customers, so that some members of the bargaining unit work only when orders are high.) The union then goes on strike over those three issues. Bond files a Section 8(b)(6) charge, claiming that vacation pay, severance pay, and especially call-in pay are, by definition, payments for which no services are performed. Assuming the Regional Director issues a complaint, how should the Administrative Law Judge rule in this case? See Cox, "Some Aspects of the Labor–Management Relations Act, 1947," 61 Harv.L.Rev. 288–89 (1947).

**2.** ABC Company was responsible for supervising construction work at a building site, and did so through three employees who worked as civil engineers; ABC undertook no construction work directly. The Teamsters have insisted that ABC hire an on-site steward, who would be available to haul construction materials, coordinate deliveries and do other construction-related work at the site. ABC asserts that it has no need for such an employee, given its role providing supervision rather than construction services. The Teamsters have called a strike to pressure ABC to hire the steward. Has it violated section 8(b)(6)? *See* Local 282, Teamsters (TDX Constr. Corp.), 332 NLRB No. 82 (2000).

––––––

## E.   VIOLENCE AND UNION RESPONSIBILITY[j]

At one time, picketing was regarded as in itself so intimidating as to constitute "moral coercion" akin to physical coercion and threats of violence. Vegelahn v. Guntner, 167 Mass. 92, 44 N.E. 1077 (1896). That view has been discarded, at first by common law judges such as Justice Holmes, then by legislatures including the federal Congress, and later by the Supreme Court which in 1940 declared in Thornhill v. Alabama, 310 U.S. 88, 60 S.Ct. 736, 84 L.Ed. 1093 (1940) that picketing represented a form of communication of information protected by the First Amendment to the Constitution. But serious violence to person and property will on occasion be committed in the course of a strike or picketing, and such violence is not constitutionally immune from governmental regulation in the public interest. Milk Wagon Drivers Union of Chicago, Local 753 v. Meadowmoor Dairies, 312 U.S. 287, 61 S.Ct. 552, 85 L.Ed. 836 (1941).

**j.** See A. Thieblot, Jr. & T. Haggard, Union Violence: The Record and the Response by Courts, Legislatures, and the NLRB (1983); Comment, Strike Violence: The NLRB's Reluctance to Wield its Broad Remedial Power, 50 Fordham L.Rev. 1371 (1982); Getman & Marshall, The Continuing Assault on the Right to Strike, 79 TEX. L. REV. 703 (2001).

Violence during a strike or picketing may subject the union and employees to several sanctions.

First, if the employees engaging in violence are employed by the company which is their object, they may be discharged or otherwise disciplined for their misconduct which, although concerted, is not within the shelter of Section 7 or 8(a)(1) of the Labor Act. See pp. 525–26, infra.

Second, state courts may enjoin or issue a judgment of damages—compensatory and punitive—against a union or individuals found to have engaged in such violence. Criminal prosecution may also be in order.

Third, if the misconduct can be charged to a union, it may be found to violate Section 8(b)(1)(A) of the Labor Act. Thus, just as with employer violence unlawful under Section 8(a)(1), a union violates Section 8(b)(1) when its agents use physical violence—or threats of physical violence—to force an employee to engage in concerted activity which he would otherwise resist. Perry Norvell Co., 80 NLRB 225 (1948). Although, as will be considered more fully at pp. 941–45, infra, NLRB jurisdiction to regulate union activity ordinarily ousts state-court jurisdiction over the same matter, the deeply felt need for local authorities to stem violence, regardless of its coexistence with a labor dispute, has been held to warrant congruent exercise of state law with Board power under Section 8(b)(1). Ordinary principles of agency law will be invoked by the NLRB to determine union responsibility for the conduct of its agents in cases of violence. Thus, if threats to strike-breakers, or physical injury to them, are effected by officers or employees of the union within the general scope of their activities on behalf of the union—even though contrary to specific instructions—the union may be held responsible under Section 8(b)(1). International Longshoremen's Union Local 6 v. Sunset Line & Twine Co., 77 F.Supp. 119 (N.D.Cal.1948)(since union business agent was acting in furtherance of the strike, and he had authority to direct the strike and picketing, union is responsible for his assault and threats against nonstrikers). Reference should also be made to Section 2(13) of the Labor Act: "In determining whether any person is acting as an 'agent' of another person so as to make such other person responsible for his acts, the question of whether the specific acts performed were actually authorized or subsequently ratified shall not be controlling."

In cases in which the union is held to violate Section 8(b)(1)(A) by causing or threatening physical violence, the Board will issue a cease-and-desist order but will not require the union to reimburse the employee victims either for loss of pay (caused by the union's blocking access to the plant) or for physical or mental injury. Although this refusal to grant monetary damages against the union is controversial and has divided the Board—particularly in cases of flagrant and aggravated violence—the Board has adhered to this policy for some thirty years. The reasons were reiterated in Union de Tronquistas Local 901 (Lock Joint Pipe & Co.), 202 NLRB 399 (1973). The Board noted that, while it deplores violence in the course of a strike or picketing, the award of substantial monetary damages against the union will unduly interfere with the policy of the Labor Act to protect concerted activities. Emotions run high in times of industrial combat; the violent conduct of isolated individuals might all too readily be attributed to the union; the large number of employees refraining from work will both create serious problems of proof as to the reasons therefor and generate the risk of enormous backpay liability for the union. The Board also asserted that remedies against the union for violation of Section 8(b)(1)(A) for strike violence were sufficient deterrent: the Board may ultimately issue a cease-and-desist order, court-enforceable through the contempt sanction; while the case is pending before the Board, an injunction may be sought under Section 10(j) in aggravated cases; and the union seeking to enforce its bargaining rights through violent action may be denied a bargaining order and forced to demonstrate its majority support in a secret-ballot election. Moreover, the employee suffering physical or mental injury may secure redress against the union in a state-court tort action.

Do you share the Board's reticence to award damages, in cases of union violence contrary to Section 8(b)(1), for loss of pay and for physical or mental injury to employees? Ought the Board make *some* exceptions to its absolute bar?

In United Mine Workers v. Bagwell, 512 U.S. 84, 114 S.Ct. 2552, 129 L.Ed.2d 642 (1994), the United States Supreme Court was called upon to decide whether fifty-two million dollars in fines levied upon the union for violent activity in contempt of an injunction was civil or criminal in nature. A proceeding in criminal contempt would require a jury trial and proof beyond a reasonable doubt; a civil contempt would not. The Court noted the traditional if often "elusive" distinction between the two: civil contempt is a sanction to coerce obedience (e.g., to pay alimony or to give testimony), while criminal contempt is punitive. And it noted the concern that the contempt power is especially liable to abuse, where the offended judge is solely responsible for identifying, prosecuting, adjudicating, and sanctioning the contumacious conduct. In the instant case, the trial court had laid down an exacting code of behavior to govern the striking union, and had later identified precise dollar amounts it would fine the union for each future violation. Under all the circumstances, the Court concluded the fines imposed were criminal in nature and could not be imposed without a jury trial.

———

## F.  Remedies for Union Unfair Labor Practices[g]

Along with the ban upon certain union-induced concerted activities, which Congress enacted in 1947 and expanded in 1959, came the revival in modified form of the labor injunction. In view of Congress's special objection to the secondary boycott (including the hot cargo agreement), strikes

**g.**  See P. Walther, J. F. Hunsicker & J.     Practices (2d ed. 1986).
Kane, NLRB Remedies for Unfair Labor

in support of work-assignment demands, and unlawfully protracted recognition picketing, Congress provided in Section 10(*l*) of the Labor Act that the Regional Director is obligated to request a temporary injunction in the event a charge is filed against a union for such violations and the charge is believed by the Regional Director to have merit. (Section 10(*l*) should be studied, with attention given to the kind of union activity it reaches, the timing of the injunction request, the function of the federal district court, the limitations upon the issuance of an injunction and the procedures to be employed.) Many cases arising from union-induced strikes and picketing are promptly handled through the injunction procedures of Section 10(*l*) and in many instances the injunction effectively terminates the dispute, without completion of the unfair labor practice proceeding before the Administrative Law Judge and the Board.

Union unfair labor practices not covered within Section 10(*l*) are subject to the injunction procedures of Section 10(j)—as are all employer unfair labor practices. Examples of union conduct which have been enjoined under Section 10(j) are strikes initiated without complying with the notification and cooling-off requirements of Section 8(d), inducement of employer discrimination against nonmembers, and violence or mass picketing in violation of Section 8(b)(1). The Section 10(j) injunction differs from that under Section 10(*l*) in two major respects: it may not be sought by the Regional Director until after a complaint has been issued at the Regional Office and only after authorization by the five-member Board, and—more important—the decision to petition for the 10(j) injunction lies within the discretion of the Regional Director and is not mandated by the Labor Act. Although the federal district court will generally issue an injunction under Section 10(*l*) whenever it is determined that there is reasonable cause to believe Section 8(b)(4) or 8(b)(7) has been violated, the court will generally require additional proof of need for the injunction when it is sought under Section 10(j). The requirements for issuance of the 10(j) injunction—and the fact that it is sought and issued very infrequently—have already been discussed, at pages 261–62, supra.

Not only did Congress in the Taft–Hartley amendments provide for the intervention of the federal district courts by way of injunction against union unfair labor practices, but it also took the unusual step of singling out union unfair labor practices under Section 8(b)(4) and declaring them in Section 303 to be federal torts which may be remedied by actions in federal and state trial courts for damages for past economic harm caused to the employer. Such an action may be brought, in the case of a secondary boycott for example, either by the "neutral" employer or by the "primary" employer. United Brick and Clay Workers v. Deena Artware, Inc., 198 F.2d 637 (6th Cir.), cert. denied, 344 U.S. 897, 73 S.Ct. 277, 97 L.Ed. 694 (1952). More generally, a cause of action has been accorded third persons who have suffered rather direct and foreseeable economic injury as a result of the union's illegal activity. Thus, recovery was permitted for business losses suffered by an exclusive area sales agent of the primary employer in a secondary-boycott situation, even though that sales agent was not the object of the unlawful picketing. W. J. Milner & Co. v. IBEW Local 349, 476

F.2d 8 (5th Cir.1973). But see UMW v. Osborne Mining Co., 279 F.2d 716 (6th Cir.1960), cert. denied, 364 U.S. 881, 81 S.Ct. 169, 5 L.Ed.2d 103 (1960).

Assuming a proper party plaintiff, common law principles developed under the law of torts dictate liability in a Section 303 action for all injuries proximately flowing from the illegal conduct. Thus, the aggrieved party may recover for loss of a lease suffered because of the illegal union activity and for loss of business profits which can be ascertained with reasonable certainty, Riverside Coal Co. v. UMW, 410 F.2d 267 (6th Cir.1969), cert. denied, 396 U.S. 846, 90 S.Ct. 89, 24 L.Ed.2d 95 (1969); for time and money spent in attempting to have the picketing stopped, Abbott v. Local Union No. 142 of United Associations of Journeymen and Apprentices of Pipe Fitting Industry, 429 F.2d 786 (5th Cir.1970); and for such losses as the rental value of idled equipment and amounts paid as salaries of supervisory personnel for the period of the work stoppage, and daily liquidated damages under a contract with a third party to the extent that late performance resulted from the boycott, Wells v. International Union of Operating Engineers, 206 F.Supp. 414 (W.D.Ky.1962), aff'd, 303 F.2d 73 (6th Cir. 1962).

Both the language and the legislative history of Section 303 demonstrate that the damages under that section are to be limited, as a matter of federal law, to compensatory damages. Punitive damages may not be awarded for violation of that section. Local 20, Teamsters v. Morton, 377 U.S. 252, 84 S.Ct. 1253, 12 L.Ed.2d 280 (1964). Nor may an injunction issue, for that form of relief may be sought or issued only by the NLRB. Amalgamated Ass'n of Street, Elec. Ry. & Motor Coach Employees v. Dixie Motor Coach Corp., 170 F.2d 902 (8th Cir.1948). If, however, the court considers along with the Section 303 claim a proper claim for violation of state law—most commonly, for violence in the course of a strike or picketing—the court does have the power to award punitive damages or an injunction, if that would be proper under state law, but only with regard to the violent conduct under consideration as distinguished from the peaceful (although illegal) conduct of the union in violation of Section 8(b)(4). The Supreme Court recently decided that attorneys' fees may not be awarded to the successful plaintiff in a Section 303 action. In Summit Valley Industries, Inc. v. Local 112, United Broth. of Carpenters and Joiners, 456 U.S. 717, 102 S.Ct. 2112, 72 L.Ed.2d 511 (1982), the Court held that that section did not clearly provide for a departure from the "American rule" barring the recovery of attorneys' fees in the ordinary case, and also that the legislative history of Section 303 compelled the conclusion that the employer's interests were sufficiently vindicated by the award of compensatory damages for its business losses.

Court remedies under Section 303 and Board remedies under Section 8(b)(4) are independent. Choosing one remedy does not constitute a waiver of the other; both remedies may be pursued simultaneously in the two different forums; and recovery under Section 303 need not await a Board determination of illegality under Section 8(b)(4). International Longshoremen's and Warehousemen's Union v. Juneau Spruce Corp., 342 U.S. 237, 72 S.Ct. 235, 96 L.Ed. 275 (1952). Indeed, it is possible that the Board will find a union not to have committed an unfair labor practice while a judge and jury will conclude that the union—in the same transaction—has violated Section 303, with both determinations being affirmed by the court of appeals. NLRB v. Deena Artware, Inc., 198 F.2d 645 (6th Cir.1952), cert. denied, 345 U.S. 906, 73 S.Ct. 644, 97 L.Ed. 1342 (1953); United Brick & Clay Workers v. Deena Artware, Inc., 198 F.2d 637 (6th Cir.1952), cert. denied 344 U.S. 897, 73 S.Ct. 277, 97 L.Ed. 694 (1952). But some courts have concluded that a union which has been held by the Board after a full and fair hearing to have violated Section 8(b)(4) will be collaterally estopped in a later proceeding under Section 303 to challenge the Board's findings. *E.g.,* Paramount Transp. Systems v. Chauffeurs, Teamsters and Helpers, Local 150, 436 F.2d 1064 (9th Cir.1971).

# PART FIVE

# ADMINISTRATION OF THE COLLECTIVE AGREEMENT

## I. THE COLLECTIVE AGREEMENT AND THE GRIEVANCE PROCEDURE[a]

---

*THE COLLECTIVE BARGAINING AGREEMENT*

The anticipated, and usual, product of collective bargaining is a written agreement between the employer and the union. In part, this agreement sets down the relationship between those two parties, for example in provisions dealing with the recognition of the union as exclusive representative for employees in the bargaining unit or dealing with the resolution of contract disputes through a grievance procedure. In greatest measure, the labor contract sets down the relationship between the employer and its employees, and among the employees themselves. Thus, the contract will normally have provisions governing wages, hours, discipline, promotions and transfers, medical and health insurance, pensions, vacations and holidays, work assignments, seniority and the like. The labor agreement is not a contract of employment; employees are hired separately and individually, but the tenure and terms of their employment once in the unit are regulated by the provisions of the collective bargaining agreement.

The collective bargaining agreement shares with the ordinary commercial contract a number of common features of form and function. But the

---

**a.** See Cox, Rights Under a Labor Agreement, 69 Harv.L.Rev. 601 (1956); Cox, The Legal Nature of Collective Bargaining Agreements, 57 Mich.L.Rev. 1 (1958); Feller, A General Theory of the Collective Bargaining Agreement, 61 Calif.L.Rev. 663 (1973); S. Slichter, J. Healy & E. Livernash, The Impact of Collective Bargaining on Management 692–738 (1960); Summers, Collective Agreements and the Law of Contracts, 78 Yale L.J. 525 (1969).

differences between the labor contract and the commercial contract are of far more profound significance. While the typical commercial contract is the creation of parties who have been joined in a voluntary arrangement sparked by mutual self-interest, the labor contract is the product of a bilateral relationship which is in large measure compelled by law, frequently against the wishes of one of the two parties. Most commercial contracts regulate the rights and duties of the parties for a single and transient transaction, or for a defined period of time. The labor contract, while fixed in duration, will usually govern the parties' relationship for a number of years and looks toward an indefinite period of continued dealing in the future. While the labor contract resembles the commercial contract in its form, in that it is technically an agreement between two signatory parties, it most pointedly shapes the rights and duties for a mass of third persons, the employees in the plant. Those employees spend a great part of their life doing the work which is the subject of the labor contract. By articulating or absorbing a host of rules and regulations for carrying on the day-to-day continuing activities of those employees, the labor contract functions more like a statute or a code of regulations than it does a bilateral agreement. Moreover, the union, although a legal entity with capacity to contract, does not speak for a single monolithic constituency but rather for an amalgam of workers who are skilled and unskilled, young and old, male and female, black and white, educated and uneducated, whose ambitions, needs and interests frequently come into conflict.

Because of many of these characteristics, the labor contract—burdened with the task of regulating a complex work community on a continuing basis—cannot reduce to writing each and every norm or rule that has been developed over time to govern the parties' activities. It is common to treat the collective bargaining agreement as comprised not only of the written and executed document but also of plant customs and industrial practices as well as of informal agreements and concessions made at the bargaining table but not reduced to writing. Moreover, many contract provisions contain purposeful ambiguities or silences, in the expectation that no dispute will arise over their meaning or that future disputes will be resolved in due course to the mutual satisfaction of the parties. The parties normally realize that resolution of contract disputes will require formal procedures, typically culminating in recourse to a neutral third party; by this process of grievance settlement and arbitration, the contract itself evolves and the process of collective bargaining continues. Both the labor contract and the commercial contract are negotiated subject to applicable rules of contract law and of public policy, but the labor contract is far more peculiarly enmeshed in a framework of regulatory laws—in part state law but always against the background of federal labor legislation, and in part conventional contract law but always against the background of the special history of labor-management relations in America. Because of this, there are a number of different decisionmaking agencies which are potentially implicated in the construction and application of the terms of the labor contract: state courts and federal courts, privately selected arbitrators, state administrative agencies, the National Labor Relations Board, and other federal agencies (such as the Equal Employment Opportunity Commission or the Department of Labor).

––––––––

*THE GRIEVANCE PROCEDURE*

Most collective bargaining agreements make express provision for resolution of contract disputes not by a lawsuit in a civil court but rather through machinery which is internal to the plant or company. Some contracts define the term "grievance" very broadly to refer, for example, to "any dispute, disagreement or difference arising between any employee or the union and the company." More often, however, grievances are more narrowly defined as disputes relating in some manner to the proper interpretation or application of the collective agreement. Such a definition does not necessarily imply that a grievance must involve a matter that is explicitly covered by some term of the contract for, as just noted, the "agreement" of the parties is commonly understood to encompass unwritten past practices and informal understandings; the parties' relationship is constantly evolving and adapting to new and changing circumstances.

The typical agreement will provide for the presentation of a grievance, often orally but sometimes in writing, by the aggrieved employee or the union to the appropriate supervisor or foreman. If unresolved, the grievance will move to a higher level of supervision, and it is common to have a three or four step grievance procedure, in which the last in-company step involves dealings between high union officials (sometimes at the international level) and company officials (commonly at companywide levels outside the plant). The great majority of grievances are generally settled at the first stage; were it otherwise, higher management and union officials could easily become overburdened with the task of reviewing complaints.

An increasing number of agreements specify time limits within which grievances must be initiated, considered, and, if necessary, appealed to higher levels. Originally, the demand for time limits emanated from union officials who sought to prevent stalling tactics by management and to avoid impatience and dissatisfaction among the employees involved. But management has also become interested in preventing delay, particularly in cases involving discharges and layoffs where retroactive pay may be required in the event that the grievance is settled favorably to the union.

Agreements commonly provide that union representatives processing grievances will be given access to the plant premises and to plant personnel in order to obtain the information needed to prosecute the grievance. In addition, special provisions may be included with respect to union representatives, such as elected shop stewards or grievance committeemen, who are also employees of the company. Thus, contracts commonly provide that such employees will be compensated for working time spent in processing grievances.

Further provisions are often included to safeguard the jobs of shop stewards or grievance committeemen and insure their continuity of service. For example, these employees may be given preferred seniority to protect them from layoffs, and management may be further restricted in transferring them to other plants or departments. (Are these forms of "job favoritism" unlawful, as discrimination which encourages union membership? See pp. 1134–39, infra.)

Although a wide variety of techniques may be employed, any grievance procedure can be expected to serve a number of distinct purposes affecting the union, the employer and the employees. The most straightforward function of the process, of course, is to provide a method for peacefully settling the complaints of employees, after mutual deliberation, and in so doing, to provide guidance for future cases by clarifying the terms of the contract. In the course of fulfilling this primary function, however, the grievance procedure may also serve other purposes. For example, the accumulation of grievances may pin-point ambiguities and trouble-spots in the agreement which can be taken up for discussion at the next contract negotiations. Moreover, the pattern of grievances may provide valuable information to higher management by identifying problems of supervision and personnel policy which may then be corrected before more serious trouble can arise. In some instances, the grievance procedure may also be used, for better or worse, as a strategic device. For example, certain unions may look upon the process as a technique with which to gradually extend the bargaining agreement by gaining concessions from management that stretch the literal provisions of the contract. In other cases, unions may press grievances with particular vigor in order to gain leverage in forthcoming contract negotiations or to satisfy constituents who are being appealed to by rival factions within the union.

In the light of experience in countless plants, it is clear beyond dispute that an effective, well-administered grievance procedure can play an indispensable role in improving the climate of labor relations and providing a measure of "industrial due process" to the individual worker. The advantages to be derived from these procedures have been summed up in the following terms by a distinguished panel of labor relations experts:[b]

"The gains from this system are especially noteworthy because of their effect on the recognition and dignity of the individual worker. This system helps prevent arbitrary action on questions of discipline, layoff, promotion, and transfer, and sets up orderly procedures for the handling of grievances. Wildcat strikes and other disorderly means of protest have been curtailed and an effective work discipline generally established. In many situations, cooperative relationships marked by mutual respect between management and labor stand as an example of what can be done."

**b.** Independent Study Group for the Committee for Economic Development, The Public Interest in National Labor Policy, p. 32 (1961).

In order that the grievance procedure may achieve these objectives, there has developed a principle which can be capsulized in the phrase "Obey, and then grieve." The employer, it may be assumed, has issued a work rule or through its supervisors has given an employee an order which violates the employer's obligations under the collective bargaining agreement. Both industrial justice and plant efficiency can be secured if the wronged employees do not take it upon themselves to ignore the improper rule or order but rather obey it and file a grievance. The reasons behind this cardinal principle were set forth by the late Harry Shulman, professor and Dean of the Yale Law School, permanent umpire under the labor contract between the Ford Motor Company and the United Auto Workers, and commonly regarded as one of the great scholar/practitioners of the art of labor arbitration. In FORD MOTOR CO., 3 Lab.Arb. 779 (1944), Dean Shulman stated:

> "The remedy under the contract for violation of right lies in the grievance procedure and only in the grievance procedure. To refuse obedience because of a claimed contract violation would be to substitute individual action for collective bargaining and to replace the grievance procedure with extra-contractual methods. And such must be the advice of the committeeman if he gives advice to employees. His advice must be that the safe and proper method is to obey supervision's instructions and to seek correction and redress through the grievance procedure. * * *

> " * * * [M]ore important, the grievance procedure is prescribed in the contract precisely because the parties anticipated that there would be claims of violations which would require adjustment. That procedure is prescribed for all grievances and not merely for doubtful ones. Nothing in the contract even suggests the idea that only doubtful violations need be processed through the grievance procedure and that clear violations can be resisted through individual self-help. The only difference between a 'clear' violation and a 'doubtful' one is that the former makes a clear grievance and the latter a doubtful one. But both must be handled in the regular prescribed manner. * * * "

---

## II.   GRIEVANCE ARBITRATION[a]

---

**a.**   See C. Barreca, A. Miller & M. Zimny, Labor Arbitrator Development: A Handbook (1983); T. Bornstein, A. Gosline & M. Greenbaum (eds.), Labor and Employment Arbitration (1997); Cox, Reflections Upon Labor Arbitration, 72 Harv.L.Rev. 1482 (1959); F. & E. Elkouri, How Arbitration Works (5th ed. 1997); Feller, The Remedy Power in Grievance Arbitration, 5 Ind.Rel.L.J. 128 (1982); R. Fleming, The Labor Arbitration Process (1965); Fuller, Collective Bargaining and the Arbitrator, 1963 Wis.L.Rev. 3; P. Hays, Labor Arbitration: A Dissenting View (1966); Nolan & Abrams, American Labor Arbitration: The Early Years, 35 U.Fla.L.Rev. 373 (1983), and The Maturing Years, 35

## A. THE NATURE AND FUNCTIONS OF LABOR ARBITRATION

It has often been observed that the solving of disputes through arbitration probably antedates recorded history. Although in the field of labor relations, the practice is of relatively recent origin, at least in this country, arbitration provisions can today be found in an estimated 96% of all agreements. The reasons for the prevalence of grievance arbitration are clear enough. In part, its use has resulted from the emergence of powerful unions able to insist upon this procedure at the bargaining table. Many unions favor arbitration both because they believe that they will receive a more sympathetic hearing from an arbitrator and because they retain a lingering distrust of courts and "legalistic" procedures originating from judicial decisions prior to the passage of the Norris–LaGuardia Act. Perhaps a stronger reason for the spread of arbitration lies in the growing recognition by management as well as labor that arbitration represents the best available alternative for settling disputes under collective agreements. Since disagreements over the interpretation or application of these agreements arise frequently, it would be intolerable to management and impossibly burdensome to unions to resort to a strike in order to resolve their differences. A possible alternative would be to bring suit in a state or federal court (and this procedure may actually be followed under agreements which make no provision for arbitration). Nevertheless, crowded dockets make the process too cumbersome to be widely accepted.

Most commonly, the arbitration is conducted before an individual, although occasionally it will be a three-person panel (with each party appointing one member of the panel more as an advocate than as a neutral). Typically, the arbitrator is selected by the parties on an ad hoc basis to decide only a single case. In some of the larger industrial bargaining units, however, in light of the volume of grievances, a permanent umpire or referee will be selected, to be paid an annual retainer and to handle all of the cases going to arbitration under a given contract or group of contracts. Arbitrators come most frequently from the ranks of the legal profession or the teaching profession (most commonly, professors of law or business administration or industrial relations), although there will sometimes be resort to a local clergyman or other respected person in the community. There are also a relatively small number of full-time professional labor arbitrators. Government or private organizations, primarily the Federal Mediation and Conciliation Service or the American Arbitration Association, facilitate the selection of an arbitrator by supplying the parties with lists of names of qualified persons from which the parties are to choose; not surprisingly, the parties will frequently research earlier arbitration decisions rendered by the persons on the list, in an effort to determine their "leanings."

U.Fla.L.Rev. 557 (1983); R. Schoonhoven (ed.), Fairweather's Practice and Procedure in Labor Arbitration (4th ed. 1999); Shulman, Reason, Contract, and Law in Labor Relations, 68 Harv.L.Rev. 999 (1955); C. Updegraff, Arbitration and Labor Relations (3d ed. 1970); A. Zack, Arbitration in Practice (1984); A. Zack & R. Bloch, Labor Agreement in Negotiation and Arbitration (1983).

There are some important differences between the ad hoc arbitrator and the permanent umpire. The latter over the course of time develops a familiarity with the parties, with the contract, with past negotiations, with the physical set-up of the plant and with plant practices. By virtue of this familiarity, he is sometimes expected by the parties (or assumes that he is expected) to consider the long-range implications of particular decisions and the overall working relationship between the parties, rather than to render a "literal" decision within the four corners of the written document. The ad hoc arbitrator, appointed to decide a single dispute, may not have this kind of familiarity and feels constrained to take a more particularistic or legalistic attitude toward the dispute, the parties and the agreement. Whether these differing attitudes are appropriate is, however, a source of considerable disagreement within the arbitral community. Some observers have pointed out another difference between the permanent and the ad hoc arbitrator, noting the greater likelihood that the ad hoc arbitrator—whose future reemployment by the parties may depend on it—will render a decision which is excessively cautious about offending one party or the other and which tends to "split the difference." Support for this claim is said to be commonly found in discharge grievances, where the arbitrator will find the discharge to have been without just cause and will order the grievant reinstated, but without imposing on the company any liability for backpay.

In any event, whether the arbitrator is designated on a permanent or an ad hoc basis, he will sometimes be required to determine whether he is properly simply a creature of the parties whose function is to determine no more than what their private-contractual intentions are, or is more like a civil judge who can (or must) consider such "external" matters as law and public policy. This issue can arise when one party relies upon an explicit provision in the agreement and the other party claims that the arbitrator must find the provision to violate the National Labor Relations Act or Title VII of the 1964 Civil Rights Act and must refuse to give it effect. Here too, arbitral opinion is sharply split. The matter is further complicated by the fact that, as noted above, many arbitrators are not trained in the law but are selected rather for their expertise in industrial relations or because they are a respected "lay" figure in the community. An added source of difficulty are the statements in a number of judicial opinions to the effect that an arbitrator's award will be subject to court reversal if the arbitrator strays from the agreement and bases his opinion solely upon the assumed requirements of statutory or case law.

On the whole arbitration proceedings are more informal, more expeditious and less costly than civil litigation. The hearing itself may take place almost anywhere—in a conference room at the plant, in an office or even a hotel room. Frequently, the parties are not represented by lawyers (but by a full-time union representative and an industrial-relations or personnel executive for the company). Formal rules of evidence do not apply, and arbitrators tend to admit "for what it is worth" a substantial amount of evidence which would normally be objectionable as immaterial or hearsay. Although evidence is elicited by questioning witnesses and submitting documents, and witnesses will generally be examined and cross-examined in a more or less orderly fashion, the presentation of written or oral evidence is commonly quite informal and unstructured. In many cases, the purpose of the proceeding is as much to "ventilate" the grievance as it is to secure a favorable decision from the arbitrator. The arbitrator's decision, usually in writing, tends to be brief, undetailed, and untechnical; it will commonly be filed with the parties less than a month after the hearing. Written briefs are not common, and in almost all cases in which they are filed, are submitted after the hearing rather than before. Many of these informal qualities—which have always made arbitration a most attractive alternative to civil litigation—have been giving way in recent years to a greater "legalization" of the arbitration process, as lawyers have been called in to serve as arbitrators and as parties have increasingly called in legal counsel to represent them at hearings.

Cox, "REFLECTIONS UPON LABOR ARBITRATION," 72 Harv.L.Rev. 1482, 1493, 1498–99 (1959): "The generalities, the deliberate ambiguities, the gaps, the unforeseen contingencies, and the need for a rule even though the agreement is silent all require a creativeness in contract administration which is quite unlike the attitude of one construing a deed, a promissory note, or a 300–page corporate trust indenture. The process of interpretation cannot be the same because the conditions which determine the character of the instruments are different. * * *

"At this point we may draw two conclusions:

"First, it is not unqualifiedly true that a collective-bargaining agreement is simply a document by which the union and employees have imposed upon management limited, express restrictions of its otherwise absolute right to manage the enterprise, so that an employee's claim must fail unless he can point to a specific contract provision upon which the claim is founded. There are too many people, too many problems, too many unforeseeable contingencies to make the words of the contract the exclusive source of rights and duties. One cannot reduce all the rules governing a community like an industrial plant to fifteen or even fifty pages. Within the sphere of collective bargaining, the institutional characteristics and the governmental nature of the collective-bargaining process demand a common law of the shop which implements and furnishes the context of the agreement. We must assume that intelligent negotiators acknowledged so plain a need unless they stated a contrary rule in plain words.

"Second, the 'interpretation and application' of a collective-bargaining agreement through grievance arbitration is not limited to documentary construction of language. The failure to recognize this truth probably explains much of the conflict between arbitral and judicial thinking. * * * Collective agreements, because of the institutional characteristics already mentioned, are less complete and more loosely drawn than many other contracts; therefore, there is much more to be supplied from the context in which they were negotiated. The governing criteria are not judge-made principles of the common law but the practices, assumptions, understandings, and aspirations of the going industrial concern. The arbitrator is not bound by conventional law although he may follow it. If we are to develop a rationale of grievance arbitration, more work should be directed towards identifying the standards which shape arbitral opinions; if the process is rational, as I assert, a partial systematization should be achievable even though scope must be left for art and intuition. I can pause only to note some of the familiar sources: legal doctrines, a sense of fairness, the national labor policy, past practice at the plant, and perhaps good industrial practice generally. Of these perhaps past practice is the most significant; witness the cases in which it is argued that a firmly established practice takes precedence even over the plain meaning of the words.''

## PROBLEM FOR DISCUSSION

In a collective bargaining agreement between Inland Container Corporation and the Paper Mill Workers, it was provided that job vacancies would be filled by management selection but that "if the qualifications are comparatively equal between two Regular Employees, seniority shall prevail." An opening appeared for a job and though a regular employee, Torres, was the only applicant, the Company considered his experience insufficient and promoted an apprentice with less seniority. Torres submitted a grievance claiming he should have at least been given a fair trial in the new job. At the outset of the arbitration hearing, however, Torres stated unequivocally that he no longer desired promotion to the new job and would not accept it even if it were offered to him. Management then moved to dismiss the proceeding, but the union asked to continue and demanded that a decision be reached. What disposition would you make as arbitrator?

## B.  DISCHARGE AND DISCIPLINE[b]

## Mallinckrodt, Inc.

83–2 CCH Arb. ¶ 8358 (Seidman 1983).

■ SEIDMAN, ARBITRATOR: These are three related discharge cases. All three grievants were discharged by the Company on September 24, 1982 for "violation of Company work rule 3–SLP–6–2, Intoxicating Liquor and Drugs". All three employees grieved with the support of the Union on the

---

**b.**  See L. Cooper, D. Nolan & R. Bales, ADR in the Workplace (2000); Edwards, Due Process Considerations in Labor Arbitration, 25 Arb.J. 141 (1970); M. Hill & A. Sinicropi, Management Rights (1986); Kadish, The Criminal Law and Industrial Discipline as Sanctioning Systems: Some Comparative Ob- servations, 17th Annual Proceedings of Nat'l Acad. of Arbitrators 125 (1964); A. Koven & S. Smith, Just Cause: The Seven Tests (2d ed. 1992); J. Redeker, Employee Discipline: Policies and Practices (1989); Summers, Indi- vidual Protection Against Unjust Dismissal: Time for a Statute, 62 Va.L.Rev. 481 (1976).

ground that by their discharge the Company violated Article 2, Section 2 of the collective bargaining agreement because it was not "for just cause", the litmus for any discipline.

\* \* \*

### [Findings of Fact]

I find that Officer [B.] testified truthfully in this proceeding. Based upon his testimony, I find that [B.] observed [Y.] smoking a marijuana cigarette. I find that [C.], [Y.] and [P.] were in the mill room of Building 204 together on that evening. I find that [C.] admitted to [B.] that he was sharing a joint with [Y.] and [P.] that evening. I find, based on [C.'s] testimony, that [P.] also shared a joint with the other two that evening.

In so doing, I rely upon my evaluation of [B.'s] credibility; his official knowledge of the odor of marijuana; his prior knowledge of the names, faces, and physical appearances of the three grievants; [B.'s] lack of any reason to falsify his testimony; and [B.'s] response to vigorous and able cross examination.

I find the testimony of the three grievants to be incredible. I visited Building 204 and its mill room. Even during the day the mill room was a dank, dark, damp, and dismal place. It was no place that anyone would go to on a break for recreational purposes. It is no place where anyone would sit in the dark simply for the purpose of rapping. It is exactly the type of place where one would go to hide in order to engage in a forbidden act. It is also a place where one would crack open a door to the outside to permit fresh air into its interior to dispel the heavy, pungent, and sweet odor of marijuana.

I further find: 1. [C.], [Y.] and [P.] agreed to go out to the mill room of Building 204 to share a marijuana joint on their break; 2. They met there at or about 9:00 p.m. and did share a joint; 3. None of them, as a result of sharing this joint, were under the influence of marijuana to such an extent that they were unfit to continue at their work; 4. While Building 204 is a no-smoking area, the fact of their smoking where they were smoking posed no threat of fire or explosion to the premises or its contents; 5. Each was discharged solely for possession and/or use of a drug, to wit, sharing a single marijuana cigarette; 6. None had ever been previously disciplined for possession or use of intoxicants or drugs.

### [Reasonableness of Penalty]

Having found that the three grievants in fact were guilty of a violation of the Company's work rule with respect to the use or possession of intoxicating liquor and drugs on Company property, the next question is whether the penalty of discharge was "for just cause" as required by the contract and claimed by the Company, or not "for just cause" because excessive, as contended by the Union. To determine this I must consider the history of the work rule, including its promulgation and enforcement.

**[History of Rule]**

The rule was first posted on February 20, 1975. Its subject was "Intoxicating Liquor and Drugs." The purpose of its posting was "to establish the policy on possession and use of intoxicating liquor and drugs." The policy was stated to be as follows:

"1. Possession of intoxicating liquor and/or drugs on Company property is strictly forbidden.

"2. Employees will not be permitted to work while under the influence of intoxicating liquor or drugs.

"3. Possession of, or being under the influence of, intoxicating liquor or drugs on the job will result in immediate disciplinary action, up to and including discharge."

On February 28, 1975 the Company under the subject of "Constructive Discipline" with the purpose: "To establish the St. Louis Plant Policy on Constructive Discipline and the handling of infractions of Plant Work Rules and other administration [sic] policy" posted the following:

Punishment is a last resort to be used only when all other corrective action has failed.

When punishment is required to maintain a high level of discipline, it will be administered in a uniform fashion throughout the plant.

Seriousness of the proven offense, the employees past record, and his length of service will always be considered in determining appropriate action.

Thereafter, on May 31, 1977, the Company posted a further notice having as its purpose the drawing of distinctions between work rules whose violation was not so serious and those whose violation was serious. Among the eight listed as "serious violations" was "Possession of Intoxicating Liquor or Drugs." The notice stated: "When the circumstances warrant, after thorough investigation, an employee found in violation of the following work rules will be discharged."

At a subsequent time, but prior to the incident herein, the company posted a further notice stating that as a producer of narcotics the Company was bound by regulations established by the Drug Enforcement Administration, among which was the following:

It is the position of DEA that employees who possess, sell, use, or divert controlled substances will subject themselves not only to State or Federal prosecution for any illicit activity, but shall immediately become the subject of independent action regarding their continued employment. The employer will assess the seriousness of the employee's violation, the position of responsibility held by the employee, past record of employment, etc., in determining whether to suspend, transfer, terminate or take other action against the employee.

Finally, on August 10, 1981, the Company and the Union issued a Joint Statement of Policy on Union–Management Employee Assistance Program which stated:

> The purpose of this program is to assist employees who develop behavioral medical problems by helping them to help themselves to arrest its advancement before the condition renders them unemployable.
>
> 1. The parties recognize alcoholism and substance abuse problems as illnesses which are treatable. Mallincrokdt, in conjunction with UAW Local 1887, intends to offer assistance in referring the employees to treatment of these and other behavioral medical problems which result in impaired job performance.

As evidence of the Company's policy in enforcing violations of this work rule when applicable to the possession or use of intoxicating liquor on Company property, the Union introduced into evidence five cases wherein the employees were found to have been guilty of violation of this work rule with the following results:

1. Three day suspension; 2. Three day suspension; 3. One day suspension; 4. Two week suspension, since this employee had previously been suspended three days for the same thing; and 5. After several previous suspensions of a like nature an employee was discharged because of alcoholism which reflected itself in absenteeism. During the grievance procedure the employee was reinstated contingent upon his completing the Joint Labor–Management Employee Assistance Program.

### [Findings as to Penalty]

Thus, the Union proved, and I find, that the employer's response to alcoholism is to utilize progressive discipline. No employee in the history of this Company has ever been discharged for the first offense of alcohol abuse.

The Union claimed that since both alcohol abuse and drug abuse are dealt with in the same work rule and are subject to the same penalty that discipline for the one should be consistent with discipline for the other. Since alcohol abuse is treated under the progressive discipline system so should drug abuse. Since no one has ever been discharged for a first offense of alcohol abuse, no one should be discharged for a first offense of drug abuse.

The Company responded that the two are different and should be treated differently. In Missouri marijuana use is a crime whereas alcohol use is not. Under Section 195.020, Revised Statutes of Missouri, 1978, as amended: "It is unlawful for any person to ... possess, have under his control ... any controlled ... substance ..." Marijuana is a Schedule 1. controlled substance, the possession of which is punishable by up to a year in jail and/or a fine not to exceed $1000. for the first offense. Second, the grievants were smoking a joint in a warehouse building which was marked with a "no-smoking" sign. Third, the plant is a licensee of the Federal

Government producing controlled substances and jeopardizes that status by having employees who use them illegally.

     \* \* \*

### [Conclusions]

     \* \* \* Alcoholism in industry, and as a social problem, is far more debilitating, costly, and destructive than marijuana. There is no rational or reasonable basis to treat them as distinct. Therefore to treat alcohol abuse with progressive discipline and treat drug abuse with immediate discharge is improper.

     Of all the cases involving marijuana, the facts herein are the least significant as posing any real threat to the Company. Three employees shared a single joint during a brief break. This was not a case of an abuse leading to a physical or mental state that threatened harm to themselves, to other persons, or to property. This was not the case of pushing marijuana or selling marijuana or having a significant cache of marijuana on Company premises. It was a simple case of recreational use.

     The employer itself released the employees after their initial interrogation to return to the plant evidencing that in the employer's mind none of the employees were under the influence of the substance to such an extent that they could not safely return to the work force. None had ever previously been involved in a like incident, either with intoxicants or drugs. No real or imagined harm befell the Company as a result of this incident. Even the D.E.A. does not mandate discharge for a first offense but counsels individuation of punishment.

     The history of treating the use or possession of marijuana as criminal has been that of persistent decriminalization. In those areas where it remains a criminal act the reduction of the act from felony to misdemeanor and the punishment from imprisonment to fine has gone on apace.

     Generally the usual form of punishment for a plea of guilty or a conviction simply of possession and use for personal benefit on a first occasion is unsupervised probation. No evidence was introduced that the State of Missouri regards the matter more significantly than this. This punishment is far less than what the Company would exact of discharge, particularly discharge regardless of the employee's length of service, regardless of the quality of the employee's service, and regardless of whether any harm came to the Company as a result of the employee's use for personal and recreational purposes of the drug. It seems strange indeed that the criminal penalty would be far less, in both kind and degree, than that imposed by the Company. In fact, if this were a criminal case, it is probable that only the conviction of [B.] would stand. [C.'s] confession would be ruled out because of *Miranda*. Even if it could be used against him, it could not be used against [P.], because of its hearsay nature.

     Discharge just was not an appropriate penalty in this case. The analogous penalty for possession and use of intoxicants on Company premises should be the guide. If these grievants had been so charged, the

Company would not have given them a disciplinary suspension which lasted beyond seven calendar days or five working days. If these grievants had admitted that they were sharing a joint at the time they were discovered by Security Officer [B.], I would have found that a seven calendar day disciplinary suspension for that offense was proper and would have reinstated them with full seniority and with appropriate back pay at the end of that suspension period.

However, these three grievants did not admit what I have found to be the facts in this matter. To the contrary, each of them, some to a greater extent, some to a lesser extent, lied to Security Officer [B.], lied to their Union Representative during the course of the grievance procedure, lied to the Company Representative at the various grievance steps, and committed perjury in front of me in continuing to lie after being placed under oath to tell the truth. There is no doubt in my mind that the grievants were guilty of violating the plant rule against possession and use of drugs on Company property. Further, there is no doubt in my mind that the grievants lied and continued to lie throughout the investigatory, grievance and arbitration phases of this matter. I do not intend to allow them to profit from their abuse of the system established by the collective bargaining contract to vindicate their rights in the case of unjust discharge. To obtain justice one must act justly.

## [Award]

I have found that the grievants were unjustly discharged. I shall remedy this contractural [sic] violation by the Company by ordering the Company to reinstate them to their former positions, without loss of seniority, on the first day of the first regular work week following receipt by the Company of this Opinion and Award. Their records shall be corrected to reflect a five working day disciplinary suspension for their offense. I shall not award them any back pay, to which they would otherwise have been entitled, for reasons noted above.

---

# Walker Manufacturing Co.

81 L.A. 1169 (C. Morgan 1983).

■ MORGAN, ARBITRATOR:—On Monday, December 13, 1982, the Grievant was placed on indefinite suspension pending further disciplinary action for smoking marijuana on Company property. On December 17, 1982, the indefinite suspension was converted to a discharge and the Grievant was so notified. A timely grievance was filed protesting the action of the Company and the matter was processed through the grievance procedure without resolution.

## Applicable Contract Provisions

* * *

*WORK RULES*

Most societies have laws, rules, or regulations to govern the conduct of persons in their everyday relationship with each other. Where rules are observed and enforced, they will normally promote a congenial work environment.

Your company has such a requirement.

The following acts or practices are expressly prohibited on company property. Where an infraction occurs the offending employee shall be subject to discharge, suspension, or a written or oral reprimand as appropriate. * * *

6. Possession, consumption, or under the influence of intoxicating beverages, and/or controlled substances, (such as uppers or downers) while on company property.

**Issue**

The issue may be stated as whether the Company had "proper cause" to discharge the Grievant.

* * *

One of the reasons urged by the Union for overturning the discharge is that the Company failed to use progressive discipline as it has in the past. Assuming that the Company has used progressive discipline in the past, it is not all offenses to which progressive discipline is applied. For example, theft from the Company would not require progressive discipline. Progressive discipline, for the most part, is used to correct relatively minor employee problems, for example, tardiness, careless workmanship, absence without permission, etc. Here the Grievant knew that what he was doing was wrong, even in the absence of a Work Rule against it, but he deliberately and intentionally set out on a course of conduct in which he violated the Work Rule at least six (6) times.

The Union urges that the Grievant was not advised of the Work Rule when he was hired. This is simply not true as Company Exhibit 5 shows that he did receive them, understood them and had read them at the time of his hire. In addition to that, however, this offense is one of those offenses which the Grievant should have known was wrong and illegal even in the absence of the Work Rule.

The Union urges that the discharge should be overturned because the Grievant's actions did not adversely affect the Company's business. This may be true, but this is not the criteria [sic] by which his actions are to be judged. What the Grievant did was illegal, constituted a criminal offense and was a violation of a reasonable Work Rule promulgated by the Company with the knowledge of the Grievant. A fist fight in a lunch room when both participants are on lunch break cannot be said to adversely affect the Company's business, and yet no one would seriously argue that the aggressor in such a situation should not be severely disciplined.

The Union urges that the discharge should be overturned because the Grievant had a clear work record. As of August 1, the approximate time when the Company first learned the identities of the participants in these activities, the Grievant had been working for the Company a little less than 11 months. During this time he had admittedly violated this Work Rule No. 6 a number of times. While a good work record may be solid ground for urging clemency in some cases, it cannot be in a situation where the only reason the work record is good is because the Grievant was not caught. This is not a game of cat and mouse. The matter of clemency is not a matter for the Arbitrator. The duty of the Arbitrator is solely to review whether or not the discipline imposed for any particular offense is too severe in light of all of the surrounding circumstances.

The Union urges that because the Grievant is 24 years old and has never been treated for any drug addiction that the discharge should be set aside. The Grievant, at 24 years of age, is or should be mature enough to know that what he did constitutes a criminal offense against the laws of the State of Ohio and the breach of his duty owed to the Company and to his fellow employees. Rules such as this are posted in the work place and enforced as much for the protection and safety of his co-workers as it is for the Company's benefit.

Lastly, the Union urges that the discharge should be set aside because the rule was not uniformly enforced. The Arbitrator respectfully disagrees with this position as the Company uniformly assessed discipline depending upon the severity of the offense. Those who were guilty of dealing in drugs were summarily dismissed; those who had breached the rule five or more times were likewise terminated; those who had breached the rule but less than five times were given 25 work days off without pay. Thus the Company made a bona fide effort to administer discipline uniformly.

The Union urges that there is a tendency to de-criminalize possession and use of marijuana in the State of Ohio. It is true that there have been modifications in the criminal law of Ohio as far as the penalties for certain offenses involving marijuana are concerned, but it is not for this Arbitrator or any other Arbitrator to say that because the State of Ohio has seen fit to reduce the criminal penalties for certain types of uses and possession of marijuana—primarily depending upon quantity—that the Company may not enforce a reasonable rule against its use on its premises.

**AWARD**

For the foregoing reasons, the grievance is denied.

---

## PROBLEMS FOR DISCUSSION

**1.** Do you think an arbitrator would likely be more sympathetic to the grievant's position in the above kind of case than would a trial-court judge? Even assuming a judge to have sustained the claim of the grievant on the merits, would he or she likely direct the employer to reinstate the grievant?

**2.** What exactly is the asserted breach of contract that is being challenged through the contract grievance procedure in the above two cases? Should the arbitrator place the burden of proof upon the union to show that the employer has violated the collective agreement, or should the arbitrator place the burden of proof upon the company to show that the grievant had engaged in wrongdoing that warranted discharge? If the latter, should the company be required to prove culpability "beyond a reasonable doubt"?

**3.** Would the outcome of the *Mallinckrodt* case likely have been different if the grievants, prior to the arbitration hearing (or prior to the discharge), had been found guilty of possession and use of a controlled substance in a criminal court? Would the outcome of the *Walker Manufacturing* case likely have been different if the grievant had previously been tried for the marijuana offense in a criminal court and acquitted of the charge? Are the results, or fact findings, in the criminal case to be treated as *res judicata* in the arbitration case, and vice versa?

**4.** Once the arbitrator in the *Mallinckrodt* case determined that the grievants had, as a factual matter, indeed been smoking marijuana on company property as charged by the company, was he not obliged to sustain the position of the company that this was "just cause" for discharge? Was the company's rule, unilaterally promulgated, that forbade drug use on company property a reasonable rule? If so, is not an employee's violation of that rule automatically cause for discharge?

**5.** How much weight should the arbitrator in a discharge case properly give to the age of the grievant? To the number of years that the grievant had worked for the company? To the grievant's prior disciplinary record? To the employer's treatment of employees who had previously committed similar infractions? Was the *Mallinckrodt* arbitrator correct in treating previous alcohol situations as similar?

**6.** What is the meaning of "constructive" or "progressive" discipline? What is its underlying rationale? Was it the arbitrator in *Mallinckrodt* or the arbitrator in *Walker* who gave the term the more appropriate reading?

**7.** If the grievants in the *Mallinckrodt* case had been employed in a section of the plant that utilized highly combustible materials, or worked along with others at large and dangerous machinery, should the arbitrator order that they be reinstated to their original position? Was it proper for the arbitrator to contemplate an award of backpay, in addition to reinstatement? If so, was it proper for the arbitrator to have denied backpay altogether because of his conclusion that the grievants had been lying from the time of discharge through the arbitration hearing? (Could a criminal court take this into account in determining guilt or innocence, or the sentence?)

**8.** How would the arbitrator in the *Walker* case have decided it had the company discharged the grievant for having been convicted of possessing and using marijuana in his home over the weekend? Would it matter if the substance in this hypothetical variation had been cocaine? Would it matter if the grievant had been selling cocaine to others? (In all of these hypotheticals, would discharge be sustained if the grievant, rather than a production worker, was a security guard employed at a manufacturing concern? was a police officer?)

———

## C.   SUBCONTRACTING[c]

———

**c.** See Dash, The Arbitration of Subcontracting Disputes, 16 Ind. & Lab.Rel.Rev. 208 (1963); Greenbaum, The Arbitration of Subcontracting Disputes: An Addendum, 16

# Allis–Chalmers Mfg. Co.

39 Lab.Arb. 1213 (1962).

■ SMITH, ARBITRATOR. [The union alleged that the Company had violated the contract by contracting out certain janitorial work on October 29 and 30, 1960 and certain work on components in early 1962.]

The initial question for decision is whether, as the Company contends, the claims made by the instant grievances fall outside the jurisdictional authority of the Referee. The Company relies upon Reference Paragraph 167 of the Agreement, which provided as follows:

The jurisdictional authority of the Impartial Referee is defined as and limited to the determination of any grievance which is a controversy between the parties or between the Company and employes covered by this agreement concerning compliance with any provision of this agreement and is submitted to him consistent with the provisions of this agreement.

The Company notes that the first step of the grievance procedure contemplates that an employee may present "any grievance concerning his employment," but asserts that this provision is much broader than the "arbitration clause" above quoted in that the latter limits arbitrable grievances to those which allege a violation of some express provision or provisions of the Agreement. The Company reasons that, inasmuch as the claim of the Union does not rest on any specific provision of the Agreement relating to the matter of subcontracting (or, more accurately, contracting out) of work encompassed by the defined bargaining unit, but, instead, rests on alleged implications derived from a composite of provisions (the definition of the bargaining unit, specified wage rates, seniority, etc.), the Referee has no jurisdiction.

This contention, in the Referee's judgment, is without merit and must be rejected. Without elaborating the point, it seems to the Referee that the Company is reading into Reference Paragraph 167 a limitation which is not there. The Paragraph does not state that a grievance must concern and involve a "provision" which explicitly touches the subject matter of the grievance. It simply says, in effect, that the grievance must involve a controversy concerning compliance with "any provision" of the Agreement. This language does not foreclose the consideration of a claim based on the theory that one or more cited provisions of the Agreement give rise to an implied limitation or restriction on managerial action. There can be no doubt that in the area of contractual obligations generally it is frequently necessary, in order to give effect to the intent of the parties, to determine whether the specific provisions of the agreement, fairly and properly construed, import obligations not specifically stated. This is true at least as much in the case of labor agreements as in the case of other kinds of contracts.

Ind. & Lab.Rel.Rev. 221 (1963); M. Hill & A. Sinicropi, Management Rights (1986); Wallen, How Issues of Subcontracting and Plant Removal Are Handled by Arbitrators, 19 Ind. & Lab.Rel.Rev. 265 (1965).

The Referee therefore concludes that the instant grievances present claims which are within his jurisdiction to decide. The basic issue is whether, from the provisions defining the bargaining unit, specifying the wage structure, providing seniority rights, and otherwise providing rights and benefits to employees, there arises an implied prohibition upon the contracting out of work of kinds normally and customarily done by employees in the bargaining unit. This is a contention which involves a controversy concerning compliance with a provision of the Agreement alleged to be implicit in the specified provisions.

Insofar as the Union's case is predicated, as it appears at least in part to be, on the broad proposition that the labor agreement, taken as a whole or in the light of the specific provisions cited, gives rise to an implied absolute and unqualified prohibition upon the contracting out of work normally and customarily performed by employees in the bargaining unit, the contention must be dismissed as untenable. The Referee considered this matter in Referee Case No. 8, 1959–1961 Agreement, Springfield Works, and there stated:

> The Referee has considered this general problem more than once. He is unable to accept as sound the broad proposition asserted by the Union that an absolute prohibition upon the contracting out of work done by bargaining unit employees can properly be implied from the "recognition," "wage" and "seniority" provisions of the contract. None of these provisions literally, historically, or in context is a guarantee to employees in the defined bargaining unit that the work which was there when the unit was first recognized will continue to be there. Rather, they assure that, insofar as persons are employed by the Company to perform work of the kinds which are included within the defined unit, there will be recognition by the Company of the Union as the bargaining representative of such persons, and that such persons will be entitled to the benefits of the wage, seniority, and other provisions of the labor agreement. * * *

Little would be gained by attempting, here, to analyze the reported decisions, either as to the particular facts involved, or as to the statements of "principle" to be found in the opinions. As Bethlehem Steel Company Umpire Ralph T. Seward stated in 30 LA 678, after he had undertaken such an examination:

> Beyond revealing that other companies and unions have faced this same question of implied obligations—have presented similar arguments and voiced similar fears—the cases show little uniformity of either theoretical argument or ultimate decision. Within each group of decisions, moreover, there are conflicts of principle and approach. The Umpire has returned from his exploration of the cases a sadder—if not a wiser—man. * * *

The present Referee, while rejecting the Union's view that there exists an absolute (implied) prohibition on the contracting out of work of kinds regularly and normally performed by bargaining unit employees, likewise rejects the Company's view that it has complete freedom in this respect. In the Springfield case he indicated that "a standard of 'good faith' may be applicable, difficult of definition as this may be." Upon further reflection, he is prepared now to say that he thinks this standard is implicit in the union-management relationship represented by the parties' Agreement, in view of the quite legitimate interests and expectations which the employees and the Union have in protecting the fruits of their negotiations with the Company.

"Past practice" in subcontracting for services and for the manufacturing of components may properly be taken into account as a factor negating the existence of any broad, implied limitation on subcontracting, but not as eliminating the restriction altogether. Moreover, an unsuccessful Union attempt to negotiate into the contract specific restrictions on subcontracting, as was the case in the parties' negotiations of their 1959–1961 Agreement, is likewise a fact which may help to support the claim that the parties have recognized that the Company has substantial latitude in the matter of subcontracting. Yet it would be unrealistic to interpret futile bargaining efforts as meaning the parties were in agreement that the Agreement implies no restriction at all. Parties frequently try to solidify through bargaining a position which they could otherwise take, or to broaden rights which otherwise might arguably exist. Thus, the Referee does not find either in the evidence of past practice, here adduced or in the history of the negotiations of the 1959–1961 Agreement, a satisfactory basis for concluding that the Company has complete, untrammeled freedom in the matter of subcontracting. Nor, incidentally, does he attach any special significance to the decisions of the National Labor Relations Board holding that the matter of subcontracting is a "bargainable" issue under the National Labor Relations Act. The parties did bargain on this subject without reaching agreement on any specific provision for inclusion in their Agreement. The question here is whether the Agreement they reached may properly be said to imply some kind of limitation on the Company's freedom to subcontract. In the Referee's judgment, some limitation may properly be implied, narrow though it may be.

Real difficulty arises, however, in attempting to lay down a set of specific criteria to be used in determining whether, in a subcontracting situation, an employer has acted in bad faith. Many arbitrators have sought to do this, and the wide variation in the results of their deliberations of itself casts some doubt on the wisdom of such efforts and suggests that detailed specification may best be left to the collective bargaining process. In general, it seems to the Referee that "good faith" is present when the managerial decision to contract out work is made on the basis of a rational consideration of factors related to the conduct of an efficient, economical operation, and with some regard for the interests, and expectations of the employees affected by the decision, and that "bad faith" is present when the decision is arbitrary (i.e., lacks any rational basis) or fails to take into account at all the interests and expectations of employees affected. Without attempting anything like a complete "catalog," the following would appear, at least prima facie, to be instances of bad faith: (1) To negotiate a collective agreement with the Union representative covering classifications of work while withholding from the Union the fact that the employer contemplates, in the immediate future, a major change in operations which will eliminate such work; (2) entering into a "subcontracting" arrangement which is a subterfuge, in the sense that the "employees" of the ostensible "subcontractor" become in substance the employees of the employer; (3) the commingling of employees of a subcontractor, working under a different set of wages or other working conditions, regularly and continuously with employees of the employer performing the same kinds of work; (4) contracting out work for the specific purpose of undermining or weakening the Union or depriving employees of employment opportunities. On the other hand, the Referee does not consider that it is *per se* arbitrary, unreasonable, or an act of bad faith to contract out work primarily to reduce production costs. After all, a prime managerial obligation is to conduct an efficient and profitable enterprise, and in doing so serve, in the long run, the best interests of employees as well as stockholders.

The observations made above do not resolve cases. The facts of the particular case must be examined, especially in relation to the considerations underlying the managerial decision to contract out the work in question. Of necessity, the Referee, having taken the position that the managerial discretion is subject to the implied limitation that it must be exercised in good faith, cannot escape the necessity and responsibility for making a judgment on this matter. As a matter of procedure, it seems evident that management should explain *why* it made the decision, and that it is then appropriate for the Union to attempt either to show that the considerations motivating the decision, as disclosed by management, indicate bad faith, or else that other considerations of a kind indicating bad faith in fact motivated the decision.

The only part of the work undertaken by Don's Window Cleaning Company on October 29 and 30, 1960, which is here protested is floor cleaning. Company testimony is to the effect that this work (in addition to other work) was "let" to the outside contractor, rather than assigned at least in part to bargaining unit employees, on an overtime basis, because of these considerations: (1) The necessity of insuring that the work would be completed over the week-end; (2) lack of certainty as to when the floor washing would take place; (3) lack of certainty as to how many people would be required to do such work; (4) the difficulty of getting unit personnel to come in "on emergencies" or on overtime; (5) the inability of some of the unit personnel to handle "scrubbing machines"; (6) the necessity of coordinating the floor cleaning with the moving and other operations involved; (7) the limitations, under State law, of the number of hours which women could be required to work consecutively; and (8) safety factors. Economic considerations, such as the overtime premium payments which would have been required, were not, apparently, involved in the determination.

The Union does not claim that these considerations were not the factors motivating the decision. Its claim is that the Company judgment concerning some of them (*e.g.,* the difficulty of coordinating the work of Company employees with the work of employees of the outside contractor) was unsound. It seems to the Referee, however, that the factors which management took into account were within the range of considerations which could rationally be taken into account, and that there is no evidence that the total judgment reached was either arbitrary or unreasonable, or failed to take into account the natural desires of unit personnel to avail themselves of an overtime opportunity. On the whole, the conclusion must be that there is no evidence of bad faith.

[The arbitrator then concluded that as to both the "operating mechanisms" and the "stationary contracts," the Company did the work through a subcontractor only because it would be less costly and more quickly completed than if the Company performed the work itself.]

As in the case of the janitorial work, the Referee concludes that the considerations which management took into account, although in these instances primarily or partially economic, indicate that its decisions were not arbitrary or unreasonable, and were not taken in bad faith. No ulterior purpose is indicated in terms either of the status of the Union or of employees in the bargaining unit, nor is there any showing, if this has relevance, that the effect of such subcontracting was to curtail bargaining unit jobs in any substantial way. The Referee repeats that, in his view, cost considerations as a basis for subcontracting, do not of themselves, necessarily indicate bad faith. Manufacturing operations commonly involve some contracting out or purchasing of components, or work thereon, and considerable flexibility in this regard is to be expected in the interest of an efficient and economically sound enterprise. It may fairly be presumed, indeed, that the Company on occasion takes contracts to supply components, or to perform work on components, for other manufacturing concerns. The existence of a substantial degree of managerial discretion, therefore, does not necessarily harm the employees of the Company. They may actually gain thereby, rather than lose, in their over-all employment opportunities.

---

Carbide and Carbon Chemicals Co., 24 Lab.Arb. 158 (1955). The union protested the subcontracting of certain painting work in 1954, although the company had contracted out over fifty maintenance jobs of various kinds without protest from the union during the preceding eight years. A majority of the tripartite panel denied the grievance. "The Parties were fully aware that this type of work was being contracted out over a period of many years and yet took no action to in any way modify the contractual language. The Board cannot do so now upon the request of one of the Parties."

Pure Oil Co., 38 Lab.Arb. 1042 (1962). The company in 1962 subcontracted various types of work, including occasional snow-plowing together with certain maintenance, roustabout and well-pulling work. Some of these jobs could have been performed by the company's employees; others were non-recurring and would have required management to obtain equipment not then owned by the company. There was no record of subcontracting by the company prior to this time. The arbitrator ruled in favor of the company. "There is a well recognized and accepted statement of management's prerogatives which is that, in the absence of statutory restrictions, the Company has all rights which have not been specifically bargained away in a collective bargaining agreement. Management is restrained only to the extent that federal or state statutes, or a collective bargaining agreement with a union has specifically limited the free exercise of its powers. * * * Since we find no restrictive language in the parties' Agreement, and particularly no evidence that the Company has been seeking to cripple or destroy the Union, we find no basis for sustaining this grievance."

## PROBLEMS FOR DISCUSSION

**1.** The *Allis-Chalmers* case involved not only a dispute about whether the subcontracting violated a substantive contractual limitation upon management's power but also a dispute about whether *that* contract issue was intended by the company and the union to be resolved by an arbitrator. The latter issue, known as "substantive arbitrability," was argued to and decided by Arbitrator Smith himself. Is it at all strange for the arbitrator himself to determine whether he has the power to decide the underlying substantive contract dispute? Does the arbitrator's determination that he has jurisdiction predetermine in any way the outcome of the case on the merits? What is the recourse of the union in the event the employer refuses to submit even the issue of substantive arbitrability to the arbitrator? (See pp. 747–63, infra.)

**2.** The arbitrator in *Allis-Chalmers* acknowledges that the employer's discretion in operating its business may be subject to limitations which are not spelled out in the labor contract in express terms. Do you agree with the following observations of the arbitrator in American Sugar Refining Co., 37 Lab.Arb. 334 (1961)?

"Arbitrators are not soothsayers and 'wise men' employed to dispense equity and good will according to their own notions of what is best for the parties, nor are they kings like Solomon with unlimited wisdom or courts of unlimited jurisdiction. Arbitrators are employed to interpret the working agreement as the parties themselves wrote it. * * * When an arbitrator finds that the parties have not dealt with the subject of contracting-out in their working agreement, but that the employer is nevertheless prohibited from contracting-out (a) unless he acts in good faith; (b) unless he acts in conformance with past practice; (c) unless he acts reasonably; (d) unless his act does not deprive a substantial number of employees of employment; (e) unless his acts were dictated by the requirements of the business; (f) if his act is barred by the recognition clause; (g) if his act is barred by the seniority provisions of the working agreement; or (h) if his act violates the spirit of the agreement, the arbitrator may be in outer space and reading the stars instead of the contract." (The arbitrator then denied the union's grievance on the ground that there was no language in the contract which mentioned subcontracting or otherwise limited management's right to operate the business efficiently.)

**3.** On the other hand, did not the arbitrator in *Allis-Chalmers* give the employer *too much* freedom to subcontract when he suggested that the employer there was free to subcontract when motivated in good faith by a desire to reduce labor costs? Why do not the typical provisions for wages, hours and workweek compel the conclusion that the employer may not lay off a worker and then use a subcontractor to get the same work performed for less (often by the very same worker who is hired by the subcontractor)? See Continental Tenn. Lines, Inc., 72 Lab.Arb. 619 (1979).

**4.** Could the union have challenged the subcontracting by going to the National Labor Relations Board? What form could such challenge take? If the union were indeed to have a choice of forum for the prosecution of its case—arbitration or Board—what factors should go into making that choice? Should the Board proceed to rule on the case if an arbitrator has not yet done so? (See pp. 828–47, infra.) Should the arbitrator proceed to rule if the Board has not yet done so? (See p. 808.)

---

## D. THE EFFECT OF PAST PRACTICE AND PUBLIC LAW[d]

It has already been noted, see pp. 691–92, supra, that the "collective bargaining agreement" is not confined to the written terms of a document executed by the company and the union. As is demonstrated by the *Allis-Chalmers* case, see p. 707 supra, the agreement contains as well a set of unspoken rights and obligations. These rights and obligations go even beyond those which are implied from the express terms. Perhaps the most significant source of these unwritten rules are the customs and usages—or past practices—which represent the accepted way that employees are treated and the production processes are ordered. Since the press of negotiations and the complexity of the rules governing the workplace make it impossible to reduce all of these rules to writing, many of the parties' understandings are expressed only in the habits of the past: a rest break in mid-morning, early close-down of machines at the end of the workweek to allow time for cleaning and servicing, two workers on a task rather than three or one, paid time off to vote on Election Day, distributing overtime opportunities on a rotational basis rather than by seniority, the distribution of turkeys at Thanksgiving. What is the legal effect of these practices? Are they as binding as are the written terms? Are they, to the contrary, modifiable at will? How does one determine which practices are binding and which are not? How and when can otherwise binding past practices be terminated? These issues will be considered in the materials immediately following.

**d.** See Edwards, Labor Arbitration at the Crossroads: The Common Law of the Shop v. External Law, 32 Arb.J. 65 (1977); Feller, The Coming End of Arbitration's Golden Age, in National Academy of Arbitrators, 29th Annual Proceedings 97 (1976); M. Hill & A. Sinicropi, Management Rights (1986); McLaughlin, Custom and Past Practice in Labor Arbitration, 18 Arb.J. 205 (1963); Meltzer, Ruminations About Ideology, Law, and Labor Arbitration, 34 U.Chi.L.Rev. 545 (1967); Mittenthal, Past Practice and the Administration of Collective Bargaining Agreements, 59 Mich.L.Rev. 1017 (1961); R. Schoonhoven, ed., Fairweather's Practice and Procedure in Labor Arbitration (4th ed. 1999).

Another source of arbitral principles lying outside the written terms of the contract—and also considered below—are the rules of law laid down by legislatures and courts to regulate the conduct of private persons; some of these rules apply to society generally, such as the broad rules of torts, contracts and criminal law, while others apply to employers and employees, such as the rules regulating industrial safety and health, the freedom of employees to organize and bargain collectively, and the abolition of employment discrimination based upon race, sex, or national origin. What should be the position of the arbitrator when it is argued that these rules of statutory or court-made law modify or actually negate the terms of the written labor agreement?

The following materials can serve only as an introduction to the role of past practices and public law in the construction and application of the collective bargaining agreement.

———

## Phillips Petroleum Co.

24 Lab.Arb. 191 (1955).

■ MERRILL, ARBITRATOR:—For many years, perhaps for more than twenty, Phillips Petroleum Company has furnished electrical energy, generated at its DeNoya Power Plant, to employees living in and around the DeNoya Plant Camp. Some of these employees lived in company owned houses, which were rented at $4.00 per room per month, including utilities. Others lived in housing owned either by themselves or by others than the Company. To these houses, a flat rate of $1.00 per month is charged for electric service. These arrangements long antedated the achievement of bargaining representation by the local union which is the grievant in this case. * * *

The contract does not specifically provide for the furnishing of electrical or other service by the Company. However, one provision states, in substance, that present rents for company housing or utility charges shall not be increased, except in connection with a general increase by the Company in such rents and charges. This provision did not appear in the first contract negotiated after the Union achieved its status as representative. It was introduced at some later time, which was not specifically identified at the hearing. Neither were the parties able to enlighten me concerning the nature of the bargaining which led to its inclusion. It appears that its presence in the contract has not made a difference in the wage rates prevailing in the bargaining unit. However, the Union asserted, and the Company did not seem to me seriously to deny, that, in bargaining negotiations, reference has been made to the availability of this service as one of the advantages resulting from employment with the Company in this area. * * *

For some time, conditions surrounding the rendition of this service have been growing unsatisfactory, certainly to the Company, perhaps to some of the "patrons". The Company's selection as Operator of the North

Burbank Water Flood Unit has imposed an additional load upon its DeNoya plant. A survey of the situation led to the conclusion that the Company, for economic reasons, should terminate the service from that plant to all employees except those living at the DeNoya Camp, itself. A notice of intention so to do, dated June 18, 1954, was mailed to all such employees, and a definitive notice, specifying November 1 as time of termination, was sent under date of October 21, 1954. * * *

### Positions of Parties

The Union, filing this grievance, declines to recognize the propriety of the discontinuance as a unilateral act by the Company. It insists that continued service is called for by the contract; that discontinuance, if desired, should have been bargained for through the procedure prescribed for amending that document; that, in any event, partial discontinuance, since the "discontinued" employees must pay a higher rate to private utilities, amounts to an increased rate for utilities which is not part of a general increase. The Company, on the other hand, contends that the electrical service, not being specifically mentioned in the contract as an emolument of employment, is a mere gratuity, which may be discontinued at any time; and that the contractual reference to charges for rents and utilities is merely a promise that, so long as the Company *does* elect to furnish these advantages, it will do so at a uniform rate to all who *are* served, but without any agreement that they shall be made available to all employees, or to all those who have received service in the past. * * *

**Arbitrators' Rulings**—* * * In a number of cases, arbitrators have regarded plant practices, even of long standing, as imposing no obligation of continuance on the employer if not embodied specifically in the collective bargaining contract. Le Roi Mfg. Co., 8 L.A. 350 (1947)(milk concession to union); Drug Products Co., 10 L.A. 804 (1948)(travel allowance to two particular employees); Globe–Union, Inc., 18 L.A. 320 (1951)(preparation of time-records by time-keepers rather than employees); American Zinc Co. of Ill., 18 L.A. 827 (1952)(helpers for skilled craftsmen); New York Trap Rock Corp., 19 L.A. 421 (1952)(extra pay for certain type of work). Of these five decisions, it is noteworthy that three are rendered by the same arbitrator, which detracts somewhat from the extent to which they should be regarded as establishing a general body of opinion. In addition, there may be added to this group a decision which ruled it a violation of a contract to change a "long existing practice or custom" without notice, though recognizing that a change on proper notice would be valid. Diamond Alkali Co., 3 La. 560 (1946).

On the other hand, a much stronger current of decision regards long standing plant practices, customs and usages as incorporated into the collective bargaining contract, unless expressly negatived by its terms. The theory upon which this view proceeds is expressed best by a few quotations:

> "A union-management contract is far more than words on paper. It is also all the oral understandings, interpretations and

mutually acceptable habits of action which have grown up around it over the course of time. * * *

"If any of these mutually acceptable methods of effectuating the contract become undesirable to either party, it should obtain the consent of the other party to revise the contract, in this larger sense, accordingly. The terms of a contract cannot be unilaterally changed during the time period it covers. * * * " Coca Cola Bottling Co., 9 La. 197 (1947) (custom to notify union and allow time for investigation before discharging employee for dishonesty).

"In the absence of a change in the contract, established practices under the old contract are given approval by the execution of the new and become, by construction, a part of the new contract." Republic Steel Corp., 3 L.A. 760 (1946)(computation of seniority). * * *

In addition to the decisions quoted from, many others apply the same doctrine. Goodyear Tire & Rubber Co., 1 L.A. 556 (1946)(wash-up time); International Shoe Co., 2 L.A. 201 (1946)(excuse of employee from Saturday work on account of religious scruples); West Pittston Iron Works, 3 L.A. 137 (1944)(paid lunch period—"plant practices and customs which existed at the time the contract was executed and which the parties did not contemplate changing, are by implication a part of the contract"); Libby, McNeill & Libby, 5 L.A. 564 (1946)(special piecework basis and standby allowances); Franklin Assn. of Chicago, 7 L.A. 614 (1947)(vacation pay, though not specified); Standard Oil Co. (Ind.), 14 L.A. 641 (1950)(job description, fixed by practice and custom); Ryan Aeronautical Co., 17 L.A. 395 (1951)(free milk); John Deere Waterloo Tractor Works, 18 L.A. 276 (1952)(clean-up time allowance to "incentive workers"); General Aniline & Film Corp., 19 L.A. 628 (1952)(job evaluation); International Minerals & Chem. Corp., 20 L.A. 248 (1953) (using production employees on construction work, when available). The principle has been applied against labor as well as against management. Cory Glass Coffee Brewer Co., 4 L.A. 426 (1946).

A third group of cases, recognizing that existing practices are accepted by contracts which do not restrict them, does not incorporate them fully into the contracts. By this view, the employer cannot, at his own volition, discontinue the prior practice. He must negotiate with the bargaining agent concerning his desire for modification or elimination. Western Air Lines, 9 La. 419 (1948)(downgrading); General Cable Corp., 17 L.A. 780 (1952)(paid supper time). If negotiations, conducted in good faith, bring no accord, the employer then may act without waiting for the close of the contractual term. Ryan Aeronautical Co., 17 L.A. 395 (1951) (free milk).

While the cases do not indicate that every last detail of existent plant practice is frozen into a collective bargaining agreement, they do not as yet seem clearly to indicate where the line is to be drawn. One arbitrator attempted to distinguish between matters affecting working conditions and gratuities. According to him, matters affecting working conditions are integrally related to time worked, or not worked, while gratuities are not so related. Gratuities may be withdrawn at will; practices as to working conditions become integral parts of the contract. As examples of matters affecting working conditions, he cites paid meal times, washing up periods, rest periods and coffee breaks. As gratuities, he cites parking spaces, music-while-you-work, Thanksgiving turkeys and free coffee. Fawick Airflex Co., 11 L.A. 666 (1948). But a comparison of the illustrations given with the items which various arbitrators have held not to be alterable unilaterally by the employer indicates that his distinction cannot be supported. Certainly, the employer's view that a practice is a gratuity is not decisive. Libby, McNeill & Libby, 5 L.A. 564 (1946); Franklin Assn. of Chicago, 7 L.A. 614 (1947). The test suggested is impracticable, because working time is not the only important consideration in working conditions. Perhaps the best test, though admittedly inexact, is that the usage, to achieve contractual status, must concern a "major condition of employment." General Aniline & Film Corp., 19 L.A. 628 (1952). And see Cox and Dunlop, "The Duty to Bargain Collectively During the Term of an Existing Agreement," 63 Harv.L.Rev. 1097, 1116–1125 (1950).

**Conclusion**—In the light of the decisions, as recited above, it seems to me that the current of opinion has set strongly in favor of the position that existing practices, in respect to major conditions of employment, are to be regarded as included within a collective bargaining contract, negotiated after the practice has become established and not repudiated or limited by it. This also seems to me the reasonable view, since the negotiators work within the frame of existent practice and must be taken to be conscious of it. Likely, they do not always think it necessary to spell it out. That principle would lead to a sustention of the grievance here involved. However, a still stronger case is presented where the contract, though not expressly embodying the practice, refers to it and contemplates its continuance. Cf. International Harvester Co., 20 L.A. 276 (1953). That, it seems to me, is the situation here. The stipulation respecting rents and utility charges recognizes an existing practice, and, by stipulating against any increase in charges except one of general application, clearly assumes that the practice will continue. I think this is borne out by the references to the practice in collective bargaining discussions and by the part it played in inducing the location of houses. Had this provision been deleted, it would have been an indication that the scope of the contract was being narrowed so as to exclude the practice. Corn Products Ref. Co., 7 L.A. 125 (1947). Cf. Connecticut Power Co., 14 L.A. 951 (1950). But here the stipulation has little significance, unless the service is to be continued, and I think that the principle applied by the arbitrators in the decisions which have been recited before supports the view that such continuance is part of the contractual obligation. * * *

Whatever may be the merits of the "negotiation rule" as applied to practices where the contract is absolutely silent, I am convinced that the "contractual incorporation" rule is the proper one when applied to a contract which contains stipulations based on and assuming the continuance of the existing practice. Any other rule, it seems to me, would defeat

the justifiable expectations of the party in whose favor the practice runs.
* * *

**Remedy**—* * * [T]he award will be, and is, that the grievance be sustained, and that the furnishing of electric service to employees outside the DeNoya Camp who have heretofore received such service in accordance with the established practice, at the rate of $1.00 per month, is declared to be a continuing obligation under the contract; that the Company shall make good its obligations to such employees to whom it has discontinued service by paying to them the difference between $1.00 per month and the rates actually charged by the utilities from whom service has been secured; that, for the future, the Company shall have the option either of restoring the service or of reimbursing the employees concerned in the same manner as provided for past service, it being understood that nothing in this award shall preclude the Company from exercising the privilege, secured to it by the contract, of instituting a general increase in its charge for this service, which, of course, must be applicable to all recipients.

----

## PROBLEMS FOR DISCUSSION

**1.** For twenty years, the Torrington Company had permitted its employees to take one hour off from work, with pay, to vote on Election Day. The policy was instituted unilaterally, and the Company continued it after the Metal Products Union was selected as the bargaining representative, even though the labor contract made no mention of it. In December 1999, when Mr. Torrington announced that this benefit would be discontinued, the Union sent a written protest. As the contract drew toward its expiration date of September 30, 2000, the parties began to negotiate a new agreement and at the first meeting, Mr. Torrington informed the Union that he did not intend to reestablish the Election Day benefit. The Union responded by including a contrary provision in its written demands at a meeting in early September. Later that month, both parties exchanged written proposals that the old contract be continued with specific amendments, but neither set of proposals mentioned the Election Day policy. When a new contract was signed in October 2000, it made no mention of the Election Day benefit. The first week in November, Mr. Torrington announced once again that there would be no paid time off to vote. The Union filed a grievance, which it has taken to arbitration. The labor contract provides for arbitration of disputes regarding "the interpretation or application of any provisions in this contract," and also provides that the arbitrator "shall have no power to add to, delete from or modify, in any way, any of the provisions of this agreement."

The Company has argued to the arbitrator that the grievance is not arbitrable and that if it is arbitrable it should be dismissed on the merits. How should the arbitrator rule? See Torrington Co. v. Metal Products Workers Union Local 1645, 362 F.2d 677 (2d Cir.1966).

**2.** Examine carefully each of the theories set forth in *Phillips Petroleum* for determining when past practices are binding on the employer and when they may be unilaterally terminated. On each of these theories, how should the arbitrator rule if an employer unilaterally discontinues the following practices of long standing? (a) Three workers have worked together to assemble a component which now, because of new technology, can be assembled by only one. (b) Workers have been given five minutes (paid) at the end of the workday to wash up, but now the use of computerized technology has eliminated the "dirty" feature of their work. (c) A Christmas bonus has been given for many years, measured by one-half of one week's wages for each employee. (d) Employees working in a plant utilizing precious metals, who were formerly permitted to leave the plant without a search, are new being subjected to electronic detection devices, in light of a substantial increase in pilferage of company materials.

---

## Mittenthal, the Role of Law in Arbitration[e]

National Academy of Arbitrators, Proceedings of the Twenty–First Annual Meeting 42 (1968).

\* \* \* My concern here is with what arbitrators should do when asked to consider the law in resolving a grievance dispute.

\* \* \* Howlett's view is based in part on the belief that "all applicable law" is, *by implication,* incorporated in "every agreement." Some courts and some arbitrators have drawn this implication. \* \* \*

I find no merit in such an argument. \* \* \* A judge has two functions to perform. He must interpret the contract; he must also determine the legal operation of the contract, that is, the legal remedies (if any) for its enforcement. He is, in other words, "concerned not only with the [contract] but also with the law that limits and governs it." It is only in connection with the legal operation of the contract that it is necessary for the judge to refer to any applicable constitution or statute. Realistically, what happens is that he interprets the contract and then imposes upon his interpretation the relevant rules of law. Given this view of judicial decision-making, there is no need to imply that the law is incorporated in the contract.

\* \* \* [J]udges concern themselves with applicable law because they exercise the coercive power of the state and must determine the legal operation of the contract. Arbitrators, unlike judges, are not an arm of the state and do not determine the legal operation of the collective bargaining contract. We determine contract rights and questions of interpretation and application, nothing more. We are the servants of the parties, not the public. We derive our powers from the contract, not from the superior authority of the law. Hence, even if courts had a rational basis for implying that law is part of the contract, arbitrators would have no justification for doing the same. \* \* \*

The typical contract does mention the law. It is not unusual for the parties to refer to statutory law regarding union security,[15] checkoff,[16]

---

e. Reprinted by permission from Proceedings of the 21st Annual Meeting, National Academy of Arbitrators, copyright 1968 by Bureau of National Affairs, Inc.

15. *E.g.,* "the foregoing provisions [union membership] shall be effective in accordance with and consistent with applicable provisions of federal and state law."

16. *E.g.,* "the provisions of this [checkoff clause] shall be effective in accordance with and consistent with applicable provisions of federal law."

reemployment of veterans,[17] and supplemental unemployment benefits.[18] Those who draft such provisions are certainly aware of the impact of law upon employee rights. Their limited reference to the law suggests that they intend a limited role for the law. Their failure to state, in these circumstances, that all applicable law is part of the contract must have some significance. Thus, Howlett's implication seems inconsistent with the language found in most contracts.

Finally, even if the implication could somehow hurdle all of these objections, it would be confronted by the arbitration clause. Ordinarily, the arbitrator is confined to the interpretation and application of the agreement and forbidden to add to or modify the terms of the agreement. If he rules that the law is part of the contract, he must read into the parties' contract a new and indeterminate set of rights and duties. By doing so, however, he would be adding to the terms of the contract and thus ignoring the limitations on his authority. The purpose of a narrow arbitration clause is to limit us to questions of private rights which arise out of the contract. That purpose would certainly be defeated if we were to draw an implication which would transform arbitration into a forum for the vindication of not just private rights but public rights as well. In the absence of any evidence that the parties intend such a drastic departure from the normal arbitration system, the implication should be rejected.

For these reasons, I find nothing in the collective bargaining contract to support the implication that the law is incorporated in the contract.

\* \* \* \*

Let me turn now to more specific problems. What should an arbitrator do where the contract and the law conflict, where an award affirming a clear contract obligation would require either party to violate a statutory command?

Professor Cox gave us an excellent example of this problem at an earlier meeting. He noted that after World War II a conflict developed between the Selective Service Act and contract seniority. This statute was interpreted by the Supreme Court to require employers to give veterans preference over nonveterans in the event of layoffs during the first year after their discharge from the armed forces. The typical contract gave veterans only the seniority they would have had if they had not been drafted. A dispute arose when an employer, in reducing the work force, retained a veteran and laid off a nonveteran even though he had more

---

**17.** *E.g.,* "the Company shall accord to each employee who applies for reemployment after conclusion of his military service with the United States such reemployment rights as he shall then be entitled to under then existing statutes."

**18.** *E.g.,* "the [SUB] Plan and all rights and duties thereunder, shall be governed, construed and administered in accordance with the laws of the State of Ohio."

contract seniority. The nonveteran grieved, relying upon the contract. The employer defended his action, relying upon the law. Who should prevail?

There are two possible points of view. Cox tells us to deny this grievance—that is, to respect the law and ignore the contract.[21] He argues that:

> * * * The parties to collective bargaining cannot avoid negotiating and carrying out their agreement within the existing legal framework. It is either futile or grossly unjust to make an award directing an employer to take action which the law forbids—futile because if the employer challenges the award the union cannot enforce it; unjust because if the employer complies he subjects himself to punishment by civil authority.

Furthermore, such an award demeans the arbitration process by inviting noncompliance, appeals to the courts, and reversal of the award.

Professor Meltzer, on the other hand, tells us to grant the grievance— that is, to respect the contract and ignore the law. His argument includes three main points, each of which deserves some comment.

First, Meltzer says:

> There is * * * no reason to credit arbitrators with any competence, let alone any special expertise, with respect to the law, as distinguished from the agreement. A good many arbitrators lack any legal training at all, and even lawyer-arbitrators do not necessarily hold themselves out as knowledgeable about the broad range of statutory and administrative materials that may be relevant in labor arbitrations.

No one can quarrel with this description. Arbitrators are not omniscient. Most of us do not have the time, the energy, or the occasion to become truly knowledgeable about the law. But some of our members—Smith, Aaron, Cox, Meltzer himself, to name but a few—surely possess the necessary expertise. Such men are well equipped to decide grievance disputes which raise both contractual and legal questions. It is not unusual for the parties to fit the arbitrator to the dispute, to choose a man qualified by experience or learning for the particular task involved. An example of this is the use of industrial engineers to arbitrate time-study or incentive issues. There is no reason why the parties, when confronted by a difficult legal question, cannot exercise this same selectivity in finding a man with experience in both the contract and the law.

Second, Meltzer says:

> * * * an analogy to administrative tribunals is instructive. Such agencies consider themselves bound by the statutes entrusted to

---

**21.** Most arbitrators followed this course and held the statute to be controlling. See, e.g., International Harvester Co., 22 L.A. 583 (1954); Dow Chemical Co., 1 L.A. 70 (1945). Another example of this problem would be a situation where the contract requires the employer or the union to discriminate against employees in a manner prohibited by the NLRA.

their administration and leave to the courts challenges to the constitutional validity of such statutes. Arbitrators should in general accord a similar respect to the agreement that is the source of their authority and should leave to the courts or other official tribunals the determination of whether the agreement contravenes a higher law.

This analogy is appealing. But another analogy can be constructed to support a different conclusion. For example, an administrative agency would refuse to enforce the terms of its enabling statute in a given case if enforcement would require conduct that is unlawful under some other statute. An arbitrator should likewise refuse to enforce a particular contract provision if enforcement would require action forbidden by the law. My point is not that Meltzer's analogy is wrong but rather that his analogy, by itself, is not sufficient reason to adopt his point of view.

Third, Meltzer says that "the parties typically call on an arbitrator to construe and not to destroy their agreement." His position is that an arbitrator is not construing the contract if he defers to the law and ignores the terms of the contract. He would adhere strictly to the contract even where it means requiring one of the parties to act unlawfully.

This is really the crux of the problem. No one would disagree with Meltzer's view that the arbitrator is supposed to construe, rather than destroy, the contract. The question is what exactly is the arbitrator doing when he takes notice of the conflict between the law and the contract and refuses to order the commission of an act required by contract but forbidden by law? Is he destroying the contract by refusing to issue such an order? I do not think so. A strong case can be made for the proposition that the arbitrator, when exercising this kind of restraint, is ordinarily construing the contract.

Consider some of the language in the typical contract. First, it is not unusual to find a "separability" or "saving" clause. Such a clause says that if any contract provision "shall be or become invalid or unenforceable" by reason of the law, "such invalidity or unenforceability shall not affect" the rest of the contract. The parties thus intend to isolate any invalidity so as to preserve the overall integrity of the contract. But they also recognize the fact that a contract provision can be held "invalid" or "unenforceable" because of a state or federal statute. They do not wish to be bound by an invalid provision. The implication seems clear that the arbitrator should not enforce a provision which is clearly unenforceable under the law.

Second, it is not unusual to find an arbitration clause which says the arbitrator's awards will be "final and binding" upon the employer, the union, and the employees concerned. If the arbitrator ignores the law and orders the employer to commit an unlawful act, he invites noncompliance and judicial intervention.[29] He knows that his award, under such circum-

---

**29.** A court would certainly set aside such an award. See Smith and Jones, "The Supreme Court and Labor Dispute Arbitra- tion: The Emerging Federal Law," 63 Mich. L.Rev. 751, 804 (1965).

stances, is not going to be "final and binding." Either the employer asks a court to reverse the award, or the employer refuses to comply and the union asks a court to affirm the award. In either event, the dispute continues beyond the grievance procedure. That could hardly be what the parties intended when they adopted arbitration as the final step in the grievance procedure as the means of terminating the dispute. The implication seems clear that the arbitrator must consider the law in this kind of situation if his award is to have the finality which the contract contemplates.[30]

Thus, it may well be that contracts can be construed to justify resort to the law to avoid an award which would require unlawful conduct.

On balance, the relevant considerations support Cox's view. The arbitrator should "look to see whether sustaining the grievance would require conduct the law forbids or would enforce an illegal contract; if so, the arbitrator should not sustain the grievance." This principle, however, should be carefully limited. It does not suggest that "an arbitrator should pass upon all the parties' legal rights and obligations" or that "an arbitrator should refuse to give effect to a contract provision merely because the courts would not enforce it." Thus, although the arbitrator's award may *permit* conduct forbidden by law but sanctioned by contract, it should not *require* conduct forbidden by law even though sanctioned by contract.

\* \* \*

---

## PROBLEM FOR DISCUSSION

The collective bargaining agreement provides: "In the interest of efficiency, order and cleanliness, no employee shall be permitted at any time anywhere on company property to distribute literature of any kind. Violators of this rule shall be subject to discipline." Three weeks prior to the election of union officers, Ralph Rebel stationed himself in the company parking lot prior to the beginning of his shift, and there distributed leaflets attacking the record of the incumbent union officials and urging the election of an insurgent slate of candidates. He was seen by a representative of the union, who informed him of the no-distribution rule in the labor contract. At the end of his shift, Rebel stationed himself in the parking lot once again, and distributed the leaflets. The union representative insisted that Rebel be disciplined, but the company has refused. The union filed a grievance, and the case is now before an arbitrator. The company has argued that the contract provision is unlawful on its face and that it cannot serve as the basis for a grievance. It therefore asks either that the grievance be declared nonarbitrable, or else that if the arbitrator reaches the merits she should rule against the union. What decision should the arbitrator render?

---

**30.** Note, however, that even if the arbitrator respects the law and refuses to order the employer to commit an unlawful act, the union might ask a court to set aside the award on the ground that the arbitrator exceeded his authority under the contract. No award is "final and binding" in the sense that it precludes parties from going to court and attempting to reverse the award on certain limited grounds.

## III.  JUDICIAL ENFORCEMENT OF COLLECTIVE AGREEMENTS[a]

Prior to the enactment of Section 301 of the Labor Management Relations Act in 1947, the state courts alone had jurisdiction over suits for breach of a collective bargaining agreement (except where there was diversity of citizenship), and any substantive rights and remedies were determined by state law. Legal rights and remedies were uncertain or ineffective or both, for a variety of reasons.

A union was not treated as a legal entity. In most jurisdictions a class action was necessary for the members to sue or be sued. Execution of a money judgment would have to be levied upon the individual property of the members. There was grave doubt whether a collective agreement was enforceable at all and, if so, by and against whom it was enforceable.

In the national debate upon labor policy leading to enactment of the Taft Hartley Act many employers and trade associations pressed for a law that would make collective bargaining agreements binding on unions. But disinterested observers were divided over the wisdom of giving the law a role to play in the enforcement of collective bargaining agreements. Dean Harry Shulman, a wise and experienced arbitrator and public member of many labor panels, urged keeping law out of the administration of collective bargaining agreements ("Reason, Contract, and Law in Labor Relations," 68 Harv.L.Rev. 999 (1955)):

> [A]rbitration is an integral part of the system of self-government. And the system is designed to aid management in its quest for efficiency, to assist union leadership in its participation in the enterprise, and to secure justice for the employees. It is a means of making collective bargaining work and thus preserving private enterprise in a free government. When it works fairly well, it does not need the sanction of the law of contracts or the law of arbitration. It is only when the system breaks down completely that the courts' aid in these respects is invoked. But the courts cannot, by occasional sporadic decision, restore the parties' continuing relationship; and their intervention in such cases may seriously affect the going systems of self-government. When their autonomous system breaks down, might not the parties better be left to the usual methods for adjustment of labor disputes rather

a.  See Bickel & Wellington, Legislative Purpose and the Judicial Process: The Lincoln Mills Case, 71 Harv.L.Rev. 1 (1957); Lesnick, Arbitration as a Limit on the Discretion of Management, Union, and NLRB: The Year's Major Developments, N.Y.U. 18th Annual Conf. on Labor 7 (1966); Smith & Jones, The Impact of the Emerging Federal Law of Grievance Arbitration on Judges, Arbitrators, and Parties, 52 Va.L.Rev. 831 (1966).

A significant and highly controversial appraisal of labor arbitration and the role of the courts in contract enforcement can be found in P. Hays, Labor Arbitration: A Dissenting View (1966); the author was an arbitrator himself, as well as a professor of labor law and later a federal circuit judge. The book is critically reviewed in Aaron, 42 Wash.L.Rev. 969 (1967); Dunau, 35 Amer.Scholar 774 (1966); Wallen, 81 Harv.L.Rev. 507 (1967).

than to court actions on the contract or on the arbitration award? I suggest that the law stay out—but, mind you, not the lawyers.

Professor Cox, writing shortly after LMRA Section 301 became law, expressed a somewhat different view:

> Litigation will not establish sound industrial relations. One unfortunate consequence of the enactment of Section 301 may be that it will temporarily encourage some employers to rush to court. It is comparatively rare, however, for persons to exercise their right to sue when, as a practical matter, they are bound in a continuing personal or commercial relationship, and there seems no reason to suppose that the practice would be different in the industrial world. But even though judicial processes are rarely invoked to enforce collective bargaining agreements, the voluntary acceptance of the mutual responsibilities to which collective bargaining gives rise should be encouraged by the law's recognition of the binding character of such agreements.[b]

> It is difficult to make an accurate appraisal, but casual observation leads me to the conclusion that in the overwhelming proportion of cases employers and labor unions accept arbitration in good faith and scrupulously comply with arbitration agreements and awards. Yet for a few years longer we will be unable to rely on honesty and good will as the sanction for all undertakings, and the absence of a statutory remedy allows any party with preponderant economic power to disregard the grievance procedures if he chooses. If a decline in business activity should reduce the economic power of unions, more companies might succumb to the temptation to refuse to arbitrate doubtful cases. Conversely, it is not outside the realm of possibility for a union with a stranglehold on a business to assert its economic power in disregard of the agreement.[c]

---

# Textile Workers Union v. Lincoln Mills of Alabama

353 U.S. 448, 77 S.Ct. 923, 1 L.Ed.2d 972 (1957).

■ Mr. Justice Douglas delivered the opinion of the Court.

Petitioner-union entered into a collective bargaining agreement in 1953 with respondent-employer, the agreement to run one year and from year to year thereafter, unless terminated on specified notices. The agreement provided that there would be no strikes or work stoppages and that grievances would be handled pursuant to a specified procedure. The last

---

**b.** Cox, Some Aspects of the Labor Management Relations Act, 1947, 61 Harv. L.Rev. 274, 313 (1948).

**c.** Cox, Grievance Arbitration in the Federal Courts, 67 Harv.L.Rev. 591, 605–606 (1954).

step in the grievance procedure—a step that could be taken by either party—was arbitration.

This controversy involves several grievances that concern work loads and work assignments. The grievances were processed through the various steps in the grievance procedure and were finally denied by the employer. The union requested arbitration, and the employer refused. Thereupon the union brought this suit in the District Court to compel arbitration.

The District Court concluded that it had jurisdiction and ordered the employer to comply with the grievance arbitration provisions of the collective bargaining agreement. The Court of Appeals reversed by a divided vote. 230 F.2d 81. * * *

There has been considerable litigation involving § 301 [of the Labor Management Relations Act of 1947] and courts have construed it different-ly. There is one view that § 301(a) merely gives federal district courts jurisdiction in controversies that involve labor organizations in industries affecting commerce, without regard to diversity of citizenship or the amount in controversy. Under that view § 301(a) would not be the source of substantive law; it would neither supply federal law to resolve these controversies nor turn the federal judges to state law for answers to the questions. Other courts—the overwhelming number of them—hold that § 301(a) is more than jurisdictional—that it authorizes federal courts to fashion a body of federal law for the enforcement of these collective bargaining agreements and includes within that federal law specific perfor-mance of promises to arbitrate grievances under collective bargaining agreements. Perhaps the leading decision representing that point of view is the one rendered by Judge Wyzanski in Textile Workers Union of America (C.I.O.) v. American Thread Co., D.C., 113 F.Supp. 137. That is our construction of § 301(a), which means that the agreement to arbitrate grievance disputes, contained in this collective bargaining agreement, should be specifically enforced.

From the face of the Act it is apparent that § 301(a) and § 301(b) supplement one another. Section 301(b) makes it possible for a labor organization, representing employees in an industry affecting commerce, to sue and be sued as an entity in the federal courts. Section 301(b) in other words provides the procedural remedy lacking at common law. Section 301(a) certainly does something more than that. Plainly, it supplies the basis upon which the federal district courts may take jurisdiction and apply the procedural rule of § 301(b). The question is whether § 301(a) is more than jurisdictional.

The legislative history of § 301 is somewhat cloudy and confusing. But there are a few shafts of light that illuminate our problem.

The bills, as they passed the House and the Senate, contained provi-sions which would have made the failure to abide by an agreement to arbitrate an unfair labor practice. S.Rep. No. 105, 80th Cong., 1st Sess., pp. 20–21, 23; H.R.Rep. No. 245, 80th Cong., 1st Sess., p. 21. This feature of the law was dropped in Conference. As the Conference's Report stated,

"Once parties have made a collective bargaining contract, the enforcement of that contract should be left to the usual processes of the law and not to the National Labor Relations Board." H.Conf.Rep. No. 510, 80th Cong., 1st Sess., p. 42.

Both the Senate and the House took pains to provide for "the usual processes of the law" by provisions which were the substantial equivalent of § 301(a) in its present form. Both the Senate Report and the House Report indicate a primary concern that unions as well as employees should be bound to collective bargaining contracts. But there was also a broader concern—a concern with a procedure for making such agreements enforceable in the courts by either party. * * *

Congress was also interested in promoting collective bargaining that ended with agreements not to strike. The Senate Report, supra, p. 16 states:

> "If unions can break agreements with relative impunity, then such agreements do not tend to stabilize industrial relations. The execution of an agreement does not by itself promote industrial peace. The chief advantage which an employer can reasonably expect from a collective labor agreement is assurance of uninterrupted operation during the term of the agreement. Without some effective method of assuring freedom from economic warfare for the term of the agreement, there is little reason why an employer would desire to sign such a contract.

> "Consequently, to encourage the making of agreements and to promote industrial peace through faithful performance by the parties, collective agreements affecting interstate commerce should be enforceable in the Federal courts. Our amendment would provide for suits by unions as legal entities and against unions as legal entities in the Federal courts in disputes affecting commerce."

Thus collective bargaining contracts were made "equally binding and enforceable on both parties." Id., p. 15. As stated in the House Report, supra, p. 6, the new provision "makes labor organizations equally responsible with employers for contract violation and provides for suit by either against the other in the United States district courts." To repeat, the Senate Report, supra, p. 17, summed up the philosophy of § 301 as follows: "Statutory recognition of the collective agreement as a valid, binding, and enforceable contract is a logical and necessary step. It will promote a higher degree of responsibility upon the parties to such agreements, and will thereby promote industrial peace."

Plainly the agreement to arbitrate grievance disputes is the *quid pro quo* for an agreement not to strike. Viewed in this light, the legislation does more than confer jurisdiction in the federal courts over labor organizations. It expresses a federal policy that federal courts should enforce these agreements on behalf of or against labor organizations and that industrial peace can be best obtained only in that way. * * *

It seems, therefore, clear to us that Congress adopted a policy which placed sanctions behind agreements to arbitrate grievance disputes, by implication rejecting the common-law rule, discussed in Red Cross Line v. Atlantic Fruit Co., 264 U.S. 109, 44 S.Ct. 274, 68 L.Ed. 582, against enforcement of executory agreements to arbitrate. We would undercut the Act and defeat its policy if we read § 301 narrowly as only conferring jurisdiction over labor organizations.

The question then is, what is the substantive law to be applied in suits under § 301(a)? We conclude that the substantive law to apply in suits under § 301(a) is federal law which the courts must fashion from the policy of our national labor laws. See Mendelsohn, Enforceability of Arbitration Agreements Under Taft–Hartley Section 301, 66 Yale L.J. 167. The Labor Management Relations Act expressly furnishes some substantive law. It points out what the parties may or may not do in certain situations. Other problems will lie in the penumbra of express statutory mandates. Some will lack express statutory sanction but will be solved by looking at the policy of the legislation and fashioning a remedy that will effectuate that policy. The range of judicial inventiveness will be determined by the nature of the problem. See Board of Commissioners of Jackson County v. United States, 308 U.S. 343, 351, 60 S.Ct. 285, 288, 84 L.Ed. 313. Federal interpretation of the federal law will govern, not state law. Cf. Jerome v. United States, 318 U.S. 101, 104, 63 S.Ct. 483, 485, 87 L.Ed. 640. But state law, if compatible with the purpose of § 301, may be resorted to in order to find the rule that will best effectuate the federal policy. See Board of Commissioners of Jackson County v. United States, supra, 308 U.S. at pages 351–352, 60 S.Ct. at pages 288–289. Any state law applied, however, will be absorbed as federal law and will not be an independent source of private rights.

It is not uncommon for federal courts to fashion federal law where federal rights are concerned. See Clearfield Trust Co. v. United States, 318 U.S. 363, 366–367, 63 S.Ct. 573, 574–575, 87 L.Ed. 838; National Metropolitan Bank v. United States, 323 U.S. 454, 65 S.Ct. 354, 89 L.Ed. 383. Congress has indicated by § 301(a) the purpose to follow that course here. There is no constitutional difficulty. Article III, § 2 extends the judicial power to cases "arising under * * * the Laws of the United States * * *." The power of Congress to regulate these labor-management controversies under the Commerce Clause is plain. Houston East & West Texas R. Co. v. United States, 234 U.S. 342, 34 S.Ct. 833, 58 L.Ed. 1341; National Labor Relations Board v. Jones & Laughlin Corp., 301 U.S. 1, 57 S.Ct. 615, 81 L.Ed. 893. A case or controversy arising under § 301(a) is, therefore, one within the purview of judicial power as defined in Article III.

The question remains whether jurisdiction to compel arbitration of grievance disputes is withdrawn by the Norris–LaGuardia Act, 47 Stat. 70, 29 U.S.C. § 101 et seq., 29 U.S.C.A. § 101 et seq. Section 7 of that Act prescribes stiff procedural requirements for issuing an injunction in a labor dispute. The kinds of acts which had given rise to abuse of the power to enjoin are listed in § 4. The failure to arbitrate was not a part and parcel of the abuses against which the Act was aimed. Section 8 of the Norris–

LaGuardia Act does, indeed, indicate a congressional policy toward settlement of labor disputes by arbitration, for it denies injunctive relief to any person who has failed to make "every reasonable effort" to settle the dispute by negotiation, mediation, or "voluntary arbitration." Though a literal reading might bring the dispute within the terms of the Act (see Cox, Grievance Arbitration in the Federal Courts, 67 Harv.L.Rev. 591, 602–604), we see no justification in policy for restricting § 301(a) to damage suits, leaving specific performance of a contract to arbitrate grievance disputes to the inapposite procedural requirements of that Act. * * * The congressional policy in favor of the enforcement of agreements to arbitrate grievance disputes being clear, there is no reason to submit them to the requirements of § 7 of the Norris–LaGuardia Act. * * *

■ MR. JUSTICE BURTON, whom MR. JUSTICE HARLAN joins, concurring in the result.

This suit was brought in a United States District Court under § 301 of the Labor Management Relations Act of 1947, 61 Stat. 156, 29 U.S.C. § 185, 29 U.S.C.A. § 185, seeking specific enforcement of the arbitration provisions of a collective-bargaining contract. * * * Having jurisdiction over the suit, the court was not powerless to fashion an appropriate federal remedy. The power to decree specific performance of a collectively bargained agreement to arbitrate finds its source in § 301 itself, and in a Federal District Court's inherent equitable powers, nurtured by a congressional policy to encourage and enforce labor arbitration in industries affecting commerce.

I do not subscribe to the conclusion of the Court that the substantive law to be applied in a suit under § 301 is federal law. At the same time, I agree with Judge Magruder in International Brotherhood v. W.L. Mead, Inc., 1 Cir., 230 F.2d 576, that some federal rights may necessarily be involved in a § 301 case, and hence that the constitutionality of § 301 can be upheld as a congressional grant to Federal District Courts of what has been called "protective jurisdiction."

[MR. JUSTICE FRANKFURTER dissented and MR. JUSTICE BLACK did not participate.]

---

*FEDERALISM AND THE PEACEFUL ADJUSTMENT OF GRIEVANCES*

The Supreme Court addressed other important questions of federalism in the interpretation of labor agreements in two 1962 decisions. In Charles Dowd Box Co. v. Courtney, 368 U.S. 502, 82 S.Ct. 519, 7 L.Ed.2d 483 (1962), the Court held that section 301 was not designed to oust state courts of their traditional jurisdiction to enforce labor-contract promises, and that actions under that section may be brought either in state or in federal court.

In LOCAL 174, TEAMSTERS V. LUCAS FLOUR CO., 369 U.S. 95, 82 S.Ct. 571, 7 L.Ed.2d 593 (1962), the Court held that state courts enforcing such promises must, however, refrain from applying local rules of contract law and must apply instead the principles of federal law devised under the mandate of *Lincoln Mills.* In *Lucas Flour,* a union called an eight-day strike to protest the discharge of an employee and also invoked the arbitration clause of the labor agreement. In spite of the absence in the contract of any express promise by the union not to strike during the term of the agreement (a not unusual arrangement in Teamster agreements), the employer commenced an action against the union in the state court for damages measured by its business losses during the strike. The state court purported to apply state rules of contract interpretation, held the strike to violate the collective agreement, and awarded money damages. The Supreme Court held that the state court was obligated, in the interest of national uniformity, to apply federal rules of contract construction.

> The possibility that individual contract terms might have different meanings under state and federal law would inevitably exert a disruptive influence upon both the negotiation and administration of collective agreements. Because neither party could be certain of the rights which it had obtained or conceded, the process of negotiating an agreement would be made immeasurably more difficult by the necessity of trying to formulate contract provisions in such a way as to contain the same meaning under two or more systems of law which might someday be invoked in enforcing the contract. Once the collective bargain was made, the possibility of conflicting substantive interpretation under competing legal systems would tend to stimulate and prolong disputes as to its interpretation. Indeed, the existence of possibly conflicting legal concepts might substantially impede the parties' willingness to agree to contract terms providing for final arbitral or judicial resolution of disputes.... [W]e cannot but conclude that in enacting section 301 Congress intended doctrines of federal labor law uniformly to prevail over inconsistent local rules.

The Court then (over the forceful dissent of Justice Black) proceeded to announce a fundamental principle of federal labor-contract law: "[A] strike to settle a dispute which a collective bargaining agreement provides shall be settled exclusively and finally by compulsory arbitration constitutes a violation of the agreement." Implying a no-strike promise commensurate with the arbitration clause was thought to be required by "accepted principles of traditional contract law" as well as by "the basic policy of national labor legislation to promote the arbitral process as a substitute for economic warfare." (Presumably, the parties are free by clear and explicit language to reserve to the union the right to strike concerning grievances subject to the arbitration clause.) Justice Black condemned the majority for "chang[ing] completely the nature of a contract by adding new promises that the parties themselves refused to make in order that the new court-made contract might better fit into whatever social, economic, or legal policies the courts believe to be so important that they should have been taken out of the realm of voluntary contract by the legislative body and furthered by compulsory legislation." See Wellington, *Freedom of Contract and the Collective Bargaining Agreement,* 112 U.Pa.L.Rev. 467 (1964).

In GROVES V. RING SCREW WORKS, 498 U.S. 168, 111 S.Ct. 498, 112 L.Ed.2d 508 (1990), the collective bargaining agreement prohibited discharge except for "just cause," and provided a multi-step grievance procedure ending in a joint union-management conference. No provision was made for arbitration; but there was a "no strike" clause prohibiting strikes during the term of the agreement "until all negotiations have failed through the grievance procedure." The discharge of two employees was grieved through the procedure but, upon the company's failure to agree, the union declined to strike and the employees sued under § 301 to secure a judicial determination of whether or not they were discharged for cause. The Supreme Court held the suit justiciable under § 301. The Company argued that the contract reserved the strike as the exclusive remedy in the event negotiations over the grievance failed. The Court agreed that the plain language of a collective bargaining contract could reserve the use of force to resolve grievances, but declined to find such to be the case here:

> Of course, the parties may expressly agree to resort to economic warfare rather than to mediation, arbitration, or judicial review, but the statute surely does not favor such an agreement. For in most situations a strike or a lockout, though it may be a method of ending the impasse, is not a method of resolving the merits of the dispute over the application or meaning of the contract. Rather, it is simply a method by which one party imposes its will upon its adversary. Such a method is the antithesis of the peaceful methods of dispute resolution envisaged by Congress when it passed the Taft–Hartley Act.

---

# United Steelworkers of America v. American Mfg. Co.

363 U.S. 564, 80 S.Ct. 1343, 4 L.Ed.2d 1403 (1960).

■ MR. JUSTICE DOUGLAS delivered the opinion of the Court.

This suit was brought by petitioner union in the District Court to compel arbitration of a "grievance" that petitioner, acting for one Sparks, a union member, had filed with the respondent, Sparks' employer. * * * The agreement provided that during its term there would be "no strike," unless the employer refused to abide by a decision of the arbitrator. The agreement sets out a detailed grievance procedure with a provision for arbitration (regarded as the standard form) of all disputes between the parties "as to the meaning, interpretation and application of the provisions of this agreement."[1]

---

**1.** The relevant arbitration provisions read as follows:

"Any disputes, misunderstandings, differences or grievances arising between the

The agreement also reserves to the management power to suspend or discharge any employee "for cause."[2] It also contains a provision that the employer will employ and promote employees on the principle of seniority "where ability and efficiency are equal."[3] Sparks left his work due to an injury and while off work brought an action for compensation benefits. The case was settled, Sparks' physician expressing the opinion that the injury had made him 25% permanently partially disabled. That was on September 9. Two weeks later the union filed a grievance which charged that Sparks was entitled to return to his job by virtue of the seniority provision of the collective bargaining agreement. Respondent refused to arbitrate and this action was brought. The District Court held that Sparks, having accepted the settlement on the basis of permanent partial disability, was estopped to claim any seniority or employment rights and granted the motion for summary judgment. The Court of Appeals affirmed, 264 F.2d 624, for different reasons. After reviewing the evidence it held that the grievance is "a frivolous, patently baseless one, not subject to arbitration under the collective bargaining agreement." Id., at page 628. The case is here on a writ of certiorari, 361 U.S. 881, 80 S.Ct. 152, 4 L.Ed.2d 118.

Section 203(d) of the Labor Management Relations Act, 1947, 61 Stat. 154, 29 U.S.C. § 173(d), 29 U.S.C.A. § 173(d) states, "Final adjustment by a method agreed upon by the parties is hereby declared to be the desirable method for settlement of grievance disputes arising over the application or interpretation of an existing collective-bargaining agreement. * * * " That policy can be effectuated only if the means chosen by the parties for settlement of their differences under a collective bargaining agreement is given full play.

A state decision that held to the contrary announced a principle that could only have a crippling effect on grievance arbitration. The case was

parties as to the meaning, interpretation and application of the provisions of this agreement, which are not adjusted as herein provided, may be submitted to the Board of Arbitration for decision. * * *

"The arbitrator may interpret this agreement and apply it to the particular case under consideration but shall, however, have no authority to add to, subtract from, or modify the terms of the agreement. Disputes relating to discharges or such matters as might involve a loss of pay for employees may carry an award of back pay in whole or in part as may be determined by the Board of Arbitration.

"The decision of the Board of Arbitration shall be final and conclusively binding upon both parties, and the parties agree to observe and abide by same. * * * "

**2.** "The Management of the works, the direction of the working force, plant layout and routine of work, including the right to hire, suspend, transfer, discharge or otherwise discipline any employee for cause, such cause being: infraction of company rules, inefficiency, insubordination, contagious disease harmful to others, and any other ground or reason that would tend to reduce or impair the efficiency of plant operation; and to lay off employees because of lack of work, is reserved to the Company, provided it does not conflict with this agreement. * * * "

**3.** This provision provides in relevant part:

"The Company and the Union fully recognize the principle of seniority as a factor on the selection of employees for promotion, transfer, lay-off, re-employment, and filling of vacancies, where ability and efficiency are equal. It is the policy of the Company to promote employees on that basis."

International Ass'n of Machinists v. Cutler–Hammer, Inc., 271 App.Div. 917, 67 N.Y.S.2d 317, affirmed 297 N.Y. 519, 74 N.E.2d 464. It held that "If the meaning of the provision of the contract sought to be arbitrated is beyond dispute, there cannot be anything to arbitrate and the contract cannot be said to provide for arbitration." 271 App.Div. at page 918, 67 N.Y.S.2d at page 318. The lower courts in the instant case had a like preoccupation with ordinary contract law. The collective agreement requires arbitration of claims that courts might be unwilling to entertain. Yet in the context of the plant or industry the grievance may assume proportions of which judges are ignorant. Moreover, the agreement is to submit all grievances to arbitration, not merely those that a court may deem to be meritorious. There is no exception in the "no strike" clause and none therefore should be read into the grievance clause, since one is the *quid pro quo* for the other. The question is not whether in the mind of a court there is equity in the claim. Arbitration is a stabilizing influence only as it serves as a vehicle for handling every and all disputes that arise under the agreement.

The collective agreement calls for the submission of grievances in the categories which it describes irrespective of whether a court may deem them to be meritorious. In our role of developing a meaningful body of law to govern the interpretation and enforcement of collective bargaining agreements, we think special heed should be given to the context in which collective bargaining agreements are negotiated and the purpose which they are intended to serve. See Lewis v. Benedict Coal Corp., 361 U.S. 459, 468, 80 S.Ct. 489, 495, 4 L.Ed.2d 442. The function of the court is very limited when the parties have agreed to submit all questions of contract interpretation to the arbitrator. It is then confined to ascertaining whether the party seeking arbitration is making a claim which on its face is governed by the contract. Whether the moving party is right or wrong is a question of contract interpretation for the arbitrator. In these circumstances the moving party should not be deprived of the arbitrator's judgment, when it was his judgment and all that it connotes that was bargained for.

The courts therefore have no business weighing the merits of the grievance considering whether there is equity in a particular claim, or determining whether there is particular language in the written instrument which will support the claim. The agreement is to submit all grievances to arbitration, not merely those the court will deem meritorious. The processing of even frivolous claims may have therapeutic values of which those who are not a part of the plant environment may be quite unaware.[6]

---

**6.** Cox, Current Problems in the Law of Grievance Arbitration, 30 Rocky Mt.L.Rev. 247, 261 (1958) writes:

"The typical arbitration clause is written in words which cover, without limitation, all disputes concerning the interpretation or application of a collective bargaining agreement. Its words do not restrict its scope to meritorious disputes or two-sided disputes, still less are they limited to disputes which a judge will consider two-sided. Frivolous cases are often taken, and are expected to be taken, to arbitration. What one man considers frivolous another may find meritorious, and it is

The union claimed in this case that the company had violated a specific provision of the contract. The company took the position that it had not violated that clause. There was, therefore, a dispute between the parties as to "the meaning, interpretation and application" of the collective bargaining agreement. Arbitration should have been ordered. When the judiciary undertakes to determine the merits of a grievance under the guise of interpreting the grievance procedure of collective bargaining agreements, it usurps a function which under that regime is entrusted to the arbitration tribunal.

Reversed.

MR. JUSTICE BRENNAN, MR. JUSTICE HARLAN, and MR. JUSTICE FRANKFURTER concurred (see page 761 infra).

[MR. JUSTICE WHITTAKER concurred in a separate opinion, and MR. JUSTICE BLACK took no part in the consideration of the case.]

------

## United Steelworkers of America v. Warrior & Gulf Navigation Co.

363 U.S. 574, 80 S.Ct. 1347, 4 L.Ed.2d 1409 (1960).

■ MR. JUSTICE DOUGLAS delivered the opinion of the Court.

Respondent transports steel and steel products by barge and maintains a terminal at Chicasaw, Alabama, where it performs maintenance and repair work on its barges. The employees at that terminal constitute a bargaining unit covered by a collective bargaining agreement negotiated by petitioner union. Respondent between 1956 and 1958 laid off some employees, reducing the bargaining unit from 42 to 23 men. This reduction was due in part to respondent contracting maintenance work, previously done by its employees, to other companies. The latter used respondent's supervisors to lay out the work and hired some of the laid-off employees of respondent (at reduced wages). Some were in fact assigned to work on respondent's barges. A number of employees signed a grievance which petitioner presented to respondent, the grievance reading:

> "We are hereby protesting the Company's actions, of arbitrarily and unreasonably contracting out work to other concerns, that could and previously has been performed by Company employees.

> "This practice becomes unreasonable, unjust and discriminatory in view of the fact that at present there are a number of

common knowledge in industrial relations circles that grievance arbitration often serves as a safety valve for troublesome complaints. Under these circumstances it seems proper to read the typical arbitration clause as a promise to arbitrate every claim, meritorious or frivolous, which the complainant bases upon the contract. The objection that equity will not order a party to do a useless act is outweighed by the cathartic value of arbitrating even a frivolous grievance and by the dangers of excessive judicial intervention."

employees that have been laid off for about 1 and ½ years or more for allegedly lack of work.

"Confronted with these facts we charge that the Company is in violation of the contract by inducing a partial lockout, of a number of the employees who would otherwise be working were it not for this unfair practice."

The collective agreement had both a "no strike" and a "no lockout" provision. It also had a grievance procedure which provided in relevant part as follows:

"Issues which conflict with any Federal statute in its application as established by Court procedure or matters which are strictly a function of management shall not be subject to arbitration under this section.

"Should differences arise between the Company and the Union or its members employed by the Company as to the meaning and application of the provisions of this Agreement, or should any local trouble of any kind arise, there shall be no suspension of work on account of such differences, but an earnest effort shall be made to settle such differences immediately [through a five-step grievance procedure culminating in arbitration] * * *."

Settlement of this grievance was not had and respondent refused arbitration. This suit was then commenced by the union to compel it.

The District Court granted respondent's motion to dismiss the complaint. * * * The Court of Appeals affirmed by a divided vote, 269 F.2d 633, 635, the majority holding that the collective agreement had withdrawn from the grievance procedure "matters which are strictly a function of management" and that contracting-out fell in that exception. The case is here on a writ of certiorari. 361 U.S. 912, 80 S.Ct. 255, 4 L.Ed.2d 183.

We held in Textile Workers v. Lincoln Mills, 353 U.S. 448, 77 S.Ct. 912, 920, 1 L.Ed.2d 972, that a grievance arbitration provision in a collective agreement could be enforced by reason of § 301(a) of the Labor Management Relations Act and that the policy to be applied in enforcing this type of arbitration was that reflected in our national labor laws. Id., 353 U.S. at pages 456–457, 77 S.Ct. at pages 917–918. The present federal policy is to promote industrial stabilization through the collective bargaining agreement. Id., 353 U.S. at pages 453–454, 77 S.Ct. at page 916. A major factor in achieving industrial peace is the inclusion of a provision for arbitration of grievances in the collective bargaining agreement.[4]

Thus the run of arbitration cases, illustrated by Wilko v. Swan, 346 U.S. 427, 74 S.Ct. 182, 98 L.Ed. 168 become irrelevant to our problem. There the choice is between the adjudication of cases or controversies in

---

**4.** Complete effectuation of the federal policy is achieved when the agreement contains both an arbitration provision for all unresolved grievances and an absolute prohibition of strikes, the arbitration agreement being the *"quid pro quo"* for the agreement not to strike. Textile Workers v. Lincoln Mills, 353 U.S. 448, 455, 77 S.Ct. 912, 917.

courts with established procedures or even special statutory safeguards on the one hand and the settlement of them in the more informal arbitration tribunal on the other. In the commercial case, arbitration is the substitute for litigation. Here arbitration is the substitute for industrial strife. Since arbitration of labor disputes has quite different functions from arbitration under an ordinary commercial agreement, the hostility evinced by courts toward arbitration of commercial agreements has no place here. For arbitration of labor disputes under collective bargaining agreements is part and parcel of the collective bargaining process itself.

The collective bargaining agreement states the rights and duties of the parties. It is more than a contract; it is a generalized code to govern a myriad of cases which the draftsmen cannot wholly anticipate. See Shulman, Reason, Contract, and Law in Labor Relations, 68 Harv.L.Rev. 999, 1004–1005. The collective agreement covers the whole employment relationship. It calls into being a new common law—the common law of a particular industry or of a particular plant. As one observer has put it:[6]

> " * * * [I]t is not unqualifiedly true that a collective-bargaining agreement is simply a document by which the union and employees have imposed upon management limited, express restrictions of its otherwise absolute right to manage the enterprise, so that an employee's claim must fail unless he can point to a specific contract provision upon which the claim is founded. There are too many people, too many problems, too many unforeseeable contingencies to make the words of the contract the exclusive source of rights and duties. One cannot reduce all the rules governing a community like an industrial plant to fifteen or even fifty pages. Within the sphere of collective bargaining, the institutional characteristics and the governmental nature of the collective-bargaining process demand a common law of the shop which implements and furnishes the context of the agreement. We must assume that intelligent negotiators acknowledged so plain a need unless they stated a contrary rule in plain words."

A collective bargaining agreement is an effort to erect a system of industrial self-government. When most parties enter into [a] contractual relationship they do so voluntarily, in the sense that there is no real compulsion to deal with one another, as opposed to dealing with other parties. This is not true of the labor agreement. The choice is generally not between entering or refusing to enter into a relationship, for that in all probability pre-exists the negotiations. Rather it is between having that relationship governed by an agreed upon rule of law or leaving each and every matter subject to a temporary resolution dependent solely upon the relative strength, at any given moment, of the contending forces. The mature labor agreement may attempt to regulate all aspects of the complicated relationship, from the most crucial to the most minute over an extended period of time. Because of the compulsion to reach agreement and

**6.**  Cox, Reflections Upon Labor Arbitration, 72 Harv.L.Rev. 1482, 1498–1499 (1959).

the breadth of the matters covered, as well as the need for a fairly concise and readable instrument, the product of negotiations (the written document) is, in the words of the late Dean Shulman, "a compilation of diverse provisions: some provide objective criteria almost automatically applicable; some provide more or less specific standards which require reason and judgment in their application; and some do little more than leave problems to future consideration with an expression of hope and good faith." Shulman, supra, at 1005. Gaps may be left to be filled in by reference to the practices of the particular industry and of the various shops covered by the agreement. Many of the specific practices which underlie the agreement may be unknown, except in hazy form, even to the negotiators. Courts and arbitration in the context of most commercial contracts are resorted to because there has been a breakdown in the working relationship of the parties; such resort is the unwanted exception. But the grievance machinery under a collective bargaining agreement is at the very heart of the system of industrial self-government. Arbitration is the means of solving the unforeseeable by molding a system of private law for all the problems which may arise and to provide for their solution in a way which will generally accord with the variant needs and desires of the parties. The processing of disputes through the grievance machinery is actually a vehicle by which meaning and content is given to the collective bargaining agreement.

Apart from matters that the parties specifically exclude, all of the questions on which the parties disagree must therefore come within the scope of the grievance and arbitration provisions of the collective agreement. The grievance procedure is, in other words, a part of the continuous collective bargaining process. It, rather than a strike, is the terminal point of a disagreement.

> "A proper conception of the arbitrator's function is basic. He is not a public tribunal imposed upon the parties by superior authority which the parties are obliged to accept. He has no general charter to administer justice for a community which transcends the parties. He is rather part of a system of self-government created by and confined to the parties. * * * " Shulman, supra, at 1016.

The labor arbitrator performs functions which are not normal to the courts; the considerations which help him fashion judgments may indeed be foreign to the competence of courts. The labor arbitrator's source of law is not confined to the express provisions of the contract, as the industrial common law—the practices of the industry and the shop—is equally a part of the collective bargaining agreement although not expressed in it. The labor arbitrator is usually chosen because of the parties' confidence in his knowledge of the common law of the shop and their trust in his personal judgment to bring to bear considerations which are not expressed in the contract as criteria for judgment. The parties expect that his judgment of a particular grievance will reflect not only what the contract says but, insofar as the collective bargaining agreement permits, such factors as the effect upon productivity of a particular result, its consequence to the morale of the shop, his judgment whether tensions will be heightened or diminished. For the parties' objective in using the arbitration process is primarily to further their common goal of uninterrupted production under the agreement, to make the agreement serve their specialized needs. The ablest judge cannot be expected to bring the same experience and competence to bear upon the determination of a grievance, because he cannot be similarly informed.

The Congress, however, has by § 301 of the Labor Management Relations Act, assigned the courts the duty of determining whether the reluctant party has breached his promise to arbitrate. For arbitration is a matter of contract and a party cannot be required to submit to arbitration any dispute which he has not agreed so to submit. Yet, to be consistent with congressional policy in favor of settlement of disputes by the parties through the machinery of arbitration, the judicial inquiry under § 301 must be strictly confined to the question whether the reluctant party did agree to arbitrate the grievance or agreed to give the arbitrator power to make the award he made. An order to arbitrate the particular grievance should not be denied unless it may be said with positive assurance that the arbitration clause is not susceptible to an interpretation that covers the asserted dispute. Doubts should be resolved in favor of coverage.[7]

We do not agree with the lower courts that contracting-out grievances were necessarily excepted from the grievance procedure of this agreement. To be sure the agreement provides that "matters which are strictly a function of management shall not be subject to arbitration." But it goes on to say that if "differences" arise or if "any local trouble of any kind" arises, the grievance procedure shall be applicable.

Collective bargaining agreements regulate or restrict the exercise of management functions; they do not oust management from the performance of them. Management hires and fires, pays and promotes, supervises and plans. All these are part of its function, and absent a collective bargaining agreement, it may be exercised freely except as limited by public law and by the willingness of employees to work under the particular, unilaterally imposed conditions. A collective bargaining agreement may treat only with certain specific practices, leaving the rest to management but subject to the possibility of work stoppages. When, however, an absolute no-strike clause is included in the agreement, then in a very real sense everything that management does is subject to the agreement, for either management is prohibited or limited in the action it takes, or if not, it is protected from interference by strikes. This comprehensive reach of the

---

7. It is clear that under both the agreement in this case and that involved in American Manufacturing Co., 363 U.S. 564, 80 S.Ct. 1343, 4 L.Ed.2d 1403, the question of arbitrability is for the courts to decide. Cf. Cox, Reflections Upon Labor Arbitration, 72 Harv.L.Rev. 1482, 1508–1509. Where the assertion by the claimant is that the parties excluded from court determination not merely the decision of the merits of the grievance but also the question of its arbitrability, vesting power to make both decisions in the arbitrator, the claimant must bear the burden of a clear demonstration of that purpose.

collective bargaining agreement does not mean, however, that the language, "strictly a function of management" has no meaning.

"Strictly a function of management" might be thought to refer to any practice of management in which, under particular circumstances prescribed by the agreement, it is permitted to indulge. But if courts, in order to determine arbitrability, were allowed to determine what is permitted and what is not, the arbitration clause would be swallowed up by the exception. Every grievance in a sense involves a claim that management has violated some provision of the agreement.

Accordingly, "strictly a function of management" must be interpreted as referring only to that over which the contract gives management complete control and unfettered discretion. Respondent claims that the contracting-out of work falls within this category. Contracting-out work is the basis of many grievances; and that type of claim is grist in the mills of the arbitrators. A specific collective bargaining agreement may exclude contracting-out from the grievance procedure. Or a written collateral agreement may make clear that contracting-out was not a matter for arbitration. In such a case a grievance based solely on contracting-out would not be arbitrable. Here, however, there is no such provision. Nor is there any showing that the parties designed the phrase "strictly a function of management" to encompass any and all forms of contracting-out. In the absence of any express provision excluding a particular grievance from arbitration, we think only the most forceful evidence of a purpose to exclude the claim from arbitration can prevail, particularly where, as here, the exclusion clause is vague and the arbitration clause quite broad. Since any attempt by a court to infer such a purpose necessarily comprehends the merits, the court should view with suspicion an attempt to persuade it to become entangled in the construction of the substantive provisions of a labor agreement, even through the back door of interpreting the arbitration clause, when the alternative is to utilize the services of an arbitrator.

The grievance alleged that the contracting-out was a violation of the collective bargaining agreement. There was, therefore, a dispute "as to the meaning and application of the provisions of this Agreement" which the parties had agreed would be determined by arbitration.

The judiciary sits in these cases to bring into operation an arbitral process which substitutes a regime of peaceful settlement for the older regime of industrial conflict. Whether contracting-out in the present case violated the agreement is the question. It is a question for the arbiter, not for the courts.

Reversed.

■ Mr. Justice Brennan, Mr. Justice Harlan and Mr. Justice Frankfurter, concurring. The issue in the Warrior Case is essentially no different from that in American, that is, it is whether the company agreed to arbitrate a particular grievance. In contrast to American, however, the arbitration promise here excludes a particular area from arbitration—"matters which are strictly a function of management." Because the arbitration promise is different, the scope of the court's inquiry may be broader. Here, a court may be required to examine the substantive provisions of the contract to ascertain whether the parties have provided that contracting out shall be a "function of management." If a court may delve into the merits to the extent of inquiring whether the parties have expressly agreed whether or not contracting out was a "function of management," why was it error for the lower court here to evaluate the evidence of bargaining history for the same purpose? Neat logical distinctions do not provide the answer. The Court rightly concludes that appropriate regard for the national labor policy and the special factors relevant to the labor arbitral process, admonish that judicial inquiry into the merits of this grievance should be limited to the search for an explicit provision which brings the grievance under the cover of the exclusion clause since "the exclusion clause is vague and arbitration clause quite broad." The hazard of going further into the merits is amply demonstrated by what the courts below did. On the basis of inconclusive evidence, those courts found that Warrior was in no way limited by any implied covenants of good faith and fair dealing from contracting out as it pleased—which would necessarily mean that Warrior was free completely to destroy the collective bargaining agreement by contracting out all the work.

The very ambiguity of the Warrior exclusion clause suggests that the parties were generally more concerned with having an arbitrator render decisions as to the meaning of the contract than they were in restricting the arbitrator's jurisdiction. The case might of course be otherwise were the arbitration clause very narrow, or the exclusion clause quite specific, for the inference might then be permissible that the parties had manifested a greater interest in confining the arbitrator; the presumption of arbitrability would then not have the same force and the Court would be somewhat freer to examine into the merits.

The Court makes reference to an arbitration clause being the quid pro quo for a no-strike clause. I do not understand the Court to mean that the application of the principles announced today depends upon the presence of a no-strike clause in the agreement.

MR. JUSTICE BLACK took no part in the consideration or decision of this case.

■ MR. JUSTICE WHITTAKER, dissenting.

* * * With respect, I submit that there is nothing in the contract here to indicate that the employer "signified [its] willingness" (Marchant, supra, 169 N.E. at 391) to submit to arbitrators whether it must cease contracting out work. Certainly no such intention is "made manifest by plain language" [as required by prior arbitration cases not involving a collective bargaining relation]. To the contrary, the parties by their conduct over many years interpreted the contracting out of major repair work to be "strictly a function of management," and if, as the concurring opinion suggests, the words of the contract can "be understood only by reference to the background which gave rise to their inclusion," then the interpretation given by the parties over 19 years to the phrase "matters which are strictly a function of management" should logically have some significance here. By

their contract, the parties agreed that "matters which are strictly a function of management shall not be subject to arbitration." The union over the course of many years repeatedly tried to induce the employer to agree to a covenant prohibiting the contracting out of work, but was never successful. The union again made such an effort in negotiating the very contract involved here, and, failing of success, signed the contract, knowing, of course, that it did not contain any such covenant, but that, to the contrary, it contained, just as had the former contracts, a covenant that "matters which are strictly a function of management shall not be subject to arbitration." Does not this show that, instead of signifying a willingness to submit to arbitration the matter of whether the employer might continue to contract out work, the parties fairly agreed to exclude at least that matter from arbitration? * * *

---

## PROBLEMS FOR DISCUSSION

**1.** After the decision of the Supreme Court in *Warrior & Gulf,* is the arbitrator free to determine that the contract was intended to make subcontracting "strictly a function of management" and that the dispute before him is thus nonarbitrable? Assume that the arbitrator concludes that the dispute is arbitrable; is he then free to determine that subcontracting is a management function and hence not a breach of the agreement? The opinion of the arbitrator is reported at 36 Lab.Arb. 695 (1961).

**2.** Company has, for fourteen years, paid its employees a Christmas bonus, based upon each employee's regular earnings during the calendar year. Union has represented plant employees for eight years, and has negotiated contracts containing a "standard" arbitration clause, which authorizes either party to take to arbitration any unsettled "dispute regarding the meaning, interpretation or application of the provisions of this agreement" and forbids the arbitrator "to add to, subtract from, or modify the terms of the agreement." Last Christmas, the employer, claiming hard economic times, failed to give any employees a Christmas bonus. Union has unsuccessfully asserted a claim of contract breach through the grievance procedure, and has brought an action in the federal district court to compel arbitration. The Company has moved to dismiss. Should this motion be granted, on the following alternative assumptions?

(a) The contract (as have all its predecessor contracts) contains a provision: "It shall be within the complete discretion of Company whether to make gifts or pay bonuses to employees."

(b) There is no contract language at all which explicitly deals with the issue of bonuses (although there are conventional wage and other fringe-benefit provisions). See Boeing Co. v. International Union, UAW, 231 F.Supp. 930 (E.D.Pa.1964), aff'd mem., 349 F.2d 412 (3d Cir.1965).

(c) There is no contract language at all which explicitly deals with the issue of bonuses, and the Company attempts to offer evidence that during negotiations for the current contract the Union negotiator persistently sought a provision requiring Company to pay a Christmas bonus and the Company just as persistently refused. (Should the court grant Union's motion to exclude this evidence as irrelevant?)

(d) There is no contract language at all which explicitly deals with the issue of bonuses, and the Company attempts to offer evidence that during negotiations for the current contract the Union and Company negotiators agreed that disputes concerning any Company gifts or bonuses would not be sent to arbitration but would instead be finally resolved at the level of the Vice–President for Personnel Relations. (Should the court grant Union's motion to exclude this evidence as irrelevant?) See Pacific Northwest Bell Tel. Co. v. Communications Workers of America, 310 F.2d 244 (9th Cir.1962).

**3.** Assume that a labor contract contains a recognition clause in the customary form; provisions dealing with such familiar subjects as seniority, vacations, holidays, hours, wages and grievances; a provision barring "coercion, intimidation, discrimination by the employer or union against any employee because of membership or nonmembership in the union"; and an arbitration clause covering "any dispute concerning the interpretation, application, or alleged violation of any provisions of this agreement." Assume, however, that there is no explicit provision dealing with employer decisions to subcontract work or dealing with discharge for just cause, and that there is no union-security clause. Should a court require the company to arbitrate on demand of the union in the following cases?

(a) The company has subcontracted work which bargaining-unit employees have performed in the past. See Local Union No. 483, Boilermakers v. Shell Oil Co., 369 F.2d 526 (7th Cir.1966); *Allis Chalmers Mfg. Co.,* p. 729 supra.

(b) The company has discharged employee Pierce, and the union asserts that the discharge was arbitrary and unjustifiable. See Corn Belt Elec. Coop., 79 Lab.Arb. 1045 (O'Grady 1982).

———

JOHN WILEY & SONS V. LIVINGSTON, 376 U.S. 543, 84 S.Ct. 909, 11 L.Ed.2d 898 (1964). Interscience, a small publishing company, had a collective bargaining agreement with District 65 of the Retail Store Union; the agreement contained an arbitration provision, and was to expire on January 31, 1962. In October 1961, Interscience was merged into a large publishing company, John Wiley & Sons, and most of the Interscience employees were absorbed into the Wiley workforce. District 65 contended, before and after the merger, that it had the right to represent the former Interscience employees upon their employment with Wiley and that certain rights of those employees had "vested" under the Interscience contract and were therefore also binding upon Wiley after the merger. When Wiley continued to reject these contentions, the union—after the merger was effected and one week before the expiration date of the Interscience contract—brought an action against Wiley to compel arbitration.

The Supreme Court held that "the disappearance by merger of a corporate employer which has entered into a collective bargaining agreement with a union does not automatically terminate all rights of the employees covered by the agreement, and ... in appropriate circumstances, present here, the successor employer may be required to arbitrate with the union under the agreement." The circumstances to which the Court referred were the fact that Wiley's predecessor Interscience had been a party to a collective agreement containing an arbitration provision, and that there was "relevant similarity and continuity of operation across the change in ownership ... by the wholesale transfer of Interscience employees to the Wiley plant, apparently without difficulty."

Among the other defenses asserted by Wiley was that the Interscience contract required, as a prerequisite to arbitration, that the union take the grievance in a timely manner through two pre-arbitration steps of the grievance procedure, requiring a conference between affected employees or their union and some company representative; Wiley claimed that the union had not followed these steps. The Court characterized this as an issue of "procedural arbitrability" (as opposed to "substantive arbitrability," the issue raised in the *American Mfg.* and *Warrior & Gulf* cases of the so-called Steelworkers Trilogy). It concluded that although issues of substantive arbitrability are normally for the courts to determine (absent an agreement between the parties to have the arbitrator do so), issues of procedural arbitrability should be decided by the arbitrator.

The Court noted that the union's two responses to Wiley's claim that the grievance procedure had not been exhausted were that Wiley's adamance made it "utterly futile" to do so and that in any event Wiley's contract violations were "continuing" in nature and could be raised at any time. The Court saw these "procedural" disputes as raising issues that were "intertwined" with the merits of the grievance—here, whether the contract contemplated that certain employee rights were "vested" at the time of the merger; these merits were governed by the substantive terms of the labor agreement and were for the arbitrator to decide.

The Court stated: "It would be a curious rule which required that intertwined issues of 'substance' and 'procedure' growing out of a single dispute and raising the same questions on the same facts had to be carved up between two different forums, one deciding after the other. Neither logic nor considerations of policy compel such a result. Once it is determined, as we have, that the parties are obligated to submit the subject matter of a dispute to arbitration, 'procedural' questions which grow out of the dispute and bear on its final disposition should be left to the arbitrator." Moreover, were the rule otherwise, there would be too many cases in which the employer's invoking of procedural obstacles to arbitration in a proceeding before a court "may entirely eliminate the prospect of a speedy arbitrated settlement of the dispute, to the disadvantage of the parties (who, in addition, will have to bear increased costs) and contrary to the aims of national labor policy." The court therefore affirmed the decision ordering Wiley to arbitrate.

---

## PROBLEMS FOR DISCUSSION

**1.** Why is there a presumption that a court rather than the arbitrator is to determine questions of *substantive* arbitrability? Is it consistent with that presumption to presume that questions of *procedural* arbitrability are for the arbitrator rather than a court? Are the reasons for the latter presumption which are given by the Court in *Wiley* convincing? Are they not even more convincing when the issue is substantive arbitrability?

**2.**   On Wednesday, September 8, the employer, Milton Typesetters, promoted one Robert Finn to head typesetter. Michael Kingman, an employee with more seniority than Finn, felt that he should have received the promotion instead. The collective bargaining agreement provides a grievance procedure which can be instituted by an employee who believes "he or she has been unjustly dealt with provided that a grievance is filed within ten days." A grievance was filed on Kingman's behalf on Monday, September 21, the ninth working day. The employer refused to arbitrate contending that "within ten days" means not ten working days but ten calendar days and that the grievance had to have been filed by the 18th. The union has initiated a suit under Section 301 on Kingman's behalf to compel arbitration, contending that any procedural questions are to be decided by the arbitrator. Counsel for the employer contends that under *Wiley* there is the negative inference that where the merits (here seniority and promotion) and the procedural questions are not intertwined, the procedural questions are to be decided by the courts and not the arbitrator and that therefore the court should not compel the employer to arbitrate even the procedural question. How should the court rule? See Operating Engineers Local 150 v. Flair Builders, Inc., 406 U.S. 487, 92 S.Ct. 1710, 32 L.Ed.2d 248 (1972); Raceway Park, Inc. v. Local 47, SEIU, 167 F.3d 953 (6th Cir.1999).

---

## Litton Financial Printing Div. v. NLRB

501 U.S. 190, 111 S.Ct. 2215, 115 L.Ed.2d 177 (1991).

■ Justice Kennedy delivered the opinion of the Court.

This case requires us to determine whether a dispute over layoffs which occurred well after expiration of a collective-bargaining agreement must be said to arise under the agreement despite its expiration. The question arises in the context of charges brought by the National Labor Relations Board (Board) alleging an unfair labor practice in violation of §§ 8(a)(1) and (5) of the National Labor Relations Act (NLRA), 49 Stat. 449, as amended, 29 U.S.C. §§ 158(a)(1) and (5). We interpret our earlier decision in Nolde Bros., Inc. v. Bakery Workers, 430 U.S. 243, 97 S.Ct. 1067, 51 L.Ed.2d 300 (1977).

[Petitioner Litton operated a check printing plant, utilizing both cold-type and hot-type printing processes. The production workers were covered by a collective bargaining agreement with what the Supreme Court characterized as "a broad arbitration provision":

[Differences that may arise between the parties hereto regarding this Agreement and any alleged violations of the Agreement, the construction to be placed on any clause or clauses of the Agreement shall be determined by arbitration in the manner hereinafter set forth.

[The labor contract also provided that "in case of layoffs, lengths of continuous service will be the determining factor if other things such as aptitude and ability are equal." The contract expired on October 3, 1979.

Thereafter, Litton challenged the majority status of the Union, but a Union election victory was upheld by the NLRB and Litton was ordered to bargain. In the meantime, Litton eliminated its cold-type operation at the plant, and in August and September 1980, without notifying the Union, it laid off 10 of its 42 employees; those laid off had worked either primarily or exclusively with the cold-type operation, and included 6 of the 11 most senior employees in the plant.

[Despite the prior termination of the labor agreement, the Union filed grievances claiming that the layoffs violated the seniority provision, but Litton refused to submit to the grievance and arbitration procedure of the contract and also refused to negotiate its layoff decisions with the Union. In proceedings under sections 8(a)(1) and (5), the NLRB and court of appeals found, *inter alia*, that Litton had violated its duty to bargain by refusing to submit to arbitration; both the Board and the court relied principally upon a 1977 Supreme Court decision, *Nolde Bros. v. Local 358, Bakery Workers Union*, which had held that under certain circumstances an employer's promise to arbitrate grievances could be found to survive beyond the contract's termination date.]

Litton petitioned for a writ of certiorari. Because of substantial disagreement as to the proper application of our decision in *Nolde Bros.*, we granted review limited to the question of arbitrability of the layoff grievances. 498 U.S. 966, 111 S.Ct. 426, 112 L.Ed.2d 410.

## II

### A

Sections 8(a)(5) and 8(d) of the NLRA, 29 U.S.C. §§ 158(a)(5) and (d), require an employer to bargain "in good faith with respect to wages, hours, and other terms and conditions of employment." The Board has taken the position that it is difficult to bargain if, during negotiations, an employer is free to alter the very terms and conditions that are the subject of those negotiations. The Board has determined, with our acceptance, that an employer commits an unfair labor practice if, without bargaining to impasse, it effects a unilateral change of an existing term or condition of employment. See NLRB v. Katz, 369 U.S. 736, 82 S.Ct. 1107, 8 L.Ed.2d 230 (1962). * * * Litton does not question that arrangements for arbitration of disputes are a term or condition of employment and a mandatory subject of bargaining.

The Board has ruled that most mandatory subjects of bargaining are within the *Katz* prohibition on unilateral changes. The Board has identified some terms and conditions of employment, however, which do not survive expiration of an agreement for purposes of this statutory policy. For instance, it is the Board's view that union security and dues check-off provisions are excluded from the unilateral change doctrine because of statutory provisions which permit these obligations only when specified by the express terms of a collective-bargaining agreement. * * * Also, in recognition of the statutory right to strike, no-strike clauses are excluded from the unilateral change doctrine, except to the extent other dispute resolution methods survive expiration of the agreement. * * *

In *Hilton–Davis Chemical Co.,* 185 N.L.R.B. 241 (1970), the Board determined that arbitration clauses are excluded from the prohibition on unilateral changes, reasoning that the commitment to arbitrate is a "voluntary surrender of the right of final decision which Congress * * * reserved to [the] parties * * *. [A]rbitration is, at bottom, a consensual surrender of the economic power which the parties are otherwise free to utilize." * * * Since *Hilton–Davis* the Board has adhered to the view that an arbitration clause does not, by operation of the NLRA as interpreted in *Katz,* continue in effect after expiration of a collective-bargaining agreement.

### B

The Union argues that we should reject the Board's decision in *Hilton–Davis Chemical Co.,* and instead hold that arbitration provisions are within *Katz'* prohibition on unilateral changes. The unilateral change doctrine, and the exclusion of arbitration from the scope of that doctrine, represent the Board's interpretation of the NLRA requirement that parties bargain in good faith. And "[i]f the Board adopts a rule that is rational and consistent with the Act * * * then the rule is entitled to deference from the courts." * * *

We think the Board's decision in *Hilton–Davis Chemical Co.* is both rational and consistent with the Act. The rule is grounded in the strong statutory principle, found in both the language of the NLRA and its drafting history, of consensual rather than compulsory arbitration. See *Indiana & Michigan,* supra, at 57–58; *Hilton–Davis Chemical Co.,* supra. The rule conforms with our statement that "[n]o obligation to arbitrate a labor dispute arises solely by operation of law. The law compels a party to submit his grievance to arbitration only if he has contracted to do so." Gateway Coal Co. v. Mine Workers, 414 U.S. 368, 374, 94 S.Ct. 629, 635, 38 L.Ed.2d 583 (1974). We reaffirm today that under the NLRA arbitration is a matter of consent, and that it will not be imposed upon parties beyond the scope of their agreement.

In the absence of a binding method for resolution of postexpiration disputes, a party may be relegated to filing unfair labor practice charges with the Board if it believes that its counterpart has implemented a unilateral change in violation of the NLRA. If, as the Union urges, parties who favor labor arbitration during the term of a contract also desire it to resolve postexpiration disputes, the parties can consent to that arrangement by explicit agreement. Further, a collective-bargaining agreement might be drafted so as to eliminate any hiatus between expiration of the old and execution of the new agreement, or to remain in effect until the parties bargain to impasse. Unlike the Union's suggestion that we impose arbitration of postexpiration disputes upon parties once they agree to arbitrate disputes arising under a contract, these alternatives would reinforce the statutory policy that arbitration is not compulsory.

* * *

## IV

The duty not to effect unilateral changes in most terms and conditions of employment, derived from the statutory command to bargain in good faith, is not the sole source of possible constraints upon the employer after the expiration date of a collective-bargaining agreement. A similar duty may arise as well from the express or implied terms of the expired agreement itself. This, not the provisions of the NLRA, was the source of the obligation which controlled our decision in Nolde Bros., Inc. v. Bakery Workers, 430 U.S. 243, 97 S.Ct. 1067, 51 L.Ed.2d 300 (1977). We now discuss that precedent in the context of the case before us.

In *Nolde Bros.,* a union brought suit under § 301 of the Labor Management Relations Act, 29 U.S.C. § 185, to compel arbitration. Four days after termination of a collective-bargaining agreement, the employer decided to cease operations. The employer settled employee wage claims, but refused to pay severance wages called for in the agreement, and declined to arbitrate the resulting dispute. The union argued that these wages

"were in the nature of 'accrued' or 'vested' rights, earned by employees during the term of the contract on essentially the same basis as vacation pay, but payable only upon termination of employment." *Nolde Bros.,* 430 U.S., at 248, 97 S.Ct. at 1070.

We agreed that

"whatever the outcome, the resolution of that claim hinges on the interpretation ultimately given the contract clause providing for severance pay. The dispute therefore, although arising *after* the expiration of the collective-bargaining contract, clearly arises *under* that contract." Id., at 249, 97 S.Ct., at 1071 (emphasis in original).

We acknowledged that "the arbitration duty is a creature of the collective-bargaining agreement" and that the matter of arbitrability must be determined by reference to the agreement, rather than by compulsion of law. Id., at 250–251, 97 S.Ct., at 1071–1072. With this understanding, we held that the extensive obligation to arbitrate under the contract in question was not consistent with an interpretation that would eliminate all duty to arbitrate as of the date of expiration. That argument, we noted,

"would preclude the entry of a post-contract arbitration order even when the dispute arose during the life of the contract but arbitration proceedings had not begun before termination. The same would be true if arbitration processes began but were not completed, during the contract's term." Id., at 251, 97 S.Ct., at 1072.

We found "strong reasons to conclude that the parties did not intend their arbitration duties to terminate automatically with the contract," id., at 253, 97 S.Ct., at 1073, and noted that "the parties' failure to exclude from arbitrability contract disputes arising after termination * * * affords a basis for concluding that they intended to arbitrate all grievances arising out of the contractual relationship," id., at 255, 97 S.Ct., at 1074. We found a presumption in favor of postexpiration arbitration of matters unless "negated expressly or by clear implication," ibid, but that conclusion was limited by the vital qualification that arbitration was of matters and disputes arising out of the relation governed by contract.

## A

Litton argues that provisions contained in the Agreement rebut the *Nolde Bros.* presumption that the duty to arbitrate disputes arising under an agreement outlasts the date of expiration. The Agreement provides that its stipulations "shall be in effect for the time hereinafter specified," in other words, until the date of expiration and no longer. The Agreement's no-strike clause, which Litton characterizes as a *quid pro quo* for arbitration, applies only "during the term of this [a]greement," id., at 34. Finally, the Agreement provides for "interest arbitration" in case the parties are unable to conclude a successor agreement, id., at 53–55, proving that where the parties wished for arbitration other than to resolve disputes as to contract interpretation, they knew how to draft such a clause. These arguments cannot prevail. The Agreement's unlimited arbitration clause, by which the parties agreed to arbitrate all "[d]ifferences that may arise between the parties" regarding the Agreement, violations thereof, or "the construction to be placed on any clause or clauses of the Agreement," id., at 34, places it within the precise rationale of *Nolde Bros.* It follows that if a dispute arises under the contract here in question, it is subject to arbitration even in the post-contract period.

## B

With these matters resolved, we come to the crux of our inquiry. We agree with the approach of the Board and those courts which have interpreted *Nolde Bros.* to apply only where a dispute has its real source in the contract. The object of an arbitration clause is to implement a contract, not to transcend it. *Nolde Bros.* does not announce a rule that postexpiration grievances concerning terms and conditions of employment remain arbitrable. A rule of that sweep in fact would contradict the rationale of *Nolde Bros.* The *Nolde Bros.* presumption is limited to disputes arising under the contract. A postexpiration grievance can be said to arise under the contract only where it involves facts and occurrences that arose before expiration, where an action taken after expiration infringes a right that accrued or vested under the agreement, or where, under normal principles of contract interpretation, the disputed contractual right survives expiration of the remainder of the agreement.

Any other reading of *Nolde Bros.* seems to assume that postexpiration terms and conditions of employment which coincide with the contractual terms can be said to arise under an expired contract, merely because the contract would have applied to those matters had it not expired. But that interpretation fails to recognize that an expired contract has by its own terms released all its parties from their respective contractual obligations, except obligations already fixed under the contract but as yet unsatisfied. Although after expiration most terms and conditions of employment are not subject to unilateral change, in order to protect the statutory right to bargain, those terms and conditions no longer have force by virtue of the contract. * * *

The difference is as elemental as that between *Nolde Bros.* and *Katz.* Under *Katz,* terms and conditions continue in effect by operation of the NLRA. They are no longer agreed-upon terms; they are terms imposed by law, at least so far as there is no unilateral right to change them. As the Union acknowledges, the obligation not to make unilateral changes is "rooted not in the contract but in preservation of existing terms and conditions of employment and applies before any contract has been negotiated." Brief for Respondents 34, n. 21. *Katz* illustrates this point with utter clarity, for in *Katz* the employer was barred from imposing unilateral changes even though the parties had yet to execute their first collective-bargaining agreement.

* * * [C]ontractual obligations will cease, in the ordinary course, upon termination of the bargaining agreement. Exceptions are determined by contract interpretation. Rights which accrued or vested under the agreement will, as a general rule, survive termination of the agreement. And of course, if a collective-bargaining agreement provides in explicit terms that certain benefits continue after the agreement's expiration, disputes as to such continuing benefits may be found to arise under the agreement, and so become subject to the contract's arbitration provisions. See United Steelworkers of America v. Fort Pitt Steel Casting, Division of Conval–Penn, Inc., 598 F.2d 1273 (C.A.3 1979)(agreement provided for continuing medical benefits in the event of postexpiration labor dispute).

Finally, as we found in *Nolde Bros.,* structural provisions relating to remedies and dispute resolution—for example, an arbitration provision— may in some cases survive in order to enforce duties arising under the contract. *Nolde Bros.'* statement to that effect under § 301 of the LMRA is similar to the rule of contract interpretation which might apply to arbitration provisions of other commercial contracts. We presume as a matter of contract interpretation that the parties did not intend a pivotal dispute resolution provision to terminate for all purposes upon the expiration of the agreement.

## C

The Union, and Justice Stevens' dissent, argue that we err in reaching the merits of the issue whether the post-termination grievances arise under the expired agreement because, it is said, that is an issue of contract interpretation to be submitted to an arbitrator in the first instance. Whether or not a company is bound to arbitrate, as well as what issues it must arbitrate, is a matter to be determined by the court, and a party cannot be forced to "arbitrate the arbitrability issue." AT & T Technologies, Inc. v. Communications Workers of America, 475 U.S. 643, 651, 106 S.Ct. 1415, 1419–20, 89 L.Ed.2d 648. We acknowledge that where an effective bargaining agreement exists between the parties, and the agreement contains a broad arbitration clause, "there is a presumption of arbitrability in the sense that '[a]n order to arbitrate the particular grievance should not be denied unless it may be said with positive assurance that the arbitration clause is not susceptible of an interpretation that covers the asserted dispute.' " Id., at 650, 106 S.Ct., at 1419 (quoting Steelworkers v. Warrior & Gulf Navigation Co., 363 U.S. 564, 582–583, 80 S.Ct. 1343, 1353, 4 L.Ed.2d 1403 (1960)). But we refuse to apply that presumption wholesale in the context of an expired bargaining agreement, for to do so would make limitless the contractual obligation to arbitrate. Although "[d]oubts should be resolved in favor of coverage," *AT & T Technologies,* supra, 475 U.S., at 650, 106 S.Ct., at 1419, we must determine whether the parties agreed to arbitrate this dispute, and we cannot avoid that duty because it requires us to interpret a provision of a bargaining agreement.

We apply these principles to the layoff grievances in the present case. The layoffs took place almost one year after the Agreement had expired. It follows that the grievances are arbitrable only if they involve rights which accrued or vested under the Agreement, or rights which carried over after expiration of the Agreement, not as legally imposed terms and conditions of employment but as continuing obligations under the contract.

The contractual right at issue, that "in case of layoffs, lengths of continuous service will be the determining factor if other things such as aptitude and ability are equal," App. 30, involves a residual element of seniority. Seniority provisions, the Union argues, "create a form of earned advantage, accumulated over time, that can be understood as a special form of deferred compensation for time already worked." Brief for Respondents 23–25, n. 14. Leaving aside the question whether a provision requiring all layoffs to proceed in inverse order of seniority would support an analogy to the severance pay at issue in *Nolde Bros.,* which was viewed as a form of deferred compensation, the layoff provision here cannot be so construed, and cannot be said to create a right that vested or accrued during the term of the Agreement, or a contractual obligation that carries over after expiration.

The order of layoffs under the Agreement was to be determined primarily with reference to "other factors such as aptitude and ability." Only where all such factors were equal was the employer required to look to seniority. Here, any arbitration proceeding would of necessity focus upon whether aptitude and ability—and any unenumerated "other factors"— were equal long after the Agreement had expired, as of the date of the decision to lay employees off and in light of Litton's decision to close down its cold-type printing operation.

The important point is that factors such as aptitude and ability do not remain constant, but change over time. They cannot be said to vest or accrue or be understood as a form of deferred compensation. Specific aptitudes and abilities can either improve or atrophy. And the importance of any particular skill in this equation varies with the requirements of the employer's business at any given time. Aptitude and ability cannot be measured on some universal scale, but only by matching an employee to the requirements of an employer's business at that time. We cannot infer an intent on the part of the contracting parties to freeze any particular order of layoff or vest any contractual right as of the Agreement's expiration.

V

For the reasons stated, we reverse the judgment of the Court of Appeals to the extent that the Court of Appeals refused to enforce the Board's order in its entirety and remanded the cause for further proceedings.

It is so ordered.

■ JUSTICE MARSHALL, with whom JUSTICE BLACKMUN and JUSTICE SCALIA join, dissenting.

Although I agree with JUSTICE STEVENS' dissent, *post,* I write separately to emphasize the majority's mischaracterization of our decision in Nolde Bros., Inc. v. Bakery Workers, 430 U.S. 243, 97 S.Ct. 1067, 51 L.Ed.2d 300 (1977). * * * The majority grossly distorts *Nolde's* test for arbitrability by transforming the first requirement that posttermination disputes "arise under" the expired contract. The *Nolde* Court defined "arises under" by reference to the *allegations* in the grievance. In other words, a dispute "arises under" the agreement where "the resolution of [the Union's] claim hinges on the interpretation ultimately given the contract." Id., at 249, 97 S.Ct., at 1071.

By contrast, the majority today holds that a postexpiration grievance can be said to "arise under" the agreement only where the court satisfies itself (1) that the challenged action "infringes a right that accrued or vested under the agreement," or (2) that "under normal principles of contract interpretation, the disputed contractual right survives expiration of the remainder of the agreement." Ante, at 2225. Because they involve inquiry into the substantive effect of the terms of the agreement, these determinations require passing upon the merits of the underlying dispute. Yet the *Nolde* Court expressly stated that "in determining the arbitrability of the dispute, the merits of the underlying claim * * * are not before us." 430 U.S., at 249, 97 S.Ct. at 1071.

Since the proper question under *Nolde* is whether the dispute in this case "arises under" the agreement in the sense that it is "based on * * * differing perceptions of a provision in the expired collective bargaining agreement," ibid., I have no difficulty concluding that this test is met here. The Union's grievance "claim[ed] a violation of the Agreement," ante, at 2219, by petitioner's layoffs. And, as even the majority concedes, "[t]he Agreement's unlimited arbitration clause" encompasses any dispute that "arises under the contract here in question." Ante, at 2225. Thus, the dispute is arbitrable because the "presumptions favoring" arbitrability have not been "negated expressly or by clear implication." 430 U.S., at 255, 97 S.Ct., at 1074.

\* \* \* Consequently, the issue here, as it was in *Nolde,* is not whether a substantive provision of the expired collective-bargaining agreement (in this case the provision covering layoffs) remains enforceable but whether the expired agreement reflects the parties' intent to *arbitrate* the Union's contention that this provision remains enforceable. The majority itself acknowledges a general rule of contract construction by which arbitration or other dispute resolution provisions may survive the termination of a contract. Ante, at 2226, and n. 3. That is all *Nolde* stands for. \* \* \*

■ JUSTICE STEVENS, with whom JUSTICE BLACKMUN and JUSTICE SCALIA join, dissenting.

As the Court today recognizes, an employer's obligation to arbitrate postcontract termination grievances may arise by operation of labor law or by operation of the expired collective-bargaining agreement. I think the Court is correct in deferring to the National Labor Relations Board's line of cases and holding that a *statutory* duty to arbitrate grievances does not automatically continue after contract termination by operation of labor law, see ante, at 2221–2224. I also agree with the Court's recognition that notwithstanding the absence of an employer's statutory duty to arbitrate posttermination grievances, a *contractual* duty to arbitrate such grievances may nevertheless exist, see ante, at 2224–2226. I part company with the Court, however, at Part IV–C of its opinion, where it applies its analysis to the case at hand. Because I am persuaded that the issue whether the post-termination grievances in this case "arise under" the expired agreement is ultimately an issue of contract interpretation, I think that the Court errs in reaching the merits of this issue rather than submitting it to an arbitrator in the first instance, pursuant to the broad agreement of the parties to submit for arbitration any dispute regarding contract construction. \* \* \*

In my opinion, the question whether the seniority clause in fact continues to provide employees with any rights after the contract's expiration date is a separate issue concerning the merits of the dispute, not its arbitrability. Whatever the merits of the Union's contention that the seniority-rights provision survives the contract's termination date, I think that the merits should be resolved by the arbitrator, pursuant to the parties' broad contractual commitment to arbitrate all disputes concerning construction of the agreement, rather than by this Court.

I respectfully dissent.

---

## PROBLEM FOR DISCUSSION

Acme Electronics Company and the Machinists Union operated under a collective bargaining agreement that expired six months ago. One of the provisions obligated the employer, in the event of a sale of the business, to require the purchaser to assume the entire labor agreement. After the contract had expired, Acme announced its intention to sell the business; it promptly did so, but failed in the negotiation with the purchaser to extract a promise to honor the expired labor agreement. Shortly before the sale (but after the contract expiration date), Acme discharged employee Wollett on suspicion of theft. Efforts by the Machinists Union to take both the discharge and the business-purchase issues through the grievance procedure have met with complete resistance by Acme. The Union has brought an action under Section 301 seeking an order that Acme arbitrate both matters. Should the trial court order Acme to arbitrate? See Local Jt. Exec. Bd., Culinary Workers Union, Local 226 v. Royal Center, Inc., 754 F.2d 835 (9th Cir.1985); United Food & Comm. Wkrs. Intern. Union Local 7 v. Gold Star Sausage Co., 897 F.2d 1022 (10th Cir.1990).

———

# United Steelworkers of America v. Enterprise Wheel & Car Corp.[d]

363 U.S. 593, 80 S.Ct. 1358, 4 L.Ed.2d 1424 (1960).

■ MR. JUSTICE DOUGLAS delivered the opinion of the Court.

Petitioner union and respondent during the period relevant here had a collective bargaining agreement which provided that any differences "as to the meaning and application" of the agreement should be submitted to arbitration and that the arbitrator's decision "shall be final and binding on the parties." Special provisions were included concerning the suspension and discharge of employees. The agreement stated:

> "Should it be determined by the Company or by an arbitrator in accordance with the grievance procedure that the employee has been suspended unjustly or discharged in violation of the provisions of this Agreement, the Company shall reinstate the employee and pay full compensation at the employee's regular rate of pay for the time lost."

The agreement also provided:

> " * * * It is understood and agreed that neither party will institute *civil suits or legal proceedings* against the other for alleged violation of any of the provisions of this labor contract; instead all disputes will be settled in the manner outlined in this Article III—Adjustment of Grievances."

A group of employees left their jobs in protest against the discharge of one employee. A union official advised them at once to return to work. An official of respondent at their request gave them permission and then rescinded it. The next day they were told they did not have a job any more "until this thing was settled one way or the other."

A grievance was filed; and when respondent finally refused to arbitrate, this suit was brought for specific enforcement of the arbitration provisions of the agreement. The District Court ordered arbitration. The

---

**d.**  See Aaron, Judicial Intervention in Labor Arbitration, 20 Stan.L.Rev. 41 (1967); Dunau, Three Problems in Labor Arbitration, 55 Va.L.Rev. 427 (1969); Jones, The Name of the Game is Decision—Some Reflections on "Arbitrability" and "Authority" in Labor Arbitration, 46 Texas L.Rev. 865 (1968); St. Antoine, Judicial Review of Labor Arbitration Awards, 75 Mich.L.Rev. 1137 (1977).

arbitrator found that the discharge of the men was not justified, though their conduct, he said, was improper. In his view the facts warranted at most a suspension of the men for 10 days each. After their discharge and before the arbitration award the collective bargaining agreement had expired. The union, however, continued to represent the workers at the plant. The arbitrator rejected the contention that expiration of the agreement barred reinstatement of the employees. He held that the provision of the agreement above quoted imposed an unconditional obligation on the employer. He awarded reinstatement with back pay, minus pay for a 10–day suspension and such sums as these employees received from other employment.

Respondent refused to comply with the award. Petitioner moved the District Court for enforcement. The District Court directed respondent to comply. 168 F.Supp. 308. The Court of Appeals, while agreeing that the District Court had jurisdiction to enforce an arbitration award under a collective bargaining agreement held that the failure of the award to specify the amounts to be deducted from the back pay rendered the award unenforceable. That defect, it agreed, could be remedied by requiring the parties to complete the arbitration. It went on to hold, however, that an award for back pay subsequent to the date of termination of the collective bargaining agreement could not be enforced. It also held that the requirement for reinstatement of the discharged employees was likewise unenforceable because the collective agreement had expired. 269 F.2d 327.

The refusal of courts to review the merits of an arbitration award is the proper approach to arbitration under collective bargaining agreements. The federal policy of settling labor disputes by arbitration would be undermined if courts had the final say on the merits of the awards. As we stated in United Steelworkers of America v. Warrior & Gulf Navigation Co., 363 U.S. 574, 80 S.Ct. 1347, the arbitrators under these collective agreements are indispensable agencies in a continuous collective bargaining process. They sit to settle disputes at the plant level—disputes that require for their solution knowledge of the custom and practices of a particular factory or of a particular industry as reflected in particular agreements.[2]

When an arbitrator is commissioned to interpret and apply the collective bargaining agreement, he is to bring his informed judgment to bear in order to reach a fair solution of a problem. This is especially true when it

---

**2.** "Persons unfamiliar with mills and factories—farmers or professors, for example—often remark upon visiting them that they seem like another world. This is particularly true if, as in the steel industry, both tradition and technology have strongly and uniquely molded the ways men think and act when at work. The newly hired employee, the 'green hand,' is gradually initiated into what amounts to a miniature society. There he finds himself in a strange environment that assaults his senses with unusual sounds and smells and often with different 'weather conditions' such as sudden drafts of heat, cold, or humidity. He discovers that the society of which he only gradually becomes a part has of course a formal government of its own— the rules which management and the union have laid down—but that it also differs from or parallels the world outside in social classes, folklore, ritual, and traditions. * * * " Walker, Life in the Automatic Factory, 36 Harv.Bus.L.Rev. 111, 117.

comes to formulating remedies. There the need is for flexibility in meeting a wide variety of situations. The draftsmen may never have thought of what specific remedy should be awarded to meet a particular contingency. Nevertheless, an arbitrator is confined to interpretation and application of the collective bargaining agreement; he does not sit to dispense his own brand of industrial justice. He may of course look for guidance from many sources, yet his award is legitimate only so long as it draws its essence from the collective bargaining agreement. When the arbitrator's words manifest an infidelity to this obligation, courts have no choice but to refuse enforcement of the award.

The opinion of the arbitrator in this case, as it bears upon the award of back pay beyond the date of the agreement's expiration and reinstatement, is ambiguous. It may be read as based solely upon the arbitrator's view of the requirements of enacted legislation, which would mean that he exceeded the scope of the submission. Or it may be read as embodying a construction of the agreement itself, perhaps with the arbitrator looking to "the law" for help in determining the sense of the agreement. A mere ambiguity in the opinion accompanying an award, which permits the inference that the arbitrator may have exceeded his authority, is not a reason for refusing to enforce the award. Arbitrators have no obligation to the court to give their reasons for an award. To require opinions free of ambiguity may lead arbitrators to play it safe by writing no supporting opinions. This would be undesirable for a well reasoned opinion tends to engender confidence in the integrity of the process and aids in clarifying the underlying agreement. Moreover, we see no reason to assume that this arbitrator has abused the trust the parties confided in him and has not stayed within the areas marked out for his consideration. It is not apparent that he went beyond the submission. The Court of Appeals opinion refusing to enforce the reinstatement and partial back pay portions of the award was not based upon any finding that the arbitrator did not premise his award on his construction of the contract. It merely disagreed with the arbitrator's construction of it.

The collective bargaining agreement could have provided that if any of the employees were wrongfully discharged, the remedy would be reinstatement and back pay up to the date they were returned to work. Respondent's major argument seems to be that by applying correct principles of law to the interpretation of the collective bargaining agreement it can be determined that the agreement did not so provide, and that therefore the arbitrator's decision was not based upon the contract. The acceptance of this view would require courts, even under the standard arbitration clause, to review the merits of every construction of the contract. This plenary review by a court of the merits would make meaningless the provisions that the arbitrator's decision is final, for in reality it would almost never be final. This underlines the fundamental error which we have alluded to in United States Steelworkers of America v. American Manufacturing Co., 363 U.S. 564, 80 S.Ct. 1343, 4 L.Ed.2d 1403. As we there emphasized the question of interpretation of the collective bargaining agreement is a question for the arbitrator. It is the arbitrator's construction which was bargained for; and so far as the arbitrator's decision concerns construction of the contract, the courts have no business overruling him because their interpretation of the contract is different from his.

We agree with the Court of Appeals that the judgment of the District Court should be modified so that the amounts due the employees may be definitely determined by arbitration. In all other respects we think the judgment of the District Court should be affirmed.

———

MAJOR LEAGUE BASEBALL PLAYERS ASS'N. V. GARVEY, ___U.S.___ 121 S.Ct. 1724, ___ L.Ed.2d ___ (2001). An arbitrator concluded, after a hearing, that former first baseman Steve Garvey had not proved that the failure of the San Diego Padres to offer him a contract for the 1988 and 1989 baseball seasons was a product of collusion among the major league owners. The arbitrator failed to give credence to a letter written at the time of the arbitration by a former Padres executive, admitting to the collusion, because of its inconsistency with his statements of years earlier denying such collusion. The arbitrator thus dismissed Garvey's grievance. Garvey challenged this decision, and ultimately prevailed in the Court of Appeals for the Ninth Circuit, which found the decision of the arbitrator "inexplicable" and directed that the trial court issue a judgment for Garvey on the merits in the amount of his claim for $3 million. The United States Supreme Court, without briefs or oral argument, summarily reversed the decision of the Ninth Circuit, as inconsistent with the clear principles governing judicial review of arbitration awards.

The Court held that it was reversible error for the court of appeals to overturn the credibility determinations of the arbitrator and to substitute its own, and then to hold that there was only one decision on the merits that the arbitrator could rationally reach. This violated the Supreme Court's clear precedents barring judicial determination of grievances that the parties had agreed to resolve through arbitration, and barring judicial reversal of arbitration awards because of errors of fact or of interpretation. Indeed, even when an arbitrator's decision is a product of dishonesty or "affirmative misconduct," the court "must not foreclose further proceedings by settling the merits according to its own judgment of the appropriate result." Instead, the court should "simply vacate the award, thus leaving open the possibility of further proceedings if they are permitted under the terms of the agreement." The Court also went on to conclude that "In any event, no serious error on the arbitrator's part is apparent in this case."

[Because there was no division between the Circuits on a point of law, ordinarily a prerequisite for Supreme Court consideration, the Court's agreement to hear the case and its summary disposition can be taken as a strong admonition to the judiciary to adhere to the Court's teachings regarding deference to arbitration awards.]

———

## PROBLEMS FOR DISCUSSION

**1.** For twenty years, the Torrington Company granted its employees time off with pay to vote on Election Day; that benefit has not, however, been expressly mentioned in its collective bargaining agreement with the Metal Products Workers.

The month before last November's election, the Company announced in its newsletter that it was discontinuing the practice and it in fact paid no such benefits on Election Day. The Union claimed that this constituted a breach of the labor agreement, and it filed a grievance that ultimately reached an arbitrator.

The arbitrator ruled that the twenty-year Election Day practice had become a part of employee pay expectations and of the employer's obligations, which the employer could not abrogate without securing the Union's consent. She found no such consent to be manifested in the "management rights" provision of the agreement. She therefore ruled that Torrington had to pay employees an amount of money consistent with the prior Election Day practice.

The contract provides for arbitration of disputes "with respect to the meaning, interpretation or application of the provisions of this agreement," and also provides that "The arbitrator shall be bound by and must comply with all of the terms of this agreement and shall have no power to add to, delete from or modify, in any way, any of the provisions of this agreement." Torrington has petitioned a federal district court to vacate the arbitrator's award, contending that the arbitrator went outside the terms of the contract and exceeded her contractual authority. How should the court rule? Cf. Torrington Co. v. Metal Products Workers Union Local 1645, 362 F.2d 677 (2d Cir.1966). Compare Ethyl Corp. v. United Steelworkers, 768 F.2d 180 (7th Cir.1985); Edward Hines Lumber Co. v. Lumber and Sawmill Workers Local No. 2588, 764 F.2d 631 (9th Cir.1985).

**2.** A collective bargaining agreement provides that in the case of grievances about discharges, there shall first be an effort at adjustment between the union and the plant manager, and that failing resolution a demand for arbitration may be filed provided it is served in writing no later than five working days after the manager confirms the discharge decision. Failure to file within that time period "shall constitute a waiver of the grievance and a resolution on the terms set forth by management in the previous step." Greta Greeve was discharged on April 15, and the plant manager confirmed that decision after meeting with the union on April 30. Although representatives of the union immediately stated their dissatisfaction, they did not file a written demand for arbitration until June 1. At the arbitration hearing, the company challenged the arbitrator's jurisdiction by virtue of the union's untimely filing of its demand. The arbitrator ruled on that issue as follows: "The purpose of the time limits is to assure that the union takes unequivocal action in alerting management to its desire for arbitration. The union's manifested dissatisfaction after the manager confirmed the discharge, although oral, and its explicit written request 30 days later, satisfy in substance the requirement of timely filing. The grievance is therefore arbitrable." The arbitrator went on to sustain the grievance and to order reinstatement. You are the district judge in the company's action to vacate the arbitration award as beyond the arbitrator's authority. What is your ruling? See Wyandot, Inc. v. Local 227, Food Workers, 205 F.3d 922 (6th Cir.2000).

**3.** Article 28 of the collective bargaining agreement between United Package Service (UPS) and Local 1099 deals with discharge as follows:

Art. 28

Any case pertaining to a discharge or suspension shall be handled as follows: No employee(s) shall suffer suspension or discharge without the employee(s) having been given a written warning notice wherein the facts forming the grounds for such warning notice are clearly set forth. The facts therein set forth must be of the same type as those upon which such suspension or discharge is founded. (A) In cases of: (1) dishonesty; (2) drinking of alcoholic beverages while on duty; (3) recklessness resulting in a serious accident while on duty; (4) the carrying of unauthorized passengers; (5) unprovoked assault on an employee or a supervisory employee while on duty; (6) selling, transporting or uses of illegal narcotics while in the employment of the Employer; or (7) willful, wanton or malicious damage to the Employer's property, shall be dischargeable offenses without the necessity of a warning letter being in effect.

Steven Harris, a UPS employee, got into a dispute about his paycheck with a payroll clerk. He proceeded almost uncontrollably to berate the clerk using extreme profanity. He was discharged summarily—no warning notice was given—and the union took his discharge up to arbitration under the collective agreement. The arbitrator sustained the discharge. In her award, the arbitrator opined in part:

> While the arbitrator is unable to find that this [Harris'] language used rose to the level of an assault, it does rise to such insubordination and disrespect as to fall within industrially and socially disapproved conduct such as to authorize immediate dismissal without warning under Article 28. A number of acts, such as sexual harassment or drug possession on the premises, are well recognized as being dischargeable, yet these are not listed in subsection A, and there are no doubt other cardinal sins not specifically named in this CBA article which fall within the broad scope of insubordination and for which forthwith termination without benefit of warning may legitimately be imposed.

The Union has moved to vacate the award. How should the court rule? Hawaii Teamsters and Allied Workers Union, Local 996 v. United Parcel Service, 241 F.3d 1177 (9th Cir.2001).

**4.**  Sally Steward, the union's shop-floor representative responsible for dealing with employee grievances, left her work station in mid-day to complain to the plant manager about safety conditions at two work stations (not her own). The plant manager insisted that Steward had chosen an improper time to leave her post and that she should return to work immediately. When Steward refused to comply, the manager immediately imposed a two-week disciplinary suspension for insubordination, one of the forms of employee conduct listed in the labor agreement as subject to discipline including discharge. The union took Ms. Steward's case to arbitration, where the arbitrator concluded that—despite the facts as stipulated above—Steward was improperly disciplined and that she should be reinstated with full backpay. The arbitrator reasoned: "Had any other employee refused such a work order, discipline would have been appropriate. But Steward is a union representative as well as an employee. Under the National Labor Relations Act, her representation of fellow employees is given special protection. In her dealings with the plant manager, the relationship was one of co-equals in the administration of the labor agreement, and not one of subordinate to supervisor. The term 'insubordination' under the labor agreement thus does not embrace Steward's refusal to return to work. Discipline was therefore inappropriate."

The company refused to honor the award, and in the union's action to enforce, the company claimed that the arbitrator had exceeded her authority by relying on sources outside the labor contract. How should the court rule? See Roadmaster Corp. v. Production and Maintenance Employees' Local 504, 851 F.2d 886 (7th Cir.1988).

# Eastern Associated Coal Corp. v. United Mine Workers, District 17[e]

531 U.S. 57, 121 S.Ct. 462, 148 L.Ed.2d 354 (2000).

■ JUSTICE BREYER delivered the opinion of the Court.

A labor arbitrator ordered an employer to reinstate an employee truck driver who had twice tested positive for marijuana. The question before us is whether considerations of public policy require courts to refuse to enforce that arbitration award. We conclude that they do not. The courts may enforce the award. And the employer must reinstate, rather than discharge, the employee.

I

Petitioner, Eastern Associated Coal Corp., and respondent, United Mine Workers of America, are parties to a collective-bargaining agreement with arbitration provisions. The agreement specifies that, in arbitration, in order to discharge an employee, Eastern must prove it has "just cause." Otherwise the arbitrator will order the employee reinstated. The arbitrator's decision is final. App. 28–31.

James Smith worked for Eastern as a member of a road crew, a job that required him to drive heavy trucklike vehicles on public highways. As a truck driver, Smith was subject to Department of Transportation (DOT) regulations requiring random drug testing of workers engaged in "safety-sensitive" tasks. 49 CFR § § 382.301, 382.305 (1999).

In March, 1996, Smith tested positive for marijuana. Eastern sought to discharge Smith. The union went to arbitration, and the arbitrator concluded that Smith's positive drug test did not amount to "just cause" for discharge. Instead the arbitrator ordered Smith's reinstatement, provided that Smith (1) accept a suspension of 30 days without pay, (2) participate in a substance-abuse program, and (3) undergo drug tests at the discretion of Eastern (or an approved substance-abuse professional) for the next five years.

Between April, 1996 and January, 1997, Smith passed four random drug tests. But in July 1997 he again tested positive for marijuana. Eastern again sought to discharge Smith. The union again went to arbitration, and the arbitrator again concluded that Smith's use of marijuana did not amount to "just cause" for discharge, in light of two mitigating circumstances. First, Smith had been a good employee for 17 years. App. to Pet. for Cert. 26a–27a. And, second, Smith had made a credible and "very personal appeal under oath . . . concerning a personal/family problem which caused this one time lapse in drug usage." Id., at 28a.

**e.** Easterbrook, Arbitration, Contract and Public Policy, 44 Proc. of Nat'l Acad. of Arbitrators 65 (1992); Feller, Court Review of Arbitration, 43 Lab.L.J. 539 (1992); Gould, Judicial Review of Labor Arbitration Awards: The Aftermath of *AT & T* and *Misco*, 64 Notre Dame L.Rev. 464 (1989); Meltzer, After the Labor Arbitration Award: The Public Policy Defense, 10 Ind.Rel.L.J. 241 (1988).

The arbitrator ordered Smith's reinstatement provided that Smith (1) accept a new suspension without pay, this time for slightly more than three months; (2) reimburse Eastern and the union for the costs of both arbitration proceedings; (3) continue to participate in a substance abuse program; (4) continue to undergo random drug testing; and (5) provide Eastern with a signed, undated letter of resignation, to take effect if Smith again tested positive within the next five years. Id., at 29a.

Eastern brought suit in federal court seeking to have the arbitrator's award vacated, arguing that the award contravened a public policy against the operation of dangerous machinery by workers who test positive for drugs. 66 F.Supp.2d 796 (S.D.W.V.1998). The District Court, while recognizing a strong regulation-based public policy against drug use by workers who perform safety-sensitive functions, held that Smith's conditional reinstatement did not violate that policy. Id., at 804–805. And it ordered the award's enforcement. Id., at 805.

The Court of Appeals for the Fourth Circuit affirmed on the reasoning of the District Court. 188 F.3d 501, 1999 WL 635632 (1999) (unpublished). We granted certiorari in light of disagreement among the Circuits. Compare id., at *1 (holding that public policy does not prohibit "reinstatement of employees who have used illegal drugs in the past"), with, e.g., Exxon Corp. v. Esso Workers' Union, Inc., 118 F.3d 841, 852 (C.A.1 1997) (holding that public policy prohibits enforcement of a similar arbitration award). We now affirm the Fourth Circuit's determination.

## II

Eastern claims that considerations of public policy make the arbitration award unenforceable. In considering this claim, we must assume that the collective-bargaining agreement itself calls for Smith's reinstatement. That is because both employer and union have granted to the arbitrator the authority to interpret the meaning of their contract's language, including such words as "just cause." See Steelworkers v. Enterprise Wheel & Car Corp., 363 U.S. 593, 599, 80 S.Ct. 1358, 4 L.Ed.2d 1424 (1960). They have "bargained for" the "arbitrator's construction" of their agreement. Ibid. And courts will set aside the arbitrator's interpretation of what their agreement means only in rare instances. Id., at 596, 80 S.Ct. 1358. Of course, an arbitrator's award "must draw its essence from the contract and cannot simply reflect the arbitrator's own notions of industrial justice." Paperworkers v. Misco, Inc., 484 U.S. 29, 38, 108 S.Ct. 364, 98 L.Ed.2d 286 (1987). "But as long as [an honest] arbitrator is even arguably construing or applying the contract and acting within the scope of his authority," the fact that "a court is convinced he committed serious error does not suffice to overturn his decision." Ibid.; see also *Enterprise Wheel*, supra, at 596, 80 S.Ct. 1358 (the "proper" judicial approach to a labor arbitration award is to "refus[e] . . . to review the merits"). Eastern does not claim here that the arbitrator acted outside the scope of his contractually delegated authority. Hence we must treat the arbitrator's award as if it represented an agreement between Eastern and the union as to the proper meaning of the contract's words "just cause." See St. Antoine, *Judicial Review of Labor Arbitration Awards: A Second Look at Enterprise Wheel and Its Progeny*, 75 Mich. L.Rev. 1137, 1155 (1977). For present purposes, the award is not distinguishable from the contractual agreement.

We must then decide whether a contractual reinstatement requirement would fall within the legal exception that makes unenforceable "a collective bargaining agreement that is contrary to public policy." W.R. Grace & Co. v. Rubber Workers, 461 U.S. 757, 766, 103 S.Ct. 2177, 76 L.Ed.2d 298 (1983). The Court has made clear that any such public policy must be "explicit," "well defined," and "dominant." Ibid. It must be "ascertained 'by reference to the laws and legal precedents and not from general considerations of supposed public interests.' " Ibid. (quoting Muschany v. United States, 324 U.S. 49, 66, 65 S.Ct. 442, 89 L.Ed. 744 (1945)); accord, *Misco*, supra, at 43, 108 S.Ct. 364. And, of course, the question to be answered is not whether Smith's drug use itself violates public policy, but whether the agreement to reinstate him does so. To put the question more specifically, does a contractual agreement to reinstate Smith with specified conditions, see App. to Pet. for Cert. 29a, run contrary to an explicit, well-defined, and dominant public policy, as ascertained by reference to positive law and not from general considerations of supposed public interests? See Misco, supra, at 43, 108 S.Ct. 364.

## III

Eastern initially argues that the District Court erred by asking, not whether the award is "contrary to" public policy "as ascertained by reference" to positive law, but whether the award "violates" positive law, a standard Eastern says is too narrow. We believe, however, that the District Court correctly articulated the standard set out in *W.R. Grace* and *Misco*, see 66 F.Supp.2d, at 803 (quoting *Misco*, supra, at 43, 108 S.Ct. 364), and applied that standard to reach the right result.

We agree, in principle, that courts' authority to invoke the public policy exception is not limited solely to instances where the arbitration award itself violates positive law. Nevertheless, the public policy exception is narrow and must satisfy the principles set forth in *W.R. Grace* and *Misco*. Moreover, in a case like the one before us, where two political branches have created a detailed regulatory regime in a specific field, courts should approach with particular caution pleas to divine further public policy in that area.

Eastern asserts that a public policy against reinstatement of workers who use drugs can be discerned from an examination of that regulatory regime, which consists of the Omnibus Transportation Employee Testing Act of 1991 and DOT's implementing regulations. The Testing Act embodies a congressional finding that "the greatest efforts must be expended to eliminate the ... use of illegal drugs, whether on or off duty, by those individuals who are involved in [certain safety-sensitive positions, including] the operation of ... trucks." Pub.L. 102–143, § 2(3), 105 Stat. 953. The Act adds that "increased testing" is the "most effective deterrent" to "use of illegal drugs." § 2(5). It requires the Secretary of Transportation to promulgate regulations requiring "testing of operators of commercial motor vehicles for the use of a controlled substance." 49 U.S.C. § 31306(b)(1)(A) (1994 ed., Supp. III). It mandates suspension of those operators who have driven a commercial motor vehicle while under the influence of drugs. 49 U.S.C. § 31310(b)(1)(A) (requiring suspension of at least one year for a first offense); § 31310(c)(2) (requiring suspension of at least 10 years for a second offense). And DOT's implementing regulations set forth sanctions applicable to those who test positive for illegal drugs. 49 CFR § 382.605 (1999).

In Eastern's view, these provisions embody a strong public policy against drug use by transportation workers in safety-sensitive positions and in favor of random drug testing in order to detect that use. Eastern argues that reinstatement of a driver who has twice failed random drug tests would undermine that policy—to the point where a judge must set aside an employer-union agreement requiring reinstatement.

Eastern's argument, however, loses much of its force when one considers further provisions of the Act that make clear that the Act's remedial aims are complex. The Act says that "rehabilitation is a critical component of any testing program," § 2(7), 105 Stat. 953, that rehabilitation "should be made available to individuals, as appropriate," ibid., and that DOT must promulgate regulations for "rehabilitation programs," 49 U.S.C. § 31306(e). The DOT regulations specifically state that a driver who has tested positive for drugs cannot return to a safety-sensitive position until (1) the driver has been evaluated by a "substance abuse professional" to determine if treatment is needed, 49 CFR § 382.605(b) (1999); (2) the substance-abuse professional has certified that the driver has followed any rehabilitation program prescribed, § 382.605(c)(2)(i); and (3) the driver has passed a return-to-duty drug test, § 382.605(c)(1). In addition, (4) the driver must be subject to at least six random drug tests during the first year after returning to the job. § 382.605(c)(2)(ii). Neither the Act nor the regulations forbid an employer to reinstate in a safety-sensitive position an employee who fails a random drug test once or twice. The congressional and regulatory directives require only that the above-stated prerequisites to reinstatement be met.

Moreover, when promulgating these regulations, DOT decided not to require employers either to provide rehabilitation or to "hold a job open for a driver" who has tested positive, on the basis that such decisions "should be left to management/driver negotiation." 59 Fed.Reg. 7502 (1994). That determination reflects basic background labor law principles, which caution against interference with labor-management agreements about appropriate employee discipline. * * * *

The award before us is not contrary to these several policies, taken together. The award does not condone Smith's conduct or ignore the risk to public safety that drug use by truck drivers may pose. Rather, the award punishes Smith by suspending him for three months, thereby depriving him of nearly $9,000 in lost wages, Record Doc. 29, App. A, p. 2; it requires him to pay the arbitration costs of both sides; it insists upon further substance-abuse treatment and testing; and it makes clear (by requiring Smith to provide a signed letter of resignation) that one more failed test means discharge.

The award violates no specific provision of any law or regulation. It is consistent with DOT rules requiring completion of substance-abuse treatment before returning to work, see 49 CFR § 382.605(c)(2)(i) (1999), for it does not preclude Eastern from assigning Smith to a non-safety-sensitive position until Smith completes the prescribed treatment program. It is consistent with the Testing Act's 1–year and 10–year driving license suspension requirements, for those requirements apply only to drivers who, unlike Smith, actually operated vehicles under the influence of drugs. See 49 U.S.C. § § 31310(b), (c). The award is also consistent with the Act's rehabilitative concerns, for it requires substance-abuse treatment and testing before Smith can return to work.

The fact that Smith is a recidivist—that he has failed drug tests twice—is not sufficient to tip the balance in Eastern's favor. The award punishes Smith more severely for his second lapse. And that more severe punishment, which included a 90–day suspension, would have satisfied even a "recidivist" rule that DOT once proposed but did not adopt—a rule that would have punished two failed drug tests, not with discharge, but with a driving suspension of 60 days. 57 Fed.Reg. 59585 (1992). * * * *

* * * * Upon careful consideration, including public notice and comment, the Secretary has done so. Neither Congress nor the Secretary [of Transportation] has seen fit to mandate the discharge of a worker who twice tests positive for drugs. We hesitate to infer a public policy in this area that goes beyond the careful and detailed scheme Congress and the Secretary have created.

We recognize that reasonable people can differ as to whether reinstatement or discharge is the more appropriate remedy here. But both employer and union have agreed to entrust this remedial decision to an arbitrator. We cannot find in the Act, the regulations, or any other law or legal precedent an "explicit," "well defined," "dominant" public policy to which the arbitrator's decision "runs contrary." *Misco*, 484 U.S., at 43, 108 S.Ct. 364; *W.R. Grace*, 461 U.S., at 766, 103 S.Ct. 2177. We conclude that the lower courts correctly rejected Eastern's public policy claim. The judgment of the Court of Appeals is

Affirmed.

Justice SCALIA, with whom Justice THOMAS joins, concurring in the judgment.

I concur in the Court's judgment, because I agree that no public policy prevents the reinstatement of James Smith to his position as a truck driver, so long as he complies with the arbitrator's decision, and with those requirements set out in the Department of Transportation's regulations. I do not endorse, however, the Court's statement that "[w]e agree, in principle, that courts' authority to invoke the public policy exception is not limited solely to instances where the arbitration award itself violates positive law." Ante, at 467. No case is cited to support that proposition, and none could be. There is not a single decision, since this Court washed its hands of general common-lawmaking authority, see Erie R. Co. v. Tompkins, 304 U.S. 64, 58 S.Ct. 817, 82 L.Ed. 1188 (1938), in which we have refused to enforce on "public policy" grounds an agreement that did not violate, or provide for the violation of, some positive law. See, e.g., Hurd v. Hodge, 334 U.S. 24, 68 S.Ct. 847, 92 L.Ed. 1187 (1948) (refusing to enforce under the public policy doctrine a restrictive covenant that violated Rev. Stat. § 1978, at 42 U.S.C. § 1982).

After its dictum opening the door to flaccid public policy arguments of the sort presented by petitioner here, the Court immediately posts a giant "Do Not Enter" sign. "[T]he public policy exception," it says, "is narrow and must satisfy the principles set forth in *W.R. Grace*," ante, at 467, which require that the applicable public policy be "explicit," "well defined," "dominant," and "ascertained 'by reference to the laws and legal precedents and not from general considerations of supposed public interests.'" W.R. Grace & Co. v. Rubber Workers, 461 U.S. 757, 766, 103 S.Ct. 2177, 76 L.Ed.2d 298 (1983) (quoting Muschany v. United States, 324 U.S. 49, 66, 65 S.Ct. 442, 89 L.Ed. 744 (1945)). It is hard to imagine how an arbitration award could violate a public policy, identified in this fashion, without actually conflicting with positive law. If such an award could ever exist, it would surely be so rare that the benefit of preserving the courts' ability to deal with it is far outweighed by the confusion and uncertainty, and hence the obstructive litigation, that the Court's Delphic "agree[ment] in principle" will engender. * * * *

UNITED PAPERWORKERS INTERNATIONAL UNION v. MISCO, INC., 484 U.S. 29, 108 S.Ct. 364, 98 L.Ed.2d 286 (1987). After an arbitrator reinstated with full backpay and seniority an employee who had been discharged for possession and use of marijuana in violation of explicit company rules, the employer brought an action to set aside the award. The facts showed that the employee—Isiah Cooper, who worked at a dangerous slitter-rewinder machine in a paper converting plant—was found by the police, shortly before the start of his shift, sitting in the rear of a fellow employee's car, parked on the company parking lot, with a lit marijuana joint in the front ashtray and marijuana smoke permeating the vehicle. The arbitrator, in sustaining the grievance, concluded that these circumstances were inadequate to prove marijuana use or possession; he also excluded evidence proffered by the company that the police had also found marijuana in Cooper's own car, because that evidence was not known to the company at the time of the discharge and did not come to its attention until five days before the arbitration hearing, and to the union's attention until the day of the hearing. In the court action to set aside the award, the employer challenged the arbitrator's factfinding, his interpretation of the collective agreement, his exclusion of evidence, and the reinstatement award which it asserted violated the public policy against operating dangerous machinery while affected by narcotics.

The Supreme Court unanimously reversed the decision of the trial judge and the court of appeals, which had concluded that the award violated public policy. As intimated in the *Eastern Associated Coal* decision, the Court concluded that the public policy proffered by the Misco company was based only on "general considerations of supposed public interests" and not on a "well defined and dominant" policy reflected in specific laws and legal precedents. Moreover, the Court held that it was not for a court to infer from the marijuana gleanings in Cooper's car that he was a danger in the workplace and "under the influence" while there: "[This] is an exercise in fact-finding about Cooper's use of drugs and his amenability to discipline, a task that exceeds the authority of a court asked to overturn an arbitration award.... Had the arbitrator found that Cooper had possessed drugs on the property yet imposed discipline short of discharge because he found as a factual matter that Cooper could be trusted not to use them on the job, the Court of Appeals could not upset the award because of its own view that public policy about plant safety was threatened."

Apart from its discussion of the public policy defense to the enforcement of an arbitration award, the Court emphasized the very narrow role of the judiciary in overturning such awards.

> The courts are not authorized to reconsider the merits of an award even though the parties may allege that the award rests on errors of fact or on misinterpretation of the contract.... Because the parties have contracted to have disputes settled by an arbitrator chosen by them rather than by a judge, it is the arbitrator's view of the facts and of the meaning of the contract that they have agreed to accept. Courts thus do not sit to hear claims of factual or legal error by an arbitrator as an appellate court does in reviewing decisions of lower courts. To resolve disputes about the application of a collective-bargaining agreement, an arbitrator must find facts and a court may not reject those findings simply because it disagrees with them. The same is true of the arbitrator's interpretation of the contract.... So, too, where it is contemplated that the arbitrator will determine remedies for contract violations that he finds, courts have no authority to disagree with his honest judgment in that respect. If the courts were free to intervene on these grounds, the speedy resolution of grievances by private mechanisms would be greatly undermined.... [A]s long as the arbitrator is even arguably construing or applying the contract and acting within the scope of his authority, that a court is convinced he committed serious error does not suffice to overturn his decision. Of course, decisions procured by the parties through fraud or through the arbitrator's dishonesty need not be enforced. But there is nothing of that sort involved in this case.

Applying those principles, the Court concluded that it was not for the reviewing court to conclude that Cooper's presence in his friend's car on company property was ample proof of a violation of the company rule against drug possession and use. "No dishonesty [on the part of the arbitrator] is alleged; only improvident, even silly, factfinding is claimed." Nor should the lower court have challenged the arbitrator's exclusion of evidence (of marijuana in Cooper's own car) that was not relied on by the employer in ordering the discharge, particularly when neither the union nor the grievant had reason to know that the company would rely on this after-discovered evidence at the arbitration hearing. The arbitrator's approach "was consistent with the practice followed by other arbitrators" and with the Court's own rulings that " 'procedural' questions which grow out of the dispute and bear on its final disposition are to be left to the arbitrator." It was another excess of judicial authority for the court of appeals to assume that, if a violation of the company rule was indeed shown, discharge was the only correct remedy; the proper course would have been to remand to the arbitrator for reconsideration of the remedy.

———

## PROBLEMS FOR DISCUSSION

**1.** You sit on the United States Court of Appeals for your local circuit, and you are asked to rule on a number of requests to vacate or to enforce arbitration awards rendered against several different employers. In each case, the employer discharged the employee and the arbitrator (although finding the facts as alleged by the employer) ordered reinstatement without backpay. How would you rule in each of the following cases?

(a) An airline pilot, following three hours of sleep after a night of very heavy drinking, piloted a large passenger aircraft. Upon landing, he was tested for alcohol, which proved to be in excess of the limits permitted by state law for automobile drivers and far in excess of the limits permitted by the Federal Aviation Agency (which explicitly bans, by regulation, flying while under the influence of alcohol and flying within eight hours of drinking alcohol) and by explicit company policy. The arbitrator concluded that the employer's proper response was to attempt to rehabilitate the pilot rather than to punish him. (The employer argues that the award contravenes public policy in that, unlike *Misco,* the pilot was under the influence while actually engaged in his employment duties, and that the airline employer, had it known of the pilot's condition, could not lawfully have permitted him to fly.) Compare Delta Air Lines, Inc. v. Air Line Pilots Ass'n, 861 F.2d 665 (11th Cir.1988), with Northwest Airlines, Inc. v. Air Line Pilots Ass'n, 808 F.2d 76 (D.C.Cir.1987).

(b) Chrysler Company discharged one of its male employees, who stealthily approached a woman co-worker from behind, while she was at her work station, and placed his arms around her and grabbed her breasts. The union, claiming that the employee's conduct was intolerable but that discharge was too severe, and was in violation of the contractual "just cause" provision, took the case through the grievance procedure and demanded arbitration. In preparing for the arbitration, Chrysler learned that the grievant had molested four other women employees on earlier occasions.

At the arbitration hearing, the arbitrator refused to permit the Company to introduce the evidence of the earlier molestations. In light of the grievant's long service and his unblemished work record, without even a prior oral warning for misconduct, the arbitrator concluded that discipline should be regarded as corrective rather than punitive (as was the Company's practice) and that the grievant was capable of rehabilitation. He ordered Chrysler to reinstate the grievant and, because of the seriousness of the grievant's conduct, the arbitrator reduced the discipline to a thirty-day suspension; backpay was calculated accordingly.

Chrysler seeks to have the award vacated. It cites, in particular, federal law barring discrimination on the basis of sex, and regulations of the EEOC that interpret this to embrace physical sexual harassment and that make an employer liable for condoning such employee behavior. (See 29 C.F.R. § 1604.11.) It also claims that the arbitrator abused his discretion by refusing to hear evidence about the other instances of similar misbehavior. How should the court decide the case? See Weber Aircraft, Inc. v. General Warehousemen Local 767, 2001 WL 630178 (5th Cir. 2001).

[If you had been counsel to the Union, would you have felt obliged to decline pursuing the grievance when initially presented, by virtue of the Union's duty of fair representation? If instead you were counsel to Chrysler, would you have recommended that the Company save time and expense by not bringing an action to vacate the arbitrator's award, but rather—after losing in arbitration—simply by discharging the grievant for the earlier four molestations?]

**2.** The collective bargaining agreement between Company and Union provides: "Employees who do not maintain their membership in good standing in the Union shall be subject to immediate discharge." Union bylaws define "membership in good standing" to include regular attendance at Union meetings. Employee Jones is consistently absent from membership meetings, and Union insists that Company discharge him, but Company refuses. The contract has a standard arbitration clause.

(a) Union commences an action in a federal district court to compel arbitration of its grievance. Should the court order arbitration?

(b) Assume that the grievance is sent to arbitration. How should the arbitrator rule?

(c) Assume that the arbitrator rules that Jones had failed to maintain his membership in good standing, that the labor contract thus requires Company to discharge him immediately, and that Company should therefore be ordered to do so. If Company brings an action to set aside the award—or if Union brings an action to confirm it—how should the court decide? Compare Broadway Cab Co-op., Inc. v. Teamsters and Chauffeurs Local Union No. 281, 710 F.2d 1379 (9th Cir.1983); General Warehousemen and Helpers Local 767 v. Standard Brands, Inc., 579 F.2d 1282 (5th Cir.1978); with Wilmington Typog. Union No. 123 v. News–Journal Co., 513 F.Supp. 987 (D.Del.1981). See also Kaiser Steel Corp. v. Mullins, 455 U.S. 72, 102 S.Ct. 851, 70 L.Ed.2d 833 (1982).

————

*JUDICIAL ENFORCEMENT OF THE NO–STRIKE CLAUSE*

With the reintroduction in the Taft–Hartley Act of 1947 of the federal judiciary as an important agency in regulating labor-management relations, and the emphasis in the same legislation upon the peaceful resolution of disputes concerning collective bargaining agreements, it became all but inevitable that the continuing vitality of the Norris–LaGuardia Act of 1932 would have to be tested. The earlier statute had been based upon the belief that judges were ill-equipped to pass judgment upon the social and economic issues involved in labor disputes and that strikes, boycotts and picketing were part of the competitive struggle for life which society tolerates because the freedom is worth more than it costs. There was no clear congressional attempt in 1947 to reconcile these two conflicting social and juridical philosophies, and the task of compromise and adjustment fell to the courts. That task was presented most starkly when a union instituted a strike during the term of a contract which provided that grievances would be determined by arbitration and that there would be no resort to strike or lockout during the contract term. A request for an injunction against the strike in breach of contract required a determination whether Section 4 of the Norris–LaGuardia Act was to be treated as limited in any way by Section 301 of the Labor Management Relations Act.

This statutory conflict was not altogether unprecedented in the sphere of federal labor legislation. The Railway Labor Act of 1926 imposed various duties upon employers, but established no agency to enforce them and left the problem of compliance to the courts. Neither the Norris–LaGuardia Act nor the 1934 amendments to the Railway Labor Act spoke specifically to the question of the injunctive powers of the federal courts in enforcing the mandates of the Railway Labor Act. In Virginian Ry. Co. v. System Federation No. 40, 300 U.S. 515, 57 S.Ct. 592, 81 L.Ed. 789 (1937), the Supreme Court rejected the argument that a mandatory injunction compelling an employer to recognize and bargain with a union offended Section 9 of the Norris–LaGuardia Act, holding instead that that Act could not render nugatory the specific provisions of the Railway Labor Act protecting employees from the interference, restraint or coercion of employers. Some years later, in Graham v. Brotherhood of Locomotive Firemen & Enginemen, 338 U.S. 232, 70 S.Ct. 14, 94 L.Ed. 22 (1949), the Court sustained the issuance of an injunction requiring the bargaining representative to represent fairly all employees within the bargaining unit; to preclude such relief because of the Norris–LaGuardia Act would mean that Congress intended to hold before employees the illusory right to nondiscriminatory representation by their bargaining agent while denying them any remedy for its violation.

Neither of the cases mentioned above involved an injunction which prohibited a strike by a labor union—the classic situation with which the Norris–LaGuardia Act was primarily concerned. This very situation, however, eventually came before the Supreme Court in BROTHERHOOD OF R.R. TRAINMEN V. CHICAGO RIVER & IND. R. CO., 353 U.S. 30, 77 S.Ct. 635, 1 L.Ed.2d 622 (1957). There, a railroad union had asserted twenty-one contract grievances (almost all involving claims to additional compensation) which were ultimately submitted to the National Railroad Adjustment Board, and called a strike while the cases were pending before the Board. A permanent injunction was issued against the strike by a federal district court, and the union argued to the Supreme Court that the injunction violated the Norris–LaGuardia Act. The Court, however, sustained the injunction. It considered the history of the Railway Labor Act of 1926 and its failure to eliminate strikes over contract grievances (or so-called "minor disputes" under the Act), followed by the creation in 1934 of the Adjustment Board, whose jurisdiction to render binding grievance decisions could be invoked either by the railroad or the union. The Court characterized the latter provisions as erecting a system of "compulsory arbitration" and framed the question before it as whether the federal courts may enjoin a union "from striking to defeat the jurisdiction of the Adjustment Board." The Court concluded:

"We hold that the Norris–LaGuardia Act cannot be read alone in matters dealing with railway labor disputes. There must be an accommodation of that statute and the Railway Labor Act so that the obvious purpose in the enactment of each is preserved. We think that the purposes of these Acts are reconcilable.

" * * * [In the Norris–LaGuardia Act,] Congress acted to prevent the injunctions of the federal courts from upsetting the natural interplay of the competing economic forces of labor and capital. Rep. LaGuardia, during the floor debates on the 1932 Act, recognized that the machinery of the Railway Labor Act channeled these economic forces, in matters dealing with railway labor, into special processes intended to compromise them. Such controversies, therefore, are not the same as those in which the injunction strips labor of its primary weapon without substituting any reasonable alternative. * * * "

(Strikes arising from "major disputes", that is the negotiation of new contract terms, are not, however, unlawful under the Railway Labor Act, and no injunction may issue when, under Section 13(c) of the Norris–LaGuardia Act, there is a "controversy concerning terms or conditions of employment." Order of R.R. Telegraphers v. Chicago & N.W. R. Co., 362 U.S. 330, 80 S.Ct. 761, 4 L.Ed.2d 774 (1960).)

With the enactment of the Labor Management Relations Act of 1947, providing for union unfair labor practices and NLRB cease and desist orders and Board-initiated injunction actions, Congress once again narrowed the freedom from injunctive relief which had been expressed in such sweeping terms in Section 4 of the Norris–LaGuardia Act. Further possible conflicts were created by Section 301 of the LMRA, which raised the question whether the Norris–LaGuardia Act precluded the use of injunctions to enforce claims arising out of a collective bargaining agreement. In Textile Workers Union v. Lincoln Mills, at p. 747, supra, the Supreme Court held that Section 7 of the Norris–LaGuardia Act did not apply to a suit for specific enforcement of a promise to arbitrate.

When the Court then considered the more pointed issue whether a federal court could enjoin a strike in violation of a no-strike clause in a collective bargaining agreement, the Court first held that no such injunction could issue. In SINCLAIR REFINING CO. v. ATKINSON, 370 U.S. 195, 82 S.Ct. 1328, 8 L.Ed.2d 440 (1962), a divided Court affirmed a dismissal of an injunction action brought by an employer against continued work stoppages concerning contract grievances during the term of a labor contract providing for arbitration and for "no strikes or work stoppages for any cause which is or may be the subject of a grievance." The Court concluded that the contract-enforcement policy underlying Section 301 "was not intended to have any such partially repealing effect upon such a long-standing, carefully thought out and highly significant part of this country's labor legislation as the Norris–LaGuardia Act."

The Court majority, through Mr. Justice Black, refused to engage in the "accommodation" of the anti-injunction principles of the Norris–La-Guardia Act when Congress had not done so in the Labor–Management Relations Act of 1947. Justice Black pointed out that when Congress intended to supersede the Norris–LaGuardia Act it did so explicitly, witness Section 10(h) of the Labor Act, and that injunctions under the Taft–Hartley Act were uniformly to be sought by the NLRB and not by private parties. Reference was also made to congressional bills which would expressly have repealed the Norris–LaGuardia Act in actions to enforce labor contracts but which failed of passage. The Court also distinguished several cases on which the plaintiff company had relied. The *Chicago River* case under the Railway Labor Act was held inapt, principally because the strike in that case was "in defiance of an affirmative duty, imposed upon the union by the Railway Labor Act itself, compelling unions to settle disputes as to the interpretation of an existing collective bargaining agreement, not by collective union pressures on the railroad but by submitting them to the Railroad Adjustment Board as the exclusive means of final determination of such 'minor' disputes." *Lincoln Mills* was distinguished because there the injunction was sought against a refusal to arbitrate and its issuance thus "did not enjoin any one of the kinds of conduct which the specific prohibitions of the Norris–LaGuardia Act withdrew from the injunctive powers of United States courts." Finally, *Lincoln Mills* and the *Steelworkers Trilogy* were held simply to be applications of the clear statutory directives of Section 301 and not to invite the development of a judge-made policy contrary to the directives of the Norris–LaGuardia Act; "The argument to the contrary seems to rest upon the notion that injunctions against peaceful strikes are necessary to make the arbitration process effective. But whatever might be said about the merits of this argument, Congress has itself rejected it."

Three dissenting Justices, in an opinion by Mr. Justice Brennan, would have read the Norris–LaGuardia Act and Section 301 of the Labor Management Relations Act as to authorize the issuance of an injunction against the strike in breach of contract. In a dramatic reversal of position, a majority of the Court eight years after *Sinclair* adopted the views of the dissenting Justices, in the following case.

---

# Boys Markets, Inc. v. Retail Clerks Union, Local 770[f]
398 U.S. 235, 90 S.Ct. 1583, 26 L.Ed.2d 199 (1970).

■ MR. JUSTICE BRENNAN delivered the opinion of the Court.

In this case we re-examine the holding of Sinclair Refining Co. v. Atkinson, 370 U.S. 195, 82 S.Ct. 1328, 8 L.Ed.2d 440 (1962), that the anti-

**f.** See Atleson, The Circle of Boys Market: A Comment on Judicial Inventiveness, 7 Indus.Rel.L.J. 88 (1985); Atleson, Threats to Health and Safety: Employee Self–Help Un-

injunction provisions of the Norris–LaGuardia Act preclude a federal district court from enjoining a strike in breach of a no-strike obligation under a collective-bargaining agreement, even though that agreement contains provisions, enforceable under § 301(a) of the Labor Management Relations Act, 1947, for binding arbitration of the grievance dispute concerning which the strike was called. The Court of Appeals for the Ninth Circuit, considering itself bound by *Sinclair* reversed the grant by the District Court for the Central District of California of petitioner's prayer for injunctive relief. 416 F.2d 368 (1969). We granted certiorari. 396 U.S. 1000, 90 S.Ct. 572, 24 L.Ed.2d 492 (1970). Having concluded that *Sinclair* was erroneously decided and that subsequent events have undermined its continuing validity, we overrule that decision and reverse the judgment of the Court of Appeals.

I

In February, 1969, at the time of the incidents that produced this litigation, petitioner and respondent were parties to a collective-bargaining agreement which provided, *inter alia,* that all controversies concerning its interpretation or application should be resolved by adjustment and arbitration procedures set forth therein and that, during the life of the contract, there should be "no cessation or stoppage of work, lock-out, picketing or boycotts * * *." The dispute arose when petitioner's frozen foods supervisor and certain members of his crew who were not members of the bargaining unit began to rearrange merchandise in the frozen food cases of one of petitioner's supermarkets. A union representative insisted that the food cases be stripped of all merchandise and be restocked by union personnel. When petitioner did not accede to the union's demand, a strike was called and the union began to picket petitioner's establishment. Thereupon petitioner demanded that the union cease the work stoppage and picketing and sought to invoke the grievance and arbitration procedures specified in the contract.

The following day, since the strike had not been terminated, petitioner filed a complaint in California Superior Court seeking a temporary restraining order, a preliminary and permanent injunction, and specific performance of the contractual arbitration provision. The state court issued a temporary restraining order forbidding continuation of the strike and also an order to show cause why a preliminary injunction should not be granted. Shortly thereafter, the union removed the case to the Federal District

der the NLRA, 59 Minn.L.Rev. 647 (1975); Axelrod, The Application of the Boys Markets Decision in the Federal Courts, 16 B.C.Ind. & Com.L.Rev. 893 (1975); Comment, Boys Markets Injunctions Against Employers, 91 Harv. L.Rev. 715 (1978); Gould, On Labor Injunctions, Unions, and the Judges the Boys Markets Case, 1970 Sup.Ct.Rev. 215; Klare, The Public–Private Distinction in Labor Law, 130 U.Pa.L.Rev. 1358, 1388–415 (1982); Vladeck, *Boys Markets* and National Labor Policy, 24 Vand.L.Rev. 93 (1970). See also Wellington & Albert, Statutory Interpretation and the Political Process: A Comment on Sinclair v. Atkinson, 72 Yale L.J. 1547 (1963).

Court and there made a motion to quash the state court's temporary restraining order. In opposition, petitioner moved for an order compelling arbitration and enjoining continuation of the strike. Concluding that the dispute was subject to arbitration under the collective-bargaining agreement and that the strike was in violation of the contract, the District Court ordered the parties to arbitrate the underlying dispute and simultaneously enjoined the strike, all picketing in the vicinity of petitioner's supermarket, and any attempts by the union to induce the employees to strike or to refuse to perform their services.

## II

At the outset, we are met with respondent's contention that *Sinclair* ought not to be disturbed because the decision turned on a question of statutory construction which Congress can alter at any time. Since Congress has not modified our conclusions in *Sinclair,* even though it has been urged to do so,[5] respondent argues that principles of *stare decisis* should govern the present case.

We do not agree that the doctrine of *stare decisis* bars a reexamination of *Sinclair* in the circumstances of this case. We fully recognize that important policy considerations militate in favor of continuity and predictability in the law. Nevertheless, as Mr. Justice Frankfurter wrote for the Court, *"[S]tare decisis* is a principle of policy and not a mechanical formula of adherence to the latest decision, however recent and questionable, when such adherence involves collision with a prior doctrine more embracing in its scope, intrinsically sounder, and verified by experience." Helvering v. Hallock, 309 U.S. 106, 119, 60 S.Ct. 444, 451, 84 L.Ed. 604 (1940). See Swift & Co. v. Wickham, 382 U.S. 111, 116, 86 S.Ct. 258, 261, 15 L.Ed.2d 194 (1965). It is precisely because *Sinclair* stands as a significant departure from our otherwise consistent emphasis upon the congressional policy to promote the peaceful settlement of labor disputes through arbitration and our efforts to accommodate and harmonize this policy with those underlying the anti-injunction provisions of the Norris–LaGuardia Act that we believe *Sinclair* should be reconsidered. Furthermore, in light of developments subsequent to *Sinclair,* in particular our decision in Avco Corp. v. Aero Lodge 735, 390 U.S. 557, 88 S.Ct. 1235, 20 L.Ed.2d 126 (1968), it has become clear that the *Sinclair* decision does not further but rather frustrates realization of an important goal of our national labor policy.

Nor can we agree that conclusive weight should be accorded to the failure of Congress to respond to *Sinclair* on the theory that congressional silence should be interpreted as acceptance of the decision. The Court has cautioned that "[i]t is at best treacherous to find in congressional silence alone the adoption of a controlling rule of law." Girouard v. United States, 328 U.S. 61, 69, 66 S.Ct. 826, 830, 90 L.Ed. 1084 (1946). Therefore, in the absence of any persuasive circumstances evidencing a clear design that congressional inaction be taken as acceptance of *Sinclair,* the mere silence

---

**5.**  See, e.g., Report of Special Atkinson–Sinclair Committee, A.B.A. Labor Relations Law Section—Proceedings 226 (1963) [hereinafter cited as A.B.A. *Sinclair* Report].

of Congress is not a sufficient reason for refusing to reconsider the decision. Helvering v. Hallock, supra, 309 U.S. at 119–120, 60 S.Ct. at 451–452.

## III

[The Court here referred to the *Lincoln Mills* case, in which it decided that substantive federal law was to apply in suits under Section 301 and that a union could obtain specific performance of an employer's promise to arbitrate grievances, consistent with the Norris–LaGuardia Act. The *Steelworkers Trilogy* emphasized the importance of arbitration to resolve labor-management disputes. Charles Dowd Box Co. v. Courtney, 368 U.S. 502, 82 S.Ct. 519, 7 L.Ed.2d 483 (1962), held that Congress in enacting Section 301 did not intend to disturb preexisting state-court jurisdiction over suits for violation of labor contracts, but rather to supplement that jurisdiction. The Court also mentioned the holding in *Lucas Flour* that in Section 301 actions brought in state courts, substantive federal law is to displace inconsistent local rules.]

Subsequent to the decision in *Sinclair,* we held in Avco Corp. v. Aero Lodge 735, supra, that § 301(a) suits initially brought in state courts may be removed to the designated federal forum under the federal question removal jurisdiction delineated in 28 U.S.C. § 1441. In so holding, however, the Court expressly left open the questions whether state courts are bound by the anti-injunction proscriptions of the Norris–LaGuardia Act and whether federal courts, after removal of a § 301(a) action, are required to dissolve any injunctive relief previously granted by the state courts. See generally General Electric Co. v. Local Union 191, 413 F.2d 964 (5th Cir.1969)(dissolution of state injunction required). Three Justices who concurred expressed the view that *Sinclair* should be reconsidered "upon an appropriate future occasion." 390 U.S. at 562, 88 S.Ct., at 1238 (Stewart, J., concurring).

The decision in *Avco,* viewed in the context of *Lincoln Mills* and its progeny, has produced an anomalous situation which, in our view, makes urgent the reconsideration of *Sinclair.* The principal practical effect of *Avco* and *Sinclair* taken together is nothing less than to oust state courts of jurisdiction in § 301(a) suits where injunctive relief is sought for breach of a no-strike obligation. Union defendants can, as a matter of course, obtain removal to a federal court,[11] and there is obviously a compelling incentive for them to do so in order to gain the advantage of the strictures upon injunctive relief which *Sinclair* imposes on federal courts. The sanctioning of this practice, however, is wholly inconsistent with our conclusion in *Dowd Box* that the congressional purpose embodied in § 301(a) was to *supplement,* and not to encroach upon, the pre-existing jurisdiction of the state courts. It is ironic indeed that the very provision that Congress clearly intended to provide additional remedies for breach of collective-bargaining agreements has been employed to displace previously existing state reme-

---

**11.** Section 301(a) suits require neither the existence of diversity of citizenship nor a minimum jurisdictional amount in controversy. All § 301(a) suits may be removed pursuant to 28 U.S.C. § 1441.

dies. We are not at liberty thus to depart from the clearly expressed congressional policy to the contrary.

On the other hand, to the extent that widely disparate remedies theoretically remain available in state, as opposed to federal, courts, the federal policy of labor law uniformity elaborated in *Lucas Flour Co.*, is seriously offended. This policy, of course, could hardly require, as a practical matter, that labor law be administered identically in all courts, for undoubtedly a certain diversity exists among the state and federal systems in matters of procedural and remedial detail, a fact that Congress evidently took into account in deciding not to disturb the traditional jurisdiction of the States. The injunction, however, is so important a remedial device, particularly in the arbitration context, that its availability or non-availability in various courts will not only produce rampant forum shopping and maneuvering from one court to another but will also greatly frustrate any relative uniformity in the enforcement of arbitration agreements.

Furthermore, the existing scheme, with the injunction remedy technically available in the state courts but rendered inefficacious by the removal device, assigns to removal proceedings a totally unintended function. While the underlying purposes of Congress in providing for federal question removal jurisdiction remain somewhat obscure, there has never been a serious contention that Congress intended that the removal mechanism be utilized to foreclose completely remedies otherwise available in the state courts. Although federal question removal jurisdiction may well have been intended to provide a forum for the protection of federal rights where such protection was deemed necessary or to encourage the development of expertise by the federal courts in the interpretation of federal law, there is no indication that Congress intended by the removal mechanism to effect a wholesale dislocation in the allocation of judicial business between the state and federal courts. Cf. City of Greenwood, Miss. v. Peacock, 384 U.S. 808, 86 S.Ct. 1800, 16 L.Ed.2d 944 (1966).

It is undoubtedly true that each of the foregoing objections to *Sinclair-Avco* could be remedied either by overruling *Sinclair* or by extending that decision to the States. While some commentators have suggested that the solution to the present unsatisfactory situation does lie in the extension of the *Sinclair* prohibition to state court proceedings, we agree with Chief Justice Traynor of the California Supreme Court that "whether or not Congress could deprive state courts of the power to give such [injunctive] remedies when enforcing collective bargaining agreements, it has not attempted to do so either in the Norris–LaGuardia Act or section 301." McCarroll v. Los Angeles County Dist. Council of Carpenters, 49 Cal.2d 45, 63, 315 P.2d 322, 332 (1957), cert. denied, 355 U.S. 932, 78 S.Ct. 413, 2 L.Ed.2d 415 (1958). * * *

An additional reason for not resolving the existing dilemma by extending *Sinclair* to the States is the devastating implications for the enforceability of arbitration agreements and their accompanying no-strike obligations if equitable remedies were not available.[15] As we have previously indicated, a no-strike obligation, express or implied, is the *quid pro quo* for an undertaking by the employer to submit grievance disputes to the process of arbitration. See Textile Workers Union of America v. Lincoln Mills, supra, 353 U.S., at 455, 77 S.Ct. at 917. Any incentive for employers to enter into such an arrangement is necessarily dissipated if the principal and most expeditious method by which the no-strike obligation can be enforced is eliminated. While it is of course true, as respondent contends, that other avenues of redress, such as an action for damages, would remain open to an aggrieved employer, an award of damages after a dispute has been settled is no substitute for an immediate halt to an illegal strike. Furthermore, an action for damages prosecuted during or after a labor dispute would only tend to aggravate industrial strife and delay an early resolution of the difficulties between employer and union.[17]

Even if management is not encouraged by the unavailability of the injunction remedy to resist arbitration agreements, the fact remains that the effectiveness of such agreements would be greatly reduced if injunctive relief were withheld. Indeed, the very purpose of arbitration procedures is to provide a mechanism for the expeditious settlement of industrial disputes without resort to strikes, lockouts, or other self-help measures. This basic purpose is obviously largely undercut if there is no immediate, effective remedy for those very tactics that arbitration is designed to obviate. Thus, because *Sinclair,* in the aftermath of *Avco,* casts serious doubt upon the effective enforcement of a vital element of stable labor-management relations—arbitration agreements with their attendant no-strike obligations—we conclude that *Sinclair* does not make a viable contribution to federal labor policy.

## IV

We have also determined that the dissenting opinion in *Sinclair* states the correct principles concerning the accommodation necessary between the seemingly absolute terms of the Norris–LaGuardia Act and the policy considerations underlying § 301(a). 370 U.S., at 215, 82 S.Ct., at 1339.

---

**15.** It is true that about one-half of the States have enacted so-called "little Norris–LaGuardia Acts" that place various restrictions upon the granting of injunctions by state courts in labor disputes. However, because many States do not bar injunctive relief for violations of collective-bargaining agreements, in only about 14 jurisdictions is there a significant Norris–LaGuardia-type prohibition against equitable remedies for breach of no-strike obligations. * * *

**17.** As the neutral members of the A.B.A. committee on the problems raised by *Sinclair* noted in their report:

"Under existing laws, employers may maintain an action for damages resulting from a strike in breach of contract and may discipline the employees involved. In many cases, however, neither of these alternatives will be feasible. Discharge of the strikers is often inexpedient because of a lack of qualified replacements or because of the adverse effect on relationships within the plant. The damage remedy may also be unsatisfactory because the employer's losses are often hard to calculate and because the employer may hesitate to exacerbate relations with the union by bringing a damage action. Hence, injunctive relief will often be the only effective means by which to remedy the breach of the no-strike pledge and thus effectuate federal labor policy." A.B.A. *Sinclair* Report 242.

Although we need not repeat all that was there said, a few points should be emphasized at this time.

The literal terms of § 4 of the Norris–LaGuardia Act must be accommodated to the subsequently enacted provisions of § 301(a) of the Labor Management Relations Act and the purposes of arbitration. * * *

The Norris–LaGuardia Act was responsive to a situation totally different from that which exists today. In the early part of this century, the federal courts generally were regarded as allies of management in its attempt to prevent the organization and strengthening of labor unions; and in this industrial struggle the injunction became a potent weapon that was wielded against the activities of labor groups. The result was a large number of sweeping decrees, often issued *ex parte,* drawn on an *ad hoc* basis without regard to any systematic elaboration of national labor policy. See Milk Wagon Drivers' Union, etc. v. Lake Valley Co., 311 U.S. 91, 102, 61 S.Ct. 122, 127, 85 L.Ed. 63 (1940).

In 1932, Congress attempted to bring some order out of the industrial chaos that had developed and to correct the abuses that had resulted from the interjection of the federal judiciary into union-management disputes on the behalf of management. See declaration of public policy, Norris–LaGuardia Act, § 2, 47 Stat. 70. Congress, therefore, determined initially to limit severely the power of the federal courts to issue injunctions "in any case involving or growing out of any labor dispute * * *." § 4, 47 Stat. 70. Even as initially enacted, however, the prohibition against federal injunctions was by no means absolute. See Norris–LaGuardia Act, §§ 7, 8, 9, 47 Stat. 71, 72. Shortly thereafter Congress passed the Wagner Act, designed to curb various management activities that tended to discourage employee participation in collective action.

As labor organizations grew in strength and developed toward maturity, congressional emphasis shifted from protection of the nascent labor movement to the encouragement of collective bargaining and to administrative techniques for the peaceful resolution of industrial disputes. This shift in emphasis was accomplished, however, without extensive revision of many of the older enactments, including the anti-injunction section of the Norris–LaGuardia Act. Thus it became the task of the courts to accommodate, to reconcile the older statutes with the more recent ones.

A leading example of this accommodation process is Brotherhood of Railroad Trainmen v. Chicago River & Ind. R. Co., 353 U.S. 30, 77 S.Ct. 635, 1 L.Ed.2d 622 (1957). There we were confronted with a peaceful strike which violated the statutory duty to arbitrate imposed by the Railway Labor Act. The Court concluded that a strike in violation of a statutory arbitration duty was not the type of situation to which the Norris–LaGuardia Act was responsive, that an important federal policy was involved in the peaceful settlement of disputes through the statutorily mandated arbitration procedure, that this important policy was imperiled if equitable remedies were not available to implement it, and hence that Norris–LaGuardia's policy of nonintervention by the federal courts should yield to the overriding interest in the successful implementation of the arbitration process.

The principles elaborated in *Chicago River* are equally applicable to the present case. To be sure, *Chicago River* involved arbitration procedures established by statute. However, we have frequently noted, in such cases as *Lincoln Mills,* the *Steelworkers Trilogy,* and *Lucas Flour,* the importance that Congress has attached generally to the voluntary settlement of labor disputes without resort to self-help and more particularly to arbitration as a means to this end. Indeed, it has been stated that *Lincoln Mills,* in its exposition of § 301(a), "went a long way towards making arbitration the central institution in the administration of collective bargaining contracts."

The *Sinclair* decision, however, seriously undermined the effectiveness of the arbitration technique as a method peacefully to resolve industrial disputes without resort to strikes, lockouts, and similar devices. Clearly employers will be wary of assuming obligations to arbitrate specifically enforceable against them when no similarly efficacious remedy is available to enforce the concomitant undertaking of the union to refrain from striking. On the other hand, the central purpose of the Norris–LaGuardia Act to foster the growth and viability of labor organizations is hardly retarded—if anything, this goal is advanced—by a remedial device that merely enforces the obligation that the union freely undertook under a specifically enforceable agreement to submit disputes to arbitration.[22] We conclude, therefore, that the unavailability of equitable relief in the arbitration context presents a serious impediment to the congressional policy favoring the voluntary establishment of a mechanism for the peaceful resolution of labor disputes, that the core purpose of the Norris–LaGuardia Act is not sacrificed by the limited use of equitable remedies to further this important policy, and consequently that the Norris–LaGuardia Act does not bar the granting of injunctive relief in the circumstances of the instant case.

## V

Our holding in the present case is a narrow one. We do not undermine the vitality of the Norris–LaGuardia Act. We deal only with the situation in which a collective-bargaining contract contains a mandatory grievance adjustment or arbitration procedure. Nor does it follow from what we have

---

**22.** As well stated by the neutral members of the A.B.A. *Sinclair* committee: " * * * [T]he reasons behind the Norris–La-Guardia Act seem scarcely applicable to the situation * * * [in which a strike in violation of a collective-bargaining agreement is enjoined]. The Act was passed primarily because of widespread dissatisfaction with the tendency of judges to enjoin concerted activities in accordance with 'doctrines of tort law which made the lawfulness of a strike depend upon judicial views of social and economic policy.' * * * Where an injunction is used against a strike in breach of contract, the union is not subjected in this fashion to judicially created limitations on its freedom of action but is simply compelled to comply with limitations to which it has previously agreed. Moreover, where the underlying dispute is arbitrable, the union is not deprived of any practicable means of pressing its claim but is only required to submit the dispute to the impartial tribunal that it has agreed to establish for this purpose." A.B.A. *Sinclair* Report 242.

said that injunctive relief is appropriate as a matter of course in every case of a strike over an arbitrable grievance. The dissenting opinion in *Sinclair* suggested the following principles for the guidance of the district courts in determining whether to grant injunctive relief—principles that we now adopt:

> "A District Court entertaining an action under § 301 may not grant injunctive relief against concerted activity unless and until it decides that the case is one in which an injunction would be appropriate despite the Norris–LaGuardia Act. When a strike is sought to be enjoined because it is over a grievance which both parties are contractually bound to arbitrate, the District Court may issue no injunctive order until it first holds that the contract *does* have that effect; and the employer should be ordered to arbitrate, as a condition of his obtaining an injunction against the strike. Beyond this, the District Court must, of course, consider whether issuance of an injunction would be warranted under ordinary principles of equity—whether breaches are occurring and will continue, or have been threatened and will be committed; whether they have caused or will cause irreparable injury to the employer; and whether the employer will suffer more from the denial of an injunction than will the union from its issuance." 370 U.S., at 228, 82 S.Ct., at 1346. (Emphasis in original.)

In the present case there is no dispute that the grievance in question was subject to adjustment and arbitration under the collective-bargaining agreement and that the petitioner was ready to proceed with arbitration at the time an injunction against the strike was sought and obtained. The District Court also concluded that, by reason of respondent's violations of its no-strike obligation, petitioner "has suffered irreparable injury and will continue to suffer irreparable injury." Since we now overrule *Sinclair,* the holding of the Court of Appeals in reliance on *Sinclair* must be reversed. Accordingly, we reverse the judgment of the Court of Appeals and remand the case with directions to enter a judgment affirming the order of the District Court.

MR. JUSTICE MARSHALL took no part in the decision of this case.

■ MR. JUSTICE STEWART, concurring.

When Sinclair Refining Co. v. Atkinson, 370 U.S. 195, 82 S.Ct. 1328, 8 L.Ed.2d 440, was decided in 1962, I subscribed to the opinion of the Court. Before six years had passed I had reached the conclusion that the *Sinclair* holding should be reconsidered, and said so in Avco Corp. v. Aero Lodge 735, 390 U.S. 557, 562, 88 S.Ct. 1235, 1238, 20 L.Ed.2d 126 (concurring opinion). Today I join the Court in concluding "that *Sinclair* was erroneously decided and that subsequent events have undermined its continuing validity * * *."

In these circumstances the temptation is strong to embark upon a lengthy personal *apologia*. But since MR. JUSTICE BRENNAN has so clearly stated my present views in his opinion for the Court today, I simply join in that opinion and in the Court's judgment. An aphorism of Mr. Justice Frankfurter provides me refuge: "Wisdom too often never comes, and so one ought not to reject it merely because it comes late." Henslee v. Union Planters Bank, 335 U.S. 595, 600, 69 S.Ct. 290, 293, 93 L.Ed. 259 (dissenting opinion).

■ Mr. Justice Black, dissenting. * * *

Although Congress has been urged to overrule our holding in *Sinclair*, it has steadfastly refused to do so. Nothing in the language or history of the two Acts has changed. Nothing at all has changed, in fact, except the membership of the Court and the personal views of one Justice. I remain of the opinion that *Sinclair* was correctly decided, and, moreover, that the prohibition of the Norris–LaGuardia Act is close to the heart of the entire federal system of labor regulation. In my view *Sinclair* should control the disposition of this case.

Even if the majority were correct, however, in saying that *Sinclair* misinterpreted the Taft–Hartley and Norris–LaGuardia Acts, I should be compelled to dissent. I believe that both the making and the changing of laws which affect the substantial rights of the people are primarily for Congress, not this Court. Most especially is this so when the laws involved are the focus of strongly held views of powerful but antagonistic political and economic interests. The Court's function in the application and interpretation of such laws must be carefully limited to avoid encroaching on the power of Congress to determine policies and make laws to carry them out.

* * * When the law has been settled by an earlier case then any subsequent "reinterpretation" of the statute is gratuitous and neither more nor less than an amendment: it is no different in effect from a judicial alteration of language that Congress itself placed in the statute. * * * If the Congress is unhappy with these powers as this Court defined them, then the Congress may act; this Court should not. The members of the majority have simply decided that they are more sensitive to the "realization of an important goal of our national labor policy" than the Congress or their predecessors on this Court. * * *

I dissent.

■ Mr. Justice White dissents for the reasons stated in the majority opinion in Sinclair Refining Co. v. Atkinson, 370 U.S. 195, 82 S.Ct. 1328, 8 L.Ed.2d 440 (1962).

Buffalo Forge Co. v. United Steelworkers of America, 428 U.S. 397, 96 S.Ct. 3141, 49 L.Ed.2d 1022 (1976).[f] The Company operates three plant and office facilities, and had labor contracts covering its production and maintenance employees who were represented by the United Steelworkers and

---

**f.** See Cantor, Buffalo Forge and Injunctions Against Employer Breaches of Collective Bargaining Agreements, 1980 Wisc. L.Rev. 247 (1980); Gould, On Labor Injunctions Pending Arbitration: Recasting *Buffalo Forge*, 30 Stanford L.Rev. 533 (1978); Smith, The Supreme Court, *Boys Markets* Labor Injunctions, and Sympathy Work Stoppages, 44 U.Chi.L.Rev. 321 (1977).

two Steelworker locals (the Union). The contracts contained no-strike clauses ("There shall be no strikes, work stoppages or interruption or impeding of work") and a grievance and arbitration procedure which provided for arbitration of disputes concerning "the meaning and application of the provisions of this Agreement." During the term of these contracts, clerical and technical employees (represented by the United Steelworkers and two other locals) went out on strike in a dispute arising from the negotiation of their first contract with the Company. The Union endorsed a refusal by the production and maintenance workers to cross the picket lines established by the clerical and technical employees. The Company, claiming that this constituted a breach of the no-strike clause and that the Union should arbitrate whatever dispute caused this work stoppage by the production and maintenance employees, brought an action in the federal district court seeking damages and a preliminary injunction of the work stoppage. The Union asserted that its work stoppage did not violate the no-strike clause and that it was prepared promptly to submit that question to arbitration. The district court concluded that the Norris–LaGuardia Act forbade the issuance of an injunction, since the action of the production and maintenance employees was not over an arbitrable grievance but was rather a sympathetic action in aid of the clerical workers; accordingly it was not enjoinable under the *Boys Markets* case. The court of appeals affirmed the denial of the injunction and it was in turn affirmed by the Supreme Court, in a 5–4 decision.

Unlike *Boys Markets,* this was not a strike concededly in violation of the contract, with the object of avoiding arbitration of some underlying dispute with the Company. *Boys Markets* allowed of an exception to Section 4 of the Norris–LaGuardia Act only for a strike which frustrated the federal policy favoring arbitration procedures designated by the parties to resolve their contract disputes. "The District Court found, and it is not now disputed, that the strike was not *over* any dispute between the Union and the employer that was even remotely subject to the arbitration provisions of the contract. The strike at issue was a sympathy strike in support of sister unions negotiating with the employer; neither its causes nor the issue underlying it were subject to the settlement procedures provided by the contract between the employer and respondents. The strike had neither the purpose nor the effect of denying or evading an obligation to arbitrate or of depriving the employer of his bargain." (The Court also stated, in dictum, that in a labor contract silent on the right to strike, a mandatory arbitration clause would not justify implying a commitment by the Union to refrain from engaging in sympathy strikes.) Whether the Union's work stoppage violated its no-strike promise was itself a dispute to be decided by an arbitrator and not by the district court, which is deprived by Section 4 of the Norris–LaGuardia Act of the power to enjoin the strike even pending the decision of the arbitrator. It would "cut deeply into the policy of the Norris–LaGuardia Act" if the federal court could hold hearings, make findings of fact, interpret the applicable contract provisions and issue injunctions to restore the status quo ante as to any arbitrable contract breaches falling within the shelter of Section 4. Were the courts to have power to enjoin, this would improperly influence the decision of the arbitrator as to the facts and the interpretation of the contract; it would also in many instances discourage one of the parties from seeking arbitration or as a practical matter permanently settle the issue, quite in the face of the federal policy to resolve the issue through arbitration.

In a lengthy and careful dissenting opinion for four Justices, Mr. Justice Stevens argued that the district court had jurisdiction to enjoin the work stoppage by the production and maintenance employees. He contended that the central concerns of the Norris–LaGuardia Act related to union organization, recognition and contract negotiation, rather than to the enforcement of commitments already made in such contracts; that all of the reasons underlying the decision of the Court in *Boys Markets* were also applicable in the case of sympathy strikes in breach of contractual no-strike provisions; and that court-issued injunctions against such sympathy strikes pending their arbitration would not unduly interfere with the arbitral procedures designated by the parties.

---

*Individual and Union Liability Under a No–Strike Clause*

As the Supreme Court observed in the *Boys Markets* case, an employer whose business has been interrupted by a work stoppage in breach of a labor agreement may seek to secure damages in lieu of or in addition to an injunction. The Court has passed upon the question of liability of unions and their officers and members, in cases involving authorized strikes and "wildcat" strikes. Legislative guidance is provided in Sections 301(b) and (e), which the student should consult.

In Atkinson v. Sinclair Refining Co., 370 U.S. 238, 82 S.Ct. 1318, 8 L.Ed.2d 462 (1962), some 1000 employees struck, during the term of a contract with a no-strike clause, to protest the employer's docking of a total of $2.19 from the pay of three employees. The Court held that the first count of the employer's complaint, which sought damages of $12,500 from the signatory local and international unions, stated a cause of action under Section 301; the Court read the labor contract to make unavailable to the employer the grievance and arbitration procedure in the event of a contract breach by the unions, so that judicial recourse was appropriate. The second count of the complaint relied upon diversity-of-citizenship jurisdiction and claimed damages from twenty-four union committeemen as individuals for "fomenting, assisting and participating in" the strike. The Court read the third sentence of Section 301(b) as a congressional reaction to cases such as the *Danbury Hatters* case, page 33 supra, in which treble damages were awarded against union officers and members as individuals for a nationwide union-directed boycott, and foreclosure made on the homes of many of the members. "The national labor policy requires and we hold that when a union is liable for damages for violation of the no-strike clause, its officers and members are not liable for these damages."

In COMPLETE AUTO TRANSIT, INC. V. REIS, 451 U.S. 401, 101 S.Ct. 1836, 68 L.Ed.2d 248 (1981), the Court was confronted with the more difficult question whether the same immunity of individual strikers against damage actions applies when they participate in a "wildcat" strike which is unauthorized by the signatory union and for which that union can therefore not be held liable in damages. Although such individual immunity would leave the employer with no financial remedy for loss of business during the wildcat strike, a divided Court held that Section 301(b), particularly when read in light of its legislative history, "clearly reveals Congress' intent to shield individual employees from liability for damages arising from their breach of the no-strike clause of a collective-bargaining agreement, whether or not the union participated in or authorized the illegality."

The legislative history revealed that Congress had rejected the imposition of liability for damages upon individuals engaging in various kinds of unlawful work stoppages and had opted instead to render such individuals unprotected by Section 7 of the NLRA and thus susceptible to discharge and other discipline by the employer. The Court concluded that such discipline, along with other sanctions—including union discipline of the wildcat strikers, and employer recourse through damages or an injunction against a union which participated in or authorized the strike—gave the employer adequate assurance of adherence to collective bargaining agreements. Two dissenting Justices contended that these sanctions were wholly inadequate protection for the employer against wildcat strikers and that Congress did not intend, in Section 301(b), to shelter individuals from personal accountability for damages resulting from their own individual conduct as distinguished from union-authorized conduct.

The standards to be used in determining the circumstances in which a union can be held responsible for breaching a no-strike clause—either in its own right or vicariously for the breach of another union—were articulated by the Supreme Court in CARBON FUEL CO. V. UNITED MINE WORKERS, 444 U.S. 212, 100 S.Ct. 410, 62 L.Ed.2d 394 (1979). There, Carbon Fuel Company was party to a labor contract with the United Mine Workers (UMWA) and its District 17; certain locals within District 17 violated the agreement by calling a total of forty-eight unauthorized or "wildcat" strikes. The company brought an action for damages not only against the locals but also against District 17 and the UMWA on the theory that they had a duty to use all reasonable means to stop the locals' "wildcat" stoppages.

The Supreme Court held that, although the locals may be liable in damages, District 17 and the UMWA were not, absent a showing that they adopted, encouraged or prolonged the strikes or were otherwise responsible by virtue of common law principles of agency. Sections 301(b) and (e) were held to supplant both the narrower test for union liability under Section 6 of the Norris–LaGuardia Act and the broader test of responsibility for employers under Section 2(2) of the Wagner Act ("any person acting in the interest of an employer"). Since District 17 and the UMWA were not liable vicariously for the locals' stoppages, Congress must also have intended to free them of direct liability for their own failure to respond to the stoppages absent their own instigation, support, ratification or encouragement. There was thus no liability for failure to use reasonable means to control the locals' actions in breach of contract.

---

# PROBLEMS FOR DISCUSSION

**1.** The workers in the Fiume Coalmine are represented by the Mine Workers Union, which has an agreement with the company providing for the arbitration of "any disputes" arising during the contract term but lacking any no-strike clause. A recent explosion in a nearby mine, which resulted in a number of deaths, has generated considerable concern among the workers and the Union officials. Yesterday, several miners detected a heavier density of fumes than that normally perceived, and the figures reflecting the airflow in the mine were barely at the level of acceptability under federal safety regulations. A meeting of the Union was called last night, and the members overwhelmingly voted not to go into the mines until a full and impartial safety investigation was conducted and conditions in the mine approved. The company contends that the Union's action is in violation of the contract and that the appropriate manner for the Union to challenge conditions in the mine is not by a work stoppage but rather by use of the grievance and arbitration machinery. The company has instituted an action in the federal district court for an injunction, and has requested that a temporary restraining order issue. What arguments should the Union make in defense? Should the injunction issue? (Consider the relevance of Section 502 of the Labor Act.) See Gateway Coal Co. v. UMW, 414 U.S. 368, 94 S.Ct. 629, 38 L.Ed.2d 583 (1974).

**2.** In the labor contract between Power Tractors Corporation and the Auto Workers Union, there is an unqualified no-strike clause and a grievance and arbitration provision; however, because of some dissatisfaction in the past with arbitration decisions on matters of job reclassification, that issue has been explicitly excluded from the reach of the arbitration clause. During the contract term, a dispute arose on a reclassification issue and, after having exhausted the procedures for intra-company review, the Union has instituted a strike. The company has commenced an action in a state court for an injunction against the strike.

(a) Over the union's claim that *Boys Markets* is controlling and that a court may, under these facts, perhaps grant money damages, but not an injunction, the state court has in fact issued an injunction against continuation of the strike. Should the injunction be reversed on appeal?

(b) Assume, instead, that the strike concerns a grievance which is subject to the arbitration clause of the labor contract, but that the state court has refused to issue an injunction, relying on the state's "little Norris–LaGuardia Act" which has been broadly read by the courts of the state to bar strike injunctions even over arbitrable grievances. Should the court's order of dismissal be reversed?

**3.** Lever Brothers has for many years operated a soap-production plant in Baltimore, Maryland, where the employees are represented by the Chemical Workers Union. The labor contract there has an arbitration clause, and a provision which permits the company "permanently to eliminate, change or consolidate jobs, departments or divisions" and another provision which permits the company to "assign work to outside contractors" only after giving notice to the Union furnishing "full information regarding the reasons for the action." Last month, Lever Brothers advised the Union that it was permanently closing its Baltimore plant and transferring the work there to its Hammond, Indiana facility which was represented by the Oil Workers Union. The Chemical Workers Union filed a grievance, alleging violation of the "contracting out" provision (since there had been no notice or consultation), and it ultimately brought an action in the federal court. In that action, the Union sought not only an order to compel arbitration but also an injunction against the closing of the Baltimore plant and the transfer of the operations to Hammond. Should the court issue the injunction? See Local Lodge No. 1266, Intern. Ass'n of Machinists v. Panoramic Corp., 668 F.2d 276 (7th Cir.1981).

If such an injunction could issue, would the procedural prerequisites for labor injunctions set forth in Sections 7–10 of the Norris–LaGuardia Act apply? See United Parcel Serv. (N.Y.) Inc. v. Local 804, Intern. Broth. Teamsters, 698 F.2d 100 (2d Cir.1983); International Union, UAW v. LaSalle Mach. Tool, Inc., 696 F.2d 452 (6th Cir.1982).

## IV. THE ROLE OF THE NATIONAL LABOR RELATIONS BOARD AND THE ARBITRATOR DURING THE TERM OF A COLLECTIVE AGREEMENT

The execution of a collective agreement has substantial effect upon the rights and duties of employers and labor unions under the NLRA. For example, although the use of a peaceful strike or picketing in support of a claim by employees is normally protected under Section 7 of the Act, the bargaining representative may contractually waive this statutory privilege for itself and for all employees in the bargaining unit. A strike in violation of a no-strike promise will thus be treated as unprotected activity and will render the participating employees subject to discharge. Disputes between unions concerning the representation of employees in the plant, or concerning the assignment of work to employees already represented by these different unions, will normally be subject to resolution through the procedures of the National Labor Relations Board. But these procedures may be lawfully displaced if the interested parties can effect an adjustment of their claims through the collective bargaining process. An agreement waiving the right to bargain about statutory subjects or authorizing management to take unilateral action will effectively modify the employer's duties under Section 8(a)(5). It has indeed been suggested that the employer's duty to bargain has little independent significance during the life of a labor agreement, and that that duty is effectively discharged by complying with the grievance and arbitration procedures of the agreement. (Of course, as has already been noted, it has been held that there are certain statutory rights of such central significance to the legislative scheme that they cannot be effectively waived by contract. An example is the right of employees in the bargaining unit to engage in solicitation for or against unions outside of their working time. See NLRB v. Magnavox Co., at p. 120, supra. But such unwaivable statutory rights are rare.)

The reciprocal impact of the NLRA and the collective bargaining agreement is a complex subject, involving a consideration of two different sets of regulations for the conduct of the parties and two different sets of interpreting and enforcing institutions, on the one hand the Board and the federal courts of appeals and on the other the arbitrator and (or) the federal district courts. Two kinds of illustrative problems have been selected for detailed study: (1) The relationship between the Board's role in enforcing the NLRA and the arbitrator's role in enforcing the labor contract, and (2) the duty to bargain during the term of the labor contract.

---

## A.  CONDUCT WHICH ALLEGEDLY VIOLATES BOTH THE CONTRACT AND THE LABOR ACT[a]

During the term of a collective agreement the same conduct may give rise to both unfair labor practice charges (or representation issues) and an arbitrable grievance. This might be the case if an employer discharges a shop steward allegedly because of his zealous prosecution of grievances. Or, an employer may bargain with one union rather than another on behalf of certain employees, or assign work to one group of employees and thereby precipitate a work stoppage by some other group represented by a different union under a different labor agreement. Or, management without bargaining with the union may contract out electrical repairs theretofore done by the maintenance department, with resulting layoffs of maintenance electricians.

Such disputes concerning alleged discriminatory discharge, representation or work-assignment issues, and unilateral employer action can be processed by the aggrieved union either through the NLRB or the contractual grievance and arbitration procedure. May the union choose either remedy it wishes and, one failing, pursue the other? Is the arbitrator stripped of jurisdiction to decide cases which touch upon statutory matters, or conversely is the Board without power to decide cases which invite a construction of the collective bargaining agreement? If such deference is not required, should either institution defer to the other as a matter of comity?

---

### THE CONCURRENT JURISDICTION OF THE NLRB AND THE ARBITRATOR

The Supreme Court dealt with these large jurisdictional questions in the mid–1960s, shortly after its decisions in the Steelworkers Trilogy had articulated a federal policy under Section 301 of the Labor Act that was extremely hospitable to the use of arbitration procedures in collective agreements.

---

**a.**  See Atleson, Disciplinary Discharges, Arbitration and NLRB Deference, 20 Buffalo L.Rev. 355 (1971); Sovern, Section 301 and the Primary Jurisdiction of the NLRB, 76 Harv.L.Rev. 529 (1963); Wollett, The Agreement and the National Labor Relations Act: Courts, Arbitrators, and the NLRB—Who Decides What? 14 Lab.L.J. 1041 (1963).

In CAREY V. WESTINGHOUSE ELEC. CORP., 375 U.S. 261, 84 S.Ct. 401, 11 L.Ed.2d 320 (1964), the Court addressed the question whether arbitration could properly be ordered when the issue that would confront the arbitrator is one that the NLRB can decide, either as a representation issue under Section 9 of the Act or an unfair labor practice issue under Sections 8 and 10. Westinghouse had a labor agreement with the IUE covering "all production and maintenance employees" at its plant, and excluding "all salaried, technical employees." Another union, the Federation, had an agreement with Westinghouse covering salaried technical employees and excluding production and maintenance workers. IUE filed a grievance asserting that Westinghouse had improperly assigned production and maintenance work to employees in the Federation unit, and ultimately brought an action to compel arbitration. The state courts refused to order arbitration, holding that the controversy involved representation, a matter exclusively for the NLRB. The Supreme Court reversed and ordered arbitration.

The Court said that it was not altogether clear whether the parties had a work-assignment dispute (i.e., how work should be allocated between two groups of workers represented by different unions) or a representation dispute (i.e., whether certain workers should be represented by one or another union). Viewed as the former, the jurisdiction of the NLRB does not come into play until a strike occurs in violation of section 8(b)(4)(D). Thus, the Court thought that arbitration could serve a useful function of resolving the dispute without forcing it into the strike stage. The Court also noted that arbitration is frequently used to resolve work-assignment disputes and that the NLRB often gives effect to such decisions in making work-allocation awards under section 10(k) of the Act. Even though only one union may be before the arbitrator, "the arbitration may as a practical matter end the controversy or put into movement forces that will resolve it."

If the dispute is instead one regarding which union has the right to represent certain employees, this can be handled by the NLRB through refusal-to-bargain charges under section 8(a)(5) or a unit-clarification petition under section 9(c)(1). Even so, the Court thought that the contract-enforcement policies reflected in section 301 and in *Lincoln Mills* and other decisions justified sending the dispute, if covered by the contract, to the arbitrator. "[R]esort to arbitration may have a pervasive, curative effect even though one union is not a party."

If the arbitrator decides the dispute before it reaches the NLRB, "the Board shows deference to the arbitral award, provided the procedure was a fair one and the results not repugnant to the Act." Should the Board disagree with the arbitrator, the Board's ruling would of course take precedence. Fragmentation of the dispute may be avoided if the case is sent to arbitration, and the "therapy of arbitration" is brought to bear in a complicated area so as to promote industrial peace.

In NLRB v. C & C PLYWOOD CORP., 385 U.S. 421, 87 S.Ct. 559, 17 L.Ed.2d 486 (1967), the Court decided essentially the converse question—

whether the NLRB has jurisdiction to decide an unfair labor practice case that would require it to construe the provisions of a collective bargaining agreement. The Court also answered that question in the affirmative. Although the labor agreement between the company and the Plywood Workers Union contemplated a certain wage scale for "glue spreader" crews, the employer announced that it would pay crew members at a higher rate provided they met certain production standards. The company spurned the union's request to rescind the new rate, and the union filed refusal-to-bargain charges under section 8(a)(5). (The contract had a grievance procedure to resolve disputes, but no provision for arbitration.)

The employer defended its premium-pay program by invoking a provision in the labor agreement to the effect that "The Employer reserves the right to pay a premium rate over and above the contractual classified wage rate to reward any particular employee for some special fitness, skill, aptitude or the like." The NLRB, examining the contract provision and the history of negotiations between the parties, held that the provision did not authorize the employer's action, and found a violation of section 8(a)(5). The court of appeals refused to enforce the Board's order, because the dispute was based upon good-faith readings of the terms of the labor agreement and not entirely upon the provisions of the NLRA. The Supreme Court reversed.

The Court began by noting that, because the labor agreement contained no arbitration clause, the Board's assertion of jurisdiction did not undermine the role of arbitration as "an instrument of national labor policy for composing contractual differences." It noted that Congress's rejection in the 1947 Taft–Hartley amendments of a bill that would have given the NLRB jurisdiction over all breaches of labor contracts was simply a reflection of the national policy against governmental regulation of contract terms. Here, the NLRB did not construe the labor agreement to determine the extent of contract rights given to union, or to impose its own view of the meaning of contract terms; "The Board's interpretation went only so far as was necessary to determine that the union did not agree to give up [the] statutory safeguards" provided under section 8(a)(5). "Thus, the Board, in necessarily construing a labor agreement to decide this unfair labor practice case, has not exceeded the jurisdiction laid out for it by Congress." Moreover, Congress could not have intended that a union seeking to enforce its statutory rights before the NLRB would first have to institute a proceeding before a court or arbitrator to secure an interpretation of the contract, and proceed to the Board only after prevailing there.

The Court concluded by upholding the Board's determination that the wage provision in the labor agreement did not give the employer the unilateral right to institute its premium-pay plan for the glue spreader crew.

In NLRB v. Acme Industrial Co., 385 U.S. 432, 87 S.Ct. 565, 17 L.Ed.2d 495 (1967), the union feared that the company's movement of equipment from its plant threatened an imminent layoff of employees covered by the labor agreement. The union asked the company for information about the equipment removal, but the company claimed that the union was not entitled to such information, there being no violation of the agreement. The union filed a grievance and once again asked the employer for the information, but the employer once again refused, asserting among other things that whether it was obligated to turn over the information was itself a question of contract construction to be eventually determined by an arbitrator. The union's unfair labor practice claim under section 8(a)(5) was ultimately sustained by the Supreme Court.

The Court noted the employer's duty to turn over to the union requested information that is pertinent to bargaining or to the processing of grievances. The Board's order to disclose information about the employer's removal of equipment would not conflict with the policy under Section 301 of the Labor Act to resolve contract disputes through arbitration. "[T]he Board was not making a binding construction of the labor contract. It was only acting upon the probability that the desired information was relevant, and that it would be of use to the union in carrying out its statutory duties and responsibility. This discovery-type standard decided nothing about the merits of the union's contractual claims." Far from intruding upon the arbitration process, the Board's action aided such process; enforcing a statutory requirement to disclose information pertinent to grievances would, by affording the union an opportunity to evaluate the merits of its claims, facilitate the sifting out of unmeritorious claims and the resolution of grievances short of arbitration.

--------

## PROBLEM FOR DISCUSSION

The union contends that employee Williams has been delinquent in the payment of dues and that the employer is thus obligated to discharge her in accordance with the union-security provision of the labor contract. The employer, however, has refused to discharge Williams, asserting (1) that it does not believe that Williams was delinquent within the meaning of the contract and that it indeed believes that union officials have purposely made themselves unavailable to receive such dues, and (2) that in any event the union-security provision in the labor contract violates the National Labor Relations Act.

(a) If the union brings suit to compel arbitration under Section 301 of its claim that Williams must be discharged, how should the court rule?

(b) If the employer, while the Section 301 action is pending, files a charge against the union under Section 8(b)(2) of the NLRA, should the court grant a motion by the employer to stay arbitration?

(c) Should the Regional Director decline to issue a complaint against the union under Section 8(b)(2) until the arbitrator has ruled on the union's claim of contract breach?

(d) If the unfair labor practice case is actually decided by an Administrative Law Judge, adverse to the union, should the court in a Section 301 action order the employer to arbitrate? See Kentile, Inc. v. Local 457, United Rubber Workers, 228 F.Supp. 541 (E.D.N.Y.1964).

(e) If the union's claim of contract breach reaches an arbitrator, who concludes that Williams had been delinquent in her dues and that the company was required by the contract to discharge her, may the employer—in an action by the union to enforce the arbitration award—properly defend upon the ground that the award requires it to commit an unfair labor practice?

---

## NLRB DEFERENCE TO ARBITRATION

Once it was settled that both the arbitrator and the NLRB can pass upon overlapping contract and statutory claims, without automatic preemption by virtue of the other's jurisdiction, it became necessary to work out guidelines regarding mutual accommodation and deference. One such guideline was articulated by the Board in DUBO MFG. CO., 142 NLRB 431 (1963). There the Board held that it would defer processing an unfair labor practice case when a similar contract dispute was already being considered in the parties' grievance and arbitration procedure, which was likely to resolve it. Another significant Board decision regarding deference to arbitration was SPIELBERG MFG. CO., 112 NLRB 1080 (1955), in which the Board dismissed an unfair labor practice complaint arising from the discharge of four strikers whom the employer had charged with misconduct; the discharges had already been upheld in arbitration. The Board stated that the arbitration proceedings "appear to have been fair and regular, all parties had agreed to be bound, and the decision of the arbitration panel is not clearly repugnant to the purposes and policies of the Act. In these circumstances, we believe that the desirable objective of encouraging the voluntary settlement of labor disputes will be best served by our recognition of the arbitrators' award." A fuller explanation of the Board's justification for deference to arbitration is set forth in the decision excerpted below. The principal cases that follow deal with the criteria for NLRB deference to arbitration decisions already rendered and deference to arbitration procedures not yet invoked by the parties to the contract.

INTERNATIONAL HARVESTER CO., 138 NLRB 923 (1962), enf'd sub nom. Ramsey v. NLRB, 327 F.2d 784 (7th Cir.1964), cert. denied, 377 U.S. 1003, 84 S.Ct. 1938, 12 L.Ed.2d 1052 (1964). The Board held, in a case arising under Sections 8(a)(3) and 8(b)(2), that it would not reexamine the merits of a dispute already resolved in arbitration regarding the construction and application of a union-security provision of the labor agreement. The Board stated:

"There is no question that the Board is not precluded from adjudicating unfair labor practice charges even though they might have been the subject of an arbitration proceeding and award. Section 10(a) of the Act expressly makes this plain, and the courts have uniformly so held. However, it is equally well established that the Board has considerable discretion to respect an arbitration award and decline to exercise its authority over alleged unfair labor practices if to do so will serve the fundamental aims of the Act.

"The Act, as has repeatedly been stated, is primarily designed to promote industrial peace and stability by encouraging the practice and procedure of collective bargaining. Experience has demonstrated that collective-bargaining agreements that provide for final and binding arbitration of grievances and disputes arising thereunder, 'as a substitute for industrial strife,' contribute significantly to the attainment of this statutory objective. Approval of the arbitral technique, which has become an effective and expeditious means of resolving labor disputes, finds expression in Section 203(d) of the Labor Management Relations Act, 1947. That provision declares: 'Final adjustment by a method agreed upon by the parties is hereby declared to be the desirable method for settlement of grievance disputes arising over the application or interpretation of an existing collective-bargaining agreement.' The Board has often looked to this declaration as a guideline in administering its Act.

"If complete effectuation of the Federal policy is to be achieved, we firmly believe that the Board, which is entrusted with the administration of one of the many facets of national labor policy, should give hospitable acceptance to the arbitral process as 'part and parcel of the collective bargaining process itself,' and voluntarily withhold its undoubted authority to adjudicate alleged unfair labor practice charges involving the same subject matter, unless it clearly appears that the arbitration proceedings were tainted by fraud, collusion, unfairness, or serious procedural irregularities or that the award was clearly repugnant to the purpose and policies of the Act. As the Court has reminded the Board in another context but in language equally applicable to the situation here presented:

" * * * that the Board has not been commissioned to effectuate the policies of the Labor Relations Act so single-mindedly that it may wholly ignore other and equally important Congressional objectives. Frequently the entire scope of Congressional purpose calls for careful accommodation of one statutory scheme to another, and it is not too much to demand of an administrative body that it undertake this accommodation without excessive emphasis upon its immediate task.

"Consistent with this reminder, and aware of the underlying objectives of the Act, the Board in the appropriate case has not permitted parties to bypass their specially devised grievance-arbitration machinery for resolving their disputes and where an arbitration award had already been rendered has held them to it."

# Olin Corp.[b]

268 NLRB 573 (1984).

■ * * * In brief, the Union is the exclusive collective-bargaining representative of the Respondent's approximately 260 production and maintenance employees. The 1980–1983 collective-bargaining agreement contained the following provisions:

### Article XIV—Strikes and Lockouts

During the life of the Agreement, the Company will not conduct a lockout at the Plant and neither the Local Union nor the International Union, nor any officer or representative of either, will cause or permit its members to cause any strike, slowdown or stoppage (total or partial) of work or any interference, directly or indirectly, with the full operation of the plant.

Employee Salvatore B. Spatorico was president of the Union from 1976 until his termination in December 1980. On the morning of 17 December, the Respondent suspended two pipefitters for refusing to perform a job that they felt was more appropriately millwright work. A "sick out" ensued during which approximately 43 employees left work that day with medical excuses. The Respondent gave formal written reprimands to 39 of the employees who had engaged in the sick out. In a letter dated 29 December, the Respondent notified Spatorico that he was discharged based on his entire record and in particular for threatening the sick out, participating in the sick out, and failing to prevent it.

Spatorico's discharge was grieved and arbitrated. After a hearing, the arbitrator found that a sick out had occurred at the Respondent's facility on 17 December, that Spatorico "at least partially caused or participated" in it, and that he failed to try to stop it until after it had occurred. The arbitrator concluded that Spatorico's conduct contravened his obligation under article XIV of the collective-bargaining agreement set forth above. The arbitrator also stated, "Union officers implicitly have an affirmative duty not to cause strikes which are in violation of the clause, not to participate in such strikes and to try to stop them when they occur." Accordingly, the arbitrator found that Spatorico had been appropriately discharged.

Noting that the unfair labor practice charges had been referred to arbitration under Dubo Mfg. Corp., 142 NLRB 431 (1963), the arbitrator addressed these charges and found "no evidence that the company discharged the grievant for his legitimate Union activities." The arbitrator

---

**b.** See Comment, Judicial Review and the Trend Toward More Stringent NLRB Standards on Arbitral Deferrals, 129 U.Pa. L.Rev. 738 (1981); Gates & Elder, *Olin* Must Not and Will Not Survive, 38 Lab.L.J. 723 (1987); Harper, Union Waiver of Employee Rights Under the NLRA, 4 Indus.Rel.L.J. 680 (1981); Moses, Deferral to Arbitration in Individual Rights Cases: A Re-examination of *Spielberg*, 51 Tenn.L.Rev. 187 (1984); Sharpe, NLRB Deferral to Grievance—Arbitration: A General Theory, 48 Ohio State L.J. 595 (1987).

again stated his conclusion that Spatorico had been discharged for participating in and failing to stop the sick out because Spatorico "is a Union
officer but the contract's no strike clause *specifically* prohibits such activity
by Union officers." (Emphasis added.)

The judge declined to defer to the arbitration award on the grounds
that although the arbitrator referred to the unfair labor practice issue he
did not consider it "in any serious way." The judge determined that the
arbitrator was not competent to decide the unfair labor practice issue
because the award was limited to interpretation of the contract. Moreover,
he determined that the arbitrator did not explicitly refer to the statutory
right and the waiver questions raised by the unfair labor practice charge.
On the merits, however, the judge agreed with the arbitrator's conclusion
in that he found Spatorico's "participation in the strike was inconsistent
with his manifest contractual obligation to attempt to stem the tide of
unprotected activity." The judge concluded that article XIV of the collective-bargaining agreement was sufficiently clear and unmistakable to
waive, at the least, the sort of conduct in which Spatorico engaged, that,
therefore, "Spatorico exposed himself to the greater liability permitted by
the Supreme Court" in Metropolitan Edison Co. v. NLRB, 103 S.Ct. 1467
(Apr. 4, 1983), and that the Respondent did not violate Section 8(a)(3) and
(1) of the Act by discharging him while merely reprimanding other employees.

We agree with the judge that the complaint should be dismissed. We do
so, however, without reaching the merits because we would defer to the
arbitrator's award consistent with the standards set forth in *Spielberg Mfg.
Co.*[2] In its seminal decision in *Spielberg,* the Board held that it would defer
to an arbitration award where the proceedings appear to have been fair and
regular, all parties have agreed to be bound, and the decision of the
arbitrator is not clearly repugnant to the purposes and policies of the Act.
The Board in *Raytheon Co.*[3] further conditioned deferral on the arbitrator's
having considered the unfair labor practice issue. Consistent application of
the *Raytheon* requirement has proven elusive, and as illustrated by the
recent *Propoco*[4] case, its scope has expanded considerably. Accordingly, in
his dissent in *Propoco,* Member Hunter proposed certain standards limiting
the application of *Raytheon.* * * *

Accordingly, we adopt the following standard for deferral to arbitration
awards. We would find that an arbitrator has adequately considered the
unfair labor practice if (1) the contractual issue is factually parallel to the
unfair labor practice issue, and (2) the arbitrator was presented generally
with the facts relevant to resolving the unfair labor practice. In this
respect, differences, if any, between the contractual and statutory standards of review should be weighed by the Board as part of its determination

**2.**  112 NLRB 1080 (1955).

**3.**  140 NLRB 883 (1963).

**4.**  Propoco, Inc., 263 N.L.R.B. 136
(1982), enf. with unpublished, nonpreceden-
tial opinion, Case No. 83–4058 (2d Cir.1983).
See also American Freight System, 264
N.L.R.B. 126 (1982).

under the *Spielberg* standards of whether an award is "clearly repugnant" to the Act. And, with regard to the inquiry into the "clearly repugnant" standard, we would not require an arbitrator's award to be totally consistent with Board precedent. Unless the award is "palpably wrong," i.e., unless the arbitrator's decision is not susceptible to an interpretation consistent with the Act, we will defer. * * *

The dissent attempts to distort our holding here by asserting, in essence, that we are depriving employees of their statutory forum. On the contrary, the Board expressly retains and fulfills its statutory obligation to determine whether employee rights have been protected by the arbitral proceeding by our commitment to determine in each case whether the arbitrator has adequately considered the facts which would constitute unfair labor practices and whether the arbitrator's decision is clearly repugnant to the Act. We differ with our dissenting colleague concerning the scope of the inquiry into the arbitrator's consideration of unfair labor practices because our clarifications of the *Spielberg* standards are, in our view, necessary to restrict the "overzealous dissection of [arbitrators'] opinions by the NLRB" decried by the Ninth Circuit in Douglas Aircraft Co. v. NLRB, 609 F.2d 352, 355 (9th Cir.1979). That misdirected zeal has resulted in such infrequent deferral by the Board that its occasional exercise has had little substantive relationship to a mechanism which daily settles uncounted labor disputes to the satisfaction of the labor relations community.

Accordingly, the infrequent deferrals by the Board (and the General Counsel's concomitant failure to defer at the complaint stage) under the allocation of burdens set forth in Suburban Motor Freight, 247 N.L.R.B. 146 (1980), [which required that the party asserting the arbitration award as a defense had to prove that the unfair labor practice issues were fully and fairly presented to the arbitrator] lead us to the conclusion that a different allocation of burdens is more consistent with the goals of national labor policy. For these reasons we are requiring that the party seeking to have the Board reject deferral and consider the merits of a given case show that the above standards for deferral have not been met. Thus, if a respondent establishes that an arbitration concerning the matter before the Board has taken place, the burden of persuasion rests with the General Counsel to demonstrate that there are deficiencies in the arbitral process requiring the Board to ignore the determination of the arbitrator and subject the case to de novo review. * * *

Turning now to the case before us, we find that the arbitral proceeding has met the *Spielberg* standards for deferral, and that the arbitrator adequately considered the unfair labor practice issue. First, it is clear that the contractual and statutory issues were factually parallel. Indeed, the arbitrator noted that the factual questions that he was required to determine were "(1) whether or not there was a sick out and (2) whether the grievant caused, participated in or failed to attempt to stop the sick out, i.e., whether the grievant failed to meet the obligation imposed upon him by Article XIV." These factual questions are coextensive with those that would be considered by the Board in a decision on the statutory question—i.e., whether the collective-bargaining agreement clearly and unmistakably proscribed the behavior engaged in by Union President Spatorico on 17 December 1980.

Second, it is equally apparent that the arbitrator was presented generally with the facts relevant to resolving the unfair labor practice. In this respect, the General Counsel has not shown that the arbitrator was lacking any evidence relevant to the determination of the nature of the obligations imposed by the no-strike clause in the collective-bargaining agreement and to the determination of the nexus between that clause and Spatorico's conduct. Thus the evidence before the arbitrator was essentially the same evidence necessary for determination of the merits of the unfair labor practice charge.

Finally, we turn to whether the arbitrator's award is clearly repugnant to the purposes and policies of the Act.[14] In this regard, the Supreme Court in *Metropolitan Edison Co.,* above, recently addressed the merits of the substantive issue involved here. In *Metropolitan Edison* the collective-bargaining agreement contained only a general no-strike/no-lockout clause. Two arbitral awards had interpreted a similar clause in prior contracts to impose a higher duty on union officials, but the currently operative collective-bargaining agreement stated that arbitral awards were binding only for the term of the agreement. On these facts, the Court found that the Union had not clearly and explicitly waived the Section 7 rights of its employee officials, and accordingly that the employer violated Section 8(a)(3) and (1) of the Act by disciplining the officials more severely than rank-and-file employees. The Court noted, however, that a "union and an employer reasonably could choose to secure the integrity of a no-strike clause by requiring union officials to take affirmative steps to end unlawful work stoppages," and that a union lawfully may bargain away the statutory protection accorded union officials in order to secure gains it considers more valuable to its members. A union's "decision to undertake such contractual obligations," the Court added, "promotes labor peace and clearly falls within the range of reasonableness accorded bargaining representatives."

Article XIV of the parties' contract here, in addition to a general no-strike/no-lockout obligation similar to the clause in issue in *Metropolitan Edison,* includes a proscription that "neither the Local Union nor the International Union, nor any officer or representative of either, will cause or permit its members to cause any strike, slowdown or stoppage (total or partial) of work or any interference, directly or indirectly, with the full operation of the plant." Certainly, were we reviewing the merits, Board Members might differ as to the standards of specificity required for contractual language waiving statutory rights and as to whether the above language meets those standards at least as applied to employee Spatorico. The question of waiver, however, is also a question of contract interpreta-

---

**14.** No party contends that the parties had not agreed to be bound by arbitration or that the proceedings were not fair and regular.

tion. An arbitrator's interpretation of the contract is what the parties here have bargained for and, we might add, what national labor policy promotes. Particularly in view of the additional proscriptions in the no-strike clause quoted above, the arbitrator here had a reasonable basis for finding as he did, in reference to the unfair labor practice charge, that the clause "specifically prohibits" union officers from engaging in activity of the sort engaged in by Spatorico. We find that the arbitrator's contractual interpretation is not clearly repugnant to either the letter or the spirit of the Supreme Court's opinion in *Metropolitan Edison,* which held that a union may waive the right of its officials to acquiesce in unprotected work stoppages. * * *

■ Member Zimmerman, dissenting in part.

　　* * *

Very early in the Board's experience with the *Spielberg* doctrine, it became apparent that there must be some minimal proof that an unfair labor practice issue has been resolved in arbitration before the Board can defer to an arbitration award. With such proof, the Board can reasonably evaluate the award according to the *Spielberg* standards and can accommodate and encourage the arbitral process by deferring to it when the award meets those standards. Without such proof, the Board cannot defer because it has no reasonable basis for determining whether the award fulfills the Board's obligation under Section 10(a) of the Act to prevent unfair labor practices.

* * * In reality, the majority's new test involves only one step. It will presume that an arbitrator has considered both contract and unfair labor practice issues unless the General Counsel can prove that there is no factual parallel between the issues. The more broadly the Board construes the notion of factual parallelism, the more difficult the General Counsel's task becomes. * * *

* * * First, and most importantly, the new standard expands the Board's deferral policy beyond permissible statutory bounds. For all the reasons stated by the Board in the long line of cases upon which I rely, I find that the use of a presumption here to justify deferral amounts to an abdication by this Board of its obligation under Section 10(a) of the Act to protect employees' rights and the public interest by preventing and remedying unfair labor practices. Nowhere in the Act itself, its legislative history, or in its judicial interpretation is there authority for the proposition that the Federal labor policy favoring arbitration requires or permits the Board to abstain from effectuating the equally important Federal labor policy entrusted to the Board under Section 10(a).

Second, I emphasize that the overwhelming weight of judicial precedent stands for the proposition that the Board *has no authority to defer* if it does not have some affirmative proof that an unfair labor practice issue was presented to and considered by an arbitrator. Judicial rulings on this point stand in sharp contrast to the general proposition that the Board has broad discretionary authority to defer to the grievance and arbitration process. * * *

A third unacceptable aspect of the majority's new rule is the inequity of requiring that "the party seeking to have the Board reject deferral ... show that the above standards for deferral have not been met." * * *

I suggest that the Board has reached a point where it actually discourages arbitration by the extent to which the Board defers to it. Sometimes less expensive, more informal, or more expeditious arbitration may be an attractive way to resolve minor grievances and disputes which are essentially contractual in nature. The more we force parties to resolve unfair labor practice issues in a contractual forum, however, the more we risk impairing those attributes which make arbitration attractive. Knowing the risks of failing to litigate statutory issues in arbitration, unions might best serve their duty of fair representation by insisting in collective bargaining that arbitration have all the formal procedural features of an unfair labor practice case before the Board. Even without such a development, an increase in the arbitration caseload could strain the resources of many unions, employees, and arbitrators, as well as delay the hearing and resolution of each grievance. The final irony of the stress created by a Board policy of wholesale deferral may be that one or both parties to collective-bargaining negotiations will oppose the inclusion of any form of arbitration provision in a contract.

* * *

For all the foregoing reasons, I dissent from the change in Board law made today. As a final point, however, I reiterate that no change in law was necessary to justify Board deferral to the arbitration award at issue here. I agree that the judge should have deferred to the arbitration award by applying the proper standard of *Suburban Motor Freight.* The arbitrator expressly found that Spatorico was not discharged for his legitimate union activities, but instead was discharged pursuant to the contractual no-strike clause which specifically prohibits union officers from causing work stoppages. It is clear that the arbitrator was presented with, considered, and ruled on the statutory issue. Further, I find that the arbitrator's award is not repugnant to the Act. The award is consistent with the Supreme Court's decision in Metropolitan Edison Co. v. NLRB, 103 S.Ct. 1467 (Apr. 4, 1983). The award also comports with the Board's holding in Midwest Precision Castings Co., 244 N.L.R.B. 597 (1979), that employees—be they union officers or not—who instigate unauthorized strikes are properly subject to more severe discipline than are employees who merely participate in such activity. In this case, the arbitrator found that Spatorico "at least partially caused" the work stoppage.

---

## PROBLEMS FOR DISCUSSION

**1.** Union officers who participated in a strike and picketing in violation of a collective bargaining agreement were suspended pending a discharge. They were, however, reinstated pursuant to a "last chance agreement" that prohibited them from holding any union office for the duration of the collective agreement nor any office involving direct dealing with the Company. This provision was challenged before and sustained by an arbitrator as reasonable in light of their conduct. But the General Counsel has issued a complaint that the conditions imposed violate sections 8(a)(1) and (3) of the Act. What should the Board hold? See Bethenergy Mines, Inc., 308 NLRB 1242 (1992).

**2.** The Company, an ice cream manufacturer, has had a bargaining relationship with the Union for 50 years. It notified the Union that it would discontinue the over-the-road delivery portion of its business and subcontract that work. The Union filed a grievance and a charge alleging violation of §§ 8(a)(1) and (5) of the Act. The Regional Director issued a complaint, but deferred proceeding on it until the grievance was arbitrated. The Arbitrator held that the collective agreement did not prohibit the Company from subcontracting that operation and did not subject that decision to any bargaining obligation. His award stated:

> [T]he Employer has shown that the subcontracting in this case was done for legitimate business reasons. The evidence in the record overwhelmingly supports the Employer's assertions that it terminated the over-the-road operations because the operations did not fit in with the Company's strategic goals, the personalized service of the over-the-road drivers was no longer necessary, and the legal risks and associated costs were too high to continue the over-the-road operations. The evidence does not support a conclusion that the discontinuance of the operations was done to avoid the Employer's contractual responsibilities or that the decision was based on any anti-union animus.

Nevertheless, a majority of a three-member panel of the Board held the Company's motion for summary judgment on the basis of arbitral deferral should be denied: "[A]n arbitral determination that a contract does not prohibit an employer action is not tantamount to a finding that the parties have contractually agreed to permit that action." Nor, in their view, did the arbitrator effectively resolve the statutory issue "by implicitly finding the ... [subcontracting] decision was not a mandatory bargaining subject." Kohler Mix Specialties, Inc., 332 NLRB No. 61 (2000). Has the Board retreated from *Olin*?

---

PLUMBERS & PIPEFITTERS LOCAL 520 v. NLRB (C–CATALYTIC INC.), 955 F.2d 744 (D.C.Cir.1992), cert. denied, 506 U.S. 817, 113 S.Ct. 61, 121 L.Ed.2d 29 (1992). The company had a collective bargaining agreement with a group of fourteen international construction unions. The contract, among other things, empowered the company to discharge or discipline employees for "proper cause," prohibited work stoppages, and had a grievance procedure with three steps leading to possible arbitration. At the third step, both the company and the aggrieved international union present their cases to a committee (GPC) which includes a representative of each of the signatory unions (but no employer representative); if the employer does not agree with the GPC decision, the aggrieved union may take the case to arbitration. In the instant case, the company discharged employee Berry, who was also a union steward; Berry had advised certain other employees to refuse to work when assigned to a new shift. The company claimed that this was insubordination that provided "cause" for discharge, while the union claimed anti-union animus and filed both a grievance under the labor agreement and an unfair labor practice charge with the NLRB.

An unfair labor practice complaint under section 8(a)(3) was issued, but not until a year and a half later. In the meantime, the grievance was processed to the third step of the contract procedure, at which the GPC held a hearing and concluded that Berry should be rehired without any backpay; both the company and the union accepted that determination. More than a year later, an ALJ of the Board concluded that he would not defer to the grievance settlement (which had been made by the international union, the party to the contract, over the objection of Berry and his local union); he conducted a hearing, found that the asserted insubordination was a pretext for an anti-union discharge, and recommended reinstatement with full backpay. The NLRB, however, reversed, and held that it would defer to the settlement and dismiss the unfair labor practice complaint. The court of appeals enforced the Board's order—but instructed the NLRB to clarify the "theoretical underpinnings" of its policy of deferring to grievance settlements.

The court noted that the NLRB had supplemented its policy of deferring to arbitration awards that satisfied the *Spielberg-Olin* criteria with a similar policy of deferring to pre-arbitration grievance settlements, provided four criteria are satisfied: (1) the settlement is reached through a collective bargaining process which is "fair and regular"; (2) the parties agreed to be bound by the terms of the settlement agreement; (3) the outcome reached is not "palpably wrong" (meaning that both sides have compromised to some degree); and (4) the unfair labor practice issue was "considered" in the settlement process, in that the contractual and unfair labor practice issues are factually parallel and both parties were generally aware of the relevant facts.

The court held the policy of deferring to pre-arbitration grievance settlements, pursuant to the four criteria, was rational and consistent with the Labor Act, in particular with the NLRA promotion of the peaceful resolution of disputes through voluntarily agreed upon techniques of collective bargaining—at least when the statutory right being asserted is one which is "waivable" through union negotiations (including, as was involved here, a union official's susceptibility to "selective discipline" for promoting what was in effect a work stoppage in violation of the labor contract).

The court also held that the Board's application of its policy in this case, leading to its dismissal of the 8(a)(3) complaint, was not an abuse of its discretion. Even if Berry and his local union resisted the settlement, it was reached by the two parties to the labor contract, and even though Berry did not appear before the GPC (and the GPC had set forth no written reasons for its decision), his case was fully presented there by a representative of the international union. Nor was the settlement "palpably wrong" when tested against the NLRA, for the very scope of the NLRA rights to strike and to be a union official were defined by the terms of the labor contract and settlement concerning "proper cause," which lawfully "waived" rights that Berry might otherwise have had. The issues under both the labor contract and the NLRA were in effect identical: whether the company was justified in terminating Berry based upon his alleged insubordination—so that both the third and fourth NLRB criteria for deference were satisfied.

Despite upholding both the Board deference policy and its application here, the court admonished the Board that the "theoretical underpinnings" of that policy were questionable and should be reassessed in order to avoid future reversals. In particular, the court thought that the "palpably wrong" criterion, understood by the Board to require both parties to have made concessions in the settlement agreement, was not consistent with the "contractual waiver" doctrine that underpins the Board's deference policy. The latter policy should result in the Board's never deferring to a pre-arbitration settlement when the asserted statutory right is non-waivable, and always deferring when that right is waivable—and yet the Board appears to do otherwise, in a manner that the court suggested resulted in standardless decisions.

---

# PROBLEMS  FOR  DISCUSSION

**1.**  Are the reasons for deferring to an arbitration award, fully elaborated in *Olin Corp.*, roughly as compelling when deference is sought to a negotiated grievance settlement? Consider, at the least, the nature of the factual record presented to the arbitrator, the airing of arguments and counter-arguments, the usual explication of reasons in the arbitrator's award. Although some of these were present in the instant case in the proceeding before the GPC at step three, some were not—and most are not in the typical pre-arbitration settlements regularly worked out by management and union representatives. Should the Board therefore defer to such settlements only after giving them some form of "heightened scrutiny"? Should the Board therefore not defer to them at all?

**2.**  Does the court of appeals in *C-Catalytic* too quickly sustain the parties' contractual definition of Berry's rights as a shop steward as a substitute for the rights that he is entitled to under the NLRA? What if a union's relinquishment of certain claims on his behalf was based upon a misunderstanding of the NLRA, and an inadequate appreciation of the extent of the rights afforded union representatives? What if the union, at the time it decided to settle Berry's grievance, viewed his aggressiveness when dealing with his foreman over the work-shift dispute in a manner different from that of the General Counsel when issuing a complaint? What if the union's assessment of a fair remedy (i.e., reinstatement without backpay) falls far short of what the Board would order to vindicate the policies of section 8(a)(3)? Should any of these suppositions warrant a conclusion that the NLRB should have decided the unfair labor practice claim?

---

## *NLRB DEFERENCE IN REPRESENTATION CASES*

Following the Supreme Court decision in Carey v. Westinghouse Elec. Corp., p. 808 supra, that the arbitrator had jurisdiction to decide the grievance arising from the assignment of work that was allegedly "production and maintenance" work, the company filed with the NLRB a motion to clarify the certifications of the competing unions (IUE and Federation). The Board, however, chose to defer action pending the outcome of the arbitration proceeding. The arbitrator, resting his decision principally upon the wage level of the affected group of employees, determined that some of them should be treated as production and maintenance employees, to be represented by IUE, and the others as technical employees to be represented by Federation. After the rendition of the arbitrator's award, the Board assumed jurisdiction to clarify the unions' certifications. WESTINGHOUSE ELEC. CORP., 162 NLRB 768 (1967). The initial question addressed by the Board was the weight properly to be accorded an arbitration award which purported to resolve competing claims under two different labor contracts with one of the competing unions not a party to the arbitration proceeding, and which applied criteria other than those generally applied by the Board in making unit determinations. The Board decided that it was not appropriate to defer to the award of the arbitrator, as "the ultimate issue of representation could not be decided by the Arbitrator on the basis of his interpreting the contract under which he was authorized to act, but could only be resolved by utilization of Board criteria for making unit determinations." It was necessary, to warrant deference, that the arbitrator's award reflect use of Board standards and be consistent with them. "In this case apparently not all the evidence concerning all these standards was available to the Arbitrator for his consideration and appraisal, and his award reflects this deficiency." The Board concluded that the arbitrator's award rested solely on one criterion, an estimate of the skills of the employees involved, and neglected other significant factors usually considered in unit-determination cases, such as bargaining history, integration of operations within the group, and the progression of employees within the group from lower to higher grades. The Board, concluding that "while we give some consideration to the award, we do not think it would effectuate statutory policy to defer to it entirely," held that the disputed group of employees ought not be split and that they should be absorbed within the existing unit represented by the Federation.

---

*JUDICIAL DEFERENCE TO ARBITRATION UNDER TITLE VII?*

Title VII of the Civil Rights Act of 1964, 42 U.S.C.A. § 2000e et seq., bars discrimination in employment on the basis (among other things) of race, and provides for a lawsuit by the aggrieved employee after there has been an opportunity for conciliation by the Equal Employment Opportunity Commission. In ALEXANDER V. GARDNER-DENVER CO., 415 U.S. 36, 94 S.Ct. 1011, 39 L.Ed.2d 147 (1974), the Supreme Court considered a case in which an employer covered by the Act had a collective bargaining agreement which also barred discrimination on the basis of race, barred discharge without "just cause," and provided for arbitration of grievances. An employee who was discharged, allegedly for poor work, challenged the discharge through the grievance procedure; although the issue of race discrimination was presented to the arbitrator, he made no mention of it in his decision sustaining the discharge as based on "just cause" on account of poor work. The Supreme Court held that when the employee thereafter pursued an action in a federal court for violation of Title VII, he was entitled to a trial de novo on the issue of race discrimination.

The Court held that prior resort to arbitration did not constitute an election of remedies or a waiver of judicial relief, and also that trial courts in Title VII actions were not obligated to "defer" to arbitration decisions which ruled upon the same transaction. Noting the analogy to the National Labor Relations Act, the Court stated that the employee's rights under the Civil Rights Act and under the labor contract were of a "distinctly separate nature" entitled to separate vindication; it also noted that the arbitrator's task was merely to effectuate the intent of the parties to the contract and not to invoke public laws. The Court stated that the arbitrator's task was to construe the law of the shop and not the law of the land; that the arbitrator was generally chosen for his familiarity with industrial relations and not with public law; that arbitration procedures were informal and did not accord the evidentiary guarantees present in civil trials; and that a principle of judicial deference to arbitration might induce employees to circumvent arbitration in race discrimination cases. The Court concluded: "The federal court should consider the employee's claim de novo. The arbitral decision may be admitted as evidence and accorded such weight as the court deems appropriate." See also Barrentine v. Arkansas–Best Freight System, Inc., 450 U.S. 728, 101 S.Ct. 1437, 67 L.Ed.2d 641 (1981)(wage claim under Fair Labor Standards Act); McDonald v. West Branch, 466 U.S. 284, 104 S.Ct. 1799, 80 L.Ed.2d 302 (1984)(§ 1983 claim by discharged police officer).

Some fifteen years after *Gardner-Denver* was decided, the Supreme Court manifested an altogether different attitude regarding the capacity of arbitrators to rule on statutory claims. In Gilmer v. Interstate/Johnson Lane Corp., 500 U.S. 20, 111 S.Ct. 1647, 114 L.Ed.2d 26 (1991), the Court held that the rules of the New York Stock Exchange, requiring registered representatives to arbitrate "any controversy ... arising out of employment or termination of employment," were enforceable under the Federal Arbitration Act (FAA), 9 U.S.C. § 1 et seq. The Court also held that an employee's claim that his termination was in violation of the Age Discrimination in Employment Act was subject to the arbitration rule, incorporated as part of his employment agreement. The Court found no inconsistency between the congressional purpose to protect workers against age discrimination, usually through federal court litigation, and the enforcement of such a right through a workplace arbitration arrangement agreed to by a worker at the time of employment and covering all potential termination disputes.

The majority opinion, written by Justice White, distinguished the *Gardner–Denver* line of cases:

First, those cases did not involve the issue of the enforceability of an agreement to arbitrate statutory claims. Rather, they involved the quite different issue whether arbitration of contract-based claims precluded subsequent judicial resolution of statutory claims. Since the employees there had not agreed to arbitrate their statutory claims, and the labor arbitrators were not authorized to resolve such claims, the arbitration in those cases understandably was held not to preclude subsequent statutory actions. Second, because the arbitration in those cases occurred in the context of a collective-bargaining agreement, the claimants there were represented by their unions in the arbitration proceedings. An important concern therefore was the tension between collective representation and individual statutory rights, a concern not applicable to the present case. Finally, those cases were not decided under the FAA, which, as discussed above, reflects a "liberal federal policy favoring arbitration agreements." ... Therefore, those cases provide no basis for refusing to enforce Gilmer's agreement to arbitrate his ADEA claim.

----

## PROBLEMS FOR DISCUSSION

**1.** Are the characterizations of the arbitration process, made by the Supreme Court in the *Gardner-Denver* case, equally apt when the issue is NLRB deference to arbitral awards? Is the strongly deferential policy articulated by the Board in *Olin* consistent with the *Gardner-Denver* decision? See Taylor v. NLRB, 786 F.2d 1516 (11th Cir.1986).

**2.** Note that in the *Olin* case, the issue that would have been before the Board, had it considered the merits, was whether the no-strike clause of the labor agreement constituted a waiver of the usual statutory protection that a union official has against differential discipline. In short, the unfair labor practice decision turned principally upon an issue of contract construction. Should the *Olin* decision be properly limited to such a situation? Or does it apply just as much to the case where discipline is challenged simply under a "just cause" provision of the labor contract, and later under Section 8(a)(3) barring discrimination on account of union activity? Cf. West Penn Power Co., 274 NLRB 1160 (1985).

**3.** Are unions well advised—in light of the Board's deference to arbitration awards—to introduce before the arbitrator all claims, facts, theories and legal precedents that are possibly pertinent to both the labor agreement and the NLRA? Are arbitrators, likewise, well advised to hear (and induce the parties to proffer) all such claims, facts, theories and legal precedents? What are the arguments favoring such a development? What are the arguments opposing such a development?

On the other hand, will a union or individual with both a plausible statutory claim and a plausible contract-breach claim now be more inclined to avoid arbitration and resort directly to the NLRB? (After reading the next major case, assess what the Board would likely do in such a situation.)

**4.** A collective bargaining agreement governing employees at an atomic energy plant "reserves the right to the Company to draft reasonable safety rules for employees and to insist on observance of such rules." The company unilaterally instituted drug testing rules for those employees who had unrestricted access to the nuclear reactor. The union filed charges of violation of section 8(a)(5), which the Regional Director held in abeyance pending deferral to arbitration. The arbitrator held the rules to be contractually permissible, but did not address the "clear and unmistakable waiver" standard applied by the Board in Johnson–Bateman, 295 N.L.R.B. 180 (1989), at 856 infra. Should the Board defer to the arbitration? See Utility Workers, Local 246 v. NLRB, 39 F.3d 1210 (D.C.Cir.1994).

**5.**  The Cafeteria Employees Union was on the ballot and unsuccessful in four successive representation elections among the New York City restaurants of the Horn and Hardart Company. Subsequently, Horn and Hardart, convinced that the Union actually did have majority support, executed a three-year labor contract recognizing it as bargaining representative for all full-time and regular part-time employees "at all Company locations in the New York metropolitan area." Horn and Hardart subsequently opened a cafeteria in Suffolk County, Long Island, and another in northern New Jersey. When the Cafeteria Employees Union claimed that these locations were within the coverage of the labor contract, Horn and Hardart protested, and the issue was submitted to arbitration. While arbitration was pending, the Retail Clerks Union presented a claim of representation to the Company for both locations, but neither that Union nor any Suffolk County or New Jersey employees were parties to the arbitration proceeding.

Shortly after the arbitrator rendered her decision sustaining the claim of the Cafeteria Employees Union, the Retail Clerks filed a petition for separate representation elections at the Suffolk County and northern New Jersey locations. In both NLRB proceedings, the Company (and the Cafeteria Employees Union as intervenor) moved to dismiss, asserting that the contract as construed by the arbitrator constituted a bar to a representation election. Should the Board dismiss the petitions for this reason? See NLRB v. Horn & Hardart Co., 439 F.2d 674 (2d Cir.1971).

**6.**  The Ace Manufacturing Company discharged two shop stewards, Alyce Adolph and Zelda Zink. Alyce, who had previously been permitted to pursue her grievance investigations on behalf of unit employees at any time during the work day, was told by her supervisor that henceforth she could leave her work station for this purpose only during a designated half-hour in the morning. When Alyce went to management to complain, she was told to leave the plant, but she refused, and she was discharged for insubordination. An arbitrator concluded that Alyce was promoting her interests as a representative of the employees and therefore she should not have been discharged; she was ordered reinstated, but because of her intemperate insubordination the arbitrator concluded that her behavior was only "partially" protected and he declined to award backpay.

Zelda, employed in another part of the plant in a different bargaining unit, was also discharged for persistently demanding that the company process her grievances immediately, before any other company activity. An arbitrator ordered her reinstatement with backpay (particularly because she was new to the position of shop steward), but—fearing future friction—he provided that her continued employment was to be conditioned on her refraining for a period of three years from holding a shop steward position or any other union office. Six months later, Zelda was elected union president, and Ace discharged her.

Alyce and Zelda have filed charges of violations of section 8(a)(3), and Ace has asserted that the NLRB should decline to exercise its jurisdiction, in deference to the awards of the arbitrators. Should the General Counsel issue a complaint? If so, how should the ALJ and the Board decide the case? See Barton Brands Ltd., 298 NLRB 976 (1990); Cone Mills Corp., 298 NLRB 661 (1990); United Cable Television Corp., 299 NLRB 138 (1990).

Wright v. Universal Maritime Serv. Corp., 525 U.S. 70, 119 S.Ct. 391, 142 L.Ed.2d 361 (1998). Under facts strikingly similar to those in the *American Mfg. Co.* case of the *Steelworkers Trilogy*, p. 753 supra, Caesar Wright—who was represented by the International Longshoremen's Association—was injured while working for a stevedoring company. He sought compensation for permanent disability, and ultimately settled his claim for $250,000 and attorney's fees; he also received Social Security disability benefits. Later, he returned to the union hiring hall and was referred for work, but the stevedoring companies declined to accept Wright for employment because he had been certified as permanently disabled. The union declared that this was a breach of the no-lockout provision of the labor contract with a multi-employer group of stevedoring companies. But the union did not invoke the contractual grievance procedure culminating in arbitration of "matters under dispute"; nor did it seek to present Wright's claim under another agreement, the so-called Longshore Seniority Plan, which provided for resolution by a two-person committee of "any dispute involving the interpretation or application of this Agreement." Instead, it advised Wright to sue in federal court for discrimination in violation of the Americans with Disabilities Act (ADA). The district and appellate court dismissed that action for failure to exhaust Wright's contractual remedies; reliance was placed upon the Supreme Court decision in *Gilmer*.

A unanimous Supreme Court reversed. The Court noted that there was "some tension" between its decision in *Gardner-Denver*, which stated that "an employee's rights under Title VII are not susceptible of prospective waiver" in arbitration, and its decision in *Gilmer*, which held that the right to a federal judicial forum for an Age Discrimination claim could be waived in an agreement to arbitrate. Petitioner Wright would resolve the tension by opting for the application of *Gardner-Denver*, where the arbitration provision was negotiated by a union rather than by the individual employee; while the employer stevedoring group proffered the *Gilmer* decision as an expression of the Court's increasing support over time for arbitral resolution of statutory disputes. The Court, however, held that "we find it unnecessary to resolve the question of the validity of a union-negotiated waiver, since it is apparent to us, on the facts and arguments presented here, that no such waiver has occurred."

In asserting the existence of an agreement to arbitrate the ADA claim, respondents rely upon the presumption of arbitrability this Court has found in § 301 of the Labor Management Relations Act * * * * That presumption, however, does not extend beyond the reach of the principal rationale that justifies it, which is that arbitrators are in a better position than courts *to interpret the terms of a CBA.* * * * The dispute in the present case, however, ultimately concerns not the application or interpretation of any CBA, but the meaning of a federal statute. * * * To be sure, respondents argue that Wright is not qualified for his position as the CBA requires, but even if that were true he would *still* prevail if the refusal to hire violated the ADA.

Aside from the unavailability to the employers of the presumption of arbitrability of Wright's ADA claim, the Court also held that the waiver of an employee's statutory right to a judicial forum for claims of employment discrimination must be "clear and unmistakable," and the CBA in this case "does not meet that standard." The CBA lacked any explicit incorporation of statutory antidiscrimination requirements, and indeed lacked any express contractual ban on discrimination; and the contracts' arbitration provisions were very general and, in the case of the Longshore Seniority Plan, were specifically limited to disputes related to that contract itself.

The Court therefore concluded: "We hold that the collective-bargaining agreement in this case does not contain a clear and unmistakable waiver of the covered employees' rights to a judicial forum for federal claims of employment discrimination. We do not reach the question whether such a waiver would be enforceable."

———

## PROBLEM FOR DISCUSSION

Note that, in effect, *Wright* reverses the presumption of arbitrability established by the *Steelworkers Trilogy*: Contractual issues are presumptively subject to the grievance-arbitration clause; but statutory labor protection claims require a "clear and unmistakable" waiver of resort to a judicial forum. Even then, the Court reserves judgment on whether such a provision should be given effect. In Circuit City Stores, Inc. v. Adams, ___ U.S. ___, 121 S.Ct. 1302, 149 L.Ed.2d 234 (2001), the United States Supreme Court held, by 5 to 4 vote, that the provision of the Federal Arbitration Act excluding from its scope "contracts of employment of seamen, railroad employees, or any other class of workers engaged in foreign or interstate commerce" applies only to those employees who actually transport goods or passengers across state lines; all other employees—a truck driver, for example, who only makes local deliveries—are included. Conjoined with the *Gilmer* decision, *Circuit City* extends the Federal Arbitration Act to "boilerplate" forms whereby applicants for employment are required to submit all work-related disputes, often including an enumerated list of labor protective statutes, to an arbitration system unilaterally established by the employer.

Return to the question the *Wright* Court refused to pass upon. If such a provision for arbitration of statutory claims is enforceable when contained in a contract of adhesion, a job application form or an employee handbook, should it be any less so when negotiated by a collective bargaining representative? Is an arbitrator selected under a CBA to resolve a statutory issue any more or less likely to be informed, competent and objective? What would the employee's rights be if the union declines to arbitrate an employment discrimination claim?

———

## United Technologies Corp.[c]

268 NLRB 557 (1984).

[The complaint charged a violation of Section 8(a)(1) by virtue of an alleged threat directed against employee Sherfield. Ms. Sherfield had filed a grievance, which the company's General Foreman denied at the first step of the grievance procedure. When Ms. Sherfield and her shop steward indicated that they would appeal to the second step, the General Foreman allegedly implied that her persistence might result in discipline. The company denied the charge in the unfair labor practice proceeding, and contended in any event that the Board should defer the exercise of its jurisdiction to the available grievance-arbitration procedures of the parties' labor agreement. The Board, overruling prior authority, upheld the company's position.]

Arbitration as a means of resolving labor disputes has gained widespread acceptance over the years and now occupies a respected and firmly established place in Federal labor policy. The reason for its success is the underlying conviction that the parties to a collective-bargaining agreement are in the best position to resolve, with the help of a neutral third party if necessary, disputes concerning the correct interpretation of their contract. Congressional intent regarding the use of arbitration is abundantly clear:

> Final adjustment by a method agreed upon by the parties is hereby declared to be the desirable method for settlement of grievance disputes arising over the application or interpretation of an existing collective-bargaining agreement.[5]

It is this congressional mandate on which the Supreme Court has consistently relied in sanctioning arbitration as a preferred instrument for preserving industrial peace.

Similarly, the concept of judicial and administrative deference to the arbitral process and the notion that courts should support, rather than interfere with, this method of dispute resolution have become entrenched in American jurisprudence. Over the years, the Board has played a key role in fostering a climate in which arbitration could flourish. Thus, as early as 1943[7] the Board announced its sympathy with the concept of prospective deference to contractual grievance machinery. In *Consolidated Aircraft* the Board stated:

---

**c.** See Getman, Collyer Insulated Wire: A Case of Misplaced Modesty, 49 Ind.L.J. 57 (1973); Lynch, Deferral, Waiver and Arbitration Under the NLRA: From Status to Contract and Back Again, 44 U.Miami L.Rev. 237 (1989); Nash, Wilder & Banov, The Development of the *Collyer* Deferral Doctrine, 27 Vand.L.Rev. 23 (1974); Note, The Contractual Waiver of Individual Rights Under the NLRA, 31 N.Y.L.S. L.Rev. 793 (1986); Schatzki, NLRB Resolution of Contract Disputes Under Section 8(a)(5), 50 Texas L.Rev. 225 (1972); Zimmer, Wired for Collyer: Rationalizing NLRB and Arbitration Jurisdiction, 48 Ind.L.J. 141 (1973).

**5.** Sec. 203(d) of the Act, 29 U.S.C. § 173(d)(1976).

**7.** Consolidated Aircraft Corp., 47 NLRB 694, 706 (1943), enfd. in pertinent part 141 F.2d 785 (9th Cir.1944).

We are of the opinion ... that it will not effectuate the statutory policy of "encouraging the practice and procedure of collective bargaining" for the Board to assume the role of policing collective contracts between employers and labor organizations by attempting to decide whether disputes as to the meaning and administration of such contracts constitute unfair labor practices under the Act. On the contrary, we believe that parties to collective contracts would thereby be encouraged to abandon their efforts to dispose of disputes under the contracts through collective bargaining or through the settlement procedures mutually agreed upon by them, and to remit the interpretation and administration of their contracts to the Board. We therefore do not deem it wise to exercise our jurisdiction in such a case, where the parties have not exhausted their rights and remedies under the contract as to which the dispute has arisen.

The Board endowed this sound approach with renewed vigor in the seminal case of *Collyer Insulated Wire*,[8] in which the Board dismissed a complaint alleging unilateral changes in wages and working conditions in violation of Section 8(a)(5) in deference to the parties' grievance-arbitration machinery. The *Collyer* majority articulated several factors favoring deferral: The dispute arose within the confines of a long and productive collective-bargaining relationship; there was no claim of employer animosity to the employees' exercise of protected rights; the parties' contract provided for arbitration in a very broad range of disputes; the arbitration clause clearly encompassed the dispute at issue; the employer had asserted its willingness to utilize arbitration to resolve the dispute; and the dispute was eminently well suited to resolution by arbitration. In these circumstances, deferral to the arbitral process merely gave full effect to the parties' agreement to submit disputes to arbitration. In essence, the *Collyer* majority was holding the parties to their bargain by directing them to avoid substituting the Board's processes for their own mutually agreed-upon method for dispute resolution.

The experience under *Collyer* was extremely positive. The *Collyer* deferral doctrine was endorsed by the courts of appeals and was quoted favorably by the Supreme Court. In the years following the issuance of *Collyer* the Board further refined the deferral doctrine and applied it to other situations. In *National Radio*[11] the Board extended the deferral policy to cases involving 8(a)(3) allegations. In that case the complaint alleged, inter alia, the disciplinary suspension and discharge of an active union adherent in violation of Section 8(a)(3) as well as various changes in terms and conditions of employment in violation of Section 8(a)(5). Thus, that case presented a situation where the resolution of the unilateral change issues by an arbitrator would not necessarily have resolved the 8(a)(3) issues raised by the complaint. Nevertheless, the Board decided that deferral to the grievance procedure prior to the issuance of the arbitrator's

**8.** 192 NLRB 837 (1971).

**11.** National Radio Co., 198 N.L.R.B. 527 (1972).

award was warranted. The Board concluded that the same fundamental considerations were present in *National Radio* as in *Collyer* \* \* \*. Following *National Radio,* the Board routinely dismissed complaints alleging violations of Section 8(a)(3) and (1) in deference to the arbitral forum.

\* \* \*

Despite the universal judicial acceptance of the *Collyer* doctrine, however, the Board in *General American Transportation*[15] abruptly changed course and adopted a different standard for arbitral deferral, one that we believe ignores the important policy considerations in favor of deferral. Indeed, by deciding to decline to defer cases alleging violations of Sections 8(a)(1) and (3) and 8(b)(1)(A) and (2), the *General American Transportation* majority essentially emasculated the Board's deferral policy, a policy that had favorably withstood the tests of judicial scrutiny and of practical application. And they did so for reasons that are largely unsupportable. Simply stated, *Collyer* worked well because it was premised on sound legal and pragmatic considerations. Accordingly, we believe it deserves to be resurrected and infused with renewed life.

It is fundamental to the concept of collective bargaining that the parties to a collective-bargaining agreement are bound by the terms of their contract. Where an employer and a union have voluntarily elected to create dispute resolution machinery culminating in final and binding arbitration, it is contrary to the basic principles of the Act for the Board to jump into the fray prior to an honest attempt by the parties to resolve their disputes through that machinery. For dispute resolution under the grievance-arbitration process is as much a part of collective bargaining as the act of negotiating the contract. In our view, the statutory purpose of encouraging the practice and procedure of collective bargaining is ill-served by permitting the parties to ignore their agreement and to petition this Board in the first instance for remedial relief. \* \* \*

The *Collyer* policy we embrace today is one that has been applied with the rule of reason. In their dissenting opinion in *General American Transportation, supra,* former Members Penello and Walther observed:

> The Board has not deferred cases to arbitration in an indiscriminate manner, nor has it been insensitive to the statutory rights of employees in deciding whether to defer and whether to give effect to an arbitration award. The standard it has used is reasonable belief that arbitration procedures would resolve the dispute in a manner consistent with the criteria of *Spielberg*. Thus, it has refused to defer where the interests of the union which might be expected to represent the employee filing the unfair labor practice charge are adverse to those of the employee, or where the respondent's conduct constitutes a rejection of the principles of collective bargaining. And where, after deferral, the respondent has refused to proceed to arbitration, the Board has rescinded the deferral and decided the case on the merits. Finally, if for any reason the

---

**15.** 228 N.L.R.B. 808 (1977).

arbitrator's award fails to meet the *Spielberg* standards, as for example, that it is repugnant to the policies of the Act, the Board will not give it effect. [Citation omitted.]

We shall continue to be guided by these principles.

The facts of the instant case make it eminently well suited for deferral. The dispute centers on a statement a single foreman made to a single employee and a shop steward during the course of a routine first-step grievance meeting allegedly concerning possible adverse consequences that might flow from a decision by the employee to process her grievance to the next step. The statement is alleged to be a threat violative of Section 8(a)(1). It is also, however, clearly cognizable under the broad grievance-arbitration provision of section VII of the collective-bargaining agreement.[20] Moreover, the Respondent has expressed its willingness, indeed its eagerness, to arbitrate the dispute.[21]

In view of the foregoing, we believe it would best effectuate the purposes and policies of the Act to defer this case to the arbitral forum. Accordingly, we conclude that the issues raised by the complaint in Case 39–CA–968 should be deferred to the grievance-arbitration provisions of the collective-bargaining agreement under the principles of *Collyer,* supra, and *National Radio,* supra. We shall so order.[22]

## ORDER

The complaint is dismissed, provided that:

Jurisdiction of this proceeding is hereby retained for the limited purpose of entertaining an appropriate and timely motion for further consideration upon a proper showing that either (a) the dispute has not, with reasonable promptness after the issuance of this Decision and Order, either been resolved by amicable settlement in the grievance procedure or submitted promptly to arbitration, or (b) the grievance or arbitration

**20.** In this regard, we note that art. IV of the contract states that "the company and the union recognize that employees covered by this agreement may not be discriminated against in violation of the provisions of the Labor Management Relations Act, 1947 as amended...." It is manifest, therefore, that the parties contemplated that disputes such as the one here be resolved under the grievance-arbitration machinery.

**21.** Although the instant dispute arose in the context of the processing of another grievance, the alleged misconduct "does not appear to be of such character as to render the use of [the grievance-arbitration] machinery unpromising or futile." United Aircraft Corp., 204 NLRB 879, supra. Indeed, both the Respondent and the Union continued to file and process grievances. Thus the record

"demonstrates full acceptance by the parties of the grievance and arbitration route to the resolution of disputes." Community Convalescent Hospital, 199 NLRB 840, 841 fn. 2 (1972), and "demonstrates the existence of a workable and freely resorted to grievance procedure," Postal Service, supra, 210 NLRB at 560 fn. 1. Accordingly, we find that Ram Construction Co., 228 NLRB 769 (1977), cited by the judge, and Joseph T. Ryerson & Sons, 199 NLRB 461 (1972), are not controlling.

**22.** The Respondent must, of course, waive any timeliness provisions of the grievance-arbitration clauses of the collective-bargaining agreement so that the Union's grievance may be processed in accordance with the following Order.

procedures have not been fair and regular or have reached a result which is repugnant to the Act.

■ Member Zimmerman, dissenting. * * *

I readily acknowledge the existence of a salutary Federal labor law policy favoring the resolution of collective-bargaining disputes through grievance and arbitration procedures. I also fully endorse the Board's general policy of accommodating private dispute resolution systems, as that policy has been expressed in three landmark cases: Spielberg Mfg. Co., 112 NLRB 1080 (1955); Dubo Mfg. Corp., 142 NLRB 431 (1963); and Collyer Insulated Wire, 192 NLRB 837 (1971). The decisions made today, however, go well beyond those cases, and make changes in deferral policy which transgress proper limits on the Board's discretionary authority to defer. With particular respect to *Collyer,* the determination to "Collyerize" the type of unfair labor practice claims at issue here needlessly sacrifices basic safeguards for individual employee rights under the Act.

Contrary to my colleagues in the majority, I would continue to adhere to the law of deferral to the arbitral process as that law was represented in the concurring opinion of former Chairman Murphy in *General American Transportation,* supra. * * * [There, she explained] the fundamental reasons for a pre-arbitral deferral policy which distinguishes between unfair labor practices involving disputes between contracting parties about their collective-bargaining agreement and unfair labor practices involving disputes about individual employees' statutory rights:

> [T]he Board should stay its processes in favor of the parties' grievance arbitration machinery only in those situations where the dispute is essentially between the contracting parties and where there is no alleged interference with individual employees' basic rights under Section 7 of the Act. Complaints alleging violations of Section 8(a)(5) and 8(b)(3) fall squarely into this category, while complaints alleging violations of Section 8(a)(3), (a)(1), (b)(1)(A), and (b)(2) clearly do not. As discussed more fully below, in the former category the dispute is principally between the contracting parties—the employer and the union—while in the latter the dispute is between the employee on the one hand and the employer and/or the union on the other. In cases alleging violations of Section 8(a)(5) and 8(b)(3), based on conduct assertedly in derogation of the contract, the principal issue is whether the complained-of conduct is permitted by the parties' contract. Such issues are eminently suited to the arbitral process, and resolution of the contract issue by an arbitrator will, as a rule, dispose of the unfair labor practice issue. On the other hand, in cases alleging violations of Section 8(a)(1), (a)(3), (b)(1)(A), and (b)(2), although arguably also involving a contract violation, the determinative issue is not whether the conduct is permitted by the contract, but whether the conduct was unlawfully motivated or whether it otherwise interfered with, restrained, or coerced employees in the exercise of the rights guaranteed them by Section 7 of the Act. In these situa-

tions, an arbitrator's resolution of the contract issue will not dispose of the unfair labor practice allegation. Nor is the arbitration process suited for resolving employee complaints of discrimination under Section 7.

Now, after 6 years of experience under the deferral policy of *General American Transportation,* without any intervening judicial criticism, the majority has overruled that case and has returned to *National Radio.* The majority cites no specific evidence that *General American Transportation* actually has had any adverse effect on private grievance and arbitration systems. * * *

First, the majority opinion overstates the case for its return to *National Radio* when it attempts to place this action under the umbrella of the "universal judicial acceptance of the *Collyer* doctrine." While there is judicial acceptance for the proposition that the Board has broad discretionary authority to defer cases to the arbitral process, there is, equally, judicial acceptance of the proposition that the Board has broad authority to decline to defer. In this regard, several circuit courts of appeals have approved the Board's determination not to defer under its *General American Transportation* policy. * * *

While the national labor policy favoring the private resolution of disputes that has evolved in a series of court cases, notably the Steelworkers Trilogy, requires the Federal judiciary to give a broad degree of deference to grievance and arbitration systems in the resolution of contract issues, the Supreme Court has made clear that the same degree of deference does not apply—indeed cannot be applied—to such systems by the Board (and reviewing courts) where statutory issues are at stake. In NLRB v. Acme Industrial Co., 385 U.S. 432 (1967), the Supreme Court clearly stated at 436–437 that the "relationship of the Board to the arbitration process is of a quite different order.... Thus, to view the *Steelworkers* decisions as automatically requiring the Board in this case to defer to the primary determination of an arbitrator is to overlook important distinctions between those cases and this one."

More recent decisions by the Court indicate that the most important distinction between judicial deferral to arbitration of contract disputes and Board deferral under *Collyer* involves the existence of noncontractual, statutory, individual rights which the Board expressly is required to protect. In Barrentine v. Arkansas–Best Freight System, 450 U.S. 728 (1981), the * * * Court stated, supra at 737:

> Not all disputes between an employee and his employer are suited for binding resolution in accordance with the procedure established by collective bargaining. While courts should defer to an arbitral decision where the employee's claim is based on rights arising out of the collective bargaining agreement, different considerations apply where the employee's claim is based on rights arising out of a statute....

\* \* \* With respect to the putative supremacy of obligations flowing from the grievance and arbitration provision of a collective-bargaining agreement, my colleagues again overstate their case. Implicit in their reasoning is that an exclusive collective-bargaining representative may waive an individual employee's right to seek initial redress of interference with Section 7 rights before the Board. A union may, of course, agree to waive some individual statutory rights. But in my view a union cannot waive an individual employee's right to choose a statutory forum in which to initiate and litigate an unfair labor practice issue. Even if it could, such a waiver would have to be a "clear and unmistakable" one. Here, however, the majority forces individual employees to litigate statutory rights in a contractual forum and does so without making any determination that there has been a "clear and unmistakable" waiver of the right to resort first and exclusively to the Board. My colleagues simply assume that the mere existence of a contractual grievance and arbitration procedure proves a waiver.

Finally, it is pure conceit that the deferral doctrine announced here is mere "prudent restraint" and that *Spielberg* is a catchall safety net for those individuals whose individual rights are not protected in grievance and arbitration. The arbitration process is not designed to and is not particularly adept at protecting employee statutory or public rights. First, a union, without breaching its duty of fair representation, might not vigorously support an employee's claim in arbitration inasmuch as the union, in balancing individual and collective interests, might trade off an employee's statutory right in favor of some other benefits for employees in the bargaining unit as a whole. Second, because arbitrators' competency is primarily in "the law of the shop, not the law of the land," they may lack the competency to resolve the statutory issue(s) involved in the dispute. Third, even if the arbitrator is conversant with the Act, he is limited to determining the dispute in accordance with the parties' intent under the collective-bargaining agreement. Finally, because the arbitrator's function is to effectuate the parties' intent rather than to enforce the Act, he may issue a ruling that is inimical to the public policies underlying the Act, thereby depriving an employee of his protected statutory rights.

\* \* \*

Even the limited guarantee which *Spielberg* has provided for *Collyer* becomes less certain when the Board will no longer require the party seeking deferral to an arbitration award to prove that the unfair labor practice issue has been presented to and considered by the arbitrator. Yet that is exactly what the Board's postarbitral deferral policy will be under the new standard announced today in *Olin Corp.*

For all of the foregoing reasons, I dissent from the majority's overruling of *General American Transportation* and its unwarranted extension of the original *Collyer* doctrine. Assuming, however, the propriety of the majority's overruling of that case, I believe its decision to defer here is unwarranted. The basis for the alleged violation of Section 8(a)(1) in this case is a threat of retaliation against employee Sherfield for participating in the grievance-arbitration procedure. * * * Therefore, contrary to the majority, I would find controlling the Board's decision in Joseph T. Ryerson & Sons, 199 NLRB 461 (1972) * * *:

> [T]he violation with which this Respondent is charged, if committed, strikes at the foundation of that grievance and arbitration mechanism upon which we have relied in the formulation of our *Collyer* doctrine. If we are to foster the national policy favoring collective bargaining and arbitration as a primary arena for the resolution of industrial disputes, as we sought to do in *Collyer,* by declining to intervene in disputes best settled elsewhere, we must assure ourselves that those alternative procedures are not only "fair and regular" but that they are or were open, in fact, for use by the disputants. These considerations caution against our abstention on a claim that a respondent has sought, by prohibited means, to inhibit or preclude access to the grievance procedures. It is this consideration which persuades us that the issues of arbitrability and contract coverage, discussed above, should not here be left to resolution by the arbitrator as might be appropriate under other circumstances. [Footnote and citation omitted.]

Accordingly, even were I to join my colleagues in overruling *General American Transportation,* I would not defer. * * *

----

# Hammontree v. NLRB

925 F.2d 1486 (D.C.Cir.1991)(en banc).

■ WALD, CIRCUIT JUDGE:

Paul Hammontree challenges a National Labor Relations Board ("NLRB" or "Board") order that requires him to exhaust grievance remedies established by a collective bargaining agreement before the Board considers his unfair labor practice complaint. Hammontree contends that such an exhaustion requirement is both inconsistent with the Board's authority under the National Labor Relations Act ("NLRA") and the Labor Management Relations Act ("LMRA"), and a departure from the Board's past policy. We find that the NLRA and the LMRA permit the Board to require an individual employee to exhaust his grievance remedies prior to the filing of an unfair labor practice charge and that the Board's order was both reasonable and consistent with its established practices. Accordingly, we deny Hammontree's petition for review.

## I.   Background

### A.   *Factual Background*

Hammontree is employed as a truck driver by intervenor Consolidated Freightways ("CF"); he drives "peddle" runs—short roundtrips of less than 200 miles.[1] In 1982, when CF first offered peddle runs out of its Memphis, Tennessee terminal, it established a "choice of runs" policy under which available runs were posted and drivers chose runs in order of seniority. Although under this system senior drivers could choose longer (and thus more lucrative) runs, no driver knew the departure time of his or her run; as a result, drivers often "babysat the telephone." Later that year, CF and Hammontree's union local reached an oral agreement: CF would post departure times for peddle runs, but would eliminate the seniority-based "choice of runs." As part of this *quid pro quo,* the union also agreed to withdraw any grievances that might be filed by drivers claiming choice of runs.

In February, 1985, as the union's collective bargaining agreement ("CBA") with CF was expiring, Jimmy Carrington, the local's newly-elected president, wrote a letter to CF which stated that "any agreements [between the union and CF] become null and void [on] March 31, 1985." The new CBA, which became effective in April 1985, included a maintenance of standards provision[2] and required that any local standards not already included in the CBA be "reduce[d] to writing." The new contract failed to specify procedures for the assignment of peddle runs and the *quid pro quo* agreement exchanging departure times for seniority rights was not reduced to writing.

In late 1985, Hammontree filed a grievance ("Grievance 180") claiming that his seniority rights had been violated by peddle-run assignment practices. Pursuant to the CBA, Hammontree's grievance was heard by a "Multi–State Grievance Committee" composed of an equal number of union and management representatives. This committee failed to resolve the grievance, which Hammontree then pursued to the next level, the Southern Area Grievance Committee. That committee sustained Hammontree's claim and awarded him damages.

Thereafter, CF stopped posting run departure times. Hammontree then filed a second grievance ("Grievance 101") claiming, *inter alia,* that the removal of run times violated the maintenance of standards provision. The first-level grievance committee denied the claim. Hammontree then filed an unfair labor practice ("ULP") charge, and the NLRB's General Counsel issued a complaint, alleging that by removing departure times in response to Hammontree's exercise of his grievance rights (in Grievance

---

**1.** Throughout the dissent, Hammontree is characterized as a "dissident member of the union," Dissent ("Diss.") at 1505, and as "at odds with his union's leadership," id. at 1516. These characterizations, if true, are atmospherics only; the record contains absolutely no evidence of any hostility between Hammontree and the union in regard to this dispute. As discussed below, infra Part II. B. 1, this lack of hostility is indeed significant to our analysis.

**2.** Article 6 of the CBA provides, in relevant part:

> The Employer agrees, subject to the following provisions, that all conditions of employment in his individual operation relating to * * * working conditions shall be maintained at not less than the highest standards in effect at the time of the signing of this Agreement * * *.

180) and by assigning Hammontree less desirable runs, CF had violated §§ 8(a)(1) and 8(a)(3) of the NLRA.

* * * CF contended [that] the Board should refer the claim to the grievance procedures established under the CBA, because the contract, like § 8(a), bars discrimination against union members.... The Board held that under its policy set forth in *United Technologies Corp.*, 268 N.L.R.B. 557 (1984), Hammontree was required to exhaust the grievance procedures established by the CBA. *Consolidated Freightways Corp.*, 288 N.L.R.B. 1252 (1988). Hammontree seeks review of the Board's order.

B.  *The NLRB's "Deferral" Policies*

This case concerns one of the Board's two "deferral" policies, its so-called "pre-arbitral deferral" policy. Under this policy, the Board refers complaints filed by the General Counsel to arbitration procedures established in the governing CBA; in doing so, the Board *defers* or delays its consideration of the complaint. Under a separate, so-called "post-arbitral deferral" policy, not directly implicated in this case, the Board shows limited *deference* to decisions made through grievance and arbitration processes pursuant to collective bargaining provisions.[7]

As this discussion suggests, the Board's two "deferral" policies operate in different ways and serve different purposes. Pre-arbitral deferral (what we will, for clarity's sake, call *"deferment"*) resembles the exhaustion requirements often found in administrative regimes and the abstention doctrines employed by federal courts. Post-arbitral deferral (what we will call *"deference"*) resembles appellate judicial deference. * * *

II.  Analysis

The central issue in this case, whether the Board may require an individual employee to exhaust grievance procedures prior to filing a ULP charge, is governed by the now-familiar two-step analysis set forth in Chevron U.S.A., Inc. v. Natural Resources Defense Council, 467 U.S. 837, 104 S.Ct. 2778, 81 L.Ed.2d 694 (1984). Under *Chevron,* we first determine "whether Congress has directly spoken to the precise question at issue"; if it has, then "that intention is the law and must be given effect." *Chevron,* 467 U.S. at 842–43 & n. 9, 104 S.Ct. at 2781–82 & n. 9. If the statute is "silent or ambiguous with respect to the specific issue," and if "the agency's answer is based on a permissible construction of the statute," we must defer. Id. at 843, 104 S.Ct. at 2782. Part A reviews the petitioner's *"Chevron I"* contentions that the NLRA and the LMRA affirmatively prohibit Board deferment in this case. Part B considers the petitioner's

---

7. The CBA in this case provides for multiple levels of grievance proceedings, but does not provide for final and binding arbitration by a neutral arbitrator. Nonetheless, in this court and others, "bipartite committee grievance resolution procedures and decisions have been upheld as equivalent to arbitra- tion." American Freight System, Inc. v. NLRB, 722 F.2d 828, 830 n. 4 (D.C.Cir.1983)(collecting authorities). There- fore, references to "arbitration" in this opin- ion should be read to include grievance pro- ceedings such as those at issue in this case.

*"Chevron II"* arguments that the Board's decision was an impermissible exercise of its discretion and a departure from established Board policy.

A.   Chevron I *Analysis*

1.   *Section 10(a) of the NLRA*

Section 10(a) of the NLRA provides that the Board's power to "prevent * * * unfair labor practice[s]" "shall not be affected by any other means of adjustment or prevention that has been or may be established by agreement, law, or otherwise * * *." 29 U.S.C. § 160(a). Relying on his reading of the plain meaning and legislative history of § 10(a), Hammontree argues that this section prohibits Board deferment of his claim. We disagree and find that § 10(a) does not reflect any express congressional intention to preclude the Board's imposition of exhaustion requirements in cases such as Hammontree's.

Hammontree first contends that the plain language of § 10(a) prohibits Board deferment of his claim; he reads that section as providing that no one (not even the Board itself) may diminish the Board's authority to resolve and prevent ULPs in the first instance. Although read literally and in isolation, § 10(a) might permit such an interpretation, a far more natural reading is that § 10(a) is an affirmative grant of authority to the Board, not an express limitation on the Board's authority. In other words, a more plausible reading of § 10(a) is that no one *other than* the Board shall diminish the Board's authority over ULP claims.

This latter interpretation is supported by a contemporary congressional analysis which explained that the contested sentence "is intended to make it clear that although *other* agencies may be established by code, agreement, or law to handle labor disputes, such *other* agencies can never divest the National Labor Relations Board of jurisdiction which it would otherwise have." Staff of Senate Comm. on Education and Labor, 74th Cong., 1st Sess., Comparison of S. 2926 (73d Congress) and S. 1958 (74th Congress) at 3 (Comm. Print 1935)(emphasis supplied) [hereinafter "Comparison"] reprinted in NLRB, 1 Legislative History of the National Labor Relations Act 1319, 1323 (1949) [hereinafter "Leg.Hist. of the NLRS"]. As that analysis indicates, Congress was concerned about other entities—such as states or industrial boards—infringing upon the Board's jurisdiction; Congress was not concerned about the Board itself deferring the exercise of its own jurisdiction. Thus, contrary to Hammontree's contention, § 10(a) is most logically read as an affirmative grant of power, firmly establishing the Board as the "Supreme Court of Labor." Comparison at 30, reprinted in 1 Leg.Hist. of the NLRA at 1357. * * *

For these reasons, we must disagree with the petitioner's contention that § 10(a) evidences a clear intent to preclude the Board from deferring consideration of a ULP claim until the claimant has exhausted grievance remedies under the CBA.

## 2. *Section 203(d) of the LMRA*

Hammontree also argues that the Board's deferment authority is limited by § 203(d) of the LMRA, which provides that "[f]inal adjustment by a method agreed upon by the parties is declared to be the desirable method for settlement of grievance disputes *arising over the application or interpretation* of an existing collective-bargaining agreement." 29 U.S.C. § 173(d)(emphasis supplied). Hammontree contends that his claim does not "arise over" the interpretation of the CBA and thus that deferment of his claim is not authorized by § 203(d)'s mandate. We conclude, however, that Hammontree's claim falls squarely within the scope of § 203(d) and accordingly that that section in no way precludes the Board's deferment of Hammontree's claim. * * *

Initially, we observe that § 203(d) reads most naturally as a general policy statement in favor of private dispute resolution, not as any kind of limitation on Board authority. But even if we were to assume *arguendo* that § 203(d) does in some way limit the Board's deferment authority, Hammontree's argument fails on its own terms, for his § 8(a)(3) claim *does* "aris[e] over [contract] application or interpretation." Hammontree's discrimination claim, although raised under §§ 8(a)(1) and 8(a)(3), is also actionable under the contract. Article 21 of the CBA prohibits "discrimination against any employee because of Union membership or activities" and Article 37 of the CBA bars "discriminatory acts prohibited by law." These provisions led the Board to conclude that the alleged discrimination "is clearly prohibited by the contract." 288 N.L.R.B. at 1255. * * *

Hammontree cannot nullify his contractual claim simply by choosing to pursue his statutory claim. Such an interpretation of the law would severely undermine Congress' "decided preference for private settlement of labor disputes without the intervention of government" as reflected in § 203(d). United Paperworkers International Union v. Misco, Inc., 484 U.S. 29, 37, 108 S.Ct. 364, 370, 98 L.Ed.2d 286 (1987). If a party could unilaterally release itself from a contractual pledge to submit complaints to arbitration simply because it had a parallel claim under the statute, then the pro-private dispute resolution policies of § 203(d) would be substantially abrogated.[15]

Hammontree's complaint, therefore, clearly arises under Articles 21 and 37 of the CBA. As such, any limitations on the Board's deferment

---

**15.** The dissent's suggestion that § 203(d)'s preference for private dispute resolution is only involved when "the [individual] employee has [ ] *voluntarily* submitted his [ ]claim to arbitration," Diss. at 1510 (emphasis supplied), is similarly infirm. To contend that Congress' "decided preference"— and a collectively bargained arbitration clause—can be automatically defeated at the option of an aggrieved employee is not only contrary to congressional intent, but also in-

consistent with the fundamental tenet of labor law that a sound collective-bargaining agreement binds all employees. Moreover, as the Board noted, the dissent's view "would mean * * * that a union could circumvent the contractual grievance procedure by the simple expedient of having the individual employee, instead of the union, file the charge with the Board." *Consolidated Freightways Corp.*, 288 N.L.R.B. 1252, 1255 (1988).

authority arguably created by § 203(d) do not affect Hammontree's claim, and § 203(d) does not preclude Board deferment of that claim. * * *

B.   Chevron II *Analysis*

1.   *Limitations on the Board's Deferment Authority*

Hammontree argues under the second prong of *Chevron* that, even if Congress did not expressly limit the Board's deferment authority in the NLRA and the LMRA, its action in his case is based on an impermissible construction of the Board's authority under those statutes. Hammontree contends that Board deferment in cases in which individual employee rights are at stake is inconsistent with a series of Supreme Court decisions beginning with Alexander v. Gardner–Denver Co., 415 U.S. 36, 94 S.Ct. 1011, 39 L.Ed.2d 147 (1974). We find the alleged conflict illusory.

In *Alexander,* the Supreme Court held that Title VII creates individual statutory rights that supplement, rather than supplant, contractual rights under a CBA. Accordingly, the Court held that an employee's use of arbitration procedures did not bar a subsequent action, based on the same facts, brought in federal court under Title VII. The Court reached a similar conclusion in Barrentine v. Arkansas–Best Freight System, Inc., 450 U.S. 728, 101 S.Ct. 1437, 67 L.Ed.2d 641 (1981)(considering an analogous claim brought under the Fair Labor Standards Act ("FLSA")) and in McDonald v. West Branch, 466 U.S. 284, 104 S.Ct. 1799, 80 L.Ed.2d 302 (1984)(considering a first amendment claim brought under 42 U.S.C. § 1983). In each of these cases, the Court ruled that Congress (in Title VII, the FLSA, and § 1983) provided a public forum for individual-rights claims and that participation in private arbitration must not diminish one's right to such a forum. Hammontree reads these cases broadly, for the proposition that "individual statutory rights cannot be sacrificed on the altar of arbitration." Thus, Hammontree maintains that these cases limit the Board's discretion to defer claims in which an individual seeks to vindicate personal rights under the NLRA.

We disagree. In *Alexander, Barrentine,* and *McDonald,* the Supreme Court held that, when individual statutory rights are at stake, arbitration of a contractual claim does not preclude a subsequent statutory claim. In this case, however, we consider not the preclusive effect of arbitration awards but rather the Board's authority to require the exhaustion of arbitration remedies. These issues are analytically distinct. To give an arbitration award preclusive effect would destroy an individual's right to a public forum for the protection of her statutory rights; Board deferment does not similarly nullify an employee's rights under the Act. As the Board has stated:

> [D]eferral is not akin to abdication. It is merely the prudent exercise of restraint, a postponement of the use of the Board's processes to give the parties' own dispute resolution machinery a chance to succeed.

*United Technologies,* 268 N.L.R.B. at 560. Deferment does not diminish Hammontree's right to a public forum; it merely delays it.

Moreover, cases following *Alexander* and suggesting that an exhaustion requirement would be inconsistent with Title VII are also not dispositive, for Title VII and the NLRA differ in several critical ways. First, under Title VII, Congress has expressly recognized that private dispute resolution and statutory relief are distinct and independent remedies; in contrast, under the NLRA, Congress has expressly legislated a preference for the use of private remedies, whenever feasible, before the resort to public remedies. * * *

We, like the Board, recognize that in some circumstances justice deferred could be justice denied. As we emphasized in approving the Board's *Collyer* policy, deferment is a "balancing rule which requires deferral to arbitration only where a balance of * * * policies favors deferral." *Local Union No. 2188,* 494 F.2d at 1090. Thus, if deferment posed "an undue financial burden upon one of the parties," or "prevent[ed] an orderly exposition of the law," or if "anti-union animus [indicated] that deferral * * * would be a futile gesture," or if arbitration would render a subsequent statutory claim untimely, then deferment might be impermissible. See *Local Union No. 2188,* 494 F.2d at 1091. As evidenced by the multi-factor analysis in its *Collyer* and *United Technologies* doctrines, the Board has also long recognized these limitations. However, in this case there is no indication that Board deferment taken along [sic] will prejudice Hammontree's right to a public forum should his claim be denied at grievance proceedings.

We also recognize that Board deferment may be impermissible if charges are filed by an individual employee and the interests of the charging party are so inimical to those of the union as to render arbitration an empty exercise. Like our dissenting colleague, we are sensitive to the "possibility that [in some cases] the interests of the union may diverge from those of the employee." Diss. at 1516. Board abstention in such cases might indeed "constitute[ ]not deference, but abdication." *Local Union No. 2188,* 494 F.2d at 1091. Thus, the Board only defers if it holds a " 'reasonable belief that arbitration procedures would resolve the dispute' " and has " 'refused to defer where the interests of the union * * * are adverse to those of the employee.' " *United Technologies,* 268 N.L.R.B. at 560 ... In this case, however, the record contains no suggestion of such hostility between the union and Hammontree and, as a result, the grievance procedures offer some hope of resolving Hammontree's discrimination claim.[32]

More broadly, we find that the Board's policy of deferment represents a reasonable construction of the Board's statutory duties and authority

---

**32.** There is absolutely no evidence in the record to support the dissent's assertion that the dispute-resolution mechanism in this case is "a sham grievance proceeding," Diss. at 1515, or a meaningless "drumhead pro- ceeding," id. at 1516. Empirically, it seems most unlikely, for, as noted above, Hammontree's first grievance was, in fact, *successfully* resolved in his favor.

under the NLRA and the LMRA. Courts have long recognized a "principle of deference" in reviewing agency actions " 'involv[ing] reconciling [potentially] conflicting policies.' " *Chevron*, 467 U.S. at 844, 104 S.Ct. at 2782 (citations omitted). * * * The Board's deferment policy simultaneously recognizes the need for the prompt resolution of ULP claims, the importance of individual statutory rights, the limitations on Board resources, and the salutary effects of arbitration and minimal governmental intervention in labor disputes. Accordingly, the Board's deferment policy constitutes a reasonable accommodation of its multiple statutory obligations. * * *

III.   Conclusion

In summary, we find that the NLRA and the LMRA do not preclude the Board from requiring a claimant to exhaust contractual grievance remedies before the Board hears a § 8(a)(3) discrimination claim. We also find that the Board's deferment policy is reasonable and is informed by a permissible construction of the Board's various statutory obligations, and that the Board's order in this case was wholly consistent with that policy. Accordingly, we deny the petition for review.

■ EDWARDS, CIRCUIT JUDGE, concurring.

I do not view the issue posed in this case as raising a difficult question. Indeed, in light of well established legal precedent (including the case law commanding deference to the judgment of the Board on the issue at hand), I think that no serious challenge can be raised to the Board's policy of deferment with respect to arbitral issues. I write separately, however, to indicate why, in my view, this is not a difficult issue, and also to underscore certain points that I believe to be critical to our disposition of this case. * * *

Although it seems clear that there can be no requirement of arbitral deferment under *Alexander* and its progeny, it is equally clear that the *Alexander* line of authority is easily distinguishable from the case at hand. The distinction rests on the fundamental differences between the National Labor Relations Act, as amended, 29 U.S.C. §§ 151–69 (1988)("NLRA"), and the Labor Management Relations Act of 1947, as amended, 29 U.S.C. §§ 141–67, 171–87 (1988)("LMRA"), and the statutes at issue in *Alexander, Barrentine, McDonald, et al.*

Under Title VII, the FLSA and section 1983, Congress emphasized that private dispute resolution mechanisms and statutory claims are separate and independent remedies; under the collective bargaining statutes, however, as manifested in section 203(d) of the LMRA, 29 U.S.C. § 173(d) (1988), Congress expressed a strong preference for the use of private remedies. And while rights protected by Title VII, the FLSA and section 1983 are individual in nature, the NLRA and the LMRA are designed to protect both individual and collective rights, and have as their paramount goal the promotion of labor peace through the collective efforts of labor and management. Thus, while courts have the undivided responsibility to adjudicate claims of individual discrimination under Title VII and section 1983, the Board is charged with fostering the overall well-being of labor-management relations, which may be best accomplished by requiring the parties to seek to resolve their disputes through contractual dispute resolution mechanisms.

Most tellingly, in the *Alexander* line of cases, the Supreme Court has flatly rejected arguments suggesting that statutory rights may be waived by an agreement to arbitrate disputes arising under a collective bargaining agreement. . . .

In stark contrast, the Court has explicitly recognized that, because a union represents collective interests, it may waive certain NLRA rights of its members. In Metropolitan Edison Co. v. NLRB, 460 U.S. 693, 103 S.Ct. 1467, 75 L.Ed.2d 387 (1983), the Court stated that it had long "recognized that a union may waive a member's statutorily protected rights * * *. Such waivers are valid because they rest on the premise of fair representation and presuppose that the selection of the bargaining representative remains free * * *. Thus a union may bargain away its members' economic rights, but it may not surrender rights that impair the employees' choice of their bargaining representative." Id. at 705–06, 103 S.Ct. at 1476 (quotation marks omitted). The Court rejected the argument that only collective, as opposed to individual, NLRA rights are subject to union waiver, expressly distinguishing its holding in *Alexander* that a union cannot waive its employees' individual Title VII rights. The Court indicated that the possibility of waiver of statutory rights depends upon the "purposes of the statute at issue," and stated that, unlike Title VII, the NLRA "contemplates that individual rights may be waived by the union so long as the union does not breach its duty of good-faith representation." Id. at 706–07 n. 11, 103 S.Ct. at 1476 n. 11.

* * * Consistent with these cases, I believe that, in light of the parties' agreement prohibiting discrimination and requiring arbitration, Hammontree was properly required by the Board to arbitrate his grievance pursuant to the terms of the collective bargaining contract. The parties to the collective agreement chose to supplant statutory rights with analogous rights created under the contract, and they provided that disputes concerning those rights would be resolved pursuant to an agreed-upon grievance procedure. Giving legal effect to that agreement respects the private ordering of rights and responsibilities established through collective bargaining, and fosters the strong labor policy of promoting industrial peace through arbitration. Consequently, Board deferment in the case is clearly permissible.

* * * If a union has the acknowledged power to "bargain away" its employees' "statutorily protected rights" under the NLRA, the Board can certainly decline to exercise its jurisdiction when the union takes the lesser step of simply agreeing to have its members' rights vindicated in an arbitral, rather than Board, forum. Accordingly, Board deferment in this case is hardly problematic. * * *

■ Mikva, Chief Judge, dissenting: * * *

Discussion

This case involves the intersection of two congressional policies: preventing unfair labor practices and fostering the collective bargaining process. Because the collective bargaining agreement between the Teamsters Union and Consolidated contains two provisions forbidding unlawful company discrimination against employees for exercising union rights, the court holds that deferring Hammontree's discrimination charges to arbitration was proper. However, since Hammontree did not pursue his claims under the non-discrimination clauses in the contract, and never consented to arbitration of his statutory claims, this is a straightforward example of the Board abdicating its responsibility to protect rank-and-file workers from their own unions as well as their employers.

A.  *Congressional Enactments*

1.  The Wagner Act.

There can be no dispute that the Wagner Act gave the Board exclusive power to prevent unfair labor practices. Section 10(a) of the Act, 29 U.S.C. § 160(a)(1988), provides in pertinent part:

> The Board is empowered to prevent * * * any person from engaging in any unfair labor practice (listed in Section 8) affecting commerce. This power shall not be affected by any other means of adjustment or prevention that has been or may be established by agreement, law, or otherwise * * *.

The court contends that the section merely "empowers" the Board and in no way constrains its discretion to defer disputes to private arbitration. If this is correct, it is hard to understand why the proviso in the second sentence was even necessary. In fact, a review of the Act's legislative history demonstrates an alternative motivation, namely a clear directive *not* to let private parties interfere with the Board's congressionally mandated function. Furthermore, contrary to the majority's suggestion, the legislative history of the Act and its subsequent amendments confirms that there is no generalized preference for arbitration that would trump an individual employee's right under § 10(a) to have the Board consider his discrimination charges. * * *

2.  The Taft–Hartley Act.

The preference for arbitration of disputes involving the application or interpretation of a collective bargaining agreement was added by § 203(d) of the Labor–Management Relations ("Taft–Hartley") Act in 1947. After initially charging the Board with preventing unfair labor practices through the Wagner Act, Congress subsequently carved out a limited preference for allowing parties to a collective bargaining agreement to resolve any disputes over that agreement in a manner agreed upon by them. * * *

But this case does not require any application or interpretation of the collective bargaining agreement, and Hammontree never agreed to give up his statutory protections against discrimination by the very parties to the collective bargaining agreement. There is nothing that would dilute the unambiguous command of § 10(a). * * *

The preference for arbitration is simply not involved in a case where the employee has not voluntarily submitted his discrimination claim to arbitration. The court's reasoning may well encourage the routine inclusion of contract provisions that merely incorporate the National Labor Relations Act by reference. If this does not wipe out the statutory rights guaranteed to rank-and-file workers, it certainly assures that their vindication will be substantially diminished and unnecessarily delayed * * * *

### 3. The Landrum–Griffin Act.

Perhaps nowhere is congressional concern for the well-being of the individual employee vis-a-vis the powerful union more manifest than in the Landrum–Griffin Act (the Labor–Management Reporting and Disclosure Act of 1959). The Act was passed at a time when union corruption was perceived to be widespread and individual employees were powerless to prevent abusive union tactics. In response, title I of Landrum–Griffin created a bill of rights for union members guaranteeing equal rights for all employees, including freedom of speech and the right to sue. See 29 U.S.C. § 411 (1988). It is clear from the legislative history of Landrum–Griffin that Congress no longer was willing to assume that the rights of individual employees would be adequately protected by the unions. * * *

* * * Thus, the Board's current policy of deferring individual unfair labor practice claims to grievance committees composed of company and union representatives interdicts its primary statutory responsibility to protect the rights of individual employees. * * *

### B. *Statutory Interpretation and Agency Practice*

The court has to overcome all of the plain language and legislative history hurdles described above to even reach the question of whether the Board's interpretation of the statute was reasonable and entitled to deference. * * * When the language of § 10(a) is viewed in tandem with legislative intent and with other parts of the Act (especially in light of the Landrum–Griffin amendments), the statutory question can be settled under step one of *Chevron* rather than shunted into the lazy deference of step two. I believe that the Board violated Congress' clear intent when it deferred Hammontree's statutory claims. Even if we must proceed to step two, however, the court errs in ignoring *Chevron's* requirement that a court gauge the reasonableness of an agency's interpretation by looking at the statute as a whole.

* * * [U]ntil this case, no court has ever sanctioned deferral where the employee did *not* request arbitration and no portion of the claims rested upon a contractual matter. * * * In this case, Hammontree did *not* agree to arbitration of his discrimination claims and those claims are wholly separate from any questions of contract interpretation. The union merely created an additional procedure whereby it could arbitrate statutory claims. Absent a conscious waiver by the employee of those statutory rights or a

decision to effectuate those rights under the parallel non-discrimination provisions of the collective bargaining agreement, Board deferral was inappropriate. * * *

## C.   *The Waiver Doctrine*

No one disputes the fact that Hammontree's unfair labor practice charges properly arise under the substantive prohibitions contained in sections 7 and 8(a) of the Act, 29 U.S.C. §§ 157, 158(a)(1) & (3), although counsel for the Board now suggests that the inclusion of parallel non-discrimination provisions in the parties' collective bargaining agreement may have waived Hammontree's statutory right to be free from discrimination for engaging in protected activity. A waiver of an employee's statutory rights may not be found unless it is "established clearly and unmistakably." * * * Nor does the arbitration provision by itself waive the statutory rights that might be settled in a grievance proceeding. * * *

The majority maintains that because Articles 21 and 37 in the collective bargaining agreement parallel the nondiscrimination guarantees in the Act, Hammontree's claims of retaliation can properly be submitted to arbitration. However, the fact that the union claims to have bolstered employees' protection against discrimination by negotiating the inclusion of these provisions in the contract would not deprive Hammontree of his preexisting statutory right to bring a claim under section 8(a)(1) and (3) before the Board. An individual's right to freely engage in union activities without fear of retaliation exists independently of any contract and cannot be diminished or diffused by its reiteration in a collective bargaining agreement. * * *

In analogous contexts, the Supreme Court has repeatedly made it clear that the statutory rights of individual employees to present their grievances before a public forum could not be denied by the existence of a private dispute resolution mechanism. [Judge Mikva discussed *Gardner–Denver, Barrentine,* and *McDonald.*] The majority distinguishes these decisions as based on other statutes, but the court thereby ignores the Supreme Court's clear teachings on the general question of deferring employees' claims to arbitration. * * *

One of the reasons for not deferring to arbitration in these cases was the possibility that the union would not fully pursue an employee's statutory rights. * * * Certainly, the joint labor-management arbitration committees at issue here might well choose to address a particular employee's grievances through a generalized give-and-take of union/employee interests, instead of by conscientiously enforcing the terms of the statute. The majority fails to fully appreciate the possibility that the interests of the union may diverge from those of the employee. Indeed, Hammontree was at odds with his union's leadership; restricting him to a drumhead proceeding where his antagonists are viewed as his protectors frustrates the goals of the Act.

D. *Exhaustion of Remedies*

The court contends that this is solely an exhaustion of remedies question and does not foreclose subsequent judicial review in case the grievance committee rejects Hammontree's unfair labor practice claim and the Board summarily affirms that decision. While that characterization may ease the court's conscience, it ignores reality. The Board's precedents amply suggest what will happen if Hammontree's grievance proceeding is ever concluded: it will no doubt defer yet again, according significant deference to the arbitrator's decision. A challenger to an arbitration decision bears the burden of showing that it was repugnant to the Act or that the statutory issues were not fairly decided. See *Olin Corp.,* 268 N.L.R.B. 573 (1984). An individual's right to have the Board review an arbitrator's decision under *Olin*'s highly deferential standard is fundamentally unlike the right to *de novo* consideration of an unfair labor practice claim by the Board. * * *

There are other deficiencies in the Teamsters' grievance mechanism that may well hamper effective review after exhaustion. This is not arbitration in the traditional sense where parties submit their dispute to a neutral third party. After hearing the individual's claim, the joint committee meets in private and either grants or denies the claim without a word of explanation for its decision. Since no record is kept, there is simply no way of knowing that the individual's claim has been fairly decided, let alone the grounds for the curt decision. Such a scenario is particularly unacceptable if the individual employee is, as in this case, at odds with his union leadership. * * *

* * * Deferral to arbitration is perfectly legitimate when the issues submitted to the arbitrator require interpretation of a contract, or when the employee consents to arbitration of his unfair labor practice claim. However, when an unfair labor practice against an employee is involved, and the employee brings the charge before the Board, we ought not allow Board deferral to a potentially hostile or indifferent agent for enforcement of the employee's statutory rights. * * *

---

# PROBLEMS FOR DISCUSSION

**1.** Which opinion in *Hammontree* is ultimately the most convincing? Is it not sufficient justification for pre-arbitral deference that an arbitrator *might* render a decision to which the Board will ultimately defer under the *Olin Corp.* case?

**2.** Will the Board's decision in *United Technologies*—taken along with its decision in *Olin*—all but guarantee that arbitrators will, in any case containing a hint of a potential unfair labor practice, address the issue of statutory violation? Is that a salutary development? Is it likely to have been within the contemplation of those Justices who initially extolled the virtues of labor arbitration and arbitral expertise?

**3.** The company and the union operate under a collective bargaining agreement that provides for promotions on the basis of strict seniority, unless the junior job-bidder is "substantially more qualified" than his or her seniors. When a high-paying production job recently became vacant, a number of employees bid on the job, including Tom Tuff, a member of a dissident movement within the union and an outspoken critic of the current union leadership. The job was awarded to the senior bidder, but Tuff believes that he is "substantially more qualified" than the awardee. He believes that the company discriminated against him because of his activities relating to the union. Tuff has filed a charge with the NLRB under Section 8(a)(3). The company has asked that the Regional Director decline to issue a complaint, in view of the available arbitration procedures under the labor agreement. What advice would you give the Regional Director? (Should it matter whether Tuff has filed a grievance? Should it matter whether the union has, or has not, declined to process any such grievance?) See General Counsel Memorandum 84–10 (June 7, 1984), at 1984 Lab.Rel.Yearbk. (BNA) 360.

**4.** When the Supreme Court in the *Carey* case, p. 808 supra, ordered that arbitration should proceed in the dispute between the IUE and the Federation, and the Company thereafter asked the Board to clarify the certifications of those competing unions, ought the Board have stayed its proceedings pending the outcome of the arbitration? Consider as well the Horn & Hardart problem (problem 5 at p. 825 supra); if the representation petition had been filed before the arbitrator had rendered her decision construing the recognition clause of the labor contract, ought the Board have deferred action on the petition pending arbitration?

**5.** An employee, a union negotiator, was discharged for a rule violation. She alleged it was due to her supervisor's learning of a derogatory report she made about him during management-union negotiations. The grievance-arbitration procedure available under the current collective agreement limits an arbitrator's remedial authority in discharge cases to reinstatement with no more than twenty days' backpay. In light of *C-Catalytic*, *United Technologies*, and *Hammontree*, should the Board refer the case to arbitration? See NLRB v. Roswil, Inc., 55 F.3d 382 (8th Cir.1995).

---

## B.   THE DUTY TO BARGAIN DURING THE TERM OF AN EXISTING AGREEMENT[d]

The major thrust of Section 8(a)(5) when it was originally enacted in 1935 was to compel the employer, after a union had been properly designated as majority employee representative, to acknowledge it as a partner in setting wages, hours and working conditions. The employer was not to be permitted to frustrate the employees' designation simply by refusing outright to recognize and bargain with the union. The question remains whether the duty to bargain is thus discharged upon the execution of the labor contract or whether it imposes upon the parties obligations independent of the contract during the contract term.

During congressional consideration of the Taft–Hartley amendments of 1947, it was suggested that any contract breach should be treated as an unfair labor practice, remediable by the NLRB (in contrast to an arbitra-

**d.** Nelson & Howard, The Duty to Bargain During the Term of an Existing Agreement, 27 Lab.L.J. 573 (1976); Note, Mid– Term Modifications of Terms and Conditions of Employment, 1972 Duke L.J. 813.

tor), but that proposal was rejected. Section 8(d), enacted in 1947, defines the duty to bargain collectively as including the duty to "confer in good faith" with respect to "any question arising" under a labor contract; it also forbids either party during the contract term to "terminate or modify such contract" unless notice is given to the other party sixty days prior to the contract termination date (with notice to federal and state mediation agencies to follow within thirty days) and all contract terms maintained in full force, without strike or lockout, until the expiration of a cooling-off period. Section 8(d) also provides that

> "the duties so imposed shall not be construed as requiring either party to discuss or agree to any modification of the terms and conditions contained in a contract for a fixed period, if such modification is to become effective before such terms and conditions can be reopened under the provisions of the contract."

While it is obvious that Congress intended that the labor contract is to serve as an instrument of stability and repose during its term, it has never been altogether clear how much the Board—in contrast to the arbitrator and the courts—was to play a role in implementing that congressional intention. Thus, while an employer refusal to arbitrate a contract grievance might arguably be a refusal to "confer in good faith" on a "question arising" under the contract, the normal procedure is to treat this simply as the breach of a contract promise to arbitrate, remediable by a court action under Section 301. Similarly, while a strike during the term of a contract in support of demands which an arbitrator would not sustain might be viewed as a strike to "modify" the contract—called without complying with the notice and cooling-off provisions of Section 8(d)—most such strikes are treated as union efforts to support a good-faith claim as to the meaning of the contract terms (and not their "modification"), which are actionable, if at all, not through the NLRB but through the grievance and arbitration procedures of the contract.

The National Labor Relations Board has itself given considerable credibility to the assertion that midterm conduct by the employer or the union should properly be challenged through contract-breach procedures rather than through unfair labor practice procedures. That, indeed, is the thrust of the Board's "deferral" jurisprudence, particularly its decision in *Collyer Insulated Wire,* see pp. 829–31 supra.

There are, however, a number of significant situations in which Section 8(a)(5) plays a role in determining the powers and duties of the employer during the contract term. Does the employer have a duty, for example, to bargain in good faith over "mandatory" mid-term contract proposals presented by the union—even as to matters resolved or discussed at the bargaining table when the present contract was negotiated? Does the statute curtail the employer's freedom to modify the express terms of the contract, even after bargaining with the union in good faith to impasse? These and related matters are the issues explored in the following cases.

————

# Jacobs Manufacturing Co.

94 NLRB 1214 (1951).

■ * * * In July 1948, the Respondent and the Union executed a 2–year bargaining contract which, by its terms, could be reopened 1 year after its execution date for discussion of "wage rates." In July 1949 the Union invoked the reopening clause of the 1948 contract, and thereafter gave the Respondent written notice of its "wage demands." In addition to a request for a wage increase, these demands included a request that the Respondent undertake the entire cost of an existing group insurance program, and another request for the establishment of a pension plan for the Respondent's employees. When the parties met thereafter to consider the Union's demands, the Respondent refused to discuss the Union's pension and insurance requests on the ground that they were not appropriate items of discussion under the reopening clause of the 1948 contract.

The group insurance program to which the Union alluded in its demands was established by the Respondent before 1948. It was underwritten by an insurance company, and provided life, accident, health, surgical, and hospital protection. All the Respondent's employees were eligible to participate in the program, and the employees shared its costs with the Respondent. When the 1948 contract was being negotiated, the Respondent and the Union had discussed changes in this *insurance program,* and had agreed to increase certain of the benefits as well as the costs. However, neither the changes thereby effected, nor the insurance program itself, was mentioned in the 1948 contract.

As indicated by the Union's request, there was no pension plan for the Respondent's employees in existence in 1949. The subject of *pensions,* moreover, had not been discussed during the 1948 negotiations; and, like insurance, that subject is not mentioned in the 1948 contract.

a. For the reasons stated below, Chairman Herzog and Members Houston and Styles agree with the Trial Examiner's conclusion that the Respondent violated Section 8(a)(5) of the Act by refusing to discuss the matter of *pensions* with the Union. * * *

We are satisfied * * * that the 1948 contract did not in itself impose on the Respondent any obligation to discuss pensions or insurance. The reopening clause of that contract refers to *wage rates,* and thus its intention appears to have been narrowly limited to matters directly related to the amount and manner of compensation for work. For that reason, a requirement to discuss pensions or insurance cannot be predicated on the language of the contract.

On the other hand, a majority of the Board believes that, regardless of the character of the reopening clause, the Act itself imposed upon the Respondent the duty to discuss *pensions* with the Union during the period in question.

It is now established as a principle of law that the matter of pensions is a subject which falls within the area where the statute requires bargaining.

And, as noted above, the 1948 contract between the Respondent and the Union was silent with respect to the subject of pensions; indeed, the matter had never been raised or discussed by the parties. The issue raised, therefore, is whether the Respondent was absolved of the obligation to discuss pensions because of the limitation contained in Section 8(d) of the amended Act dealing with the duty to discuss or agree to the modification of an existing bargaining contract. The pertinent portion of Section 8(d) of the Act provides:

> * * * the duties so imposed shall not be construed as requiring either party to discuss or agree to any modification of the terms and conditions contained in a contract for a fixed period, if such modification is to become effective before such terms and conditions can be reopened under the provisions of the contract.

* * * The crucial point at issue here * * * is the construction to be given the phrase "terms and conditions *contained in* a contract." (Emphasis supplied.) The Board, in the *Tide Water* case [Tide Water Assoc. Oil Co., 85 N.L.R.B. 1096], concluded that the pertinent portion of Section 8(d)

> *refers to terms and conditions which have been integrated and embodied into a writing.* * * * With respect to unwritten terms dealing with "wages, hours and other terms and conditions of employment," the obligation remains on both parties to bargain continuously.

Thus, as already construed by this Board in the *Tide Water* case, Section 8(d) does not itself license a party to a bargaining contract to refuse, during the life of the contract, to discuss a bargainable subject unless it has been made a part of the agreement itself. Applied here, therefore, the *Tide Water* construction of Section 8(d) means that the Respondent was obligated to discuss the Union's pension demand.

Members Houston and Styles have carefully reexamined the Board's construction of Section 8(d) in the *Tide Water* case, and are persuaded that the view the Board adopted in the *Tide Water* case best effectuates the declared policy of the Act. Chairman Herzog, while joining in the result with respect to the obligation to bargain here concerning pensions—never previously discussed by the parties—joins in the rationale herein *only* to the extent that it is consistent with his views separately recited below, concerning the insurance program.

By making mandatory the discussion of bargainable subjects not already covered by a contract, the parties to the contract are encouraged to arrive at joint decisions with respect to bargainable matters, that, at least to the party requesting discussion, appear at the time to be of some importance. The Act's policy of "encouraging the practice and procedure of collective bargaining" is consequently furthered. A different construction of Section 8(d) in the circumstances—one that would permit a party to a bargaining contract to avoid discussion when it was sought on subject matters not contained in the contract—would serve, at its best, only to dissipate whatever the good will that had been engendered by the previous bargaining negotiations that led to the execution of a bargaining contract; at its worst, it could bring about the industrial strife and the production interruptions that the policy of the Act also seeks to avert.

The significance of this point cannot be overemphasized. It goes to the heart of our disagreement with our dissenting colleague, Member Reynolds. His dissent stresses the need for "contract stability," and asserts that the furtherance of sound collective bargaining requires that the collective bargaining agreement be viewed as fixing, for the term of the contract, all aspects of the employer-employee relationship, and as absolving either party of the obligation to discuss, during that term, even those matters which had never been raised, or discussed in the past. We could hardly take issue with the virtue of "contract stability," at least in the abstract, and we would certainly agree that everyone is better off when, in negotiating an agreement, the parties have been able to foresee what all the future problems may be, to discuss those problems, and either to embody a resolution of them in the contract, or to provide that they may not be raised again during the contract. But we are here concerned with the kind of case in which, for one reason or another, this has *not* been done, and the question is what best effectuates the policies of the Act in *such* a case.
* * *

The construction of Section 8(d) adopted by the Board in the *Tide Water* case serves also to simplify, and thus to speed, the bargaining process. It eliminates the pressure upon the parties at the time when a contract is being negotiated to raise those subjects that may not then be of controlling importance, but which might in the future assume a more significant status. It also assures to both unions and employers that, if future conditions require some agreement as to matters about which the parties have not sought, or have not been able to obtain agreement, then some discussion of those matters will be forthcoming when necessary.

We cannot believe that Congress was unaware of the foregoing considerations when it amended the Act by inserting Section 8(d), or that it sought, by the provision in question, to freeze the bargaining relationship by eliminating any mandatory discussion that might lead to the addition of new subject matter to an existing contract. What Section 8(d) does do is to reject the pronouncements contained in some pre–1947 Board and court decisions—sometimes *dicta,* sometimes necessary to the holding—to the effect that the duty to bargain continues even as to those matters upon which the parties have reached agreement and which are set forth in the terms of a written contract. But we believe it does no more. Those bargainable issues which have never been discussed by the parties, and which are in no way treated in the contract, remain matters which both the union and the employer are obliged to discuss at any time.

In so holding, we emphasize that under this rule, no less than in any other circumstance, the duty to bargain implies only an obligation to *discuss* the matter in question in good faith with a sincere purpose of reaching some agreement. It does not require that either side agree, or make concessions. And if the parties originally desire to avoid later discussion with respect to matters not specifically covered in the terms of an executed contract, they need only so specify in the terms of the contract itself. Nothing in our construction of Section 8(d) precludes such an agreement, entered into in good faith, from foreclosing future discussion of matters not contained in the agreement.[13]

b.  Chairman Herzog, for reasons set forth in his separate opinion, believes that—unlike the pensions issue—the Respondent was under no obligation to bargain concerning the *group insurance program.*[14]

However, Members Houston and Styles—a minority of the Board on this issue—are of the further opinion that the considerations discussed above leading to the conclusion that the Respondent was obligated to discuss the matter of pensions, also impel the conclusion that the Respondent was obligated to discuss the Union's group insurance demand. * * *

Members Houston and Styles believe, moreover, that the view adopted by Chairman Herzog on the insurance issue is subject to the same basic criticism as is the view of Member Reynolds—it exalts "contract stability" over industrial peace; it eliminates mandatory collective bargaining on subjects about which one of the parties *now* wants discussion, and concerning which it may well be willing to take economic action if discussion is denied, solely because the matter has once been discussed in a manner which may warrant an inference that the failure to mention that subject in the contract was part of the bargain. Members Houston and Styles are constrained to reject the view of Chairman Herzog for the further reason that it would establish a rule which is administratively unworkable, and would inject dangerous uncertainty into the process of collective bargaining. Apart from the extremely difficult problems of proof—illustrated in this very case—which would constantly confront the Board in cases of this type, the parties to collective bargaining negotiations would always be faced with this question after a subject has been *discussed*—"Have we really *negotiated,* or are we under an obligation to discuss the subject further if asked to?" To this query the rule of the *Tide Water* case gives a clear and

---

**13.** For an example of a contract in which such a provision was incorporated, see the contract between United Automobile Workers of America and General Motors Corporation, which states:

> (154) The parties acknowledge that during the negotiations which resulted in this agreement, each had the unlimited right and opportunity to make demands and proposals with respect to any subject or matter not removed by law from the area of collective bargaining, and that the understandings and agreements arrived at by the parties after the exercise of that right and opportunity are set forth in this agreement. Therefore, the Corporation and the Union, for the life of this agreement, each voluntarily and un-

qualifiedly waives the right, and each agrees that the other shall not be obligated, to bargain collectively with respect to any subject or matter not specifically referred to or covered in this agreement, even though such subjects or matter may not have been within the knowledge or contemplation of either or both of the parties at the time that they negotiated or signed this agreement.

**14.** *Members Reynolds* and *Murdock* would also find that the Respondent was not obligated to discuss the group insurance program. Their views on the matter likewise are set forth in their separate opinions * * *. The complaint is therefore *dismissed* as to this aspect of the case.

concise answer: "You are obligated to discuss any bargainable subject upon request unless you have reduced your agreement on that subject to writing or unless you have agreed in writing not to bargain about it during the term of the contract." Members Houston and Styles would apply that rule without deviation. * * *

■ CHAIRMAN HERZOG, concurring in part:

I believe that this Respondent was *not* under a duty to discuss the Union's *group insurance* demand. The individual views which lead me, by a different road, to the result reached on this issue by Members Reynolds and Murdock, are as follows:

Unlike the issue of pensions, concerning which the contract is silent and the parties did not negotiate at all in 1948, the subject of group insurance was fully discussed while the Respondent and the Union were negotiating the agreement. True, that agreement is silent on the subject, so it cannot literally be said that there is a term "contained in" the 1948 contract relating to the group insurance program. The fact remains that during the negotiations which preceded its execution, the issue was consciously explored. The record reveals that the Union expressly requested that the preexisting program be changed so that the Respondent would assume its entire cost, the very proposal that was again made as part of the 1949 midterm demand which gave rise to this case. The Respondent rejected the basic proposal on this first occasion, but agreement was then reached—although outside the written contract—to increase certain benefits under the group insurance program.

In my opinion, it is only reasonable to assume that rejection of the Union's basic proposal, coupled in this particular instance with enhancement of the substantive benefits, constituted a part of the contemporaneous "bargain" which the parties made when they negotiated the entire 1948 contract. In the face of this record as to what the parties discussed and did, I believe that it would be an abuse of this Board's mandate to throw the weight of Government sanction behind the Union's attempt to disturb, in midterm, a bargain sealed when the original agreement was reached.

To hold otherwise would encourage a labor organization—or, in a Section 8(b)(3) case, an employer—to come back, time without number, during the term of a contract, to demand resumed discussion of issues which, although perhaps not always incorporated in the written agreement, the other party had every good reason to believe were put at rest for a definite period. * * * That would serve only to stimulate uncertainty and evasion of commitments at a time when stability should be the order of the day.

■ MEMBER REYNOLDS, concurring separately and dissenting in part:

* * * [I]t is my opinion that Section 8(d) imposes no obligation on either party to a contract to bargain on any matter during the term of the contract except as the express provisions of the contract may demand. This is a result reasonably compatible with the particular Section 8(d) language

involved, as well as with Section 8(d) as a whole. Moreover, not only does the result accord stability and dignity to collective bargaining agreements, but it also gives substance to the practice and procedure of collective bargaining.

It is well established that the function of collective bargaining agreements is to contribute stability, so essential to sound industrial relations. Contractually stabilized industrial relations enable employers, because of fixed labor costs, to engage in sound long-range production planning, and employees, because of fixed wage, seniority, promotion, and grievance provisions, to anticipate secure employment tenure. Hence, when an employer and a labor organization have through the processes of collective bargaining negotiated an agreement containing the terms and conditions of employment for a definite period of time, their total rights and obligations emanating from the employer-employee relationship should remain fixed for that time. Stabilized therefore are the rights and obligations of the parties with respect to all bargainable subjects whether the subjects are or are not specifically set forth in the contract. To hold otherwise and prescribe bargaining on unmentioned subjects would result in continued alteration of the total rights and obligations under the contract, thus rendering meaningless the concept of contract stability.

That a collective bargaining agreement stabilizes all rights and conditions of employment is consonant with the generally accepted concept of the nature of such an agreement. The basic terms and conditions of employment existing at the time the collective bargaining agreement is executed, and which are not specifically altered by, or mentioned in, the agreement, are part of the *status quo* which the parties, by implication, consider as being adopted as an essential element of the agreement. This view is termed "reasonable and logical," and its widespread endorsement as sound industrial relations practice makes it a general rule followed in the arbitration of disputes arising during the term of a contract. The reasonableness of the approach is apparent upon an understanding of collective bargaining techniques. Many items are not mentioned in a collective bargaining agreement either because of concessions at the bargaining table or because one of the parties may have considered it propitious to forego raising one subject in the hope of securing a more advantageous deal on another. Subjects traded off or foregone should, under these circumstances, be as irrevocably settled as those specifically covered and settled by the agreement. To require bargaining on such subjects during midterm debases initial contract negotiations. * * *

Eliminating the duty to bargain in midterm concerning items not mentioned in the contract does not mean that the collective bargaining process ends with the negotiation of the contract. Day-to-day grievances and other disputes arising out of the employer-employee relationship are ever present. The settlement of these matters is part and parcel of the collective bargaining process, and it is in this regard that there remains upon the parties the continuing duty to bargain collectively. * * * Collective bargaining during the term of the contract therefore would be mandatory only with respect to administering or interpreting the terms of the contract in accordance with the procedure outlined in the contract. * * *

■ MEMBER MURDOCK, dissenting in part:

I am unable to agree with my colleagues of the majority that by refusing to discuss pensions and insurance with the Union under the particular circumstances of this case, the Respondent violated Section 8(a)(5) of the Act.

Despite the fact that the reopening clause in the contract which the Union here invoked was limited to "wage rates," the Union included insurance and pensions in its demands thereunder in addition to a wage increase. In my view the Respondent properly took the position that the parties were meeting pursuant to the reopening provision of the contract to discuss wage *rates* and that pensions and insurance were not negotiable thereunder and would not be discussed at that time. * * *

[In NLRB v. JACOBS MFG. Co., 196 F.2d 680 (2d Cir.1952), the court of appeals agreed that the company was obligated to bargain about pensions because that issue was not mentioned in the written agreement and had not been discussed in negotiations. The court did not, however, decide whether discussion of a subject during negotiations relieves the employer of the duty to bargain, upon union request, for the insertion of a new contract provision in mid-term. The Board has generally held that a union in the latter situation will not be deemed to have "waived" its right to have the employer discuss a subject in mid-term unless it has rather clearly manifested an intention to relinquish that right, for example through explicit statements at the bargaining table or by explicit contract provisions; but the Board's application of this principle, and even its adherence to it, has been far from consistent. See Pepsi–Cola Distrib. Co., 241 NLRB 869 (1979).]

## PROBLEM FOR DISCUSSION

Assume that, pursuant to the Board's decision, the Jacobs Co. bargains with the union upon request concerning a pension plan, and that an impasse is reached after two months. (The date is still in the midst of the contract term.) May the union strike? May the union strike after it gives the appropriate notices required under Section 8(d)? Compare United Packinghouse Workers, 89 NLRB 310 (1950), with Local No. 3 United Packinghouse Workers v. NLRB, 210 F.2d 325 (8th Cir.1954), cert. denied, 348 U.S. 822, 75 S.Ct. 36, 99 L.Ed. 648 (1954).

## Johnson–Bateman Co.

295 NLRB 180 (1989).

[The Company announced its unilateral adoption of mandatory alcohol and drug testing of all employees who are injured and require treatment.

The NLRB held that such a policy governing the incumbent complement of employees is a mandatory subject of bargaining. The Board's attention then turned to whether the union had waived its right to bargain. The collective agreement's management-rights clause provided in pertinent part that, "[T]he Company reserves and retains, soley [sic] and exclusively, all of the rights, privileges and prerogatives which it would have in the absence of this Agreement, except to the extent that such rights, privileges and prerogatives are specifically and clearly abridged by express provision [sic] of this Agreement." Further, the contract provision governing discharge provided that "The term 'just cause' shall include ... drinking or possessing any alcoholic beverages on company premises or on company time or reporting for work while under the influence of alcohol or drugs."]

### ■ a. *General Principles*

It is well settled that the waiver of a statutory right will not be inferred from general contractual provisions; rather, such waivers must be clear and unmistakable. Accordingly, the Board has repeatedly held that generally worded management rights clauses or "zipper" clauses will not be construed as waivers of statutory bargaining rights.[23] * * *

Waiver of a statutory right may be evidenced by bargaining history, but the Board requires the matter at issue to have been fully discussed and consciously explored during negotiations and the union to have consciously yielded or clearly and unmistakably waived its interest in the matter.

\* \* \*

Applying these principles to the instant case, we note that the provision in the Management's Rights clause permitting the Respondent unilaterally to issue, enforce, and change company rules is couched in the most general of terms and makes no reference to any particular subject areas, much less a specific reference to drug/alcohol testing.[27] Accordingly, we find

---

**23.** Suffolk Child Development Center, 277 N.L.R.B. 1345, 1350 (1985); Kansas National Education Assn., 275 N.L.R.B. 638, 639 (1985). Cf. Rockford Manor Care Facility, 279 N.L.R.B. 1170 (1986)(employer's unilateral substitution of new health insurance plan not unlawful; union waived right to bargain about carrier-induced changes in health insurance by virtue of contractual agreement to a "highly detailed 'zipper clause' ... and an equally comprehensive management rights clause" demonstrating mutual intent to waive bargaining during term of contract with respect to all subjects left unregulated within the four corners of the contract, and constituting an "incisive, direct, and specific ... assault on the existence of any negotiating responsibility during the term of the contract," thus committing unresolved issues to management prerogative).

**27.** In addition to giving the Respondent the right unilaterally to issue, enforce, and change rules, the Management's Rights clause also reserves to the Respondent the right to discipline or discharge employees for just cause. There is a written work rule specifying that drinking or possessing any alcoholic beverages on company premises or on company time or reporting for work while under the influence of alcohol or drugs constitutes just cause for discharge. However, this work rule is not incorporated or otherwise referred to in the collective-bargaining agreement, but was instead unilaterally promulgated and implemented by the Respondent (albeit without subsequent objection from the Union). There was no discussion or mention during negotiations for the collective-bargaining agreement about the possibility of drug/alcohol testing being used as a method of enforcement of the

that neither the Management's Rights nor zipper clauses * * * constitutes an express, clear, unequivocal, and unmistakable waiver by the Union of its statutory right to bargain about the Respondent's implementation of the instant drug/alcohol testing requirement.

b.  *Contract Interpretation*

We also find, contrary to the Respondent's assertions, that its unilateral implementation of the drug/alcohol testing requirement is not beyond the scope of our consideration as an unfair labor practice on the basis that this issue presents solely a matter of contract interpretation. * * *

Although in the instant case there is no separately negotiated plan dealing with drug/alcohol testing of employees injured while working * * *, we nevertheless find that the express, general provisions of the Management's Rights clause, even standing alone, do not provide the Respondent with a "sound arguable basis" for ascribing to that clause a specific privilege to implement unilaterally the drug/alcohol testing requirement. We have not, therefore, improperly entered this dispute merely to serve the function of an arbitrator who determines a correct interpretation of a contract.

c.  *Contract Negotiations*

Nor is there anything in the bargaining history of the contract to show that the meaning and potential implications of the Management's Rights clause in general, or drug/alcohol testing in particular, were "fully discussed and consciously explored" during negotiations, or that the Union "consciously yielded or clearly and unmistakably waived its interest" in regard to bargaining about the drug/alcohol testing requirement. Indeed, there is nothing in the record to show that drug/alcohol testing was even mentioned, much less discussed, during contract negotiations. According to Union Business Representative Bill Phillips, drug/alcohol testing was not discussed during negotiations for the current collective-bargaining agreement. The Respondent proposed an addition to the seniority clause that would have reserved to the Respondent the right to require laid-off employees to undergo a physical examination as a condition of recall. The Respondent subsequently withdrew this proposal. According to the Respondent's vice president, Larry Johnson, during the negotiations over this proposal there was no discussion of drug testing of employees who had suffered industrial accidents. During the same negotiations, the Respondent proposed to add a new section, entitled "Discharge and Discipline," to the current contract. This proposed section would have reserved to the Respondent the "absolute right" to suspend or discharge employees for,

rule against drug/alcohol use, possession, or influence. Under these circumstances, we find, contrary to our dissenting colleague, that the general contractual rights of the Respondent to make and enforce rules, and to discipline or discharge for just cause, do not constitute a clear and unmistakable waiv-er by the Union of its right to bargain about the implementation of the instant drug/alcohol testing requirement, even if those general contractual rights are coupled with the extra-contractual, unilaterally implemented categorization of the above aspects of drug and alcohol use as just causes for discharge.

inter alia, intoxication or possession of narcotics or alcoholic beverages during working hours. The Respondent also subsequently withdrew this proposal. Johnson did not testify about whether the parties discussed drug/alcohol testing in the context of this proposal.

Further, the Respondent's president, Lewis Johnson, testified that there was never any discussion during contract negotiations "to the effect that" the Management's Rights clause "could not be used for drug testing." We infer from this that there was also no discussion about whether the Management's Rights clause *could* be used for drug testing; again, there is no evidence of any such discussion. In sum, there is no evidence that the parties engaged in any discussion of drug/alcohol testing during contract negotiations, in this or any other context.

Thus, in light of the complete absence of any evidence that the parties discussed drug/alcohol testing during negotiations for the instant collective-bargaining agreement, we will not infer a waiver by the Union of its right to bargain about that subject.

### d. *Arbitration Award*

We also do not find that the 1983 arbitration award * * * constitutes, or is evidence of, a waiver by the Union of its right to bargain about the drug/alcohol testing requirement or in any other way privileged the Respondent's unilateral implementation of that requirement. First, in finding that the Respondent "has a right to make rules to manage the plant, provided that those rules do not violate the collective bargaining agreement," the arbitration award does not give the Respondent a right that is any broader or more inclusive than the rights expressly reserved to the Respondent under the contractual Management's Rights clause itself. We have, of course, already found that this clause itself does not constitute a waiver by the Union of its right to bargain about the instant drug/alcohol testing requirement. Consequently, we find that the 1983 arbitration award does not constitute such a waiver by the Union.

Second, the extra-contractual written work rule involved in the 1983 arbitration—that employees who are unable to work scheduled overtime must provide advance written notice of and reasons for that inability—was found by the arbitrator to be directly related to, consistent with, and a reasonable refinement of the specific express contractual provision that employees would not unreasonably refuse to work scheduled overtime. Here, on the other hand, the extra-contractual written rule requiring drug/alcohol testing of employees who are injured while working is not related to any express term or provision in the collective-bargaining agreement. Indeed, as seen, the only contractual basis asserted by the Respondent as justification for its unilateral implementation of drug/alcohol testing is the Management's Rights clause itself—a basis which we have found not to support this claim.[32]

* * *

---

**32.** The Supreme Court's opinion in Metropolitan Edison Co. v. NLRB, 460 U.S. 693 (1983), is relevant to this aspect of our discussion. There, the Court held that the

e.  *Past Practices*

Finally, we do not find that the Union's acquiescence in either the Respondent's unilateral implementation of the requirement that new employees undergo drug/alcohol testing at the time of their hiring, or the Respondent's unilateral implementation of numerous work rules * * * constitutes a waiver by the Union of its right to bargain about the drug/alcohol testing requirement for employees who are injured while working. First, as to the requirement that new employees undergo drug/alcohol testing, a union's past acquiescence in an employer's unilateral action on a particular subject generally does not, without more, constitute a waiver by that union of any right it may have to bargain about future action by the employer in that matter. As the Board majority found in Owens–Corning Fiberglas, 282 N.L.R.B. 609 (1987), the fact that an employer previously changed the terms of a particular program without bargaining does not preclude a union from effectively demanding to bargain over the most recent change in the program: "A union's acquiescence in previous unilateral changes does not operate as a waiver of its right to bargain over such changes for all time." Id. (citations omitted). Thus, we find that the Union's acquiescence in the drug/alcohol testing requirement for new employees at time of hiring does not constitute a waiver of its right to bargain about drug/alcohol testing of injured employees.[33]

A fortiori, the Union's acquiescence in the Respondent's past unilateral implementation of other work rules, not involving drug/alcohol testing, does not constitute a waiver of the Union's right to bargain about the Respondent's new rule imposing drug/alcohol testing. * * *

f.  *Conclusion*

Accordingly, in light of all the above considerations, we conclude that drug/alcohol testing of employees who require treatment for injuries re-

---

union's failure affirmatively to seek modification of the contractual no-strike clause, in the face of two earlier arbitration decisions upholding the employer's disparately severe punishment of certain union officials for their participation in unlawful strikes, did not constitute a waiver by the union of the statutory protection of employees against disparate treatment on the basis of their union activities. The Court held, inter alia, that an arbitration decision may be relevant to establishing a waiver of the statutory right in question where (1) the arbitrator has stated that the collective-bargaining agreement itself clearly and unmistakably imposed an explicit duty on union officials to end unlawful work stoppages, or (2)(absent such an express statement by the arbitrator) there is a clear and consistent pattern of arbitration decisions, and circumstances exist under which it

could be said that the parties have incorporated those decisions into subsequent bargaining agreements. 460 U.S. at 709 fn. 13. Quite clearly, no such circumstances as suggested by the Court exist in the instant case, which involves only one arbitration decision, on a matter not related to the subject at hand. Indeed, the Court itself stated, with reference to the facts before it in *Metropolitan Edison,* that "We do not think that two arbitration awards establish a pattern of decisions clear enough to convert the union's silence into binding waiver." Id. at 709.

**33.** As noted above, the question of whether drug/alcohol testing of applicants for employment or of new employees at time of hire is a mandatory subject of bargaining is not at issue here. That issue is addressed in *Star Tribune,* 295 NLRB No. 63.

ceived while on the job is a mandatory subject of bargaining; that the Union has not waived its right to bargain with the Respondent about this subject; and that the Respondent's unilateral implementation of the requirement for such testing, without providing the Union with prior notice and an opportunity to bargain, violated Section 8(a)(5) and (1) of the Act, as alleged.

\* \* \*

[Member Johansen dissented in part.]

-------

## Milwaukee Spring Div. of Illinois Coil Spring Co.[e]

268 NLRB 601 (1984), enf'd sub nom. International Union, UAW v. NLRB, 765 F.2d 175 (D.C.Cir.1985).

[The employer was charged with violating Section 8(a)(5) by deciding without the union's consent, in the midst of the contract term, to transfer certain operations from its unionized Milwaukee Spring facility to its non-union McHenry Spring facility. The employer had informed the union that the higher wage rates in Milwaukee necessitated the transfer, and it urged the union to forgo a wage increase scheduled under the labor agreement and to make other contract concessions, but the union rejected the proposal. Although the employer then made specific proposals for alternatives to relocation, the union rejected these proposals as well and declined to bargain further over the decision to transfer operations. The employer then announced its relocation decision, which the union was willing to concede was economically motivated and not the result of anti-union animus. In the Section 8(a)(5) proceeding, the union stipulated that the company had satisfied its obligation to bargain with the union over the decision itself as well as its effects upon the Milwaukee employees. Initially, the Board found that the employer had violated the Act by transferring its operations in violation of obligations "contained in" the labor agreement, in particular the wage provision and the provision recognizing the union as bargaining agent at the Milwaukee plant. 265 N.L.R.B. 206 (1982). After cross-petitions were filed with the court of appeals, the Board—with new members appointed by President Reagan—secured a remand for additional consideration. The Board decided to reverse its "Milwaukee I" decision, and to dismiss the complaint.]

■ II. Midterm Modification of Contracts Under Section 8(d)

### A.

Sections 8(a)(5) and 8(d) establish an employer's obligation to bargain in good faith with respect to "wages, hours, and other terms and conditions

---

**e.**  See O'Keefe & Touhey, Economically Motivated Relocations of Work and an Employer's Duties Under Section 8(d) of the NLRA: A Three–Step Analysis, 11 Fordham Urb.L.J. 795 (1983); Wachter & Cohen, The Law and Economics of Collective Bargaining: An Introduction and Application to the Problems of Subcontracting, Partial Closure, and Relocation, 136 U.Pa.L.Rev. 1349 (1988).

of employment." Generally, an employer may not unilaterally institute changes regarding these mandatory subjects before reaching a good-faith impasse in bargaining.[6] Section 8(d) imposes an additional requirement when a collective-bargaining agreement is in effect and an employer seeks to "modif[y] ... the terms and conditions contained in" the contract: the employer must obtain the union's consent before implementing the change.[7] If the employment conditions the employer seeks to change are not "contained in" the contract, however, the employer's obligation remains the general one of bargaining in good faith to impasse over the subject before instituting the proposed change.

Applying these principles to the instant case, before the Board may hold that Respondent violated Section 8(d), the Board first must identify a specific term "contained in" the contract that the Company's decision to relocate modified. In *Milwaukee Spring I,* the Board never specified the contract term that was modified by Respondent's decision to relocate the assembly operations. The Board's failure to do so is not surprising, for we have searched the contract in vain for a provision requiring bargaining unit work to remain in Milwaukee.

*Milwaukee Spring I* suggests, however, that the Board may have concluded that Respondent's relocation decision, because it was motivated by a desire to obtain relief from the Milwaukee contract's labor costs, modified that contract's wage and benefits provisions. We believe this reasoning is flawed. While it is true that the Company proposed modifying the wage and benefits provisions of the contract, the Union rejected the proposals. Following its failure to obtain the Union's consent, Respondent, in accord with Section 8(d), abandoned the proposals to modify the contract's wage and benefits provisions. Instead, Respondent decided to transfer the assembly operations to a different plant where different workers (who were not subject to the contract) would perform the work. In short, Respondent did not disturb the wages and benefits at its Milwaukee facility, and consequently did not violate Section 8(d) by modifying, without the Union's consent, the wage and benefits provisions contained in the contract.[9]

Nor do we find that Respondent's relocation decision modified the contract's recognition clause. In two previous cases, the Board construed recognition clauses to encompass the duties performed by bargaining unit employees and held that employers' reassignment of work modified those

---

**6.** See NLRB v. Katz, 369 U.S. 736 (1962).

**7.** Oak Cliff–Golman Baking Co., 207 N.L.R.B. 1063 (1973), enfd. 505 F.2d 1302 (5th Cir.1974), cert. denied 423 U.S. 826 (1975).

**9.** *Oak Cliff–Golman* illustrates a midterm modification of wage provisions. In that case, the contract contained wage rates that the respondent unilaterally reduced during the life of the contract. Respondent in the instant case, having unsuccessfully sought the Union's consent to modify the contractual wages and benefits, left those provisions intact.

*Oak Cliff–Golman* also discussed the appropriateness of deferral to contractual grievance and arbitration procedures. We need not make any finding in this case regarding deferral.

clauses. In both instances, reviewing courts found no basis for reading jurisdictional rights into standard clauses that merely recognized the contracts' coverage of specified employees. Boeing Co., 230 N.L.R.B. 696 (1977), enf. denied 581 F.2d 793 (9th Cir.1978); University of Chicago, 210 N.L.R.B. 190 (1974), enf. denied 514 F.2d 942 (7th Cir.1975). We agree with the courts' reasoning.

Language recognizing the Union as the bargaining agent "for all production and maintenance employees in the Company's plant at Milwaukee, Wisconsin," does not state that the functions that the unit performs must remain in Milwaukee. No doubt parties could draft such a clause; indeed, work-preservation clauses are commonplace. It is not for the Board, however, to create an implied work-preservation clause in every American labor agreement based on wage and benefits or recognition provisions, and we expressly decline to do so.

In sum, we find in the instant case that neither wage and benefits provisions nor the recognition clause contained in the collective-bargaining agreement preserves bargaining unit work at the Milwaukee facility for the duration of the contract, and that Respondent did not modify these contract terms when it decided to relocate its assembly operations. Further, we find that no other term contained in the contract restricts Respondent's decision-making regarding relocation.

B.

Our dissenting colleague and the decision in *Milwaukee Spring I* fail to recognize that decision's substantial departure from NLRB textbook law that an employer need not obtain a union's consent on a matter not contained in the body of a collective-bargaining agreement even though the subject is a mandatory subject of bargaining. See, *e.g.*, Ozark Trailers, 161 NLRB 561 (1966). Although the Board found a violation in *Ozark*, it did so grounded on the employer's failure to bargain over its decision to close a part of its operation during the collective-bargaining agreement, transfer equipment to another of its plants, and subcontract out work which had been performed at the Ozark plant. Even though the Board's ultimate conclusion in that case may not here survive the Supreme Court's analysis in *First National Corp.*, it is instructive to note the Board's recognition that the employer's obligation, absent a specific provision in the contract restricting its rights, was to *bargain* with the union over its decision:

> In the first place, however, as we have pointed out time and time again, an employer's obligation to bargain does not include the obligation to agree, but solely to engage in a full and frank discussion with the collective-bargaining representative in which a bona fide effort will be made to explore possible alternatives, if any, that may achieve a mutually satisfactory accommodation of the interests of both the employer and the employees. If such efforts fail, the employer is wholly free to make and effectuate his decision. [161 NLRB at 568. Footnote omitted.] * * *

In making its conclusion in *Ozark* the Board recognized that it was common practice for unions and employers to negotiate concerning work relocation, subcontracting, contracting out, etc., and that such negotiations had resulted in contractual language in some contracts which restricted the employer's right to contract out unit work. Consequently, the General Counsel's assertion at oral argument and the implication of our dissenting colleague that to reverse *Milwaukee Spring I* would change the whole course of collective bargaining set forth throughout the years of the National Labor Relations Act is not accurate. Rather, it was *Milwaukee Spring I* which was a radical departure * * *

The rationale of our dissenting colleague adds to the collective-bargaining agreement terms not agreed to by the parties and forecloses the exercise of rational economic discussion and decision-making which ultimately accrue to the benefit of all parties.

## C.

Accordingly, we conclude that Respondent's decision to relocate did not modify the collective-bargaining agreement in violation of Section 8(d). In view of the parties' stipulation that Respondent satisfied its obligation to bargain over the decision, we also conclude that Respondent did not violate Section 8(a)(5).[13]

[The Board then reexamined, and decided to overrule, two earlier decisions—*Los Angeles Marine Hardware Co.* and *University of Chicago*—that had found Section 8(a)(5) violations for midterm relocations.]

### IV. THE SECTION 8(a)(3) ISSUE

In *Milwaukee Spring I,* the Board also found that Respondent's laying off employees as a consequence of its relocation decision violated Section 8(a)(3) notwithstanding that the parties stipulated that there was no union animus. Invoking the "inherently destructive" doctrine of *Great Dane*

---

**13.** The dissent's references to "contract avoidance" and "do[ing] indirectly what cannot be done directly" are misleading and deflect the reader's attention from the language of Sec. 8(d). Respondent's action is branded unlawful, even though the dissent fails to identify any term or condition contained in the contract that Respondent modified.

As we stated in the body of this opinion, we believe that, under Sec. 8(d), an employer must obtain a union's consent before implementing a change during the life of a contract only if the change is in a mandatory term or condition "contained in" the contract. Contrary to the dissent, because we can identify no term or condition contained in the contract that Respondent modified, we characterize Respondent's conduct as doing directly what lawfully can be done directly, i.e., deciding to relocate unit work after bargaining with the Union in good faith to impasse.

The dissent claims that Respondent's work relocation decision would indirectly modify contractual wage rates. Thus, the dissent would imply a work-preservation clause from the mere fact that an employer and a union have agreed on a wage scale. This revolutionary concept, if adopted, would affect virtually every American collective-bargaining agreement and would undoubtedly come as a surprise to parties that have labored at the bargaining table over work-preservation proposals. An agreed-upon wage scale, standing by itself, means only that the employer will pay the stated wages to the extent that the employer assigns work to the covered employees.

*Trailers,* the Board apparently held that the 8(a)(3) violation flowed from the finding that the relocation decision violated Section 8(a)(5). Accepting this logic for the purposes of our decision only, we conclude that, having found that Respondent complied with its statutory obligation before deciding to relocate and did not violate Section 8(a)(5), there is no factual or legal basis for finding that the consequent layoff of employees violated Section 8(a)(3).

## V. REALISTIC AND MEANINGFUL COLLECTIVE BARGAINING

*Los Angeles Marine* and *Milwaukee Spring I* discourage truthful midterm bargaining over decisions to transfer unit work. Under those decisions [which had forbidden relocation of facilities based on high contract wage rates], an employer contemplating a plant relocation for several reasons, one of which is labor costs, would be likely to admit only the reasons unrelated to labor costs in order to avoid granting the union veto power over the decision. The union, unaware that labor costs were a factor in the employer's decision, would be unlikely to volunteer wage or other appropriate concessions. Even if the union offered to consider wage concessions, the employer might hesitate to discuss such suggestions for fear that bargaining with the union over the union's proposals would be used as evidence that labor costs had motivated the relocation decision.

We believe our holding today avoids this dilemma and will encourage the realistic and meaningful collective bargaining that the Act contemplates. Under our decision, an employer does not risk giving a union veto power over its decision regarding relocation and should therefore be willing to disclose all factors affecting its decision. Consequently, the union will be in a better position to evaluate whether to make concessions. Because both parties will no longer have an incentive to refrain from frank bargaining, the likelihood that they will be able to resolve their differences is greatly enhanced.

## VI. CONCLUSION

Accordingly, for all the foregoing reasons, we reverse our original Decision and Order and dismiss the complaint.

■ MEMBER ZIMMERMAN, dissenting.

* * * I find that Respondent's midterm relocation decision was proscribed under Section 8(d) of the Act. Such decision, admittedly motivated solely to avoid the contractual wage rates, was simply an attempt to modify the wage rate provisions in the contract, albeit indirectly. Respondent voluntarily obligated itself to pay a certain amount of wages to employees performing assembly work during the term of the contract, and it cannot avoid this obligation merely by unilaterally relocating the work to another of its facilities, just as it could not by unilaterally reducing the wage rate. It is disingenuous to argue, as do my colleagues, that Respondent's relocation decision did not disturb the contractual wages and benefits at the Milwaukee facility. If Respondent had implemented its decision, there would be no assembly employees at the Milwaukee facility to receive the contractual

wages and benefits. Rather, all assembly work would be performed at McHenry where Respondent would pay its employees less for the same work. Under these circumstances, my colleagues' conclusion that Respondent left the wage and benefit provisions "intact" at Milwaukee is illogical and without legal significance.

Similarly, their claim that my affirmation of the 8(d) mandate implies a work-preservation clause in virtually every labor contract is equally unfounded. Although a valid work-preservation clause could serve to bar a relocation of bargaining unit work motivated for reasons other than avoidance of contractual terms, that circumstance is unrelated to the instant case. Here, Respondent does seek to modify the contractual wage provision, a result that is prohibited by Section 8(d) itself and is not dependent on any work-preservation clause. It is hardly "revolutionary," as my colleagues assert, simply to apply the contractual terms to which the parties voluntarily agreed.

At the same time, my views of the narrow reach of Section 8(d) brings me into partial agreement with my colleagues in this case. In agreement with them, I would not endorse the approach utilized by the Board in its *University of Chicago* and *Boeing* decisions that employer midterm transfers of work abrogate the contractual recognition clause. Such clauses are "merely the parties' descriptive recitation of the physical location of the facilities at the time of the negotiations," and do not create an implied prohibition against the transfer or relocation of work away from the bargaining unit regardless of the employer's motivation.

Neither do I endorse the Board's decisions in *University of Chicago* and *Boeing* to the extent that the Board found that an employer's midterm relocation decision motivated by reasons unrelated to a desire to avoid the contractual wage rates is proscribed by Section 8(d). As the motivation for the employers' action in those cases was a desire to increase productivity, I concur in the court opinions in those cases that the employers' actions did not violate Section 8(d).

In my view, the determinative factor in deciding whether an employer's midterm relocation decision is proscribed under Section 8(d) is the employer's motive. Where, as here, the decision is controlled by a desire to avoid a contractual term with regard to a mandatory subject of bargaining, such as wages, then the decision is violative under Sections 8(d) and 8(a)(5), and the employer may not implement the decision during the term of the contract without the union's consent. But where the decision is motivated by reasons unrelated to contract avoidance, then the employer may unilaterally implement its decision after bargaining to impasse with the union.

My colleagues claim that this approach encourages employers to deny that a relocation decision is motivated by a desire to reduce labor costs. I disagree. An employer considering relocation to reduce labor costs has substantial incentive to tell the union why it needs relief and how much relief it needs: relocation will usually involve the transfer of equipment and management personnel, as well as the training of new employees to perform the relocated work. An employer who can avoid these kinds of disruption to production by bargaining with the union for contract concessions will likely do so. See First National Corp. v. NLRB, 452 U.S. at 682. Indeed, Respondent's actions illustrate this point. Respondent, whose relocation decision was admittedly motivated by its desire to reduce labor costs, informed the Union of its plan and its reasons, and engaged in concessions bargaining, which, if successful, would have resulted in the assembly operations remaining in Milwaukee. * * *

---

## PROBLEMS FOR DISCUSSION

**1.** Because the parties had presented their case to the Board on the assumption that the company's relocation/transfer decision was a mandatory subject of bargaining, the Board stated that it was not necessary to decide that issue. Had the company contended that its decision was a merely permissive subject of bargaining, under *First National Maintenance*, see page 458, supra, how would the Board have decided?

**2.** The *Jacobs Manufacturing* case considered whether Section 8(d) can be used as a shield against union demands for midterm negotiations at the *union's* initiative. *Milwaukee Spring* deals with the impact of Section 8(d) when the *employer* wishes to institute certain midterm changes. Consider, then, the following hypothetical situations regarding Jacobs's efforts—in the middle of the contract term—to alter the employee share of premiums for the health insurance plan and to change the benefit structure.

Can Jacobs make such a change without notifying or bargaining with the union? Does the *Katz* decision make such a change unlawful? Does Section 8(d)(particularly the "termination or modification" provisions) make such a change unlawful? Conversely, would the *Jacobs* decision itself make the change *lawful*? Would the change be validated by virtue of the "integration clause" at footnote 13? Can Jacobs make such a change after first notifying the union and giving the union every effort to negotiate about the matter (which the union declines to do)?

**3.** Suppose that a labor contract sets forth the terms of a pension and retirement plan and that, during the contract term, the employer declares that it will thereafter terminate the payment of pension moneys to retirees and will instead devote them to the construction of a convalescent home for aged former employees. Would such action violate Section 8(a)(5)? If not, would there be any legal recourse for aggrieved parties, and who would have standing to pursue that legal recourse? See *Allied Chem. Workers v. Pittsburgh Plate Glass Co.,* p. 481 supra.

---

*THE LABOR AGREEMENT AND THE BANKRUPTCY LAWS*

Ordinarily, an employer's total repudiation of a labor agreement is a violation of Section 8(a)(5). During the recessionary period around 1980, this general rule created a problem of particular concern for companies seeking to undergo reorganization through bankruptcy proceedings. A number of courts were called upon to resolve the seemingly unresolvable tension between the rehabilitative policies of the federal bankruptcy laws, which empower the trustee or "debtor in possession" unilaterally to reject executory contracts, and the contract-enforcement policies embodied in the National Labor Relations Act. The Supreme Court definitively (albeit only temporarily) resolved the issue in NLRB v. BILDISCO & BILDISCO, 465 U.S. 513, 104 S.Ct. 1188, 79 L.Ed.2d 482 (1984).

The Bildisco partnership was a New Jersey company in the business of distributing building supplies. Nearly half of its employees were represented by Teamsters Local 408 and were covered by a labor agreement due to expire on April 30, 1982. Beginning in January 1980, the company failed to meet certain obligations under the labor agreement, in particular the payment of health and pension benefits and the remittance of membership dues to the union. In April 1980, it filed a petition in bankruptcy for reorganization under Chapter 11 of the Bankruptcy Code, and the following month it refused to pay wage increases called for in the labor agreement. After being authorized by the Bankruptcy Court to operate its business as a "debtor in possession" (akin to a trustee in bankruptcy), the company in that capacity in December 1980 invoked 11 U.S.C. § 365(a), which permits a trustee, subject to the approval of the Bankruptcy Court, to "assume or reject any executory contract * * * of the debtor." It requested permission from the Court to reject its collective bargaining agreement. After a hearing, the Court in January 1981 granted Bildisco permission to reject the labor agreement and allowed the union thirty days in which to file a claim for damages as a creditor of Bildisco as a result of the contract rejection. On the basis of unfair labor practice charges filed in mid–1980, the NLRB determined that Bildisco's failure to meet its financial commitments to the union under the labor agreement, and its unilateral changing of the contract's terms, violated Section 8(a)(5).

Appeals from the decisions of the Bankruptcy Court and the NLRB were consolidated before the Court of Appeals for the Third Circuit. The court remanded to the Bankruptcy Court for reconsideration of the contract rejection in light of new criteria articulated by the appeals court, and refused enforcement of the NLRB order. The two issues—the proper standard for a bankrupt's rejection of a labor agreement, and the circumstances in which rejection might violate Section 8(a)(5)—were placed before the Supreme Court. On the first issue, the Court was unanimous; on the second issue, it divided 5–to–4.

The Court held that a collective bargaining agreement was an "executory contract" which could be rejected under Section 365(a) of the Bankruptcy Code. The standard to be applied by the Bankruptcy Court for granting permission to do so was somewhere between the fairly lenient "business judgment" test normally applicable to ordinary commercial contracts and the very strict requirement that the debtor in possession demonstrate that its reorganization will fail unless rejection is permitted. "[T]he Bankruptcy Court should permit rejection of a collective-bargaining agreement under § 365(a) of the Bankruptcy Code if the debtor can show that the collective-bargaining agreement burdens the estate, and that after careful scrutiny, the equities balance in favor of rejecting the labor contract." Before acting on the debtor's petition, however, the Bankruptcy Court "should be persuaded that reasonable efforts to negotiate a voluntary modification have been made and are not likely to produce a prompt and satisfactory solution. The NLRA requires no less." The union remains the bargaining representative with which the debtor-in-possession must deal, but if the Court concludes that "the parties' inability to reach [a modified] agreement threatens to impede the success of the debtor's reorganization," even if no formal "impasse" has been reached under the NLRA precedents, the Bankruptcy Court may permit rejection. The Supreme Court thus affirmed the court of appeals remand of this issue to the Bankruptcy Court.

A Court majority also affirmed the lower court's determination that Bildisco's unilateral rejection or modification of the terms of the labor agreement between the date it filed its petition and the date the Bankruptcy Court authorized rejection of the agreement was not an unfair labor practice. After analyzing various provisions of the Bankruptcy Code, the majority concluded that from the date of filing of the petition in bankruptcy, the labor agreement became immediately unenforceable; for the NLRB to enforce its terms pursuant to Section 8(d) would directly contradict the letter and purposes of the Code. Although the union argued that the debtor-in-possession should at the least be expected to bargain to impasse prior to seeking rejection, that too would conflict with the exigencies of bankruptcy; so to condition the rejection "will simply divert the Bankruptcy Court from its customary area of expertise into a field in which it presumably has little or none."

The four dissenting Justices, in an opinion by Justice Brennan, concluded that the majority had given too little weight to the policies underlying Section 8(d) of the NLRA; they would find that Bildisco had committed an unfair labor practice by unilaterally altering the terms of the labor agreement prior to the date when the Bankruptcy Court formally authorized such modification or termination.

Within a matter of weeks, Congress amended the Bankruptcy Code so as to impose stricter procedures and conditions for the debtor-in-possession seeking to modify a collective bargaining agreement. See Note, Nobody Likes Rejection Unless You're a Debtor in Chapter 11: Rejection of Collective Bargaining Agreements Under 11 U.S.C. § 1113, 34 N.Y.L.S.L.Rev. 169 (1989); Note, Rejection of Collective Bargaining Agreements in Bankruptcy: Finding a Balance in 11 U.S.C. § 1113, 56 Fordham L.Rev. 1233 (1988).

11 U.S.C. § 1113 now requires that the debtor or trustee maintain the labor agreement in effect while presenting to the union (and conferring with it in good faith about) a proposal for modifications in employee benefits and protections. The proposed modifications must be "necessary to permit the reorganization of the debtor" and must assure fair and equitable treatment of all affected parties; and they must be communicated to the union before filing an application seeking rejection of the labor agreement.

If the court finds that the debtor or trustee has complied with this requirement, and that the union has refused to accept the modification proposal "without good cause," and that the balance of the equities "clearly favors" rejection, then it shall approve such an application for rejection.

The court must hold a hearing on the satisfaction of these conditions no later than fourteen days after the filing of the debtor's application for rejection of the labor contract, and must rule on the application within thirty days after the commencement of the hearing. (If the court delays, then the trustee may alter or terminate the contract's terms pending the court's ruling.) The court may permit the debtor or trustee to implement "interim changes" in the contract's terms only if it concludes, after notice and hearing, that this is "essential to the continuation of the debtor's business, or in order to avoid irreparable damage to the estate."

Since the enactment of the statute, there has been disagreement among the courts of appeals over the proper interpretation of the "necessity" requirement for proposed contract modifications. In Wheeling–Pittsburgh Steel Corp. v. United Steelworkers, 791 F.2d 1074 (3d Cir.1986), the Third Circuit concluded that "necessary" was synonymous with "essential." The court held that necessity must "be construed strictly to signify only modifications that the trustee is constrained to accept because they are directly related to the Company's financial position and its reorganization."

In a decision that has been generally followed by other courts of appeals and by bankruptcy courts, e.g., Sheet Metal Wkrs. v. Mile Hi Metal Sys., Inc., 899 F.2d 887 (10th Cir.1990), the Second Circuit refused to adopt such a strict construction of the term "necessary." In Truck Drivers Local 807 v. Carey Transp., Inc., 816 F.2d 82 (2d Cir.1987), that court concluded that "necessary" does not mean "essential" or "bare minimum." Instead, proposed changes must "contain necessary but not absolutely minimal, changes that will enable the debtor to complete the reorganization process successfully." Thus, proposed modifications "need not be limited to bare bones relief that will keep [the debtor] going." And the same court, in its decision in In re Royal Composing Room, Inc., 848 F.2d 345, 350 (2d Cir.1988), concluded that a proposed modification must be considered as a whole and thus held that rejection of a collective bargaining agreement is not precluded by the fact that any single element of the proposal might not be "necessary." Rejection of the agreement is therefore still possible if the proposal considered as a whole can be shown to be "necessary."

Although the language of 11 U.S.C. § 1113 directly refers to modifications in employee benefits, the statute has been found to apply to the protection of retiree interests. See, *e.g.,* In re Unimet Corp., 842 F.2d 879 (6th Cir.1988); In re Century Brass Products, Inc., 795 F.2d 265 (2d Cir.1986). In *Century Brass,* the court held that prior to seeking rejection of a collective bargaining agreement, the employer was required to make proposals for alterations of the vested rights of retirees in a retirement plan.

Empirical studies have shown that, whatever definition of "necessary" courts choose to use, more often than not bankrupt parties are able to get out of their commitments under collective bargaining agreements. In 54 cases decided between 1974 and the enactment of § 1113 ten years later, courts allowed employers to set aside such agreements approximately 67% of the time; in 38 cases after the passage of § 1113, courts so acted approximately 58% of the time. (The bulk of these cases were decided in the late 1980s and involved bankruptcies of airlines and their subsidiaries, typically covered by the Railway Labor Act.) Cameron, How "Necessary" Became the Mother of Rejection: An Empirical Look at the Fate of Collective Bargaining Agreements on the Tenth Anniversary of Bankruptcy Code Section 1113, 34 Santa Clara L.Rev. 841 (1994).

If it is determined that an employer has improperly modified or repudiated a collective bargaining agreement in the course of a bankruptcy proceeding, the question remains whether the injured employees are to be allowed any special priority for their wages and benefits. Some courts have held that § 1113 grants such claims a "superpriority" status over other claims, United Steelworkers v. Unimet Corp., 842 F.2d 879 (6th Cir.1988); although other courts have held to the contrary, In re Roth American, Inc., 975 F.2d 949 (3d Cir.1992). See generally In re Kitty Hawk, Inc., 255 B.R. 428 (Bkrtcy. N.D. Tex. 2000). Courts have also held—in light of the language of § 1113, its placement in the Code or its legislative history— that the elaborate arrangements created by that section for rejection and modification of collective agreements do not apply to bankruptcy proceedings instituted under Chapters 7 and 9 of the Bankruptcy Code. In re Rufener Constr. Co., 53 F.3d 1064 (9th Cir.1995); In re County of Orange, 179 B.R. 177 (Bkrtcy.Cal.1995). See generally UFCW, Local 211 v. Family Snacks, Inc., 257 B.R. 884 (8th Cir.2001).

On the issue of bankruptcy and collective bargaining agreements, see generally Keating, The Continuing Puzzle of Collective Bargaining Agreements, 35 Wm. & Mary L.Rev. 503 (1994).

# PART SIX

# SUCCESSORSHIP[a]

## R. Gorman, Basic Text on Labor Law: Unionization and Collective Bargaining

120–124 (1976).

[In NLRB v. Burns Int'l Security Services, Inc., 406 U.S. 272, 92 S.Ct. 1571, 32 L.Ed.2d 61 (1972)] Wackenhut provided plant protection services for Lockheed at a California airport, under a contract to terminate on June 30, 1967. On March 8, the United Plant Guard Workers (UPG) was certified as bargaining representative for Wackenhut employees and a three-year labor contract was executed on April 29. Lockheed invited bids for a new protection-services contract, informing all bidders of the UPG certification and contract with Wackenhut, and although Wackenhut submitted a bid, Lockheed awarded the contract to Burns, effective July 1. Burns retained 27 of the Wackenhut guards, and brought in 15 of its own guards from other locations, but refused to bargain with the UPG or honor its labor contract; indeed, it recognized a rival union, American Federation of Guards (AFG), which represented Burns employees elsewhere. The Board found the Lockheed plant to be an appropriate bargaining unit, and held Burns to be a successor under section 8(a)(5) both to Wackenhut's duty to bargain with the UPG (within four months of its certification) and to its labor contract with UPG. The Supreme Court, by a vote of 5 to 4 sustained the Board's order to bargain with the UPG, but unanimously refused to enforce the Board's order to honor the labor contract. It established a number of significant principles on the question of the duty of a successor to bargain with the predecessor's union.

a. See Goldberg, The Labor Law Obligations of a Successor Employer, 63 Nw. L.Rev. 735 (1969); H. Northrup & P. Miscimarra, Government Protection of Employees Involved in Mergers and Acquisitions (1989); Note, Contract Rights and the Successor Employer: The Impact of *Burns Security*, 71 Mich.L.Rev. 571 (1973); Slicker, A Reconsideration of the Doctrine of Employer Successorship—A Step Toward a Rational Approach, 57 Minn.L.Rev. 1051 (1973).

(1) When a company hires as a majority of its workforce (in an appropriate bargaining unit) employees who had worked for a unionized company, and these employees continue to perform the same work in the same setting, the successor company is obligated to recognize and bargain with the predecessor's union during the same period of time as the predecessor would be obligated to do. . . .  The Supreme Court did note that Burns had not merely retained former Wackenhut employees as a majority of its own workforce at the Lockheed plant, but had also used them to perform the same tasks under supervision organized as before (although the particular supervisors were not those used by Wackenhut). But these latter factors were, if not altogether ignored, clearly treated as less significant than the successor majority comprised of former Wackenhut employees.  Indeed, the Court expressly held:

> Burns' obligation to bargain with the union over terms and conditions of employment stemmed from its hiring of Wackenhut's employees and from the recent election and Board certification.  It has been consistently held that a mere change of employers or of ownership in the employing industry is not such an "unusual circumstance" as to affect the force of the Board's certification within the normal operative period if a majority of employees after the change of ownership or management were employed by the preceding employer.

\* \* \*

The Court majority was thus not deterred by the observation of the four dissenting Justices that this might well require the successor to bargain with a union which in fact was at no time the freely selected representative of a majority of its employees, since for example of the fifty-one percent of the successor's workforce who had worked for the predecessor only a bare majority in turn might have voted for the union; indeed, a random selection of the predecessor's employees might bring to the successor only a very small proportion of those who had supported the predecessor's union. . . .

The Supreme Court decision in *Burns* made it clear that the duty to bargain would not carry over to a company acquiring a unionized business in any of three (at least) situations:  (a) when recruitment by the successor employer results in, for example, "an almost complete turnover of employees," provided of course that the successor does not purposely avoid hiring predecessor employees because they are union members, for such would violate section 8(a)(3) of the Labor Act;  or (b) when—even if all of the predecessor's employees are retained—because the successor's "operational structure and practices" differ from those of the predecessor, the former bargaining unit is no longer appropriate (*e.g.,* if the former Wackenhut employees had been dispersed among Burns employees at other locations and the Lockheed location had thus become an "accretion" to a larger Burns–AFG bargaining unit);  or (c) when, for other reasons, the successor nurtures in good faith a reasonable doubt that the union continues to represent a majority within the unit, for this defense would have been available even to the predecessor employer had there been no transfer of ownership (but even then such a doubt would presumably be conclusively inapt within the year following the certification of the union)....

At the heart of the Court's opinion in *Burns* is its willingness to free the successor of any obligation actually to hire the predecessor's employees, provided it recruits its new workforce without discrimination against union members; any contrary suggestions in earlier Board decisions are thus overruled. Also at the heart of the Court's opinion, at least impliedly, is its indifference to the question whether the business was acquired by merger or by sale of assets or by any other consensual arrangement between the two employers, or was indeed acquired—as in *Burns* itself—by direct competitive bidding and without any contract between predecessor and successor. (This indifference contrasted sharply with the position of four dissenting Justices, who would have required as a condition of a continued duty to bargain that there be some assets transferred to the successor by the predecessor, and not merely "a naked transfer of employees.")

(2) The second essential principle established by the Court in *Burns* is that the duty to bargain ordinarily does not commence *until* the successor has hired as a majority of its workforce the former employees of the predecessor, such that the status quo from which bargaining is to begin is that which obtains between the successor and its own workforce at that time (rather than the earlier status quo between the predecessor and *its* workforce). The Court thus repudiated the Board's earlier position that the predecessor's collective bargaining agreement—even if expired or for other reasons deemed not independently binding on the successor—set the successor's starting wages and working conditions which could be altered only after bargaining with the predecessor's union to an impasse. The Court in *Burns* held that the successor was ordinarily empowered to establish its own starting wages and working conditions, to offer them directly to all job applicants including those then working for the predecessor, and to implement them after the takeover, with the duty to bargain arising only as to future changes and only after the hiring of a majority of the unit from the predecessor's workforce:

> The terms on which Burns hired employees for service after July 1 may have differed from the terms extended by Wackenhut and required by the collective-bargaining contract, but it does not follow that Burns changed *its* terms and conditions of employment when it specified the initial basis on which employees were hired on July 1.

The Court did, however, proceed in dictum to outline a situation where the substantive terms of the predecessor's labor contract will serve as the status quo which binds the successor until it bargains to impasse with the union:

> Although a successor employer is ordinarily free to set initial terms on which it will hire the employees of a predecessor, there will be instances in which it is perfectly clear that the new employer plans to retain all of the employees in the unit and in

which it will be appropriate to have him initially consult with the employees' bargaining representative before he fixes terms. In other situations, however, it may not be clear until the successor employer has hired his full complement of employees that he has a duty to bargain with a union, since it will not be evident until then that the bargaining representative represents a majority of the employees in the unit as required by § 9(a) of the Act.

(3) The short-lived Board doctrine that section 8(a)(5) requires the successor employer not only to recognize and bargain with the predecessor's union but also to honor its labor contract was flatly rejected by a unanimous Court. The Court found in the Labor Act a strong policy favoring the voluntary establishment of contract terms by bargaining between the parties, free of government dictation of those terms. An obligation to abide by the predecessor's contract must be found in some express or implied assumption of such an obligation by the successor, and cannot rest merely on the retention of a majority of former employees without consensual dealings between the parties.... The *Burns* Court ... placed preeminent emphasis upon the need of employers freely to transfer and rearrange physical and human resources in an effort to resuscitate ailing businesses:

> A potential employer may be willing to take over a moribund business only if he can make changes in corporate structure, composition of the labor force, work location, task assignment, and nature of supervision. Saddling such an employer with the terms and conditions of employment contained in the old collective-bargaining contract may make these changes impossible and may discourage and inhibit the transfer of capital. On the other hand, a union may have made concessions to a small or failing employer that it would be unwilling to make to a large or economically successful firm.

Both successor and union should be free to renegotiate working conditions, with economic power rather than the old contract (including many implied terms unknown to the successor) determining the content of the bargain.

    \* \* \*

-------

# Fall River Dyeing & Finishing Corp. v. NLRB

482 U.S. 27, 107 S.Ct. 2225, 96 L.Ed.2d 22 (1987).

■ JUSTICE BLACKMUN delivered the opinion of the Court.

In this case we are confronted with the issue whether the National Labor Relations Board's decision is consistent with NLRB v. Burns International Security Services, Inc., 406 U.S. 272, 92 S.Ct. 1571, 32 L.Ed.2d 61 (1972). In *Burns,* this Court ruled that the new employer, succeeding to the business of another, had an obligation to bargain with the union representing the predecessor's employees. Id., at 278–279, 92 S.Ct., at

1577. We first must decide whether *Burns* is limited to a situation where the union only recently was certified before the transition in employers, or whether that decision also applies where the union is entitled to a presumption of majority support. Our inquiry then proceeds to three questions that concern rules the Labor Board has developed in the successorship context. First, we must determine whether there is substantial record evidence to support the Board's conclusion that petitioner was a "successor" to Sterlingwale Corp., its business predecessor. Second, we must decide whether the Board's "substantial and representative complement" rule, designed to identify the date when a successor's obligation to bargain with the predecessor's employees' union arises, is consistent with *Burns,* is reasonable, and was applied properly in this case. Finally, we must examine the Board's "continuing demand" principle to the effect that, if a union has presented to a successor a premature demand for bargaining, this demand continues in effect until the successor acquires the "substantial and representative complement" of employees that triggers its obligation to bargain.

I

For over 30 years before 1982, Sterlingwale operated a textile dyeing and finishing plant in Fall River, Mass. Its business consisted basically of two types of dyeing, called, respectively, "converting" and "commission." Under the converting process, which in 1981 accounted for 60% to 70% of its business, Sterlingwale bought unfinished fabrics for its own account, dyed and finished them, and then sold them to apparel manufacturers. In commission dyeing, which accounted for the remainder of its business, Sterlingwale dyed and finished fabrics owned by customers according to their specifications. The financing and marketing aspects of converting and commission dyeing are different. Converting requires capital to purchase fabrics and a sales force to promote the finished products. The production process, however, is the same for both converting and commission dyeing. * * *

[Starting in the late 1970s the textile dyeing business, including Sterlingwale's, began to suffer. As long as Sterlingwale had been in existence, its production and maintenance employees had been represented by the United Textile Workers of America, AFL–CIO. The union agreed to extend its contract, due to expire in 1981, to 1982 without any wage increase. But in February 1982, Sterlingwale laid off all its production employees. By late summer, it went out of business. A professional liquidator was hired to dispose of all the company's remaining assets, mostly inventory, at auction.]

During this same period, a former Sterlingwale employee and officer, Herbert Chace, and Arthur Friedman, president of one of Sterlingwale's major customers, Marcamy Sales Corporation (Marcamy), formed petitioner Fall River Dyeing & Finishing Corp. Chace, who had resigned from Sterlingwale in February 1982, had worked there for 27 years, had been vice-president in charge of sales at the time of his departure, and had participated in collective bargaining with the Union during his tenure at Sterlingwale.  Chace and Friedman formed petitioner with the intention of engaging strictly in the commission-dyeing business and of taking advantage of the availability of Sterlingwale's assets and workforce.  Accordingly, Friedman had Marcamy acquire * * * Sterlingwale's plant, real property, and equipment, and convey them to petitioner.  Petitioner also obtained some of Sterlingwale's remaining inventory at the liquidator's auction. Chace became petitioner's vice president in charge of operations and Friedman became its president.

In September 1982, petitioner began operating out of Sterlingwale's former facilities and began hiring employees.  It advertised for workers and supervisors in a local newspaper, and Chace personally got in touch with several prospective supervisors.  Petitioner hired 12 supervisors, of whom 8 had been supervisors with Sterlingwale and 3 had been production employees there.  In its hiring decisions for production employees, petitioner took into consideration recommendations from these supervisors and a prospective employee's former employment with Sterlingwale.  Petitioner's initial hiring goal was to attain one full shift of workers, which meant from 55 to 60 employees.  Petitioner planned to "see how business would be" after this initial goal had been met and, if business permitted, to expand to two shifts.  The employees who were hired first spent approximately four to six weeks in start-up operations and an additional month in experimental production.

By letter dated October 19, 1982, the Union requested petitioner to recognize it as the bargaining agent for petitioner's employees and to begin collective bargaining.  Petitioner refused the request, stating that, in its view, the request had "no legal basis."  At that time, 18 of petitioner's 21 employees were former employees of Sterlingwale.  See 272 N.L.R.B. 839, 840 (1984).  By November of that year, petitioner had employees in a complete range of jobs, had its production process in operation, and was handling customer orders; by mid-January 1983, it had attained its initial goal of one shift of workers.  Of the 55 workers in this initial shift, a number that represented over half the workers petitioner would eventually hire, 36 were former Sterlingwale employees.  Petitioner continued to expand its workforce, and by mid-April 1983 it had reached two full shifts. For the first time, ex-Sterlingwale employees were in the minority but just barely so (52 or 53 out of 107 employees).

Although petitioner engaged exclusively in commission dyeing, the employees experienced the same conditions they had when they were working for Sterlingwale.  The production process was unchanged and the employees worked on the same machines, in the same building, with the same job classifications, under virtually the same supervisors.  Over half the volume of petitioner's business came from former Sterlingwale customers, and, in particular, Marcamy.  * * *

[On November 1, 1982, the Union filed an unfair labor practice charge with the NLRB for the company's refusal to bargain.  The ALJ held the company to be a successor to Sterlingwale, and that a duty to bargain commenced from mid-January when the company had a "representative complement" of employees. The Board affirmed and the Court of Appeals for the First Circuit enforced, albeit by a divided vote.]

## II

Fifteen years ago in NLRB v. Burns International Security Services, Inc., 406 U.S. 272, 92 S.Ct. 1571, 32 L.Ed.2d 61 (1972), this Court first dealt with the issue of a successor employer's obligation to bargain with a union that had represented the employees of its predecessor....

\* \* \*

[The Court made clear that the policy at work in *Burns* was predicated not only upon the fact of a recent certification, under which the union enjoys an irrebuttable presumption of majority support for a year, but also upon the continuing presumption of majority support a union enjoys thereafter.]

These presumptions are based not so much on an absolute certainty that the union's majority status will not erode following certification, as on a particular policy decision. The overriding policy of the NLRA is "industrial peace." Brooks v. NLRB, 348 U.S., at 103, 75 S.Ct., at 181. The presumptions of majority support further this policy by "promot[ing] stability in collective-bargaining relationships, without impairing the free choice of employees." Terrell Machine Co., 173 N.L.R.B. 1480, 1480 (1969), enf'd, 427 F.2d 1088 (CA4), cert. denied, 398 U.S. 929, 90 S.Ct. 1821, 26 L.Ed.2d 91 (1970). In essence, they enable a union to concentrate on obtaining and fairly administering a collective-bargaining agreement without worrying that, unless it produces immediate results, it will lose majority support and will be decertified. See Brooks v. NLRB, 348 U.S., at 100, 75 S.Ct., at 179. The presumptions also remove any temptation on the part of the employer to avoid good-faith bargaining in the hope that, by delaying, it will undermine the union's support among the employees. See ibid.; see also R. Gorman, Labor Law 53 (1976). The upshot of the presumptions is to permit unions to develop stable bargaining relationships with employers, which will enable the unions to pursue the goals of their members, and this pursuit, in turn, will further industrial peace.

The rationale behind the presumptions is particularly pertinent in the successorship situation and so it is understandable that the Court in *Burns* referred to them. During a transition between employers, a union is in a peculiarly vulnerable position. It has no formal and established bargaining relationship with the new employer, is uncertain about the new employer's plans, and cannot be sure if or when the new employer must bargain with it. While being concerned with the future of its members with the new employer, the union also must protect whatever rights still exist for its members under the collective-bargaining agreement with the predecessor employer.[6] Accordingly, during this unsettling transition period, the union

---

**6.** The difficulty a union faces during an employer-transition period is graphically exhibited by the facts of this case. The Union was confronted with the layoff. App. 64.

needs the presumptions of majority status to which it is entitled to safeguard its members' rights and to develop a relationship with the successor.

The position of the employees also supports the application of the presumptions in the successorship situation. If the employees find themselves in a new enterprise that substantially resembles the old, but without their chosen bargaining representative, they may well feel that their choice of a union is subject to the vagaries of an enterprise's transformation. This feeling is not conducive to industrial peace. In addition, after being hired by a new company following a layoff from the old, employees initially will be concerned primarily with maintaining their new jobs. In fact, they might be inclined to shun support for their former union, especially if they believe that such support will jeopardize their jobs with the successor or if they are inclined to blame the union for their layoff and problems associated with it. Without the presumptions of majority support and with the wide variety of corporate transformations possible, an employer could use a successor enterprise as a way of getting rid of a labor contract and of exploiting the employees' hesitant attitude towards the union to eliminate its continuing presence.

In addition to recognizing the traditional presumptions of union majority status, however, the Court in *Burns* was careful to safeguard " 'the rightful prerogative of owners independently to rearrange their businesses.' " Golden State Bottling Co. v. NLRB, 414 U.S. 168, 182, 94 S.Ct. 414, 424, 38 L.Ed.2d 388 (1973), quoting John Wiley & Sons, Inc. v. Livingston, 376 U.S. 543, 549, 84 S.Ct. 909, 914, 11 L.Ed.2d 898 (1964). We observed in *Burns* that, although the successor has an obligation to bargain with the union, it "is ordinarily free to set initial terms on which it will hire the employees of a predecessor," 406 U.S., at 294, 92 S.Ct., at 1585, and it is not bound by the substantive provisions of the predecessor's collective-bargaining agreement. Id., at 284, 92 S.Ct., at 1580. We further explained that the successor is under no obligation to hire the employees of its predecessor, subject, of course, to the restriction that it not discriminate against union employees in its hiring. Id., at 280, and n. 5, 92 S.Ct., at 1578, and n. 5; see also Howard Johnson Co. v. Hotel Employees, 417 U.S. 249, 262, and n. 8, 94 S.Ct. 2236, 2243, and n. 8, 41 L.Ed.2d 46 (1974). Thus, to a substantial extent the applicability of *Burns* rests in the hands of the successor. If the new employer makes a conscious decision to maintain generally the same business and to hire a majority of its employees from the predecessor, then the bargaining obligation of § 8(a)(5) is activated. This makes sense when one considers that the employer *intends* to take advantage of the trained workforce of its predecessor.[8]

Although officials at Sterlingwale were willing to meet with it, the Union unsuccessfully attempted to have Sterlingwale honor its commitments under the collective-bargaining agreement, particularly those dealing with health benefits. Id., at 78–86. Moreover, despite the Union's desire to participate in the transition between employers, it was left entirely in the dark about petitioner's acquisition. Id., at 68–69.

**8.** If, during negotiations, a successor questions a union's continuing majority status, the successor "may lawfully withdraw

Accordingly, in *Burns* we acknowledged the interest of the successor in its freedom to structure its business and the interest of the employees in continued representation by the union. We now hold that a successor's obligation to bargain is not limited to a situation where the union in question has been recently certified. Where, as here, the union has a rebuttable presumption of majority status, this status continues despite the change in employers. And the new employer has an obligation to bargain with that union so long as the new employer is in fact a successor of the old employer and the majority of its employees were employed by its predecessor.

### III

We turn now to the three rules, as well as to their application to the facts of this case, that the Board has adopted for the successorship situation. The Board, of course, is given considerable authority to interpret the provisions of the NLRA. See NLRB v. Financial Institution Employees, 475 U.S. 192, ___, 106 S.Ct. 1007, 1013, 89 L.Ed.2d 151 (1986). If the Board adopts a rule that is rational and consistent with the Act, see ibid., then the rule is entitled to deference from the courts. Moreover, if the Board's application of such a rational rule is supported by substantial evidence on the record, courts should enforce the Board's order. See Beth Israel Hospital v. NLRB, 437 U.S. 483, 501, 98 S.Ct. 2463, 2473, 57 L.Ed.2d 370 (1978); Universal Camera Corp. v. NLRB, 340 U.S. 474, 488, 71 S.Ct. 456, 464, 95 L.Ed. 456 (1951). These principles also guide our review of the Board's action in a successorship case. See, *e.g.,* Golden State Bottling Co. v. NLRB, 414 U.S., at 181, 94 S.Ct., at 423.

### A

In *Burns* we approved the approach taken by the Board and accepted by courts with respect to determining whether a new company was indeed the successor to the old. 406 U.S., at 280–281, and n. 4, 92 S.Ct., at 1578–1579, and n. 4. This approach, which is primarily factual in nature and is based upon the totality of the circumstances of a given situation, requires that the Board focus on whether the new company has "acquired substantial assets of its predecessor and continued, without interruption or substantial change, the predecessor's business operations." Golden State Bottling Co. v. NLRB, 414 U.S., at 184, 94 S.Ct., at 425. Hence, the focus is on whether there is "substantial continuity" between the enterprises. Under this approach, the Board examines a number of factors: whether the

from negotiation at any time following recognition if it can show that the union had in fact lost its majority status at the time of the refusal to bargain or that the refusal to bargain was grounded on a good-faith doubt based on objective factors that the union continued to command majority support." Harley–Davidson Transp. Co., 273 N.L.R.B. 1531, 1531 (1985). The ALJ made no express finding on the issue of petitioner's good-faith doubt. Moreover, an employer, unsure of a union's continued majority support, may petition the Board for another election. See NLRB v. Financial Institution Employees, 475 U.S. 192, ___, 106 S.Ct. 1007, 1011, 89 L.Ed.2d 151 (1986); Brooks v. NLRB, 348 U.S. 96, 101, 75 S.Ct. 176, 180, 99 L.Ed. 125 (1954). Petitioner did not request an election.

business of both employers is essentially the same;  whether the employees of the new company are doing the same jobs in the same working conditions under the same supervisors;  and whether the new entity has the same production process, produces the same products, and basically has the same body of customers.  See Burns, 406 U.S., at 280, n. 4, 92 S.Ct., at 1578, n. 4;  Aircraft Magnesium, 265 N.L.R.B. 1344, 1345 (1982), enf'd, 730 F.2d 767 (C.A.9 1984);  Premium Foods, Inc., 260 N.L.R.B. 708, 714 (1982), enf'd, 709 F.2d 623 (C.A.9 1983).

In conducting the analysis, the Board keeps in mind the question whether "those employees who have been retained will understandably view their job situations as essentially unaltered."  See Golden State Bottling Co., 414 U.S., at 184, 94 S.Ct., at 425;  NLRB v. Jeffries Lithograph Co., 752 F.2d 459, 464 (C.A.9 1985).  This emphasis on the employees' perspective furthers the Act's policy of industrial peace.  If the employees find themselves in essentially the same jobs after the employer transition and if their legitimate expectations in continued representation by their union are thwarted, their dissatisfaction may lead to labor unrest. See Golden State Bottling Co., 414 U.S., at 184, 94 S.Ct., at 425.

Although petitioner does not challenge the Board's "substantial continuity" approach, it does contest the application of the rule to the facts of this case.  * * * Petitioner acquired most of Sterlingwale's real property, its machinery and equipment, and much of its inventory and materials.[10] It introduced no new product line.  Of particular significance is the fact that, from the perspective of the employees, their jobs did not change. Although petitioner abandoned converting dyeing in exclusive favor of commission dyeing, this change did not alter the essential nature of the employees' jobs, because both types of dyeing involved the same production process.  The job classifications of petitioner were the same as those of Sterlingwale;  petitioners' employees worked on the same machines under the direction of supervisors most of whom were former supervisors of Sterlingwale.  The record, in fact, is clear that petitioner acquired Sterlingwale's assets with the express purpose of taking advantage of its predecessor's workforce.

We do not find determinative of the successorship question the fact that there was a 7–month hiatus between Sterlingwale's demise and petitioner's start-up.  Petitioner argues that this hiatus, coupled with the fact that its employees were hired through newspaper advertisements—not through Sterlingwale employment records, which were not transferred to

---

**10.**  Petitioner makes much of the fact that it purchased the assets of Sterlingwale on the "open market."  Brief for Petitioner 17.  Petitioner, however, overlooks the fact that it was formed with the express purpose of acquiring Sterlingwale's assets, a purpose it accomplished by having its parent company acquire some of Sterlingwale's major assets and then transferring them to petitioner.  So long as there are other indicia of "substantial

continuity," the way in which a successor obtains the predecessor's assets is generally not determinative of the "substantial continuity" question.  See Howard Johnson Co. v. Hotel Employees, 417 U.S. 249, 257, 94 S.Ct. 2236, 2241, 41 L.Ed.2d 46 (1974);  Golden State Bottling Co. v. NLRB, 414 U.S. 168, 182, n. 5, 94 S.Ct. 414, 424, n. 5, 38 L.Ed.2d 388 (1973);  see also R. Gorman, Labor Law 122 (1976).

it—resolves in its favor the "substantial continuity" question.  See Brief for Petitioner 16–17, 20–22;  see also 775 F.2d at 439 (dissenting opinion).  Yet such a hiatus is only one factor in the "substantial continuity" calculus and thus is relevant only when there are other indicia of discontinuity.  See NLRB v. Band–Age, Inc., 534 F.2d 1, 5 (CA1), cert. denied, 429 U.S. 921, 97 S.Ct. 318, 50 L.Ed.2d 288 (1976).  Conversely, if other factors indicate a continuity between the enterprises, and the hiatus is a normal start-up period, the "totality of the circumstances" will suggest that these circumstances present a successorship situation.  See NLRB v. Daneker Clock Co., 516 F.2d 315, 316 (C.A.4 1975);  C.G. Conn, Ltd., 197 N.L.R.B. 442, 446–447 (1972), enf'd, 474 F.2d 1344 (C.A.5 1973).  * * *

[The Court noted that the hiatus between the demise of Sterlingwale and the start up of the successor was less than certain, given Sterlingwale's efforts even after the lay-off to find new financing or a buyer for the company.]

### B

In *Burns,* the Court determined that the successor had an obligation to bargain with the union because a majority of its employees had been employed by Wackenhut.  406 U.S., at 278–279, 92 S.Ct., at 1577.  The "triggering" fact for the bargaining obligation was this composition of the successor's workforce.  The Court, however, did not have to consider the question *when* the successor's obligation to bargain arose: Wackenhut's contract expired on June 30 and Burns began its services with a majority of former Wackenhut guards on July 1.  See id., at 275, 92 S.Ct., at 1576.  In other situations, as in the present case, there is a start-up period by the new employer while it gradually builds its operations and hires employees.  In these situations, the Board, with the approval of the Courts of Appeals, has adopted the "substantial and representative complement" rule for fixing the moment when the determination as to the composition of the successor's workforce is to be made.  If, at this particular moment, a majority of the successor's employees had been employed by its predecessor, then the successor has an obligation to bargain with the union that represented these employees.

This rule represents an effort to balance " 'the objective of insuring maximum employee participation in the selection of a bargaining agent against the goal of permitting employees to be represented as quickly as possible.' "  775 F.2d, at 430–431, quoting NLRB v. Pre–Engineered Building Products, Inc., 603 F.2d 134, 136 (C.A.10 1979).[15]  In deciding when a

---

**15.** The "substantial and representative complement" rule originated in the context of the initial representation election when, faced with an expanding or contracting workforce, the Board had to determine the appropriate time for an election.  See, *e.g.,* Clement–Blythe Companies, 182 N.L.R.B. 502 (1970), enf'd 77 LRRM 2373 (C.A.4 1971).  The rationale for the rule was as follows:

"The Board must often balance what are sometimes conflicting *desiderata,* the insurance of maximum employee participation in the selection of a bargaining agent, and permitting employees who wish to be represented as immediate rep-

"substantial and representative complement" exists in a particular employer transition, the Board examines a number of factors. It studies "whether the job classifications designated for the operation were filled or substantially filled and whether the operation was in normal or substantially normal production." See Premium Foods, Inc. v. NLRB, 709 F.2d 623, 628 (C.A.9 1983). In addition, it takes into consideration "the size of the complement on that date and the time expected to elapse before a substantially larger complement would be at work ... as well as the relative certainty of the employer's expected expansion."

Petitioner contends that the Board's representative complement rule is unreasonable, given that it injures the representation rights of many of the successor's employees and that it places significant burdens upon the successor, which is unsure whether and when the bargaining obligation will arise. Brief for Petitioner 24–31; see also Brief for Chamber of Commerce of the United States of America as *Amicus Curiae* 21–25. According to petitioner, if majority status is determined at the "full complement" stage, all the employees will have a voice in the selection of their bargaining representative, and this will reveal if the union truly has the support of most of the successor's employees. This approach, however, focuses only on the interest in having a bargaining representative selected by the majority of the employees. It fails to take into account the significant interest of employees in being represented as soon as possible. The latter interest is especially heightened in a situation where many of the successor's employees, who were formerly represented by a union, find themselves after the employer transition in essentially the same enterprise, but without their bargaining representative. Having the new employer refuse to bargain with the chosen representative of these employees "disrupts the employees' morale, deters their organizational activities, and discourages their membership in unions." Franks Bros. Co. v. NLRB, 321 U.S. 702, 704, 64 S.Ct. 817, 818, 88 L.Ed. 1020 (1944). Accordingly, petitioner's "full complement" proposal must fail.

Nor do we believe that this "substantial and representative complement" rule places an unreasonable burden on the employer. It is true that, if an employer refuses to bargain with the employees once the representative complement has been attained, it risks violating § 8(a)(5). Furthermore, if an employer recognizes the union before this complement has been reached, this recognition could constitute a violation of § 8(a)(2), which makes it an unfair labor practice for an employer to support a labor

resentation as possible. Thus, it would unduly frustrate existing employees' choice to delay selection of a bargaining representative for months or years until the very last employee is on board. Conversely, it would be pointless to hold an election for very few employees when in a relatively short period the employee complement is expected to multiply many times." 182 N.L.R.B., at 502.

Similar reasoning applies in the successorship context. On the one hand, there is a concern to allow as many employees of the successor to participate in the selection of the union. On the other hand, the previous choice of a union by those employees of the successor who had worked for the predecessor should not be frustrated.

organization.    29 U.S.C. § 158(a)(2).    And, unlike the initial election situation, see n. 15, supra, here the employer, not the Board, applies this rule.

We conclude, however, that in this situation the successor is in the best position to follow a rule the criteria of which are straightforward.    The employer generally will know with tolerable certainty when all its job classifications have been filled or substantially filled, when it has hired a majority of the employees it intends to hire, and when it has begun normal production.  * * *[18]

* * *

We therefore hold that the Board's "substantial and representative complement" rule is reasonable in the successorship context.  * * * Although petitioner intended to expand to two shifts, and, in fact, reached this goal by mid-April, that expansion was contingent expressly upon the growth of the business.    Accordingly, as found by the Board and approved by the Court of Appeals, mid-January was the period when petitioner reached its "substantial and representative complement."    Because at that time the majority of petitioner's employees were former Sterlingwale employees, petitioner had an obligation to bargain with the Union then.

### C

We also hold that the Board's "continuing demand" rule is reasonable in the successorship situation.    The successor's duty to bargain at the "substantial and representative complement" date is triggered only when the union has made a bargaining demand.    Under the "continuing demand" rule, when a union has made a premature demand that has been rejected by the employer, this demand remains in force until the moment when the employer attains the "substantial and representative complement."    See *e.g.*, Aircraft Magnesium, 265 N.L.R.B., at 1345, n. 9; Spruce Up Corp., 209 N.L.R.B., at 197.

Such a rule, particularly when considered along with the "substantial and representative complement" rule, places a minimal burden on the successor and makes sense in light of the union's position.    Once the employer has concluded that it has reached the appropriate complement, then, in order to determine whether its duty to bargain will be triggered, it has only to see whether the union already has made a demand for bargaining.    Because the union has no established relationship with the

---

**18.**  In addition, even if an employer were to err as to the "substantial and representative complement" date and thus were to recognize the union prematurely, its good-faith violation of § 8(a)(2) would be subject only to a remedial order.  See Garment Workers v. NLRB, 366 U.S. 731, 740, 81 S.Ct. 1603, 1608, 6 L.Ed.2d 762 (1961).  Similarly, we assume that if the employer were to refuse to recognize a union on the basis of its reasonable good-faith belief that it had not yet hired a "substantial and representative complement," the Board would likewise enter a remedial order, see ibid., with no collateral consequences such as a decertification bar. Finally, if the employer has a good-faith doubt about the union's continuing majority status, it has several remedies available to it. See n. 8, supra.

successor and because it is unaware of the successor's plans for its operations and hiring, it is likely that, in many cases, a union's bargaining demand will be premature.  It makes no sense to require the union repeatedly to renew its bargaining demand in the hope of having it correspond with the "substantial and representative complement" date, when, with little trouble, the employer can regard a previous demand as a continuing one.  * * *

The judgment of the Court of Appeals is affirmed.

It is so ordered.

■ JUSTICE POWELL, with whom THE CHIEF JUSTICE and JUSTICE O'CONNOR join, dissenting.

* * *

In this case the undisputed evidence shows that petitioner is a completely separate entity from Sterlingwale.  There was a clear break between the time Sterlingwale ceased normal business operations in February 1982 and when petitioner came into existence at the end of August.  In addition, it is apparent that there was no direct contractual or other business relationship between petitioner and Sterlingwale.  Although petitioner bought some of Sterlingwale's inventory, it did so by outbidding several other buyers on the open market.  Also, the purchases at the public sale involved only tangible assets.  Petitioner did not buy Sterlingwale's trade name or good will, nor did it assume any of its liabilities.  And while over half of petitioner's business (measured in dollars) came from former Sterlingwale customers, apparently this was due to the new company's skill in marketing its services.  There was no sale or transfer of customer lists, and given the 9–month interval between the time that Sterlingwale ended production and petitioner commenced its operations in November, the natural conclusion is that the new business attracted customers through its own efforts.  No other explanation was offered.  Cf. Lincoln Private Police, Inc., 189 N.L.R.B. 717, 719 (1971)(finding it relevant to the successorship question that, while the new business acquired many of the former company's clients, "it did so by means of independent solicitation").  Any one of these facts standing alone may be insufficient to defeat a finding of successorship, but together they persuasively demonstrate that the Board's finding of "substantial continuity" was incorrect.

The Court nevertheless is unpersuaded.  It views these distinctions as not directly affecting the employees' expectations about their job status or the status of the union as their representative, even though the CBA with the defunct corporation had long since expired.  See Golden State Bottling Co. v. NLRB, supra, 414 U.S., at 184, 94 S.Ct., at 425 (emphasizing the importance of the workers' perception that their job situation continues "essentially unaltered").  Yet even from the employees' perspective, there was little objective evidence that the jobs with petitioner were simply a continuation of those at Sterlingwale.  When all of the production employees were laid off indefinitely in February 1982, there could have been little hope—and certainly no reasonable expectation—that Sterlingwale would ever reopen.  Nor was it reasonable for the employees to expect that Sterlingwale's failed textile operations would be resumed by a corporation not then in existence.  The CBA had expired in April with no serious effort to renegotiate it, and with several of the employees' benefits left unpaid. The possibility of further employment with Sterlingwale then disappeared entirely in August 1982 when the company liquidated its remaining assets. Cf. Textile Workers Union v. Darlington Manufacturing Co., 380 U.S. 263, 274, 85 S.Ct. 994, 1002, 13 L.Ed.2d 827 (1965)(the "closing of an entire business ... ends the employer-employee relationship").  After petitioner was organized, it advertised for workers in the newspaper, a move that hardly could have suggested to the old workers that they would be reinstated to their former positions.  The sum of these facts inevitably would have had a negative "effect on the employees' expectations of rehire."  See Aircraft Magnesium, 265 N.L.R.B., at 1346.  See also Radiant Fashions, Inc., 202 N.L.R.B. 938, 940 (1973).  The former employees engaged by petitioner found that the new plant was smaller, and that there would be fewer workers, fewer shifts, and more hours per shift than at their prior job.  Moreover, as petitioner did not acquire Sterlingwale's personnel records, the benefits of having a favorable work record presumably were lost to these employees.

In deferring to the NLRB's decision, the Court today extends the successorship doctrine in a manner that could not have been anticipated by either the employer or the employees.  I would hold that the successorship doctrine has no application when the break in continuity between enterprises is as complete and extensive as it was here.

II

Even if the evidence of genuine continuity were substantial, I could not agree with the Court's decision.  As we have noted in the past, if the presumption of majority support for a union is to survive a change in ownership, it must be shown that there is both a continuity of conditions *and* a continuity of work force.  Howard Johnson Co. v. Hotel Employees, 417 U.S. 249, 263, 94 S.Ct. 2236, 2244, 41 L.Ed.2d 46 (1974).  This means that unless a majority of the new company's workers had been employed by the former company, there is no justification for assuming that the new employees wish to be represented by the former union, or by any union at all.  See Spruce Up Corp., 209 N.L.R.B. 194, 196 (1974), enf'd, 529 F.2d 516 (C.A.4 1975);  209 N.L.R.B., at 200 (Member Kennedy, concurring in part and dissenting in part); Saks & Co. v. NLRB, 634 F.2d 681, 685–686 (C.A.2 1980).  Indeed, the rule hardly could be otherwise.  It would be contrary to the basic principles of the NLRA simply to presume in these cases that a majority of workers supports a union when more than half of them have never been members, and when there has been no election....

In my view, the Board's decision to measure the composition of the petitioner work force in mid-January is unsupportable.  The substantial and representative complement test can serve a useful role when the hiring process is sporadic, or the future expansion of the work force is speculative.

But as the Court recognized in *NLRB v. Burns Security Services, Inc.*, in some cases "it may not be clear until the successor employer has hired his full complement of employees that he has a duty to bargain with a union, since it will not be evident until then that the bargaining representative represents a majority of the employees in the unit." 406 U.S., at 295, 92 S.Ct., at 1586. Indeed, where it is feasible to wait and examine the full complement—as it was here—it clearly is fairer to both employer and employees to do so. The substantial complement test provides no more than an *estimate* of the percentage of employees from the old company that eventually will be part of the new business, and thus often will be an imperfect measure of continuing union support. The risks of relying on such an estimate are obvious. If the "substantial complement" examined by the Board at a particular time contains a disproportionate number of workers from the old company, the result either might be that the full work force is deprived of union representation that a majority favors, or is required to accept representation that a majority does not want. Accordingly, unless the delay or uncertainty of future expansion would frustrate the employees' legitimate interest in early representation—a situation not shown to exist here—there is every reason to wait until the full anticipated work force has been employed.

In this case the date chosen by the NLRB for measuring the substantial complement standard is unsupportable, and the Court's affirmance of this choice, curious. In prior decisions, courts and the Board have looked not only to the *number* of workers hired and positions filled on a particular date, but also to "the time expected to elapse before a substantially larger complement would be at work ... as well as the relative certainty of the employer's expected expansion." Premium Foods, Inc. v. NLRB, 709 F.2d 623, 628 (C.A.9 1983). See also St. John of God Hospital, Inc., 260 N.L.R.B. 905 (1982). Here the anticipated expansion was both imminent and reasonably definite. The record shows that in January petitioner both expected to, and in fact subsequently did, hire a significant number of new employees to staff its second shift. Although the Court finds that the growth of the work force was "contingent" on business conditions, neither the Administrative Law Judge nor the NLRB made such a finding.[7] In fact, they both noted that by January 15, the second shift already had begun limited operations. See 272 N.L.R.B., at 839, n. 1 ("[i]n mid-January [petitioner] had one shift in full operation and had started a second shift"); id., at 840. In fact, less than three months after the duty to bargain allegedly arose, petitioner had nearly doubled the size of its mid-January work force by hiring the remaining 50–odd workers it needed to reach full production. This expansion was not unexpected; instead, it closely tracked petitioner's original forecast for growth during its first few months in business. Thus there was no reasonable basis for selecting mid-

---

7. The evidence shows that in the textile industry, two shifts are necessary for proper finishing work. See 775 F.2d 425, 428 (C.A.1 1985). Thus, it was clear in mid-January that petitioner would need more employees in the immediate future.

January as the time that petitioner should have known that it should commence bargaining.[9]

As the Court notes, the substantial complement rule reflects the need to balance "the objective of insuring maximum employee participation in the selection of a bargaining agent against the goal of permitting employees to be represented as quickly as possible." The decision today "balances" these interests by over-protecting the latter and ignoring the former. In an effort to ensure that some employees will not be deprived of representation for even a short time, the Court requires petitioner to recognize a union that has never been elected or accepted by a majority of its workers. For the reasons stated, I think that the Court's decision is unfair both to petitioner, who hardly could have anticipated the date chosen by the Board, and to most of petitioner's employees, who were denied the opportunity to choose their union. I dissent.

---

## PROBLEMS FOR DISCUSSION

**1.** Food America, a food service contractor, had the contract to supply food services at Old Siwash College. Four employees performed that work. They were part of a workforce of 150 Food America employees engaged at numerous locations. The workforce comprised a single bargaining unit represented by the Food Service Workers Union under a collective bargaining agreement that ran from 1999 to 2002. Old Siwash terminated Food America's contract in May of 2001, and awarded it to Gastronomic, Inc. Gastronomic contacted each of the four previous Food America employees on June 1, 2001, and asked them to apply for employment. At the same time, it discussed the establishment of a "working manager" job with the union. Gastronomic scheduled job interviews with the four for June 23. On June 22, it informed the union that it wanted these employees to serve a probationary period. In the interviews conducted the next day, it offered each of the four a job at a substantial pay reduction. Three of the four refused. The union filed a charge under section 8(a)(5) and the General Counsel has issued a complaint. How should the Board rule? See Canteen Co., 317 NLRB 1052 (1995); NLRB v. Advanced Stretchforming Int'l, Inc., 233 F.3d 1176 (9th Cir.2000). What weight, if any, should be given to the dramatic change in the size of the bargaining unit? See NLRB v. DeBartelo Group, 241 F.3d 207 (2d Cir.2001).

If, instead, Gastronomic declined to hire any of the four former Food America employees and the General Counsel can prove that its reason for doing so was to avoid having to bargain with the Food Service Workers Union, would that be an

---

**9.** The NLRB's reliance on the substantial complement standard is particularly puzzling on these facts, since the evidence shows that the "substantial" complement examined by the Board was not truly "representative" of the work force. When the unfair labor practice hearing was held on May 2, 1983, petitioner already had hired a full complement of workers. At that point the company employed 106–109 workers, less than half of whom were former Sterlingwale employees. Rather than rely on this accurate measure of the composition of the work force, the ALJ looked back to the middle of January, and concluded that petitioner should have acted differently because it *appeared* at the time that most of the workers who eventually would be represented by the union would be ex-Sterlingwale employees. In other words, the Board ruled that petitioner violated the NLRA because it failed to make the same estimate in January that the ALJ made in May—an estimate that already had proved to be erroneous at the time that the ALJ made it.

unfair labor practice?  If so, what would the remedy be?  Could the Board properly order that Gastronomic be bound by the Food America contract until its termination in 2002?  See U.S. Marine Corp. v. NLRB, 944 F.2d 1305 (7th Cir.1991), cert. denied, 503 U.S. 936, 112 S.Ct. 1474, 117 L.Ed.2d 618 (1992).

**2.**  Phoenix Steel Company was a specialty steel mill producing a number of different low-volume, high-cost steels for specific uses.  It employed from 600 to 1,000 employees in about 134 job classifications.  The workers had been represented by the Steelworkers Union since 1943.  In March 2000, the plant closed.  The international union continued to help the workers to get job retraining, benefits, and placement services; but the union hall was closed and the local's officers either left town or were relieved of their duties.  In June 2001, a foreign investor group acquired the plant for $13 million; it modernized the plant at a cost of $25 million and reopened in February 2002.  The plant uses advanced technology to produce a few types of steel at high volume and low cost (known as a "minimill").  It began with 100 workers, hoping to reach a maximum workforce of 350.  Workers were placed in one of about 25 job classifications, which required cross-training for more than one job and the doing of much that in the past had been done by first-line supervisors (who were largely eliminated).  Two months after reopening, the plant employed 125 production and maintenance employees, a majority of whom had worked for Phoenix.  The union has demanded recognition, the company has denied it, and upon the union's charge the General Counsel has issued a complaint under section 8(a)(5).  How should the Board rule?  See CitiSteel USA v. NLRB, 53 F.3d 350 (D.C.Cir.1995).

**3.**  You are an attorney retained to advise the Acme Company, which wishes to take over the Baker Company.  Acme would like to free itself of any present obligation to bargain with the Union representing Baker employees, as well as from Baker's obligation to continue the existing terms of employment of the employees.  Is it possible for Acme to do this without violating the law?  What would you advise it to do?

**4.**  If a successor employer wrongfully refuses to bargain with the union, but a majority of employees subsequently petition the employer that they no longer wish to be represented by the union, which petition was not coerced or solicited by the employer, may the Board issue a bargaining order?  See Sullivan Industries v. NLRB, 957 F.2d 890 (D.C.Cir.1992).

---

GOLDEN STATE BOTTLING CO. v. NLRB, 414 U.S. 168, 94 S.Ct. 414, 38 L.Ed.2d 388 (1973).  Golden State, a bottler and distributor of soft drinks, was held by the NLRB to have unlawfully discharged employee Baker and was ordered to reinstate him with backpay.  Thereafter, with knowledge of these facts, All American Beverages, Inc. purchased the business and continued to carry it on without interruption or substantial changes in method of operation, employee complement, or supervisory personnel.  In the NLRB's supplemental proceeding against Golden State to determine backpay, it also named and notified All American, which was ordered to reinstate Baker and (jointly with Golden State) to pay him backpay.  The Supreme Court held that the Board had the statutory authority to treat All American, a bona fide purchaser, as a "successor" to Golden State's liability for this preexisting unfair labor practice.

All American referred to section 10(c), the remedy provision of the NLRA, which empowers the NLRB to order "any person named in the complaint" to take remedial action that "will effectuate the policies of this Act." The Court referred to some of its early decisions under the NLRA which held that a Board order directed against the perpetrator of an unfair labor practice, and its "officers, agents, successors, and assigns" may be applied to a transferee employer who has taken over "as a means of evading the judgment or for other reasons"; the sale transaction may not itself be an unfair labor practice, but the Board nonetheless "is obligated to effectuate the policies of the Act" and can do so through an order to the successor. And, interpreting Federal Rule of Civil Procedure 65(d), which makes a court injunctive order binding only upon the parties to an action "and upon those persons in active concert or participation with them," the Court concluded: "We hold that a bona fide purchaser, acquiring, with knowledge that the wrong remains unremedied, the employing enterprise which was the locus of the unfair labor practice, may be considered in privity with its predecessor for purposes of Rule 65(d)."

All American claimed that it was a denial of due process to subject it to the Board's reinstatement and backpay order. To that, the Court responded:

> In this case, All American has no complaint that it was denied due notice and a fair hearing. It was made a party to the supplemental backpay specification proceeding, given notice of the hearing, and afforded full opportunity, with the assistance of counsel, to contest the question of its successorship for purpose of the Act and its knowledge of the pendency of the unfair labor practice litigation at the time of purchase.

Turning then to the question whether the Board had properly exercised its discretion, the Court noted that the Board seeks to strike "a balance between the conflicting legitimate interests of the bona fide successor, the public, and the affected employee," and that the Board had not erred in placing special weight on the victimized employee's need for protection at a time his employer's business is changing hands and is then operated essentially unchanged. "Under these circumstances, the employees may well perceive the successor's failure to remedy the predecessor employer's unfair labor practices arising out of an unlawful discharge as a continuation of the predecessor's labor policies." Allowing this may result in labor unrest or may deter union activities and create a "leadership vacuum" in the future. Reinstatement and backpay by the successor will address these statutory concerns

> at a relatively minimal cost to the bona fide successor. Since the successor must have notice before liability can be imposed, "his potential liability for remedying the unfair labor practice is a matter which can be reflected in the price he pays for the business, or he may secure an indemnity clause in the sale contract which will indemnify him for liability arising from the seller's unfair labor practices." ... If the reinstated employee does not effectively perform, he may, of course, be discharged for cause.

## PROBLEM FOR DISCUSSION

Should a successor's liability for remedying the predecessor's unfair labor practices be conditioned on an NLRB order being issued prior to the acquisition? on charges having been filed? or merely on illegal acts having been committed by the predecessor? See NLRB v. St. Marys Foundry Co., 860 F.2d 679 (6th Cir.1988).

———

# Howard Johnson Co. v. Detroit Local Joint Executive Bd.[b]

417 U.S. 249, 94 S.Ct. 2236, 41 L.Ed.2d 46 (1974).

■ MR. JUSTICE MARSHALL delivered the opinion of the Court.

[The Grissom family owned and operated a Howard Johnson Motor Lodge and an adjacent restaurant. Its employees at the two locations were represented by the Hotel and Restaurant Employees Union in two separate bargaining units. Both collective bargaining agreements had arbitration provisions and also provided that the agreements would be binding on the employer's "successors, assigns, purchasers, lessees or transferees." The Grissoms leased their real property to the Howard Johnson Co. and sold it the personal property, Howard Johnson thus becoming the direct operator of these facilities. By letter to the seller, Howard Johnson disclaimed that it would be bound by any labor agreement. On July 9, the Grissoms notified all employees that their employment would terminate as of July 23, when operations would be transferred to Howard Johnson. Howard Johnson notified the union on July 11 that it would not recognize the union or assume any obligation of the existing collective bargaining agreements. It started hiring on July 10 and commenced operations with 45 employees, few of whom had been employed by the Grissoms. Upon the union's suit, the lower courts held that Howard Johnson was required to arbitrate with the union the extent of Howard Johnson's obligations to the former Grissom employees. The United States Supreme Court reversed.]

Both courts below relied heavily on this Court's decision in John Wiley & Sons v. Livingston, 376 U.S. 543 (1964). In *Wiley,* the union representing the employees of a corporation which had disappeared through a merger sought to compel the surviving corporation, which had hired all of the merged corporation's employees and continued to operate the enterprise in a substantially identical form after the merger, to arbitrate under the merged corporation's collective-bargaining agreement. As *Wiley* was this Court's first experience with the difficult "successorship" question, its holding was properly cautious and narrow:

---

**b.** In addition to materials cited at p. 872, supra, see Goldstein, Protecting Employee Rights in Successorship, 44 Lab.L.J. 18 (1993); Severson & Willcoxon, Successorship Under *Howard Johnson*: Short Order Justice for Employees, 64 Calif.L.Rev. 795 (1976); Silverstein, The Fate of Workers in Successor Firms: Does Law Tame the Market?, 8 Indus.Rel.L.J. 153 (1986).

"We hold that the disappearance by merger of a corporate employer which has entered into a collective bargaining agreement with a union does not automatically terminate all rights of the employees covered by the agreement, and that, in appropriate circumstances, present here, the successor employer may be required to arbitrate with the union under the agreement." Id., at 548.

Mr. Justice Harlan, writing for the Court, emphasized "the central role of arbitration in effectuating national labor policy" and preventing industrial strife, and the need to afford some protection to the interests of the employees during a change of corporate ownership. Id., at 549.

The courts below recognized that the reasoning of *Wiley* was to some extent inconsistent with our more recent decision in NLRB v. Burns International Security Services, 406 U.S. 272 (1972). * * *

We find it unnecessary, however, to decide in the circumstances of this case whether there is any irreconcilable conflict between *Wiley* and *Burns.* We believe that even on its own terms, *Wiley* does not support the decision of the courts below.  The Court in *Burns* recognized that its decision "turn[ed] to a great extent on the precise facts involved here." * * *

When the focus is placed on the facts of these cases, it becomes apparent that the decision below is an unwarranted extension of *Wiley* beyond any factual context it may have contemplated.  Although it is true that both *Wiley* and this case involve § 301 suits to compel arbitration, the similarity ends there.  *Wiley* involved a merger, as a result of which the initial employing entity completely disappeared.  In contrast, this case involves only a sale of some assets, and the initial employers remain in existence as viable corporate entities, with substantial revenues from the lease of the motor lodge and restaurant to Howard Johnson.  Although we have recognized that ordinarily there is no basis for distinguishing among mergers, consolidations, or purchases of assets in the analysis of successorship problems, see Golden State Bottling Co. v. NLRB, 414 U.S. 168, 182–183, n. 5 (1973), we think these distinctions are relevant here for two reasons.  First, the merger in *Wiley* was conducted "against a background of state law that embodied the general rule that in merger situations the surviving corporation is liable for the obligations of the disappearing corporation," *Burns,* 406 U.S., at 286, which suggests that holding Wiley bound to arbitrate under its predecessor's collective-bargaining agreement may have been fairly within the reasonable expectations of the parties.  Second, the disappearance of the original employing entity in the *Wiley* merger meant that unless the union were afforded some remedy against Wiley, it would have no means to enforce the obligations voluntarily undertaken by the merged corporation, to the extent that those obligations vested prior to the merger or to the extent that its promises were intended to survive a change of ownership.  Here, in contrast, because the Grissom corporations continue as viable entities with substantial retained assets, the Union does have a realistic remedy to enforce their contractual obligations.  Indeed, the Grissoms have agreed to arbitrate the extent of their liability to the Union and their former employees; presumably this arbitration will explore the question whether the Grissoms breached the successorship provisions of their collective-bargaining agreements, and what the remedy for this breach might be.[3]

Even more important, in *Wiley* the surviving corporation hired *all* of the employees of the disappearing corporation. Although, under *Burns*, the surviving corporation may have been entitled to make substantial changes in its operation of the enterprise, the plain fact is that it did not. As the arbitrator in *Wiley* subsequently stated:

> "Although the Wiley merger was effective on October 2, 1961, the former Interscience employees continued to perform the same work on the same products under the same management at the same work place as before the change in the corporate employer."

Interscience Encyclopedia, Inc., 55 Lab.Arb. 210, 218 (1970).[4]

The claims which the union sought to compel Wiley to arbitrate were thus the claims of Wiley's employees as to the benefits they were entitled to receive in connection with their employment. It was on this basis that the Court in *Wiley* found that there was the "substantial continuity of identity in the business enterprise," 376 U.S., at 551, which it held necessary before the successor employer could be compelled to arbitrate.

Here, however, Howard Johnson decided to select and hire its own independent work force to commence its operation of the restaurant and motor lodge.[5] It therefore hired only nine of the 53 former Grissom

**3.** The Union apparently did not explore another remedy which might have been available to it prior to the sale, i.e., moving to enjoin the sale to Howard Johnson on the ground that this was a breach by the Grissoms of the successorship clauses in the collective-bargaining agreements. See National Maritime Union v. Commerce Tankers Corp., 325 F.Supp. 360 (S.D.N.Y.1971), vacated, 457 F.2d 1127 (C.A.2 1972). The mere existence of the successorship clauses in the bargaining agreements between the Union and the Grissoms, however, cannot bind Howard Johnson either to the substantive terms of the agreements or to the arbitration clauses thereof, absent the continuity required by *Wiley*, when it is perfectly clear the Company refused to assume any obligations under the agreements.

**4.** Subsequently, the Interscience plant was closed and the former Interscience employees were integrated into Wiley's work force. The arbitrator, relying in part on the NLRB's decision in *Burns*, held that the provisions of the Interscience collective-bargaining agreement remained in effect for as long as Wiley continued to operate the former Interscience enterprise as a unit in substan-

tially the same manner as prior to the merger, but that the integration of the former Interscience employees into Wiley's operations destroyed this continuity of identity and terminated the effectiveness of the bargaining agreement. 55 Lab.Arb., at 218–220.

**5.** It is important to emphasize that this is not a case where the successor corporation is the "alter ego" of the predecessor, where it is "merely a disguised continuance of the old employer." Southport Petroleum Co. v. NLRB, 315 U.S. 100, 106, 62 S.Ct. 452, 455, 86 L.Ed. 718 (1942). Such cases involve a mere technical change in the structure or identity of the employing entity, frequently to avoid the effect of the labor laws, without any substantial change in its ownership or management. In these circumstances, the courts have had little difficulty holding that the successor is in reality the same employer and is subject to all the legal and contractual obligations of the predecessor. * * *

There is not the slightest suggestion in this case that the sale of the restaurant and motor lodge by the Grissoms to Howard Johnson was in any sense a paper transaction without meaningful impact on the ownership or operation of the enterprise. * * *

employees and none of the Grissom supervisors.  The primary purpose of the Union in seeking arbitration here with Howard Johnson is not to protect the rights of Howard Johnson's employees; rather, the Union primarily seeks arbitration on behalf of the former Grissom employees who were *not* hired by Howard Johnson.  It is the Union's position that Howard Johnson was bound by the pre-existing collective-bargaining agreement to employ all of these former Grissom employees, except those who could be dismissed in accordance with the "just cause" provision or laid off in accordance with the seniority provision.  * * *

What the Union seeks here is completely at odds with the basic principles this Court elaborated in *Burns*.  We found there that nothing in the federal labor laws "requires that an employer ... who purchases the assets of a business be obligated to hire all of the employees of the predecessor though it is possible that such an obligation might be assumed by the employer."  406 U.S., at 280 n. 5.  See also Golden State Bottling Co. v. NLRB, 414 U.S., at 184 n. 6.  *Burns* emphasized that "[a] potential employer may be willing to take over a moribund business only if he can make changes in corporate structure, composition of the labor force, ... and nature of supervision."  406 U.S., at 287–288.  We rejected the Board's position in part because "[i]t would seemingly follow that employees of the predecessor would be deemed employees of the successor, dischargeable only in accordance with provisions of the contract and subject to the grievance and arbitration provisions thereof.  Burns would not have been free to replace Wackenhut's guards with its own except as the contract permitted."  Id., at 288.  Clearly, *Burns* establishes that Howard Johnson had the right not to hire any of the former Grissom employees, if it so desired.[8]  The Union's effort to circumvent this holding by asserting its claims in a § 301 suit to compel arbitration rather than in an unfair labor practice context cannot be permitted.

We do not believe that *Wiley* requires a successor employer to arbitrate in the circumstances of this case.[9]  The Court there held that arbitration

---

**8.** See Crotona Service Corp., 200 N.L.R.B. 738 (1972).  Of course, it is an unfair labor practice for an employer to discriminate in hiring or retention of employees on the basis of union membership or activity under § 8(a)(3) of the National Labor Relations Act, 29 U.S.C. § 158(a)(3).  Thus, a new owner could not refuse to hire the employees of his predecessor solely because they were union members or to avoid having to recognize the union.  * * * There is no suggestion in this case that Howard Johnson in any way discriminated in its hiring against the former Grissom employees because of their union membership, activity, or representation.

**9.** The Court of Appeals stated that "[t]he first question we must face is whether

Howard Johnson is a successor employer," 482 F.2d, at 492, and, finding that it was, that the next question was whether a successor is required to arbitrate under the collective-bargaining agreement of its predecessor, id., at 494, which the court found was resolved by *Wiley*.  We do not believe that this artificial division between these questions is a helpful or appropriate way to approach these problems.  The question whether Howard Johnson is a "successor" is simply not meaningful in the abstract.  Howard Johnson is of course a successor employer in the sense that it succeeded to operation of a restaurant and motor lodge formerly operated by the Grissoms.  But the real question in each of these "successorship" cases is, on the particular facts, what are the legal obligations of the new employer to the employees

could not be compelled unless there was "substantial continuity of identity in the business enterprise" before and after a change of ownership, for otherwise the duty to arbitrate would be "something imposed from without, not reasonably to be found in the particular bargaining agreement and the acts of the parties involved." 376 U.S., at 551. This continuity of identity in the business enterprise necessarily includes, we think, a substantial continuity in the identity of the work force across the change in ownership. The *Wiley* Court seemingly recognized this, as it found the requisite continuity present there in reliance on the "wholesale transfer" of Interscience employees to Wiley. Ibid. This view is reflected in the emphasis most of the lower courts have placed on whether the successor employer hires a majority of the predecessor's employees in determining the legal obligations of the successor in § 301 suits under *Wiley*. This interpretation of *Wiley* is consistent also with the Court's concern with affording protection to those employees who are in fact retained in "[t]he transition from one corporate organization to another" from sudden changes in the terms and conditions of their employment, and with its belief that industrial strife would be avoided if these employees' claims were resolved by arbitration rather than by " 'the relative strength ... of the contending forces.' " Id., at 549, quoting United Steelworkers v. Warrior & Gulf Navigation Co., 363 U.S. 574, 580 (1960). At the same time, it recognizes that the employees of the terminating employer have no legal right to continued employment with the new employer, and avoids the difficulties inherent in the Union's position in this case. This holding is compelled, in our view, if the protection afforded employee interests in a change of ownership by *Wiley* is to be reconciled with the new employer's right to operate the enterprise with his own independent labor force.

Since there was plainly no substantial continuity of identity in the work force hired by Howard Johnson with that of the Grissoms, and no express or implied assumption of the agreement to arbitrate, the courts below erred in compelling the Company to arbitrate the extent of its obligations to the former Grissom employees. Accordingly, the judgment of the Court of Appeals must be

---

of the former owner or their representative? The answer to this inquiry requires analysis of the interests of the new employer and the employees and of the policies of the labor laws in light of the facts of each case and the particular legal obligation which is at issue, whether it be the duty to recognize and bargain with the union, the duty to remedy unfair labor practices, the duty to arbitrate, etc. There is, and can be, no single definition of "successor" which is applicable in every legal context. A new employer, in other words, may be a successor for some purposes and not for others. See Golden State Bottling Co. v. NLRB, 414 U.S. 168, 181 (1973); International Assn. of Machinists v.

NLRB, 134 U.S.App.D.C. 239, 244, 414 F.2d 1135, 1140 (1969)(Leventhal, J., concurring); Goldberg, The Labor Law Obligations of a Successor Employer, 63 Nw.U.L.Rev. 735 (1969); Comment, Contractual Successorship: The Impact of *Burns*, 40 U.Chi.L.Rev. 617, 619 n. 10 (1973).

Thus, our holding today is that Howard Johnson was not required to arbitrate with the Union representing the former Grissom employees in the circumstances of this case. We necessarily do not decide whether Howard Johnson is or is not a "successor employer" for any other purpose.

*Reversed.*

■ MR. JUSTICE DOUGLAS, dissenting.

* * * The contract between the Grissoms and the Union explicitly provided that successors of the Grissoms would be bound, and certainly there can be no question that there was a substantial continuity—indeed identity—of the business operation under Howard Johnson, the successor employer. Under its franchise agreement Howard Johnson had substantial control over the Grissoms' operation of the business;[2] it was no stranger to the enterprise it took over. The business continued without interruption at the same location, offering the same products and services to the same public, under the same name and in the same manner, with almost the same number of employees. The only change was Howard Johnson's replacement of the Union members with new personnel, but as the court below pointed out, petitioner's reliance upon that fact is sheer "bootstrap": "[Howard Johnson] argues that it need not arbitrate the refusal to hire Grissoms' employees because it is not a successor. It is not a successor, because it did not hire a majority of Grissoms' employees." 482 F.2d 489, 493.

As we said in *Wiley,* "[i]t would derogate from 'the federal policy of settling labor disputes by arbitration,' . . . if a change in the corporate structure or ownership of a business enterprise had the automatic consequence of removing a duty to arbitrate previously established. . . ." 376 U.S., at 549.

NLRB v. Burns International Security Services, supra, does not require any different result. * * * In distinguishing *Wiley,* we pointed out in *Burns* that unlike *Wiley* it did not involve a § 301 suit to compel arbitration, and thus was without the support of the national policy favoring arbitration. *Burns,* supra, at 286. Moreover, in *Burns* "there was no merger or sale of assets, and there were no dealings whatsoever between Wackenhut and Burns. On the contrary, they were competitors for the same work, each bidding for the service contract at Lockheed. Burns purchased nothing from Wackenhut and became liable for none of its financial obligations." Ibid.

All of the factors distinguishing *Burns* and *Wiley* call here for affirmance of the order to arbitrate. This is a § 301 suit, and Howard Johnson did purchase the assets from the Grissoms. As a matter of federal labor law, when Howard Johnson took over the operation that had been conducted by its franchisee, it seems clear that it also took over the duty to arbitrate under the collective-bargaining agreements which expressly bound the Grissoms' successors. Any other result makes nonsense of the

**2.** The motel franchise agreement provided, for example, that Howard Johnson would determine and approve standards of construction, operation, and service, and would have the right at any time to enter the premises for that purpose; that prior approval would be required for equipment and sup- plies bearing the name "Howard Johnson"; that Howard Johnson would have the first option to purchase if the business were to be sold, and that in any event Howard Johnson must approve any successor. See the District Court opinion, 81 L.R.R.M. 2329, 2330, and App. 50a et seq.

principles laid down in *Wiley*.   The majority, by making the number of
prior employees retained by the successor the sole determinative factor,
accepts petitioner's bootstrap argument.   The effect is to allow any new
employer to determine for himself whether he will be bound, by the simple
expedient of arranging for the termination of all of the prior employer's
personnel.   I cannot accept such a rule, especially when, as here, all of the
other factors point so compellingly to the conclusion that petitioner is a
successor employer who should be bound by the arbitration agreement.

## PROBLEMS FOR DISCUSSION

**1.**   What is the underlying rationale for finding one company to "succeed" to
another company's bargaining obligation?  arbitration obligation?  obligation to
remedy unfair labor practices?   Is it that the employees at the new company can
reasonably be assumed to want the union, or the contract terms, that had previously obtained?   Is it that the new company can reasonably expect to deal with the old
union or to be governed by the old contract?   To what extent does federal labor
policy dictate the result, as distinguished from the likely expectations or preferences
of the parties?

**2.**   In determining whether one company succeeds to another's duty to bargain,
*Burns* and *Fall River* emphasize the proportion of the *successor's* workforce that
had previously been employed by the predecessor.   In determining whether one
company succeeds to another's duty to arbitrate, *Howard Johnson* emphasizes the
proportion of the *predecessor's* workforce that is retained by the successor.   Are
these tests consistent?   Are they each sound?

**3.**   Recall that in the *Wiley* case, the small Interscience publishing company was
merged into the larger Wiley company; the Supreme Court held that Wiley had a
duty to arbitrate under the Interscience labor agreement.   What result would the
Court have reached had the Interscience union made a demand that Wiley bargain
with it on behalf of the absorbed Interscience employees?   (Recall, in particular, the
rules regarding the appropriate bargaining unit.)

**4.**   Weber operated a retail coal and fuel oil business in Brooklyn, New York with
24 drivers and servicemen represented by Teamsters under a collective agreement
running until December 15, which contained provisions relating to seniority,
grievances, job security, pensions, and other matters.   There was also a conventional arbitration clause.   Six months prior to the expiration date of the agreement
Humble, a fully integrated oil company with retail fuel oil customers, purchased all
the assets and good will of Weber, and hired about half of Weber's employees.   The
Weber operations and accounts were completely absorbed into Humble's business
and lost any separate identity.   Humble's 518 employees in the New York area,
including those in its retail fuel oil business, were represented by another union
under a different collective agreement.   The Teamsters demanded that Humble
comply with its contract with Weber and, when Humble declined, demanded
arbitration.   Humble refused arbitration and the Teamsters brought an action
under Section 301.   Pending the litigation the NLRB determined that the former
Weber employees had become part of the Humble bargaining unit.   The district
court, following *Wiley*, ordered arbitration.   Humble appealed.   What judgment
should be entered?   See McGuire v. Humble Oil & Refining Co., 355 F.2d 352 (2d

Cir.1966).   Cf. General Warehousemen and Helpers Local 767 v. Standard Brands, Inc., 579 F.2d 1282 (5th Cir.1978).

———————

### THE "DOUBLE BREASTED EMPLOYER"

The increased utilization of nonunion labor in the construction industry in recent years has led to the phenomenon of the "double-breasted" company.   A subcontractor that is already unionized (and drawing its workforce from the union hiring hall) may—in order to submit bids to general contractors who invite bids from nonunion subcontractors—cause the creation of a parallel nonunion entity.   The nonunion company may be spun off from the unionized company, or both may be subsidiaries of a parent holding company.   The union may contend that the two entities are really a single employer and that the collective bargaining agreement at the unionized company also governs the nonsignatory company, so that the union secures representation rights there and the employees get the economic benefits of the labor agreement.   If the double-breasted employer rejects the union and the contract in the nonunion enterprise, the union may file a refusal-to-bargain charge under Section 8(a)(5).

In such situations, the Board will undertake a two-step analysis.   First, it will determine whether the two entities are properly to be treated as a single integrated employer.   The Board looks for indicia of interrelated operations, common management, common ownership, and centralized control of labor relations; it determines whether there would be comparable arrangements found in an arm's length relationship among unintegrated companies.

Even if the Board finds that the double-breasted company is really a single employer, it does not, however, automatically follow that the union and its contract terms will be imported into the nonsignatory company. The Board must make a separate determination as to whether the two enterprises constitute a single bargaining unit.   Here, the usual "community of interest" test will be applied, in order to protect the rights of the employees of the nonsignatory company to choose their own bargaining representative.   If the Board finds that the two entities constitute a single appropriate unit, then the union will be declared the representative of all of the workers and the contract will govern the terms of employment.

This two-step approach has been endorsed by the Supreme Court. South Prairie Constr. Co. v. Operating Engineers, Local 627, 425 U.S. 800, 96 S.Ct. 1842, 48 L.Ed.2d 382 (1976).   See generally, Befort, Labor Law and the Double–Breasted Employer: A Critique of the Single Employer and Alter Ego Doctrines and a Proposed Reformulation, 1987 Wisc.L.Rev. 67; Bornstein, The Emerging Law of the "Double Breasted" Operation in the Construction Industry, 28 Lab.L.J. 77 (1977).   If the Board finds a Section 8(a)(5) violation, it can order not only recognition of the union and honoring of the contract but also backpay and other make-whole remedies.

*E.g.*, Angelus Block Co., 250 NLRB 868 (1980)(employer ordered to pay employees for past medical and dental bills).

The rights of the parties in the double-breasted situation can also be determined in a Section 301 action in which the union seeks to compel an employer to arbitrate the pertinent issues under the labor agreement. E.g., Bricklayers Local 6 v. Boyd G. Heminger, Inc., 483 F.2d 129 (6th Cir.1973); Carpenters Local 1846 v. Pratt–Farnsworth, Inc., 690 F.2d 489 (5th Cir.1982).

# PART SEVEN

# LABOR AND THE ANTITRUST LAWS[a]

It will be recalled that the Supreme Court held, in Loewe v. Lawlor, 208 U.S. 274, 28 S.Ct. 301, 52 L.Ed. 488 (1908), that the Sherman Act applied to combinations of workers, and affirmed a judgment for damages. See page 33, supra. In 1914 the Clayton Act granted private persons the right to injunctive relief against violations of the Sherman Act. Congress had in mind suits against trusts and similar corporate combinations, but the new remedy was soon seized upon by employers seeking to put a speedy end to strikes and picketing. Although Sections 6 and 20 of the Clayton Act were widely believed to curtail the labor injunction, Duplex Printing Press Co. v. Deering, p. 40, supra, limited them to disputes between an employer and its own employees. This very controversial analysis of the Clayton Act meant that the antitrust laws could still be utilized against such frequently employed union techniques as the secondary boycott and organizational picketing instigated by nonemployee union organizers (at least when these had the requisite impact on interstate commerce). Eventually, in 1932, the Norris–LaGuardia Act was broadly written so as to shelter against federal injunction a wide range of peaceful concerted activities, even those involving "strangers" to the dispute. Further protection for such activities—and imminent conflict with the Sherman Act as

**a.** See Cox, Labor and the Antitrust Laws—A Preliminary Analysis, 104 U.Pa. L.Rev. 252 (1955); Cox, Labor and the Antitrust Laws: Pennington and Jewel Tea, 46 B.U.L.Rev. 317 (1966); Gifford, Redefining the Antitrust Labor Exemption, 72 Minn. L.Rev. 1379 (1988); Handler & Zifchak, Collective Bargaining and the Antitrust Laws: The Emasculation of the Labor Exemption, 81 Colum.L.Rev. 459 (1981); Leslie, Principles of Labor Antitrust, 66 Va.L.Rev. 1183 (1980); Meltzer, Labor Unions, Collective Bargaining, and the Antitrust Laws, 32 U.Chi.L.Rev. 659 (1965); E. Miller, Antitrust Laws and Employee Relations (1984); Winter, Collective Bargaining and Competition: The Application of Antitrust Standards to Union Activities, 73 Yale L.J. 14 (1963).

applied to labor—resulted from the enactment of New Deal legislation such as the Fair Labor Standards Act and the Wagner Act.

The antitrust laws were designed to encourage manufacturers to compete for public favor at least in part through lower prices; this generated pressure on manufacturers to minimize the costs incurred for the factors of production, among which was labor. A strict application of antitrust policy would induce employers, through individualized bargaining, constantly to bid down the cost of labor (i.e., wages paid) and to secure a competent workforce at the lowest wage that the market would allow. The national labor laws, on the other hand, were based on the congressional judgment that just such individual bargaining and subsistence working conditions caused industrial strife and interruptions in the flow of interstate commerce. Congress's remedy was to foster collective bargaining, which was "anti-competitive" in at least two respects. First, wage demands were thus stabilized within a single plant, geographic area or industry; competition was removed from the labor market. Second, and as a result, competition in pricing was restricted in the product market, to the extent that product prices among competitors were determined by the costs incurred by the manufacturers in purchasing labor. In short, unionization, collective bargaining and standardization of wages and working conditions are inherently inconsistent with many of the assumptions at the heart of antitrust policy.

The reader will recall that an "accommodation" between federal labor and antitrust policies was effectively reached through the creative analysis of Justice Stone in *Apex Hosiery Co. v. Leader,* p. 56 supra. That decision should be re-examined at this time, along with the accompanying Problems for Discussion. So too should the decision of a divided Supreme Court in *United States v. Hutcheson,* at page 58 supra. These two decisions appear to leave rather little room for the application of the federal antitrust laws to labor union activity. The *Allen–Bradley* case, excerpted below, represents what is generally regarded as a particularly objectionable form of union participation in company antitrust violations. (That decision has had at least as much impact upon the evolution of the law of secondary boycotts under the federal labor acts as it has had upon the evolution of the antitrust laws.) The accommodation of the federal labor and antitrust laws remains a bone of contention, as the divided decisions of the Supreme Court in the following cases demonstrate.

ALLEN BRADLEY CO. v. LOCAL UNION No. 3, IBEW, 325 U.S. 797, 65 S.Ct. 1533, 89 L.Ed. 1939 (1945). Local 3 of the International Brotherhood of Electrical Workers had jurisdiction over the metropolitan district of New York only. Some of its members were employed by New York manufacturers of electrical equipment and others by contractors engaged in installing such equipment in the New York area. In order to enlarge employment opportunities for union members working in local manufacturing establishments, the union obtained closed-shop contracts with those manufacturers. In addition, by means of strikes and boycotts, it put pressure on the contractors to agree not to purchase equipment except from local manufacturers having such contracts. These agreements with individual employers were subsequently expanded into a local industry-wide understanding which resulted in the setting up of agencies composed of representatives of the unions, the manufacturers and the contractors for the purpose of boycotting recalcitrant local manufacturers and contractors and excluding from the metropolitan area all equipment manufactured elsewhere, including that manufactured in factories which had collective bargaining agreements with other locals of the IBEW. Plaintiffs, manufacturers of electrical equipment in other cities, brought suit in a federal court against the New York local union, its officials and members, and obtained both a declaratory judgment to the effect that the combination of the union and the employers was a violation of the Sherman Act and a broadly phrased injunction, which included a provision forbidding all persons, including union officials, to induce union members not to install plaintiff's products. This decision was reversed by the Circuit Court of Appeals for the Second Circuit, which held "the activities which cannot be forbidden to Local 3 acting by itself are not to be interdicted because other groups join with them to the same end." 145 F.2d 215.

The Supreme Court held that the Sherman Act had been violated, but that the injunction should be limited to activities in which the union engaged in combination "with any person, firm or corporation which is a non-labor group." Mr. Justice Black, writing for himself and six other members of the Court, stated—

"Aside from the fact that the labor union here acted in combination with the contractors and manufacturers, the means it adopted to contribute to the combination's purpose fall squarely within the 'specified acts' declared by § 20 not to be violations of federal law. For the union's contribution to the trade boycott was accomplished through threats that unless their employers bought their goods from local manufacturers the union laborers would terminate the 'relation of employment' with them and cease to perform 'work or labor' for them; and through their 'recommending, advising, or persuading others by peaceful and lawful means' not to 'patronize' sellers of the boycotted electrical equipment. Consequently, under our holdings in the *Hutcheson* case and other cases which followed it, had there been no union-contractor-manufacturer combination the union's actions here, coming as they did within the exemptions of the Clayton and Norris–LaGuardia Acts, would not have been violations of the Sherman Act. * * *

"We have been pointed to no language in any act of Congress or in its reports or debates, nor have we found any, which indicates that it was ever suggested, considered, or legislatively determined that labor unions should be granted an immunity such as is sought in the present case. It has been argued that this immunity can be inferred from the union's right to make bargaining agreements with its employer. Since union members can without violating the Sherman Act strike to enforce a union boycott of goods, it is said they may settle the strike by getting their employers to agree to refuse to buy the goods. Employers and the union did here make bargaining agreements in which the employers agreed not to buy goods manufactured by companies which did not employ the members of Local No. 3.  We may assume that such an agreement standing alone would not have violated the Sherman Act.  But it did not stand alone.  It was but one element in a far larger program in which contractors and manufacturers united with one another to monopolize all the business in New York City, to bar all other business men from that area, and to charge the public prices above a competitive level.  It is true that victory of the union in its disputes, even had the union acted alone, might have added to the cost of goods, or might have resulted in individual refusals of all of their employers to buy electrical equipment not made by Local No. 3.  So far as the union might have achieved this result acting alone, it would have been the natural consequence of labor union activities exempted by the Clayton Act from the coverage of the Sherman Act.  But when the unions participated with a combination of business men who had complete power to eliminate all competition among themselves and to prevent all competition from others, a situation was created not included within the exemptions of the Clayton and Norris–LaGuardia Acts.''

---

## United Mine Workers of America v. Pennington

381 U.S. 657, 85 S.Ct. 1585, 14 L.Ed.2d 626 (1965).

■ Mr. Justice White delivered the opinion of the Court.  * * *

[In an action against the Phillips Brothers Coal Company, brought by trustees of the United Mine Workers Welfare and Retirement Fund for royalty payments allegedly due under a 1950 wage agreement (as amended), the Company filed an answer and a cross claim in which it asserted that the UMW, the trustees and certain large coal operators had conspired to restrain and monopolize interstate commerce in violation of Sections 1 and 2 of the Sherman Act; the Company claimed actual damages in the amount of $100,000.]  The allegations of the cross claim were essentially as follows:  Prior to the 1950 Wage Agreement between the operators and the union, severe controversy had existed in the industry, particularly over wages, the welfare fund and the union's efforts to control the working time of its members.  Since 1950, however, relative peace has existed in the industry, all as the result of the 1950 Wage Agreement and its amendments and the additional understandings entered into between UMW and the large operators.  Allegedly the parties considered overproduction to be the critical problem of the coal industry.  The agreed solution was to be the elimination of the smaller companies, the larger companies thereby controlling the market.  More specifically, the union abandoned its efforts to control the working time of the miners, agreed not to oppose the rapid mechanization of the mines which would substantially reduce mine employment, agreed to help finance such mechanization and agreed to impose the terms of the 1950 agreement on all operators without regard to their ability to pay.  The benefit to the union was to be increased wages as productivity increased with mechanization, these increases to be demanded of the smaller companies whether mechanized or not. * * *

The complaint survived motions to dismiss and after a five-week trial before a jury, a verdict was returned in favor of Phillips and against the trustees and the union, the damages against the union being fixed in the amount of $90,000, to be trebled under 15 U.S.C.A. § 15 (1958 ed.). The trial court set aside the verdict against the trustees but overruled the union's motion for judgment notwithstanding the verdict or in the alternative for a new trial. The Court of Appeals affirmed. * * *

## I.

We first consider UMW's contention that the trial court erred in denying its motion for a directed verdict and for judgment notwithstanding the verdict, since a determination in UMW's favor on this issue would finally resolve the controversy. The question presented by this phase of the case is whether in the circumstances of this case the union is exempt from liability under the antitrust laws. We think the answer is clearly in the negative and that the union's motions were correctly denied.

The antitrust laws do not bar the existence and operation of labor unions as such. Moreover, § 20 of the Clayton Act, 38 Stat. 738, and § 4 of the Norris–LaGuardia Act, 47 Stat. 70, permit a union, acting alone, to engage in the conduct therein specified without violating the Sherman Act. United States v. Hutcheson * * *.

But neither § 20 nor § 4 expressly deals with arrangements or agreements between unions and employers. Neither section tells us whether any or all such arrangements or agreements are barred or permitted by the antitrust laws. Thus Hutcheson itself stated:

"So long as a union acts in its self-interest *and does not combine with non-labor groups,* the licit and the illicit under § 20 are not to be distinguished by any judgment regarding the wisdom or unwisdom, the rightness or wrongness, the selfishness or unselfishness of the end of which the particular union activities are the means." 312 U.S., at 232, 61 S.Ct. at 466. (Emphasis added.)

And in Allen Bradley Co. v. Local Union No. 3, IBEW, 325 U.S. 797, 65 S.Ct. 1533, 89 L.Ed. 1939, this Court made explicit what had been merely a qualifying expression in Hutcheson and held that "when the unions participated with a combination of business men who had complete power to eliminate all competition among themselves and to prevent all competition from others, a situation was created not included with the exemptions of the Clayton and Norris–LaGuardia Acts." Id., 325 U.S. at 809, 65 S.Ct. at 1540. * * *

If the UMW in this case, in order to protect its wage scale by maintaining employer income, had presented a set of prices at which the mine operators would be required to sell their coal, the union and the employers who happened to agree could not successfully defend this contract provision if it were challenged under the antitrust laws by the United States or by some party injured by the arrangement.   Cf. Allen Bradley Co. v. Local Union No. 3, IBEW, 325 U.S. 797, 65 S.Ct. 1533, 89 L.Ed. 1939; * * * In such a case, the restraint on the product market is direct and immediate, is of the type characteristically deemed unreasonable under the Sherman Act and the union gets from the promise nothing more concrete than a hope for better wages to come.

Likewise, if as is alleged in this case, the union became a party to a collusive bidding arrangement designed to drive Phillips and others from the TVA spot market, we think any claim to exemption from antitrust liability would be frivolous at best.   For this reason alone the motions of the unions were properly denied.

A major part of Phillips' case, however, was that the union entered into a conspiracy with the large operators to impose the agreed-upon wage and royalty scales upon the smaller, nonunion operators, regardless of their ability to pay and regardless of whether or not the union represented the employees of these companies, all for the purpose of eliminating them from the industry, limiting production and pre-empting the market for the large, unionized operators.   The UMW urges that since such an agreement concerned wage standards, it is exempt from the antitrust laws.

It is true that wages lie at the very heart of those subjects about which employers and unions must bargain and the law contemplates agreements on wages not only between individual employers and a union but agreements between the union and employers in a multi-employer bargaining unit.   National Labor Relations Board v. Truck Drivers Union, 353 U.S. 87, 94–96, 77 S.Ct. 643, 646–647, 1 L.Ed.2d 676.   The union benefit from the wage scale agreed upon is direct and concrete and the effect on the product market, though clearly present, results from the elimination of competition based on wages among the employers in the bargaining unit, which is not the kind of restraint Congress intended the Sherman Act to proscribe. Apex Hosiery Co. v. Leader, 310 U.S. 469, 503–504, 60 S.Ct. 982, 997, 84 L.Ed. 1311; see Adams Dairy Co. v. St. Louis Dairy Co., 260 F.2d 46 (8th Cir.1958).   We think it beyond question that a union may conclude a wage agreement with the multi-employer bargaining unit without violating the antitrust laws and that it may as a matter of its own policy, and not by agreement with all or part of the employers of that unit, seek the same wages from other employers.

This is not to say that an agreement resulting from union-employer negotiations is automatically exempt from Sherman Act scrutiny simply because the negotiations involve a compulsory subject of bargaining, regardless of the subject or the form and content of the agreement.   Unquestionably the Board's demarcation of the bounds of the duty to bargain has great relevance to any consideration of the sweep of labor's antitrust immunity, for we are concerned here with harmonizing the Sherman Act with the national policy expressed in the National Labor Relations Act of promoting "the peaceful settlement of industrial disputes by subjecting labor-management controversies to the mediatory influence of negotiation," Fibreboard Paper Prods. Corp. v. National Labor Relations Board, 379 U.S. 203, 211, 85 S.Ct. 398, 403, 13 L.Ed.2d 233. But there are limits to what a union or an employer may offer or extract in the name of wages, and because they must bargain does not mean that the agreement reached may disregard other laws. Local 24 of Intern. Broth. of Teamsters, etc. v. Oliver, 358 U.S. 283, 296, 79 S.Ct. 297, 304, 3 L.Ed.2d 312; United Brotherhood of Carpenters v. United States, 330 U.S. 395, 399–400, 67 S.Ct. 775, 778, 91 L.Ed. 973.

We have said that a union may make wage agreements with a multi-employer bargaining unit and may in pursuance of its own union interests seek to obtain the same terms from other employers. No case under the antitrust laws could be made out on evidence limited to such union behavior.[2] But we think a union forfeits its exemption from the antitrust laws when it is clearly shown that it has agreed with one set of employers to impose a certain wage scale on other bargaining units. One group of employers may not conspire to eliminate competitors from the industry and the union is liable with the employers if it becomes a party to the conspiracy. This is true even though the union's part in the scheme is an undertaking to secure the same wages, hours or other conditions of employment from the remaining employers in the industry.

We do not find anything in the national labor policy that conflicts with this conclusion. This Court has recognized that a legitimate aim of any national labor organization is to obtain uniformity of labor standards and that a consequence of such union activity may be to eliminate competition based on differences in such standards. Apex Hosiery Co. v. Leader, 310 U.S. 469, 503, 60 S.Ct. 982, 997, 84 L.Ed. 1311. But there is nothing in the labor policy indicating that the union and the employers in one bargaining unit are free to bargain about the wages, hours and working conditions of other bargaining units or to attempt to settle these matters for the entire industry. On the contrary, the duty to bargain unit by unit leads to a quite different conclusion. The union's obligation to its members would seem best served if the union retained the ability to respond to each bargaining situation as the individual circumstances might warrant, without being strait-jacketed by some prior agreement with the favored employers. * * *

On the other hand, the policy of the antitrust laws is clearly set against employer-union agreements seeking to prescribe labor standards outside the bargaining unit. One could hardly contend, for example, that one group of employers could lawfully demand that the union impose on other employers wages that were significantly higher than those paid by the

---

**2.** Unilaterally, and without agreement with any employer group to do so, a union may adopt a uniform wage policy and seek vigorously to implement it even though it may suspect that some employers cannot effectively compete if they are required to pay the wage scale demanded by the union. The union need not gear its wage demands to wages which the weakest units in the industry can afford to pay. Such union conduct is not alone sufficient evidence to maintain a union-employer conspiracy charge under the Sherman Act. There must be additional direct or indirect evidence of the conspiracy. There was, of course, other evidence in this case, but we indicate no opinion as to its sufficiency.

requesting employers, or a system of computing wages that, because of differences in methods of production, would be more costly to one set of employers than to another.   The anticompetitive potential of such a combination is obvious, but is little more severe than what is alleged to have been the purpose and effect of the conspiracy in this case to establish wages at a level that marginal producers could not pay so that they would be driven from the industry.   And if the conspiracy presently under attack were declared exempt it would hardly be possible to deny exemption to such avowedly discriminatory schemes.

From the viewpoint of antitrust policy, moreover, all such agreements between a group of employers and a union that the union will seek specified labor standards outside the bargaining unit suffer from a more basic defect, without regard to predatory intention or effect in the particular case.   For the salient characteristic of such agreements is that the union surrenders its freedom of action with respect to its bargaining policy. Prior to the agreement the union might seek uniform standards in its own self-interest but would be required to assess in each case the probable costs and gains of a strike or other collective action to that end and thus might conclude that the objective of uniform standards should temporarily give way.   After the agreement the union's interest would be bound in each case to that of the favored employer group.   It is just such restraints upon the freedom of economic units to act according to their own choice and discretion that run counter to antitrust policy.   See, e.g., Associated Press v. United States, 326 U.S. 1, 19, 65 S.Ct. 1416, 1424, 89 L.Ed. 2013; Fashion Originators' Guild v. Federal Trade Comm'n, 312 U.S. 457, 465, 61 S.Ct. 703, 706, 85 L.Ed. 949; Anderson v. Shipowners' Assn., 272 U.S. 359, 364–365, 47 S.Ct. 125, 71 L.Ed. 298.

Thus the relevant labor and antitrust policies compel us to conclude that the alleged agreement between UMW and the large operators to secure uniform labor standards throughout the industry, if proved, was not exempt from the antitrust laws.   * * *

[The decision below was nonetheless reversed and the case was remanded for further proceedings, because the trial court had erred in admitting evidence that the defendants had, as part of their conspiracy, attempted to influence the Secretary of Labor.   Eastern R.R. Presidents Conference v. Noerr Motor Freight, Inc., 365 U.S. 127, 81 S.Ct. 523, 5 L.Ed.2d 464 (1961), had held that "joint efforts to influence public officials do not violate the antitrust laws even though intended to eliminate competition."]

■ Mr. Justice Douglas, with whom Mr. Justice Black, and Mr. Justice Clark agree, concurring.

As we read the opinion of the Court, it reaffirms the principles of Allen Bradley Co. v. Local Union No. 3, IBEW, 325 U.S. 797, 65 S.Ct. 1533, 89 L.Ed. 1939, and tells the trial judge:

*First.*   On the new trial the jury should be instructed that if there were an industry-wide collective bargaining agreement whereby employers and the union agreed on a wage scale that exceeded the financial ability of some operators to pay and that if it was made for the purpose of forcing some employers out of business, the union as well as the employers who participated in the arrangement with the union should be found to have violated the antitrust laws.

*Second.*   An industry-wide agreement containing those features is prima facie evidence of a violation.

Congress can design an oligopoly for our society, if it chooses.   But business alone cannot do so as long as the antitrust laws are enforced.   Nor should business and labor working hand-in-hand be allowed to make that basic change in the design of our so-called free enterprise system.   \* \* \*

■ MR. JUSTICE GOLDBERG, with whom MR. JUSTICE HARLAN and MR. JUSTICE STEWART join, dissenting from the opinion but concurring in the reversal in [UMW v. Pennington] and concurring in the judgment of the Court in [Local 189, Meat Cutters v. Jewel Tea Co.]   [Excerpts from the opinion of Mr. Justice Goldberg relevant to the *Pennington* case are set forth here; excerpts relevant to the *Jewel Tea* case are set forth with the other opinions in that case, below.]

\* \* \* [B]oth Pennington and Jewel Tea, as the Court in Pennington, and my Brother WHITE's opinion in Jewel Tea acknowledge, involve conventional collective bargaining on wages, hours, and working conditions— mandatory subjects of bargaining under the National Labor Relations Act, 49 Stat. 452, as amended, 29 U.S.C. § 158(d)(1958 ed.).   Yet the Mine Workers' activity in Pennington was held subject to an antitrust action by two lower courts.   This decision was based upon a jury determination that the Union's economic philosophy is undesirable, and it resulted in an award against the Union of treble damages of $270,000 and $55,000 extra for respondent's attorneys' fees.   In Jewel Tea, the Union has also been subjected to an antitrust suit in which a court of appeals, with its own notions as to what butchers are legitimately interested in, would subject the Union to a treble damage judgment in an as yet undetermined amount.

Regretfully these cases, both in the lower courts and in expressions in the various opinions filed today in this Court, as I shall demonstrate, constitute a throwback to past days when courts allowed antitrust actions against unions and employers engaged in conventional collective bargaining, because "a judge considered" the union or employer conduct in question to be "socially or economically" objectionable.   Duplex Printing Press Co. v. Deering, supra, 254 U.S. at 485, 41 S.Ct. at 183 (dissenting opinion of Mr. Justice Brandeis).   It is necessary to recall that history to place the cases before us in proper perspective.

[Mr. Justice Goldberg then traced the history of the application of the Sherman Act to labor unions, adverting to the major Supreme Court decisions construing that Act and the Clayton and Norris–LaGuardia Acts. He observed that the Wagner Act sought affirmatively to protect and encourage unionization and collective bargaining and that it also sought to narrow the role of the judiciary in formulating labor policy.   He also noted that the Taft–Hartley Act outlawed certain specific union activities and did not test legality by subjective judgments of the union's purpose or effect.]

In my view, this history shows a consistent congressional purpose to limit severely judicial intervention in collective bargaining under cover of the wide umbrella of the antitrust laws, and, rather, to deal with what Congress deemed to be specific abuses on the part of labor unions by specific proscriptions in the labor statutes.  * * * Following the sound analysis of Hutcheson, the Court should hold that, in order to effectuate congressional intent, collective bargaining activity concerning mandatory subjects of bargaining under the Labor Act is not subject to the antitrust laws.  This rule flows directly from the Hutcheson holding that a union acting as a union, in the interests of its members, and not acting to fix prices or allocate markets in aid of an employer conspiracy to accomplish these objects, with only indirect union benefits, is not subject to challenge under the antitrust laws.  To hold that mandatory collective bargaining is completely protected would effectuate the congressional policies of encouraging free collective bargaining, subject only to specific restrictions contained in the labor laws, and of limiting judicial intervention in labor matters via the antitrust route—an intervention which necessarily under the Sherman Act places on judges and juries the determination of "what public policy in regard to the industrial struggle demands."  Duplex Printing Press Co. v. Deering, supra, 254 U.S., at 485, 41 S.Ct., at 183 (dissenting opinion of Mr. Justice Brandeis).  See Winter, Collective Bargaining and Competition: The Application of Antitrust Standards to Union Activities, 73 Yale L.J. 14 (1963).  * * * This national scheme would be virtually destroyed by the imposition of Sherman Act criminal and civil penalties upon employers and unions engaged in such collective bargaining. To tell the parties that they must bargain about a point but may be subject to antitrust penalties if they reach an agreement is to stultify the congressional scheme.

Moreover, mandatory subjects of bargaining are issues as to which union strikes may not be enjoined by either federal or state courts.  To say that the union can strike over such issues but that both it and the employer are subject to possible antitrust penalties for making collective bargaining agreements concerning them is to assert that Congress intended to permit the parties to collective bargaining to wage industrial warfare but to prohibit them from peacefully settling their disputes.  This would not only be irrational but would fly in the face of the clear congressional intent of promoting "the peaceful settlement of industrial disputes by subjecting labor-management controversies to the mediatory influence of negotiation."  Fibreboard Paper Prods. Corp. v. National Labor Relations Board, 379 U.S. 203, 211, 85 S.Ct. 398, 403, 13 L.Ed.2d 233.  * * *

* * * Since collective bargaining inevitably involves and requires discussion of the impact of the wage agreement reached with a particular employer or group of employers upon competing employers, the effect of the Court's decision will be to bar a basic element of collective bargaining from the conference room.  If a union and employer are prevented from

discussing and agreeing upon issues which are, in the great majority of cases, at the central core of bargaining, unilateral force will inevitably be substituted for rational discussion and agreement.  Plainly and simply, the Court would subject both unions and employers to antitrust sanctions, criminal as well as civil, if in collective bargaining they concluded a wage agreement and, as part of the agreement, the union has undertaken to use its best efforts to have this wage accepted by other employers in the industry.  Indeed, the decision today even goes beyond this.  Under settled antitrust principles which are accepted by the Court as appropriate and applicable, which were the basis for jury instructions in Pennington, and which will govern it upon remand, there need not be direct evidence of an express agreement.  Rather the existence of such an agreement, express or implied, may be inferred from the conduct of the parties.

* * * The rational thing for an employer to do, when faced with union demands he thinks he cannot meet, is to explain why, in economic terms, he believes that he cannot agree to the union requests.  Indeed, the Labor Act's compulsion to bargain in good faith requires that he meaningfully address himself to the union's requests.  See National Labor Relations Board v. Truitt Mfg. Co., 351 U.S. 149, 76 S.Ct. 753, 100 L.Ed. 1027.  A recurring and most understandable reason given by employers for their resistance to union demands is that competitive factors prevent them from accepting the union's proposed terms.  Under the Court's holding today, however, such a statement by an employer may start both the employer and union on the road to antitrust sanctions, criminal and civil.  For a jury may well interpret such discussion and subsequent union action as showing an implicit or secret agreement to impose uniform standards on other employers.  * * *

Furthermore, in order to determine whether, under the Court's standard, a union is acting unilaterally or pursuant to an agreement with employers, judges and juries will inevitably be drawn to try to determine the purpose and motive of union and employer collective bargaining activities.  The history I have set out, however, makes clear that Congress intended to foreclose judges and juries from roaming at large in the area of collective bargaining, under cover of the antitrust laws, by inquiry into the purpose and motive of the employer and union bargaining on mandatory subjects.  Such roaming at large, experience shows, leads to a substitution of judicial for congressional judgment as to how collective bargaining should operate.  * * *

In Pennington, central to the alleged conspiracy is the claim that hourly wage rates and fringe benefits were set at a level designed to eliminate the competition of the smaller nonunion companies by making the labor cost too high for them to pay.  Indeed, the trial judge charged that there was no violation of the Sherman Act in the establishing of wages and welfare payments through the national contract, "provided" the mine workers and the major coal producers had not agreed to fix "high" rates "in order to drive the small coal operators out of business."  Under such an instruction, if the jury found the wage scale too "high" it could impute to the union the unlawful purpose of putting the nonunion operators out of business.  It is clear that the effect of the instruction therefore, was to invite 12 jurymen to become arbiters of the economic desirability of the wage scale in the Nation's coal industry.  The Court would sustain the judgment based on this charge and thereby put its stamp of approval on this role for courts and juries.  * * * It is clear, as experience shows, that judges and juries neither have the aptitude nor possess the criteria for making this kind of judgment.  * * *

* * * [L]abor contracts establishing more or less standardized wages, hours, and other terms and conditions of employment in a given industry or market area are often secured either through bargaining with multi-employer associations or through bargaining with market leaders that sets a "pattern" for agreements on labor standards with other employers.  These are two similar systems used to achieve the identical result of fostering labor peace through the negotiation of uniform labor standards in an industry.  Yet the Court makes antitrust liability for both unions and employers turn on which of these two systems is used.  It states that uniform wage agreements may be made with multi-employer units but an agreement cannot be made to affect employers outside the formal bargaining unit.  I do not believe that the Court understands the effect of its ruling in terms of the practical realities of the automobile, steel, rubber, shipbuilding, and numerous other industries which follow the policy of pattern collective bargaining.  See Chamberlain, Collective Bargaining 259–263 (1951) * * *.  I also do not understand why antitrust liability should turn on the form of unit determination rather than the substance of the collective bargaining impact on the industry.  * * *

* * * Where there is an "agreement" to seek uniform wages in an industry, in what item is competition restrained?  The answer to this question can only be that competition is restrained in employee wage standards.  * * *

As I have already discussed, however, if one thing is clear, it is that Congress has repudiated the view that labor is a commodity and thus there should be competition to see who can supply it at the cheapest price.  * * * The kind of competition which is suppressed by employer-union agreement on uniform wages can only be competition between unions to see which union will agree to supply labor at a lower rate, or competition between employers in the sale of their products based on differences in labor costs.  Neither type of "suppression," I submit, can be supported as a restraint of trade condemned by the antitrust laws.  No one, I think, believes that Congress intended that there be an economic system under which unions would compete with each other to supply labor at the lowest possible cost. * * *

---

## PROBLEMS FOR DISCUSSION

**1.** In their comprehensive article, "Collective Bargaining and the Antitrust Laws: The Emasculation of the Labor Exemption," 81 Colum.L.Rev. 459, 508–09 (1981),

Handler and Zifchak criticize what they view as Justice White's suggestion in *Pennington* that a privately negotiated restraint on the bargaining freedom of either of the parties to a collective bargaining agreement is not merely nonexempt, but a per se violation of the Sherman Act.

> This is pernicious principle, without redeeming virtue. Every contract restrains one party vis-a-vis the other in certain respects. If a supplier grants an exclusive franchise to a retailer, he has disabled himself from dealing with third parties. In the labor-relations context a prohibition on subcontracting precludes the employer from dealing with a certain category of enterprises. A work preservation agreement has like consequences. Taken literally, Justice White's formulation would condemn all such agreements, although they are mandatory subjects of bargaining. His apparent opposition to bargaining with reference to other units also flies in the face of the realities of collective bargaining.

Is Justice White's position as characterized by the authors? Is their criticism convincing?

**2.** Embry Aeronautical University, having submitted the low bid, is announced to be the successor of its competitor Ross Aviation, Inc. to a contract with the Army for the rendering of flight-training services. Prior to Embry's succession, Ross abandons its longstanding resistance to the unionization of its employees and negotiates a high-wage contract with Local 2003, International Association of Machinists. It is expected by Embry, the Army, Ross and Ross's employees that Embry will employ all or most of the Ross employees, as did Ross with respect to the workforce of its predecessor. However, given the low bid which won it the Army contract, Embry cannot afford the costly wage agreement. Both Ross and the union are aware of this fact; Ross hopes to regain the Army contract for itself by inducing a default by Embry. Embry does indeed default and brings suit against Ross and the union alleging that the wage agreement is a violation of the anti-trust laws. The union raises the labor exemption as its defense and distinguishes the *Pennington* case on two grounds: (1) here the wage contract was only with Ross, a single employer, and thus was not part of a multiemployer conspiracy; (2) the contract was simply to be extended to Embry, a successor employer in the same bargaining unit, and thus had no "extra-unit" impact. What result? See Embry–Riddle Aeronautical Univ. v. Ross Aviation, Inc., 504 F.2d 896 (5th Cir.1974); Mid–America Regional Bargaining Ass'n v. Will County Carpenters Dist. Council, 675 F.2d 881 (7th Cir.1982), cert. denied, 459 U.S. 860, 103 S.Ct. 132, 74 L.Ed.2d 114 (1982).

**3.** The Milk Drivers Union represents delivery employees of dairies and milk dealers in the Chicago area. Associated Milk Dealers, Inc. (AMDI) is a nonprofit association which represents independently owned milk dealers in negotiating collective bargaining agreements. When the Union and AMDI agree upon an area contract, individual milk dealers (not AMDI) sign the agreement. The current three-year contract, which covers wages, hours, contributions to benefit funds, arbitration of disputes, etc., was concluded after negotiations attended by the Union, AMDI, Chicago Area Dairymen's Association (another employer association) and a number of individual employers. The contract also contains a "most favored nation" clause which permits a signatory milk dealer automatically to adopt the terms of an agreement between the Union and any other milk dealer if such terms are more advantageous to the other milk dealer than are the terms of the standard contract. The reason for the clause is apparent in a market of one union and numerous employers: it allows those employers who sign the contract to do so without fear of prejudice which might result to them if the union then turns to remaining employers and agrees to a different contract more favorable to the latter. Diamond Food Stores has just entered the Chicago milk processing market and its subdivision Hillfarm Dairy has signed a contract with the Union on terms allegedly more favorable than those of the standard contract. AMDI wishes to invoke the "most favored nation" clause and adopt the terms of the Hillfarm agreement. The Union contends that the anti-trust laws prohibit the enforcement of the "most favored nation" clause. Is the Union's contention correct? Associated Milk Dealers, Inc. v. Milk Drivers Union Local 753, 422 F.2d 546 (7th Cir.1970).

------

## Local Union No. 189, Amalgamated Meat Cutters v. Jewel Tea Co.

381 U.S. 676, 85 S.Ct. 1596, 14 L.Ed.2d 640 (1965).

■ MR. JUSTICE WHITE announced the judgment of the Court and delivered an opinion in which THE CHIEF JUSTICE and MR. JUSTICE BRENNAN join.

Like United Mine Workers of America v. Pennington, this case presents questions regarding the application of §§ 1 and 2 of the Sherman Antitrust Act, 26 Stat. 209, as amended, 15 U.S.C.A. §§ 1–2 (1958 ed.), to activities of labor unions. In particular, it concerns the lawfulness of the following restriction on the operating hours of food store meat departments contained in a collective agreement executed after joint multi-employer, multi-union negotiations:

> "Market operating hours shall be 9:00 a.m. to 6:00 p.m. Monday through Saturday, inclusive. No customer shall be served who comes into the market before or after the hours set forth above."

[Since shortly after the turn of the century, the working hours of Chicago butchers have been a source of great contention. A strike in 1919 eliminated the 81–hour, 7–day week, and subsequent labor contracts reduced working hours by 1947 to the 9 a.m. to 6 p.m. period contained in current agreements. Since 1920, the labor agreements similarly provided for a limitation upon the hours during which customers could be served. In the 1957 contract negotiations between locals of the Amalgamated Meat Cutters and representatives of Chicago retailers of fresh meat (both "self-service" markets, where meat was available for sale on a prepackaged self-service basis, and "service" markets, where meat could be custom-cut), an agreement was reached on the marketing-hour restrictions between the unions and the Associated Food Retailers of Greater Chicago, representing *inter alia* 300 meat dealers. Jewel Tea Co., however, sought a modification of the marketing-hour provision so as to allow for Friday night operations, but it relented and signed the standard agreement when the unions threatened to strike. In 1958, Jewel brought suit against the unions, certain union officers, Associated and one of its officers, seeking invalidation of the contract provision as a violation of Sections 1 and 2 of the Sherman Act. The gist of the complaint was an alleged conspiracy between the unions and Associated to prevent the retail sale of fresh meat after 6 p.m.]

The complaint stated that in recent years the prepackaged, self-service system of marketing meat had come into vogue, that 174 of Jewel's 196 stores were equipped to vend meat in this manner, and that a butcher need not be on duty in a self-service market at the time meat purchases were actually made. The prohibition of night meat marketing, it was alleged, unlawfully impeded Jewel in the use of its property and adversely affected the general public in that many persons find it inconvenient to shop during the day. An injunction, treble damages and attorney's fees were demanded.

The trial judge held the allegations of the complaint sufficient to withstand a motion to dismiss made on the grounds, *inter alia,* that (a) the "alleged restraint [was] within the exclusive regulatory scope of the National Labor Relations Act and [was] therefore outside the jurisdiction of the Court" and (b) the controversy was within the labor exemption to the antitrust laws. That ruling was sustained on appeal. Jewel Tea Co. v. Local Unions Nos. 189, etc., Amalgamated Meat Cutters, AFL–CIO, 274 F.2d 217 (7th Cir.1960), cert. denied, 362 U.S. 936, 80 S.Ct. 757, 4 L.Ed.2d 747. After trial, however, the District Judge ruled the "record was devoid of any evidence to support a finding of a conspiracy" between Associated and the unions to force the restrictive provision on Jewel. Testing the unions' action standing alone, the trial court found that even in self-service markets removal of the limitation on marketing hours either would inaugurate longer hours and night work for the butchers or would result in butchers' work being done by others unskilled in the trade. Thus, the court concluded, the unions had imposed the marketing hours limitation to serve their own interests respecting conditions of employment, and such action was clearly within the labor exemption of the Sherman Act established by Hunt v. Crumboch, 325 U.S. 821, 65 S.Ct. 1545, 89 L.Ed. 1954; United States v. Hutcheson, 312 U.S. 219, 61 S.Ct. 463, 85 L.Ed. 788; United States v. American Federation of Musicians, 318 U.S. 741, 63 S.Ct. 665, 87 L.Ed. 1120. Alternatively, the District Court ruled that even if this was not the case, the arrangement did not amount to an unreasonable restraint of trade in violation of the Sherman Act.

The Court of Appeals reversed the dismissal of the complaint as to both the unions and Associated.  * * * We granted certiorari on the unions' petition, 379 U.S. 813, 85 S.Ct. 66, and now reverse the Court of Appeals.

[The Court opened its opinion by rejecting the union's argument that the case was within the exclusive primary jurisdiction of the NLRB.]

## II.

Here, as in United Mine Workers v. Pennington, 381 U.S. 657, 85 S.Ct. 1585, the claim is made that the agreement under attack is exempt from the antitrust laws. We agree, but not on the broad grounds urged by the union.

It is well at the outset to emphasize that this case comes to us stripped of any claim of a union-employer conspiracy against Jewel. The trial court found no evidence to sustain Jewel's conspiracy claim and this finding was not disturbed by the Court of Appeals. We therefore have a situation where the unions, having obtained a marketing-hours agreement from one group of employers, has successfully sought the same terms from a single employer, Jewel, not as a result of a bargain between the unions and some employers directed against other employers, but pursuant to what the unions deemed to be in their own labor union interests. * * *

We pointed out in Pennington that exemption for union-employer agreements is very much a matter of accommodating the coverage of the Sherman Act to the policy of the labor laws. Employers and unions are required to bargain about wages, hours and working conditions, and this fact weighs heavily in favor of antitrust exemption for agreements on these subjects. But neither party need bargain about other matters and either party commits an unfair labor practice if it conditions its bargaining upon discussions of a nonmandatory subject. National Labor Relations Board v. Division of Wooster Borg–Warner Corp., 356 U.S. 342, 78 S.Ct. 718. Jewel, for example, need not have bargained about or agreed to a schedule of prices at which its meat would be sold and the union could not legally have insisted that it do so. But if the union had made such a demand, Jewel had agreed and the United States or an injured party had challenged the agreement under the antitrust laws, we seriously doubt that either the union or Jewel could claim immunity by reason of the labor exemption, whatever substantive questions of violation there might be.

Thus the issue in this case is whether the marketing-hours restriction, like wages, and unlike prices, is so intimately related to wages, hours and working conditions that the unions' successful attempt to obtain that provision through bona fide, arms-length bargaining in pursuit of its own labor union policies, and not at the behest of or in combination with nonlabor groups, falls within the protection of the national labor policy and is therefore exempt from the Sherman Act.[5] We think that it is.

The Court of Appeals would classify the marketing hours restriction with the product-pricing provision and place both within the reach of the Sherman Act. In its view, labor has a legitimate interest in the number of

---

**5.** The crucial determinant is not the form of the agreement—e.g., prices or wages—but its relative impact on the product market and the interests of union members. Thus in Teamsters Union v. Oliver, 358 U.S. 283, 79 S.Ct. 297, we held that federal labor policy precluded application of state antitrust laws to an employer-union agreement that when leased trucks were driven by their owners, such owner-drivers should receive, in addition to the union wage, not less than a prescribed minimum rental. Though in form a scheme fixing prices for the supply of leased vehicles, the agreement was designed "to protect the negotiated wage scale against the possible undermining through diminution of the owner's wages for driving which might result from a rental which did not cover his operating costs." Id., at 293–294. As the agreement did not embody a " 'remote and indirect approach to the subject of wages' * * * but a direct frontal attack upon a problem thought to threaten the maintenance of the basic wage structure established by the collective bargaining contract," id., at 294, the paramount federal policy of encouraging collective bargaining proscribed application of the state law.

hours it must work but no interest in whether the hours fall in the daytime, in the nighttime or on Sundays. "[T]he furnishing of a place and advantageous hours of employment for the butchers to supply meat to customers are the prerogatives of the employer." 331 F.2d 547, 549. That reasoning would invalidate with respect to both service and self-service markets the 1957 provision that "eight hours shall constitute the basic work day, Monday through Saturday; *work to begin at 9:00 a.m. and stop at 6:00 p.m.* \* \* \*'" as well as the marketing hours restriction.

Contrary to the Court of Appeals, we think that the particular hours of the day and the particular days of the week during which employees shall be required to work are subjects well within the realm of "wages, hours, and other terms and conditions of employment" about which employers and unions must bargain. National Labor Relations Act § 8(d); see Timken Roller Bearing Co., 70 N.L.R.B. 500, 504, 515–516, 521 (1946), rev'd on other grounds, 161 F.2d 949 (C.A.6th Cir.1947)(employer's unilateral imposition of Sunday work was refusal to bargain); Massey Gin & Machine Works, Inc., 78 N.L.R.B. 189, 195, 199 (1948)(same; change in starting and quitting time); Camp & McInnes, Inc., 100 N.L.R.B. 524, 532 (1952) (same; reduction of lunch hour and advancement of quitting time). And, although the effect on competition is apparent and real, perhaps more so than in the case of the wage agreement, the concern of union members is immediate and direct. Weighing the respective interests involved, we think the national labor policy expressed in the National Labor Relations Act places beyond the reach of the Sherman Act union-employer agreements on when, as well as how long, employees must work. An agreement on these subjects between the union and the employers in a bargaining unit is not illegal under the Sherman Act, nor is the union's unilateral demand for the same contract of other employers in the industry.

Disposing of the case, as it did, on the broad grounds we have indicated, the Court of Appeals did not deal separately with the marketing hours provision, as distinguished from hours of work, in connection with either service or self-service markets. The dispute here pertains principally to self-service markets. \* \* \*

If it were true that self-service markets could actually operate without butchers, at least for a few hours after 6 p.m., that no encroachment on butchers' work would result and that the workload of butchers during normal working hours would not be substantially increased, Jewel's position would have considerable merit. For then the obvious restraint on the product market—the exclusion of self-service stores from the evening market for meat—would stand alone, unmitigated and unjustified by the vital interests of the union butchers which are relied upon in this case. In such event the limitation imposed by the union might well be reduced to nothing but an effort by the union to protect one group of employers from competition by another, which is conduct that is not exempt from the Sherman Act. Whether there would be a violation of §§ 1 and 2 would then depend on whether the elements of a conspiracy in restraint of trade or an attempt to monopolize had been proved.[6]

Thus the dispute between Jewel and the unions essentially concerns a narrow factual question: Are night operations without butchers, and without infringement of butchers' interests, feasible?  The District Court resolved this factual dispute in favor of the unions.  It found that "in stores where meat is sold at night it is impractical to operate without either butchers or other employees.  Someone must arrange, replenish and clean the counters and supply customer services."  Operating without butchers would mean that "their work would be done by others unskilled in the trade," and "would involve an increase in workload in preparing for the night work and cleaning the next morning."  215 F.Supp., at 846.  Those findings were not disturbed by the Court of Appeals, which, as previously noted, proceeded on a broader ground.  Our function is limited to reviewing the record to satisfy ourselves that the trial judge's findings are not clearly erroneous.  Fed.Rules Civ.Proc., 52(a).

The trial court had before it evidence concerning the history of the unions' opposition to night work, the development of the provisions respecting night work and night operations, the course of collective negotiations in 1957, 1959, and 1961 with regard to those provisions, and the characteristics of meat marketing insofar as they bore on the feasibility of night operations without butchers.  * * *

The unions' evidence with regard to the practicability of night operations without butchers was accurately summarized by the trial judge as follows:

> "[I]n most of plaintiff's stores outside Chicago, where night operations exist, meat cutters are on duty whenever a meat department is open after 6 P.M.  * * *  Even in self-service departments, ostensibly operated without employees on duty after 6 P.M., there was evidence that requisite customer services in connection with meat sales were performed by grocery clerks.  In the same vein, defendants adduced evidence that in the sale of delicatessen items, which could be made after 6 P.M. from self-service cases under the contract, 'practically' always during the time the market was open the manager, or other employees, would be rearranging and restocking the cases.  There was also evidence that even if it were practical to operate a self-service meat market after 6 P.M. without employees, the night operations would add to the workload in getting the meats prepared for night sales and in putting the counters in order the next day."  215 F.Supp., at 844.

---

**6.** One issue, for example, would be whether the restraint was unreasonable.  Judicial pronouncements regarding the reasonableness of restraints on hours of business are relatively few.  Some cases appear to have viewed such restraints as tantamount to limits on hours of work and thus reasonable, even though contained in agreements among competitors.  * * *

The decided cases * * * do not appear to offer any easy answer to the question whether in a particular case an operating hours restraint is unreasonable.

[The Justices concluded that the findings of the district judge were not clearly erroneous.]

Reversed.

◼ MR. JUSTICE DOUGLAS, with whom MR. JUSTICE BLACK and MR. JUSTICE CLARK concur, dissenting.

If we followed Allen Bradley Co. v. Local Union No. 3, 325 U.S. 797, 65 S.Ct. 1533, 89 L.Ed. 1939, we would hold with the Court of Appeals that this multi-employer agreement with the union not to sell meat between 6 p.m. and 9 a.m. was not immunized from the antitrust laws and that respondent's evidence made out a prima facie case that it was in fact a violation of the Sherman Act.

If, in the present case, the employers alone agreed not to sell meat from 6 p.m. to 9 a.m., they would be guilty of an anticompetitive practice, barred by the antitrust laws.  * * * In the circumstances of this case the collective bargaining agreement itself, of which the District Court said there was clear proof, was evidence of a conspiracy among the employers with the unions to impose the marketing-hours restriction on Jewel via a strike threat by the unions.  This tended to take from the merchants who agreed among themselves their freedom to work their own hours and to subject all who, like Jewel, wanted to sell meat after 6 p.m. to the coercion of threatened strikes, all of which if done in concert only by businessmen would violate the antitrust laws.  * * * Some merchants relied chiefly on price competition to draw trade; others employed courtesy, quick service, and keeping their doors open long hours to meet the convenience of customers.  The unions here induced a large group of merchants to use their collective strength to hurt others who wanted the competitive advantage of selling meat after 6 p.m.  Unless Allen Bradley is either overruled or greatly impaired, the unions can no more aid a group of businessmen to force their competitors to follow uniform store marketing hours than to force them to sell at fixed prices.  Both practices take away the freedom of traders to carry on their business in their own competitive fashion.  * * *

◼ JUSTICE GOLDBERG, JUSTICE STEWART and JUSTICE HARLAN, concurring.

* * * The judicial expressions in *Jewel Tea* represent another example of the reluctance of judges to give full effect to congressional purpose in this area and the substitution by judges of their views for those of Congress as to how free collective bargaining should operate.  In this case the Court of Appeals would have held the Union liable for the Sherman Act's criminal and civil penalties because in the court's social and economic judgment, the determination of the hours at which meat is to be sold is a "proprietary" matter within the exclusive control of management and thus the Union had no legitimate interest in bargaining over it.  My Brother DOUGLAS, joined by MR. JUSTICE BLACK and MR. JUSTICE CLARK, would affirm this judgment apparently because the agreement was reached through a multi-employer bargaining unit.  But, as I have demonstrated above, there is nothing even remotely illegal about such bargaining.  Even if an independent conspiracy test were applicable to the Jewel Tea situation, the simple fact is that

multi-employer bargaining conducted at arm's length does not constitute union abetment of a business combination.  It is often a self-defensive form of employer bargaining designed to match union strength.

My Brother WHITE, joined by THE CHIEF JUSTICE and MR. JUSTICE BRENNAN, while not agreeing with my Brother DOUGLAS, would reverse the Court of Appeals.  He also, however, refuses to give full effect to the congressional intent that judges should not, under cover of the Sherman Act umbrella, substitute their economic and social policies for free collective bargaining.  My Brother WHITE recognizes that the issue of the hours of sale of meat concerns a mandatory subject of bargaining based on the trial court's findings that it directly affected the hours of work of the butchers in the self-service markets, and therefore, since there was a finding that the Union was not abetting an independent employer conspiracy, he joins in reversing the Court of Appeals.  In doing so, however, he apparently draws lines among mandatory subjects of bargaining, presumably based on a judicial determination of their importance to the worker, and states that not all agreements resulting from collective bargaining based on mandatory subjects of bargaining are immune from the antitrust laws, even absent evidence of union abetment of an independent conspiracy of employers. Following this reasoning, my Brother WHITE indicates that he would sustain a judgment here, even absent evidence of union abetment of an independent conspiracy of employers, if the trial court had found "that self-service markets could actually operate without butchers, at least for a few hours after 6 p.m., that no encroachment on butchers' work would result and that the workload of butchers during normal working hours would not be substantially increased * * *."  Such a view seems to me to be unsupportable.  It represents a narrow, confining view of what labor unions have a legitimate interest in preserving and thus bargaining about.  Even if the self-service markets could operate after 6 p.m., without their butchers and without increasing the work of their butchers at other times, the result of such operation can reasonably be expected to be either that the small, independent, service markets would have to remain open in order to compete, thus requiring their union butchers to work at night, or that the small, independent, service markets would not be able to operate at night and thus would be put at a competitive disadvantage.  Since it is clear that the large, automated self-service markets employ less butchers per volume of sales than service markets do, the Union certainly has a legitimate interest in keeping service markets competitive so as to preserve jobs.  Job security of this kind has been recognized to be a legitimate subject of union interest.  * * * Putting the opinion of the Court in Pennington together with the opinions of my Brothers DOUGLAS and WHITE in Jewel Tea, it would seem that unions are damned if their collective bargaining philosophy involves acceptance of automation (Pennington) and are equally damned if their collective bargaining philosophy involves resistance to automation (Jewel Tea).  Again, the wisdom of a union adopting either philosophy is not for judicial determination.  * * *

My view that Congress intended that collective bargaining activity on mandatory subjects of bargaining under the Labor Act not be subject to the antitrust laws does not mean that I believe that Congress intended that activity involving all nonmandatory subjects of bargaining be similarly exempt.   That direct and overriding interest of unions in such subjects as wages, hours, and other working conditions, which Congress has recognized in making them subjects of mandatory bargaining is clearly lacking where the subject of the agreement is price-fixing and market allocation.   Moreover, such activities are at the core of the type of anticompetitive commercial restraint at which the antitrust laws are directed.   * * *

## PROBLEMS FOR DISCUSSION

**1.**  In the *National Woodwork* case, at page 672 supra, the full text of Rule 17 in the labor contract between the Union and the general contractor Frouge provided: "No employee shall work on any job on which cabinet work, fixtures, millwork, sash, doors, trim or other detailed millwork is used unless the same is Union-made and bears the Union Label of the United Brotherhood of Carpenters and Joiners of America.   No member of this District Council will handle material coming from a mill where cutting out and fitting has been done for butts, locks, letter plates, or hardware of any description, nor any doors or transoms which have been fitted prior to being furnished on the job, including base, chair, rail, picture moulding, which has been previously fitted."   [The NLRB held that the first sentence was a union-signatory provision which violated Section 8(e), and the Union did not challenge that conclusion on judicial review.   The second sentence was, of course, upheld by the Supreme Court.]

Consider the following questions under the antitrust laws:

(a)  Had the association of general contractors, with which the Union was negotiating, refused to include Rule 17 in their labor contract, and had the Union struck and picketed the contractors, could the Union's conduct have been enjoined as a violation of the Sherman Act?   Would the Union be liable for treble damages?

(b)  Could the general contractors (or Frouge as an individual contractor), once having agreed to include Rule 17 in the labor contract, successfully invalidate it by an action under the Sherman Act?   Might your answer to this question depend upon whether this provision had been included in the contract with the general contractors at the urging of manufacturers of cabinets, fixtures and the like, whose sales had been increasingly undercut by cheaper cabinets, etc. supplied by nonunion manufacturers (and who had informed the Union that they could not continue to pay union wages while losing these sales)—as opposed to having been incorporated at the insistence of the Union?   See United States v. Brims, 272 U.S. 549, 47 S.Ct. 169, 71 L.Ed. 403 (1926).

(Is the sentence in Rule 17 which is more obviously unlawful under Section 8(e) for that reason more obviously lawful under the Sherman Act?   At the least, is it sound to argue that the more moderate remedies provided for unlawful hot cargo provisions under Section 8(e) should be deemed to "preempt" the more severe sanctions available under the Sherman Act?)

(c)  If these refusal-to-handle provisions had not been incorporated in the labor contract, but had instead been for many years a part of the constitution of the Carpenters' Union and thus binding on its members, could they be invalidated under the Sherman Act?   Would a refusal to handle, actually carried out at the job site pursuant to the Union's constitution, violate the Sherman Act?  See Bedford Cut Stone Co. v. Journeymen Stone Cutters' Ass'n, 274 U.S. 37, 47 S.Ct. 522, 71 L.Ed. 916 (1927).

Reconsider all of these questions after studying the *Connell* case, immediately below.

**2.**  Some years ago a new firm, Adams Dairy Company, began business in the St. Louis metropolitan area.  While most dairy companies were then principally engaged in door-to-door sales, Adams devoted its energies to high-volume sales, in half-gallon and gallon paper cartons, to food markets.  By spending less on containers and utilizing many fewer drivers than its competitors, Adams was able to charge prices substantially below prevailing levels for home-delivered milk.  After Adams was organized by the Milk Drivers Union, the union began contract negotiations on behalf of the milk wagon drivers employed by the St. Louis dairies including Adams (which were members of a multiemployer association).  The union has insisted upon dramatic wage increases at various increasing levels of quantity of milk delivered, such that the wages and commissions of the Adams deliverymen would be doubled as a result of the new agreement.  The union has argued that higher pay is needed to compensate for the strain imposed by virtue of the heavy loading and unloading required by Adams, even though none of the drivers has complained and even though the drivers are already earning almost $40,000 a year; moreover, the union claims that its wage demands are also a valid means of work-spreading and generating more jobs.  Adams believes that the union is simply trying to make it economically impossible to continue to charge low prices.  It also believes that the other dairies are prepared to sign the agreement, since (because of their low-bulk deliveries) they will not be seriously injured by the sharply graduated pay scale sought by the union.

Adams wishes to know:  (a) Whether there is any way that the union can be prevented from striking to enforce its demands, and (b) whether, if the other dairies sign the proposed contract, a court action is available to challenge the wage provision.  See Adams Dairy Co. v. St. Louis Dairy Co., 260 F.2d 46 (8th Cir.1958).

**3.**  The retail automobile dealers in the city of Franklin are members of the Franklin Auto Dealers Association.  Last year, the Salespersons' Union sought to organize the sales staff at the new car dealerships in Franklin.  The principal aim of the Union's militant campaign was to reduce sharply working hours at night and on weekends, without any loss of pay; it has also demanded bargaining on a multiemployer basis.  The Union made extensive use of organizational picketing and consumer handbilling.  In response, members of the Dealers Association agreed among themselves permanently to close their showrooms all day on Saturdays and on three weekday evenings, in order to defeat organizing and forestall collective bargaining.  The strategy was successful, and the Union suffered a precipitous decline in support among salespersons.  The Union has brought a federal court action challenging the Association's activities on antitrust grounds.  Evaluate the Union's chances of success.  See Detroit Auto Dealers Ass'n v. Federal Trade Comm., 955 F.2d 457 (6th Cir.1992), cert. denied, 506 U.S. 973, 113 S.Ct. 461, 121 L.Ed.2d 369 (1992).

**4.**  If a union agrees with an employer group selectively to subsidize the wages of union workers, in order to allow their employers successfully to bid on jobs in competition with non-union employers, would the agreement be exempt from antitrust challenge? See Phoenix Electric Co. v. National Elec. Contractors Ass'n, 81 F.3d 858 (9th Cir.1996).

--------

### *THE NONSTATUTORY ANTITRUST EXEMPTION AND PROFESSIONAL SPORTS*

The most active area of litigation in recent years concerning the nonstatutory antitrust exemption has been professional sports. All team players in baseball, football, basketball and hockey are organized into players' associations, which bargain with the teams on a multiemployer basis. For many years, collective bargaining agreements in each sport have dealt with such matters as team compensation (including so-called salary caps), the rights of players to move from team to team (including so-called free agency), and the systematic team selection of new players (the so-called draft system). When these arrangements—which eliminate competition among teams with respect to the recruitment and compensation of players—are incorporated with the consent of the players' association into a collective bargaining agreement, it is undisputed that the nonstatutory exemption from the antitrust laws applies. As in the *Jewel Tea* case, these are generally recognized as mandatory subjects of bargaining that affect only bargaining-unit employees; and the policies of the NLRA fostering bargaining and agreement on such matters are thought to supersede any policies of the antitrust laws.

A number of cases have arisen in which a labor agreement has expired, bargaining has been pursued, and the multi-team association has been unyielding on a proposed term that is objectionable to the players' association. The players have argued in several cases—principally in football and basketball, in light of baseball's historically rooted exemption from the Sherman Act—that once the contract expires, so too does the nonstatutory exemption derived from cases such as *Jewel Tea*, thus rendering the teams' united front on such matters as salary caps and free agency subject to antitrust liability, including of course treble damages and injunctive relief. (Curiously, no court ruling on such matters has held flatly that a common bargaining position within a multiemployer unit with respect to wages and working conditions constitutes a restraint only in the labor market and not at all in the "product market" for sport services, so that Section 6 of the Clayton Act renders such restraint altogether beyond the reach of the Sherman Act. This was, of course, the thrust of the Supreme Court decision in Apex Hosiery Co. v. Leader, at p. 56 supra, which has never been thought to carry the day in these professional sport antitrust actions. Is there any reason why this is do?)

The outcomes in the decided cases have not been consistent. Some courts have held that the nonstatutory exemption does indeed terminate when the collective agreement does. Most courts have resisted this conclusion, among other reasons because it would altogether rest such exemption upon the consent of the union, which would give the union a bargaining weapon of enormous proportions. Other courts have taken what might be labeled a "middle ground," holding either that the exemption continues until the parties reach a bargaining impasse over the disputed issue or that it continues until the employer no longer has reason to believe that the disputed contract term will be incorporated in any forthcoming labor contract.

The Supreme Court dispelled the confusion, quite unambiguously, in its 1996 decision in BROWN v. PRO FOOTBALL, INC., 518 U.S. 231, 116 S.Ct. 2116, 135 L.Ed.2d 521 (1996), which favored a broad application of the nonstatutory labor exemption throughout the multi-employer collective bargaining process.  There, the League and the Players Association were negotiating, among other things, about the salaries to be paid to players on so-called development squads, who played in practice games and substituted for injured players.  The teams of the League agreed among themselves and insisted in bargaining that there would be a uniform weekly salary of $1,000 for each of these players, while the union insisted that the development-squad players should get the same economic terms as regular players and should be allowed to negotiate those terms individually with their teams.  After an impasse was reached, the League implemented its program of paying all such players $1,000 per week.  The players brought an antitrust action which ultimately resulted in a jury verdict and treble-damage award in excess of $30 million.  The Court of Appeals for the District of Columbia Circuit reversed, and the Supreme Court (in an 8–1 decision by Justice Breyer) affirmed the court of appeals.

The Court considered the history of the 1914 Clayton Act and the 1935 Labor Act and concluded that Congress "hoped to prevent judicial use of antitrust law to resolve labor disputes—a kind of dispute normally inappropriate for antitrust law resolution."

> The implicit ("nonstatutory") exemption interprets the labor statutes in accordance with this intent, namely, as limiting an antitrust court's authority to determine, in the area of industrial conflict, what is or is not a "reasonable" practice.  It thereby substitutes legislative and administrative labor-related determinations for judicial antitrust-related determinations as to the appropriate legal limits of industrial conflict.

The Court noted that multiemployer bargaining "is a well-established, important, pervasive method of collective bargaining, offering advantages to both management and labor."  (Such bargaining was stated to account for more than 40% of major collective-bargaining agreements).  At the core of such bargaining is the capability that cooperating employers have to discuss and establish a common bargaining strategy before and during negotiations and after an impasse is reached.  The Court also referred to the many NLRB and court decisions allowing an employer to implement after impasse terms already offered to the union at the bargaining table, just as the National Football League had done here.

> [T]o permit antitrust liability here threatens to introduce instability and uncertainty into the collective-bargaining process, for antitrust law [which discourages anticompetitive behavior] often for-

bids or discourages the kinds of joint discussions and behavior that the collective-bargaining process invites or requires.... The labor laws give the Board, not antitrust courts, primary responsibility for policing the collective-bargaining process.

The Court then turned to a number of proposed termination points for the antitrust exemption—among them, when the collective agreement terminates, or when impasse is reached, or when after impasse the teams impose substantive terms rather than merely agree upon "tactics"—and firmly rejected them all. It also rejected the players' claims that, as specially talented individuals accustomed to individualized salary bargaining, they should be given preferred treatment under the antitrust laws to "transport works, coal miners, or meat packers."

> For these reasons, we hold that the implicit ("nonstatutory") antitrust exemption applies to the employer conduct at issue here. That conduct took place during and immediately after a collective-bargaining negotiation. It grew out of, and was directly related to, the lawful operation of the bargaining process. It involved a matter that the parties were required to negotiate collectively. And it concerned only the parties to the collective-bargaining relationship.

The Court acknowledged that perhaps the antitrust laws might come into play for the joint imposition of contract terms if "an agreement among employers [were] sufficiently distant in time and in circumstances from the collective-bargaining process"; but it declined to opine whether, or where, such a line would be drawn in the range between a union's decertification and the "defunctness" of the multiemployer unit.

---

## Connell Constr. Co. v. Plumbers and Steamfitters Local Union No. 100[b]

421 U.S. 616, 95 S.Ct. 1830, 44 L.Ed.2d 418 (1975).

■ MR. JUSTICE POWELL delivered the opinion of the Court.

The building trades union in this case supported its efforts to organize mechanical subcontractors by picketing certain general contractors, including Petitioner. The union's sole objective was to compel the general contractors to agree that in letting subcontracts for mechanical work they would deal only with firms that were parties to the union's current collective-bargaining agreement. The union disclaimed any interest in

---

**b.** Comment, Broadening Labor's Antitrust Liability While Narrowing its Construction Industry Proviso Protection, 27 Cath. U.L.Rev. 305 (1978); Handler & Zifchak, Collective Bargaining and the Antitrust Laws: The Emasculation of the Labor Exemption, 81 Colum.L.Rev. 459 (1981); King & Smith, Labor Relations and Antitrust: Developments After *Connell*, 3 Ind.Rel.L.J. 605 (1979); Leslie, Principles of Labor Antitrust, 66 Va.L.Rev. 1183 (1980); St. Antoine, *Connell:* Antitrust Law at the Expense of Labor Law, 62 Va.L.Rev. 603 (1976).

representing the general contractors' employees.  In this case the picketing succeeded, and Petitioner seeks to annul the resulting agreement as an illegal restraint on competition under federal and state law.  The union claims immunity from federal antitrust statutes and argues that federal labor regulation pre-empts state law.

## I

Local 100 is the bargaining representative for workers in the plumbing and mechanical trades in Dallas.  When this litigation began, it was party to a multiemployer bargaining agreement with the Mechanical Contractors Association of Dallas, a group of about 75 mechanical contractors.  That contract contained a "most favored nation" clause, by which the union agreed that if it granted a more favorable contract to any other employer it would extend the same terms to all members of the Association.

Connell Construction Company is a general building contractor in Dallas.  It obtains jobs by competitive bidding and subcontracts all plumbing and mechanical work.  Connell has followed a policy of awarding these subcontracts on the basis of competitive bids, and it has done business with both union and nonunion subcontractors.  Connell's employees are represented by various building trade unions.  Local 100 has never sought to represent them or to bargain with Connell on their behalf.

In November 1970, Local 100 asked Connell to agree that it would subcontract mechanical work [to be performed at the construction site] only to firms that had a current contract with the union.  * * * When Connell refused to sign this agreement, Local 100 stationed a single picket at one of Connell's major construction sites.  About 150 workers walked off the job, and construction halted.  Connell filed suit in state court to enjoin the picketing as a violation of Texas antitrust laws.  Local 100 removed the case to federal court.  Connell then signed the subcontracting agreement under protest.  It amended its complaint to claim that the agreement violated §§ 1 and 2 of the Sherman Act, 15 U.S.C. §§ 1, 2, and was therefore invalid.  Connell sought a declaration to this effect and an injunction against any further efforts to force it to sign such an agreement.

By the time the case went to trial, Local 100 had submitted identical agreements to a number of other general contractors in Dallas.  Five others had signed, and the union was waging a selective picketing campaign against those who resisted.

The District Court held that the subcontracting agreement was exempt from federal antitrust laws because it was authorized by the construction industry proviso to § 8(e) of the National Labor Relations Act, 29 U.S.C. § 158(e).  The court also held that federal labor legislation pre-empted the State's antitrust laws.  78 L.R.R.M. 3012 (N.D.Tex.1971).  The Court of Appeals for the Fifth Circuit affirmed, 483 F.2d 1154 (C.A.5 1973), with one judge dissenting.  It held that Local 100's goal of organizing nonunion subcontractors was a legitimate union interest and that its efforts toward that goal were therefore exempt from federal antitrust laws.  On the second issue, it held that state law was pre-empted under San Diego

Building Trades Council v. Garmon, 359 U.S. 236, 79 S.Ct. 773, 3 L.Ed.2d 775 (1959). We granted certiorari on Connell's petition. 416 U.S. 981, 94 S.Ct. 2381, 40 L.Ed.2d 757 (1974). We reverse on the question of federal antitrust immunity and affirm the ruling on state law pre-emption.

## II

The basic sources of organized labor's exemption from federal antitrust laws are §§ 6 and 20 of the Clayton Act, 15 U.S.C. § 17 and 29 U.S.C. § 52, and the Norris–LaGuardia Act, 29 U.S.C. §§ 104, 105, and 113. These statutes declare that labor unions are not combinations or conspiracies in restraint of trade, and exempt specific union activities, including secondary picketing and boycotts, from the operation of the antitrust laws. See United States v. Hutcheson, 312 U.S. 219, 61 S.Ct. 463, 85 L.Ed. 788 (1941). They do not exempt concerted action or agreements between unions and nonlabor parties. UMW v. Pennington, 381 U.S. 657, 662, 85 S.Ct. 1585, 1589, 14 L.Ed.2d 626 (1965). The Court has recognized, however, that a proper accommodation between the congressional policy favoring collective bargaining under the NLRA and the congressional policy favoring free competition in business markets requires that some union-employer agreements be accorded a limited nonstatutory exemption from antitrust sanctions. Meat Cutters Local 189 v. Jewel Tea Co., 381 U.S. 676, 85 S.Ct. 1596, 14 L.Ed.2d 640 (1965).

The nonstatutory exemption has its source in the strong labor policy favoring the association of employees to eliminate competition over wages and working conditions. Union success in organizing workers and standardizing wages ultimately will affect price competition among employers, but the goals of federal labor law never could be achieved if this effect on business competition were held a violation of the antitrust laws. The Court therefore has acknowledged that labor policy requires tolerance for the lessening of business competition based on differences in wages and working conditions. See UMW v. Pennington, supra, 381 U.S. at 666, 85 S.Ct. at 1591; *Jewel Tea,* supra, 381 U.S. at 692–693, 85 S.Ct. at 1603–1604 (opinion of Mr. Justice White). Labor policy clearly does not require, however, that a union have freedom to impose direct restraints on competition among those who employ its members. Thus, while the statutory exemption allows unions to accomplish some restraints by acting unilaterally, *e.g.,* American Federation of Musicians v. Carroll, 391 U.S. 99, 88 S.Ct. 1562, 20 L.Ed.2d 460 (1968), the nonstatutory exemption offers no similar protection when a union and a nonlabor party agree to restrain competition in a business market. See Allen Bradley Co. v. IBEW Local 3, 325 U.S. 797, 806–811, 65 S.Ct. 1533, 1538–1541, 89 L.Ed. 1939 (1945); Cox, Labor and the Antitrust Laws—A Preliminary Analysis, 104 U.Pa.L.Rev. 252 (1955); Meltzer, Labor Unions, Collective Bargaining, and the Antitrust Laws, 32 U.Chi.L.Rev. 659 (1965).

In this case Local 100 used direct restraints on the business market to support its organizing campaign. The agreements with Connell and other general contractors indiscriminately excluded nonunion subcontractors from a portion of the market, even if their competitive advantages were not derived from substandard wages and working conditions but rather from more efficient operating methods. Curtailment of competition based on efficiency is neither a goal of federal labor policy nor a necessary effect of the elimination of competition among workers. Moreover, competition based on efficiency is a positive value that the antitrust laws strive to protect.

The multiemployer bargaining agreement between Local 100 and the Association, though not challenged in this suit, is relevant in determining the effect that the agreement between Local 100 and Connell would have on the business market. The "most favored nation" clause in the multiemployer agreement promised to eliminate competition between members of the Association and any other subcontractors that Local 100 might organize. By giving members of the Association a contractual right to insist on terms as favorable as those given any competitor, it guaranteed that the union would make no agreement that would give an unaffiliated contractor a competitive advantage over members of the Association. Subcontractors in the Association thus stood to benefit from any extension of Local 100's organization, but the method Local 100 chose also had the effect of sheltering them from outside competition in that portion of the market covered by subcontracting agreements between general contractors and Local 100. In that portion of the market, the restriction on subcontracting would eliminate competition on all subjects covered by the multiemployer agreement, even on subjects unrelated to wages, hours and working conditions.

Success in exacting agreements from general contractors would also give Local 100 power to control access to the market for mechanical subcontracting work. The agreements with general contractors did not simply prohibit subcontracting to any nonunion firm; they prohibited subcontracting to any firm that did not have a contract with Local 100. The union thus had complete control over subcontract work offered by general contractors that had signed these agreements. Such control could result in significant adverse effects on the market and on consumers, effects unrelated to the union's legitimate goals of organizing workers and standardizing working conditions. For example, if the union thought the interests of its members would be served by having fewer subcontractors competing for the available work, it could refuse to sign collective-bargaining agreements with marginal firms. Cf. UMW v. Pennington, supra. Or, since Local 100 has a well-defined geographical jurisdiction, it could exclude "travelling" subcontractors by refusing to deal with them. Local 100 thus might be able to create a geographical enclave for local contractors, similar to the closed market in *Allen–Bradley,* supra.

This record contains no evidence that the union's goal was anything other than organizing as many subcontractors as possible.[2] This goal was

---

**2.** There was no evidence that Local 100's organizing campaign was connected with any agreement with members of the multiemployer bargaining unit, and the only

legal, even though a successful organizing campaign ultimately would reduce the competition that unionized employers face from nonunion firms. But the methods the union chose are not immune from antitrust sanctions simply because the goal is legal.  Here Local 100, by agreement with several contractors, made nonunion subcontractors ineligible to compete for a portion of the available work.  This kind of direct restraint on the business market has substantial anti-competitive effects, both actual and potential, that would not follow naturally from the elimination of competition over wages and working conditions.  It contravenes antitrust policies to a degree not justified by congressional labor policy, and therefore cannot claim a nonstatutory exemption from the antitrust laws.

There can be no argument in this case, whatever its force in other contexts, that a restraint of this magnitude might be entitled to an antitrust exemption if it were included in a lawful collective-bargaining agreement.  Cf. UMW v. Pennington, supra, 381 U.S. at 664–665, 85 S.Ct. at 1590, 1591; *Jewel Tea,* supra, 381 U.S. at 689–690, 85 S.Ct. at 1601–1602 (opinion of Mr. Justice White); id., at 709–713, 732–733, 85 S.Ct. 1614, 1616, 1626–1627 (opinion of Mr. Justice Goldberg).  In this case, Local 100 had no interest in representing Connell's employees.  The federal policy favoring collective bargaining therefore can offer no shelter for the union's coercive action against Connell or its campaign to exclude nonunion firms from the subcontracting market.

[In Part III of the Court's opinion, Justice Powell considered the union's claim that its contract was explicitly allowed by the construction-industry proviso to Section 8(e), which removes from the ban of that Section "hot cargo" clauses relating to the subcontracting of work to be performed at a construction site.  Observing that the scope of Section 8(e) was not exclusively to be determined by the NLRB and that a court could do so in the context of a federal antitrust action, the Court held that Section 8(e) "does not allow this type of agreement."  The Court studied the legislative history of that Section and found that the permission to use "hot cargo" agreements for jobsite work was not for the purpose of entitling unions "to use subcontracting agreements as a broad organizational weapon" but rather "to alleviate the frictions that may arise when union men work continuously alongside nonunion men on the same construction site."]

Local 100 does not suggest that its subcontracting agreement is related to any of these policies.  * * * The union admits that it sought the agreement solely as a way of pressuring mechanical subcontractors in the Dallas area to recognize it as the representative of their employees.

If we agreed with Local 100 that the construction industry proviso authorizes subcontracting agreements with "stranger" contractors, not

evidence of agreement among those subcontractors was the "most favored nation" clause in the collective-bargaining agreement. In fact, Connell has not argued the case on a theory of conspiracy between the union and unionized subcontractors.  It has simply relied on the multiemployer agreement as a factor enhancing the restraint of trade implicit in the subcontracting agreement it signed.

limited to any particular jobsite, our ruling would give construction unions an almost unlimited organizational weapon. The unions would be free to enlist any general contractor to bring economic pressure on nonunion subcontractors, as long as the agreement recited that it only covered work to be performed on some jobsite somewhere. The proviso's jobsite restriction then would serve only to prohibit agreements relating to subcontractors that deliver their work complete to the jobsite.

It is highly improbable that Congress intended such a result. One of the major aims of the 1959 Act was to limit "top-down" organizing campaigns, in which unions used economic weapons to force recognition from an employer regardless of the wishes of his employees. * * *

These careful limits on the economic pressure unions may use in aid of their organizational campaigns would be undermined seriously if the proviso to § 8(e) were construed to allow unions to seek subcontracting agreements, at large, from any general contractor vulnerable to picketing. Absent a clear indication that Congress intended to leave such a glaring loophole in its restrictions on "top-down" organizing, we are unwilling to read the construction industry proviso as broadly as Local 100 suggests. Instead, we think its authorization extends only to agreements in the context of collective-bargaining relationships and in light of congressional references to the *Denver Building Trades* problem, possibly to common-situs relationships on particular jobsites as well.

Finally, Local 100 contends that even if the subcontracting agreement is not sanctioned by the construction industry proviso and therefore is illegal under § 8(e), it cannot be the basis for antitrust liability because the remedies in the NLRA are exclusive. This argument is grounded in the legislative history of the 1947 Taft–Hartley amendments. Congress rejected attempts to regulate secondary activities by repealing the antitrust exemptions in the Clayton and Norris–LaGuardia Acts, and created special remedies under the labor law instead. It made secondary activities unfair labor practices under § 8(b)(4), and drafted special provisions for preliminary injunctions at the suit of the NLRB and for recovery of actual damages in the district courts. Sections 10(*l*), 303; 29 U.S.C. §§ 160(*l*), 187. But whatever significance this legislative choice has for antitrust suits based on those secondary activities prohibited by § 8(b)(4), it has no relevance to the question whether Congress meant to preclude antitrust suits based on the "hot-cargo" agreements that it outlawed in 1959. There is no legislative history in the 1959 Congress suggesting that labor-law remedies for § 8(e) violations were intended to be exclusive, or that Congress thought allowing antitrust remedies in cases like the present one would be inconsistent with the remedial scheme of the NLRA.

We therefore hold that this agreement, which is outside the context of a collective-bargaining relationship and not restricted to a particular jobsite, but which nonetheless obligates Connell to subcontract work only to firms that have a contract with Local 100, may be the basis of a federal antitrust suit because it has a potential for restraining competition in the business market in ways that would not follow naturally from elimination of competition over wages and working conditions.

[In Part IV of its opinion, the Court held that although the agreement between the union and Connell was subject to federal antitrust law, state antitrust law was to be preempted. "Because employee organization is central to federal labor policy and regulation of organizational procedures is comprehensive, federal law does not admit the use of state antitrust law to regulate union activity that is closely related to organizational goals. * * * Of course, other agreements between unions and nonlabor parties may yet be subject to state antitrust laws. See Teamsters Local 24 v. Oliver, supra, 358 U.S. at 295–297, 79 S.Ct. at 304–305. The governing factor is the risk of conflict with the NLRA or with federal labor policy."]

### V

Neither the District Court nor the Court of Appeals decided whether the agreement between Local 100 and Connell, if subject to the antitrust laws, would constitute an agreement that restrains trade within the meaning of the Sherman Act. The issue was not briefed and argued fully in this Court. Accordingly, we remand for consideration whether the agreement violated the Sherman Act.[19]

Reversed in part and remanded.

[The dissenting opinions of JUSTICES DOUGLAS and STEWART, on behalf of a total of four justices, have been omitted.]

---

*THE DISTINCTION BETWEEN NON-EXEMPTION AND SUBSTANTIVE ANTITRUST LIABILITY*

The following passages are from Handler & Zifchak, "Collective Bargaining and the Antitrust Laws: The Emasculation of the Labor Exemption," 81 Colum.L.Rev. 459, 510–13 (1981):

"Assuming the antitrust laws do apply to labor conduct that constitutes a restraint on trade, what should be the standard of legality? * * *

---

**19.** In addition to seeking a declaratory judgment that the agreement with Local 100 violated the antitrust laws, Connell sought a permanent injunction against further picketing to coerce execution of the contract in litigation. Connell obtained a temporary restraining order against the picketing on January 21, 1971, and thereafter executed the contract—under protest—with Local 100 on March 28, 1971. So far as the record in this case reveals, there has been no further picketing at Connell's construction sites. Accordingly, there is no occasion for us to consider whether the Norris–LaGuardia Act forbids such an injunction where the specific agreement sought by the union is illegal, or to determine whether, within the meaning of the Norris–LaGuardia Act, there was a "labor dispute" between these parties. If the Norris–LaGuardia Act were applicable to this picketing, injunctive relief would not be available under the antitrust laws. See United States v. Hutcheson, 312 U.S. 219, 61 S.Ct. 463, 85 L.Ed. 788 (1941). If the agreement in question is held on remand to be invalid under federal antitrust laws, we cannot anticipate that Local 100 will resume picketing to obtain or enforce an illegal agreement.

*Connell* and other Supreme Court decisions strongly suggest that union conduct should be measured by the rule of reason in recognition of the peculiar labor relations context in which the restraint arises even if, in a nonlabor context, similar conduct might be per se unlawful. * * * [T]o invoke a per se rule upon a lifting of the exemption would bring antitrust and its panoply of sanctions to bear with a vengeance. The factors to be considered in determining the existence of an antitrust *exemption* are separate and distinct from those bearing on the presence of an antitrust *infraction.* We have seen a variety of union conduct held not immune to antitrust: hot cargo agreements that violate section 8(e) and possibly other acts constituting unfair labor practices; restraints on a party's bargaining freedom; and permissive bargaining subjects. But once such conduct is deemed not exempt, it is incumbent upon the decisionmaker to consider the relative anti–competitiveness of the conduct before imposing antitrust liability. Does the conduct restrain commercial competition? Does it do so unreasonably? How strong is the union in the labor market, and how strong is the employer in its market? What is the bargaining history, and what is the purpose behind the challenged restraint? Is the purpose to prey upon an employer's competitor, or only to minimize competition in the labor market? Finally, what interest, if any, of national labor policy does the restraint serve?

"On the one hand, merely because a restraint violates labor law does not mean that it is a pernicious commercial restraint, per se unlawful. While the particular means utilized by a union to achieve its goal may be unlawful under the labor law for reasons unique to that body of law—for example, a secondary boycott, which implicates neutrals in a labor dispute and hence is viewed as an unfair tactic—the union's overall objective may be legitimate in a broader sense, in that it promotes unionization and the betterment of terms and conditions of employment through collective bargaining. Therefore, once an antitrust exemption is denied to conduct interdicted by the labor laws, the conduct should be measured by the rule of reason. In such an inquiry the broad objectives sanctioned by labor policy should be carefully balanced against antitrust's concern with the preservation of market or product competition. The adverse market effects of a restraint must be of serious dimension to outweigh the legitimate labor-related motives of a union in imposing the restraint. In this regard, it is most significant that provisos to section 8(e) *sanction* hot cargo agreements, with adverse secondary objectives, in the construction and garment industries. It is difficult to believe that Congress would have condoned hot cargo agreements in two specific industries if they were viewed as so inherently pernicious and without redeeming virtue as to merit per se illegality under the Sherman Act."

———

## PROBLEMS FOR DISCUSSION

**1.** If Connell had sought injunctive relief not against the enforcement of the disputed contract clause but rather against the union's picketing to secure that clause, would the Norris–LaGuardia Act forbid the issuance of such an injunction?

**2.** Is the Court's objection to the union's tactics rooted principally in anti-trust policy or principally in a disdain for coercive "top-down" organizing campaigns? If it is the latter, ought not the appropriate remedies be those provided in the Labor Act rather than those provided in the Sherman Act? (What exactly would the remedies be under either statute?) Can the result in *Connell* be squared with the Court's earlier decision in *Apex Hosiery*?

**3.** Unions in the clothing industry have, over time, been unsuccessful in organizing employees of contractors, who receive fabric from the jobbers or manufacturers and cut and sew it to make a finished garment which is then returned to the jobbers or manufacturers. Organization is difficult because the contractors work in out-of-the-way lofts, are extremely mobile (since their primary capital equipment is sewing machines) and do not work on any one project for too long a time. This has permitted the non-union contractors to pay very little, to require long hours and generally to operate under "sweatshop" conditions. To organize the contractors effectively, the unions in the "needle trade" have entered into agreements with the jobbers or manufacturers (who *can* be organized) containing provisions barring the use of nonunion contractors. One such agreement is that between the National Skirt and Sportswear Association (the Association) and the International Ladies' Garment Workers' Union (the Union). It provides that the employer members of the Association are to maintain a union shop for employees doing manufacturing work on the employer's premises; that if manufacturing work is contracted out, it will be sent only to contractors operating union shops organized by the ILGWU; and that payments to contractors are to be sufficient to pay their workers in accordance with the agreement between the Association and the Union and in addition a reasonable amount to cover overhead. Certain manufacturers who are party to the agreement have brought an action in a federal court seeking a declaration that these contract provisions are illegal and unenforceable, and an injunction against their enforcement by the Union. What should be the court's disposition of the case? See Jou–Jou Designs v. International Ladies Garment Workers Union, 643 F.2d 905 (2d Cir.1981); Greenstein v. National Skirt & Sportswear Ass'n, 178 F.Supp. 681 (S.D.N.Y.1959).

**4.** Long John Silver's (Silver's) is a fast-food seafood restaurant chain, which has had two restaurants in the Pittsburgh area built by Muko Builders, Inc., a non-union company. During construction of the two buildings, and subsequently during their operation, they were picketed by representatives of the Southwestern Pennsylvania Building and Construction Trades Council (Trades Council), an association of construction unions. The president of Silver's requested a meeting with representatives of the Trades Council, in an effort to terminate the picketing. The result of the meeting was an agreement that Silver's would invite bids for the construction of future restaurant buildings only from unionized contractors certified by the Trades Council; the Trades Council in turn terminated the picketing. Silver's asked Muko if it would build as a union contractor, but Muko refused, and it subsequently was not asked to bid on any further jobs for Silver's. Silver's subsequently built twelve additional restaurants, all by union contractors. Muko can show that the prices for those new restaurants aggregated over $250,000 more than Muko would have charged (while projecting a significant profit); that Muko's employees (who function primarily as supervisors, with the actual construction being done through subcontractors) are paid at prevailing wage rates; and that the Trades Council has never made any effort to organize Muko's employees.

Muko has brought an action against Silver's and the Trades Council under the federal antitrust laws, seeking an injunction and treble damages. The defendants have moved for summary judgment. Should the motion be granted? See Larry V.

Muko, Inc. v. Southwestern Pennsylvania Bldg. & Constr. Trades Council, 609 F.2d 1368 (3d Cir.1979)("*Muko I*"), and 670 F.2d 421 (3d Cir.1982)("*Muko II*"), cert. denied, 459 U.S. 916, 103 S.Ct. 229, 74 L.Ed.2d 182(1982).

----

AMERICAN FEDERATION OF MUSICIANS v. CARROLL, 391 U.S. 99, 88 S.Ct. 1562, 20 L.Ed.2d 460 (1968).  The AFM has bylaws and regulations governing so-called "club date" engagements (one-time engagements such as weddings and commencements) of its members, some of whom function as band leaders (usually playing an instrument as well) and some of whom function as instrumentalists or "sidemen."  Among other things, the union bylaws and regulations required leaders to engage a minimum number of sidemen;  required leaders to charge purchasers of music (*e.g.,* the father of the bride) a minimum price, composed of union-scale wages for sidemen, twice that for the leader, and an additional eight percent to cover taxes, insurance, and other expenses of the leader;  required leaders to use a specific contract form in dealing with purchasers of music;  required a leader to charge an additional ten percent when his band played outside its territory.  In effect, these regulations substituted for collective bargaining agreements with one-time music purchasers, since such agreements would be impracticable.  The AFM provisions were challenged by certain union members who functioned principally as band leaders, and who brought an action for injunctive relief and treble damages under the Sherman Act.

The Supreme Court agreed with the lower courts that the union's bylaws and regulations did not constitute a combination with a "non-labor group" but rather were exempt as affecting only a "labor" group within the Norris–LaGuardia Act, and that the complaint was properly dismissed.  Although the band leaders were functioning technically as independent contractors in arranging performing dates, and as employers of the sidemen, they were properly treated as a labor group, given their competition with "employee" members of the union regarding jobs, wages and the like.

The Court stated:  "The District Court found that the orchestra leaders performed work and functions which actually or potentially affected the hours, wages, job security, and working conditions of [AFM] members.  These findings have substantial support in the evidence and in the light of the job and wage competition thus established, both courts correctly held that it was lawful for petitioners to pressure the orchestra leaders to become union members, * * * to insist upon a closed shop, * * * to impose the minimum employment quotas complained of, * * * to require the orchestra leaders to use the Form B contract, * * * and to favor local musicians by requiring that higher wages be paid to musicians from outside a local's jurisdiction * * *."

The court of appeals had disagreed with the trial court as to the legality of the "price list," holding it beyond the labor exemption because of its concern with "prices" rather than "wages."  The Supreme Court, however, stated that it was "not dispositive of the question that petitioners' regulation in form establishes price floors.  The critical inquiry is whether the price floors in actuality operate to protect the wages of the * * * sidemen." If the leaders were themselves to undercut the wage scale or other union regulations, this would put pressure on the union members they compete with to correspondingly lower their own demands. Even when the band leader was simply leading a group in a club-date engagement and not performing on an instrument and displacing an employee-musician, the price list was within the exemption from the antitrust laws. By fixing a reasonable amount over the sum of the minimum wages paid the sidemen, to cover the leader's costs in setting up the engagement, the union's price list insured that no part of the labor costs of the leader or the sidemen would be diverted for overhead or other non-labor costs. "In other words, the price of the product—here the price for an orchestra for a club-date—represents almost entirely the scale wages of the sidemen and the leader. Unlike most industries, except for the 8% charge, there are no other costs contributing to the price. Therefore, if leaders cut prices, inevitably wages must be cut." The Court viewed its analysis as supported by the opinions of Justices White and Goldberg in the *Jewel Tea* case (as well as by the opinion of the Court in Teamsters Union v. Oliver, see page 950, infra).

---

## PROBLEMS FOR DISCUSSION

**1.** A number of lawyers in private practice in Washington, D.C., have regularly made themselves available for assignment as counsel in criminal cases, when staff lawyers from the local defender association are unavailable. These private attorneys are paid for their services by the District of Columbia, at the hourly rate of $30. They have created an organization known as the Trial Lawyers Association (TLA), the principal purpose of which is to communicate to Congress and the courts on matters of interest to the attorneys. When TLA lobbying efforts recently failed to secure an increase in their hourly fee to $40, the attorneys agreed among themselves to refuse all case assignments until the fee is increased. This has had a serious adverse impact upon the criminal justice system in the District. Is this illegal price fixing in violation of the antitrust laws? Is it sheltered by the labor exemption? (Is it ethical?) See Federal Trade Com'n v. Superior Court Trial Lawyers Ass'n, 493 U.S. 411, 110 S.Ct. 768, 107 L.Ed.2d 851 (1990).

**2.** Paper companies with mills in the area of Mobile, Alabama, secure their supplies of pulpwood from various parties known as "dealers" who in turn obtain their supply from pulpwood "producers." The "producers"—working ordinarily with a crew of up to three other persons whom they employ—cut, load and haul cord wood designated by the "dealer," who generally acquires rights from the landowner to cut standing timber. The dealer leases trucks, saws and other necessary equipment to the producer (who ordinarily cannot afford to buy them), and gives the producer credit (against future moneys owed to the producers for wood supplied) for gas, tires, and the like. The dealers also deduct from the price they pay the producers for wood amounts required by law for workmen's compensation, liability insurance and the like. Producers do not sell directly to the paper mills but must do business through a dealer.

The producers have organized themselves as the Gulf Coast Pulpwood Association, and have engaged in a work stoppage and picketing of the dealers, in support of demands concerning the price and conditions of sale of pulpwood. The paper companies bring an action under the Sherman Act to enjoin the activities of the Association. May an injunction issue? See Scott Paper Co. v. Gulf Coast Pulpwood Ass'n, 85 L.R.R.M. 2978, 72 CCH Lab.Cas. ¶ 14,031 (S.D.Ala.1973), affirmed 491 F.2d 119 (5th Cir.1974).

(After thirty days, could a meritorious charge be filed with the NLRB against the Association for violation of Section 8(b)(7)? Could the paper companies proceed both in court and before the NLRB?)

**3.** In the theater world, it is customary (if not essential) for actors to secure employment through agents. The actors' union, Actors' Equity, has unilaterally established a licensing system regulating the fees charged actors by theatrical agents for the referral of union members; these agents' fees are calculated as a percentage of the actor's wage. Equity's rules forbid members to contract with agents not licensed by the union. Has Actors' Equity violated the antitrust laws? See H.A. Artists & Assocs. v. Actors' Equity Ass'n, 451 U.S. 704, 101 S.Ct. 2102, 68 L.Ed.2d 558 (1981).

# PART EIGHT

# FEDERALISM AND LABOR RELATIONS[a]

---

## I. PREEMPTION OF STATE LABOR LAW: AN OVERVIEW

Congress has since the founding of the nation been accorded the power, by Article I, Section 8 of the Constitution, "To regulate Commerce * * * among the several States" and "To make all Laws which shall be necessary and proper for carrying into Execution the foregoing Powers." The entire residue of regulatory power, as far as it may affect labor relations, was left to the states. Throughout the nineteenth century and for the first third of this century, the principal body of legal rules regulating the relationships among employers, workers and unions was formulated through common law decisionmaking by state-court judges. The focus of those rules was the legality of concerted activities by workers, in particular the means that could be utilized and the objectives that could be sought.

Although the Constitution also provided, in the Supremacy Clause in the second paragraph of Article VI, that "This Constitution, and the Laws of the United States which shall be made in Pursuance thereof * * * shall be the supreme Law of the Land; and the Judges in every State shall be bound thereby, any Thing in the Constitution or Laws of any State to the

---

**a.** See Cox, Federalism in the Law of Labor Relations, 67 Harv.L.Rev. 1297 (1954); Cox, Labor Law Preemption Revisited, 85 Harv.L.Rev. 1337 (1972); Cox, Recent Developments in Federal Labor Law Preemption, 41 Ohio St.L.J. 277 (1980); Drummonds, The Sister Sovereign States: Preemption and the Second Twentieth Century Revolution in the Law of the American Workplace, 62 Fordham L.Rev. 469 (1993); Gottesman, Rethinking Labor Law Preemption: State Laws Facilitating Unionization, 7 Yale J. on Reg. 355 (1990); Lesnick, Preemption Reconsidered: The Apparent Reaffirmation of *Garmon*, 72 Colum.L.Rev. 469 (1972); Meltzer, The Supreme Court, Congress and State Jurisdiction Over Labor Relations, 59 Columbia L.Rev. 6, 269 (1959); Michelman, State Power to Govern Concerted Employee Activities, 74 Harv. L.Rev. 641 (1961); Silverstein, Against Preemption in Labor Law, 24 Conn.L.Rev. 1 (1991); Stone, The Legacy of Industrial Pluralism: The Tension Between Individual Employment Rights and the New Deal Collective Bargaining System, 59 U. Chi. L.Rev. 575 (1992).

contrary notwithstanding," little attention was paid throughout this period to limitations imposed by our federal system upon state lawmaking in the area of labor relations.

Until the mid–1930s, it was assumed that the relations between labor and management were in fact essentially beyond the power of Congress to regulate. In 1908, for example, the Supreme Court held in Adair v. United States, 208 U.S. 161, 28 S.Ct. 277, 52 L.Ed. 436 (1908), that the federal government could not constitutionally protect organizational activities on interstate railroads because there was no "possible legal or logical connection * * * between an employee's membership in a labor organization and the carrying on of interstate commerce." As late as 1936, the Court declared in Carter v. Carter Coal Co., 298 U.S. 238, 56 S.Ct. 855, 80 L.Ed. 1160 (1936), that Congress lacked power to regulate the labor standards under which bituminous coal was produced. By that time, the body of state law in this field was considerable; it consisted mostly of a mass of restrictions upon strikes, picketing and other concerted activities, and rather little protection of union organizing.

The status of this body of state law was potentially unsettled once the Supreme Court modified its approach toward the federal regulation of interstate commerce by declaring, in NLRB v. Jones & Laughlin Steel Corp., 301 U.S. 1, 57 S.Ct. 615, 81 L.Ed. 893 (1937), that it was within the constitutional powers of Congress to regulate, in the National Labor Relations Act of 1935, labor relations in production industries. Subsequent decisions of the Court have vastly increased the scope of Congress's power to regulate even seemingly local enterprises, as witness the decision in Howell Chevrolet Co. v. NLRB, 346 U.S. 482, 74 S.Ct. 214, 98 L.Ed. 215 (1953), which upheld the application of the NLRA to small local retailers of automobiles. See Stern, "The Commerce Clause and the National Economy, 1933–1946," 59 Harv.L.Rev. 645, 883 (1946).

Congress clearly, then, has the power to regulate labor relations in most American businesses and to exclude (expressly or impliedly) the application of state laws whether statutory or judge-made. But this power is permissive only, and need not be fully exercised by Congress. Neither the allocation of constitutional power to Congress nor even the actual enactment of federal legislation necessarily excludes the jurisdiction of state tribunals or the application of state law. Thus, the enormous expansion of national power over industrial relations which began in 1937 raised three groups of questions.

First, how far out along the range of infinitely small gradations from interstate railroads and basic steel producers to corner drugstores and delicatessens should actual federal regulation of labor relations extend? Although in the early years of the administration of the NLRA, it was assumed that the Board's jurisdiction was congruent with Congress's power under the Constitution to regulate interstate commerce, the burden on the Board that would accompany the exercise of such a vast jurisdiction (as well as the budgetary implications) convinced the Board to decline to exercise its jurisdiction over smaller businesses having only local signifi-

cance.   In 1959, Congress as part of the Landrum–Griffin Act declared in
Section 14(c) of the NLRA that the Board was not to contract its jurisdiction beneath the levels announced in 1958.   The jurisdictional standards
now utilized by the Board are set forth in detail at page 94–95, supra.

A second major question bearing on federalism in labor law is what
tribunals have jurisdiction and what law applies to the labor relations of
those businesses over which the NLRB can, but declines to, exercise
jurisdiction?   When the Board in the 1950s set its own jurisdiction at a
level beneath that which it could statutorily assert over interstate commerce, it assumed that state tribunals and state law would regulate the
business which it declined to regulate.   But in Guss v. Utah Labor
Relations Bd., 353 U.S. 1, 77 S.Ct. 598, 1 L.Ed.2d 601 (1957), the Supreme
Court held this assumption to be incorrect, thus creating a "no man's
land" in which the federal agency declined to act (partly from choice but
partly for lack of funds and personnel) but from which the states were
excluded by federal legislation.   The Board's response was to announce
expanded jurisdictional guidelines in 1958, in order that "more individuals,
labor organizations and employers may invoke the rights and protections
afforded by the statute."   Siemons Mailing Service, 122 NLRB 81 (1958).
As to the "no man's land" that still remained, Congress in 1959 declared in
Section 14(c) that state courts and agencies may assert jurisdiction over
labor disputes which the Board declines to regulate as outside its discretionary jurisdiction.   Although Congress did not explicitly declare whether
state tribunals are in these proceedings to apply federal or local law, it is
generally understood that state law may be applied.   E.g., Kempf v.
Carpenters and Joiners Local Union No. 1273, 229 Or. 337, 367 P.2d 436
(1961).[b]

Alternatively, it is permissible under a proviso to section 10(a) for the
NLRB to negotiate an agreement with a state agency to cede jurisdiction to
the latter if the state law is consistent with the federal act.   The Supreme
Court has read that section to require that the state statute's provisions
parallel those of the federal act.   Algoma Plywood & Veneer Co. v.
Wisconsin Employment Relations Board, 336 U.S. 301, 69 S.Ct. 584, 93
L.Ed. 691 (1949).   The NLRB has required that the state law be "substantially identical."   See Produce Magic, Inc., 318 NLRB 1171 (1995)(Chairman Gould and Member Browning dissenting, opining that that requirement has rendered the proviso a nullity and observing that no cession
agreements have been made by the Board since the proviso was added in
1947).

The third issue of federalism in labor law is the most vexing.   How far
does actual federal regulation of the labor relations of a business exclude

**b.**  On occasion, the question will be
raised before the state court or agency
whether a given employer actually fails to
meet the NLRB's jurisdictional standards.
The Board has thus far left state tribunals
free to determine this question, and thus
their own jurisdiction, under Section 14(c),
but has arranged to render advisory opinions
in particular cases at the request of either of
the parties to the proceeding or the state
court or agency involved.   NLRB Rules &
Regulations, 29 C.F.R. § 102.98.

the application of inconsistent, parallel, or supplementary state law? To the extent that federal law is exclusive, where does one draw the line between the "labor relations" subject only to federal law and the permissible subjects of state regulation? These basic questions take form in any number of factual settings—from the freedom of employees to select their bargaining representative, to the use of concerted activities, to the negotiation and enforcement of a collective bargaining agreement.

Initially, little attention was given to the potential conflict between state labor-relations law and the provisions of the 1935 Wagner Act because the principal concern of state law was the regulation of strikes, picketing and boycotts, while the principal concerns of the federal act were questions of representation and employer unfair labor practices rather than limitations upon unions. (It is now apparent that Section 7 created a federal right to engage in concerted activities immune from state interference but this implication of the NLRA passed virtually unnoticed until 1949.) By 1947—when Congress did outlaw certain union activity, and by which time the Supreme Court had vastly expanded the effective reach of the federal labor laws and of the NLRB—duplication and collision between state and federal law were becoming common. According to conventional "preemption" theory, the courts in determining whether state regulation is allowable in the face of federal legislation attempt to divine "the intent of Congress." Although Supreme Court decisions left Congress free to determine the reach of state authority over labor-management relations, Congress—with such limited exceptions as Section 14(b) of the Taft–Hartley Act, permitting individual states to outlaw union-shop provisions which would otherwise be valid under the NLRA—remained silent, thus transferring the issue back to the Court.

Federal-state preemption issues are difficult to resolve in most substantive areas of the law, but they are particularly complicated in the area of labor-management relations. Superimposed upon the general clash between centralized and local authorities are two added factors: the existence of a presumably expert and experienced federal administrative agency, charged since the enactment of the NLRA in 1935 with the tasks of regulating representation elections and conducting unfair labor practice proceedings; and the historically rooted suspicion of judges (all judges, but particularly state-court judges) for their alleged insensitivity, if not hostility, to the goals of the labor movement.

No legal issue in the field of collective bargaining has been presented to the Supreme Court more frequently in the past thirty years than that of the preemption of state law, and perhaps no other legal issue has been left in quite as much confusion. The Court has stated its strong preference for a single coherent principle that can be readily applied in general categories of cases, rather than for ad hoc balancing of federal and state interests on a case-by-case basis. The Court has, in fact, articulated two broad theories that, applied to their fullest, would have an all-encompassing preemptive effect on state labor-relations law. These two theories will be summarized immediately below. However—particularly in the period since 1980—the

Court has with increasing frequency sustained state law, relying upon a number of analytical approaches that, in their totality, have resulted in rather little certainty and predictability for parties seeking to formulate conduct outside the courtroom or their litigative posture within.

One theory—which might be referred to as the "substantive rights" theory—holds that state courts and state law may not curtail conduct of employers or unions which Congress seeks affirmatively to protect or at least to permit. A state court could not, for example, enjoin a peaceful strike by a lawfully recognized union asserting wage demands in a contract renegotiation. Nor could a state outlaw, for example, a no-subcontracting provision which is the product of lawful mandatory bargaining under the National Labor Relations Act. This "substantive rights" theory does not rely for its applicability upon the existence or nonexistence of an expert administrative agency enforcing the NLRA; the inferred curtailment of state authority would follow even had the enforcement of the NLRA been left with the federal courts. Notice too that this theory appears not to impair the authority of the states to provide sanctions for employer or union conduct which is prohibited under the unfair labor practice provisions of the NLRA; additional state remedies would not impair any protection or permission afforded by federal law.

A second theory which has been articulated in the Supreme Court decisions might be called the "primary jurisdiction" theory. It assumes that Congress in the NLRA not only protected certain conduct and prohibited other conduct, but also created an administrative agency—expert, experienced, peculiarly sensitive to federal values in the area of labor-management relations, and possessed of delicately balanced remedial authority. Under this theory, states could not regulate conduct which is clearly protected, or even conduct which is clearly prohibited. Indeed, conduct which is arguably but not clearly protected would also have to go unregulated, since it is the NLRB which is the designated agency for making this determination; the same is true for conduct which is arguably but not clearly prohibited by the unfair labor practice provisions of the Act.

Despite the broad preemptive potential of these two theories applied in combination, the Supreme Court has been willing to sustain state laws by applying any one of a number of contrary hypotheses: that the issue is "deeply rooted in local feeling and responsibility," or that it is "a merely peripheral concern" of the federal labor laws; that the state's law is one of "general applicability" rather than one directly focusing upon relations among employers, workers and unions; that Congress has expressly manifested its willingness to tolerate state regulation; or that, properly understood, federal regulatory policy can be narrowly construed and the state policy readily accommodated. For some, this retreat from a broad preemption philosophy conjures up images of a return to unwanted and unsympathetic judicial intrusion in peaceful industrial confrontations, generally to the disadvantage of the union movement. For others, this trend reflects a just desire to afford some fair forum and expeditious relief against clear violations of private rights, as well as a recognition of the significant interests of state and local governments in regulating an increasingly complex workplace environment. The latter is punctuated by the rise of state law, legislative and judicial, regulating the individual employment relationship—laws or decisions prohibiting discharge for reasons violative of some public policy, or that afford protection for individual reputation, privacy, or dignity. The question is how these laws fit in the federal structure and how they relate to the enforcement of collective agreements under section 301 of the Act.

In what follows, the general outline of preemption is presented through the principal cases. Separate attention will then be given to the main areas of intersection: selection of a bargaining representative, collective bargaining, and enforcement of collective agreements.

---

## San Diego Building Trades Council v. Garmon

359 U.S. 236, 79 S.Ct. 773, 3 L.Ed.2d 775 (1959).

■ MR. JUSTICE FRANKFURTER delivered the opinion of the Court.

This case is before us for the second time. The present litigation began with a dispute between the petitioning unions and respondents, co-partners in the business of selling lumber and other materials in California. Respondents began an action in the Superior Court for the County of San Diego, asking for an injunction and damages. Upon hearing, the trial court found the following facts. In March of 1953 the unions sought from respondents an agreement to retain in their employ only those workers who were already members of the unions, or who applied for membership within thirty days. Respondents refused, claiming that none of their employees had shown a desire to join a union, and that, in any event, they could not accept such an arrangement until one of the unions had been designated by the employees as a collective bargaining agent. The unions began at once peacefully to picket the respondents' place of business, and to exert pressure on customers and suppliers in order to persuade them to stop dealing with respondents. The sole purpose of these pressures was to compel execution of the proposed contract. The unions contested this finding, claiming that the only purpose of their activities was to educate the workers and persuade them to become members. On the basis of its findings, the court enjoined the unions from picketing and from the use of other pressures to force an agreement, until one of them had been properly designated as a collective bargaining agent. The court also awarded $1,000 damages for losses found to have been sustained.

[The California state court concluded that the unions were violating Section 8(b)(2) of the NLRA, so that their conduct was not privileged; it issued an injunction and awarded damages. In a certiorari proceeding, the United States Supreme Court reversed, holding that the state injunction would conflict with the authority of the NLRB to issue cease-and-desist orders. On remand, the California court sustained the award of damages for violation of state law, and the Supreme Court once again granted certiorari "to determine whether the California court had jurisdiction to award damages arising out of peaceful union activity which it could not enjoin."]

In determining the extent to which state regulation must yield to subordinating federal authority, * * * [w]e have necessarily been concerned with the potential conflict of two law-enforcing authorities, with the disharmonies inherent in two systems, one federal, the other state, of inconsistent standards of substantive law and differing remedial schemes. But the unifying consideration of our decisions has been regard to the fact that Congress has entrusted administration of the labor policy for the Nation to a centralized administrative agency, armed with its own procedures, and equipped with its specialized knowledge and cumulative experience * * *.

Administration is more than a means of regulation; administration is regulation. We have been concerned with conflict in its broadest sense; conflict with a complex and interrelated federal scheme of law, remedy, and administration. Thus, judicial concern has necessarily focused on the nature of the activities which the States have sought to regulate, rather than on the method of regulation adopted. When the exercise of state power over a particular area of activity threatened interference with the clearly indicated policy of industrial relations, it has been judicially necessary to preclude the States from acting. However, due regard for the presuppositions of our embracing federal system, including the principle of diffusion of power not as a matter of doctrinaire localism but as a promoter of democracy, has required us not to find withdrawal from the States of power to regulate where the activity regulated was a merely peripheral concern of the Labor Management Relations Act. See International Ass'n of Machinists v. Gonzales, 356 U.S. 617, 78 S.Ct. 923, 2 L.Ed.2d 1018. Or where the regulated conduct touched interests so deeply rooted in local feeling and responsibility that, in the absence of compelling congressional direction, we could not infer that Congress had deprived the States of the power to act.

When it is clear or may fairly be assumed that the activities which a State purports to regulate are protected by § 7 of the National Labor Relations Act, or constitute an unfair labor practice under § 8, due regard for the federal enactment requires that state jurisdiction must yield. To leave the States free to regulate conduct so plainly within the central aim of federal regulation involves too great a danger of conflict between power asserted by Congress and requirements imposed by state law. Nor has it mattered whether the States have acted through laws of broad general application rather than laws specifically directed towards the governance of industrial relations. Regardless of the mode adopted, to allow the States to control conduct which is the subject of national regulation would create potential frustration of national purposes.

At times it has not been clear whether the particular activity regulated by the States was governed by § 7 or § 8 or was, perhaps, outside both these sections. But courts are not primary tribunals to adjudicate such issues. It is essential to the administration of the Act that these determinations be left in the first instance to the National Labor Relations Board. What is outside the scope of this Court's authority cannot remain within a State's power and state jurisdiction too must yield to the exclusive primary competence of the Board. See, *e.g.,* Garner v. Teamsters, etc. Union, 346 U.S. 485, especially at pages 489–491, 74 S.Ct. 161, at pages 165–166, 98 L.Ed. 228; Weber v. Anheuser–Busch, Inc., 348 U.S. 468, 75 S.Ct. 480, 99 L.Ed. 546.

The case before us is such a case. The adjudication in California has throughout been based on the assumption that the behavior of the petitioning unions constituted an unfair labor practice. This conclusion was derived by the California courts from the facts as well as from their view of the Act. It is not for us to decide whether the National Labor Relations Board would have, or should have, decided these questions in the same manner. When an activity is arguably subject to § 7 or § 8 of the Act, the States as well as the federal courts must defer to the exclusive competence of the National Labor Relations Board if the danger of state interference with national policy is to be averted.

To require the States to yield to the primary jurisdiction of the National Board does not ensure Board adjudication of the status of a disputed activity. If the Board decides, subject to appropriate federal judicial review, that conduct is protected by § 7, or prohibited by § 8, then the matter is at an end, and the States are ousted of all jurisdiction. Or, the Board may decide that an activity is neither protected nor prohibited, and thereby raise the question whether such activity may be regulated by the States.[4] However, the Board may also fail to determine the status of the disputed conduct by declining to assert jurisdiction, or by refusal of the General Counsel to file a charge, or by adopting some other disposition which does not define the nature of the activity with unclouded legal significance. This was the basic problem underlying our decision in Guss v. Utah Labor Relations Board, 353 U.S. 1, 77 S.Ct. 598, 609, 1 L.Ed.2d 601. In that case we held that the failure of the National Labor Relations Board to assume jurisdiction did not leave the States free to regulate activities they would otherwise be precluded from regulating. It follows that the failure of the Board to define the legal significance under the Act of a particular activity does not give the States the power to act. In the absence of the Board's clear determination that an activity is neither protected nor prohibited or of compelling precedent applied to essentially undisputed facts, it is not for this Court to decide whether such activities are subject to state jurisdiction. The withdrawal of this narrow area from possible state activity follows from our decisions in Weber and Guss. The governing consideration is that to allow the States to control activities that

4. See International Union, United Auto. Workers, etc. v. Wisconsin Employment Relations Board, 336 U.S. 245, 69 S.Ct. 516, 93 L.Ed. 651. The approach taken in that case, in which the Court undertook for itself to determine the status of the disputed activity, has not been followed in later decisions, and is no longer of general application.

are potentially subject to federal regulation involves too great a danger of conflict with national labor policy.

In the light of these principles the case before us is clear. Since the National Labor Relations Board has not adjudicated the status of the conduct for which the State of California seeks to give a remedy in damages, and since such activity is arguably within the compass of § 7 or § 8 of the Act, the State's jurisdiction is displaced.

Nor is it significant that California asserted its power to give damages rather than to enjoin what the Board may restrain though it could not compensate. Our concern is with delimiting areas of conduct which must be free from state regulation if national policy is to be left unhampered. Such regulation can be as effectively exerted through an award of damages as through some form of preventive relief. The obligation to pay compensation can be, indeed is designed to be, a potent method of governing conduct and controlling policy. Even the States' salutary effort to redress private wrongs or grant compensation for past harm cannot be exerted to regulate activities that are potentially subject to the exclusive federal regulatory scheme. See Garner v. Teamsters, etc. Union, 346 U.S. 485, 492–497, 74 S.Ct. 161, 166–169, 98 L.Ed. 228. It may be that an award of damages in a particular situation will not, in fact, conflict with the active assertion of federal authority. The same may be true of the incidence of a particular state injunction. To sanction either involves a conflict with federal policy in that it involves allowing two law-making sources to govern. In fact, since remedies form an ingredient of any integrated scheme of regulation, to allow the State to grant a remedy here which has been withheld from the National Labor Relations Board only accentuates the danger of conflict.

It is true that we have allowed the States to grant compensation for the consequences, as defined by the traditional law of torts, of conduct marked by violence and imminent threats to the public order. International Union, United Automobile, Aircraft and Agricultural Implement Workers, etc. v. Russell, 356 U.S. 634, 78 S.Ct. 932, 2 L.Ed.2d 1030; United Construction Workers, etc. v. Laburnum Const. Corp., 347 U.S. 656, 74 S.Ct. 833, 98 L.Ed. 1025. We have also allowed the States to enjoin such conduct. Youngdahl v. Rainfair, Inc., 355 U.S. 131, 78 S.Ct. 206, 2 L.Ed.2d 151; United Automobile Aircraft and Agricultural Implement Workers, etc. v. Wisconsin Employment Relations Board, 351 U.S. 266, 76 S.Ct. 794, 100 L.Ed. 1162. State jurisdiction has prevailed in these situations because the compelling state interest, in the scheme of our federalism, in the maintenance of domestic peace is not overridden in the absence of clearly expressed congressional direction. We recognize that the opinion in United Construction Workers, etc. v. Laburnum Const. Corp., 347 U.S. 656, 74 S.Ct. 833, 835, 98 L.Ed. 1025, found support in the fact that the state remedy had no federal counterpart. But that decision was determined, as is demonstrated by the question to which review was restricted, by the "type of conduct" involved, i.e., "intimidation and threats of violence." In the present case there is no such compelling state interest.

The judgment below is reversed.

Reversed.

■ [Mr. Justice Harlan concurred, for himself and three other Justices, not because the union's activity was an unfair labor practice but rather because it was arguably protected by Section 7. He stated that "The threshold question in every labor pre-emption case is whether the conduct with respect to which a State has sought to act is, or may fairly be regarded as, federally protected activity," since such activity must be beyond the reach of state power. He claimed that the Court majority had read the *Russell* and *Laburnum* cases too narrowly in construing them to mean that state tort law was not preempted because it was violence that the state was regulating. Rather, the violence in those cases was relevant for a broader reason: it rendered the defendants' conduct beyond the protection of Section 7. Assuming this conduct to have been prohibited and thus within the regulatory power of the NLRB, a strict theory of primary jurisdiction would have dictated displacement of state power to grant relief; but the Court in those two earlier cases probed further in order to determine whether there was any conflict between state remedies and the NLRA, and concluded that there was none, since the NLRB affords no remedy for past injury caused by violent unfair labor practices. State remedies for conduct not protected by Section 7 should thus survive if there is no conflict between them and federal administrative remedies. "The Court's opinion in this case cuts deeply into the ability of States to furnish an effective remedy under their own laws for the redress of past nonviolent tortious conduct which is not federally protected, but which may be deemed to be, or is, federally prohibited. Henceforth the States must withhold access to their courts until the National Labor Relations Board has determined that such unprotected conduct is not an unfair labor practice, a course which, because of unavoidable Board delays, may render state redress ineffective. And in instances in which the Board declines to exercise its jurisdiction, the States are entirely deprived of power to afford any relief. * * * Solely because it is fairly debatable whether the conduct here involved is federally protected, I concur in the result of today's decision."]

------

## PROBLEMS FOR DISCUSSION

**1.** The Milwaukee Gas & Light Company has for many years negotiated labor agreements with the Electrical Workers Union. The Company is privately owned, and the Union initially secured bargaining rights through an election supervised by the NLRB. When the most recent contract negotiations reached an impasse, the Union announced its intention to strike, and the Company promptly initiated a proceeding with the Wisconsin Employment Relations Board; the Board in turn secured a state-court restraining order requiring the union to "desist and refrain" from going on strike. This order was entered pursuant to the state's Public Utility Anti–Strike Law which states, in part: "It shall be unlawful for any group of employees of a public utility employer acting in concert to call a strike or go out on strike, or to cause any work stoppage or slowdown which would cause an interruption of an essential service." The union has appealed the issuance of the injunction. Should the injunction be vacated? See Amalgamated Ass'n of Street Employees Div. 998 v. Wisconsin Employment Rel. Bd., 340 U.S. 383, 71 S.Ct. 359, 95 L.Ed. 364 (1951).

**2.** Shortly after the Meat Cutters began an organizing campaign among the employees of the meat department of the Jack and Jill Supermarket, the company began to interrogate the employees coercively, to engage in surveillance of union meetings and to threaten the most active union supporters with discharge. The union filed charges against the company under Section 8(a)(1), which were sustained by the Administrative Law Judge; it also set up a picket line at the store advising the public that it was protesting the company's unfair labor practices. The company thereupon sought an injunction from a state court, claiming that there was mass picketing and intimidation of customers, in violation of state law. Although the state court found no violence or breach of the peace, it issued an injunction which limited the number of pickets at the store and which enjoined the picketers from handing out certain handbills and conversing with customers. Meanwhile, the Board adopted the findings of the Administrative Law Judge, found that the company had violated Section 8(a)(1) and issued a cease and desist order. It also filed suit in a federal district court seeking to restrain the enforcement of the state injunction and claiming that the NLRB had exclusive jurisdiction. Should the district court issue such an order? See NLRB v. Nash–Finch Co., 404 U.S. 138, 92 S.Ct. 373, 30 L.Ed.2d 328 (1971).

Assume, in the above case, that as soon as the company commenced its state-court action for an injunction against the union, the union filed a complaint in the federal district court seeking an order to the employer to withdraw its injunction action. Should the federal court so order? See Amalgamated Clothing Workers v. Richman Bros., 348 U.S. 511, 75 S.Ct. 452, 99 L.Ed. 600 (1955).

**3.** The State of Wisconsin has enacted a statute that requires the state's Department of Industry to maintain a current list of persons or firms that have been found by the NLRB to have violated the National Labor Relations Act on three separate occasions in the preceding five-year period. The statute also provides that the state's Department of Administration "shall not purchase any product known to be manufactured or sold by any person or firm included on the list of labor law violators" (subject to certain limited exceptions). State procurement agencies have informed the Ace Manufacturing Company, which is on the list of labor law violators, that the state will enter into no further purchase contracts with Ace until its name is removed in due course from the list.

Ace has brought an action against appropriate state agencies and officials seeking injunctive and declaratory relief against the enforcement of the statute. What are the strongest arguments to be made by the State of Wisconsin? What result should the court reach? See Wisconsin Dept. of Industry v. Gould Inc., 475 U.S. 282, 106 S.Ct. 1057, 89 L.Ed.2d 223 (1986).

AMALGAMATED ASS'N OF STREET, ELEC. RY. AND MOTOR COACH EMPLOYEES V. LOCKRIDGE, 403 U.S. 274, 91 S.Ct. 1909, 29 L.Ed.2d 473 (1971). Lockridge's union dues were to be paid by the end of October 1959, but he neglected to pay them, tendering the sum ten days later. The union refused to accept the tender and had the employer, Greyhound, discharge Lockridge pursuant to the union security provision of the labor agreement. Lockridge filed suit in state court for breach of the contract between the member and the union, embodied in the union's constitution and by-laws. The constitution provided that a fifteen-day delinquency in dues payment rendered the member "not in good standing," and a two-month delinquency resulted in suspension. The state court ordered reinstatement to union membership and damages in the amount of lost wages. The United States Supreme Court reversed, relying principally on *Garmon*.

Justice Harlan wrote for the majority. That Lockridge's complaint charged a breach of contract rather than an unfair labor practice, he opined, is beside the point, since "it is the conduct being regulated, not the formal description of governing legal standards, that is the proper focus of concern." Moreover the state, in purporting to interpret contractual terms, was not dealing with an issue different from that which would be presented to the NLRB, i.e., the Union's discrimination against Lockridge. Had the Board attempted to determine whether Lockridge's discharge was for reasons other than nonpayment of dues, it would routinely inquire into the proper construction of the Union constitution and bylaws in order to ascertain whether the Union properly found him to have been delinquent in his dues-paying responsibilities; had a violation of Section 8(b)(2) been made out, the Board would not treat the Union's good-faith misapplication of its rules as a defense.

Justice White wrote a dissenting opinion, in which the Chief Justice joined. "Here, Lockridge was discharged for alleged nonpayment of dues in accordance with the union constitution and brought suit alleging that he had in fact not been unduly tardy and that union's action was a breach of the contract. The face of the complaint did not implicate federal law. If the Idaho court were allowed to proceed, it would not have purported to adjudicate an unfair labor practice by reference to federal law, but, if it found the conduct unprotected by federal law, * * * would have enforced rights and obligations created by the union constitution." To hold that the NLRB must have exclusive power to adjudicate this case because the union's alleged conduct is, or may be, an unfair labor practice is "wooden logic."

Nor should Idaho's jurisdiction be preempted by the fact that the union's conduct might arguably have been protected under Section 7; the "arguably protected" branch of the *Garmon* doctrine should be rejected, urged Justice White for it "blindly preempts other tribunals" even though it is virtually impossible to secure an NLRB determination on this question in the first instance unless the employer deliberately commits an unfair labor practice through coercion or discrimination. Conduct arguably prohibited can be brought before the NLRB by the aggrieved party by filing a charge, but the Board will not determine whether employee or union conduct is actually *protected* unless the employer resorts to self-help in the hope that an unfair labor practice charge will be filed and the Board will find the union or employee conduct to be unprotected. "There seems little point in a doctrine that, in the name of national policy encourages the commission of unfair labor practices * * *. I would permit the state court to entertain the action and if the union defends on the ground that its conduct is protected by federal law, to pass on that claim at the outset of the proceeding.  If the federal law immunizes the challenged union action, the case is terminated; but if not, the case is adjudicated under state law."

---

## PROBLEMS FOR DISCUSSION

**1.** *Garmon* and *Lockridge* suggest that a defendant in a state court case will maximize its chances for a dismissal if it concedes that its conduct is an unfair labor practice under Section 8(b).  Is the defendant's attorney well advised to make such a concession?  Can it be used adversely in a later-filed unfair labor practice case before the NLRB?

If the defendant's conduct is concededly prohibited under the NLRA, then the only reluctance to uphold state court jurisdiction will stem from a concern about differing remedies.  Is that generally a strong enough concern to warrant preemption of state relief?  Would *Garmon* and *Lockridge* therefore have been better articulated as "substantive right" cases rather than "primary jurisdiction" cases?

**2.** *Garmon* and *Lockridge* conclude that when the defendant's conduct is only *arguably* prohibited, state court jurisdiction should be preempted because it is for the expert NLRB to determine whether the conduct is actually prohibited (and to order proper remedies) rather than the inexpert state courts.  Might not a better rationale have been that state courts may err by holding actually prohibited some conduct which is in fact actually *protected*—so that once again the "substantive right" theory would better explain these decisions, rather than the "primary jurisdiction" theory?  (By the way, is the Court's fear consistent with the fact that Congress in Section 303 has given jurisdiction to state judges and juries to rule upon secondary boycott cases, perhaps the most complex category of unfair labor practice cases under the NLRA?)

---

## Farmer v. United Brotherhood of Carpenters and Joiners, Local 25

430 U.S. 290, 97 S.Ct. 1056, 51 L.Ed.2d 338 (1977).

■ MR. JUSTICE POWELL delivered the opinion of the Court.

The issue in this case is whether the National Labor Relations Act, as amended, pre-empts a tort action brought in state court by a union member against the union and its officials to recover damages for the intentional infliction of emotional distress.

I

Petitioner Richard T. Hill[1] was a carpenter and a member of Local 25 of the United Brotherhood of Carpenters and Joiners of America.  Local 25

---

1. Hill died after the petition for a writ of certiorari was granted.  On June 1, 1976, Joy A. Farmer, special administrator of Hill's estate, was substituted as petitioner.  We will refer to Hill as the petitioner.

(the Union) operates an exclusive hiring hall for employment referral of carpenters in the Los Angeles area. In 1965, Hill was elected to a three-year term as vice president of the Union. Shortly thereafter sharp disagreement developed between Hill and the Union Business Agent, Earl Daley, and other Union officials over various internal Union policies. According to Hill, the Union then began to discriminate against him in referrals to employers, prompting him to complain about the hiring hall operation within the Union and to the District Council and the International Union. Hill claims that as a result of these complaints he was subjected to a campaign of personal abuse and harassment in addition to continued discrimination in referrals from the hiring hall.[2]

In April of 1969 petitioner filed in Superior Court for the County of Los Angeles an action for damages against the Union, the District Council and the International with which the Union was affiliated, and certain officials of the Union, including Business Agent Daley. In count two of his amended complaint, Hill alleged that the defendants had intentionally engaged in outrageous conduct, threats, and intimidation, and had thereby caused him to suffer grievous emotional distress resulting in bodily injury. In three other counts, he alleged that the Union had discriminated against him in referrals for employment because of his dissident intra-Union political activities, that the Union had breached the hiring hall provisions of the collective-bargaining agreement between it and a contractors association by failing to refer him on a nondiscriminatory basis, and that the failure to comply with the collective-bargaining agreement also constituted a breach of his membership contract with the Union. He sought $500,000 in actual, and $500,000 in punitive, damages.

The Superior Court sustained a demurrer to the allegations of discrimination and breach of contract on the ground that federal law pre-empted state jurisdiction over them, but allowed the case to go to trial on the allegations in count two. Hill attempted to prove that the Union's campaign against him included "frequent public ridicule," "incessant verbal abuse," and refusals to refer him to jobs in accordance with the rules of the hiring hall. The defendants countered with evidence that the hiring hall was operated in a nondiscriminatory manner. The trial court instructed the jury that in order to recover damages Hill had to prove by a preponderance of the evidence that the defendants intentionally and by outrageous conduct had caused him to suffer severe emotional distress. The court defined severe emotional distress as "any highly unpleasant mental reaction such as fright, grief, shame, humiliation, embarrassment, anger, chagrin, disappointment, or worr[y]." The injury had to be "severe," which in this context meant

"substantial or enduring, as distinguished from transitory or trivial. It must be of such a substantial quantity or enduring quality

---

2. According to Hill, the Union accomplished this discrimination by removing his name from the top of the out-of-work list and placing it at the bottom, by referring him to jobs of short duration when more desirable work was available, and by referring him to jobs for which he was not qualified.

that no reasonable man in a civilized society should be expected to endure it. Liability does not extend to mere insults, indignities, annoyances, petty or other trivialities."

The court also instructed that the National Labor Relations Board (the Board) would not have jurisdiction to compensate petitioner for injuries such as emotional distress, pain and suffering, and medical expenses, nor would it have authority to award punitive damages. The court refused to give a requested instruction to the effect that the jury could not consider any evidence regarding discrimination with respect to employment opportunities or hiring procedures.

The jury returned a verdict of $7,500 actual damages and $175,000 punitive damages against the Union, the District Council, and Business Agent Daley, and the trial court entered a judgment on the verdict.

The California Court of Appeal reversed. * * * [I]t held that the state courts had no jurisdiction over the complaint since the "crux" of the action concerned employment relations and involved conduct arguably subject to the jurisdiction of the National Labor Relations Board. The Court remanded "with instructions to render judgment for the defendants and dismiss the action." 49 Cal.App.3d, at 631, 122 Cal.Rptr., at 732. The California Supreme Court denied review.

We granted certiorari to consider the applicability of the preemption doctrine to cases of this nature, 423 U.S. 1086, 96 S.Ct. 876, 47 L.Ed.2d 96 (1976). For the reasons set forth below we vacate the judgment of the Court of Appeal and remand for further proceedings.

## II

* * * Judicial experience with numerous approaches to the pre-emption problem in the labor law area eventually led to the general rule set forth in *Garmon,* 359 U.S., at 244, 79 S.Ct., at 779, and recently reaffirmed in both *Lockridge,* 403 U.S., at 291, 91 S.Ct., at 1920, and Lodge 76, International Association of Machinists and Aerospace Workers v. Wisconsin Employment Relations Comm'n, 427 U.S. 132, 138–141, 96 S.Ct. 2548, 2552–2553, 49 L.Ed.2d 396 (1976):

> "When it is clear or may fairly be assumed that the activities which a State purports to regulate are protected by § 7 of the National Labor Relations Act, or constitute an unfair labor practice under § 8, due regard for the federal enactment requires that state jurisdiction must yield. To leave the States free to regulate conduct so plainly within the central aim of federal regulation involves too great a danger of conflict between power asserted by Congress and requirements imposed by state law." 359 U.S., at 244, 79 S.Ct., at 779.

But the same considerations that underlie the *Garmon* rule have led the Court to recognize exceptions in appropriate classes of cases. * * *

The nature of the inquiry is perhaps best illustrated by Linn v. Plant Guard Workers, 383 U.S. 53, 86 S.Ct. 657, 15 L.Ed.2d 582 (1966). Linn, an assistant manager of Pinkerton's National Detective Agency, filed a diversity action in federal court against a union, two of its officers, and a Pinkerton employee, alleging that the defendants had circulated a defamatory statement about him in violation of state law. If unfair labor practice charges had been filed, the Board might have found that the union violated § 8 by intentionally circulating false statements during an organizational campaign, or that the issuance of the malicious statements during the campaign had such a significant effect as to require that the election be set aside. Under a formalistic application of *Garmon,* the libel suit could have been pre-empted.

But a number of factors influenced the Court to depart from the *Garmon* rule. First, the Court noted that the underlying conduct—the intentional circulation of defamatory material known to be false—was not protected under the Act, 383 U.S., at 61, 86 S.Ct., at 662, and there was thus no risk that permitting the state cause of action to proceed would result in state regulation of conduct that Congress intended to protect. Second, the Court recognized that there was " 'an overriding state interest' " in protecting residents from malicious libels, and that this state interest was " 'deeply rooted in local feeling and responsibility.' " Id., at 61, 62, 86 S.Ct., at 663. Third, the Court reasoned that there was little risk that the state cause of action would interfere with the effective administration of national labor policy. The Board's § 8 unfair labor practice proceeding would focus only on whether the statements were misleading or coercive; whether the statements also were defamatory would be of no relevance to the Board's performance of its functions. Id., at 63, 86 S.Ct., at 663. Moreover, the Board would lack authority to provide the defamed individual with damages or other relief. Ibid. Conversely, the state law action would be unconcerned with whether the statements were coercive or misleading in the labor context, and in any event the court would have power to award Linn relief only if the statements were defamatory. Taken together, these factors justified an exception to the pre-emption rule.

The Court was careful, however, to limit the scope of that exception. To minimize the possibility that state libel suits would either dampen the free discussion characteristic of labor disputes or become a weapon of economic coercion, the Court adopted by analogy the standards enunciated in New York Times Co. v. Sullivan, 376 U.S. 254, 84 S.Ct. 710, 11 L.Ed.2d 686 (1964), and held that state damage actions in this context would escape pre-emption only if limited to defamatory statements published with knowledge or reckless disregard of their falsity. The Court also held that a complainant could recover damages only upon proof that the statements had caused him injury, including general injury to reputation, consequent mental suffering, alienation of associates, specific items of pecuniary loss, or any other form of harm recognized by state tort law. The Court stressed the responsibility of the trial judge to assure that damages were not excessive.

Similar reasoning underlies the exception to the pre-emption rule in cases involving violent tortious activity. Nothing in the federal labor statutes protects or immunizes from state action violence or the threat of violence in a labor dispute, Automobile Workers v. Russell, 356 U.S. 634, 640, 78 S.Ct. 932, 935, 2 L.Ed.2d 1030 (1958); id., at 649, 78 S.Ct., at 941 (Warren, C.J., dissenting); United Construction Workers v. Laburnum Construction Corp., 347 U.S. 656, 666, 74 S.Ct. 833, 838, 98 L.Ed. 1025 (1954), and thus there is no risk that state damage actions will fetter the exercise of rights protected by the NLRA. On the other hand, our cases consistently have recognized the historic state interest in "such traditionally local matters as public safety and order and the use of streets and highways." Allen–Bradley Local v. Wisconsin Employment Relations Board, 315 U.S. 740, 749, 62 S.Ct. 820, 825, 86 L.Ed. 1154 (1942). And, as with the defamation actions preserved by *Linn*, state court actions to redress injuries caused by violence or threats of violence are consistent with effective administration of the federal scheme: such actions can be adjudicated without regard to the merits of the underlying labor controversy. Automobile Workers v. Russell, supra, 356 U.S., at 649, 78 S.Ct., at 941 (Warren, C.J., dissenting).

Although cases like *Linn* and *Russell* involve state law principles with only incidental application to conduct occurring in the course of a labor dispute, it is well settled that the general applicability of a state cause of action is not sufficient to exempt it from pre-emption. "[I]t [has not] mattered whether the States have acted through laws of broad general application rather than laws specifically directed towards the governance of industrial relations."[9] *Garmon*, 359 U.S., at 246, 79 S.Ct., at 779. Instead, the cases reflect a balanced inquiry into such factors as the nature of the federal and state interests in regulation and the potential for interference with federal regulation. * * *

### III

In count two of his amended complaint, Hill alleged that the defendants had intentionally engaged in "outrageous conduct, threats, intimi-

**9.** In Local 100 of United Ass'n v. Borden, 373 U.S. 690, 83 S.Ct. 1423, 10 L.Ed.2d 638 (1963), for example, an employee sued his union, which operated a hiring hall, claiming that the union had arbitrarily refused to refer him for employment on one particular occasion. He alleged that the union's conduct constituted both tortious interference with his right to contract for employment and breach of a promise, implicit in his membership arrangement with the union, not to discriminate unfairly against any member or deny him the right to work. Under these circumstances, concurrent state court jurisdiction would have impaired significantly the functioning of the federal system.

If unfair labor practice charges had been filed, the Board might have concluded that the refusal to refer Borden was due to a lawful hiring hall practice, see Teamsters Local 357 v. Labor Board, 365 U.S. 667, 81 S.Ct. 835, 6 L.Ed.2d 11 (1961). Board approval of various hiring hall practices would be meaningless if state courts could declare those procedures violative of the contractual rights implicit between a member and his union. Accordingly, the state cause of action was pre-empted under *Garmon*. Similar reasoning prompted the Court to apply the *Garmon* rule in the companion case of Iron Workers v. Perko, 373 U.S. 701, 83 S.Ct. 1429, 10 L.Ed.2d 646 (1963).

dation, and words" which caused Hill to suffer "grievous mental and emotional distress as well as great physical damage." In the context of Hill's other allegations of discrimination in hiring hall referrals, these allegations of tortious conduct might form the basis for unfair labor practice charges before the Board. On this basis a rigid application of the *Garmon* doctrine might support the conclusion of the California courts that Hill's entire action was preempted by federal law. Our cases indicate, however, that inflexible application of the doctrine is to be avoided, especially where the state has a substantial interest in regulation of the conduct at issue and the State's interest is one that does not threaten undue interference with the federal regulatory scheme. With respect to Hill's claims of intentional infliction of emotional distress, we cannot conclude that Congress intended exclusive jurisdiction to lie in the Board.

No provision of the National Labor Relations Act protects the "outrageous conduct" complained of by petitioner Hill in the second count of the complaint. Regardless of whether the operation of the hiring hall was lawful or unlawful under federal statutes, there is no federal protection for conduct on the part of union officers which is so outrageous that "no reasonable man in a civilized society should be expected to endure it." Thus, as in Linn v. Plant Guard Workers, 383 U.S. 53, 86 S.Ct. 657, 15 L.Ed.2d 582 (1966), and Automobile Workers v. Russell, 356 U.S. 634, 78 S.Ct. 932, 2 L.Ed.2d 1030 (1958), permitting the exercise of state jurisdiction over such complaints does not result in state regulation of federally protected conduct.

The State, on the other hand, has a substantial interest in protecting its citizens from the kind of abuse of which Hill complained. That interest is no less worthy of recognition because it concerns protection from emotional distress caused by outrageous conduct, rather than protection from physical injury, as in *Russell,* or damage to reputation, as in *Linn.* Although recognition of the tort of intentional infliction of emotional distress is a comparatively recent development in state law, see Prosser, Law of Torts, 49–50, 56 (4th ed.), our decisions permitting the exercise of state jurisdiction in tort actions based on violence or defamation have not rested on the history of the tort at issue, but rather on the nature of the State's interest in protecting the health and well-being of its citizens.

There is, to be sure, some risk that the state cause of action for infliction of emotional distress will touch on an area of primary federal concern. Hill's complaint itself highlights this risk. [It charged union discrimination in hiring-hall referrals and work assignments, which standing alone might well be preempted.] * * * The occurrence of the abusive conduct, with which the state tort action is concerned, in such a context of federally prohibited discrimination suggests a potential for interference with the federal scheme of regulation.

Viewed, however, in light of the discrete concerns of the federal scheme and the state tort law, that potential for interference is insufficient to counterbalance the legitimate and substantial interest of the State in protecting its citizens. If the charges in Hill's complaint were filed with the Board, the focus of any unfair labor practice proceeding would be on whether the statements or conduct on the part of union officials discriminated or threatened discrimination against him in employment referrals for reasons other than failure to pay union dues. Whether the statements or conduct of the respondents also caused Hill severe emotional distress and physical injury would play no role in the Board's disposition of the case, and the Board could not award Hill damages for pain, suffering, or medical expenses. Conversely, the state court tort action can be adjudicated without resolution of the "merits" of the underlying labor dispute. Recovery for the tort of emotional distress under California law requires proof that the defendant intentionally engaged in outrageous conduct causing the plaintiff to sustain mental distress. State Rubbish Collectors Assn. v. Siliznoff, 38 Cal.2d 330, 240 P.2d 282 (1952); Alcorn v. Anbro Engineering, Inc., 2 Cal.3d 493, 86 Cal.Rptr. 88, 468 P.2d 216 (1970). The state court need not consider, much less resolve, whether a union discriminated or threatened to discriminate against an employee in terms of employment opportunities. To the contrary, the tort action can be resolved without reference to any accommodation of the special interests of unions and members in the hiring hall context.

On balance, we cannot conclude that Congress intended to oust state court jurisdiction over actions for tortious activity such as that alleged in this case. At the same time, we reiterate that concurrent state court jurisdiction cannot be permitted where there is a realistic threat of interference with the federal regulatory scheme. Union discrimination in employment opportunities cannot itself form the underlying "outrageous" conduct on which the state court tort action is based; to hold otherwise would undermine the pre-emption principle. Nor can threats of such discrimination suffice to sustain state court jurisdiction. It may well be that the threat, or actuality, of employment discrimination will cause a union member considerable emotional distress and anxiety. But something more is required before concurrent state court jurisdiction can be permitted. Simply stated, it is essential that the state tort be either unrelated to employment discrimination or a function of the particularly abusive manner in which the discrimination is accomplished or threatened rather than a function of the actual or threatened discrimination itself.[13]

Two further limitations deserve emphasis. Our decision rests in part on our understanding that California law permits recovery only for emotional distress sustained as a result of "outrageous" conduct. The potential for undue interference with federal regulation would be intolerable if state tort recoveries could be based on the type of robust language and clash of strong personalities that may be commonplace in various labor

---

**13.** In view of the potential for interference with the federal scheme of regulation, the trial court should be sensitive to the need to minimize the jury's exposure to evidence of employment discrimination in cases of this sort. Where evidence of discrimination is necessary to establish the context in which the state claim arose, the trial court should instruct the jury that the fact of employment discrimination (as distinguished from attendant tortious conduct under state law) should not enter into the determination of liability or damages.

contexts. We also repeat that state trial courts have the responsibility in cases of this kind to assure that the damages awarded are not excessive. See Linn v. Plant Guard Workers, 383 U.S., at 65–66, 86 S.Ct., at 664.

## IV

Although the second count of petitioner's complaint alleged the intentional infliction of emotional distress, it is clear from the record that the trial of that claim was not in accord with the standards discussed above. The evidence supporting the verdict in Hill's favor focuses less on the alleged campaign of harassment, public ridicule, and verbal abuse, than on the discriminatory refusal to dispatch him to any but the briefest and least desirable jobs; and no appropriate instruction distinguishing the two categories of evidence was given to the jury. See n. 13, supra. The consequent risk that the jury verdict represented damages for employment discrimination rather than for instances of intentional infliction of emotional distress precludes reinstatement of the judgment of the Superior Court.

The Judgment of the Court of Appeal is vacated, and the case is remanded to that court for further proceedings not inconsistent with this opinion.

It is so ordered.

---

## PROBLEMS FOR DISCUSSION

**1.** In determining whether or not the Union is liable in tort, will most juries succeed in separating the Union's discriminatory referral practices, as such, from the abusive manner in which those practices were implemented? In determining compensatory damages, will most juries succeed in ignoring the wronged employee's loss of earnings, resulting from hiring hall non-referrals?

Does the Court's decision not invite resort to state courts and juries to determine substantially the same issues which the NLRB would address in a Section 8(b)(2) proceeding? If so, is this at all salutary? Is it constitutional?

**2.** In the *Lockridge* case, the complaint was in two counts, one charging that the suspension from union membership was a contractual violation of the union constitution and bylaws, and the other charging that the union "acted wantonly, wilfully and wrongfully and without just cause, and * * * deprived plaintiff of his * * * employment with Greyhound Corporation * * * and plaintiff has been harassed and subject to mental anguish." Had the trial court sustained the jury's verdict under the latter theory (rather than under the theory of contract breach), should the Supreme Court have decided the case differently?

**3.** After studying the materials on the Duty of Fair Representation, infra, the student should consider the following question: Could Hill (or Lockridge) have sued, in a state court, for breach of the duty of fair representation, and claimed among other elements of relief money damages for emotional suffering? If this would permit the jury to address both the "discrimination" and "abusive manner" issues, and to award full damages, why did the Court in *Farmer* struggle so hard to justify state-court jurisdiction?

**4.** Note that in both *Linn* and *Farmer,* the Court—although perhaps technically sustaining the application of state tort law—was "re-shaping" the state law so as to take federal labor policy into account. Is this "federalization" of defamation and emotional-injury law, when applied in an industrial-relations context, a preferred alternative to outright preemption or outright application of state tort law?

**5.** In the proceedings below in *Farmer,* the state trial court entered a judgment, based on a jury verdict, in the amount of $7,500 actual damages and $175,000 punitive damages. Had the issue been properly raised on appeal, should the judgment for punitive damages have been reversed? Compare IBEW v. Foust, page 1047 infra, which holds that punitive damages may not be awarded against a union for violating its duty of fair representation.

**6.** A union, recently certified as bargaining representative for the company's production and maintenance workers, initiated a vigorous campaign to organize those within the bargaining unit who had not yet become members. Part of its campaign was the publication in its newsletter of a list of names of those in the unit who had not yet applied for membership, with the term "Scabs" predominantly displayed at the head of the list. After having twice seen his name on this list, Austin, a nonunion employee, informed union officials that he intended to sue the union if this coercive listing was continued. Thereafter, the list appeared again, this time with a definition, borrowed from the author Jack London: "After God had finished the rattlesnake, the toad and the vampire, He had some awful substance left with which He made a scab. A scab is a two-legged animal with a corkscrew soul, a water brain and a combination backbone of jelly and glue * * *." Austin promptly instituted an action against the union in the state court for defamation. The union moved to dismiss, arguing that state-court jurisdiction was preempted by the National Labor Relations Act. Should the union's motion be granted? See Old Dominion Branch No. 496, National Ass'n of Letter Carriers v. Austin, 418 U.S. 264, 94 S.Ct. 2770, 41 L.Ed.2d 745 (1974).

**7.** Sandra Thomson, a registered nurse, has worked at Doctors' Hospital for fifteen years. She has started a drive to unionize the nursing staff. The hospital has retained a law firm to assist it in resisting that effort. After Thomson protested the posting of anti-union literature, she was discharged. She has filed a charge with the Regional Director of the NLRB. She has also sued the hospital's law firm in state court for intentional interference in a business relationship and the intentional infliction of emotional distress. (The former claim would encompass the causing of a termination of an at-will employment relationship if accomplished by "improper methods" or if done for "socially unjustifiable reasons.") Is either claim, or both, preempted? See Richardson v. Kruchko & Fries, 966 F.2d 153 (4th Cir.1992).

---

SEARS, ROEBUCK & CO. v. SAN DIEGO COUNTY DIST. COUNCIL OF CARPENTERS, 436 U.S. 180, 98 S.Ct. 1745, 56 L.Ed.2d 209 (1978). The union picketed in Sears' parking lot to protest Sears' assignment of carpentry work in its store to a subcontractor who had neither used the union hiring hall nor agreed in writing to abide by the terms of the union's master agreement. The picketing was enjoined in state court as violative of state trespass law.

Justice Stevens, writing for the Court, noted that the conduct was either "arguably prohibited"—under section 8(b)(4)(D) or section 8(b)(7)(C)—or "arguably protected" as area standards picketing under section 7. Turning to the former, he noted that the issues before the state court would not be the same as the issues before the Labor Board had unfair labor practice charges been filed—the former involves only the location of the picketing, not the reasons it was undertaken. Thus there was no "realistic risk of interference" with the Board's primary jurisdiction. On the "arguably protected" theory, he noted that there was a greater concern for federal supremacy: "Prior to granting relief from the Union's continuing trespass, the state court was obligated to decide that the trespass was not actually protected by federal law, a determination which might entail an accommodation of Sears' property rights and the Union's § 7 rights. In an unfair labor practice proceeding initiated by the Union, the Board might have been required to make the same accommodation." But, he reasoned, the union could have had the Board reach that question by filing unfair labor practice charges when Sears demanded that it remove its pickets, which the union declined to do. Thus the state action was not pre-empted. "As long as the union has a fair opportunity to present the protection issue to the Labor Board, it retains meaningful protection against the risk of error in a state tribunal. * * * Whatever risk of an erroneous state court adjudication does exist is outweighed by the anomalous consequence of a rule which would deny the employer access to any forum in which to litigate either the trespass issue or the protection issue in those cases in which the disputed conduct is least likely to be protected by § 7."

Justices Brennan, Stewart, and Marshall dissented, arguing that the case was a "classic one for pre-emption."

> To decide whether the location of the Union's picketing rendered it unlawful, the state court here had to address a host of exceedingly complex labor law questions, which implicated nearly every aspect of the Union's labor dispute with Sears and which were uniquely within the province of the Board. Because it [the state court] had to assess the "relative strength of the § 7 right" ... its first task necessarily was to determine the nature of the Union's picketing.... Obviously, since even the Court admits that the characterization of the picketing "entail[s] relatively complex factual and legal determinations," there is a substantial danger that the state court, lacking the Board's expertise and specialized sensitivity to labor relations matters, would err at the outset and effectively deny respondent the right to engage in any effective § 7 communication.

------

## PROBLEMS FOR DISCUSSION

**1.** Is it fair to conclude that, after *Sears,* if conduct is *arguably* protected (and what concerted activity, except for the most egregious, will not be?), state courts will have jurisdiction to construe Section 7 and all NLRB and judicial precedents thereunder; jurisdiction to construe them erroneously, subject only to the remote and long-delayed possibility of correction by the United States Supreme Court; and jurisdiction to issue an injunction mistakenly—unless and until the union "invokes the jurisdiction" of the National Labor Relations Board?   Is this consistent with prior Supreme Court decisions?

Is it fair to conclude that, after *Farmer* and *Sears,* the only clearly preempted cases are those in which the plaintiff concedes that the defendant's conduct is clearly protected under Section 7 (and that these cases will be very rare indeed)?   Is this consistent with prior Supreme Court decisions?

**2.**   When would the state trespass proceeding become pre-empted?   When the General Counsel issues a complaint?   When the union files a charge?   Compare Davis Supermarkets v. NLRB, 2 F.3d 1162 (D.C.Cir.1993) with UMW v. Waters, 200 W.Va. 289, 489 S.E.2d 266 (1997).

**3.**   During contract negotiations between the Steelworkers and the Pepsi–Cola Company covering workers at the Miami plant, several employees participated in a work slowdown and were immediately discharged.   This triggered a march by nearly 100 employees away from their work stations and to the office of the plant manager.   After listening to the employee protests concerning the discharges, the plant manager announced that the discharged employees would not be reinstated and he demanded that the workers return to their work stations or leave the plant. The workers returned to their stations but remained there, without working, for the few hours remaining in their shift.   They did not attempt to damage or to seize the plant machinery or property, and left the plant at the end of their shift when ordered to do so by police officers called by the employer.   The employer, alleging that the union and employees had engaged in an unlawful trespassory "sitdown" strike, brought an action for damages.   The defendants have moved to dismiss the action as beyond the jurisdiction of the state court.   Should the action be dismissed? Cf. NLRB v. Pepsi–Cola Bottling Co., 449 F.2d 824 (5th Cir.1971), cert. denied, 407 U.S. 910, 92 S.Ct. 2434, 32 L.Ed.2d 683 (1972).

Would your analysis be affected if the company could prove that certain minor damage was done to some plant machinery when the employees resisted the attempts of certain foremen to drag them physically from their work stations?

-----

## Lodge 76, International Ass'n of Machinists v. Wisconsin Employment Relations Com'n

427 U.S. 132, 96 S.Ct. 2548, 49 L.Ed.2d 396 (1976).

■ MR. JUSTICE BRENNAN delivered the opinion of the Court.

The question to be decided in this case is whether federal labor policy pre-empts the authority of a state labor relations board to grant an employer covered by the National Labor Relations Act an order enjoining a union and its members from continuing to refuse to work overtime pursuant to a union policy to put economic pressure on the employer in negotiations for renewal of an expired collective-bargaining agreement.

[During the more than yearlong negotiations for a new labor contract, a particularly controverted issue was the employer's demand that the provision of the expired agreement under which, as for the prior 17 years, the basic workday was seven and one-half hours, Monday through Friday, and the basic workweek was 37½ hours, be replaced with a new provision providing a basic workday of eight hours and a basic workweek of 40 hours, and that the terms on which overtime rates of pay were payable be changed accordingly.  When the employer announced its intention to implement such a change unilaterally, the Union membership adopted and implemented a resolution binding union members to refuse to work any overtime, defined as work in excess of seven and one-half hours in any day or 37½ hours in any week.  The employer did not discipline any employees for refusing to work overtime.]

Instead, while negotiations continued, the employer filed a charge with the National Labor Relations Board that the Union's resolution violated § 8(b)(3) of the National Labor Relations Act, 29 U.S.C. § 158(b)(3).  The Regional Director dismissed the charge on the ground that the "policy prohibiting overtime work by its member employees does not appear to be in violation of the Act" and therefore was not conduct cognizable by the Board under NLRB v. Insurance Agents Intern'l Union, 361 U.S. 477, 80 S.Ct. 419, 4 L.Ed.2d 454 (1960).  However, the employer also filed a complaint before the Wisconsin Employment Relations Commission charging that the refusal to work overtime constituted an unfair labor practice under state law.  The Union filed a motion before the Commission to dismiss the complaint for want of "jurisdiction over the subject matter" in that jurisdiction over "the activity of the [union] complained of [is] preempted by" the National Labor Relations Act.  App. 11.  The motion was denied and the Commission adopted the Conclusion of Law of its Examiner that "the concerted refusal to work overtime is not an activity which is arguably protected under Section 7 or arguably prohibited under Section 8 of the National Labor Relations Act, as amended and * * * therefore the * * * Commission is not preempted from asserting its jurisdiction to regulate said conduct."  The Commission also adopted the further Conclusion of Law that the Union "by authorizing * * * the concerted refusal to work overtime * * * engaged in a concerted effort to interfere with production and * * * committed an unfair labor practice within the meaning of Section 111.06(2)(h) * * *."[1]  The Commission thereupon entered an order that the Union, *inter alia,* "[i]mmediately cease and desist from authorizing, encouraging or condoning any concerted refusal to accept overtime assignments * * *."  The Wisconsin Circuit Court affirmed and entered judgment enforcing the Commission's order.  The Wisconsin Supreme Court affirmed the Circuit Court.  67 Wis.2d 13, 226 N.W.2d 203 (1975).  We granted certiorari, 423 U.S. 890, 96 S.Ct. 186, 46 L.Ed.2d 121 (1975).  We reverse.

## I

* * * "[I]n referring to decisions holding state laws preempted by the NLRA, care must be taken to distinguish preemption based on federal

---

1.  Wis.Stat. § 111.06(2) provides:

"It shall be an unfair labor practice for an employee individually or in concert with others: * * *

"(h) To take unauthorized possession of the property of the employer or to engage in any concerted effort to interfere with production except by leaving the premises in an orderly manner for the purpose of going on strike."

protection of the conduct in question * * * from that based predominantly on the primary jurisdiction of the National Labor Relations Board * * *, although the two are often not easily separable." Brotherhood of Railroad Trainmen v. Jacksonville Terminal Co., 394 U.S. 369, 383 n. 19, 89 S.Ct. 1109, 1118, 22 L.Ed.2d 344 (1969). Each of these distinct aspects of labor law pre-emption has had its own history in our decisions to which we now turn.

We consider first pre-emption based predominantly on the primary jurisdiction of the Board. This line of pre-emption analysis was developed in San Diego Unions v. Garmon, 359 U.S. 236, 79 S.Ct. 773, 3 L.Ed.2d 775, and its history was recently summarized in Amalgamated Association of Street, Electric Railway & Motor Coach Employees v. Lockridge, 403 U.S. 274, 290–291, 91 S.Ct. 1909, 1920, 29 L.Ed.2d 473 (1971) * * *.

However, a second line of pre-emption analysis has been developed in cases focusing upon the crucial inquiry whether Congress intended that the conduct involved be unregulated because left "to be controlled by the free play of economic forces." NLRB v. Nash–Finch Co., 404 U.S. 138, 144, 92 S.Ct. 373, 377, 30 L.Ed.2d 328 (1971).[4] Concededly this inquiry was not made in 1949 in the so-called *Briggs-Stratton* case, Automobile Workers v. Wisconsin Board, 336 U.S. 245, 69 S.Ct. 516, 93 L.Ed. 651 (1949), the decision of this Court heavily relied upon by the court below in reaching its decision that state regulation of the conduct at issue is not pre-empted by national labor law. In *Briggs-Stratton,* the union, in order to bring pressure on the employer during negotiations, adopted a plan whereby union meetings were called at irregular times during working hours without advance notice to the employer or any notice as to whether or when the workers would return. In a proceeding under the Wisconsin Employment Peace Act, the Wisconsin Employment Relations Board issued an order forbidding the union and its members from engaging in concerted efforts to interfere with production by those methods. This Court did not inquire

---

**4.** See Cox, Labor Law Preemption Revisited, 85 Harv.L.Rev. 1337, 1352 (1972):

"An appreciation of the true character of the national labor policy expressed in the NLRA and the LMRA indicates that in providing a legal framework for union organization, collective bargaining, and the conduct of labor disputes, Congress struck a balance of protection, prohibition, and laissez-faire in respect to union organization, collective bargaining, and labor disputes that would be upset if a state could enforce statutes or rules of decision resting upon its views concerning accommodation of the same interests."

Cf. Lesnick, Preemption Reconsidered: The Apparent Reaffirmation of *Garmon,* 72 Col.L.Rev. 469, 478, 480 (1972):

"[T]he failure of Congress to prohibit a certain conduct * * * warrant[s a] * * * negative inference that it was deemed proper, indeed desirable—at least, desirable to be left for the free play of contending economic forces. Thus, the state is not merely filling a gap when it outlaws what federal law fails to outlaw; it is denying one party to an economic contest a weapon that Congress meant him to have available.

* * *

"The premise is * * * that Congress judged whether the conduct was illicit or legitimate, and that 'legitimate' connotes, not simply that federal law is neutral, but that the conduct is to be assimilated to the large residual area in which a regime of free collective bargaining—'economic warfare' if you prefer—is thought to be the course of regulatory wisdom."

whether Congress meant that such methods should be reserved to the union "to be controlled by the free play of economic forces." Rather, because these methods were "neither made a right under federal law nor a violation of it" the Court held that there "was no basis for denying to Wisconsin the power, in governing her internal affairs, to regulate" such conduct. Id., at 265, 69 S.Ct., at 527.

However, the *Briggs-Stratton* holding that state power is not preempted as to peaceful conduct neither protected by § 7 nor prohibited by § 8 of the federal Act, a holding premised on the statement that "[t]his conduct is either governable by the State or it is entirely ungoverned," id., at 254, 69 S.Ct., at 521, was undercut by subsequent decisions of this Court. For the Court soon recognized that a particular activity might be "protected" by federal law not only where it fell within § 7, but also when it was an activity that Congress intended to be "unrestricted by *any* governmental power to regulate" because it was among the permissible "economic weapons in reserve * * * actual exercise [of which] on occasion by the parties is part and parcel of the system that the Wagner and Taft–Hartley Acts have recognized." NLRB v. Insurance Agents, 361 U.S., at 488, 489, 80 S.Ct., at 426, 427 (emphasis added). "[T]he legislative purpose may * * * dictate that certain activity 'neither protected nor prohibited' be privileged against state regulation." Hanna Mining Co. v. Marine Engineers, 382 U.S., at 187, 86 S.Ct., at 331.

## II

*Insurance Agents,* supra, involved a charge of a refusal by the union to bargain in good faith in violation of § 8(b)(3) of the Act. * * * [The Court here discussed, and quoted at length from, its opinion in *Insurance Agents;* see p. 405, supra.] We noted further that "Congress has been rather specific when it has come to outlaw particular economic weapons on the part of unions" and "the activities here involved have never been specifically outlawed by Congress." Id., at 498, 80 S.Ct., at 432. Accordingly, the Board's claim "to power * * * to distinguish among various economic pressure tactics and brand the ones at bar inconsistent with good-faith collective bargaining," id., at 492, 80 S.Ct., at 428, was simply inconsistent with the design of the federal scheme in which "the use of economic pressure by the parties to a labor dispute is * * * part and parcel of the process of collective bargaining." Id., at 495, 80 S.Ct., at 430.

The Court had earlier recognized in pre-emption cases that Congress meant to leave some activities unregulated and to be controlled by the free play of economic forces. Garner v. Teamsters, Chauffeurs and Helpers Local Union, 346 U.S. 485, 74 S.Ct. 161, 98 L.Ed. 228, in finding preempted state power to restrict peaceful recognitional picketing, said:

> "The detailed prescription of a procedure for restraint of specified types of picketing would seem to imply that other picketing is to be free of other methods and sources of restraint. For the policy of the Labor Management Relations Act is not to condemn all picketing but only that ascertained by its prescribed process to fall

within its prohibition. Otherwise it is implicit in the Act that the public interest is served by freedom of labor to use the weapon of picketing. For a state to impinge on the area of labor combat designed to be free is quite as much an obstruction of federal policy as if the state were to declare picketing free for purposes or by methods which the federal Act prohibits." Id., at 499–500, 74 S.Ct., at 170–171.

* * * [T]he analysis of *Garner* and *Insurance Agents* came full bloom in the pre-emption area in Local 20, Teamsters, Chauffeurs & Helpers Union v. Morton, 377 U.S. 252, 84 S.Ct. 1253, 12 L.Ed.2d 280 (1964), which held pre-empted the application of state law to award damages for peaceful union secondary picketing. Although *Morton* involved conduct neither "protected nor prohibited" by § 7 or § 8 of the NLRA, we recognized the necessity of an inquiry whether " 'Congress occupied the field and closed it to state regulation.' " Id., at 258, 84 S.Ct., at 1257. Central to *Morton's* analysis was the observation that "[i]n selecting which forms of economic pressure should be prohibited * * *, Congress struck the 'balance * * * between the uncontrolled power of management and labor to further their respective interests,' " id., at 258–259, 84 S.Ct., at 1258, and that:

> "This weapon of self-help, permitted by federal law, formed an integral part of the petitioner's effort to achieve its bargaining goals during negotiations with the respondent. Allowing its use is a part of the balance struck by Congress between the conflicting interests of the union, the employees, the employer and the community. * * * If the Ohio law of secondary boycott can be applied to proscribe the same type of conduct which Congress focused upon but did not proscribe when it enacted § 303, the inevitable result would be to frustrate the congressional determination to leave this weapon of self-help available, and to upset the balance of power between labor and management expressed in our national labor policy. * * *"

Although many of our past decisions concerning conduct left by Congress to the free play of economic forces address the question in the context of union and employee activities, self-help is of course also the prerogative of the employer because he too may properly employ economic weapons Congress meant to be unregulable. * * * "[R]esort to economic weapons should more peaceful measures not avail" is the right of the employer as well as the employee, American Ship Building Co. v. NLRB, 380 U.S., at 317, 85 S.Ct., at 966, and the State may not prohibit the use of such weapons or "add to an employer's federal legal obligations in collective bargaining" any more than in the case of employees. Cox, Labor Law Preemption Revisited, 85 Harv.L.Rev. 1337, 1365 (1972). See, *e.g.* Beasley v. Food Fair, Inc., 416 U.S. 653, 94 S.Ct. 2023, 40 L.Ed.2d 443 (1974). Whether self-help economic activities are employed by employer or union, the crucial inquiry regarding pre-emption is the same: whether "the exercise of plenary state authority to curtail or entirely prohibit self-help would frustrate effective implementation of the Act's processes." Railroad Trainmen v. Jacksonville Terminal Co., 394 U.S., at 380, 89 S.Ct., at 1116.

## III

There is simply no question that the Act's processes would be frustrated in the instant case were the State's ruling permitted to stand. The employer in this case invoked the Wisconsin law because unable to overcome the union tactic with its own economic self-help means. Although it did employ economic weapons putting pressure on the union when it terminated the previous agreement, * * * it apparently lacked sufficient economic strength to secure its bargaining demands under "the balance of power between labor and management expressed in our national labor policy," Teamsters Union v. Morton, 377 U.S., at 260, 84 S.Ct., at 1258.[10] But the economic weakness of the affected party cannot justify state aid contrary to federal law for, "as we have developed, the use of economic pressure by the parties to a labor dispute is not a grudging exception [under] * * * the [federal] Act; it is part and parcel of the process of collective bargaining." *Insurance Agents,* 361 U.S., at 495, 80 S.Ct., at 430. The state action in this case is not filling "a regulatory void which Congress plainly assumed would not exist," Hanna Mining Co. v. Marine Engineers, 382 U.S., at 196, 86 S.Ct., at 335 (Brennan, J., concurring). Rather, it is clear beyond question that Wisconsin "[entered] into the substantive aspects of the bargaining process to an extent Congress has not countenanced." NLRB v. Insurance Agents, supra, at 498, 80 S.Ct., at 432.

Our decisions hold that Congress meant that these activities, whether of employer or employees, were not to be regulable by States any more than by the NLRB, for neither States nor the Board are "afforded flexibility in picking and choosing which economic devices of labor and management would be branded as unlawful." Ibid. Rather, both are without authority to attempt to "introduce some standard of properly 'balanced' bargaining power," id., at 497, 80 S.Ct., at 431, or to define "what economic sanctions might be permitted negotiating parties in an 'ideal' or 'balanced' state of collective bargaining." Id., at 500, 80 S.Ct., at 433. To sanction state regulation of such economic pressure deemed by the federal Act "desirabl[y] * * * left for the free play of contending economic forces, * * * is not merely [to fill] a gap [by] outlaw[ing] what federal law fails to outlaw; it is denying to one party to an economic contest a weapon that Congress meant him to have available." Lesnick, Preemption Reconsidered: The Apparent Reaffirmation of *Garmon,* 72 Col.L.Rev. 469, 478 (1972). Accordingly, such regulation by the State is impermissible because it " 'stands as an obstacle to the accomplishment and execution of the full purposes and

---

**10.** Cf. *Cox,* supra, n. 4, at 1347:

"[In *Briggs-Stratton,*] the Court was beguiled by the fallacy of supposing that a Congress which allowed an employer to discharge his employees for engaging in a series of 'quickie' strikes surely would not preclude the employer's pursuing what the Court regarded as the relatively mild sanction of legal redress through state courts. In fact, most employers facing a union with the strength and discipline to call a series of 'quickie' strikes would lack the economic power to discharge union members, leaving legal redress the more efficient sanction."

objectives of Congress.' "  Hill v. Florida, 325 U.S. 538, 542, 65 S.Ct. 1373, 1375, 89 L.Ed. 1782 (1945).

## IV

There remains the question of the continuing vitality of *Briggs-Stratton*.  San Diego Unions v. Garmon, 359 U.S., at 245 n. 4, 79 S.Ct., at 780, made clear that the *Briggs-Stratton* approach to pre-emption is "no longer of general application."  See also *Insurance Agents,* 361 U.S. at 493 n. 23, 80 S.Ct., at 429.  We hold today that the ruling of *Briggs-Stratton,* permitting state regulation of partial strike activities such as are involved in this case is likewise "no longer of general application."  * * * [S]ince our later decisions make plain that *Briggs-Stratton* "does not further but rather frustrates realization of an important goal of our national labor policy," *Boys Markets,* supra, at 241, 90 S.Ct., at 1587, *Briggs-Stratton* is expressly overruled.

■ MR. JUSTICE POWELL, with whom THE CHIEF JUSTICE joins, concurring.

* * * I write to make clear my understanding that the Court's opinion does not * * * preclude the States from enforcing, in the context of a labor dispute, "neutral" state statutes or rules of decision: state laws that are not directed toward altering the bargaining positions of employers or unions but which may have an incidental effect on relative bargaining strength.  Except where Congress has specifically provided otherwise, the States generally should remain free to enforce, for example, their law of torts or of contracts, and other laws reflecting neutral public policy.*  See Cox, Labor Law Preemption Revisited, 85 Harv.L.Rev. 1337, 1355–1356 (1972).

With this understanding, I join the opinion of the Court.

■ MR. JUSTICE STEVENS, with whom MR. JUSTICE STEWART and MR. JUSTICE REHNQUIST join, dissenting.  * * *

If Congress had focused on the problems presented by partial strike activity, and enacted special legislation dealing with this subject matter, but left the form of the activity disclosed by this record unregulated, the Court's conclusion would be supported by Teamsters Union v. Morton, 377 U.S. 252, 84 S.Ct. 1253, 12 L.Ed.2d 280.  But this is not such a case. Despite the numerous statements in the Court's opinion about Congress' intent to leave partial strike activity wholly unregulated, I have found no legislative expression of any such intent nor any evidence that Congress has scrutinized such activity.  * * *

If adherence to the rule of *Briggs-Stratton* would permit the States substantially to disrupt the balance Congress has struck between union and employer, I would readily join in overruling it.  But I am not persuaded

---

* State laws should not be regarded as neutral if they reflect an accommodation of the special interests of employers, unions, or the public in areas such as employee self-organization, labor disputes, or collective bargaining.

that partial strike activity is so essential to the bargaining process that the States should not be free to make it illegal. * * *

---

## PROBLEM FOR DISCUSSION

**1.** The Golden Gate Cab Company has been operating taxicabs in San Francisco under a franchise granted three years ago by the city council. Its application for franchise renewal is currently before the council. The labor agreement between Golden Gate and the Teamsters has expired and the drivers are on strike. Union representatives have appeared before the city council, arguing that no franchise should be granted until the strike has ended. The city council is considering adopting a resolution that would bar the renewal of the Golden Gate Cab franchise unless a new labor agreement is executed within thirty days. You are an attorney in the office of the City Solicitor, and you have been asked whether such a resolution could constitutionally be adopted. What is your advice? See Golden State Transit Corp. v. City of Los Angeles, 475 U.S. 608, 106 S.Ct. 1395, 89 L.Ed.2d 616 (1986).

**2.** State law requires that all bidders on state construction projects must pay the "prevailing wage" for construction in each locality as determined by the state. These wages are calculated periodically by the State Department of Industrial Relations on the basis of a sample of collective bargaining agreements in each county; they cover each craft separately and deal with both wages (which must be paid hourly) and benefits. The Board of Supervisors of Knox County, in addition, has enacted an ordinance that no construction permit will be issued for any project in the county, public or private, in excess of $500,000 unless the contractor shows compliance by it and by all of its subcontractors with the state's "prevailing wage" law. Is this state law, or county ordinance, preempted? See Building & Constr. Trades Council of the Metropolitan Dist. v. Associated Builders & Contractors of Mass./R.I., 507 U.S. 218, 113 S.Ct. 1190, 122 L.Ed.2d 565 (1993); Chamber of Commerce v. Bragdon, 64 F.3d 497 (9th Cir.1995).

**3.** The state has enacted the Protection of Displaced Workers Act, governing private contractors who employ 25 or more persons to perform "food, janitorial, maintenance, or nonprofessional health care services." The Act requires contractors to "retain, for a 90–day transition period, employees who have been employed by the previous contractor for the preceding eight months or longer at the site or sites covered by the contract." The stated purpose of the Act is to "provide a measure of employment security to certain low-wage service workers who are frequently displaced when their employers lose contracts." Is the statute preempted by the NLRA? See Washington Serv. Contractors Coalition v. District of Columbia, 54 F.3d 811 (D.C.Cir.1995). May a state statute require a successor employer to hire its predecessor's workforce and observe the terms of the predecessor's collective agreement if the agreement contains a successorship clause imposing those obligations? *See* Commonwealth Edison Co. v. IBEW, Local 15, 961 F.Supp. 1169 (N.D.Ill.1997).

---

## II. SPECIFIC APPLICATIONS: REPRESENTATION, BARGAINING AND CONCERTED ACTIVITIES

Direct intervention by state courts or agencies in deciding questions of representation in any business within the jurisdiction of the NLRB will not be tolerated.   Representation cases turn upon administrative policy concerning the time for and fairness of elections, the composition of the bargaining unit, and the eligibility of voters.  Were a state agency to decide these matters, there might be established a pattern of representation inconsistent with federal policy, even though the NLRB has not acted in the particular case.  See, *e.g.*, Bethlehem Steel Co. v. New York State Labor Rel. Bd., 330 U.S. 767, 67 S.Ct. 1026, 91 L.Ed. 1234 (1947);  La Crosse Tel. Corp. v. Wisconsin Employment Rel. Bd., 336 U.S. 18, 69 S.Ct. 379, 93 L.Ed. 463 (1949).   Nor may a state purport to adjudicate and remedy employer unfair labor practices in any such business.  In Plankinton Packing Co. v. Wisconsin Employment Rel. Bd., 338 U.S. 953, 70 S.Ct. 491, 94 L.Ed. 588 (1950), Wisconsin had found a packinghouse guilty of discriminatory discharges and ordered reinstatement and backpay;  the Supreme Court set the order aside without opinion.  There is no reason for distinguishing between this unfair labor practice and others, whether committed by an employer or by a union.

State intervention does not, however, ordinarily take such blatant forms.  State laws of varying forms may touch upon labor-management relations at all stages:  from the selection of the bargaining representative, through negotiations for and enforcement of a collective bargaining agreement, to the use of economic force outside the bargaining room.  To what extent can states, in aid of a local policy, limit the employees' choice of their bargaining representative or their union officials?  To what extent can states regulate the processes of collective bargaining, or the substantive terms of the labor agreement and their enforcement?  Can states properly affect the "balance of power" in the use of economic weapons, for example, by granting compensation benefits to workers on strike, by removing pickets from property owned by the employer (or by third persons), or by regulating the respective contract rights of strikers and strike replacements?  These are the issues explored in the following cases.

----

## A.   SELECTION OF BARGAINING REPRESENTATIVE

----

## Brown v. Hotel & Restaurant Employees, International Union Local 54

468 U.S. 491, 104 S.Ct. 3179, 82 L.Ed.2d 373 (1984).

[The New Jersey Casino Control Act provides for the licensing of owners, operators and suppliers of casino hotels, and for the licensing or registration of casino hotel employees, including bartenders, waiters and waitresses.  Section 86 of the Act bars the registration of casino licensees or employees who have been convicted of any one of a number of enumerated offenses or of "any other offense which indicates that licensure ...

would be inimical to the policy of this act and to casino operations." Section 93(a) requires labor organizations that represent or seek to represent casino-hotel employees to register annually with the Casino Control Commission, an independent state administrative body.  Section 93(b) provides that no such labor organization shall receive dues from any such employees, or administer any pension or welfare funds, if any of the union's officers are disqualified under Section 86.

[Local 54 of the Hotel and Restaurant Employees Union represents approximately 12,000 employees, 8,000 of whom are employed in casino hotels in Atlantic City.  When in 1978 it filed the annual registration statement required by Section 93(a), an investigation was undertaken by the Casino Control Commission regarding the disqualification of the local president and other union officials.  After a hearing, the Commission concluded that the president and others were disqualified under Section 86 for association with members of organized crime or for criminal convictions.  The Commission therefore ordered that these individuals be removed from office in the local union, failing which the union would be barred from collecting dues from any of its licensed or registered members. Thereafter, in a federal court injunction proceeding brought initially by the union to enjoin the Commission's proceedings, the Court of Appeals for the Third Circuit decided that Section 93 was preempted by Section 7 of the NLRA.]

■ JUSTICE O'CONNOR delivered the opinion of the Court.

* * * If employee conduct is protected under § 7, then state law which interferes with the exercise of these federally protected rights creates an actual conflict and is preempted by direct operation of the Supremacy Clause.  * * * We turn, therefore, to consider whether New Jersey's Act actually conflicts with the casino industry employees' § 7 rights.

Section 7 guarantees to employees various rights, among them the right "to bargain collectively through representatives of their own choosing."  29 U.S.C. § 157.  In a straightforward analysis, the Court of Appeals found that this express right of employees to choose their collective-bargaining representatives encompasses an unqualified right to choose the officials of these representatives.  Because § 93(b) of the Act precludes casino industry employees from selecting as union officials individuals who do not meet the § 86 disqualification criteria, the Court of Appeals determined that this provision clearly and directly conflicts with § 7 and, under traditional pre-emption analysis, must be held pre-empted.

The Court of Appeals relied heavily on this Court's decision in Hill v. Florida, 325 U.S. 538, 65 S.Ct. 1373, 89 L.Ed. 1782 (1945), as support for the threshold proposition that § 7 confers an unfettered right on employees to choose the officials of their own bargaining representatives.  Hill involved a Florida statute that provided for state licensing of union business agents and prohibited the licensing of individuals who had not been citizens for more than 10 years, who had been convicted of a felony, or who were not of "good moral character."  The statute also required the unions to file annual reports.  Pursuant to this law, the Florida Attorney General obtained injunctions against a union and its business agent, restraining them from functioning until they had complied with the statute.

On review, the Court found that Florida's statute as applied conflicted with § 7, explaining:

> "The declared purpose of the Wagner Act, as shown in its first section, is to encourage collective bargaining, and to protect the 'full freedom' of workers in the selection of bargaining representatives of their own choice. To this end Congress made it illegal for an employer to interfere with, restrain or coerce employees in selecting their representatives. Congress attached no conditions whatsoever to their freedom of choice in this respect. Their own best judgment, not that of someone else, was to be their guide. 'Full freedom' to choose an agent means freedom to pass upon that agent's qualifications." 325 U.S. at 541, 65 S.Ct., at 1374.

The decision in Hill does not control the present case, however, because Congress has, in our view, subsequently disclaimed any intent to pre-empt all state regulation which touches upon the specific right of employees to decide which individuals will serve as officials of their bargaining representatives. As originally enacted, and as interpreted by the Court in Hill, § 7 imposed no restrictions whatsoever on employees' freedom to choose the officials of their bargaining representatives. In 1959, however, Congress enacted the Labor–Management Reporting and Disclosure Act (LMRDA), designed in large part to address the growing problems of racketeering, crime, and corruption in the labor movement.   \* \* \*

[The Court examined section 504(a) of the LMRDA, which bars persons convicted of certain enumerated state-law crimes from serving as union officer, trustee, business agent or organizer for five years after such conviction or term of imprisonment. Section 603(a) of the LMRDA was read to disclaim preemption of state laws that regulate the responsibilities of union officials. The Court thus viewed Congress as willing to allow variant state laws to regulate the responsibilities and qualifications of union officials. The purpose behind the federal legislation—the need to police against crime and corruption in unions, particularly local unions—allowed the Court to "presume that Congress would allow a State to adopt different and more stringent qualification requirements for union officials to effectuate this important goal." The Court also relied upon an earlier decision, which had sustained a New York statute that prohibited unions representing waterfront employees from collecting dues if any of its officers or agents had been convicted of a felony; this statute had been enacted as part of an interstate compact, approved by Congress, between New York and New Jersey to combat crime and corruption on their waterfronts. The Court noted that both the New York statute and the challenged New Jersey casino-regulation statute had the common purpose, implicitly approved by Congress, of vindicating the compelling state interest in combatting local crime infesting particular industries.]

\* \* \* In its enactment of LMRDA and its awareness of New York's comparable restrictions when approving the bi-state compact, Congress has at least indicated both that employees do not have an unqualified right to choose their union officials and that certain state disqualification requirements are compatible with § 7. * * * In the absence of a more specific congressional intent to the contrary, we therefore conclude that New Jersey's regulation of the qualifications of casino industry union officials does not actually conflict with § 7 and so is not pre-empted by the NLRA.

We emphasize that this conclusion does not implicate the employees' express § 7 right to select a particular labor union as their collective-bargaining representative, but only their subsidiary right to select the officials of that union organization. While the Court in Hill v. Florida, 325 U.S. 538, 65 S.Ct. 1373, 89 L.Ed. 1782 (1945), apparently assumed that the two rights were undifferentiated and equally protected, our reading of subsequent legislative action indicates that Congress has since distinguished between the two and has accorded less than absolute protection to the employees' right to choose their union officials. In this litigation, the casino industry employees' freedom in the first instance to select Local 54 to represent them in collective bargaining is simply not affected by the qualification criteria of New Jersey's Act.

Although the NLRA does not preclude § 93(b)'s imposition of qualification standards on casino industry union officials, also at issue is the separate validity of that provision's dues collection ban imposed by the Commission to effect the removal of these disqualified persons from their union positions. As in Hill v. Florida, supra, a sanction for noncompliance with an otherwise valid state regulation must, for preemption purposes, be assessed independently in terms of its potential conflict with the federal enactment. The Court in Hill concluded that Florida's filing requirement, while itself unobjectionable, could not be enforced by an injunction against the union's "functioning as a labor union" without contravening the NLRA. See 325 U.S., at 543, 65 S.Ct., at 1375. Appellees vigorously contend that imposition of the § 93(b)'s dues collection sanction will similarly prohibit Local 54 from functioning as the employees' bargaining representative, thereby directly abridging the employees' separate § 7 rights to organize and bargain collectively. According to affidavits submitted in District Court, 85% of Local 54's monthly income comes from membership dues paid by casino hotel employees. Without these payments, Local 54 claims that it could no longer process employee grievances, administer collective bargaining agreements, bargain for new agreements, organize the unorganized, or perform the other responsibilities of a collective bargaining agent. * * *

Unfortunately, because of the procedural posture of this litigation, we cannot decide this issue. Appellees' factual allegations were never addressed by the District Court and the Court of Appeals. We * * * remand so that the District Court can make the requisite findings of fact to determine whether imposition of the dues collection ban will so incapacitate Local 54 as to prevent it from performing its functions as the employees' chosen collective-bargaining agent. * * *

■ Justice Brennan and Justice Marshall took no part in the decision of these cases.

■ JUSTICE WHITE, with whom JUSTICE POWELL and JUSTICE STEVENS join, dissenting.

* * * [A]s the Court amply demonstrates, Congress' actions in enacting the LMRDA indicate that federal labor law does not preempt state laws which prevent certain types of individuals from serving as union officials. However, § 93(b) is not directed at the individuals who are disqualified under § 86. It imposes sanctions on the union itself and, in so doing, infringes on the employees' federally-protected rights.

Section 7 of the NLRA grants covered employees the right "to bargain collectively through representatives of their own choosing." 29 U.S.C. § 157.[3] * * * The employees whose rights are involved in these cases have exercised this right by selecting Local 54 as their bargaining representative. The state, acting pursuant to § 93(b), has sought to prohibit Local 54 from collecting dues from these employees, thereby effectively preventing the union from carrying out the collective bargaining function and nullifying the employees' exercise of their § 7 right.

In Hill v. Florida, supra, the Court held that federal labor policy prohibits a state from enforcing permissible regulations by the use of sanctions that prevent the union "from functioning as a labor union." Id., at 543, 65 S.Ct., at 1375. * * * Unlike the Court, I see no need to remand these cases in order to determine whether, as a factual matter, Local 54 is so dependent on dues that it will be prevented from effectively functioning as a bargaining representative if that source of revenue is cut off. I am willing to hold that, as a matter of law, a statute like § 93(b), which prohibits a union from collecting dues from its members, impairs the union's ability to represent those members to such an extent that it infringes on their § 7 right to bargain through the representative of their choice. Since the Court refuses to strike down the statute on this ground, I respectfully dissent.

---

**3.** The Court correctly recognizes that there is a fundamental difference between the employees' absolute § 7 right to choose which labor organization will act as their bargaining representative and their less-absolute right to determine who will serve as officers in that organization. One need only examine the actual workings of most unions in order to realize that the two rights are not co-extensive. For example, while a non-union employee in an agency shop retains his § 7 right to participate in the selection of the bargaining representative, he often has no say in who will serve as officers of the union that represents him in the bargaining process since such decisions are generally made by union members only. Similarly, while only the members of a particular collective bargaining unit are empowered to decide which union will act as their bargaining representative, all members of the union, even those not in the particular bargaining unit, are generally free to participate in the process of electing union officials. Thus, in a large union, it is possible that a substantial majority of the members of a particular bargaining unit may vote against the union official who is eventually elected. Even though the members of the bargaining unit are unable to select the union official of their choice in such situations, there would be no legitimate claim that this somehow interfered with their § 7 right to bargain through the representative of their choice.

## PROBLEMS FOR DISCUSSION

**1.** After this decision, can a state now: (a) require all labor organizations and their officials to register with a state labor-relations agency, upon pain of being fined for failure to do so?  (b) require that all officers of unions representing employees within the state be "of good moral character" and be United States citizens for no less than ten years?

**2.** Do you agree with the majority and the dissenters that the selection of union leadership—as distinguished from the selection of the union itself as bargaining representative—is not a right secured by Section 7 of the NLRA?  What arguments can you make to the contrary?

**3.** Was it necessary for the Court to remand for further findings on the issue of the union's ability to function without the collection of dues from its members?  Is not the position of the dissenting Justices compelling on this point?

**4.** Could a state enact a law requiring employers to deal with any representative designated by employees for that purpose; that is, to require the employer to deal with a lawyer on behalf of his or her employee clients concerning their wages, hours, or other terms or conditions of employment, or to require the employer to deal with any organization so designated on behalf of each of its members?  (Such a representational structure is further explored in Part Nine, infra, dealing with the contemporary situation of organized labor.)

———

## B.  COLLECTIVE BARGAINING

———

## Local 24, International Teamsters v. Oliver

358 U.S. 283, 79 S.Ct. 297, 3 L.Ed.2d 312 (1959).

[This action was commenced in an Ohio state court by one Revel Oliver, a member of Teamsters Local 24, who worked as a truck-driver of a truck owned by him.  He secured employment by leasing his truck to certain interstate carriers, which paid him both for his driving services and for the truck rental.  Collective bargaining in the trucking industry in the midwest, including Ohio, was carried out between an association of motor carriers and a council of Teamster locals.  The labor contract, effective February 1, 1955, contained an Article XXXII which regulated the minimum rental (and certain other terms) when a motor vehicle was leased to a carrier by an independent owner-driver working in the carrier's service.  Since 1938, the union had sought some control over the terms of such truck rentals, since the union claimed that the carriers were undermining the wage scale of the drivers employed by them, and for whom the union negotiated, by leasing vehicles from an owner-driver at a rental which returned to the owner-driver less than his actual costs of operation; as a result, the net wage received by the owner-driver (although nominally he received the negotiated wage) was actually a wage reduced by the excess of his operating expenses over the rental he received.  The negotiated minimum rental had been a compromise between the union's desire to abolish all owner-operators (who were allegedly using part of their wages for the upkeep of their vehicles) and the carriers' desire to have no limitations at all.

[Oliver, seeking to have the Ohio court strike down the minimum-rental provision in the labor contract, brought an action against both the Teamsters council and the carrier association. The court held Article XXXII to violate the Ohio antitrust law, since it constituted a price-fixing agreement between a union and a nonlabor group which imposed restrictions upon articles of commerce (i.e., the leased vehicles) and barred an owner of those articles from reasonable freedom of action in dealing with them. (At trial, the carriers joined with Oliver in attacking Article XXXII.) To the union's claim that Ohio could not overturn an agreement made pursuant to the duty to bargain under the National Labor Relations Act, the state court held that the Labor Act could not "be reasonably construed to permit this remote and indirect approach to the subject of wages." The state court issued a permanent injunction barring the use of Article XXXII or of any future contract to alter Oliver's present rental agreement with the carriers or to determine the rate to be charged for the use of Oliver's equipment. The Supreme Court granted certiorari.]

■ MR. JUSTICE BRENNAN delivered the opinion of the Court.

* * * [T]he point of the Article is obviously not price fixing but wages. The regulations embody not the "remote and indirect approach to the subject of wages" perceived by the Court of Common Pleas but a direct frontal attack upon a problem thought to threaten the maintenance of the basic wage structure established by the collective bargaining contract. The inadequacy of a rental which means that the owner makes up his excess costs from his driver's wages not only clearly bears a close relation to labor's efforts to improve working conditions but is in fact of vital concern to the carrier's employed drivers; an inadequate rental might mean the progressive curtailment of jobs through withdrawal of more and more carrier-owned vehicles from service. Cf. Bakery and Pastry Drivers and Helpers Local 802 of International Brotherhood of Teamsters v. Wohl, 315 U.S. 769, 771, 62 S.Ct. 816, 817, 86 L.Ed. 1178. It is not necessary to attempt to set precise outside limits to the subject matter properly included within the scope of mandatory collective bargaining, cf. National Labor Relations Board v. Wooster Division of Borg–Warner Corp., 356 U.S. 342, 78 S.Ct. 718, 2 L.Ed.2d 823, to hold, as we do, that the obligation under § 8(d) on the carriers and their employees to bargain collectively "with respect to wages, hours, and other terms and conditions of employment" and to embody their understanding in "a written contract incorporating any agreement reached," found an expression in the subject matter of Article XXXII. See Timken Roller Bearing Co., 70 N.L.R.B. 500, 518, reversed on other grounds, 6 Cir., 161 F.2d 949. And certainly bargaining on this subject through their representatives was a right of the employees protected by § 7 of the Act.

*Second.* We must decide whether Ohio's antitrust law may be applied to prevent the contracting parties from carrying out their agreement upon a subject matter as to which federal law directs them to bargain. Little extended discussion is necessary to show that Ohio law cannot be so applied. We need not concern ourselves today with a contractual provision dealing with a subject matter that the parties were under no obligation to discuss; the carriers as employers were under a duty to bargain collectively with the union as to the subject matter of the Article, as we have shown. The goal of federal labor policy, as expressed in the Wagner and Taft–Hartley Acts, is the promotion of collective bargaining; to encourage the employer and the representative of the employees to establish, through collective negotiation, their own charter for the ordering of industrial relations, and thereby to minimize industrial strife. See National Labor Relations Board v. Jones & Laughlin Steel Corp., 301 U.S. 1, 45, 57 S.Ct. 615, 628, 81 L.Ed. 893; National Labor Relations Board v. American National Ins. Co., 343 U.S. 395, 401–402, 72 S.Ct. 824, 828, 96 L.Ed. 1027. Within the area in which collective bargaining was required, Congress was not concerned with the substantive terms upon which the parties agreed. Cf. Terminal Railroad Ass'n of St. Louis v. Brotherhood of Railroad Trainmen, 318 U.S. 1, 6, 63 S.Ct. 420, 423, 87 L.Ed. 571. The purposes of the Acts are served by bringing the parties together and establishing conditions under which they are to work out their agreement themselves. To allow the application of the Ohio antitrust law here would wholly defeat the full realization of the congressional purpose. The application would frustrate the parties' solution of a problem which Congress has required them to negotiate in good faith toward solving, and in the solution of which it imposed no limitations relevant here. * * * We believe that there is no room in this scheme for the application here of this state policy limiting the solutions that the parties' agreement can provide to the problems of wages and working conditions. Cf. State of California v. Taylor, 353 U.S. 553, 566, 567, 77 S.Ct. 1037, 1044, 1045, 1 L.Ed.2d 1034. Since the federal law operates here, in an area where its authority is paramount to leave the parties free, the inconsistent application of state law is necessarily outside the power of the State. * * * Of course, the paramount force of the federal law remains even though it is expressed in the details of a contract federal law empowers the parties to make, rather than in terms in an enactment of Congress. See Railway Employees' Dept. v. Hanson, 351 U.S. 225, 232, 76 S.Ct. 714, 718, 100 L.Ed. 1112. Clearly it is immaterial that the conflict is between federal labor law and the application of what the State characterizes as an antitrust law. "* * * Congress has sufficiently expressed its purpose to * * * exclude state prohibition, even though that with which the federal law is concerned as a matter of labor relations be related by the State to the more inclusive area of restraint of trade." Weber v. Anheuser–Busch, Inc., 348 U.S. 468, 481, 75 S.Ct. 480, 488, 99 L.Ed. 546. We have not here a case of a collective bargaining agreement in conflict with a local health or safety regulation; the conflict here is between the federally sanctioned agreement and state policy which seeks specifically to adjust relationships in the world of commerce. If there is to be this sort of limitation on the arrangements that unions and employers may make with regard to these subjects, pursuant to the collective bargaining provisions of the Wagner and Taft–Hartley Acts, it is for Congress, not the States, to provide it.

Reversed.

[The dissenting opinion of MR. JUSTICE WHITTAKER is omitted.]

■ The CHIEF JUSTICE, MR. JUSTICE FRANKFURTER and MR. JUSTICE STEWART took no part in the consideration or decision of this case.

---

## Metropolitan Life Ins. Co. v. Commonwealth of Massachusetts

471 U.S. 724, 105 S.Ct. 2380, 85 L.Ed.2d 728 (1985).

■ JUSTICE BLACKMUN delivered the opinion of the Court.

[Chapter 175, Section 47B of the Massachusetts General Laws provides that a Massachusetts resident who is insured under a general insurance policy, an accident or sickness insurance policy, or an employee health-care plan that covers hospital and surgical expenses must be afforded specified minimum mental health-care benefits. Any such policy must provide sixty days of coverage for confinement in a mental hospital, coverage for confinement in a general hospital for mental-health care equal to that provided by the policy for non-mental illness, and certain minimum outpatient benefits. This is known as a "mandated-benefit statute," and is part of the state's broad-ranging regulation—typical of all states—of the insurance industry. In the words of the Supreme Court, Section 47B "was intended to help safeguard the public against the high costs of comprehensive inpatient and outpatient mental-health care, reduce non-psychiatric medical-care expenditures for mentally-related illness, shift the delivery of treatment from inpatient to outpatient services, and relieve the Commonwealth of some of the financial burden it otherwise would encounter with respect to mental-health problems."

[Metropolitan Life Insurance Company and Travelers Insurance Company, located in New York and Connecticut respectively, issue group-health policies providing hospital and surgical coverage to employers or unions having employees or members residing in Massachusetts. The Attorney General of Massachusetts brought an action in a state court seeking to require those insurance companies to comply with the mandated-benefit provisions of Section 47B. The insurers contended that the Massachusetts law was preempted by ERISA (the Employee Retirement Income Security Act of 1974), and also by the National Labor Relations Act in view of the status of insurance benefits as a mandatory subject of bargaining under Sections 8(a)(5) and 8(b)(3). The state courts concluded that the Massachusetts law was not preempted by either federal statute, and the Supreme Court unanimously agreed. The Court found controlling the ERISA provision preserving (in the face of an explicit preemption provision in the Act) any state law "which regulates insurance." The Court then proceeded to discuss the claim of preemption under the NLRA.]

## IV

### A

Unlike ERISA, the NLRA contains no statutory preemption provision. Still, as in any pre-emption analysis, " '[t]he purpose of Congress is the ultimate touchstone.' " Malone v. White Motor Corp., 435 U.S. 497, 504, 98 S.Ct. 1185, 1190, 55 L.Ed.2d 443 (1978), quoting Retail Clerks v. Schermerhorn, 375 U.S. 96, 103, 84 S.Ct. 219, 222, 11 L.Ed.2d 179 (1963). Where the pre-emptive effect of federal enactments is not explicit, "courts sustain a local regulation 'unless it conflicts with federal law or would frustrate the federal scheme, or unless the courts discern from the totality of the circumstances that Congress sought to occupy the field to the exclusion of the States.' " Allis–Chalmers Corp. v. Lueck, 471 U.S. 202, 209, 105 S.Ct. 1904, 1910, 85 L.Ed.2d 206 (1985), quoting Malone v. White Motor Corp., supra, 435 U.S., at 504, 98 S.Ct., at 1190.

Appellants contend first that because mandated-benefit laws require benefit plans whose terms are arrived at through collective bargaining to purchase certain benefits the parties may not have wished to purchase, such laws in effect mandate terms of collective-bargaining agreements. The Supreme Judicial Court of Massachusetts correctly found that "[b]ecause a plan that purchases insurance has no choice but to provide mental health care benefits, the insurance provisions of § 47B effectively control the content of insured welfare benefit plans." 385 Mass., at 605, 433 N.E.2d, at 1227. More precisely, faced with § 47B, parties to a collective-bargaining agreement providing for health insurance are forced to make a choice: either they must purchase the mandated benefit, decide not to provide health coverage at all, or decide to become self-insured, assuming they are in a financial position to make that choice.

The question then becomes whether this kind of interference with collective bargaining is forbidden by federal law. Appellants argue that because Congress intended to leave the choice of terms in collective-bargaining agreements to the free play of economic forces, not subject either to state law or to the control of the National Labor Relations Board (NLRB), mandated-benefit laws should be pre-empted by the NLRA.

The Court has articulated two distinct NLRA pre-emption principles. The so-called Garmon rule, see San Diego Building Trades Council v. Garmon, 359 U.S. 236, 79 S.Ct. 773, 3 L.Ed.2d 775 (1959), protects the primary jurisdiction of the NLRB to determine in the first instance what kind of conduct is either prohibited or protected by the NLRA. There is no claim here that Massachusetts has sought to regulate or prohibit any conduct subject to the regulatory jurisdiction of the NLRB, since the Act is silent as to the substantive provisions of welfare-benefit plans.

A second pre-emption doctrine protects against state interference with policies implicated by the structure of the Act itself, by pre-empting state law and state causes of action concerning conduct that Congress intended to be unregulated.  * * *  [The Court discussed Teamsters v. Morton, Machinists v. Wisc. Employment Rel. Bd., and New York Tel. Co. v. New York Labor Dept. (upholding New York's grant of unemployment compensation to strikers).]

These cases rely on the understanding that in providing in the NLRA a framework for self-organization and collective bargaining, Congress determined both how much the conduct of unions and employers should be regulated, and how much it should be left unregulated:

"The States have no more authority than the Board to upset the balance that Congress has struck between labor and management in the collective-bargaining relationship.  'For a state to impinge on the area of labor combat designed to be free is quite as much an obstruction of federal policy as if the state were to declare picketing free for purposes or by methods which the federal Act prohibits.' "  New York Tel. Co. v. New York Labor Department, 440 U.S., at 554, 99 S.Ct., at 1348 (dissenting opinion), quoting Garner v. Teamsters, 346 U.S. 485, 500, 74 S.Ct. 161, 171, 98 L.Ed. 228 (1953).

All parties correctly understand this case to involve Machinists pre-emption.

## B

Here, however, appellants do not suggest that § 47B alters the balance of power between the parties to the labor contract.  Instead, appellants argue that, not only did Congress establish a balance of bargaining power between labor and management in the Act, but it also intended to prevent the States from establishing minimum employment standards that labor and management would otherwise have been required to negotiate from their federally protected bargaining positions, and would otherwise have been permitted to set at a lower level than that mandated by state law.  Appellants assert that such state regulation is permissible only when Congress has authorized its enactment.  Because welfare benefits are a mandatory subject of bargaining under the labor law, see Chemical & Alkali Workers v. Pittsburgh Plate Glass Co., 404 U.S. 157, 159, and n. 1, 92 S.Ct. 383, 387, and n. 1, 30 L.Ed.2d 341 (1971), and because Congress has never given States the authority to enact health regulations that affect the terms of bargaining agreements, appellants urge that the NLRA pre-empts any state attempt to impose minimum-benefit terms on the parties.[29]

**29.** Even if we were to accept appellants' argument that state laws mandating contract terms on collectively bargained contracts are pre-empted unless Congress authorizes their imposition, we would still find § 47B not pre-empted here.  For mandated-benefit laws are laws "regulating the business of insurance," see n. 21, supra, and Congress in the McCarran–Ferguson Act expressly left to the States the power to enact such regulation.  15 U.S.C. § 1012(a).  That Act states: "No Act of Congress shall be construed to invalidate, impair, or supersede any law enacted by any State for the purpose

Appellants assume that Congress' ultimate concern in the NLRA was in leaving the parties free to reach agreement about contract terms. The framework established in the NLRA was merely a means to allow the parties to reach such agreement fairly. A law that interferes with the end-result of bargaining is, therefore, even worse than a law that interferes with the bargaining process. Thus, it is argued, this case is *a fortiori* to cases like Morton, Machinists, and New York Telephone. * * * Upon close analysis, however, we find that Morton, Machinists, and New York Telephone all rest on a sound understanding of the purpose and operation of the Act that is incompatible with appellants' position here.

## C

Congress apparently did not consider the question whether state laws of general application affecting terms of collective-bargaining agreements subject to mandatory bargaining were to be pre-empted.[30] That being so, "the Court must construe the Act and determine its impact on state law in light of the wider contours of federal labor policy." Belknap, Inc. v. Hale, 463 U.S. 491, 520, n. 4, 103 S.Ct. 3172, 3188, n. 4, 77 L.Ed.2d 798 (1983)(opinion concurring in the judgment).

The NLRA is concerned primarily with establishing an equitable process for determining terms and conditions of employment, and not with particular substantive terms of the bargain that is struck when the parties are negotiating from relatively equal positions. See Cox, Recent Developments in Federal Labor Law Preemption, 41 Ohio St. L.J. 277, 297 (1980). The NLRA's declared purpose is to remedy "[t]he inequality of bargaining power between employees who do not possess full freedom of association or actual liberty of contract, and employers who are organized in the corporate or other forms of ownership association." § 1, 29 U.S.C. § 151. * * *

One of the ultimate goals of the Act was the resolution of the problem of "depress[ed] wage rates and the purchasing power of wage earners in industry," 29 U.S.C. § 151, and "the widening gap between wages and profits," 79 Cong.Rec. 2371 (1935)(remarks of Sen. Wagner), thought to be the cause of economic decline and depression. Congress hoped to accomplish this by establishing procedures for more equitable private bargaining.

The evil Congress was addressing thus was entirely unrelated to local or federal regulation establishing minimum terms of employment. Neither inequality of bargaining power nor the resultant depressed wage rates were thought to result from the choice between having terms of employment set

---

of regulating the business of insurance." § 1012(b). * * *

**30.** We have found no relevant legislative history on the specific question. The right to bargain collectively was only gradually understood to include the right to bargain about each subject that the Board found to be comprehended by the phrase "wages, hours and other terms and conditions of employment." § 8(d), 29 U.S.C. § 158(d). Thus, Congress could not easily have anticipated the claim that a state labor standard would be pre-empted as a result of the right to bargain. See Cox and Seidman, Federalism and Labor Relations, 64 Harv.L.Rev. 211, 242 (1950).

by public law or having them set by private agreement.  No incompatibility exists, therefore, between federal rules designed to restore the equality of bargaining power, and state or federal legislation that imposes minimal substantive requirements on contract terms negotiated between parties to labor agreements, at least so long as the purpose of the state legislation is not incompatible with these general goals of the NLRA.

Accordingly, it never has been argued successfully that minimal labor standards imposed by other *federal* laws were not to apply to unionized employers and employees.  See, *e.g.,* Barrentine v. Arkansas–Best Freight System, Inc., 450 U.S. 728, 737, 739, 101 S.Ct. 1437, 1443–1444, 67 L.Ed.2d 641 (1981).  Cf. Alexander v. Gardner–Denver Co., 415 U.S. 36, 51, 94 S.Ct. 1011, 1021, 39 L.Ed.2d 147 (1974).  Nor has Congress ever seen fit to exclude unionized workers and employers from laws establishing federal minimal employment standards.  We see no reason to believe that for this purpose Congress intended state minimum labor standards to be treated differently from minimum federal standards.

Minimum state labor standards affect union and nonunion employees equally, and neither encourage nor discourage the collective-bargaining processes that are the subject of the NLRA.  Nor do they have any but the most indirect effect on the right of self-organization established in the Act.  Unlike the NLRA, mandated-benefit laws are not laws designed to encourage or discourage employees in the promotion of their interest collectively; rather, they are in part "designed to give specific minimum protections to *individual* workers and to ensure that *each* employee covered by the Act would receive" the mandated health insurance coverage.  Barrentine, 450 U.S., at 739, 101 S.Ct., at 1444 (emphasis in original).  Nor do these laws even inadvertently affect these interests implicated in the NLRA.  Rather, they are minimum standards "independent of the collective-bargaining process [that] devolve on [employees] as individual workers, not as members of a collective organization."  Id., at 745, 101 S.Ct., at 1447.

It would further few of the purposes of the Act to allow unions and employers to bargain for terms of employment that state law forbids employers to establish unilaterally.  "Such a rule of law would delegate to unions and unionized employers the power to exempt themselves from whatever state labor standards they disfavored."  Allis–Chalmers Corp. v. Lueck, 471 U.S., at 212, 105 S.Ct., at 1911–1912.  It would turn the policy that animated the Wagner Act on its head to understand it to have penalized workers who have chosen to join a union by preventing them from benefiting from state labor regulations imposing minimal standards on nonunion employers.

### D

Most significantly, there is no suggestion in the legislative history of the Act that Congress intended to disturb the myriad state laws then in existence that set minimum labor standards, but were unrelated in any way to the processes of bargaining self-organization.  To the contrary, we believe that Congress developed the framework for self-organization and collective bargaining of the NLRA within the larger body of state law promoting public health and safety. The States traditionally have had great latitude under their police powers to legislate as "to the protection of the lives, limbs, health, comfort, and quiet of all persons." Slaughter–House Cases, 16 Wall, 36, 62, 21 L.Ed. 394 (1873), quoting Thorpe v. Rutland & Burlington R. Co., 27 Vt. 140, 149 (1855). "States possess broad authority under their police powers to regulate the employment relationship to protect workers within the State. Child labor laws, minimum and other wage laws, laws affecting occupational health and safety ... are only a few examples." DeCanas v. Bica, 424 U.S. 351, 356, 96 S.Ct. 933, 937, 47 L.Ed.2d 43 (1976). State laws requiring that employers contribute to unemployment and workmen's compensation funds, laws prescribing mandatory state holidays, and those dictating payment to employees for time spent at the polls or on jury duty all have withstood scrutiny. See, *e.g.*, Day–Brite Lighting, Inc. v. Missouri, 342 U.S. 421, 72 S.Ct. 405, 96 L.Ed. 469 (1952).

Federal labor law in this sense is interstitial, supplementing state law where compatible, and supplanting it only when it prevents the accomplishment of the purposes of the federal act. Hines v. Davidowitz, 312 U.S. 52, 67, n. 20, 61 S.Ct. 399, 404, n. 20, 85 L.Ed. 581 (1941); Allen–Bradley Local 1111 v. Wisconsin Employment Relations Bd., 315 U.S. 740, 749–751, 62 S.Ct. 820, 825–826, 86 L.Ed. 1154 (1942); Malone v. White Motor Corp., 435 U.S., at 504, 98 S.Ct., at 1189. Thus the Court has recognized that it "cannot declare pre-empted all local regulation that touches or concerns in any way the complex interrelationships between employees, employers, and unions; obviously, much of this is left to the States." Motor Coach Employees v. Lockridge, 403 U.S. 274, 289, 91 S.Ct. 1909, 1919, 29 L.Ed.2d 473 (1971). When a state law establishes a minimal employment standard not inconsistent with the general legislative goals of the NLRA, it conflicts with none of the purposes of the Act. * * *[32]

Massachusetts' mandated-benefit law is an insurance regulation designed to implement the Commonwealth's policy on mental-health care, and as such is a valid and unexceptional exercise of the Commonwealth's police power. It was designed in part to ensure that the less-wealthy residents of the Commonwealth would be provided adequate mental-health treatment should they require it. Though § 47B, like many laws affecting

---

**32.** The Court previously has addressed this same issue in the related context of the Railway Labor Act, 44 Stat. 577, as amended, 45 U.S.C. § 151 et seq.:

"The Railway Labor Act, like the National Labor Relations Act, does not undertake governmental regulation of wages, hours, or working conditions. Instead it seeks to provide a means by which agreement may be reached with respect to them. The national interest expressed by those Acts is not primarily in the working conditions as such....

"State laws have long regulated a great variety of conditions in transportation and industry....

"But it cannot be that the minimum requirements laid down by state authority are all set aside. We hold that the enactment by Congress of the Railway Labor Act was not a preemption of the field of regulating working conditions themselves and did not preclude the State ... from making the order in question." Terminal Assn. v. Trainmen, 318 U.S. 1, 6–7 (1943)(footnote omitted).

terms of employment, potentially limits an employee's right to choose one thing by requiring that he be provided with something else, it does not limit the rights of self-organization or collective bargaining protected by the NLRA, and is not pre-empted by that Act.

\* \* \*

In FORT HALIFAX PACKING CO., INC. V. COYNE, 482 U.S. 1, 107 S.Ct. 2211, 96 L.Ed.2d 1 (1987), the Court confronted a Maine statute that, in effect, mandated severance pay in the event of plant closing but allowed the statutory schedule of payment to be mitigated for employees covered by an express contractual severance pay provision. The Court sustained the statute against preemption challenge under both the express (and sweeping) preemption provision of the Employee Retirement Income Security Act (ERISA) and under the Labor Act. (Chief Justice Rehnquist and Justices O'Connor and Scalia dissented on the former issue.) The Court saw the Labor Act issue as controlled by *Metropolitan Life.*

> It is true that the Maine statute gives employees something for which they otherwise might have to bargain. That is true, however, with regard to any state law that substantively regulates employment conditions. Both employers and employees come to the bargaining table with rights under state law that form a " 'backdrop' " for their negotiations.... Absent a collective bargaining agreement, for instance, state common law generally permits an employer to run the workplace as it wishes. The employer enjoys this authority without having to bargain for it. The parties may enter negotiations designed to alter this state of affairs, but, if impasse is reached, the employer may rely on pre-existing state law to justify its authority to make employment decisions; that same state law defines the rights and duties of employees. Similarly, Maine provides that employer and employees may negotiate with the intention of establishing severance pay terms. If impasse is reached, however, pre-existing state law determines the right of employees to a certain level of severance pay and the duty of the employer to provide it. Thus, the mere fact that a state statute pertains to matters over which the parties are free to bargain cannot support a claim of preemption, for "there is nothing in the NLRA ... which expressly forecloses all state regulatory power with respect to those issues ... that may be the subject of collective bargaining."

In 1987, Montana became the first state to enact a general law of fair dismissal, the Wrongful Discharge From Employment Act, Mont.Code §§ 39–2–901 to –915. (See excerpts in statutory supplement to the casebook.). It provides that any employee dismissed without good cause is entitled to lost wages and fringe benefits for a period not to exceed four years from the date of discharge less mitigation. Exempt from the law, however, is the discharge "of an employee covered by a written collective bargaining agreement." The Act was declared constitutional by the Supreme Court of Montana in the face of challenges based on provisions of the Montana Constitution. Meech v. Hillhaven West, Inc., 238 Mont. 21, 776 P.2d 488 (1989). Justice Sheehy dissented on the ground *inter alia* that the Act discriminated in favor of unionized workers; that is, by exempting employees covered by collective agreements, the law leaves available to them a full range of tort remedies that the Act—by virtue of its provisions broadly preempting all other tort and contract relief—denies to non-unionized employees. "Thus a union worker who is discharged for 'whistle blowing' has larger rights of recovery than a non-union worker discharged for the same reason." Does the Act, as a consequence, offend the federal scheme? Note, however, that in the more common case, that of a claim simply of a discharge without just cause, the non-unionized employee has a statutory right to have the case adjudicated while the unionized employee has only the right to have the union decide whether or not the case will be submitted to arbitration. In that case, the non-unionized have greater rights than the unionized. Does the Act offend the federal scheme on that account?

---

## PROBLEMS FOR DISCUSSION

**1.** The Court in the *Metropolitan Life* case says nothing of its earlier decision in *Teamsters v. Oliver*. Can one infer that the Court regarded that earlier decision as essentially on point but now no longer controlling? Or, rather, can one infer that the Court regarded that decision as so clearly dealing with an unrelated issue as not to warrant any attention? If the Court *had* discussed the pertinence of the *Oliver* case, what should it have said?

**2.** Was it appropriate for the Court to treat as effectively controlling the fact that *Congress* has regularly enacted legislation touching squarely upon workplace benefits, such as wage and hour laws, retirement, and health and safety? Apart from the obvious fact that the Supremacy Clause does not apply to this legislation, is it appropriate for the Court to infer an "intention" on the part of Congress that state laws in these areas can properly afford higher protections than those accorded by Congress—and then to transplant that "intention" into the National Labor Relations Act?

**3.** In holding irrelevant the *Garmon* basis for preemption, the Court states: "There is no claim here that Massachusetts has sought to regulate or prohibit any conduct subject to the regulatory jurisdiction of the NLRB, since the Act is silent as to the substantive provisions of welfare-benefit plans." Is there any sense to be made of this declaration, given the fact that the issue in dispute related to a mandatory subject of bargaining, which the parties are not merely permitted by the NLRA to bargain about but are required to bargain about? Although it is indeed true that the NLRA does not dictate substantive contract terms but leaves their determination to private bargaining, is that not an argument *against* state substantive regulation rather than in support of it?

**4.** The *Oliver* decision, in dictum, had acknowledged that the parties' agreement on mandatory subjects could be made subject to the states' "local health or safety regulation." In the *Metropolitan Life* case, the Court appears to expand this to all exercises of the state's "police power." What exactly is this power and how broad is it? Does it encompass state laws regarding working uniforms? regarding working hours? regarding retirement age? regarding minimum vacation time?

**5.** It is clear, is it not, that a state could not constitutionally declare unlawful the insistence in bargaining upon a mandatory subject of bargaining? It is also clear, is it not, that a state could not constitutionally require that, in the event of impasse in bargaining about a mandatory subject, the employer and union (in private industry) must submit their dispute to resolution on the merits by an arbitrator appointed by the state? Why is it any more tolerable an intrusion upon federal policy when a state dictates a term (even a "minimum" term) of the labor agreement regarding a mandatory subject such as health insurance or severance pay? (Indeed, is not the "compulsory arbitration" requirement a form of state regulation that intrudes less upon federal labor-relations policy?)

Assume that because of a strike by cemetery workers a number of decedents remained unburied, several of whom were of religions that require immediate or swift burial. Could the state legislate a "religiously required interment" law, requiring interment in those cases by workers from a labor pool to be negotiated by the cemetery authority and the union? See Cannon v. Edgar, 33 F.3d 880 (7th Cir.1994).

---

# New York Tel. Co. v. New York State Dept. of Labor

440 U.S. 519, 99 S.Ct. 1328, 59 L.Ed.2d 553 (1979).

■ MR. JUSTICE STEVENS announced the judgment of the Court and an opinion in which MR. JUSTICE WHITE and MR. JUSTICE REHNQUIST joined.

The question presented is whether the National Labor Relations Act, as amended, implicitly prohibits the State of New York from paying unemployment compensation to strikers.

Communication Workers of America, AFL–CIO (CWA) represents about 70% of the nonmanagement employees of companies affiliated with the Bell Telephone Company. In June of 1971, when contract negotiations had reached an impasse, CWA recommended a nationwide strike. The strike commenced on July 14, 1971, and, for most workers, lasted only a week. In New York, however, the 38,000 CWA members employed by petitioners remained on strike for seven months.

New York's unemployment insurance law normally authorizes the payment of benefits after approximately one week of unemployment. If a claimant's loss of employment is caused by "a strike, lockout, or other industrial controversy in the establishment in which he was employed," § 592.1 of the law suspends the payment of benefits for an additional seven-week period. In 1971, the maximum weekly benefit of $75 was payable to an employee whose base salary was at least $149 per week.

After the eight-week waiting period, petitioners' striking employees began to collect unemployment compensation. During the ensuing five months more than $49 million in benefits were paid to about 33,000 striking employees at an average rate of somewhat less than $75 per week. Because New York's unemployment insurance system is financed primarily by employer contributions based on the benefits paid to former employees of each employer in past years, a substantial part of the cost of these benefits was ultimately imposed on petitioners.

Petitioners brought suit in the United States District Court for the Southern District of New York against the state officials responsible for the administration of the unemployment compensation fund. They sought a declaration that the New York statute authorizing the payment of benefits to strikers conflicts with federal law and is therefore invalid, an injunction against the enforcement of § 592.1, and an award recouping the increased taxes paid in consequence of the disbursement of funds to their striking employees. After an eight-day trial, the District Court granted the requested relief. * * * The Court of Appeals for the Second Circuit reversed. * * *

The importance of the question led us to grant certiorari. 435 U.S. 941. We now affirm. Our decision is ultimately governed by our understanding of the intent of the Congress that enacted the National Labor Relations Act on July 5, 1935, and the Social Security Act on August 14 of the same year. * * *

## I

* * * [T]here is no claim in this case that New York has sought to regulate or prohibit any conduct subject to the regulatory jurisdiction of the Labor Board under § 8. Nor are the petitioning employers pursuing any claim of interference with employee rights protected by § 7. The State simply authorized striking employees to receive unemployment benefits, and assessed a tax against the struck employers to pay for some of those benefits, once the economic warfare between the two groups reached its ninth week. Accordingly, beyond identifying the interest in national uniformity underlying the doctrine, the cases comprising the main body of labor pre-emption law are of little relevance in deciding this case.

There is, however, a pair of decisions in which the Court has held that Congress intended to forbid state regulation of economic warfare between labor and management, even though it was clear that none of the regulated conduct on either side was covered by the federal statute. [The Court here summarized its decisions in Teamsters v. Morton and Lodge 76, Machinists v. Wisconsin Employment Rel. Bd.]

The economic weapons employed by labor and management in Morton, Lodge 76, and the present case are similar, and petitioners rely heavily on the statutory policy, emphasized in the former two cases, of allowing the free play of economic forces to operate during the bargaining process. Moreover, because of the two-fold impact of § 592.1, which not only provides financial support to striking employees but also adds to the burdens of the struck employers, we must accept the District Court's finding that New York's law, like the state action involved in Morton and

Lodge 76, has altered the economic balance between labor and management.

But there is not a complete unity of state regulation in the three cases. Unlike Morton and Lodge 76, as well as the main body of labor pre-emption cases, the case before us today does not involve any attempt by the State to regulate or prohibit private conduct in the labor-management field. It involves a state program for the distribution of benefits to certain members of the public. Although the class benefited is primarily made up of employees in the State and the class providing the benefits is primarily made up of employers in the State, and although some of the members of each class are occasionally engaged in labor disputes, the general purport of the program is not to regulate the bargaining relationships between the two classes but instead to provide an efficient means of insuring employment security in the State. It is therefore clear that even though the statutory policy underlying Morton and Lodge 76 lends support to petitioners' claim, the holdings in those cases are not controlling. The Court is being asked to extend the doctrine of labor law pre-emption into a new area.

## II

The differences between state laws regulating private conduct and the unemployment benefits program at issue here are important from a pre-emption perspective. For a variety of reasons, they suggest an affinity between this case and others in which the Court has shown a reluctance to infer a pre-emptive congressional intent.

Section 591.1 is not a "State law regulating the relations between employees, their union and their employer," as to which the reasons underlying the pre-emption doctrine have their "greatest force." Sears, [Roebuck & Co. v. Carpenters, 436 U.S. 180,] at 193, 98 S.Ct., at 1755. Instead, as discussed below, the statute is a law of general applicability. Although that is not a sufficient reason to exempt it from pre-emption, Farmer v. Carpenters, 430 U.S. 290, 300, 97 S.Ct. 1056, 1063, 51 L.Ed.2d 338, our cases have consistently recognized that a congressional intent to deprive the States of their power to enforce such general laws is more difficult to infer than an intent to pre-empt laws directed specifically at concerted activity. See Farmer, supra, at 302, 97 S.Ct., at 1064; Sears, supra, 436 U.S., at 194–195, 98 S.Ct., at 1756–1757; Cox, [Labor Law Pre-emption Revisited, 85 Harv.L.Rev. 1337,], at 1356–1357.

Because New York's program, like those in other States, is financed in part by taxes assessed against employers, it is not strictly speaking a public welfare program. It nevertheless remains true that the payments to the strikers implement a broad state policy that does not primarily concern labor-management relations, but is implicated whenever members of the labor force become unemployed. Unlike most States, New York has concluded that the community interest in the security of persons directly affected by a strike outweighs the interest in avoiding any impact on a particular labor dispute. * * *

New York's program differs from State statutes expressly regulating labor-management relations for another reason. The program is structured to comply with a federal statute, and as a consequence is financed, in part, with federal funds. The federal subsidy mitigates the impact on the employer of any distribution of benefits. More importantly, as the Court has pointed out in the past, the federal statute authorizing the subsidy provides additional evidence of Congress' reluctance to limit the States' authority in this area. * * *

Title IX of the Social Security Act of 1935, supra, established the participatory federal unemployment compensation scheme. The statute authorizes the provision of federal funds to States having programs approved by the Secretary of Labor. * * * The voluminous history of the Social Security Act [makes] it abundantly clear that Congress intended the several States to have broad freedom in setting up the types of unemployment compensation that they wish. * * * Congress has been sensitive to the importance of the States' interest in fashioning their own unemployment compensation programs and especially their own eligibility criteria.[32] It is therefore appropriate to treat New York's statute with the same deference that we have afforded analogous state laws of general applicability that protect interests "deeply rooted in local feeling and responsibility." With respect to such laws, we have stated "that, in the absence of compelling congressional direction, we could not infer that Congress had deprived the States of the power to act." San Diego Building Trades Council v. Garmon, 359 U.S. 236, 244, 79 S.Ct. 773, 779, 3 L.Ed.2d 775.

### III

Pre-emption of state law is sometimes required by the terms of a federal statute. See, *e.g.,* Ray v. Atlantic Richfield, 435 U.S. 151, 173–179, 98 S.Ct. 988, 1002–1005, 55 L.Ed.2d 179. This, of course, is not such a case. Even when there is no express pre-emption, any proper application of the doctrine must give effect to the intent of Congress. Malone v. White Motor Co., 435 U.S. 497, 504, 98 S.Ct. 1185, 1190, 55 L.Ed.2d 443. In this case there is no evidence that the Congress that enacted the National Labor Relations Act in 1935 intended to deny the States the power to provide unemployment benefits for strikers. Cf. Hodory, 431 U.S., at 482, 97 S.Ct., at 1905. Far from the compelling congressional direction on which pre-emption in this case would have to be predicated, the silence of Congress in 1935 actually supports the contrary inference that Congress intended to allow the States to make this policy determination for themselves.

New York was one of the five States that had an unemployment insurance law before Congress passed the Social Security and the Wagner

---

**32.** The force of the legislative history discussed in [earlier court decisions dealing with the Social Security Act] comes close to removing this case from the pre-emption setting altogether. In light of those decisions, the case may be viewed as presenting a potential conflict between two federal statutes—Title IX of the Social Security Act and the NLRA—rather than between federal and state regulatory statutes. But however the conflict is viewed, its ultimate resolution depends on an analysis of congressional intent.

Acts in the summer of 1935. Although the New York law did not then assess taxes against employers on the basis of their individual experience, it did authorize the payment of benefits to strikers out of a general fund financed by assessments against all employers in the State. The junior Senator from New York, Robert Wagner, was a principal sponsor of both the National Labor Relations Act and the Social Security Act; the two statutes were considered in Congress simultaneously and enacted into law within five weeks of one another; and the Senate Report on the Social Security Bill, in the midst of discussing the States' freedom of choice with regard to their unemployment compensation laws, expressly referred to the New York statute as a qualifying example. Even though that reference did not mention the subject of benefits for strikers, it is difficult to believe that Senator Wagner and his colleagues were unaware of such a controversial provision, particularly at a time when both unemployment and labor unrest were matters of vital national concern.   * * *

Subsequent events confirm our conclusion that the congressional silence in 1935 was not evidence of an intent to pre-empt the States' power to make this policy choice. On several occasions since the 1930's Congress has expressly addressed the question of paying benefits to strikers, and especially the effect of such payments on federal labor policy. On none of these occasions has it suggested that such payments were already prohibited by an implicit federal rule of law. Nor, on any of these occasions has it been willing to supply the prohibition. The fact that the problem has been discussed so often supports the inference that Congress was well aware of the issue when the Wagner Act was passed in 1935, and that it chose, as it has done since, to leave this aspect of unemployment compensation eligibility to the States.

In all events, a State's power to fashion its own policy concerning the payment of unemployment compensation is not to be denied on the basis of speculation about the unexpressed intent of Congress. New York has not sought to regulate private conduct that is subject to the regulatory jurisdiction of the National Labor Relations Board. Nor, indeed, has it sought to regulate any private conduct of the parties to a labor dispute. Instead, it has sought to administer its unemployment compensation program in a manner that it believes best effectuates the purposes of that scheme. In an area in which Congress has decided to tolerate a substantial measure of diversity, the fact that the implementation of this general state policy affects the relative strength of the antagonists in a bargaining dispute is not a sufficient reason for concluding that Congress intended to pre-empt that exercise of State power.

The judgment of the Court of Appeals is

Affirmed.

[In a separate concurring opinion, Mr. Justice Brennan concluded that the legislative histories of the NLRA and the Social Security Act provided sufficient evidence of congressional intent not to pre-empt state unemployment compensation laws providing for payments to strikers. He therefore disclaimed reliance upon the more general preemption principles emanating from the *Morton* and *Machinists* cases.  He questioned Justice Stevens' distinguishing of those cases on the ground that they dealt with statutes regulating private conduct rather than conferring public benefits; Justice Brennan could not understand why the former kind of statute should be subjected to greater scrutiny.  Nor could Justice Brennan agree with Justice Stevens that the New York statute was clearly a "law of general applicability" (even assuming that to be relevant to preemption analysis). Justice Brennan joined more enthusiastically in the assertion of Justice Stevens that the New York law was of the kind which evinced a policy "deeply rooted in local feeling and responsibility," and in his suggestion that this case was more one of conflicting federal statutes than of federal-state preemption.]

■ MR. JUSTICE BLACKMUN, with whom MR. JUSTICE MARSHALL joins, concurring in the judgment.

I concur in the result.  I agree with that portion of Part III of the Court's opinion where the conclusion is reached that Congress has made its decision to permit a State to pay unemployment benefits to strikers. (Whether Congress has made that decision wisely is not for this Court to say.)  Because I am not at all certain that the Court's opinion is fully consistent with the principles recently enunciated in Machinists v. Wisconsin Emp. Rel. Comm'n, 427 U.S. 132, 96 S.Ct. 2548, 49 L.Ed.2d 396 (1976), I refrain from joining the opinion's pre-emption analysis.  * * *

[The] requirement that petitioner must demonstrate "compelling congressional direction" in order to establish pre-emption is not, I believe, consistent with the pre-emption principles laid down in Machinists.  * * * Where the exercise of state authority to curtail, prohibit, or enhance self-help " 'would frustrate effective implementation of the Act's processes,' " 427 U.S., at 148, 96 S.Ct., at 2557, quoting Railroad Trainmen v. Jacksonville Terminal Co., 394 U.S. 369, 380, 89 S.Ct. 1109, 1116, 22 L.Ed.2d 344 (1969), I believe Machinists compels the conclusion that Congress intended to pre-empt such state activity, unless there is evidence of congressional intent to tolerate it.

　　　* * *

I believe this conclusion to be applicable to a case where a State alters the balance struck by Congress by conferring a benefit on a broadly defined class of citizens rather than by regulating more explicitly the conduct of parties to a labor-management dispute.  The crucial inquiry is whether the exercise of state authority "frustrates the effective implementation of the Act's processes," not whether the State's purpose was to confer a benefit on a class of citizens.  * * *

In summary, in the adjudication of this case, I would not depart from the path marked out by the Court's decision in Machinists.  Because, however, I believe the evidence justifies the conclusion that Congress has decided to permit New York's unemployment compensation law, notwithstanding its impact on the balance of bargaining power, I concur in the Court's judgment.

■ Mr. Justice Powell, with whom The Chief Justice and Mr. Justice Stewart join, dissenting.

The Court's decision substantially alters, in the State of New York, the balance of advantage between management and labor prescribed by the National Labor Relations Act (the NLRA). It sustains a New York law that requires the employer, after a specified time, to pay striking employees as much as 50% of their normal wages. In so holding, the Court substantially rewrites the principles of pre-emption that have been developed to protect the free collective bargaining which is the essence of federal labor law.
* * *

## II

* * * Nothing in the NLRA or its legislative history indicates that Congress intended unemployment compensation for strikers, let alone employer financing of such compensation, to be part of the legal structure of collective bargaining. The New York law therefore alters significantly the bargaining balance prescribed by Congress in that law. The decision upholding it cannot be squared with Morton and Lodge 76, where far less intrusive state statutes were invalidated because they "upset the balance of power between labor and management expressed in our national labor policy." Morton, supra, at 260.

The Court's opinion seeks to avoid this conclusion by ignoring the fact that the petitioners are not challenging the entire New York unemployment compensation law but only that portion of it that provides for benefits for striking employees. Although the Court characterizes the State's unemployment compensation law as "a law of general applicability" that "implement[s] a broad state policy that does not primarily concern labor-management relations," this description bears no relation to reality when applied to the challenged provisions of the law. Those provisions are "of general applicability" only if that term means—contrary to what the Court itself says—generally applicable only to labor-management relations. It would be difficult to think of a law more specifically focused on labor-management relations than one that compels an employer to finance a strike against itself.

Even if the challenged portion of the New York statute properly could be viewed as part of a law of "general applicability," this generality of the law would have little or nothing to do with whether it is pre-empted by the NLRA. * * * The "crucial inquiry regarding pre-emption" is whether the application of the state law in question " 'would frustrate the effective implementation of the NLRA's processes.' " Lodge 76, 427 U.S., at 147–148, quoting Railroad Trainmen v. Jacksonville Terminal Co., 394 U.S. 369, 380, 89 S.Ct. 1109, 1116, 22 L.Ed.2d 344 (1969). * * * It is self-evident that the "potential [of the New York law] for interference" (Morton, supra, at 260) with the federally protected economic balance between management and labor is direct and substantial.

The Court has identified several categories of state laws whose application is unlikely to interfere with federal regulatory policy under the NLRA.

\* \* \* [The Court here] mistakenly treats New York's requirement that employers pay benefits to striking employees as state action "deeply rooted in local feeling and responsibility." But the broad language from Garmon has been applied only to a narrow class of cases. \* \* \* The provisions of the New York law at issue here have nothing in common with the state laws protecting against personal torts or violence to property that have defined the "local feeling and responsibility" exception to pre-emption.

### III

The challenged provisions of the New York law cannot, consistently with prior decisions of this Court, be brought within the "local feeling and responsibility" exception to the pre-emption doctrine. The principles of Morton and Lodge 76 therefore require pre-emption in this case unless in some other law Congress has modified the policy of the NLRA. The Court, acknowledging the need to look beyond the NLRA to support its conclusion, relies primarily on the Social Security Act. In that Act, adopted only five weeks after the passage of the NLRA, it finds an indication that Congress did intend that the States be free to make unemployment compensation payments part of the collective-bargaining relationship structured by the NLRA. But it is extremely unlikely that little over a month after enacting a detailed and carefully designed statute to structure industrial relations, the Congress would alter so dramatically the balance struck in that law. It would be even more remarkable if such a change were made, as the Court suggests, without any explicit statutory expression, and indeed absent any congressional discussion whatever of the problem. \* \* \*

A much more cautious approach to implied amendments of the NLRA is required if the Court is to give proper effect to the legislative judgments of the Congress. Having once resolved the balance to be struck in the collective-bargaining relationship, and having embodied that balance in the NLRA, Congress should not be expected by the Court to reaffirm the balance explicitly each time it later enacts legislation that may touch in some way on the collective-bargaining relationship. Absent explicit modification of the NLRA, or clear inconsistency between the terms of the NLRA and a subsequent statute, the Court should assume that Congress intended to leave the NLRA unaltered. This assumption is especially appropriate in considering the intent of Congress when it enacted the Social Security Act just five weeks after completing its deliberations on the NLRA.

### IV

\* \* \* I would hold, as it seems to me our prior decisions compel, that the New York statute contravenes federal law. It would then be open to the elected representatives of the people in Congress to address this issue in the way that our system contemplates.

––––––––

In LYNG v. INTERNATIONAL UNION, UNITED AUTOMOBILE WORKERS, 485 U.S. 360, 108 S.Ct. 1184, 99 L.Ed.2d 380 (1988), the Supreme Court upheld against constitutional attack provisions of the federal Food Stamp Act that bar strikers and their families from participating in the food stamp program. As to possible impairment of the strikers' constitutionally protected right of association, the Court stated: "Strikers and their union would be much better off if food stamps were available, but the strikers' right of association does not require the Government to furnish funds to maximize the exercise of that right." As to possible impairment of the right of expression, the statute does not coerce employees in their expression regarding matters of importance to the union; "It merely declines to extend additional food stamp assistance to striking individuals merely because the decision to strike inevitably leads to a decline in their income."

The Court proceeded to determine whether the provisions of the statute adversely affecting strikers are "rationally related to a legitimate governmental interest." It found three valid congressional objectives: to cut federal expenditures, to use limited food-stamp funds for those most in need, and to avoid providing "one-sided support" in labor strikes. As to the latter objective, the Court quoted from the pertinent Senate Report, which stated: "Union strike funds should be responsible for providing support and benefits to strikers during labor-management disputes." The Court continued: "It was no part of the purposes of the Food Stamp Act to establish a program that would serve as a weapon in labor disputes; the Act was passed to alleviate hunger and malnutrition.... We are not authorized to ignore Congress' considered efforts to avoid favoritism in labor disputes...."

Justice Marshall dissented (joined by Justices Brennan and Blackmun). Among his observations in his extended opinion, he stated: "[T]he withdrawal of the ... support of food stamps—a support critical to the continued life and health of an individual worker and his or her family—cannot be seen as a 'neutral' act. Altering the backdrop of governmental support in this one-sided and devastating way amounts to a penalty on strikers, not neutrality."

In BAKER V. GENERAL MOTORS CORP., 478 U.S. 621, 106 S.Ct. 3129, 92 L.Ed.2d 504 (1986), the Court was confronted with the question whether a similar state statute was preempted by federal labor law. There, the state law barred unemployment compensation for employees providing "financing" for strikes that cause their unemployment. The Court held that the statute was not preempted. It concluded that states are free to decide whether or not to compensate employees who voluntarily cause their own unemployment, and that the state restriction did not impair the rights of strikers under section 7 of the Labor Act.

————

## PROBLEMS FOR DISCUSSION

**1.** Had there been no specific legislative history evincing congressional toleration of variant state unemployment-compensation policies, how would the *New York Telephone* case have been decided in the Supreme Court, and by what vote?

**2.** Assume that New York (or some other state) were to amend its unemployment compensation law to provide for the payment of benefits equal to 100 percent of strikers' wages, to commence with the first day of the strike. Would the Court conclude that this state law was valid?

**3.** The mill workers have struck International Paper's plant in Jay, Maine. The company has hired over 500 replacements and housed them in 52 mobile homes next to the plant. The Jay town council has, in turn, passed three local ordinances. The first, the Temporary Housing Ordinance, prohibits Jay property owners from constructing temporary or movable living quarters to house ten or more persons, except pursuant to Maine's Mobile Home Parks statute and Land Subdivisions statute. Property owners are granted a compliance grace period equal to one-half the time their temporary or movable housing existed prior to the passage of the ordinance. Post-grace period violations are punishable by fines of up to $2500 per day for each person housed in the temporary or movable quarters. International Paper would thus be subject to a maximum $1.2 million in fines per day.

The second ordinance, the Professional Strikebreaker Ordinance, prohibits persons and corporations from hiring or offering to hire employees who have twice before been hired for jobs ordinarily performed by striking workers. Violations are subject to injunction in civil proceedings. The third, the Environmental Protection Ordinance, requires Jay officials to take extra care to enforce existing federal, state and local environmental protection laws, and creates a special fund to finance the increased enforcement efforts. The company has proceeded in federal district court to secure a declaratory judgment that the three ordinances are void. How should the court rule? See International Paper Co. v. Inhabitants of the Town of Jay, 672 F.Supp. 29 (D.Me.1987).

---

# Belknap, Inc. v. Hale[a]

463 U.S. 491, 103 S.Ct. 3172, 77 L.Ed.2d 798 (1983).

■ JUSTICE WHITE delivered the opinion of the Court.

The federal labor relations laws recognize both economic strikes and strikes to protest unfair labor practices. Where employees have engaged in an economic strike, the employer may hire permanent replacements whom it need not discharge even if the strikers offer to return to work unconditionally. If the work stoppage is an unfair labor practice strike, the employer must discharge any replacements in order to accommodate returning strikers. In this case we must decide whether the National Labor Relations Act (NLRA or Act) pre-empts a misrepresentation and breach-of-contract action against the employer brought in state court by strike replacements who were displaced by reinstated strikers after having been offered and accepted jobs on a permanent basis and assured they would not be fired to accommodate returning strikers.

**a.** See Estreicher, Strikers and Replacements, 3 Lab.Law. 897 (1987); Finkin, Labor Policy and the Enervation of the Economic Strike, 1990 U.Ill.L.Rev. 547.

## I

Petitioner Belknap, Inc., is a corporation engaged in the sale of hardware products and certain building materials. A bargaining unit consisting of all of Belknap's warehouse and maintenance employees selected International Brotherhood of Teamsters Local No. 89 (Union) as their collective-bargaining representative. In 1975, the Union and Belknap entered into an agreement which was to expire on January 31, 1978. The two opened negotiations for a new contract shortly before the expiration of the 1975 agreement, but reached an impasse. On February 1, 1978, approximately 400 Belknap employees represented by the Union went out on strike. Belknap then granted a wage increase, effective February 1, for union employees who stayed on the job.

Shortly after the strike began, Belknap placed an advertisement in a local newspaper seeking applicants to "permanently replace striking warehouse and maintenance employees." A large number of people responded to the offer and were hired. After each replacement was hired, Belknap presented to the replacement the following statement for his signature:

> "I, the undersigned, acknowledge and agree that I as of this date have been employed by Belknap, Inc. at its Louisville, Kentucky, facility as a regular full time permanent replacement to permanently replace _____ in the job classification of _____."

On March 7, the Union filed unfair labor practice charges against petitioner Belknap. The charge was based on the unilateral wage increase granted by Belknap. Belknap countered with charges of its own. On April 4, the company distributed a letter which said, in relevant part:

> "TO ALL PERMANENT REPLACEMENT EMPLOYEES
>
> * * *
>
> "We recognize that many of you continue to be concerned about your status as an employee. The Company's position on this matter has not changed nor do we expect it to change. You will continue to be permanent replacement employees so long as you conduct yourselves in accordance with the policies and practices that are in effect here at Belknap.
>
> * * *
>
> "We continue to meet and negotiate in good faith with the Union. It is our hope and desire that a mutually acceptable agreement can be reached in the near future. However, we have made it clear to the Union that we have no intention of getting rid of the permanent replacement employees just in order to provide jobs for the replaced strikers if and when the Union calls off the strike."

On April 27, the Regional Director issued a complaint against Belknap, asserting that the unilateral increase violated §§ 8(a)(1), 8(a)(3), and 8(a)(5) of the Act. Also on April 27, the company again addressed the strike replacements:

"We want to make it perfectly clear, once again, that there will be no change in your employment status as a result of the charge by the National Labor Relations Board, which has been reported in this week's newspapers.

"We do not believe there is any substance to the charge and we feel confident we can prove in the courts satisfaction that our intent and actions are completely within the law."

A hearing on the unfair labor practice charges was scheduled for July 19. The Regional Director convened a settlement conference shortly before the hearing was to take place. He explained that if a strike settlement could be reached, he would agree to the withdrawal and dismissal of the unfair labor practice charges and complaints against both the company and the Union. During these discussions the parties made various concessions, leaving one major issue unresolved, the recall of the striking workers. The parties finally agreed that the company would, at a minimum, reinstate 35 strikers per week. The settlement agreement was then reduced to writing. Petitioner laid off the replacements, including the 12 respondents, in order to make room for the returning strikers.

Respondents sued Belknap in the Jefferson County, Ky., Circuit Court for misrepresentation and breach of contract. Belknap, they alleged, had proclaimed that it was hiring permanent employees, knowing both that the assertion was false and that respondents would detrimentally rely on it. The alternative claim was that Belknap was liable for breaching its contracts with respondents by firing them as a result of its agreement with the Union. Each respondent asked for $250,000 in compensatory damages, and an equal amount in punitive damages.

Belknap, after unsuccessfully seeking to remove the suit to federal court, moved for summary judgment, on the ground that respondents' causes of action were pre-empted by the NLRA. The trial court agreed and granted summary judgment. The Kentucky Court of Appeals reversed.
\* \* \*

We granted Belknap's petition for certiorari, 457 U.S. 1131, 102 S.Ct. 2956, 73 L.Ed.2d 1347 (1982). We affirm.
\* \* \*

### III

It is asserted that Congress intended the respective conduct of the Union and Belknap during the strike beginning on February 1 " 'to be controlled by the free play of economic forces,' " Machinists v. Wisconsin Employment Relations Comm'n, supra, at 140, 96 S.Ct., at 2553, quoting NLRB v. Nash–Finch Co., 404 U.S. 138, 144, 92 S.Ct. 373, 377, 30 L.Ed.2d 328 (1971), and that entertaining the action against Belknap was an impermissible attempt by the Kentucky courts to regulate and burden one of the employer's primary weapons during an economic strike, that is, the right to hire permanent replacements. To permit the suit filed in this case to proceed would upset the delicate balance of forces established by the federal law.  Subjecting the employer to costly suits for damages under state law for entering into settlements calling for the return of strikers would also conflict with the federal labor policy favoring the settlement of labor disputes.  These arguments, it is urged, are valid whether or not a strike is an economic strike.

We are unpersuaded.  It is true that the federal law permits, but does not require, the employer to hire replacements during a strike, replacements that it need not discharge in order to reinstate strikers if it hires the replacements on a "permanent" basis within the meaning of the federal labor law.  But when an employer attempts to exercise this very privilege by promising the replacements that they will not be discharged to make room for returning strikers, it surely does not follow that the employer's otherwise valid promises of permanent employment are nullified by federal law and its otherwise actionable misrepresentations may not be pursued. * * * It is one thing to hold that the federal law intended to leave the employer and the union free to use their economic weapons against one another, but it is quite another to hold that either the employer or the union is also free to injure innocent third parties without regard to the normal rules of law governing those relationships.  We cannot agree with the dissent that Congress intended such a lawless regime.

* * * We do not think that the normal contractual rights and other usual legal interests of the replacements can be so easily disposed of by broad-brush assertions that no legal rights may accrue to them during a strike because the federal law has privileged the "permanent" hiring of replacements and encourages settlement.

In defense of this position, Belknap, supported by the Board in an *amicus* brief, urges that permitting the state suit where employers may, after the beginning of a strike, either be ordered to reinstate strikers or find it advisable to sign agreements providing for reinstatement of strikers, will deter employers from making permanent offers of employment or at the very least force them to condition their offer by stating the circumstances under which replacements must be fired.  This would considerably weaken the employer's position during the strike, it is said, because without assuring permanent employment, it would be difficult to secure sufficient replacements to keep the business operating.  Indeed, as the Board interprets the law, the employer must reinstate strikers at the conclusion of even a purely economic strike unless it has hired "permanent" replacements, that is, hired in a manner that would "show that the men [and women] who replaced the strikers were regarded by themselves and the [employer] as having received their jobs on a permanent basis." * * *

We remain unconvinced.  If serious detriment will result to the employer from conditioning offers so as to avoid a breach of contract if the employer is forced by Board order to reinstate strikers or if the employer settles on terms requiring such reinstatement, much the same result would follow from Belknap's and the Board's construction of the Act.  Their view is that, as a matter of federal law, an employer may terminate replacements, without liability to them, in the event of settlement or Board decision that the strike is an unfair labor practice strike. Any offer of permanent employment to replacements is thus necessarily conditional and nonpermanent. This view of the law would inevitably become widely known and would deter honest employers from making promises that they know they are not legally obligated to keep. Also, many putative replacements would know that the proffered job is, in important respects, nonpermanent and may not accept employment for that reason. It is doubtful, with respect to the employer's ability to hire, that there would be a substantial difference between the effect of the Board's preferred rule and a rule that would subject the employer to damages liability unless it suitably conditions its offers of employment made to replacements.

Belknap counters that conditioning offers in such manner will render replacements nonpermanent employees subject to discharge to make way for strikers at the conclusion or settlement of a purely economic strike, which would not be the case if replacements had been hired on a "permanent" basis as the Board now understands that term. The balance of power would thus be distorted if the employer is forced to condition its offers for its own protection. * * *

An employment contract with a replacement promising permanent employment, subject only to settlement with its employees' union and to a Board unfair labor practice order directing reinstatement of strikers, would not in itself render the replacement a temporary employee subject to displacement by a striker over the employer's objection during or at the end of what is proved to be a purely economic strike. * * * [T]he protection is of great moment if the employer is not found guilty of unfair practices, does not settle with the union, or settles without a promise to reinstate. * * * Those contracts, it seems to us, create a sufficiently permanent arrangement to permit the prevailing employer to abide by his promises.

We perceive no substantial impact on the availability of settlement of economic or unfair labor practice strikes if the employer is careful to protect itself against suits like this in the course of contracting with strike replacements. Its risk of liability if it discharges replacements pursuant to a settlement or to a Board order would then be minimal. We fail to understand why in such circumstances the employer would be any less willing to settle the strike than it would be under the regime proposed by Belknap and the Board, which as a matter of law, would permit it to settle without liability for misrepresentation or for breach of contract.

Belknap and its supporters, the Board and the AFL–CIO, offer no substantial case authority for the proposition that the *Machinists* [*v. Wisconsin Employment Rel. Bd.*] rationale forecloses this suit. Surely *Machinists* did not deal with solemn promises of permanent employment, made to innocent replacements, that the employer was free to make and keep under federal law. J.I. Case, Co. v. NLRB, 321 U.S. 332, 64 S.Ct. 576, 88 L.Ed. 762 (1944), suggests that individual contracts of employment must give way to otherwise valid provisions of the collective-bargaining contract, id., at 336–339, 64 S.Ct., at 579–581 but it was careful to say that the Board "has no power to adjudicate the validity or effect of such contracts except as to their effect on matters within its jurisdiction," id., at 340, 64 S.Ct., at 581. There, the cease-and-desist order, as modified, stated that the discontinuance of the individual contracts was "without prejudice to the assertion of any legal rights the employee may have acquired under such contract or to any defenses thereto by the employer." Id., at 342, 64 S.Ct., at 582 * * *.

There is still another variant or refinement of the argument that the employer and the Union should be privileged to settle their dispute and provide for striker reinstatement free of burdensome lawsuits such as this. It is said that respondent replacements are employees within the bargaining unit, that the Union is the bargaining representative of petitioner's employees, and the replacements are thus bound by the terms of the settlement negotiated between the employer and "their" representative. The argument is not only that as a matter of federal law the employer cannot be foreclosed from discharging the replacements pursuant to a contract with a bargaining agent, but also that by virtue of the agreement with the Union it is relieved from responding in damages for its knowing breach of contract—that is, that the contracts are not only not specifically enforceable but also may be breached free from liability for damages. We need not address the former issue—the issue of specific performance—since the respondents ask only damages. As to the damages issue, as we have said above, such an argument was rejected in *J.I. Case*.

If federal law forecloses this suit, more specific and persuasive reasons than those based on *Machinists* must be identified to support any such result. Belknap insists that the rationale of the *Garmon* decision, properly construed and applied, furnishes these reasons.

### IV

The complaint issued by the Regional Director alleged that on or about February 1, Belknap unilaterally put into effect a 50per-hour wage increase, that such action constituted unfair labor practices under §§ 8(a)(1), 8(a)(3), and 8(a)(5), and that the strike was prolonged by these violations. If these allegations could have been sustained, the strike would have been an unfair labor practice strike almost from the very start. From that time forward, Belknap's advertised offers of permanent employment to replacements would arguably have been unfair labor practices since they could be viewed as threats to refuse to reinstate unfair labor practice strikers. See NLRB v. Laredo Coca Cola Bottling Co., 613 F.2d 1338, 1341 (CA5), cert. denied, 449 U.S. 889, 101 S.Ct. 246, 66 L.Ed.2d 115 (1980). Furthermore, if the strike had been an unfair labor practice strike, Belknap would have been forced to reinstate the strikers rather than keep replacements on the job. Mastro Plastics Corp. v. NLRB, 350 U.S. 270, 278, 76 S.Ct. 349, 355, 100 L.Ed. 309 (1956). Belknap submits that its offers of permanent employment to respondents were therefore arguably unfair labor practices, the adjudication of which were within the exclusive jurisdiction of the

Board, and that discharging respondents to make way for strikers was protected activity since it was no more than the federal law required in the event the unfair labor practices were proved.[12] * * *

[In *Sears, Roebuck & Co. v. Carpenters*], we emphasized that a critical inquiry in applying the *Garmon* rules, where the conduct at issue in the state litigation is said to be arguably prohibited by the Act and hence within the exclusive jurisdiction of the NLRB, is whether the controversy presented to the state court is identical with that which could be presented to the Board. There the state-court and Board controversies could not fairly be called identical. This is also the case here.

Belknap contends that the misrepresentation suit is preempted because it related to the offers and contracts for permanent employment, conduct that was part and parcel of an arguable unfair labor practice. It is true that whether the strike was an unfair labor practice strike and whether the offer to replacements was the kind of offer forbidden during such a dispute were matters for the Board. The focus of these determinations, however, would be on whether the rights of strikers were being infringed. Neither controversy would have anything in common with the question whether Belknap made misrepresentations to replacements that were actionable under state law. The Board would be concerned with the impact on strikers not with whether the employer deceived replacements. * * * [I]t appears to us that maintaining the misrepresentation action would not interfere with the Board's determination of matters within its jurisdiction and that such an action is of no more than peripheral concern to the Board and the federal law. At the same time, Kentucky surely has a substantial interest in protecting its citizens from misrepresentations that have caused them grievous harm. It is no less true here than it was in

---

**12.** The dissent makes the same ineffective argument, ineffective because it cannot explain in any convincing way why the breach, if required by federal law, should not be subject to a damages remedy. It is not easy to grasp why the employer who settles a purely economic strike (such as one in which no unfair labor practice charge is filed) and fires permanent replacements to make way for returning strikers could be made to respond in damages; yet the employer who violates the labor laws is for that reason insulated from damages liability when it discharges replacements to whom it has promised permanent employment. The dissent asserts that to subject the unfair labor practice employer to damages suits would cause intolerable confusion, but as we see it there would be no interference with the Board's authority to impose its remedy for violating the federal labor law. Performing that function neither requires nor suggests that the replacements must be deprived of their remedy for breach of contract. See supra, at 500.

Of course, here there was no adjudication of an unfair practice. The employer settled short of that possible outcome. That action was *not* required by federal law. We do not share the dissent's apparent view that federal labor policy favoring settlement privileges the employer to make and break contracts with innocent third parties at will. Nor do we understand why the threat of liability to discharged replacements, in the event the employer loses the unfair labor practice case and discharges them, would deter the employer from settling with the Board where it thinks the unfair labor practice charge will be sustained. Settling would not increase its potential liability to replacements. It may be that the employer would prefer to settle even a case that it is quite confident it could win, but that is surely no reason to deprive the replacements of their contract. Nor in such a case do the equities favor the strikers over the replacements, who would be entitled to stay unless the employer has violated the federal law.

Linn v. Plant Guard Workers, supra, at 63, 86 S.Ct., at 663, that "[t]he injury" remedied by the state law "has no relevance to the Board's function" and that "[t]he Board can award no damages, impose no penalty, or give any other relief" to the plaintiffs in this case. The state interests involved in this case clearly outweigh any possible interference with the Board's function that may result from permitting the action for misrepresentation to proceed.

* * * We have already concluded that the federal law does not expressly or impliedly privilege an employer, as part of a settlement with a union, to discharge replacements in breach of its promises of permanent employment. Also, even had there been no settlement and the Board had ordered reinstatement of what it held to be unfair labor practice strikers, the suit for damages for breach of contract could still be maintained without in any way prejudicing the jurisdiction of the Board or the interest of the federal law in insuring the replacement of strikers. The interests of the Board and the NLRA, on the one hand, and the interest of the State in providing a remedy to its citizens for breach of contract, on the other, are "discrete" concerns, cf. Farmer v. Carpenters, supra, 430 U.S., at 304, 97 S.Ct., at 1065. We see no basis for holding that permitting the contract cause of action will conflict with the rights of either the strikers or the employer or would frustrate any policy of the federal labor laws.

### V

Because neither the misrepresentation nor the breach-of-contract cause of action is pre-empted under *Garmon* or *Machinists*, the decision of the Kentucky Court of Appeals is

Affirmed.

[The concurring opinion of JUSTICE BLACKMUN is omitted.]

■ JUSTICE BRENNAN, with whom JUSTICE MARSHALL and JUSTICE POWELL join, dissenting.

* * *

Despite the conceded difficulty of this case, I cannot agree with the Court's conclusion that neither respondents' breach-of-contract claim nor their misrepresentation claim is preempted by federal law. * * * In my view these claims go to the core of federal labor policy. If respondents are allowed to pursue their claims in state court, employers will be subject to potentially conflicting state and federal regulation of their activities; the efficient administration of the National Labor Relations Act will be threatened; and the structure of the economic weapons Congress has provided to parties to a labor dispute will be altered. In short, the purposes and policies of federal law will be frustrated. I, therefore, respectfully dissent.

* * *

### II

Respondents' breach-of-contract claim is based on the allegation that petitioner breached its contracts with them by entering into a settlement agreement with the union that called for the gradual reinstatement of the strikers respondents had replaced.  See App. 3–5.  The strike involved in this case, however, arguably was converted into an unfair labor practice strike almost immediately after it started.  * * * If the strike was converted into an unfair labor practice strike, the striking employees were entitled to reinstatement irrespective of petitioner's decision to hire permanent replacements.  See NLRB v. Johnson Sheet Metal, Inc., 442 F.2d 1056, 1061 (C.A.10, 1971);  Philip Carey Mfg. Co. v. NLRB, 331 F.2d 720, 728–729 (C.A.6 1964).  See also Fleetwood Trailer Co., 389 U.S., at 379, n. 5, 88 S.Ct., at 546, n. 5;  Mastro Plastics Corp., 350 U.S., at 278, 76 S.Ct., at 355; supra, at 3192.  Under these circumstances, federal law would have required petitioner to reinstate the striking employees and to discharge the replacements.  In this light, it is clear that petitioner's decision to breach its contracts with respondents was arguably *required* by federal law.

* * * [The basic principles announced in the *Garmon* decision] compel a conclusion that respondents' breach-of-contract claim is pre-empted.  The potential for conflicting regulation clearly exists in this case.  Respondents' breach-of-contract claim seeks to regulate activity that may well have been required by federal law.  Petitioner may have to answer in damages for taking such an action.  This sort of conflicting regulation is intolerable. * * *

Prohibiting specific enforcement, but permitting a damages award, does nothing to eliminate the conflict between state and federal law in this context.  The Court fails to recognize that "regulation can be as effectively exerted through an award of damages as through some form of preventive relief."  *Garmon*, 359 U.S., at 247, 79 S.Ct., at 780.  "The obligation to pay compensation can be, indeed is designed to be, a potent method of governing conduct and controlling policy."  Ibid.  The force of these observations is apparent in this case.  If an employer is confronted with potential liability for discharging workers he has hired to replace striking employees, he is likely to be much less willing to enter into a settlement agreement calling for the dismissal of unfair labor practice charges and for the reinstatement of strikers.  Instead, he is much more likely to refuse to settle and to litigate the charges at issue while retaining the replacements.  Such developments would frustrate the strong federal interest in ending strikes and in settling labor disputes.  In addition, the National Labor Relations Board has suggested that any impediment to the settlement of unfair labor practice charges would have a serious adverse effect on the Board's administration of the Act.  Brief for NLRB as Amicus Curiae 13, n. 6.  Finally, any obstacle to strike settlement agreements clearly affects adversely the interest of striking employees in returning to work, to say nothing of the public interest in ending labor strife.  Consideration of these factors leads to the clear conclusion that respondents' breach-of-contract claim must be pre-empted.[7]

---

7.  Even assuming that such analysis is necessary, this claim clearly does not fall within the exceptions to the pre-emption doctrine described in *Garmon*.  See supra, n. 1.  The claim at issue here hardly can be said to relate to activity that is "a merely peripheral

## III

Respondents' misrepresentation claim stands on a somewhat different footing than their breach-of-contract claim. There is no sense in which it can be said that federal law required petitioner to misrepresent to respondents the terms on which they were hired. Permitting respondents to pursue their misrepresentation claim in state court, therefore, does not present the same potential for directly conflicting regulation of employer activity as permitting respondents to pursue their breach-of-contract claim. Nor can it be said that petitioner's alleged misrepresentation was "arguably protected" under *Garmon*. While it is arguable that petitioner's alleged offers of permanent employment were prohibited by the Act and therefore pre-empted under *Garmon*, see n. 1, supra, careful analysis yields the conclusion that this is not a sufficient ground for pre-empting respondents' misrepresentation claim.[8] In my view, however, respondents' misrepresentation claim is pre-empted under the analysis articulated principally in Machinists v. Wisconsin Emp. Rel. Comm'n, 427 U.S. 132, 96 S.Ct. 2548, 49 L.Ed.2d 396 (1976).

* * * [E]mployers have the right to hire replacements for striking employees. This is an economic weapon that the employer may use to combat pressure brought to bear by the union. Permitting the use of this weapon is part of the balance struck by the Act between labor and management. There is no doubt that respondents' misrepresentation claim, involving as it does the potential for substantial employer liability, burdens an employer's right to resort to this weapon. This is especially apparent when one considers the fact that the character of a strike is often unclear. * * *

In order to avoid misrepresentation claims, an employer might decide not to hire replacements on a permanent basis or to hire permanent replacements only in cases in which it is absolutely clear that the strike is an economic one. Either of these developments would mean that employers were being inhibited by state law from making full use of an economic weapon available to them under federal law. Moreover, if an employer decided not to hire replacements on a permanent basis, his ability to hire replacements might be affected adversely. An employer also might decide

concern of the ... Act." *Garmon*, 359 U.S., at 243, 79 S.Ct., at 779. Moreover, the conduct at issue here does not touch "interests so deeply rooted in local feeling and responsibility that, in the absence of compelling congressional direction, we could not infer that Congress had deprived the States of the power to act." Id., at 244, 79 S.Ct., at 779 * * *.

**8.** If this strike was converted into an unfair labor practice strike almost immediately after it started, * * *, petitioner's offers of permanent employment to replacements may have constituted additional unfair labor practices under § 8(a)(1), 29 U.S.C.

§ 158(a)(1). See NLRB v. Laredo Coca Cola Bottling Co., 613 F.2d 1338, 1341 (C.A.5 1980) * * *. Sears, Roebuck & Co. v. Carpenters, 436 U.S. 180, 98 S.Ct. 1745, 56 L.Ed.2d 209 (1978), suggests, however, that this is not a sufficient ground for pre-emption under the "arguably prohibited" branch of *Garmon*. Unfair labor practice proceedings before the Board based on this arguably prohibited conduct would not be identical to the state-court action involving respondents' misrepresentation claim. See 436 U.S., at 196–197, 98 S.Ct., at 1757.

to disclose to prospective replacements the possibility, even if it is remote, that the strike might be determined to have been an unfair labor practice strike and that he might be ordered to reinstate the strikers and to discharge the replacements. This course of action, however, might limit an employer's ability to hire replacements, and it might have the further effect of rendering the replacements temporary under federal law, in which case the strikers would be entitled to reinstatement regardless of the nature of the strike. See supra, at 526–527.

Based on this analysis, it is clear that permitting respondents to pursue their misrepresentation claim in state court would limit and substantially burden an employer's resort to an economic weapon available to him under federal law. This would have the inevitable effect of distorting the delicate balance struck by the Act between the rights of labor and management in labor disputes. For these reasons, respondents' misrepresentation claim must be pre-empted.[12]

\* \* \*

It might be a better world if strike replacements were afforded greater protection. But if accomplishing this end requires an alteration of the balance of power between labor and management or an erosion of the right to strike, this Court should not pursue it. \* \* \*

---

## PROBLEMS FOR DISCUSSION

**1.** If you were a state court judge, how would you rule, on the facts of this case, regarding the strike replacements' claim for misrepresentation? (For example, would they be able to prove that the employer had the requisite state of mind?) How would you rule on the breach-of-contract claim? (For example, should the parties be presumed to know what the law is regarding the right of unfair labor practice strikers to "bump" their replacements?) Compare Verway v. Blincoe Packing Co., 108 Idaho 315, 698 P.2d 377 (App.1985), with Bubbel v. Wien Air Alaska, Inc., 682 P.2d 374 (Alaska 1984).

**2.** The Supreme Court in *Belknap* was unanimous in its belief that the state courts could not, as a remedy for either state cause of action, order that reinstated unfair labor practice strikers must be ousted from their positions to make way for the wronged strike replacements. If that would be such a clear affront to federal labor policy, how can it be that awarding them money damages is completely consistent with such federal policy? Had the reinstated strikers at Belknap been *economic* strikers, could a state court freely order the employer to oust them to make way for the wronged strike replacements?

**3.** Is it so clear that the employer in *J.I. Case*, at page 363 supra, should be subject to breach-of-contract actions by individual employees who lose special job privileges by virtue of the later-negotiated collective bargaining agreement? Is it material

---

**12.** It is also true that the prospect of facing misrepresentation claims would make an employer less likely to enter into an agreement settling a strike for the same reasons that were discussed with respect to the breach-of-contract claim. \* \* \* This would also undermine the policies of the Act and affect adversely its administration. \* \* \*

that at the time the individual employment contracts were made, the union was not yet on the scene? *Cf.* Barbiczi v. United Tech. Corp., 771 A. 2d 915 (Conn.2001).

**4.**  Does it follow from the *Belknap* decision that the ousted strike replacements may sue the *union* in a state court, perhaps for inducement of the company's breach of contract?  Is the union's conduct arguably protected?  Arguably prohibited? With so many significant federal labor policies implicated, should a state-court action against the union be tolerated?  If you conclude that there is a convincing case for preemption of the state claim against the union, is it not untenable to sustain the application of state law in the action against the employer?

**5.**  Is the Court suggesting that, in the event of economic combat between a company and its union, the economic interests of injured third parties can always freely be regulated by state law?  If so, has the Court quietly worked a major revolution in the law of secondary boycotts?

**6.**  The National Labor Relations Board appeared amicus curiae in the *Belknap* case, arguing that the application of state law would have a significantly adverse impact on federal statutory rights of employers and strikers, as well as upon the efficient operations of the NLRB and its regional offices.  How much weight should be given by the Supreme Court to the Board and its expertise on these matters?

**7.**  Assume that a state were to enact a Striker Replacement Act that would make it an unlawful labor practice for an employer:

> To grant or offer to grant the status of permanent replacement employee to a person for performing bargaining unit work for an employer during a lockout of employees in a labor organization or during a strike of employees in a labor organization authorized by a representative of employees.

Would such a statute be enforceable, consistent with Belknap, Inc. v. Hale?  See Kapiolani Med. Center v. State, 82 F.Supp.2d 1151 (D.Hawai'i 2000), and State v. Labor Ready, Inc., 14 P.3d 828 (Wash.App.2001).

**8.**  Section 1128 of the State Labor and Employment Code provides in pertinent part:

> (a) If a party to a collective bargaining agreement prevails in a court action to compel arbitration of disputes concerning the collective bargaining agreement, the court shall award attorney's fees to the prevailing party unless the other party has raised substantial and credible issues involving complex or significant questions of law or fact regarding whether or not the dispute is arbitrable under the agreement.

> (b) If a party to a collective bargaining agreement appeals the decision of an arbitrator regarding disputes concerning the collective bargaining agreement, the court shall award attorney's fees to the prevailing appellee unless the appellant has raised substantial issues involving complex or significant questions of law.

The Company and the Union have arbitrated a dispute under their labor contract concerning the assignment of overtime. After the arbitrator denied the grievance, the Union moved to vacate the award on the ground that the arbitrator had exceeded her authority by grossly misinterpreting the contract language. The trial court denied the Union's petition and granted the Company's petition to confirm the award. The Company has now moved for attorney's fees and the Union has objected on the ground of preemption. How should the court rule? See

Warehouse Union, Local 26 v. Hugo Neu Proler Co., 65 Cal.App.4th 732, 76 Cal.Rptr.2d 814 (1998).

———

## C.   ENFORCEMENT OF COLLECTIVE AGREEMENTS[b]

ALLIS–CHALMERS CORP. V. LUECK, 471 U.S. 202, 105 S.Ct. 1904, 85 L.Ed.2d 206 (1985).   Plaintiff Lueck was an employee of the Allis–Chalmers Corporation, which had a collective bargaining agreement with Local 248 of the United Automobile Workers.   The labor contract incorporated by reference a separately negotiated group health and disability plan administered by Aetna Life & Casualty Company;  the plan provided for disability benefits even for injuries suffered away from the job.   Disputes regarding insurance coverage were to be submitted to a grievance procedure culminating in arbitration.   Lueck suffered a back injury away from the job and filed a disability claim with Aetna, which began to make periodic payments. According to Lueck, however, Allis–Chalmers frequently and in bad faith ordered Aetna to interrupt such payments and otherwise "harassed" him. Although all insurance payments were ultimately made, Lueck brought an action in the Wisconsin court against both Allis–Chalmers and Aetna, alleging bad faith and unreasonable failure to make disability payments, resulting in his economic, physical and emotional injury;  he sought both compensatory and punitive damages.

Although the lower state courts found the claim to be preempted by Section 301 of the Labor Management Relations Act, the Wisconsin Supreme Court held that Lueck's suit did not arise under the collective bargaining agreement but was rather based on the state tort law of bad faith, which was altogether different from a contract claim and was therefore not preempted either by Section 301 or by Section 8(a)(5) of the NLRA.   The United States Supreme Court framed the issue as "whether § 301 of the Labor Management Relations Act preempts a state-law tort action for bad-faith delay in making disability-benefit payments due under a collective-bargaining agreement."   The Court held that it does, and reversed the state court decision.

The Court recalled that, under its earlier decision in *Lucas Flour,* page 752 supra, claims of violation of labor-contract provisions must be determined under Section 301 by reference to federal law.   The same policies of predictable and uniform construction require that, even in suits alleging violations of non-contractual rights, "the meaning given to a contract phrase or term be subject to uniform federal interpretation.   * * * Of

---

**b.** See Note, Labor Law Preemption Under Section 301: New Rules for an Old Game, 40 Syrac.L.Rev. 1279 (1990); White, Section 301's Preemption of State Law Claims: A Model for Analysis, 41 Ala.L.Rev. 377 (1990); Stein, Preserving Unionized Employees' Individual Employment Rights: An Argument Against Section 301 Preemption, 17 Berkeley J. Emp. & Lab. L. 1 (1996); Bales, The Discord Between Collective Bargaining and Individual Employment Rights: Theoretical Origins and a Proposed Solution, 77 B.U. L. Rev. 687 (1997).

course, not every dispute concerning employment, or tangentially involving a provision of a collective-bargaining agreement, is pre-empted by § 301 or other provisions of the federal labor law. * * * In extending the pre-emptive effect of § 301 beyond suits for breach of contract, it would be inconsistent with congressional intent under that section to pre-empt state rules that proscribe conduct, or establish rights and obligations, independent of a labor contract." The Court therefore had to decide "whether the Wisconsin tort action for breach of the duty of good faith as applied here confers non-negotiable state law rights on employers or employees independent of any right established by contract, or, instead, whether evaluation of the tort claim is inextricably intertwined with consideration of the terms of the labor contract. If the state tort law purports to define the meaning of the contract relationship, that law is pre-empted."

The state court had assumed that Lueck's claim was based on state tort law independent of the labor agreement because there was no express reference in that agreement to the duty to treat the insured in good faith. But "the assumption that the labor contract creates no implied rights is not one that state law may make. Rather, it is a question of federal contract interpretation whether there was an obligation under this labor contract to provide the payments in a timely manner, and, if so, whether Allis–Chalmers' conduct breached that implied contract provision." The Court concluded that any implied duty to act in good faith, as much as the express duty to make disability payments, was based upon the labor agreement, was governed by federal law, and was subject to the contractual grievance procedure. (The parties were free, for example, contractually to negate any state tort-law obligation to handle Lueck's disability claim in a particular manner.) "Because the right asserted not only derives from the contract, but is defined by the contractual obligation of good faith, any attempt to assess liability here inevitably will involve contract interpretation. * * * Since the state tort purports to give life to these terms in a different environment, it is pre-empted."

The Court asserted a final reason for preempting this tort action by virtue of Section 301: to permit a state-court action without first exhausting the contractual grievance procedures would deprive the parties to the contract of their right under federal law to have disputes resolved through the grievance procedure and would thus affront the strong federal policy supporting arbitration of industrial disputes.

Since nearly any alleged willful breach of contract can be restated as a tort claim for breach of a good-faith obligation under a contract, the arbitrator's role in every case could be by-passed easily if § 301 is not understood to pre-empt such claims. Claims involving vacation or overtime pay, work assignment, unfair discharge—in short, the whole range of disputes traditionally resolved through arbitration—could be brought in the first instance in state court by a complaint in tort rather than in contract. A rule that permitted an individual to side-step available grievance

procedures would cause arbitration to lose most of its effectiveness
* * *.

[We do not] hold that every state-law suit asserting a right
that related in some way to a provision in a collective-bargaining
agreement, or more generally to the parties to such an agreement,
necessarily is pre-empted by § 301. The full scope of the pre-
emptive effect of federal labor-contract law remains to be fleshed
out on a case-by-case basis. We do hold that when resolution of a
state-law claim is substantially dependent upon analysis of the
terms of an agreement made between the parties in a labor
contract, that claim must either be treated as a § 301 claim * * *
or dismissed as pre-empted by federal labor-contract law. This
complaint should have been dismissed for failure to make use of
the grievance procedure established in the collective-bargaining
agreement, * * * or dismissed as pre-empted by § 301.

---

## Lingle v. Norge Div. of Magic Chef, Inc.

486 U.S. 399, 108 S.Ct. 1877, 100 L.Ed.2d 410 (1988).

■ Justice Stevens delivered the opinion of the Court.

In Illinois an employee who is discharged for filing a worker's compensation claim may recover compensatory and punitive damages from her
employer. The question presented in this case is whether an employee
covered by a collective-bargaining agreement that provides her with a
contractual remedy for discharge without just cause may enforce her state
law remedy for retaliatory discharge. The Court of Appeals held that the
application of the state tort remedy was preempted by § 301 of the Labor
Management Relations Act of 1947, 61 Stat. 156, 29 U.S.C. § 185. 823
F.2d 1031 (C.A.7 1987)(en banc). We disagree.

### I

Petitioner was employed in respondent's manufacturing plant in Herrin, Illinois. On December 5, 1984, she notified respondent that she had
been injured in the course of her employment and requested compensation
for her medical expenses pursuant to the Illinois Workers' Compensation
Act. On December 11, 1984, respondent discharged her for filing a "false
worker's compensation claim." 823 F.2d, at 1033.

The union representing petitioner promptly filed a grievance pursuant
to the collective-bargaining agreement that covered all production and
maintenance employees in the Herrin plant. The agreement protected
those employees, including petitioner, from discharge except for "proper"
or "just" cause, App. 13–14, and established a procedure for the arbitration
of grievances, id., at 10–11. The term grievance was broadly defined to
encompass "any dispute between ... the Employer and any employee,
concerning the effect, interpretation, application, claim of breach or viola-

tion of this Agreement." Id., at 10. Ultimately, an arbitrator ruled in petitioner's favor and ordered respondent to reinstate her with full back pay. See id., at 25–26.

Meanwhile, on July 9, 1985, petitioner commenced this action against respondent by filing a complaint in the Illinois Circuit Court for Williamson County, alleging that she had been discharged for exercising her rights under the Illinois worker's compensation laws. App. 2–4; see Kelsay v. Motorola, Inc., 74 Ill.2d 172, 23 Ill.Dec. 559, 384 N.E.2d 353 (1978); Midgett v. Sackett–Chicago, Inc., 105 Ill.2d 143, 85 Ill.Dec. 475, 473 N.E.2d 1280 (1984); see also Ill.Rev.Stat., ch. 48, ¶ 138.4(h) (1987). Respondent removed the case to the Federal District Court on the basis of diversity of citizenship, and then filed a motion praying that the Court either dismiss the case on preemption grounds or stay further proceedings pending the completion of the arbitration. Record, Doc. No. 7. Relying on our decision in Allis–Chalmers Corp. v. Lueck, 471 U.S. 202, 105 S.Ct. 1904, 85 L.Ed.2d 206 (1985), the District Court dismissed the complaint. It concluded that the "claim for retaliatory discharge is 'inextricably intertwined' with the collective bargaining provision prohibiting wrongful discharge or discharge without just cause" and that allowing the state-law action to proceed would undermine the arbitration procedures set forth in the parties' contract. 618 F.Supp. 1448, 1449 (S.D.Ill.1985).

The Court of Appeals agreed that the state-law claim was preempted by § 301. In an en banc opinion, over the dissent of two judges, it rejected petitioner's argument that the tort action was not "inextricably intertwined" with the collective-bargaining agreement because the disposition of a retaliatory discharge claim in Illinois does not depend upon an interpretation of the agreement; on the contrary, the Court concluded that "the same analysis of the facts" was implicated under both procedures. 823 F.2d, at 1046. It took note of, and declined to follow, contrary decisions in the Tenth, Third, and Second Circuits. We granted certiorari to resolve the conflict in the Circuits. 484 U.S. 895, 108 S.Ct. 226, 98 L.Ed.2d 185 (1987).

\* \* \*

### III

Illinois courts have recognized the tort of retaliatory discharge for filing a worker's compensation claim, Kelsay v. Motorola, Inc., 74 Ill.2d 172, 23 Ill.Dec. 559, 384 N.E.2d 353 (1978),[6] and have held that it is

---

**6.** Although the cause of action was not based on any specific statutory provision, the following section of the Illinois Workers' Compensation Act expresses the public policy underlying the common-law development:

"It shall be unlawful for any employer, insurance company or service or adjustment company to interfere with, restrain or coerce an employee in any manner whatsoever in the exercise of the rights or remedies granted to him or her by this Act or to discriminate, attempt to discriminate, or threaten to discriminate against an employee in any way because of the exercise of his or her rights granted to him or her by this Act.

"It shall be unlawful for any employer, individually or through any insurance

applicable to employees covered by union contracts, Midgett v. Sackett–Chicago, Inc., 105 Ill.2d 143, 85 Ill.Dec. 475, 473 N.E.2d 1280 (1984), cert. denied, 474 U.S. 909, 106 S.Ct. 278, 88 L.Ed.2d 243 (1985). "[T]o show retaliatory discharge, the plaintiff must set forth sufficient facts from which it can be inferred that (1) he was discharged or threatened with discharge and (2) the employer's motive in discharging or threatening to discharge him was to deter him from exercising his rights under the Act or to interfere with his exercise of those rights." Horton v. Miller Chemical Co., 776 F.2d 1351, 1356 (C.A.7 1985) (summarizing Illinois state court decisions), cert. denied, 475 U.S. 1122, 106 S.Ct. 1641, 90 L.Ed.2d 186 (1986); see Gonzalez v. Prestress Engineering Corp., 115 Ill.2d 1, 104 Ill.Dec. 751, 503 N.E.2d 308 (1986). Each of these purely factual questions pertains to the conduct of the employee and the conduct and motivation of the employer. Neither of the elements requires a court to interpret any term of a collective-bargaining agreement. To defend against a retaliatory discharge claim, an employer must show that it had a nonretaliatory reason for the discharge, cf. Loyola University of Chicago v. Illinois Human Rights Comm'n, 149 Ill.App.3d 8, 102 Ill.Dec. 746, 500 N.E.2d 639 (1986); this purely factual inquiry likewise does not turn on the meaning of any provision of a collective-bargaining agreement. Thus, the state-law remedy in this case is "independent" of the collective-bargaining agreement in the sense of "independent" that matters for § 301 pre-emption purposes: resolution of the state-law claim does not require construing the collective-bargaining agreement.[7]

The Court of Appeals seems to have relied upon a different way in which a state-law claim may be considered "independent" of a collective-bargaining agreement. The court wrote that "the just cause provision in the collective-bargaining agreement may well prohibit such retaliatory discharge," and went on to say that if the state law cause of action could go forward, "a state court would be deciding precisely the *same issue* as would an arbitrator: whether there was 'just cause' to discharge the worker." 823 F.2d, at 1046 (emphasis added). The Court concluded, "the state tort of retaliatory discharge is inextricably intertwined with the collective-

company or service or adjustment company, to discharge or threaten to discharge, or to refuse to rehire or recall to active service in a suitable capacity an employee because of the exercise of his or her rights or remedies granted him or her by this Act." Ill.Rev.Stat., ch. 48, ¶ 138.4(h)(1987).

**7.** Petitioner points to the fact that the Illinois right to be free from retaliatory discharge is nonnegotiable and applies to unionized and nonunionized workers alike. While it may be true that most state laws that are not pre-empted by § 301 will grant nonnegotiable rights that are shared by all state workers, we note that neither condition en-

sures nonpre-emption. It is conceivable that a State could create a remedy that, although nonnegotiable, nonetheless turned on the interpretation of a collective-bargaining agreement for its application. Such a remedy would be pre-empted by § 301. Similarly, if a law applied to all state workers but required, at least in certain instances, collective-bargaining agreement interpretation, the application of the law in those instances would be pre-empted. Conversely, a law could cover only unionized workers but remain unpre-empted if no collective-bargaining agreement interpretation was needed to resolve claims brought thereunder.

bargaining agreements here, because it implicates the *same analysis of the facts* as would an inquiry under the just cause provisions of the agreements." Ibid. (emphasis added).  We agree with the Court's explanation that the state-law analysis might well involve attention to the same factual considerations as the contractual determination of whether Lingle was fired for just cause.  But we disagree with the Court's conclusion that such parallelism renders the state-law analysis dependent upon the contractual analysis.  For while there may be instances in which the National Labor Relations Act pre-empts state law on the basis of the subject matter of the law in question, § 301 pre-emption merely ensures that federal law will be the basis for interpreting collective-bargaining agreements, and says nothing about the substantive rights a State may provide to workers when adjudication of those rights does not depend upon the interpretation of such agreements.[9]  In other words, even if dispute resolution pursuant to a collective-bargaining agreement, on the one hand, and state law, on the other, would require addressing precisely the same set of facts, as long as the state-law claim can be resolved without interpreting the agreement itself, the claim is "independent" of the agreement for § 301 pre-emption purposes.

## IV

The result we reach today is consistent both with the policy of fostering uniform, certain adjudication of disputes over the meaning of collective-bargaining agreements and with cases that have permitted separate fonts of substantive rights to remain unpre-empted by other federal labor-law statutes.

First, as we explained in *Lueck,* "[t]he need to preserve the effectiveness of arbitration was one of the central reasons that underlay the Court's holding in *Lucas Flour.*" 471 U.S., at 219, 105 S.Ct., at 1915.  "A rule that permitted an individual to sidestep available grievance procedures would cause arbitration to lose most of its effectiveness, . . . as well as eviscerate a central tenet of federal labor contract law under § 301 that it is the arbitrator, not the court, who has the responsibility to interpret the labor contract in the first instance."  Id., at 220, 105 S.Ct., at 1916.  See Paperworkers v. Misco, Inc., 484 U.S. 29, 108 S.Ct. 364, 98 L.Ed.2d 286 (1987); Steelworkers v. Enterprise Wheel & Car Corp., 363 U.S. 593, 80 S.Ct. 1358, 4 L.Ed.2d 1424 (1960).  Today's decision should make clear that

---

**9.** Whether a union may *waive* its members' individual, nonpre-empted state-law rights, is, likewise, a question distinct from that of whether a claim is pre-empted under § 301, and is another issue we need not resolve today.  We note that under Illinois law, the parties to a collective-bargaining agreement may not waive the prohibition against retaliatory discharge nor may they alter a worker's rights under the state worker's compensation scheme.  Byrd v. Aetna Casualty & Surety Co., 152 Ill.App.3d 292, 298, 105 Ill.Dec. 347, 352, 504 N.E.2d 216, 221, app. denied, 115 Ill.2d 539, 110 Ill.Dec. 454, 511 N.E.2d 426 (1987).  Before deciding whether such a state law bar to waiver could be pre-empted under federal law by the parties to a collective-bargaining agreement, we would require "clear and unmistakable" evidence, see Metropolitan Edison Co. v. NLRB, 460 U.S. 693, 708, 103 S.Ct. 1467, 1477, 75 L.Ed.2d 387 (1983), in order to conclude that such a waiver had been intended.  No such evidence is available in this case.

interpretation of collective-bargaining agreements remains firmly in the arbitral realm; judges can determine questions of state law involving labor-management relations only if such questions do not require construing collective-bargaining agreements.

Second, there is nothing novel about recognizing that substantive rights in the labor relations context can exist without interpreting collective-bargaining agreements.

> "This Court has, on numerous occasions, declined to hold that individual employees are, because of the availability of arbitration, barred from bringing claims under federal statutes. See, *e.g.,* McDonald v. West Branch, 466 U.S. 284 [104 S.Ct. 1799, 80 L.Ed.2d 302] (1984); Barrentine v. Arkansas–Best Freight System, Inc., 450 U.S. 728 [101 S.Ct. 1437, 67 L.Ed.2d 641] (1981); Alexander v. Gardner–Denver Co., 415 U.S. 36 [94 S.Ct. 1011, 39 L.Ed.2d 147] (1974). Although the analysis of the question under each statute is quite distinct, the theory running through these cases is that notwithstanding the strong policies encouraging arbitration, 'different considerations apply *where the employee's claim is based on rights arising out of a statute designed to provide minimum substantive guarantees to individual workers.' Barrentine,* supra, 450 U.S., at 737 [101 S.Ct. at 1443]." Atchison, T. & S.F.R. Co. v. Buell, 480 U.S. 557, 564, 107 S.Ct. 1410, 1415, 94 L.Ed.2d 563 (1987)(emphasis added).

Although our comments in *Buell,* construing the scope of Railway Labor Act pre-emption, referred to independent *federal* statutory rights, we subsequently rejected a claim that federal labor law pre-empted a *state* statute providing a one-time severance benefit to employees in the event of a plant closing. In Fort Halifax Packing Co. v. Coyne, 482 U.S. 1, ___, 107 S.Ct. 2211, ___, 96 L.Ed.2d 1 (1987), we emphasized that "pre-emption should not be lightly inferred in this area, since the establishment of labor standards falls within the traditional police power of the State." We specifically held that the Maine law in question was not pre-empted by the NLRA, "since its establishment of a minimum labor standard does not impermissibly intrude upon the collective-bargaining process." Id., at ___, 107 S.Ct., at 2215.

The Court of Appeals "recognize[d] that § 301 does not pre-empt state anti-discrimination laws, even though a suit under these laws, like a suit alleging retaliatory discharge, requires a state court to determine whether just cause existed to justify the discharge." 823 F.2d, at 1046, n. 17. The court distinguished those laws because Congress has affirmatively endorsed state antidiscrimination remedies in Title VII of the Civil Rights Act of 1964, 78 Stat. 241, see 42 U.S.C. §§ 2000e–5(c) and 2000e–7, whereas there is no such explicit endorsement of state worker's compensation laws. As should be plain from our discussion in Part III, supra, this distinction is unnecessary for determining whether § 301 preempts the state law in question. The operation of the anti-discrimination laws does, however, illustrate the relevant point for § 301 pre-emption analysis that the mere fact that a broad contractual protection against discriminatory—or retaliatory—discharge may provide a remedy for conduct that coincidentally violates state law does not make the existence or the contours of the state law violation dependent upon the terms of the private contract.  For even if an arbitrator should conclude that the contract does not prohibit a particular discriminatory or retaliatory discharge, that conclusion might or might not be consistent with a proper interpretation of state law.  In the typical case a state tribunal could resolve either a discriminatory or retaliatory discharge claim without interpreting the "just cause" language of a collective-bargaining agreement.

## V

In sum, we hold that an application of state law is pre-empted by § 301 of the Labor Management Relations Act of 1947 only if such application requires the interpretation of a collective-bargaining agreement.[12]

The judgment of the Court of Appeals is reversed.

―――――

In LIVADAS v. BRADSHAW, 512 U.S. 107, 114 S.Ct. 2068, 129 L.Ed.2d 93 (1994), the United States Supreme Court confronted the policy of the California Commissioner of Labor to differentiate between non-unionized and unionized workers in the enforcement of the State's wage payment law.  The law requires the prompt payment of all wages due an employee upon discharge, subject to enforcement by the Commissioner.  The Commissioner, however, adopted a policy declining to seek enforcement of any wage claim "concerning the interpretation or application of any collective bargaining agreement containing an arbitration clause."  Justice Souter, writing for a unanimous Court, held that policy to be preempted.  The Court considered two separate lines of argument.

First, it was argued that the policy was compelled by preemption doctrine.  The Court rejected this as resting upon a misunderstanding of *Lueck* and *Lingle*.  In those cases the Court had "stressed that it is the legal character of a claim, as 'independent' of rights under the collective-bargaining agreement ... and not whether a grievance arising from precisely the same set of facts could be pursued ... that decides whether a state cause of action may go forward."  The Court made clear that "when

---

**12.** A collective-bargaining agreement may, of course, contain information such as rate of pay and other economic benefits that might be helpful in determining the damages to which a worker prevailing in a state law suit is entitled.  See Baldracchi v. Pratt & Whitney Aircraft Div., United Technologies Corp., 814 F.2d 102, 106 (C.A.2 1987).  Although federal law would govern the interpretation of the agreement to determine the proper damages, the underlying state law claim, not otherwise pre-empted, would stand.  Thus, as a general proposition, a state law claim may depend for its resolution upon both the interpretation of a collective-bargaining agreement and a separate state law analysis that does not turn on the agreement.  In such a case, federal law would govern the interpretation of the agreement, but the separate state law analysis would not be thereby pre-empted.  As we said in Allis–Chalmers Corp. v. Lueck, 471 U.S., at 211, 105 S.Ct., at 1911, "not every dispute ... tangentially involving a provision of a collective-bargaining agreement is pre-empted by § 301...."

the meaning of contract terms is not the subject of dispute, the bare fact that a collective-bargaining agreement will be consulted in the course of state-law litigation plainly does not require the claim to be extinguished." The issue in the statutory claim was of prompt payment, the primary text for which decision was the calendar not the collective agreement. The mere need to "look to" the collective agreement for the damage computation does not preempt the claim.

Second, it was also argued that the "hands off" policy was justified either: (1) to husband enforcement resources to those more in need of them—the non-unionized who lacked the institutional presence of a union and an available grievance-arbitration system; or, (2) to encourage collective bargaining and arbitral processes favored by federal law. The former would penalize workers who chose union representation by denying them the protection given to the non-unionized. Of the latter, the Court observed that the law's favorableness toward collective bargaining is scarcely fostered by requiring employees to bargain for what they are otherwise entitled to under state law.

———

## PROBLEMS FOR DISCUSSION

**1.** Several states have adopted "whistleblower" laws—laws that protect an employee's right to complain within the corporate hierarchy or to some public body; they provide the employee a remedy for discharge or discipline imposed in violation of the law. New York protects an employee's complaint of a violation of law that "presents a substantial and specific danger to the public health and safety." New York Labor Law § 740(2). It provides, however, that the institution of an action under the law "shall be deemed a waiver of the rights and remedies available under any ... collective bargaining agreement...." Id. § 740(7). Is this provision operative?

**2.** Sally Watt was employed as an electrical apprentice by the Power and Light Company. The Electrical Workers Union is the bargaining representative for the company's employees. It has a collective bargaining agreement that among other things provides for a joint safety committee and provides for the employer strictly to enforce safety rules. The union also has a "side agreement" with the company governing the assignment of electrical apprentices. The company assigned Sally to a job that, she alleges, required her to perform tasks beyond her competence and resulted in her being injured. She has sued the union in state court for negligence, in failing to provide her with necessary training, in failing to enforce safety rules, and in exposing her to a dangerous work environment. Is her suit preempted by § 301? See IBEW v. Heckler, 481 U.S. 851, 107 S.Ct. 2161, 95 L.Ed.2d 791 (1987).

**3.** In 1985, Peter Petzel was hired as a production worker by Continental Container at its San Leandro, California facility. The company has had a long-standing bargaining relationship with the Container Workers Union. In 1990 Petzel was promoted out of the bargaining unit into a managerial job. Because Petzel was fearful of losing job security as a unit member, management repeatedly assured him that if the San Leandro facility closed, he would be given a salaried position at another of the company's facilities. In 2001, due to an economic downturn, Petzel was downgraded from a salaried to an hourly position and so returned to the bargaining unit. He was told that the demotion was temporary. The following year the company closed the San Leandro facility and Petzel was placed on permanent layoff. May he sue the company in state court for its refusal to transfer him to another salaried position? See Caterpillar Inc. v. Williams, 482 U.S. 386, 107 S.Ct. 2425, 96 L.Ed.2d 318 (1987); McCarty v. Reynolds Metals Co., 883 F.Supp. 356 (S.D.Ind.1995); cf. Trans Penn Wax Corp. v. McCandless, 50 F.3d 217 (3d Cir.1995).

**4.** A group of employees discover a hidden video camera directed to observe the employees' restroom. They have sued the employer for invasion of privacy and the infliction of emotional distress. The employer has moved to dismiss on the grounds of section 301 preemption. How should the court rule? Assume that the collective agreement has no provision dealing with video surveillance, but it does have a broad management rights clause. Should it make a difference whether or not such an installation is criminally actionable? See Cramer v. Consolidated Freightways, Inc., 209 F.3d 1122 (9th Cir.2000), reh'g en banc granted 2001 WL 668923 (9th Cir.2001). If preemption applies, is the state cause of action totally extinguished? See Brazinski v. Amoco Petroleum Additives Co., 6 F.3d 1176 (7th Cir.1993).

**5.** Jack Spratt has been discharged by the Winona Trucking Company. He filed a grievance with the union representing Winona's drivers alleging discharge without just cause. He filed a charge of unfair labor practice with the Regional Director of the NLRB alleging discharge "because of his union and concerted activities" in protesting the assignment of unsafe trucks. And he has filed a lawsuit alleging a violation of state law forbidding retaliation against employees who make safety complaints. The joint union-management grievance committee established under the collective agreement has upheld the discharge as for just cause, for failure to complete an alcohol rehabilitation program. The NLRB's regional director has declined to issue a complaint on grounds of insufficient evidence. And the Company has moved to dismiss the lawsuit on preemption grounds. How should the court rule? Compare Platt v. Jack Cooper Transport Co., Inc., 959 F.2d 91 (8th Cir.1992), with Maher v. New Jersey Transit Rail Operations, Inc., 125 N.J. 455, 593 A.2d 750 (1991).

**6.** Under the State's Mechanics Lien law, employees "are entitled to have and hold a first and prior lien," on (1) the employer's property and (2) on the earnings of the corporation, for wages. Wages are defined to include inter alia pay for accrued vacations. This lien is given first priority vis-a-vis other creditors.

The collective bargaining agreement between Old Sawmill Furniture and the Woodworkers Union provides for vacation time to accrue depending on years of service with the company. A petition for involuntary bankruptcy was filed against Old Sawmill by Bank Ten, its primary secured creditor. The employees of Old Sawmill have filed liens under state law for all wages due, including accrued vacation pay, and have filed a petition in bankruptcy court for first priority under their lien to wages and vacation pay naming Bank Ten and Old Sawmill as defendants. The defendants have moved to dismiss on grounds of § 301 preemption. Assume the collective agreement has a grievance-arbitration procedure set forth as the contractually "sole and exclusive" means whereby any claim to wages or benefits may be made. Assume further that the company contests the eligibility of some employees to vacation pay and the amounts due. How should the court rule? Dismiss the case as one for a claim to wages and benefits which can be heard only through the grievance arbitration procedure? What if there is no dispute about the sum due because (a) the parties agree or (b) because it has already been arbitrated? In re Bentz Metal Prods. Co., ___ F.3d ___, 2001 WL 624863 (7th Cir. 2001) (*en banc*).

---

## *The retaliatory lawsuit*

If a person brings an action grounded in a non-preempted state-law theory, for the purpose of retaliating against the defendant for exercising rights protected under the Labor Act, may the lawsuit itself be found to be an unfair labor practice and enjoined?   That question was presented to the Supreme Court in Bill Johnson's Restaurants, Inc. v. NLRB, 461 U.S. 731, 103 S.Ct. 2161, 76 L.Ed.2d 277 (1983).

There, one Helton, a waitress in a restaurant, filed unfair labor practice charges alleging that she had been fired because of her efforts to organize a union.   When Helton and others began to picket and leaflet at the restaurant, her employer instituted an action in an Arizona state court for damages and an injunction, alleging that the defendants had harassed customers, blocked access to the restaurant, created a threat to public safety, and libeled the restaurant owners.   Helton promptly filed a second unfair labor practice charge with the NLRB, claiming that her employer's lawsuit was in retaliation for her initial NLRB charges and her protected concerted activities, such that the lawsuit violated Sections 8(a)(1) and (4) of the Labor Act.   The Administrative Law Judge examined into the merits of the state-court action and, finding it to lack "reasonable basis," concluded that it must have been intended as retaliation and that it violated the Labor Act;  the NLRB agreed.   The prevailing NLRB doctrine had been set forth in Power Systems, Inc., 239 NLRB 445 (1978), in which it held that it was an unfair labor practice to sue with a retaliatory motive;  it was not significant whether the lawsuit was baseless or was meritorious.

The Supreme Court acknowledged that a vindictive lawsuit could readily chill employees' exercise of rights under the Labor Act, but it also acknowledged that the right of access to a court is an aspect of the First Amendment right to petition government for redress of grievances and that states do have significant local interests in the maintenance of domestic peace.   The Court therefore concluded that "the filing and prosecution of a *well-founded* lawsuit may not be enjoined as an unfair labor practice, even if it would not have been commenced but for the plaintiff's desire to retaliate against the defendant for exercising rights protected by the Act" (emphasis added);  but that it is an unfair labor practice, which the NLRB may order to be stopped, to prosecute a *baseless* lawsuit with such retaliatory intent.   "[A]lthough it is an unfair labor practice to prosecute an unmeritorious lawsuit for a retaliatory purpose, the offense is not enjoinable unless the suit lacks a reasonable basis."

The Court concluded that if the ALJ was confronted in the unfair labor practice proceeding with "a genuine issue of material fact that turns on the credibility of witnesses or on the proper inferences to be drawn from undisputed facts," it would be improper for the Board to enjoin the state lawsuit; the unfair labor practice proceeding should be stayed until the state suit has been concluded. The same result should follow if the ALJ determines that there are genuinely disputed legal questions under the state law. "[I]f the state plaintiff can show that such genuine material factual or legal issues exist, the Board must await the results of the state-court adjudication with respect to the merits of the state suit. If the state proceedings result in a judgment adverse to the plaintiff, the Board may then consider the matter further and, if it is found that the lawsuit was filed with retaliatory intent, the Board may find a violation and order appropriate relief." Such appropriate relief could include reimbursement of the wrongfully sued employees for their attorneys' fees and other expenses.

------

## PROBLEM FOR DISCUSSION

The Union has been locked in an intense conflict with a nursing home chain. It has handbilled the facilities alleging unsafe and unhealthful conditions for the residents, *e.g.*,

> One of the most dangerous problems we have is that the hot water in the kitchen and laundry is not hot enough to sterilize and sanitize the dishes, linens and clothes. The water is not warm enough to give the residents a hot bath or shower.

The Union has also run radio spots alleging that hundreds of unfair labor practices have been filed against the Company which has attempted to "gag" workers and has refused to acknowledge "worker concerns about improving staffing and patient care." The Company has sued the Union in state court for defamation. The Union has filed a charge of violation of § 8(a)(1) flowing from the lawsuit. Should the Board require the Company to stay its lawsuit? Beverly Health and Rehabilitation Services, 331 N.L.R.B. No. 121 (2000).

------

*STATE REGULATION OF UNIONIZATION BY SUPERVISORS*

Section 2(3) of the National Labor Relations Act excludes from the coverage of the Act "any individual employed as a supervisor," a term which is defined in Section 2(11). At the same time as supervisors were excluded, Congress in 1947 provided, in Section 14(a), that "Nothing herein shall prohibit any individual employed as a supervisor from becoming or remaining a member of a labor organization, but no employer subject to this Act shall be com lled to deem individuals defined herein as supervisors as employees fo the purpose of any law, either national or local, relating to collective bargaining." The implications of these sections for the continued vitality of state law governing unionization and collective bargaining by supervisors have been considered by the Supreme Court in several cases.

In Marine Engineers Beneficial Ass'n v. Interlake S.S. Co., 370 U.S. 173, 82 S.Ct. 1237, 8 L.Ed.2d 418 (1962), the union (MEBA) had picketed one of Interlake's ships, causing longshore employees of another company to refuse to unload the vessel. The picketing was enjoined by a state court, in spite of claims of NLRA preemption, on the ground that MEBA represented "supervisors" and hence was not a "labor organization" subject to the Act at all. On certiorari, the Supreme Court reversed. There was some question whether MEBA was clearly outside the latter statutory definition, since it to some extent represented employees as well; in fact, the NLRB had already ruled in other cases (one arising under Section 8(b) and the other a representation election proceeding) that MEBA was a "labor organization." The Court held that the task of deciding what is a "labor organization" requires the same expertise that the NLRB must bring to bear in deciding the applicability of Sections 7 and 8 of the Act. Hence, the courts must defer to the Board whenever a reasonably arguable case can be made that a union is a "labor organization" within the meaning of the Act. See also International Longshoremen's Ass'n v. Davis, 476 U.S. 380, 106 S.Ct. 1904, 90 L.Ed.2d 389 (1986)(union claiming that individual is not a "supervisor" must present "at least an arguable case" and cannot merely rely on the fact that the NLRB has not determined his status).

Preemption problems continue, however, even after there has been a definitive determination that particular workers are "supervisors" outside of the coverage of the NLRA, as is the union in which they seek to organize.

In Hanna Mining Co. v. District 2, Marine Engineers Beneficial Ass'n, 382 U.S. 181, 86 S.Ct. 327, 15 L.Ed.2d 254 (1965), Hanna operated a fleet of vessels and was involved in a dispute with a union (MEBA) seeking to continue its representation of licensed marine engineers. The NLRB dismissed MEBA's election petition, as well as Hanna's charges of unlawful picketing by the union, on the ground that the engineers were "supervisors" excluded from the coverage of the NLRA by virtue of Section 2(11). Hanna thereupon sought to enjoin the picketing in a Wisconsin state court, claiming that the picketing had the improper objective of forcing MEBA's representation on unwilling engineers. The state court action was dismissed for lack of jurisdiction, but the Supreme Court reversed and remanded.

Because of the statutory exclusion of supervisors, the Court concluded that "activity designed to secure organization or recognition of supervisors cannot be protected by § 7 of the Act, arguably or otherwise," and that picketing to compel representation of supervisors is not prohibited by Section 8(b). Therefore, the *Garmon* decision would not require preemption of state regulation. But "the question arises whether Congress nonetheless desired that in their peaceful facets these efforts remain free from state regulation as well as Board authority." MEBA argued that the 1947 exclusion of supervisors from the NLRA, and the concurrent enactment of Section 14(a) disclaiming congressional intent to prohibit union membership by supervisors, signified "a federal policy of *laissez-faire* toward supervisors ousting state as well as Board authority, and more particularly, that to allow the Wisconsin injunction would obliterate the opportunity for supervisor unions that Congress expressly reserved." The Supreme Court rejected this argument, and held that Wisconsin courts had the jurisdiction to enjoin the MEBA picketing.

"This broad argument fails utterly in light of the legislative history, for the Committee reports reveal that Congress' propelling intention was to relieve employers from any compulsion under the Act and under state law to countenance or bargain with any union of supervisory employees. Whether the legislators fully realized that their method of achieving this result incidentally freed supervisors' unions from certain limitations under the newly enacted § 8(b) is not wholly clear, but certainly Congress made no considered decision generally to exclude state limitations on supervisory organizing. As to the portion of § 14(a) quoted above, some legislative history suggests that it was not meant to immunize any conduct at all but only to make it 'clear that the amendments to the act do not prohibit supervisors from joining unions * * *.' S.Rep. No. 105, 80th Cong., 1st Sess., p. 28; H.R.Conf.Rep. No. 510, 80th Cong., 1st Sess., p. 60 ('[T]he first part of this provision [§ 14(a)] was included presumably out of an abundance of caution.'). However, even assuming that § 14(a) also itself intended to make it clear that state law could not prohibit supervisors from joining unions, the section would have no application to the present facts; for picketing by a minority union to extract recognition by force of such pressures is decidedly not a *sine qua non* of collective bargaining, as indeed its limitation by § 8(b)(7) in nonsupervisor situations attests."

In a converse situation—in which supervisors seeking to unionize commenced a state-court action against employer resort to self-help measures (there, discharge of the supervisors)—the Supreme Court held that state remedies *were* barred, by inference from federal law. Despite the surface inconsistency with *Hanna Mining*, the outcome and reasoning of the Court in BEASLEY v. FOOD FAIR OF NORTH CAROLINA, INC., 416 U.S. 653, 94 S.Ct. 2023, 40 L.Ed.2d 443 (1974), are in reality quite consistent with the earlier case.

In *Beasley*, the plaintiffs (petitioners for certiorari) were managers of meat departments in Food Fair supermarkets in the Winston–Salem, North Carolina area. Shortly after the Meat Cutters union won a representation election among the meat department employees, and the petitioners had joined the union, Food Fair discharged them, allegedly for their union membership. The union filed unfair labor practice charges with the NLRB, but the Regional Director and the General Counsel refused to issue a complaint, stating that the petitioners were "supervisors" excluded from the protection of the NLRA. Petitioners then brought an action against Food Fair for damages for violation of North Carolina's right-to-work law, which provides: "No person shall be required by an employer to abstain or refrain from membership in any labor union or labor organization as a condition of employment or continuation of employment." The North

Carolina Supreme Court affirmed a summary judgment for Food Fair, concluding that Section 14(a) of the Labor Act ("no employer * * * shall be compelled to deem individuals defined herein as supervisors as employees for the purpose of any law, either national or local, relating to collective bargaining") prohibited the supervisors' enforcement of the North Carolina Law. The Supreme Court affirmed.

The Court, finding that the Labor Act provided no protection for supervisors against discharge because of union membership, formulated the question before it as whether Congress "should be taken as having also precluded North Carolina from affording petitioners its state damages remedy for such discharges." The Court found Section 14(a) to accord the employer freedom—under federal and state law—to decline to deal with unionized supervisors. That Section, along with the exclusion of supervisors effected through the 1947 amendments of Sections 2(3) and 2(11), rested on Congress's belief that supervisors were "management obliged to be loyal to their employer's interests" whose loyalty might be impaired by unionization (especially when in the same unit or union with rank-and-file employees). Congress intended to free the employer from the "perceived imbalance in labor-management relationships" that came when supervisors served "two masters with opposed interests." The Court concluded that the North Carolina right-to-work law would improperly pressure Food Fair to treat the petitioner-managers as employees, and endorsed the position of the North Carolina Supreme Court: "To permit a state law to deprive an employer of his right to discharge his supervisor for membership in a union would completely frustrate the congressional determination to leave this weapon of self-help to the employer."

---

## PROBLEMS FOR DISCUSSION

**1.** In light of the Court's analysis in the *Wisconsin Employment Relations Commission* case, page 958, supra, do you think that the Court would today justify its decision in *Hanna* in somewhat different terms? Does the *Wisconsin* case provide a principle regarding the allowable role of State law that would embrace both *Hanna* and *Beasley*?

**2.** Frank Foreman, a supervisor for Railcar Repair Services in Daggett, California, has been discharged. He has sued his former employer in state court for the tort of discharge for a reason violative of public policy, alleging that he was discharged: (1) for complaining about the employer's failure to adhere to occupational health and safety standards and for his refusal to cooperate in actions violative of state occupational safety and health law; and (2) his refusal of company orders to make up false reasons for the discharge of probationary employees to prevent them from joining the Steelworkers' Union, with which the company has a collective bargaining agreement. The company has moved for summary judgment on the ground of federal preemption. How should the court rule? See Balog v. LRJV, Inc., 204 Cal.App.3d 1295, 250 Cal.Rptr. 766 (1988).

# PART NINE

# RECONSIDERING THE LABOR ACT IN THE CONTEMPORARY CONTEXT

It has been estimated that union density (the percentage of the civilian, non-agricultural labor force that is unionized) at the time the Labor Act became law in 1935 stood at about 12%. That rose to a high of over 35% in the mid–1950s, under perhaps unique economic conditions both globally and domestically, but it has declined continuously ever since. Currently, private sector union density stands at under 10%.

Consequently, a question presented by the decline in union density is the contemporary relevance of the Labor Act—whether the changes that have occurred over the past half century, singularly or cumulatively, should cause a rethinking of the basic propositions upon which the Act rests: (1) that collectivization in the employment relationship is necessary to redress an imbalance in bargaining power between corporate employers and individual employees; (2) that collectivization will conduce toward greater industrial stability and labor peace; (3) that collectivization will work a needed increase in purchasing power and so benefit the economy; (4) that the participation of employees by way of an organization of "their own choosing" in the determination of wages, hours, and working conditions is essential to the achievement of "industrial democracy" as a good in itself; and, (5) that the better realization of democracy in the larger body politic requires the active participation of workers, and that there is accordingly an intimate connection between the realization of industrial democracy and the better realization of political democracy.

Before addressing the economic, demographic and social changes that have occurred since the Labor Act was passed and that might contribute to union decline, the strength of these assumptions should be tested. A leading study by the economists Richard Freeman and James Medoff, What

Do Unions Do? (1984), drew a number of conclusions, some of the more salient for purposes here being:

1.  On the wage side, unions have a substantial monopoly wage impact, but there is no single union/nonunion wage differential. The union wage effect is greater for less educated than more educated workers, for younger than for prime-age workers, and for junior than for senior workers, and it is greater in heavily organized industries and in regulated industries than in others. It increased in the 1970s as unionized workers won wage gains exceeding those of their nonunion peers. Most importantly, the social costs of the monopoly wage gains of unionism appear to be relatively modest, on the order of .3 percent of gross national product, or less.

2.  In addition to raising wages, unions alter the entire package of compensation, substantially increasing the proportion of compensation allotted to fringe benefits, particularly to deferred benefits such as pensions and life, accident and health insurance, which are favored by older workers. These changes are, on balance, to be viewed as a social plus.

3.  The claim that unions increase wage inequality is not true. It is true that unions raise the wages of organized blue-collar workers relative to the wages of unorganized blue-collar workers, and thus increase that aspect of inequality. But they also raise blue-collar earnings relative to the higher white-collar earnings, thus reducing inequality between those groups. Moreover, by adopting pay policies that limit managerial discretion in wage-setting, they reduce inequality among workers in the same establishments and among different establishments. Quantitatively, the inequality-reducing effects of unionism outweigh the inequality-increasing effects, so that on balance unions are a force for equality in the distribution of wages among individual workers.

4.  By providing workers with a voice in determining rules and conditions of work, by instituting grievance and arbitration procedures for appealing supervisors' decisions, and by negotiating seniority clauses desired by workers, unionism greatly reduces the probability that workers will quit their jobs. As a result, unionized workforces are more stable than nonunion workforces paid the same compensation.

5.  Unionism alters the way in which firms respond to swings in the economy. In cyclical downturns, unionized firms make more use of temporary layoffs and less use of cuts in wage growth than do nonunion firms, while in cyclical upturns, unionized firms recall relatively more workers and nonunion firms tend to hire new employees. In a decline that threatens the jobs of senior employees, unions negotiate wage and work-rule concessions of substantial magnitudes.

6.   Union workplaces operate under rules that are both different from and more explicit than nonunion workplaces. Seniority is more important in union settings, with unionized senior workers obtaining relatively greater protection against job loss and relatively greater chance of promotion than nonunion senior workers. In addition, management in union companies generally operates more "by the book," with less subjectivity and also less flexibility, than does management in nonunion companies, and in more professional, less paternalistic or authoritarian ways.

7.   Some nonunion workers, namely those in large nonunion firms that are trying to avoid unions through "positive labor relations," obtain higher wages and better working conditions as a result of the existence of trade unions. The average employed nonunion blue-collar worker may enjoy a slight increase in well-being because the threat of unionism forces his or her firm to offer better wages and work conditions, but the average white-collar worker appears essentially unaffected by the existence of blue-collar unionization. Some workers, however, may suffer from greater joblessness as a result of higher union wages in their city or their industry.

8.   Paradoxically, while unionized workers are less willing to leave their employers than nonunion workers, unionized workers often report themselves less satisfied with their jobs than nonunion workers. Unionists are especially dissatisfied with their work conditions and their relations with supervisors. One explanation is that unions galvanize worker discontent in order to make a strong case in negotiations with management. To be effective, voice must be heard.

9.   The view of unions as a major deterrent to productivity is erroneous. In many sectors, unionized establishments are more productive than nonunion establishments, while in only a few are they less productive. The higher productivity is due in part to the lower rate of turnover under unionism, improved managerial performance in response to the union challenge, and generally cooperative labor-management relations at the plant level. When labor-management relations are bad, so too is productivity in organized plants.

10.   Unionized employers tend to earn a lower rate of return per dollar of capital than do nonunion employers. The return is lower under unionism because the increase in wages and the greater amount of capital used per worker are not compensated for by the higher productivity of labor associated with unionism. The reduction in profitability, however, is centered in highly concentrated and otherwise historically highly profitable sectors of the economy.

11.   Unions have had mixed success in the political arena. Legislators representing highly unionized districts or receiving

considerable union campaign support tend to support unions' political goals in the Congress, but legislators representing less unionized districts or receiving more support from business and other interest groups often oppose union political goals. In the important area of major labor legislation, bills opposed by unions have been enacted while bills favored by unions have been voted down. In general unions have managed to *preserve* laws augmenting monopoly powers in specific sectors but have not been able to use the law to *expand* their monopoly power. Most union political successes have come in the areas of general labor and social goals that benefit workers as a whole rather than unionists alone.

In sum, the evidence seems to bear out some of the aspirations the drafters had for the Act, if only partially and not without some negative externalities: Greater purchasing power, lessened levels of wage inequality, more "voice" and fairness in treatment, greater productivity, and greater political influence, albeit on issues of larger social significance rather than of parochial union self-interest. These, however, at the cost of lower corporate profitability (or shareholder value), possibly a higher rate of inflation, but certainly less managerial flexibility—the latter especially concerning management's ability to react to changing economic conditions. Some of these are explored below.

## I.  THE CHANGING CONTEXT

### A.  ECONOMIC

A persistent refrain in the current reassessment of the role of unions is the "globalization" of the economy. This has had several consequences for the effectiveness of the Labor Act in terms of its policy goals. First, to the extent that wages comprise a significant component of the cost of production and a lower wage advantage is not off-set by higher insurance and transportation costs and poorer work quality, manufacturing (and some services) can relocate from higher wage countries to lower wage ones or, to use the European formulation, can engage in "social dumping." Managements have been quick to argue the futility of unionization to their workforces and to advert, lawfully or otherwise, to the prospect of plant relocation to the third world, as a powerful argument against unionization.

Second, economic "globalization" undercuts the Keynesian rationale that was one underpinning of the Labor Act. Increased wages may well be spent upon the consumption of imported as much as domestically produced goods.

Third, is a related shift in public attitude.

Whereas traditional wage bargaining and generous social welfare benefits once were regarded as public goods, they are viewed now as a drag on national efficiency, and not only by conservative economists. The alternative supposedly is to make welfare benefits more "realistic" and to tie compensation more closely to enterprise conditions; these trends are ongoing throughout the OECD (Organization for Economic Cooperation and Development) nations.

Sanford Jacoby, *Social Dimensions of Global Economic Integration*, *in* THE WORKERS OF NATIONS: INDUSTRIAL RELATIONS IN A GLOBAL ECONOMY 3 (Sanford Jacoby ed., 1995) (references omitted).

## B.   DEMOGRAPHIC

The occupational distribution of jobs in the workforce has undergone enormous change. There has been a major shift away from the production of goods to the performance of services and, consequently, an occupational redistribution. This is significant because earnings vary significantly by sector and the resulting shift has contributed to the well-documented widening gap in income inequality set out below.

Hourly wages for all workers by wage percentile, 1973–99 (1999 dollars)

| Year | Percentile | | | | | | | | | |
|---|---|---|---|---|---|---|---|---|---|---|
| | 10 | 20 | 30 | 40 | 50 | 60 | 70 | 80 | 90 | 95 |
| Real hourly wage | | | | | | | | | | |
| 1973 | $6.30 | $7.60 | $9.04 | $10.51 | $12.05 | $13.80 | $16.05 | $18.35 | $23.06 | $28.94 |
| 1999 | 6.05 | 7.35 | 8.72 | 10.10 | 11.87 | 13.93 | 16.45 | 19.93 | 26.05 | 33.25 |
| Percent change | | | | | | | | | | |
| 1979–99 | –9.3 | –3.3 | –2.4 | –3.9 | –0.2 | 1.1 | 1.0 | 4.9 | 11.7 | 17.6 |

Source: MISCHEL, BERNSTEIN & SCHMITT, THE STATE OF WORKING AMERICA 2000/2001, Table 2.6, at p. 124 (2001).

As the authors of this study explain, inequality is evidenced not only between groups of workers by occupation, educational level, and the like, but is increasingly evidenced within these groups. *Id.* at 123. In addition, some observers have noted the rise of "winner-take-all" labor markets: The ratio of median CEO pay to worker pay in 1962 was 20 to 1; in 1999, it was 107 to 1. *Id.* at 5. The rise in inequality affects the attitudes and involvements of those who are better off vis-a-vis those who are worse off, JAMES GALBRAITH, CREATED UNEQUAL: THE CRISIS IN AMERICAN PAY 15–16 (1998), and this in turn may contribute to the documented decline in "social capital"—the willingness of Americans to devote time to and participate in collective endeavors. *See generally* ROBERT PUTNAM, BOWLING ALONE: THE COLLAPSE AND REVIVAL OF AMERICAN COMMUNITY (2000).

In sum, the labor market is far more complex than it was in 1935. It is characterized increasingly on the one hand by highly trained people who value their own skills, merits (and mobility) more than collective action and, on the other hand, by low-wage poorly educated service workers, often immigrant, with high turnover. *See generally*, PAUL OSTERMAN, SECURING PROSPERITY 170–171 (1999). Both groups have tended to prove resistant to unionization, though for very different reasons.

## C.  EMPLOYER POLICIES[a]

Change in the nature of the work being generated has been accompanied by change in the conditions governing its performance. After World War II and, in part, in consequence of unionization in large mass-production industries, there was a growing assumption that workers would be retained by commitments to job security, an array of company benefits, and internal lines of promotion and progression, *i.e.*, by the creation of an "internal" labor market, one with limited "ports of entry" into the firm and where, once in, incumbent employees did not compete for their jobs with those waiting at the gate. Non-union firms, wishing to remain non-union, often emulated the pattern created in unionized industry. This shift is evidenced in the widespread adoption of employee handbooks, manuals, or employer policy compendia setting out the "web of rules." Finkin, The Bureaucratization of Work: Employer Policies and Contract Law, 1986 WIS. L. REV. 733, 741–743. And many of these policies contained rules providing for progressive discipline, fair evaluation, or just cause for discharge—rules that replicate in form the protections afforded by collective bargaining agreements—in part to maintain a stable complement of satisfied and so productive employees, and in part to avoid unionization. One consequence was the widespread expectation—and reality—of job security in a great many non-unionized jobs. *See* Hall, *The Importance of Lifetime Jobs in the U.S. Economy*, 72 AM. ECON. REV. 716 (1982). Another was an increased dependence as people came to rely upon the job not only for a steady income, but for medical insurance and other vital benefits, to the point of creating, in the view of some critics, a new "industrial feudalism."

Since the early 90s there has been a return to "market mediated" employment arrangements: An increased use of part-time employees, short-time hires (often on a project specific basis and sometimes legally characterized as "independent contractors"), agency temporaries or "leased" workers, casual or "on call" workers, and of subcontractors. It has been estimated that perhaps 10% of the labor market is now made up of such "market mediated work," and that these arrangements are growing more rapidly than permanent full-time employment. Katherine Abraham, *Restructuring the Employment Relationship: The Growth of Market–Mediated Work Arrangements*, in NEW DEVELOPMENTS IN THE LABOR MARKET: TOWARD A NEW INSTITUTIONAL PARADIGM 85 (K. Abraham & R. McKersie eds., 1990). *See*

**a.** *Compare* S. JACOBY, MODERN MANORS: (1997), *with* PETER CAPPELLI, THE NEW DEAL AT WELFARE CAPITALISM SINCE THE NEW DEAL   WORK (1999).

Stewart Schwab, The Diversity of Contingent Workers and the Need for Nuanced Policy, 52 Wash. & Lee L. Rev. 915 (1995), and Gillian Lester, Careers and Contingency, 51 Stan. L. Rev. 73 (1998).

In other words, there has been a diminution in the corporate commitment to "internal labor markets" and a concomitant shifting of risk on to the worker (who may—may not—be a statutory "employee"): for upgrading his or her skills and for the potential of job loss. This heightened concern for mobility—more for future employability than for current job security—undermines a basic premise of unionization under the Labor Act, *i.e.* of a stable "bargaining unit" centered on a single employer for the bulk of the employee's working life. *See* Virginia du Rivage, Francoise Carré & Chris Tilly, *Making Labor Law Work for Part–Time and Contingent Workers, in* Contingent Work 163 (Kathleen Banker & Kathleen Christensen eds., 1998). At the same time, a number of employers have adopted policies to create a "high performance workplace" that not only involves workers in making decisions about the organization and performance of work, but seeks to instill in workers the sense of themselves as integral elements of a cooperative work system. Eileen Appelbaum, Thomas Bailey & Peter Berg, Manufacturing Advantage: Why High-Performance Work Systems Pay Off (2000). The former blurs the distinction between employee and manager; the latter makes an appeal by an "outside" organization difficult to sustain.

## D.  Law

When in the debate on the Norris–LaGuardia Act Representative Oliver adverted to "the field of American freedom where laws do not govern but men alone reign," his characterization of the employment relationship was on firm legal ground. Apart from some state protective legislation for women and children, "truck" laws requiring payment for work in United States currency at regular and frequent intervals, factory safety and inspection laws, and worker compensation laws for industrial injury, it was assumed that employment, in the absence of a contract for a fixed duration, was to be utterly unregulated and "at will." The employer could fire for any reason, no reason, or even a morally repugnant reason without legal recourse, just as the employee was equally free to quit. Moreover, the courts were reluctant to find implied contracts affording job security. In some jurisdictions, a commitment not to discharge except for just cause was treated as a contract of "lifetime" employment, which required consideration additional to the performance of service in order to be enforceable.

Since the passage of the Labor Act, however, and at an accelerating pace over the past two decades, federal and state laws have increasingly regulated the employment relationship. At the federal level, the Fair Labor Standards Act, regulating wages and hours, was enacted in 1938. In 1963 the Equal Pay Act required that men and women be paid at the same rate for jobs that were substantially the same; and, in the following year, Title VII of the Civil Rights Act was enacted comprehensively prohibiting discrimination in employment (and by unions) on grounds of race, sex, religion, and national origin. Age discrimination in employment was legislated against in 1967. As a result, the "at will" rule has become substantially modified. At least theoretically, any member of a statutorily protected class can claim that a particular impermissible ground supplied the basis for an adverse employment decision, so to shift the burden to the employer in litigation to articulate a valid, non-discriminatory reason. More recently, discrimination on the basis of handicap (Americans With Disabilities Act of 1990) and citizenship (Immigration Reform and Control Act of 1986) have been added.

Health and safety on the job were comprehensively (and, some argue, ineffectively) dealt with by the Occupational Safety and Health Act in 1970, and welfare and pension benefits were regulated by the Employee Retirement Income Security Act in 1974. In addition, federal laws protect employees from retaliation by their employers on a variety of grounds— serving on a federal jury, once having one's wages garnished, filing for bankruptcy, or complaining through official channels of employer violations of certain health or safety laws, *e.g.*, mine or atomic safety, toxic substances, clean water, and the like. The use of polygraphs in employment was sharply restricted in 1988 (Employee Polygraph Protection Act); a federal law requiring 60–day notice of plant closing or mass layoff took effect in 1989 (Worker Adjustment and Retraining Notification Act); and in 1993 Congress enacted the Family and Medical Leave Act.

Often more far-reaching state legislation has been enacted, variously requiring, for example, employee access to personnel records and mandatory severance pay in the event of plant closing, limiting the employer's ability to engage in random drug testing, forbidding the use of polygraphs, and, in the case of Montana, requiring just cause to dismiss employees (excluding those who are covered by collective agreements or who are serving under contracts of express duration). The Montana development underlines—and was in response to—what many state courts had been doing as a matter of common law. A majority of courts have held that employee rulebooks and manuals that provide for progressive discipline or require cause to discharge are capable of rising to contractual status, though the force of these holdings has been limited if not eviscerated by the willingness of the courts to defer to boilerplate disclaimers of contractual obligation. A majority of courts have also held that a discharge for a reason violative of some clearly articulated public policy is a tort. Such "public policy" has been found in the state constitution, legislation, administrative rules, and, in some jurisdictions, in judge-made doctrine as well. In addition, a minority of jurisdictions have held that the "covenant of good faith and fair dealing" applicable to contracts in general is applicable to employment contracts as well; but the content of the duty has varied from a limited obligation to refrain from "opportunistic" behavior—*e.g.*, a discharge to defeat the vesting of a salesman's commission—to a more expansive obligation, in effect, not to dismiss without good cause. Finally, the courts have applied other aspects of the common law governing the protection of dignitary interests to the employment setting—affording, for example, tort relief for invasions of privacy or the infliction of emotional distress caused by an extraordinarily abusive work environment or a discharge effected by outrageous means.

In sum, employment has become a field where laws *do* govern, but the laws are often a crazy-quilt of federal and state legislation, and common law doctrine that varies significantly from state to state. And the effectiveness of these various laws to realize their ends in the workplace remains to be seen.

---

## PROBLEM FOR DISCUSSION

Much office work has become computerized in consequence of which the worker is subject to persistent computerized monitoring of her work. *See generally* OFFICE OF TECHNOLOGY ASSESSMENT, THE ELECTRONIC SWEATSHOP (1987). Is the introduction and use of this technology of concern to the workers? How is it to be decided whether workers should be made an object of continuous electronic observation, and, if so, what uses will be made of such observations? How fast should the pace of work be, and at what cost not only in employee turnover and training to the employer, but also in physical and emotional stress on the employee? Will the data produced be compiled on an individual or group basis and, if the latter, what group? For how long will these data be kept? Who shall have access to them? Are these questions of societal concern or should they be left to market forces? Do they call for rules? If so, who should devise them—the employer, the legislature, an administrative agency, the courts? How should compliance be monitored?

---

## II.   THE "REPRESENTATION GAP"

A multi-year effort, the Worker Representation and Participation Survey (WRPS) by Richard Freeman and Joel Rogers, WHAT WORKERS WANT (1999), made some "basic findings":

- American workers want more of a say/influence/representation/participation/voice (call it what you will) at the workplace than they now have. . . .

- Employees want greater say both because they think it will directly improve the quality of their working lives and because they think it will make their firm more productive and successful (which also enhances their work lives over the long run).

- Employees want greater workplace participation as individuals and as part of a group as well. . . . [O]n many issues they prefer to deal with management individually. But on other issues, for example, workplace health and safety, pay and benefit plans—where problems affect workers as a group—, workers want to speak as a group. . . .

- Workers want *cooperative relations* with management.... [T]he vast majority think that a workplace organization can only be effective if it enjoys management participation and support....

- Workers want some measure of *independence and protection of that independence* in their dealings with management.... Union members want to maintain union representation, and many nonunion workers also favor a union. An even larger share of workers want some form of a labor-management committee that stops short of collective bargaining but in which they have some significant independence in selecting representatives and resolving disputes....

- Workers believe that *management resistance* is the primary reason they do not have their desired level of influence at the workplace.... They know that management would fight them if they tried to form a union, and many believe that management opposes independent worker representatives even in advisory workplace committees.

*Id.* at 4–5 (emphases in original). Freeman and Rogers conclude that most unionized workers continue to support their unions and that about a third of non-union employees would vote for a union. In other words, over 40% of American workers wish to be represented by a union, but less than 10% are—producing a "representation gap" of 30%. *I.e.* about 30,000,000 workers want to be represented, and aren't.

One of the Survey's investigator's argued earlier that there is a mismatch between the law—which allows only the form of exclusive representation by majority rule—and contemporary needs: Management is limited in its ability to support new forms of worker participation; workers are denied the choice of these other forms; and the nation suffers lost productivity, growth, a rising inequality, ineffective enforcement of labor standards, and the "erosion of democratic norms." Joel Rogers, *United States: Lessons from Abroad and Home, in* Works Councils: Consultation, Representation, and Cooperation in Industrial Relations 375, 377 (J. Rogers & W. Streeck eds., 1995).

## III. Labor Law Reform[b]

The foregoing developments have occasioned a reconsideration of the effectiveness of the Labor Act and a search for alternatives. Proposals for reform cluster around four major themes: (1) strengthen the current system of exclusive representation by majority rule; (2) by modifying

b. Several symposia have been published of papers useful in themselves and valuable for the additional references supplied. See 34 Indus. Relations No. 3 (1995) ("Special Issue: Labor Law Reform"); Restoring the Promise of American Labor Law (Sheldon Friedman *et al.* eds., 1994); The Legal Future of Employee Representation (Matthew Finkin ed., 1994); Employee Representation: Alternatives and Future Directions (Bruce Kaufman & Morris Kleiner eds., 1993); 31 Indus. Rel. No. 1 (1992) ("Symposium: Labor Market Institution and the Future Role of Unions"). *See also* Michael C. Harper, A Framework for the Rejuvenation of the American Labor Movement, 76 Ind. L.J. 103 (2001).

section 8(a)(2), allow the employer greater flexibility for instituting alternative forms of employee representation; (3) provide for a statutorily mandated system of employee participation; or, (4) provide for the non-majority representation of individuals and groups.

Other observers look at the problem from a different angle. Some see a more or less permanently diminished workplace role for unions (that employer-sponsored committees cannot fill). The gap is being filled substantively by increasing legal regulation mandating conditions that heretofore might have been determined by collective bargaining; but these laws are as yet imperfectly implemented. Thus, some commentators see unions altering their focus from workplace bargainers to legal service providers. *See, e.g.*, Robert Rabin, The Role of Unions in the Rights–Based Workplace, 25 U.S.F.L. Rev. 169 (1991); *cf.* Clyde Summers, Effective Remedies for Employment Rights: Preliminary Guidelines and Proposals, 141 U. Pa. L. Rev. 457 (1992). As with all the proposed "reforms," there are drawbacks as well as benefits arguably to be derived from an increasing resort to litigation and the reader may wish to ponder both with respect to this alternative. Suffice it to say, however, this is the one "reform" that requires no change in law.

Some observers see the infirmity to lie in our system of corporate governance which is increasingly driven by shareholder demands for higher and higher returns on investment and which, absent countervailing power—that is, unions—tends to treat employees as disposable factors of production. *See, e.g.*, Marleen A. O'Connor, The Human Capital Era: Reconceptualizing Corporate Law to Facilitate Labor–Management Cooperation, 78 Cornell L. Rev. 899 (1993). The debate on this question is quite rich, but the legal reforms discussed lie in corporate law, not labor law. It is to the latter that attention turns here.

## A.   Strengthening the Labor Act

A commission was appointed jointly by the Secretaries of Labor and Commerce in March of 1993, charged with reporting on a series of questions including recommending changes in the legal framework of collective bargaining, the eponymous Dunlop Commission. It issued a Fact Finding Report in May 1994 and a Final Report in December 1994. After reviewing evidence and testimony bearing upon the efficacy of the Labor Act as currently implemented, the Commission recommended three changes in the statute:

> [No. 4] Providing for prompt elections after the NLRB determines that sufficient employees have expressed a desire to be represented by a union. Such elections should generally be held within two weeks. To accomplish this objective we propose that challenges to bargaining units and other legal disputes be resolved after the elections are held.

Beyond the reversal of the Supreme Court's decision in *Lechmere* so that employees may have access to union organizers in privately-owned but publicly-used spaces such as shopping malls, access questions are best left to the NLRB. The Commission urges the Board to strive to afford employees the most equal and democratic dialogue possible.

[No. 5] Requiring by statute that the NLRB obtain prompt injunctions to remedy discriminatory actions against employees that occur during an organizing campaign or negotiations for a first contract.

[No. 6] Assisting employers and newly certified unions in achieving first contracts through an upgraded dispute resolution system which provides for mediation and empowers a tripartite advisory board to use a variety of options to resolve disputes ranging from self-help (strike or lockout) to binding arbitration for relatively few disputes.

Commission on the Future of Worker–Management Relations, Report and Recommendations xviii (1994). These recommendations are based upon the Commission's compilation of the data which it summarized *inter alia* as follows:

—The number of NLRB elections held, the number of workers in elections, and the number in units certified for collective bargaining has diminished.

—Representation elections as currently constituted are a highly conflictual activity for workers, unions, and firms. This means that many new collective bargaining relationships start off in an environment that is highly adversarial.

—The probability that a worker will be discharged or otherwise unfairly discriminated against for exercising legal rights under the NLRA has increased over time. Unions as well as firms have engaged in unfair labor practices under the NLRA. The bulk of meritorious charges are for employer unfair practices.

—Roughly a third of workplaces that vote to be represented by a union do not obtain a collective bargaining contract with their employer.

Commission on the Future of Worker–Management Relations, Fact Finding Report 79 (1994).

Legislated card-check recognition, immediate or five-day elections, employer neutrality in organizing efforts, first contract arbitration, severe and immediate penalties for anti-union discrimination and the elimination of the rule allowing the permanent replacement of economic strikers have been "the centerpiece" of organized labor's legislative reform efforts since the mid–1970s. Charles McDonald, *U.S. Union Membership in Future Decades: A Trade Unionist's Perspective*, 31 INDUS. REL. 13, 25 (1991). But the effectiveness of these measures (arguably useful in themselves) significantly to close the representation gap has been questioned on two grounds. First, it is argued that these reforms are unlikely effectively to mitigate managerial resistance which is a major reason for the gap, as a comparison with Europe shows. In Europe, political parties allied with labor have sought to legislate in matters that are the subject of bargaining on an enterprise basis in the United States—medical care, pensions, vacations, and work hours. Moreover, bargaining on major economic issues with unions there is often done on a sectoral basis, *e.g.* including an entire industry, the results of which may be extended by governmental order even to non-unionized companies. There would accordingly be less reason for European managers to resist unionization. Further, in several European countries, notably Germany, much that is done to represent workers on the shop floor by unions here is done by elected works councils mandated by law and which are independent of the unions, though they enjoy a close if often complex relationship with them.

Second, it has been argued that reform of the Labor Act, to make it more accessible, is unresponsive to the economic, demographic and business organization changes that places in question the viability of the Act's very premises and structure. Consequently, broader proposals have been assayed on the question of how employees might be represented.

## B.  MODIFYING THE RESTRICTION ON COMPANY SUPPORT OF LABOR ORGANIZATIONS

The Dunlop Commission was generally supportive of "employee involvement." It opined that such programs should not be ruled unlawful because they involve "discussion of terms and conditions of work or compensation where such discussion is incidental to the broad purposes of these programs." Report and Recommendations at 8. But the House of Representatives Committee on Economic and Educational Opportunities went a good deal further. On September 18, 1995, it reported out the "Teamwork for Employees and Managers Act," H.R. 743 (104th Cong., 1st Sess.) which, after reciting the need to facilitate "legitimate employee involvement programs" would add the following proviso to section 8(a)(2):

> Provided further, That it shall not constitute or be evidence of an unfair labor practice under this paragraph for an employer to establish, assist, maintain, or participate in any organization or entity of any kind, in which employees participate, to address matters of mutual interest, including, but not limited to, issues of quality, productivity, efficiency, and safety and health, and which does not have, claim, or seek authority to be the exclusive bargaining representative of the employees or to negotiate or enter into collective bargaining agreements with the employer or to amend existing collective bargaining agreements between the employer and any labor organization, except that in a case in which a labor

organization is the representative of such employees as provided in section 9(a), this proviso shall not apply.

Whether a loosening of the "company union" prohibition would be a good or bad policy has been richly debated. Views favorable to a modification include Samuel Estreicher, Employee Involvement and the "Company Union" Prohibition: The Case for a Partial Repeal of Section 8(a)(2), 69 N.Y.U. L. Rev. 125 (1994), and Michael LeRoy, Employee Participation in the New Millennium: Redefining a Labor Organization Under Section 8(a)(2) of the NLRA, 72 S. Cal. L. Rev. 1651 (1999). Those more skeptical include Robert Moberly, The Worker Participation Conundrum: Does Prohibiting Employer Assisted Labor Organization Prevent Labor–Management Cooperation?, 69 Wash. L. Rev. 331 (1994), and Michael Harper, The Continuing Relevance of Section 8(a)(2) to the Contemporary Workplace, 96 Mich. L. Rev. 2322 (1998).

## PROBLEM FOR DISCUSSION

Return to the conclusions of What Workers Want. Would enactment of the *Teamwork for Employees and Managers Act* be more likely to give employees the kind of organization they want to have or the kind of organization employers want them to have?

## C.   Works Councils or Employee Participation Committees

Professor Paul Weiler has been the most prominent advocate for a statutory provision for employee participation committees (EPC) modeled roughly upon the works council mandated under German law. He has put the proposal in a nutshell:

[A] single committee would represent all the employees in both the plant and the office, including professionals and lower echelon managers. A proportional electoral system would be designed to guarantee representation of each of the key employee constituencies. The committee's jurisdiction would cover a wide range of employment issues, involving the right to be consulted before management could make material changes in workplace conditions (e.g., via the introduction of new technology or the adoption of cost sharing or cost containment programs in health insurance). In addition, the EPC would play the front-line role in administering the growing number of regulatory programs for the workplace, ranging from OSHA to wrongful dismissal rights. . . .

Every EPC would be entitled to the extensive information necessary for performing its representation role for the employees, just as management must now provide the data needed by boards of directors representing shareholders. The committee would also be entitled to a defined level of financial resources—contributed jointly by the firm and the employees according to a statutory per capita formula—so that the committee could draw on the advice of people and organizations with experience and expertise in relevant subject matters. A prominent source of such assistance would likely be the trade union in that sector, but so also would be women's action committees, injured worker groups, and the like. Where a union already enjoyed bargaining rights in a workplace, the local union would function as the EPC, assuming the same responsibility and resources to represent the interests of its unit members.

Paul Weiler, Governing the Workplace: Employee Representation in the Eyes of the Law, *in* EMPLOYEE REPRESENTATION: ALTERNATIVES AND FUTURE DIRECTION 81, 97–98 (Bruce Kaufman & Morris Kleiner eds., 1993).

Four arguments have been made to require or, alternatively, legally to allow EPCs:

First, participation is a win-win process: both efficiency and employee satisfaction gain. Plant-and company-wide EPCs are logical extensions of various already legal forms of workplace participation such as quality circles and work teams. EPCs would deal with organization-wide issues impossible to resolve on a departmental level.

Second, EPCs are needed to fill a "representation gap." Under the present law, workers have a choice between U.S.-style unions or not being represented at all. They can't choose EPCs, for example, or being represented by the Gay–Lesbian–Hispanic Alliance. Thus, it is argued, non-unionized workers are deprived of any real voice and of any opportunity to contribute their ideas for organizational improvement (aside perhaps from suggestion systems, hot lines, and e-mail)....

Third, EPCs might serve as way stations toward independent unions. The United Steelworkers evolved out of the employee representation plans of the 1930s.... [M]any once docile company unions have become quite militant. Further, the experience of German unions with works councils might be repeated. These unions were hostile to these councils at first, viewing them as rival unions. But over time these unions took control of major councils and so have strengthened their shop-level position....

Finally, in contrast to the third argument, some conclude that traditional adversarial unionism is out-of-date except in a limited number of situations. So EPCs are not just way stations, but the final destination.

George Strauss, Is the New Deal Collapsing? With What Might It Be Replaced?, 34 INDUS. REL. 329, 339–340 (1995) (reference omitted). For a discussion of the legal system of works councils in Germany, *see generally* WORKS COUNCILS (J. Rogers & W. Streeck eds., 1995).

---

## PROBLEM FOR DISCUSSION

Eighteen states currently require the establishment of workplace safety committees. *See* Matthew Finkin, Bridging the "Representation Gap," 3 U. PA. J. LAB. & EMP. L. 391 (2001). These statutes often entitle workers to equal representation with management and give them the right to elect their representatives. Are these laws preempted by the Labor Act? Absent close policing of these provisions by the state, how would these bodies be established? If established, what would make management want to cooperate with them? *See generally* David Weil, Implementing Employment Regulation: Insights on the Determinants of Regulatory Performance, *in* GOVERNMENT REGULATION OF THE EMPLOYMENT RELATIONSHIP 429 (Bruce Kaufman ed., 1997).

## D. NON–MAJORITY REPRESENTATION

The Dunlop Commission's Fact–Finding Report identified as among the questions to be addressed: "Should the labor law seek to provide workers who want representation but who are a minority at a workplace a greater option for non-exclusive representation?" *Id.* at 80. But the Commission's final Report and Recommendations declined to address it.

George Strauss has discussed the prospect of a new form of unionism that takes into account the trend adverted to at the outset—of the rise of a class of short term hires, subcontracted employees, and professionals concerned more for future employability than with current job security. These employees need representation in their occupations; organizations should be prepared accordingly to provide minority representation rather than be concerned with exclusive bargaining rights in static bargaining units. Strauss, Is the New Deal Collapsing?, *supra.* Such organizations could also provide other services in job training and placement. *See* Rogers, A Strategy for Labor, 34 INDUS. REL. 367 (1995).

The idea of non-majority or "members only" representation was one of the most hotly contested issues in the framing of the Labor Act. A very early, precommittee draft provided that: "Where no representatives have been selected by the majority as provided in the above paragraph, the representatives chosen by any group of two or more employees shall represent such group for the purpose of dealing with employers." Kenneth Casebeer, Drafting Wagner's Act: Leon Keyserling and the Precommittee Drafts of the Labor Disputes Act and the National Labor Relations Act, 11 INDUS. REL. L.J. 73, 113 (1989). But this approach was rejected in favor of exclusive representation by majority rule.

Under a "members only" system all the representative need supply to establish its right to represent employees is their membership or authorization to that effect; there need be no petitions, elections or election campaigns, and the adversarial climate engendered by bitter contests would be avoided. Similarly, the representative's right of access to pertinent information would also accrue upon its submission.

The drawbacks of the proposal now, as in 1934, are two. The first argues to the likely weakness inherent in organizations representing only their members who otherwise lack a strategic situation in the workplace. Indeed, it is possible that the majority of such relationships would be the "worse case" scenario essayed by Freeman and Rogers in their study of employee attitudes—of a weak organization confronting a hostile employer. The second goes to workability, to a prospect of an employer having to deal with a multiplicity of such "members only" groups. It has been argued, however, that that problem can be dealt with statutorily in light of the experience under the Labor Act. Finkin, The Road Not Taken: Some Thoughts on Nonmajority Employee Representation, *in* THE LEGAL FUTURE OF EMPLOYEE REPRESENTATION 191 (Matthew Finkin ed., 1994). But others have been (to put it charitably) dubious. Gottesman, In Despair, Starting Over: Imagining a Labor Law for Unorganized Workers, *id.* at 57.

# PART TEN

# The Individual and the Union

## INTRODUCTION

After the passage of the Railway Labor Act and the National Labor Relations Act, our national labor policy was preoccupied for a number of years with the formation of unions and the operation of collective bargaining as a system of labor-management relations. The interests of the union were widely assumed to be synonymous with those of the employees it represented; any concern with individual rights and internal union affairs tended to be submerged by the overriding need to strengthen labor organizations so that they might better support the interests of the workers. Hence, the relationships between union officials and their organization and between the organization and its members were largely left to State courts, where trade unions were lumped in the general category of voluntary unincorporated associations along with churches, social clubs and fraternal organizations.

As unions increased in wealth and size in the friendly environment of the Wagner Act, a growing concern was expressed that the power of unions might be improperly used to further the private ends of union leaders. Warnings were also uttered to the effect that union power could sometimes be employed to run roughshod over the rights of the individual worker. Some recognition was given to these dangers by the Supreme Court in *Steele v. Louisville & Nashville R. Co.*, p. 378, supra, where the Court implied a duty on the part of the exclusive bargaining representative to represent fairly all members of the bargaining unit. On the other hand, Congress paid little heed to these problems. Legislative proposals were sometimes advanced to protect the individual union member, but they evoked scant interest. During the nineteen fifties, however, increasing attention was paid to the internal affairs of unions. At last, the entire subject erupted before the public through a series of revelations elicited by a Select Committee of the Senate (the McClellan Committee) during an investigation of union activities. In the course of these hearings, witnesses provided numerous examples of the misuse of union funds by labor leaders, the signing of "sweetheart" contracts by union officials in return for bribes from employers, the use of violence and fraud in union elections and similar abuses. Though only a small fraction of American unions were tainted, the impression on the public was vivid and there was increasing clamor for corrective legislation.

Following these events, Congress enacted legislation regulating the internal affairs of unions. This statute, entitled the Labor and Management Reporting and Disclosure Act (LMRDA), was built on certain basic premises: (1) union leaders had abused their power in the ways described; (2) because the government had been partially responsible for the growth of unions and for their power over those they represented, the government had an obligation to see that the abuses were eliminated; and (3) responsibility for reform should rest predominantly with unions and their members, in the interest of preserving the initiative and self-determination of the labor movement.

The LMRDA thus placed primary emphasis upon democratic processes within unions as an instrument of reform. Periodic, fair, and fully participatory elections were required. Unions and union officials were required to disclose information that could bear upon financial irregularities and conflicts of interest. Congress also specifically forbade certain actions on the part of union officials: the expenditure of union funds for purposes not authorized in the union constitution, the holding of union office by persons recently convicted of specified crimes, and the making of loans by unions in excess of two thousand dollars to their officers and employees, and similar questionable behavior.

The materials in this part explore the complex relationships between the union and its members.

The first chapter deals with the minimum obligation of a bargaining representative to represent fairly all of the employees whom it represents within the bargaining unit. The second chapter is devoted to the problem of "union security," i.e., the membership and financial obligations that a union may exact; as well as the legality of job benefits for union officials and those referred through the union hiring hall. The third chapter takes up the question of the powers that unions have to discipline their members, under three bodies of law (the National Labor Relations Act, the 1959 LMRDA, and state common law). The fourth chapter describes the LMRDA requirements for the election of union officers. The final chapter considers additional LMRDA safeguards to prevent corruption and related abuses by union officials.

---

# I.  THE RIGHT TO FAIR REPRESENTATION

---

## A. THE SOURCE AND ENFORCEMENT OF THE UNION'S DUTY[a]

Collective bargaining inevitably involves conflicts of interests between different groups of workers within the bargaining unit. Even when the unit is defined by the NLRB so as to assure homogeneity, the workers within cannot be exactly alike. The negotiation and administration of labor agreements involve repeated decisions by the union as to whose interests to prefer. Shall there be provision for more liberal pensions or for a larger wage increase? How large a wage premium should be given to skilled members of the unit? Should employees displaced by a plant closing be put at the bottom of the seniority list at the plant to which they transfer? Should the union seek to balance the seniority factor in promotions and layoffs with affirmative-action considerations? Should the union's resources be expended on the processing of grievances that have only minor significance for the bulk of the unit? To what extent should the law scrutinize such decisions by the union, and by what criteria should those decisions be judged?

Two decisions rendered by the United States Supreme Court in 1944 set the fundamental guidelines for the resolution of these very perplexing problems. In J.I. CASE CO. v. NLRB, 321 U.S. 332, 64 S.Ct. 576, 88 L.Ed. 762 (1944) at page 353 supra, the Court concluded that the collective agreement took priority over, and displaced, individual contracts of employment negotiated by the employer; that the best interests of the collectivity were to be assessed not by the employer but by the bargaining representative, accommodating conflicting interests within the bargaining unit; and that even employees who might otherwise be in a position to secure favored treatment through individual dealings must sacrifice such treatment for the good of the collective. In STEELE v. LOUISVILLE & NASHVILLE R. CO., 323 U.S. 192, 65 S.Ct. 226, 89 L.Ed. 173 (1944), at page 378 supra, the Court inferred—by virtue of the powers of the union as exclusive bargaining representative—a correlative duty to represent all employees within the bargaining unit "without hostile discrimination, fairly, impartially, and in good faith." (The same obligation as the court inferred in that case from the Railway Labor Act was inferred under the National Labor Relations Act in Ford Motor Co. v. Huffman, 345 U.S. 330, 73 S.Ct. 681, 97 L.Ed. 1048 (1953), at page 372 supra; and Syres v. Oil Workers International Union Local No. 23, 350 U.S. 892, 76 S.Ct. 152, 100 L.Ed. 785 (1955)(per curiam).) The student is encouraged to review these leading Supreme Court decisions at this point, and the accompanying Problems for Discussion.

In what forum is this duty enforceable? The *Steele* decision held that the duty of fair representation was enforceable by an action for damages and injunction in the federal courts. The Railway Labor Act has no enforcing agency akin to the National Labor Relations Act; and even the NLRB, at the time of the *Steele* decision, had no unfair labor practice

---

**a.** In addition to the materials cited at page 378 supra, see Axelrod & Kaufman, Mansion House—Bekins—Handy Andy: The National Labor Relations Board's Role in Ra- cial Discrimination Cases, 45 Geo.Wash. L.Rev. 675 (1977); Leiken, The Current and Potential Equal Employment Role of the NLRB, 1971 Duke L.J. 833.

jurisdiction over labor organizations. Nearly two decades passed after *Steele* before the NLRB in fact held that a breach of the duty of fair representation was an unfair labor practice. Of course, if a union induced an employer to discipline an employee because he or she was not a member of the union, that would violate Sections 8(a)(3) and 8(b)(2). It was in NLRB v. MIRANDA FUEL Co., 140 NLRB 181 (1962), enf't denied, 326 F.2d 172 (2d Cir.1963), that the Board held that such union-induced discipline is also an unfair labor practice when the individual employee is targeted for invidious or capricious reasons apart from nonmembership. The Board concluded that the freedom of employees from such union conduct was a right impliedly granted by Section 7 of the NLRA, and that such union conduct foreseeably encouraged union membership. The breach of the duty of fair representation thus violated Sections 8(b)(1)(A) and 8(b)(2). A divided court of appeals denied enforcement, but mustered no majority on the question whether the union's breach was indeed an unfair labor practice.

Even the Board itself continued to be divided on the issue, as demonstrated by the opinions in INDEPENDENT METAL WORKERS, LOCAL 1 (HUGHES TOOL Co.), 147 NLRB 1573 (1964). There, the Board found that the racially segregated bargaining representative had improperly declined to process an employee's grievance because he was black. In its capacity as a decision-maker on questions of representation, the Board unanimously decided that it would, as a sanction for the union's breach of its duty of fair representation, rescind its certification. A three-member majority also concluded that the union's breach was a violation of Sections 8(b)(1), (2) and (3). Although the other two members agreed that Section 8(b)(1)(A) had been violated— because the union's race discrimination was also in effect discrimination because of the employee's nonmembership in the union—they challenged the conclusion that a union's failure to process a grievance on the basis of race alone could be an unfair labor practice. They argued that no duty of fair representation could properly be found within the original Wagner Act (which regulated only employer conduct); that Congress never saw fit in writing the Taft–Hartley Act, three years after *Steele*, and the later Landrum–Griffin Act, to make it an unfair labor practice for a union to breach such a duty; that the enforcement of such a duty would involve the Board improperly in scrutinizing the substance of union positions in negotiating and grievance-processing; that the union-respondent could not have violated Section 8(b)(2), because it merely declined to press a grievance and did not cause the employer to discriminate in any way; and that the union's duties under Section 8(b)(3) run only to the employer and not to the employees in the bargaining unit.

Despite these troubling criticisms, the Board adhered to its position that the union's breach of its DFR (as it has come to be known) is an unfair labor practice, and this position has been endorsed by every court of appeals that has considered the matter. It is also uniformly acknowledged that the Board-enforceable duty obtains both when the union negotiates a collective bargaining agreement and when it processes a grievance. Although the Supreme Court has not squarely so ruled, it has in a number of major decisions assumed that NLRB jurisdiction exists without raising any doubts about the matter.

When a union has been found by the NLRB to violate the duty of fair representation by discriminating on the basis of race or sex, the Board may as a remedy revoke the union's certification. Moreover, although a labor agreement executed by a majority union will normally bar the holding of a representation election during its term (up to three years), the Board will dispense with this contract-bar rule when the agreement contains provisions that are racially discriminatory on their face. Pioneer Bus Co., 140 NLRB 54 (1962). (These principles, however, may be of little concern to the incumbent union, which might still have an entrenched majority position—and thus continued bargaining rights—in spite of the dropping of the contract bar or the revocation of certification.)

For a brief time, the Board held that a union's illegally discriminatory policy as to membership criteria could be shown by the employer as a bar to initial certification. In Bekins Moving & Storage Co., 211 NLRB 138 (1974), a divided Board found that certification of such a union would be tantamount to unconstitutional *governmental* discrimination. The Board soon overruled this position, in Handy Andy, Inc., 228 NLRB 447 (1977), in which it concluded that it would be premature to withhold a union's certification before it had an opportunity to demonstrate its freedom from discrimination based on race, sex or national origin in negotiation and in grievance processing. Certification merely confirms the fact of majority status; a later violation of the DFR could be challenged in unfair labor practice proceedings and remedied, in part, by revocation of the certification. The Board's position has had a mixed reception in the courts of appeals. In Bell & Howell Co. v. NLRB, 598 F.2d 136 (D.C.Cir.1979), cert. denied, 442 U.S. 942, 99 S.Ct. 2885, 61 L.Ed.2d 312 (1979), the court held that alleged sex discrimination by a union should be examined in unfair labor practice proceedings rather than in a challenge to initial certification. Two other courts of appeals, however, have concluded that the Constitution compels the Board not only to withhold certification from a union that illegally discriminates in membership or representation, but also to permit an employer to assert such discrimination by way of defense to that union's refusal-to-bargain charge under Section 8(a)(5). See NLRB v. Mansion House Center Mgt. Corp., 473 F.2d 471 (8th Cir.1973); NLRB v. Heavy Lift Serv., Inc., 607 F.2d 1121 (5th Cir.1979), cert. denied, 449 U.S. 822, 101 S.Ct. 82, 66 L.Ed.2d 25 (1980).

---

DelCostello v. International Bhd. of Teamsters, 462 U.S. 151, 103 S.Ct. 2281, 76 L.Ed.2d 476 (1983). In the two cases before the Court, grievants—having lost their arbitration cases—brought suit against their employers for breach of the labor agreement and against their unions for breach of the duty of fair representation. (As will be seen below, in *Vaca v. Sipes*, an individual may sue the employer directly on the labor agreement provided it can be shown that the union handled the grievance in a bad-faith, arbitrary or perfunctory manner.) In one case, the action was brought just short of six months from the effective date of the arbitration award; in the other, some eleven months after. In the former case, the federal district court dismissed both claims by virtue of the "borrowed" state statute of limitations for actions to vacate arbitration awards, which required suit within thirty days. The court of appeals affirmed. In the latter case, a different court of appeals held that the local ninety-day statute should indeed be borrowed in the lawsuit against the employer, but that the pertinent limitations period in the action against the union for breach of the DFR was the state's three-year period for malpractice actions. It therefore affirmed the dismissal of the contract claim against the employer but permitted the suit against the union. Both courts relied upon an earlier decision of the Supreme Court, United Parcel Service, Inc. v. Mitchell, 451 U.S. 56, 101 S.Ct. 1559, 67 L.Ed.2d 732 (1981), which had held, in a suit against an employer alone, that there was no federal statute of limitations for an action under Section 301 and that the proper state statute to "borrow" was that for vacating an arbitration award (in most states, only ninety days) and not that for contract breach.

The Court in *DelCostello* distinguished *United Parcel Service*, and concluded that both the Section 301 action against the employer and the DFR action against the union are to be governed by an implied federal statute of limitations and that the pertinent period—borrowed from Section 10(b) of the NLRA for unfair labor practice charges—is to be six months.

The Court acknowledged that when a federal statute has no explicit period of limitations, it is proper for a court to borrow the most closely analogous statute of limitations under state law. On occasions, however, the state limitations period is an "unsatisfactory vehicle" because it is "at odds with the purpose or operation of federal substantive law." In such cases, timeliness rules are to be drawn from "either express limitations periods from related federal statutes, or such alternatives as laches." The Court also acknowledged that the analogy drawn in *United Parcel Service*, to proceedings to set aside commercial arbitration awards, was "imperfect in operation." A central distinction is that in the labor setting, "the employee will often be unsophisticated in collective-bargaining matters, and he will almost always be represented solely by the union," and not his own counsel. "He is called upon, within the limitations period, to evaluate the adequacy of the union's representation, to retain counsel, to investigate substantial matters that were not at issue in the arbitration proceeding, and to frame his suit." In view of the very short limitations periods in most states for vacating arbitration awards, the Court concluded that their application would "fail to provide an aggrieved employee with a satisfactory opportunity to vindicate his rights under § 301 and the fair representation doctrine." Moreover, the DFR action against the union was never the subject of the arbitration award under the labor agreement, so that the DFR plaintiff is not asking that any such award be undone. In such cases, the application of a state malpractice limitations period (in most states, somewhere between two years and ten years) would also frustrate federal policy, for it "would preclude the relatively rapid final resolution of labor disputes favored by federal law—a problem not present when a party to a commercial arbitration sues his lawyer.''

The Court therefore concluded that a federal limitations period was appropriate for both the claim against the employer and the claim against the union, by "an analogy to the present lawsuit more apt than any of the suggested state-law parallels. We refer to § 10(b) of the National Labor Relations Act, which establishes a six-month period for making charges of unfair labor practices to the NLRB." The Court reasoned as follows:

"The NLRB has consistently held that all breaches of a union's duty of fair representation *are* in fact unfair labor practices. *E.g.*, Miranda Fuel Co., 140 N.L.R.B. 181 (1962), enforcement denied, 326 F.2d 172 (C.A.2 1963). We have twice declined to decide the correctness of the Board's position, and we need not address that question today. Even if not all breaches of the duty are unfair labor practices, however, the family resemblance is undeniable, and indeed there is a substantial overlap. Many fair representation claims * * * include allegations of discrimination based on membership status or dissident views, which would be unfair labor practices under § 8(b)(1) or (2). Aside from these clear cases, duty-of-fair-representation claims are allegations of unfair, arbitrary, or discriminatory treatment of workers by unions—as are virtually all unfair labor practice charges made by workers against unions. See generally R. Gorman, Labor Law 698–701 (1976). Similarly, it may be the case that alleged violations by an employer of a collective bargaining agreement will also amount to unfair labor practices. See id., at 729–734."

"At least as important as the similarity of the rights asserted in the two contexts, however, is the close similarity of the considerations relevant to the choice of a limitations period. As Justice Stewart observed in *Mitchell*:

"In § 10(b) of the NLRA, Congress established a limitations period attuned to what it viewed as the proper balance between the national interests in stable bargaining relationships and finality of private settlements, and an employee's interest in setting aside what he views as an unjust settlement under the collective-bargaining system. That is precisely the balance at issue in this case. The employee's interest in setting aside the "final and binding" determination of a grievance through the method established by the collective-bargaining agreement unquestionably implicates "those consensual processes that federal labor law is chiefly designed to promote—the formation of the * * * agreement and the private settlement of disputes under it." *Hoosier*, 383 U.S., at 702, 86 S.Ct., at 1111. Accordingly, "[t]he need for uniformity" among procedures followed for similar claims, ibid., as well as the clear congressional indication of the proper balance between the interests at stake, counsels the adoption of § 10(b) of the NLRA as the appropriate limitations period for lawsuits such as this.' " 451 U.S., at 70–71, 101 S.Ct., at 1567–1568 (opinion concurring in the judgment) (footnote omitted).

In INTERNATIONAL BHD. OF ELEC. WORKERS v. FOUST, 442 U.S. 42, 99 S.Ct. 2121, 60 L.Ed.2d 698 (1979), the Supreme Court held (in a decision that was clearly intended to construe the NLRA as well) that the Railway Labor Act does not contemplate the award of punitive damages against a union which violates its duty of fair representation (in this case, by untimely filing a grievance for a discharged employee).

Respondent Foust was discharged for alleged medical reasons; the collective bargaining agreement required the presentation of grievances within sixty days from the occurrence giving rise thereto. Foust's attorney first contacted the union about the grievance fifty-two days after the discharge, and by the time intra-union communications were undertaken and the grievance filed, ten more days had elapsed. The railroad and the National Railroad Adjustment Board denied the grievance as untimely. Foust sued the union for breach of the duty of fair representation, and the district court entered a judgment, based on a jury verdict, for $40,000 actual damages and $75,000 punitive damages. The court of appeals held that punitive damages could be awarded but only if the union acted wantonly or in reckless disregard of an employee's rights. The Supreme Court granted certiorari to resolve a conflict in the circuits regarding punitive damages in fair representation cases (and therefore, did not review either the finding of breach of that duty in this case or the award of compensatory damages).

In an opinion by Justice Marshall, for five Justices, the Court concluded that any positive value to be served by permitting punitive damage awards was offset by "the possibility that punitive awards could impair the financial stability of unions and unsettle the careful balance of individual and collective interest which this Court has previously articulated in the unfair representation area." The Court read earlier cases to adopt a principle of compensation of wronged individual employees in fair-representation cases "without compromising the collective interest of union members in protecting limited funds." The broad discretion of juries to award punitive damages would make the "impact of these windfall recoveries * * * unpredictable and potentially substantial." The depletion of union treasuries, with the resulting impairment of the union's effectiveness as collective bargaining representative, "is simply too great a price for whatever deterrent effect punitive damages may have."

The Court also feared that the threat of punitive damages would unduly interfere with the salutary exercise of union discretion in handling and settling grievances, and with the resulting strengthening of employer confidence in the union. Unions would be pressured to process frivolous grievances or resist fair settlements, threatening disruption of the "responsible decision-making essential to peaceful labor relations."

Treating the NLRA and the Railway Labor Act as articulating the same basic policies on this issue, the Court concluded: "[W]e hold that such [punitive] damages may not be assessed against a union that breaches its duty of fair representation by failing properly to pursue a grievance."

Four Justices, in a concurring opinion by Justice Blackmun, agreed that punitive damages ought not be awarded in the present case, where the union's delinquency was at worst negligent or grossly negligent. When, however, the union's breach of its duty of fair representation is rooted, for example, in intentional racial discrimination or deliberate personal animus, punitive damages would serve as a deterrent, an acceptable objective in duty of fair representation cases. The concurring Justices criticized the Court for announcing a per se rule barring punitive damages when the record did not necessitate such a broad (and unsound) disposition.

---

## PROBLEMS FOR DISCUSSION

**1.** It is obvious that the Supreme Court by now has endorsed, without formally considering the issue, the Board's conclusion that breach of the duty of fair representation is an unfair labor practice. If the issue were in fact to be fully considered by the Court, what conclusion should the Court reach, and on what grounds? For example, precisely which subsections of Section 8(b) are violated? Does your answer depend on whether the breach of the duty takes place in negotiating a new contract or in processing grievances under the present contract?

**2.** Assuming that an individual does have recourse either to the NLRB or to a federal (or state) court action for breach of the DFR, what factors will shape his or her judgment in deciding which forum to choose? Does your answer depend on whether the breach of the duty takes place in negotiating a new contract or in processing grievances under the present contract?

If access to a jury trial were to be available in a court action (but, of course, not in a proceeding before the NLRB), would this likely affect the choice of forum? How? The Supreme Court has held that in a DFR action seeking backpay, the plaintiff has a constitutional right under the Seventh Amendment to trial by jury. See Teamsters Local 391 v. Terry, 494 U.S. 558, 110 S.Ct. 1339, 108 L.Ed.2d 519 (1990).

**3.** Should the NLRB consider claims that the union seeking representation discriminates either in its membership or in its negotiating practices on the basis of race, sex or national origin? If so, at which stage of the representation proceeding—when it files a petition or after the election and before certification? Would certification represent an unconstitutional participation by the federal government in the union's discriminatory practices? Should actual discriminatory practices within a bargaining unit by an incumbent union justify stripping its certification, or justify an employer's refusal to bargain? (Note that discrimination on the basis of race, sex, and national origin on the part of a union in admitting workers to membership—a practice that was commonly featured in the earlier DFR cases—has since been outlawed under Title VII of the Civil Rights Act, enforceable by the Equal Employment Opportunity Commission and the federal courts.)

**4.** Does the duty of fair representation require that the union not merely abstain from making negotiating decisions and grievance-processing decisions that are themselves hostilely motivated but also take affirmative steps to redress discriminatory practices on the part of the employer? If, for example, an employer arguably continues to maintain racially segregated eating or sanitary facilities, or to favor male employees in promotions, does the union have a duty affirmatively to formulate grievances or contract proposals to eliminate such practices?

**5.**   The union representing hotel employees at a number of hotels and motels in Southern California counts among its members a substantial number of Mexican-born workers who have come to this country only recently and who understand very little English; nor are they acquainted with the practices of American labor-management relations. These workers have complained to the union that the union meetings ought not be conducted exclusively in English, that a Spanish-language copy of the collective bargaining agreement should be prepared and made available to all employees, and that a Spanish-speaking individual should be designated by the union to assist the employees in their adjustment to the workplace and in the understanding of their rights under the labor contract. The union officials have refused to take such steps, and have noted that neither the union nor the company discriminates against any members of the union in the negotiation or administration of the labor contract. A Spanish-speaking member of the union has filed a complaint against the union in a federal court, alleging the above facts, and the union has moved to dismiss the action. How should the court rule? See Retana v. Apartment, Motel, Hotel & Elevator Operators Union Local No. 14, 453 F.2d 1018 (9th Cir.1972).

**6.**   Do you find the reasons for applying the six-month limitations period of Section 10(b) equally compelling as to both the action against the employer and the action against the union? Are they equally compelling with regard to DFR suits arising from bad-faith negotiating and DFR suits arising from bad-faith processing of grievances?

**7.**   To the extent there was disagreement within the Supreme Court in the *Foust* case, which group of Justices has the more sound position?

---

In WOODDELL v. INTERNATIONAL BROTHERHOOD OF ELEC. WORKERS, LOCAL 71, 502 U.S. 93, 112 S.Ct. 494, 116 L.Ed.2d 419 (1991), the plaintiff claimed that the local union's discriminatory refusal to refer him from its hiring hall violated the parent union's constitution which required locals to "live up to all collective bargaining agreements." The Supreme Court held the claim to be justiciable in federal court under § 301. It noted that a parent union's constitution was held to be a contract between the parent and the local. Accordingly, the suit could be brought under § 301 by the plaintiff as a beneficiary of a contract between two labor organizations. It also held, following Teamsters Local 391 v. Terry, supra p. 1043, that the plaintiff was entitled to a jury trial on the § 301 claim.

---

## B.   THE UNION'S DUTY IN CONTRACT-MAKING[b]

The Problems immediately above begin to focus the reader's attention on a possible distinction between the duty of fair representation as applied

**b.**   Finkin, The Limits of Majority Rule in Collective Bargaining, 64 Minn.L.Rev. 183

to contract-making and as applied to contract-administration and grievance processing. Although the earliest significant Supreme Court decisions sketched out the contours of the DFR in cases of contract-making, these have today become the less frequently litigated category of DFR situations. With the more blatant forms of discrimination in contract-making on the basis of union membership, and race or sex, being clearly outlawed either by the NLRA or Title VII of the Civil Rights Act, scrutiny of union negotiating practices under the DFR theory has turned to more subtle practices in which arguably well-intentioned unions pay heed to the negotiating preferences of a majority within the bargaining unit. The *Steele* and *Huffman* cases, pages 378 and 382, supra, affirm that distinctions among groups within the unit must of necessity be drawn by a union in formulating its bargaining policy, and that reasonable work-related criteria for making such distinctions will be sustained. The practical implementation of this principle is, however, often most vexing, as the following cases indicate.

--------

## Air Line Pilots Ass'n, Intern. v. O'Neill

499 U.S. 65, 111 S.Ct. 1127, 113 L.Ed.2d 51 (1991).

■ JUSTICE STEVENS delivered the opinion of the Court.

     * * *

This case arose out of a bitter confrontation between Continental Airlines, Inc. (Continental) and the union representing its pilots, the Air Line Pilots Association, International (ALPA). On September 24, 1983, Continental filed a petition for reorganization under Chapter 11 of the Bankruptcy Code. Immediately thereafter, with the approval of the Bankruptcy Court, Continental repudiated its collective-bargaining agreement with ALPA and unilaterally reduced its pilots' salaries and benefits by more than half. ALPA responded by calling a strike that lasted for over two years.

Of the approximately 2,000 pilots employed by Continental, all but about 200 supported the strike. By the time the strike ended, about 400 strikers had "crossed over" and been accepted for reemployment in order of reapplication. By trimming its operations and hiring about 1,000 replacements, Continental was able to continue in business. By August 1985, there were 1,600 working pilots and only 1,000 strikers. * * *

(1980); Freed, Polsby & Spitzer, Unions, Fairness, and the Conundrums of Collective Choice, 56 So.Calif.L.Rev. 461 (1983); Hyde, Can Judges Identify Fair Bargaining Procedures? : A Comment on Freed, Polsby & Spitzer, 57 So.Calif.L.Rev. 415 (1984); Freed, Polsby & Spitzer, A Reply to Hyde, 57 So.Calif.L.Rev. 425 (1984); Hyde, Democracy in Collective Bargaining, 93 Yale L.J. 793 (1984); Leffler, Piercing the Duty of Fair Representation: The Dichotomy Between Negotiations and Grievance Handling, 1979 U.Ill.L.F. 35; Note, Union Obligations to Disclose Information Under the Duty of Fair Representation: A Survey, 25 Duquesne L.Rev. 959 (1987).

For many years Continental had used a "system bid" procedure for assigning pilots to new positions. Bids were typically posted well in advance in order to allow time for necessary training without interfering with current service. When a group of vacancies was posted, any pilot could submit a bid specifying his or her preferred position (Captain, First Officer, or Second Officer), base of operations, and aircraft type. In the past, vacant positions had been awarded on the basis of seniority, determined by the date the pilot first flew for Continental. The 85–5 bid covered an unusually large number of anticipated vacancies—441 future Captain and First Officer positions and an undetermined number of Second Officer vacancies. Pilots were given nine days—until September 18, 1985—to submit their bids.

Fearing that this bid might effectively lock the striking pilots out of jobs for the indefinite future, ALPA authorized the strikers to submit bids. Although Continental initially accepted bids from both groups, it soon became concerned about the bona fides of the striking pilots' offer to return to work at a future date. It therefore challenged the strikers' bids in court and announced that all of the 85–5 bid positions had been awarded to working pilots.

At this juncture, ALPA intensified its negotiations for a complete settlement. ALPA's negotiating committee and Continental reached an agreement, which was entered as an order by the Bankruptcy Court on October 31, 1985. The agreement provided for an end to the strike, the disposition of all pending litigation, and reallocation of the positions covered by the 85–5 bid.

The agreement offered the striking pilots three options. Under the first, pilots who settled all outstanding claims with Continental were eligible to participate in the allocation of the 85–5 bid positions. Under the second option, pilots who elected not to return to work received severance pay.... Under the third option, striking pilots retained their individual claims against Continental and were eligible to return to work only after all the first option pilots had been reinstated.

Pilots who chose the first option were thus entitled to some of the 85–5 bid positions that, according to Continental, had previously been awarded to working pilots. The first 100 Captain positions were allocated to working pilots and the next 70 Captain positions were awarded, in order of seniority, to returning strikers who chose option one. Thereafter, striking and nonstriking pilots were eligible for Captain positions on a one-to-one ratio. The initial base and aircraft type for a returning striker was assigned by Continental, but the assignments for working pilots were determined by their bids. After the initial assignment, future changes in bases and equipment were determined by seniority, and striking pilots who were in active service when the strike began received seniority credit for the period of the strike.

[A class of former striking pilots brought suit against ALPA for breach of the duty of fair representation. The district court granted ALPA's motion for summary judgment. The Court of Appeals reversed.]

III

ALPA's central argument is that the duty of fair representation requires only that a union act in good faith and treat its members equally and in a nondiscriminatory fashion. The duty, the union argues, does not impose any obligation to provide *adequate* representation. The District Court found that there was no evidence that ALPA acted other than in good faith and without discrimination.[7] Because of its view of the limited scope of the duty, ALPA contends that the District Court's finding, which the Court of Appeals did not question, is sufficient to support summary judgment.

The union maintains, not without some merit, that its view that courts are not authorized to review the rationality of good-faith, nondiscriminatory union decisions is consonant with federal labor policy. The Government has generally regulated only "the process of collective bargaining," H.K. Porter Co. v. NLRB, 397 U.S. 99, 102, 90 S.Ct. 821, 823, 25 L.Ed.2d 146 (1970)(emphasis added), but relied on private negotiation between the parties to establish "their own charter for the ordering of industrial relations," Teamsters v. Oliver, 358 U.S. 283, 295, 79 S.Ct. 297, 304, 3 L.Ed.2d 312 (1959). As we stated in NLRB v. Insurance Agents, 361 U.S. 477, 488, 80 S.Ct. 419, 426, 4 L.Ed.2d 454 (1960), Congress "intended that the parties should have wide latitude in their negotiations, unrestricted by any governmental power to regulate the substantive solution of their differences." See also Carbon Fuel Co. v. Mine Workers, 444 U.S. 212, 219, 100 S.Ct. 410, 415, 62 L.Ed.2d 394 (1979).

There is, however, a critical difference between governmental modification of the terms of a private agreement and an examination of those terms in search for evidence that a union did not fairly and adequately represent its constituency. Our decisions have long recognized that the need for such an examination proceeds directly from the union's statutory role as exclusive bargaining agent. "[T]he exercise of a granted power to act in behalf of others involves the assumption toward them of a duty to exercise the power in their interest and behalf." Steele v. Louisville & Nashville R. Co., 323 U.S. 192, 202, 65 S.Ct. 226, 232, 89 L.Ed. 173 (1944).

The duty of fair representation is thus akin to the duty owed by other fiduciaries to their beneficiaries. For example, some Members of the Court have analogized the duty a union owes to the employees it represents to the duty a trustee owes to trust beneficiaries. See Teamsters v. Terry, 494 U.S. 558, ___, 110 S.Ct. 1339, ___, 108 L.Ed.2d 519 (1990); id., at ___, 110 S.Ct., at ___ (KENNEDY, J., dissenting). Others have likened the relationship between union and employee to that between attorney and client. See id., at ___, 110 S.Ct., at ___ (STEVENS, J., concurring in part and concurring in judgment). The fair representation duty also parallels the responsibilities of corporate officers and directors toward shareholders. Just as these fiducia-

---

**7.** "There is nothing to indicate that the Union made any choices among the Union members or the strikers who were not Union members other than on the best deal that the Union thought it could construct; that the deal is somewhat less than not particularly satisfactory is not relevant to the issue of fair representation." App. 74.

ries owe their beneficiaries a duty of care as well as a duty of loyalty, a union owes employees a duty to represent them adequately as well as honestly and in good faith. See, *e.g.,* Restatement (Second) of Trusts § 174 (1959)(trustee's duty of care); Strickland v. Washington, 466 U.S. 668, 686, 104 S.Ct. 2052, 2063, 80 L.Ed.2d 674 (1984)(lawyer must render ''adequate legal assistance''); Hanson Trust PLC v. ML SCM Acquisition Inc., 781 F.2d 264, 274 (C.A.2 1986) (directors owe duty of care as well as loyalty).

ALPA suggests that a union need owe no enforceable duty of adequate representation because employees are protected from inadequate representation by the union political process. ALPA argues, as has the Seventh Circuit, that employees ''do not need * * * protection against representation that is inept but not invidious'' because if a ''union does an incompetent job * * * its members can vote in new officers who will do a better job or they can vote in another union.'' Dober v. Roadway Express, Inc., 707 F.2d 292, 295 (C.A.7 1983). In *Steele,* the case in which we first recognized the duty of fair representation, we also analogized a union's role to that of a legislature. See 323 U.S., at 198, 65 S.Ct., at 230. Even legislatures, however, are subject to *some* judicial review of the rationality of their actions. See, e.g., United States v. Carolene Products Co., 304 U.S. 144, 58 S.Ct. 778, 82 L.Ed. 1234 (1938); United States Dept. of Agriculture v. Moreno, 413 U.S. 528, 93 S.Ct. 2821, 37 L.Ed.2d 782 (1973).

ALPA relies heavily on language in Ford Motor Co. v. Huffman, 345 U.S. 330, 73 S.Ct. 681, 97 L.Ed. 1048 (1953), which, according to the union, suggests that no review of the substantive terms of a settlement between labor and management is permissible. In particular, ALPA stresses our comment in the case that ''[a] wide range of reasonableness must be allowed a statutory bargaining representative in serving the unit it represents, subject always to complete good faith and honesty of purpose in the exercise of its discretion.'' Id., at 338, 73 S.Ct., at 686. Unlike ALPA, we do not read this passage to limit review of a union's actions to ''good faith and honesty of purpose,'' but rather to recognize that a union's conduct must also be within ''[a] wide range of reasonableness.''

Although there is admittedly some variation in the way in which our opinions have described the unions' duty of fair representation, we have repeatedly identified three components of the duty, including a prohibition against ''arbitrary'' conduct. Writing for the Court in the leading case in this area of the law, Justice White explained:

> ''The statutory duty of fair representation was developed over 20 years ago in a series of cases involving alleged racial discrimination by unions certified as exclusive bargaining representatives under the Railway Labor Act, see Steele v. Louisville & N.R. Co., 323 U.S. 192 [65 S.Ct. 226]; Tunstall v. Brotherhood of Locomotive Firemen, 323 U.S. 210 [65 S.Ct. 235, 89 L.Ed. 187 (1944) ], and was soon extended to unions certified under the N.L.R.A., see *Ford Motor Co. v. Huffman, supra.* Under this doctrine, the exclusive agent's statutory authority to represent all members of a designated unit includes a statutory obligation to serve the interests of all

members without hostility or discrimination toward any, to exercise its discretion with complete good faith and honesty, and to avoid arbitrary conduct. Humphrey v. Moore, 375 U.S. [335], at 342 [84 S.Ct. 363, at 367, 11 L.Ed.2d 370 (1964) ]. It is obvious that Owens' complaint alleged a breach by the Union of a duty grounded in federal statutes, and that federal law therefore governs his cause of action." Vaca v. Sipes, 386 U.S., at 177, 87 S.Ct., at 910.

This description of the "duty grounded in federal statutes" has been accepted without question by Congress and in a line of our decisions spanning almost a quarter of a century.[8]

The union correctly points out, however, that virtually all of those cases can be distinguished because they involved contract administration or enforcement rather than contract negotiation. ALPA argues that the policy against substantive review of contract terms applies directly only in the negotiation area. Although this is a possible basis for distinction, none of our opinions has suggested that the duty is governed by a double standard. Indeed, we have repeatedly noted that the *Vaca v. Sipes* standard applies to "challenges leveled not only at a union's contract administration and enforcement efforts but at its negotiation activities as well." Communications Workers v. Beck, 487 U.S. 735, 743, 108 S.Ct. 2641, 2647, 101 L.Ed.2d 634 (1988)(internal citation omitted); see also Electrical Workers v. Foust, 442 U.S. 42, 47, 99 S.Ct. 2121, 2125, 60 L.Ed.2d 698 (1979); Vaca v. Sipes, 386 U.S., at 177, 87 S.Ct., at 909–10. We have also held that the duty applies in other instances in which a union is acting in its representative role, such as when the union operates a hiring hall. See Breininger v. Sheet Metal Workers, 493 U.S. 67, ___, 110 S.Ct. 424, ___, 107 L.Ed.2d 388 (1989).

We doubt, moreover, that a bright line could be drawn between contract administration and contract negotiation. Industrial grievances may precipitate settlement negotiations leading to contract amendments, and some strikes and strike settlement agreements may focus entirely on questions of contract interpretation. See Conley v. Gibson, 355 U.S. 41, 46, 78 S.Ct. 99, 102, 2 L.Ed.2d 80 (1957); Steelworkers v. Warrior & Gulf Navigation Co., 363 U.S. 574, 581, 80 S.Ct. 1347, 1352, 4 L.Ed.2d 1409 (1960). Finally, some union activities subject to the duty of fair representation fall into neither category. See *Breininger,* 493 U.S., at ___, 110 S.Ct. at ___.

We are, therefore, satisfied that the Court of Appeals correctly concluded that the tripartite standard announced in *Vaca v. Sipes* applies to a union in its negotiating capacity. We are persuaded, however, that the Court of Appeals' further refinement of the arbitrariness component of the

---

**8.** See, *e.g.,* Teamsters v. Terry, 494 U.S. 558, ___, 110 S.Ct. 1339, ___, 108 L.Ed.2d 519 (1990); Electrical Workers v. Foust, 442 U.S. 42, 47, 99 S.Ct. 2121, 2125, 60 L.Ed.2d 698 (1979); Hines v. Anchor Motor Freight, Inc., 424 U.S. 554, 564, 96 S.Ct. 1048, 1056, 47 L.Ed.2d 231 (1976).

standard authorizes more judicial review of the substance of negotiated agreements than is consistent with national labor policy.

As we acknowledged above, Congress did not intend judicial review of a union's performance to permit the court to substitute its own view of the proper bargain for that reached by the union. Rather, Congress envisioned the relationship between the courts and labor unions as similar to that between the courts and the legislature. Any substantive examination of a union's performance, therefore, must be highly deferential, recognizing the wide latitude that negotiators need for the effective performance of their bargaining responsibilities. Cf. Day–Brite Lighting, Inc. v. Missouri, 342 U.S. 421, 423, 72 S.Ct. 405, 407, 96 L.Ed. 469 (1952)(court does "not sit as a superlegislature to weigh the wisdom of legislation nor to decide whether the policy which it expresses offends the public welfare"); United States v. Carolene Products, 304 U.S., at 154, 58 S.Ct., at 784 (where "question is at least debatable," "decision was for Congress"). For that reason, the final product of the bargaining process may constitute evidence of a breach of duty only if it can be fairly characterized as so far outside a "wide range of reasonableness," Ford Motor Co. v. Huffman, 345 U.S., at 338, 73 S.Ct., at 686, that it is wholly "irrational" or "arbitrary."

The approach of the Court of Appeals is particularly flawed because it fails to take into account either the strong policy favoring the peaceful settlement of labor disputes, see, *e.g.*, Groves v. Ring Screw Works, Ferndale Fastener Div., 498 U.S. 168, ___, 111 S.Ct. 498, ___, 112 L.Ed.2d 508 (1990), or the importance of evaluating the rationality of a union's decision in the light of both the facts and the legal climate that confronted the negotiators at the time the decision was made. As we shall explain, these factors convince us that ALPA's agreement to settle the strike was not arbitrary for either of the reasons posited by the Court of Appeals.

IV

The Court of Appeals placed great stress on the fact that the deal struck by ALPA was worse than the result the union would have obtained by unilateral termination of the strike. Indeed, the court held that a jury finding that the settlement was worse than surrender could alone support a judgment that the union had acted arbitrarily and irrationally. See 886 F.2d, at 1445–1446. This holding unduly constrains the "wide range of reasonableness," 345 U.S., at 338, 73 S.Ct., at 686, within which unions may act without breaching their fair representation duty.

For purposes of decision, we may assume that the Court of Appeals was correct in its conclusion that, if ALPA had simply surrendered and voluntarily terminated the strike, the striking pilots would have been entitled to reemployment in the order of seniority. Moreover, we may assume that Continental would have responded to such action by rescinding its assignment of all of the 85-5 bid positions to working pilots. After all, it did rescind about half of those assignments pursuant to the terms of the settlement. Thus, we assume that the union made a bad settlement— one that was even worse than a unilateral termination of the strike.

Nevertheless, the settlement was by no means irrational. A settlement is not irrational simply because it turns out *in retrospect* to have been a bad settlement. Viewed in light of the legal landscape at the time of the settlement, ALPA's decision to settle rather than give up was certainly not illogical. At the time of the settlement, Continental had notified the union that all of the 85–5 bid positions had been awarded to working pilots and was maintaining that none of the strikers had any claim on any of those jobs.

A comparable position had been asserted by United Air Lines in litigation in the Northern District of Illinois.[9] Because the District Court in that case had decided that such vacancies were not filled until pilots were trained and actually working in their new assignments, the Court of Appeals here concluded that the issue had been resolved in ALPA's favor when it agreed to the settlement with Continental. *See* 886 F.2d, at 1446. But this reasoning overlooks the fact that the validity of the District Court's ruling in the other case was then being challenged on appeal.[10]

Moreover, even if the law had been clear that the 85–5 bid positions were vacancies, the Court of Appeals erroneously assumed that the existing law was also clarion that the striking pilots had a right to those vacancies because they had more seniority than the cross-over and replacement workers. The court relied for the latter proposition solely on our cases interpreting the National Labor Relations Act. See 886 F.2d, at 1445. We have made clear, however, that National Labor Relations Act cases are not necessarily controlling in situations, such as this one, which are governed by the Railway Labor Act. See Railroad Trainmen v. Jacksonville Terminal Co., 394 U.S. 369, 383, 89 S.Ct. 1109, 1117–18, 22 L.Ed.2d 344 (1969).

Given the background of determined resistance by Continental at all stages of this strike, it would certainly have been rational for ALPA to recognize the possibility that an attempted voluntary return to work would merely precipitate litigation over the right to the 85–5 bid positions. Because such a return would not have disposed of any of the individual claims of the pilots who ultimately elected option one or option two of the settlement, there was certainly a realistic possibility that Continental would not abandon its bargaining position without a complete settlement.

At the very least, the settlement produced certain and prompt access to a share of the new jobs and avoided the costs and risks associated with

---

**9.** Air Line Pilots Assn. Int'l v. United Air Lines, Inc., 614 F.Supp. 1020 (N.D.Ill. 1985).

**10.** Even if the Seventh Circuit had already affirmed the District Court's holding in the *United Air Lines* case, the Court of Appeals would have erred in its conclusion that the law was so assuredly in ALPA's favor that the settlement was irrational. First, a Seventh Circuit case would not have controlled the outcome in this dispute, which arose in the Fifth Circuit. Second, even if the

*United Air Lines* decision had been a Fifth Circuit case, it was factually distinguishable and therefore might not have dictated the outcome regarding the 85–5 bid positions. In *United Air Lines,* the Fifth Circuit affirmed on the basis of the District Court's finding that the carrier's action was taken in bad faith, motivated by antiunion animus. 802 F.2d, at 898; 614 F.Supp., at 1046. An equivalent finding was by no means certain in this case.

major litigation. Moreover, since almost a third of the striking pilots chose the lump-sum severance payment rather than reinstatement, see n. 1, supra, the settlement was presumably more advantageous than a surrender to a significant number of striking pilots. In labor disputes, as in other kinds of litigation, even a bad settlement may be more advantageous in the long run than a good lawsuit. In all events, the resolution of the dispute over the 85–5 bid vacancies was well within the "wide range of reasonableness," 345 U.S., at 338, 73 S.Ct., at 686, that a union is allowed in its bargaining.

The suggestion that the "discrimination" between striking and working pilots represented a breach of the duty of fair representation also fails. If we are correct in our conclusion that it was rational for ALPA to accept a compromise between the claims of the two groups of pilots to the 85–5 bid positions, some form of allocation was inevitable. A rational compromise on the initial allocation of the positions was not invidious "discrimination" of the kind prohibited by the duty of fair representation. Unlike the grant of "super seniority" to the cross-over and replacement workers in NLRB v. Erie Resistor Corp., 373 U.S. 221, 83 S.Ct. 1139, 10 L.Ed.2d 308 (1963), this agreement preserved the seniority of the striking pilots after their initial reinstatement. In *Erie,* the grant of extra seniority enabled the replacement workers to keep their jobs while more senior strikers lost theirs during a layoff subsequent to the strike. See id., at 223–224, 83 S.Ct., at 1142–1143. The agreement here only provided the order and mechanism for the reintegration of the returning strikers but did not permanently alter the seniority system. This case therefore more closely resembles our decision in Trans World Airlines, Inc. v. Flight Attendants, 489 U.S. 426, 109 S.Ct. 1225, 103 L.Ed.2d 456 (1989), in which we held that an airline's refusal, after a strike, to displace cross-over workers with more senior strikers was not unlawful discrimination.

The judgment of the Court of Appeals is reversed and the case is remanded for further proceedings consistent with this opinion.

It is so ordered.

———

Prior to *O'Neill,* several decisions had expanded upon the duty of fair representation in contract-making, both substantively and procedurally. On the former, for example, the District of Columbia Circuit considered the Labor Board's approach to the merger of seniority lists resulting from the acquisition—by a company with fifty employees—of a company with thirty employees. The larger number were represented by the Union of Transportation Employees (UTE); the smaller by the Teamsters. The Board ordered an election to decide who would represent the merged unit, after the company announced the closing of the terminal represented by the Teamsters. During the campaign, the UTE took the position that, if chosen as the bargaining representative, it would not agree to a dovetailing of seniority lists, as would be the case if the Teamsters won. The Board concluded that this campaign conduct amounted to an announced intention to breach the duty of fair presentation. The District of Columbia Circuit agreed:

> UTE has renounced any good faith effort to reconcile the interests of the [two groups]. It raised no questions with respect to the merits of dovetailing, such as that some jobs are more difficult of execution or require more training than others.... UTE has, in sum, failed to come forward with any reason at all for preferring the [favored] employees other than the purely political motive of winning an election by a promise of preferential representation to the numerically larger number of voters.

Truck Drivers Local 568 v. NLRB (Red Ball Motor Freight, Inc.), 379 F.2d 137 (D.C.Cir.1967).

On the latter, the procedural limb, the same court was later to consider the decision of the postal workers' union to allow union locals to decide work schedules by a vote of their members only. The Board held the union to have established working conditions in a manner that encouraged union membership; but the Court of Appeals enforced the Board's order on a different basis—that a vote that excluded nonmembers breached the duty of fair representation owed to them:

> In most cases a general familiarity with the working environment may allow a representative of some experience to appreciate adequately the perspective of all employees. There must be communication access for employees with a divergent view, although there is no requirement of formal procedures. Where, as here, it appears to the Board that as a practical matter one segment of the bargaining unit has been excluded from consideration, it may find a breach of the duty of fair representation.

Branch 6000, Nat'l Ass'n of Letter Carriers v. NLRB, 595 F.2d 808, 813 (D.C.Cir.1979).

The vitality of both elements—at least in the strong form taken in these cases—now remains to be seen. In RAKESTRAW v. UNITED AIRLINES, INC., 981 F.2d 1524 (7th Cir.1992), cert. denied, 510 U.S. 906, 114 S.Ct. 286, 126 L.Ed.2d 236 (1993), the court upheld, as consistent with the duty of fair representation, two union bargaining positions at United and TWA Airlines: (1) after a strike at United, the union negotiated for relative seniority dates that favored pilot trainees who for the most part honored the union picket lines, over fully qualified pilots who came to work for United as permanent strike replacements; and (2) after TWA acquired the assets of Ozark Airlines, the union "dovetailed" pilot seniority lists according to seniority at either airline company, although this was alleged to disfavor the Ozark pilots, who overall had less seniority and who constituted only a small minority within the union ranks. As to the former case, the court held that even if the union had acted partially out of deep hostility to the qualified pilots for their strikebreaking, its action was nonetheless a reasonable effort to restore preexisting seniority arrangements, and was therefore not a violation of the duty of fair representation. As to the latter dispute, the court held that such a "dovetailing" constituted equal treatment and was fair and reasonable, in a passage that seems to cede much more discretion to the union's internal politics than did *Red Ball Motor Freight*:

> A rational person could conclude that dovetailing seniority lists in a merger, treating service at either firm as of equal weight, without quotas or other preferences for either group of employees, serves the interests of labor as a whole. Seniority lists sometimes are endtailed. That is, the employees of the smaller firm are given seniority only from the date of the acquisition, effectively added at the end of the larger firm's seniority roster. Contentions that endtailing violates the union's duty have been unsuccessful.... The propriety of dovetailing, treating the two groups identically, follows directly. If the union's leaders took account of the fact that the workers at the larger firm preferred this outcome, so what? Majority rule is the norm. Equal treatment does not become forbidden because the majority prefers equality, even if formal equality bears more harshly on the minority.

*Id.* at 1533 (citations omitted).

And in Burkevich v. Air Line Pilots Ass'n Int'l, 894 F.2d 346 (9th Cir.1990), the Ninth Circuit held that the union did not breach the duty of fair representation when it endorsed an employer plan for reorganization in bankruptcy that disadvantaged a group of pilots without any prior consultation with the disadvantaged group; the failure to consult was neither discriminatory nor in bad faith. It does not breach the duty to restrict a ratification vote on the collective bargaining agreement to the union's membership; nor is the union prohibited from excluding non-members from discussions formulating the union's bargaining position. American Postal Workers Union (U.S. Postal Service), 300 NLRB 34 (1990).

———

## PROBLEMS FOR DISCUSSION

**1.** A collective bargaining agreement prohibited strikes and provided a grievance-arbitration procedure for discharge. When twelve workers were discharged, 200 went out on strike in support. All were replaced and the union took the discharges to arbitration. The arbitrator awarded preferential rehiring of the strikers in order of seniority. The collective agreement thereafter expired and the Company insisted—to the point of being willing to "take a strike"—on a new seniority clause that would extinguish the arbitrator's award. Without consulting the strikers or putting the contract to a ratification vote of the membership (there being no such requirement in the union's constitution or by-laws), the union agreed. Has it violated the duty of fair representation owed to the strikers? See Strick Corp., 241 NLRB 210 (1979).

**2.** Rule 12(c) of the collective bargaining agreement governing a multi-employer bargaining unit in the dairy industry provides:

In all consolidations of branches or plants, company craft group seniority shall prevail for the purpose of layoffs, vacations, bidding and in all other usual respects.

If the Employer acquires all or any part of a milk business ... and merges or consolidates the same with its own business, or handles the same in any other manner, ... the Employer shall be required to assume responsibility for the employment of the employees who elect to or who are transferred to the new Employer as provided herein who shall enjoy craft group seniority, on the basis of the period of employment in the business acquired for the purpose of layoffs, vacations, bidding and in all other usual respects.

The union's by-laws require that all collective bargaining agreements be subject to a ratification vote of the union's membership.

Agfab Dairies, an aggressive newly formed company and party to the agreement, employs 200 workers. It is negotiating to acquire Archer Dairy, a much older company with 100 workers, most of whom have much more company seniority than do the Agfab workers; it, too, is party to the agreement.

The union president, who is shortly up for re-election, has been negotiating with Agfab on the acquisition, especially Agfab's assumption of Archer's unfunded pension liability. On advice of counsel, he has told Agfab that he has the authority to waive any provision in the collective bargaining agreement that might be an obstacle to the acquisition and has agreed that the Archer workers would be endtailed. In meetings with Archer employees, however, he has stated that Agfab's acquisition would work a merger under Rule 12(c) resulting in the dovetailing of their seniority; he urged them to stay on the job.

Agfab purchased Archer, closed Archer's dairy, and offered to hire Archer employees in order of seniority at Archer but by placing them in that order at the bottom of Agfab's seniority list. The shop steward at Archer has demanded that the union dovetail those employees according to Rule 12(c), but the union has refused. Has the union violated the duty of fair representation? If so, what should be the remedy? See Lewis v. Tuscan Dairy Farms, Inc., 25 F.3d 1138 (2d Cir.1994), on remand, 907 F.Supp. 740 (S.D.N.Y.1995); Thomas v. Bakery Workers Local 433, 982 F.2d 1215 (8th Cir.1992), cert. denied, 508 U.S. 972, 113 S.Ct. 2961, 125 L.Ed.2d 661 (1993). *See also* Spellacy v. Airline Pilots Ass'n-Int'l, 156 F.3d 120 (2d Cir.1998).

**3.**   In the recessionary economy of the early 1980s, when many companies were faced with unprecedented financial losses and the serious threat of bankruptcy, many unions were called upon to negotiate "give-backs" or concessions in new labor agreements or through mid-term modifications. How would you appraise the legal validity of the following alternative arrangements?

(a) Present wage rates are maintained for employees presently at work in the bargaining unit. Newly hired employees and employees recalled from long-term layoffs, however, are to be paid according to a newly negotiated significantly lower scale of pay. See Note, "Two–Tier Wage Discrimination and the Duty of Fair Representation," 98 Harv.L.Rev. 631 (1985).

(b) In the event of production cutbacks, employees are not to be laid off in order of least seniority as provided by the present agreement; rather, working hours for all employees are to be uniformly reduced to the extent necessary to keep all on the job.

(c) In the event of production cutbacks, junior employees are to be laid off first as provided by the contract; but the wages of the senior retained employees are to be "frozen" and their contemplated wage increases are to be paid instead into a fund to be used to defray emergency expenses of the displaced workers. Cf. Atkinson v. Superior Ct. of Calif., 310 P.2d 145 (Cal.App.1957), vacated, 49 Cal.2d 338, 316 P.2d 960 (1957).

---

## C. THE INDIVIDUAL AND HIS GRIEVANCE[c]

### Vaca v. Sipes

386 U.S. 171, 87 S.Ct. 903, 17 L.Ed.2d 842 (1967).

■ MR. JUSTICE WHITE delivered the opinion of the Court.

On February 13, 1962, Benjamin Owens filed this class action against petitioners, as officers and representatives of the National Brotherhood of Packinghouse Workers and of its Kansas City Local No. 12 (the Union), in the Circuit Court of Jackson County, Missouri. Owens, a Union member, alleged that he had been discharged from his employment at Swift & Company's (Swift) Kansas City Meat Packing Plant in violation of the collective bargaining agreement then in force between Swift and the Union, and that the Union had "arbitrarily, capriciously and without just or reasonable reason or cause" refused to take his grievance with Swift to arbitration under the fifth step of the bargaining agreement's grievance procedures. * * *

### I.

In mid–1959, Owens, a long-time high blood pressure patient, became sick and entered a hospital on sick leave from his employment with Swift. After a long rest during which his weight and blood pressure were reduced, Owens was certified by his family physician as fit to resume his heavy work in the packing plant. However, Swift's company doctor examined Owens upon his return and concluded that his blood pressure was too high to permit reinstatement. After securing a second authorization from another outside doctor, Owens returned to the plant, and a nurse permitted him to resume work on January 6, 1960. However, on January 8, when the doctor

---

c. See Cheit, Competing Models of Fair Representation: The Perfunctory Processing Cases, 24 B.C.L.Rev. 1 (1982); Cox, Rights Under a Labor Agreement, 69 Harv.L.Rev. 601 (1956); Feller, A General Theory of the Collective Bargaining Agreement, 61 Calif.L.Rev. 663 (1973); Sherman, the Role and Rights of the Individual in Labor Arbitration, 15 Wm. Mitchell L.Rev. 379 (1989); Summers, The Individual Employee's Rights Under the Collective Agreement: What Constitutes Fair Representation, 126 U.Pa.L.Rev. 251 (1977); VanderVelde, A Fair Process Model for the Union's Fair Representation Duty, 67 Minn.L.Rev. 1079 (1983).

discovered Owens' return, he was permanently discharged on the ground of poor health. * * *

## II.

Petitioners challenge the jurisdiction of the Missouri courts on the ground that the alleged conduct of the Union was arguably an unfair labor practice and within the exclusive jurisdiction of the NLRB. * * * For the reasons which follow, we reject this argument.

It is now well established that, as the exclusive bargaining representative of the employees in Owens' bargaining unit, the Union had a statutory duty fairly to represent all of those employees, both in its collective bargaining with Swift, see Ford Motor Co. v. Huffman, 345 U.S. 330, 73 S.Ct. 681, 97 L.Ed. 1048; Syres v. Oil Workers International Union, 350 U.S. 892, 76 S.Ct. 152, 100 L.Ed. 785, and in its enforcement of the resulting collective bargaining agreement, see Humphrey v. Moore, 375 U.S. 335, 84 S.Ct. 363, 11 L.Ed.2d 370. * * * Under this doctrine, the exclusive agent's statutory authority to represent all members of a designated unit includes a statutory obligation to serve the interests of all members without hostility or discrimination toward any, to exercise its discretion with complete good faith and honesty, and to avoid arbitrary conduct. Humphrey v. Moore, 375 U.S., at 342, 84 S.Ct., at 367. It is obvious that Owens' complaint alleged a breach by the Union of a duty grounded in federal statutes, and that federal law therefore governs his cause of action. *E.g.*, Ford Motor Co. v. Huffman, supra.

Although N.L.R.A. § 8(b) was enacted in 1947, the NLRB did not until *Miranda Fuel* interpret a breach of a union's duty of fair representation as an unfair labor practice. * * * [P]etitioners argue that Owens' state court action was based upon Union conduct that is arguably proscribed by N.L.R.A. § 8(b), was potentially enforceable by the NLRB, and was therefore pre-empted under the *Garmon* line of decisions.

A. * * * [A]s a general rule, neither state nor federal courts have jurisdiction over suits directly involving "activity [which] is arguably subject to § 7 or § 8 of the Act." San Diego Building Trades Council v. Garmon, 359 U.S., at 245, 79 S.Ct., at 780.

This pre-emption doctrine, however, has never been rigidly applied to cases where it could not fairly be inferred that Congress intended exclusive jurisdiction to lie with the NLRB. Congress itself has carved out exceptions to the Board's exclusive jurisdiction: [Justice White here enumerated actions under Section 303 of the LMRA, claims of contract breach under Section 301, actions in which the NLRB declines to assert jurisdiction by virtue of Section 14 of the Act, and cases involving a "merely peripheral concern" of the Act or "deeply rooted" state interests. He then pointed out that a basic assumption underlying preemption—the need to develop uniform labor-relations law by an expert administrative agency—is not applicable in DFR cases. First, the DFR doctrine was judicially developed in *Steele*, and was applied before the Board was given unfair labor practice jurisdiction over unions in 1947 and long before the Board asserted DFR jurisdiction in *NLRB v. Miranda Fuel Co.*, see page 981, supra, when it decided to adopt the doctrine as it had been developed by the federal courts. Moreover, it is doubtful that the NLRB has special expertise in DFR cases (especially as relates to assessing the content of union positions in contract-making and grievance processing). Finally, the General Counsel has unreviewable discretion to refuse to issue an unfair labor practice complaint, and "the existence of even a small group of cases in which the Board would be unwilling or unable to remedy a union's breach of duty would frustrate the basic purposes" underlying the DFR doctrine.]

B.   There are also some intensely practical considerations which foreclose pre-emption of judicial cognizance of fair representation duty suits, considerations which emerge from the intricate relationship between the duty of fair representation and the enforcement of collective bargaining contracts. For the fact is that the question of whether a union has breached its duty of fair representation will in many cases be a critical issue in a suit under L.M.R.A. § 301 charging an employer with a breach of contract. To illustrate, let us assume a collective bargaining agreement that limits discharges to those for good cause and that contains no grievance, arbitration or other provisions purporting to restrict access to the courts. If an employee is discharged without cause, either the union or the employee may sue the employer under L.M.R.A. § 301. * * *

* * * [I]f the wrongfully discharged employee himself resorts to the courts before the grievance procedures have been fully exhausted, the employer may well defend on the ground that the exclusive remedies provided by such a contract have not been exhausted. Since the employee's claim is based upon breach of the collective bargaining agreement, he is bound by terms of that agreement which govern the manner in which contractual rights may be enforced. For this reason, it is settled that the employee must at least attempt to exhaust exclusive grievance and arbitration procedures established by the bargaining agreement. Republic Steel Corp. v. Maddox, 379 U.S. 650, 85 S.Ct. 614, 13 L.Ed.2d 580. However, because these contractual remedies have been devised and are often controlled by the union and the employer, they may well prove unsatisfactory or unworkable for the individual grievant. The problem then is to determine under what circumstances the individual employee may obtain judicial review of his breach-of-contract claim despite his failure to secure relief through the contractual remedial procedures. * * *

We think that [one] situation when the employee may seek judicial enforcement of his contractual rights arises if, as is true here, the union has sole power under the contract to invoke the higher stages of the grievance procedure, *and* if, as is alleged here, the employee-plaintiff has been prevented from exhausting his contractual remedies by the union's *wrongful* refusal to process the grievance. It is true that the employer in such a situation may have done nothing to prevent exhaustion of the exclusive contractual remedies to which he agreed in the collective bargaining agreement. But the employer has committed a wrongful discharge in breach of that agreement, a breach which could be remedied through the grievance process to the employee-plaintiff's benefit were it not for the union's breach of its statutory duty of fair representation to the employee. To leave the employee remediless in such circumstances would, in our opinion, be a great injustice. We cannot believe that Congress, in conferring upon employers and unions the power to establish exclusive grievance procedures, intended to confer upon unions such unlimited discretion to deprive injured employees of all remedies for breach of contract. Nor do we think that Congress intended to shield employers from the natural consequences of their breaches of bargaining agreements by wrongful union conduct in the enforcement of such agreements. Cf. Richardson v. Texas & N.O.R.R., 242 F.2d 230, 235–236 (C.A.5th Cir.).

For these reasons, we think the wrongfully discharged employee may bring an action against his employer in the face of a defense based upon the failure to exhaust contractual remedies, provided the employee can prove that the union as bargaining agent breached its duty of fair representation in its handling of the employee's grievance. We may assume for present purposes that such a breach of duty by the union is an unfair labor practice, as the NLRB and the Fifth Circuit have held. The employee's suit against the employer, however, remains a § 301 suit, and the jurisdiction of the courts is no more destroyed by the fact that the employee, as part and parcel of his § 301 action, finds it necessary to prove an unfair labor practice by the union, than it is by the fact that the suit may involve an unfair labor practice by the employer himself. The court is free to determine whether the employee is barred by the actions of his union representative, and, if not, to proceed with the case. And if, to facilitate his case, the employee joins the union as a defendant, the situation is not substantially changed. The action is still a § 301 suit, and the jurisdiction of the courts is not pre-empted under the *Garmon* principle. * * * And, insofar as adjudication of the union's breach of duty is concerned, the result should be no different if the employee, as Owens did here, sues the employer and the union in separate actions. There would be very little to commend a rule which would permit the Missouri courts to adjudicate the Union's conduct in an action against Swift but not in an action against the Union itself.

For the above reasons, it is obvious that the courts will be compelled to pass upon whether there has been a breach of the duty of fair representation in the context of many § 301 breach-of-contract actions. If a breach of duty by the union and a breach of contract by the employer are proven, the court must fashion an appropriate remedy. Presumably, in at least some cases, the union's breach of duty will have enhanced or contributed to the employee's injury. What possible sense could there be in a rule which would permit a court that has litigated the fault of employer and union to fashion a remedy only with respect to the employer? Under such a rule, either the employer would be compelled by the court to pay for the union's wrong— slight deterrence, indeed, to future union misconduct—or the injured employee would be forced to go to two tribunals to repair a single injury. Moreover, the Board would be compelled in many cases either to remedy injuries arising out of a breach of contract, a task which Congress has not assigned to it, or to leave the individual employee without remedy for the union's wrong. Given the strong reasons for not pre-empting duty of fair representation suits in general, and the fact that the courts in many § 301 suits must adjudicate whether the union has breached its duty, we conclude that the courts may also fashion remedies for such a breach of duty.

It follows from the above that the Missouri courts had jurisdiction in this case. * * *

### III.

Petitioners contend, as they did in their motion for judgment notwithstanding the jury's verdict, that Owens failed to prove that the Union breached its duty of fair representation in its handling of Owens' grievance. Petitioners also argue that the Supreme Court of Missouri, in rejecting this contention, applied a standard that is inconsistent with governing principles of federal law with respect to the Union's duty to an individual employee in its processing of grievances under the collective bargaining agreement with Swift. We agree with both contentions.

### A.

* * * [T]he question which the Missouri Supreme Court thought dispositive of the issue of liability was whether the evidence supported Owens' assertion that he had been wrongfully discharged by Swift, regardless of the Union's good faith in reaching a contrary conclusion. This was also the major concern of the plaintiff at trial: the bulk of Owens' evidence was directed at whether he was medically fit at the time of discharge and whether he had performed heavy work after that discharge.

A breach of the statutory duty of fair representation occurs only when a union's conduct toward a member of the collective bargaining unit is arbitrary, discriminatory, or in bad faith. * * * Though we accept the proposition that a union may not arbitrarily ignore a meritorious grievance or process it in perfunctory fashion, we do not agree that the individual employee has an absolute right to have his grievance taken to arbitration regardless of the provisions of the applicable collective bargaining agreement. In L.M.R.A. § 203(d), 61 Stat. 154, 29 U.S.C. § 173(d), Congress declared that "Final adjustment by a method agreed upon by the parties is * * * the desirable method for settlement of grievance disputes arising over the application or interpretation of an existing collective-bargaining agreement." In providing for a grievance and arbitration procedure which gives the union discretion to supervise the grievance machinery and to invoke arbitration, the employer and the union contemplate that each will endeavor in good faith to settle grievances short of arbitration. Through this settlement process, frivolous grievances are ended prior to the most costly and time-consuming step in the grievance procedures. Moreover, both sides are assured that similar complaints will be treated consistently, and major problem areas in the interpretation of the collective bargaining contract can be isolated and perhaps resolved. And finally, the settlement process furthers the interest of the union as statutory agent and as coauthor of the bargaining agreement in representing the employees in the enforcement of that agreement. See Cox, Rights Under a Labor Agreement, 69 Harv.L.Rev. 601 (1956).

If the individual employee could compel arbitration of his grievance regardless of its merit, the settlement machinery provided by the contract would be substantially undermined, thus destroying the employer's confidence in the union's authority and returning the individual grievant to the vagaries of independent and unsystematic negotiation. Moreover, under such a rule, a significantly greater number of grievances would proceed to arbitration. This would greatly increase the cost of the grievance machinery and could so overburden the arbitration process as to prevent it from functioning successfully. See NLRB v. Acme Ind. Co., 385 U.S. 432, 438, 87 S.Ct. 565, 569, 17 L.Ed.2d 495; Ross, Distressed Grievance Procedures and Their Rehabilitation, in Labor Arbitration and Industrial Change, Proceedings of the 16th Annual Meeting, National Academy of Arbitrators 104 (1963). It can well be doubted whether the parties to collective bargaining agreements would long continue to provide for detailed grievance and arbitration procedures of the kind encouraged by L.M.R.A. § 203(d), supra, if their power to settle the majority of grievances short of the costlier and more time-consuming steps was limited by a rule permitting the grievant unilaterally to invoke arbitration. Nor do we see substantial danger to the interests of the individual employee if his statutory agent is given the contractual power honestly and in good faith to settle grievances short of arbitration. For these reasons, we conclude that a union does not breach its duty of fair representation, and thereby open up a suit by the employee for breach of contract, merely because it settled the grievance short of arbitration. * * *

For these same reasons, the standard applied here by the Missouri Supreme Court cannot be sustained. For if a union's decision that a particular grievance lacks sufficient merit to justify arbitration would constitute a breach of the duty of fair representation because a judge or jury later found the grievance meritorious, the union's incentive to settle such grievances short of arbitration would be seriously reduced. The dampening effect on the entire grievance procedure of this reduction of the union's freedom to settle claims in good faith would surely be substantial. Since the union's statutory duty of fair representation protects the individual employee from arbitrary abuses of the settlement device by providing him with recourse against both employer (in a § 301 suit) and union, this severe limitation on the power to settle grievances is neither necessary nor desirable. Therefore, we conclude that the Supreme Court of Missouri erred in upholding the verdict in this case solely on the ground that the evidence supported Owens' claim that he had been wrongfully discharged.

## B.

Applying the proper standard of union liability to the facts of this case, we cannot uphold the jury's award, for we conclude that as a matter of federal law the evidence does not support a verdict that the Union breached its duty of fair representation. * * *

In administering the grievance and arbitration machinery as statutory agent of the employees, a union must, in good faith and in a nonarbitrary manner make decisions as to the merits of particular grievances. See Humphrey v. Moore, 375 U.S. 335, 349–350, 84 S.Ct. 363, 371–372, 11 L.Ed.2d 370; Ford Motor Co. v. Huffman, 345 U.S. 330, 337–339, 73 S.Ct. 681, 685–687, 97 L.Ed. 1048. In a case such as this, when Owens supplied the Union with medical evidence supporting his position, the Union might well have breached its duty had it ignored Owens' complaint or had it processed the grievance in a perfunctory manner. See Cox, Rights under a Labor Agreement, 69 Harv.L.Rev., at 632–634. But here the Union processed the grievance into the fourth step, attempted to gather sufficient evidence to prove Owens' case, attempted to secure for Owens less vigorous work at the plant, and joined in the employer's efforts to have Owens rehabilitated. Only when these efforts all proved unsuccessful did the Union conclude both that arbitration would be fruitless and that the grievance should be dismissed. There was no evidence that any Union officer was personally hostile to Owens or that the Union acted at any time other than in good faith. Having concluded that the individual employee has no absolute right to have his grievance arbitrated under the collective bargaining agreement at issue, and that a breach of the duty of fair representation is not established merely by proof that the underlying grievance was meritorious, we must conclude that that duty was not breached here.

[The Court also held that it was improper to enter a judgment against the union for compensatory damages in the amount of $6,500 for earnings lost by virtue of the employer's breach of contract, along with $3,000 punitive damages. If the union's failure to take Owens's case to arbitration was a breach of its DFR, "there is no reason to exempt the employer from contractual damages which he would otherwise have had to pay. The difficulty lies in fashioning an appropriate scheme of remedies." The Court held that one appropriate remedy might be an order compelling the employer and union to arbitrate the grievance. But because an arbitrator will normally have no power to award damages against a union, and because sometimes the arbitrable issues will have already been substantially resolved in the course of the DFR lawsuit, "the court should be free to decide the contractual claim and to award the employee appropriate damages or equitable relief." In determining how to apportion damages, "may an award against a union include, as it did here, damages attributable solely to the employer's breach of contract? We think not. Though the union has violated a statutory duty in failing to press the grievance, it is the employer's unrelated breach of contract which triggered the controversy and which caused this portion of the employee's damages. * * * It could be a real hardship on the union to pay these damages, even if the union were given a right of indemnification against the employer."]

The governing principle, then, is to apportion liability between the employer and the union according to the damage caused by the fault of each. Thus, damages attributable solely to the employer's breach of contract should not be charged to the union, but increases if any in those damages caused by the union's refusal to process the grievance should not be charged to the employer. In this case, even if the Union had breached its duty, all or almost all of Owens' damages would still be attributable to his allegedly wrongful discharge by Swift. For these reasons, even if the Union here had properly been found liable for a breach of duty, it is clear that the damage award was improper.

Reversed.

■ MR. JUSTICE FORTAS, with whom THE CHIEF JUSTICE and MR. JUSTICE HARLAN join, concurring in the result.

* * * There is no basis for failure to apply the pre-emption principles in the present case * * *. The employee's claim against the union is not a claim under the collective bargaining agreement, but a claim that the union has breached its statutory duty of fair representation. This claim, I submit, is a claim of unfair labor practice and it is within the exclusive jurisdiction of the NLRB. * * * As the Court in effect acknowledges, we are concerned with the subtleties of a union's statutory duty faithfully to represent employees in the unit, including those who may not be members of the union. The Court—regrettably, in my opinion—ventures to state judgments as to the metes and bounds of the reciprocal duties involved in the relationship between the union and the employee. In my opinion, this is precisely and especially the kind of judgment that Congress intended to entrust to the Board and which is well within the pre-emption doctrine that this Court has prudently stated. * * *

■ MR. JUSTICE BLACK, dissenting.

The Court today opens slightly the courthouse door to an employee's incidental claim against his union for breach of its duty of fair representation, only to shut it in his face when he seeks direct judicial relief for his underlying and more valuable breach-of-contract claim against his employer. This result follows from the Court's announcement in this case, involving an employee's suit against his union, of a new rule to govern an employee's suit against his employer. The rule is that before an employee can sue his employer under § 301 of the L.M.R.A. for a simple breach of his employment contract, the employee must prove not only that he attempted to exhaust his contractual remedies, but that his attempt to exhaust them was frustrated by "arbitrary, discriminatory or * * * bad faith" conduct on the part of his union. With this new rule and its result, I cannot agree.

The Court recognizes as it must, that the jury in this case found at least that Benjamin Owens was fit for work, that his grievance against Swift was meritorious, and that Swift breached the collective bargaining agreement when it wrongfully discharged him. * * * Owens, who now has obtained a judicial determination that he was wrongfully discharged, is left remediless, and Swift, having breached its contract, is allowed to hide behind, and is shielded by, the union's conduct. I simply fail to see how it should make one iota of difference, as far as the "unrelated breach-of-contract" by Swift is concerned, whether the union's conduct is wrongful or rightful. Neither precedent nor logic support the Court's new announcement that it does.

Certainly, nothing in Republic Steel Corp. v. Maddox, 379 U.S. 650, 85 S.Ct. 614, supports this new rule. * * * [T]he Court there held that the employee "must *attempt* use of the contract grievance procedure," id., at 652, 85 S.Ct. at 616, and "must afford the union the opportunity to act on his behalf," id., at 653, 85 S.Ct. at 616. * * * Here, of course, Benjamin Owens did not "completely sidestep available grievance procedures in favor of a lawsuit." With complete respect for the union's authority and deference to the contract grievance procedures, he not only gave the union a chance to act on his behalf, but in every way possible tried to convince it that his claim was meritorious and should be carried through the fifth step to arbitration. In short, he did everything the Court's opinion in *Maddox* said he should do, and yet now the Court says so much is not enough.

* * * If the Court here were satisfied with merely holding that in this situation the employee cannot recover damages from the union unless the union breached its duty of fair representation, then it would be one thing to say that the union did not do so in making a good-faith decision not to take the employee's grievance to arbitration. But if, as the Court goes on to hold, the employee cannot sue his employer for breach of contract unless his failure to exhaust contractual remedies is due to the union's breach of its duty of fair representation, then I am quite unwilling to say that the union's refusal to exhaust such remedies—however non-arbitrary—does not amount to a breach of its duty. Either the employee should be able to sue his employer for breach of contract after having attempted to exhaust his contractual remedies, or the union should have an absolute duty to exhaust contractual remedies on his behalf. The merits of an employee's grievance would thus be determined by either a jury or an arbitrator. Under today's decision it will never be determined by either.

* * * The Court suggests three reasons for giving the union this almost unlimited discretion to deprive injured employees of all remedies for breach of contract. The first is that "frivolous grievances" will be ended prior to time-consuming and costly arbitration. But here no one, not even the union, suggests that Benjamin Owens' grievance was frivolous. The union decided not to take it to arbitration simply because the union doubted the chance of success. Even if this was a good-faith doubt, I think the union had the duty to present this contested, but serious claim to the arbitrator whose very function is to decide such claims on the basis of what he believes to be right. Second, the Court says that allowing the union to settle grievances prior to arbitration will assure consistent treatment of "major problem areas in interpretation of collective bargaining contracts." But can it be argued that whether Owens was "fit to work" presents a major problem in the interpretation of the collective bargaining agreement? The problem here was one of interpreting medical reports, not a collective bargaining agreement, and of evaluating other evidence of Owens' physical condition. I doubt whether consistency is either possible or desirable in determining whether a particular employee is able to perform a particular

job. Finally, the Court suggests that its decision "furthers the interests of the union as statutory agent." I think this is the real reason for today's decision which entirely overlooks the interests of the injured employee, the only one who has anything to lose. Of course, anything which gives the union life and death power over those whom it is supposed to represent furthers its "interests." I simply fail to see how the union's legitimate role as statutory agent is undermined by requiring it to prosecute all serious grievances to a conclusion or by allowing the injured employee to sue his employer after he has given the union a chance to act on his behalf.

* * * [T]oday's decision, requiring the individual employee to take on both the employer and the union in every suit against the employer and to prove not only that the employer breached its contract, but that the union acted arbitrarily, converts what would otherwise be a simple breach-of-contract action into a three-ring donnybrook. It puts an intolerable burden on employees with meritorious grievances and means they will frequently be left with no remedy. Today's decision, while giving the worker an ephemeral right to sue his union for breach of its duty of fair representation, creates insurmountable obstacles to block his far more valuable right to sue his employer for breach of the collective bargaining agreement.

---

Breininger v. Sheet Metal Workers, Local 6, 493 U.S. 67, 110 S.Ct. 424, 107 L.Ed.2d 388 (1989). Breininger was denied job referrals by certain Union officials at the Union's hiring hall, established under a multiemployer collective bargaining agreement. Alleging that the action was in retaliation for his opposition to those officials in a recent Union election—and was arbitrary, discriminatory and in bad faith—Breininger brought an action in federal court for breach of the duty of fair representation. The district court and the court of appeals held that they lacked jurisdiction, the latter court holding that DFR claims based on an employee's intra-union activities were properly to be asserted to the NLRB and that in any event the DFR claim would fail because Breininger did not simultaneously allege that his employer had violated the collective bargaining agreement. The Supreme Court reversed.

The Court began by reiterating its holding in *Vaca v. Sipes* that the Board's assertion of jurisdiction in the *Miranda Fuel* case to remedy DFR violations under sections 8(b)(1) and (b)(2) does not oust the courts of jurisdiction to enforce the duty as well; the reasons that normally support exclusive jurisdiction in the Board lack force here. The Court went on to reject the Union's argument that an exception to the prevailing rule of nonpre-emption should apply in the context of hiring-hall referrals, an area in which the Board has had long experience. "[W]e have never suggested that the *Vaca* rule contains exceptions based on the subject matter of the fair representation claim presented, the relative expertise of the NLRB in the particular area of labor law involved, or any other factor. We are unwilling to begin the process of carving out exceptions now, especially since we see no limiting principle to such an approach.... Adopting a rule that NLRB expertise bars federal jurisdiction would remove an unacceptably large number of fair representation claims from federal courts," among them claims of discrimination by the Union based on lack of union membership, intraunion dissent, and racial and gender considerations. Unlike state law claims based upon tort, contract and other legal theories developed independently of federal labor law, the DFR is part of federal labor policy and indeed predates the 1947 enumeration of union unfair labor practices.

The Court then considered, and rejected, the contention that a DFR claim must fail absent an allegation that the employer has violated the labor contract; there was no such allegation in this case. Although relief against an employer for contract breach cannot be secured absent a union breach of the DFR in administering the contract, "our reasoning in *Vaca* in no way implies, however, that a fair representation action *requires* a concomitant claim against an employer for breach of contract. Indeed, the earliest fair representation suits involved claims against unions for breach of the duty in *negotiating* a collective bargaining agreement, a context in which no breach-of-contract action against an employer is possible."

The Union argued that where there is no contract claim under section 301 against the employer, and the employer violates section 8(a)(3) by participating in a discriminatory nonreferral by a union, there is a policy favoring joining the claims against union and employer and that can only be done before the NLRB. The Court, however, concluded: "The fact that an employee *may* bring his fair representation claim in federal court in order to join it with a § 301 claim does not mean that he *must* bring the fair representation claim before the Board in order to 'join' it with a hypothetical unfair-labor-practice case against the employer that was never actually filed." Federal court jurisdiction to hear DFR cases stems from 28 U.S.C. § 1337(a), because the NLRA is an act regulating commerce; this is true whether or not that claim is accompanied by one against the employer.

The Union then argued, even assuming there is jurisdiction over Breininger's DFR claim, that he failed on the merits to allege such a claim. First, the Union contended that the DFR should be understood as coincident with section 8(b)(2) which, the Union argued, bars only union discrimination on the basis of union membership or lack thereof—which was not alleged here. The Court declined to rule upon whether it is an unfair labor practice for a union to induce employer discrimination even for reasons other than union membership—such as for any unfair, irrelevant or invidious consideration—because it concluded that "we reject the proposition that the duty of fair representation should be defined in terms of what is an unfair labor practice. . . . The duty of fair representation is not intended to mirror the contours of § 8(b); rather, it arises independently from the grant under § 9(a) of the NLRA ... of the union's exclusive power to represent all employees" and protects those employees against arbitrary union conduct. *Miranda Fuel* treated breaches of the DFR as unfair labor practices in order to *expand* the remedies available to employees, and there is no justification for using the unfair labor practice provisions so as to *restrict* employee rights.

Finally, the Court rejected the Union's claim that it could not violate the DFR because in operating the hiring hall it was functioning essentially as an employer and not as the employees' bargaining agent. The Court noted that it is only through the union's status as bargaining representative with the attendant powers granted by the labor agreement that the union gains the ability to refer workers for employment. "That the particular function of job referral resembles a task that an employer might perform is of no consequence. The key is that the union is administering a provision of the contract, something that we have always held is subject to the duty of fair representation." Because the individual employee would otherwise confront, unprotected, the union acting as employer as well, "if a union does wield additional power in a hiring hall by assuming the employer's role, its responsibility to exercise that power fairly *increases* rather than *decreases*. We reject [the Union's] contention that [Breininger's] complaint fails to state a fair representation claim."

———

UNION NEWS CO. v. HILDRETH, 295 F.2d 658 (6th Cir.1961). Plaintiff Gladys Hildreth had been employed for ten years at the soda and lunch counter of the defendant Union News Company in a Detroit railroad station. The labor contract between the Company and the Hotel and Restaurant Employees Union provided that no employee was to be discharged except for just cause. Between early 1957 and early 1958, the Company noted cash shortages at the lunch counter; an examination by Union representatives of the Company's business records caused them to concur in the Company's judgment that one or more of the counter employees was being dishonest in handling money. Although the Company's manager suggested that the entire counter crew (of eleven or twelve employees) should be terminated, the Union prevailed upon the Company not to take such drastic action; instead, both Company and Union agreed to a temporary layoff and replacement of five of the counter employees for the purpose of seeing whether the cash picture would improve. Plaintiff Hildreth was among the five employees thus laid off in March 1958. When the cash picture improved in March and April, the Union agreed that the Company's experiment had proved its point, and that the replacement of the five employees could be made permanent. Ms. Hildreth met with Union officials—including the grievance committee and ultimately the executive board—in an effort to convince them that her discharge was unjust, but the Union chose not to press a grievance on her behalf. The Company did not acquiesce in demands by Ms. Hildreth's attorney to permit her to process her grievance directly. Ms. Hildreth secured a jury verdict in the amount of $5,000 in her action for wrongful discharge in breach of the collective bargaining agreement. The judgment of the trial court was, however, reversed on appeal.

Although the court of appeals found no evidence that Ms. Hildreth had acted dishonestly, it also found no evidence that the Union and the Company had acted fraudulently, collusively or in bad faith. The court thus concluded that, by virtue of the Union's authority as exclusive bargaining representative, the Union and the Company could "mutually conclude, as a part of the bargaining process, that the circumstances shown by the evidence provided just cause for the layoff and discharge of plaintiff and other of defendant's employees. * * * Unless such bilateral decisions, made in good faith, and after unhurried consideration between a Union and an employer, be sustained in court, the bargaining process is a mirage, without the efficacy contemplated by the philosophy of the law which makes its use compulsory." The court noted that the parties were obligated by law to continue the process of collective bargaining even during the contract term, in the interpretation and administration of that contract. It held that the parties did not, "through retroactive compromise, settle or wipe out a vested and already existing grievance or cause of action of an employee," which would be beyond the Union's power; rather, the Union agreed with the employer that the "just cause" provision of the contract was properly construed to embrace the situation at the Company's lunch counter. The labor contract itself gave the Union the responsibility to construe its terms on behalf of the employees. "We consider that the Union was acting in the *collective* interest of those who by law and contract the Union was charged with protecting. * * * Under the philosophy of collective responsibility an employer who bargains in good faith should be entitled to rely upon the promises and agreements of the Union representatives with whom he must deal under the compulsion of law and contract. The collective bargaining process should be carried on between parties who can mutually respect and rely upon the authority of each other."

SIMMONS v. UNION NEWS CO., 382 U.S. 884, 86 S.Ct. 165, 15 L.Ed.2d 125 (1965). The Supreme Court denied certiorari to review a court of appeals decision for the Union News Company in a case, brought by one Simmons, arising from the same incident of "group discharge" that was litigated in the *Hildreth* case. Mr. Justice Black wrote an opinion, in which Chief Justice Warren concurred, dissenting from the denial of certiorari. Excerpts from his opinion follow.

"This case points up with great emphasis the kind of injustice that can occur to an individual employee when the employer and the union have such power over the employee's claim for breach of contract. Here no one has claimed from the beginning to the end of the Hildreth lawsuit or this lawsuit that either of these individuals was guilty of any kind of misconduct justifying her discharge. * * * Moreover, petitioner alleges that she was prepared to show that subsequent to her discharge, the office girl who counted the money received at the lunch counter was found to be embezzling those funds and was discharged for it. Miss Hildreth had worked for respondent for nine and one-half years, and petitioner for fifteen years, prior to their discharges. There is no evidence that respondent had ever been dissatisfied with their work before the company became disappointed with its lunch counter about a year prior to the discharges. Yet both were discharged for 'just cause,' as determined not by a court but by an agreement of the company and the union."

"I would not construe the National Labor Relations Act as giving a union and an employer any such power over workers. In this case there has been no bargain made on behalf of all the workers represented by the union. Rather there has been a sacrifice of the rights of a group of employees based on the belief that some of them might possibly have been guilty of some kind of misconduct that would reduce the employer's profits. Fully recognizing the right of the collective bargaining representative to make a contract on the part of the workers for the future, I cannot believe that those who passed the Act intended to give the union the right to negotiate away alleged breaches of a contract claimed by individual employees."

———

At the heart of Mr. Justice Black's disagreement with the Court in Vaca v. Sipes and Simmons v. Union News Co. is a felt distinction between the negotiation of new contract terms and the settlement of grievances arising under an existing labor agreement. New contract terms are of a "legislative" quality, which speak broadly and prospectively to issues of general import for whole classes of employees, and which are formulated, declared and ratified typically in an open and visible manner; the orderly adjustment of interests within the bargaining unit requires that the union be the exclusive representative and that individual negotiations be outlawed. (Such was the philosophy articulated in J.I. Case Co. v. NLRB, 321 U.S. 332, 64 S.Ct. 576, 88 L.Ed. 762 (1944).) On the other hand, claims arising under an existing agreement have a more "vested" quality about them; they may arise under fairly clear contractual provisions, on which individuals have rested their expectations; grievance adjustment will often arise from such idiosyncratic fact situations that no broad contractual norms will be at stake and no other substantial employee interests undermined. Grievance settlements by the union may often be ad hoc and achieved through informal processes of low visibility. It is said that all of these elements make it appropriate—and not at all disruptive—to permit the aggrieved employee to pursue his or her contract claim directly against the employer, either by lawsuit or by the contractual grievance machinery culminating in arbitration. Indeed, there are references in a number of judicial decisions, including those of Justice Black, to the proviso to Section 9(a) of the Labor Act, which some have read to *entitle* aggrieved employees to press their contract claims directly whenever the union declines to do so (even in good faith). See, *e.g.,* Hughes Tool Co., 56 NLRB 981 (1944), enforced 147 F.2d 69 (5th Cir.1945); Donnelly v. United Fruit Co., 40 N.J. 61, 190 A.2d 825 (1963). But it is clear that this interpretation of the proviso has been rejected by the Supreme Court in *Vaca v. Sipes,* and also more recently and explicitly in *Emporium Capwell Co. v. Western Addition Community Organization,* supra page 371, note 12.

Consider also the broader underlying distinction between contract negotiation and grievance adjustment, and the suggestion that the union's authority in the latter process is much more restricted. Justice Goldberg spoke to this issue in his concurring opinion in HUMPHREY V. MOORE, 375 U.S. 335, 352–53, 84 S.Ct. 363, 373–74, 11 L.Ed.2d 370 (1964), a case in which a joint union-management panel resolved a contract grievance by agreeing to construe a provision in the labor contract to allow dovetailing of seniority rosters (when there was a serious issue as to the effect of the provision):

> A mutually acceptable grievance settlement between an employer and a union, which is what the decision of the Joint Committee was, cannot be challenged by an individual dissenting employee under § 301(a) on the ground that the parties exceeded their contractual powers in making the settlement. * * * [T]he existing labor contract is the touchstone of an arbitrator's powers. But the power of the union and the employer jointly to settle a grievance dispute is not so limited. The parties are free by joint action to modify, amend and supplement their original collective bargaining agreement. They are equally free, since "[t]he grievance procedure is * * * a part of the continuous collective bargaining process," to settle grievances not falling within the scope of the contract. [United Steelworkers v. Warrior & Gulf Navigation Co., 363 U.S. 574, 581, 80 S.Ct. 1347, 1352, 4 L.Ed.2d 1409 (1960).] In this case, for example, had the dispute gone to arbitration, the arbitrator would have been bound to apply the existing agreement and to determine whether the merger-absorption clause applied. However, even in the absence of such a clause, the contracting parties—the multiemployer unit and the union—were free to resolve the dispute by amending the contract to dovetail seniority lists or to achieve the same result by entering into a grievance settlement. The presence of the merger-absorption clause did not restrict the right of the parties to resolve their dispute by joint agreement applying, interpreting, or amending the contract. There are too many unforeseeable contingencies in a collective bargaining relationship to justify making the words of the contract the exclusive source of rights and duties.

> * * * If collective bargaining is to remain a flexible process, the power to amend by agreement and the power to interpret by agreement must be coequal.

> It is wholly inconsistent with this Court's recognition that "[t]he grievance procedure is * * * a part of the continuous collective bargaining process," to limit the parties' power to settle grievances to the confines of the existing labor agreement, or to assert, as the Court now does, that an individual employee can claim that the collective bargaining contract is violated because the parties have made a grievance settlement going beyond the strict terms of the existing contract.

———

## PROBLEMS FOR DISCUSSION

**1.** Suppose that Johnson, a carpenter in a plant-wide unit covered by a collective bargaining agreement, was called out to do maintenance work on a high roof on Labor Day as a result of hurricane damage. He worked from 7:00 a.m. to 7:00 p.m. His usual rate of pay is $10.00 an hour. The collective bargaining agreement contains the following provisions:

> "Eight hours' work between the hours of 8 o'clock a.m. and 5 o'clock p.m. shall constitute the regularly scheduled workday.

> "All work in excess of eight hours a day and work performed outside of the regularly scheduled working hours shall be paid at time and a half the regular rate of pay.

> "When maintenance men are required to perform work at heights above 50 feet, they shall be paid double time.

> "Double time shall be paid for all work on the following holidays: New Year's Day, Memorial Day * * * Labor Day. * * * *"

The company paid Johnson $20.00 an hour for this work. It might be contended that he should have been paid $40.00 for each of eight hours between 8 a.m. and 5 p.m., $60.00 for the ninth hour, and $90.00 for the work outside normal hours, a total of $470 for the day. Various other interpretations and calculations are possible that would reduce the pyramiding.

(a) May the company discuss the grievance with Johnson alone?

(b) If Johnson refuses to sign a grievance form, has the union any remedy under the grievance procedure?

(c) If Johnson accepts a compromise, does it bind the union?

(d) If the union accepts a compromise in grievance discussions (for example, an interpretation that gives Johnson only the premiums for high and holiday work), does it bind Johnson? If not, what recourse does Johnson have?

**2.** Assume that in the *Hildreth* or *Simmons* case, the dischargee proceeded initially against the union for breach of the duty of fair representation, by filing a charge under Section 8(b)(1) with the NLRB. Assume too that the NLRB concludes that the union committed no unfair labor practice. In the event the dischargee then sues the Union News Company for breach of the labor contract, can the company successfully assert the NLRB determination as a defense? (Might it depend on whether the NLRB determination took the form of a refusal by the General Counsel to issue a complaint or was instead a judgment on the merits by an administrative law judge and the full Board?)

Conversely, if the NLRB found that the union had violated its duty of fair representation, will that finding be preclusive in an action under Section 301 against the company?

———

HINES v. ANCHOR MOTOR FREIGHT, INC., 424 U.S. 554, 96 S.Ct. 1048, 47 L.Ed.2d 231 (1976). Anchor discharged eight truckdrivers for dishonesty, claiming that in seeking reimbursement for overnight motel expenses, they had presented to the company receipts which overstated their actual room charges. At a later meeting attended by the drivers and their union, the company produced these receipts along with motel registration cards showing a lower room rate for the night in question, a notarized statement of the motel clerk asserting that the registration cards were accurate, and the motel owner's affidavit containing the same assertion as well as his statement that the drivers had been furnished with inflated receipts. The union claimed that the drivers were innocent and that their discharge was not for "just cause" as required by the collective bargaining agreement; and it asked that the case be submitted to the joint company-union arbitration committee. The union took no steps to investigate the motel, and at the hearing no evidence other than the drivers' assertion of their own innocence was presented by the union to challenge the company's documents.

The committee denied the grievance. The drivers then retained an attorney who secured a statement from the motel owner to the effect that the discrepancy between the receipts and the registration cards could in theory have been attributable to the motel clerk's intentional understatement on the cards and his pocketing of the difference.

The drivers brought an action against Anchor for unjust discharge in breach of contract, and against the union for breach of its duty of fair representation by virtue of its alleged failure, arbitrarily and in bad faith, to investigate their case properly. A deposition of the motel clerk revealed that he had in fact falsified the registration records and that it was he and not the drivers who had pocketed the difference between the sum on the registration cards and the sum on the receipts.

Although the District Judge granted summary judgment for both Anchor and the union (holding that at worst the union's conduct exhibited bad judgment), the court of appeals reversed the judgment as to the union, finding sufficient facts to sustain a possible inference of bad faith or arbitrary conduct. The higher court, however, affirmed the summary judgment for Anchor; it relied on the labor-contract provision making a grievance-committee decision "final and binding," and it concluded that the company had engaged in no misconduct in the grievance procedure.

The Supreme Court, assuming without deciding that the reversal of the summary judgment for the union was correct, held (6–2) that it necessarily followed that the summary judgment for Anchor had to be reversed, and that the finality provisions of the labor contract were no defense. Relying on *Vaca v. Sipes,* the Court concluded that just as the union's breach of the duty of fair representation in settling a grievance before arbitration relieves the employee in the Section 301 action against the employer of the duty to exhaust the grievance procedures, so too does the union's subversion of the arbitration process itself remove the bar of the arbitrator's decision.

The Court stated:

"Under the rule announced by the Court of Appeals, unless the employer is implicated in the Union's malfeasance or has otherwise caused the arbitral process to err, petitioners would have no remedy against Anchor even though they are successful in proving the Union's bad faith, the falsity of the charges against them and the breach of contract by Anchor by discharging without cause. This rule would apparently govern even in circumstances where it is shown that a union has manufactured the evidence and knows from the start that it is false; or even if, unbeknownst to the employer, the union has corrupted the arbitrator to the detriment of disfavored union members. As is the case where there has been a failure to exhaust, however, we cannot believe that Congress intended to foreclose the employee from his § 301 remedy otherwise available against the employer if the contractual processes have been seriously flawed by the union's breach of its duty to represent employees honestly and in good faith and without invidious discrimination or arbitrary conduct. * * *

"Petitioners are not entitled to relitigate their discharge merely because they offer newly discovered evidence that the charges against them were false and that in fact they were fired without cause. The grievance processes cannot be expected to be error-free. The finality provision has sufficient force to surmount occasional instances of mistake. But it is quite another matter to suggest that erroneous arbitration decisions must stand even though the employee's representation by the Union has been dishonest, in bad faith or discriminatory; for in that event error and injustice of the grossest sort would multiply. The contractual system would then cease to qualify as an adequate mechanism to secure individual redress for damaging failure of the employer to abide by the contract. Congress has put its blessing on private dispute settlement arrangements provided in collective agreements, but it was anticipated, we are sure, that the contractual machinery would operate within some minimum levels of integrity. In our view, enforcement of the finality provision where the arbitrator has erred is conditioned upon the Union's having satisfied its statutory duty fairly to represent the employee in connection with the arbitration proceedings. Wrongfully discharged employees would be left without jobs and without a fair opportunity to secure an adequate remedy. * * *

"Petitioners, if they prove an erroneous discharge and the Union's breach of duty tainting the decision of the joint committee, are entitled to an appropriate remedy against the employer as well as the Union. * * *"

---

In NLRB v. Local 299, Teamsters, 782 F.2d 46 (6th Cir.1986), the union reacted to company layoffs by calling a meeting of employees when they should have been at work. The collective bargaining agreement prohibited most work stoppages, and provided that the company could discipline employees for engaging in a work stoppage not properly authorized by the union. Treating the "meeting" as a work stoppage in breach of contract, the company suspended the 58 participants for 30 days each. The union filed a grievance, but the statewide joint arbitration committee found that the grievants had indeed engaged in an unauthorized work stoppage. One of them filed charges against the union with the NLRB, claiming a breach of the duty of fair representation. The Board concluded that the union's position, that the "meeting" was not a work stoppage, was not taken in good faith and that the union had misled the employees about their susceptibility to discipline; the employees "had a right to expect that the union would not encourage them to violate the contract in a way that would expose them to a loss of income or even employment." The NLRB found a breach of the duty of fair representation in violation of section 8(b)(1)(A).

The court refused to enforce the Board order. It concluded that the essence of all earlier cases in which the duty of fair representation was found to be violated involved singling out an individual or a group of employees for disparate treatment among their fellow workers. "The Board apparently argues that this statutory duty prohibits *any* bad faith or arbitrary action taken by a union. It further asserts that the duty of fair representation imposes an affirmative obligation on a union to inform its members of possible disciplinary consequences for participating in at least some forms of union activity.... This position would require us to extend the duty to cover a situation involving a work stoppage rather than collective bargaining or grievance processing, and where a member or group was not singled out for different treatment. In other words, the duty would be expanded to include an undefined fiduciary duty which a union owes to its unit as a whole.... We decline to extend the duty so far, since we believe the duty of fair representation was never intended to be a 'catch all' for undesirable union activity."

The same conclusion was reached on similar facts—a strike that exposed all employees to discharge because of failure to abide by the notification requirements of section 8(d)—in Le'Mon v. NLRB, 902 F.2d 810 (10th Cir.1990). The case was thereafter remanded by the United States Supreme Court—at 499 U.S. 933, 111 S.Ct. 1383, 113 L.Ed.2d 440 (1991)—for reconsideration in light of United Steelworkers of America v. Rawson, p. 1076 infra, and Air Line Pilots Ass'n, Intern. v. O'Neill. On remand, the Tenth Circuit held that *O'Neill*'s holding, that fair representation applied to "all union activity," vitiated the circuit court's earlier reasoning that the duty did not apply when the union's action affected all the members of the bargaining unit. Nevertheless, the court of appeals accepted the NLRB's position that negligence does not amount to breach of the duty, even when that negligence consisted of urging workers to continue a strike after the union had learned of its possible illegality. Le'Mon v. NLRB, 952 F.2d 1203 (10th Cir.1991), cert. denied, 506 U.S. 830, 113 S.Ct. 93, 121 L.Ed.2d 55 (1992).

In CAMACHO V. RITZ-CARLTON WATER TOWER, 786 F.2d 242 (7th Cir.1986), the court addressed the question whether a union violates the DFR in handling an employee grievance in a "perfunctory" manner, or whether it is necessary to demonstrate that the union has engaged in "intentional misconduct." Employee Camacho, a hotel waiter, was discharged for prematurely leaving the dining room at the end of his workday; because of his conduct and earlier similar incidents, the company adhered to its decision even after a grievance hearing at which Camacho was represented by his union. When the union declined to take his case to arbitration, Camacho brought this action against the company, claiming that the resolution of his grievance should be set aside because of the union's perfunctory handling in breach of its duty of fair representation.

The court of appeals affirmed the summary judgment awarded to the company because the record did not support any finding of "intentional misconduct" as required in the earlier decisions of the Seventh Circuit. The court held that a union breaches its DFR by discriminating against an employee "for forbidden reasons (such as race or politics, including the employee's position on the union and its leaders)"; but there is no remedy "for careless or bone-headed conduct. When the prohibition is directed against the motive rather than the result, it is necessary to use the standard of intent or recklessness (from which intent may be inferred)." The court concluded that an assessment whether perfunctory handling caused an employee to lose a meritorious grievance would necessarily and improperly implicate the judiciary in passing upon the merits of grievances, contrary to the national policy favoring non-judicial disposition of labor disputes which the parties intend to resolve through grievance and arbitration procedures. Another reason the court gave for adhering to its "intentional or reckless" standard is that in suits such as this, where only the employer is the defendant, it can only guess at why the union handled the grievance in the manner it did, and the union will generally be disinclined to provide the company with the pertinent facts; the steep burden imposed upon the plaintiff "helps to protect employers from the risk of [union] error, a risk magnified when the employer must justify acts it may find inscrutable."

The court also resorted to a measure of economic analysis to support its conclusion.

The use of a standard based on causation or negligence also would interfere with employees' right to choose the level of care for which they are willing to pay. Business agents such as Grossman usually have many duties in addition to handling grievances. They are not lawyers or private investigators. They may know the ins and outs of the collective bargaining agreement without having a trial lawyer's skills. A union could secure the skills and perseverance of a good litigation team only by paying the steep fees these skills command in the market. A union may choose to rely on part-time, untrained, overworked grievers—with the inevitable difference in the outcome of some cases—rather than purchase a higher quality of representation. A union may conclude that its limited resources should go into a strike fund or toward negotiating the next contract. "A wide range of reasonableness must be allowed a statutory bargaining representative in serving the unit it represents", Ford Motor Co. v. Huffman, 345 U.S. 330, 338, 73 S.Ct. 681, 686, 97 L.Ed. 1048 (1953), and one part of this "wide range" is the choice between better grievance machinery and other things the employees value.

... An unqualified prohibition of "perfunctory" representation would compel unions to change the allocation of their resources and to be more belicose. Both results would undercut employees' rights to control their own destiny; both could do more harm than good, as the employees see things.... True, the casual handling of grievances may not be what the employees want, but if perfunctory representation defeats rather than implements the wishes of the employees, they may install a new team of grievers.

The Supreme Court has—rather casually—endorsed this legal principle, in UNITED STEELWORKERS V. RAWSON, 495 U.S. 362, 110 S.Ct. 1904, 109 L.Ed.2d 362 (1990). There, after 91 miners were killed in an underground fire, their survivors brought an action in a state court against the union, which allegedly assumed certain safety obligations to the workers by virtue of provisions in the collective bargaining agreement. Because the Supreme Court concluded that the plaintiffs' claims were not independently based upon state tort law but rather upon the labor agreement, it held that the governing law was federal law and not state law. Because the complaint charged the union only with negligence, the union argued that this was insufficient to sustain a claim for breach of the duty of fair representation, and the Supreme Court agreed. Its complete discussion of the issue was as follows: "[A] breach [of the DFR] occurs 'only when a union's conduct toward a member of the collective bargaining unit is arbitrary, discriminatory, or in bad faith.' [*Vaca v. Sipes.*] The courts have in general assumed that mere negligence, even in the enforcement of a collective-bargaining agreement, would not state a claim for breach of the duty of fair representation, and we endorse that view today." The Court therefore held that any negligence by the union in carrying out safety inspections could not violate its duty of fair representation. (The Court also concluded that, although a labor agreement might possibly impose upon the union a more rigorous duty of conduct running to the workers in the bargaining unit, the contract had not explicitly enough done so in this case.)

Do you agree with the conclusion of the Supreme Court regarding the content of the duty of fair representation, and with the supporting reasons offered by the court of appeals in *Camacho?* Does the Court's rejection of the "mere negligence" standard indeed stem from *Vaca v. Sipes* and from other Supreme Court cases like *Hines v. Anchor Motor Freight?*

————

## PROBLEMS FOR DISCUSSION

**1.** The Court in *Hines* did not consider whether the union had in fact violated its duty of fair representation in its preparation and presentation of the discharge grievance before the arbitrator. Given the manner in which the Court defines that duty in this case, did the Union in fact violate it? Did the union violate its duty as defined in the *Rawson* case? If the union is indeed found liable, what remedies should a court order? Curtis v. United Transportation Union, 700 F.2d 457 (8th Cir.1983); NLRB v. American Postal Workers Union, 618 F.2d 1249 (8th Cir.1980).

**2.** The chairman of the union's grievance committee has come to you for advice. A grievance initiated by employee Curth has been processed through the first three steps of the contractual grievance procedure; it remains unsettled, and arbitration is now available to the union on demand. Although the grievance committee believes there is some merit to Curth's grievance, it has concluded that it ought not proceed to arbitration. This judgment was based on the fact that the Curth grievance arose in a somewhat unique factual setting, that an arbitration victory will therefore not be of important precedential value, and, most important, that the union is in serious financial straits and an arbitration will consume a substantial proportion of its funds. The committee decided that it was more important to conserve those funds either for a grievance of more general significance or for the next collective bargaining negotiation. The chairman of the committee wishes to know whether, on these facts, the union is free to decline to take Curth's grievance to arbitration. What is your response? See Barrentine v. Arkansas–Best Freight System, Inc., 450 U.S. 728, 742, 101 S.Ct. 1437, 1445, 67 L.Ed.2d 641 (1981); Curth v. Faraday, Inc., 401 F.Supp. 678 (E.D.Mich.1975). (If a court were to find this action by the union to be a violation of the duty of fair representation, what remedy should be ordered?)

**3.** Pete Velasquez has been a member of the International Longshoremen's Association and served as an official in an ILA local for two years. In June, the employers' association which bargained with and signed a labor contract with the ILA instituted a grievance proceeding, charging that Velasquez had been responsible for instigating illegal work stoppages. In October, the claim was considered by an arbitrator, and was upheld; the award of the arbitrator "deregistered" Velasquez, which had the effect of depriving him of longshore work anywhere on the Pacific coast. On the same day, the same arbitrator rendered a decision in another grievance, this time in the union's favor, which limited the amount of lifting of heavy sacks to be done by all employees covered by the labor contract. Velasquez has secured information which leads him to believe that the two arbitration decisions were the product of an informal "swapping" agreement between the union and the employers, with the union sacrificing the Velasquez case in order to secure a decision that would benefit all workers in the unit. He has instituted an action against the union in a federal court, claiming breach of the duty of fair representation and alleging the above facts; the union has moved to dismiss the complaint. Should the motion be granted? See Local 13, Intern. Longshoremen's and Warehousemen's Union v. Pacific Maritime Ass'n, 441 F.2d 1061 (9th Cir.1971), cert. denied, 404 U.S. 1016, 92 S.Ct. 677, 30 L.Ed.2d 664 (1972).

If the case were to go to trial, would Velasquez prevail if he could demonstrate that the "swapping" was done because he was disliked by union officials? Would it be *necessary* to prove this?

Would the union's conduct be any less subject to challenge had the "swapping" of grievances been effected informally between union and company representatives at the third step of the grievance procedure, prior to any arbitration proceedings?

Could the union win the case by demonstrating that the Velasquez grievance lacked merit?

**4.** Employee Janice Wilson was admonished two months ago for insubordinate behavior in refusing a work order; a written warning of more serious possible discipline was put in her personnel file, and neither she nor her union filed a grievance. Last month, after another episode of insubordination, Ms. Wilson was given a three-day suspension, with a warning that the next such episode would result in her termination. Wilson sent a note to her shop steward, asking that he file a grievance on her behalf challenging the suspension. The labor agreement provides that grievances must be filed (either by the union representative or the aggrieved employee) within ten days of the occurrence giving rise thereto. The steward let the ten-day period go by, and Wilson has asked you whether she has any recourse against the union or the employer. Give her an answer, making the following alternative assumptions:

(a) The steward put her note in the trunk of his car, went off on a hunting vacation for a week, and forgot about the note.

(b) The steward read the note, promptly inquired of Wilson's supervisor regarding the circumstances leading to the suspension, decided that Wilson's complaint lacked merit, and absent-mindedly failed so to inform her.

(c) The facts are the same as in (b), but the shop steward purposely neglected to inform Wilson until the ten-day period had passed, on account of a long-time grudge between them.

See Dober v. Roadway Express, Inc., 707 F.2d 292 (7th Cir.1983); Harrison v. United Transp. Union, 530 F.2d 558 (4th Cir.1975), cert. denied, 425 U.S. 958, 96 S.Ct. 1739, 48 L.Ed.2d 203 (1976); Office & Professional Employees, Local 2, 268 NLRB 1353 (1984); Vencl v. International Union of Operating Engineers, Local 18, 137 F.3d 420 (6th Cir.1998).

**5.** Employee Holodnak had published a letter in a local newspaper of a political group and was discharged for violating a company rule barring false or malicious statements concerning the company; the letter had attacked, among others, the company, the union, judges and arbitrators. The union assisted Holodnak in challenging his discharge through the grievance procedure, and provided an attorney to represent him in arbitration. At the arbitration proceeding, the attorney conceded the validity of the company's rule; he did not urge the arbitrator to construe the rule strictly; he did not assert that the rule posed problems under the First Amendment, in view of the fact that almost all of the company's work was done pursuant to defense contracts with the United States Government; and he failed to intercede when the arbitrator on several occasions subjected Holodnak to questioning which Holodnak found offensive, inquisitorial and biased. The arbitrator ultimately sustained the discharge and denied the grievance. Holodnak now brings an action against the union for violation of its duty of fair representation, claiming that the attorney's performance was grossly inadequate. Should the court grant the union's motion for summary judgment? See Holodnak v. Avco Corp., Avco–Lycoming Div., 381 F.Supp. 191 (D.Conn.1974), modified on other grounds, 514 F.2d 285 (2d Cir.1975); Freeman v. O'Neal Steel, Inc., 609 F.2d 1123 (5th Cir.1980), cert. denied, 449 U.S. 833, 101 S.Ct. 104, 66 L.Ed.2d 39 (1980). (If the court were to find the union's conduct to be a violation of the duty of fair representation, what remedy should be ordered?)

**6.** The labor contract between the Hussmann Refrigerator Company and Local 138 of the Steelworkers Union provides: "The Company recognizes the principle of seniority based upon the total length of continuous service with the Company. Seniority, skill and ability to perform the work required shall be considered by the Company in making promotions, transfers, layoffs and recalls. Where skill and ability to perform are substantially equal, seniority shall govern." The Company posted four job openings, and ultimately decided—after reviewing the personnel files of the eight employees bidding for the promotion—to award the positions to employees Morris, Newcomb, Oliver and Parker. These four had less seniority than four other bidders, Archer, Biddle, Carrington and DeVito, all of whom claimed that they had skill and ability equal to the successful bidders and all of whom convinced the Local to file grievances on their behalf. The union's grievance committee decided ultimately to proceed to arbitration. The union gave no notice of the hearing date to Morris, Newcomb, Oliver and Parker, and they did not appear before the arbitrator. The foreman, however, did testify on behalf of the Company, and gave the reasons why he believed that those four had skill and ability "head and shoulders" above the grievants, who testified on their own behalf. The arbitrator concluded that grievants Carrington and DeVito possessed skill and ability substantially equal to the four awardees, and directed the Company to promote them. The Company did so, by "bumping" and demoting Oliver and Parker.

Oliver and Parker have brought an action in a federal court against the Company for breach of contract and against the Local for breach of the duty of fair representation.

(a) Assume that the union decided to press the grievance of Archer, Biddle, Carrington and DeVito solely on the grounds that they were the four most senior bidders, that seniority is an objective principle for which unions have long fought, and that the claim that the awardees have greater skill and ability is not for the union to assess but rather for the employer to demonstrate before the arbitrator. Has the union violated its duty of fair representation? See Smith v. Hussmann Refrigerator Co., 619 F.2d 1229 (8th Cir.1980)(en banc), cert. denied, 449 U.S. 839, 101 S.Ct. 116, 66 L.Ed.2d 46 (1980).

(b) Assume, instead, that the union made a thorough investigation of the skill and ability of grievants Archer, Biddle, Carrington and DeVito, and decided to press the grievance of these senior employees only after concluding that they were equal in skill and ability to the four awardees. In arguing that the union nonetheless violated its duty of fair representation, Oliver and Parker have asserted: "Where the interests of two groups of employees are diametrically opposed to each other and the union espouses the cause of one in the arbitration, it follows as a matter of law that there has been no fair representation of the other group. This is true even though, in choosing the cause of which group to espouse, the union acts completely objectively and with the best of motives. The old adage, that one cannot serve two masters, is particularly applicable to such a situation." Are Oliver and Parker correct? See Clark v. Hein–Werner Corp., 8 Wis.2d 264, 99 N.W.2d 132 (1959).

(c) Did the union breach the duty of fair representation by failing to inform Oliver and Parker of the arbitration hearing and by failing to afford them an opportunity to testify there?

(d) Assume that the court concludes that there has been a breach of the union's duty of fair representation. Should the court then decide for itself (with a jury?) whether Oliver and Parker have substantially greater skill and ability than grievants Carrington and DeVito? What weight if any should be given the decision of the arbitrator?

(e) Assume that the court agrees with the arbitrator, finds that plaintiff-awardees Oliver and Parker were properly bumped and demoted, and that the employer did not breach the labor contract by doing so. Does this mean that, although the union may have violated its duty of fair representation, it is not liable for any remedy?

In a significant and controversial article, Professor Clyde W. Summers has, by examining the decided cases and reasoning from first principles, elicited the following "emerging principles of fair representation." See "The Individual Employee's Rights Under the Collective Agreement: What Constitutes Fair Representation?", 126 U.Pa.L.Rev. 251, 279 (1977). Do you agree with Professor Summers that these principles "protect the individual's right to representation in grievance handling, and, at the same time, allow the union sufficient freedom to fulfill its function in administering the agreement"?

1.  The individual employee has a right to have clear and unquestioned terms of the collective agreement that have been made for his benefit, followed and enforced until the agreement is properly amended. For the union to refuse to follow and enforce the rules and standards it has established on behalf of those it represents is arbitrary and constitutes a violation of its fiduciary obligation.

2.  The individual employee has no right to insist on any particular interpretation of an ambiguous provision in a collective agreement, for the union must be free to settle a grievance in accordance with any reasonable interpretation of the ambiguous provision. However, the individual has a right that ambiguous provisions be applied consistently and that the provision mean the same when applied to him as when applied to other employees. Settlement of similar grievances on different terms is discriminatory and violates the union's duty to represent all employees equally.

3.  The union has no duty to carry every grievance to arbitration; the union can sift out grievances that are trivial or lacking in merit. However, the individual's right to equal treatment includes equal access to the grievance procedure and arbitration for similar grievances of equal merit.

4.  The individual employee has a right to have his grievance decided on its own merits. The union violates its duty to represent fairly when it trades an individual's meritorious grievance for the benefit of another individual or of the group. Majority vote does not necessarily validate grievance settlements, but may instead, make the settlement suspect as based on political power and not the merits of the grievance.

5.  Settlement of grievances for improper motives such as personal hostility, political opposition, or racial prejudice constitutes bad faith regardless of the merit of the grievance. The union thereby violates its duty to represent fairly by refusing to process the grievance even though the employer may not have violated the agreement.

6.  The union can make good faith judgments in determining the merits of a grievance, but it owes the employees it represents the duty to use reasonable care and diligence both in investigating grievances in order to make that judgment, and in processing and presenting grievances on their behalf.

# Bowen v. United States Postal Service[d]

459 U.S. 212, 103 S.Ct. 588, 74 L.Ed.2d 402 (1983).

■ JUSTICE POWELL delivered the opinion of the Court.

The issue is whether a union may be held primarily liable for that part of a wrongfully discharged employee's damages caused by his union's breach of its duty of fair representation.

[Bowen was discharged following an altercation with another employee, and his union—the American Postal Workers Union—declined to take his grievance to arbitration. Bowen sued both the Postal Service and the Union in a federal district court, seeking damages and injunctive relief. The district court put to the jury a series of questions to be answered as a special verdict, including the apportionment of damages between the Service and the Union; apportionment was left primarily to the jury's discretion. The court suggested to the jury that they might determine a hypothetical arbitration date at which time the Service would have reinstated Bowen had the Union not violated the DFR, and might then impose on the Service damages incurred before that date and on the Union damages incurred thereafter.

[Upon return of the special verdict, the district court entered judgment against the Service for discharging Bowen without just cause and against the Union for handling Bowen's "apparently meritorious grievance ... in an arbitrary and perfunctory manner." The court, pursuant to the jury's apportionment, entered judgment against the Service for $22,954 and against the Union for $30,000. The court of appeals, although it agreed with the trial court regarding the total amount of Bowen's injury ($52,954), held that the Union could not be held responsible for any part of Bowen's lost earnings, which were exclusively the responsibility of the Postal Service; it therefore affirmed the judgment against the Service in the amount of $22,954, but overturned the award against the Union.]

In Vaca v. Sipes, 386 U.S. 171, 87 S.Ct. 903, 17 L.Ed.2d 842 (1967), the Court held that an employee such as Bowen, who proves that his employer violated the labor agreement and his union breached its duty of fair representation, may be entitled to recover damages from both the union and the employer. The Court explained that the award must be apportioned according to fault:

> "The governing principle, then, is to apportion liability between the employer and the union according to the damage caused by the fault of each. Thus, damages attributable solely to the employer's breach of contract should not be charged to the union, but increases if any in those damages caused by the union's refusal to process the grievance should not be charged to the employer." Id., at 197–198, 87 S.Ct., at 920–921.

\* \* \*

---

**d.** See VanderVelde, Making Good on *Vaca*'s Promise: Apportioning Back Pay to Achieve Remedial Goals, 32 UCLA L.Rev. 302 (1984).

The interests * * * identified in Vaca provide a measure of its principle for apportioning damages. Of paramount importance is the right of the employee, who has been injured by both the employer's and the union's breach, to be made whole. In determining the degree to which the employer or the union should bear the employee's damages, the Court held that the employer should not be shielded from the "natural consequences" of its breach by wrongful union conduct. Id., at 186, 87 S.Ct., at 914. The Court noted, however, that the employer may have done nothing to prevent exhaustion. Were it not for the union's failure to represent the employee fairly, the employer's breach "could [have been] remedied through the grievance process to the employee-plaintiff's benefit." The fault that justifies dropping the bar to the employee's suit for damages also requires the union to bear some responsibility for increases in the employee's damages resulting from its breach. To hold otherwise would make the employer alone liable for the consequences of the union's breach of duty.

* * * It is true that the employer discharged the employee wrongfully and remains liable for the employee's backpay. See *Vaca*, supra, at 197, 87 S.Ct., at 920. The union's breach of its duty of fair representation, however, caused the grievance procedure to malfunction resulting in an increase in the employee's damages. Even though both the employer and the union have caused the damage suffered by the employee, the union is responsible for the increase in damages and, as between the two wrongdoers, should bear its portion of the damages.[12] * * *

Although each party participates in the grievance procedure, the union plays a pivotal role in the process since it assumes the responsibility of determining whether to press an employee's claims. The employer, for its part, must rely on the union's decision not to pursue an employee's grievance. * * * When the union, as the exclusive agent of the employee, waives arbitration or fails to seek review of an adverse decision, the employer should be in substantially the same position as if the employee had had the right to act on his own behalf and had done so. Indeed, if the employer could not rely on the union's decision, the grievance procedure would not provide the "uniform and exclusive method for [the] orderly settlement of employee grievances," which the Court has recognized is essential to the national labor policy.[15] See Clayton v. International Union

---

**12.** Although the union remains primarily responsible for the portion of the damages resulting from its default, Vaca made clear that the union's breach does not absolve the employer of liability. Thus if the petitioner in this case does not collect the damages apportioned against the Union, the Service remains secondarily liable for the full loss of backpay.

**15.** Under the dissent's analysis, the employer may not rely on the union's decision not to pursue a grievance. Rather it can prevent continued liability only by reinstating the discharged employee. See post, at 603.

This leaves the employer with a dubious option: it must either reinstate the employee promptly or leave itself exposed to open-ended liability. If this were the rule, the very purpose of the grievance procedure would be defeated. It is precisely to provide the exclusive means of resolving this kind of dispute that the parties agree to such a procedure and national labor policy strongly encourages its use. See Republic Steel, supra, at 653, 85 S.Ct., at 616.

When the union has breached its duty of fair representation, the dissent justifies its rule by arguing that "only the employer ha[s]

Automobile, Aerospace & Agricultural Implement Workers, 451 U.S. 679, 686–687, 101 S.Ct. 2088, 2093–2094, 68 L.Ed.2d 538 (1981).

The principle announced in *Vaca* reflects this allocation of responsibilities in the grievance procedure—a procedure that contemplates that both employer and union will perform their respective obligations. In the absence of damages apportionment where the default of both parties contributes to the employee's injury, incentives to comply with the grievance procedure will be diminished. Indeed, imposing total liability solely on the employer could well affect the willingness of employers to agree to arbitration clauses as they are customarily written.

Nor will requiring the union to pay damages impose a burden on the union inconsistent with national labor policy.[16] It will provide an additional incentive for the union to process its members' claims where warranted. See *Vaca*, supra, at 187, 87 S.Ct., at 915. This is wholly consistent with a union's interest. It is a duty owed to its members as well as consistent with the union's commitment to the employer under the arbitration clause. See Republic Steel, supra, at 653, 85 S.Ct., at 616.

\* \* \*

In this case, the findings of the District Court, accepted by the Court of Appeals, establish that the damages sustained by petitioner were caused initially by the Service's unlawful discharge and increased by the Union's breach of its duty of fair representation. Accordingly, apportionment of the damages was required by Vaca. We reverse the judgment of the Court of Appeals and remand for entry of judgment allocating damages against both the Service and the Union consistent with this opinion.

It is so ordered.

■ JUSTICE WHITE, with whom JUSTICE MARSHALL, JUSTICE BLACKMUN, and JUSTICE REHNQUIST, join, concurring in part in the judgment and dissenting in part.

\* \* \* [The Court's conclusion,] which heretofore has been rejected by every Court of Appeals that has squarely considered it, does not give due

---

the continuing ability to right the wrong by reinstating" the employee, an ability that the union lacks. See post, at 604. But an employer has no way of knowing that a failure to carry a grievance to arbitration constitutes a breach of duty. Rather than rehiring, as the dissent suggests, the employer reasonably could assume that the union had concluded the discharge was justified. The union would have the option, if it realized it had committed an arguable breach of duty, to bring its default to the employer's attention. Our holding today would not prevent a jury from taking such action into account. See infra, n. 19. \* \* \*

**16.** Requiring the union to pay its share of the damages is consistent with the interests recognized in International Brotherhood of Electrical Workers v. Foust, 442 U.S. 42, 99 S.Ct. 2121, 60 L.Ed.2d 698 (1979). In Foust, we found that a union was not liable for punitive damages. The interest in deterring future breaches by the union was outweighed by the debilitating impact that "unpredictable and potentially substantial" awards of punitive damages would have on the union treasury and the union's exercise of discretion in deciding what claims to pursue. Id., at 50–52, 99 S.Ct., at 2126–2127. An award of compensatory damages, however, normally will be limited and finite. \* \* \*

regard to our prior precedents, to equitable principles, or to the national labor policy. I therefore respectfully dissent. For the following reasons, I believe that the employer should be primarily liable for all backpay.

* * * Vaca made clear that, with respect to an *employer,* the only consequence of a union's breach of a fair-representation duty to an *employee* is that it provides the employee with the means of defeating the employer's "defense based upon the failure to exhaust contractual remedies," ibid., in a § 301 suit. * * *

Thus, under [both *Vaca* and *Hines*], as far as the employer is concerned, a union's breach of a fair-representation duty does no more than remove the procedural exhaustion-of-remedies bar to a § 301 suit by an aggrieved employee. The union's breach does not affect the employer's potential liability, including backpay liability, if the employee prevails in the § 301 judicial proceedings by showing that the employer had breached its contract in discharging him. * * *

Of course, this does not mean that the union escapes liability for the "natural consequences," Vaca, 386 U.S., at 186, 87 S.Ct., at 914, of *its* wrongful conduct.

* * * What, then, is the proper measure of the union's damages in a hybrid § 301/breach-of-duty suit? We considered this question in Czosek v. O'Mara, 397 U.S. 25, 29, 90 S.Ct. 770, 773, 25 L.Ed.2d 21 (1970), and concluded that, under the Vaca rule, the union is liable in damages to the extent that its misconduct "add[s] to the difficulty and expense of collecting from the employer." * * *

It is true that, under the Vaca–Czosek rule, the union may sometimes only have de minimis liability, and we unanimously acknowledged this fact in Electrical Workers v. Foust, 442 U.S. 42, 48, 50, 99 S.Ct. 2121, 2125, 2126, 60 L.Ed.2d 698 (1979). "The damages a union will have to pay in a typical unfair representation suit are minimal; under Vaca's apportionment formula, the bulk of the award will be paid by the employer, the perpetrator of the wrongful discharge, in a parallel § 301 action." Id., at 57, 99 S.Ct., at 2130 (Blackmun, J., concurring in result; joined by Burger, C.J., Rehnquist, and Stevens, JJ.). The Foust majority nevertheless reaffirmed Vaca and, moreover, further insulated unions from liability by holding that punitive damages could not be assessed in an action for breach of the duty of fair representation. In reaching these conclusions, the Court relied on the policy of affording individual employees redress for injuries caused by union misconduct without compromising the collective interests of union members in protecting limited union funds. As in Vaca, considerations of deterrence were deemed insufficient to risk endangering union "financial stability." Id., at 50–51, 99 S.Ct., at 2126–2127.[6]

---

**6.** Even though Foust requires that punitive damages not be assessed against a union, the Vaca rule nevertheless provides for a credible deterrent against wrongful union conduct. Attorney's fees and other litigation expenses have been assessed as damages against unions, because such damages measure the extent by which the union's breach of duty adds to the difficulty and expense of collecting from the employer. See, e.g., Sey-

\* \* \* It cannot be denied that, contrary to Vaca and its progeny, under the Court's new rule, the "bulk of the award" for backpay in a hybrid § 301/breach-of-duty suit will have to be borne by the union, not the employer. In the present case, for example, the jury, which was instructed in accordance with the Court's new test, assessed $30,000 in compensatory damages against the union, and only $17,000 against the employer. The union should well consider itself fortunate that this dispute proceeded to trial less than three years after the cessation of petitioner Bowen's employment. Most of the cases of this nature that have been reviewed by this Court have taken the better part of a decade to run their course. Because the hypothetical arbitration date will usually be less than one year after the discharge, \* \* \* it is readily apparent that, under the Court's rule, in many cases the union will be subject to large liability, far greater than that of the employer, the extent of which will not be in any way related to the union's comparative culpability. Nor will the union have any readily apparent way to limit its constantly increasing liability.

Bowen and the Postal Service argue that the employer is not the "cause" of an employee's lost earnings after the date on which an arbitral decision would have reinstated or otherwise compensated the employee. In the "but for" sense, of course, this is patently false, as the Court concedes. \* \* \*

It bears re-emphasizing that both before and after the hypothetical arbitration date, the union did not in any way prevent the employer from reinstating Bowen, and that the employer could reinstate him. Under these circumstances, it is bizarre to hold, as the Court does, that the relatively impotent union is *exclusively* liable for the bulk of the backpay. The Court, in effect, sustains the employer's protest to the union that "you should be liable for all damages flowing from my wrong from and after a certain time, because you should have caught and rectified my wrong by that time." Seymour v. Olin Corp., 666 F.2d 202, 215 (C.A.5 1982). The employer's wrongful conduct clearly was the generating cause of Bowen's loss, and only the employer had the continuing ability to right the wrong and limit liability by reinstating Bowen. The employer has the sole duty to pay wages, and it should be responsible for all back wages to which Bowen is entitled.

\* \* \*

The Court also contends \* \* \* that its rule will better enable grievance procedures to provide the uniform and exclusive method for the orderly settlement of employee grievances, because a contrary rule "could well affect the willingness of employers to agree to arbitration clauses as they are customarily written." Why the Court's rule will not "affect the willingness" of *unions* to agree to such clauses is left unexplained. More importantly, since the practical consequence of today's holding is that unions will take many unmeritorious grievances to arbitration simply to avoid expo-

mour v. Olin Corp., 666 F.2d, at 215; Scott v. Teamsters Local 377, 548 F.2d 1244 (C.A.6), cert. denied 431 U.S. 968, 97 S.Ct. 2927, 53 L.Ed.2d 1064 (1977).

sure to the new breach-of-duty liability, the Court's rule actually impairs the ability of the grievance machinery to provide for orderly dispute resolution. * * *

* * * Accordingly, I would affirm the Court of Appeals' judgment that the union was not liable for backpay damages, but I would reverse the remainder of the judgment and remand the case with instructions that the District Court be directed to enter judgment against the Postal Service for the entire amount of Bowen's backpay loss.

[JUSTICE REHNQUIST's dissenting opinion is omitted.]

———

CLAYTON v. INTERNATIONAL UNION, UNITED AUTOMOBILE WORKERS, 451 U.S. 679, 101 S.Ct. 2088, 68 L.Ed.2d 538 (1981). The employer, ITT Gilfillan, discharged employee Clayton for violation of a plant rule, and the union chose not to take his grievance to arbitration. Clayton brought an action against both the employer, for breach of the labor contract, and the union, for breach of the DFR. He did not, however, avail himself of the union's internal appeal procedures before bringing his lawsuit. Under the constitution of the United Automobile Workers, any union member "who feels aggrieved by any action, decision, or penalty imposed upon him" by the union must, before initiating legal action, seek relief from the membership of the local; if not satisfied there, the member may further appeal to the UAW International Executive Board, and eventually to either the Constitutional Convention Appeals Committee or to a Public Review Board composed of "impartial persons of good public repute" who are not members or employees of the union. In Clayton's lawsuit, both the company and the union pleaded as an affirmative defense his failure to exhaust the internal union appeals procedure, and for this reason the district court dismissed both suits.

The Supreme Court held (5-to-4) that this was improper. It acknowledged that the aggrieved employee had to exhaust the *contractual* grievance procedure before bringing a § 301 action against the employer; but it concluded that it was not always necessary that the employee also exhaust the *union's* procedures for internal review. "We hold that where an internal union appeals procedure cannot result in reactivation of the employee's grievance or an award of the complete relief sought in his § 301 suit, exhaustion will not be required with respect to either the suit against the employer or the suit against the union."

The defendants argued that an exhaustion requirement was dictated by the basic federal policies of avoiding judicial intrusion in internal union affairs and encouraging private resolution of labor-contract disputes. As to the former policy, the Court found it inapplicable to DFR actions based on statutory interests as distinguished from internal union matters involving the interpretation or application of a union constitution. And, despite the fact that exhaustion of internal union appeals procedures might in many cases result in private non-judicial dispute resolution, "we decline to impose a universal exhaustion requirement lest employees with meritorious § 301 claims be forced to exhaust themselves and their resources by submitting their claims to potentially lengthy internal union procedures that may not be adequate to redress their underlying grievances." The Court stated that such exhaustion would be inappropriate either where union officials were so hostile to the employee that no fair hearing could be expected, or where the appeals procedures could not reactivate the employee's grievance or award him the full relief sought against the employer, or where exhaustion would unreasonably delay the employee's opportunity to obtain a judicial hearing on the merits of his claim.

Here, the second circumstance existed. Clayton's lawsuit sought reinstatement and monetary relief. Although the UAW Public Review Board is empowered to award backpay, the union had no power to reinstate Clayton in his job or reactivate his grievance (which lapsed for failure to comply with a fifteen-day filing requirement in the labor agreement).

> [W]e conclude that these restrictions on the relief available through the internal UAW procedures render those procedures inadequate.
>
> Where internal appeals procedures can result in either complete relief to an aggrieved employee or reactivation of his grievance, exhaustion would advance the national labor policy of encouraging private resolution of contractual labor disputes. * * * [Otherwise, however,] national labor policy would not be served by requiring exhaustion of internal remedies. In such cases, exhaustion would be a useless gesture: it would delay judicial consideration of the employee's § 301 action, but would not eliminate it. The employee would still be required to pursue judicial means to obtain the relief he seeks under § 301.

The union argued that even if exhaustion of union appeals should not necessarily be required as a condition to an action against the employer, it should be required as a condition of the DFR action against the union. The Court rejected this proposition. If such a distinction were to obtain, trial courts would be confronted with two undesirable alternatives: either to stay the action against the employer pending internal union appeals (which would of course in effect constitute an improper exhaustion requirement in the § 301 action) or proceed with the lawsuit against the employer with the possibility of confronting much later a new lawsuit against the union based on the same facts. Thus, Clayton's failure to exhaust the internal UAW appeals procedures ought not dictate the dismissal of his suit against either defendant.

Four Justices dissented. Justice Powell concluded that until the internal UAW procedures had been exhausted the union had made no final determination whether to pursue arbitration on Clayton's behalf; his claim against both defendants could therefore not mature until that time. Justice Rehnquist believed that an exhaustion requirement could effectively lead in many cases to the resolution of the dispute—by convincing an employee his case lacked merit, or by convincing a union that it had merit, or by convincing an employer to reactivate the grievance and arbitration procedures of the labor agreement. Moreover, such a requirement "promotes union democracy and self-government as well as the broader policy of non-interference with internal union affairs."

## PROBLEMS FOR DISCUSSION

**1.** The Master Collective Bargaining Agreement with the union prohibits the company from closing a facility and the reopening of it as a non-union shop. The company, however, did exactly that with one of its facilities: terminating its workforce, paying them severance pay, and re-opening later with a lower-paid non-union workforce. The union did nothing to protest or stop that action. The terminated employees have brought a class action against both the company and the union. Has the union violated its duty of fair representation? If so, what would the damages be? How should they be apportioned between the company and the union? See Aguinaga v. United Food and Commercial Workers Int'l, 720 F.Supp. 862 (D.Kan.1989). If, instead of bringing suit, the employees sought relief from the NLRB under *Miranda Fuel*, should the union be liable for all the employees' lost wages? *See* Iron Workers Local Union 377, 326 NLRB 375 (1998).

**2.** You have been consulted by a company and by the union representing its employees. They acknowledge that on occasion an aggrieved employee might have a meritorious claim that is resisted or ignored, in good faith, by the employer or by the union. They want to minimize the likelihood of litigation in such situations, and would like to provide a fair set of grievance procedures and intra-union appeals procedures which could serve as the employee's exclusive recourse. They want you to propose language for the grievance procedure and for the union's constitution or bylaws that would achieve this objective. Can you help them?

## II. UNION SECURITY AND THE ENCOURAGEMENT OF UNION ACTIVITY

Unions in this country have traditionally faced a major problem in maintaining and increasing their membership. They have been met with greater and more persistent opposition from employers than their counterparts have faced in most other industrialized, democratic countries. And even apart from employer resistance, it is probably correct to state that employees in this country have generally been less easy to organize than has been true abroad. Finally, the labor movement in the United States has been marked throughout most of its history by rivalries between individual unions, and these rivalries have often taken the form of spirited contests to obtain new members at the expense of other labor organizations. For all these reasons, unions in this country have long striven to achieve 100% membership and to obtain this goal through contractual arrangements with employers which would make union membership a condition of employment for each employee in the unit. The notion of compulsory membership has inevitably created troublesome questions of principle—questions which have been raised not only by employers wishing to weaken the power of unions but by others not immediately involved in the field of labor relations in this country. With this background, the law has responded in a variety of ways to regulate the use of union security arrangements.

The materials below deal with the following issues:

(1) Under what circumstances may an employer and union lawfully agree that all employees shall, as a condition of employment, become members of the union or contribute financial support to the union? Are any limits imposed by the federal Constitution or by the Labor Act upon the use that may be made by a union of moneys contributed pursuant to a union security agreement?

(2) What power may be exercised by the states to limit the use of union security agreements?

(3) To what extent may unions lawfully exert control over the hiring process through the negotiation with the employer of hiring-hall agreements?

(4) To what extent, if any, may union officials be accorded preferred job status under the collective bargaining agreement?

---

## A. UNION SECURITY AND THE USE OF UNION DUES[a]

---

# NLRB v. General Motors Corp.

373 U.S. 734, 83 S.Ct. 1453, 10 L.Ed.2d 670 (1963).

■ MR. JUSTICE WHITE delivered the opinion of the Court.

The issue here is whether an employer commits an unfair labor practice (National Labor Relations Act, § 8(a)(5)), when he refuses to bargain with a certified union over the union's proposal for the adoption of the "agency shop." More narrowly, since the employer is not obliged to bargain over a proposal that he commit an unfair labor practice, the question is whether the agency shop is an unfair labor practice under § 8(a)(3) of the Act or else is exempted from the prohibitions of that section by the proviso thereto. We have concluded that this type of arrangement does not constitute an unfair labor practice and that it is not prohibited by § 8.

Respondent's employees are represented by the United Automobile, Aerospace and Agricultural Implement Workers of America, UAW, in a single, multi-plant, company-wide unit. The 1958 agreement between union and company provides for maintenance of membership and the union shop.

---

a. See T. Haggard, Compulsory Unionism, the NLRB, and the Courts (1977); Hopfl, The Agency Shop Question, 49 Cornell L.Q. 478 (1964); Mayer, Union Security and the Taft–Hartley Act, 1961 Duke L.J. 505; Rosenthal, The National Labor Relations Act and Compulsory Unionism, 1954 Wis.L.Rev. 53.

These provisions were not operative, however, in such states as Indiana where state law prohibited making union membership a condition of employment.

In June 1959, the Indiana intermediate appellate court held that an agency shop arrangement would not violate the state right-to-work law. Meade Elec. Co. v. Hagberg, 129 Ind.App. 631, 159 N.E.2d 408 (1959). As defined in that opinion, the term "agency shop" applies to an arrangement under which all employees are required as a condition of employment to pay dues to the union and pay the union's initiation fee, but they need not actually become union members. The union thereafter sent respondent a letter proposing the negotiation of a contractual provision covering Indiana plants "generally similar to that set forth" in the *Meade* case. Continued employment in the Indiana plants would be conditioned upon the payment of sums equal to the initiation fee and regular monthly dues paid by the union members. The intent of the proposal, the NLRB concluded, was not to require membership but to make membership available at the employees' option and on nondiscriminatory terms. Employees choosing not to join would make the required payments and, in accordance with union custom, would share in union expenditures for strike benefits, educational and retired member benefits, and union publications and promotional activities, but they would not be entitled to attend union meetings, vote upon ratification of agreements negotiated by the union, or have a voice in the internal affairs of the union. The respondent made no counterproposal, but replied to the union's letter that the proposed agreement would violate the National Labor Relations Act and that respondent must therefore "respectfully decline to comply with your request for a meeting" to bargain over the proposal.

[The NLRB held the agency shop provision lawful under Section 8(a)(3) and a subject of mandatory bargaining; the employer was held to violate Section 8(a)(5) and was ordered to bargain about the provision. The court of appeals, however, set aside the Board's order. It held that a provision requiring the payment of an agency fee equivalent to union dues as a condition of employment was not within the proviso to Section 8(a)(3) permitting a requirement of "membership" as a condition of employment. It found the agency shop provision to be unlawful and concluded that the employer was not required to bargain concerning its inclusion in the labor contract.]

Section 8(3) under the Wagner Act was the predecessor to § 8(a)(3) of the present law. Like § 8(a)(3), § 8(3) forbade employers to discriminate against employees to compel them to join a union. Because it was feared that § 8(3) and § 7, if nothing were added to qualify them, might be held to outlaw union-security arrangements such as the closed shop, see 79 Cong. Rec. 7570 (statement of Senator Wagner), 7674 (statement of Senator Walsh); H.R.Rep. No. 972, p. 17; H.R.Rep. No. 1147, p. 19, the proviso to § 8(3) was added expressly declaring:

> "*Provided*, That nothing in this act * * * or in any other statute of the United States, shall preclude an employer from

making an agreement with a labor organization * * * to require as
a condition of employment membership therein, if such labor
organization is the representative of the employees as provided in
section 9(a) * * *."

The prevailing administrative and judicial view under the Wagner Act
was or came to be that the proviso to § 8(3) covered both the closed and
union shop, as well as less onerous union security arrangements, if they
were otherwise legal. The NLRB construed the proviso as shielding from an
unfair labor practice charge less severe forms of union-security arrangements than the closed or the union shop, including an arrangement in
Public Service Co. of Colorado, 89 NLRB 418, requiring nonunion members
to pay to the union $2 a month "for the support of the bargaining unit."
And in Algoma Plywood & Veneer Co. v. Wisconsin Employment Relations
Board, 336 U.S. 301, 307, 93 L.Ed. 691, 69 S.Ct. 584 (1949), which involved
a maintenance of membership agreement, the Court, in commenting on
petitioner's contention that the proviso of § 8(3) affirmatively protected
arrangements within its scope, cf. Garner v. Teamsters, C. & H. Union, 346
U.S. 485, 98 L.Ed. 228, 74 S.Ct. 161 (1953), said of its purpose: "The short
answer is that § 8(3) merely disclaims a national policy hostile to the closed
shop *or other forms of union-security agreement.*" (Emphasis added.)

When Congress enacted the Taft–Hartley Act, it added * * * to the
language of the original proviso to § 8(3) * * *. These additions were
intended to accomplish twin purposes. On the one hand, the most serious
abuses of compulsory unionism were eliminated by abolishing the closed
shop. On the other hand, Congress recognized that in the absence of a
union-security provision "many employees sharing the benefits of what
unions are able to accomplish, like collective bargaining, will refuse to pay
their share of the cost." S.Rep. No. 105, 80th Cong., 1st Sess., p. 6, 1
Leg.Hist.L.M.R.A. 412. Consequently, under the new law "employers would
still be permitted to enter into agreements requiring all employees in a
given bargaining unit to become members thirty days after being hired"
but "expulsion from a union cannot be a ground of compulsory discharge if
the worker is not delinquent in paying his initiation fees or dues". S.Rep.
No. 105, p. 7, 1 Leg.Hist.L.M.R.A. 413. The amendments were intended
only to "remedy the most serious abuses of compulsory union membership
and yet give employers and unions who feel that such agreements promoted
stability by eliminating 'free riders' the right to continue such arrangements." Ibid. As far as the federal law was concerned, all employees could
be required to pay their way. The bill "abolishes the closed shop but
permits voluntary agreements for requiring such forms of compulsory
membership as the union shop or maintenance of membership * * *."
S.Rep. No. 105, p. 3, 1, Leg.Hist.L.M.R.A. 409.

We find nothing in the legislative history of the Act indicating that
Congress intended the amended proviso to § 8(a)(3) to validate only the
union shop and simultaneously to abolish, in addition to the closed shop, all
other union-security arrangements permissible under state law. There is
much to be said for the Board's view that, if Congress desired in the

Wagner Act to permit a closed or union shop and in the Taft–Hartley Act
the union shop, then it also intended to preserve the status of less vigorous,
less compulsory contracts, which demanded less adherence to the union.

Respondent, however, relies upon the express words of the proviso
which allow employment to be conditioned upon "membership": since the
union's proposal here does not require actual membership but demands
only initiation fees and monthly dues it is not saved by the proviso. * * *
[T]he 1947 amendments not only abolished the closed shop but also made
significant alterations in the meaning of "membership" for the purposes of
union security contracts. Under the second proviso to § 8(a)(3), the burdens of membership upon which employment may be conditioned are
expressly limited to the payment of initiation fees and monthly dues. It is
permissible to condition employment upon membership, but membership
insofar as it has significance to employment rights, may in turn be
conditioned only upon payment of fees and dues. "Membership" as a
condition of employment is whittled down to its financial core. This Court
has said as much before in Radio Officers' Union v. NLRB, 347 U.S. 17, 41,
98 L.Ed. 455, 74 S.Ct. 323 (1954):

> " * * * This legislative history clearly indicates that Congress
> intended to prevent utilization of union security agreements for
> any purpose other than to compel payment of union dues and fees.
> Thus, Congress recognized the validity of unions' concern about
> 'free riders,' i.e., employees who receive the benefits of union
> representation but are unwilling to contribute their fair share of
> financial support to such union, and gave the unions the power to
> contract to meet that problem while withholding from unions the
> power to cause the discharge of employees for any other reason
> * * *."

We are therefore confident that the proposal made by the union here
conditioned employment upon the practical equivalent of union "membership," as Congress used that term in the proviso to § 8(a)(3). The proposal
for requiring the payment of dues and fees imposes no burdens not imposed
by a permissible union shop contract and compels the performance of only
those duties of membership which are enforceable by discharge under a
union shop arrangement. If an employee in a union shop unit refuses to
respect any union-imposed obligations other than the duty to pay dues and
fees, and membership in the union is therefore denied or terminated, the
condition of "membership" for § 8(a)(3) purposes is nevertheless satisfied
and the employee may not be discharged for nonmembership even though
he is not a formal member. * * *

In short, the employer categorically refused to bargain with the union
over a proposal for an agreement within the proviso to § 8(a)(3) and as
such, lawful, for the purposes of this case. By the same token, § 7, and
derivatively § 8(a)(1), cannot be deemed to forbid the employer to enter
such agreements, since it too is expressly limited by the § 8(a)(3) proviso.
We hold that the employer was not excused from his duty to bargain over

the proposal on the theory that his acceding to it would necessarily involve him in an unfair labor practice. * * *

Reversed and remanded.

MR. JUSTICE GOLDBERG took no part in the consideration or decision of this case.

––––––––––

## PROBLEMS FOR DISCUSSION

**1.**   Note the three kinds of union security provisions mentioned at the outset of the Court's opinion: the union shop, maintenance of membership, and the agency shop. What do each of these different clauses provide? (What kind of provision is incorporated in the illustrative labor agreement set forth in the Statutory Supplement to the casebook?) After the *General Motors* decision, is there any difference among these three provisions in substantive legal impact?

**2.**   The Court in *General Motors* held that the employer in a refusal-to-bargain proceeding under Section 8(a)(5) could not rely as a defense upon the alleged illegality of the agency shop provision. Did the Court also hold that the provision is a mandatory subject of bargaining? Do the reasons underlying such a clause, as articulated by the Court, suggest that it should be treated as mandatory, or as merely permissive?

**3.**   Martin was employed by the Eclipse Lumber Company and was a member of the Woodworkers Union; the labor contract contained no union security provision. During the term of that contract, Martin refused to pay to the Union an amount which the Union had assessed against all members in order to create a fund for contributions to certain political candidates for state office; for this he was fined, and rather than pay the fine he resigned from membership. Some years later, the Company and the Union negotiated a labor contract which contained a provision requiring all employees to become and remain members of the Union. Although Martin applied for membership, he was told that membership would be extended only if he paid the fine. He refused to pay the fine, and the company discharged him upon the Union's request. Has the Labor Act been violated? See NLRB v. Eclipse Lumber Co., 199 F.2d 684 (9th Cir.1952).

**4.**   The contract between the Smith Mfg. Co. and the Electrical Workers Union contains a union shop provision, and employee Gray joined the Union thirty days after being placed on the payroll. Union dues are $10 per month, but members who attend monthly Union meetings are granted a $2 refund at the meeting. Gray has thus insisted on tendering no more than $8 to the Union each month in satisfaction of his dues obligation, asserting that the other $2 is actually a fine for nonattendance at Union meetings. The Union has refused the tender of $8 and has asked the Company to discharge Gray. The Company wishes to know whether it may do so without violating the Labor Act. May it? Is Section 8(b)(5) of the Act pertinent? Compare NLRB v. Leece–Neville Co., 140 NLRB 56 (1963), enforced, 330 F.2d 242 (6th Cir.1964), cert. denied, 379 U.S. 819, 85 S.Ct. 41, 13 L.Ed.2d 31 (1964), with Local 171, Ass'n of Western Pulp Workers (Boise Cascade Corp.), 165 NLRB 971 (1967).

**5.**   For years, the contract between Triangle Publications and the Television Broadcasters Union has contained a union shop provision; the Union initiation fee for all new employees (who generally receive roughly $400 per week) has been $200.

The Union has become concerned about the loss of work for its members resulting from the Company's greater use of part-time employees. In order to curtail this practice, the Union recently raised its initiation fee to $1,000, payable $500 immediately and $250 in two monthly payments. This has made it extremely difficult for part-time employees to become Union members as required by the collective bargaining agreement. The Company has filed a charge against the Union for violation of Sections 8(b)(2) and (5) of the Labor Act. Has the Union violated either Section? See NLRB v. Television and Radio Broadcasting Studio Employees, Local 804, 315 F.2d 398 (3d Cir.1963).

————

### PRE-HIRE AGREEMENTS

In one industry—building and construction—the statute takes account of special circumstances and reduces the grace period for acquiring union "membership" under a union shop provision or for beginning to pay union dues under an agency shop provision. In the building and construction industry, a given employer works on different jobs in different localities, performs work of brief duration and hires a transient workforce (often through a union-controlled hiring hall) typically highly organized along craft lines. A construction employer also must be in a position to know what wage rates to anticipate in different places in order that it may intelligently compute its contract bids. These factors render unsuitable the full-dressed representation election conducted by the NLRB and the usual month-long statutory grace period for union security provisions and invite dealing with a particular union even before the employee complement has been hired. Congress therefore, in the Landrum–Griffin amendments of 1959, enacted Section 8(f) of the Labor Act in order to broaden the powers of construction employers and unions to make union security agreements (like all others, subject to outlawry by state right-to-work laws) in two pertinent respects: The agreement will be lawful even if:

> (1) the majority status of such labor organization has not been established under the provisions of section 9 of this Act prior to the making of such agreement, or (2) such agreement requires as a condition of employment, membership in such labor organization after the seventh day following the beginning of such employment or the effective date of the agreement, whichever is later * * *.

Since these union shop arrangements may be negotiated before the union demonstrates majority support within the employer's bargaining unit, and indeed before employees are hired at all, they are known as "pre-hire agreements." The NLRB has through the years vacillated on such questions as whether pre-hire agreements are fully enforceable during their term and whether the employer must continue to recognize the union during and after the life of the contract. The Board's present views are set forth in Deklewa, 282 NLRB 1375 (1987), enf'd sub nom. International Ass'n of Bridge Workers, Local 3, 843 F.2d 770 (3d Cir.1988), cert. denied, 488 U.S. 889, 109 S.Ct. 222, 102 L.Ed.2d 213 (1988). The courts have upheld the Board, e.g., Laborers' Int'l Union v. Foster Wheeler Corp., 26

F.3d 375 (3d Cir.1994), cert. denied, 513 U.S. 946, 115 S.Ct. 357, 130 L.Ed.2d 311 (1994); Mesa Verde Constr. Co. v. Northern Cal. Dist. Council, 861 F.2d 1124 (9th Cir.1988)(en banc).

--------

# International Association of Machinists v. Street

367 U.S. 740, 81 S.Ct. 1784, 6 L.Ed.2d 1141 (1961).

■ MR. JUSTICE BRENNAN delivered the opinion of the Court.

A group of labor organizations, appellants here, and the carriers comprising the Southern Railway System, entered into a union-shop agreement pursuant to the authority of § 2, Eleventh of the Railway Labor Act.[1] The agreement requires each of the appellees, employees of the carriers, as a condition of continued employment, to pay the appellant union representing his particular class or craft the dues, initiation fees and assessments uniformly required as a condition of acquiring or retaining union membership. The appellees, in behalf of themselves and of employees similarly situated, brought this action in the Superior Court of Bibb County, Georgia, alleging that the money each was thus compelled to pay to hold his job was in substantial part used to finance the campaigns of candidates for federal and state offices whom he opposed, and to promote the propagation of political and economic doctrines, concepts and ideologies with which he disagreed. The Superior Court found that the allegations were fully proved and entered a judgment and decree enjoining the enforcement of the union-shop agreement on the ground that § 2, Eleventh violates the Federal Constitution to the extent that it permits such use by the appellants of the funds exacted from employees. The Supreme Court of Georgia affirmed, 215 Ga. 27, 108 S.E.2d 796. On appeal to this Court under 28 U.S.C. § 1257(1), 28 U.S.C.A. § 1257(1), we noted probable jurisdiction, 361 U.S. 807, 80 S.Ct. 84, 4 L.Ed.2d 54.

**1.** 64 Stat. 1238, 45 U.S.C. § 152, Eleventh, 45 U.S.C.A. § 152, Eleventh. The section provides:

"Eleventh. Notwithstanding any other provisions of this chapter, or of any other statute or law of the United States, or Territory thereof, or of any State, any carrier or carriers as defined in this chapter and a labor organization or labor organizations duly designated and authorized to represent employees in accordance with the requirements of this chapter shall be permitted—

"(a) to make agreements, requiring, as a condition of continued employment, that within sixty days following the beginning of such employment, or the effective date of such agreements, whichever is the later, all employees shall become members of the labor organization representing their craft or class: *Provided,* That no such agreement shall require such condition of employment with respect to employees to whom membership is not available upon the same terms and conditions as are generally applicable to any other member or with respect to employees to whom membership was denied or terminated for any reason other than the failure of the employee to tender the periodic dues, initiation fees, and assessments (not including fines and penalties) uniformly required as a condition of acquiring or retaining membership. * * * "

I.

The Hanson Decision.

We held in Railway Employes' Dept. v. Hanson, 351 U.S. 225, 76 S.Ct. 714, 100 L.Ed. 1112, that enactment of the provision of § 2, Eleventh authorizing union-shop agreements between interstate railroads and unions of their employees was a valid exercise by Congress of its powers under the Commerce Clause and did not violate the First Amendment or the Due Process Clause of the Fifth Amendment. It is argued that our disposition of the First Amendment claims in Hanson disposes of appellees' constitutional claims in this case adversely to their contentions. We disagree. As appears from its history, that case decided only that § 2, Eleventh, in authorizing collective agreements conditioning employees' continued employment on payment of union dues, initiation fees and assessments, did not on its face impinge upon protected rights of association. * * * We said: "It is argued that compulsory membership will be used to impair freedom of expression. But that problem is not presented by this record. * * * [I]f the exaction of dues, initiation fees, or assessments is used as a cover for forcing ideological conformity or other action in contravention of the First Amendment, this judgment will not prejudice the decision in that case. For we pass narrowly on § 2, Eleventh of the Railway Labor Act. We only hold that the requirement for financial support of the collective-bargaining agency by all who receive the benefits of its work is within the power of Congress under the Commerce Clause and does not violate either the First or the Fifth Amendment." * * *

The record in this case is adequate squarely to present the constitutional questions reserved in Hanson. These are questions of the utmost gravity. However, the restraints against unnecessary constitutional decisions counsel against their determination unless we must conclude that Congress, in authorizing a union shop under § 2, Eleventh, also meant that the labor organization receiving an employee's money should be free, despite that employee's objection, to spend his money for political causes which he opposes. Federal statutes are to be so construed as to avoid serious doubt of their constitutionality. "When the validity of an act of the Congress is drawn in question, and even if a serious doubt of constitutionality is raised, it is a cardinal principle that this Court will first ascertain whether a construction of the statute is fairly possible by which the question may be avoided." Crowell v. Benson, 285 U.S. 22, 62, 52 S.Ct. 285, 296, 76 L.Ed. 598. Each named appellee in this action has made known to the union representing his craft or class his dissent from the use of his money for political causes which he opposes. We have therefore examined the legislative history of § 2, Eleventh in the context of the development of unionism in the railroad industry under the regulatory scheme created by the Railway Labor Act to determine whether a construction is "fairly possible" which denies the authority to a union, over the employee's objection, to spend his money for political causes which he opposes. We conclude that such a construction is not only "fairly possible" but entirely reasonable, and we therefore find it unnecessary to decide the correctness of the constitutional determinations made by the Georgia courts.

## II.

### The Rail Unions and Union Security.

The history of union security in the railway industry is marked *first,* by a strong and long-standing tradition of voluntary unionism on the part of the standard rail unions; *second,* by the declaration in 1934 of a congressional policy of complete freedom of choice of employees to join or not to join a union; *third,* by the modification of the firm legislative policy against compulsion, but only as a specific response to the recognition of the expenses and burdens incurred by the unions in the administration of the complex scheme of the Railway Labor Act. * * *

[Mr. Justice Brennan recounted the history leading to the amendment of the Railway Labor Act in 1934. The "regular" train unions urged that they be allowed to enter into labor contracts requiring membership in them as a condition of employment but that this privilege be denied to "company" unions. This proposal was, however, rejected by Congress, which approved the principle of freedom of choice for all railroad workers regarding union membership; the amended Act forbade all carriers to "require any person seeking employment to sign any contract or agreement promising to join or not to join a labor organization." During World War II, when major contract negotiations reached an impasse, in part over the issue of union security, a Presidential Emergency Board recommended against a membership requirement, concluding that it was both illegal under the Railway Labor Act and also unnecessary, in light of the unions' membership strength and their recognition by the carriers. When the issue of union security was revived in Congress in 1950, it was viewed in light of Congress's rejection of the principle of compulsory arbitration of new contract terms in the railroad industry and its emphasis upon the amicable adjustment of disputes between carriers and unions through free collective bargaining leading to a labor contract. Although this policy had been embodied in the Railway Labor Act since 1926, with its provisions requiring bargaining and resort to the National Mediation Board to assist in the resolution of impasses, new responsibilities had been imposed on rail unions in 1934, when Congress provided for representation elections, for exclusive representation on behalf of all employees in the craft or class, and for arbitration of contract grievances before the National Railroad Adjustment Board to which the unions were to appoint representatives.]

Performance of these functions entails the expenditure of considerable funds. Moreover, this Court has held that under the statutory scheme, a union's status as exclusive bargaining representative carries with it the duty fairly and equitably to represent all employees of the craft or class, union and nonunion. Steele v. Louisville & N.R. Co., 323 U.S. 192, 65 S.Ct. 226; Tunstall v. Brotherhood of Locomotive Firemen & Enginemen, 323 U.S. 210, 65 S.Ct. 235, 89 L.Ed. 187. The principal argument made by the unions in 1950 was based on their role in this regulatory framework. They maintained that because of the expense of performing their duties in the congressional scheme, fairness justified the spreading of the costs to all employees who benefited. They thus advanced as their purpose the elimination of the "free riders"—those employees who obtained the benefits of the unions' participation in the machinery of the Act without financially supporting the unions. * * *

This argument was decisive with Congress. * * *

These considerations overbore the arguments in favor of the earlier policy of complete individual freedom of choice. As we said in Railway Employes' Dept. v. Hanson, supra, 351 U.S. at page 235, 76 S.Ct. at page 720, "[t]o require, rather than to induce, the beneficiaries of trade unionism to contribute to its costs may not be the wisest course. But Congress might well believe that it would help insure the right to work in and along the arteries of interstate commerce. No more has been attempted here. * * * The financial support required relates * * * to the work of the union in the realm of collective bargaining." The conclusion to which this history clearly points is that § 2, Eleventh contemplated compulsory unionism to force employees to share the costs of negotiating and administering collective agreements, and the costs of the adjustment and settlement of disputes. One looks in vain for any suggestion that Congress also meant in § 2, Eleventh to provide the unions with a means for forcing employees, over their objection, to support political causes which they oppose.

### III.

### The Safeguarding of Rights of Dissent.

To the contrary, Congress incorporated safeguards in the statute to protect dissenters' interests. Congress became concerned during the hearings and debates that the union shop might be used to abridge freedom of speech and beliefs. The original proposal for authorization of the union shop was qualified in only one respect. It provided "That no such agreement shall require such condition of employment with respect to employees to whom membership is not available upon the same terms and conditions as are generally applicable to any other member * * *." This was primarily designed to prevent discharge of employees for nonmembership where the union did not admit the employee to membership on racial grounds. See House Hearings, p. 68; Senate Hearings, pp. 22–25. But it was strenuously protested that the proposal provided no protection for an employee who disagreed with union policies or leadership. It was argued, for example, that "the right of free speech is at stake. * * * A man could feel that he was no longer able freely to express himself because he could be dismissed on account of criticism of the union * * *." House Hearings, p. 115; see also Senate Hearings, pp. 167–169, 320. Objections of this kind led the rail unions to propose an addition to the proviso to § 2, Eleventh to prevent loss of job for lack of union membership "with respect to employees to whom membership was denied or terminated for any reason other than the failure of the employee to tender the periodic dues, fees, and assessments uniformly required as a condition of acquiring or retaining membership." House Hearings, p. 247. * * *

A congressional concern over possible impingements on the interests of individual dissenters from union policies is therefore discernible. It is true that opponents of the union shop urged that Congress should not allow it without explicitly regulating the amount of dues which might be exacted or prescribing the uses for which the dues might be expended. We may assume that Congress was also fully conversant with the long history of intensive involvement of the railroad unions in political activities. But it does not follow that § 2, Eleventh places no restriction on the use of an employee's money, over his objection, to support political causes he opposes merely because Congress did not enact a comprehensive regulatory scheme governing expenditures. For it is abundantly clear that Congress did not completely abandon the policy of full freedom of choice embodied in the 1934 Act, but rather made inroads on it for the limited purpose of eliminating the problems created by the "free rider." That policy survives in § 2, Eleventh in the safeguards intended to protect freedom of dissent. Congress was aware of the conflicting interests involved in the question of the union shop and sought to achieve their accommodation. * * * We respect this congressional purpose when we construe § 2, Eleventh as not vesting the unions with unlimited power to spend exacted money. We are not called upon to delineate the precise limits of that power in this case. We have before us only the question whether the power is restricted to the extent of denying the unions the right, over the employee's objection, to use his money to support political causes which he opposes. Its use to support candidates for public office, and advance political programs, is not a use which helps defray the expenses of the negotiation or administration of collective agreements, or the expenses entailed in the adjustment of grievances and disputes. In other words, it is a use which falls clearly outside the reasons advanced by the unions and accepted by Congress why authority to make union-shop agreements was justified. On the other hand, it is equally clear that it is a use to support activities within the area of dissenters' interests which Congress enacted the proviso to protect. We give § 2, Eleventh the construction which achieves both congressional purposes when we hold, as we do, that § 2, Eleventh is to be construed to deny the unions, over an employee's objection, the power to use his exacted funds to support political causes which he opposes. * * *

[As to the proper remedy, the Court pointed out that—although the unions were without power thereafter to spend upon political causes any moneys collected from objecting employees—the union shop agreement itself was not unlawful. "If their money were used for purposes contemplated by § 2, Eleventh, the appellees would have no grievance at all. We think that an injunction restraining enforcement of the union-shop agreement is therefore plainly not a remedy appropriate to the violation of the Act's restriction on expenditures." An injunction against the provision itself would also impair the unions' performance of their statutory duties.

[The Court also concluded that it would be improper to issue an injunction against political expenditures generally. "[M]any of the expenditures involved in the present case are made for the purpose of disseminating information as to candidates and programs and publicizing the positions of the unions on them. As to such expenditures an injunction would work a restraint on the expression of political ideas which might be offensive to the First Amendment. For the majority also has an interest in stating its views without being silenced by the dissenters." The Court suggested two possible methods for structuring a remedy against the unions, but only for the benefit of employees who affirmatively make known to union officials their desire not to have funds spent on objectionable political causes. "One remedy would be an injunction against expenditure for political causes opposed by each complaining employee of a sum, from those moneys to be spent by the union for political purposes, which is so much of the moneys exacted from him as is the proportion of the union's total expenditures made for such political activities to the union's total budget. * * * A second remedy would be restitution to each individual employee of that portion of his money which the union expended, despite his notification, for the political causes to which he had advised the union he was opposed."]

The judgment is reversed and the case is remanded to the court below for proceedings not inconsistent with this opinion.

■ MR. JUSTICE DOUGLAS, concurring.

* * * If an association is compelled, the individual should not be forced to surrender any matters of conscience, belief, or expression. * * * [H]e should not be required to finance the promotion of causes with which he disagrees. * * *

The collection of dues for paying the costs of collective bargaining of which each member is a beneficiary is one thing. If, however, dues are used, or assessments are made, to promote or oppose birth control, to repeal or increase the taxes on cosmetics, to promote or oppose the admission of Red China into the United Nations, and the like, then the group compels an individual to support with his money causes beyond what gave rise to the need for group action.

I think the same must be said when union dues or assessments are used to elect a Governor, a Congressman, a Senator, or a President. It may be said that the election of a Franklin D. Roosevelt rather than a Calvin Coolidge might be the best possible way to serve the cause of collective bargaining. But even such a selective use of union funds for political purposes subordinates the individual's First Amendment rights to the views of the majority. I do not see how that can be done, even though the objector retains his rights to campaign, to speak, to vote as he chooses. For when union funds are used for that purpose, the individual is required to finance political projects against which he may be in rebellion. The furtherance of the common cause leaves some leeway for the leadership of the group. As long as they act to promote the cause which justified bringing the group together, the individual cannot withdraw his financial support merely because he disagrees with the group's strategy. If that were allowed, we would be reversing the Hanson case *sub silentio*. * * *

■ MR. JUSTICE BLACK, dissenting.

* * * I think the Court is once more "carrying the doctrine of avoiding constitutional questions to a wholly unjustifiable extreme." In fact, I think the Court is actually rewriting § 2, Eleventh to make it mean exactly what Congress refused to make it mean. The very legislative history relied on by the Court appears to me to prove that its interpretation of § 2, Eleventh is without justification. For that history shows that Congress with its eyes wide open passed that section, knowing that its broad language would permit the use of union dues to advocate causes, doctrines, laws, candidates and parties, whether individual members objected or not. Under such circumstances I think Congress has a right to a determination of the constitutionality of the statute it passed, rather than to have the Court rewrite the statute in the name of avoiding decision of constitutional questions. * * *

There is, of course, no constitutional reason why a union or other private group may not spend its funds for political or ideological causes if its members voluntarily join it and can voluntarily get out of it. * * * But a different situation arises when a federal law steps in and authorizes such a group to carry on activities at the expense of persons who do not choose to be members of the group as well as those who do. Such a law, even though validly passed by Congress, cannot be used in a way that abridges the specifically defined freedoms of the First Amendment. And whether there is such abridgment depends not only on how the law is written but also on how it works.

There can be no doubt that the federally sanctioned union-shop contract here, as it actually works, takes a part of the earnings of some men and turns it over to others, who spend a substantial part of the funds so received in efforts to thwart the political, economic and ideological hopes of those whose money has been forced from them under authority of law. This injects federal compulsion into the political and ideological processes, a result which I have supposed everyone would agree the First Amendment was particularly intended to prevent. And it makes no difference if, as is urged, political and legislative activities are helpful adjuncts of collective bargaining. * * *

I would therefore hold that § 2, Eleventh of the Railway Labor Act, in authorizing application of the union-shop contract to the named protesting employees who are appellees here, violates the freedom of speech guarantee of the First Amendment. * * *

■ MR. JUSTICE FRANKFURTER, whom MR. JUSTICE HARLAN joins, dissenting.

* * * I completely defer to the guiding principle that this Court will abstain from entertaining a serious constitutional question when a statute may fairly be construed so as to avoid the issue, but am unable to accept the restrictive interpretation that the Court gives to § 2, Eleventh of the Railway Labor Act. * * *

The statutory provision cannot be meaningfully construed except against the background and presupposition of what is loosely called political activity of American trade unions in general and railroad unions in particular—activity indissolubly relating to the immediate economic and social concerns that are the *raison d'être* of unions. It would be pedantic heavily to document this familiar truth of industrial history and commonplace of trade-union life. To write the history of the Brotherhoods, the United Mine Workers, the Steel Workers, the Amalgamated Clothing Workers, the International Ladies Garment Workers, the United Auto Workers, and leave out their so-called political activities and expenditures for them, would be sheer mutilation. Suffice it to recall a few illustrative manifestations. The AFL, surely the conservative labor group, sponsored as early as 1893 an extensive program of political demands calling for compulsory education, an eight-hour day, employer tort liability, and other social reforms. * * * More specifically, the weekly publication "Labor"—an expenditure under attack in this case—has since 1919 been the organ of the railroad brotherhoods which finance it. Its files through the years show its preoccupation with legislative measures that touch the vitals of labor's interests and with the men and parties who effectuate them. This aspect—call it the political side—is as organic, as inured a part of the philosophy and practice of railway unions as their immediate bread-and-butter concerns.

Viewed in this light, there is a total absence in the text, the context, the history and the purpose of the legislation under review of any indication that Congress, in authorizing union-shop agreements, attributed to unions and restricted them to an artificial, non-prevalent scope of activities in the expenditure of their funds. An inference that Congress legislated regarding expenditure control in contradiction to prevailing practices ought to be better founded than on complete silence. The aim of the 1951 legislation, clearly stated in the congressional reports, was to eliminate "free riders" in the industry—to make possible "the sharing of the burden of maintenance by all of the beneficiaries of union activity." To suggest that this language covertly meant to encompass any less than the maintenance of those activities normally engaged in by unions is to withdraw life from law and to say that Congress dealt with artificialities and not with railway unions as they were and as they functioned. * * *

I cannot attribute to Congress that *sub silentio* it meant to bar railway unions under a union-shop agreement from expending their funds in their traditional manner. How easy it would have been to give at least a hint that such was its purpose. The claim that these expenditures infringe the appellees' constitutional rights under the First Amendment must therefore be faced. * * *

[W]e unanimously held that the plaintiffs in Hanson had not been denied any right protected by the First Amendment. Despite our holding, the gist of the complaint here is that the expenditure of a portion of mandatory funds for political objectives denies free speech—the right to speak or to remain silent—to members who oppose, against the constituted authority of union desires, this use of their union dues. No one's desire or power to speak his mind is checked or curbed. The individual member may express his views in any public or private forum as freely as he could before the union collected his dues. Federal taxes also may diminish the vigor with which a citizen can give partisan support to a political belief, but as yet no one would place such an impediment to making one's views effective within the reach of constitutionally protected "free speech." * * *

But were we to assume, *arguendo,* that the plaintiffs have alleged a valid constitutional objection if Congress had specifically ordered the result, we must consider the difference between such compulsion and the absence of compulsion when Congress acts as platonically as it did, in a wholly non-coercive way. Congress has not commanded that the railroads shall employ only those workers who are members of authorized unions. Congress has only given leave to a bargaining representative, democratically elected by a majority of workers, to enter into a particular contractual provision arrived at under the give-and-take of duly safeguarded bargaining procedures. * * * When we speak of the Government "acting" in permitting the union shop, the scope and force of what Congress has done must be heeded. There is not a trace of compulsion involved—no exercise of restriction by Congress on the freedom of the carriers and the unions. On the contrary, Congress expanded their freedom of action. Congress lifted limitations upon free action by parties bargaining at arm's length.

The plaintiffs have not been deprived of the right to participate in determining union policies or to assert their respective weight in defining the purposes for which union dues may be expended. * * *

In conclusion, then, we are asked by union members who oppose these expenditures to protect their right to free speech—although they are as free to speak as ever—against governmental action which has permitted a union elected by democratic process to bargain for a union shop and to expend the funds thereby collected for purposes which are controlled by internal union choice. To do so would be to mutilate a scheme designed by Congress for the purpose of equitably sharing the cost of securing the benefits of union exertions; it would greatly embarrass if not frustrate conventional labor activities which have become institutionalized through time. To do so is to give constitutional sanction to doctrinaire views and to grant a miniscule claim constitutional recognition.

　　　* * *

[The separate opinion of Mr. Justice Whittaker is omitted.]

———

Communications Workers v. Beck, 487 U.S. 735, 108 S.Ct. 2641, 101 L.Ed.2d 634 (1988).[b] The Court considered the question whether the same restrictions placed by the *Street* decision upon union expenditure of agency

**b.** See Brudney, Association, Advocacy, and the First Amendment, 4 Wm. & Mary Bill of Rights J. 1 (1995); Dau–Schmidt, Union Security Agreements Under the NLRA: The Statute, the Constitution, and the Court's Opinion in *Beck*, 27 Harv.J. on Leg. 51 (1990).

fees under the Railway Labor Act also apply under the National Labor Relations Act. A divided Court answered in the affirmative. It noted that the union shop provisions of the Railway Labor Act (section 2, Eleventh) were added by Congress in 1951, and that they were patterned essentially verbatim upon the provisos to NLRA section 8(a)(3) which Congress enacted in the 1947 Taft–Hartley amendments to the NLRA.

The Court stated: "Our decision in *Street* . . . is far more than merely instructive here: we believe it is controlling, for § 8(a)(3) and § 2, Eleventh are in all material respects identical. . . . [I]n amending the RLA in 1951, Congress expressly modeled § 2, Eleventh on § 8(a)(3) . . . and repeatedly emphasized that it was extending 'to railroad labor the same rights and privileges of the union shop that are contained in the Taft–Hartley Act.' . . . We have [recently affirmed] that 'Congress' essential justification for authoring the union shop' limits the expenditures that may properly be charged to nonmembers under § 2, Eleventh to those 'necessarily or reasonably incurred for the purpose of performing the duties of an exclusive [bargaining] representative.' . . . Given the parallel purpose, structure, and language of § 8(a)(3), we must interpret that provision in the same manner. Like § 2, Eleventh, § 8(a)(3) permits the collection of 'periodic dues and initiation fees uniformly required as a condition of acquiring or retaining membership' in the union, and like its counterpart in the RLA, § 8(a)(3) was designed to remedy the inequities posed by 'free riders' who would otherwise unfairly profit from the Taft–Hartley Act's abolition of the closed shop. In the face of such statutory congruity, only the most compelling evidence could persuade us that Congress intended the nearly identical language of these two provisions to have different meanings. Petitioners have not proffered such evidence here."

Justice Blackmun dissented (for Justice O'Connor and Scalia as well), stating: "Throughout the hearings and lengthy debate on one of the most hotly contested issues that confronted the 1947 Congress, not once did any member of Congress suggest that § 8(a)(3) did not leave employers and unions free to adopt and enforce union-security agreements requiring all employees in the bargaining unit to pay an amount equal to full union dues and standard initiation fees. Nor did anyone suggest that § 8(a)(3) affected a union's expenditure of such funds." The purpose behind the provisos to section 8(a)(3) was to protect workers' *employment* rights against capricious actions by union leaders, and not to regulate how the union itself spent the dues uniformly collected from all workers in the bargaining unit.

---

## PROBLEMS FOR DISCUSSION

**1.** The Company and the Union have entered into a collective bargaining agreement containing a union security provision that allows an employee either to join the Union or to pay an agency fee "not in excess of that allowed by the pertinent case law." The exact amount is to be negotiated between the Company and the Union and, if they cannot agree, "the issue will be submitted to an arbitrator." In the ensuing negotiations, the Company proposed that the agency fee be 20% of union dues, which figure the Union rejected. The Company then demanded a detailed breakdown of all revenues and expenditures over the past three years from both the Local and the International. The Union refused. The Company invoked the arbitration clause and filed a charge of unfair labor practice for the Union's refusal to supply the information. How should the Board rule? See North Bay Development Disabilities Services, Inc. v. NLRB, 905 F.2d 476 (D.C.Cir.1990), cert. denied, 498 U.S. 1082, 111 S.Ct. 952, 112 L.Ed.2d 1041 (1991).

**2.** In ABOOD v. DETROIT BOARD OF EDUCATION, 431 U.S. 209, 97 S.Ct. 1782, 52 L.Ed.2d 261 (1977), the Court was confronted with the constitutional issue it sought to avoid in *Street* by statutory construction. Under Michigan law, public sector employers and unions are authorized to agree to agency shop provisions; the Michigan Court of Appeals construed the state statute to authorize the expenditure of such agency fees for political, professional and economic programs not limited to collective bargaining. The Supreme Court concluded that such expenditures, over the protests of involuntary dues payers, interfered with their First Amendment rights and was unconstitutional. The Court acknowledged that the same legislative justifications found in the *Hanson* and *Street* cases applied in the public sector when "the service charge is used to finance expenditures by the Union for the purpose of collective bargaining, contract administration, and grievance adjustment." The complaining teachers could, however, "constitutionally prevent the Union's spending a part of their required service fees to contribute to political candidates and to express political views unrelated to its duties as exclusive bargaining representative. * * * For at the heart of the First Amendment is the notion that an individual should be free to believe as he will, and that in a free society one's beliefs should be shaped by his mind and his conscience rather than coerced by the State. * * * [These principles] prohibit the [school board] from requiring any of the appellants to contribute to the support of an ideological cause he may oppose as a condition of holding a job as a public school teacher."

Does the public-sector setting of the *Abood* case make the objecting employees' case stronger or weaker than in the private sector? That is, the case for the application of First Amendment limitations may be greater when the employer is an arm of state or local government; but is not the scope of union activities properly to be treated as related to collective bargaining far broader in the public sector (*e.g.,* school board elections, bond issues, and the like)?

**3.** William Buckley is a noted newspaper and television journalist, author, and sometime political candidate. He is a member of the bargaining unit at his television station which is represented by AFTRA (American Federation of Television and Radio Artists); AFTRA and the company have negotiated a collective bargaining agreement which requires all employees in the bargaining unit to become members of the union. Buckley claims that thus conditioning his right to continued employment in the media upon his joining AFTRA is an infringement of the rights accorded him by the First Amendment to the Federal Constitution. He brings an action against AFTRA and his employer to enjoin their enforcement of the union shop provision. What defenses do you believe should be raised by the defendants? How should the case be decided? See Buckley v. AFTRA, 496 F.2d 305 (2d Cir.1974), cert. denied, 419 U.S. 1093, 95 S.Ct. 688, 42 L.Ed.2d 687 (1974).

**4.** In 1974, Congress brought within the coverage of the Labor Act nonprofit health care institutions (which had formerly been explicitly excluded from the definition of "employer" in Section 2(2)). At the same time, Congress enacted a new Section 19, which announced an exception to the principles normally governing union security agreements. Section 19 as presently written exempts members of a bona fide religious organization, which has historically held conscientious objections to joining or financially supporting labor organizations, from the obligation to join or pay moneys to the bargaining representative—provided such persons pay an equal sum to a nonreligious charity. (The section also authorizes the union to charge any such conscientious objector the reasonable cost of pursuing a grievance at his or her request.) The apparent reason underlying Section 19 was to avoid disrupting charitable hospitals controlled by Seventh Day Adventists, for so long outside the union security provisions of the NLRA (by virtue of the earlier health-care exclusion), by subjecting employees there to discharge. Can you formulate any constitutional challenges to Section 19? Could that section be put to good use (by which party) in the action by Mr. Buckley in Problem 3? See Wilson v. NLRB, 920 F.2d 1282 (6th Cir.1990), cert. denied, 505 U.S. 1218, 112 S.Ct. 3025, 120 L.Ed.2d 896 (1992).

**5.** The student should be aware that union expenditures in political campaigns are regulated not only under the *Street* decision but also under various statutory enactments. Thus, Section 321 of the Federal Election Campaign Act of 1976 (which can be traced back to Section 304 of the 1947 Taft–Hartley Act) prohibits unions from spending dues moneys for "contributions or expenditures in connection with" any caucus, political convention, primary election, or election determining the selection or election of the President, Vice President, or a United States Senator or Congressional Representative. 29 U.S.C. § 441b(a). (Some states have enacted similar statutes regulating union political contributions in elections for state offices.) Under the federal act, however, unions may establish separate funds to be used for contributions in connection with federal elections, provided such funds are financed by voluntary contributions from the members of the union. 29 U.S.C. § 441b(b).

Does such legislation make more compelling—or less compelling—the case against union expenditures in connection with lobbying for legislative proposals (as distinguished from campaigns of political candidates)?

**6.** Mollie Member is a member of the United Auto Workers, which has negotiated an agency-shop provision in the labor contract with her employer. She is active in union affairs, often as a dissenter, and she is often heard on the floor of the union meeting hall and has been an unsuccessful candidate for union office. She wishes to remain a union member and to exercise these rights—as well as the right to vote whether or not to ratify collective bargaining agreements—but she objects to having a substantial part of her union dues devoted to political causes with which she is unsympathetic. Mollie has consulted you, and you have informed her that she can secure an appropriate rebate of a portion of her dues if she resigns from membership in the union and invokes the rights given nonmembers under the *Beck* decision. She, however, asserts that she should not have to be forced, in order to protest and secure a rebate for expenses unrelated to collective bargaining, to forgo the crucial rights of participation afforded to union members.

Does her claim have merit? See Kidwell v. Transportation Communications Intern. Union, 946 F.2d 283 (4th Cir.1991), cert. denied, 503 U.S. 1005, 112 S.Ct. 1760, 118 L.Ed.2d 423 (1992).

# Marquez v. Screen Actors Guild, Inc.

525 U.S. 33, 119 S.Ct. 292, 142 L.Ed.2d 242 (1998).

■ Justice O'Connor delivered the opinion of the Court.

Section 8(a)(3) of the National Labor Relations Act (NLRA), 49 Stat. 452, as added, 61 Stat. 140, 29 U.S.C. § 158(a)(3), permits unions and employers to negotiate an agreement that requires union "membership" as a condition of employment for all employees. We have interpreted a proviso to this language to mean that the only "membership" that a union can require is the payment of fees and dues, NLRB v. General Motors Corp., 373 U.S. 734, 742, 83 S. Ct. 1453, 10 L.Ed.2d 670 (1963), and we have held that § 8(a)(3) allows unions to collect and expend funds over the objection of nonmembers only to the extent they are used for collective bargaining, contract administration, and grievance adjustment activities, Communications Workers v. Beck, 487 U.S. 735, 745, 762–763, 108 S. Ct. 2641, 101 L.Ed.2d 634 (1988). In this case, we must determine whether a union breaches its duty of fair representation when it negotiates a union security clause that tracks the language of § 8(a)(3) without explaining, in the agreement, this Court's interpretation of that language. We conclude that it does not.

We are also asked to review the Court of Appeals' decision that the District Court did not have jurisdiction to decide a claim that a union breached the duty of fair representation by negotiating a clause that was inconsistent with the statute. We conclude that because this challenge to the union security clause was based purely on an alleged inconsistency with the statute, the Court of Appeals correctly held that this claim was within the primary jurisdiction of the National Labor Relations Board (NLRB).

## I

### A

The language of § 8(a)(3) is at the heart of this case. In pertinent part, it provides as follows:

> "It shall be an unfair labor practice for an employer—" (3) by discrimination in regard to hire or tenure of employment . . . to encourage or discourage membership in any labor organization: *Provided*, That nothing in this subchapter, or in any other statute of the United States, shall preclude an employer from making an agreement with a labor organization . . . to require as a condition of employment membership therein on or after the thirtieth day following the beginning of such employment or the effective date of such agreement, whichever is the later. . . . *Provided further*, "That no employer shall justify any discrimination against an employee for nonmembership in a labor organization . . . if he has reasonable grounds for believing that membership was denied or terminated for reasons other than the failure of the employee to tender the periodic dues and the initiation fees uniformly required

as a condition of acquiring or retaining membership." 29 U.S.C. § 158(a)(3).

This section is the statutory authorization for "union security clauses," clauses that require employees to become "member[s]" of a union as a condition of employment. *See* Communications Workers v. Beck, *supra*, at 744–745, 108 S. Ct. 2641.

The conclusion that § 8(a)(3) permits union security clauses is not the end of the story. This Court has had several occasions to interpret § 8(a)(3), and two of our conclusions about the language of that subsection bear directly on this case. First, in NLRB v. General Motors Corp., *supra*, at 742–743, 83 S. Ct. 1453 (*citing* Radio Officers v. NLRB, 347 U.S. 17, 41, 74 S. Ct. 323, 98 L.Ed. 455 (1954)), we held that although § 8(a)(3) states that unions may negotiate a clause requiring "membership" in the union, an employee can satisfy the membership condition merely by paying to the union an amount equal to the union's initiation fees and dues. *See also* Pattern Makers v. NLRB, 473 U.S. 95, 106, n. 16, 108, 105 S. Ct. 3064, 87 L.Ed.2d 68 (1985). In other words, the membership that may be required "as a condition of employment is whittled down to its financial core." NLRB v. General Motors Corp., *supra*, at 742, 83 S. Ct. 1453,. Second, in *Communications Workers v. Beck*, *supra*, we considered whether the employee's "financial core" obligation included a duty to pay for support of union activities beyond those activities undertaken by the union as the exclusive bargaining representative. We held that the language of § 8(a)(3) does not permit unions to exact dues or fees from employees for activities that are not germane to collective bargaining, grievance adjustment, or contract administration. *Id.* at 745, 762–763, 108 S. Ct. 2641. As a result of these two conclusions, § 8(a)(3) permits unions and employers to require only that employees pay the fees and dues necessary to support the union's activities as the employees' exclusive bargaining representative.

## B

Respondent Screen Actors Guild (SAG) is a labor organization that represents performers in the entertainment industry. In 1994, respondent Lakeside Productions (Lakeside) signed a collective bargaining agreement with SAG, making SAG the exclusive bargaining agent for the performers that Lakeside hired for its productions. This agreement contained a standard union security clause, providing that any performer who worked under the agreement must be "a member of the Union in good standing." App. 28. Tracking the language of § 8(a)(3), the clause also provided:

> "The foregoing [section], requiring as a condition of employment membership in the Union, shall not apply until on or after the thirtieth day following the beginning of such employment or the effective date of this Agreement, whichever is the later; the Union and the Producers interpret this sentence to mean that membership in the Union cannot be required of any performer by a Producer as a condition of employment until thirty (30) days after his first employment as a performer in the motion picture indus-

try. . . . The Producer shall not be held to have violated this paragraph if it employs a performer who is not a member of the Union in good standing . . . if the Producer has reasonable grounds for believing that membership in the Union was denied to such performer or such performer's membership in the Union was terminated for reasons other than the failure of the performer to tender the periodic dues and the initiation fee uniformly required as a condition of acquiring or retaining membership in the Union. . . ." *Id.* at 28–29.

The present dispute arose when petitioner, a part-time actress, successfully auditioned for a one-line role in an episode of the television series, "Medicine Ball," which was produced by Lakeside. Petitioner accepted the part, and pursuant to the collective bargaining agreement, Lakeside's casting director called SAG to verify that petitioner met the requirements of the union security clause. Because petitioner had previously worked in the motion picture industry for more than 30 days, the union security clause was triggered and petitioner was required to pay the union fees before she could begin working for Lakeside. There is some dispute whether the SAG representative told Lakeside's casting director that petitioner had to "join" or had to "pay" the union; regardless, petitioner understood from the casting director that she had to pay SAG before she could work for Lakeside. Petitioner called SAG's local office and learned that the fees that she would have to pay to join the union would be around $500.

Over the next few days, petitioner attempted to negotiate an agreement with SAG that would allow her to pay the union fees after she was paid for her work by Lakeside. When these negotiations failed to produce an acceptable compromise and petitioner had not paid the required fees by the day before her part was to be filmed, Lakeside hired a different actress to fill the part. At some point after Lakeside hired the new actress, SAG faxed a letter to Lakeside stating that it had no objection to petitioner working in the production. The letter was too late for petitioner; filming proceeded on schedule with the replacement actress.

Petitioner filed suit against Lakeside and SAG alleging, among other things, that SAG had breached the duty of fair representation. According to petitioner, SAG had breached its duty by negotiating and enforcing a union security clause with two basic flaws. First, the union security clause required union "membership" and the payment of full fees and dues when those terms could not be legally enforced under *General Motors* and *Beck*. Petitioner argued that the collective bargaining agreement should have contained language, in addition to the statutory language, informing her of her right not to join the union and of her right, under *Beck*, to pay only for the union's representational activities. Second, the union security clause contained a term that interpreted the 30–day grace period provision to begin running with any employment in the industry. According to petitioner, this interpretation of the grace period provision contravened the express language of § 8(a)(3), which requires that employees be given a 30–day grace period from the beginning of "such employment." She interprets "such employment" to require a new grace period with each employment relationship. Finally, in addition to these claims about the language of the union security clause, petitioner alleged that SAG had violated the duty of fair representation by failing to notify her truthfully about her rights under the NLRA as defined in *Beck* and *General Motors*. . . .

We granted certiorari to resolve the conflict over the facial validity of a union security clause that tracks the language of § 8(a)(3), and to clarify the standards for defining the primary jurisdiction of the NLRB. 523 U.S. ___, 118 S. Ct. 1298, 140 L.Ed.2d 465 (1998).

## II

### A

This case presents a narrow question: Does a union breach its duty of fair representation merely by negotiating a union security clause that tracks the language of § 8(a)(3)? . . . There is no disagreement about the substance of the union's obligations: If a union negotiates a union security clause, it must notify workers that they may satisfy the membership requirement by paying fees to support the union's representational activities, and it must enforce the clause in conformity with this notification. The only question presented by this case is whether a union breaches the duty of fair representation merely by negotiating a union security clause that uses the statutory language without expressly explaining, in the agreement, the refinements introduced by our decisions in *General Motors* and *Beck*. To rephrase the question slightly, petitioner's claim is that even if the union has an exemplary notification procedure and even if the union enforces the union security clause in perfect conformity with federal law, the mere negotiation of a union security clause that tracks the language of the NLRA breaches the duty of fair representation. We hold that it does not.

### B

When a labor organization has been selected as the exclusive representative of the employees in a bargaining unit, it has a duty, implied from its status under § 9(a) of the NLRA as the exclusive representative of the employees in the unit, to represent all members fairly. *See, e.g.*, Ford Motor Co. v. Huffman, 345 U.S. 330, 337, 73 S. Ct. 681, 97 L.Ed. 1048 (1953); Vaca v. Sipes, 386 U.S. 171, 177, 87 S. Ct. 903, 17 L.Ed.2d 842 (1967). As we described this duty in *Vaca v. Sipes*, the duty of fair representation requires a union "to serve the interests of all members without hostility or discrimination toward any, to exercise its discretion with complete good faith and honesty, and to avoid arbitrary conduct." *Ibid*. In other words, a union breaches the duty of fair representation when its conduct toward a member of the bargaining unit is arbitrary, discriminatory, or in bad faith. *Id*. at 190, 87 S. Ct. 903. *See also* Air Line Pilots v. O'Neill, 499 U.S. 65, 67, 111 S. Ct. 1127, 113 L.Ed.2d 51 (1991) (reaffirming this tripartite standard). In this case, petitioner does not argue that SAG's negotiation of the union security clause was discriminatory, so we only consider whether SAG's conduct was arbitrary or in bad faith.

... [In *Air Line Pilots*,] decided three years after *Beck*, we specifically considered the appropriate standard for evaluating conduct under the "arbitrary" prong of the duty of fair representation. We held that under the "arbitrary" prong, a union's actions breach the duty of fair representation "only if [the union's conduct] can be fairly characterized as so far outside a 'wide range of reasonableness' that it is wholly 'irrational' or 'arbitrary.'" 499 U.S. at 78, 111 S. Ct. 1127 (*quoting Ford Motor Co. v. Huffman, supra*, at 338, 73 S. Ct. 681). This "wide range of reasonableness" gives the union room to make discretionary decisions and choices, even if those judgments are ultimately wrong. In *Air Line Pilots*, for example, the union had negotiated a settlement agreement with the employer, which in retrospect proved to be a bad deal for the employees. The fact that the union had not negotiated the best agreement for its workers, however, was insufficient to support a holding that the union's conduct was arbitrary. 499 U.S. at 78–81, 111 S. Ct. 1127. A union's conduct can be classified as arbitrary only when it is irrational, when it is without a rational basis or explanation. *Ibid*.

Under this standard, SAG's negotiation of a union security clause with language derived from the NLRA section authorizing such a clause is far from arbitrary. Petitioner argues that it is irrational to negotiate a clause that cannot be enforced as written. But this clause can be enforced as written, because by tracking the statutory language, the clause incorporates all of the refinements that have become associated with that language. When we interpreted § 8(a)(3) in *General Motors* and *Beck*, we held that the section, fairly read, included the rights that we found. To the extent that these interpretations are not obvious, the relevant provisions of § 8(a)(3) have become terms of art; the words and phrasing of the section now encompass the rights that we announced in *General Motors* and *Beck*. After we stated that the statutory language incorporates an employee's right not to "join" the union (except by paying fees and dues) and an employee's right to pay for only representational activities, we cannot fault SAG for using this very language to convey these very concepts.

Petitioner also invites us to conclude that the union's conduct in negotiating the union security clause breached the duty of fair representation because it was done in bad faith. She argues that the negotiation of this clause was in bad faith because the union had no reason to use the statutory language except to mislead employees about their rights under *Beck* and *General Motors*.... According to petitioner, even if the union always informs workers of their rights and even if it enforces the union security clause in conformity with federal law, it is bad faith for a union to use the statutory language in the collective bargaining agreement because such use can only mislead employees. Petitioner's argument fails because it is so broad. It is difficult to conclude that a union acts in bad faith by notifying workers of their rights through more effective means of communication and by using a term of art to describe those rights in a contract workers are unlikely to read. . . .

In sum, on this record, the union's conduct in negotiating a union security clause that tracked the statutory language cannot be said to have been either arbitrary or in bad faith. The Court of Appeals correctly rejected petitioner's argument that, by negotiating this clause, the union breached its duty of fair representation.

## III

The Court of Appeals also correctly refused to exercise jurisdiction over petitioner's challenge to the 30–day grace period provision of the union security clause. Petitioner argues that all duty of fair representation claims are cognizable in federal court, and that because she couched her claim as a breach of the duty of fair representation, her claim by definition can be heard in federal court. . . .

. . . As we noted in *Beck*, "[e]mployees . . . may not circumvent the primary jurisdiction of the NLRB simply by casting statutory claims as violations of the union's duty of fair representation." 487 U.S. at 743, 108 S. Ct. 2641. When a plaintiff's only claim is that the union violated the NLRA, the plaintiff cannot avoid the jurisdiction of the NLRB by characterizing this alleged statutory violation as a breach of the duty of fair representation. To invoke federal jurisdiction when the claim is based in part on a violation of the NLRA, there must be something more than just a claim that the union violated the statute. The plaintiff must adduce facts suggesting that the union's violation of the statute was arbitrary, discriminatory, or in bad faith. * * * *

Applying these principles in this case, petitioner's challenge to SAG's grace period provision falls squarely within the primary jurisdiction of the NLRB. Her claim is that SAG employed a term in the collective bargaining agreement that was inconsistent with the NLRA. This allegation, although framed by the recitation that this act breached the duty of fair representation, is at base a claim that SAG's conduct violated § 8(a)(3) [sic]. * * * *

Accordingly, the judgment of the United States Court of Appeals for the Ninth Circuit is affirmed.

■ JUSTICE KENNEDY, with whom JUSTICE THOMAS joins, concurring.

I join the opinion of the Court and offer these further observations.

. . . The security [sic] clause at issue required, as conditions of employment, "member[ship] in good standing," *id*. at 28, and payment of "the periodic dues and the initiation fee uniformly required as a condition of acquiring or retaining membership in the Union," *id*. at 29. As recognized by other courts and by members of the National Labor Relations Board, language like this can facilitate deception. *See, e.g.,* Bloom v. NLRB, 153 F.3d 844, 850–851 (C.A.8 1998) ("As Bloom can well attest, when an employee who is approached regarding union membership expresses reluctance, a union frequently will produce or invoke the collective bargaining agreement. . . . The employee, unschooled in semantic legal fictions, cannot possibly discern his rights from a document that has been designed by the union to conceal them. In such a context, 'member' is not a term of 'art,'

... but one of deception''); Wegscheid v. Local 2911, Int'l Union, United Automobile, Aerospace and Agricultural Implement Workers, 117 F.3d 986, 990 (C.A.7 1997) ("[T]he only realistic explanation for the retention of the statutory language in collective bargaining agreements ... is to mislead employees about their right not to join the union''); Monsoon Trucking, Inc., 324 N.L.R.B. No. 149, pp. 6–8 (Chairman Gould, concurring) ("[A] collective-bargaining agreement that speaks in terms of 'membership' or 'membership in good standing' without further definition misleads employees into believing that they can be terminated if they do not become formal, full-fledged union members''). As I understand the Court's opinion, there is no basis in our holding today for an inference that inclusion of the statutory language is somehow a defense when a violation of the fair-representation duty has been alleged and facts in addition to the bare language of the contract have been adduced to show the violation. Rather, our holding reflects only the conclusion that the negotiation of a security clause containing such language does not necessarily, or in all circumstances, violate this duty....

———

## PROBLEMS FOR DISCUSSION

**1.** If all of the Justices (and particularly Justices Kennedy and Thomas) believe that the language of the typical union security provision misleadingly induces employees to give more to the union than is required by law, and if it is obvious that most if not all employees will be thoroughly unfamiliar with the limiting decisions announced over the years by the Supreme Court, why should the Court tolerate the inclusion of such a provision in collective agreements? What other possible purpose could the Union have in negotiating such a provision than thus to mislead? Is that "fair representation"? (Incidentally, was Ms. Marquez given "fair representation" when SAG insisted that she pay her $500 membership fee before (and as a condition of) performing, and being paid for, her one-line television role, rather than after?)

**2.** Assume you have been asked to re-draft the union security provision contained in the sample collective bargaining agreement in the Casebook's Statutory Supplement. What fair, concise, intelligible and accurate language would you insert instead? (On February 17, 2001, President George W. Bush signed an executive order requiring all federal contractors to post conspicuous notices informing employees of their rights under the *Beck* decision, in prescribed detailed language. Failure to do so may result in the cancellation of the federal contract.)

———

ELLIS v. BROTHERHOOD OF RAILWAY, AIRLINE AND S.S. CLERKS, 466 U.S. 435, 104 S.Ct. 1883, 80 L.Ed.2d 428 (1984). The collective bargaining agreement between Western Airlines and the Brotherhood (BRAC) requires the payment by clerical employees of agency fees equal to union dues; the union provides for rebates to members who object to the use of their contributions for political or ideological activities. Several present or former employees brought an action challenging the adequacy of the rebate scheme and also challenging six specific union expenses which the Supreme Court characterized as falling between those for which "free riders" could clearly be taxed (i.e., negotiating agreements and settling grievances) and those clearly relating to the union's political activities. The Court held that the union's rebate scheme was inadequate, and that dues-paying members could under the Railway Labor Act properly object to only some of the challenged union expenditures.

As to the manner in which objecting dues payers were to secure a reduction in their dues for statutorily objectionable expenditures, the Court said as follows:

> As the Court of Appeals pointed out, there is language in this Court's cases to support the validity of a rebate program. *Street* suggested "restitution to each individual employee of that portion of his money which the union expended, despite his notification, for the political causes to which he had advised the union he was opposed." 367 U.S., at 775, 81 S.Ct., at 1803. See also Abood v. Detroit Board of Education, 431 U.S. 209, 238, 97 S.Ct. 1782, 1801, 52 L.Ed.2d 261 (1977). On the other hand, we suggested a more precise advance reduction scheme in Railway Clerks v. Allen, 373 U.S. 113, 122, 83 S.Ct. 1158, 1163, 10 L.Ed.2d 235 (1963), where we described a "practical decree" comprising a refund of exacted funds in the proportion that union political expenditures bore to total union expenditures and the reduction of future exactions by the same proportion. Those opinions did not, nor did they purport to, pass upon the statutory or constitutional adequacy of the suggested remedies. Doing so now, we hold that the pure rebate approach is inadequate.

> By exacting and using full dues, then refunding months later the portion that it was not allowed to exact in the first place, the union effectively charges the employees for activities that are outside the scope of the statutory authorization. The cost to the employee is, of course, much less than if the money was never returned, but this is a difference of degree only. The harm would be reduced were the union to pay interest on the amount refunded, but respondents did not do so. Even then the union obtains an involuntary loan for purposes to which the employee objects.

> The only justification for this union borrowing would be administrative convenience. But there are readily available alternatives, such as advance reduction of dues and/or interest-bearing escrow accounts, that place only the slightest additional burden, if any, on the union. Given the existence of acceptable alternatives, the union cannot be allowed to commit dissenters' funds to improper uses even temporarily. A rebate scheme reduces but does not eliminate the statutory violation.

As to the employees' claim that the use of their fees for the challenged expenditures violated the First Amendment, the Court reasserted the position taken in *Street* that the proper approach was to construe the statute so as to narrow the union's spending power to accord with the statutory purpose: "We remain convinced that Congress' essential justification for authorizing the union shop was the desire to eliminate free riders—employees in the bargaining unit on whose behalf the union was obliged to perform its statutory functions, but who refused to contribute to the cost thereof." Thus, "objecting employees may be compelled to pay their fair share of not only the direct costs of negotiating and administering a collective-bargaining contract and of settling grievances and disputes, but also the expenses of activities or undertakings normally or reasonably employed to implement or effectuate the duties of the union as exclusive representative of the employees in the bargaining unit."

The Court then separately considered the challenged expenses.

(1) *BRAC Conventions.* "Every four years, BRAC holds a national convention at which the members elect officers, establish bargaining goals and priorities, and formulate overall union policy. We have very little trouble in holding that petitioners must help defray the costs of these conventions." Congress was fully aware that these conventions are "normal events ... essential to the union's discharge of its duties as bargaining agent"; they guide the union's approach to, and relate directly to its effectiveness in, bargaining.

(2) *Social Activities.* Seven-tenths of one percent of union expenditures go toward purchasing refreshments for business meetings and occasional social activities. Although such expenses are not central to collective bargaining, the Court emphasized that they were *de minimis,* that they are a "standard feature of union operations," and that they "are important to the union's members because they bring about harmonious working relationships, promote closer ties among employees, and create a more pleasant environment for union meetings." Accordingly, they are within the scope of the statute and can be charged to objecting members.

(3) *Publications.* The union's monthly magazine—paid for out of the union treasury—includes articles about negotiations, strikes, employee benefits, pending or enacted legislation, general news, boycotted products, and recreational and social activities. Under the union's voluntary rebate policy, objecting employees are not charged for that portion of the magazine devoted to "political causes." The Court held that the costs of publication (subject to the political-cause exception) were statutorily sanctioned. Congress knew this to be "an accepted and basic union activity," related to its representation obligations and to worker education.

(4) *Organizing.* The Supreme Court disagreed with the conclusion of the court of appeals that organizing expenses contributed to a stronger union and greater success at the bargaining table and could thus be charged to objecting employees. Congress did not intend the union shop to aid the union in recruiting new members. Moreover, the dues would obviously be used to organize workers outside the bargaining unit (those within the unit already being obliged to join) and any resulting benefits for unit members would necessarily be highly attenuated. Like union contributions to pro-labor political candidates (excluded from the statute in the *Street* case), organizing outside the bargaining unit is hardly designed to deal with the "free rider" problem at which the statute was aimed. Even

so, the Board has held that union organizing expenses are chargeable to objectors where that activity is in the same competitive market as the objectors' bargaining unit; but the Court of Appeals for the Ninth Circuit has rejected this position as flatly inconsistent with the Supreme Court decisions in *Ellis* and *Beck*. UFCW, Local 1036 v. NLRB, 249 F.3d 1115 (9th Cir.2001).

(5) *Litigation*. Expenses of litigation before courts and agencies—on such matters as negotiating, grievance processing, duty of fair representation, and jurisdictional disputes—are chargeable to objecting members only to the extent "the Western Airlines bargaining unit is directly concerned." This would not include "the costs of the union's challenge to the legality of the airline industry mutual aid pact [utilized in the event of a strike against a particular airline]; of litigation seeking to protect the rights of airline employees generally during bankruptcy proceedings; or of defending suits alleging violation of the non-discrimination requirements of Title VII."

(6) *Death Benefits*. BRAC pays from its general funds a $300 death benefit to the designated beneficiary of any member or compulsory dues payor. The court of appeals found this benefit sufficiently related to the union's statutory functions: it affects BRAC's financial demands at the bargaining table, strengthens the employee's ties to the union, and has historically played an important role in labor organizations. For technical reasons, the Supreme Court found it unnecessary to rule on this issue.

Having thus construed the Railway Labor Act, the Court concluded that the expenses it found to be chargeable to objecting members—even those (like conventions and publications) that "have direct communicative content and involve the expression of ideas"—did not infringe upon the objectors' First Amendment rights; in any event, such expenses were justified by the same governmental interest (i.e., overriding the free-rider problem) that sustains the power to compel dues payments under the union shop itself. See generally Note, Agency Shops and the First Amendment: A Balancing Test in Need of Unweighted Scales, 18 Rutgers L.J. 833 (1987).

———

## PROBLEMS FOR DISCUSSION

**1.**  Consider the conclusion of the Supreme Court on each of the six challenged union expenditures—particularly for organizing efforts and litigation outside the bargaining unit. What are the strongest arguments you can make to the contrary? Are they convincing arguments?

**2.**  Is a union of airline pilots obligated to rebate the portion of agency fees paid by non-members that is spent to support strikes by union members at other airlines? Would it matter whether there has historically been parallel wage-and-benefit outcomes in contracts reached at the different airlines? See Crawford v. Air Line Pilots Ass'n, 992 F.2d 1295 (4th Cir. en banc), cert. denied, 510 U.S. 869, 114 S.Ct. 195, 126 L.Ed.2d 153 (1993).

**3.**  In Lehnert v. Ferris Faculty Ass'n, 500 U.S. 507, 111 S.Ct. 1950, 114 L.Ed.2d 572 (1991), the Supreme Court once again considered the extent to which dissenting fee payers may lawfully be charged their pro rata share of certain union expenses.

Although the case involved a public-sector union operating under Michigan law, the Court—which split into a number of camps, with three separate partial concurrences and partial dissents—invoked its earlier private-sector decisions under the Railway Labor Act. Writing for five Justices, Justice Blackmun stated:

> Hanson and Street and their progeny teach that chargeable activities must (1) be "germane" to collective-bargaining activity; (2) be justified by the government's vital policy interest in labor peace and avoiding "free riders;" and (3) not significantly add to the burdening of free speech that is inherent in the allowance of an agency or union shop.

The Court held that the dissenting members of the local union could be charged with certain convention, publication and "program" expenditures relating to the state and national affiliates, information services regarding such matters as professional development and job opportunities, and expenses incurred to prepare for a strike that had it taken place would have been in violation of state law; but that they could not be charged with the union's program to secure funds for public education in Michigan, litigation not concerning the local unit, public relations efforts designed to enhance the reputation of the teaching profession, and lobbying, electoral and political activities not bearing upon the ratification or implementation of a collective agreement.

Had you been a member of the Court, how would you have voted with respect to the chargeability to nonmembers of each of these union expenditure items?

---

CALIFORNIA SAW & KNIFE WORKS, 320 NLRB 224 (1995), enf'd sub. nom. Int'l Ass'n of Machinists v. NLRB, 133 F.3d 1012 (7th Cir.1998). The NLRB consolidated twelve cases that raised questions relating to the obligations of a union to notify, and to provide dues-reduction procedures for, nonmember dues-paying employees who are entitled under the Beck decision to challenge union expenditures going beyond collective bargaining, grievance adjustment, and contract administration. All of the cases involved the International Association of Machinists and its three-tier structure of Grand Lodge (i.e., international), District Lodges (six in number) and Local Lodges (some 1400 in number). The IAM has approximately 800,000 members—and approximately 12,000 nonmembers—covered by some 6500 to 8000 collective bargaining agreements. At least half of those agreements contain union-security clauses requiring the payment of dues and fees; these are paid typically to the local, which forwards some moneys to the Grand and District Lodges in return for their services to the local. Nonmembers who make such payments may invoke the IAM "Beck policy" (in fact established two years before that Supreme Court decision) to challenge union expenditures and proportionally limit dues collection.

The IAM publishes notice of its Beck policy in the December issue of its monthly magazine, The Machinist, which is mailed to all represented employees, both members and nonmembers. Nonmembers objecting to dues payments for nonrepresentational activities must send a written notice of their objection by certified mail (one objection per envelope) to the IAM secretary-treasurer either in January or within the first thirty days of becoming subject to the union-security provision. On receipt of the objection, the union automatically reduces the employee's dues according to past expenditure allocations and establishes an escrow account; the dues objector is also provided with notice of the major categories of union expenses and an explanation of how the reduced dues are calculated (at all three union levels). Independent accountants provide an audit report that is used to calculate dues reductions for the Grand Lodge, and an IAM in-house auditing staff does the same for the District and Local Lodges in a single overall audit. Objectors may challenge the surveys and thus have their own individual lodges audited; they may also participate in an annual consolidated arbitration of all such challenges, the costs of which are borne by the IAM.

The General Counsel raised a number of challenges to the IAM practices as falling short of what is required under the *Beck* decision to protect the rights of nonmember dues payers. The Board first determined that the pertinent source of limits upon the union's authority to collect and spend is not the Constitution—as was true in the public-sector cases such as *Abood* and *Lehnert* and the Railway Labor Act cases such as *Hanson* and *Street*. Rather, it is the duty of fair representation, enforceable by the NLRA under § 8(b)(1)(A), which is violated by union action that is arbitrary, discriminatory or in bad faith. Applying that standard, the Board reached the following conclusions:

(1) The union must give a "*Beck* rights notice" to newly hired nonmember employees at the time the union seeks to obligate those newly hired employees to pay dues. The union must inform such employees that they have the rights: to object to paying for union activities not germane to the union's duties as bargaining agent and to obtain a reduction in fees for such activities; to be given sufficient information to enable them intelligently to decide whether to object; and to be apprised of any internal union procedures for filing objections. If an employee chooses to object, he or she must be told of the percentage of the reduction, the basis for the calculation, and the right to challenge these figures. Failure to provide such notice of *Beck* rights is arbitrary and in bad faith, and violates the duty of fair representation.

(2) As for current employees, the union seeking to subject them to an obligation to pay dues must also provide notice of their *Beck* rights. This is adequately done when the IAM publishes such a notice in the December issue of The Machinist, which is mailed to the employees' last known address, whether or not they are members of the union. (The Board rejected the contention of the General Counsel that the cover of the issue must clearly state that it includes the *Beck* notice; the notice is conspicuously placed within the issue, and would be readily found by the reader.) It is therefore not necessary to give additional notice to current employees who are union members upon their resignation from membership (unless they have not been sent a copy of The Machinist).

(3) As has been provided under earlier Board decisions, before a union may seek the discharge of an employee for the failure to tender dues and fees, it must at a minimum give the employee reasonable notice of the delinquency, including a statement of the precise amount and months for which dues are owed and of the method used to compute this amount, tell

the employee when to make the required payments, and explain to the employee that failure to pay will result in discharge.

(4) Limiting an employee's right to register "a *Beck* objection" to the month of January impermissibly burdens the resignation rights of those who resign their union membership following that "window" period. "A unit employee may exercise *Beck* rights only when he or she is not a member of the union. An employee who resigns union membership outside the window period is thereafter effectively compelled to continue to pay full dues even though no longer a union member, and the window period in this circumstance operates as an arbitrary restriction on the right to refrain from union membership and from supporting nonrepresentational expenditures." It is also an arbitrary impediment to the exercise of *Beck* rights that objections must be sent to the union only by certified mail and only in individual envelopes. The Seventh Circuit has disagreed that a "window" period was an impermissible limit on *Beck* rights. Nielsen v. International Ass'n of Machinists, 94 F.3d 1107 (7th Cir.1996). Would it be unlawful for a union to require that employees give written notice—every year—within a 35–day window period of their desire to opt out of membership and into fee-payer status (rather than allow them to rely upon a single notice of continuing objection)? *See* Shea v. IAM, 154 F.3d 508 (5th Cir.1998).

(5) Although the General Counsel contended that objecting nonmembers may lawfully be charged only for those expenses incurred in the union's representational activities "in the objector's individual bargaining unit," the Board held otherwise. The Board noted that expenses incurred at the national level, for example for research pertinent to collective bargaining, are efficiently expended there for the benefit of locals generally. The IAM is not required to calculate its *Beck* dues reductions on a unit-by-unit basis; nor need the union allocate and disclose its chargeable expenses on a unit-by-unit basis. Expenses made outside the objector's bargaining unit are properly chargeable if they "ultimately inure to the benefit of the members of the local union by virtue of their membership in the parent organization"; if an objector does not accept the union's assertion to that effect, he or she may challenge it in the arbitration proceeding the IAM has provided for in its Beck policy.

(6) Nor need unit-by-unit accounting be done for litigation outside the objector's unit, provided it is ultimately germane to the union's role in collective bargaining, contract administration, and grievance adjustment in that unit. Examples can be lawsuits involving labor-contract interpretation or NLRB proceedings involving the union's jurisdictional claims to disputed work. (The Supreme Court decisions announcing a narrower rule for the chargeability of extra-unit litigation in the public sector and under the Railway Labor Act were distinguished.)

(7) The form of information provided to objectors by the IAM was found to be adequate in achieving the purposes of disclosure. It is necessary to set forth only "major categories of union expenditures," and the union may lawfully denote that certain of those categories were "mixed," i.e., only partially chargeable, without setting forth a more detailed breakdown.

(The mixed categories may, however, be challenged through individual objections.) Contrary to the Board, the District of Columbia Circuit held that the notice must include more than the nineteen categories of expenditure given by the union: It must indicate for each category the percentage reduction in dues that would result from a *Beck* objection as well as how funds disbursed to affiliates were expended by them. Penrod v. NLRB, 203 F.3d 41 (D.C.Cir.2000).

(8) The Board made clear that the union must supply an "audit," as that is understood in the accounting profession; a professionally prepared "compilation" will not do. American Fed. Tel. & Recording Artists, 327 NLRB 474 (1999). The Board explained:

> A compilation is a financial statement prepared by an accountant based solely on information supplied by the reported entity. In performing a review, an accountant would similarly rely on the representations of the reported entity, but would further analyze the information for consistency and question the reported entity's management concerning any information which appeared to deviate from expected norms. An audit involves an accountant's independent confirmation of the reliability of the financial information contained in the financial report through such procedures as gathering information from outside entities and testing of selected information.

The Board opined in *California Saw & Knife* that the use of in-house union auditors, rather than independent certified accountants, to verify the expenses of District and Local Lodges, and the allocation of those expenses between chargeable and nonchargeable, was not arbitrary or in bad faith and thus did not violate the duty of fair representation. The District of Columbia Circuit rejected the Labor Board's acceptance of in-house auditors in lieu of requiring an "independent auditor." Ferriso v. NLRB, 125 F.3d 865 (D.C.Cir.1997). It concluded that an independent audit was a "minimal guarantee of the trustworthiness" of the calculations upon which the union's fee is based; and it grounded its rejection of the Board's position in the legislative history of the LMRDA. The court provided further guidance on both the requirement of "independence," which would bar an audit by a person or entity that had otherwise been employed by the union within a relevant period of time, and on the professional qualification of the "auditor," who need not necessarily be a certified public accountant in contradistinction to a licensed public accountant.

(9) All challenges to the IAM's dues-reduction calculations are consolidated for arbitration once each year—and the procedures utilized there (with the union bearing the burden of proof), and the requirement that objectors bear their own travel costs, "fall well within the wide range of reasonableness afforded a union in discharging its duty of fair representation."

The NLRB applied all of these principles to the twelve consolidated cases before it, found some unfair labor practices, and issued an order requiring that certain *Beck* notices be given and certain amounts of dues moneys be refunded to objecting employees.

———

Air Line Pilots Ass'n v. Miller, 523 U.S. 866, 118 S.Ct. 1761, 140 L.Ed.2d 1070 (1998). The collective agreement between ALPA and Delta Air Lines pilots includes an agency-shop clause requiring nonunion Delta pilots to pay ALPA a monthly service charge for representing them. When in 1992, ALPA began to allocate its expenses for fee payors, it concluded that 81 percent of its expenses were germane to collective bargaining and imposed its agency-fee charge accordingly. In this case, 153 Delta pilots challenged the accuracy of this charge by bringing suit in a federal district court. Under ALPA's internal policies and procedures, pilots who object to the fee calculation may do so by requesting arbitration under procedures of a neutral appointing body, the American Arbitration Association. When 174 Delta pilots (including 91 of the plaintiffs here) objected to the 1992 agency-fee calculation, ALPA referred them to an AAA arbitrator, who proceeded to hear the matter despite the ongoing litigation. The district court in turn held that the internal ALPA arbitration procedure should be exhausted, but the court of appeals reversed, a decision with which the Supreme Court agreed (in a 7–to–2 decision).

A major issue was what to make of the Supreme Court decision in a public-sector case, Teachers v. Hudson, 475 U.S. 292, 106 S.Ct. 1066, 89 L.Ed.2d 232 (1986), in which the Court held, among other things, that the First Amendment required that nonunion workers who object to agency-fee calculations must be afforded "a reasonably prompt opportunity to challenge the amount of the fee before an impartial decisionmaker." (The parties did not challenge the application of the *Hudson* principle to unions and employees governed by the Railway Labor Act, such as the pilots here.) The Court in *ALPA v. Miller* concluded that this requirement "aims to protect the interest of objectors by affording them access to a neutral forum in which their objections can be resolved swiftly; nothing in our decision purports to compel objectors to pursue that remedy." Ordinarily, arbitration is a matter of contract, and no party should be forced to arbitrate when he has not agreed to do so. Forcing arbitration as a prerequisite to a federal court action by the objectors would in fact frustrate the objective announced in *Hudson* of having a swift, fair and final settlement of the objectors' claims. The Court rejected the dissenters' (Justices Breyer and Stevens) contentions that arbitration would facilitate the resolution of disputes, would avoid the possible multiplicity of lawsuits by different groups of objectors with different outcomes, and would aid any later court in narrowing the dispute and handling complicated financial issues. "[G]enuine as the Union's interest in avoiding multiple proceedings may be, that interest does not overwhelm objectors' resistance to arbitration to which they did not consent, and their election to proceed immediately to court for adjudication of their federal rights. We hold that, unless they agree to the procedure, agency-fee objectors may not be required to exhaust an arbitration remedy before bringing their claims in federal court."

———

## B.   STATE RIGHT-TO-WORK LAWS[c]

Between 1944 and 1947—when the proviso to Section 8(3) of the Wagner Act sheltered union security agreements as potent as the closed shop—twelve states enacted so-called right-to-work laws (either by statute or by constitutional amendment) which provided in substance that employees were not to be required to join a union as a condition of receiving or retaining a job. Today, such laws obtain in twenty-one states, most of them in the more agricultural states of the south and midwest. (These states are Alabama, Arizona, Arkansas, Florida, Georgia, Idaho, Iowa, Kansas, Louisiana, Mississippi, Nebraska, Nevada, North Carolina, North Dakota, South Carolina, South Dakota, Tennessee, Texas, Utah, Virginia, and Wyoming.) The wording of these state provisions varies a good deal. Some states, for example, bar discrimination in employment so as to encourage union membership, while others bar an employment or "monopoly" by a labor union "combinations" or "conspiracies" to deprive persons of employment because of nonmembership. Most right-to-work states simply declare unlawful any agreement which conflicts with the policy that the right of persons to work shall not be denied or abridged on account of membership or nonmembership in any labor organization, or any agreement requiring union membership (or paying dues to a union) as a condition of employment. The remedy provided under most such state laws is damages for persons injured by the violation; many provide for injunctive relief; and some make violations a misdemeanor subject to criminal penalties.

The purpose of these laws appears in part to be the protection of employee freedom and in part to be the attraction of new business to a union-free and thus presumably lower-wage environment. The question whether these state laws could flourish under a federal law that authorized the union shop as a force for industrial stability was definitively addressed by Congress in the Taft–Hartley amendments of 1947. In spite of the strong preemptive implications of the Wagner Act (not articulated to any substantial degree by the Supreme Court until the mid–1950's), Congress established a preserve for state right-to-work laws by enacting Section 14(b) of the Labor Act:

> Nothing in this Act shall be construed as authorizing the execution or application of agreements requiring membership in a labor organization as a condition of employment in any State or Territory in which such execution or application is prohibited by State or Territorial law.

Shortly after the Taft–Hartley Act, a union's constitutional attack on a state right-to-work law was rebuffed by the Supreme Court in Lincoln Fed. Labor Union 19129 v. Northwestern Iron & Metal Co., 335 U.S. 525, 69

---

c.   See Grodin & Beeson, State Right-to-Work Laws and Federal Labor Policy, 52 Calif.L.Rev. 95 (1964); Henderson, The Confrontation of Federal Preemption and State Right to Work Laws, 1967 Duke L.J. 1079; Kuhn, Right-to-Work Laws—Symbols or Substance?, 14 Ind. & Lab.Rel.Rev. 587 (1961); F. Meyers, Right to Work in Practice (1959); P. Sultan, Right-to-Work Laws (1958).

S.Ct. 251, 93 L.Ed. 212 (1949). Just as, some years before, the Court had endorsed the union argument that a state constitutionally could, in the reasonable pursuit of industrial peace, outlaw contracts which *forbade* joining a union (the so-called yellow dog contract), the Court now marshalled the same considerations to reject the union argument that states could not constitutionally outlaw contracts which *compelled* the joining of a union. It only remained to determine how these state laws were to be interwoven with the federal statutory fabric, and on this issue the Supreme Court was to speak in two 1963 decisions, once again giving rather broad scope to the right-to-work laws.

In RETAIL CLERKS, INTERN. ASS'N, LOCAL 1625 v. SCHERMERHORN, 373 U.S. 746, 83 S.Ct. 1461, 10 L.Ed.2d 678 (1963), the state court had interpreted its right-to-work law to outlaw not only the union shop (requiring employees to become members) but also the agency shop (requiring employees to give the union only financial support). The union argued that Section 14(b) did not cede to the states the power to invalidate the agency shop since this was not an agreement "requiring membership in a labor organization." The Court quickly rejected this argument, holding that the only kind of "membership" which may lawfully be demanded of an employee is his payment of a service fee to the union measured by periodic dues and initiation fees, and that thus the agency shop is the "practical equivalent" of an agreement requiring "membership," both under the proviso to Section 8(a)(3), NLRB v. General Motors, 373 U.S. 734, 83 S.Ct. 1453, 10 L.Ed.2d 670 (1963), which made the agency shop lawful under federal law, and under Section 14(b), which authorized states to prohibit it. The Court proceeded to address the union's second argument which was that, even if its agency shop provision was invalid—because banned by the state right-to-work law—its execution and enforcement would violate Sections 8(a)(3) and 8(b)(2) and could thus be addressed only by the National Labor Relations Board. By 1963, the law of federal preemption had indeed been sufficiently developed and rather clearly compelled the ouster of state-court jurisdiction over conduct which arguably or actually was a federal unfair labor practice. San Diego Bldg. Trades Council v. Garmon, 359 U.S. 236, 79 S.Ct. 773, 3 L.Ed.2d 775 (1959). On this issue, the Court sought the benefit of reargument and the views of the NLRB.

After reargument, the Court, in RETAIL CLERKS INTERN. ASS'N, LOCAL 1625 v. SCHERMERHORN, 375 U.S. 96, 84 S.Ct. 219, 11 L.Ed.2d 179 (1963), concluded that the state-court injunction against the enforcement of the agency shop agreement was a valid remedy. Congress, by acknowledging that states could prohibit union security agreements which the federal law would protect, "chose to abandon any search for uniformity in dealing with the problems of state laws barring the execution and application of agreements authorized by Section 14(b) and decided to suffer a medley of attitudes and philosophies on the subject." Congress gave the states such overriding power that it would be anomalous to conclude that only the NLRB had the power to implement state policy. But the Court was cautious to note that the state-court injunction may run only against the "execution or application" (in the words of Section 14(b)) of a union security agreement; the state is not free to enjoin a strike or picketing the object of which is to *secure* a union shop or agency shop agreement. While it may seem strange to direct the states to permit concerted activity for a contract clause while authorizing the states to enjoin the enforcement of the clause after the concerted activity has been successful, the Court took no note of the anomaly and merely reiterated that state power "begins *only with actual negotiation and execution of the type of agreement described by Section 14(b).* Absent such an agreement, conduct arguably an unfair labor practice would be a matter for the National Labor Relations Board under *Garmon.*" Perhaps the Court was concerned that certain concerted activity which Congress clearly sought to protect—such as peaceful picketing designed to induce employees to become members, at least when not outlawed by Section 8(b)(7), and peaceful informational picketing designed to communicate to the public that a company is nonunion—would be too readily outlawed by state courts, particularly when a number of state right-to-work laws are extremely broadly drawn and provide in some instances for severe sanctions (including criminal penalties).

A continuing campaign has been waged both for and against the enactment of state "right to work" laws authorized by Section 14(b). Unions have stressed several points in resisting such legislation. Primary emphasis, of course, has been placed upon the argument that unions—unlike other voluntary associations—must represent members and non-members alike so that those who do not join are "free riders," accepting valuable benefits without cost. Unions also stress the fact that the National Labor Relations Act prohibits various abuses of union security and reduces the union shop to little more than an obligation to pay dues. Reference is frequently made to the experience under the union shop authorization elections that were required for a time under the NLRA; in the 46,117 authorization elections, the union shop prevailed in 97.1% of the contests with 91% of the employees voting in favor. Finally, unions argue that the union shop contributes to harmonious labor-management relations by minimizing the insecurity of labor representatives and reducing the temptation of the employer to undermine the union and thus exacerbate the relationship.

Employers respond to these arguments by stressing "the basic rights of an individual to get and keep a job without having to pay tribute to any organization in order to make a living." In answer to the unions' "free-loader" argument, it is urged that many employees may wish to refrain from joining a union or paying dues for genuine reasons of conscience. Regardless of the size of the majority favoring compulsory union membership, the rights of these individuals should be respected. In addition to this question of principle, employers argue that unions are already too powerful and will become more so if "right to work" laws are repealed. Finally, the argument is often made that the right of employees to shift allegiance to a different union will be impaired, as a practical matter, if all must become members of the incumbent union. As a result, corrupt and ineffective unions will be perpetuated to the detriment of the employees involved.

## PROBLEMS FOR DISCUSSION

**1.** In the collective bargaining agreement between the General Contractors Association in Houston, Texas and the Laborers Union, there is a provision for hiring exclusively through referrals by the union-operated hiring hall. The hiring-hall provision expressly bars discrimination in referrals because of union membership or nonmembership, giving priority to workers with greatest seniority in service for the contractors and general work experience in the trade. Smith works as a laborer, but has for years strongly resisted becoming a member of the Union. He believes as a matter of principle that hiring should be done by the employers and not controlled by the Union, and that Union control over the hiring process exerts subtle and unlawful pressures on workers to become union members. He points to the Texas right-to-work law, barring hiring on the basis of union membership or nonmembership. He wishes to know whether he can successfully attack the contractual hiring-hall provision in the Texas courts as in violation of state law. What advice would you give him? See NLRB v. Houston Chapter, Assoc. Gen. Contractors, 349 F.2d 449 (5th Cir.1965), cert. denied, 382 U.S. 1026, 86 S.Ct. 648, 15 L.Ed.2d 540 (1966).

**2.** In negotiations last year for a new collective bargaining agreement, the Union insisted that the Company agree to a provision requiring employees, as a condition of their employment, to pay $20 per month to the Union, whether or not they were members of the Union, simply to cover their pro rata share of the Union's expenses in administering the labor agreement. The fee was considerably less than the amount of dues that Union members would have had to pay under the prevailing formula for dues calculation, and was not to be assessed in periods when the contract was not in effect.

The Company refused to include such a provision in the contract under negotiation, pointing out that Mississippi law (constitutional and statutory) provides: "No employer shall require any person, as a condition of employment or continuation of employment to pay any dues, fees or other charges of any kind to any labor union or labor organization." When the Union commenced picketing in support of its demand for what it called "representation fees," the Company filed charges with the NLRB under Section 8(b)(3), claiming that the Union was insisting upon a provision which, under Section 14(b) of the Act, was invalidated by virtue of Mississippi law. What should be the decision of the NLRB? See International Union of United Ass'n of Journeymen & Apprentices of Plumbing & Pipefitting Industry v. NLRB, 675 F.2d 1257 (D.C.Cir.1982), cert. denied, 459 U.S. 1171, 103 S.Ct. 816, 74 L.Ed.2d 1014 (1983).

———

## C.  The Union Hiring Hall[d]

In certain industries—most notably, maritime, longshoring and construction—unions provide what is in effect a job-referral service and act as a clearinghouse between employees seeking work and employers seeking workers. These industries are characterized by irregular and short-lived employment opportunities. For example, an electrical subcontractor in the construction business may have no regular employee force but rather seek

**d.**  See Fenton, Union Hiring Halls Under the Taft–Hartley Act, 9 Lab.L.J. 505 (1958); Rains, Construction Trades Hiring Halls, 10 Lab.L.J. 363 (1959).

qualified electricians to go to the jobsite on one date to install wires across the studded substructure of the house and will later send electricians (not always the same ones) back after the walls have been completed in order to install switchplates and fixtures. A shipowner may seek to employ a crew for a transoceanic run and return, or for a shorter run to some port along the same coast; after a long time at sea, the crewmen may not wish to ship out again but may rather prefer some days on shore to be spent with family or friends. It would be time-consuming and uneconomical for the many employers in these industries to hire on their own and for the many employees individually to search for employment.

The solution that has been worked out over time is the union-operated hiring hall, which receives from the employers requests for workers and provides workers who are qualified and available. The service can be rendered at no cost to the employer, and the union recoups its cost from membership dues and hiring-hall fees of nonmembers. The union and employer may agree that the hiring hall is "nonexclusive," that is, that the employer is free to reject persons referred by the union and may hire from other sources; or may agree to make the hiring hall the exclusive method of recruitment. The union is expected to distribute work opportunities in accordance with some equitable principle; work on board ship will commonly be assigned in accordance with the seniority of the workers in their service within the hall's jurisdiction, and work on shore in loading and unloading ships will commonly be on a rotary basis, with work assigned to the employees who earliest completed their last preceding job and are thus at the top of a first-come first-served list. In industries where seniority with a given employer cannot be utilized to achieve job security, the union hiring hall can afford comparable benefits.

Union control over the referral process has frequently, however, tempted union officials to engage in invidious discrimination—to give preference in referrals to union members rather than to nonmembers, or to give preference to those union members who are most zealous in their attendance at meetings or in their support of the incumbent officials, or simply to friends, relatives or persons of the same color. The union-operated hiring hall thus frequently went hand-in-hand with the closed shop, where union membership in good standing was a condition of referral and thus of employment; the union could control the volume and qualifications of the work force at the source. To the extent that the parties make union membership a condition of referral and employment, such an agreement would clearly constitute a violation by the employer of Section 8(a)(3)— since it would lack the thirty-day grace period for joining the union, which makes the union shop lawful under the proviso to that section—and a violation of Section 8(b)(2) by the union. But exclusive referral or preference of union members is not a necessary adjunct of the union-operated hiring hall, and it has been the task of the Board and the courts to test the hiring hall against the directive in those two sections barring "discrimination." The key issue is thus whether the hiring hall arrangement, as written or as implemented in practice, works a union-induced discrimination which encourages union membership.

————

## Local 357, International Broth. of Teamsters v. NLRB

365 U.S. 667, 81 S.Ct. 835, 6 L.Ed.2d 11 (1961).

■ Mr. Justice Douglas delivered the opinion of the Court.

Petitioner union (along with the International Brotherhood of Teamsters and a number of other affiliated local unions) executed a three-year collective bargaining agreement with California Trucking Associations which represented a group of motor truck operators in California. The provisions of the contract relating to hiring of casual or temporary employees were as follows:

"Casual employees shall, wherever the Union maintains a dispatching service, be employed only on a seniority basis in the Industry whenever such senior employees are available. An available list with seniority status will be kept by the Unions, and employees requested will be dispatched upon call to any employer who is a party to this Agreement. Seniority rating of such employees shall begin with a minimum of three months service in the Industry, *irrespective of whether such employee is or is not a member of the Union.*

"Discharge of any employee by any employer shall be grounds for removal of any employee from seniority status. No casual employee shall be employed by any employer who is a party to this Agreement in violation of seniority status if such employees are available and if the dispatching service for such employees is available. The employer shall first call the Union or the dispatching hall designated by the Union for such help. In the event the employer is notified that such help is not available, or in the event the employees called for do not appear for work at the time designated by the employer, the employer may hire from any other available source." (Emphasis added.)

Accordingly the union maintained a hiring hall for casual employees. One Slater was a member of the union and had customarily used the hiring hall. But in August 1955 he obtained casual employment with an employer who was party to the hiring-hall agreement without being dispatched by the union. He worked until sometime in November of that year, when he was discharged by the employer on complaint of the union that he had not been referred through the hiring-hall arrangement.

Slater made charges against the union and the employer. Though, as plain from the terms of the contract, there was an express provision that employees would not be discriminated against because they were or were not union members, the Board found that the hiring-hall provision was unlawful *per se* and that the discharge of Slater on the union's request constituted a violation by the employer of § 8(a)(1) and § 8(a)(3) and a violation by the union of § 8(b)(2) and § 8(b)(1)(A) of the National Labor Relations Act, as amended by the Taft–Hartley Act, 61 Stat. 140–141, as amended, 29 U.S.C. § 158, 29 U.S.C.A. § 158. The Board ordered, *inter alia,* that the company and the union cease giving any effect to the hiring-hall agreement; that they jointly and severally reimburse Slater for any loss sustained by him as a result of his discharge; and that they jointly and severally reimburse all casual employees for fees and dues paid by them to the union beginning six months prior to the date of the filing of the charge. 121 N.L.R.B. 1629.

The union petitioned the Court of Appeals for review of the Board's action, and the Board made a cross-application for enforcement. That court set aside the portion of the order requiring a general reimbursement of dues and fees. By a divided vote it upheld the Board in ruling that the hiring-hall agreement was illegal *per se.* 107 U.S.App.D.C. 188, 275 F.2d 646. Those rulings are here on certiorari, 363 U.S. 837, 80 S.Ct. 1610, 4 L.Ed.2d 1723, one on the petition of the union, the other on petition of the Board.

Our decision in Local 60, United Broth. of Carpenters, etc., v. National Labor Relations Board, 365 U.S. 651, 81 S.Ct. 875, 6 L.Ed.2d 1, is dispositive of the petition of the Board that asks us to direct enforcement of the order of reimbursement. [The Supreme Court in that case found that the reimbursement remedy was "punitive" and hence beyond the Board's remedial power under Section 10(c) since there was no basis for concluding that all the casual employees involved, many of whom were union members of long standing, would have refused to pay dues to the union had it refrained from committing unlawful acts under Section 8(b)(2).]

The other aspect of the case goes back to the Board's ruling in Mountain Pacific Chapter, 119 N.L.R.B. 883. That decision, rendered in 1958, departed from earlier rulings and held, Abe Murdock dissenting, that the hiring-hall agreement, despite the inclusion of a nondiscrimination clause, was illegal *per se:*

"Here the very grant of work at all depends solely upon union sponsorship, and it is reasonable to infer that the arrangement displays and enhances the Union's power and control over the employment status. Here all that appears is unilateral union determination and subservient employer action with no above-board explanation as to the reason for it, and it is reasonable to infer that the Union will be guided in its concession by an eye towards winning compliance with a membership obligation or union fealty in some other respect. The Employers here have surrendered all hiring authority to the Union and have given advance notice via the established hiring hall to the world at large that the Union is arbitrary master and is contractually guaranteed to remain so. From the final authority over hiring vested in the Respondent Union by the three AGC chapters, the inference of the encouragement of union membership is inescapable." Id., 896.

The Board went on to say that a hiring-hall arrangement to be lawful must contain protective provisions. Its views were stated as follows:

"We believe, however, that the inherent and unlawful encouragement of union membership that stems from unfettered union control over the hiring process would be negated, and we would find an agreement to be non-discriminatory on its face, only if the agreement explicitly provided that:

"(1) Selection of applicants for referral to jobs shall be on a nondiscriminatory basis and shall not be based on, or in any way affected by, union membership, bylaws, rules, regulations, constitutional provisions, or any other aspect or obligation of union membership, policies, or requirements.

"(2) The employer retains the right to reject any job applicant referred by the union.

"(3) The parties to the agreement post in places where notices to employees and applicants for employment are customarily posted, all provisions relating to the functioning of the hiring arrangement, including the safeguards that we deem essential to the legality of an exclusive hiring agreement." Id., 897.

The Board recognizes that the hiring hall came into being "to eliminate wasteful, time-consuming, and repetitive scouting for jobs by individual workmen and haphazard uneconomical searches by employers." Id., 896, n. 8. The hiring hall at times has been a useful adjunct to the closed shop. But Congress may have thought that it need not serve that cause, that in fact it has served well both labor and management—particularly in the maritime field and in the building and construction industry. In the latter the contractor who frequently is a stranger to the area where the work is done requires a "central source" for his employment needs; and a man looking for a job finds in the hiring hall "at least a minimum guarantee of continued employment."

Congress has not outlawed the hiring hall, though it has outlawed the closed shop except within the limits prescribed in the *provisos* to § 8(a)(3). Senator Taft made clear his views that hiring halls are useful, that they are not illegal *per se,* that unions should be able to operate them so long as they are not used to create a closed shop:

"In order to make clear the real intention of Congress, it should be clearly stated that the hiring hall is not necessarily illegal. The employer should be able to make a contract with the union as an employment agency. The union frequently is the best employment agency. The employer should be able to give notice of vacancies, and in the normal course of events to accept men sent to him by the hiring hall. He should not be able to bind himself, however, to reject nonunion men if they apply to him * * *.

" * * * Neither the law nor [NLRB and court] decisions forbid hiring halls, even hiring halls operated by the unions as long as they are not so operated as to create a closed shop with all of the abuses possible under such an arrangement, including discrimination against employees, prospective employees, members of union minority groups, and operation of a closed union." S.Rep. No. 1827, 81st Cong., 2d Sess., pp. 13, 14.

There being no express ban of hiring halls in any provisions of the Act, those who add one, whether it be the Board or the courts, engage in a legislative act. The Act deals with discrimination either by the employers or unions that encourages or discourages union membership. As respects § 8(a)(3) we said in Radio Officers, etc., v. National Labor Relations Board, 347 U.S. 17, 42–43, 74 S.Ct. 323, 337, 98 L.Ed. 455:

> "The language of § 8(a)(3) is not ambiguous. The unfair labor practice is for an employer to encourage or discourage membership by means of discrimination. Thus this section does not outlaw all encouragement or discouragement of membership in labor organizations; only such as is accomplished by discrimination is prohibited. Nor does this section outlaw discrimination in employment as such; only such discrimination as encourages or discourages membership in a labor organization is proscribed."

It is the "true purpose" or "real motive" in hiring or firing that constitutes the test. Id., 347 U.S. 43, 74 S.Ct. 337. Some conduct may by its very nature contain the implications of the required intent; the natural foreseeable consequences of certain action may warrant the inference. Id., 347 U.S. 45, 74 S.Ct. 338. And see Republic Aviation Corp. v. National Labor Relations Board, 324 U.S. 793, 65 S.Ct. 982, 89 L.Ed. 1372. The existence of discrimination may at times be inferred by the Board, for "it is permissible to draw on experience in factual inquiries." Radio Officers, etc., v. National Labor Relations Board, supra, 347 U.S. 49, 74 S.Ct. 340.

But surely discrimination cannot be inferred from the face of the instrument when the instrument specifically provides that there will be no discrimination against "casual employees" because of the presence or absence of union membership. The only complaint in the case was by Slater, a union member, who sought to circumvent the hiring-hall agreement. When an employer and the union enforce the agreement against union members, we cannot say without more that either indulges in the kind of discrimination to which the Act is addressed.

It may be that the very existence of the hiring hall encourages union membership. We may assume that it does. The very existence of the union has the same influence. When a union engages in collective bargaining and obtains increased wages and improved working conditions, its prestige doubtless rises and, one may assume, more workers are drawn to it. When a union negotiates collective bargaining agreements that include arbitration clauses and supervises the functioning of those provisions so as to get equitable adjustments of grievances, union membership may also be encouraged. The truth is that the union is a service agency that probably encourages membership whenever it does its job well. But as we said in Radio Officers, etc., v. National Labor Relations Board, supra, the only encouragement or discouragement of union membership banned by the Act is that which is "accomplished by discrimination." 347 U.S. at page 43, 74 S.Ct. at page 337.

Nothing is inferable from the present hiring-hall provision, except that employer and union alike sought to route "casual employees" through the union hiring hall and required a union member who circumvented it to adhere to it.

It may be that hiring halls need more regulation than the Act presently affords. * * * Perhaps the conditions which the Board attaches to hiring-hall arrangements will in time appeal to the Congress. Yet where Congress has adopted a selective system for dealing with evils, the Board is confined to that system. * * * Where, as here, Congress has aimed its sanctions only at specific discriminatory practices, the Board cannot go farther and establish a broader, more pervasive regulatory scheme.

The present agreement for a union hiring hall has a protective clause in it, as we have said; and there is no evidence that it was in fact used unlawfully. We cannot assume that a union conducts its operations in violation of law or that the parties to this contract did not intend to adhere to its express language. Yet we would have to make those assumptions to agree with the Board that it is reasonable to infer the union will act discriminatorily. * * *

Reversed.

■ Mr. Justice Frankfurter took no part in the consideration or decision of this case.

■ Mr. Justice Harlan, whom Mr. Justice Stewart joins, concurring. * * *

While I agree with the opinion of the Court that the Board could not infer from the mere existence of the "hiring hall" clause an intent on the part of employer or union to discriminate in favor of union status, I think it was within the realm of Board expertness to say that the natural and foreseeable effect of this clause is to make employees and job applicants think that union status will be favored. For it is surely scarcely less than a fact of life that a certain number of job applicants will believe that joining the union would increase their chances of hire when the union is exercising the hiring function.

What in my view is wrong with the Board's position in these cases is that a mere showing of foreseeable encouragement of union status is not a sufficient basis for a finding of violation of the statute. It has long been recognized that an employer can make reasonable business decisions, unmotivated by an intent to discourage union membership or protected concerted activities, although the foreseeable effect of these decisions may be to discourage what the act protects. For example, an employer may discharge an employee because he is not performing his work adequately, whether or not the employee happens to be a union organizer. See National Labor Relations Board v. Universal Camera Corp., 2 Cir., 190 F.2d 429. Yet a court could hardly reverse a Board finding that such firing would foreseeably tend to discourage union activity. Again, an employer can properly make the existence or amount of a year-end bonus depend upon the productivity of a unit of the plant, although this will foreseeably tend to discourage the protected activity of striking. Pittsburgh–Des Moines Steel Co. v. National Labor Relations Board, 9 Cir., 284 F.2d 74. A union, too, is privileged to make decisions which are reasonably calculated to further the welfare of all the employees it represents, nonunion as well as union, even though a foreseeable result of the decision may be to encourage union membership.

This Court's interpretation of the relevant statutory provisions has recognized that Congress did not mean to limit the range of either employer or union decision to those possible actions which had *no* foreseeable tendency to encourage or discourage union membership or concerted activities. In general, this Court has assumed that a finding of a violation of §§ 8(a)3 or 8(b)2 requires an affirmative showing of a *motivation* of encouraging or discouraging union status or activity. * * *

Considered in this light, I do not think we can sustain the Board's holding that the "hiring hall" clause is forbidden by the Taft–Hartley Act. The Board has not found that this clause was without substantial justification in terms of legitimate employer or union purposes. * * * The Board has not, in my view, made the type of showing of an actual motive of encouraging union membership that is required * * *.

■ MR. JUSTICE CLARK, dissenting in part. * * *

[T]he employer's "true purpose" and "real motive" [are] to be tested by the "natural consequences" and "foreseeable result" of his resort, however justifiably taken, to an institution so closely allied to the closed shop. I believe, as this Court has recognized, that "the desire of employees to unionize is directly proportional to the advantages *thought to be* obtained * * *." Radio Officers, supra, 347 U.S. at page 46, 74 S.Ct. at page 339. (Emphasis added.) I therefore ask, "Does the ordinary applicant for casual employment, who walks into the union hall at the direction of his prospective employer, consider his chances of getting dispatched for work diminished because of his non-union status or his default in dues payment?" Lester Slater testified—and it is uncontradicted—that "He [the applicant] had to be a union member; otherwise he wouldn't be working there; * * * you got to have your dues paid up to date and so forth." When asked how he knew this, Slater replied, "I have always knew that." Such was the sum of his impressions gained from contact with the hall from 1953 or 1954 when he started to 1958 when he ended. The misunderstanding—if it is that—of this common worker, who had the courage to complain, is, I am sure, representative of many more who were afraid to protest or, worse, were unaware of their right to do so.

Of the gravity of such a situation the Board is the best arbiter and best equipped to find a solution. It is, after all, "permissible [for the Board] to draw on experience in factual inquiries." * * *

* * * I need not go so far as to presume that the union has set itself upon an illegal course, conditioning referral on the unlawful criterion of union membership in good standing (which inference the majority today

says cannot be drawn), to reach the same result. I need only assume that, by thousands of common workers like Slater, the contract and its conditioning of casual employment upon union referral will work a misunderstanding as to the significance of union affiliation unless the employer's abdication of his role be made less than total and some note of the true function of the hiring hall be posted where all may see and read. The tide of encouragement may not be turned, but it will in part at least be stemmed. As an added dividend, the inherent probability of the free-wheeling operation of the union hiring hall resulting in arbitrary dispatching of job seekers would to some significant extent be diminished.

I would hold that there is not only a reasonable likelihood, but that it must inescapably be concluded under this record, that, without the safeguards at issue, a contract, conditioning employment *solely upon union referral,* encourages membership in the union by that very distinction itself. * * *

----

## PROBLEMS FOR DISCUSSION

**1.**  Which of the opinions in the *Local 357* case most accords with the more recent approach of the Court articulated in such cases as *Great Dane Trailers,* p. 565, supra? Is that more recent decision pertinent on the question of the employer's discretion in hiring or firing individual workers?

**2.**  The labor contract between the Operating Engineers and the Associated General Contractors of Illinois (AGC) provides that job referrals through the union-operated hiring hall shall be nondiscriminatory and shall be based on length of service in the area with contractors who are members of the AGC. When the jobsite on which one Parker worked was temporarily closed down because of the contractor's financial situation, Parker was laid off; he is not a union member and does not maintain a permanent residence in the area. When the jobsite opens up again, Parker is not recalled, the union informing him that this is because there are others available with longer employment experience with contractors who are parties to the labor agreement. Does the union's refusal to refer violate the Labor Act? See Robertson v. NLRB, 597 F.2d 1331 (10th Cir.1979); J–M Co., 173 NLRB 1461 (1969).

**3.**  The labor contract between the local Association of General Contractors and Operating Engineers local provides for exclusive hiring through a "nondiscriminatory" hiring hall. The union incurs administrative expenses in the operation of the hall, and requires that all persons who wish to be listed for referral and who are not members of the union must pay a monthly charge of $18.00 to defray the expenses of the union's services. The union has declined to register one Hender for referral and has refused to refer him for any job openings, claiming that he has consistently refused to tender the $18.00 monthly service fee. Hender has objected that no union member must pay that fee, but the union has rejoined that union members already pay, in addition to their initiation fees and assessments, monthly dues of $20.00 (of which $2.00 is remitted to the International). Would you advise Hender to file charges with the NLRB against the union local for violation of Section 8(b)(2)? See Local 825, Operating Engineers, 137 NLRB 1043 (1962).

---

## D.   BENEFITS FOR UNION OFFICIALS

### Local 900, International Union of Electrical Workers v. NLRB (Gulton Electro–Voice, Inc.)

727 F.2d 1184 (D.C.Cir.1984).

■ McGOWAN, SENIOR CIRCUIT JUDGE:

Petitioner Local 900 (the "union" or "Local 900") seeks reversal of a decision of the National Labor Relations Board (the "Board" or "NLRB"), and the Board cross-petitions for enforcement of that order. The Board held unlawful a contract clause that granted superseniority, with regard to layoff and recall, to the union's Financial Secretary and Recording Secretary. In doing so, the Board overruled prior precedent and established that superseniority with regard to layoff and recall is lawful only when extended to union officers who are involved in on-the-job contract administration, such as grievance processing. We uphold the Board's new principle and enforce the order in its entirety.

I

* * * Local 900 is the collective bargaining agent of the employees of Gulton Electro–Voice, Inc. The collective bargaining agreement has long contained a clause granting superseniority as to layoff and recall to a number of union officers. Pursuant to membership suggestion, the 1975 contract limited superseniority coverage to a smaller number of union officials, including the Recording Secretary and the Financial Secretary. The formal duties of the Recording Secretary involve keeping minutes of union meetings, preparing union correspondence, maintaining union records, and keeping the union membership and mailing list up to date. The formal duties of the Financial Secretary are to receive and account for union funds, pay union bills, furnish supplies, and transmit dues to the parent international union. The union does not dispute that neither of these officers engages in grievance resolution.

The parties stipulated that in the year preceding the General Counsel's charges the operation of the superseniority clause on behalf of the Financial Secretary did not affect any other employees, but the grant of superseniority to the Recording Secretary on various occasions, including November 5 and 6, 1980, caused some employees to be laid off when they otherwise would not have been. Local 900 has agreed to a moratorium on the exercise of superseniority for these officers pending the resolution of the present charges.

The General Counsel filed unfair labor practice charges against the union and Gulton Electro–Voice in 1981, alleging that the grant of super-seniority to these two officers unjustifiably discriminated against employees on the basis of union involvement, contrary to section 7 of the National Labor Relations Act ("NLRA"), 29 U.S.C. § 157 (1976). After a hearing, the ALJ dismissed the complaint. In an extensive opinion tracing the shifting lines of Board precedent in this area, the ALJ concluded that superseniority for these officers served the lawful purpose of promoting both effective representation and the collective bargaining relationship. The Board reversed his decision 4–0. We now review the Board's decision under the familiar limitation that we must uphold the Board's action if it is reasonable and supported by the record. See Ford Motor Co. v. NLRB, 441 U.S. 488, 497, 99 S.Ct. 1842, 1849, 60 L.Ed.2d 420 (1979); Automobile Salesmen's Union Local 1095 v. NLRB, 711 F.2d 383, 385–86 (D.C.Cir. 1983).

## II

Section 7 of the NLRA protects the rights of employees to engage in concerted activity to promote mutual interests, but it also protects employees' rights to refrain from such concerted activity. 29 U.S.C. § 157 (1976). In so doing, section 7 preserves an employee's right to be a "good, bad, or indifferent" union member. See Radio Officers' Union v. NLRB, 347 U.S. 17, 40, 74 S.Ct. 323, 335, 98 L.Ed. 455 (1954). Unions and employers may be held liable to employees for infringing their right to refrain from union activity. Coercive or discriminatory action by employers based on the exercise of section 7 rights may be unfair labor practices under section 8(a)(3), and similar action when performed by unions may violate section 8(b)(2). See id. at 39–42, 74 S.Ct. at 335–336. In some instances, however, discriminatory treatment may be permitted because it furthers other substantial statutory or business purposes. See NLRB v. Great Dane Trailers, Inc., 388 U.S. 26, 34, 87 S.Ct. 1792, 1797, 18 L.Ed.2d 1027 (1967).

Unions have long included in collective bargaining agreements provisions granting superseniority to various union officials. The Board did not address the possibility that the operation of such clauses may infringe section 7 rights until 1975. In Dairylea Cooperative Inc., 219 N.L.R.B. 656 (1975), enforced sub nom. NLRB v. Milk Drivers & Dairy Employees, Local 338, 531 F.2d 1162 (2d Cir.1976), the Board was faced with a clause that gave the union-selected steward top seniority in his craft, which in effect gave the steward first choice in route selection, overtime assignments, vacation time, and shift, hour, and day-off selection, as well as priority with regard to layoff and recall. Id. at 657. The General Counsel did not contest the use of superseniority for purposes of layoff and recall, but he charged that the remainder of the clause "unlawfully encourages union activism and discriminates with respect to on-the-job benefits against employees who ... prefer to refrain from [section 7] activity." Id. In contrast, the union argued that there could be no violation of the Act because the employees who would arguably be prejudiced by the clause had ratified it as part of their contract. Alternatively, the union contended that the General

Counsel had the burden of proving that the clause had a discriminatory purpose.

The Board agreed with the General Counsel, finding that it was reasonable to assume that the union would select as stewards only employees who were enthusiastic union members. By thus tying benefits to union activity, the clause created "a dependent relationship essentially at odds with the policy of the Act." Id. at 658. The General Counsel had not challenged the use of superseniority for layoff and recall, but the Board addressed the issue nevertheless, approving the practice and distinguishing it from providing on-the-job benefits. Both practices tie job benefits to union activity, but superseniority for stewards for layoff and recall is lawful, the Board said, because "it furthers the effective administration of bargaining agreements on the plant level by encouraging the continued presence of the steward on the job. It thereby not only serves a legitimate statutory purpose but also redounds ... to the benefit of all unit employees." Id. The rule that emerged from *Dairylea*, therefore, was that steward superseniority that is not limited to layoff and recall is "presumptively unlawful," subject to proof by the party urging its legality to show that the clause is justified by a legitimate statutory purpose. Id. at 658–59.

In 1977, the Board addressed the broader issue of superseniority not just for stewards, but for "functional union officer[s]." United Electrical, Radio & Machine Workers of America, Local 623 (Limpco), 230 N.L.R.B. 406 (1977), *enforced sub nom.* D'Amico v. NLRB, 582 F.2d 820 (3d Cir. 1978). The officer in *Limpco* was the local's Recording Secretary, who officially had no grievance adjustment or on-the-job contract administration obligations, although she did participate informally in such activities.[2] The *Limpco* decision was by aggregate majority. Two members concluded that superseniority regarding layoff and recall for functional union officers is presumptively lawful, id. at 407–08, while Member Murphy, casting the decisive vote, limited the presumption of legality to superseniority for "stewards and officers whose functions relate in general to furthering the bargaining relationship," id. at 408 n. 12. Two members dissented, concluding that "the only proper objective of superseniority is to retain those union officials responsible for the processing of grievances on the job, and whose presence on the job is therefore required for the proper performance of this functions [sic]." Id. at 409 (Jenkins & Penello, dissenting).

In enforcing the Board's order, the Third Circuit considered the Board to have required the union to provide "credible proof that the individual in question was *officially assigned* duties which helped to implement the collective bargaining agreement in a meaningful way." 582 F.2d at 825 (emphasis added). The court appeared to have found the clause lawful at least in part because of the informal role the Recording Secretary played in the grievance process. Id. It is not at all clear that the grievance role was decisive for the Board, but the Third Circuit's limiting language was one

---

**2.** The Recording Secretary participated informally in grievance processing, and she assisted stewards in writing grievances, advised stewards and shop foremen in contract interpretation, and posted notices of union meetings. 230 N.L.R.B. at 408.

reason for the Board's decision in American Can Co., 244 N.L.R.B. 736, 737 (1979), *enforced,* 658 F.2d 746 (10th Cir.1981), which again was by aggregate majority with Member Murphy again providing the decisive vote. Two members concluded that the superseniority clause was invalid on its face, for it "applies to all union officers without regard to whether they act as stewards." Id. at 739 (Jenkins & Penello, concurring). Member Murphy found the clause lawful on its face, but concluded that the General Counsel had met his burden to prove that the application of the clause to the particular officers was not justified because the officers' activities did not further the bargaining relationship. Id. at 740. The two dissenting members went so far as to reject *Dairylea* and its progeny. Because the benefits of superseniority are too "remote and contingent" to have any significant effect on employees' exercise of their section 7 rights, the dissent would have found that superseniority provisions for any union official "which are duly negotiated by the parties and contained in their bargaining agreements are presumptively lawful." Id. (Fanning & Truesdale, dissenting). The Tenth Circuit's enforcement, like the Third Circuit's in *Limpco,* rested on the union's failure to show substantial justification for granting superseniority to the particular union officials involved. See 658 F.2d at 757.

Although the Board addressed superseniority clauses in a number of contexts in other cases, the cases described above demonstrate the principal arguments surrounding the issue as well as the principal contours of the Board's decisions. After *Limpco,* despite the varying rationales of the Board's members, the decisions generally followed this pattern: So long as a superseniority clause was limited to layoff and recall and pertained to functional union officers, the Board would presume it lawful, and the General Counsel would have the burden of proving that the clause was unfairly discriminatory. If the General Counsel succeeded, the union and employer could still avoid liability by showing that the clause served a substantial, legitimate purpose. Although some courts, in enforcing Board orders, may have suggested that the unions bore an initial burden of justifying such clauses, the Board imposed that burden only when the clause extended beyond layoff and recall.

After further changes in the composition of the Board, the present case arose. The Board reviewed its previous decisions, weighed the arguments that had been presented on all sides of the issue, and returned to a position closer to that suggested in *Dairylea,* limiting the presumption of validity to layoff-and-recall superseniority for stewards and those officers with steward-like functions.

The Board started from the proposition that any form of superseniority for union officials is inherently at odds with section 7's guarantee of a disjunction between employment terms and union activity. Because of "the immediacy of attention that stewards can offer," because their attention benefits all employees, and because the stewards "need to maintain an on-the-job presence" in order to carry out their functions, superseniority for them, limited to layoff and recall, is justified. *Gulton,* 266 N.L.R.B. No. 84, at 10. Facilitating the stewards' role in this way, moreover, is consonant with one purpose identified in the title of the Labor Management Relations Act, Pub.L. No. 80–101, 61 Stat. 136, 136 (1947), namely, "to provide additional facilities for the mediation of labor disputes." See 266 N.L.R.B. No. 84, at 10. Finally, it followed from the Board's restrictive rationale that it would find lawful "only those superseniority provisions limited to employees who, as agents of the union, must be on the job to accomplish their duties directly related to administering the collective-bargaining agreement." Id. at 13.

The Board explicitly rejected the argument that superseniority was justified for other officers because it helped to maintain an effective and efficient bargaining relationship, an argument at the heart of the *Limpco* decision. The Board concluded that, however legitimate that goal might be, the NLRA precludes achieving it by linking job rights to union activity. Similarly, to the extent that superseniority serves this goal by attracting better union representatives, the method is illegitimate, for it is up to the union by its own devices, and not by job benefits, to achieve the quantum and quality of representation it deems appropriate. See id. at 10–12. See also Milk Drivers, 531 F.2d at 1166–67 (union should provide own incentives to attract qualified officers). Finally, the Board rejected the broad proposition that job retention was necessary for officers without on-the-job union duties in order to continue effective representation. In doing so, the Board relied on the following conclusions: (1) a laid-off officer can continue to serve in office; (2) the lay-off of officers is not unbearably disruptive; (3) unions often change officers in any event, so any replacement of officers due to lay-offs cannot be held inherently to disrupt adequate union representation. See 266 N.L.R.B. No. 84, at 12.

As noted at the outset, we must uphold defensible Board decisions, regardless of how we might have decided the matter in the first instance. The Board in this case addressed all considerations relevant to the issue before it and frankly overruled any prior inconsistent precedent. Such is its prerogative, and the Board exercised it with a unanimity not seen since *Dairylea*. It surely has arrived at one reasonable resolution of the problem in a reasonable manner. We will not substitute our judgment on a question of policy when four members of the Board have brought their expert knowledge of labor relations to bear and have reached a unanimous conclusion. We therefore affirm the Board's new presumption of legality restricted to layoff-and-recall superseniority for union officials who must be on the job to administer the collective bargaining agreement.

### III

The union does not contest that there is ample evidence to support the Board's application of the new rule in this case: The Recording Secretary had no union duties at the plant, and although the Financial Secretary had to meet with company officers once a month to go over the dues-withholding plan, performing this duty while at work was a matter of convenience, not necessity, and lay-off would in no way interfere with her continued performance of it. See id. at 14. The union does, however, challenge the application of the rule in this case on [the ground of] waiver * * *.

A. *Waiver*

Local 900 argues that, even if its superseniority clause as applied to these two officers is discriminatory under section 7, the employees waived the protection of section 7 by ratifying the contract that included the clause. Indeed, at the instigation of employees in 1975, the clause had been narrowed to include fewer officers, suggesting that the waiver, if it is such, was full and knowing. The union relies primarily on a line of cases, including one from this circuit, Fournelle v. NLRB, 670 F.2d 331, 337–38 (D.C.Cir.1982), whose basic conclusion was reaffirmed by the Supreme Court with the following language:

> Such waivers are valid because they "rest on 'the premise of fair representation' and presuppose that the selection of the bargaining representative 'remains free.'" ... Thus a union may bargain away its members' economic rights but it may not surrender rights that impair the employees' choice of their bargaining representative.

Metropolitan Edison Co. v. NLRB, 460 U.S. 693, 706, 103 S.Ct. 1467, 1476, 75 L.Ed.2d 387 (1983)(citations omitted).

The union's reliance on *Metropolitan Edison* and the waiver principle is misplaced. *Metropolitan Edison* and *Fournelle* were cases in which union officers were singled out for more severe sanctions for violation of their collective bargaining agreements' no-strike pledges. The courts upheld these discriminatory measures as necessary for the enforcement of the unions' lawful waivers of the economic right to strike. See Metropolitan Edison, 103 S.Ct. at 1476–77; *Fournelle,* 670 F.2d at 341. The disciplinary measures would not inhibit employees from becoming union members or officers, but only from participating in strike activity which they legally foreswore in their contract.

The right at stake in the present case, however, is not economic, but rather is said to affect employees' choices with regard to their level of participation in union affairs. Superseniority presumably encourages employees to become active supporters of the incumbent union in the hope that their efforts will win them union office and, thereby, greater job security. Thus superseniority can coerce employees in deciding whether to support the union, and the Supreme Court has held that such rights are not waivable, see NLRB v. Magnavox Co., 415 U.S. 322, 325–26, 94 S.Ct. 1099, 1102, 39 L.Ed.2d 358 (1974). * * *

---

# PROBLEMS FOR DISCUSSION

**1.** Assuming that the *Local 357* and *Great Dane* cases represent the views of the current Supreme Court, how would that Court decide the *Gulton* case? Would the outcome in *Dairylea* be different if the charge against the union were to be formulated in terms of breach of the duty of fair representation?

**2.** Would a superseniority provision such as that in the *Gulton* case fall within the prohibition of state right-to-work laws such as those described above at pages 1090–90?

**3.** The collective bargaining agreement between Company and Local Union provides: "The highest seniority preference shall be given to Officers and Union stewards in regard to layoffs provided they are capable of performing the available work in their unit." Patricia Jenkins is the Recording Secretary of the local union, and pursuant to the agreement she was kept on the job when Anna D'Amico, an employee with two years more seniority at the Company, was laid off. Ms. D'Amico filed charges under Sections 8(b)(1)(A) and (2) of the NLRA. At the hearing before the Administrative Law Judge, after the General Counsel presented evidence of the labor agreement, the union introduced in evidence its constitution, which defined the functions of the Recording Secretary precisely the same way as in the *Gulton* case. The union also proved that in addition to performing those tasks, Ms. Jenkins from time to time undertook the tasks referred to in footnote 2 of that case. The union then rested its case before the ALJ, and the General Counsel introduced no further evidence, choosing to rely upon a presumption that the superseniority provision in the labor agreement was invalid. How should the Judge decide the case? See Pattern Makers' Ass'n of Detroit v. NLRB, 622 F.2d 267 (6th Cir.1980); D'Amico v. NLRB, 582 F.2d 820 (3d Cir.1978).

**4.** The same collective bargaining agreement also provides that union stewards (who are paid $500 per year by the Union for their services) are to receive a wage differential on the job of five cents per hour. The Company and the Union agreed that this was a rough approximation of the expenses incurred by the stewards for such matters as telephone calls, gasoline and stationery used in the processing of grievances. The Union has also stated that such additional wage payment is designed to provide some added incentive to employees to take on the "headaches" of being a steward. Should the contractual wage differential withstand attack under Sections 8(a)(3) and 8(b)(2)? See Teamsters Local 20 v. Seaway Food Town, Inc., 235 NLRB 1554 (1978).

---

# III.  DISCIPLINE OF UNION MEMBERS

## A.  THE EFFECT OF THE NATIONAL LABOR RELATIONS ACT[a]

### NLRB v. Allis–Chalmers Mfg. Co.

388 U.S. 175, 87 S.Ct. 2001, 18 L.Ed.2d 1123 (1967).

■ MR. JUSTICE BRENNAN delivered the opinion of the Court.

\* \* \*

**a.** See Archer, Allis–Chalmers Recycled: A Current View of a Union's Right to Fine Employees for Crossing a Picket Line, 7 Indiana L.Rev. 498 (1974); Atleson, Union Fines and Picket Lines: The NLRA and Union Disciplinary Power, 17 U.C.L.A.L.Rev. 681 (1970); Craver, The *Boeing* Decision: A Blow to Federalism, Individual Rights and Stare Decisis, 122 U.Pa.L.Rev. 556 (1974); Gould, Some Limitations Upon Union Discipline Under the National Labor Relations Act: The Radiations of *Allis-Chalmers,* 1970 Duke L.J. 1067; Note, The Contractual Waiver of Individual Rights Under the NLRA, 31 N.Y.L.S.L.Rev. 793 (1986); Note, Section 8(b)(1)(A) from *Allis-Chalmers* to *Pattern*

Employees at the West Allis and La Crosse, Wisconsin, plants of respondent Allis–Chalmers Manufacturing Company were represented by locals of the United Automobile Workers. Lawful economic strikes were conducted at both plants in support of new contract demands. In compliance with the UAW constitution, the strikes were called with the approval of the International Union after at least two-thirds of the members of each local voted by secret ballot to strike. Some members of each local crossed the picket lines and worked during the strikes. After the strikes were over, the locals brought proceedings against these members charging them with violation of the International constitution and bylaws. The charges were heard by local trial committees in proceedings at which the charged members were represented by counsel. No claim of unfairness in the proceedings is made. The trials resulted in each charged member being found guilty of "conduct unbecoming a Union-member" and being fined in a sum from $20 to $100. Some of the fined members did not pay the fines and one of the locals obtained a judgment in the amount of the fine against one of its members, Benjamin Natzke, in a test suit brought in the Milwaukee County Court. An appeal from the judgment is pending in the Wisconsin Supreme Court.

Allis–Chalmers filed unfair labor practice charges against the locals alleging violation of § 8(b)(1)(A). [The National Labor Relations Board dismissed the complaint. The Seventh Circuit set the order aside, holding that the locals had violated § 8(b)(1)(A). The Supreme Court granted certiorari.]

### I.

The panel and the majority *en banc* of the Court of Appeals thought that reversal of the NLRB order would be required under a literal reading of §§ 7 and 8(b)(1)(A); under that reading union members who cross their own picket lines would be regarded as exercising their rights under § 7 to refrain from engaging in a particular concerted activity, and union discipline in the form of fines for such activity would therefore "restrain or coerce" in violation of § 8(b)(1)(A) if the section's proviso is read to sanction no form of discipline other than expulsion from the union. The panel rejected that literal reading. The majority *en banc* adopted it, stating that the panel "mistakenly took the position that such a literal reading was unwarranted in the light of the history and purposes" of the sections, 358 F.2d 659, and holding that "The statutes in question present no ambigui-

*Makers' League*: A Case Study in Judicial Legislation, 74 Calif.L.Rev. 1409 (1986); Silard, Labor Board Regulation of Union Discipline After Allis–Chalmers, Marine Workers, and Scofield, 38 Geo.Wash.L.Rev. 187 (1969).

ties whatsoever, and therefore do not require recourse to legislative history for clarification." Id., p. 660.

It is highly unrealistic to regard § 8(b)(1), and particularly its words "restrain or coerce," as precisely and unambiguously covering the union conduct involved in this case. On its face court enforcement of fines imposed on members for violation of membership obligations is no more conduct to "restrain or coerce" satisfaction of such obligations than court enforcement of penalties imposed on citizens for violation of their obligations as citizens to pay income taxes, or court awards of damages against a contracting party for nonperformance of a contractual obligation voluntarily undertaken. But even if the inherent imprecision of the words "restrain or coerce" may be overlooked, recourse to legislative history to determine the sense in which Congress used the words is not foreclosed. * * *

National labor policy has been built on the premise that by pooling their economic strength and acting through a labor organization freely chosen by the majority, the employees of an appropriate unit have the most effective means of bargaining for improvements in wages, hours, and working conditions. The policy therefore extinguishes the individual employee's power to order his own relations with his employer and creates a power vested in the chosen representative to act in the interests of all employees. * * *

Integral to this federal labor policy has been the power in the chosen union to protect against erosion its status under that policy through reasonable discipline of members who violate rules and regulations governing membership. That power is particularly vital when the members engage in strikes. The economic strike against the employer is the ultimate weapon in labor's arsenal for achieving agreement upon its terms, and "the power to fine or expel strikebreakers is essential if the union is to be an effective bargaining agent * * *." Provisions in union constitutions and bylaws for fines and expulsion of recalcitrants, including strikebreakers, are therefore commonplace and were commonplace at the time of the Taft–Hartley amendments.

In addition, the judicial view current at the time § 8(b)(1)(A) was passed was that provisions defining punishable conduct and the procedures for trial and appeal constituted part of the contract between member and union and that "The courts' role is but to enforce the contract." * * *

To say that Congress meant in 1947 by the § 7 amendments and § 8(b)(1)(A) to strip unions of the power to fine members for strikebreaking, however lawful the strike vote, and however fair the disciplinary procedures and penalty, is to say that Congress preceded the Landrum–Griffin amendments with an even more pervasive regulation of the internal affairs of unions. It is also to attribute to Congress an intent at war with the understanding of the union-membership relation which has been at the heart of its effort "to fashion a coherent labor policy" and which has been a predicate underlying action by this Court and the state courts. More importantly, it is to say that Congress limited unions in the powers necessary to the discharge of their role as exclusive statutory bargaining agents by impairing the usefulness of labor's cherished strike weapon. It is no answer that the proviso to § 8(b)(1)(A) preserves to the union the power to expel the offending member. Where the union is strong and membership therefore valuable, to require expulsion of the member visits a far more severe penalty upon the member than a reasonable fine. Where the union is weak, and membership therefore of little value, the union faced with further depletion of its ranks may have no real choice except to condone the member's disobedience. Yet it is just such weak unions for which the power to execute union decisions taken for the benefit of all employees is most critical to effective discharge of its statutory function.

Congressional meaning is of course ordinarily to be discerned in the words Congress uses. But when the literal application of the imprecise words "restrain or coerce" Congress employed in § 8(b)(1)(A) produce the extraordinary results we have mentioned we should determine whether this meaning is confirmed in the legislative history of the section.

## II.

The explicit wording of § 8(b)(2), which is concerned with union powers to affect a member's employment, is in sharp contrast with the imprecise words of § 8(b)(1)(A). Section 8(b)(2) limits union power to compel an employer to discharge a terminated member other than for "failure of the employee to tender the periodic dues and initiation fees uniformly required as a condition of acquiring or retaining membership." It is significant that Congress expressly disclaimed in this connection any intention to interfere with union self-government or to regulate a union's internal affairs. The Senate Report stated:

> "The committee did not desire to limit the labor organization with respect to either its selection of membership or expulsion therefrom. But the committee did wish to protect the employee in his job if unreasonably expelled or denied membership. The tests provided by the amendment are based upon facts readily ascertainable and *do not require the employer to inquire into the internal affairs of the union.*" (S.Rep. No. 105, 80th Cong., 1st Sess., 20, I 1947 Leg.Hist. 426.) (Emphasis supplied.)

> * * *

What legislative materials there are dealing with § 8(b)(1)(A) contain not a single word referring to the application of its prohibitions to traditional internal union discipline in general, or disciplinary fines in particular. On the contrary there are a number of assurances by its sponsors that the section was not meant to regulate the internal affairs of unions.

* * * The first suggestion that restraint or coercion of employees in the exercise of § 7 rights should be an unfair labor practice appears in the Statement of Supplemental Views to the Senate Report, in which a minority of the Senate Committee, including Senators Ball, Taft, and Smith, concurred. The mischief against which the Statement inveighed was re-

straint and coercion by unions in *organizational campaigns.* "The committee heard many instances of union coercion of employees such as that brought about by threats of reprisal against employees and their families in the course of organizing campaigns; also direct interference by mass picketing and other violence." S.Rep. No. 105, supra, at 50, I Leg.Hist. 456.
* * *

Cogent support for an interpretation of the body of § 8(b)(1) as not reaching the imposition of fines and attempts at court enforcement is the proviso to § 8(b)(1). It states that nothing in the section shall "impair the right of a labor organization to prescribe its own rules with respect to the acquisition or retention of membership therein * * *." * * * At the very least it can be said that the proviso preserves the rights of unions to impose fines, as a lesser penalty than expulsion, and to impose fines which carry the explicit or implicit threat of expulsion for nonpayment. Therefore, under the proviso the rule in the UAW constitution governing fines is valid and the fines themselves and expulsion for nonpayment would not be an unfair labor practice. Assuming that the proviso cannot also be read to authorize court enforcement of fines, a question we need not reach, the fact remains that to interpret the body of § 8(b)(1) to apply to the imposition and collection of fines would be to impute to Congress a concern with the permissible *means* of enforcement of union fines and to attribute to Congress a narrow and discreet interest in banning court enforcement of such fines. Yet there is not one word of the legislative history evidencing any such congressional concern. And as we have pointed out, a distinction between court enforcement and expulsion would have been anomalous for several reasons. First Congress was operating within the context of the "contract theory" of the union-member relationship which widely prevailed at that time. The efficacy of a contract is precisely its legal enforceability. A lawsuit is and has been the ordinary way by which performance of private money obligations is compelled. Second, as we have noted, such a distinction would visit upon the member of a strong union a potentially more severe punishment than court enforcement of fines, while impairing the bargaining facility of the weak union by requiring it either to condone misconduct or deplete its ranks. * * *

The 1959 Landrum–Griffin amendments, thought to be the first comprehensive regulation by Congress of the conduct of internal union affairs, also negate the reach given § 8(b)(1)(A) by the majority *en banc* below. "To be sure, what Congress did in 1959 does not establish what it meant in 1947. However, as another major step in an evolving pattern of regulation of union conduct, the 1959 Act is a relevant consideration. Courts may properly take into account the later Act when asked to extend the reach of the earlier Act's vague language to the limits which, read literally, the words might permit." National Labor Relations Board v. Drivers, etc., Local Union No. 639, 362 U.S. 274, 291–292, 80 S.Ct. 706, 4 L.Ed.2d 710. In 1959 Congress did seek to protect union members in their relationship to the union by adopting measures to insure the provision of democratic processes in the conduct of union affairs and procedural due process to members subjected to discipline. Even then, some Senators emphasized that "in establishing and enforcing statutory standards great care should be taken not to undermine union self-government or weaken unions in their role as collective-bargaining agents." S.Rep. No. 187, 86th Cong., 1st Sess., 7. The Eighty-sixth Congress was thus plainly of the view that union self-government was not regulated in 1947. Indeed, that Congress expressly recognized that a union member may be "fined, suspended, expelled, or otherwise disciplined," and enacted only procedural requirements to be observed. 73 Stat. 523, 29 U.S.C. § 411(a)(5). Moreover, Congress added a proviso to the guarantee of freedom of speech and assembly disclaiming any intent "to impair the right of a labor organization to adopt and enforce reasonable rules as to the responsibility of every member toward the organization as an institution * * *." 29 U.S.C. § 411(a)(2).

* * *

### III.

The collective bargaining agreements with the locals incorporate union security clauses. Full union membership is not compelled by the clauses: an employee is required only to become and remain "a member of the union to the extent of paying his monthly dues * * *." The majority *en banc* below nevertheless regarded full membership to be "the result not of individual voluntary choice but of the insertion of [this] union security provision in the contract under which a substantial minority of the employees may have been forced into membership." 358 F.2d, at 660. * * * Whether those prohibitions would apply if the locals had imposed fines on members whose membership was in fact limited to the obligation of paying monthly dues is a question not before us and upon which we intimate no view.

* * *

■ Mr. Justice Black, whom Mr. Justice Douglas, Mr. Justice Harlan, and Mr. Justice Stewart join, dissenting.

* * * The real reason for the Court's decision is its policy judgment that unions, especially weak ones, need the power to impose fines on strikebreakers and to enforce those fines in court. It is not enough, says the Court, that the unions have the power to expel those members who refuse to participate in a strike or who fail to pay fines imposed on them for such failure to participate; it is essential that weak unions have the choice between expulsion and court-enforced fines, simply because the latter are more effective in the sense of being more punitive. Though the entire mood of Congress in 1947 was to curtail the power of unions, as it had previously curtailed the power of employers, in order to equalize the power of the two, the Court is unwilling to believe that Congress intended to impair "the usefulness of labor's cherished strike weapon." I cannot agree with this conclusion or subscribe to the Court's unarticulated premise that the Court has power to add a new weapon to the union's economic arsenal whenever the Court believes that the union needs that weapon. That is a job for Congress, not this Court.

Though the Court recognizes that a union fine is in fact coercive, it seeks support for its holding—that court-enforced fines are not prohibited by § 8(b)(1)(A)—by reference to the proviso which authorizes a union to prescribe its own rules with respect to the retention of membership. * * * Just because a union might be free, under the proviso, to expel a member for crossing a picket line does not mean that Congress left unions free to threaten their members with fines. Even though a member may later discover that the threatened fine is only enforceable by expulsion, and in that sense a "lesser penalty," the direct threat of a fine, to a member normally unaware of the method the union might resort to for compelling its payment, would often be more coercive than a threat of expulsion.

Even on the assumption that § 8(a)(1)(A) permits a union to fine a member as long as the fine is only enforceable by expulsion, the fundamental error of the Court's opinion is its failure to recognize the practical and theoretical difference between a court-enforced fine, as here, and a fine enforced by expulsion or less drastic intra-union means. As the Court recognizes, expulsion for nonpayment of a fine may, especially in the case of a strong union, be more severe than judicial collection of the fine. But, if the union membership has little value and if the fine is great, then court-enforcement of the fine may be more effective punishment, and that is precisely why the Court desires to provide weak unions with this alternative to expulsion, an alternative which is similar to a criminal court's power to imprison defendants who fail to pay fines. * * *

The Court disposes of this tremendous practical difference between court-enforced and union-enforced fines by suggesting that Congress was not concerned with "the permissible means of enforcement of union fines" and that court-enforcement of fines is a necessary consequence of the "contract theory" of the union-member relationship. * * * At the very least Congress intended to preclude a union's use of certain means to collect fines. It is clear, as the Court recognizes, that Congress in enacting § 8(b)(2) was concerned with insulating an employee's job from his union membership. If the union here had attempted to enforce the payment of the fines by persuading the employer to discharge the nonpaying employees or to withhold the fines from their wages, it would have clearly been guilty of an unfair labor practice under § 8(b)(2). If the union here, operating under a union shop contract, had applied the employees' dues to the satisfaction of the fines and then charged them extra dues, that, under Board decisions, would have been a violation of § 8(b)(1)(A), since it jeopardized the employees' jobs. Yet here the union has resorted to equally effective outside assistance to enforce the payment of its fines, and the Court holds that within the ambit of "internal union discipline." I have already pointed to the impact that $100 per day court-enforced fines may have on an employee's job—they would totally discourage him from working at all—and I fail to see how court enforcement of union fines is any more "internal" than employer enforcement. The undeniable fact is that the union resorts to outside help when it is not strong enough to enforce obedience internally. And even if the union does not resort to outside help but uses threats of physical violence by its officers or other members to compel payment of its fines, I do not doubt that this too would be a violation of § 8(b)(1)(A).

Finally, the Court attempts to justify court-enforcement of fines by comparing it to judicial enforcement of the provisions of an ordinary commercial contract—a comparison which, according to the Court's own authority, is simply "a legal fabrication." The contractual theory of union membership, at least until recently, was a fiction used by the courts to justify judicial intervention into union affairs to protect employees, not to help unions. I cannot believe that Congress intended the effectiveness of § 8(b)(1)(A) to be impaired by such a fiction, or that it was content to rely on the state courts' use of this fiction to protect members from union coercion. Particularly is that so where the "contract" between the union and the employee is the involuntary product of a union shop. * * *

The union here had a union security clause in its contract with Chalmers. That clause made it necessary for all employees, including the ones involved here, to pay dues and fees to the union. But § 8(a)(3) and § 8(b)(2) make it clear that "Congress intended to prevent utilization of union security agreements for any purpose other than to compel payment of union dues and fees." Radio Officers' Union, etc. v. National Labor Relations Board, 347 U.S. 17, 41, 74 S.Ct. 323, 336, 98 L.Ed. 455. If the union uses the union security clause to compel employees to pay dues, characterizes such employees as members, and then uses such membership as a basis for imposing court-enforced fines upon those employees unwilling to participate in a union strike, then the union security clause is being used for a purpose other than "to compel payment of union dues and fees." It is being used to coerce employees to join in union activity in violation of § 8(b)(2).

The Court suggests that this problem is not present here, because the fined employees failed to prove they enjoyed other than full union membership, that their role in the union was not in fact limited to the obligation of paying dues. For several reasons, I am unable to agree with the Court's approach. Few employees forced to become "members" of the union by virtue of the union security clause will be aware of the fact that they must somehow "limit" their membership to avoid the union's court-enforced fines. Even those who are brash enough to attempt to do so may be unfamiliar with how to do it. Must they refrain from doing anything but paying dues, or will signing the routine union pledge still leave them with less than full membership? And finally, it is clear that what restrains the employee from going to work during a union strike is the union's threat that it will fine him and collect those fines from him in court. How many employees in a union shop whose names appear on the union's membership rolls will be willing to ignore that threat in the hope that they will later be able to convince the Labor Board or the state court that they were not full members of the union? By refusing to decide whether § 8(b)(1)(A) prohibits the union from fining an employee who does nothing more than pay union dues as a condition to retaining his job in a union shop, the Court adds coercive impetus to the union's threat of fines. Today's decision makes it

highly dangerous for an employee in a union shop to exercise his § 7 right
to refrain from participating in a strike called by a union in which he is a
member by name only.

    * * *

---

# PROBLEM FOR DISCUSSION

Jones is an employee of the ABC Company which has incorporated a union
shop provision in its contract with the Truckers Union, which represents all of the
Company's employees. The provision, legal in this state, requires that all employees
must—as a condition of continued employment—become a member of the Union.
Jones initially protested this membership requirement but has over the years
continued to pay the dues required for membership; he has attended no Union
meetings and has not otherwise participated in the activities of the Union. In a
recent strike during contract negotiations, Jones reported to work through the
Union picket lines, in spite of warnings by Union officials that this was contrary to
provisions of the Union constitution. At the conclusion of the strike, Union
disciplinary proceedings were instituted against Jones, and a $1000 fine imposed for
strikebreaking. Jones has consulted you to determine whether he must pay the fine
and whether there are any steps he may take to overturn the fine (and any similar
fines in the future). What advice can you give him?

---

# Scofield v. NLRB

394 U.S. 423, 89 S.Ct. 1154, 22 L.Ed.2d 385 (1969).

■ MR. JUSTICE WHITE delivered the opinion of the Court.

    * * *

[The union has represented production employees of the Wisconsin
Motor Corporation since 1937. For the substantial number of workers in
the unit who are paid on a piecework or incentive basis, the labor contract
sets a minimum hourly "machine rate" (based on the productivity of an
average employee working at a reasonable pace) which may be exceeded by
a faster worker. Since 1938, the union has implemented among its members a ceiling on the production for which members would accept immediate piecework pay; although members may produce as much as they like
each day, they may draw pay only up to the ceiling rate and any balance is
"banked" by the company, to be paid out later for days on which the
member does not reach the production ceiling. If a member demands
immediate payment for work over the ceiling rate during the pay period,
the company will comply, but the union assesses a fine of up to $100 for
repeated violators. The apparent purpose of the production ceiling is to
protect negotiated rest periods for the workers. Both the "machine rate"
and the "ceiling rate" have been negotiated between the company and the
union, with the union gradually over the years agreeing to increase the
margin between the two but not acceding to the company's demands to

eliminate the ceiling altogether. The company opens its work records to the union to permit a check on members' compliance with the ceiling, and the ceiling rate has been used in computing piece-rate increases and in settling grievances. In 1961, the union imposed fines of $50 to $100 (and a one-year suspension from union membership) on several employees, and sued in state court to collect the fines. Charges of unfair labor practices were rejected by the trial examiner, the NLRB, the court of appeals, and ultimately by the Supreme Court.]

## II.

Based on the legislative history of [Section 8(b)(1)(A)], including its proviso, the Court in NLRB v. Allis–Chalmers Mfg. Co., 388 U.S. 175, 195, 87 S.Ct. 2001, 2014, 18 L.Ed.2d 1123 (1967) * * * essentially accepted the position of the National Labor Relations Board dating from Minneapolis Star and Tribune Co., 109 N.L.R.B. 727 (1954) where the Board also distinguished internal from external enforcement in holding that a union could fine a member for violating a rule against working during a strike but that the same rule could not be enforced by causing the employer to exclude him from the work force or by affecting his seniority without triggering violations of §§ 8(b)(1), 8(b)(2), 8(a)(1), 8(a)(2), and 8(a)(3). These sections form a web, of which § 8(b)(1)(A) is only a strand, preventing the union from inducing the employer to use the emoluments of the job to enforce the union's rules.[5] * * *

Although the Board's construction of the section emphasizes the sanction imposed, rather than the rule itself, and does not involve the Board in judging the fairness or wisdom of particular union rules, it has become clear that if the rule invades or frustrates an overriding policy of the labor laws the rule may not be enforced, even by fine or expulsion, without violating § 8(b)(1). In both *Skura*[7] and *Marine Workers*,[8] the Board was concerned with union rules requiring a member to exhaust union remedies before filing an unfair labor practice charge with the Board. That rule, in the Board's view, frustrated the enforcement scheme established by the statute and the union would commit an unfair labor practice by fining or expelling members who violated the rule.

The *Marine Workers* case came here[9] and the result reached by the Board was sustained, the Court agreeing that the rule in question was

---

**5.** The Court has held that the "policy of the Act is to insulate employees' jobs from their organizational rights." Radio Officers' Union v. National Labor Relations Board, 347 U.S. 17, 40, 74 S.Ct. 323, 335, 98 L.Ed. 455 (1954). As an employee, he may be a "good, bad, or indifferent" member so long as he meets the financial obligations of the union security contract. Thus the Board has found an unfair labor practice by union and employer where an employee was discharged for violation of a union rule limiting production. Printz Leather Co., 94 N.L.R.B. 1312 (1951). But as a union member, so long as he chooses to remain one, he is subject to union discipline.

**7.** Local 138, International Union of Operating Engineers, 148 N.L.R.B. 679 (1964).

**8.** Industrial Union of Marine and Shipbuilding Workers of America, 159 N.L.R.B. 1065 (1966).

**9.** National Labor Relations Board v. Industrial Union of Marine & Shipbuilding Workers, 391 U.S. 418, 88 S.Ct. 1717, 20 L.Ed.2d 706 (1968).

contrary to the plain policy of the Act to keep employees completely free from coercion against making complaints to the Board. Frustrating this policy was beyond the legitimate interest of the labor organization, at least where the member's complaint concerned conduct of the employer as well as the union.

Under this dual approach, § 8(b)(1) leaves a union free to enforce a properly adopted rule which reflects a legitimate union interest, impairs no policy Congress has imbedded in the labor laws, and is reasonably enforced against union members who are free to leave the union and escape the rule. This view of the statute must be applied here.

### III.

In the case at hand, there is no showing in the record that the fines were unreasonable or the mere fiat of a union leader, or that the membership of petitioners in the union was involuntary. Moreover, the enforcement of the rule was not carried out through means unacceptable in themselves, such as violence or employer discrimination. It was enforced solely through the internal technique of union fines, collected by threat of expulsion or judicial action. The inquiry must therefore focus on the legitimacy of the union interest vindicated by the rule and the extent to which any policy of the Act may be violated by the union-imposed production ceiling.

As both the trial examiner and the Court of Appeals noted, union opposition to unlimited piecework pay systems is historic. Union apprehension, not without foundation, is that such systems will drive up employee productivity and in turn create pressures to lower the piecework rate so that at the new, higher level of output employees are earning little more than they did before. The fear is that the competitive pressure generated will endanger workers' health, foment jealousies, and reduce the work force. In addition, the findings of the trial examiner were that the ceiling served as a yardstick for the settlement of job allowance grievances, that it has played an important role in negotiating the minimum hourly rate and that it is the standard for "factoring" the hourly rate raises into the piecework rate. The view of the trial examiner was that "[i]n terms of a union's traditional function of trying to serve the economic interests of the group as a whole, the union has a very real, immediate, and direct interest in it." 145 N.L.R.B., at 1135. * * *

[The Court rejected the employees' claim that the union rule impeded collective bargaining. The union acknowledges that its ceiling is a bargainable issue, it has bargained about it in the past, and it has in fact agreed to raise the ceiling in return for an increase in the piece rate. Nor does the ceiling or compliance with it violate the labor agreement, which established a guaranteed minimum rate (the rate of production of an average efficient worker) that is well below the union ceiling. Nor does the ceiling violate any statutory policy against "featherbedding." Section 8(b)(6) outlaws only exacting pay for performing no work and Congress has refrained from determining "where the area between shiftlessness and over-work should lie," leaving such matters to private negotiation.] In light of this, and the acceptable manner in which the rule was enforced, vindicating a legitimate union interest, it is impossible to say that it contravened any policy of the Act.

We affirm, holding that the union rule is valid and that its enforcement by reasonable fines does not constitute the restraint or coercion proscribed by § 8(b)(1)(A).

Affirmed.

[MR. JUSTICE BLACK dissented for reasons set forth in his *Allis-Chalmers* dissent.]

———

NLRB v. BOEING CO., 412 U.S. 67, 93 S.Ct. 1952, 36 L.Ed.2d 752 (1973). During an 18–day strike, some 143 employees out of 1900 production and maintenance workers crossed the union's picket lines, which resulted in their being fined by the union when the strike was settled and a new labor contract signed. The base weekly income of the employees fined ranged from $95 to $145; they were fined $450 and barred from holding union office for five years. No union member paid in full, and the union sued nine employees in state court to collect the fines and attorneys' fees. The company's claim that the fines were excessive and thus in violation of Section 8(b)(1)(A) was rejected by the NLRB, which concluded that Congress did not give it authority to regulate the size of union fines or establish standards for their reasonableness. A divided Supreme Court agreed.

Justice Rehnquist for the Court conceded that all union fines are "coercive" in some degree but noted that the fines in *Allis-Chalmers* and *Scofield* were sustained not because they were "reasonable" but rather because Congress did not intend Section 8(b)(1)(A) to outlaw union fines not affecting the employer-employee relationship and not otherwise prohibited by the Act. Were the NLRB to attempt to pass upon the reasonableness of the amount of a fine, it would have to consider the motivation of union leaders and thus "delve into internal union affairs in a manner which we have previously held Congress did not intend." The Court majority rejected the argument that Congress contemplated Board scrutiny of the amount of fines as a way of providing labor expertise and uniformity of decisions. State courts have for many years been enforcing union fines in conventional contract actions, and "state courts applying state law are quite willing to determine whether disciplinary fines are reasonable in amount. Indeed, the expertise required for a determination of reasonableness may well be more evident in a judicial forum that is called upon to assess reasonableness in varying factual contexts than it is in a specialized agency. In assessing the reasonableness of disciplinary fines, for example, state courts are often able to draw on their experience in areas of the law apart from labor relations." And, even assuming uniformity of decisions is thought to be desirable in this area, giving the NLRB authority to determine the reasonableness of fines in an unfair labor practice proceeding will not oust continued state-court jurisdiction to make such a determination in the context of an action by a union to enforce a fine.

In a dissenting opinion, Chief Justice Burger pointed out the irony of the union's supporting state-court jurisdiction to determine reasonable union fines given the long history of union opposition to state-court "intervention" in industrial disputes and consistent union claims of NLRB "expertise." The Board has the experience and sensitivity to devise uniform national rules which draw the line between legitimate union interests and oppressively retributive fines. In another dissenting opinion, Justice Douglas (for a total of three Justices, including the Chief Justice) pointed out that by fining the strikebreakers in excess of their earnings during the strike, the union was in substance effecting their post-strike suspension without pay, which would have clearly been unlawful had the union induced Boeing to take such action. In any event, it is no consolation to tell the union member that an oppressive fine can be contested in a state-court suit, since the individual member is typically unsophisticated and without adequate financial resources; in an NLRB case, the union member is represented without cost by the General Counsel. Moreover, the Board has the expertise in labor-management relations which state judges lack.

---

## PROBLEMS FOR DISCUSSION

**1.** Under *Allis-Chalmers* and *Scofield,* will the validity of union discipline turn upon whether it "restrains and coerces" union members in the exercise of their statutory rights? Will it turn upon whether the discipline takes the form of affecting only "the acquisition or retention of membership" as opposed to court-enforceable fines or loss of job rights? Does the formula articulated in these two cases comport at all with the language of Section 8(b)(1)(A)?

Evaluate the following proposition: "The text of Section 8(b)(1)(A) is of no greater assistance in deciding specific cases of union coercion than is the text of Section 8(a)(1) in cases of employer coercion. When a union disciplines a member for purposes of strengthening the union in a strike or collective bargaining situation, it is using an economic weapon much as the employer does when pressuring employees by replacement or lockout. The validity of the union discipline is determined in the same manner—by balancing the substantiality of the union's interest against the severity of the impact on significant employee rights. That is essentially a lawmaking function, and the NLRB should be accorded great deference in striking the balance."

**2.** Strawson is a member of the International Molders Union, which is the certified bargaining representative for production employees at the Blackhawk Tanning Company. Strawson, along with several other employees, is unhappy with the policies of the Union, and after some weeks of gathering signed cards requesting a new election she has filed a petition with the NLRB for a decertification election. If these facts are found after a Union disciplinary proceeding instituted against Strawson, what action may the Union take?

(a) May it induce the Blackhawk Company to discharge her?

(b) May it expel her from the Union? *See* Sandia Nat'l Laboratories, 331 NLRB No. 193 (2000).

(c) May it impose a fine upon her in the amount of $100? (Does it matter whether nonpayment of the fine will lead to Strawson's expulsion from the Union, or will lead instead to a lawsuit to collect the fine?) See International Molders Local 125 (Blackhawk Tanning Co.), 178 NLRB 208 (1969), enf'd, 442 F.2d 92 (7th Cir.1971).

**3.** McCloskey is an officer of the Aluminum Workers Union, which represents employees at the Deluxe Canning Company. Several months ago, the Company suspended two employees, each for ten days, because of their alleged violation of Company rules; these employees filed a grievance and the case ultimately went to arbitration. McCloskey gave testimony in support of the Company's case before the arbitrator, and the suspensions were upheld. The Union brought charges against McCloskey, and after a hearing removed him from union office. Has the union violated Section 8(b)(1)(A)?

Would it matter if the union could demonstrate that the testimony given by McCloskey was knowingly false? Compare Teamsters Local 788 (San Juan Islands Cannery), 190 NLRB 24 (1971), with United Lodge 66, IAM (Smith–Lee Co.), 182 NLRB 849 (1970).

**4.** Lombardi is a member of a traveling orchestra and is also a member in good standing of the American Federation of Musicians. At a one-night engagement in Salina, Kansas, Lombardi played alongside a musician who was called in as a last-minute substitute and who was not a member of the Federation (and Lombardi was aware of this fact). Lombardi was charged with violating Federation bylaws prohibiting a member from working alongside a nonmember and, after due proceedings, he was fined $50. Has the union committed an unfair labor practice? Would your analysis be different if Lombardi served that night as the orchestra leader and was thus (while still a member of the Federation) considered an employer? See Glasser v. NLRB, 395 F.2d 401 (2d Cir.1968).

**5.** Is it lawful for a union to discipline (by fine or suspension from membership) a member who, contrary to the union constitution, crosses a union picket line to report for work when there is a collective bargaining agreement in effect and that agreement forbids strikes and picketing by the union during the contract term? See Glaziers Local 1162 (Tusco Glass, Inc.), 177 NLRB 393 (1969).

———

# Pattern Makers' League of North America v. NLRB[b]

473 U.S. 95, 105 S.Ct. 3064, 87 L.Ed.2d 68 (1985).

■ JUSTICE POWELL delivered the opinion of the Court.

The Pattern Makers' League of North America, AFL–CIO (the League), a labor union, provides in its constitution that resignations are not permitted during a strike or when a strike is imminent. The League fined 10 of its members who, in violation of this provision, resigned during a strike and returned to work. The National Labor Relations Board held

**b.** Comment, Section 8(b)(1)(A) from *Allis-Chalmers* to *Pattern Makers' League*: A    Case Study in Judicial Legislation, 74 Calif.L.Rev. 1409 (1986).

that these fines were imposed in violation of § 8(b)(1)(A) of the National Labor Relations Act, 29 U.S.C. § 158(b)(1)(A). We granted a petition for a writ of certiorari in order to decide whether § 8(b)(1)(A) reasonably may be construed by the Board as prohibiting a union from fining members who have tendered resignations invalid under the union constitution.

I

The League is a national union composed of local associations (locals). In May 1976, its constitution was amended to provide that:

"No resignation or withdrawal from an Association, or from the League, shall be accepted during a strike or lockout, or at a time when a strike or lockout appears imminent."

This amendment, known as League Law 13, became effective in October 1976, after being ratified by the League's locals. On May 5, 1977, when a collective-bargaining agreement expired, two locals began an economic strike against several manufacturing companies in Rockford, Illinois and Beloit, Wisconsin. Forty-three of the two locals' members participated. In early September 1977, after the locals formally rejected a contract offer, a striking union member submitted a letter of resignation to the Beloit association. He returned to work the following day. During the next three months, 10 more union members resigned from the Rockford and Beloit locals and returned to work. On December 19, 1977, the strike ended when the parties signed a new collective-bargaining agreement. The locals notified 10 employees who had resigned that their resignations had been rejected as violative of League Law 13. The locals further informed the employees that, as union members, they were subject to sanctions for returning to work. Each was fined approximately the equivalent of his earnings during the strike.

The Rockford–Beloit Pattern Jobbers' Association (the Association) had represented the employers throughout the collective-bargaining process. It filed charges with the Board against the League and its two locals, the petitioners. Relying on § 8(b)(1)(A), the Association claimed that levying fines against employees who had resigned was an unfair labor practice. Following a hearing, an Administrative Law Judge found that the petitioners had violated § 8(b)(1)(A) by fining employees for returning to work after tendering resignations. Pattern Makers' League of North America, 265 N.L.R.B. 1332, 1339 (1982)(decision of G. Wacknov, ALJ). The Board agreed that § 8(b)(1)(A) prohibited the union from imposing sanctions on the 10 employees. *Pattern Makers' League of North America,* supra. In holding that League Law 13 did not justify the imposition of fines on the members who attempted to resign, the Board relied on its earlier decision in Machinists Local 1327 (Dalmo Victor II), 263 N.L.R.B. 984 (1982), enf. denied, 725 F.2d 1212 (C.A.9 1984).

The United States Court of Appeals for the Seventh Circuit enforced the Board's order. 724 F.2d 57 (1983). * * *

We granted a petition for a writ of certiorari, 469 U.S. 814, 105 S.Ct. 79, 83 L.Ed.2d 27 (1984), to resolve the conflict between the Courts of Appeals over the validity of restrictions on union members' right to resign. The Board has held that such restrictions are invalid and do not justify imposing sanctions on employees who have attempted to resign from the union. Because of the Board's "special competence" in the field of labor relations, its interpretation of the Act is accorded substantial deference. NLRB v. J. Weingarten, Inc., 420 U.S. 251, 266, 95 S.Ct. 959, 968, 43 L.Ed.2d 171 (1975). The question for decision today is thus narrowed to whether the Board's construction of § 8(b)(1)(A) is reasonable. NLRB v. City Disposal Systems, Inc., 465 U.S. 822, 830, 104 S.Ct. 1505, 1510, 79 L.Ed.2d 839 (1984). We believe that § 8(b)(1)(A) properly may be construed as prohibiting the fining of employees who have tendered resignations ineffective under a restriction in the union constitution. We therefore affirm the judgment of the Court of Appeals enforcing the Board's order.

## II

### A

Section 7 of the Act, 29 U.S.C. § 157, grants employees the right to "refrain from any or all [concerted] ... activities...." This general right is implemented by § 8(b)(1)(A). The latter section provides that a union commits an unfair labor practice if it "restrain[s] or coerce[s] employees in the exercise" of their § 7 rights. When employee members of a union refuse to support a strike (whether or not a rule prohibits returning to work during a strike), they are refraining from "concerted activity." Therefore, imposing fines on these employees for returning to work "restrain[s]" the exercise of their § 7 rights. Indeed, if the terms "refrain" and "restrain or coerce" are interpreted literally, fining employees to enforce compliance with any union rule or policy would violate the Act.

Despite this language from the Act, the Court in NLRB v. Allis–Chalmers, 388 U.S. 175, 87 S.Ct. 2001, 18 L.Ed.2d 1123 (1967), held that § 8(b)(1)(A) does not prohibit labor organizations from fining current members. In NLRB v. Textile Workers, [409 U.S. 213, 93 S.Ct. 385, 34 L.Ed.2d 422 (1972)], and Machinists & Aerospace Workers v. NLRB, 412 U.S. 84, 93 S.Ct. 1961, 36 L.Ed.2d 764 (1973)(*per curiam*), the Court found as a corollary that unions may not fine former members who have resigned lawfully. Neither *Textile Workers,* supra, nor *Machinists,* supra, however, involved a provision like League Law 13, restricting the members' right to resign. We decide today whether a union is precluded from fining employees who have attempted to resign when resignations are prohibited by the union's constitution.

### B

The Court's reasoning in *Allis-Chalmers,* supra, supports the Board's conclusion that petitioners in this case violated § 8(b)(1)(A). In *Allis-Chalmers,* the Court held that imposing court-enforceable fines against current union members does not "restrain or coerce" the workers in the exercise of their § 7 rights. In so concluding, the Court relied on the legislative history of the Taft–Hartley Act. It noted that the sponsor of § 8(b)(1)(A) never intended for that provision " 'to interfere with the internal affairs or organization of unions,' " 388 U.S., at 187, 87 S.Ct., at 2010, quoting 93 Cong.Rec. 4272 (1947) (statement of Sen. Ball), and that other proponents of the measure likewise disclaimed an intent to interfere with unions' "internal affairs." 388 U.S., at 187–190, 87 S.Ct., at 2010–2012. From the legislative history, the Court reasoned that Congress did not intend to prohibit unions from fining present members, as this was an internal matter. The Court has emphasized that the crux of *Allis–Chalmers'* holding was the distinction between "internal and external enforcement of union rules...." Scofield v. NLRB, 394 U.S., at 428, 89 S.Ct., at 1157. See also NLRB v. Boeing Co., 412 U.S. 67, 73, 93 S.Ct. 1952, 1956, 36 L.Ed.2d 752 (1973).

The Congressional purpose to preserve unions' control over their own "internal affairs" does not suggest an intent to authorize restrictions on the right to resign. Traditionally, union members were free to resign and escape union discipline.[11] In 1947, union constitutional provisions restricting the right to resign were uncommon, if not unknown.[12] Therefore, allowing unions to "extend an employee's membership obligation through restrictions on resignation" would "expan[d] the definition of internal action" beyond the contours envisioned by the Taft–Hartley Congress. International Assn. of Machinists, Local 1414 (Neufeld Porsche–Audi, Inc.), 270 N.L.R.B. No. 209, p. 11 (1984).

## C

Language and reasoning from other opinions of this Court confirm that the Board's construction of § 8(b)(1)(A) is reasonable. In Scofield v. NLRB, 394 U.S. 423, 89 S.Ct. 1154, 22 L.Ed.2d 385 (1969), the Court upheld a union rule setting a ceiling on the daily wages that members working on an incentive basis could earn. The union members' freedom to resign was

---

**11.** See Bossert v. Dhuy, 221 N.Y. 342, 365, 117 N.E. 582, 587 (1917) ("The members of the organization ... who are not willing to obey the orders of the organization are at liberty to withdraw therefrom"); Barker Painting Co. v. Brotherhood of Painters, 57 App.D.C. 322, 324, 23 F.2d 743, 745, cert. denied, 276 U.S. 631, 48 S.Ct. 324, 72 L.Ed. 741 (1928)(It is "not unlawful for ... unions to punish a member by fine, suspension, or expulsion for an infraction of the union rules, since membership in the union is purely voluntary"); Bayer v. Brotherhood of Painters, Decorators and Paperhangers of America, Local 301, 108 N.J.Eq. 257, 262, 154 A. 759, 761 (1931)("association is a voluntary one, and the workmen may decline to become members or withdraw from membership, if dissatisfied with the conduct of its affairs"); Mische

v. Kaminski, 127 Pa.Super. 66, 91–92, 193 A. 410, 421 (1937) (members "had a right to leave the union"); Longshore Printing Co. v. Howell, 26 Ore. 527, 540, 38 P. 547, 551 (1894)("No resort can be had to compulsory methods of any kind either to increase, keep up, or retain such membership").

**12.** Our attention has not been called to any provision limiting the right to resign in a union constitution extant in 1947. Indeed, even by the 1970's, very few unions had such restrictions in their constitutions. See Millan, Disciplinary Developments Under § 8(b)(1)(A) of the National Labor Relations Act, 20 Loyola L.Rev. 245, 269 (1974); Wellington, Union Fines and Workers' Rights, 85 Yale L.J. 1022, 1042 (1976).

critical to the Court's decision that the union rule did not "restrain or coerce" the employees within the meaning of § 8(b)(1)(A). It stated that the rule was "reasonably enforced against union members who [were] free to leave the union and escape the rule." *Id.*, at 430, 89 S.Ct., at 1158. The Court deemed it important that if members were unable to take full advantage of their contractual right to earn additional pay, it was because they had "chosen to become *and remain* union members." Id., at 435, 89 S.Ct., at 1160 (emphasis added).

The decision in NLRB v. Textile Workers, 409 U.S. 213, 93 S.Ct. 385, 34 L.Ed.2d 422 (1972), also supports the Board's view that § 8(b)(1)(A) prohibits unions from punishing members not free to resign. There, 31 employees resigned their union membership and resumed working during a strike. We held that fining these former members "restrained or coerced" them, within the meaning of § 8(b)(1)(A). In reaching this conclusion, we said that "the vitality of § 7 requires that the member be free to refrain in November from the actions he endorsed in May." Id., at 217–218, 93 S.Ct., at 387. Restrictions on the right to resign curtail the freedom that the *Textile Workers* Court deemed so important. See also *Machinists*, supra.

### III

Section 8(b)(1)(A) allows unions to enforce only those rules that "impai[r] no policy Congress has imbedded in the labor laws...." *Scofield,* supra, \* \* \* We believe that the inconsistency between union restrictions on the right to resign and the policy of voluntary unionism supports the Board's conclusion that League Law 13 is invalid.

Closed shop agreements, legalized by the Wagner Act in 1935, became quite common in the early 1940's. Under these agreements, employers could hire and retain in their employ only union members in good standing. R. Gorman, Labor Law, ch. 28, § 1, p. 639 (1976). Full union membership was thus compulsory in a closed shop; in order to keep their jobs, employees were required to attend union meetings, support union leaders, and otherwise adhere to union rules. Because of mounting objections to the closed shop, in 1947—after hearings and full consideration—Congress enacted the Taft–Hartley Act. Section 8(a)(3) of that Act effectively eliminated compulsory union membership by outlawing the closed shop. The union security agreements permitted by § 8(a)(3) require employees to pay dues, but an employee cannot be discharged for failing to abide by union rules or policies with which he disagrees.[16]

Full union membership thus no longer can be a requirement of employment. If a new employee refuses formally to join a union and subject himself to its discipline, he cannot be fired. Moreover, no employee can be discharged if he initially joins a union, and subsequently resigns. We think

---

**16.** Under § 8(a)(3), the only aspect of union membership that can be required pursuant to a union shop agreement is the payment of dues. \* \* \* Therefore, an employee required by a union security agreement to assume financial "membership" is not subject to union discipline. Such an employee is a "member" of the union only in the most limited sense.

it noteworthy that § 8(a)(3) protects the employment rights of the dissatisfied member, as well as those of the worker who never assumed full union
membership. By allowing employees to resign from a union at any time,
§ 8(a)(3) protects the employee whose views come to diverge from those of
his union.

League Law 13 curtails this freedom to resign from full union membership. Nevertheless, the petitioners contend that League Law 13 does not
contravene the policy of voluntary unionism imbedded in the Act. They
assert that this provision does not interfere with workers' employment
rights because offending members are not discharged, but only fined. We
find this argument unpersuasive, for a union has not left a "worker's
employment rights inviolate when it exacts [his entire] paycheck in satisfaction of a fine imposed for working." Wellington, Union Fines and
Workers' Rights, 85 Yale L.J. 1022, 1023 (1976). Congress in 1947 sought
to eliminate completely any requirement that the employee maintain full
union membership.[17] Therefore, the Board was justified in concluding that
by restricting the right of employees to resign, League Law 13 impairs the
policy of voluntary unionism.

## IV

We now consider specifically three arguments advanced by petitioners:
(i) union rules restricting the right to resign are protected by the proviso to
§ 8(b)(1)(A); (ii) the legislative history of the Act shows that Congress did
not intend to protect the right of union members to resign; and (iii) labor
unions should be allowed to restrict the right to resign because other
voluntary associations are permitted to do so.

## A

Petitioners first argue that the proviso to § 8(b)(1)(A) expressly allows
unions to place restrictions on the right to resign. The proviso states that
nothing in § 8(b)(1)(A) shall "impair the right of a labor organization to
prescribe its own rules with respect to the acquisition or retention of
membership therein." 29 U.S.C. § 158(b)(1)(A). Petitioners contend that
because League Law 13 places restrictions on the right to withdraw from
the union, it is a "rul[e] with respect to the . . . retention of membership,"
within the meaning of the proviso.[19]

---

**17.** The focus of § 8(a)(3) on employment rights is understandable because union
restrictions on the right to resign were not
an issue in 1947. See n. 12, supra, and accompanying text. Senator Taft, for example, stated that § 8(a)(3), 29 U.S.C. § 158(a)(3), was
designed to prevent the discharge of workers
for reasons other than nonpayment of dues,
93 Cong.Rec. 4885–4886 (1947), because this
was "the usual type of abuse, and is the only
type of abuse testified to." Id., at 4886.

**19.** Justice Blackmun's dissent asserts
that League Law 13 is protected by the proviso because the rule "literally involv[es] the
acquisition and retention of membership."
* * *. This interpretation of the proviso
would authorize *any* union restriction on
the right to resign. The dissent does say
that restrictions on resignation would not be
permitted if they "furthered none of the
purposes of collective action and self-organization." Post, at 3084, n. 5. This limitation
is illusory. An absolute restriction on resig-

Neither the Board nor this Court has ever interpreted the proviso as allowing unions to make rules restricting the right to resign. Rather, the Court has assumed that "rules with respect to the . . . retention of membership" are those that provide for the expulsion of employees from the union. The legislative history of the Taft–Hartley Act is consistent with this interpretation. Senator Holland, the proviso's sponsor, stated that § 8(b)(1)(A) should not outlaw union rules "which ha[ve] to do with the admission *or the expulsion* of members." 93 Cong.Rec. 4271 (1947) (emphasis added). Senator Taft accepted the proviso, for he likewise believed that a union should be free to "refuse [a] man admission to the union, or *expel him from the union.*" Id., at 4272 (emphasis added). Furthermore, the legislative history of the Labor–Management Reporting and Disclosure Act of 1959, 29 U.S.C. § 401 et seq., confirms that the proviso was intended to protect union rules involving admission and expulsion. Accordingly, we find no basis for refusing to defer to the Board's conclusion that League Law 13 is not a "rule with respect to the retention of membership," within the meaning of the proviso.

### B

The petitioners next argue that the legislative history of the Taft–Hartley Act shows that Congress made a considered decision not to protect union members' right to resign. Section 8(c) of the House bill contained a detailed "bill of rights" for labor union members. H.R. 3020, § 8(c), 80th Cong., 1st Sess., at pp. 22–26 (1947). Included was a provision making it an unfair labor practice to "deny to any [union] member the right to resign from the organization at any time." H.R. 3020, supra, § 8(c)(4), at 23. The Senate bill, on the other hand, did not set forth specific employee rights, but stated more generally that it was an unfair labor practice to "restrain or coerce" employees in the exercise of their § 7 rights. H.R. 3020, 80th Cong., 1st Sess., § 8(b)(1)(A), p. 81 (1947)(as passed Senate). The Taft–Hartley Act contains the Senate bill's general language rather than the more specific House prohibitions. See 29 U.S.C. § 158(b)(1)(A). The petitioners contend that the omission of the House provision shows that Congress expressly decided not to protect the "right to resign."

The legislative history does not support this contention. The "right to resign" apparently was included in the original House bill to protect workers unable to resign because of "closed shop" agreements. Union constitutions limiting the right to resign were uncommon in 1947, see n. 12, supra; closed shop agreements, however, often impeded union resignations. The House Report, H.R.Rep. No. 245, 80th Cong., 1st Sess. (1947), confirms that closed shop agreements provided the impetus for the inclusion of a right to resign in the House bill. The report simply states that even under the proposed legislation, employees could be required to pay dues pursuant to union security agreements. Id., at 32. Because the closed

nations would enhance a union's collective bargaining power, as would a rule that prohibited resignations during the life of the collective bargaining agreement. In short, there is no limiting principle to the dissent's reading of the proviso.

shop was outlawed by the Taft–Hartley Act, see § 8(a)(3), 29 U.S.C. § 158(a)(3), it is not surprising that Congress thought it unnecessary explicitly to preserve the right to resign.

Even if § 8(c)(4) of the House bill, H.R. 3020, § 8(c)(4), supra, was directed at restrictive union rules, its omission from the Taft–Hartley Act does not convince us that the Board's construction of § 8(b)(1)(A) is unreasonable. * * * Congress must have been aware that the broad language of § 8(b)(1)(A) would reach some of the same union conduct proscribed by the detailed "bill of rights."

* * * The ambiguous legislative history upon which the petitioners rely falls far short of showing that the Board's interpretation of the Act is unreasonable.

### C

* * * The Court's decision in NLRB v. Marine & Shipbuilding Workers, 391 U.S. 418, 88 S.Ct. 1717, 20 L.Ed.2d 706 (1968), demonstrates that many union rules, although valid under the common law of associations, run afoul of § 8(b)(1)(A) of the Act.[26] There the union expelled a member who failed to comply with a rule requiring the "exhaust[ion of] all remedies and appeals within the Union ... before ... resort to any court or other tribunal outside of the Union." Id., at 421, 88 S.Ct., at 1720. Under the common law, associations may require their members to exhaust all internal remedies. See, *e.g.,* Medical Soc. of Mobile Cty. v. Walker, 245 Ala. 135, 16 So.2d 321 (1944). Nevertheless, the *Marine Workers* Court held that "considerations of public policy" mandated a holding that the union rule requiring exhaustion violated § 8(b)(1)(A), 29 U.S.C. § 158(b)(1)(A). 391 U.S., at 424, 88 S.Ct., at 1721; see also Scofield v. NLRB, 394 U.S., at 430, 89 S.Ct., at 1158 (union rule is invalid under § 8(b)(1)(A) if it "impairs [a] policy Congress has imbedded in the labor laws").

The Board reasonably has concluded that League Law 13 "restrains or coerces" employees, see § 8(b)(1)(A), and is inconsistent with the congres-

---

**26.** Justice Blackmun's dissent suggests that the relationship between a union and its members should be governed by contract law. Post, at 3077. The rationale of this theory is that a member, by joining the union, "enters into a contract, the terms of which are expressed in the union constitution and by laws." Summers, Legal Limitations on Union Discipline, 64 Harv.L.Rev. 1049, 1054 (1951). Marine Workers, 391 U.S. 418, 88 S.Ct. 1717, 20 L.Ed.2d 706, shows, of course, that union discipline cannot be analyzed primarily in terms of the common law of contracts.

The dissent repeatedly refers to the "promise" made by the employees involved in this case. Post, at 3083. Because they were members of the union when League Law 13 was adopted, the dissent reasons that the employees "promised" not to resign during a strike. But the "promise" to which the dissent refers is unlike any other in traditional contract law. As a commentator has recognized:

"Membership in a union contemplates a continuing relationship with changing obligations as the union legislates in monthly meetings or in annual conventions. It creates a complex cluster of rights and duties expressed in a constitution. In short, membership is a special relationship. It is as far removed from the main channel of contract law as the relationships created by marriage, the purchase of a stock certificate, or the hiring of a servant."

Summers, supra, at 1055–1056.

sional policy of voluntary unionism. Therefore, whatever may have been the common law, the Board's interpretation of the Act merits our deference.

## V

The Board has the primary responsibility for applying " 'the general provisions of the Act to the complexities of industrial life.' " * * * Where the Board's construction of the Act is reasonable, it should not be rejected "merely because the courts might prefer another view of the statute." Ford Motor Co. v. NLRB, supra, 441 U.S., at 497, 99 S.Ct., at 1849. In this case, two factors suggest that we should be particularly reluctant to hold that the Board's interpretation of the Act is impermissible. First, in related cases this Court invariably has yielded to Board decisions on whether fines imposed by a union "restrain or coerce" employees. Second, the Board consistently has construed § 8(b)(1)(A) as prohibiting the imposition of fines on employees who have tendered resignations invalid under a union constitution. Therefore, we conclude that the Board's decision here is entitled to our deference. * * *

■ JUSTICE BLACKMUN, with whom JUSTICE BRENNAN and JUSTICE MARSHALL join, dissenting.

Today the Court supinely defers to a divided-vote determination by the National Labor Relations Board that a union commits an unfair labor practice when it enforces a worker's promise to his fellow workers not to resign from his union and return to work during a strike, even though the worker freely made the decision to join the union and freely made the promise not to resign at such a time, and even though union members democratically made the decision to strike in full awareness of that promise. The Court appears to adopt the NLRB's rule that enforcement of any such promise, no matter how limited and no matter how reasonable, violates the breaching worker's right to refrain from concerted activity. The Board's rule, however, finds no support in either the language of §§ 7 and 8(b)(1)(A) of the National Labor Relations Act on which the Court purports to rely, or in the general goals of the Act, which it ignores. Accordingly, the undeserved deference accorded that rule has produced a holding that improperly restricts a union's federally protected right to make and enforce its own rules, and at the same time traduces the broader aim of federal labor policy implicated by this right: to preserve the balance of power between labor and management by guaranteeing workers an effective right to strike.

## I

### A

* * * Sensitive to both the Act's central goal of facilitating collective action, and the Taft–Hartley Act's protection against coercion of employees, the Court previously has interpreted the proviso to distinguish between two kinds of union rules. Reasonable union rules that represent obligations voluntarily incurred by members were intended to be free from federal

regulation under § 8, while union rules that seek to coerce an employee by utilizing the employer's power over his employment status, or otherwise compel him to take on duties or join in concerted activities he never consented to, were intended to be subject to regulation by the Board. Because rules that regulate the relationship between the union and his employer could be used to coerce an employee into becoming involved with the union in order to protect his job, such rules would impair the employee's free association rights. "[T]he repeated refrain throughout the debates on § 8(b)(1)(A) and other sections [was] that Congress did not propose any limitations with respect to the internal affairs of unions, aside from barring enforcement of a union's internal regulations to affect a member's employment status." *Allis-Chalmers,* 388 U.S., at 195, 87 S.Ct., at 2014. * * *

League Law 13 is an internal union rule, a "rule with respect to the acquisition or retention of membership" protected by the proviso to § 8(b)(1)(A). It requires that employees who freely choose to join the union promise to remain members during a strike or lockout, as well as during the time when a strike or lockout appears imminent. In other words, the rule imposes a condition upon members of the bargaining unit who would like to acquire membership rights. The rule stands for the proposition that to become a union member one must be willing to incur a certain obligation upon which others may rely; as such, it is a rule literally involving the acquisition and retention of membership. Conversely, League Law 13 does not in any way affect the relationship between the employee and the employer. An employee who violates the rule does not risk losing his job, and the union cannot seek an employer's coercive assistance in collecting any fine that is imposed. The rule neither coerces a worker to become a union member against his will, nor affects an employee's status as an employee under the Act. Thus, it clearly falls within the powers of any voluntary association to enact and enforce "the requirements and standards of membership itself," so as to permit the association effectively to pursue collective goals. 93 Cong.Rec. 4433 (1947)(remarks of Sen. Ball).

### B

* * * Congress explicitly has rejected the Court's interpretation of §§ 7 and 8(b)(1)(A). The "right to refrain" language upon which the Court relies was contained in § 7(a) of the House version of the Act, H.R. 3020, 80th Cong., 1st Sess. (1947)(House bill). Section 7 of the House bill was divided into subsection (a), granting "employees" the right to refrain from concerted activity, and subsection (b), granting "members of any labor organization" rights concerning the "affairs of the organization." Corresponding to these provisions were § 8(b), which made it an unfair labor practice for anyone to interfere with an employee's § 7(a) rights, and § 8(c), which made it an unfair labor practice to interfere with an employee's § 7(b) rights. In particular, § 8(c) created a bill of rights for union members in their dealings with their union, establishing 10 unfair labor practices which regulated the major facets of the member-union relationship. Among these specifically enumerated rights was § 8(c)(4), which

made it an unfair labor practice "to deny to any member the right to resign from the organization at any time." * * *

It is critical to an understanding of the Taft–Hartley bill, therefore, to recognize that the Senate explicitly *rejected* the House bill's §§ 7(b) and 8(c). It did so not, as the Court intimates, because it considered the specific provisions of §§ 7(b) and 8(c) to encompass the "right to refrain" language adopted from § 7(a), but because it decided that "the formulation of a code of rights for individual members of trade unions ... should receive more extended study by a special joint congressional committee." S.Rep. No. 105, 80th Cong., 1st Sess., 2 (1947). * * * In the face of this substantial legislative history indicating that the House provisions were rejected on the merits, the Court's treatment of that history, see ante, is both inaccurate and inadequate.[1] * * *

The Court also attempts to justify its result by suggesting that League Law 13 impairs a federal labor policy mandating "voluntary unionism" implicit in § 8(a)(3) of the Act, and thus is unenforceable under § 8(a)(1) of the Act. * * *

The Court, however, again ignores the distinction between internal and external rules fashioned in its prior cases, and so misunderstands the concept of "voluntary unionism" implicated by the Act. The purpose of the union unfair labor practice provisions added to § 8(a)(3) was to "preven[t] the union from inducing the employer to use the emoluments of the job to enforce the union's rules." *Scofield*, 394 U.S., at 429, 89 S.Ct., at 1157. * * *

The proviso serves a fundamentally different purpose—to make manifest that § 8 did not grant the Board the authority to impair the basic right of all membership associations to establish their own reasonable membership rules. League Law 13 is such a rule. It binds members to a reciprocal promise not to resign and return to work during a strike. It does not involve use of the employer's power or affect an individual's employment status, and so does not implicate § 8(a)(3). A member who violates the union rule may be fined, or even expelled from the union, but his employment status remains unaffected. Despite the Court's suggestions to the contrary, "voluntary unionism" does not require that an employee who has freely chosen to join a union and retain his membership therein, in full knowledge that by those decisions he has accepted specified obligations to other members, nevertheless has a federally protected right to disregard those obligations at will, regardless of the acts of others taken in reliance on them. * * *

---

**1.** Moreover, any claim that the language of § 8(b)(1)(A) as enacted is broad enough to allow the Board to find in it a prohibition on union rules governing the right to resign ignores the fact that the Senate also rejected the House's broader version of *that* section that at least would have lent some support for that assertion. In particular, the Senate rejected the House's proscription on union efforts "by intimidating practices ... to compel or seek to compel any individual to become *or remain* a member of any labor organization." See H.R. 3020, 80th Cong., 1st Sess., § 8(b)(1)(1947)(emphasis added).

## II

Congress' decision not to intervene in the internal affairs of a union reflects Congress' understanding that membership in a union—if not a precondition for one's right to employment—is a freely chosen membership in a voluntary association. The Court therefore has looked to "the law which normally is reflected in our free institutions" to determine whether any given membership rule is lawful. NLRB v. Textile Workers, 409 U.S., at 216, 93 S.Ct., at 387. And the common law of associations establishes that an association may place reasonable restrictions on its members' right to resign where such restrictions are designed to further a basic purpose for which the association was formed—here, where the restriction "reflects a legitimate union interest." *Scofield,* 394 U.S., at 430, 89 S.Ct., at 1158. The Pattern Makers evidently promulgated League Law 13 to protect the common interest in maintaining a united front during an economic strike. Such a rule protects individual union members' decisions to place their own and their families' welfare at risk in reliance on the reciprocal decisions of their fellow workers, and furthers the union's ability to bargain with the employer on equal terms, as envisioned by the Act. As such, the rule comports with the broader goals of federal labor policy, which guarantees workers the right to collective action and, in particular, the right to strike. * * * As such, League Law 13 is a condition on union membership that a union might reasonably impose to advance its legitimate ends, and so is an internal union rule protected by the proviso preserving a union's right to enact reasonable rules defining the conditions of union membership. * * *

[The separate concurring opinion of Justice White and the separate dissenting opinion of Justice Stevens are omitted.]

---

## PROBLEM FOR DISCUSSION

Would the Board and Supreme Court in the *Pattern Makers* case have concluded that the union acted lawfully had it—rather than impose a fine—subjected the resigning members to suspension of or expulsion from membership, such that they would be barred from becoming union members for a fixed or indefinite future period? See Food & Commercial Workers Local 81 (MacDonald Meat Co.), 284 NLRB 1084 (1987).

---

### UNION DISCIPLINE OF SUPERVISORS

In certain industries, most notably in construction, supervisors are typically members of the union that represents the rank-and-file workers. This is largely so because jobs are mobile and short-lived and a person working one day as a supervisor may work the next in a nonsupervisory position; supervisors retain their membership because it carries with it economic benefits in the form of pensions, life insurance, and death benefits which have been accruing while working in the rank and file. On occasion, a supervisor is placed in a position of conflicting loyalties when service to an employer is condemned by the union and results in union disciplinary action such as expulsion, suspension or fines. This will often happen when the supervisor reports to work through a picket line in the course of a strike.

Neither the supervisor nor the employer can properly file a charge under § 8(b)(1)(A), because that protects only "employees" against union coercion. Nonetheless, redress against union discipline can be available under § 8(b)(1)(B), which proscribes union coercion or restraint of "an employer in the selection of his representatives for the purposes of collective bargaining or the adjustment of grievances." Core examples of violations of that section, as cited in the legislative history of the Taft–Hartley Act of 1947, are a union's coercing an employer into joining or resigning from an employer association that negotiates labor contracts, or a union's insistence upon the removal of a personnel director or supervisor who has the function of settling grievances.

After some twenty years of thus literally construing § 8(b)(1)(B), the NLRB—in SAN FRANCISCO-OAKLAND MAILERS' UNION 18, 172 NLRB 2173 (1968)—applied the section more broadly to outlaw union fines of members who, acting as foremen, had interpreted the labor contract to authorize their assigning work to persons outside the bargaining unit. The union was held to have exerted pressure on the employer through indirection, by attempting through fining the supervisors to force a change in their attitudes rather than a change of persons assigned by the employer to such positions.

This broadening of the ban in § 8(b)(1)(B) beyond its literal language has been considered by the Supreme Court in three cases (each involving a divided Court), each testing the limits of the union's power to discipline supervisors in different factual situations.

In FLORIDA POWER & LIGHT CO. v. ELECTRICAL WORKERS, 417 U.S. 790, 94 S.Ct. 2737, 41 L.Ed.2d 477 (1974), the Court set aside a Board order and held that a union could lawfully impose fines upon supervisor-members who report to work during a strike in order to perform "rank-and-file work" that would otherwise be done by the strikers. The Court assumed, without deciding, the correctness of the *Oakland Mailers* principle that § 8(b)(1)(B) could be violated by disciplinary action against supervisor-members rather than by direct union pressure on the employer. But this would be so, held the Court, "only when that discipline may adversely affect the supervisor's conduct in performing the duties of, and acting in his capacity as, grievance adjuster or collective bargainer on behalf of the employer." That was not so in the case before the Court. Even though the fines for doing struck work might induce a more attenuated loyalty to the employer, that was not the precise concern for employer interests manifested by Congress in the statute.

The congressional concern was, however, found by the Court to be implicated in its decision, soon after, in AMERICAN BROADCASTING COMPANIES, INC. v. WRITERS GUILD OF AMERICA, WEST, INC., 437 U.S. 411, 98 S.Ct. 2423, 57

L.Ed.2d 313 (1978). There, a union imposed sanctions including expulsion and suspension from membership, and heavy fines, upon members who, as television and film directors, did supervisory work during a strike, including handling grievances of actors and writers. The Court held that the Board's use of the *Oakland Mailers* principle to forbid union discipline of supervisor-members for actually engaging in grievance adjustment represented an "acceptable reading of the statutory language and a reasonable implementation" of the statute's purposes. Although a union generally has the right to impose economic sanctions on members during a strike, "an employer also has economic rights during a strike, and the statute declares that, in the unrestrained freedom to select a grievance-adjustment and collective-bargaining representative, the employer's rights dominate. * * * Union pressure on supervisors can affect either their willingness to serve as grievance adjustors or collective bargainers, or the manner in which they fulfill these functions; and either effect impermissibly coerces the employer in his choice of representative."

Nearly ten years later, however, the Court concluded that the NLRB had gone too far in expanding the application of § 8(b)(1)(B) to bar certain union discipline of supervisors. In NLRB v. IBEW, LOCAL 340 (ROYAL ELECTRIC), 481 U.S. 573, 107 S.Ct. 2002, 95 L.Ed.2d 557 (1987), the union fined two members who, working as supervisors, violated a provision in the union constitution barring work for any employer that did not have a collective bargaining relationship with that union; the supervisor-members had worked for two companies whose employees were represented by another union, and they had done work of a general supervisory nature without doing any collective bargaining or grievance adjustment. The NLRB applied its so-called reservoir doctrine: present supervisors provide the reservoir from which the employer will in the future select persons to do such bargaining and grievance adjustment, so that were the present supervisors to respond to the union's fines by giving up their work for their employers, the latter would be deprived of their grievance-adjustment services in the future.

The Court found this series of suppositions to be far too speculative and the impact on employer selection of bargainers and grievance adjusters too remote. The reservoir doctrine would reach so far as to outlaw union pressure against all supervisors, while the sheltered supervisory cadre in § 8(b)(1)(B) is meant to be far smaller. Moreover, the Court noted that the union in question had no bargaining relationship with the employers, and was seeking none. That was another reason why any impact on bargaining or grievance-adjusting services was much too speculative.

The Court in *Royal Electric* concluded by observing that even if the union's fines did create a conflict of loyalties for the supervisor-members, this was of the employers' own making. The statute gives the employer the right to eliminate such conflict by hiring as supervisors only persons who are not union members or by requiring union members promptly to resign their membership (a member's right upheld by the Court in the *Pattern Makers* case, supra). It could well be—if the Court were to pursue this point to its logical conclusion—that § 8(b)(1)(B) would not be violated at all by union discipline of supervisors, regardless of the kind of work they do, and that it would be violated only by direct union pressure on an employer to change its bargaining or grievance-adjustment representatives. Would that outcome be truer to the statutory language and purpose? Would it be an altogether fair outcome?

---

## B.  JUDICIAL SUPERVISION OF UNION DISCIPLINE[c]

Although the Labor Management Reporting and Disclosure Act does not insulate the member against all forms of unreasonable or arbitrary union discipline, Section 101 of the Act does protect members in exercising a number of political rights within the union, *e.g.*, by requiring that they be given equal rights to nominate candidates and to vote, and that all members be given the right to attend meetings, to express their views on union business and so forth. In addition, Section 101(a)(5) of the LMRDA requires that before any union member may be expelled or disciplined for any reason other than non-payment of dues he must receive specific written charges, be given a reasonable time to prepare his defense and be afforded a "full and fair hearing."

For many years prior to the passage of the LMRDA, state courts had undertaken to review the disciplinary action of labor unions. In so doing, state courts have often been guided by very similar principles to those now embodied in Section 101 of the LMRDA, but they have also exercised still broader powers of review either by insisting that disciplinary action conform to the provisions of the union constitution and by-laws or by declaring certain types of disciplinary action to be void as contrary to public policy. As a result, bearing in mind that Section 103 of the LMRDA leaves the jurisdiction of state courts undisturbed, the "common law" of union disciplinary action deserves to be considered together with the case law under the federal act.

The materials that follow have been divided into three sections. The first section is devoted to the problems that have arisen in interpreting Section 101 of the LMRDA. These problems fall into three general categories: the kind of union action that constitutes "discipline" within the reach of the Act; the kind of member conduct which a union may properly subject to discipline; and the procedures which the union must utilize before imposing discipline. The second section deals with the regulation of union discipline by state courts, through the application of common law principles. As just noted, these principles may go beyond those of the LMRDA in limiting such discipline. The third section takes up the requirement that internal union remedies be exhausted prior to bringing suit to challenge

---

**c.** For a general discussion see Summers, Legal Limitations on Union Discipline, 64 Harv.L.Rev. 1049 (1951); and, by the same author, The Law of Union Discipline: What the Courts Do in Fact, 70 Yale L.J. 175 (1960).

union discipline—a requirement commonly observed by state courts and carried forward in a modified form under the LMRDA.

---

## 1.   THE DISCIPLINE OF UNION MEMBERS UNDER THE LABOR–MANAGEMENT REPORTING AND DISCLOSURE ACT[d]

Section 101(a)(5) of the Landrum–Griffin Act requires the union to observe the procedural safeguards of a "full and fair hearing" before a member is "fined, suspended, expelled, or otherwise disciplined" by the union or its officers. Section 609 makes it unlawful for the union "to fine, suspend, expel or otherwise discipline" any member for exercising rights provided him under the Act. What, then, is "discipline" within the meaning of these provisions?

To constitute "discipline," first of all, it is necessary that the alleged sanction be imposed by union officers acting in their official capacities. As for the nature of the sanction itself, some courts have suggested that "discipline" exists only when the member is injured or deprived in such a way as to affect his rights *qua* union member. Under this view, no "discipline" would result from the failure of union officials to protest the discharge of a member by an employer or even from a union official's request that the employer suspend a member from work. See, *e.g.,* Turner v. Local Lodge No. 455 of the Intern. Broth. of Boilermakers, 755 F.2d 866 (11th Cir.1985); Allen v. Armored Car Chauffeurs and Guards, Local 820, 185 F.Supp. 492 (D.N.J.1960). Other courts, however, have taken a broader view; they would interpret "discipline" under Section 609 to include any union action which harms a member in retaliation for the exercise of his rights under the Act. The same courts would interpret "discipline" under Section 101(a)(5) to include any action imposing any detriment upon a member because of his conduct as a union member. See, *e.g.,* Scovile v. Watson, 338 F.2d 678 (7th Cir.1964), cert. denied, 380 U.S. 963, 85 S.Ct. 1107, 14 L.Ed.2d 154 (1965). Which is the preferable reading of the LMRDA?

---

**d.** See Aaron, The Labor–Management Reporting & Disclosure Act of 1959, 73 Harv. L.Rev. 851 (1960); Atleson, A Union Member's Right of Free Speech and Assembly: Institutional Interests and Individual Rights, 51 Minn.L.Rev. 403 (1967); Beaird & Player, Free Speech and the Landrum–Griffin Act, 25 Ala.L.Rev. 577 (1973); Beaird & Player, Union Discipline of its Membership Under Section 101(a)(5) of Landrum–Griffin: What is "Discipline" and How Much Process is Due?, 9 Ga.L.Rev. 383 (1975); Bellace & Berkowitz, The Landrum–Griffin Act—Twenty Years of Federal Protection of Union Members' Rights (1979); Cox, Internal Affairs of Labor Unions Under the Labor Reform Act of 1959, 58 Mich.L.Rev. 819 (1960); Etelson & Smith, Union Discipline Under the Landrum–Griffin Act, 82 Harv.L.Rev. 727 (1969); McLaughlin & Schoomaker, The Landrum–Griffin Act and Union Democracy (1979); Summers, The Law of Union Discipline: What the Courts Do in Fact, 70 Yale L.J. 175 (1960); Summers, Legal Limitations on Union Discipline, 64 Harv.L.Rev. 1049 (1951).

# Finnegan v. Leu

456 U.S. 431, 102 S.Ct. 1867, 72 L.Ed.2d 239 (1982).

■ Chief Justice Burger delivered the opinion of the Court.

The question presented in this case is whether the discharge of a union's appointed business agents by the union president, following his election over the candidate supported by the business agents, violated the Labor Management Reporting and Disclosure Act of 1959, 73 Stat. 534, 29 U.S.C. § 401 et seq. The Court of Appeals held that the Act did not protect the business agents from discharge. We granted certiorari to resolve circuit conflicts. 454 U.S. 813, 102 S.Ct. 89, 70 L.Ed.2d 82 (1981), and we affirm.

## I

In December 1977, respondent Harold Leu defeated Omar Brown in an election for the presidency of Local 20 of the International Brotherhood of Teamsters, Chauffeurs, Warehousemen and Helpers of America, a labor organization representing workers in a 14 county area of northwestern Ohio. During the vigorously contested campaign, petitioners, then business agents of Local 20, openly supported the incumbent President, Brown. Upon assuming office in January 1978, Leu discharged petitioners and the Local's other business agents, all of whom had been appointed by Brown following his election in 1975. Leu explained that he felt the agents were loyal to Brown, not to him, and therefore would be unable to follow and implement his policies and programs.

Local 20's Bylaws—which were adopted by, and may be amended by, a vote of the union membership—provide that the President shall have authority to appoint, direct, and discharge the Union's business agents. Bylaws of Teamsters, Chauffeurs, Warehousemen and Helpers Union Local No. 20, Art. IX, § 3D, Joint Exhibit 1, at 15. The duties of the business agents include participation in the negotiating of collective bargaining agreements, organizing of union members, and processing of grievances. In addition, the business agents, along with the President, other elected officers, and shop stewards, sit as members of the Stewards Council, the legislative assembly of the Union. Petitioners had come up through the union ranks, and as business agents they were also members of Local 20. Discharge from their positions as business agents did not render petitioners ineligible to continue their union membership.

Petitioners filed suit in the United States District Court, alleging that they had been terminated from their appointed positions in violation of the Labor Management Reporting and Disclosure Act, 29 U.S.C. §§ 411(a)(1), 411(a)(2), 412, and 529. The District Court granted summary judgment for respondents Leu and Local 20, holding that the Act does not protect a union employee from discharge by the president of the union if the employee's rights as a union member are not affected. 469 F.Supp. 832. The United States Court of Appeals for the Sixth Circuit affirmed, concluding "that a union president should be able to work with those who will cooperate with his program and carry out his directives, and that these business agents, who served at the pleasure of the union president, and actively supported the president's opponent could be removed from their employment as union business agents." App. to Pet. for Cert. A3.

## II

\* \* \*

Sections 101(a)(1) and (2) of the Act, 29 U.S.C. §§ 411(a)(1) and (2), on which petitioners rely, guarantee equal voting rights, and rights of speech and assembly, to "[e]very *member* of a labor organization" (emphasis added). In addition, § 609 of the Act, 29 U.S.C. § 529, renders it unlawful for a union or its representatives "to fine, suspend, expel, or otherwise discipline any of its *members* for exercising any right to which he is entitled under the provisions of [the Act]." (Emphasis added). It is readily apparent, both from the language of these provisions and from the legislative history of Title I, that it was rank and file union members—not union officers or employees, as such—whom Congress sought to protect.

Petitioners held a dual status as both employees and members of the Union. As *members* of Local 20, petitioners undoubtedly had a protected right to campaign for Brown and support his candidacy. At issue here is whether they were thereby immunized from discharge at the pleasure of the President from their positions as appointed union *employees*.

## III

Petitioners contend that discharge from a position as a union employee constitutes "discipline" within the meaning of § 609; and that termination of union employment is therefore unlawful when predicated upon an employee's exercise of rights guaranteed to members under the Act. However, we conclude that the term "discipline," as used in § 609, refers only to retaliatory actions that affect a union member's rights or status *as a member* of the union. Section 609 speaks in terms of disciplining "members"; and the three disciplinary sanctions specifically enumerated—fine, suspension, and expulsion—are all punitive actions taken against union members as members. In contrast, discharge from union employment does not impinge upon the incidents of union membership, and affects union members only to the extent that they happen also to be union employees. See Sheridan v. Carpenters Local No. 626, 306 F.2d 152, 156 (C.A.3 1962). We discern nothing in § 609, or its legislative history, to support petitioners' claim that Congress intended to establish a system of job security or tenure for appointed union employees.

Congress used essentially the same language elsewhere in the Act with the specific intent not to protect a member's status as a union employee or officer. Section 101(a)(5), 29 U.S.C. § 411(a)(5), states that "[n]o member of any labor organization may be fined, suspended, expelled, or otherwise disciplined" without enumerated procedural protections. The Conference Report accompanying S. 1555 as finally enacted, H.R.Rep. 1147, 86th Cong., 1st Sess. 31 (1959), I Leg.Hist. 935, explains that this "prohibition on suspension without observing certain safeguards applies only to suspension of membership in the union; *it does not refer to suspension of a member's status as an officer of the union*" (emphasis added). This too is a persuasive indication that the virtually identical language in § 609 was likewise meant to refer only to punitive actions diminishing membership rights, and not to termination of a member's status as an appointed union employee.

We hold, therefore, that removal from appointive union employment is not within the scope of those union sanctions explicitly prohibited by § 609.

## IV

Our analysis is complicated, however, by the fact that § 102, 29 U.S.C. § 412, provides independent authority for a suit against a union based on an alleged violation of Title I of the Act. Section 102 states that

> "[a]ny person whose rights secured by the provisions of this subchapter [Title I of the Act] have been infringed by any violation of this subchapter may bring a civil action in a district court of the United States for such relief (including injunctions) as may be appropriate."

Although the intended relationship between §§ 102 and 609 is not entirely clear, it seems evident that a litigant may maintain an action under § 102—to redress an "infringement" of "rights secured" under Title I— without necessarily stating a violation of § 609.

The question still remains, however, whether petitioners' "rights secured" under Title I were "infringed" by the termination of their union employment. Petitioners, as union members, had a right under §§ 101(a)(1) and (2) to campaign for Brown and to vote in the union election, but they were not prevented from exercising those rights. Rather, petitioners allege only an *indirect* interference with their membership rights, maintaining that they were forced to "choos[e] between the right to free expression * * * and their jobs." See Retail Clerks Union Local 648 v. Retail Clerks International Ass'n, 299 F.Supp. 1012, 1021 (D.D.C.1969).

We need not decide whether the retaliatory discharge of a union member from union office—even though not "discipline" prohibited under § 609—might ever give rise to a cause of action under § 102. For whatever limits Title I places on a union's authority to utilize dismissal from union office as "part of a purposeful and deliberate attempt to suppress dissent within the union," cf. Schonfeld v. Penza, 477 F.2d 899, 904 (C.A.2 1973), it does not restrict the freedom of an elected union leader to choose a staff whose views are compatible with his own.[11] Indeed, neither the language nor the legislative history of the Act suggests that it was intended even to address the issue of union patronage.[12] To the contrary, the Act's over-

---

**11.** We leave open the question whether a different result might obtain in a case involving nonpolicymaking and nonconfidential employees.

**12.** We think it virtually inconceivable that Congress would have prohibited the longstanding practice of union patronage without any discussion in the legislative history of the Act. See Wood v. Dennis, 489 F.2d

riding objective was to ensure that unions would be democratically governed, and responsive to the will of the union membership as expressed in open, periodic elections. See Wirtz v. Hotel Employees, Local 6, 391 U.S. 492, 497, 88 S.Ct. 1743, 1746, 20 L.Ed.2d 763 (1968). Far from being inconsistent with this purpose, the ability of an elected union president to select his own administrators is an integral part of ensuring a union administration's responsiveness to the mandate of the union election. * * *

No doubt this poses a dilemma for some union employees; if they refuse to campaign for the incumbent they risk his displeasure, and by supporting him risk the displeasure of his successor. However, in enacting Title I of the Act, Congress simply was not concerned with perpetuating appointed union employees in office at the expense of an elected president's freedom to choose his own staff. Rather, its concerns were with promoting union democracy, and protecting the rights of union *members* from arbitrary action by the union or its officers.

We therefore conclude that petitioners have failed to establish a violation of the Act. Accordingly, the decision of the Court of Appeals is affirmed.

[The concurring opinion of JUSTICE BLACKMUN is omitted.]

---

## Sheet Metal Workers' Int'l Ass'n v. Lynn

488 U.S. 347, 109 S.Ct. 639, 102 L.Ed.2d 700 (1989).

■ JUSTICE MARSHALL delivered the opinion of the Court.

In Finnegan v. Leu, 456 U.S. 431, 102 S.Ct. 1867, 72 L.Ed.2d 239 (1982), we held that the discharge of a union's appointed business agents by the union president, following his election over the incumbent for whom the business agents had campaigned, did not violate the Labor–Management Reporting and Disclosure Act of 1959 (LMRDA or Act), 73 Stat. 519, 29 U.S.C. § 401 et seq. The question presented in this case is whether the removal of an elected business agent, in retaliation for statements he made at a union meeting in opposition to a dues increase sought by the union trustee, violated the LMRDA. * * *

I

In June, 1981, respondent Edward Lynn was elected to a 3–year term as a business representative of petitioner Local 75 of the Sheet Metal Workers' International Association (Local), an affiliate of petitioner Sheet Metal Workers' International Association (International). Lynn was instrumental in organizing fellow members of the Local who were concerned

---

849, 858 (C.A.7 1973)(en banc)(Stevens, J., concurring). Had such a result been contemplated, it undoubtedly would have encountered substantial resistance. Moreover, Congress likely would have made some express accommodation to the needs of union employers to appoint and remove policymaking officials. See id.

about a financial crisis plaguing the Local. These members, who called themselves the Sheet Metal Club Local 75 (Club), published leaflets that demonstrated, on the basis of Department of Labor statistics, that the Local's officials were spending far more than the officials of two other sheet metal locals in the area. The Club urged the Local's officials to reduce expenditures rather than increase dues in order to alleviate the Local's financial problems. A majority of the Local's members apparently agreed, for they defeated three successive proposals to increase dues.

Following the third vote, in June 1982, the Local's 17 officials, including Lynn, sent a letter to the International's General President, requesting that he "immediately take whatever action [is] . . . necessary including, but not limited to, trusteeship to put this local on a sound financial basis." App. 14. Invoking his authority under the International's constitution, the General President responded by placing the Local under a trusteeship and by delegating to the trustee, Richard Hawkins, the authority "to supervise and direct" the affairs of the Local, "including, but not limited to, the authority to suspend local union . . . officers, business managers, or business representatives." Art. 3, § 2(c), Constitution and Ritual of the Sheet Metal Workers' International Association, Revised and Amended by Authority of the Thirty–Fifth General Convention, St. Louis, Missouri (1978).

Within a month of his appointment, Hawkins decided that a dues increase was needed to rectify the Local's financial situation. Recognizing that he lacked authority to impose a dues increase unilaterally, Hawkins prepared a proposal to that effect which he submitted to and which was approved by the Local's executive board. A special meeting was then convened to put the dues proposal to a membership vote. Prior to the meeting, Hawkins advised Lynn that he expected Lynn's support. Lynn responded that he first wanted a commitment to reduce expenditures, which Hawkins declined to provide. Lynn thus spoke in opposition to the dues proposal at the special meeting. The proposal was defeated by the members in a secret ballot vote. Five days later, Hawkins notified Lynn that he was being removed "indefinitely" from his position as business representative specifically because of his outspoken opposition to the dues increase. App. 20.

After exhausting his intraunion remedies, Lynn brought suit in District Court under § 102 of the LMRDA, 29 U.S.C. § 412, claiming *inter alia* that his removal from office violated § 101(a)(2), the free speech provision of Title I of the LMRDA, 29 U.S.C. § 411(a)(2).[2] The District Court granted

---

**2.** Section 101(a)(2) of the LMRDA, titled "Freedom of Speech and Assembly," provides:

"Every member of any labor organization shall have the right to meet and assemble freely with other members; and to express any views, arguments, or opinions; and to express at meetings of the labor organization his views, upon candidates in an election of the labor organization or upon any business properly before the meeting, subject to the organization's established and reasonable rules pertaining to the conduct of meetings: *Provided*, That nothing herein shall be construed to impair the right of a labor organization to adopt and enforce reasonable rules as to the responsibility of

summary judgment for petitioners, reasoning that, under Finnegan v. Leu, supra, "[a] union member's statutory right to oppose union policies affords him no protection against dismissal from employment as an agent of the union because of such opposition." App. to Pet. for Cert. 36a.

The Court of Appeals for the Ninth Circuit reversed. * * *

## II

The LMRDA "was the product of congressional concern with widespread abuses of power by union leadership." *Finnegan,* 456 U.S., at 435, 102 S.Ct., at 1870. The major reform bills originally introduced in the Senate, as well as the bill ultimately reported out of the Committee on Labor and Public Welfare, S. 1555, 86th Cong., 1st Sess. (1959), dealt primarily with disclosure requirements, elections, and trusteeships. The legislation that evolved into Title I of the LMRDA, the "Bill of Rights of Members of Labor Organizations," was adopted as an amendment on the Senate floor by "legislators [who] feared that the bill did not go far enough because it did not provide general protection to union members who spoke out against the union leadership." Steelworkers v. Sadlowski, 457 U.S. 102, 109, 102 S.Ct. 2339, 2344, 72 L.Ed.2d 707 (1982). "[D]esigned to guarantee every member equal voting rights, rights of free speech and assembly, and a right to sue," ibid., the amendment was "aimed at enlarged protection for members of unions paralleling certain rights guaranteed by the Federal Constitution." *Finnegan,* 456 U.S., at 435, 102 S.Ct., at 1870. In providing such protection, Congress sought to further the basic objective of the LMRDA: "ensuring that unions [are] democratically governed and responsive to the will of their memberships." * * *

We considered this basic objective in *Finnegan,* where several members of a local union who held staff positions as business agents were discharged by the local's newly elected president. The business agents had been appointed by the incumbent president and had openly supported him in his unsuccessful re-election campaign. They subsequently sought relief under § 102 of the LMRDA, claiming that discharge from their appointed positions constituted an "infringement" of their free speech and equal voting rights as guaranteed by Title I.

We held that the business agents could not establish a violation of § 102 because their claims were inconsistent with the LMRDA's "overriding objective" of democratic union governance. 456 U.S., at 441, 102 S.Ct., at 1873. Permitting a victorious candidate to appoint his own staff did not frustrate that objective; rather, it ensured a union's "responsiveness to the mandate of the union election." Ibid. We thus concluded that

---

every member toward the organization as an institution and to his refraining from conduct that would interfere with its performance of its legal or contractual obligations." 73 Stat. 522.

Section 102 provides in relevant part:

"Any person whose rights secured by the provisions of this title have been infringed by any violation of this title may bring a civil action in a district court of the United States for such relief (including injunctions) as may be appropriate." Id., at 523.

the LMRDA did not "restrict the freedom of an elected union leader to choose a staff whose views are compatible with his own." Ibid. In rejecting the business agents' claim, we did not consider whether the retaliatory removal of an elected official violates the LMRDA and, if so, whether it is significant that the removal is carried out under a validly imposed trusteeship. It is to these questions that we now turn.

### A

Petitioners argue that Lynn's Title I rights were not "infringed" for purposes of § 102 because Lynn, like other members of the Local, was not prevented from attending the special meeting, expressing his views on Hawkins' dues proposal, or casting his vote, and because he remains a member of the Local. Under this view, Lynn's status as an elected, rather than an appointed, official is essentially immaterial and the loss of union employment cannot amount to a Title I violation.

This argument is unpersuasive. In the first place, we acknowledged in *Finnegan* that the business agents' Title I rights had been interfered with, albeit indirectly, because the agents had been forced to choose between their rights and their jobs. See id., at 440, 442, 102 S.Ct., at 1872, 1873. This was so even though the business agents were not actually prevented from exercising their Title I rights. The same is true here. Lynn was able to attend the special meeting, to express views in opposition to Hawkins' dues proposal, and to cast his vote. In taking these actions, Lynn "was exercising . . . membership right[s] protected by section 101(a)." 804 F.2d, at 1479. Given that Lynn was removed from his post as a direct result of his decision to express disagreement with Hawkins' dues proposal at the special meeting, and that his removal presumably discouraged him from speaking out in the future, Lynn paid a price for the exercise of his membership rights.

This is not, of course, the end of the analysis. Whether such interference with Title I rights gives rise to a cause of action under § 102 must be judged by reference to the LMRDA's basic objective: "to ensure that unions [are] democratically governed, and responsive to the will of the union membership as expressed in open, periodic elections." *Finnegan,* 456 U.S., at 441, 102 S.Ct., at 1873. In *Finnegan,* this goal was furthered when the newly elected union president discharged the appointed staff of the ousted incumbent. Indeed, the basis for the *Finnegan* holding was the recognition that the newly elected president's victory might be rendered meaningless if a disloyal staff were able to thwart the implementation of his programs. While such patronage-related discharges had some chilling effect on the free speech rights of the business agents, we found this concern outweighed by the need to vindicate the democratic choice made by the union electorate.

The consequences of the removal of an elected official are much different. To begin with, when an elected official like Lynn is removed from his post, the union members are denied the representative of their choice. Indeed, Lynn's removal deprived the membership of his leadership, knowledge and advice at a critical time for the Local. His removal, therefore, hardly was "an integral part of ensuring a union administration's responsiveness to the mandate of the union election." Ibid.; see also Wirtz v. Hotel Employees, 391 U.S. 492, 497, 88 S.Ct. 1743, 1746–47, 20 L.Ed.2d 763 (1968).

Furthermore, the potential chilling effect of Title I free speech rights is more pronounced when elected officials are discharged. Not only is the fired official likely to be chilled in the exercise of his own free speech rights, but so are the members who voted for him. See Hall v. Cole, 412 U.S. 1, 8, 93 S.Ct. 1943, 1947–48, 36 L.Ed.2d 702 (1973). Seeing Lynn removed from his post just five days after he led the fight to defeat yet another dues increase proposal, other members of the Local may well have concluded that one challenged the union's hierarchy, if at all, at one's peril. This is precisely what Congress sought to prevent when it passed the LMRDA. "It recognized that democracy would be assured only if union members are free to discuss union policies and criticize the leadership without fear of reprisal." *Sadlowski,* 457 U.S., at 112, 102 S.Ct., at 2346. We thus hold that Lynn's retaliatory removal stated a cause of action under § 102.

### B

Petitioners next contend that, even if the removal of an elected official for the exercise of his Title I rights ordinarily states a cause of action under § 102, a different result obtains here because Lynn was removed during a trusteeship lawfully imposed under Title III of the LMRDA, 73 Stat. 530–532, 29 U.S.C. §§ 461–466.

We disagree. In the first place, we find nothing in the language of the LMRDA or its legislative history to suggest that Congress intended Title I rights to fall by the wayside whenever a trusteeship is imposed. Had Congress contemplated such a result, we would expect to find some discussion of it in the text of the LMRDA or its legislative history. Given Congress' silence on this point, a trustee's authority under Title III ordinarily should be construed in a manner consistent with the protections provided in Title I. * * *

* * * In order to ensure that the union members' democratic right to decide on a dues proposal is meaningful, the right to exchange views on the advantages and disadvantages of such a measure must be protected. A trustee should not be able to control the debate over an issue which, by statute, is beyond his control. * * * Thus, at the special meeting, Lynn was free to express the view apparently shared by a majority of the Local's members that the best solution to the Local's financial problems was not an increase in dues, but a reduction in expenditures. Under these circumstances, Hawkins violated Lynn's Title I rights when he removed Lynn from his post.

### III

For the reasons stated herein, we conclude that Lynn's removal from his position as business representative constituted a violation of Title I of the LMRDA. Accordingly, the judgment of the Court of Appeals is AF-FIRMED.

[JUSTICE WHITE concurred in the judgment, in a separate opinion.]

---

## PROBLEMS FOR DISCUSSION

**1.** Employee Nance works at the Vernor plant of the Chrysler Corporation, and has been serving as the appointed chairman of the Union's Fair Employment Practices Committee; as chairman, he investigated and reported to management any claims of discrimination on the basis of race, sex, or handicap. When employee Adams was discharged for excessive absenteeism, Nance investigated the case and concluded that the absenteeism was due to Adams's alcoholism, such that discharge was in violation of Michigan law providing protection to the handicapped. When the Union declined to support Nance's position on the Adams discharge, Nance—without exhausting the intra-union appeals procedure—filed an unfair labor practice charge against the Union with the National Labor Relations Board.

Union officials thereupon removed Nance from his position as chairman of the Fair Employment Practices Committee. No salary or employment seniority was lost as a result. Nance claims that he has been disciplined in violation of the LMRDA. The Union claims that it has the right to remove an appointed official "who ignores his duty to represent the Union by filing a meritless charge that disparages the Union he had a duty to serve"; it argues that the policy considerations endorsed by the Supreme Court in the *Finnegan* case also apply here. Should Nance prevail? Would it matter if Nance had been elected as chairman by the union membership?

If Nance had instead filed an unfair labor practice charge with the NLRB, challenging his removal from the committee chairmanship as an unfair labor practice, how should the Board rule? See NLRB v. Local 212, International Union, United Automobile Workers, 690 F.2d 82 (6th Cir.1982).

**2.** Bill Brash, a member of the Sheet Metal Workers Union, typically secures work by referral through the union-operated hiring hall, created pursuant to a multiemployer collective bargaining agreement. The Union, as obliged by law, refers members and nonmembers on a nondiscriminatory basis; and employers can turn down workers referred by the Union, and workers can seek employment through means other than the hiring hall, i.e., the hiring hall is "nonexclusive." Because Brash, in a recent election of Union officials, outspokenly opposed the incumbent Business Manager and Business Agent, the latter have since the election declined to refer Brash through the hiring hall for work. Brash has commenced an action in the federal court for violation of sections 101(a)(5) and 609 of the LMRDA, claiming that the Union—although it has not fined, suspended or expelled him for exercising his right to speak out on election issues—has "otherwise disciplined" him. The Union argues that there has been no "discipline" because of the nonexclusive nature of the hiring hall, and that there is lacking the kind of formal institutional Union action (as opposed to the informal retaliatory action of some Union officers) that the LMRDA calls for in order to found a violation. Has Brash asserted a valid statutory claim? See Breininger v. Sheet Metal Workers Intern. Ass'n Local Union No. 6, 493 U.S. 67, 110 S.Ct. 424, 107 L.Ed.2d 388 (1989).

Does a union impose "discipline," challengeable under the LMRDA, when it disqualifies a member from running in an election for union office on account of his failure to pay an assessment to a fund for the assistance of strikers? See Department of Labor v. Aluminum Workers Local 200, 941 F.2d 1172 (11th Cir.1991).

———

## Salzhandler v. Caputo
316 F.2d 445 (2d Cir.1963).

■ LUMBARD, CHIEF JUDGE. Solomon Salzhandler, a member of Local 442, Brotherhood of Painters, Decorators & Paperhangers of America, brought suit in the district court following the decision of a Trial Board of the union's New York District Council No. 9 that he had untruthfully accused Isadore Webman, the president of the local, of the crime of larceny. The Trial Board found that Salzhandler's "unsupported accusations" violated the union's constitution which prohibited "conduct unbecoming a member * * * ", "acts detrimental to * * * interests of the Brotherhood", "libeling, slandering * * * fellow members [or] officers of local unions" and "acts and conduct * * * inconsistent with the duties, obligations and fealty of a member."

Salzhandler's complaint alleged that his charges against Webman were an exercise of his rights as a member of the union and that the action of the Trial Board was in violation of the provisions of the LMRDA under which he was entitled to relief. * * *

[Salzhandler was serving as financial secretary of Local 442, an elective office, in November 1960, at which time he reviewed the union's checks for purposes of an audit. He found two checks, in the amounts of $800 and $375, which had been used by Webman and by the local's business agent at two union conventions; he also found two union checks, each in the amount of $6.00, representing a refund of union dues (normally paid to the widow) upon the death of the local's business agent. Salzhandler, in a leaflet distributed to members of the local, charged that the larger checks represented expenses well in excess of those to which Webman was entitled, that there was no indication that any part of those checks was used to reimburse the expenses of the business agent, and that the two $6.00 checks were improperly diverted by Webman to unauthorized purposes. The leaflet referred to Webman as a "petty robber," unworthy of trust, and accused him of having referred to union members as "thieves, scabs, robbers, scabby bosses, bums, pimps, f-bums and jail birds." In December 1960, Webman filed charges against Salzhandler with New York District Council No. 9 of the union, alleging that Salzhandler had violated the union constitution by libeling him, that Salzhandler was guilty of conduct inconsistent with his duties as a member and officer of the union, and that Salzhandler had untruthfully accused him of the crime of larceny. A six-hour hearing was conducted in February 1961 before a five-member Trial Board of the District Council, with evidence being presented by both Webman and Salzhandler (who was represented by a union member who was not a lawyer). In early April 1961, Salzhandler was informed by the Trial Board that he was to be removed from office, that he was no longer to participate in the affairs of any local within the union for five years, and that he was to be barred from union meetings, from speaking on the floor at any meetings and from running for any office in any local or in the District Council. Salzhandler filed intraunion appeals, as so provided in the union constitution, but there was no disposition of those appeals at the time he commenced his action in the federal district court. Salzhandler was also prevented from attending a union meeting; he claimed that Webman assaulted him and used violence in removing him. Salzhandler's action pursuant to Section 102 of the LMRDA sought a nullification of the Trial Board's order, reinstatement as financial secretary, and damages.]

Judge Wham dismissed the complaint holding that the Trial Board's conclusion that the leaflet was libelous was sufficiently supported by the evidence. He went further, however, and made an independent finding that the statements were, in fact, libelous. The court held, as a matter of law, that "The rights accorded members of labor unions under Title I of the Labor–Management Reporting and Disclosure Act of 1959 * * * do not include the right of a union member to libel or slander officers of the union." We do not agree.

The LMRDA of 1959 was designed to protect the rights of union members to discuss freely and criticize the management of their unions and the conduct of their officers. The legislative history and the extensive hearings which preceded the enactment of the statute abundantly evidence the intention of the Congress to prevent union officials from using their disciplinary powers to silence criticism and punish those who dare to question and complain. The statute is clear and explicit. [The court here quoted sections 101(a)(1), 101(a)(2), 102, and 609 of the LMRDA.]

Appellees argue that just as constitutionally protected speech does not include libelous utterances, Beauharnais v. Illinois, 343 U.S. 250, 266, 72 S.Ct. 725, 96 L.Ed. 919 (1952), the speech protected by the statute likewise does not include libel and slander. The analogy to the First Amendment is not convincing. In Beauharnais, the Supreme Court recognized the possibility that state action might stifle criticism under the guise of punishing libel. However, because it felt that abuses could be prevented by the exercise of judicial authority, 343 U.S. at 263–264, 72 S.Ct. at 733–734, 96 L.Ed. 919, the court sustained a state criminal libel statute. But the union is not a political unit to whose disinterested tribunals an alleged defamer can look for an impartial review of his "crime." It is an economic action group, the success of which depends in large measure on a unity of purpose and sense of solidarity among its members.

The Trial Board in the instant case consisted of union officials, not judges. It was a group to which the delicate problems of truth or falsehood, privilege, and "fair comment" were not familiar. Its procedure is peculiarly unsuited for drawing the fine line between criticism and defamation, yet, were we to adopt the view of the appellees, each charge of libel would be given a trial de novo in the federal court—an impractical result not likely contemplated by Congress, see 105 Cong.Rec. 6026 (daily ed. April 25, 1959)(colloquy between Senator Goldwater and Senator Clark)—and such a

Trial Board would be the final arbiter of the extent of the union member's protection under § 101(a)(2).[7]

In a proviso to § 101(a)(2), there are two express exceptions to the broad rule of free expression. One relates to "the responsibility of every member toward the organization as an institution." The other deals with interference with the union's legal and contractual obligations.

While the inclusion of only two exceptions, without more, does not mean that others were intentionally excluded, we believe that the legislative history supports the conclusion that Congress intended only those exceptions which were expressed.[8]

The expression of views by Salzhandler did not come within either exception in the proviso to § 101(a)(2). The leaflet did not interfere in any way with the union's legal or contractual obligations and the union has never claimed that it did. Nor could Salzhandler's charges against Webman be construed as a violation of the "responsibility of every member toward the organization as an institution." Quite the contrary; it would seem clearly in the interest of proper and honest management of union affairs to permit members to question the manner in which the union's officials handle the union's funds and how they treat the union's members. It is that interest which motivated the enactment of the statute and which would be immeasurably frustrated were we to interpret it so as to compel each dissatisfied and questioning member to draw, at the peril of union discipline, the thin and tenuous line between what is libelous and what is

---

**7.** See Summers, American Legislation for Union Democracy, 25 Mod.L.Rev. 273, 287:

"The most difficult problem arises when a member is expelled for 'slandering a union officer.' Union debates are characterized by vitriol and calumny, and campaigns for office are salted with overstated accusations. Defining the scope of fair comment in political contests is never easy, and in this context is nearly impossible. To allow the union to decide this issue in the first instance is to invite retaliation and repression and to frustrate one of the principal reasons for protecting this right—to enable members to oust corrupt leadership through the democratic process." [Editor's note—The usual disciplinary procedure provides for a trial board—consisting either of the union's executive board or of members appointed by the President, elected by the members, or selected by lot. A hearing is held after notice to the respondent member and both sides can sometimes use counsel selected from among the membership. The trial board then decides, usually by majority vote, and presents its verdict to the membership which may accept, reject or modify the board's recommendations. As a rule, either

side may appeal this decision to the international president, executive board, and/or the international union convention.]

**8.** As initially introduced before the Senate, the freedom of speech section was absolute in form. See 105 Cong.Rec. 5810 (daily ed. April 22, 1959). The section was in fact passed in that form. Id. at 5827. Later the question came to be reconsidered and the free speech section was amended to include the two express exceptions. Id. at 6030 (daily ed. April 25, 1959). In effect, the section as initially passed took away the power of unions to punish for expressions of views. The subsequent amendment restored that power in only two situations.

We are referred to certain statements made during the debate in the Senate which allegedly indicate that "reasonable restraints" on speech were intended. See: *e.g.*, 105 Cong.Rec. 6022 (daily ed. April 25, 1959) (remarks of Senator Kuchel). We find these statements to be ambiguous and we are not persuaded that exceptions other than those specified were intended.

not. This is especially so when we consider that the Act was designed largely to curtail such vices as the mismanagement of union funds, criticism of which by union members is always likely to be viewed by union officials as defamatory.

The union argues that there is a public interest in promoting the monolithic character of unions in their dealings with employers. But the Congress weighed this factor and decided that the desirability of protecting the democratic process within the unions outweighs any possible weakening of unions in their dealings with employers which may result from the freer expression of opinions within the unions.

The democratic and free expression of opinion in any group necessarily develops disagreements and divergent opinions. Freedom of expression would be stifled if those in power could claim that any charges against them were libelous and then proceed to discipline those responsible on a finding that the charges were false. That is precisely what Webman and the Trial Board did here when they punished Salzhandler with a five-year ban of silence and stripped him of his office.

So far as union discipline is concerned Salzhandler had a right to speak his mind and spread his opinions regarding the union's officers, regardless of whether his statements were true or false. It was wholly immaterial to Salzhandler's cause of action under the LMRDA whether he spoke truthfully or not, and accordingly Judge Wham's views on whether Salzhandler's statements were true are beside the point. Here Salzhandler's charges against Webman related to the handling of union funds; they concerned the way the union was managed. The Congress has decided that it is in the public interest that unions be democratically governed and toward that end that discussion should be free and untrammeled and that reprisals within the union for the expression of views should be prohibited. It follows that although libelous statements may be made the basis of civil suit between those concerned, the union may not subject a member to any disciplinary action on a finding by its governing board that such statements are libelous. The district court erred in dismissing the complaint.

Accordingly, we reverse the judgment of the district court and direct entry of judgment for the plaintiff which, among other things, should assess damages and enjoin the defendants from carrying out any punishment imposed by the District Council Trial Board.

---

## PROBLEMS FOR DISCUSSION

**1.** If Caputo were to bring a libel action against Salzhandler in a state court, as the Second Circuit suggests, would the policies of the LMRDA articulated by the federal court limit the ability of the state court to fashion and apply its rules of defamation? If so, is the suggestion of the Second Circuit merely illusory? Cf. Linn v. United Plant Guard Workers, Local 114, 383 U.S. 53, 86 S.Ct. 657, 15 L.Ed.2d 582 (1966).

**2.**  Is any of the following conduct of a union member a lawful basis, under the LMRDA, for suspension or expulsion from the union?

(a) crossing a picket line established by the union allegedly in breach of contract?

(b) urging members to strike during a collective bargaining negotiation despite the union officers' admonitions to continue to work because a tentative agreement has been reached with the employer? See Falcone v. Dantinne, 288 F.Supp. 719 (E.D.Pa.1968), rev'd, 420 F.2d 1157 (3d Cir.1969).

(c) urging members not to pay a union assessment which has been held by a trial court to be unlawful? See Farowitz v. Associated Musicians, Local 802, 330 F.2d 999 (2d Cir.1964).

(d) testifying adversely to the union in grievance arbitration?

(e) campaigning on behalf of (and being an officer of) another union competing in an NLRB election? Compare Ferguson v. International Ass'n of Iron Workers, 854 F.2d 1169 (9th Cir.1988), with Airline Maintenance Lodge 702 v. Loudermilk, 444 F.2d 719 (5th Cir.1971).

(f) writing letters to state legislators urging the enactment of a right-to-work law (forbidding an agreement to make union membership a condition of employment)?

(g) refusing to march with union members in a Labor Day parade?

(h) being a member of the Communist Party (or the Ku Klux Klan)?

(i) threatening a union officer, at a heated union meeting, to "step outside to settle this matter"? Compare Kelsey v. Philadelphia Local 8, International Alliance of Theatrical Stage Employees, 294 F.Supp. 1368 (E.D.Pa.1968), aff'd, 419 F.2d 491 (3d Cir.1969), cert. denied, 397 U.S. 1064, 90 S.Ct. 1501, 25 L.Ed.2d 685 (1970), with Reyes v. Laborers' Local 16, 327 F.Supp. 978 (D.N.M.1971), aff'd, 464 F.2d 595 (10th Cir.1972), cert. denied, 411 U.S. 915, 93 S.Ct. 1542, 36 L.Ed.2d 307 (1973).

––––––––

# International Brotherhood of Boilermakers v. Hardeman

401 U.S. 233, 91 S.Ct. 609, 28 L.Ed.2d 10 (1971).

■ MR. JUSTICE BRENNAN delivered the opinion of the Court.

Section 102 of the Labor–Management Reporting and Disclosure Act (hereafter LMRDA) provides that a union member who charges that his union violated his rights under Title I of the Act may bring a civil action against the union in a district court of the United States for appropriate relief. Respondent was expelled from membership in petitioner union and brought this action under § 102 in the District Court for the Southern District of Alabama. He alleged that in expelling him the petitioner violated § 101(a)(5) of the Act, 73 Stat. 523, 29 U.S.C. § 411(a)(5) which provides: "No member of any labor organization may be fined, suspended, expelled, or otherwise disciplined except for nonpayment of dues by such organization or by any officer thereof unless such member has been (A) served with written specific charges; (B) given a reasonable time to prepare his defense;

(C) afforded a full and fair hearing." A jury awarded respondent damages of $152,150. The Court of Appeals for the Fifth Circuit affirmed. 420 F.2d 485 (1969). We granted certiorari limited to the questions whether the subject matter of the suit was preempted because exclusively within the competence of the National Labor Relations Board and, if not preempted, whether the courts below had applied the proper standard of review to the union proceedings, 398 U.S. 926, 90 S.Ct. 1816, 26 L.Ed.2d 88 (1970). We reverse.

The case arises out of events in the early part of October 1960. Respondent, George Hardeman, is a boilermaker. He was then a member of petitioner's Local Lodge 112. On October 3, he went to the union hiring hall to see Herman Wise, business manager of the Local Lodge and the official responsible for referring workmen for jobs. Hardeman had talked to a friend of his, an employer who had promised to ask for him by name for a job in the vicinity. He sought assurance from Wise that he would be referred for the job. When Wise refused to make a definite commitment, Hardeman threatened violence if no work was forthcoming in the next few days.

On October 4, Hardeman returned to the hiring hall and waited for a referral. None was forthcoming. The next day, in his words, he "went to the hall * * * and waited from the time the hall opened until we had the trouble. I tried to make up my mind what to do, whether to sue the Local or Wise or beat hell out of Wise, and then I made up my mind." When Wise came out of his office to go to a local jobsite, as required by his duties as business manager, Hardeman handed him a copy of a telegram asking for Hardeman by name. As Wise was reading the telegram, Hardeman began punching him in the face.

Hardeman was tried for this conduct on charges of creating dissension and working against the interest and harmony of the Local Lodge, and of threatening and using force to restrain an officer of the Local Lodge from properly discharging the duties of his office. The trial committee found him "guilty as charged," and the Local Lodge sustained the finding and voted his expulsion for an indefinite period. Internal union review of this action, instituted by Hardeman, modified neither the verdict nor the penalty. Five years later, Hardeman brought this suit alleging that petitioner violated § 101(a)(5) by denying him a full and fair hearing in the union disciplinary proceedings.

## I

We consider first the union's claim that the subject matter of this lawsuit is, in the first instance, within the exclusive competence of the National Labor Relations Board. * * * We hold that this claim was not within the exclusive competence of the National Labor Relations Board. * * * [T]he critical question in this action is whether Hardeman was afforded the rights guaranteed him by § 101(a)(5) of the LMRDA. If he was denied them, Congress has said that he is entitled to damages for the consequences of that denial. Since these questions are irrelevant to the legality of conduct under the National Labor Relations Act, there is no danger of conflicting interpretation of its provisions. And since the law applied is federal law explicitly made applicable to such circumstances by Congress, there is no danger that state law may come in through the back door to regulate conduct that has been removed by Congress from state control. Accordingly, this action was within the competence of the District Court.

## II

Two charges were brought against Hardeman in the union disciplinary proceedings. He was charged with violation of Art. XIII, § 1, of the Subordinate Lodge Constitution, which forbids attempting to create dissension or working against the interest and harmony of the union, and carries a penalty of expulsion. He was also charged with violation of Art. XII, § 1, of the Subordinate Lodge By–Laws, which forbids the threat or use of force against any officer of the union in order to prevent him from properly discharging the duties of his office; violation may be punished "as warranted by the offense." Hardeman's conviction on both charges was upheld in internal union procedures for review.

The trial judge instructed the jury that "whether or not he [respondent] was rightfully or wrongfully discharged or expelled is a pure question of law for me to determine." He assumed, but did not decide, that the transcript of the union disciplinary hearing contained evidence adequate to support conviction of violating Art. XII. He held, however, that there was no evidence at all in the transcript of the union disciplinary proceedings to support the charge of violating Art. XIII. This holding appears to have been based on the Fifth Circuit's decision in International Brotherhood of Boilermakers v. Braswell, 388 F.2d 193 (C.A.5 1968). There the Court of Appeals for the Fifth Circuit had reasoned that "penal provisions in union constitutions must be strictly construed," and that as so construed Art. XIII was directed only to "threats to the union as an organization and to the effective carrying out of the union's aims," not to merely personal altercations. 388 F.2d at 199. Since the union tribunal had returned only a general verdict, and since one of the charges was thought to be supported by no evidence whatsoever, the trial judge held that Hardeman had been deprived of the full and fair hearing guaranteed by § 101(a)(5). The Court of Appeals affirmed, simply citing *Braswell.* 420 F.2d 485 (C.A.5 1969).

We find nothing in either the language or the legislative history of § 101(a)(5) that could justify such a substitution of judicial for union authority to interpret the union's regulations in order to determine the scope of offenses warranting discipline of union members. Section 101(a)(5) began life as a floor amendment to S. 1555, the Kennedy–Ervin Bill, in the 86th Congress. As proposed by Senator McClellan, and as adopted by the Senate on April 22, 1959, the amendment would have forbidden discipline of union members "except for breach of a published written rule of [the union]." 105 Cong.Rec. 6476, 6492–6493. But this language did not long survive. Two days later, a substitute amendment was offered by Senator

Kuchel, who explained that further study of the McClellan amendment had raised "some rather vexing questions." Id., at 6720. The Kuchel substitute, adopted the following day, deleted the requirement that charges be based upon a previously published, written union rule; it transformed Senator McClellan's amendment, in relevant part, into the present language of § 101(a)(5). Id., at 6720, 6727. As so amended, S. 1555 passed the Senate on April 25. Id., at 6745. Identical language was adopted by the House, Id., at 15884, 15891, and appears in the statute as finally enacted.

The Congress understood that Senator Kuchel's amendment was intended to make substantive changes in Senator McClellan's proposal. Senator Kennedy had specifically objected to the McClellan amendment because

> "In the case of * * * the * * * official who bribed a judge, unless there were a specific prohibition against bribery of judicial officers written into the constitution of the union, then no union could take disciplinary action against [an] officer or member guilty of bribery.
>
> * * *
>
> "It seems to me that we can trust union officers to run their affairs better than that." Id., at 6491.

Senator Kuchel described his substitute as merely providing "the usual reasonable constitutional basis" for union disciplinary proceedings: union members were to have "constitutionally reasonable notice and a reasonable hearing." Id., at 6720. After the Kuchel amendment passed the Senate, Senator Goldwater explained it to the House Committee on Labor and Education as follows:

> "[T]he bill of rights in the Senate bill requires that the union member be served with written specific charges prior to any disciplinary proceedings but it does not require that these charges, to be valid, must be based on activity that the union had proscribed prior to the union member having engaged in such activity." Labor–Management Reform Legislation, Hearings before a Joint Subcommittee of the House Committee on Education and Labor, 86th Cong., 1st Sess., pt. 4, p. 1595 (1959).

And Senator McClellan's testimony was to the same effect. Id., pt. 5, pp. 2235–2236, 2251, 2285.

We think that this is sufficient to indicate that § 101(a)(5) was not intended to authorize courts to determine the scope of offenses for which a union may discipline its members.[11] And if a union may discipline its members for offenses not proscribed by written rules at all, it is surely a

---

11. State law, in many circumstances, may go further. See Summers, The Law of Union Discipline: What the Courts Do in Fact, 70 Yale L.J. 175 (1960). But Congress, which preserved state law remedies by § 103 of the LMRDA, 29 U.S.C. § 413, was well aware that even the broad language of Senator McClellan's original proposal was more limited in scope than much state law. See 105 Cong.Rec. 6481–6489 (1959).

futile exercise for a court to construe the written rules in order to determine whether particular conduct falls within or without their scope.

Of course, § 101(a)(5)(A) requires that a member subject to discipline be "served with written specific charges." These charges must be, in Senator McClellan's words, "specific enough to inform the accused member of the offense that he has allegedly committed." Where, as here, the union's charges make reference to specific written provisions, § 101(a)(5)(A) obviously empowers the federal courts to examine those provisions and determine whether the union member had been misled or otherwise prejudiced in the presentation of his defense. But it gives courts no warrant to scrutinize the union regulations in order to determine whether particular conduct may be punished at all.

Respondent does not suggest, and we cannot discern, any possibility of prejudice in the present case. Although the notice of charges with which he was served does not appear as such in the record, the transcript of the union hearing indicates that the notice did not confine itself to a mere statement or citation of the written regulations that Hardeman was said to have violated: the notice appears to have contained a detailed statement of the facts relating to the fight that formed the basis for the disciplinary action. Section 101(a)(5) requires no more.

### III

There remains only the question whether the evidence in the union disciplinary proceeding was sufficient to support the finding of guilt. Section 101(a)(5)(C) of the LMRDA guarantees union members a "full and fair" disciplinary hearing, and the parties and the lower federal courts are in full agreement that this guarantee requires the charging party to provide some evidence at the disciplinary hearing to support the charges made. This is the proper standard of judicial review. We have repeatedly held that conviction on charges unsupported by any evidence is a denial of due process * * *; and we feel that § 101(a)(5)(C) may fairly be said to import a similar requirement into union disciplinary proceedings. Senator Kuchel, who first introduced the provision, characterized it on the Senate floor as requiring the "usual reasonable constitutional basis" for disciplinary action, 105 Cong.Rec. 6720, and any lesser standard would make useless § 101(a)(5)(A)'s requirement of written, specific charges. A stricter standard, on the other hand, would be inconsistent with the apparent congressional intent to allow unions to govern their own affairs, and would require courts to judge the credibility of witnesses on the basis of what would be at best a cold record.

Applying this standard to the present case, we think there is no question that the charges were adequately supported. Respondent was charged with having attacked Wise without warning, and with continuing to beat him for some time. Wise so testified at the disciplinary hearing, and his testimony was fully corroborated by one other witness to the altercation. Even Hardeman, although he claimed he was thereafter held and beaten, admitted having struck the first blow. On such a record there is no question but that the charges were supported by "some evidence."

Reversed.

[The concurring opinion of MR. JUSTICE WHITE and the dissenting opinion of MR. JUSTICE DOUGLAS have been omitted.]

———

ANDERSON v. UNITED BROTHERHOOD OF CARPENTERS, 47 CCH Lab.Cases par. 18,400 (D.Minn.1963). Plaintiff was expelled from defendant union for having attended Communist Party meetings in the 1940's and 1950's and for answering "No" to questions concerning whether he was a Communist or sympathetic to communist philosophy upon his application for union membership in 1948. At his hearing before the union trial committee, plaintiff was allowed to testify and to present witnesses, but he was not allowed to confront or cross-examine his accusers or witnesses against him. After exhausting internal union remedies, plaintiff brought suit for reinstatement under Section 102. *Held,* plaintiff is entitled to immediate reinstatement. The proceedings before the trial committee did not constitute a "full and fair hearing" under Section 101(a)(5) of the LMRDA in view of the absence of confrontation and the right to cross-examine.

SMITH v. GENERAL TRUCK DRIVERS, LOCAL 467, 181 F.Supp. 14 (S.D.Cal. 1960). Plaintiff was issued an honorable withdrawal card because he was no longer engaged in the trade or occupation covered by the jurisdiction of the defendant local. In a suit under Section 101 of the Labor–Management Reporting and Disclosure Act for an injunction and damages, *held, inter alia,* that plaintiff was not entitled to be represented by counsel. "The answer to the contention lies in the statement of the fundamental principle that the right to be represented by counsel, guaranteed by the Sixth Amendment to the Constitution of the United States, does not apply to hearings before labor unions. The reason is obvious. All that a union member is entitled to in any controversy between him and the union is a fair hearing. This means only that before any action is taken against him he must be informed of the charges and be given an opportunity to hear them and refute them. * * * This satisfies the constitutional concept as to all administrative proceedings. * * * Except in rare instances of illegality the general concept of due process applicable in criminal prosecutions is not applied to members of a union."

———

## 2.  UNION DISCIPLINE UNDER THE COMMON LAW

State courts in actions at common law have affirmed the power of unions to expel, suspend or otherwise discipline their members for a wide variety of reasons. For example, disciplinary action has been upheld against members who have failed to pay initiation fees, dues or assessments; or who have violated union work rules by working in a non-union shop or by accepting less than the union wage. Penalties have likewise been upheld against members for engaging in a wildcat strike or for strike breaking or for aiding or promoting a rival union. Inevitably, however, unions have sought to discipline members in order to promote objectives which have been considered as offensive to public policy, and courts have generally struck down such discipline. Thus, courts have enjoined a union from punishing those who refused to join in an illegal strike, and similar action was taken against the Railroad Trainmen for expelling a member who merely voted for a rival union in an election carried out pursuant to the Railway Labor Act. The case which follows is designed to suggest some of the problems that may arise in seeking to draw a line between proper and improper disciplinary action.

## Mitchell v. International Association of Machinists

196 Cal.App.2d 796, 16 Cal.Rptr. 813 (Dist.Ct.App.1961).

■ Fox, P.J. This appeal is from a judgment denying a petition for a writ of mandate. Petitioners seek reinstatement in respondent union, having been expelled for "conduct unbecoming a member." The conduct involved is their "peaceable, open, public, active, and vigorous campaign and support" for Proposition 18, the "right-to-work" law, in contravention of the expressed official policy of the union. (Respondents will be referred to in the singular.)

Petitioner Mitchell was a member of respondent from 1942 to July 8, 1959, the date of his expulsion. Petitioner Mulgrew was a member from 1953 until his expulsion on July 8, 1959. Both petitioners have been continuously employed by the California Division of Lockheed Aircraft from 1942 and 1953 respectively to the present time. Pursuant to an agreement between respondent union and Lockheed, the former is the exclusive bargaining representative of the company's employees in the bargaining unit described therein. Petitioners are within that bargaining unit. Neither lost his job as a result of the expulsion. The trial court found that the expulsion has not interfered with or threatened interference with petitioners' employment, nor is their opportunity for continued employment with Lockheed uncertain as a result of their expulsion. Lockheed is engaged in interstate commerce and the Taft–Hartley Act applies to it.

Proposition 18 was an initiative measure placed on the 1958 ballot for the general election held in California on November 4. It sought to alter the state Constitution so that both closed shops and union shops would be prohibited in this state. The proposition was defeated by a majority of the voters. The trial court found that respondent was reasonable and justified in regarding the effect of the initiative measure as a serious threat to its best interests, strength, welfare, and existence.

It was further found that petitioners, as individual citizens and "as union members" supported Proposition 18 in the manner stated above by, among other things, issuing releases to the press, distributing handbills, and making speeches on television and before groups in various parts of the State of California. It was not found that they purported to represent their union. They conducted their campaign although they were aware of the union's opposition to the measure and the union's recommendation that its members oppose adoption in every possible legal way.

Petitioners were charged with conduct unbecoming a member of the union and tried on January 13, 1959. They were found guilty as charged. Petitioners waived in open court any claims relating to the regularity of the internal union trial or appeal procedure. The trial court affirmed the union's determination that petitioners' acts constituted conduct unbecoming a member and concluded as a matter of law that the expulsions were justified and not in contravention of public policy or petitioners' constitutional rights.

Once again a court is asked to choose between rights which conflict. On the one hand there is a voluntary, private organization that insists it has the right to determine its membership, which includes the right to expel members whom it considers obnoxious so long as the union constitution and by-laws are complied with. On the other hand there is the individual member, insisting that he has the right to express himself on political matters as he will, without interference from his group. Viewing this conflict from a first row seat is the community, certainly not without interest in the outcome of the dispute.

It would seem proper to begin by dispelling two troublesome illusions. The first is that unions are purely voluntary organizations like Republicans, Democrats, Elks, and church groups. A modern labor union, both in structure and in function, bears little resemblance to other voluntary associations. (Summers, Legal Limitations on Union Discipline, 64 Harv. L.Rev. 1049, 1051.) "It is this omnipotent analogy that leads the courts astray." (Williams, The Political Liberties of Labor Union Members, 32 Tex.L.Rev. 826, 829.) Unions can be distinguished from other voluntary organizations in many respects. Most importantly, a large part of their power and authority is derived from government which makes it exclusive bargaining agent. Further, they are not primarily social groups which require homogeneous views in order to retain smooth functioning. They are large, heterogeneous groups, whose members may agree on one thing only—they want improved working conditions and greater economic benefits. The union's power, when considered together with its source, imposes upon it reciprocal responsibilities toward its membership and the public generally that other voluntary organizations do not bear. James v. Marinship Corp., 25 Cal.2d 721, 731, 155 P.2d 329, 160 A.L.R. 900; Chavez v. Sargent, 52 Cal.2d 162, 339 P.2d 801; Betts v. Easley, 161 Kan. 459, 169 P.2d 831, 166 A.L.R. 342.

Secondly, it cannot be assumed that the only value in membership is job retention. Even though a member may keep his job when expelled, his expulsion causes him to suffer a detriment the apprehension of which would no doubt have a coercive effect on the membership. First of all, it is not clear what his rights would be if he quit his job to seek another, at least in intrastate commerce. Also, he has a financial stake in the strike fund, perhaps a pension fund, and other funds to which he has contributed. Further, he is denied the right to participate in his union "government." Although the union is required by law to represent him impartially (Steele v. Louisville & N.R. Co., 323 U.S. 192, 65 S.Ct. 226, 89 L.Ed. 173), he has no voice in how that representation is to be conducted. In addition, there are frequently social ramifications for a nonmember working among members that cannot be overlooked. All this is solely for the purpose of demonstrating that there *is* a real conflict which cannot be dismissed by the assertion that since a member is assured by federal legislation that loss of membership for a reason other than nonpayment of dues does not mean loss of job, he is free to do as he wishes.

A review of the case law in and around this area will serve to orient the reader. * * *

Other groups of cases involving the question of the extent of the limitation on personal rights imposed by union membership have been fairly well categorized by the writers. At one extreme there are the "treason" cases in which an individual's acts are patently antagonistic to the continued existence of the union as a collective bargaining agent. Company spies and dual unionists are two examples. See *Summers,* supra, at p. 1059 et seq. See also Davis v. International Alliance etc. Employees, 60 Cal.App.2d 713, 141 P.2d 486. Similar cases are those in which members impair adherence to the collective bargaining agreement by violating work rules, working below scale, and engaging in wildcat strikes. See *Williams,* supra, at p. 831. The courts lose no time in such cases in upholding union discipline. At the other extreme are cases in which the courts frustrated union attempts to interfere with specific citizenship obligations. The Barbers were enjoined from expelling a member for enforcing Sunday laws against a fellow member (Manning v. Klein, 1 Pa.Super. 210). The Plumbers were prevented from expelling a member who, as a public official, refused to appoint another member as a plumbing inspector (Schneider v. Local Union No. 60, 116 La. 270, 40 So. 700, 5 L.R.A.N.S., 891). Another union was compelled to reinstate a member who testified before the Interstate Commerce Commission against safety devices sought by the union (Abdon v. Wallace, 95 Ind.App. 604, 165 N.E. 68). Other unions have been ordered to reinstate members who testified against the union in court (Angrisani v. Stearn, 167 Misc. 731, 3 N.Y.S.2d 701; Thompson v. Grand International Brotherhood of Locomotive Engineers, 41 Tex.Civ.App. 176, 91 S.W. 834).

Somewhere between these two extremes lies the small group of cases involving political activity by members, obligatory only in the moral sense, which the union as a whole opposes. * * *

In deciding whether a union may, *under these facts,* be permitted to penalize a member for engaging in political activity which the union opposes, certain considerations must be brought to light: (1) the interest of the community and the individual in the latter's membership; (2) the importance to the community of the individual's untrammeled right to express himself on political questions; (3) the interest of the union in excluding obnoxious members; (4) the interest of the union in speaking with one voice; (5) the nature of the political activity and the manner of its conduct. As to the first consideration, the value of membership to the individual has already been demonstrated. And to the extent that industrial democracy is important to the community, its interest is also manifest. (Cox, Law and the National Labor Policy [1960] p. 110.)

With respect to the second, few subjects in the history of western civilization have drawn such a unanimity of support. In a dissenting opinion Mr. Justice Brandeis observed, "The right of a citizen of the United States to take part, for his own or the country's benefit, in the making of federal laws and the conduct of the Government, necessarily includes the right to speak or write about them; * * * Full and free exercise of this right * * * is ordinarily also his duty; for its exercise is more important to the Nation than it is to himself." Gilbert v. State of Minnesota, 254 U.S. 325, 337–338, 41 S.Ct. 125, 129, 65 L.Ed. 287. * * * Further quotation is unnecessary. Suffice it to say that the unlimited freedom to express political views is the very heart of a democratic body, pumping the lifeblood of ideas without which our system could not survive.

As to the union's interest in excluding obnoxious members, it would be completely unrealistic to assume that unions are composed of like-thinking individuals. It is only when dissident views are expressed in a forum where they have a chance of acceptance that the member becomes "undesirable." But expulsion cannot serve to quiet the individual. It can only serve to intimidate those who remain. While this, too, might be a legitimate objective under some circumstances, the very question to be decided is whether the community ought to tolerate that result in *these* circumstances.

As to the interest of the union in presenting a unified front, this cannot be gainsaid. And where activity of the union is directly designed to attain economic goals, such as the decision to strike or not to strike, or adherence to the collective bargaining agreement, judicial regard for this interest has already been demonstrated. And it is no doubt true that economic and political objectives of unions frequently cannot be treated as completely separate things. * * * But still a distinction should be made in this context. Where purely economic activity is concerned, the community interest is not so deeply involved as it would be if the entire union membership in the nation were limited in its political expression (on matters of legitimate union interest) to the opinions of the majority or the union leadership. If this were the case we would be deprived of an immeasurably important source of political thought. Furthermore, so long as the individual member purports to represent only himself, and not his union, the union's public position is not diluted.

This brings us to the question of the nature of the political doctrine propounded and the manner in which it is advocated. We are not called upon to decide what the result would be if a member was expelled for advocating repeal of the Wagner Act or the abolition of unions. Only the right-to-work law is here involved. The union argues that it may reasonably consider such a law seriously inimical to its interests. This is certainly not an unreasonable position * * *. But there is a substantial respectable opinion to the contrary. Cox, [Law and National Labor Policy (1960),] at page 110 says, "The member who acts as a strikebreaker may be guilty of treason, but one can believe in right-to-work laws and remain a good trade-unionist." * * * There being such a disparity of opinion as to the long-run effect of voluntary unionism, the question becomes not whether the union is justified in its opinion, but whether the point is sufficiently debatable so that society's interest in the debate, together with the individual's right to speak freely on political matters, outweighs the union's interest in subduing public dissent among union members.

With respect to the manner in which the campaign was conducted, petitioners did speak as union members. But they did not purport to represent their union * * *.

It could not be more apparent where the balance lies. On this point, Cox, supra, page 111, has this to say: "It needs no argument to demonstrate the importance of freedom to pursue personal political activities. It begs the question to say that a man has a right to engage in whatever political activity he wishes but no right to be a union member. The question is whether there will be an excessive loss of freedom if unions are permitted to make political conformity the price of membership. Bearing in mind the size and importance of unions in industry as well as their growing interest in politics, it seems apparent that the total loss would be great indeed if a significant number of large labor organizations adopted the attitude of the International Association of Machinists. It would also work serious changes in our political system if individuals can be insulated from direct political action by the decisions of organized groups even though the decisions are reached by majority rule." It is therefore clear that, at least where the political activity of the member is not patently in conflict with the union's best interests, the union should not be permitted to use its power over the individual to curb the advocacy of his political views. * * *

---

## PROBLEMS FOR DISCUSSION

**1.** Consider the grounds for expulsion from union membership set forth in Problem 2 at p. 1182, supra. Under the principles announced in the *Mitchell* case, would these be valid grounds for expulsion at common law? See Anderson v. Los Angeles County Employee Rels. Comm'n, 229 Cal.App.3d 817, 280 Cal.Rptr. 415 (2d Dist.Ct.of App.1991).

**2.** If it were determined that any particular ground for expulsion was valid under the LMRDA, would it follow that the expelled member could not secure reinstatement to membership by an action in a state court? If it were determined that any particular ground for expulsion was valid under Section 8(b)(1)(A) of the Labor Act, would it follow that the expelled member could not secure reinstatement to membership by an action in a state court? For example, assume that a member is expelled for crossing a lawful union picket line or for filing a decertification petition against his own union, and assume that expulsion does not violate the NLRA; can it be held to violate state law and to furnish a basis for reinstatement to membership?

**3.**   Assume that an expelled member has a claim for reinstatement to membership that may be pursued under Section 8(b)(1)(A) of the Labor Act, Section 101(a) of the LMRDA and state common law. What factors should be considered in determining the forum in which to seek relief?

––––––––

3.   EXHAUSTION OF INTERNAL UNION REMEDIES

## Falsetti v. Local Union No. 2026, United Mine Workers

400 Pa. 145, 161 A.2d 882 (1960).

■ COHEN, J. This is an appeal from the order of the Court of Common Pleas of Allegheny County dismissing appellant's Bill in Equity on preliminary objections. Appellant's amended complaint alleged that he was a dues-paying member in good standing in appellee Local No. 2026, United Mine Workers of America (Union); that he was employed by appellee Pittsburgh Consolidation Coal Company (Company) with seniority from 1939; that on January 8, 1954, in violation of appellant's seniority rights under the collective bargaining agreement between Union and Company, he was laid off by the Company while at least one, and possibly more, employees with less seniority than he were retained; that appellee Company continues to employ such employee or employees and has rehired others with less seniority than appellant; that appellant's loss of seniority rights came about as a result of an unlawful conspiracy between appellee Company and the named individual appellees (Union officials) under the pretext that appellant was no longer able to fulfill his job obligations; that after appellant filed the original complaint in this action he was expelled from the Union; that he has demanded to be restored to Union membership, but appellee Union has refused, and that all remedies under the Union constitution and collective bargaining agreement between the Union and the Company have been exhausted and further resort thereto would be futile. In his prayer for relief, appellant asks that the Union be compelled to restore appellant's membership; that the appellee Company be compelled to reinstate appellant in his employment with the same job classification he had before the alleged discharge; that damages be awarded appellant for loss of wages; and that such other and further relief that may be just and equitable be allowed. * * *

* * * First, we will consider appellant's claim that he was wrongfully expelled from appellee Union. Appellees contend in this regard that appellant has failed to exhaust his internal remedies within the Union and therefore the issue presented is not "ripe" for adjudication by our courts. * * *

At this late date in the history of labor-management relations, it is but pointing out the obvious to state that autonomous, self-disciplining labor unions are beneficial to the public. The rule of exhaustion of internal remedies, applicable when a dispute arises between an association and a member thereof, evolved by our courts through the years and applicable to all "voluntary" unincorporated associations, serves to promote the desired autonomy and to encourage the establishment of fair procedures for maintaining internal discipline. Although this court has often relied on the contract rationale that a member, by voluntarily joining an association, has bound himself perpetually to abide by its constitution and by-laws, there are today other and more justifiable policy reasons for applying the exhaustion rule. * * *

* * * [W]e find the doctrine of exhaustion of internal remedies to be a necessary and proper incentive for achieving true association democracy.

In intra-association disputes, there are three sets of interests to be considered: (1) the interest of the association as such, (2) the interest of the members of the association, and (3) the interest of the courts. There is as well an over-riding *public* interest in promoting well-managed autonomous associations which are able to perform their functions effectively and still provide internally for the fair treatment of individual members who must be disciplined. See Chafee, op. cit. supra. The exhaustion rule is beneficial to the association in that by encouraging intra-association resolution of internal disputes, it permits officials in positions of higher authority within the association to carry out a uniform application of the association's policies. The association, in this manner, is able to prevent its "dirty linen" from being washed in public. Moreover, such a rule often saves the association the unnecessary burden and expense of litigation.

The exhaustion rule is beneficial as well to the vast majority of association members. Since very few members are willing to appeal beyond the association level when they are required to exhaust their internal remedies, the majority of members are benefited for the same reasons as the association in having disputes resolved within the association. The rule, when properly applied, will also tend to improve the machinery of the intra-association appellate system and make it a more responsible and efficient means of settling problems of discipline.

We are fully cognizant of the tremendous burden that premature judicial intervention into internal association-member disputes would place on already overcrowded court dockets. The exhaustion rule reduces litigation by forcing disputes through a private system where they may be settled before reaching the courts. This undoubtedly eliminates a needless waste of judicial time and duplication of litigation. The aggrieved member will quite often obtain satisfaction within the association's hierarchy, thereby terminating the dispute before it ripens into a full-blown legal contest. The rule, in summary, is extremely valuable in encouraging private adjustment, self-correction, and fair internal procedures.

This is not to say, of course, that the interests of the majority should persuade the courts to ignore the rights and interests of an occasional member who, with good cause, has ignored the association's internal procedure. But in holding that a case falls within one of the narrow exceptions to the exhaustion rule, we must be overly careful not to completely undercut it. Such exceptions as there are should be narrowly construed in line with the beneficial purposes of the rule itself. The exceptions are few and should be mentioned at this point.

First and foremost, a person will not be required to take intra-association appeals which cannot in fact yield remedies. If a remedy exists in theory only, it can well be considered illusory. Secondly, there is no need for a member to exhaust his internal remedies where the association officials have, by their own actions, precluded the member from having a fair or effective trial or appeal. See Heasley v. Operative P. & C.F.I. Assn., 324 Pa. 257, 188 A. 206 (1936); Weiss v. The Musical Protective Union, 189 Pa. 446, 42 A. 118 (1899). This includes those situations in which a member is not given due notice, right of hearing or review (see *e.g.* Labor Management Reporting and Disclosure Act of 1959, Sec. 101(a)(5)), and those where the association's officials are obviously biased or have pre-judged the member's case before hearing it. See Blenko v. Schmeltz, 362 Pa. 365, 67 A.2d 99 (1949).

Still another exception to the rule is where to insist that a member exhaust the appellate procedure would be unreasonably burdensome, *e.g.*, if the appellate procedure requires a member to appeal to a national convention which does not convene for several years.[11] See O'Neill v. United Plumbers, 348 Pa. 531, 36 A.2d 325 (1944); Heasley v. Operative P. & C.F.I. Assn., supra. In this regard, for all situations which arise subsequent to the passage of the new "Labor Bill of Rights" contained in the Labor Management Reporting and Disclosure Act of 1959, Sec. 101(a)(4) and to which the Act is applicable a member of a labor organization may be required to exhaust internal remedies *only if* such hearing procedures are "reasonable" and if they are completed within four months.

And finally there are instances where the requirement of exhaustion of remedies would subject a member to an injury that is in a practical sense irreparable. Such a situation would arise where a person expelled from a union and suing for re-admittance would, during the interim of his appeal, be barred from working in a union shop. Our courts are aptly armed, however, to prevent such irreparable injury to plaintiffs without destroying the vitality of the exhaustion rule.[13]

---

**11.** On its face, certainly, the two or three step appellate procedure provided for in the constitution of the International Union is not so burdensome or time-consuming as to justify immediate judicial intervention in an internal dispute.

**13.** Many associations voluntarily stay the imposition of penalty themselves, but if the association fails to do so, our courts are empowered to issue a temporary injunction staying the imposition of penalty while the member is taking an intra-association appeal. Such injunction must be based upon proof of a potential severe injury to the member and a colorable claim for relief. There need be no fear of dilatory tactics by the plaintiff since the injunction can be expressly conditioned upon his prompt exhaustion of all available internal remedies. The injunction *pendente lite,* of course, should be used but sparingly.

We hasten to emphasize, at this point, that the subject matter of the plaintiff's complaint, the harm complained of, should have little bearing on whether at that instant our courts may exercise jurisdiction. * * *

We are not unaware of the strong emphasis now being accorded the problem of internal union democracy. It is with a view toward the recent important steps taken legislatively to safeguard in the federal courts the rights of individual members against organizational excesses that we today elevate the rule of exhaustion to such a prominent position in our jurisdictional scheme. The Labor Management Reporting and Disclosure Act of 1959, Title I—Bill of Rights of Members of Labor Organizations, is not an attempt by the Congress of the United States to control the internal affairs of labor organizations. Rather, it represents the establishment of certain channels within which union activities which affect membership rights may proceed. * * * Rather than adopt judicial rules that would discourage resort to union processes which now must meet detailed elementary standards of fairness, we will attempt in every way to encourage the steady evolution of internal democracy. A strict adherence to the rule of exhaustion will go far toward placing the initial responsibility where it rightfully belongs—on the association itself. It is only when an issue has become fully "ripe" for adjudication that our courts will enter the picture.

[The court concluded that the plaintiff had failed to make an adequate case for avoiding the exhaustion of internal union remedies. His "mere allegation of futility or illusoriness," without substantial supporting evidence, will not establish the court's jurisdiction. The fact that the union had persistently declined to take the plaintiff's case to arbitration against the employer does not constitute a demonstration "that the Union will not provide an effective forum and internal procedure whereby appellant may fairly resolve a subsequent Union-member disciplinary dispute."]

---

## Kowaleviocz v. Local 333, International Longshoremen's Association

942 F.2d 285 (4th Cir.1991)

■ ERVIN, CHIEF JUDGE:

Union member Joseph M. Kowaleviocz appeals a fine and 10–year suspension from union membership imposed on him by the general membership of Local 333, International Longshoremen's Association (AFL–CIO)("Local 333" or "union"). The penalty stems from a charge that Kowaleviocz used profanity toward a union officer at a union meeting and on the docks. The district court granted summary judgment to the union on the union's claim that federal jurisdiction was lacking by virtue of Kowaleviocz's failure to exhaust internal union remedies before filing his appeal in federal district court. Finding that the union's illegal disciplinary action in

See Summers, supra at 1096–97; Comment,    65 Yale L.J. 369, 383–85 (1956).

violation of Kowaleviocz's free speech rights rendered the exhaustion requirement unnecessary, we reverse and remand this case to the district court with instructions to take jurisdiction.

I.

Since September 1984, Maryland longshoreman Joseph Kowaleviocz and Local 333 officer Garris McFadden had engaged in a long-running dispute concerning the propriety of an increase in local union dues that McFadden had proposed and secured. Kowaleviocz also became involved in an attempt to secure from McFadden the payment of wages to Local 333's recording secretary. As a result of these controversies, a number of hostile interchanges between Kowaleviocz and McFadden occurred in union meetings throughout 1984. These culminated in a December 6, 1984 motion by McFadden, approved by the membership, to fine Kowaleviocz $100 and suspend him for 10 years from all rights and privileges except work. Kowaleviocz appealed this action to the union's Baltimore District Council. Having been advised by union counsel that Kowaleviocz had been denied due process and that the penalties imposed were too harsh for the offense, the District Council overturned the disciplinary action against Kowaleviocz.

In January, 1985, McFadden filed charges with the union's Executive Board against Kowaleviocz for alleged profanity directed toward McFadden during the District Council appeal and on the docks. The Executive Board heard these charges and dismissed them on July 24, 1985.

On August 6, 1985, at a general membership meeting, McFadden orally appealed the Executive Board's dismissal of the charges against Kowaleviocz to the membership present. Kowaleviocz was present at the meeting but had received no prior notice that McFadden planned to appeal the Executive Board's dismissal of the charges against him. The membership voted to reverse the Executive Board's decision, determining that Kowaleviocz was guilty of the charges McFadden had made against him. Kowaleviocz's objections to the taking of the vote were rejected by Local 333's president, Edward Howell. No vote was taken for the imposition of a penalty. Kowaleviocz did not receive an official written notice from the union that he was fined $100 and suspended for 10 years until September 10, 1985.

The union's constitution provides that all appeals shall be made within 30 days after the rendition of the decision from which the appeal is taken. Kowaleviocz filed his appeal on October 4, 1985—within 30 days of his receipt of official notice of his penalty, but almost two months after the August 6 general membership meeting. The union rejected Kowaleviocz's appeal as having been untimely filed.

Kowaleviocz then filed an action in the United States District Court for the District of Maryland against Local 333, McFadden, and Howell for violation of his rights and privileges under the Labor Management Reporting and Disclosure Act of 1959 ("LMRDA"), 29 U.S.C. ss 401 et seq., specifically Sections 411(a)(2), 411(a)(5), 412, and 529. Local 333 responded with a motion for summary judgment, on the basis that under Section

411(a)(4) federal jurisdiction was lacking because Kowaleviocz had failed to exhaust internal union remedies regarding the disciplinary action taken against him. Kowaleviocz filed an opposition to the motion requesting the district court to excuse the exhaustion requirement while claiming that he had, in fact, exhausted his remedies by filing a timely appeal of the disciplinary action.

The district court granted the union's motion for summary judgment. The court determined that Kowaleviocz had failed to exhaust internal remedies and that such failure was not excusable by reason of either illegal union action or protection of Kowaleviocz's free speech rights. * * *

### III.

This appeal is grounded in Subchapter II of the LMRDA, which is entitled the Bill of Rights of Members of Labor Organizations. This portion of the LMRDA was designed to protect the rights of union members to discuss freely and criticize the management of their unions and the conduct of their officers. Salzhandler v. Caputo, 316 F.2d 445, 448–49 (2d Cir.), cert. denied, 375 U.S. 946, 84 S.Ct. 344, 11 L.Ed.2d 275 (1963). To further that goal, the statute attempts to ensure procedural due process to members subjected to union discipline and to provide for democratic processes in the conduct of union affairs. Maxwell v. United Auto., Aerospace & Agricultural Implement Workers of America, Local 1306, 489 F.Supp. 745, 748 (C.D.Ill.1980)(citing NLRB v. Allis–Chalmers Mfg. Co., 388 U.S. 175, 194, 87 S.Ct. 2001, 2013, 18 L.Ed.2d 1123, 1135–36 (1967)).

Section 411 enumerates specific rights which every member of any labor organization shall have, including the rights to meet and assemble freely with other members and to express any views, arguments, or opinions. 29 U.S.C.A. s 411(a)(2)(West 1985). By provision of Section 412, any worker whose rights under the Bill of Rights of union membership have been infringed may file a civil action in federal court. 29 U.S.C.A. s 412 (West 1985). Section 411(a)(4) stipulates that the labor organization shall not infringe any member's right to pursue such an action, but adds that the labor organization may require that members exhaust reasonable internal hearing procedures prior to instituting an action in federal court. 29 U.S.C.A. s 411(a)(4)(West 1985).

It is well established, however, that the exhaustion provision of Section 411(a)(4) is not mandatory, and that the statute leaves the ultimate decision whether to require exhaustion in a particular case to the sound discretion of the courts. See, e.g., Detroy v. Am. Guild of Variety Artists, 286 F.2d 75, 78 (2d Cir.), cert. denied, 366 U.S. 929, 81 S.Ct. 1650, 6 L.Ed.2d 388 (1961); Rollison v. Hotel, Motel, Restaurant & Constr. Camp Employees, Local 879, 677 F.2d 741, 745 (9th Cir.1982). If the court determines that the disciplinary action taken by the union against a member was indisputably illegal or "void," the failure to exhaust administrative remedies will be excused. Keeffe Bros. v. Teamsters Local Union No. 592, 562 F.2d 298, 303 (4th Cir.1977)(citing Simmons v. Avisco, Local 713, 350 F.2d 1012, 1016 (4th Cir.1965)); Maxwell, supra, 489 F.Supp. at 749 (holding that voidness, alone, justifies not requiring further exhaustion). A union's action is void where it constitutes "proceedings where no proper notice was given, where the tribunal was biased, where the offense charged was not one specified in the union constitution, or where there have been other substantial jurisdictional defects or a lack of fundamental fairness." Simmons, supra, 350 F.2d at 1016–17. Voidness is found in a particular case when conceded or easily determined facts show a serious violation of the member's rights. Id. at 1017.

The copy of the union's constitution and by-laws which Kowaleviocz submitted to the district court in opposition to the union's summary judgment motion is, standing alone, sufficient to show that the union's action through McFadden in orally appealing the Executive Board's decision to the general membership without proper notice to Kowaleviocz was illegal and therefore void for exhaustion purposes.

Article XV Section 5 of Local 333's by-laws provides that appeals from the decision of the Executive Board may be taken in accordance with the union's constitution. That constitution requires the following: All appeals shall be in writing, shall contain a brief statement of the facts and the grounds for the appeal and shall be filed with the secretary of the body to which they are addressed within thirty days, or such longer period as such body may permit, after the rendition of the decision from which the appeal is taken. The secretary with whom the appeal is filed shall promptly transmit copies thereof, together with a notice of the date of hearing thereon, ... to the parties to the appeal. International Longshoremen's Assoc. Const. art. XIX s 3 (1979)(emphasis added). This provision applies to all appeals, including those of an action of the Executive Board of a local union to a membership meeting of that local union. Id., art. XIX s 1(b).

If, as the union alleges, Kowaleviocz's internal appeal was indeed untimely filed, such procedural failure can hardly be sufficient to overcome the fact that McFadden's appeal of the Executive Board's dismissal of charges against Kowaleviocz was clearly a substantive violation of Article XIX Section 3 of the union constitution. First, the appeal was oral and not in writing as the union constitution explicitly requires. Second, Kowaleviocz did not receive written notice from the secretary of the Local specifying the "facts and the grounds for the appeal." Further, the omission of notice to Kowaleviocz violated Section 411(a)(5) of the LMRDA, which provides that no member of any labor organization may be fined, suspended, or otherwise disciplined unless he has been served with written specific charges, given a reasonable time to prepare his defense, and afforded a full and fair hearing. 29 U.S.C.A. s 411(a)(5)(West 1985).

The district court held that this was not the kind of void union action which is so ultra vires as to constitute "indisputably illegal" union conduct excusing failure to exhaust. Our precedent, however, refutes this conclusion in no uncertain terms. We have held that proceedings where no proper notice was given constitute union action that is void. Keeffe, supra, 562 F.2d at 303; Simmons, supra, 350 F.2d at 1016–17. Moreover, it is clear that exhaustion of intra-union remedies is excused when conceded or easily determined facts show a serious violation of the plaintiff's rights. See, e.g., Simmons, supra, 350 F.2d at 1017; Keeffe, supra, 562 F.2d at 303; Wiglesworth v. Teamsters Local Union No. 592, 552 F.2d 1027, 1030 (4th Cir.1976), cert. denied, 431 U.S. 955, 97 S.Ct. 2676, 53 L.Ed.2d 271 (1977)(citing Libutti v. DiBrizzi, 337 F.2d 216, 219 (2d Cir.1964)). In this case, easily determinable facts concerning the substance of the charge against Kowaleviocz indicate that the disciplinary action was in violation of Section 411(a)(2), which guarantees union members the right to freely express their views and opinions. See Keeffe, supra (court rejected union's failure-to-exhaust argument where it was obvious that union acted to penalize member for exercise of right of free speech).

The district court found that Kowaleviocz's speech did not constitute the expression of an opinion or view, characterizing it instead as profanity directed personally against McFadden. Yet it is undisputed that, regardless of any personal animosity between the men, Kowaleviocz had a history of opposition to certain official actions taken by McFadden. The union itself described the speech at issue as an "assault on the institution of the presidency and the district council." The speech as charged occurred not only at the docks but at the meeting of the District Council concerning the appeal of the penalty that had been imposed on Kowaleviocz in December 1984. Thus, the speech is protected by Section 411(a)(2) as an expression "at meetings of the labor organization" of "[the union member's] views ... upon any business properly before the meeting." 29 U.S.C.A. s 411(a)(2)(West 1985). Disciplinary action instituted to inhibit criticism of local union leadership constitutes a serious violation of a union member's rights. Bradford v. TWA Local 1093, 563 F.2d 1138, 1141 (4th Cir.1977); Maxwell, supra, 489 F.Supp. at 749.

The fact that Kowaleviocz's speech was offensive to McFadden and to the district court does not remove it from the protection of the LMRDA. The law is explicit that Section 411(a)(2) protects the conduct of union members, no matter how offensive that conduct may be to other union members. See, e.g., Rollison, supra, 677 F.2d at 746 (affirming grant of summary judgment for union member in charges involving use of obscene language toward union officers); Keeffe, supra, 562 F.2d at 304; Salzhandler, supra, 316 F.2d at 451 (holding that LMRDA protects allegedly libellous statements).

The union's actions in this case are unquestionably void. If Kowaleviocz failed to exhaust intra-union remedies, such failure must be excused. Because the granting of summary judgment to the union was inappropriate, we reverse the district court's action and remand this case to the district court for proceedings consistent with this opinion.

———

## PROBLEMS FOR DISCUSSION

**1.** Consider the reasons—particularly those set forth in the *Falsetti* case—underlying the requirement that a member must exhaust internal union remedies before initiating judicial proceedings for wrongful disciplinary action by the union. Were those reasons given due attention by the court in the *Kowaleviocz* case? Given all of the exceptions to the exhaustion proviso in § 101(a)(4), as recounted in the latter case, have the federal courts effectively obliterated that proviso?

**2.** Why should the fact that "conceded or easily determined facts show a serious violation" of a member's rights justify immediate judicial intervention, rather than an opportunity for rectification directly by the union? Assuming that insulting and provocative speech by the member, directed at a union official partly at a union meeting and partly "on the docks," is protected by LMRDA, is it futile to give the union an opportunity to correct the initial disciplinary action by its local officers or membership? (Consider this in the particular factual context of the case, and the earlier instances in which Kowaleviocz pressed intra-union appeals.)

# IV. UNION ELECTIONS[a]

The election of officers is the heart of union democracy. The policies of any large organization must be formulated and administered by a small group of officials. Their responsiveness to the members depends upon the frequency of elections, a fair opportunity to nominate and vote for candidates, and an honest count of the ballots. Local unions and international unions have traditionally provided for election procedures in their constitutions and bylaws. Does a union member have any legal redress if those internal union documents are violated when an election is conducted, or if those documents are themselves so designed as to endorse grossly unfair procedures or outcomes?

As with most claims by members of voluntary associations against the associations themselves, claims of union election irregularities have historically been triable in state common law courts. But the common law in the area has had an uneven development. Relief has been frequently barred by anachronistic rules requiring proof of actual damages or proof that a "property" interest has been impaired. *E.g.,* Stanton v. Harris, 152 Fla. 736, 13 So.2d 17 (1943); State ex rel. Givens v. Marion County Superior Ct., 233 Ind. 235, 117 N.E.2d 553 (1954). Other courts have devised fictions to get around such obstacles, or have altogether ignored nice questions of the basis for jurisdiction. *E.g.,* Raevsky v. Upholsterers' Intern. Union, 38 Pa. D. & C. 187 (1940); O'Neill v. United Ass'n of Journeymen Plumbers, 348 Pa. 531, 36 A.2d 325 (1944).

**a.** For a detailed discussion of the regulation of union elections by the state courts of New York, see Summers, Judicial Regulation of Union Elections, 70 Yale L.J. 1221 (1961); and for a study of union elections under the Landrum–Griffin Act, see Beaird, Union Officer Election Provisions of the LMRDA of 1959, 51 Va.L.Rev. 1306 (1965); Bellace & Berkowitz, The Landrum–Griffin Act—Twenty Years of Federal Protection of Union Members' Rights (1979); Comment, Union Elections and the LMRDA: Thirteen Years of Use and Abuse, 81 Yale L.J. 407 (1972); Harris, Titles I and IV of the LMRDA: A Resolution of the Conflict of Remedies, 42 U.Chi.L.Rev. 166 (1974); McLaughlin & Schoomaker, The Landrum–Griffin Act and Union Democracy (1979); Note, Pre–Election Remedies Under the Landrum–Griffin Act, 74 Colum.L.Rev. 1105 (1974); Topol, Union Elections Under the LMRDA, 74 Yale L.J. 1282 (1965).

In states permitting a cause of action, a wide variety of challenges have been entertained. In New York alone, courts have insisted that the names of candidates improperly stricken be restored to the ballot; that candidates receive equal access to the union newspaper and to voting lists; that proper notice of an election or nomination meeting be given; that voters not be intimidated from making nominations; and that the election district be properly drawn.[b] After elections have been held, the New York courts have been willing to examine the qualifications of candidates, to review challenged ballots and to consider such questions as the improper use of the union newspaper by the incumbent officers.[c]

Despite the willingness of judges in some states to intervene, various obstacles have hindered the courts in playing an effective role to insure democratic union elections. A court lacks authority to do much more than enforce the union's own constitution and bylaws. True, a court may invalidate a constitutional provision which is contrary to public policy, but even this will do little to enforce democratic control, for a court cannot always provide a substitute for the provisions which it invalidates. Ambiguous provisions or gaps in the union constitution can sometimes be resolved or filled in by reference to traditional notions of fair play and democratic principles, and courts have not hesitated to act in this manner in order to improve election procedures.[d] Nevertheless, a court cannot write a union constitution. Without the consent of the union, it cannot prescribe the time, place, and frequency of elections, create machinery for nominations, or define the electorate. In short, in the absence of legislation, the common law may be hard put to supply minimum electoral guarantees if they are missing from a union constitution.

A court is also a clumsy instrument for supervising an election. The judicial process may be suitable for determining the validity of an election which has already been held; but if it is found invalid, or if no election has been held, judges have few facilities for providing an effective remedy. Merely to order an election might turn the authority to conduct the balloting over to the very same officers whose misconduct gave rise to the litigation. The court has no tellers, watchers, or similar officials. It would become mired in the details of the electoral process. Probably it is the consciousness of these weaknesses that has made judges so reluctant to exercise broad supervision over union elections, for few elections seem to have been held under the direction of the courts.[e] One alternative is to

**b.** See, respectively, Di Bucci v. Uhrich, 21 Misc.2d 1069, 189 N.Y.S.2d 717 (1959); Contes v. Ross, 125 N.Y.L.J. June 12, 1951, p. 2175 col. 5; Fisher v. Kempter, 25 L.R.R.M. 2189 (N.Y.S.Ct.1949); Alaimo v. Rossiter, S.Ct. Erie Cty., May 23, 1941 cited in Summers, Judicial Regulation of Union Elections, 70 Yale L.J. 1221, 1230, n. 52 (1961); Caliendo v. McFarland, 13 Misc.2d 183, 175 N.Y.S.2d 869 (S.Ct.1958); Litwin v. Novak, 9 A.D.2d 789, 193 N.Y.S.2d 310 (1959).

**c.** See, respectively, Litwin v. Novak, 9 A.D.2d 789, 193 N.Y.S.2d 310 (1959); Carey v. International Bhd. of Paper Makers, 123 Misc. 680, 206 N.Y.S. 73 (S.Ct.1924); Ford v. Curran, 36 L.R.R.M. 2407 (S.Ct.1955).

**d.** See Irwin v. Possehl, 143 Misc. 855, 257 N.Y.S. 597 (S.Ct.1932); Caliendo v. McFarland, 13 Misc.2d 183, 175 N.Y.S.2d 869 (S.Ct.1958).

**e.** See Dusing v. Nuzzo, 177 Misc. 35, 29 N.Y.S.2d 882 (S.Ct.1941), mod'd, 263 App. Div. 59, 31 N.Y.S.2d 849 (1941); O'Neill v.

conduct an election under the supervision of a master appointed by the court, but this device has actually been employed in only a few instances.[f]

In the face of all these problems, Congress enacted the Labor Management Reporting and Disclosure Act which established comprehensive requirements for the conduct of union elections. Under this statute, local officers must be elected every three years or more often by a secret ballot. (LMRDA § 401(b)) International officers must be elected every five years or more often by a secret ballot of the members or by a convention of delegates chosen by secret ballot. (§ 401(a)) There are appropriate guarantees of the right to nominate and support candidates, to run for office, to get written notice of the election, and to vote without "improper interference or reprisal of any kind." (§ 401(e)) Every member is guaranteed one vote, a provision which not only invalidates the practice of limiting the vote to a special class of members but which also assures apprentices and even employers a voice in the selection of the officers of any labor organization to which they may belong. The statute assures honest elections by giving each candidate the right to have an observer at the polls and at the counting of the ballots, and by requiring separate publication of the results of the balloting in each local union. The latter requirement is pertinent to international elections. The division of sentiment in a single local is usually well enough known to its members to reveal any serious dishonesty in counting the ballots, provided that the figures are not concealed by lumping them into a single total with the results in other local unions. The Act makes compliance with the union's constitution and bylaws a statutory obligation in order that a federal remedy may be available for violations. (§ 401(e), (f))

To prevent union officials from gaining improper advantage in union elections Section 401(c) requires the union to distribute any candidate's campaign literature at his expense and to refrain from discrimination between candidates. Section 401(g) prohibits using union funds to promote the candidacy of any person. The administration of the latter provision will require delicate judgments. When a union president visits major locals on union business during the months before an election, he is not unmindful of his political fences. The international representative who goes to another city to handle grievances may be expected to discuss an impending election. The incumbents invariably command more space in the union newspaper than the opposition. Compare Hodgson v. United Mine Workers, 344 F.Supp. 17 (D.D.C.1972), with New Watch–Dog Committee v. New York City Taxi Drivers Union, Local 3036, 438 F.Supp. 1242 (S.D.N.Y.1977). Legislation can no more wipe out these advantages than it can prevent a President's dramatic move toward world peace from aiding his campaign for re-election. Nevertheless the statute can help to eliminate such grossly

United Ass'n of Journeymen Plumbers, 348 Pa. 531, 36 A.2d 325 (1944); Wilson v. Miller, 194 Tenn. 390, 250 S.W.2d 575 (1952).

    **f.** See Holdeman v. International Org. of Masters, 7 A.D.2d 1021, 184 N.Y.S.2d 698

(1959), aff'd, 6 N.Y.2d 869, 188 N.Y.S.2d 987, 160 N.E.2d 119 (1959); Yellin v. Schaefer, 46 L.R.R.M. 2723 (N.Y.S.Ct.1960).

unfair tactics as hiring additional organizers to campaign for the re-election of incumbent officials or using the union treasury to send out election propaganda.

In INTERNATIONAL ORGANIZATION OF MASTERS, MATES & PILOTS v. BROWN, 498 U.S. 466, 111 S.Ct. 880, 112 L.Ed.2d 991 (1991), the Supreme Court struck down a union rule that made mailing labels unavailable to candidates for office until after the union's nominating convention. The Court held that section 401(c) of the LMRDA requires the union to accede to such a request if the *request* is reasonable (which the Court found it to be); the pertinent issue is therefore not whether the union *rule* might be reasonable.

The demand that all candidates be given access to the union's membership list produced sharp debate in Congress because two irreconcilable principles were at stake. Since a candidate seeking to defeat the incumbent would be seriously hampered by the lack of a voting list, access to membership lists became a symbol of truly democratic elections in the eyes of those congressmen who would not count it a loss if labor unions were damaged in the process. On the other hand, the unions attach great importance to the secrecy of their membership lists because employers or rival unions have often used the lists for improper purposes. Under present conditions the need for secrecy is probably exaggerated, but one friendly to the labor movement could hardly ignore the strength of the tradition or the force of experience even though driven to acknowledge that the preservation of secrecy diminished the fairness of the election. In the end a compromise was reached which gives a candidate the right to inspect a list of members who are employed under union security contracts, once within thirty days of the election and without copying the list. This limited privilege can hardly be abused. (LMRDA § 401(c))

Enforcement of the election requirements is vested in the Secretary of Labor. A member desiring to challenge an election must first invoke his or her remedies within the organization. After they are exhausted or if three months elapse without a decision, the member may file a complaint with the Secretary who, upon investigation, will either dismiss the complaint or file an action in the federal court to set aside the election. The complaint is to be upheld only if it appears that the violation of the statute "may have affected the outcome of the election." (§ 402(c)) It would be wasteful to set aside an election for violations which could not have affected the result, but obviously proof that the outcome would have been different is not required. If an election is set aside, the Secretary is to conduct a new election. (Ibid.)

In three decisions, the Supreme Court has addressed procedural questions of significance in the administration of the provisions of the LMRDA concerning post-election attack by the Secretary of Labor.

In HODGSON v. LOCAL 6799, UNITED STEELWORKERS, 403 U.S. 333, 91 S.Ct. 1841, 29 L.Ed.2d 510 (1971), internal union appeals were exhausted by an unsuccessful candidate for local union president, who claimed that union facilities had been used to prepare campaign material for the incumbent president who was reelected. In his complaint to the Secretary of Labor, the member asserted not only that impropriety but also a claim that it was unreasonable for the union to condition eligibility for office upon attendance at one-half of the local's meetings. Although the Secretary of Labor brought an action to challenge the election on both grounds—and the District Court found that Section 401(g) was violated by the use of union facilities to aid the incumbent (and thus ordered a new election)—the Supreme Court held that the Secretary could properly sue only for violations raised by the union member during his internal union appeals. The Court observed: "[T]he primary objective of the exhaustion requirement [in Section 402(a) ]is to preserve the vitality of internal union mechanisms for resolving election disputes—mechanisms to decide complaints brought by members of the union themselves. To accept [the Secretary's] contention that a union member, who is aware of the facts underlying an alleged violation, need not first protest this violation to his union before complaining to the Secretary would be needlessly to weaken union self-government. Plainly [the Secretary's] approach slights the interest in protecting union self-regulation and is out of harmony with the congressional purpose reflected in § 402(a)." See Hodgson v. Local 734, Teamsters, 336 F.Supp. 1243 (N.D.Ill.1972): "[I]f the member presented an inartfully drawn protest to the union which can be said to cover several violations, the Secretary may litigate other claims arguably covered by the protest when the union can be charged with knowledge thereof under the heavy duty placed upon it by *Local 6799* to discern all various violations that a member might be asserting. * * * [T]he Secretary is allowed to litigate an alleged § 401 violation relating to and arising from the same series of transactions about which a union member did internally protest but which specific violation the member did not internally protest because of his ignorance of the facts as to the scope of the violations at the time that he filed his protest."

Later, the Court placed certain limitations upon the discretion of the Secretary in deciding not to bring a post-election action under Title IV of the LMRDA and in actually controlling any litigation brought. Although the Secretary asserted that his discretion not to bring an action to set aside a union election was not subject to judicial review, the Court held to the contrary in DUNLOP v. BACHOWSKI, 421 U.S. 560, 95 S.Ct. 1851, 44 L.Ed.2d 377 (1975). While conceding that the Secretary need not sue *whenever* the information before him suggests a suit *might* be successful, and that he may in deciding not to sue exercise his judgment about the probability of success, the Court held that a district court could review such action to assure that it is not arbitrary or capricious. To police this requirement, the Court held that the complainant was entitled to a statement of reasons from the Secretary to support his decision not to sue. Such a statement—setting forth the grounds of decision and the essential facts—would also "promote thought" by the Secretary and would compel him to "cover the relevant points and eschew irrelevancies." Judicial review, however, is to be sharply limited. The court is (except in "the rare case") simply to examine the statement of reasons to see whether on its face it "is so irrational as to constitute the decision arbitrary and capricious." There is to be no trial of any claim by the complainant that the Secretary lacks factual support for concluding that no violation occurred or that any violation did not affect the outcome of the election. Judicial scrutiny would go further only when the Secretary's action is "plainly beyond the bounds of the Act," such as an outright refusal to assume his enforcement responsibilities, or his prosecution of complaints in a constitutionally discriminatory manner.

In a third decision, TRBOVICH v. UNITED MINE WORKERS, 404 U.S. 528, 92 S.Ct. 630, 30 L.Ed.2d 686 (1972), the Court held that once the Secretary commences an action to set aside a union election, affected union members may intervene as parties. Although Section 402 of the LMRDA makes it clear that the only party who may sue to overturn an election already held is the Secretary of Labor—and the legislative history makes it clear that such lawsuits are not to be initiated by aggrieved union members—the Court concluded that it was not inconsistent to permit a union member to intervene in the Secretary's lawsuit. The Court held that Congress gave the Secretary the exclusive right to sue after elections for two reasons: "(1) to protect unions from frivolous litigation and unnecessary judicial interference with their elections, and (2) to centralize in a single proceeding such litigation as might be warranted with respect to a single election." Once the Secretary has screened out frivolous complaints and has consolidated all meritorious complaints in a single proceeding, there is no reason to believe Congress was opposed to participation by union members in the litigation. The Court, however, limited the participation of the intervening members to the presentation of evidence and argument in support of only those grounds for setting aside the union election which are mentioned in the Secretary's complaint; to permit the intervenor to assert additional grounds in the lawsuit "would be to circumvent the screening function assigned by statute to the Secretary" and would be to subject the union to claims determined by the Secretary to lack merit.

Though the foregoing provisions of the Act and Court decisions go far to guarantee free and fair union elections, they leave unsettled a number of important issues of election regulation. One of those issues—the relationship between Title IV and the guarantee of equal rights to vote and to nominate candidates under Section 101(a)—is treated in the following opinion of the Supreme Court.

———

## Calhoon v. Harvey

379 U.S. 134, 85 S.Ct. 292, 13 L.Ed.2d 190 (1964).

■ MR. JUSTICE BLACK delivered the opinion of the Court.

This case raises important questions concerning the powers of the Secretary of Labor and federal courts to protect rights of employees guaranteed by the Labor–Management Reporting and Disclosure Act of 1959.

The respondents, three members of District No. 1, National Marine Engineers' Beneficial Association, filed a complaint in Federal District Court against the union, its president and its secretary-treasurer, alleging that certain provisions of the union's bylaws and national constitution violated the Act in that they infringed "the right of members of defendant District No. 1, NMEBA, to nominate candidates in elections of defendant, which right is guaranteed to each member of defendant, and to each plaintiff, by Section 101(a)(1) of the LMRDA * * *." It was alleged that § 102 of Title I of the Act gave the District Court jurisdiction to adjudicate the controversy. The union bylaws complained of deprived a member of the right to nominate anyone for office but himself. The national constitution in turn provided that no member could be eligible for nomination or election to a full-time elective office unless he had been a member of the national union for five years and had served 180 days or more of seatime in each of two of the preceding three years on vessels covered by collective bargaining agreements with the national or its subsidiary bodies. On the basis of these allegations respondents asked that the union be enjoined from preparing for or conducting any election until it revised its system of elections so as to afford each of its members a fair opportunity to nominate any persons "meeting fair and reasonable eligibility requirements for any or all offices to be filled by such election."

The union moved to dismiss the complaint on the grounds that (1) the court lacked jurisdiction over the subject matter, and (2) the complaint failed to state a claim upon which relief could be granted. The District Court dismissed for want of "jurisdiction," holding that the alleged conduct of the union, even if true, failed to show a denial of the equal rights of all members of the union to vote for or nominate candidates guaranteed by § 101(a)(1) of Title I of the Act, so as to give the District Court jurisdiction of the controversy under § 102. The allegations, said the court, showed at most imposition of qualifications of eligibility for nomination and election so restrictive that they might violate § 401(e) of Title IV by denying members a reasonable opportunity to nominate and vote for candidates. The District Court further held that it could not exercise jurisdiction to protect § 401(e) rights because § 402(a) of Title IV provides a remedy, declared by § 403 to be "exclusive," authorizing members to vindicate such rights by challenging elections after they have been held, and then only by (1) first exhausting all remedies available with the union, (2) filing a complaint with the Secretary of Labor, who (3) may, after investigating the violation alleged in the complaint, bring suit in a United States District Court to attack the validity of the election. The Court of Appeals reversed, holding that "the complaint alleged a violation of § 101(a)(1) and that federal jurisdiction existed under § 102." 324 F.2d 486, 487. Because of the importance of the questions presented and conflicting views in the courts of appeals and the district courts, we granted certiorari, 375 U.S. 991, 84 S.Ct. 633, 11 L.Ed.2d 478.

Jurisdiction of the District Court under § 102 of Title I depends entirely upon whether this complaint showed a violation of rights guaranteed by § 101(a)(1), for we disagree with the Court of Appeals' holding that jurisdiction under § 102 can be upheld by reliance in whole or in part on allegations which in substance charge a breach of Title IV rights. An analysis and understanding of the meaning of § 101(a)(1) and of the charges of the complaint is therefore essential to a determination of this issue. Respondents charge that the bylaws and constitutional provisions referred to above infringed their right guaranteed by § 101(a)(1) to nominate candidates. The result of their allegations here, however, is an attempt to sweep into the ambit of their right to sue in federal court if they are denied an equal opportunity to nominate candidates under § 101(a)(1), a right to sue if they are not allowed to nominate anyone they choose regardless of his eligibility and qualifications under union restrictions. But Title IV, not Title I, sets standards for eligibility and qualifications of candidates and officials and provides its own separate and different administrative and judicial procedure for challenging those standards. And the equal-rights language of § 101(a)(1) would have to be stretched far beyond its normal meaning to hold that it guarantees members not just a right to "nominate candidates," but a right to nominate anyone without regard to valid union rules. All that § 101(a)(1) guarantees is that

> every member of a labor organization shall have equal rights and privileges * * * to nominate candidates, to vote in elections or referendums of the labor organizations * * * and to participate in the deliberations and voting * * * subject to reasonable rules and regulations in such organization's constitution and bylaws.

Plainly, this is no more than a command that members and classes of members shall not be discriminated against in their right to nominate and vote. And Congress carefully prescribed that even this right against discrimination is "subject to reasonable rules and regulations" by the union. The complaining union members here have not been discriminated against in any way and have been denied no privilege or right to vote or nominate which the union has granted to others. They have indeed taken full advantage of the uniform rule limiting nominations by nominating themselves for office. It is true that they were denied their request to be candidates, but that denial was not a discrimination against their right to nominate, since the same qualifications were required equally of all members. Whether the eligibility requirements set by the union's constitution and bylaws were reasonable and valid is a question separate and distinct from whether the right to nominate on an equal basis given by § 101(a)(1) was violated. The District Court therefore was without jurisdiction to grant the relief requested here unless, as the Court of Appeals held, the "*combined* effect of the eligibility requirements and the restriction to self-nomination" are to be considered in determining whether § 101(a)(1) has been violated.

We hold that possible violations of Title IV of the Act regarding eligibility are not relevant in determining whether or not a district court has jurisdiction under § 102 of Title I of the Act. Title IV sets up a statutory scheme governing the election of union officers, fixing the terms during which they hold office, requiring that elections be by secret ballot, regulating the handling of campaign literature, requiring a reasonable opportunity for the nomination of candidates, authorizing unions to fix "reasonable qualifications uniformly imposed" for candidates, and attempting to guarantee fair union elections in which all the members are allowed to participate. Section 402 of Title IV, as has been pointed out, sets up an exclusive method for protecting Title IV rights, by permitting individual members to file a complaint with the Secretary of Labor challenging the validity of any election because of violations of Title IV. Upon complaint the Secretary investigates and if he finds probable cause to believe that Title IV has been violated, he may file suit in the appropriate district court. It is apparent that Congress decided to utilize the special knowledge and discretion of the Secretary of Labor in order best to serve the public interest. Cf. San Diego Building Trades Council v. Garmon, 359 U.S. 236, 242, 79 S.Ct. 773, 778, 3 L.Ed.2d 775, 781. In so doing Congress, with one exception not here relevant,[13] decided not to permit individuals to block or delay union elections by filing federal court suits for violations of Title IV. Reliance on the discretion of the Secretary is in harmony with the general congressional policy to allow unions great latitude in resolving their own internal controversies, and, where that fails, to utilize the agencies of government most familiar with union problems to aid in bringing about a settlement through discussion before resort to the courts. Without setting out the lengthy legislative history which preceded the passage of this measure, it is sufficient to say that we are satisfied that the Act itself shows clearly by its structure and language that the disputes here, basically relating as they do to eligibility of candidates for office, fall squarely within Title IV of the Act and are to be resolved by the administrative and judicial procedures set out in that Title.

Accordingly, the judgment of the Court of Appeals is reversed and that of the District Court is affirmed.

It is so ordered.

■ MR. JUSTICE STEWART, whom MR. JUSTICE HARLAN joins, concurring.

This case marks the first interpretation by this Court of the significant changes wrought by the Labor–Management Reporting and Disclosure Act of 1959 increasing federal supervision of internal union affairs. At issue are subtle questions concerning the interplay between Title I and Title IV of that Act. In part, both seem to deal with the same subject matter: Title I guarantees "equal rights and privileges * * * to nominate candidates"; Title IV provides that "a reasonable opportunity shall be given for the nomination of candidates." Where the two Titles of the legislation differ most substantially is in the remedies they provide. If a Title I right is at issue, the allegedly aggrieved union member has direct, virtually immediate recourse to a federal court to obtain an adjudication of his claim and an injunction if his complaint has merit. 73 Stat. 523, 29 U.S.C. § 412 (1958

---

**13.** Section 401(c) of the Act permits suits prior to election in the United States District Courts by any bona fide candidate for union office to enforce the rights, guaranteed by that section, to equal treatment in the distribution of campaign literature and access to membership lists. 73 Stat. 532, 29 U.S.C. § 481(c).

ed., Supp. V). Vindication of claims under Title IV may be much more onerous. Federal court suits can be brought only by the Secretary of Labor, and then, only after the election has been held. * * *

The Court precludes the District Court from asserting jurisdiction over this complaint by focusing on the fact that one of the [restrictions imposed by the union] speaks in terms of eligibility. And since these are "possible violations of Title IV of the Act regarding eligibility" they "are not relevant in determining whether or not a district court has jurisdiction under § 102 of Title I of the Act." By this reasoning, the Court forecloses early adjudication of claims concerning participation in the election process. But there are occasions when eligibility provisions can infringe upon the right to nominate. Had the NMEBA issued a regulation that only Jesse Calhoon was eligible for office, no one could place great store on the right to self-nomination left to the rest of the membership. * * *

After today, simply by framing its discriminatory rules in terms of eligibility, a union can immunize itself from pre-election attack in a federal court even though it makes deep incursions on the equal right of its members to nominate, to vote, and to participate in the union's internal affairs. * * *

Nonetheless, the Court finds a "general congressional policy" to avoid judicial resolution of internal union disputes. That policy, the Court says, was designed to limit the power of individuals to block and delay elections by seeking injunctive relief. Such an appraisal might have been accurate before the addition of Title I, but it does not explain the emphasis on prompt judicial remedies there provided. In addition to the injunctive relief authorized by § 102 and the savings provisions of § 103, § 101(a)(4) modifies the traditional requirement of exhausting internal remedies before resort to litigation. Even § 403 is not conclusive on the elimination of pre-election remedies. At the least, state court actions may be brought in advance of an election to "enforce the constitution and bylaws." And as to federal courts, it is certainly arguable that recourse through the Secretary of Labor is the exclusive remedy only after the election has been held.[6] By reading Title I rights so narrowly, and by construing Title IV to foreclose absolutely pre-election litigation in the federal courts, the Court sharply reduces meaningful protection for many of the rights which Congress was so assiduous to create. By so simplifying the tangled provisions of the Act, the Court renders it virtually impossible for the aggrieved union member to gain a hearing when it is most necessary—when there is still an opportunity to make the union's rules comport with the requirements of the Act.

My difference with the Court does not reach to the disposition of this particular case. Whether stated in terms of restrictions on the right to nominate, or in terms of limitations on eligibility for union office, I think the rules of a labor organization would operate illegally to curtail the

---

**6.** See Summers, Pre–Emption and the Labor Reform Act—Dual Rights and Remedies, 22 Ohio St.L.J. 119, 138–139 (1961). It would be strange indeed if only state courts were available to enforce the federal law created by the Act during the pre-election period.

members' equal right to nominate within the meaning of Title I only if those rules effectively distorted the basic democratic process. The line might be a shadowy one in some cases. But I think that in this case the respondents did not allege in their complaint nor demonstrate in their affidavits that this line was crossed. I would therefore remand the case to the District Court with directions to dismiss the complaint for failure to state a claim for relief.

■ MR. JUSTICE DOUGLAS would affirm the judgment of the Court of Appeals for the reasons stated in its opinion as reported in 324 F.2d 486.

---

PROBLEMS FOR DISCUSSION

**1.** Which of the two positions in the *Calhoon* case finds support in Section 403 of the LMRDA, which deals with remedies in union election cases?

**2.** After a union election was conducted, but before the ballots were tallied, one of the ballot boxes mysteriously disappeared for several hours. When the box reappeared and the votes were about to be tallied, several union members instituted an action in a federal court for an injunction to restrain the counting of ballots. The complaint alleged that the ballots in the temporarily missing box were tampered with, and either the ballots validly cast by the plaintiffs were removed from the box before it was returned or a completely new ballot box (with different ballots) was substituted. The plaintiffs base their claim for relief on Section 101(a)(1), asserting that the tampering has effectively deprived them of their right under that Section as members of the union to vote. The union officials named as defendants have moved to dismiss the action as beyond the jurisdiction of the federal district court. Should the motion to dismiss be granted? See Beckman v. Local No. 46, Intern. Ass'n of Bridge, Structural and Ornamental Iron Workers, 314 F.2d 848 (7th Cir.1963).

**3.** Shortly before an election for the presidency of the United Mine Workers International, membership lists were being used to send to all members copies of the union newspaper known as the Journal. The paper, like all union newspapers, was sent to members on a regular basis and, like all union newspapers, it tended to focus on the constructive activities of incumbent union officials. As the election approached, more coverage than usual—pictorially and textually—was given in the Journal to the activities of the incumbent International president, Tony Boyle; for some five months, no reference was made to the activities of Jock Yablonski, who was running against Boyle. While Yablonski concedes that the Journal's format is not materially different from that of the past, or from that of other union newspapers, he claims that the LMRDA requires the union to cease discriminating by using the Journal as a campaign instrument for Boyle. Claiming that delay until the Secretary of Labor can sue after the election will be an inadequate remedy, Yablonski brings an action in the federal district court (asserting jurisdiction under Sections 401(c) and 501 of the LMRDA) seeking a preliminary injunction against the union requiring the Journal to provide sufficient coverage in future issues for Yablonski's positions and actions, to give Yablonski equal space in the Journal until the election is held, and to print copy supplied by Yablonski for the next two issues. Should the district court issue such an injunction? Could comparable relief be secured at the suit of the Secretary of Labor after the election in the event Boyle wins? Could the district court in advance of the election grant some other relief to

Yablonski that would help him communicate directly with union members? See Yablonski v. United Mine Workers of America, 305 F.Supp. 868 (D.D.C.1969).

---

## Local 3489, United Steelworkers of America v. Usery

429 U.S. 305, 97 S.Ct. 611, 50 L.Ed.2d 502 (1977).

■ MR. JUSTICE BRENNAN delivered the opinion of the Court.

The Secretary of Labor brought this action in the District Court for the Southern District of Indiana under § 402(b) of the Labor–Management Reporting and Disclosure Act of 1959 (LMRDA), 73 Stat. 534, 29 U.S.C. § 482(b), to invalidate the 1970 election of officers of Local 3489, United Steelworkers of America. The Secretary alleged that a provision of the Steelworkers' International Constitution, binding on the Local, that limits eligibility for local union office to members who have attended at least one-half of the regular meetings of the local for three years previous to the election (unless prevented by union activities or working hours), violated § 401(e) of the LMRDA, 29 U.S.C. § 481(e). The District Court dismissed the complaint, finding no violation of the Act. The Court of Appeals for the Seventh Circuit reversed. 520 F.2d 516 (1975). We granted certiorari to resolve a conflict between circuits over whether the Steelworkers' constitutional provision violates § 401(e). 424 U.S. 907, 96 S.Ct. 1100, 47 L.Ed.2d 311 (1976). We affirm.

### I

At the time of the challenged election, there were approximately 660 members in good standing of Local 3489. The Court of Appeals found that 96.5% of these members were ineligible to hold office, because of failure to satisfy the meeting attendance rule. Of the 23 eligible members, nine were incumbent union officers. The Secretary argues, and the Court of Appeals held, that the failure of 96.5% of the local members to satisfy the meeting attendance requirement, and the rule's effect of requiring potential insurgent candidates to plan their candidacies as early as 18 months in advance of the election when the reasons for their opposition might not have yet emerged,[5] established that the requirement has a substantial anti-democratic effect on local union elections. Petitioners argue that the rule is reasonable because it serves valid union purposes, imposes no very burdensome obligation on the members, and has not proved to be a device that entrenches a particular clique of incumbent officers in the local.

### II

The opinions in three cases decided in 1968 have identified the considerations pertinent to the determination whether the attendance rule vio-

---

**5.** Regular meetings were held on a monthly basis. Thus, in order to attend half of the meetings in a three-year period, a previously inactive member desiring to run for office would have to begin attending 18 months before the election.

lates § 401(e). Wirtz v. Hotel Employees, 391 U.S. 492, 88 S.Ct. 1743, 20 L.Ed.2d 763; Wirtz v. Bottle Blowers Assn., 389 U.S. 463, 88 S.Ct. 643, 19 L.Ed.2d 705; Wirtz v. Laborers' Union, 389 U.S. 477, 88 S.Ct. 639, 19 L.Ed.2d 716.

LMRDA does not render unions powerless to restrict candidacies for union office. The injunction in § 401(e) that "every member in good standing shall be eligible to be a candidate and to hold office" is made expressly "subject to * * * reasonable qualifications uniformly imposed." But "Congress plainly did not intend that the authorization * * * of 'reasonable qualifications * * *' should be given a broad reach. The contrary is implicit in the legislative history of the section and its wording * * *." Wirtz v. Hotel Employees, supra, 391 U.S., at 499, 88 S.Ct., at 1748. The basic objective of Title IV of LMRDA is to guarantee "free and democratic" union elections modeled on "political elections in this country" where "the assumption is that voters will exercise common sense and judgment in casting their ballots." 391 U.S., at 504, 88 S.Ct., at 1750. Thus, Title IV is not designed merely to protect the right of a union member to run for a particular office in a particular election. " * * * Congress emphatically asserted a vital public interest in assuring free and democratic union elections that transcends the narrower interest of the complaining union member." Wirtz v. Bottle Blowers Assn., supra, at 475, 88 S.Ct., at 650; Wirtz v. Local 125, Laborers' Union, supra, 389 U.S., at 483, 88 S.Ct., at 642. The goal was to "protect the rights of rank-and-file members to participate fully in the operation of their union through processes of democratic self-government, and, through the election process, to keep the union leadership responsive to the membership." Wirtz v. Hotel Employees, supra, 391 U.S., at 497, 88 S.Ct., at 1747.

Whether a particular qualification is "reasonable" within the meaning of § 401(e) must therefore "be measured in terms of its consistency with the Act's command to unions to conduct 'free and democratic' union elections." 391 U.S., at 499, 88 S.Ct., at 1748. Congress was not concerned only with corrupt union leadership. Congress chose the goal of "free and democratic" union elections as a preventive measure "to curb the possibility of abuse by benevolent as well as malevolent entrenched leadership." Id., at 503, 88 S.Ct., at 1750. *Hotel Employees* expressly held that that check was seriously impaired by candidacy qualifications which substantially deplete the ranks of those who might run in opposition to incumbents, and therefore held invalid the candidacy limitation there involved that restricted candidacies for certain positions to members who had previously held union office. "Plainly, given the objective of Title IV, a candidacy limitation which renders 93% of union members ineligible for office can hardly be a 'reasonable qualification.' " Id., at 502, 88 S.Ct., at 1749.

### III

Applying these principles to this case, we conclude that here too the antidemocratic effects of the meeting attendance rule outweigh the interests urged in its support. Like the by-law in *Hotel Employees,* an attendance requirement that results in the exclusion of 96.5% of the members from candidacy for union office hardly seems to be a "reasonable qualification" consistent with the goal of free and democratic elections. A requirement having that result obviously severely restricts the free choice of the membership in selecting their leaders.

Petitioners argue however that the by-law held violative of § 401(e) in *Hotel Employees* differs significantly from the attendance rule here. Under the *Hotel Employees* by-law no member could assure by his own efforts that he would be eligible for union office, since others controlled the criterion for eligibility. Here, on the other hand, a member can assure himself of eligibility for candidacy by attending some 18 brief meetings over a three-year period. In other words, the union would have its rule treated not as excluding a category of member from eligibility, but simply as mandating a procedure to be followed by any member who wishes to be a candidate.

Even examined from this perspective, however, the rule has a restrictive effect on union democracy. In the absence of a permanent "opposition party" within the union, opposition to the incumbent leadership is likely to emerge in response to particular issues at different times, and member interest in changing union leadership is therefore likely to be at its highest only shortly before elections. Thus it is probable that to require that a member decide upon a potential candidacy at least 18 months in advance of an election when no issues exist to prompt that decision may not foster but discourage candidacies and to that extent impair the general membership's freedom to oust incumbents in favor of new leadership.

Nor are we persuaded by the Union's argument that the Secretary has failed to show an antidemocratic effect because he has not shown that the incumbent leaders of the Union became "entrenched" in their offices as a consequence of the operation of the attendance rule. The reasons why leaderships become entrenched are difficult to isolate. The election of the same officers year after year may be a signal that antidemocratic election rules have prevented an effective challenge to the regime, or might well signal only that the members are satisfied with their stewardship; if elections are uncontested, opposition factions may have been denied access to the ballot, or competing interests may have compromised differences before the election to maintain a front of unity. Conversely, significant turnover in offices may result from an open political process, or from a competition so limited as to offer no real opposition to an entrenched establishment. But Congress did not saddle the courts with the duty to search out and remove improperly entrenched union leaderships. Rather, Congress chose to guarantee union democracy by regulating not the results of a union's electoral procedure, but the procedure itself. Congress decided that if the elections are "free and democratic," the members themselves are able to correct abuse of power by entrenched leadership. Procedures that unduly restrict free choice among candidates are forbidden without regard to their success or failure in maintaining corrupt leadership.

Petitioners next argue that the rule is reasonable within § 401(e) because it encourages attendance at union meetings, and assures more qualified officers by limiting election to those who have demonstrated an interest in union affairs, and are familiar with union problems. But the rule has plainly not served these goals. It has obviously done little to encourage attendance at meetings, which continue to attract only a handful of members.[8] Even as to the more limited goal of encouraging the attendance of potential dissident candidates, very few members, as we have said, are likely to see themselves as such sufficiently far in advance of the election to be spurred to attendance by the rule.

As for assuring the election of knowledgeable and dedicated leaders, the election provisions of LMRDA express a congressional determination that the best means to this end is to leave the choice of leaders to the membership in open democratic elections, unfettered by arbitrary exclusions. Pursuing this goal by excluding the bulk of the membership from eligibility for office, and thus limiting the possibility of dissident candidacies, run directly counter to the basic premise of the statute. We therefore conclude that Congress, in guaranteeing every union member the opportunity to hold office, subject only to "reasonable qualifications," disabled unions from establishing eligibility qualifications as sharply restrictive of the openness of the union political process as is petitioners' attendance rule. * * *

Affirmed.

■ MR. JUSTICE POWELL, with whom MR. JUSTICE STEWART and MR. JUSTICE REHNQUIST join, dissenting.

* * * As this holding seems to me to be an unwarranted interference with the right of the union to manage its own internal affairs, I dissent. * * *

The Court * * *, relying heavily on *Hotel Employees,* holds that this rule imposes an unreasonable qualification, violative of § 401(e). *Hotel Employees* involved a "prior office" rule that limited candidates for local union office to members who previously had held elective union office. The Court's opinion in that case emphasized that the effect of the prior office rule was to disqualify 93.1% of the union's membership. In this case, the Government argues that *Hotel Employees* enunciated a *per se* "effects" rule, requiring invalidation of union elections whenever an eligibility rule disqualifies all but a small percentage of the union's membership. Although the Court today does not in terms adopt a *per se* "effects" analysis, it comes close to doing so. The fact that 96.5% of Local 3489's members chose not to comply with its rule was given controlling weight.

In my view, the Court has extended the reach of *Hotel Employees* far beyond the holding and basic rationale of that case. Indeed, the rule there involved was acknowledged to be a sport—"virtually unique in trade union practice." 391 U.S., at 505, 88 S.Ct., at 1751. It was a rule deliberately designed, as intimated by the Court's opinion, to entrench union leader-

---

**8.** Attendance at Local 3489's meetings averages 47 out of approximately 660 members. There is no indication in the record that this total represents a significant increase over attendance before the institution of the challenged rule.

ship. Id., at 499, 88 S.Ct., at 1748. Moreover, the general effect of the rule in *Hotel Employees* was predictable at the time the rule was adopted. By limiting eligibility to members who held or previously had held elective office, the disqualification of a large proportion of the membership was a purposeful and inevitable effect of the structure of the rule itself. The attendance rule before the Court today has no comparable feature. No member is precluded from establishing eligibility. Nor can the effect of the rule be predicted, as any member who demonstrates the requisite interest in union affairs is eligible to seek office. In short, the only common factor between the prior office rule in *Hotel Employees* and that before the Court today is the similarity in the percentage of ineligible members. But in one case the effect was predetermined for the purpose of perpetuating control of a few insiders, whereas here the effect resulted from the free choice— perhaps the indifference—of the rank and file membership.

\* \* \* [I believe that the union's attendance rule, at least facially, serves] legitimate and meritorious union purposes: (i) encouraging attendance at meetings; (ii) requiring candidates for office to demonstrate a meaningful interest in the union and its affairs; and (iii) assuring that members who seek office have had an opportunity to become informed as to union affairs. One may argue that requiring attendance at 18 of the 36 meetings prior to the election goes beyond what may be necessary to serve these purposes. But this is a "judgment call" best left to the unions themselves absent a stronger showing of potential for abuse than has been made in this case.

The record in this case is instructive. Twenty-three members were eligible to run for office in the 1970 election. These were members who were nominated and who also had complied with the attendance requirement. The record does not show, and indeed no one knows, how many members were eligible under the rule but who were not nominated. Three candidates competed for the office of president, four for the three trustee offices, and six ran unopposed for the remaining offices. Of the 10 officers elected, six were incumbents. Nonincumbents were elected to the offices of vice president, treasurer, recording secretary, and the minor office of guide. There was no history of entrenched leadership and no evidence of restrictive union practices precluding free and democratic elections. Indeed, the record is to the contrary. Five different presidents had been elected during the preceding 10 years, and an estimated 40 changes in officers had occurred in the course of four separate elections. Bernard Frye, who initiated this case by complaint to the Secretary, won the presidency in an election subsequent to 1970 and thereafter lost it.

In the final analysis, respondent, which bears the burden of proving that the rule is "unreasonable," rests its entire case on a facial attack upon the attendance rule itself, an attack supported by a statistical "effects test" that at best is ambiguous and one that could invalidate almost any attendance requirement that served legitimate union purposes. In my view, the respondent has failed to prove that the rule is unreasonable. For these reasons, I would reverse the judgment of the Court of Appeals.

WIRTZ v. LOCAL 153, GLASS BOTTLE BLOWERS ASS'N, 389 U.S. 463, 88 S.Ct. 643, 19 L.Ed.2d 705 (1968). The Secretary of Labor brought suit to void a local union election and direct a new election under his supervision on the basis of a member's complaint that the union violated Section 401(e) by its bylaw requiring as a prerequisite to run for union office that a member have attended at least 75% of the Local's regular meetings in the two years' prior to the election. The union argued that the case was mooted because the next biennial local union election had already been conducted while the suit was still being appealed. On certiorari, *held,* the decision of the Court of Appeals declaring the Secretary's action moot is reversed. The union "argues that granting the Secretary's relief after a supervening election would terminate the new officers' tenure prematurely on mere suspicion." Congress, however, concluded that there was a substantial risk that officials, once improperly elected, would exert enough influence over subsequent elections to perpetuate themselves or their supporters in office. "The only assurance that the new officers do in fact hold office by reason of a truly fair and democratic vote is to do what the Act requires, rerun the election under the Secretary's supervision." In concluding that it would serve no practical purpose to void an old election after the terms of office conferred therein had been terminated by a new election, the Court of Appeals "seems to view the Act as designed merely to protect the right of a union member to run for a particular office in a particular election. But the Act is not so limited, for Congress emphatically asserted a vital public interest in assuming free and democratic union elections that transcends the narrower interest of the complaining union member."

----

## PROBLEMS FOR DISCUSSION

**1.**  The Steelworkers now require, as a condition of eligibility for office, attendance at one-third of the meetings which the member could have attended in the twenty-four months preceding an election. Will that rule withstand attack under the LMRDA? Is there *any* reasonable rule which a union can lawfully adopt to assure that its candidates for office will be familiar with the operations and affairs of the union? If that union purpose will normally be inadequate to shelter candidacy requirements, will any other purpose suffice?

**2.**  Given the emphasis of the Court in *Steelworkers Local 3489* upon the percentage, pure and simple, of union members disqualified for candidacy, can a union know with any confidence at the time it promulgates requirements for candidates whether those requirements will be valid? *Compare* Herman v. Local 1011, United Steelworkers, 207 F.3d 924 (7th Cir.2000) (provision in union constitution limiting eligibility for local office to union members who have attended at least eight regular monthly meetings in previous two years that disqualified 92% of Local 1011's 3000 members is presumed unreasonable), *with* Herman v. Springfield Mass. Area, Local 497, Postal Workers, 201 F.3d 1 (1st Cir.2000) (union candidacy requirement of attendance at three regular monthly meetings in the 12–month period before the nominating meeting is reasonable, although it disqualified 96% of membership). How, if at all, might such "guesswork" be eliminated?

**3.** The Illinois Education Association, a state affiliate of the National Education Association, is a labor organization within the coverage of the Landrum–Griffin Act. It numbers some 50,000 members, most of them teachers in public elementary and secondary schools. The members elect a Representative Assembly of some 600 members, and the Assembly elects a Board of Directors which until recently has numbered 50. In 1974, by majority vote of its members, the Association amended its by-laws in two respects. First, members of four minority groups (black, Asians, Hispanics, American Indians) were guaranteed eight percent of the seats in the Representative Assembly; if this percentage were not elected through the normal election process, the Board of Directors was directed to appoint enough additional members to the Assembly to reach the desired percentage. Second, the Board of Directors was increased to 54 members, the four new places to be reserved for members of the specified minority groups; these reserved places were in addition to any that minority members might obtain in the normal election process.

The Secretary of Labor has brought an action challenging these by-laws as in violation of Section 401(e) of the LMRDA, on the grounds that they limit both eligibility of non-minority members for election to the Assembly and to the Board, and the right to vote for candidates of one's choice. The membership of the Association (which approved the by-laws) is overwhelmingly white. The alleged reason for their action was to "raise the consciousness" of the membership and to provide diversity of representation.

The Secretary has moved for an injunction against the implementation of these by-laws in a forthcoming election, and for summary judgment. How should the district court rule? See Donovan v. Illinois Education Association, 667 F.2d 638 (7th Cir.1982).

**4.** The Laborers' International Union has a provision in its Uniform Local Union Constitution which states that a candidate for office "shall be literate and otherwise competent to perform the duties of the office for which he is a candidate." Prior to its meeting to nominate candidates for union election, the Executive Board of Local 120 appointed three Judges of Election to screen candidates. When, at that meeting, Laurence Rose was nominated for the position of Secretary–Treasurer of the local, a member in attendance protested the nomination on the ground that Mr. Rose was incompetent for the office. The Judges of Election subsequently disqualified Rose for that reason, and his appeal of that decision to the General Executive Board of the International Union was denied. The election was held, and the Secretary of Labor has brought an action to invalidate the election for Secretary–Treasurer, claiming that the "competency" rule is a violation of Section 401(e) of the LMRDA.

The Secretary of Labor claims that the rule is not "reasonable" because it is vague and because applications of the rule are to be made by persons appointed by the incumbent executive board. He also claims that the rule cannot be "uniformly imposed," because it is so subjective. He contends that judgments regarding a member's "competence" for union office are to be made by the membership in a democratic election. The Union, however, contends that the rule does not effect a disqualification from office of a major proportion of the union membership, and that it in other respects complies with Section 401(e).

Should the "competence" rule be sustained? See Donovan v. Local Union No. 120, Laborers' Intern. Union, 683 F.2d 1095 (7th Cir.1982).

# United Steelworkers of America v. Sadlowski

457 U.S. 102, 102 S.Ct. 2339, 72 L.Ed.2d 707 (1982).

■ JUSTICE MARSHALL delivered the opinion of the Court.

In this case, we confront the question whether § 101(a)(2) of the Labor–Management Reporting and Disclosure Act of 1959 (LMRDA), 29 U.S.C. § 411(a)(2), precludes the membership of a union from adopting a rule that prohibits candidates for union office from accepting campaign contributions from nonmembers. The United States Court of Appeals for the District of Columbia held that such a rule violated § 101(a)(2). Sadlowski v. United Steelworkers of America, 645 F.2d 1114 (1981). We granted certiorari, 454 U.S. 962, 102 S.Ct. 500, 70 L.Ed.2d 376 (1981), and now reverse.

I

A

Petitioner United Steelworkers of America (USWA), a labor organization with 1,300,000 members, conducts elections for union president and other top union officers every four years. The elections for these officers are decided by referendum vote of the membership. In the 1977 election, which was hotly contested, two candidates ran for president: respondent Edward Sadlowski, Jr., the Director of USWA's largest District, and Lloyd McBride, another District Director. Both Sadlowski and McBride headed a slate of candidates for the other top union positions.

McBride was endorsed by the incumbent union leadership, and received substantial financial support from union officers and staff. Sadlowski, on the other hand, received much of his financial support from sources outside the union. During the campaign, the question whether candidates should accept contributions from persons who were not members of the union was vigorously debated. The McBride slate contended that outsider participation in USWA elections was dangerous for the union. App. 27 n. 2, 298. See also id., at 129, 398; see generally id., at 40–48. McBride ultimately defeated Sadlowski by a fairly wide margin—57% to 43%. The other candidates on the McBride slate won by similar margins.

After the elections, union members continued to debate the question whether outsider participation in union campaigns was desirable. This debate was finally resolved in 1978, when USWA held its biennial Convention. The Convention, which consists of approximately 5,000 delegates elected by members of USWA's local unions, is USWA's highest governing body. At the 1978 Convention, several local unions submitted resolutions recommending amendment of the USWA Constitution to include an "outsider rule" prohibiting campaign contributions by nonmembers. The union's International Executive Board also recommended a ban on nonmember contributions. Acting on the basis of these recommendations, the Convention's Constitution Committee proposed to the Convention that it adopt an outsider rule. After a debate on the floor of the Convention, the delegates by a margin of roughly 10 to 1, voted to include such a rule in the Constitution. Id., at 35–36, 81–105.

The outsider rule, Article V, § 27 of the USWA Constitution, provides in pertinent part:

> "Sec. 27. No candidate (including a prospective candidate) for any position set forth in Article IV, Section 1, and supporter of a candidate may solicit or accept financial support, or any other direct or indirect support of any kind (except an individual's own volunteered personal time) from any non-member." USWA Const. Art. V, § 27.

Section 27 confers authority upon the International Executive Board to adopt regulations necessary to implement the provision. It also creates a Campaign Contribution Administrative Committee, consisting of three "distinguished, impartial" nonmembers to administer and enforce the provision. Id. The Committee may order a candidate to cease and desist from conduct that breaches § 27, and may declare a candidate disqualified. Its decisions are final and binding.

## B

In October, 1979, Sadlowski and several other individuals filed suit against USWA in the United States District Court for the District of Columbia. [The court granted the plaintiffs' motion for summary judgment and the court of appeals affirmed, relying on both § 101(a)(2) of the LMRDA (the "freedom of speech and assembly" provision) and § 101(a)(4) (the "right to sue" provision).]

## II

Section 101(a)(2) is contained in Title I of the LMRDA, the "Bill of Rights of Members of Labor Organizations." See 29 U.S.C. §§ 411–415. It provides:

> *"Freedom of speech and assembly.*—Every member of any labor organization shall have the right to meet and assemble freely with other members; and to express any views, arguments, or opinions; and to express at meetings of the labor organization his views, upon candidates in an election of the labor organization or upon any business properly before the meeting, subject to the organization's established and reasonable rules pertaining to the conduct of meetings: *Provided,* That nothing herein shall be construed to impair the right of a labor organization to adopt and enforce reasonable rules as to the responsibility of every member toward the organization as an institution and to his refraining from conduct that would interfere with its performance of its legal or contractual obligations."

We must decide whether this statute is violated by a union rule that prohibits candidates for union office from accepting campaign contributions from individuals who are not members of the union.

A

At the outset, we address respondents' contention that this case can be resolved simply by reference to First Amendment law. Respondents claim that § 101(a)(2) confers upon union members rights equivalent to the rights established by the First Amendment. They further argue that in the context of a political election, a rule that placed substantial restrictions on a candidate's freedom to receive campaign contributions would violate the First Amendment. Thus, a rule that substantially restricts contributions in union campaigns must violate § 101(a)(2). We are not persuaded by this argument. In light of the legislative history, we do not believe that § 101(a)(2) should be read as incorporating the entire body of First Amendment law, so that the scope of protections afforded by the statute coincides with the protections afforded by the Constitution. * * * Rather, Congress' decision to include a proviso covering "reasonable" rules refutes that proposition. First Amendment freedoms may not be infringed absent a compelling governmental interest. Even then, any government regulation must be carefully tailored, so that rights are not needlessly impaired. Brown v. Hartlage, 456 U.S. 45, 54, 102 S.Ct. 1523, 1529, 71 L.Ed.2d 732 (1982). Union rules, by contrast, are valid under § 101(a)(2) so long as they are reasonable; they need not pass the stringent tests applied in the First Amendment context.

B

To determine whether a union rule is valid under the statute, we first consider whether the rule interferes with an interest protected by the first section of § 101(a)(2). If it does, we then determine whether the rule is "reasonable" and thus sheltered by the proviso to § 101(a)(2). * * *

Applying this form of analysis here, we conclude that the outsider rule is valid. Although it may limit somewhat the ability of insurgent union members to wage an effective campaign, an interest deserving some protection under the statute, it is rationally related to the union's legitimate interest in reducing outsider interference with union affairs.

(1)

An examination of the policies underlying the LMRDA indicates that the outsider rule may have some impact on interests that Congress intended to protect under § 101(a)(2). Congress adopted the freedom of speech and assembly provision in order to promote union democracy. See supra, at 2344–2345; see also S.Rep. No. 187, 86th Cong., 1st Sess. 2 (1959), 1 Leg.Hist. 398; H.R.Rep. No. 741, 86th Cong., 1st Sess. 2 (1959), 1 Leg.Hist. 760. It recognized that democracy would be assured only if union members are free to discuss union policies and criticize the leadership without fear of reprisal. Congress also recognized that this freedom is particularly critical, and deserves vigorous protection, in the context of election campaigns. For it is in elections that members can wield their power, and directly express their approval or disapproval of the union leadership. See S.Rep. No. 187, supra, at 2–5, 7, 2 Leg.Hist. 398–401, 416; H.R.Rep. No. 741, supra, at 1–7, 15–16, 1 Leg.Hist. 759–765, 773–774.

The interest in fostering vigorous debate during election campaigns may be affected by the outsider rule. If candidates are not permitted to accept contributions from persons outside the union, their ability to criticize union policies and to mount effective challenges to union leadership may be weakened. Restrictions that limit access to funds may reduce the number of issues discussed, the attention that is devoted to each issue, and the size of the audience reached. * * *

Although the outsider rule does affect rights protected by the statute, as a practical matter the impact may not be substantial. Respondents, as well as the Court of Appeals, suggest that incumbents have a large advantage because they can rely on their union staff during election campaigns. Challengers cannot counter this power simply by seeking funds from union members; the rank-and-file cannot provide sufficient support. Thus, they must be permitted to seek funds from outsiders. In fact, however, the rank-and-file probably can provide support. The USWA is a very large union whose members earn sufficient income to make campaign contributions. See App. 118–120. Requiring candidates to rely solely on contributions from members will not unduly limit their ability to raise campaign funds. Uncontradicted record evidence discloses that challengers have been able to defeat incumbents or administration-backed candidates, despite the absence of financial support from nonmembers. See id., 25, 118–119.

In addition, although there are undoubtedly advantages to incumbency, see Hall v. Cole, 412 U.S., at 13, 93 S.Ct., at 631, respondents and the Court of Appeals may overstate those advantages. Staff employees are forbidden by § 401(g) of the LMRDA, 29 U.S.C. § 481(g), and by internal USWA rules from campaigning on union time or from using union funds, facilities, or equipment for campaign purposes. App. 110–117; see 29 CFR § 452.76 (1981). Staff officers have a contractual right to choose whether or not to participate in any USWA campaign without being subjected to discipline or reprisal for their decision. See App. 107–110, 115–117, 228, 384–385. Indeed, USWA elections have frequently involved challenges to incumbents by members of the staff. Many of these challenges have been successful. Id., at 108, 201–216.

The impact of the outsider rule on rights protected under § 101(a)(2) is limited in another important respect. The union has stated that the rule would not prohibit union members who are not involved in a campaign from using outside funds to address particular issues. That is, members could solicit funds from outsiders in order to focus the attention of the rank-and-file on a specific problem. The fact that union members remain free to seek funds for this purpose will serve as a counter to the power of entrenched leadership, and ensures that debate on issues that are important to the membership will never be stifled.

(2)

Although the outsider rule may implicate rights protected by § 101(a)(2), it serves a legitimate purpose that is clearly protected under the statute. The union adopted the rule because it wanted to ensure that nonmembers do not unduly influence union affairs. USWA feared that officers who received campaign contributions from nonmembers might be beholden to those individuals and might allow their decisions to be influenced by considerations other than the best interests of the union. The union wanted to ensure that the union leadership remained responsive to the membership. See id., at 210; see also id., 61–62, 81–97, 275, 303, 304.[9] An examination of the policies underlying the LMRDA reveals that this is a legitimate purpose that Congress meant to protect.

Evidence that Congress regarded the desire to minimize outsider influence as a legitimate purpose is provided by the history to Title I. On the Senate floor, Senator McClellan argued that a bill of rights for union members was necessary because some unions had been "invaded" or "infiltrated" by outsiders who had no interest in the members but rather had seized control for their own purposes. 2 Leg.Hist. 1097–1100. He stated that the strongest support for the bill of rights provisions "should come from traditional union leaders. It will protect them from the assaults of those who would capture their unions." Id., at 1097. * * * It is true that Senator McClellan was particularly concerned about infiltration of unions by racketeers: he described situations in which "thugs and hoodlums" had taken over unions so that they could exploit the members for pecuniary gain. Id., at 1097. However, his statements also indicate a more general desire to ensure that union members, and not outsiders, control the affairs of their union.

Additional evidence that Congress regarded the union's desire to maintain control over its own affairs as legitimate is provided by the history of other sections of the LMRDA. In drafting Titles II through VI, Congress was guided by the general principle that unions should be left free to "operate their own affairs, as far as possible." S.Rep. No. 1684, 85th Cong., 2d Sess. 4–5 (1958). It believed that only essential standards should be imposed by legislation, and that in establishing those standards, great care should be taken not to undermine union self-government. Given certain minimum standards, "individual members are fully competent to regulate union affairs." Id. Thus, for example, in Title IV, which regulates the conduct of union elections, Congress simply set forth certain minimum standards. So long as unions conform with these standards, they are free "to run their own elections." Wirtz v. Glass Bottle Blowers, 389 U.S., at 471, 88 S.Ct., at 648. Congress' desire to permit unions to regulate their

---

**9.** Respondents allege that the rule was forced upon the union members by high union officers, who wanted to ensure that they were insulated from effective challenges in future elections. However, the record does not support respondents' claims. The outsider rule was adopted through democratic processes, and was favored by an overwhelming majority of the delegates to the 1978 Convention. * * * These delegates had been elected by the rank-and-file. See App. 301–302.

own affairs and to minimize governmental intervention suggests that it would have endorsed union efforts to reduce outsider influence.

Indeed, specific provisions contained in Title IV provide support for our conclusion that the outsider rule serves a legitimate and protected purpose. Section 401(g), 29 U.S.C. § 481(g), prohibits the use of employer as well as union funds in election campaigns. This ban reflects a desire to minimize the danger that employers will influence the outcome of union elections. A union rule that seeks to reduce the influence of outsiders other than employers is clearly consistent with that goal. See also § 403 of Title IV of the LMRDA, 29 U.S.C. § 843 (authorizing unions to establish their own election rules).[10]

\* \* \*

Finally, respondents contend that USWA could simply have required that candidates for union office reveal the sources of their funds. But a disclosure rule, by itself, would not have solved the problem. Candidates who received such funds might still be beholden to outsiders. A disclosure requirement ensures only that union members know about this possibility when they cast their votes. It does not eradicate the threat of outside influence.

### III

As an alternative basis for sustaining the result below, respondents ask this Court to hold that the outsider rule impermissibly encroaches upon its members' right, guaranteed by § 101(a)(4) of the LMRDA, to institute legal proceedings, and that the appropriate remedy for this violation is an injunction striking down the rule en toto. However, unlike the District Court and the Court of Appeals, we do not believe that the union's rule violates the right to sue provision.

Section 101(a)(4) provides that a union may not "limit the right of any member thereof to institute an action in any court, or in a proceeding before any administrative agency." 29 U.S.C. § 411(a)(4). The outsider rule would clearly violate this provision if it prohibited union members from accepting financial or other support from nonmembers for the purpose of conducting campaign-related litigation. In our view, however, the outsider rule simply does not apply where a member uses funds from outsiders to finance litigation.

The language of the rule contains no reference to litigation. In addition, the debates leading up to the passage of the rule do not contain any

---

**10.** Section 403 provides "No labor organization shall be required by law to conduct elections of officers with greater frequency or in a different form or manner than is required by its own constitution or bylaws, except as otherwise provided by [Title IV]." The union argues that the outsider rule can be justified solely on the basis of this provision, since the rule is otherwise consistent with Title IV. We are not persuaded by this argument. Section 403 must be interpreted in light of the provisions of Title I, which were adopted precisely because Congress feared that Titles II through VI did not provide sufficient protection to union members. Thus, even if the rule satisfies § 403, it must also satisfy Title I.

indication that the union intended the rule to apply in this context. But what is most persuasive, the Campaign Contribution Administration Committee (the Committee)—which was given authority to make final and binding interpretations of the outsider rule—has issued an opinion concerning the impact of the outsider rule on the right to sue. In this opinion, it holds that "the limitations imposed by Section 27 do not apply to the financing of lawsuits by nonmembers for the purpose of asserting the legal rights of candidates or other union members in connection with elections." App. 455; see also id., 456–458. * * *[16]

* * * We reverse the decision below and remand for further proceedings consistent with this opinion.

■ JUSTICE WHITE, with whom THE CHIEF JUSTICE, JUSTICE BRENNAN, and JUSTICE BLACKMUN join, dissenting.

The question before us is what Congress intended when in 1959 it passed § 101(a)(2), the Bill of Rights provision of the LMRDA. That question is best answered by identifying the problem that Congress intended to solve by adopting the provision. The answer, in turn, is not at all difficult to discover.

After long and careful examination and hearings dealing with the labor union movement, Congress found that too often unions were run by entrenched, corrupt leaders who maintained themselves and discouraged challenge by any means available, including violence and threats. As Senator McClellan explained: "[T]he records of our committee's investigations show over and over again that a rank-and-file member dare not risk any opposition to a corrupt or autocratic leadership. If he does, he may be beaten, his family threatened, his property destroyed or damaged, and he may be forced out of his job—all of these things can happen and have happened." 105 Cong.Rec. 5806 (1959). And again, "Members had better not offer any competition. They had better not seek election. That had better not aspire to the presidency or the secretaryship, or they will be expelled or disciplined." Id., at 6478.

This was the problem that Congress meant to solve. As Senator McClellan stated, its goal was to end "autocratic rule by placing the ultimate power in the hands of the members, where it rightfully belongs so that they may be ruled by their free consent, may bring about a regeneration of union leadership. I believe the union should be returned to those whom they were designed to serve; they should not be left to the hands of those who act as masters." 2 Legislative History of the LMRDA (NLRB 1959) 1099.

---

**16.** Respondents also argue that the decision below can be affirmed on the ground that the outsider rule violates the First Amendment because it interferes with members' and non-members' Constitutional rights of free speech and free association. However, the union's decision to adopt an outsider rule does not involve state action. See United Steelworkers of America v. Weber, 443 U.S. 193, 200, 99 S.Ct. 2721, 2726, 61 L.Ed.2d 480 (1979).

What Congress then did was to guarantee the union member's right to run for election, § 401(e), and to guarantee him freedom of speech and assembly. § 101(a)(2). There is no question, and the Court concedes as much, that the Act created statutory protection for the union member's right effectively to run for union office. Without doubt, § 101(a)(2) was not only aimed at protecting the member who speaks his mind on union affairs, even if critical of the leadership, but was also "specifically designed to protect the union member's right to seek higher office within the union." Hall v. Cole, 412 U.S. 1, 14, 93 S.Ct. 1943, 1951, 36 L.Ed.2d 702 (1973). The LMRDA was a major effort by Congress "to insure union democracy."
* * *

The member's right to run for office and to speak and assemble was to be subject to reasonable union rules, but the reasonableness of a particular rule must surely be judged with reference to the paradigmatic situation that Congress intended to address by guaranteeing free elections: a large union with entrenched, autocratic leadership bent on maintaining itself by fair means or foul. We do not by any means suggest that the USWA had or has the characteristics that led to the enactment of § 101(a)(2), but it is clear that the section should be construed with reference to those unions with the kind of leadership that caused the congressional response. Such a leadership is not only determined to discourage opposition; it also has at its disposal all of the advantages of incumbency for doing so, including the facilities of the union. Those leaders have normally appointed the union staff, the bureaucracy that makes the union run. The staff is dependent upon and totally loyal to the leadership. It amounts to a built-in campaign organization that can be relied upon to make substantial contributions and to solicit others for more. Such a management is in control of the union's communication system and has immediate access to membership lists and to the members themselves. Obviously, even if the incumbents eschew violence, threats or intimidation, mounting an effective challenge would be a large and difficult endeavor. And if those in office are as unscrupulous as Congress often found them to be, the dimensions of the task facing the insurgent are exceedingly large. But Congress intended to help the members help solve these very difficulties by guaranteeing them the right to run for office and to have free and open elections in the American tradition.

It is incredible to me that the union rule at issue in this case can be found to be a reasonable restriction on the right of Edward Sadlowski to speak, assemble, and run for union office in a free and democratic election. The scope and stringency of the rule cannot be doubted. It forbids any candidate for union office and his supporters from soliciting or accepting financial support from any non-member. The candidate cannot accept contributions from members of his family, relatives, friends, or well-wishers unless they are members of the union. Retired members such as Edward Sadlowski, Sr., may not contribute; neither may members not in good standing. Even a fully secured loan from a nonmember with a standard rate of interest is forbidden under the rule. The rule goes even further. It forbids the acceptance of "any other direct or indirect support of any kind

from any non-member'', except an individual's volunteered personal time.
* * *

It goes without saying that running for office in a union with 1.3 million members spread throughout the United States and Canada requires a substantial war chest if the campaign is to be effective and to have any reasonable chance of succeeding. Attempting to unseat the incumbents of union office is a substantial undertaking. As we noted in Steelworkers v. Usery, 429 U.S., at 311, 97 S.Ct., at 615, there is no permanent opposition party within the union. There is only a one-party system consisting of the union's incumbent officers and hired staff all controlled from the top down. "The full-time officers collectively, under the direction of the top officer, constitute the sole political machine for the preservation of their offices and power." Edelstein and Warner, Comparative Union Democracy, p. 39 (1979). The union involved in this case has some 30 elected positions, its presidents appoints [sic] more than 1,500 office and field staff and salaries and expenses for union personnel in 1978 totalled over 37 million dollars. App. 141.

Thus, in the best of circumstances, the role of the challenger is very difficult. And if one keeps in mind that Congress intended to give the challenger a fair chance even in a union controlled by unscrupulous leaders with an iron grip on the staff and a willingness to employ means both within and without the law, it is wholly unrealistic to confine the challenger to financial support garnered within the union. Surely, Congress never intended that a union should be permitted to impose such a limitation. As Clyde Summers, a recognized authority in this field, stated in this case on behalf of Sadlowski:

"* * * In my opinion, the practical effect of prohibiting all contributions to union election campaigns except those made by union members would be to gravely damage, if not destroy the possibility of democratic elections in unions, particularly in large local unions and in international unions—if opposition groups are barred from getting any help from outside, they can, in most situations, have no hopes of mounting an effective campaign." Id., at 160.

In addressing itself to union elections, Congress forbade union and employer contributions, but went no further in restricting contributions or expenditures to or on behalf of union candidates for office. The majority emphasizes that Congress was concerned about the control of unions by outsiders and asserts that the challenged rule serves the congressional purpose. It is true, as Senator McClellan explained, that "impositions and abuses * * * have been perpetrated upon the working people of many of our states by the thugs who have muscled into positions of power in labor unions and who masquerade [as] labor leaders and as friends of working people. * * *" 2 Leg.Hist. of the LMRDA 1097. But the remedy which he proposed and which was adopted was to end "autocractic rule by placing the ultimate power in the hands of the members," id., at 1099, and by giving them sufficient statutory protection to participate in a fair election to unseat an entrenched leadership.

Yet the majority somehow finds the absolute, unbending, no-contribution rule to be a reasonable regulation of a member's right to seek office and of the free and open elections that Congress anticipated. This, in spite of the availability of other means to satisfy the union's legitimate concerns about outsiders controlling their affairs through those whose campaigns they have financed. A requirement of disclosure of all contributions, together with a ceiling on contributions, would avoid outside corruption without trampling on the rights of members to raise reasonable sums for election campaigns. Such rules would honor both purposes of the legislation: protecting against outside influence and empowering members to express their views and to challenge established leadership. As I see it, the rule at issue contradicts the values the statute was designed to protect and thwarts its purpose.

I respectfully dissent.

## V.   CORRUPTION AND RELATED ABUSES[a]

### Highway Truck Drivers and Helpers Local 107 v. Cohen

182 F.Supp. 608 (E.D.Pa.1960), affirmed, 284 F.2d 162 (3d Cir.1960), cert. denied, 365 U.S. 833, 81 S.Ct. 747, 5 L.Ed.2d 744 (1961).

*OPINION OF THE DISTRICT COURT*

■ CLARY, DISTRICT JUDGE. This is a private suit brought under the recently enacted Labor Management Reporting and Disclosure Act of 1959, Public Law 86–257 (hereinafter referred to as the "Act"), 29 U.S.C.A. § 401 et seq. That Act establishes a fiduciary responsibility on the part of officers of a labor organization [§ 501(a) ], and further provided for a suit in a Federal district court to enforce these responsibilities [§ 501(b)]. The present suit has been brought under § 501(b) to enforce certain of these duties.

The moving parties are nine rank-and-file members of Highway Truck Drivers and Helpers, Local 107, of the International Brotherhood of Teamsters, Chauffeurs, Warehousemen and Helpers of America (hereinafter referred to as "Local 107"), who were given leave by this Court on November 12, 1959 to file a complaint against the defendants, the governing officers of Local 107. The complaint charged the defendants with a continuing mass conspiracy to cheat and defraud the union of large sums of

---

**a.**  See Clark, The Fiduciary Duties of Union Officials Under Section 501 of the LMRDA, 52 Minn.L.Rev. 437 (1967); Note, The Fiduciary Duty of Union Officers Under the LMRDA: A Guide to the Interpretation of Section 501, 37 N.Y.U.L.Rev. 486 (1962).

money—the conspiracy alleged to have begun in 1954 and continued to the present time.

The defendants have yet to answer these very serious charges. Having been unsuccessful in first opposing the plaintiffs' petition for leave of this Court to sue,[2] defendants now move to have the complaint dismissed. They are supported in this motion by counsel for Local 107, which has been allowed to intervene as a party defendant. This motion to dismiss is presently before the Court along with the plaintiffs' prayer for a preliminary injunction to prohibit the defendants from using union funds to defray the legal costs and other expenses being incurred by the defendants (and several other members of Local 107) in the defense of civil and criminal actions brought against them in the Courts of Pennsylvania and also the present suit in our own Court. * * * The charges in those cases, in essence, grow out of alleged misappropriation of funds by the officers, and the plaintiffs maintain that such expenditures are in violation of the fiduciary duties imposed upon officers of a labor union by Section 501(a) of the Act, supra, and that unless such expenditures are enjoined the union will suffer irreparable harm thereby.

Shortly after the effective date of the Act and the institution of suits, criminal and civil, in the local Courts against the defendants, the union at a regular monthly meeting, with few dissenting votes, adopted a resolution authorizing the union to bear "Legal costs of such actions [against the officers] which are in reality not directed at our officers but are directed at us, the members of Local 107, our good contracts, our good wages and our good working conditions."

The question, therefore, which faces us is: Does the expenditure of union funds to pay for legal fees in the defense of both criminal and civil actions brought against the various defendant officers for an alleged conspiracy to cheat and defraud their union of large sums of money constitute a breach of that fiduciary duty imposed upon them by Section 501(a), supra, notwithstanding the purported authorization of such expenditures by a resolution of the union membership passed at a regular union meeting? * * *

Section 501, with which we are particularly concerned, is entitled "Fiduciary responsibility of officers of labor organizations." This section * * * attempts to define in the broadest terms possible the duty which the new federal law imposes upon a union official. Congress made no attempt to "codify" the law in this area. It appears evident to us that they intended the federal courts to fashion a new federal labor law in this area, in much the same way that the federal courts have fashioned a new substantive law of collective bargaining contracts under § 301(a) of the Taft–Hartley Act, 29 U.S.C.A. § 185(a). See Textile Workers Union of America v. Lincoln Mills, 1957, 353 U.S. 448, 77 S.Ct. 923, 1 L.Ed.2d 972. In undertaking this task the federal courts will necessarily rely heavily upon the common law of

---

**2.** 501(b) specifically provides that "No such proceeding shall be brought except upon leave of the court obtained upon verified application and for good cause shown * * * ".

the various states. Where that law is lacking or where it in any way conflicts with the policy expressed in our national labor laws, the latter will of course be our guide.

We turn then to Section 501, not expecting to find a detailed command or prohibition as to the particular act complained of, but rather to find a general guide which, properly developed, will lead us to an answer. We feel that that answer here must be in plaintiffs' favor.

In determining whether or not the expenditures now sought to be enjoined violate the fiduciary responsibility of an officer of a labor organization we must necessarily determine the legal effect of the September 20th Resolution. This goes to the heart of the present problem and appears to be the main ground on which the defendants seek to avoid the injunction.

The plaintiffs assert that the Resolution authorizing such expenditures is encompassed within the express prohibition of § 501(a) against any "general exculpatory resolution". Although not expressly purporting to absolve the defendants of guilt, plaintiffs argue that the Resolution *in effect* does just this. Unfortunately the Act does not define the phrase "general exculpatory resolution".

* * * [I]t is not necessary for a resolution to read "The officers are hereby absolved of all responsibility created by the Act" before a court will strike it down as "exculpatory" under § 501(a). Nor must a court accept at face value the stated purpose of a resolution when reason and common sense clearly dictate a different purpose. Nevertheless in my interpretation of § 501(a), the Resolution under discussion is *not* one "purporting to relieve any [officer] of liability for breach of the duties declared by this section * * *."

We must distinguish between a resolution which purports to *authorize* action which is beyond the power of the union to do and for that reason in violation of § 501(a) when done by an officer (such as the present Resolution) and a resolution which purports to *relieve* an officer of liability for breach of the duties declared in § 501(a). At times this distinction may be a fine one. Very often the result will be the same. Nevertheless we feel that such a distinction should be made here unless the "exculpatory" provision is to be read as a mere "catch-all" phrase.

We turn then to the question of whether the September 20th Resolution is valid, i.e., conforms with the law of Pennsylvania and the Federal Labor laws. See International Union of Operating Engineers, A.F.L.–C.I.O. v. Pierce, Tex.Civ.App., 1959, 321 S.W.2d 914, at page 917–918. If it is inconsistent with either, we think it follows that the present expenditures by the defendants violate that provision in § 501(a) which imposes upon them a strict duty to "expend [union funds] in accordance with its constitution and bylaws and any resolutions of the governing bodies adopted thereunder * * *."—since we read this sentence to authorize only those expenditures made pursuant to a *lawful* bylaw or resolution.

[The Court here concluded that the Resolution was beyond the powers of the Union as set forth in its Constitution and that the Local could not authorize the expenditures in question by a mere majority vote taken at a regular union meeting. Hence, the Resolution was not valid under Pennsylvania law.]

There is a further reason why the present Resolution is no defense here. Aside from its validity under Pennsylvania law, it is inconsistent with the aims and purposes of the Labor Management Reporting and Disclosure Act and violates the spirit of that Act. A stated purpose of the Act is "to *eliminate* * * * improper practices on the part of labor organizations * * * and their officers". (Emphasis added.) To allow a union officer to use the power and wealth of the very union which he is accused of pilfering, to defend himself against such charges, is totally inconsistent with Congress' effort to eliminate the undesirable element which has been uncovered in the labor-management field. To allow even a majority of members in that union to authorize such action when, if the charges made against these defendants are true, it is these very members whom the officers have deceived, would be equally inconsistent with the Act. If some of those members have not been deceived by the defendants, but because of the immediate gains in their income and working conditions which Local 107 has won for them, they are content to accept as officers anyone who produces immediate results, regardless of what other wrongs those officers may commit in so doing, this Court would still not feel constrained to bow to their will in the light of its duty both to those members of Local 107 who place honesty above material gain as well as to the millions of others in the labor movement whose cause would be seriously injured by such an attitude.

Although we have not attempted to treat defendants' arguments individually, since we feel they are satisfactorily answered in this opinion, something should be said concerning their argument that the plaintiffs are here asking us to do that which Congress specifically refused to do when it failed to adopt Subsection 107(b) of the original Senate version of the Labor Bill (The Kennedy–Ives Bill), which specifically prohibited "both unions and employers from directly or indirectly paying or advancing the costs of defense, of any of their officers * * * who [are] indicted for * * * any violation of any provision of the Bill." S.Rep. No. 187, 86th Cong., First Session, 1959, U.S.Code Cong. and Adm.News 1959, p. 2318. * * * [T]here are reasons why we are not persuaded by their argument here.

First, the language contained in the Kennedy–Ives Bill is much broader than our holding in the present case. It is essential to an understanding of our position in this case that this point be made clear. That section quoted above would foreclose financial aid by the union to an officer in suits under the Act, under *any* circumstances. In our case we have expressly limited our holding *to the facts before us*. In the light of all of these facts we do not feel that the several actions brought against the defendants involve any question of sufficient interest to Local 107 to warrant their expending large sums of union money to pay the legal costs of the defendants in these suits. That Congress refused to foreclose the right of a union under *any* circumstances to lend financial aid to an officer when sued under any section of the Kennedy–Ives Bill is not, we feel, a strong argument for the conclusion that under *no* circumstances could a union be prohibited from lending financial aid to an accused officer.

* * * Finally, even assuming that Congress intended to leave a union free to use its funds for the purpose of paying its officers legal expenses in actions brought against them under the new Act, if under the law of Pennsylvania, the state in which the union membership contractual relationship arose, such expenditures are illegal, a union officer could not consistent with his duty to the union (which duties ultimately flow from its Constitution) expend union funds for this purpose. This would follow unless we interpret the omission of this prohibition as creating an affirmative federal right in a union to so spend its funds, which right is intended to supersede any state law to the contrary. We flatly reject such an interpretation of the new Act. * * *

HOLDEMAN v. SHELDON, 204 F.Supp. 890 (S.D.N.Y.1962), aff'd, 311 F.2d 2 (2d Cir.1962). The president of a local union brought action under Section 501 of the LMRDA against two officers of the union for making unauthorized salary payments to two persons who were not union employees. The complaint alleged: (1) that the officers were not authorized by the union constitution to execute the checks in question, and (2) that the money was paid for services never performed. The defendants controverted both allegations. The district court granted plaintiff's motion to enjoin the defendants from using counsel employed by the union under an annual retainer to defend them and also denied the union's motion to intervene and file a common answer with the defendants. "[A] blanket condemnation of intervention in cases of this type is not warranted. However, in the instant case, it seems clear that the union has no interest other than the protection of the two defendants. * * * Counsel for the proposed intervenors earnestly contended during the argument and in briefs that this case would be defended at no extra cost to the union since counsel is paid on an annual retainer. The court does not accept this argument as persuasive. Although cost to the union is a factor, more important is the idea that in a suit of this type a person who is charged with a violation of his fiduciary responsibility to the union should not be given the opportunity to overwhelm his opponent by putting at his disposal the power and resources of the union. The evils which Sec. 501 was designed to cure would often continue unchecked if a union official was to be permitted to use the power of the union to protect himself whenever he is accused of a wrongful act. It could very well be that the officer so charged with the offense is in a position to control the union machinery." On appeal, *held,* the judgment of the district court is affirmed. In a per curiam opinion the court of appeals declared: "We specifically note approval of the court's suggestion that on motions for injunctions of this sort, the district court should, after a preliminary hearing if necessary, determine whether the plaintiff has made a reasonable showing that he is likely to succeed, and whether the conduct of the defendants is in conflict with the interests of the Union. This, in combination with a policy of permitting a union to reimburse a defendant if he is successful in his defense, or perhaps even where his actions were based on a reasonable judgment as to appropriate procedures and do not evidence bad faith, should provide sufficient financial protection of union officials against nuisance suits."

———

In addition to providing regulations and safeguards pertaining to elections, union discipline and individual rights, the LMRDA contains a number of other provisions designed to eliminate abuses disclosed during the McClellan Committee hearings.[b] Certain of these provisions, requiring the filing of various sorts of information, are founded on the premise that public opinion and democratic processes within the union can curb much abuse if information concerning union activities is systematically collected and made available. Other provisions in the LMRDA, however, operate more directly by simply prohibiting certain types of conduct on the part of union officials.

## A.   DISCLOSURE OF INFORMATION

Section 201(a) of the LMRDA requires every labor organization to file with the Secretary of Labor information setting forth, *inter alia:* the name and address of the organization; the names of its officers; the initiation fees and dues that it charges; its procedures with regard to membership qualifications, financial audits, selection of officers, discipline of members and officers, etc. Section 201(b) requires the filing of information setting forth the assets and liabilities of the organization (specifying all receipts of any kind), the emoluments, both direct and indirect, received by union officers; loans received by any officer, employee or member; and loans extended by the organization to any business enterprise and other disbursements made. Pursuant to Section 201(c), all the information referred to above must be made available to members of the union, and members are also given the right to examine all records and reports on which this information is based.

Since these filing requirements apply to all unions, there is some danger that an overwhelming load of paper work may be imposed upon small unions. Power is conferred upon the Secretary of Labor, however, to alleviate this problem by permitting any union to file simplified reports whenever this procedure will effectuate the purposes of the Act.

Filing requirements are also imposed upon officers and employees (other than clerical or custodial) of labor organizations. Section 202(a) provides that each such person shall file with the Secretary of Labor a

**b.** For general discussions see Aaron, The Labor–Management Reporting and Disclosure Act of 1959, 73 Harv.L.Rev. 581 (1960); Cox, Internal Affairs of Labor Unions Under the Labor Reform Act of 1959, 58 Mich.L.Rev. 819 (1960).

report listing all income or other property received by himself, his spouse or minor child from any employers with whom his union deals, either commercially or as a bargaining representative. The effect of this provision is to compel disclosure of transactions which might involve the union official or employee in a conflict of interest.

Finally, Section 203 of the Act requires employers to report every payment or loan (and every agreement to make a payment or loan) to any official, agent or other representative of a labor union. Employers must also report any expenditure designed to interfere with or restrain or coerce employees in the exercise of their right to organize and bargain collectively. In addition, reports must be filed of any agreement with a labor relations consultant or other outside organization[c] whereby the latter undertakes to influence employees in the exercise of their right to organize and bargain collectively. Employers must also disclose any expenditures or agreements with outside consultants or organizations[d] designed to obtain information concerning the activities of employees or of a labor organization in connection with a labor dispute in which that employer is involved (unless the information is needed for use in an arbitration or in a court or administrative proceeding).

Section 209 of the Act imposes a fine of not more than ten thousand dollars or a prison term of not more than one year, or both, on anyone who wilfully violates Title II or who knowingly falsely represents a material fact or fails to disclose such a fact in his required reports or who wilfully conceals or destroys essential records. In addition, Section 210 empowers the Secretary of Labor to bring a civil action in federal district court to enjoin or otherwise remedy past or threatened violations of Title II. Enforcement of the various filing requirements is facilitated by Section 601 which empowers the Secretary to inspect any records and question such persons as he considers necessary in order to determine whether any individual has violated, or is about to violate, any provision of the LMRDA (other than Title I or amendments made by the LMRDA of other statutes).

## B. LIMITATIONS ON UNION OFFICIALS

In Title V of the LMRDA, various limitations are placed directly upon union officials. Of prime importance is Section 501(a) which states that it is the duty of all officers and representatives of a labor organization "taking into account the special problems and functions of a labor organization, to hold its money and property solely for the benefit of the organization and its members and to manage, invest and expend the same in accordance with

---

**c.** Section 203(e) exempts the employer from reporting payments to his officers, supervisors, and employees for their regular services.

**d.** Section 203(b) requires such consultants or organizations to report to the Secretary of Labor within thirty days concerning any arrangement with an employer to enter into any of the activities mentioned above.

its constitution and bylaws * * *.'' Some concern was voiced by union spokesmen that the effect of this provision might be to curtail various expenditures for a variety of economic and social objectives not directly connected with the aims and activities of the union making the donation. A careful reading of the section, however, together with its legislative history, suggests that save, perhaps, in extreme situations such as the *Cohen* case, supra, the law does not limit the purposes for which expenditures may be made so long as the expenditure conforms to the constitution and by-laws of the organization.

Section 501 goes on to make clear that each representative is under a duty not to acquire financial or other interests which conflict with his responsibilities to his union, and the final sentence of subsection (a) declares that no provision in the constitution or by-laws nor any resolution of the governing body of a union which seeks to circumvent the above-mentioned duties shall have legal validity. Section 501(b) provides that any member may sue a representative of his union for violating the duties set forth in Section 501(a) and may receive damages or an accounting or other appropriate relief. As a safeguard against harassing or frivolous suits, prior permission to bring suit must be sought from the court, and in order to satisfy the court the prospective plaintiff must make a showing of good cause. The final safeguard provided by Section 501 is set forth in subsection (c) which declares that any officer or employee of a union who embezzles or steals funds or other properties of his labor organization shall be punished by a fine of ten thousand dollars and/or imprisonment for five years.

Section 504(a) prohibits any person who has been a member of the Communist Party within the past five years or who has been convicted within the past five years of any one of several specified crimes from serving as an officer, representative or employee (other than clerical or custodial) of a labor organization. The constitutionality of Section 504(a) was not altogether free from doubt, particularly the disqualification of persons who have been Communist Party members within the past five years. The Supreme Court had ruled that a union may be denied access to the National Labor Relations Board if its officials have not filed an affidavit denying membership or affiliation with the Communist Party. American Communications Ass'n v. Douds, 339 U.S. 382, 70 S.Ct. 674, 94 L.Ed. 925 (1950)(upholding the constitutionality of Section 9(h) of the National Labor Relations Act which has since been repealed). Nevertheless, Section 504(a) imposes a criminal penalty upon union officers violating this provision rather than an administrative restraint upon the union. Relying in part on this distinction, the Supreme Court declared Section 504(a) as originally written unconstitutional as a bill of attainder. United States v. Brown, 381 U.S. 437, 85 S.Ct. 1707, 14 L.Ed.2d 484 (1965).

## C.  Trusteeships[e]

Title III of the LMRDA deals with the problem of trusteeships. The constitutions of many international unions authorize the international officers to suspend the normal government of a constituent local union, assume control of its property, and conduct its affairs. Under some constitutions charges must be filed against the local and a hearing must be held before the international intervenes. Others allow the General President to take over a local without a hearing, subject to the approval of the General Executive Board after a hearing. Apparently there are still a few international unions which make no provision for a hearing.

Any thoughtful discussion of trusteeships must recognize their indispensability. Trusteeships provide one device by which international officers can keep the labor movement strong and free from subversion or corruption. Thus, a trusteeship may be imposed to prevent embezzlement or misuse of funds, to restore democracy to an autocratic local, to curb irresponsible strikes or contract violations by local leaders or to revivify a moribund organization.

Unfortunately trusteeships have also been a virulent source of political autocracy and financial corruption, and the abuses which have been perpetrated with the aid of this device are familiar to every student of labor history. There appear to be four chief motivations for the imposition of improper trusteeships.

(1) The opportunity to loot rich local treasuries has been a significant temptation.

(2) The desire to control the policies of a local union may stem from honorable motives but in a good many cases there has been evidence of a desire to use union position for personal advantage.

(3) Other trusteeships have been imposed in order to keep in office men friendly to the international union. The McClellan Committee reported that when a Teamsters' local in Pontiac, Michigan revolted against four officials who had been accused of extortion, the international put the local under the trusteeship of James Hoffa, who then appointed two of the four officials as business agents to run the affairs of the local.

(4) The imposition of a trusteeship may be a method of controlling an international convention. Frequently the trustee appoints the delegates of the local union under his control. Since the General President will name a trustee friendly to himself, the trustee may be expected to follow the president's suggestions in choosing delegates, and the delegates themselves will not be blind to their dependence upon the president's good will. With ten or twenty per cent of the membership in trusteeships the international officers would have a strong bloc of votes.

---

e.  Note, a Fair Hearing Requirement for Union Trusteeships Under the LMRDA, 40 U.Chi.L.Rev. 873 (1973); Beaird, Union Trusteeship Provisions of the Labor–Management Reporting and Disclosure Act of 1959, 2 Ga.L.Rev. 469 (1968).

In order to curb the abuses of trusteeship, section 302 of the LMRDA declares that:

> "Trusteeships shall be established and administered by a labor organization over a subordinate body only in accordance with the constitution and by laws of the organization which has assumed trusteeship over the subordinate body and for the purpose of correcting corruption or financial malpractice, assuring the performance of collective bargaining agreements or other duties of a bargaining representative, restoring democratic procedures or otherwise carrying out the legitimate objects of such labor organization."

In addition, section 303 prohibits the counting of any votes from trusteed locals in a convention or election of a national officer unless the delegates from such a local have been chosen by secret ballot in an election in which all local members in good standing were eligible to participate. Moreover, no funds may be transferred from the local to the national union in excess of the normal assessments levied upon other locals which are not in trusteeship. In order to facilitate the enforcement of these provisions, section 301(c) requires that every labor organization which assumes trusteeship must file a report with the Secretary of Labor within thirty days setting forth the reasons for the trusteeship, the means by which it is carried out, the extent of participation by the trusteed local in national conventions and elections, etc. Similar reports must be filed semi-annually until the trusteeship is removed. Any member or subordinate body of the union imposing a trusteeship may either sue in a federal court or request investigation and suit by the Secretary of Labor in order to enforce the rules set forth in sections 302 and 303. If suit is brought, a trusteeship established in accord with the constitution and by-laws of the union shall be presumed valid for a period of eighteen months from the date of its establishment and shall not be subject to attack "except upon clear and convincing proof that the trusteeship was not established or maintained in good faith for a purpose allowable under section 302." After eighteen months, the opposite presumption prevails.

---

## PROBLEM FOR DISCUSSION

Local 1735 of the Brewery Bottlers Union has functioned as an autonomous local union for more than 75 years. Ten years ago, Local 1735 and several other sister locals became affiliated with the Teamsters. Last month, the Executive Board of the Teamsters announced that Local 1735 and seven other locals would be merged into two large groups, a production local and a delivery local. The members of Local 1735 are violently opposed to the merger and fear that their Local will lose its autonomy and become subject to officials of the larger group who will simply carry out policies dictated by the International. The International, however, declares that the "urgent need for today is a unified, powerful and streamlined organization; one that can successfully negotiate with the Industry and police the contracts after they are signed; * * * Only this type of merged organization can hope to meet the growing problems of automation, merger of companies and labor-saving programs which threaten the job-security of every member of our local unions." Can the members of Local 1735 prevent the merger under Section 302 of the LMRDA? See Brewery Bottlers and Drivers Union, Local 1345 v. International Brotherhood of Teamsters, 202 F.Supp. 464 (E.D.N.Y.1962).

# INDEX

†